A
CHEMICAL
LOVE STORY

Alexander
Shulgin

Ann
Shulgin

TRANSFORM
PRESS

For information, contact:
Transform Press
PO Box 11552
Berkeley, CA 94712
vm: (925) 934-2675
fax: (925) 934-5999
www.transformpress.com

Copublished with
Synergetic Press
1 Blue Bird Court
Santa Fe, NM 85708
(505) 424-0237
www.synergeticpress.com

Edited by Dan Joy
Cover by Pamela Engebretson

First Edition, Twentieth Printing
ISBN: 0-9630096-0-5
ISBN 13: 978-0-9630096-0-9

phen-ethyl-amine \ fen-'eth-al-a-,mēn \ n. [*phen*yl fr. F. phène, fr. Gk. phainein, to show (from its occurrence in illuminating gas)+ ethyl (*eth*er + *yl*) + amine fr. NL ammonia] 1: A naturally occurring compound found in both the animal and plant kingdoms. It is an endogenous component of the human brain. 2: Any of a series of compounds containing the phenethylamine skeleton, and modified by chemical constituents at appropriate positions in the molecule.

TABLE OF CONTENTS

FOREWORD

This book will be different things to different people. There has never been a work like it, and since recent legislative acts in this country have closed off the avenues of inquiry that made this one possible we may not soon, if ever, see another of its kind. Although it is doubtful that it will ever make the best seller list, no library of psychedelic literature will henceforth be complete without a copy of PIHKAL.

For nearly thirty years one of the authors, Dr. Alexander Shulgin, affectionately known to his friends as Sasha, has been the only person in the world to synthesize, then evaluate in himself, his wife Ann, and in a dedicated group of close friends, nearly 200 never-before-known chemical structures, materials expected to have effects in man similar to those of the mind-altering psychedelic drugs, mescaline, psilocybin and LSD. On the west coast, Sasha has assumed almost folk-hero status. Others regard him variously as courageous, foolhardy, or downright dangerous, depending mostly on the political persuasion of the critic. However, all would have to agree that Sasha Shulgin is a most remarkable individual. This writing collaboration with his wife Ann will be enjoyed, not only by their friends, but also by those who have heard about "Sasha" but don't have a clue as to who he really is. More importantly, this is a tale of self-discovery, accompanied by the faint stirrings of a technology that is yet to be fully born, much less developed.

The beginning of PIHKAL is autobiographical, detailing the lives of two fictional characters, Dr. Alexander Borodin, known to his friends by the Russian diminutive "Shura," and Alice, later his wife. In the first two parts, Shura and Alice describe the individual life paths which led each of them to a fascination with psychedelics and, ultimately, to their fascination with each other. In Part III, they chronicle more than a decade of their adventures together, journeys often catalyzed by the ingestion of one of Shura's new chemical compounds.

One cannot be certain of the exact extent to which Shura and Alice mirror Sasha and Ann, but the richness of imagery, detail of thought, openly expressed emotions, and moments of intimacy clearly give insight into the personalities of the two people I know. These details serve to show that Shura and Alice's research has been an honest search for meaning in life. Their pain in lost relationships, in failed marriages, and their love and caring for each other paint a picture of two extraordinary and very feeling human beings.

The second half of the book is an almost encyclopedic compendium of synthetic methods, dosages, durations of action, and commentaries for 179 different chemical materials. These essentially represent transcriptions of Sasha's laboratory notebooks, with some additional material culled from the scientific literature. Some day in the future, when it may again be acceptable to use chemical tools to study the mind, this book will be a treasure-house, a sort of sorcerer's book of spells, to delight and enchant the psychiatrist/shaman of tomorrow.

David E. Nichols, Ph. D.
Professor of Medicinal Chemistry
West Lafayette, Indiana

NOTE TO THE READER

With this book, PIHKAL, we are making available a body of information concerning the conception, synthesis, definition, and appropriate use of certain consciousness-changing chemical compounds which we are convinced are valuable tools for the study of the human mind and psyche.

At the present time, restrictive laws are in force in the United States and it is very difficult for researchers to abide by the regulations which govern efforts to obtain legal approval to do work with these compounds in human beings. Consequently there has been almost no clinical research conducted in this area for almost thirty years. However, animal studies can be done by the approved and qualified scientist who finds sources of research funding and who appeals to and obtains his supplies of drugs from an appropriate government agency such as the National Institute on Drug Abuse.

Approximately half of the recipes in Book II of PIHKAL have already been published in a number of respected scientific journals. The rest will be submitted for publication in the near future.

No one who is lacking legal authorization should attempt the synthesis of any of the compounds described in the second half of this book, with intent to give them to man. To do so is to risk legal action which might lead to the tragic ruination of a life. It should also be noted that any person anywhere who experiments on himself, or on another human being, with any one of the drugs described herein, without being familiar with that drug's action and aware of the physical and/or mental disturbance or harm it might cause, is acting irresponsibly and immorally, whether or not he is doing so within the bounds of the law.

We strongly urge that a continuing effort be made by those who care about freedom of inquiry and the search for knowledge, to work toward changes in the present drug laws, particularly in the United States. Open inquiry, and creative exploration of this important area of research, must be not only allowed but encouraged. It is essential that our present negative propaganda regarding psychedelic drugs be replaced with honesty and truthfulness about their effects, both good and bad.

There is much that we need to understand about the human psyche, and this book is dedicated to the pursuit of that understanding.

SEARCH FOR A TITLE

In trying to settle on a title for his book, a writer aims for something which both author and reader will find appropriate and easy to remember. For this book, I had originally considered something more academic than autobiographical, like "Hallucinogenic Phenethylamines," (hard to pronounce or remember, unless you're a chemist), but not only does that bear a close resemblance to "The Hallucinogens," by Hoffer and Osmond, it makes use of a word neither Ann nor I feel is appropriate in describing the effects of these materials. "Hallucinogenic," is probably the most commonly misused word in this field, so why reinforce what we regard as an inaccuracy and a misconception?

A title such as "The Psychedelic Phenethylamines," also very academic-sounding, was too close to books like "The Psychedelics," by Osmond, or "Psychedelics Encyclopedia," by Stafford; besides, with the loaded word, "psychedelics," in its title, such a book might prove difficult to stock in the bookstores of the Mid-West, even less likely in those of Russia; in Canada, quite impossible.

So when the words, "Phenethylamines I Have Known and Loved," popped into my mind, and I realized that the acronym was PIHKAL — which looks and sounds manageable — I got up from my desk and went to find Ann. I asked her, "What comes to mind when you hear the word, Pihkal?" She repeated, "Pea-KAHL? An ancient Mayan city in Guatemala, of course. Why?"

"No," I replied, "That's Tikal. Pihkal was the ruling lord of Palenque. He was entombed with six human sacrifices and a pile of jade, as I'm sure you now recall."

"Why do I have this funny feeling that you're not telling the absolutely precise truth?" asked Ann, who used to believe implicitly every word I uttered.

"You're right," I said, "I got carried away there, for a moment."

When I told her what P-I-H-K-A-L really did stand for, it took a while for her to stop laughing, leading me to the inevitable conclusion that my quest for a title was finally at an end.

PREFACE

The book should actually be titled "Phenethylamines And Other Things I Have Known and Loved," because, although Book II contains only information on phenethylamines, the story includes some descriptions of the effects of other classes of psychedelic drugs, as well.

Part I is told in the voice of Shura Borodin, a character based on myself, and traces the story of my life from childhood through the death of my first wife.

Part II is told in the voice of Alice Parr, later Borodin, a character based on my wife, Ann, and tells the story of our relationship, and the development of our love for each other.

Part III takes both of us, our voices alternating, through the later years and certain experiences from which we, and members of our research group, continued to learn about ourselves, gaining insight and knowledge through changes of consciousness which were sometimes aided by the psychedelics and at other times catalyzed by no drug at all.

Book II should be of interest to chemists and all who love chemistry, but the comments at the end of each recipe might also prove interesting to the reader who understands no chemistry whatsoever.

Most of the names in this story have been changed to protect personal privacy and to allow us freedom in the telling of our tale. Certain characters are composites.

INTRODUCTION

THE PHILOSOPHY BEHIND THE WRITING OF PIHKAL

I am a pharmacologist and a chemist. I have spent most of my adult life investigating the action of drugs; how they are discovered, what they are, what they do, how they can be helpful — or harmful. But my interests lie somewhat outside the mainstream of pharmacology, in the area I have found most fascinating and rewarding, that of the psychedelic drugs. Psychedelics might best be defined as physically non-addictive compounds which temporarily alter the state of one's consciousness.

The prevailing opinion in this country is that there are drugs that have legal status and are either relatively safe or at least have acceptable risks, and there are other drugs that are illegal and have no legitimate place at all in our society. Although this opinion is widely held and vigorously promoted, I sincerely believe that it is wrong. It is an effort to paint things either black or white, when, in this area, as in most of real life, truth is colored grey.

Let me give the reasons for my belief.

Every drug, legal or illegal, provides some reward. Every drug presents some risk. And every drug can be abused. Ultimately, in my opinion, it is up to each of us to measure the reward against the risk and decide which outweighs the other. The rewards cover a wide spectrum. They include such things as the curing of disease, the softening of physical and emotional pain, intoxication, and relaxation. Certain drugs — those known as the psychedelics — allow for increased personal insight and expansion of one's mental and emotional horizons.

The risks are equally varied, ranging from physical damage to psychological disruption, dependency, and violation of the law. Just as there are different rewards with different people, there are also different risks. An adult must make his own decision as to whether or not he should expose himself to a specific drug, be it available by prescription or proscribed by law, by measuring the potential good and bad with his own personal yardstick. And it is here that being well informed plays an indispensable role. My philosophy can be distilled into four words: be informed, then choose.

I personally have chosen some drugs to be of sufficient value to be worth the risks; others, I deem not to be of sufficient value. For instance, I use a moderate amount of alcohol, generally in the form of wine, and — at the present time — my liver function tests are completely normal. I do not smoke tobacco. I used to, quite heavily, then gave it up. It was not the health risk that swayed me, but rather the fact that I had become completely dependent upon it. That was, in my view, a case of the price being unacceptably high.

Each such decision is my own, based on what I know of the drug and what I know about myself.

Among the drugs that are currently illegal, I have chosen not to use marijuana, as I feel the light-headed intoxication and benign alteration of consciousness does not adequately compensate for an uncomfortable feeling that I am wasting time.

I have tried heroin. This drug, of course, is one of the major concerns in our society, at the present time. In me, it produces a dreamy peacefulness, with no rough edges of worry, stress or concern. But there is also a loss of motivation, of alertness, and of the urge to get things done. It is not any fear of addiction that causes me to decide against heroin; it is the fact that, under its influence, nothing seems to be particularly important to me.

I have also tried cocaine. This drug, particularly in its notorious "crack" form, is the cause celebre of today. To me, cocaine is an aggressive pusher, a stimulant which gives me a sense of power and of being completely with it, on top of the world. But there is also the inescapable knowledge, underneath, that it is not true power, that I am not really on top of the world, and that, when the drug's effects have disappeared, I will have gained nothing. There is a strange sense of falseness about the state. There is no insight. There is no learning. In its own distinctive way, I find cocaine to be as much an escape drug as heroin. With either one, you escape from who you are, or — even more to the point — from who you are not. In either case, you are relieved for a short time from awareness of your inadequacies. I frankly would rather address mine than escape them; there is, ultimately, far greater satisfaction that way.

With the psychedelic drugs, I believe that, for me, the modest risks (an occasional difficult experience or perhaps some body malaise) are more than balanced by the potential for learning. And that is why I have chosen to explore this particular area of pharmacology.

What do I mean when I say there is a potential for learning? It is a potential, not a certainty. I can learn, but I'm not forced to do so; I can gain insight into possible ways of improving the quality of my life, but only my own efforts will bring about the desired changes.

Let me try to make clear some of the reasons that I find the psychedelic experience a personal treasure.

I am completely convinced that there is a wealth of information built into us, with miles of intuitive knowledge tucked away in the genetic material of every one of our cells. Something akin to a library containing uncountable reference volumes, but without any obvious route of entry. And, without some means of access, there is no way to even begin to guess at the extent and quality of what is there. The psychedelic drugs allow exploration of this interior world, and insights into its nature.

Our generation is the first, ever, to have made the search for self-awareness a crime, if it is done with the use of plants or chemical compounds as the means of opening the psychic doors. But the urge to become aware is always present, and it increases in intensity as one grows older.

One day, looking into the face of a newborn grandchild, you find yourself thinking that her birth has made a seamless tapestry of time as it flows from yesterday to tomorrow. You realize that life continuously appears in different forms and in different identities, but that whatever it is that gives shape to each new expression does not change at all.

"From where did her unique soul come?" you wonder, "And, to where will my own unique soul go? Is there really something else out there, after death? Is there a purpose to it all? Is there an overriding order and structure that makes sense of everything, or would, if only I could see it?" You feel the urge to ask, to probe, to use what little time might be left to you, to search for ways to tie together all the loose ends, to understand what demands to be understood.

This is the search that has been part of human life from the very first moments of consciousness. The knowledge of his own mortality — knowledge which places him apart from his fellow animals — is what gives Man the right, the license, to explore the nature of his own soul and spirit, to discover what he can about the components of the human psyche.

Each of us, at some time in his life, will feel himself a stranger in the strange land of his own existence, needing answers to questions which have risen from deep within his soul and will not go away.

Both the questions and their answers have the same source: oneself.

This source, this part of ourselves, has been called by many names throughout human history, the most recent being "the unconscious." Freudians distrust it and Jungians are enraptured by it. It is the part inside you that keeps watch when your conscious mind has drifted, that gives you the sense of what to do in a crisis, when there is no time available for logical reasoning and decision-making. It is the place wherein are to be found demons and angels and everything in between.

This is one of the reasons I hold the psychedelic drugs to be treasures. They can provide access to the parts of us which have answers. They can, but again, they need not and probably will not, unless that is the purpose for which they are being used.

It is up to you to use these tools well, and in the right way. A psychedelic drug might be compared to television. It can be very revealing, very instructive, and — with thoughtful care in the selection of channels — the means by which extraordinary insights can be achieved. But to many people, psychedelic drugs are simply another form of entertainment; nothing profound is looked for, thus — usually — nothing profound is experienced.

The potential of the psychedelic drugs to provide access to the interior universe, is, I believe, their most valuable property.

From the earliest days of his time on earth, Man has sought out and used specific plants which have had the effect of altering the way he interacts with his world and communicates with his gods and with himself. For many thousands of years, in every known culture, there has been some percentage of the population — usually the shamans, the curenderos, the medicine men — which has used this or that plant to achieve a transformation in its state of consciousness. These people have used the altered state to sharpen their diagnostic abilities and to enable them to draw upon the healing energies to be found in the world of the spirits. The tribal leaders (in later civilizations, the royal families) presumably used the psychoactive plants to increase their insight and wisdom as rulers, or perhaps simply to call upon the forces of destructive power as allies in forthcoming battles.

Many plants have been found to meet specific human needs. Unwanted pain has been with mankind forever. Just as we today have our heroin (or Fentanyl or Demerol) users, for centuries past this analgesic role has been played by opium of the Old World and datura of the New World, mandragora in Europe and North Africa, as well as henbane, belladonna and mandrake, to name a few. Countless people have used this way of deadening pain (physical and psychic), which involves escape into a dream world. And, although these tools have had many users, it apparently has been only a minority that has abused them. Historically, every culture has spun these plants into its daily life, and has had more benefit than harm from them. We have, in our own society, learned to deaden physical pain and debilitating anxiety with the medical use of drugs which have been developed in imitation of the alkaloids in these plants.

The need to search out sources of additional energy has also been with us forever. And, as we have our caffeine and cocaine users, for centuries the natural sources have been mate tea and the coca plant of the New World, the khat plant of Asia Minor, the kola tree of North Africa, kavakava and the betel nut from Eastern Asia, and ephedra from all parts of the world. Again, many kinds of people — the peasant, stooped under a bundle of firewood, trudging for hours on a mountain path; the doctor on emergency duty for two days without sleep; the soldier under fire at the front, unable to rest — have sought the push and prod of stimulation. And, as always, there have been a few who have chosen to abuse the process.

Then, there is the need to explore the world that lies just beyond the immediate limits of our senses and our understanding; that, too, has been with mankind from the first. But in this case, our non-native North American society has not given its acceptance to the plants, the chemicals, that open up our seeing and feeling skills. Other civilizations, for many hundreds of years, have used the peyote cactus and the psilocybin-containing mushroom, the ayahuasca, cohoba and yajé of the New World, the harmala, cannabis and soma of the Old World, and the iboga of Africa, for this inquiry into the human unconscious. But our modern medical profession, as a whole, has never acknowledged these tools for insight or for therapy, and they have remained generally unacceptable. In the establishment of a balance of power between those who heal us and those who govern us, it has been agreed that the possession and use of these remarkable plants shall be a crime. And that the use of any chemical compounds which have been developed in imitation of these plants, even though they might show improved safety and consistency of action, shall also be a crime.

We are a great nation with one of the highest standards of living ever known. We are proud of an extraordinary Constitution that protects us from the tyranny that has torn apart lesser nations. We are rich in the heritage of English law that assumes our innocence and assures us our personal privacy. One of the major strengths of our country has been in its traditional respect for the individual. Each and every one of us is free — or so we have always believed — to follow whatever religious or spiritual path he chooses; free to inquire, to explore, to seek information and pursue truth wherever and however he wishes, as long as he accepts full responsibility for his actions and their effects on others.

How is it, then, that the leaders of our society have seen fit to try to eliminate this one very important means of learning and self-discovery, this means which has been used, respected, and honored for thousands of years, in every human culture of which we have a record? Why has peyote, for instance, which has served for centuries as a means by which a person may open his soul to an experience of God, been classified by our government as a Schedule I material, along with heroin and PCP? Is this kind of legal condemnation the result of ignorance, pressure from organized religion, or a growing urge to force conformity upon the population? Part of the answer may lie in an increasing trend in our culture towards both paternalism and provincialism.

Paternalism is the name for a system in which the authorities supply our needs, and — in exchange — are allowed to dictate our conduct, both public and private. Provincialism is narrowness of outlook, social unification by the acceptance of a single code of ethics, the limiting of interests and forms of experience to those already established as traditional.

However, the prejudice against the use of consciousness-opening plants and drugs has the major part of its origin in racial intolerance and the accumulation of political power. In the latter part of the last century, once the Intercontinental Railway had been built and the Chinese laborers were no longer needed, they were increasingly portrayed as subhuman and uncivilized; they were yellow-skinned, slant-eyed, dangerous aliens who frequented opium dens.

Peyote was described, in various publications of the late 19th century, as the cause of murder, mayhem and insanity among the shiftless American Indians. The Bureau of Indian Affairs was determined to stamp out the use of peyote, (which it consistently confused with mescal and the mescal bean, in its publications), and one of the most consistent pressures behind its efforts is made clear in this partial quotation from a letter written by the Reverend B. V. Gassaway in 1903 to the BIA, "... The Sabbath is the principal day for our preaching services and if the Indians are first made drunk on mescal (peyote) they cannot then be benefitted by the gospel."

It was only with tremendous effort and courage on the part of many people of conscience that the use of peyote as a sacrament in the Native American Church was permitted to continue. There is now underway, as you know, a renewed effort on the part of our present government to eliminate the religious use of peyote by our Native Americans.

In the 1930's, there was an effort to deport Mexican laborers from southern agricultural states, and racial prejudice was again deliberately encouraged, with the Mexicans being described as lazy, dirty, and users of that dangerous stuff called marijuana. The intolerance of black people in the United States was aided and abetted by stories of marijuana and heroin use among black musicians. It should be noted that nobody remarked on such drug use by black people until their new music, which they called jazz, began to attract the attention of whites — at first only white nightclub patrons — and there began the first stirrings of awareness of the indignities and injustices being suffered by black Americans.

We, in this country, are all too painfully aware of our past sins in regard to the rights of various minorities, but we are less conscious of the way in which the public attitude toward certain drugs has been manipulated. New positions of political power and, eventually, thousands of new jobs, were created on the basis of the perceived threat to public health and safety posed by plants and drugs whose sole function was to change perceptions, to open the way to exploration of the unconscious mind, and

— for many — to allow a direct experience of the numinous.

The 1960's, of course, delivered a powerful blow to the psychedelics. These drugs were being used as part and parcel of a massive rebellion against governmental authority and what was believed to be an immoral and unnecessary war in Vietnam. Also, there were too many loud and authoritative voices claiming that there was a need for a new kind of spirituality, and urging the use of psychedelics to make direct contact with one's God, without the intervention of priest, minister or rabbi.

The voices of psychiatrists, writers and philosophers, and many thoughtful members of the clergy, pleaded for study and investigation of the effects of psychedelics, and of what they could reveal about the nature and function of the human mind and psyche. They were ignored in the clamor against flagrant abuse and misuse, of which there was more than ample evidence. The government and the Church decided that psychedelic drugs were dangerous to society, and with the help of the press, it was made clear that this was the way to social chaos and spiritual disaster.

What was unstated, of course, was the oldest rule of all: "Thou shalt not oppose nor embarrass those in power without being punished."

I have stated some of my reasons for holding the view that psychedelic drugs are treasures. There are others, and many of them are spun into the texture of this story. There is, for instance, the effect they have on my perception of colors, which is completely remarkable. Also, there is the deepening of my emotional rapport with another person, which can become an exquisitely beautiful experience, with eroticism of sublime intensity. I enjoy the enhancement of the senses of touch, smell and taste, and the fascinating changes in my perception of the flow of time.

I deem myself blessed, in that I have experienced, however briefly, the existence of God. I have felt a sacred oneness with creation and its Creator, and — most precious of all — I have touched the core of my own soul.

It is for these reasons that I have dedicated my life to this area of inquiry. Someday I may understand how these simple catalysts do what they do. In the meantime, I am forever in their debt. And I will forever be their champion.

THE PROCESS OF DISCOVERY

The second most often asked question, after, "Why do you do the work you do?" is: "How do you determine the activity of a new drug?"

How does one go about discovering the action, the nature of the effect on the central nervous system, of a chemical which has just been synthesized, but not yet put into a living organism? I start by explaining that it must be understood, first of all, that the newborn chemical is as free of pharmacological activity as a newborn babe is free of prejudice.

At the moment of a person's conception, many fates have been sealed, from physical features to gender and intelligence. But many things have not been decided. Subtleties of personality, belief systems, countless other characteristics, are not established at birth. In the eyes of every newborn, there is a universality of innocence and godliness which changes gradually as interactions take place with parents, siblings and the environment. The adult product is shaped from repeated contacts with pains and pleasures, and what finally emerges is the fatalist, the egocentric, or the rescuer. And the traveling companions of this person during his development from undefined infant to well-defined adult, all have contributed to and have been, in turn, modified by these interactions.

So it is also with a chemical. When the idea of a new substance is conceived, nothing exists but symbols, a collage of odd atoms hooked together with bonds, all scribbled out on a blackboard or a napkin at the dinner table. The structure, of course, and perhaps even some spectral characteristics and physical properties are inescapably pre-ordained. But its character in man, the nature of its pharmacological action or even the class of the action it might eventually display can only be guessed at. These properties cannot yet be known, for at this stage they do not yet exist.

Even when the compound emerges as a new substance, tangible, palpable, weighable, it is still a tabula rasa in the pharmacological sense, in that nothing is known, nothing can be known, about its action in man, since it has never been in man. It is only with the development of a relationship between the thing tested and the tester himself that this aspect of character will emerge, and the tester is as much a contributor to the final definition of the drug's action as is the drug itself. The process of establishing the nature of a compound's action is synonymous with the process of developing that action.

Other researchers who taste your material will include some (most, you hope) who make separate evaluations after the fact and will agree with your evaluations, and it will then appear that you defined (developed) the properties accurately. Other researchers (only a few, you hope) will disagree, and they will privately tend to wonder why they failed to evaluate the material more accurately. You might call this a no-lose situation, and it is the reward for personally following all three parts of this process, namely conception, creation, and definition.

But it must be kept in mind that the interaction goes both ways; the tester, as well as the compound being tested, is molded by it.

I determine activity in the most ancient and time-honored way, established and practiced for thousands of years by medicine men and shamans who had to know the effects of plants which might prove useful in healing. The method is obvious to anyone who gives the matter some thought.

Although most of the compounds I investigate are created in the laboratory, and I seldom taste plants or fungi found in nature, there is still only one way to do it, a way that minimizes the risk, while maximizing the quality of the information obtained. I take the compound myself. I test its physical effects in my own body and I stay attentive to any mental effects which might be present.

Before I elaborate on this old-fashioned method of discovering a new drug's activity, let me explain how I feel about animal testing and why I no longer rely on it in my own research.

I used to use animals, when I worked at Dole, to detect toxicity. Obviously, drugs which promise to have clinical utility must, and should, go through the established procedures of IND (Investigation of New Drug) permits and clinical trials prior to large-scale studies in humans. But I have not killed mice experimentally for two decades, and cannot foresee any need to do so again. My reasons for having decided against the use of test animals are as follows.

During the time when I routinely tested every new, potentially psychoactive drug in mice to establish the LD-50 (the dosage level at which 50% of the test animals die), two generalities became obvious. All of the LD-50's seemed to group in the area between 50 and 150 milligrams per kilogram of body weight. For a 25 gram mouse, that would be somewhere around five milligrams. And, secondly, the number gives no prediction of the potency or character of action the drug could eventually show in man. Nevertheless, numerous compounds have been "established" in the scientific literature as being psychedelic in their action solely on the basis of animal assays, without any human evaluation having been performed. I believe totally that assays such as nest building among mice, disruption of conditioned response, grooming, maze running, or motor-activity have no value in determining the psychedelic potential of a compound.

One form of animal study does indeed have merit, and that is the cardiovascular monitoring and eventual pathological examination of an experimental animal which has been given an increasingly large dosage of a test compound. The animal I have used has usually been the dog. This form of testing is certainly useful in determining the nature of toxic effects that should be watched for, but it is still of no value in defining the subjective effects of a psychoactive drug in a human.

My usual starting point with a new drug is some 10 to 50 times less, by weight, than the known active level of its closest analog. If I have any doubts, I go down by a factor of 10 again. Some compounds that are closely related to previously assayed drugs of low potency have been started at the milligram level. But there are other compounds — those of an entirely new, unexplored class — which I may start nibbling at levels even below a microgram.

There is no completely safe procedure. Different lines of reasoning may lead to different predictions of a dosage level likely to be inactive in man. A prudent researcher begins his exploration at the lowest of these. However, there is always the question, "Yes, but what if —?" One can argue AFTER the fact that — in chemist's jargon — the ethyl group increased the potency over the methyl group because of lipophilicity, or decreased the potency because of ineffective enzymatic demethylation. My decisions, therefore, have had to be a mixture of intuition and probabilities.

There are very few drugs that, upon structural change by a single carbon atom (this is called homologation), change their pharmacological potency by an order of magnitude. There are very few compounds that are orally active at levels much below 50 micrograms. And I have discovered that the very few drugs that are active in the human central nervous system which turn out to be dangerous to the investigator at effective dosages, have usually given some preliminary warnings at threshold levels. If you intend to continue being a live, healthy investigator, you get to know those warning signals well, and immediately abandon further investigation of any drug that presents you with one or more of them. In my research, I am usually looking less for indications of danger than for signs that the new drug may have effects that are simply not useful or interesting to me.

For instance: if I'm trying a new drug at a low dosage level and find myself showing signs of hyper-reflexia, an over-sensitivity to ordinary stimuli — getting jumpy, in plain English — this could be a warning that the drug might, at higher levels, cause convulsions. Convulsants are used in animal research and have their legitimate role in medicine, but they just don't happen to be my cup of tea. A tendency to drift into reverie might be a warning sign; daydreaming is normal behavior when I'm tired or bored, but not when I've just taken a smidgin of a brand new drug and am watching for indications of activity. Or perhaps I become aware that I've been falling into brief episodes of sleep — micro-naps. Either of these signs could lead me to suspect that the drug might be a sedative-hypnotic or a narcotic. Such drugs certainly have their place in medicine, but — again — they're not what I'm looking for.

Once it's been established that the chosen initial dose has been without effect of any kind, I increase the dosage on alternate days, in increments of about a factor of times two at low levels, and perhaps times one and a half at higher levels.

One has to keep in mind that, if a drug is assayed too often, a tolerance to it might develop, even if there is no perceived activity, so that increasing doses may incorrectly appear to be inactive. To minimize this potential loss of sensitivity, no drug is repeated on sequential days. In addition, I periodically give myself a week to being completely drug free. This is especially important if a number of different drugs of similar structural properties are being screened within the same period.

The problem of cross-tolerance — the body having become tolerant because of a recent exposure to a close relative of the drug — is thus avoided.

Over the years, I evolved a method of assigning symbols which refer exclusively to the perceived strength or intensity of the experience, not to the content, which is evaluated separately in my research notes. It could just as well apply to other classes of psychoactive drugs, such as sedative-hypnotics or anti- depressants. I use a system of five levels of effect, symbolized by pluses and minuses. There is one additional level I will describe, but it stands by itself, and is not comparable to the others.

(-) or Minus. There is no effect noted, of any nature, which can be ascribed to the drug in question. This condition is also called "baseline," which is my normal state. So, if the effect of the drug is minus, it means I am in exactly the same state of mind and body I was in before taking the experimental drug.

(±) or Plus-minus. I am feeling a move off baseline, but I can't be absolutely sure it's a drug-effect. There are a lot of false positives in this category, and often my report concludes that what I interpreted as signs of activity were, in fact, products of my imagination.

Here, I will describe briefly something called the "alert." It is some small sign which serves to remind me (in case I have become distracted by phone call or conversation) that I had, indeed, taken a drug. It comes early in the experiment, and is the prelude to further developments. Each member of our research group has his own individual form of alert; one notes a decongestion of the sinuses, another has a tingling at the back of the neck, still another gets a brief runny nose, and I, personally, become aware that my chronic tinnitus has disappeared.

(+) or Plus-one. There is a real effect, and I can track the duration of that effect, but I can't tell anything about the nature of the experience. Depending on the drug, there might be early signs of activity, which can include nausea, even active vomiting (although these are extremely rare). There could be less disturbing effects, such as lightheadedness, compulsive yawning, restlessness, or the wish to remain motionless. These early physical signs, if they arise at all, usually dissipate within the first hour, but they must be considered real, not imaginary. There can be a mental change, but it is not definable as to character. There are seldom false positives in this category.

(++) or Plus-two. The effect of the drug is unmistakable, and not only can its duration be perceived, so can its nature. It's at this level that the first attempts at classification are made, and my notes might read something like this: "There is considerable visual enhancement and much tactile sensitivity, despite a light anaesthesia." (Which means that, although my fingertips might be less than usually responsive to heat or cold or pain, my sense of touch is definitely heightened.) At a plus-two, I would drive a car only in a life-or-death situation. I can still answer the phone with ease, and handle the call competently, but I would much prefer not to have to do so. My cognitive faculties are still intact, and if something unexpected should arise, I would be able to suppress the drug effects without much difficulty until the problem had been taken care of.

It's at this stage, plus-two, that I usually bring in another experimental subject, my wife, Ann. The effects of the drug are distinct enough at this level for her to be able to evaluate them in her own body and mind. She has a metabolism quite unlike my own, and of course a very different mind, so her reactions and responses constitute important information.

(+++) or Plus-three. This is the maximum intensity of drug effect. The full potential of the drug is realized. Its character can be fully appreciated (assuming that amnesia is not one of its properties) and it is possible to define the chronological pattern exactly. In other words, I can tell how soon I get an alert, when the transition stage ends, how long the plateau — or full activity — is in effect before I sense the beginning of a decline, and precisely how steep or gentle the decline to baseline is. I know what the nature of the drug's effects are on my body and mind. Answering the phone is out of the question, simply because it would require too much effort for me to maintain the required normalcy of voice and response. I would be able to handle an emergency, but suppression of the drug effects would require close concentration.

After Ann and I have explored the plus-three range of the new drug, establishing the range of dosage levels at which we get this intensity of effect, we call the research group together and share the drug with them. More will be said about this group in a moment. It is after the members of the research group have submitted their reports on the experience that the synthesis of the new drug and its human pharmacology is ready to be written up for inclusion in a scientific publication.

(++++) or Plus-four. This is a separate and very special category, in a class by itself. The four pluses do not imply in any way that it is more than, or comparable to, a plus-three. It is a serene and magical state which is largely independent of what drug is used — if any drug at all — and might be called a "peak experience," in the terminology of the psychiatrist, Abe Maslow. It cannot be repeated at will with a repetition of the experiment. Plus-four is that one-of-a-kind, mystical or even religious experience which will never be forgotten. It tends to bring about a deep change of perspective or life-direction in the person who is graced with it.

Some 30 years ago, I shared my new discoveries with an informal group of about seven friends; we didn't meet together as a single group, but usually in clusters of three to five, on occasional weekends, when they could spare the time. Most of my exploration was done, at that time, by myself on myself. These original seven have gone on to other things; a few of them have left the Bay Area and dropped out of touch, others have remained good friends whom I see occasionally, but now for dinners and reminiscences, not for drug explorations.

The present research group is a team which numbers eleven when everyone is present, but since two of them live quite far from the Bay Area and cannot always join us, we are usually nine. They are volunteers, some of them scientists, some psychologists, all of them experienced in the effects of a wide number of psychotropic drugs. They know the territory, and these particular people have been working with me for about 15 years. They are a close-knit family whose experience in this area allows them to make direct comparisons to other, familiar altered states, and to equate or critically compare some particular property of a drug's effect. I owe them all immense gratitude for having given me many years of trust in their willingness to explore unknown territory.

The question of informed consent is completely different in the context of this kind of research group, doing this type of exploration. All of our members are aware of the risks, as well as the potential benefits, to be expected in each experiment. The idea of malpractice or legal redress is without meaning within this volunteer group. Every one of us understands that any form of damage, either physical or psychological, suffered by any member as a result of experimentation with a new drug, would be responded to by all other members of the group in any way required, and for as long as it would take for the injured person to regain health. All of us would give financial aid, emotional support, and any other kind of assistance needed, without reservations. But let me add that exactly the same kind of support and care would be given to any member of the group in need, if the circumstances had no relation whatsoever to drug experimentation. In other words, we are close friends.

It should be noted here that, over the course of these 15 years, no physical or mental damage has occurred to any member of the group as a result of drug experimentation. There have been a few times of mental and emotional distress, but the person has always recovered by the time the drug's effects had dissipated.

How does a researcher rank the intensity of a drug's effects, as he perceives them to be? Ideally, such measurements should be objective, free of any opinion or bias on the part of the observer. And the experimental subject should be ignorant of the identity and the expected nature of action. But in the case of drugs like these — psychoactive drugs — the effects can be seen only within the subject's sensorium. Only he can observe and report the degree and nature of the drug's action. Hence, the subject is the observer, and objectivity in the classic sense is impossible. There can be no blind studies.

The question of blind studies, especially double-blind studies, is pointless and, in my opinion, verges upon the unethical, in this area of research. The reason for "blindness," in an experiment is to protect against possible subjective bias on the part of the subject, and objectivity — as I explained earlier — is not possible in this kind of exploration. The subject may well be promoted into an altered state of consciousness, and I consider the idea of failing to advise him of this possibility to be completely improper.

Since the subject in such an experiment has been advised as to the identity of the drug, and the general kind of action which can be expected at the dosage levels which Ann and I have found to be active, and since he knows the time and place of the experiment, and his own dosage, I use the term "double-conscious," instead of "double-blind." This term was originated by Dr. Gordon Alles, a scientist who also explored the realms of altered states with new drugs.

Certain rules are strictly observed. There must be at least three days free of any drug use before the experiment; if one of us is suffering from any kind of illness, no matter how mild, and especially if he is taking medication for it, it is understood that he will not participate in the taking of the experimental drug, even though he might choose to be present during the session.

We meet at the home of one or another of the group, and each of us brings food or drink of some kind. In most cases, the host is prepared for everyone to stay overnight, and we bring sleeping bags or mats. There must be sufficient room to allow for any one of us to separate from the rest of the group if he or she wishes to be alone for a while. The homes we use have garden space where any of us may go to spend time among plants in the fresh air. There are music tapes and art books for whoever might wish to make use of them during the experience.

There are only two procedural demands enforced. It is understood that the words, "Hand in the air," (always accompanied by an actual raising of the speaker's hand) preceding a statement means that whatever is stated is a reality-based concern or problem. If I call out, "Hand in the air," and then go on to state that I smell smoke, it means I am genuinely worried about a real smell of smoke, and not playing some sort of word-game or pursuing a fantasy of some kind. This rule is re-stated at the beginning of each session and is strictly observed.

The second is the concept of veto. If anyone in the group feels discomfort or anxiety about a particular proposal concerning the way the session might go, the power of the veto is complete and is respected by all. For instance, if one person suggests the playing of music at a certain time in the experiment, and is joined by others who like the idea, it is understood that the vote must be unanimous; one person feeling uncomfortable about hearing music assures that it won't be played for the group. This rule doesn't give rise to the problems one might expect, because in most houses which are large enough to accommodate a group of eleven people for such an experiment, there is usually an extra room in which music can be played without disturbing the quiet of other rooms.

There should be something said here about sexual behavior. In our group, it was clearly stated many years ago, and has been understood and observed ever since, that there will be no acting out of sexual impulses or feelings which may arise during an experiment, between people who are not married or in an ongoing relationship with each other. It is the same rule that applies in psychotherapy; sexual feelings can be discussed, if there is a desire to do so, but there will be no physical acting out of such feelings with another member of the group who is not the appropriate object. Of course, if an established couple wishes to retire to a private room to make love, they are free to do so with the blessings (and probably the envy) of the rest of us.

There is the same understanding in regard to feelings of anger or impulses of violence, should they arise. This allows for an openness of expression, and a complete trust that, no matter what kind of unexpected feeling or emotion comes onto the scene, no one will act in such a way as to cause regret or embarrassment, at that time or in the future, to any or all of us.

The researchers are used to treating disagreements or negative feelings the same way they would deal with them in group therapy — by exploring the reasons for the discomfort or anger or irritation. It has long been understood by all of them that exploration of the psychological and emotional effects of a psychoactive drug are, inevitably, synonymous with exploration of their individual psychological and emotional dynamics.

If everyone is healthy, there is no one in the group who does not participate. An exception was made in the case of a long-time participant, a psychologist in his 70's who made a decision during one experimental session to stop taking experimental drugs. He wished, however, to continue participating in the sessions with the rest of us, and we welcomed his presence with enthusiasm. He had a fine time with what is known as a "contact high," until his death a few years later, following heart surgery. We loved him and miss him still.

It's an admittedly unusual structure, but it has worked well in the evaluation of over one hundred psychoactive drugs, many of which have found their way into psychotherapeutic practice of a new and different kind.

Alexander Shulgin, Ph.D.

BOOK I

THE
LOVE
STORY

Part One:

Shura's Voice

CHAPTER 1. THUMB

I was born on June 17, 1925, in the progressive city of Berkeley, California.

My father was Theodore Stevens Borodin, born in the early 1890's. He was the first son of Stevens Alexander Borodin, who was, with the strange logic of the naming hierarchy of the Russian culture, the first son of Alexander Theodore Borodin. As I was a first son, I received my great-grandfather's name, and also became Alexander Theodore. And, in keeping with the Russian custom of giving feminine diminutives to all children (as well as to pets and other loved ones regardless of their sex) I answered to the name of Shura Borodin.

My father was the stern parent who was assigned the role of disciplinarian, although I can't remember his ever having used the oft-threatened belt on me. He had authority, however, and he kept it honed as a teacher of history and literature in Oakland, where the students were mostly Portuguese, and he also taught gardening to the rowdy, school-hating kids. He must have impressed them somehow, because the school garden produced magnificent flowers and you took your life in your hands if you stepped on one of the plants that his students had cultivated and tended.

My father's friends were mostly Russian emigres who had come to this country at the same time he had, in the early twenties. Most of them had escaped Bolshevism by moving eastwards through Manchuria, then south to Japan. And with the opening of the immigration doors by President Harding, many came to San Francisco to start a new life. In this circle there were also the families of his friends, the wives and children. My parents moved in these spheres, which had a Russian flavor, and so did I. I cannot remember any personal friends of my mother, apart from these allies of my father.

I truly believe my father was proud of me, but I'm not sure just why I'm left with that impression. He liked to refer to me as his "son and hair," but he never told me anything about his childhood or his private thoughts. All I knew about his family was that he had five brothers and six sisters, all of whom had been raised in Chelyabinsk, and all of whom were still in Russia. He read avidly, most easily in Russian, and always from pulp-paper books with imprints on the inside cover that said Riga or Moscow. The house was scattered with these plain brownish paperbacks with stark titles, published in some unknown country.

My mother, Henrietta D.D. (for Dorothy Dot), was also born in the early 1890's, in a small town in Illinois. Her studies were in literature, at the state college in Pullman, Washington. She had traveled widely, and chose to express herself with the writing of poetry. Her writing was done on a giant typewriter with a fast unevenness which she always claimed was sufficiently distinct that it would serve her as well as any signature. She had one brother and two sisters, all living in California. In fact, one sister (and her husband and two children) lived near us in Berkeley, on Milvia Street, but we hardly ever saw them. One Christmas, when we were over at their house, I discovered the basement, and there I found the greatest of all possible subterranean treasures — a complete pipe organ in ten million pieces. I dreamed of putting it together some day without telling anyone, finding and connecting an air compressor, and then hitting and holding a full stop B-flat minor chord in the middle of the night, just to see how long it would take to empty the house. I asked Uncle David where the organ came from, and he said he had no idea; it had been there when he bought the house. When he died, the house was torn down for an apartment building, and the beautiful pipe organ pieces were lost and gone forever.

Most of my impressions of my father came from stories told and retold to me by my mother. There was a trip we had all taken when I was very young, to the Great Lakes area, where we picked up a brand new car in Detroit. We drove across the southern tip of Ontario and re-entered the United States at Niagara Falls, in upstate New York. Apparently the immigration people were alerted by the fact that we were driving a spanking new car, and they stopped us and asked questions.

"Are you American citizens?" asked the official at the border station.

"We are," answered my father, who had a clear, distinctly Russian, accent.

"Oh," said the official, aiming his question directly at my father, "Where were you born?"

"Chelyabinsk," was the answer, with an unmistakable touch of pride.

"And where is that?"

"In Russia." I can imitate the accent when speaking the word, but in writing, it's not easy. It comes out with a lightly tongue-trilled "R," followed by a broad, extended vowel, with the texture of the letter "A" in the word "cart." Something like "Rashia," or, better, "Rrraaaashia."

My mother spoke up, trying to explain that my father was indeed born in Russia, but that he had come here in the early '20's and he had sought and received American citizenship. That did it. We were invited to come into the shack that was the immigration office, and answer more questions. Apparently, suspicions are aroused when a wife answers the questions posed to her husband.

"Do you have your naturalization papers with you?"

"No, there is no reason to carry them everywhere," said my father.

"What is the number on your citizenship paper?"

"I have no idea."

"What evidence do you have that you are a citizen?"

"I am a member of the California School Teachers Association. You have to be a citizen to teach in the California public schools."

"How do I know that?"

"Everyone knows that!"

The conversation came around to our Canadian entry. The final exchange was a classic.

"If you are carrying no evidence of U.S. citizenship," asked the aggressive official, "How is it that the Canadian authorities allowed you to enter their country in the first place?"

My father's response was clear and unanswerable, "Because the Canadian authorities are gentlemen."

That did it. Apparently the government man simply hung up his jock, realizing that no one but a genuine American citizen would display that particular kind of arrogance. We were very quickly on our way, in our crisp new 1929 Model A Ford.

Another incident involving my parents painted a somewhat different picture of my father. Around the time I was ten or so, there may have been a period when my father was involved with another woman. I did not know the meaning of the word, "involved," in that context, nor the meaning of "another woman," but something was going on which was uncomfortable for my mother. I was enlisted in a strange little plot. We drove to a motel on San Pablo Avenue, down near the border between Berkeley and Oakland, and my mother asked me to go up to a certain car parked there and to let the air out of one of its tires. That done, we drove back home. Much later that evening, my father returned from his school board meeting with the complaint of having been held up by an unexpected flat tire. I was mystified. Were there some exciting goings-on about which I knew nothing? It was all very intriguing, but it involved my father in some unknown way, and that wasn't comfortable for me.

Again, as with the border incident story, I was seeing my father through my mother's eyes, and now, viewing all these things from the point of view of an older man, it seems to me that they give me as much a measure of her as of my father, some insight, for instance, into her insecurities and her dependence on others.

My pre-college schooling occupied the expected amount of time minus a couple of years for skipped classes, but most of it is lost in a sort of amnesic cloud. Big hand-waving events can be recalled, probably because of re-telling and thus reinforcement, but the day-to-day detail is totally gone.

I can remember which schools I went to, but not a single classmate's name, and there were only three teachers whom I now remember. My mother taught my junior high school English class one year, and my mother's brother, Uncle Harry, taught my algebra class in high school. I also remember that when he had completed the writing of the rough draft of an algebra text to be published for his students, he asked me to read through it and look for errors, which was quite a compliment. The third teacher, Mr. Frederick Carter, was not a relative, but he taught all the music classes, conducted the school orchestra, and led the ROTC band. Music has always been a valuable part of my life.

Come to think of it, there is one student's name that pops up out of the fog. Rick Mundy. He was a noisy show-off, who loved doing suggestive things with uncooked hot dogs at the little lunch counter across Grove Street from University High.

Before high school, I was a little-too-tall, little-too-young, little-too-smart kid who slipped over from the comfortable "me" of pre-adolescence into the terrifying "I" of being a real person who existed apart from everyone else. I didn't see it coming and I wasn't really aware of it when it occurred, but somehow, very gradually, there was a change. Where, earlier, I might get hit by something while playing and I would look down at my leg and think, "Oh, there's blood; the stick did that and my leg hurts," now I began to think in terms of, "I've been hit by that stick; I am bleeding, and I've got a painful leg."

The terrifying aspect of it was the realization that I had to take responsibility for what happened to me. Before, it had always been my parents who fixed things, solved problems, and took care of me. As the ego-awareness (if that's what it's called) came about, I interacted less passively with other people.

I was a child prodigy. I never thought of myself in terms of intellect or intelligence, but I knew that my mother considered me quite advanced and more capable than the others in my age group. I could do this and that on the piano and the violin, and I wrote poetry. As I was growing up, the atmosphere around me always carried a certain expectation that I could do more and do it better.

I hated fights. I saw nothing wrong in getting away as fast as I could from any situation that was building up to one, because physical violence wasn't part of my world; it didn't belong in it, and if I was called names for leaving the scene of a battle, that was okay. I just didn't get any satisfaction out of hitting or getting hit.

Somewhere around age five or six I discovered marbles. There was a marble run next to the fence in the school yard. The structure was the classic one: three holes out from home, then back, then out again and one more, then home (and if you're first, you win some marbles from the other kids). I had a good span, so I could get a slight advantage on my second shot. And some days I would win an aggie, a real aggie. You couldn't tell if your marble was a real aggie unless it would break an ordinary marble, and if it was yours that broke, it wasn't an aggie and you were out a marble for trying.

There were too many older kids there at the school, so I made a marbles course of my own at home in my back yard. After putting a lot of work into it, I had a course superior to the one at school, and I became quite proficient.

My back yard had a fence that ran between our place and the back yard next door. It was completely covered with honeysuckle so that the fence couldn't be seen. The plant held up the fence more than the other way around. It was an immensely high, immensely thick, immensely long mass of what appeared to be free-standing honeysuckle vine, covered with small leaves that grew in opposite directions from one-another, and millions of tiny flowers everywhere.

Of course, I knew that there was really a fence under it all, because I had a secret entry to my tunnels inside the honeysuckle mass, tunnels that no one else knew anything about. This was my own private place. I would go inside my tunnel on one side, through a small hole where a few fence boards had disappeared, to a parallel tunnel on the other side. When I was in there, inside my capsule, I would nip off the base of a blossom and taste the droplet of sweet nectar that oozed out. It was absolutely quiet; even the street-cars that normally rattled up and down Rose Street couldn't be heard. I did not need to move my eyes to see everywhere about me. I didn't need to breathe. I could see no one, and no one could see me. There was no time here. Little bugs that should have been crawling along the stems or on the old, broken boards simply didn't move. Of course, when I would pay attention to something else, then look back, they were in a different place, but while I was looking at them, they didn't move. The only things moving were fantasies, and memory pictures of my past and future, when I was in the honeysuckle place.

The taste of the honeysuckle was a magical connection with this world where every leaf and insect was a friend and I was an intimate part of everything.

Someone decided, one day, that the fence was just too rotten and that everything, old wood and old plants, had to be replaced with something new and clean and certainly safer. I was devastated. When I cried, no one understood why.

But there were other places where I could go and be in my private world. I became a specialist in basements. My mother called it hiding, but I thought of it as escape. From what? Well, for instance, from having to practice the piano. Every day, as soon as I had completed an assignment, a practice run-through of an exercise which was supposed to be done twenty times daily, I could move another toothpick from the right hand treble clef ledge to the left hand bass clef ledge. But my mother never seemed to look at the size of the "completed" pile; she only looked at the shrinking "to be done" pile. It wouldn't have been ethical to move a toothpick from one ledge to the other — that would have been cheating — but if a toothpick accidentally slipped down between the keys, my conscience was clear, and that did seem to happen occasionally.

Other than my uncle David's basement, the first one I truly got to know well was that of our neighbor, the co-owner of the honeysuckle fence. It belonged to an old, old man whose name was Mr. Smythe, pronounced with a long "i" and a soft "th" to rhyme with blithe or scythe.

He was a book dealer, and the agent through whom my father bought his pulp-paper books. But he had received many volumes of Russian literature through Mr. Smythe as well. I remember the complete writings of Tolstoi, some fifty thick volumes of footnotes and memos and laundry-lists, in which just about the only words I could read were the non-Cyrillic imprint of the publisher on the first page which stated that the volumes were the *Edition d'Etat* and were published in *Moscou*. My ancient neighbor lived with his daughter, and some of her family as well. I never got to know any of them.

But I certainly got to know the unbelievably large collection of books in the basement of that house. Thousands of books, all in dusty rows side by side, in neatly stacked wooden orange crates. Every nook and cranny revealed something new. I was always welcome to snoop and explore, and when I would run into Mr. Smythe he would always say: "Shake my hand, young man, and you will be able to say that you have shaken the hand that shook the hand of Mr. Lincoln." It seems that when he had been a small child, his father had taken him to Lincoln's inauguration. So I would shake his hand, and smile, and run away to wait for another day to continue my exploration of his magic collection.

At about this time, I had developed a passion for stamps and stamp-collecting. I routinely visited the big offices of the Bank of Italy (it is now the Bank of America, I believe) and the secretaries would allow me to sift through the wastebaskets and tear off and take the big denomination stamps that never came in the day-to-day mail that my parents received. My mother had many letters and covers saved from her college days at Pullman and from her visit to Egypt, and these had really old stamps, from before I was born, which I carefully floated off and identified in the Scott's catalog. Then I discovered the wastebasket beside the desk of Mr. Smythe, and it was filled with the wrappers of books shipped from around the world. Stamps from Czechoslovakia, Hungary, Yugoslavia, and many other unimaginable places.

Mr. Smythe caught me one time with my nose down in his wastebasket. I was petrified that he would think me a spy or a misbehaver of some sort, but to my great relief he was amused that anyone would find value in the mailing covers of books rather than in the books themselves. He said that he would be happy to tear off the stamps from his mailings and save them for me in a little box that he put on a shelf alongside his desk. I would always look in that box when I wanted to further the stamp exploring adventure, and it was always filled with marvels of strange faces and strange country names. I don't think I said "Thank-you," but I certainly added many new, unknown countries to my collection.

I have for the last few years kept a small cardboard box in the closet of my office, and whenever I receive an interesting cover or package through the mail, I take my scissors and clip off the stamps that are on it and slip the clipping into this box. Someday, somebody visiting me here just might have a six or eight year old along with him who has discovered the miracle of stamps. He will get the whole thing as a present from an old man to a little kid. He may remember me only as that funny old gray-haired person who had a lot of books in his office and got a lot of mail from around the world.

And maybe, I just might shake his hand as well, and tell him that he will now be able to say that he had shaken the hand that shook the hand that shook the hand of Mr. Lincoln.

We had a basement in our own house as well. In this well-explored space, the front part was a concrete room where I set up my first chemistry lab. I think it was called Gilbert Chemistry Set and it contained real chemicals such as bicarbonate of soda and dilute acetic acid, and unfathomable mysteries such as logwood. I haven't, to this day, figured out what logwood is or what one is supposed to do with it. But I kept adding everything I could find to this collection. Stuff from the grocery store down the block, powders and liquids I found in garages and hardware stores. Things would fizz, and smell, and burn, and turn colors. I knew that if I could gather together enough different chemicals, every combination would be new, and would produce wonderful new results.

The back of our basement, the area under the front of the house, was a somewhat mysterious place, and pretty much out of bounds. A friend of my father, a Mr. Peremov, was in some kind of furniture making business, and in our basement he kept large gunny sacks full of hardwood scraps, in many different shapes and sizes. That part of the basement had a bare dirt floor which sloped downward, and the big sacks promised magnificent things — stacking and building and all sorts of great possibilities — but when I tried to put their contents to use, my father found me and I was told the sacks were not to be touched, although I was never given a reason why. I developed a theory that basements were places where treasures could be found, be they pipe organs, stamps, or wooden blocks, especially in the back corners.

Just four houses up the block was another basement, and it was so dark and scary that I persuaded a friend named Jack to go with me and we managed to find and light a small kerosene lantern and we explored the place to the very back wall. No treasures were to be found that time, but we were very lucky anyway, because when my mother found us later, we were both soaked to the skin with kerosene and it was a miracle we hadn't ignited ourselves. The axe came down pretty heavily about basements in general, for a while.

Some years later, I was offered the chance for a private tour of a basement across the street from my uncle's house. The invitation was extended by a girl who was a couple of years older than I, and I was scared in an entirely new way, but intrigued and ready to explore the new kinds of mysterious things that might turn up. But my mother again appeared on the scene and the program was aborted.

A psychologist with nothing better to do might have fun explaining why I decided to put three basements in the house I helped my parents build, just before World War II, here in Almond.

My violin teacher was a Russian gentleman, a compatriot of my father, and connected with the Orthodox Church. I had to play in recitals in strange living-rooms, and turn pages for the accompanists to the first-generation Russian-American daughters who sang. My Russian language tutor was one of my father's co-emigres, and it was not until my fourth (and final) lesson that I provoked him to such fury that he tried to kick me (I had retreated under his dining room table) and I succeeding in biting him on the shin. What had triggered all this violence had been his insistence on my learning the structure of the female gander, and it was only much later that I unraveled the whole thing and realized that what he meant was, of course, gender.

I had another favorite escape which was also a self-challenge, and that was to try to get from Spruce Street clear down to Walnut Street, through Live Oak Park, going from branch to branch in the tops of the trees, without letting my feet touch the ground at all, except for when I had to cross under the street to get to the other side. Once, I grabbed a branch that wouldn't hold my weight and fell with it to the ground and scratched up my knee, but I didn't mention it to anyone.

One day, I went into the men's room in the park. There were remarkable pictures drawn on the walls, and I felt an uneasy guilt at having seen them. I never told anyone about that, either.

I think my parents were in absolute terror that I might possibly learn any little something about whatever went on in the area of sex. Each felt that this aspect of my education was the responsibility of the other. I tried to piece it all together from the obvious mechanisms of masturbation, but there was nothing I could find in my parents' library that brought the female half of it into any logical focus. It was a time of prudery and total modesty and there were no clues, or, if there were, I didn't recognize them.

I slept in a wide bed on the sun-deck on the west side of the top floor, in our house at Rose and Spruce. It was half open to the elements, and the other half was covered and protected. My father slept on a narrower bed across from me, and my mother had her double bed in the big bedroom just inside. They never slept together, to my knowledge.

I had no close friends my own age, and I probably wasn't considered anyone else's best friend, either, but I knew some interesting older people. When I was around eight, there was a boy named Franklin who lived down on Oxford Street and he was all of 14. He built fantastic model planes made of balsa wood and rice paper, held together with airplane cement, which he flew overhead in the air. He would go across the street to Live Oak Park and turn the propeller around and around, until the internal rubber band was triple knotted, then he would put a little magical liquid paraffin on the tail surfaces and strike a match and start a small fire. When it was properly burning, he would let it go and we would watch the streak of orange going across the sky to crash in flames.

My mother had felt it best that I attend the schools that reflected the system's dedication to the "modern" aspects of education, such as experimental teaching methods and child psychology. There was one school at each level that was assigned this state-of-the-art role, and I hit each one. Most of these avant-guard experiments eventually went belly-up, along with the other experimental phenomena which were, and still are, so much a part of the Berkeley philosophy.

Like most other bright kids, I learned not to volunteer answers in class when it was obvious that no one else had them. It caused resentment and fierce looks from my classmates, and made me stand out, and I didn't want that. So I challenged myself in a way that nobody else had to know about. I would try to come up with answers at test time without having more than glanced at any of my books, relying only on what I'd learned from the blackboard and discussions in class.

In Junior High, my only pleasure was in the music and poetry classes.

And mechanical drawing. I can't remember anything else.

In high school, I did well in everything that was simple and obvious (such as chemistry and physics and mathematics and, as I have already mentioned, music) which would flow with no work at all, but anything that required arbitrary and illogical organization (such as grammar and history and spelling) would defeat me, since they were unpredictable and capricious.

An interesting measure of this dichotomy could be seen in my senior year of high school, where I took two examinations in preparation for college. One was called Subject A, a University of California requirement, given to everyone who might actually be admitted to the university, to assure the admission committee of one's basic literacy. Can you spell? Can you make subject and verb agree? Do you split infinitives? Can you write an essay? I totally failed this exam, so I had the pleasure of looking forward to the taking of "Bone-head English" in my freshman year at Berkeley if, indeed, I were to go to the University of California.

However, the second exam was a competitive contest for a National Collegiate Scholarship for a tuition-paid enrollment at Harvard University. This one I managed to pass; in fact, I passed it with a sufficiently high score to win an all expense paid scholarship to Harvard. I accepted the scholarship and went east to Cambridge, Massachusetts. I was 16 years old.

At Cambridge I took lodgings in Wigglesworth Hall right on the Harvard campus itself, and enrolled in freshman courses in math, chemistry, physics and psychology, with a secret desire to really connect with organic chemistry. I found myself a student in a social system which was completely alien to me. Everything was measured on the basis of who your family was, where you'd taken your preparatory studies, and just how much money your family had. My family was unknown, I had gone to a public high school, and neither my parents, as teachers, nor I, as the son of teachers, had any wealth or any immediate prospect of acquiring it. Hence, I rated as a non-person. Furthermore, I was younger than most of the others, so I spent the year without developing personal relationships with anyone. I was a fish out of water, and I was miserable.

The United States was involved in World War II, and the armed services gave the music of adultness and independence. In my second year at Harvard I joined the U. S. Navy's V-12 officer's training program, which would lead to a commission if I could only complete my baccalaureate in some subject. But my scholastic record was abysmal, and I knew I could never survive another two years. I abandoned officerial hopes and found myself at Pier 92, the enlisted man's gathering point in New York City. I survived six weeks of mid-winter boot camp at Sampson, New York, and manipulated myself into a training course at Norfolk, Virginia, emerging with a third-class fire-control rating.

My involvement in World War II was an experience that included some adventures, certainly, but there were so many negatives that I would just as soon not recall most of it. One event, however, I will always remember, because it led to an observation that shaped the rest of my life. I discovered the remarkable world of psychopharmacology and, most important of all, the power of the mind over the body.

I was on a destroyer escort (the USS Pope, DE-134) in the middle of the Atlantic in the middle of winter, in the middle of the anti-U-boat campaign, in the middle of the war. We had just finished making an anti-submarine search in the area of the Azores. All during this part of the war in the Atlantic, one of the centers of military activity was the port of Ponta Delgada, in the Azores, where the United States made available a large supply of fuel to the neutral Portuguese who, in turn, made it available to anyone who chose to pay for it. So the German U-boats came in and fueled, then the U.S. destroyers came in and fueled. The only rule was that no two different flags could fly in the harbor within 24 hours of one another. The cat and mouse game in the Atlantic, just outside the harbor, was extremely dicey, and led to all kinds of nasty military interactions. But, now, having fueled up and gotten back out to the open sea intact, we set a course for England. There was a lot of boredom, and some moments of acute fright, then something happened in the way of a personal trauma. About a thousand miles off the coast of England, I developed a severe infection, from some unknown source, on the face of my left thumb. It localized itself at this unusual place and went down through the flesh and tissue directly to the bone. It was very painful, and I was being attended to by our ship's medical corpsman, affectionately referred to as the Chancre's Mate.

The course of treatment had a simple goal: I was to be protected from pain. Surgery was said to be absolutely necessary, and there was no way to perform it at sea. So my thumb problem got worse and worse, as did the chop in the Irish Sea as we approached England, and I was given, with regularity, modest injections of morphine.

This was my introduction to the effect of a drug on the perception of pain. The man with the needle would interrupt a good rolling poker game to ask me how I was feeling. I would look at my thumb and say, "It's a little worse," or "It's a little better," and put my arm out for another morphine shot, then immerse myself again in the poker game. I knew the pain was there, and I could report on the intensity of it with accuracy, but it didn't bother me. I could play poker, I could deal, I could judge the opposition, and I could bet shrewdly, and I came out ahead more than behind. My left thumb was viciously painful, but the pain just didn't get in my way. It was fascinating to me that one could be hurting, in agony, and that the administering of a little bit of a chemical that came from some poppy flowers somewhere, could make it all quite unimportant. This is what is meant by central analgesia. The pain is not deadened; it is still there. The site of action is not the thumb but, rather, the brain. The problem is simply no longer of concern. Morphine is a pretty remarkable drug.

When we docked at Liverpool, I learned that the Navy hospital no longer existed and that the Army was now running things. Their hospital was located at Watertown, near Manchester, which was quite a way inland. I was scheduled to be taken there by ambulance — not right away, but pretty soon. In the meantime, my own personal home, the USS Pope, was tied up just outboard to the British counterpart vessel, a frigate which had been christened the HMS Wren. And since I was a petty officer, and there were allied petty officers aboard the Wren, I was invited aboard to share rum and companionship.

I remember myself in snug quarters, rum in hand, being given moral support for my imminent relocation to some remote hospital owned and operated by the Army. The memory is of friendship and laughter. Rum, too, is a pretty effective drug.

Then came a big monster of an ambulance which took me from Liverpool to Watertown and delivered me to a white-coated Army staff. A young nurse volunteered to make me comfortable with a glass of orange juice, to relieve my thirst, but at the bottom of the orange juice I saw an unmistakable layer of undissolved white crystalline solids. I wasn't going to be hoodwinked by a bunch of soldiers! The juice was obviously a sophisticated cover-up for the administration of some dramatic sedative or presurgical anesthetic which was expected to render me placid and unconcerned about the medical procedures they had planned for me.

I resolved to prove my masculinity and control of the situation by simply denying the white crystals their power. I would drink the whole mixture down, but I would stay awake and alert. I would be wheeled into the surgical bay as an attentive sailor who would challenge the Army surgeons with analytical perception and penetrating questions which would reveal to them the integrity of my mental status.

It didn't work. The drug that rested undissolved under my orange juice was undeniably a pretty effective drug, because I succumbed to it and went completely unconscious. I have no memory of the intravenous Pentothal anesthetic that was administered to me for my surgery. And I was later told of the unprecedented half-hour I required for recovery from it.

The bone infection was surgically removed, and to this day my left thumb is almost a half-inch shorter than my right.

Now I found myself somehow attached to the Army during my convalescence, stationed far from the coast of England and, again, a fish out of water. I was a sailor in an Army installation. I discovered that the Army pay-code identification number was exactly one number longer than that of the Navy pay-code, so I quite logically added one number to my identification and spent Army money in all the local bars. The people who lived in the area were familiar with the Army crowd, but not used to a Navy uniform in their neighborhood. However, since I was wandering about without any attention from the local military police, it was presumed that I was with some allied military force — the Dutch, maybe, or the Free-French. In any case, there was no way that I might be one of the enemy. And since my left hand and arm were all bundled up in a monster sling and bandage, I was undoubtedly someone *hors de combat* and the buying of a drink for me by the local gentry was the least they could do for a swab who had given his left arm for the Motherland. Nice duty. Eventually I healed, and had to become reoriented to military reality, but in the meantime I had learned a couple of facts.

The first was simple and not exactly surprising: there was no communication between the Army and the Navy, which meant that the pay chaos which I had instituted by the addition of a small integer was safely lost in the shuffle.

The second fact was not expected at all, and it was this that started me on my career as a psychopharmacologist. I was told that the white "drug" which was undissolved at the bottom of my orange juice glass, and which had finally plopped me over the line from being an alert and defensive surgery candidate to being a comatose subject available to any and all manipulation by the operating physician, was nothing but undissolved sugar.

A fraction of a gram of sugar had rendered me unconscious, because I had truly believed that it could do just that. The power of a simple placebo to radically alter my state of consciousness impressed me deeply. The contribution of the mind to the observed action of a drug was certainly real, and I decided it was possible that this contribution was a major one.

Over the intervening years, I have come to believe that the mind is *the* major factor in defining a psychoactive drug's action. One has been taught to assign the power of a drug to the drug itself, without considering the person into whom it goes. A drug by itself can be a powder, a spoonful of sugar, without any curative value whatsoever. But there is a personal reality of the recipient of the drug that plays a major role in the definition of the eventual interaction. Each of us has his own reality, and each of us will construct his own unique drug-person relationship.

The shock of the orange juice sugar caper led me to try to explore any and all tools that I might use to define that relationship. And when the tools that are needed are not, in fact, known, they must be discovered or created. They might be drugs that alter the states of consciousness (such as sugar when it is believed to be not-sugar), or they might be states of transcendence reached in meditation. They might be moments of orgasm, or fugue states, or day-dreams that take you momentarily to a rewarding fantasy and escape from responsibility. All of these are treasures of the spirit or psyche that allow exploration along paths which are undefined and completely individual.

I decided right then, and with total conviction, that drugs probably represented the most predictable and reliable tools for such studies. So I would become a pharmacologist. And, considering that all of the action was located upstairs in the brain, I'd better make that a psychopharmacologist.

I eventually returned to the West Coast and entered the University of California at Berkeley. They had lost all records of my Subject A trial, and allowed me to repeat it. I failed it again, but — pleading various stresses and infirmities expected of a World War II veteran — I was permitted to let it drift for another year. My third effort was a rousing success, as I was by then completely familiar with the structure that was expected. My prepared essay (it dealt with a hypothetical pre-Egyptian nuclear civilization) was perfect in tense and subject agreement, and immaculate in punctuation.

CHAPTER 2. MESCALINE

Mescaline: a magic name and a magic compound. My first encounter with this word was just after World War II, when I returned to Berkeley and managed to work my way into the University of California, finally to become located in the Chemistry Department. The usual process for undergraduate students in chemistry was to pursue a mountain of highly technical courses, and get a B.S. in Chemistry, within the College of Chemistry. I chose, rather, to explore a wider variety of topics, and to accept an A.B. in the College of Letters and Science. From there, I wandered over towards the more medically directed disciplines, and explored the area of biochemistry.

I had learned a valuable lesson as a violin player who loved to play in string quartettes. There are a lot of violinists, and most of them are very good. But every quartette needs one violist, and there really aren't enough of them. As a so-so fiddler, I was hard-put to participate in chamber music, but as a so-so violist I got a lot of invitations to play. The parallel to chemistry is exact. As a so-so chemist, I found myself accepted but rarely in demand. But in the area of biochemistry there were very few chemists (at least at that time) and I became a top-flight student. After a few years of courses and an uninspired research project, I wrote a dull thesis and emerged with a Ph.D. degree from a major academic institution, the University of California.

During this 1940-1950 period, there was almost no attention being given to the alkaloid, mescaline. In fact, the entire family of compounds of which mescaline is a part was virtually unknown. A few articles had appeared which talked about the "mescaline psychosis," and several publications had been widely circulated decrying the evils of Peyote as made evident by the ruin which had befallen the "simple" American Indians. In the area of serious and thoughtful texts, there were the writings and the famous maps of Alexander Rouhier in 1926. There was the treatise by Kurt Beringer, which described the responses of many scores of subjects to effective doses of mescaline, administered almost always by injection. His book, "Der Meskalinrausche siene Geschichte und Erscheinungsweise," (1927) has never been translated into English. Weston La Barre wrote in 1938 of the Peyote religion. That was pretty much it.

I was completely intrigued. Here were cultural, psychological, and religious describers of the action of a compound that appeared to have magical properties. The material could be easily synthesized. But I remained obedient to an invisible hand which rested on my shoulder and said, "No, do not taste yet." I read all the more recent literature about it that had appeared, the essays of Aldous Huxley in the mid-1950's (the exuberant Doors of Perception and the more cautious Heaven and Hell) and the generally negative reflections of Henri Michaux (Miserable Miracle). But it was not until April of 1960 that a psychologist friend of mine, Terry Major, and a friend of his who was studying medicine, Sam Golding, reinforced my interest and provided me with the opportunity to be "babysat" on an experience with 400 milligrams of mescaline sulfate. It was a day that will remain blazingly vivid in my memory, and one which unquestionably confirmed the entire direction of my life.

The details of that day were hopelessly complex and will remain buried in my notes, but the distillation, the essence of the experience, was this. I saw a world that presented itself in several guises. It had a marvel of color that was, for me, without precedent, for I had never particularly noticed the world of color. The rainbow had always provided me with all the hues I could respond to. Here, suddenly, I had hundreds of nuances of color which were new to me, and which I have never, even today, forgotten.

This world was also marvelous in its detail. I could see the intimate structure of a bee putting something into a sack on its hind leg to take to its hive, yet I was completely at peace with the bee's closeness to my face.

The world was a wonder of interpretive insight. I saw people as caricatures which revealed both their pains and their hopes, and they seemed not to mind my seeing them this way.

More than anything else, the world amazed me, in that I saw it as I had when I was a child. I had forgotten the beauty and the magic and the knowingness of it and me. I was in familiar territory, a space wherein I had once roamed as an immortal explorer, and I was recalling everything that had been authentically known to me then, and which I had abandoned, then forgotten, with my coming of age. Like the touchstone that recalls a dream to sudden presence, this experience reaffirmed a miracle of excitement that I had known in my childhood but had been pressured to forget.

The most compelling insight of that day was that this awesome recall had been brought about by a fraction of a gram of a white solid, but that in no way whatsoever could it be argued that these memories had been contained within the white solid. Everything I had recognized came from the depths of my memory and my psyche.

I understood that our entire universe is contained in the mind and the spirit. We may choose not to find access to it, we may even deny its existence, but it is indeed there inside us, and there are chemicals that can catalyze its availability.

It is now a matter of history that I decided to devote whatever energies and skills I might possess to unraveling the nature of these tools for self-exposure. It has been said that wisdom is the ability to understand others; it is the understanding of yourself that is enlightenment.

I had found my learning path.

CHAPTER 3. BURT

In the late 1940's I married a fellow-student at University of California named Helen. We were both active members of a small social collection, a Tower-and-Flame/Honor-Student/Phi-Beta-Kappa group, that had a couple of small meeting rooms buried in an old campus building known as California Hall. In fact, we called ourselves the Cal Hall crowd, and we all shared the common characteristics of being reasonably intelligent and socially awkward. The beginning of my relationship with Helen, interestingly, had a certain chemical component, in that one day I came into Cal Hall reeking of vanillin (the essential component of the extract of vanilla) which I had been using in large quantities up in the chemistry labs. She liked the smell, and we soon became a going-steady twosome. She was also a single child, of Scottish descent, and she had red hair.

We were married in the face of some rather strong parental objections on both sides, and about a year later, we had a son whom we would have named Stevens Alexander, had we followed the old Russian traditions dealing with the first-born. But we decided on Theodore Alexander instead, in honor of my father, and the nickname Theo has stuck. When, a few years later, I earned my Ph.D. in Biochemistry, Helen graduated with a A.B., having majored in Slavic Languages. Her Russian was very good; in fact, it was a lot better than mine.

I was offered, and accepted, a position as a chemist with Dole Chemical Company, and within the first couple of years I made the powers that be very happy by predicting the structure of, and synthesizing, an insecticide that actually went into commercial production. In return for this they granted me freedom to research and develop anything I wished. This is the ultimate reward for any chemist.

And what I wished to do, as a result of my remarkable mescaline experience, was to explore the world of centrally active drugs, with a special emphasis on the psychedelic drugs. I launched into a number of synthetic variations of the mescaline molecule, but a most unusual problem was becoming apparent. There is no animal model that has ever been developed or, as far as I can predict, will ever be developed, for the characterization and evaluation of a psychedelic drug. Thus, all discovery must use the human animal and I was, by default, that animal. Quite simply, as I developed new structures that might show some interesting action in the realms of thought or perception, I used myself as the experimental test subject to determine these actions. Although there were a few of the people I worked with who were aware of my tasting techniques, most were not. I had to construct some scientifically justifiable procedures that could be looked at, discussed, and rationalized as providing the evidence that might at least seem to answer the question, "How much does it take?" And that would be an infinitely easier question to pretend to answer than the obvious follow-up, "What does it do?"

I read what little literature there was, on the effects of LSD-like drugs on experimental animals. I needed some scientific looking experimental structure, so that when the research director would bring by some visitors whom he wished to impress, he could point to the laboratory and tell the visiting firemen, "Here is where all the research on psychedelic drugs is done!" The two most popular small-animal demonstrations of the time were Siamese fighting fish and spiders. The spiders were reported to weave dose-dependent construction errors into their webs as a measure of the intoxication of LSD. And the fish (they were called *Beta splendens*, as I remember) were presumably quite sensitive to LSD, and would do something strange when small amounts of it were put in their water; swim backwards or upside down, or something else equally bizarre.

Not wishing to set up cobwebs, I chose the fish route, and sent off to Van Waters and Rogers for several big battery jars, to the local pet store for a supply of fighting fish, and to the Swiss pharmaceutical house, Sandoz, for a gram of LSD. Everything arrived promptly, and along with it all came my dear friend Burt from the analytical department. He was a careful and most conservative gentleman, but he was also the most naturally curious person in the whole building. He had a continuing fascination with the strange goings-on in this "psychedelic" laboratory. He had seen the opened package from Sandoz Labs, which contained a small double-ended vial which, in turn, contained a glass ampule labeled, "Lysergide, an experimental compound, etc." He helped me in trying to establish normal behavior patterns with the fighting fish so that abnormal changes might be seen that would reflect exposure to a drug. He became, as a matter of fact, my constant companion.

Well, the lab soon looked like an aquarium. Bell jars on all lab benches. Aerators bubbling and lights shining. Fish were being transferred here and there, in a very scientific manner, from the big tanks into beakers with graded amounts of LSD in them, while Burt and I watched and watched. We never saw anything occur that was even slightly suggestive of a drug effect.

One thing that did become rapidly apparent, though, was that the growth of algae was not inhibited in the least by either the fish or the LSD, and soon the tanks were thickly green with fuzz. This led to the discovery that small snails could control the algae, but there was nothing that could control the snails. Anyone guiding a tour of the lab had to somehow improvise quite creatively to explain the assay procedures being used in the exploration of psychedelic drugs, since the fish could no longer be seen for the forest of competing wildlife which had taken over.

At about this time, I had need of a reference sample of psilocybin, so again I called upon Sandoz for a gift. In a few days, Burt wandered into the lab carrying a small double-ended vial that contained, in turn, a glass ampule labeled, "Psilocybin, for experimental use, etc." My gram had arrived. We fed it in varying amounts to the fish-algae-snails, but it did no better than the LSD.

One morning, a couple of weeks later, I took a small, double-ended vial to Burt in his analytical lab down the hall, and asked him to please weigh out for me a small quantity of material into a separate container. The actual amount was not important, a few milligrams; what was important was that I wanted the weight accurate to four places. He disappeared for a few minutes, then reappeared with the vial I had given him and also a weighing container holding a small amount of an almost white powder.

"Here is 3.032 milligrams, exactly," he said, adding, "And it's slightly bitter."

"How do you know?" asked I.

"After I weighed out the psilocybin, there was a trace of dust on the spatula, so I licked it off. Slightly bitter."

I asked him, "Did you read the label carefully?"

"It's the vial of psilocybin you just received, isn't it?" he asked, looking at the funny-shaped tube still in his hand. He read the label. It said Lysergide. He said, "Oh."

We spent the next several minutes trying to reconstruct just how much LSD might have been on the end of the spatula, and decided that it was probably not more than a few score micrograms. But a few score micrograms can be pretty effective, especially in a curious but conservative analytical chemist who is totally drug naive.

"Well," I said to him, "This should damned well be a fascinating day."

And indeed it was. The first effects were clearly noted in about twenty minutes, and during the transition stage that took place over the following forty minutes, we wandered outside and walked around the pilot plant behind the main laboratory building. It was a completely joyful day for Burt. Every trivial thing had a magical quality. The stainless steel Pfaudler reactors were giant ripe melons about to be harvested; the brightly colored steam and chemical pipes were avant-garde spaghetti with appropriate smells, and the engineers wandering about were chefs preparing a royal banquet. No threats anywhere, simply hilarious entertainment. We wandered everywhere else on the grounds, but the theme of food and its sensory rewards continued to be the leitmotif of the day.

In the late afternoon, Burt said he was substantially back to the real world, but when I asked him if he thought he could drive, he admitted that it would probably be wise to wait a bit longer. By 5:00 PM, he seemed to be happily back together again, and after a trial run — a sort of figure-eight in the almost empty parking lot — he embarked on his short drive home.

Burt never again, to my knowledge, participated in any form of personal drug investigation, but he maintained a close and intimate interest in my research and was always appreciative of the slowly evolving picture of the delicate balance between chemical structure and pharmacological action, which I continued to share with him while I remained at Dole.

One periodically hears some lecturer holding forth on the subject of psychedelic drugs, and you may hear him give voice to that old rubric that LSD is an odorless, colorless and tasteless drug. Don't believe it. Odorless yes, and colorless when completely pure, yes, but tasteless, no. It is slightly bitter.

And if you ever hear a rumor that marine snails can be used to assay psychedelic drugs, don't believe that, either. It was probably started by one of the visiting firemen touring my lab.

CHAPTER 4. TMA

It is 1960. Here I am, with my mescaline experience dramatically fresh in mind, a burning desire to explain its profound action to myself and the rest of mankind, and there is a total world inventory of, at best, a dozen such drugs known. And only two of them, TMA and MDA, have phenethylamine structures that in any way resemble mescaline. (Actually only one was known to me at this time, since the book in which the MDA report appeared didn't get into my hands for another two years.)

So there was one analogue of mescaline known, and what was known about it? TMA had first been synthesized some 12 years earlier by a chemist named P. Hey at the University of Leeds. His literature presentation was pure, cold chemistry, but he must have tasted it, for the Peretz and Smythies group in Canada alluded in its report to a private communication from Dr. Hey that he had been impressed with its euphoric properties. In the Canadian study, TMA was administered in the 50 to 100 milligram range to nine subjects. There was noted at about an hour a transient headache and slight nausea which could be avoided by pretreatment with Dramamine. At two hours there was the onset of giddiness, an increase in movement and communication and some loss of inhibition. Some later trials involving dosages of up to 125 milligrams were coupled with studies involving stroboscope-induced "hallucinations. "

So this is where I started. The drug was easily synthesized, and my preliminary assays largely paralleled the Canadians' findings. At the 140 milligram level, I watched three close friends have three distinctly different experiences. Terry Major had a brief period of nausea, which evolved into a very euphoric and responsive mood. The talking of the two others bothered him and he spoke sharply to them; his exact words were, "Please shut up!" This was his only show of aggression. Sam Golding was free of nausea, and had much eyes-closed patterning. At about the four hour point, he became extremely talkative, and was the primary inspiration for

Terry's spurt of irritability. These periods of talkativeness alternated with periods of reverie and ceiling-staring. Sam's over-all conclusion was that the drug was not completely pleasant, as it allowed him too intimate a view of himself. I refrained from editorializing on this remark, though sorely tempted. Paris Mateo, a psychiatrist, was also free of nausea, but he was very lightly affected. His major interest seemed to be in my reactions to his reactions (I was the control observer in this experiment, forgoing any personal imbibing). The consensus of all three was that the effects were of a potency almost twice that of mescaline, and that mescaline was to be preferred.

About a month later, I took 225 milligrams of TMA, having already taken 50 milligrams of Marezine (an anti-nausea drug) one hour earlier. This drug mixture is a process that I have long since abandoned. If nausea is to be part of the drug's effect, then let it be experienced and assigned. And when one is exploring a new drug, why complicate any observations by superimposing a second drug? Drug-drug interactions are a complex study unto themselves.

I had two baby-sitters, Helen and my old friend, Terry Major, again.

About three-quarters of an hour after taking the TMA, I experienced a moderately severe nausea, but this didn't last long. During the period of peak intoxication (from about the one and a half hour point to about four hours) there was only a modest color enhancement, and several of the other mescaline-like features were also noted. There was some slight change in the perception of motion and time, and some loss of physical coordination. But it was my mental attitude, and responses to, and identification with external stimuli (primarily musical) that were the most startling. While reading Bernstein's "Joy of Music," I felt, with great delight, that I could actually hear every musical phrase mentioned, but Helen claimed that I was making pugnacious and condemnatory remarks about what I was reading.

I turned on the radio to a music station, curled up and closed my eyes. Rachmaninoff's second piano concerto provided me a structure from which I could suspend myself so as not to touch the ground, holding on to the finely woven strands of arpeggios which were knotted with chords.

Then, after some commercials which annoyed me, came the rather noisy and strident music-poem, "Slaughter on 10th Avenue," which proved to be an unfortunate choice, because I went somewhat sociopathic. Helen remarked on the don't-cross-me-if-you-know-what's-good-for-you look on my face.

I was handed a rose (which under mescaline would have been precious and entrancing) and was asked if I could hurt it. I crushed it without hesitation. At that point, Terry asked me if I might consider taking a small amount of a tranquilizing medication. My response was a thinly veiled threat to push him downstairs if he tried to medicate me. He didn't pursue the subject.

Shortly thereafter we all headed for the open spaces of Tilden Park (I remarked grimly that it was just as well there was a car which could serve to protect other people from me) and, once there, I discharged the anger with a couple of thrown rocks and a stick (barely missing Terry's car, not out of consideration for him, but because I knew that making a dent in it would cause me all sorts of problems later, such as having to pay for the damage). This acting-out period passed and the nicer aspects — visual fun and games, for the most part — remained uppermost for the rest of the day.

This was an immensely important learning experience for me. My earlier mescaline experiment had been full of beauty and light, and I had rejoiced that this was what my soul contained, deep within, that this sensitivity and compassion was what had been brought to the surface by that simple catalyst. Yet here was a substantially identical molecule that produced something, at least in me, quite opposite. It was only after a great deal of introspection that I realized that mescaline no more produced beauty than TMA produced anger. Just as the beauty was always within me, so was the anger.

Different drugs may sometimes open different doors in a person, but all of those doors lead out of the same unconscious.

Paris conducted twelve additional experiments with TMA in South America, all in the 150 to 200 milligram range. He sent back reports that strongly emphasized color effects, and made considerable comparisons to LSD, equating the effects to the one hundred to two hundred microgram range of the latter drug.

All of these findings, taken together, led to a research paper that was published in the British journal Nature, in which the psychedelic properties were discussed for audience appeal, but the aggressive potential was specifically mentioned as an observed reaction. It was my first publication in the area of the action of psychedelics in man.

Some 17 years later, with more experience behind me, I tried TMA again to get a feeling of just how I might have changed in my responses over time and with repeated exposures to these materials. This recalibration is a process that I do periodically. It is something like going to the firing range or your internist once every ten years or so, but always with the same pistol (and the same body). It is good to get an objective evaluation of changes that have occurred in yourself as you age. This is especially true when the response to a drug is strongly colored by attitudes and interpretations, which are invariably tempered by the passing of the years.

Anyway, I re-titrated TMA from the lowest levels all over again, and got to a plus two at 130 milligrams, the very level at which my three allies had found it interesting but not particularly exciting. The observed chronology was unchanged, but the qualitative aspects of the experience were indeed not too pleasant. Two adjectives are sometimes used interchangeably: psychedelic and psychotomimetic, the first denoting a fundamentally benign alteration of consciousness, and the other (literally, the imitation of psychosis) implying a lack of empathy and caring. I have limited my use of the latter to titles of articles that are to be published in journals that might look upon the use of the term "psychedelic" as advocative. But I still feel that TMA might show hints of the latter meaning.

I was also aware of a considerable body discomfort and physical side-effects such as muscular twitching, and I was relieved when the experiment was over. Having safely exited the world of TMA, I could think of no compelling reason to enter it ever again.

CHAPTER 5. BLACKWOOD ARSENAL

It was somewhere around 1960 that I met a brilliant neurologist, Harry Bush, who had become totally fascinated by lichens, and had invested much effort in their identification and characterization. I learned much from him about the symbiosis between algae and fungi, and I learned that some of the chemicals contained in lichens can easily be brought to react with certain essential oils from natural sources, to make a synthetic tetra-hydrocannabinol or THC (the active component of marijuana). There was considerable satisfaction for me, and more than a little humor, in the knowledge that, by wandering around a camp ground and mixing an extract of the colored scabs flicked off a big rock with some orange peels from the nearest garbage can, in the presence of phosphorus oxychloride (you would have to bring that yourself), and finally putting the cleaned-up product on parsley and rolling it into a kind of cigarette, you could produce a potentially psychoactive smoke.

All this led me to a lot of literature searching and quite a bit of chemical diddling (I was still working at Dole), and it was through this that I was introduced to the wonderful world of plant products. I was already well aware of the strongly alkaline compounds known as the alkaloids. These were the nitrogen-containing products most often responsible for the bio-logical activity of the plant. Drugs such as nicotine, strychnine and quinine are famous, and even the psychedelic area is well represented by indoles such as DMT, 5-methoxy-DMT, psilocin, psilocybin, and our archetypal phenethylamine, mescaline. But I began to appreciate other families, usu-ally neutral compounds that were inactive, but which smelled nice and were potential starting materials for chemical synthesis. There were ter-penes which are the sharp smells of conifers and camphor. And there are the magnificent essential oils that are the smells of the spice cabinet; the oils of nutmeg, clove, parsley, dill, and apiole. And on and on. This little-studied collection of chemicals proved to be an unending source of ideas in the psychedelic area.

Then, three things occurred in rapid sequence. First (and of interest mostly to people who fool around with chemistry), I sharpened up the lichen/orange peel strategy and found that the condensation product from olivetol (which could actually be isolated from certain lichens that I collected just north of Ottawa) and pulegone (a terpene from pennyroyal, a peppermint-like plant that can be found growing profusely near Alamogordo in New Mexico), produced a sizable quantity of the marijuana-like material resembling THC. The groundwork for this chemistry was laid by Roger Adams, at the University of Illinois, before World War II. He, and A. R. Todd at the University of Manchester, in England, had a vigorous rivalry being waged in the chemical literature as to who could get closer to the chemical duplication and animal demonstration of the active components of marijuana. The culmination of Adam's work was the preparation of a mixture of synthetic products that proved, in his dog model, to be many times more potent than the natural drug. This has been called, "Adam's nine-carbon compound," since it has, not surprisingly, a nine-carbon unit in the terpene half of the molecule. This point is mentioned here only because it will reappear a little later in this account. An interesting sidelight is the fact that the precise structure of THC was still unknown at this time (some twenty years after the conclusion of Adam's work).

Secondly, it occurred to me that Mother Nature, which thoroughly loves alkaloids, kind of blew it in letting the Cannabis plant make a psychoactive compound devoid of nitrogen (the necessary component of an alkaloid). What would THC look like pharmacologically if it were a phenethylamine? I said to myself, "Let's make it!" So I hied myself off to the library to begin unraveling some possible paths to the synthesis.

And thirdly, a group of researchers (men with cautious faces, wearing proper suits and ties) from the Blackwood Arsenal, the chemical and biological warfare branch of the U. S. military, visited Dole to meet with some of the company's scientists in a brain-storming session. The visitors had some synthetic problems which could only be stated in the most general of terms, as they involved compounds that could not be explicitly described, having been assigned some classified information status, and some of us who were present did not have any kind of security clearance.

Anyway, the sum total of their query was neatly organized on a slide which showed a reaction scheme down the left-hand side of the screen, leading to the penultimate compound A, and another scheme down the right-hand side of the screen, leading to the penultimate compound B. The product (from A reacting with B) was not on the screen at all, since it was considered secret. Their questions centered on the two displayed sequences. Could any of us come up with some jazzy ideas for easier or better syntheses of either A or B?

Ideas were bounced around for a while, then I got into one of my more manic moods and grabbed some chalk. I said, in essence, that although none of our visitors were prepared to say just why it was they wanted efficient ways of making A and B, it seemed an interesting coincidence that the simple coupling of A and B (using the phosphorus oxychloride procedure that worked so well with the lichens and citrus fruit) would surely produce "Adam's nine-carbon compound," which was (in case they were not aware of it) some five hundred and twelve times more potent in the dog motor ataxia test than the synthetic THC analog which was being used at the time as a reference standard.

Silence.

I bubbled on — having written the structure of this obviously classified compound on the blackboard — that if one were to conduct the synthesis as had been suggested on the slide in any way other than the explicit procedure described by Adams, one would end up with a mixture of products which would (due to the fact that there are several optically active centers involved) produce a mixture containing a total of eight isomers. And if any deviation were to be made from the original synthesis, the ratio of these isomers just might be radically changed, with a resulting biological activity that might be radically different from that observed by Adams (the 512 times potency job).

The silence was thicker.

More manic yet, I went on to say that, to be completely scientific about it all, these eight compounds should each be explicitly synthesized as individuals, and should each be separately assayed as unique entities. And, as a throw-away, I mentioned that if they really wanted to remedy Nature's sloppiness, they should consider synthesizing this unnameable target compound with a nitrogen atom in it, so as to emulate an alkaloid. That, I added in conclusion, might be a really super-potent phenethylamine!

The silence persisted for a few moments, and when the talking eventually resumed, it wended its way into other areas, and eventually the visitors returned to Maryland.

The entire incident was forgotten with the trauma that accompanied the unexpected and untimely death of my mother, while she and my father were at their summer cabin at Lake Tahoe, high in the Sierra Nevadas. It was a difficult transition for Helen and me, but especially so for Theo, who had developed a close and intimate relationship with his grandmother. As to my father, I noted signs of a subtle deterioration which we all saw as progressively robbing him of both spirit and motivation.

Finally, I said Enough! Let's all go on some sort of short get-away, to give ourselves a chance to repair. Where should we go? It didn't matter, I said; I'll take care of it. So my father put a clean pair of socks and a change of underwear into a satchel, and all four of us set out for San Francisco, supposedly headed for San Diego. In actuality, unbeknownst to my father, I had arranged to have the house sealed off for a long absence, and I'd gotten tickets on the P & O ship Chusan for a trip, not just to San Diego, but past it to Panama, then to Trinidad, Barbados, the Canary Islands, England, and on to France, where we would stay for a year. The true unrest cure, as in the wonderful short story by H. H. Munro.

(The plan worked. My father had to buy a whole new wardrobe; he re-established contacts with Russian-speaking friends whom he hadn't seen for a quarter of a century; he completely severed himself from his grief-obligations, rediscovered his identity and his energy, and he later remarried, opened a restaurant, and lived another fifteen years. But that, as they say, is another story.)

Back to the beginning of our trip. We were about a day out of Port-au-Prince when the first bird from the Blackwood Arsenal nest came home to roost. It was about five in the morning, and Helen and I were sound asleep in our dark inside stateroom on D-deck, when there was a rapping at the door. I got up and uttered a very bad word; I had forgotten I was in the upper bunk, so my step down to the floor was a four-foot jolt. I opened the door to meet, face to face for the first time, Mr. Munoz of the radio room.

"I have a radio communication from RCA International for you," he said, handing it to me. I found a flashlight and read it. Some 500 words from a Dr. Frederick Pearsman at A.R.L. Company in Cambridge, Mass., saying — nay, demanding — that I call him from Trinidad collect when I arrived (we were due there the next day). I had no sooner gotten back to sleep, than there was another knock on the door. Mr. Munoz, again. He said that he had just received another radio communication for me, this time via ITT or something, but not to bother reading it as it was, word for word, identical to the first one. "Okay, okay," I muttered, "I've got it: I'm supposed to make a call from Trinidad."

Morning came, and with it came Trinidad, along with heat and humidity. I spent almost an hour in a telephone booth, talking to Fred Pearsman at A.R.L.

Dr. Pearsman said something like this, "We have been asked to submit a contract proposal, by a group which we can't really identify, to synthesize a nitrogen-containing phenethylamine analog of THC. You will be arriving in London at such and such a time on such and such a day (he was correct to the minute) and we want you to please send us a complete synthetic procedure at that time by airmail special delivery the very minute you arrive. It will get to us here just in time for our submission."

"But," I protested, "I'm aboard a luxury liner, and the most up-to-date reference book in its library is an 1894 edition of Roget's Thesaurus!"

"Then write it out from memory," said he, and that was that. I cannot begin to describe what forty minutes in a Trinidad telephone booth at 90%

humidity and 92 degrees temperature can do to one's rational defenses.

So, for the rest of the way across the Atlantic Ocean, I reviewed, with what modest photographic recall I could muster, the appropriate texts of Beilstein and Chemical Abstracts, and put together a chemical flow-sheet and proposal for the phenethylamine analogues of THC. It was mailed from London and got to A.R.L. Company apparently in time for the contract proposal to be awarded to them. It must have been somewhat successful in showing CNS activity, since Dr. Pearsman left A.R.L. and became the founder of a consulting group in Boston that promoted nitrogen-containing THC analogs to industry, apparently with some success.

I got my name on a patent that was subsequently issued to the Simpson Winter Corporation, and for which I received a token dollar; that is the way things are done when one works for industry. I never found out what the connection was between Blackwood Arsenal, A.R.L. and Simpson Winter. I also never met the man I privately dubbed "Frantic Freddy," although I did run into people at several scientific meetings in following years who knew him. His company has continued to grow, and today it is pursuing a large number of research projects in the area of pharmaceuticals. Their work occasionally touches the THC molecule with imaginative variations, but as to the putting of a nitrogen atom in there, not much more has been done. I did put out a few more materials with that THC-nitrogen combination from my own lab sometime later, which earned me a trip to Sweden. But I found nothing of psychedelic interest. Maybe nature wasn't being sloppy by leaving it out. I suspect she knew it wasn't worth it and was simply saving her energies.

The rest of the ocean passage to Europe (the time not spent in writing the rough draft of the government grant) was spent in developing the art of playing Ping-Pong on a rolling ship, and learning about the initiation rites of obscure African tribes from our radioman Mr. Munoz, who evolved into an interesting and constant pre-dinner cocktail companion.

I have lost all touch with Mr. Munoz; I do not know if he is even alive today. The P & O Lines certainly did not survive.

CHAPTER 6. MMDA

I had a number of projects that I wished to pursue in France. I wanted to learn to speak the language, I wanted to break my father loose from his grief over the death of my mother, and especially, I wanted to put a methylenedioxy group in place of two of the methoxy groups in TMA. The three methoxy groups of mescaline and of TMA have oxygen atoms that are sticking out from the benzene ring all isolated like islands. They are not interconnected. If two adjacent ones were to get a bridge between them, be tied together, then a very subtle change in the geometry of the molecule would result. The name of the bridged analogue would be MMDA.

All of this grew out of nutmeg. At Dole, having seen the effectiveness of TMA, I put myself to searching in catalogs, in books, on shelves, in plants, for anything that resembled it and which thus might indicate where I should go next. I discovered a few mentions in the literature of an intriguing compound called elemicin. It was an essential oil (a new term to me) which was one of a large class of compounds responsible for the flavors (the essences) of many of our food stuffs. So it looked as if plants were the direction to go.

Elemicin looked (in the structural sense) almost identical to TMA. Through the magic of blackboard and chalk, I could add a molecule of ammonia to a molecule of elemicin and get a molecule of TMA. And if it could be done on a blackboard, maybe it could be done in the liver. Was there any suggestion or report, I wondered, anywhere at all, suggesting that elemicin had psychoactive properties?

Off I went to an exciting few days in the published literature, during which I learned a great amount about the intriguing world of essential oils. They were everywhere, wonderful structures to be found in spices and related plants, with names that often reflected their origins: elemicin, api-ole, dill-apiole, safrole, eugenol, anol, croweasin, myristicin, asarone, and on and on. A wealth of obscure, unexpectedly magical chemistry completely ripe for exploration and exploitation.

Well, although I could find no specific mention of any psychopharmacology of elemicin, it is one of the major components of nutmeg, and there was a vast anecdotal literature concerning nutmeg. It had been used for everything from inducing abortions and reinstating missed menstrual periods, to attempted suicide and curing baldness. And bingo! It also had a wide reputation as an intoxicant.

Apparently, nutmeg has been used as a "kitchen narcotic," in prisons, and a scatter of medical reports have appeared describing several patterns of drunkenness or psychic disorder. It contains elemicin, which is structurally almost identical to TMA. What else might be in nutmeg that could cause or contribute to its folklore reputation? I pursued the answer by the straightforward process of buying ten pounds of high quality Oil of Nutmeg, and fractionally distilling it through a super-efficient still into some three score fractions. What a treasure of compounds! In fact, several of them had never been observed in this plant extract before.

A major component present was myristicin, a known close relative of elemicin. If one could stir simple household ammonia into elemicin to convert it to the strange and challenging psychedelic TMA (at least in theory), then a similar stirring of ammonia into myristicin should give rise to the unknown base, 3-methoxy-4,5-methylenedioxyamphetamine, or MMDA.

In principle, I thought the synthesis of MMDA should be simple and straightforward. Just take the correct starting aldehyde, myristicinaldehyde, and follow the standard procedures. Which is something like the famous recipe for hippopotamus soup: take a mature hippopotamus and follow the standard procedures. There is no obvious way of getting hold of a hippo, and I was going to discover that there was a similar problem in the getting of myristicinaldehyde. It was simply not available, and extraordinarily difficult to make. But I was totally determined to make MMDA and discover whether it was active and, if so, just what the action would be.

Arrival for a year's stay in France can be somewhat traumatic even if there are reservations and arrangements and places to go and people to contact. In this case, there were practically no plans whatsoever. We (my wife Helen, my son Theo, and my grieving father) found our way to London to pick up a new Volkswagon (that much had been arranged), and we piled all our belongings on top of it and headed for the English Channel. Across it we went, on the night ferry, and roared south to Paris the following day.

So there we were, with no place to go and no person to contact. We found the American Express office up near the Opera, and there were no messages for us. But, then, we hadn't really expected any. Clearly, we had to spend a year in some location, but the most immediate problem was where to spend a night while we searched for the place to spend a year.

It was already late afternoon. I vaguely remembered that there were some neat hotels somewhere around St. Germain des Pres, and we found that the Hotel aux Deux Continents had a room on the fifth floor. On the top of the Volkswagen we had a giant tea case and three suitcases, which carried all of our needs for the year. I managed to convey to the manager of the hotel that my father had an extremely weak heart (necessity is the mother of many little fibs) and that his walking up to the fifth floor and down again might seriously threaten him. And certainly his carrying baggage to the fifth floor would be even riskier. The manager then just happened to discover a room on the ground floor which, by good fortune, had a large window which opened out onto the street, so we passed in all the luggage from the sidewalk through it, and settled in for a while until we could find an apartment.

The complete absence of available downtown Paris rentals soon became apparent, so we finally located ourselves in the suburb of Meudon. I immediately set out on the quest for myristicinaldehyde and a laboratory where I might convert it to MMDA. What I found was that the French have a way of regarding academic positions and related research projects in a framework that is completely alien to an American. One cannot simply go into a university and say, "I am me, and I would like to meet you." All doors are locked and no one responds to telephone calls. One *must* go through channels.

My breakthrough came at the Pasteur Institute, where I ran into a post-doc who was a visiting scientist there for a year from the United States; he had, in that time, pretty well unraveled the French academic pecking order. His advice to me was, "Devote a few days to getting introduced to people who might be willing to meet you. Let's start at the lowest possible level, and work our way up." We did just that, and gave it a lot of patience.

First, I let him introduce me to a number of his peers. He had told me that one of them would try to establish his somewhat more prestigious position in the scientific community by introducing me to one of *his* peers. My post-doc had advised me: dump everyone else including the presumptuous introducer, and let the somewhat higher level person take you on the rounds of *his* peers. After a few introductions over a couple of days, the shift upwards will happen all over again. Dump, and follow the new Very Important Person.

It was a fascinating social structure and it produced, in a couple of weeks, a meeting with a Dr. Richard Sett, who had his own laboratory associated with the Sorbonne. He also had some extra space for a visiting nut such as I. He had a marvelous compassion for people who wanted to research new areas. He was at Gif-sur-Yvette, outside of Paris, but still part of the Sorbonne, and I now had my place for the investigation of my obsession, MMDA.

Almost immediately I made the astounding discovery that myristicinaldehyde was commercially available at a chemical supply house in Paris. I placed an urgent order for 100 grams and was pleasantly surprised to have it in my hands within the week. But there are unexpected surprises to be found in the French language, as well, which became clear when I discovered that the terms myristicinaldehyde and myristaldehyde are interchangeable in French. I had the latter compound which was totally unrelated to MMDA. I could find no use for it at all.

So the time I had invested advanced the cause of MMDA not a whit, and I spent the rest of my year in the chemistry of Dr. Sett's favorite project, the organic reactions of elemental cesium. And we conducted similarly intensive investigations into the comparative merits of all the local wines and pate's within a twenty-mile radius of Gif-sur-Yvette.

At the mid-point of our stay, Helen's father died and she returned to the United States. Theo and my father took advantage of my son's still being under 12 and thus able to get half-fare, and off they went, back to the United States the long way — around the world — on another P & O Line ship, the Canberra. I was left to have the unparalleled experience of breaking a lease in pidgin French. I escaped intact, returned to the U.S., and to my research position at the Dole Chemical Company.

I decided to use nutmeg as my raw material, and everything fit together beautifully. I got my myristicin from the natural oil, and its conversion to MMDA was without trauma.

MMDA was a truly fascinating compound. It did not have the bells and whistles, the drama of mescaline, but was considerably more benign. It was (I thought at the time) my first truly new discovery, and I moved very carefully with it into my small group of colleagues.

The most moving description of its effects was made by a very close friend of mine, a poet who took approximately 160 milligrams orally, in a group of several friends, and he sent me this report.

MMDA / Miniature High

I use the word *miniature* in the same sense that I would describe a piece by the jazz pianist Bud Powell as a miniature.

Comparing a Beethoven piano sonata with *Autumn in New York* as played by Powell would be analogous to comparing mescaline and MMDA. MMDA comes through as a miniature high — everything is there but in lesser quantity and duration.

MMDA stops barely short of the Olympian Universe of time-ceasing and the appearance of organic and inorganic radiances. The immediate part of the high is about two and one half hours in duration. Rather than a cessation of time as there is with mescaline or psilocybin, there is a kind of *timelessness* during the first malaise-like hour of the high. There is more a feeling of stupefaction than there is with most highs.

In a car climbing the Berkeley foothills I went into a terrible fear. It only lasted a few minutes — but it did not matter in the timelessness how long the panic lasted — it was eternal. I looked out onto the grassy hillside at the dead silver-brown grass. In the expanse of field I could see each separate blade of grass gleaming and the trillions of brown-silver blades blended together into a vast wavering fur. Far below was the panorama of foggy Berkeley and Oakland and the bay. It all began to loom in timelessness and beauty. I thought that I was going to enter the Olympian Universe. I WAS NOT PREPARED FOR THE OLYMPIAN UNIVERSE. I had been expecting something like a marijuana high. I realized that if I entered the Olympian that I hadn't yet recovered sufficiently from the last high to hold myself together.

Heat swelled in my genitals and rose to my stomach. I felt agonizing and perfect fear. I wanted to ask the others to go back so I could take Thorazine. I couldn't talk. The car swerved around a hairpin bend in the road giving me another view of the silver-brown grass-fur and the vast *unwanted* dearness of the view.

Suddenly I was fighting with 'Captain Zero' — I mean the whole disordered and eternity-seeking consciousness that is no longer mammalian in nature but belongs to the order of molecules and inert matter! I decided that all I could do was to go with it — to let Zero take over, but then I was sure that I would not come back. I tried to hold back the high but realized I would do myself damage that way. Then I tried to get on top of the whole high and control it. All in all, I tried perhaps fifteen or twenty unrecallable or almost indescribable means to control or escape the high.

During this time I believed that I was going to pieces and I would possibly never be with the human-world again. My insides were going wild and my conscious mind seemed to be the only force holding me together. At one point I managed to ask how the dosage had been figured. I was reassured by comparing the dosage to mescaline dosage. For a moment I grasped the fact that I could go through three hours of the fear. Then my insides and mind went wilder. *Jesus, I could not enter Olympia again.*

When the car stopped, I was in control and the aroused molecular consciousness had dissipated. The number of exits and ordinary animal powers that I tried had given me control. I account the sudden gaining of sureness to experience with hallucinogens. I don't think that any of the methods that I tried worked — but the number of possibilities gave me an assurance that I could control me even in Olympia.

I told the others what had happened and felt that I could enjoy some of the day, and in a moment I felt the joy of relief. (Interestingly, none of the other participants got to the Olympian Universe during the high. I account the fact that I touched the body of it due to the predisposition deposited in my body chemistry through earlier experiments with peyote and psilocybin.)

As we walked up the footpath over golden brown dust I saw footprints of birds, tennis shoes, and bare feet. The frightening nature of tracks and artifacts began to overwhelm me. As I walked I tried to insulate myself from the sight. To my right was the dream panorama of hundreds of square miles of enchanted cities and dream-reality of fog pouring upon them from the bay. I was not interested and only cared about keeping myself together and not slipping back to meet Captain Zero.

The short, eternal, uphill walk exhausted us and we fell on the ground in a tiny stand of trees. I still wanted the experience to end and to return to the meanings of daily loves and realities. I had adjusted enough to make it through the high. My companions closed their eyes and began having brain movies. (Earlier my eyes had been forced shut many times by the euphoric hallucination pleasure.) Now I held my eyes open not wanting brain movies or visions. When I closed my eyes experimentally I saw only glorious and pleasing blackness.

We talked desultorily and dozefully and I realized that I was able to see through the eyes of my companions. They were seeing stark reality exactly as I saw it. I wanted to talk to Terry and find out who he was. I found talking too difficult. My eyes were beginning to close again with exhaustion and pleasure.

When I lit cigarettes, I could not find my lips well and they were numbed. Matches kept blowing out in a wind that was not strong enough to blow them out. We wobbled as we walked.

We stayed in a little stand of trees. I sat for a while, then got up and sat in another place. Then I got up again & etc.

Except for visual sensation which was just on the verge of mescaline or psilocybin in vision and clarity, I seemed to be sealed from sensation and living in a kind of hyper-lucidity of sense — a pleasant paradox.

I lay back and closed my eyes and practiced raising the goddess Kundalini (The Serpent Power) from the base *chakra* and through my body. I succeeded in raising the power, for the first time, past my shoulders and into my head. I realized, as I did it, that I was not truly raising the Serpent Power but rather cleaning the nerve tubes. However, I achieved grayish-clear affective pictures of the *chakra* nerve centers. It was a good feeling.

The crystal clear air gave bright green sharpness to the evergreens. Looking at trees, or leaves of plants, was like a mild mescaline high. Fir trees became living, green, modern sculptures of strange Indian rococo beasts — as if the sculptor Lipschitz worked at their trimming.

The malaise-like feeling began to end and the dozeful feeling left with it.

I walked to a redwood copse where other members of the party were sitting. I was struck by the absolute and superb beauty and clarity of the people and the trees and air and the music that played over the portable radio. I felt close to the children and admired their beauty. At this point I realized that I was simply sitting and enjoying a Sunday noon in its full pleasantness. Ordinarily I would have been bored without more to do. The next couple of hours became a pleasant and beautiful picnic. The comedown was abrupt but not unpleasant. I was ready. Time passed with swift rapidity for the rest of the day. Two hour periods would flash by. Late that night I was kept from sleep for half an hour by brain movies — little crocodiles running across dusty roads through spotlights in the darkness, magic evergreen trees fading into and out of reality, and anecdotal sequences of brain visions.

AN OBSCURE FOOTNOTE

A week after taking MMDA I woke in the middle of the night and as I awakened I felt that there would be no reality but only nothingness. I was horrified and threw myself bolt upright in bed and opened my eyes instantaneously.

Shelley says:

> Lift not the painted veil which those who live
> Call life; though unreal shapes be pictured there,
> And it but mimic all we would believe
> With colors idly spread, — behind, lurk Fear
> And Hope, twin Destinies; who ever weave
> Their shadows, o'er the chasm, sightless and drear.

The awakening I had was definitely a reaction to the MMDA. Yesterday I talked with a man who had taken too much LSD. I tried to avoid speaking on hallucinogens but he was insistent. As I described some post-hallucinogen states of extreme anxiety regarding the nature of reality the man began to writhe in his chair, wring his hands, and temporarily lost the ability to speak. I have been in that state. While speaking with Sam he identified it as an anxiety state and pointed out that it is not only related to hallucinogens, but is a not uncommon state for those who have not had drugs.

Sam accounts the state to an arising of unconscious material to the surface.

That seems fine and true enough — as good a name for what is happening as any other. What it does not clear up is the intuitions that I have that strengthen and contradict each other. I am aware of two feelings: That the 'material' is of a repressed psychological nature in the Freudian-Reichian sense, and that it is also another order of 'material' confronted. The other order is that of the molecular level of consciousness. I mean a part of ourselves more

related to the *philosophical consciousness* of sea urchins and sponges
— who are no more than the tugs of their desires and hungers and
the consciousness of their motions and withdrawals — who are an
actual conscious part of the physical universe and the actual being
of their protoplasm in the 'Surge of Life.' It would be interesting if
what we so surely call the 'Unconscious' were in reality two *or more*
vastly divided parts of our being that are commonly inaccessible.

I am not saying this to strengthen my argument that I confronted
the molecular consciousness on MMDA. I was in too much of a
fear state to be definite of anything when I think of it now two
weeks later.

But I am intuitively sure that we are meeting two unknown areas
— both repressions and a molecular-philosophical-Universe consciousness. I have a strong feeling that the second of these should
be left untouched by both psychiatry and happy-day investigations.
We mess with some structure that should remain unknown, because it *is* known by *being*. Unless the experimenter is aware of the
risk and goes slowly in an investigatory manner with caution.

———————————————

This report was a treasure to me, in that it gave an articulate and
unmistakable "outside" verification that MMDA was indeed a psychedelic.
It was (at least, for that time) a drug of unprecedented potency, and proved
that it was not only mescaline that had psychological complexities. I have
personal reports from perhaps another half-dozen subjects who have explored the 160 to 200 milligram range, and the psychiatrist C. Naranjo
devotes nearly a fourth of his book, "The Healing Journey," to his clinical
experiences with MMDA.
     But the story of MMDA closes on a poignant note of sadness. I had
learned that the world-renowned psychopharmacologist, Gordon Alles
(the discoverer of the action of amphetamine and of MDA) had been
following exactly the same reasoning path as I, and had independently
worked up nutmeg and synthesized MMDA. He had actually given it the
same initials I had, and had discovered its action in himself. It was with
joyful anticipation that we made a date to meet and talk about the many
interests I am sure we shared.
     A month before our appointed meeting, I heard of his unexpected and
tragic death, apparently of complications of diabetes. As he numbered
among his accomplishments not only an enthusiastic interest in self-experimentation, but a broad reputation as an expert on insulin, I speculated

(futilely) about what he might have been assaying at the time. I contacted his graduate student but he had no idea, and I fear I shall never know either. Through his widow's private physician, I extended an offer to organize and publish his research notes in a commemorative volume under his own name, but these efforts were rebuffed. I fear that all the ideas and observations he had had are now never to be found. I regard his death as a severe personal loss, although I never met him.

CHAPTER 7. THE CAPTAIN

It was the mid-1960's and the time had come to change my employer. I had worked for the Dole Chemical Company for ten years; during that time I had developed a comfortable stride as a chemist, and added a lot of words to my vocabulary in the languages of research and laboratory technique. But it was becoming gradually apparent that both of us — Dole as employer and I as employee — were no longer entirely at peace with our relationship.

No one could deny that I was extremely productive. A continuous flow of new and potentially patentable compounds were being synthesized and spun into the biological screening processes. These were the intermediates which were the stepping stones to the target materials that I really wanted to make and explore. But the final products themselves, compounds that briefly modified the sensory world of the consumer and perhaps his interpretation of it, were unmarketable. Not that there wasn't a market out there for psychedelic drugs; it was just not the kind of market that could be openly courted by a kosher industrial giant that created and manufactured insecticides for the agricultural world and polymers for the artificial fiber world, as well as herbicides for the military world. This was, after all, the era of our Vietnam adventure, and immense pressures were being brought to bear on big industries everywhere throughout the country, to direct all their energies towards the government's needs. Psychedelic drugs were not exactly what Washington had in mind.

From my point of view, it was becoming increasingly clear that the corporate attitudes toward my work were shifting from encouragement to tolerance, which would in time — I suspected — become disapproval and eventually, of course, outright prohibition. Since my end products were seen to be of no exploitable value, there had been no restrictions on publication, and I had in fact published, in several first class scientific journals, a goodly number of papers describing the chemistry and the activity in humans of new psychedelic drugs (I still called them psychotomimetic drugs in those days because that was the scientifically accepted euphemism). But the point at which the writing on the wall became obvious was the day I was asked to no longer use Dole's address on my publications. What I held to be exciting and creative was clearly being seen by management as something that would reflect badly on the corporate image.

So I started putting my home address on scientific publications. And, since this implied that the research was being done at home, it seemed like a great idea to begin setting up a personal laboratory on the Farm, which I had long dreamt of doing. And if I were to actually do the research at home — so went my reasoning — I would no longer be working for Dole, but for a new employer. Me. That would be quite a move to make. I would retire myself from Dole, which is to say I would be self-employed, which is to say I would become a consultant, which is to say (as I eventually discovered) that I would emerge in a totally new role: unemployed scientist.

I left Dole at the end of 1966, with all the usual parting rituals observed when a long-time employee retires. There were goodbye lunches with many drinks, there were certificates of acknowledgment with many signatures, and presumably there was the customary changing of all the outside locks.

I had quite a number of plans already in mind. The first was to broaden my educational basis. Having always been a test-tube and Bunsen burner person, I knew that I had the art in hand for making new and fascinating compounds. But I had very little background for evaluating the biology of their action. Since the scene of that action was the human body, one of my earliest plans was to go to medical school and study the where's and the why's of the complex wiring patterns in the human brain and nervous system, all of which play vital roles in this activity.

I realized that if I hoped to survive as a consultant I would have to acquire some vocabulary in a number of fields such as biology, medicine and psychology, so I applied for, and received, a government grant to help pay the tuition. Helen was completely supportive; she said she wanted me to follow the path I believed in. She was working as a librarian at the University of California at Berkeley, loving the job and the economic independence it gave her. Between my grant and her salary, we figured we would manage adequately for the time necessary.

The next two years were totally committed to the San Francisco campus of the University of California, as I learned what I could of medicine.

But there was yet another language, that of power and politics, which I was destined to learn in a totally unexpected way. I had completed two years of medical studies which equipped me with a sound understanding of the normal functions of the cerebral red and green wires, and was on the verge of deciding whether or not to continue with the next two years (which would have given me a look at their abnormal functioning) when the decision was, in a sense, made for me.

I received an offer to become a consultant in the area of research in psychedelic drugs. It came from a gentleman I'd never heard of, who ran a one-man analytical laboratory located in a storefront down on the San Francisco Peninsula.

My first response was that I had no particular desire to become involved with someone else's lab, doing what might be interpreted as controversial research at a time when it seemed the whole nation was becoming increasingly polarized against recreational drug use. It was being broadly associated with hippies and liberals and academic intellectual types who were against the war in Southeast Asia. But when I finally talked with this person, I discovered that his role was only that of a finder — what is now known as a "head-hunter." He told me that he had been retained by a big government operation specifically to locate scientists from many disciplines as potential members of a research team for an unusual project that was of super-importance.

He explained, carefully: "There will be situations in the future in which astronauts might well be exposed to long periods of sensory isolation and all the potential mental developments that might come along with that particular territory. There is being set up a research program geared to develop chemicals which could be used to train those astronauts who might be subjected to long bouts of sensory deprivation. Teach them to roll with the altered states of consciousness that could very well be a consequence of that isolation."

He emphasized that I would have a free hand to establish instrumentation, choose personnel, and equip my own laboratory. Would I be interested in setting up a research project to develop such chemicals and describe their activity and maybe even to contribute to the design of the clinical experiments?

Does a bear like to shit in the woods? Yes, yes, most certainly yes!

Of course, my local contact, the store-front laboratory gentleman, was not the person who was running this astronaut-in-outer-space project. The head honcho was a Captain B. Lauder Pinkerton, who was the central hub of many different branches of biological research at the major laboratory for space research, called the San Carlos Aerospace Laboratory, which was under contract to the National Aeronautics and Space Administration, or NASA. This was located nearby, in a town called Sunnyvale.

Captain Pinkerton was many things; he was a Captain in some branch of the military, he was an intelligence officer in some corner of the government, possibly NSA (National Security Agency) and he was a millionaire, thanks to genes he shared with the inventor of a famously successful household appliance. We met, we talked, and I think it safe to say that — at the time — we had the good instincts to respect one another, but not to indulge in anything as inappropriate as mutual trust.

Having taken the bait, I was off into a new area of interaction. I was now a consultant, successfully launched on my new career.

At Aerospace, I was hailed as the shining light of psychotropic medicine. There was a whirlwind of accolades as, one after another, people came up to me and said they had been reading my articles for years and thought I was doing important and fascinating work.

So I materialized at Aerospace every morning, and began ordering glassware and instruments and mechanical things for the new laboratory, which I was told was not yet available, but would be shortly, as soon as certain necessary shifts and changes had been made. In the meantime, I explored every hallway and workroom and lab, meeting and interacting with some of the resident scientists, most of whom seemed to be gentle old-timers who had been there for years. Gradually, it became apparent that there were two entirely different worlds in coexistence at Aerospace, both under the very firm direction of Captain Pinkerton.

One of these was the new-lab-spectroscopy-psychedelic-drug-outer-space world, most of which had not yet taken any kind of tangible form (but undoubtedly would very soon), and this world included a regular weekly summons into Pinkerton's office for an intense, highly charged conversation on some topic that was always unexpected, and sometimes completely off the wall.

I might find myself having to deal with the nature and structure of scientific imagination and how it could be channeled. Or Pinkerton might bring up the subject of mental telepathy and the possibility of successfully influencing another person's thought processes or behavior from a distance. Once, it was an exploration of the kind of mental role-playing one might have to do in order to understand somebody else's perspective and motives, as symbolized by the old saying, "It takes a thief to catch a thief," or another old saying (which was new to me), "It takes a Turk to know a Turk."

This was rich and tantalizing fare, as entertaining as it was unpredictable, but somehow it never seemed quite appropriate to the role that I understood myself to be playing, as an organizer of a research center for creativity in the development of psychedelic drugs, among other heady things. Was I being used as a sounding board for Pinkerton's strange flights of fancy? Or was I being probed as to my positions on some kinds of moral or ethical questions tucked in between the lines? I thought it probably wisest to be supportive of the concepts he expressed unless I disagreed, in which case I chose to remain silent.

The only things I was totally sure of were that Captain Pinkerton was a shrewd, intelligent man, and that I hadn't a clue as to what was really going on.

But there was the other world to be seen and explored. This was composed of the many biological research projects in other areas, which had already been established by Pinkerton. Here were arcane projects such as black membrane dynamics, and studies of the influence of gravity on plant growth, the relationship between magnetic fields and the blood-brain barrier, and the effects of radiation on fertility. All were intriguing studies, and all were being run in well equipped laboratories by extremely competent scientists. But I found myself being reminded of an old-person's home. There was activity, but there was a prevalent sense of disinterest. The excellent quality of the work on the workbench was obvious, but when I would go to lunch with one of the resident mavens, the talk would be of such stuff as his forthcoming retirement. There was no excitement; just a sense of tiredness. Remarkable, I thought; all this under the same leadership as the psychedelic project?

The glassware and laboratory equipment were slow in arriving, I was told, and things hadn't quite straightened out yet in the assignment of space for my new lab, but it would all come together soon. Just be patient, they said. I ran a few experiments on equipment available in other labs, and kept busy.

A few months into my employment at Aerospace, I was invited to Pinkerton's home, which was located in the wealthy suburb of Santa Maria, to share a dinner with him, his wife, and what I was given to understand was his "acceptable" son, a boy in his late 'teens. But it so happened that, this particular evening, his other child — the twenty-year-old-hippie-druggie who had been at some point outcast and disenfranchised — had taken it into his head to drop by. (He himself told me, many years later, that it was not accidental at all; he had heard about me and decided to check things out for himself.)

It also happened that he played excellent Ping-Pong, and I was informed that he routinely beat his father (there were hints that Father found this intolerable) and by flukey chance I just happened to beat the son with serves which were only marginally legal. So, a dissymmetry was established between Pinkerton and me by the inference that I could probably beat him at Ping-Pong (this was never tested, by the way). I am sure all of this was completely incidental to the direction that our relationship soon took, but the memory of that evening does nonetheless persist.

Within the week I was called into the office of an administrative ally of Pinkerton, who had been pleasant and friendly to me and with whom I'd had several energetic conversations. He told me that he was required to process everyone who was a consultant on any of the Captain's research projects for some sort of secret clearance. The clearance level had a color or a letter attached to it, I don't remember which. Apparently (so I was told) all the people who were presently employed at Aerospace had already received it, except for me.

This security clearance would allow me access to all research related to my own that had already been done. But it was clear that my access to these unknown treasures could only be had in exchange for my agreeing to allow my own thoughts and creative processes to be similarly classified and controlled. I also knew that a security clearance mandates one's absolute silence for the rest of one's life in regard to anything and everything seen, heard and experienced during the time of employment by the government agency giving the clearance. I had no choice. I declined the opportunity.

In a few days I was gently informed that I was no longer a part of the research group.

In the months that followed, I maintained contact with some of the other scientists I had come to know at Aerospace, and eventually I learned that the funds which were available from NASA for this psychedelic study were most probably from the Department of Defense, although nobody had absolute proof, of course. In retrospect, I could see where much of the research that was going on there might well be of interest to the military and chemical warfare side of things.

I also began to understand why the promised laboratory, glassware and equipment — not to speak of astronauts — had never materialized. Whatever it was that Pinkerton thought I might bring to his program — or add to his own professional luster — had first to be wrapped safely, tied down and secured with the ropes called Secret and Classified.

I left with questions that are yet to be answered, and most probably never will be. Was my Captain Pinkerton a recruiter of scientific minds for what he saw as patriotic necessities? Was he a modern-day Machiavelli with some personal agenda that he chose not to share with anyone? Maybe he was simply a selfish collector of interesting and colorful people, like the art lover who has five original Van Gogh's in his personal gallery, where no one else can see them.

In any case, I was out of the San Carlos Aerospace Laboratories, and I was out of the academic world as well. By good fortune, I had continued to build and use my own private laboratory during the time I was at Sunnyvale, so my die was cast; I was now officially a scientific consultant, and I was going to have to make every effort to survive in that role.

CHAPTER 8. MEM

Just what is a C-natural quarter note? A musician might define it as a little solid-black circle with a vertical arm sticking up from it, located on a line below the treble staff. But then he is stuck with having to define words such as natural, and staff. A physicist might try using the image of a sinusoidal wave on the oscilloscope with a period of something under 4 milliseconds lasting for a short while. But what is a sinusoidal, and what is a millisecond? From the neurologist, one might hear something yet different involving hairs on the cochlea and neurons in the auditory cortex area. A yet different view with a different and equally arcane jargon. All are right, and yet each can be incomprehensible without extensive further definition.

I am faced with an equally difficult problem when I am asked, just what is mescaline? The person who swallowed it might recount its effects, the distributor who packaged it might describe its taste and color, and the chemist who synthesized it might speak in terms of molecular structure. Perhaps it is my prejudice, but I always tend to the molecular structure as I truly believe that it is one of the few consistent and incontestable definitions. But, oh my, it does require a certain leap of faith to accept the picture that is offered!

The molecule is the smallest chunk of something that still is that something. Anything smaller, and there appears a bunch of atoms with a complete loss of the original identity. You don't see a molecule. It has an atomic connection scheme that is inferred from a lot of reasoning and a century of experimentation. But it remains the only valid vocabulary for the design of new drugs. I don't want to launch into a lecture in chemistry, yet I truly want to share the magic of the "4-position."

Chemistry is a maddeningly discontinuous art. Things can only change by whole atomic jumps. There are no smooth, continuous variations. A compound (drug, chemical, solvent, gas, smell) is composed of unimaginably large numbers of molecules, all of them identical. If you looked at just one of them through some alchemist's microscope, you would see, maybe, 35 atoms all hooked together in some cohesive way. Some would be carbon atoms, and others would be hydrogens. In the case of TMA, you would find one nitrogen atom and three oxygen atoms as well. The identity of a compound depends on exactly how many atoms there are in that invisible minimum piece of it, and on exactly how they are hooked together.

The number of atoms must change by a whole numbers; this is what is meant by the absence of any continuous variation. One cannot make a molecule larger by a little bit of an atom. You can add an entire oxygen atom, but there is no meaning to adding 17% of an oxygen atom. A homologue of a given compound is a new compound that has been made bigger (or smaller) by the addition (or subtraction) of three atoms, one carbon and two hydrogens. Nothing can ever be created that lies part way between a drug and its immediate homologue.

Or, if one were to keep the number and identity of the atoms the same, a new compound can result simply by changing the way that they are hooked together. Move an atom or a bunch of atoms from here to there. An isomer of a given compound is a new compound that has an identical weight (at the molecular level) but the atoms have been reorganized.

My earliest manipulations of molecular structure had concentrated on making isomers, on rearranging the locations of atoms rather than adding or taking away specific atoms. The ring component of TMA (called a benzene ring) has five different positions where atoms can be located. The count starts at the one-position, where the rest of the molecule is attached. Thus the second is identical to the sixth position (both at 2 or 10 o'clock), the third is identical to the fifth (both at 4 or 8 o'clock) and the fourth (at 6 o'clock) is as far from the rest of the molecule as you can get. This is the 4-position.

TMA (like mescaline) has a bunch of atoms (called methoxy groups) at the 3-, the 4- and the 5-positions. I synthesized isomers, with these three bunches in all the other possible locations. There were two patterns that really boosted the potency of the resulting amphetamine. One was when the groups were in the 2-, 4- and 5-positions (TMA-2) and another when the groups were in the 2-, 4- and 6-positions (TMA-6). TMA-2 was the new and most satisfying discovery, being some ten times more potent than TMA. Settling for a while on this particular ordering of groups, why not try using the homologue argument and add a three atom chunk to each of these methoxy groups? Thus, one has ethoxy homologues, with the ethyl group at either the 2-, the 4- or the 5-position. If one were to call a methoxy an "M", and an ethoxy an "E", and if one were to name a compound around the ring as the groups appeared (from the 2- to the 4- to the 5-positions), one would have EMM, MEM, and MME as code names. The middle letter is, of course, the group at the 4-position.

I had completed the teutonic discipline of preparing all the three possible ethoxy homologs of TMA-2 at just about the same time that I decided to leave Dole and go to medical school. Suddenly, I didn't have a worried administration looking over my shoulder as to the chemistry and its patentability but also, by this same argument, I had no base of operations from which I could begin to document pharmacology, and especially psychopharmacology.

Since much of the synthetic work, at least of the M's and E's, had been done while I was still at Dole, I supposed that all this chemistry was still their property. But I also concluded that they were undoubtedly so relieved to be rid of me — especially as the parting had been friendly and at my own request — they probably wouldn't mind at all if I were to assume the synthesis and ownership of the M's and E's. So this would be my first solo flight, and I would not only publish from my home address from now on, I would do the chemistry there as well.

The early trials of the mono-ethoxy compounds, EMM, MEM and MME, showed no mental activity. EMM was inactive in the twenties-of-milligrams, and I took it on up to 50 milligrams, still with no effects apparent. MME was also inactive in the twenties-of-milligrams, but at 40 milligrams it gave me a 1.5 plus.

The treasure turned out to be MEM, with the ethoxy in the 4-position. Perhaps the term, "4-position," which comes up again and again in this chemical story, may be now a little less mysterious. Again, it is the place on the ring, opposite the rest of the big collection of atoms on the molecule, where the action takes place. There is true magic there, and it was with the MEM that it first became apparent. MEM was clearly active at 10 milligrams. The activity was only marginal, but it was unquestionable.

Just before a full half-hour had passed following the taking of 10 milligrams, I felt a dizziness, and had to get up and move about to offset some tension in my legs. There was no nausea. About 15 minutes later, I was clearly intoxicated (in the ethanol sense) but there were absolutely no apprehensions. There was a very slight eye dilation. From the two-hour period on, at least at this dosage, I felt that I was pretty much repairing mentally, but could not seem to shake a slight residual physical distress. I knew I had an active material here, and that I should proceed with caution.

The first thing I did was to give a good supply of it to my psychiatrist friend, Paris Mateo, with whom I had worked with TMA. He had a long history of fruitful investigations into the uses of psychoactive drugs of various kinds in therapy. Paris explored MEM with seven willing patients. He reported the effective range to be from 10 to 40 milligrams. He concluded that it was certainly more potent than TMA-2 quantitatively, and that it produced a more defended attitude than TMA-2 in his patients.

My friend the psychologist, Terry Major (also familiar with TMA), assayed MEM at 20 milligrams, and reported the chronology as peaking somewhere around the third hour, and out at about the eighth hour. The qualitative effects, he said, were along the psychedelic line (color, visual intensity, wavering of the visual field, emotional euphoria), but that he was also aware of slight but real extra-pyramidal tremors.

This was clearly the most active of the mono-ethoxy compounds. I wrote up a short note in which I described all eight possible permutations of M's and E's, and sent it to the Journal of Medicinal Chemistry. It was accepted.

I explored MEM quite thoroughly in the 20 to 30 milligram area, in these early years, and found it to be a most impressive psychedelic. In 1977, I went up to 60 milligrams and found it not to be the profound self-analysis drug I had hoped it would be, at least not for me. But I also became aware that I was a little bit insensitive to this material, so I learned to recommend dosages in the 20 to 30 milligrams area for other explorers.

From late 1977 to mid-1980, I did eleven experiments with MEM with a total of nine members of my research group (usually in threes and fours), all in the 25 to 50 milligram range. In general, we found that there was always some body discomfort, extreme anorexia (loss of appetite) and frequent reports of color enrichment and eyes-closed fantasy. The material insists on being complex, but seems nonetheless to leave you in charge. In general, the effects drop off between the sixth and tenth hour, but sleep — even some hours later — can include disturbing dreams. It was not too restful for a number of the experimenters.

I abandoned MEM in 1980, choosing to spend my time on other more intriguing compounds, but not before a couple of important experiences had taken place with the drug. One involved another psychiatrist friend of mine, who was so impressed with his observations of an opening of easy communication, that he decided to spin MEM into his practice, in a very limited way, using it with those patients he felt might benefit from it.

The other was a day I will never forget, a day that I spent with a woman in her late forties, Miriam O. She had had a few, largely unimpressive, earlier experiences with psychedelics, but her interest in working with psychoactive drugs had been rekindled by an experience with MDMA. She wanted to try something new, and I suggested MEM. I met her in Marin County one clear and not very cold December morning. I took 50 milligrams and she took 25. I had already asked her if there was any particular question she wished to address, and she said no, it was simply to be an adventure in altered spaces. The results were a reminder of the old but good maxim in the area of psychedelics: there are no casual experiments.

At about the one hour point, we were well into the effects, around a plus one and a half. We wandered into the Green Gulch Zen Center just in time to attend a half-hour meditation session and to buy a loaf of home-baked bread. Thence on to Muir Beach and to a rolling plus-three.

For a while, it was theater time. Sam Goldwyn was running the show, directing Miriam's poses and gestures, her entrances and exits, while I played the role of the laughing audience. When we were tired of making movies, we started up toward the top of a hill overlooking the Pacific Ocean, with a broad view of the surf below. After climbing a bit, we turned toward the ocean and came upon a barbed-wire fence. I suggested we crawl through it and find a place to sit and look at everything and talk

"I can't," was the reply, "My legs don't seem to work."

Her step was wobbly, and once she had reached the fence, it was clear she was having a really difficult time getting a foot raised to stick it between the two strands of wire.

"I've lost control of my bottom half!"

I helped her through, despite her apparent inability to make anything work too well, and we reached a sitting down place on the grass and sand.

"My legs are paralyzed," Miriam said, "I'm being poisoned, and I want out."

Something was developing, and I didn't know what it was she was headed for, but this "paralysis" and "poisoning" was obviously part of what was on its way up to the surface.

"Well," I offered, rather unsympathetically, "If you really want to dump the poison, concentrate it into one place, and if it's high enough, you can vomit it out, and if it's low enough, you can shit it out."

"I'm not fooling around," Miriam protested, "I'm really being poisoned and I want out."

"Then get yourself out. You're in charge."

There was no comment for a minute. Then she said it.

"Can you give yourself cancer?"

"You certainly can. Almost everyone who has cancer has gotten it for some reason that seems quite adequate. Where is yours?"

"In my stomach."

With her "paralyzed" legs stretched out in front of her, she gently touched her stomach to indicate the site of the enemy. She then unfolded one of the most complex stories I had ever heard, all of which boiled down to the fact that she'd had stomach cancer for some time, and always carried around in her purse some thirty Dilaudid tablets, so that if the pain got too much, she could end the whole thing.

I asked the only question that occurred to me.

"Why do you need cancer?"

That broke the dam. She dissolved in tears and blurted out her secret. Many years before, her mother had suffered from cancer of the stomach and was in such intractable pain that, finally, Miriam and her stepfather had smothered her with a pillow, releasing her from the agony. She was a teenager and she had helped kill her mother. She told me that she'd had total amnesia for all events in her life from that time until her early 20's.

I wept with her.

Later, we retraced our steps down the hill, reintegrating by revisiting each locale along the way which represented stages of the drug development, until we were back to the point where the entire experiment had started.

Of course, Miriam did not have cancer of the stomach. She also had no residual leg paralysis. What she emerged with was an understanding of how the repressed grief and guilt had planted itself in her own body, giving symptoms which were signals to her of something dark which needed to be exposed and opened up to consciousness before she did, indeed, succeed in giving herself her mother's cancer.

When we talked again, several days later, she told me — almost casually — that she had thrown away the Dilaudid. I could only say a heartfelt thank you.

I had developed a keen respect for MEM.

CHAPTER 9. DOM

DOM appeared on the street in the 1960's under the name of STP and it proved to be for quite a while my hair shirt or, as Albert Hofmann would say later about his discovery, LSD, my problem child.

In the early 1960's, when I had satisfied myself that the effectiveness of TMA-2 was intensified by the structural change that gave MEM (but not EMM or MME), it seemed a logical question to ask: was this because of the nature of that group in the magical 4-position? This 4-position substituted drug might have maintained its activity specifically because of the fragile nature of these groups, which would allow their easy removal by the body (or within the body) and the formation of some metabolic product that just happened to be much more potent. The human body has excellent facilities for changing molecules, and it usually changes them to make something less threatening. But in this case the change just might have achieved some upgrading of potency.

Or maybe that group at the 4-position was not easily gotten rid of. Then one could argue that an indestructible molecule got settled in the receptor site, and simply stayed there. The new compound is fully as potent as the old one, because it gets in there and cannot be removed metabolically for some time. The easiest way of answering this question was to construct a molecule with a group at that position which could not be easily displaced or changed.

I said to myself, let's replace the 4-methoxy group (of TMA-2) (or the 4-ethoxy group of MEM) with a methyl group. We will call it DOM (for TMA-2 without an oxygen atom but with a methyl group, desoxymethyl). The methyl group (at the 4-position) cannot be removed easily by any of the usual metabolic procedures. Thus, if this compound (DOM) is of reduced activity, the metabolic removal of some 4-position group seems a reasonable explanation of biological activity. And if the compound (DOM) maintains activity, it would argue that TMA-2 and MEM are intrinsically active, and something in the 4-position is instrumental to the expression of central action. In simple terms, the 4-methoxy group is fragile, and the 4-methyl group is solid. If the active 4-methoxy compound (TMA-2) becomes inactive with a 4-methyl group (if DOM is of decreased potency) then fragility (metabolic change) is needed for activity and the intrinsically active form is to be found somewhere down the metabolic pathway. If, on the other hand, the activity is maintained with the 4-methyl group (if DOM is fully potent) then the primary agents (TMA-2 or DOM) are the responsible factors, and metabolism only serves to inactivate these drugs.

The very first step toward this noble end-product DOM was actually taken by my son, Theo, who was with me late one evening at Dole, on June 22, 1963, to be exact. Having him with me was probably against all the rules, but he was in a period when he wanted to become a chemist, so at about 9:00 p.m., with my blessings, he dumped 100 grams of 2,5-dimethoxy-toluene into a mixture of 225 grams of N-methyl-formanilide and 255 grams of phosphorus oxychloride, thus launching the synthesis of a pre-cursor for what was eventually to be DOM. He ended up in the early hours of the morning with some 54.9 grams of an aromatic aldehyde that did the job. We had our precursor.

(Theo's interests in chemistry have largely flagged and he has found his metier in marine biology and superb poetry, with a garden full of lovingly tended chrysanthemums and dahlias affording him hours of peaceful contact with the earth and his own inner being.)

I completed the nitrostyrene synthesis on July 7th, and finally got back to this project on the 30th of November, to finish the reduction to the final amine. The next day, at 3:22 p.m., I tried 200 micrograms of the white solid and, as there was no effect whatsoever, I let the whole matter drift over the holidays. On January 4th of the new year, I rather heroically upped the dosage to a milligram and, to my total surprise, found activity there. This was the first time ever that a phenethylamine had been observed to be centrally active at such a miniscule dose.

Although there was no response by the end of the first hour, I noted a dryness of the mouth at around the third hour, and my eyes were extremely dilated. I had an eerie over-all feeling that lasted for a couple of additional hours, but eating seemed to clear it up, for the most part. By the seventh hour, everything was repaired, back to normal, and I decided to doubt the validity of any of it.

I noted some residual muscular pains which I readily ascribed to having hiked six miles the previous day. It was during this period of my employment at Dole that I established patterns of hiking to work, and then driving — each on alternate days. I would meet with other co-workers who were also outdoor types along the way, and, unbeknownst to them, I would often have a new level of a new compound on board. We would pick up Al at the drainage ditch, Bob at the edge of the Bainbridge Ranch, and all of us hiked along the canal until we were opposite the back parking lots of Dole. We would cut in opposite the electron accelerator and head for fresh coffee, they with wet feet and incipient muscle tiredness, I with wet feet, incipient muscle tiredness and a possible plus-one or plus-two altered space.

Five days later, I tried a slightly increased level of DOM and recorded in my notes what was probably my first plus-2 experience on a material that was this much a stranger to mescaline. At about the 1-1/4 hour point, I was talking to a friend in his office when I became aware of a warm flushing and tingling sensation in my genitals, which occasionally was a prelude to nausea. My mouth was dry. The nausea did not develop. At the 2-hour point, my teeth were what I call "rubby," which means that I'm suddenly aware of them and they have the feel of being squeaky clean. I was aware of some pressure in the ears.

Two points deserve comment here. One is that with every new drug, at the low levels where there is clearly some action, but the nature of that action cannot yet be defined, one reads every unknown possible complication into one's responses, often recording a syndrome that can never be repeated. The second point is that, at the time, I was still most naive in the area of drug effects, and just a bit frightened, so I'm sure that I often mentally promoted signs and symptoms that were not valid.

Between the third and fourth hour, I wandered out to the little greenhouse I had put in near the parking lot, where I had planted some *Salvia divinorum*, and relaxed in the pleasure of watching things grow. I knew that at higher dosages plants would creep and crawl, but now they were just visibly growing. Between the seventh and tenth hour, I recovered a good baseline and brought my notes to a close, before heading home.

Through the year 1964, DOM was being evaluated by several of my allies, in the dosage range of 2 to 4 milligrams. I was still dedicated to marginal threshold dosage evaluations, unwilling to dip into the spring deeply. I admire, to this day, the brave souls who worked with me to explore the nature of this material. My friend, Terry, evaluated 2.3 milligrams. and reported an extraordinary mood elevation, with no indication of any nausea whatsoever. In the third hour, he found a pronounced enhancement of odors and of emotional interactions, with a richness of empathy. At the eighth hour there was an unmistakable decline, and a 3/4 grain of seconal was needed for sleep at the tenth hour. He did a later experiment with 3.8 milligrams and reported that it showed its maximum effect at the fifth hour, with a peaking from there to the eighth hour, and a gradual decline on into the 12th hour. This was the first clear portrayal of the very long time course that this drug shows.

The first full "psychedelic" experience of DOM was reported by another friend, Mark, at 4.1 milligrams. For him, the effects were noted at about half an hour, and between 1-1/2 and 3 hours there was a matter-of-fact but impressive recounting of visual and interpretative effects similar to those of mescaline. It wasn't until his fifth hour that these really broke through, and his notes are replete with superlatives. For him, there were colors and textures without precedent, as he had no past experience with color effects from mescaline.

It was many years later, in 1967, that some unknown enterprising chemist introduced DOM onto the street, where it was called STP and, unfortunately, it was distributed in doses of up to 20 milligrams. When you consider that the active level, a plus three effect, is closer to 5 milligrams, it is not surprising that the emergency wards of numerous hospitals began seeing young people in states of confusion and panic. They had taken the new drug and, when nothing seemed to happen within the first hour, some of them believed they had taken too low a dose, and took another pill. The hippies and street people were used to drugs like LSD, which come on relatively quickly and are completely developed by one hour. The person responsible for this debacle must have realized his error, because within a relatively short period of time, he had put out new tablets which were only 10 milligrams each. This was still a whopping amount.

While I was in medical school, I heard the rumors and the reports about something called STP and wondered, along with everyone else, what it was. Initially it was thought to be some scopolamine-like drug, but then its nature became more evident. In time I learned that it was, indeed, DOM. Maybe it had became known from a seminar I gave at Johns Hopkins, months earlier, in Baltimore. Maybe the patents had been read and duplicated. Maybe someone had followed the same quite reasonable line of reasoning that I had. But, my challenge to the meaning of the 4-position was now public property, and there was no remaining question as to mechanistic logic. The unchangeable group at the 4-position gave a compound not just of similar potency, but of greatly enhanced potency. Clearly, that 4-position needs to remain untouched, metabolically, (for a while), if a compound is to be active.

In going through my files recently, I discovered a handwritten note that had come to me not long after the first trials with this material. It was short and impressive. I have no idea from whom it came, so no answer could ever be sent It implied an experience that had several faces:

"If on this page I shall have expressed it to you, then it is true that DOM has the glory and the doom sealed up in it. All that's needed to unseal it is to surround it with a warm living human for a few hours. For that human, for those hours, all the dark things are made clear."

CHAPTER 10. PETER MILLE

A few years after I had left Dole and taken the initially rather scary step of setting myself up as a scientific consultant, I had completed the creation of my own small laboratory in what remained of the basement of my parents' original home on this gentle hill; the house had burned down during one dry August, leaving only a few charred pine trees and the big stone basement room with its fireplace. I covered the room with a roof of 2x4's and aluminum sheeting, then moved in a solid table that was my chemical workbench. Next came water by way of plastic pipe. Finally, I built a rack of cross-hatched tubing out of inexpensive gas pipe from the local hardware store. The laboratory quickly became, and has remained, a place of exploration and excitement, resembling — according to Alice — one of those late-night-movie laboratories in which a mad scientist with wild hair and blazing eyes attempts to wrest from the gods that which no mortal can be allowed to discover, et cetera. She says the only difference is that there are no piles of dried leaves on the floor in the movie labs. There certainly are in mine.

Not long after I'd put the lab together, I received a call from a colleague in Sweden who said that he was currently the scientific organizer of an international symposium on marijuana, to be held in Stockholm. He said that he would love to have me come and present a paper on my work. As modesty has never been one of my strong points, I gave dark and subtle hints that of course I had successfully tied the marijuana world to that of the phenethylamines (this was the substance of the Trinidad adventure aboard the Chusan). However, I told my caller, I just didn't have the money needed to accept his offer.

I was unaware of the fact that the Swedish Government had just nationalized the pharmacy industry, and one of the rationalizations they had advanced for this heavy-handed action was that now the profits from this health-industry could be directed towards research and education. "Research" included such things as sponsoring international meetings on drug-related projects. And "drug-related" included such things as marijuana.

I received a call back in a couple of days saying that a round-trip ticket was on its way, that hotel reservations for a five-day meeting had been made for me, and that they were looking forward to my research report on nitrogen analogues of marijuana. I was screwed.

So, for the next two-score days, I squirreled myself away in the lab thinking up, making, and tasting new compounds that could be seen as nitrogen analogues of marijuana. I didn't want to rekindle the in-the-ring structures which had been the principal actors in the A.R.L. and Frantic Freddie circus, so I designed a new class of analogues with the nitrogen atom outside of any ring. These would be THC-like compounds with the phenethylamine chain hanging off the aromatic ring. I put together a series of furanyl and pyranyl analogs and wrote it all up as a paper to present in Stockholm. None of the compounds had any activity, so it had to sail on its chemistry, and that was frankly not too well polished.

As with most such ventures, the real reward came from an unexpected direction. After I had given my paper, I was approached by a middle-aged gentleman, wearing a tie and expensive clothes, who spoke excellent English. He said that he was most appreciative of work such as mine, in part because it had been carried out in a private laboratory, without outside financial support.

I acknowledged his appreciation and volunteered that, should he be in the United States some day, he might like to visit my place. He accepted my offer, but then told me that he had a lab of his own, and would be most honored if I would visit it. Alarm bells rang; I did not really wish to be caught in the basement of some brownstone residence outside of Stockholm, admiring a bubbling flask filled with LSD.

Well, I said, someday maybe, eventually, next time, when we are all under less social pressure. No problem, my well-dressed gentleman said; now was the perfect time.

So here I found myself, being swept out of the conference room and into his car. We dropped by the Karolinska Institute to visit my friend and colleague who worked there. He knew my companion, so I had my very first hint that his invitation was on the up-and-up. We left the institute and drove on into the center of the city, and the next thing I knew, we were pulling up in front of a two-storey building in downtown Stockholm. A guard ran out to the car, opened the door for us, and let us into the building that was surely a block by a block in size. A little while later it all became clear. I had just been given a midnight tour of the Swedish equivalent of the FBI laboratories. My host was Peter Mille, the head of the Narcotics Lab in Stockholm, and what he had called "my own little lab" was the state Big Thing!

I had never seen so many instruments, so much equipment, so many reference samples and such a professional dedication to excellence. There were instruments which would document indentations from scratch pads, and which could lift fingerprints from Styrofoam cups. There were the spectra of dust from carpet sweepings, and the chromatograms of the fumes from arson cases. But I was especially taken by a display of drawer after drawer of tablets, pills and capsules which he showed me. In Sweden, he said, there are, or have been, some 70,000 varieties of items that have been legally available for health purposes. Here, he said, embracing the entire collection with a flourish of his hand, is a reference sample of each. I was totally seduced. When I finally got back to the United States, I vowed that I would make such a collection, from the prescription world, from the over-the-counter shelves in the local drug store, and certainly from the health food suppliers and supermarket outlets that were, after all, the major distributors of our popular medicines. Get one of everything. I found out that we had in the United States, not thousands, but millions of different types of pills and capsules easily available. I have collected and organized a few thousand of them, but my collection is far from being complete, and I now know that my project is too large to ever be completed. The numbers are immense. We are truly a nation of drugs.

The personal treasure of the experience was Dr. Mille's invitation afterwards to come to his house, meet his wife Celia, and share dinner. After a modest but excellent meal, I went upstairs to Celia's private quarters where there was a piano and several musical instruments. Peter lowered a canoe-like structure from the ceiling and lit a large number of candles in it. I tuned up the violin that their daughter had left behind when she went off to school, and Celia and I played Mozart violin sonatas for several hours while Peter listened quietly from the downstairs living room.

Years later, I did indeed have the pleasure of showing my friend Peter my laboratory, here on the Farm. It was certainly more modest than his, but no less loved by its owner.

CHAPTER 11. ANDREW

One evening, in the late 1950's, I was invited to a musical soiree at an old, comfortable home in the Berkeley Hills. I brought my viola with me, as there was a promise of some string quartet sight-reading. The only person I remember from that evening was a handsome, proper gentleman with a small gray moustache and the residues of an English accent. During coffee, after the music playing was over, he struck up a conversation. He asked me if I had ever heard of the Owl Club, in San Francisco?

I had not, so he began painting a picture of a rather fascinating group, with many interests in all areas of art, drama and music. He mentioned that there was a need for a viola in their symphonic orchestra, and would I want to sit in for a couple of evenings (they met once a week for a little bit of rehearsal, a lot of talk, and too much gourmet food and wine) to see if I liked them and they liked me. It sounded like quite an adventure, so I readily said yes.

The Club proved to be a group of gentlemen from a broad array of political and professional backgrounds, leaning somewhat towards the political right and the well-to-do. The regular members carried the major share of the operating expenses, but for the actual participants in stage and concert shows, playwrights and composers, those who contributed time and effort to Club activities such as the orchestra, a couple of bands, and a chorus, the costs were largely subsidized by the Club itself. I found the camaraderie to be extraordinary. The modest time investment was completely rewarding, and I developed a number of close friends.

On my first evening at the Club, I met a Dr. Andrew Walker Scott, who proved to be an interesting collection of contradictions. Among the rituals attendant upon joining this group of rather conservative gentlemen — with whom I still regularly break both bread and Bach — was the indoctrinating lecture explaining the rather rigid behavior patterns expected of new members. Andrew was appointed my *pater familias*. He was a retired member of the medical community and had the stern, authoritative demeanor necessary to thoroughly intimidate a young, impressionable neophyte.

I eventually saw the human side of Andrew. One year, at the summer Owl Encampment (which takes place in a quiet forest preserve about two hours from the Bay Area and lasts two weeks), he came up to me (I had been in the Club for a few years, by then, and although still relatively young I was not the neophyte anymore) and asked if I would like to play a Beethoven quartette.

"Sure!" I knew he was a dedicated amateur (in both the English and American senses of the word) second violin player, but had in recent years been finding fewer and fewer volunteering co-quartetters with whom to share his enthusiasm, possibly because he was not the world's best violinist, to put it gently. He often explained that the difficulties he was having were due to the fact that he was sight-reading the music (for non-musicians, this means you're seeing it for the first time and playing it as you read).

I grabbed my viola and we were joined by two others for a little chamber work.

"What shall we play?" he asked.

"Whatever you'd like, Andrew," I replied, "Perhaps one of the middle quartettes?"

"No," he said, "Since I've never seen those quartettes before, maybe better an early one; it's probably easier. How about Opus 18, Number four? I just happen to have the music here with me."

"Sounds good to me," said I. We started sawing away, and about halfway through the first movement, during a brief lull, I glanced at his music sheet and saw that all the bowing and fingering had been carefully written in for the second violin part, and in Andrew's very own hand. Sight-reading indeed! I was careful not to let my eyes stray in that direction again, but found myself smiling at the thought of this very proper old gentleman's little pride-saving maneuver.

But I also had the pleasure of seeing his innocent side.

With my mother's death and the year's stay with my father, wife and son in Europe, I had arranged an extended leave of absence from the Club which, as it worked out, evolved into a period of several years. This was, in effect, tantamount to a resignation.

During these years, I was uncertain as to just how I should carry on my research work in the area of the psychedelic drugs. There were good arguments for remaining above-ground, publishing everything, and staying in intimate touch with the positives and negatives of the scientific community. There were also good arguments for going underground — the political climate being what it was — suffering isolation from fellow scientists, but never again required to explain, justify or defend my interests.

I had not yet made my decision.

About this time, I received a request to give testimony to Representative Claude Pepper's traveling road show, the House Committee on Crime in America, which was holding a series of public forums across the country. Did I say "request?" I should have said that I received a subpoena to present myself and answer questions. It was my first, and presumably my last, opportunity to get a close-up view of the body politic in full function.

I had the pleasure of meeting the investigating counsel in his office ahead of time. He sat behind a desk in an anteroom to the public hearing chamber (all this was on one of the top floors of the Federal Building in San Francisco), and as I sat there, an aide brought him a mountain of papers. I guessed that they had something to do with me. The lawyer began leafing through the stack. A court reporter sat nearby with fingers poised over the keys of his magic machine. I watched and waited.

He raised his head and glanced at me, "You know that you have the right to have a lawyer present with you?"

"Why would I need a lawyer?"

He didn't bother answering; I hadn't expected him to. With an efficient sweep of head and hands, he returned again to browsing through his paper mountain, while the secretary tap-tap-tapped, recording these priceless comments for history.

A photograph came out of the mountain. It was handed to me; a picture of the already rather famous Augustus Owsley Stanley, being led in handcuffs from his Orinda LSD lab in a recent arrest.

"Do you recognize this man?"

"I believe that is the picture of Mr. Stanley which appeared in the San Francisco Chronicle a few days ago, in conjunction with his arrest."

"Why would you invite a known felon to your home?"

"Who?"

"Mr. Stanley," said the lawyer.

"Mr. Stanley has never been to my home," I said calmly and truthfully.

Our eyes met. The only sound was the tapping of the court reporter's keys. Then another paper from the stack. This one was not shown to me, and there was no way I could see it.

"Why would you turn down six million dollars to set up a lab in Jamaica?"

Well, well, well, thought I. The question had brought back an interesting memory. A few years earlier, when I was still employed at Dole, I'd had a visit from a couple of rather young entrepreneurs, one small and dark, the other tall and red-bearded. They told me they were interested in setting up a "legal" laboratory for the production of psychedelic drugs known and unknown, and they were offering me the chance to do the setting up. It would be on the island of Jamaica, and I was to be paid three million dollars now and three million more upon completion of an operational lab.

When I asked who was proposing to pay for this venture, my visitors said that it was a group of businessmen. They didn't volunteer names, and I didn't ask for any, since I wouldn't have recognized them anyway. I didn't have much information about the world of business. But I did have instincts, and they were telling me that there was something not exactly kosher about either the young men or their proposal.

Although Barbarossa tried to convince me that this was the chance of a lifetime, I declined, very politely. I had a perfectly fine job, I said, with a very good chemical company, and didn't really want to relocate to another country right at the moment.

Not until now, staring across the desk at the hard-faced lawyer, had I been given a clue as to the true source of the offer! I wondered what department of the government had set up what was probably some sort of "sting", and what exactly they had expected to accomplish.

My reply to the lawyer was simple, "What would I do with six million dollars?"

The flavor of my forthcoming testimony had been established.

The actual hearings were well attended, but I suspect that the audience was not completely unbiased. This was San Francisco, after all. The act directly ahead of me was the testimony of the famous Art Linkletter, at that time widely regarded as an expert on LSD use, due to the tragedy of his daughter's death, which — although it had occurred some time after her taking of the drug — was blamed by her father and the press on an experiment with LSD.

I was nervous and didn't pay much attention to his testimony, except for an exchange concerning hippies and long hair.

Mr. Linkletter asked the congressmen if they knew why all hippies had long hair, held tightly with a rubber band?

"No," replied a suddenly interested Honorable Claude Pepper, "I've often wondered about that."

The audience sensed something dramatic about to happen, and began quieting down.

"It is really rather straightforward," said Mr. Linkletter, "It has to do with psychedelic drugs."

The audience was completely quiet now.

"When the hippie gets high, he can undo the rubber band, let his hair loose in all directions, and shake his head vigorously — ," here Mr. Linkletter shook his head energetically from side to side, in view of perhaps 200 fascinated listeners, some half dozen congressmen, and one attorney, " — to unleash the windmills of the mind."

Laughter erupted across the room, and the gavel pounded for order.

I was to be the next witness. Quite an act to follow.

My testimony began with some brief formalities, such as birth, education, and employment history, then quickly got to the subject most dear to their hearts: drugs. Much of the question and answer exchange has been lost to memory; I was in a sort of shock and responding from an instinctive urge to survive. Eventually, at one point, the lawyer asked me a question that was reasonable, but he asked it in a way that gave me control.

"How can you call yourself a scientist," he demanded, "And do the type of work you do?"

Never ask a witness on the stand a question that requires more than a yes or no answer. It is called "giving the witness the chalk." He can then suggest to the magistrate (or chairman, judge, member of Congress) that to give a meaningful answer, a little background would be needed, and ask for a bit of extra time, and he will almost always receive it. I suggested, asked, and received.

I started at the beginning. I talked about the family burdens of schizophrenia, the social costs of the hospitals and the welfare costs associated with depression and alcoholism, and I might even have talked about the heartbreak of psoriasis, although I don't specifically remember. A tear for every eye. Then, on I went to tell how recent research with the neurotransmitters was starting to bring understanding of the mental processes. And how an understanding of drugs that affected the integrity of the human brain in a controlled way might give insight into the processes of mental illness which are defined by just this type of disruption. I asked that this and that paper published in the scientific literature be entered into the record. I was just getting into the actual answer to the original question itself, when a recess was called.

I had no way of knowing what was discussed during the break, but when the hearing was reconvened, I was quickly thanked for my contributions and told that my testimony had been completed.

As I started to leave the hearing room, I was approached by a tall, well-dressed man with a neatly trimmed Van Dyke beard, and an air of total self-confidence.

"I am Doctor Paul Freye, he said, extending his hand. "And I am the head of the Narcotics Lab here in the Bay Area. I very much appreciated your contributions to today's hearings, and I'm very glad to meet you."

I said hello and shook his hand. I felt an immediate liking for him. We exchanged addresses and phone numbers, and agreed to meet again in the near future. I had no way of guessing that he would become one of my closest and most valued friends over the years to come, and that we would share many delightful hours in my laboratory, where he would occasionally come on a weekend to "get his hands wet," with the chemical manipulations that continually fascinated him.

Paul loved the chemistry of the psychedelics, but was absolutely adamant in his refusal to entertain the idea of altering his own consciousness by nibbling the resulting materials. "Call me chicken," he said once, laughing, "But the very thought of taking one of these drugs makes the hair stand up on my head!" I reassured him that I had no intention of trying to persuade him to take any kind of psychedelic, and that I didn't think of him as chicken at all. We both knew that it was just as well he wasn't tempted to become that kind of explorer, because his position within the establishment would have been severely compromised by any such undertaking.

But that was the only pleasant note on what was otherwise a very difficult day.

I avoided the press and television people outside the hearing chambers, but when I got home that evening there were more of them at the entrance to the Farm. I simply drove on by and waited them out, down at a nearby coffee shop.

The next day, there was a short report on the hearings in the morning paper, with my photograph, and a brief account of the regrets of a drug researcher concerning any of his discoveries which might have become social embarrassments.

There were very few comments made to me about the hearings or the publicity that resulted, but one of those few was from my long-ago quartetting companion, Andrew. He phoned a few days later to chat, and mentioned that he had for some reason thought of me recently. He had remembered, he said, that I used to play viola in the Club, and wanted me to know that there was a need of another fiddler, and might I be interested in considering re-activating my association with them?

Here was the innocent side of my conservative friend. He had indeed seen my picture in the paper, but hadn't bothered to read the text (perhaps because members of the Club often appeared in the newspapers for a variety of reasons). With his invitation, and without being in the least aware of it, he had decided for me the above-ground/under-ground issue. I knew that in the long run, my relationships with people would be more trouble-free and much more valuable, if they could be based on honesty rather than being clouded with deception and manipulation. I wanted, and I needed, an affirmation of my own integrity. I happily rejoined the Owl Club and, to this day, I put on a polite shirt and tie and carry my viola to the City and play in the orchestra every Thursday evening, without fail.

I should add that I am the only Club member who wears, and always has worn, black sandals instead of shoes, having decided a very long time ago that sandals were infinitely healthier for my feet than the airless, moist environment offered by the kinds of footwear worn by my fellow Owlers. They are used to my sandals, by now, and they are used to me.

CHAPTER 12. MDMA

It was in 1967, Y.F.C (Year of the Flower Children), that I attended a conference on Ethnopharmacology that was held in Cole Hall, at the Medical School in San Francisco. The Medical Center was almost exactly in the center of the hippie movement, being only a very few blocks from the Haight Ashbury. The conference was conceived of by a marvelous curmudgeon and iconoclast named Daniel Efron, with whom I had an especially warm relationship. He balanced two roles with great skill. As the chief honcho of the Pharmacology Section of Psychopharmacology at the National Institute of Mental Health, he was an important voice in the directing of governmental funds to grant-seekers and, because of his influence, he was always being lionized wherever he went. But he was also very much an underminer of sacrosanct ideologies, as illustrated by the organization of this conference on ethnopharmacology. Our friendship was unique in that I had never applied for any government grant, thus had no self-serving reason to befriend him, and he knew it.

Once I had gone to a pharmacology meeting at Stanford where he was chairing one of the afternoon sessions. I sat in the audience, in the front row, and at one point caught his eye as he scanned faces. After the last talk, I met with him, whisked him away from the professional pharmacologists, and took him off to the Farm, followed by a friend, Saul Snowman, who came in his own car. Dr. Snowman was at that time an assistant professor of pharmacology at a well-known medical school on the East Coast, and this was one of our few meetings in person; most of our communication had been by letter. On the way Danny asked to stop at a store where he might find a box of candy for my wife Helen because he felt he was certainly going to be imposing upon her as a guest.

At the Farm, we all collapsed into chairs, and everyone seemed suddenly to become human again. Danny announced that, (1) he had always wanted to see my lab, and (2) he used to play the trumpet in high-school in the eastern Europe of his childhood. So we went to the lab where my son Theo had prepared a fire in the fireplace, and Danny had his first view of it. There was a nice, crackling fire. Lichens appeared to be growing on a separatory funnel (they had been glued on years ago) which I had attached to the top of a metal rack; it also bore a funny face drawn in ink by the friend who gave it to me for good luck. The combination of face and greenish-yellow lichens had caused many a stranger to take a sudden surprised step backwards at the sight. Something was stirring and bubbling in a beaker on the bench, there were empty wine jugs on the floor, and innumerable bottles of chemicals on shelves overhead. To complete the picture, there was a beautiful colony of slender-legged, fragile spiders — the kind called Daddy Long Legs — moving ever so gently over the collection of clean round-bottomed flasks. Danny stood at the doorway looking in, cane in his right hand, the left extended, like Balboa viewing the Pacific Ocean.

"I have —" he said with an accent that defies transcription, "— spent *meell*-yons of dollars in *meell*-yons of laboratories, out of which has come *nott*-ing, and here is a laboratory in which I have spent *nott*-ing out of which has come *everry*-ting!" I was flattered.

When we returned to the house, I unearthed an old trumpet of mine with valves that luckily still worked, and offered Danny a chance to loosen up with Haydn's fourth concerto, my job being the piano reduction and Saul's role being that of attentive audience. Helen looked in now and then to check on our supply of wine and nibble-food. A couple of hours later we were happily exhausted and Saul, bless his heart, drove Danny home.

With his death, in 1972, Danny's protege, Earl Usdin, carried forward many of the projects that they had worked on together, and remarkably found yet additional energy to initiate some of his own. He, too, is now part of history. These two close friends contributed in untold ways to the science of psychopharmacology in this country.

The 1967 conference was entitled, "Ethnopharmacologic Search for Psychoactive Drugs." This meeting was, to my knowledge, the first time that most of the explorers in the area of psychedelic drugs were assembled in one place. And what a collection of rich interactions came from it!

Claudio Naranjo, a psychiatrist-anthropologist who had made his way years before through South American jungles to discover the Ayahuasca vine, gave a passionate talk which transmitted the excitement he felt about the jungle images of Ayahuasca-induced intoxication. In his experience, and in the experience of his patients, according to Claudio, the taking of plant extracts that contained harmaline invariably brought about visions of jaguars and other fauna and flora associated with the jungle in which the vine grew.

Also at the meeting was the well-known and respected botanist, Richard

E. Schultes of Harvard, and I had heard from him that he had never experienced these particular types of visual images with Ayahuasca.

I had the pleasure of introducing them, and mentioned their common interests. Claudio opened the conversation:

"What do you think of the jaguars?"

"What jaguars?"

A small silence.

"Are you personally familiar with authentic Banisteriopsis caapi?" asked Claudio, his voice slightly strained.

Richard looked at him closely. "I was the person who assigned it its name."

Claudio went on. "Have you ever taken the plant decoction itself?"

"Perhaps fifteen times."

"And never jaguars?"

"Sorry, only wiggly lines."

Claudio turned away. To my knowledge, they have not talked since.

And there was Chauncey Leake who started things on a loose note, talking of the primitive state of pharmacology at the turn of the century when just about the whole practice of medicine depended on the contents of two barrels in the basement, one labelled "Antiscrof" and the other, "Antisyph." The toxicologist and explorer Bo Holmstedt reviewed the history of the discovery of medicines in plants. There was Steven Szara of DMT fame, and Andy Weil, Gordon Wasson, Nathan Kline, Harry Isbell, Danny Freedman, and piles of others who have always been interested in, and have contributed to, this area of pharmacology. Several Russians couldn't make it for political reasons and, interestingly, neither could Albert Hofmann, the discoverer of LSD, due to the company policy of Sandoz, by whom he was still employed. A book came out of all this, published by the Government Printing Office, with a gentle disclaimer from the Public Health Service section of the Department of Health, Education and Welfare. But very few outside of the group that was in attendance there really cared, and the meeting has now been virtually forgotten.

I had presented my paper on nutmeg and was wandering around the lobby outside where the real action was taking place, and a friend introduced me to a young professor of chemistry, Noel Chestnut, who expressed a general dissatisfaction with everything he had heard so far, except for one paper on essential oils and their conversion to amphetamine derivatives. He said he would like to meet the author. I said, "I am the author," and thus began a friendship which has lasted to this day.

Noel saw that the unusual potency of my drug DOM, and its deceptively simple structure, could be the basis of a hypothesis. If the compound were converted, through some form of metabolic oxidation, to a chemical class called quinones, then a reasonable end-product would be an indole.

And one of the principal neurotransmitters in the human, serotonin, is an indole. This all just might have value in the area of mental health, which could lead to new grant applications and grant awards, and thence to the funding of graduate students and post-doctorate scholars doing marvelous metabolic studies.

A young chemist who had graduated from a large university in the Midwest came to San Francisco to take a post-doctoral position with Noel at about this time. His name was Dr. David Ladder, and when we met, flint was struck and fire found. My relationship with David developed into a productive union which still exists today. He is a shy, gentle, brilliant chemist, and we have published countless papers together and will, I hope, continue doing so in the future.

While Noel was wandering around the world on lecture tours and occasional sabbatical leaves, he appointed me a sort of surrogate "daddy-in-residence," for his graduate students at the University of California in San Francisco. One of these was a dear, dear sprite appropriately named Merrie Kleinman, who told me that she had done an experiment with two very close friends of hers, and that they had used 100 milligrams of N-methylated MDA (MDMA). She shared very little about the experience, but implied that it was quite emotional, and that there had been a basically good reaction from all three of them.

This was not the first time I had heard mention of MDMA. In fact I had synthesized it back at Dole in 1965 but had never before met someone who had personally tried it. I resynthesized it and found it unlike anything I had taken before. It was not a psychedelic in the visual or interpretive sense, but the lightness and warmth of the psychedelic was present and quite remarkable. I began collecting comments concerning its effects from a number of subjects under a variety of circumstances, and I developed a great respect and admiration for the material.

I had begun giving a course in forensic toxicology on the Berkeley campus of the University of California. It usually gathered between 20 and 30 students, and over half of them managed to stay in there with me to the very end of the course. I doubt that any of them were a great deal wiser in matters of forensic toxicology, but most of them had been exposed to what I considered very useful and important information and had been adequately entertained. One of my more devoted students was a sweet youngster, a guitar player, who had the world's most devastating stutter. Just before most words that starting with a vowel (or, for that matter, with any one of several consonants), he would tie up completely until he either (1) inhaled and exhaled at a measured pace several times, or (2) jerked his head to one side and changed the starting word. His name was Klaus.

Klaus was intrigued with MDA and, for some reason, with its N-methylated homolog, MDMA. He actually arranged to find lab space somewhere in the Life Sciences Building and set up a summer project to work out useful procedures for making MDMA. He was in perennial torment with his speech impediment whenever I happened to see him — which was rarely — and after a while, I lost all contact with him.

It was some time later, as I was bouncing across campus to a meeting, that I spotted him, and — with only a moment's pause — remembered who he was.

"How are you?" I asked, awaiting the breathing pattern or the shift of head.

"In excellent spirits," came the reply, with only a suggestion of a rolled R in the word, "spirits."

"And your music?" I continued bravely, now doubting that I had identified him correctly.

"Only once in a while." The O's in "only" and "once" were each being held just a mite too long, so I was reassured that this was indeed my Klaus.

"But," he added, without breaking stride, "That methylated MDA allowed me to do new things with myself."

"What, for example?" I asked.

""Well, for one thing, I have some control over my talking for the first time. And I've decided to take up a new career."

"And that is — ?"

"Speech therapy."

I have lost track of Klaus, but I believe that his was one of the earliest clues I had that there was something akin to snake-oil — in the sense of an apparent cure for anything that ails you — about this elixir called MDMA.

Another early trial showed yet a different view of its action.

A good friend of mine, Charles Miller, had been following my research for many years, and he occasionally asked if I thought it might be useful to him to someday have an experience. I had always put such ideas off to some undefined future time, as I felt uncomfortable with what might come up from his unconscious in any opening experience. Although he was a gentle and giving person, he was strongly opinionated — actually inflexibly opinionated — and a committed alcoholic. And with his daily change of state with alcohol, there was a daily change of personality, revealing towards the end of the evening an outspoken, largely anti-everything person; especially anti-intellectual and anti-homosexual.

That is a combination that has always been a danger signal to me, and I slowly came to believe that Charlie had in some way come to peace with many of the difficulties that had surely tormented him in his youth. Not necessarily resolved them — but at least gotten them buried deeply and safely into the unconscious. And I was not at all certain that I wished to be the person who provided the instrument to unearth any of it.

His wife, Janice, had never expressed any interest in such exploration, although she too knew intellectually of my research interests. But it was she who called me one day asking if she (and her younger son) might use a few hours of my time — to answer a question or two. It was Janice who had the questions; her son was apparently coming along to give her moral support, as he was quite worldly in the drug area. I suggested that afternoon. They accepted. As I have often noted, when the time is right, it becomes unmistakably obvious that it is right.

Janice, her son, and I, all three of us, took 120 milligrams of MDMA in the early afternoon, and the son went off by himself. At about the half-hour point, the usual "awareness" time, Janice gave no indication of effects, nor were there any changes at the 40 minute nor at the 50 minute point. A few off-hand comments were offered.

"My throat is dry."

"I'll get you a glass of water." Which I did. It did no good.

"I'm having trouble breathing."

"So, breathe as best you can." I noticed by the reflection in the window where we were, at the back of the house, that she had no difficulty breathing when I wasn't watching her.

We walked up the hill, to an area I had leased out to the condominium builders on the neighboring land for the storage of lumber. There were several 'no smoking' signs around as fire warnings.

"Do you think I smoke too much?"

"Do *you* think you smoke too much?"

"I don't think so."

"Then the answer is: probably not."

It was now an hour into the experiment, and still no acknowledgment of any activity from the MDMA. Then, came the unexpected question, the "off the wall" question.

"Is it all right to be alive?"

"You bet your sweet ass it's all right be be alive! It's a grace to be alive!"

That was it. She plunged into the MDMA state, and started running down the hill, calling out that it was all right to be alive. All the greens became living greens and all the sticks and stones became vital sticks and stones. I caught up with her and her face was radiant. She told me some of her personal history which she knew well, and which I knew well, but with which she had never come to peace.

She had come into the world by an unexpected Caesarean section and her mother had died during the delivery. And for fifty years she had lived in the guilt of having had her life given her at the cost of her mother's life. She had been in therapy with her family physician for about three years, largely addressing this problem, and apparently what she needed was the acknowledgment that it was all right to be alive.

I didn't hear from her for a couple of months. When she did call, she volunteered that she still felt very much at peace, and had discontinued her therapy.

In most of my own early experimental trials, I concentrated on the area of 80 to 100 milligrams, and I used the word, "window," in my notes to describe the effects. It enabled me to see out, and to see my own insides, without distortion or reservations.

Helen and I would occasionally take a 6:00 PM Friday to 4:00 PM Sunday trip with our friends — George and Ruth Close, whom we had known from the old Cal Hall days — on a special train out of Oakland called the Reno Fun Train. As the train proceeded eastwards across the Sierras, the mass of people would get increasingly noisy, with much food and drink, and even dancing in a music car. (After some thirty hours in the gambling casinos, the return trip was considerably more subdued.) Helen was basically uncomfortable with drugs, but perfectly at ease with an occasional drink; the Closes were, at that time, naive about any altered states except those induced by alcohol. On one of our trips, during our private foursome dinner with the cracked crab and avocado dip in the noisy car, I asked them if they would be offended if I filled my glass with quinine-water and the contents of a small vial, rather than with a martini. Why? An experiment, I said. Okay, they said, why not!

It worked. It seemed that my gradual intoxication locked into theirs very smoothly. They forgot that I was using a chemical rather than vodka. So, for a while, I referred to MDMA as my low-calorie martini.

Not long after that, I met and became very close to a likeable couple of professional researchers and teachers from Germany, Ursula and Adolph Biehls, who were studying for a year with Terry Major. Dolph, as he called himself, had taken a modest dosage of LSD one day and his experience had been extraordinarily complex, difficult and frightening. He continued for several weeks having problems with reintegration.

I suggested, after considerable thought, that — although a new psychedelic experience would certainly not be appropriate — MDMA might be of some help to him. It was not a psychedelic, I emphasized, and explained the "window" concept, and why I thought he could perhaps use it to repair himself.

I shared the experience with the two of them. It was a memorable day. There was verbal honesty without reserve, and the experiment led to an intimate friendship which would last between the three of us for several years. Dolph's LSD trauma was resolved in those few hours, and he emerged, in his own words, newborn. Another hint of snake-oil. MDMA, it was beginning to be apparent, could be all things to all people.

There is another part of the MDMA story which should be told, and it concerns a kind, elderly psychologist who was everyone's idea of what a grandfather should be, both in looks and demeanor. He listened intently, laughed heartily and often, and — as Alice says — gave you the kind of hug you wanted to stay in forever.

Adam had his practice in Oakland, on the second floor of a house which had been converted into office spaces. For the most part, his therapy was of the usual fifty-minute variety, but a small part of his practice followed quite another path, and was kept secret from all but his closest friends — and those with whom he chose to do his special work — until his death. It is still kept secret by those who knew and loved him, and will undoubtedly remain so.

This quiet practice involved the use of psychoactive materials which would allow the client to step around his psychological barriers and address himself and his unconscious directly. The use of such drugs followed a technique which he had evolved over a couple of decades.

Adam would go to the house of the client for these sessions. He always arranged ahead of time that the person taking the journey would have available family photographs which could be used to stimulate associations and prod open memories of childhood. He also told his client to frame for himself, before the day of the session, questions to which he wanted answers. After the drug had been given, Adam — not taking anything himself — would sit nearby to give assurance and a comforting touch of the hand, if needed, or to help untangle any knot or problem that might arise during the experience. The hard work was up to the client, and the answers to questions had to come from within the client's own psyche.

Adam used a range of materials, from the relatively gentle MDA, to LSD or ibogaine, which he used for an all-out assault on psychological resistance. His sources of drugs were seemingly impeccable, usually reputable chemical supply houses, but it was in his nature to verify everything, and he would often call upon me to inspect a new material for final word as to identity and purity.

In 1977, age was sneaking up on Adam and he was allowing his patient load to dwindle by attrition. I knew that he was getting ready to gather in his shingle and let the lease lapse on his Oakland office. One day, he asked me to drop by to see if I wanted to accept some of the unusual mementos which he had acquired over the years. There were bits of bark from here, and strange powders from there. He had small twigs and roots of Iboga, and discovery samples of the first collections of Yajé from South America. I spent a couple of hours with him and gratefully accepted his botanical museum.

I had decided, on this occasion, to bring with me a small bottle of my "low-calorie martini," MDMA hydrochloride, to tempt him to try something new. Knowing his fondness for MDA, I assured him it had some of the virtues of MDA, without the "stoning" properties, and it had something extra, a special magic, which just might catch his attention. He told me that he might or might not try it, but that if he did, he would let me know what he thought of it.

He phoned me a few days later to tell me that he had abandoned his plans for a quiet retirement. I know none of the details of the increasingly complex network which he proceeded to develop over the following decade, but I do know that he traveled across the country, introducing MDMA to other therapists and teaching them how to use it in their therapy. They all had to begin, of course, by learning its effects in themselves. Adam believed (as do I) that no therapist has the right to give a psychoactive drug to another person unless and until he is thoroughly familiar with its effects on his own body and mind.

Many of the psychologists and psychiatrists whom Adam instructed developed small groups or enclaves of professionals who had been similarly taught, and the information and techniques he had introduced spread widely and, in time, internationally.

It is impossible to ever know the true breadth of therapeutic MDMA usage achieved by Adam during the remaining years of his life, but at his memorial service, I asked an old friend of his whether she had a guess as to the number of people Adam had introduced to this incredible tool, either directly or indirectly. She was silent for a moment, then said, "Well, I've thought about that, and I think probably somewhere around four thousand, give or take a few."

It has proven to be such a valuable psychotherapeutic adjunct, I truly believe it will persevere in therapeutic use for a long time to come, despite the structuring of the law that has come about in many countries to prohibit its use and discourage its study.

As one psychiatrist put it, "MDMA is penicillin for the soul, and you don't give up penicillin, once you've seen what it can do."

CHAPTER 13. TIME-STOP

I realize that, for many people, pot — marijuana — is of value prima-rily as a drug that relieves stress and smooths out tensions. In general, I have regarded pot as a disappointment and a waste of time. It has, for me, really only two rewards: food tastes exceptionally good under its influence, and time slows to an extent that makes it possible to play clock-stopping games.

Once, I chose to use it just as a de-stressor, after a somewhat brittle experiment with a new drug combination, and found myself — not by choice — in a time-stopping experience that was truly frightening.

This particular day in April, sometime in the 1970's, Theo was away at college and Helen was visiting a relative for a few days, so I had the house to myself. At that time I was occasionally using either of two interesting experimental procedures. One of these, which I called "priming," was the taking of an active drug at a certain interval of time following an inactive one. If the observed effects of the "active" drug (the primed drug) are different due to the presence of the inactive drug (the priming drug) then some understanding of the process of potentiation might be gotten. The other of these, which I called "piggybacking," involved the taking of an active drug during the drop-off phase of another, different, active drug. The use of such a "false supplement" can reveal differences of qualitative action that can help define both drugs more accurately.

On this occasion, the first (and active) drug was MDOH, and the piggyback drug was MDA. I had always had a feeling in the back of my mind that these two materials might somehow merge their identities in the course of being metabolized in the body; they have very similar actions and very similar structures. They differ only by the presence of an oxygen atom, and the body is quite capable of adding (or removing) an oxygen atom in the normal process of biotransformation.

So, at 2:00 PM, I had taken 100 milligrams of MDOH, and had recorded a typical chronology and response to it. Later in the afternoon, as the effects were receding — at 4:30 PM, to be exact — I took a similar dose of MDA. Would they see each other? Would the MDA be similar enough to the MDOH to act as a supplement, and rekindle the now-waning effects of the MDOH? Or would there be some refractoriness from the first material which would make the MDA relatively ineffective? Or, for that matter, might there be an exacerbation of effects that might indicate some sort of synergy?

The effects were largely additive. At the usual awareness time of MDA — about a half-hour — I noted a familiar skin-crawling, and a quiet entry into a pretty stoned state. The expected spectrum of physical annoyances common to both drugs was there, the teeth clenching and irregularities of the motor muscles of the eyes. It was quite easy to trigger nystagmus. My handwriting was going downhill, and my motor coordination on the piano was compromised.

Another hour, and I found that there was a little time-slowing and I could play some visual games; I could get the shapes created by light and shadow from the setting sun (shining through tree leaves) to take on human forms.

By 7:00 PM, I was back down to a plus-one and at 8:00 PM, I was essentially baseline, with a somewhat sore jaw from the teeth clenching, and a weary psyche from the rest of the day's activities. That is why it was one of those rare times when I chose to use a little marijuana, to escape the stress. I smoked a 200 milligram sample of a gift material which had been sitting around, unused, for a couple of years. This was at 8:15 PM, and what followed was simply incredible.

By 8:28 PM (thirteen minutes had elapsed), I was aware of the first indications of marijuana effect, which was, for me, about the expected time. This first alert was followed by a sequence of waves of sensation, each wave bringing with it an increased slowing of time. It was uncanny, how these seemed to be evenly and regularly spaced, but as I looked at the clock's second hand, I noted that the waves must have been getting closer and closer together. Actually, this impression was due to the fact that the second hand was moving ever more slowly, rather than that the waves were different in their spacing.

My note, written at 8:31 PM, stated that there was considerable subjective time passage, out of proportion to the clock's activity, but that the music on the radio had no pitch distortion at all.

The next entry was made a couple of weeks later, at 8:35 PM, and I had just felt another wave of slowing hit me. And, just as the second-hand finally made it all the way around the clock face to 8:36 PM, there was yet another wave.

I was getting scared.

What was the status of my body? I tried to take my pulse, which is a totally ridiculous thing to do, when it takes forever to go from one heartbeat to another. You lose track of one thump-pa by the time you think that another thump-pa has just taken place. And the actual thump-pa itself is, of course, spread out across the countryside and is awfully difficult to identify. Is it the thoo- or is it the ump- or is it the -pa that counts? I noticed that there were three sounds that occurred during the time that the slow second-hand moved from one mark to another, so maybe my pulse was 180. Maybe not. There was no way for me to find out.

It was now 8:38 PM and I knew intellectually that only twenty-five minutes had elapsed since I felt the first effects. Twenty-five days seemed a better estimate. I got up and went to the piano and tried some of the Chopin First Nocturne. My fingers were somewhat sloppy, but the pitch was absolutely correct. I thought, if a second takes so long to pass, why doesn't the pitch, at so many vibrations per second, seem to be way down there, basso? Could it be that the sound receptors in my ear are also somehow slowed down, so that everything is right back up there in sync again? That makes no sense.

I abandoned the piano and returned to the couch and clock. In spite of my having played for quite a while, it was now only 8:41 PM. I thought, I am so far above a plus-three, there are no valid numbers. I can't use the plus-four symbol, since that stands for something quite apart from a stoned psychedelic state, so let's call this a 3.7 plus. Try the pulse again. Now, there is nothing to be heard at all, so either the heart has stopped beating (is that what happens if time comes totally to a stop?) or the rumbly sounds are so diffuse, they cannot be identified. But, then, why should a piano sound be okay, but a heart sound be screwy? Should I call for help?

By 8:53 PM, I had made my way through miles of house to the dining room where the phone was located, and dialed the number of my friend, George Close. It was with horror and dismay that I discovered the phone was dead. There was absolutely no sound on it. I let my gaze drift around the room, looking for something to quiet the rising panic. I wasn't certain just what I was looking for; something that would tell me which way to turn, what to do. I was forever captive in the house, and as it had taken me so long a time just to go from one room to the next, I knew that I could never get as far as the car, let alone drive it! What kind of extraordinary experience would it be, to drive a car with such extreme mis-estimating of time! I certainly didn't intend to find out.

And then it happened. I was startled back into the moment by the sound of the phone ringing in my ear. The connection had just been completed, and the Close's phone was ringing. Forever went by, then there was a second ring. Forever again, then a third ring. Ruth answered and her voice sounded normal (so voices as well as music didn't observe the changed time rules).

I spoke into the phone, "I'm in a funny place, Ruth, and I'm a bit scared. Could George come out and make sure that I will be findable, if things progress much more?"

I knew that made very little sense, but Ruth assured me that George was on his way, and I decided to stay on the phone and use her voice as an anchor in this strange storm.

I had never before been involved in a conversation that lasted for a century.

Now, my self-classification was at a 3.9 plus. I remember, at one point, asking Ruth to stay on the line while I went to the office for a piece of paper and a pen, and to note how long I was gone. I wanted to get a current estimate of how long something seemed to take, having her as the objective time-keeper. She said she would hold on and wait for my return. My plan was to start my internal subjective stop-watch and try to deduce just how much time it would take me to reach the office, pick up something, and return to the phone. Then I would get the real elapsed time from Ruth, and divide one into the other to get my "slowing factor."

I put the receiver down on the table and headed in the direction of my office. There will never be a way of reconstructing the myriad thoughts that went through my mind as I walked down the hall. One thought did stick in my mind, though. How can a person address, objectively, the subjective time-passing sense? How could I attend to an internal clock with some accuracy, so that I might give Ruth a really close guess as to just how long my round-trip really took me, subjectively? Estimating seconds by the one-thousand-and-one, one-thousand-and-two process was no good, since apparently the flow-of-words clock appeared to be running at about the right rate; it was the elapsed-time clock that was slowed down.

I reached the office, and for the life of me could not remember what it was I had intended to get. I looked around for something that I might be able to use to shed light on one clock or the other. Had I intended to type something? Calculate something? Read something? The world around me was colorful and moving, but — enjoyable as visual synthesis might be — I didn't want to let it take over. I had to stay in verbal contact. Which reminded me that the phone was off the hook and Ruth was at the other end, waiting. I had completely forgotten her, and hoped that she had waited for me.

I made it back, and she was still there.

"Sorry to be so long. I got distracted."

"How long do you think you were away?"

"Twenty, thirty minutes?"

"You were gone one minute, or a few seconds more than a minute."

So the factor was about 20 to 1 between the clocks. I knew that there had been no more waves of slowing for quite a while now, and somehow I sensed that there was repair on the way. After some long and complex discussions on the phone about the essential nature of the universe, I heard George drive up, and I let Ruth go on to bed. George came through the front door in great good humor, checked my pulse (it was about 110) and in general found me to be in an okay physical place. I'm pretty sure — now — that my heart had been all right throughout the evening.

I survived. I still have no idea how two clocks (the word-sequence and pitch clock, and the apparent-elapsed-time clock) could run at such different rates at the same time, and still both always point to the same hour.

A few days later, I re-assayed the same amount of the same marijuana lot (without the other drugs on board, of course) and there was a modest intoxication, but negligible time distortion. It must have been that combination, or me that day, or the relative positions of the planets. I will probably never know.

CHAPTER 14. ALEPH-1

It was in the year 1976 that I synthesized the first sulfur-containing psychedelic, called para-DOT, working at a distance with a friend, Dr. Charles Wyndham Mantle, who was a Professor of Chemistry at a large university on the East Coast.

The name I used for this group of the 4-position sulfur-analogues of TMA-2 was the Aleph family, calling upon the Hebrew alphabet. Using this code, the first and simplest base was Aleph-1, and with the dutiful preparation of simple homologues, these could then be named in sequence, i.e., Aleph-2, Aleph-3, etc.

Aleph-1 was, as I said, the first and simplest of the group, but my experience with it was far from simple. In fact, it was my first exposure to a state that was one of the most delicious blends of inflation, paranoia and selfishness I have ever experienced. It was a rare and prized occasion, neither predictable nor repeatable.

I hadn't named the family yet, at the time that I took the drug. The name was chosen because, with a reasonably modest dosage of para-DOT, I found myself in an extraordinary place which left me quite in awe of the chemical. It proved, as one could reasonably expect, to have been a *sui generis* occasion, but at the time I thought it might be a property of para-DOT (and perhaps even of its homologs) and, if so, the effect needed a name all its own. Hence, Aleph — the first letter of the Hebrew alphabet — and the first component of a new vocabulary.

The best explanation of that Aleph experience are my notes, written in real time (during the experience) which speak for themselves. Interestingly, as to level of effect, the experiment ranked about a plus two (the character of the effect can be defined, but it does not have an intensity that interferes with speech and function), from the sensory and physical point of view. From the mental point of view, it was certainly a full plus three.

It was extraordinary because of the strength and persistence of the many concepts which paraded past me as a sequence of distinct entities. Each was fully realized in an instant, then immediately succeeded by the next. The cascade was not only unceasing throughout the several hours of the experiment; it held me in a state of continuous, exhilarating energy for which only one word seems appropriate: power.

I have not edited out any of the apparent nonsense because it belongs here as much as does the occasional valid insight.

My notes follow, including comments and explanations inserted at a later time, which are in brackets:

I took 5.0 milligrams of the hydrochloride salt of 2,5-dimethoxy-4-methylthioamphetamine, or para-DOT (Aleph-1) in water at 10:50 AM on July 2, 1976. Three hours since any food. It is now the (0:00) hour of the experiment.

(0:50)   Warmth in lower legs.

(1:10)   Walked out to the highway for the mail.

(1:35)   Warm all over. Effects developing nicely.

(1:50)   Very real effect! Quite nice. No sense modality emphasized. Not yet, anyway.

(2:30)   Sat outside and got the concrete bag to float above the ground for a moment [this was a bag of dry Portland cement, full, with a logo on it that showed a bulging bicep]. Man on sack — Act of Power — but the act is not told, or it then would be only a Tale of Power. Or at best, a Tale of an Act of Power. An Act cannot be saved, relived — only the Tale persists. The act is past.

(2:33)   How long does it take to assimilate an act? The act itself, an augenblick [a quick glance], is like a drug effect, in that to assimilate it is to recall the wave of concepts that flooded over you. They must be sifted, reconstructed, as best as can be done from memory.

But that is only the immediate drug effect. There are aspects more broad. The drug may be just the prototype of a family, the trunk of an as-yet-unexplored tree with an unknown number of limbs, more branches yet, and an infinity of leaves.

And we can explore the infinity on many levels but we all too often choose just one, the immediate present. One can pass an opened door again and again, each time seeing new things, but always the same doorway, the same door.

Go through — don't just look through. Looking is like a tale of power;

to go through is the act of power. And suddenly a new dimension of doors, each unexplored.

In this way the SCH_3 becomes the SR [*the SCH_3, a methylthio group, is a clump of atoms found on the 4-position of Aleph-1. The "R" in SR symbolizes any of an infinity of other clumps that can be located there other than the CH_3, such as ethyl, propyl, etc.*]. It was lucky that the first door, SCH_3, was the revealer of the fact that there was an infinity of additional doors that might otherwise live to blush unseen. [*Mixed metaphors are not uncommon in notes I have written under the influence.*]

I am being inundated with "concepts" which are coming too rapidly to write down. This is not a verbal material, *ergo*, tales cannot be told.

It would be exhausting to go at this pace for long. Music is being ignored. Try eyes closed. Nothing.

Why pursue new things when I have the clues at hand — discovery is no longer needed.

This is a truly conceptually exploding experience. How can one ever hope to record this kind of intellectual supernova? If I were a historian I could be busy for life, writing down these scattered-about concepts, but that would be to no avail, as they would only be tales, and who would read them and who would believe them?

(2:45)   Theo came over to the lab, and for a few minutes we discussed the problems associated with vacuum pumps. It was a laborious exchange of words when what was needed was an exchange of concepts. I knew immediately what I wanted to impart, and was terribly impatient and not too sociable. But imaginative expansion must be a private act.

There is the value of the tale. It is the history. The record contains the details, origins, interpretations and nuances — all the things that can be explored at one's leisure, later. But if the application to the real moment is valid, a simple allusion to it is all that is needed. This approaches non-verbal communication. The thumbtack which holds the message to the bulletin board. Too many people are preoccupied with the message; it is the thumbtack that is indispensable.

Can't write fast enough.

Next time try tape recorder.

With a variable speed as well as a start-stop.

No — don't need the stop.

True, I could talk faster than I could write, but talk is too slow and too noisy. Maybe just record key words and fill in the details later at leisure. But what if there were no later, since later there would be yet more key words. And who would want leisure anyway? If you did anything with it, it wouldn't be leisure. Therefore there is no leisure. Q.E.D.

Prokofiev's "Classical Symphony," on KKHI is somehow appropriate.

(3:00)   This material is truly psychedelic. There are no sensory traps to catch your attention. My searching has been for better traps, more interesting and entertaining traps. But here there are no traps. It is certainly intriguing from the neuro-anatomical point of view, to continue the studies of SARs [*SAR is the abbreviation for "structure-activity relationship," the correlation of biological action with chemical structure.*] This is the intellectual psychedelic — no seductive sidelines to capture your interest. I want an hour to expand upon each minute.

How to record concepts?

One can't even record music without a time-dimension. But concepts are in no time — timeless, thus lasting, but untellable, only actable. Therefore, concepts are acts, acts of power.

This drug, too, shall pass. I want to scream about it to the world, but that would destroy it. This drug is power. I will talk about its effects, but I must not reveal its identity. I will have to explore through the open doorway alone.

I will put these concepts down as **C**'s so that I can keep track of them later.

C: There must be an optimum RS to reveal the universal HS. [*R, again, is any of the infinity of atom collections that could be put on the sulfur atom. If it were to be metabolically removed, an H would result. Perhaps all of these unknown modifications might give rise to a single "active" product.*]

C: Maybe there is a personalized RS for every person! How can one tailor the identity of the R in the RS to fit the person, if the only endpoint is universality? Obviously, it must be done by individualizing each product. I must make all possible RS's.

(3:25)   Let me try to write this up later tonight, when things slow down. For the moment, stick with concepts.

C: Music is basically like a tale. It must be transferred from the beginning to the end over time. Music CANNOT be POWER. History also involves time in its recording as well as in its recounting. History cannot be power despite what Toynbee says.

Concept = intensity = power. Tell NO ONE about this drug so that it can never be identified and there can be no moves made to destroy it.

C: "————————————————————————." [*I apparently censored this concept because it was so personal and private, I simply refused give anyone the right to it, including myself!*]

Everything I turn to MOVES, not in the physical or visual sense, but in the conceptual and constructive sense. One can create a concept from anything, a speck of dust, an insect —.

Try eyes closed. Looks like cottage cheese, nothing there.

C: There are hints of this in all other psychedelic drugs, but always lost in some sensory dimension.

C: This is what Huxley was trying to pick out of LSD and mescaline. This is each of those — LSD and mescaline — devoid of the entertainment; pure conceptualization. It is frightening.

C: Try lab work. Why? I would merely prove I can do what I already know I can do. To what audience?

(3:38)   On the radio, there is the news. Each item gives rise to concepts worthy of an essay. Repeal of the anti-capital punishment law allows, not systematic, but ——, lost word — proceeding with capital punishment. See — there is no record of the lost word. It was an act and it's gone.

C: The record, the tale, is still needed, to provide recall. It must be valuable, otherwise why all of this scribbling? Let's try it without scribbling. Lie down a while.

(3:40)   Conceptual cascade. I must record or, like a dream, all will be lost, and any personal value would be lost too.

C: I would like to call this the infinite 40 minutes but is it 85? I know when it started, but when does it stop? Only when I start to write history, not MAKE history.

C: How can this capacity be promoted? Controlled? Held? Recorded? Valued? And not made into an intellectual bomb? Does it even HAVE value?

C: Maybe like diabetes — with no insulin one spins one's wheels in an intellectual sea of conceptual glucose. Time is needed as insulin in the uncontrolled energy of concept.

C: This drug is like uncoupling phosphorylation at the intellectual level. [The phosphate group is one of the body's ways of storing energy].

C: Other drugs have the virtue of providing their own escape hatches, the sensory diversion. Therefore, this one is especially dangerous.

C: The thing to do is to focus one's diversions into a single sense — like the western world being glued to its T.V. or radio. McLuhan had it right.

Lying down is too much. I am out of control. It is better to be ambulatory so that escape can be made with visual input.

(3:55)   La Bohéme, rather surprisingly, is not maudlin but a true friend. And accents in written French express hand movements. The accent aigu closes off a vowel sound; the accent grave extends it. My concept cascade is truly schizophrenic. I am now wondering in whom I might confide this. David would understand the chemistry but not the content. Who would understand the content?

C: I am perhaps the Rosetta stone. The chemistry translates to the concept, which translates to what? The power to act? There is a bit of tooth-rubby, and slight body warmth. Pulse is equal to Puccini exactly. Temperature is lab temperature, of course.

Maybe I had better not connect too closely with what is going on currently in the opera — locking pulse to music at the death scene?

Or is one not master of one's own fate?

BIG C: Feather. [*At this place in the notes there is a quail feather taped onto the margin*]. Here I have gone beyond my general limits. What Tim [*Leary*] said about exceeding one's genetics is right.

Music. The Sorcerer's Apprentice is appropriate. I am living my music.

C: Are we not all living our sensory environments? Not in them, but THEM (direct object).

C: And the role of words (I am going too fast again) such as Bonsai, Gestalt, Dharma! We all live our language and are captives of our language. Slaves to words which have no equivalent in another language. Therefore non-verbal is the only way.

C: I was concerned what music would come next, what mood would be next. Why not put on a tape loop? This to guarantee eternal stasis, i.e., reading history. But we'll never discover, that way. Creativity requires a knowledge of the past, then an ignoring of the past. The tape loop is the birth, growth, life, decline, death and reincarnation cycle. One must explode out of it non-verbally and instantaneously.

C: Is creativity the making of a thing or a revealing? If we have revealed it, it existed all along. We are never creating if all is contained in all of us. Only revealing. If all this is in all of us, it must be everywhere in the galaxy. And if non-verbal insight can be triggered chemically, then its chemistry must be universal. Intergalactic. The infinitely effective catalyst. This is the truly intergalactic communication — by chemistry. Not radio, or light, or X-rays, or binary codes. Chemistry.

(4:20)   The pace begins to slacken. Ziegfried Idyls playing. How appropriate.

C: Sanity, right now, is the ability to avoid concepts for awhile. Find a mental tape that is comfortable and stay in it. This all started back at (2:30) therefore 110 minutes of infinity. I must write this all down. Spin into the 110 minutes my whole life philosophy. And add appendices with details, such as THIS RS, THIS dose, THIS identity. Why a scientific paper, anyway? They must be written, but no one reads them. The main value is in the writing of them, so they are of value only to the writer.

I am feeling most benevolent and empathetic.

If I do write this, it becomes another tale of power. I must keep my ACTS personal, and powerful, and private except when needed.

(4:30)   Clearing fast. Back again. How can I go out and chop weeds without a note-pad? I might conceive of something and lose it (like so many unrecalled dreams). Maybe, all for the best. Madness would be the complete re-dreaming of one's dreams of a lifetime. At a single moment. That — the gestalt recall — would be an ACT. Power. The replay, event by event, is the TALE.

I hope I will be largely unable to decipher this later tonight.

Obviously still not down — going down maybe — not down. So, it is more than 110 minutes of infinity.

(4:40)   Why fight to change Theo? He is my own genetics. Peace be made with the little time left. We will be dust again. Make light with what intellectual glimmer we can come forth with, during our brief passage from darkness to darkness.

(4:50)   Must shut it off. Too exhausting. Call it 160 minutes of infinity.

STOP IT

— and so it came to pass. I am aware of my body, really, for the first time during these last 3 hours.

(4:55)   Note a slight tremor, slight teeth clamp, body warmth, pulse a little slow, respiration normal, music Mozart.

Coming down nicely.

LAST C: I wonder if I will have a compensatory swing to intellectual sloth as reaction to all this?

How can one ever put "last" to a Concept? And on that I will rest. One CAN put last, by physical work.

(5:10)   In good shape — toyed with a couple of concepts — dismissed them. I am repaired. My work is now ahead of me.

(1) Writing all this up as a private essay.

(2) Persisting in scientific publication in all peripheral areas as subterfuge, diversion. Keep all progressive work in my appendices. Code them "SH" — too informative.

(5.25)   Quite clear. I can recognize the intellectual counterpart of the sensory power of DOM. I will keep this aspect of paradot to myself.

(6:10)   Helen back home. All out.

And that's the body of the real-time notes from the Aleph-1 experience. I am sure a shrewd psychopathologist would have no difficulty in coming up with a clean-cut diagnosis. Of course, a second psychopathologist would probably come up with a different one.

In any event, these notes stayed completely untouched for a full decade. And it is interesting to see what that decade did bring in the area of the Aleph family. A total of three have been studied at some depth. All three are completely fascinating.

Aleph-2 (the RS where the R is the ethyl group) is a good representative to show the positives and the negatives. The effective dosage is somewhere between 5 and 8 milligrams. The individual experiences range widely from extraordinary imagery, to childhood events reliving, to hibernation, to intense intellectual confusion. Different things for different people. The dosage requirements turned out to be unpredictable as well. For instance, (and this was perhaps the stinger that put the whole area on ice for the decade) was one friend's comments on his para-dot experience. At 10 milligrams, he reported, it had mild effects, which he found rather uninteresting.

Perhaps there was a grain of truth in the concept that stated a possible need for the designing of each compound to fit each person. I abandoned the Alephs, eventually, in favor of the 2-carbon counterparts, the 2C-T's, which were thoroughly rich compounds in their own right, but a lot more predictable as to potency and quality of action.

However, for me, Aleph-1 was still the start of a whole new alphabet.

CHAPTER 15. TENNESSEE

My wife, Helen, died on Sunday, September 11, 1977. A few days earlier, she'd had a stroke, a massive pontine hemorrhage, which hit her while she sat at her desk in the university library (she had only time to say to a friend, "My arm feels funny," before she lost consciousness). She had lost all vital abilities and was put on full life-support. I watched the sensitive encephalographic instruments being used to look for traces of brain activity. None were there. Increasing the sensitivity of detection in the search for some residues of brain function, only the heart signals could be seen; it alone remained strong. Breathing was done almost entirely artificially, by a large, impersonal machine that blinked its red light at some clock-run intervals.

There was no comfort I could give by staying in the hospital. I would accept a dinner with a friend here, or a family there, or simply stay at home, but always with a phone number and my exact whereabouts being left with the supporting crew in ICU. There were heartbreaks, "Her kidneys have failed," and there were hopes, "Urine is flowing again," and with each change I would rush to her side and watch the respirator breathe for her. But there was never a hint of brain activity.

I made a decision to place a long distance call to Germany to let Ursula and Dolph know of this tragedy. I knew they were about to leave for a trip to the Sahara. I also knew, from Ursula, that they were hoping she would return from the trip pregnant, thus strengthening a sometimes faltering marriage.

All I could think of was that I had to get hold of them before they left for the desert, to warn them of what was undoubtedly going to happen while they were away, out of touch.

It was only much later that I was able to acknowledge my real motives in making that call.

Soon, I faced a third and most difficult decision. The doctor who was in attendance in ICU had the terrible task of objectively explaining to me all the likelihoods and unlikelihoods, the possibilities and impossibilities. Now, he told me, "Life may be maintained indefinitely, but there is no possible way that a dead brain will live again. What is to be done, and when it is to be done, is in your hands. I can't decide for you. No one else can decide for you."

The simplest way was to let her try to breathe without mechanical help, leaving it to her own body and soul to decide her fate. I asked to be alone with her, and I reached out to her silently, just touching her hand. It was warm, but there was no reflexive response of any kind. I asked her to tell me what to do. There was no audible reply, but her answer was there in my mind, clear and matter-of-fact, "I've done all I can for you and Theo. It's now time for me to go on to things I really want to do for myself."

I joined the doctor and said the hardest thing I've ever had to say in my life, "Take her off the machine, and let her choose," and he quietly gave the order to have the respirator removed. I stood and watched the gradual simplification and the shrinking of her heart wave on the monitor over her head. At some critical point, an alarm buzzer sounded, and my white-coated companion reached up and turned a switch. The horizontal green wave continued to flatten, until finally it was a straight line. The oxygen-starved heart had ceased to function. *Ma femme est morte.*

The next two or three days were chaos, and they will remain largely lost to memory. I cannot recall the details of any of it; the conventions of advertising of the death, the disposing of the dead or the mourning for the dead.

I was lost; I was liberated.

I felt, at times, the kind of despair that threatened a permanent darkness inside me, a grey Hell in which nothing moved, or would ever move. At other times, a surge of something came over me which I felt as liberation; it told me I was free to discover, to form new purpose, to live among the living. I didn't know which was true, which could — or should — be my reality, and for a while it didn't matter what I thought, because I had to experience whatever imposed itself on me and, in between, get up in the morning, put my clothes on and trudge to the end of Borodin Road for the Chronicle, pay the bills, eat some food, and go to sleep. I drank a lot of wine in the evenings.

Maybe I should become a hermit, stay in the lab, pretty much avoid the outside world. It would be an uncomplicated life, and most changes would be of my own making. No surprises. Set up my own schedules and find regimens that were comfortable. Or maybe not. Should I try to maintain interactions with the outside world, rejoin friends, and risk making new ones? It was a choice, a question, that I never clearly stated to myself, but it was there.

I could not foresee that I would find an answer some two weeks later, on the other side of the country.

Six months before, I had fallen deeply in love — for the first time in my life — with Ursula, the wife of Dolph Biehls, of whom I was very fond, and who considered me one of his best friends. While they had been studying with my friend Terry, for almost a year, I had found myself responding to the gentle, soulful affection that Ursula had shown me from the beginning of our friendship. When I had tried to express my confusion of feelings, perhaps hoping that she would snap me out of it with a sharp, unmistakable rejection, her response was, instead, one of passion and frank expression of desire.

Dolph and Ursula had become not only my friends, but friends of Helen as well, and I marveled at Ursula's ability to continue interacting with both Dolph and Helen as if there had been no change of any kind in her relationship with me. I learned to be casual, when the four of us were together on a beach in Mendocino County, laughing and shouting to each other over the sound of the sea, picking up driftwood and seashells, and I learned not to seek to meet her eyes, and not to hesitate in putting my arm around her as I would around the other two.

We met, Ursula and I, two or three times in some inn or private place sufficiently far away from the Bay Area to minimize the possibility of being seen by a friend or acquaintance, and I discovered for the first time what it was to feel unashamed, uncensored, joyous sexuality.

Being in love, like any other kind of consciousness alteration, makes small but real changes in the way you view things about you, and in the way you behave around others. Over the years, my friends had come to accept me as what they affectionately called a "difficult genius," and were quite used to my habitually ironic humor, cutting commentary, and somewhat sour view of the world. One of the hardest things I had to do, in my unaccustomed role of secret lover and beloved, was to avoid giving expression — in the company of family or friends — to the feelings of optimism and even outright niceness which overtook me now and then, and which I knew would cause some degree of concern if they were detected.

I knew my wife very well, and I know that she never suspected any of this. Helen and I had lived together for 30 years, and our relationship had become a comfortable, uninspired, non-confrontational acceptance of mutual disappointment, not unlike most of the marriages we saw around us. She had been supportive of everything I had wanted to do, including changes in career which might well have daunted a less courageous wife, and I was grateful for this attitude and for what I felt was her belief in my ability to succeed. But we had not shared excitement.

One day, a number of years earlier, I had been on my way to Stanford to give a lecture on something-or-other and, on the Highway 101 freeway headed south, found myself caught in impossibly slow traffic. By the time I got to Foster City I was way, way too late for the seminar, and I saw a sign on an airplane hanger, "Learn to Fly — First Lesson Free." I turned in on impulse and accepted the lesson.

Within a few weeks I had soloed and done stuff like cross-country navigating and cross-wind landing. But I also learned to say little or nothing to Helen about my progress, or about the extreme pleasure I experienced in the little training plane. She was terribly afraid of the possibility of accidental death or injury. Even going out for a day's sail on our little 20-foot sailboat was a strain on her, and after a while, she would beg off from sailing with Theo and me. I did not try to persuade her, knowing full well the phobias she lived with.

After the birth of Theo, she had told me that she did not want to go through childbirth again; it had been too painful and frightening for her. This was an immense disappointment to me, since I had been raised an only child, and had hoped to spare my son that particular kind of loneliness. We never discussed adoption. With time, even the excitement and physical openness of love-making was interpreted by her as a threat, with her fear of physical or emotional vulnerability, and our relationship in this respect had become, sadly, more and more careful and restricted.

So it was that, after her death, I relived the shutting off of Helen's support system with more than the usual agony. I had, after all, been emotionally opened by my relationship with Ursula, and although I knew deeply and surely that the decision I had made in the hospital had been unavoidable, there was a persistent cloud of doubt that further darkened my grief, forcing me to wonder how pure my motives had been. I was always asking myself questions such as, would I conceivably have decided differently, if I had never developed an emotional intimacy with Ursula? I always worked through to the same answer. There could not have been a different decision, given Helen's state. But the dark doubts would still descend on me when I least expected them.

Some time before Helen's death, I had accepted an invitation to participate in a seminar in Birmingham, Alabama, with the understanding that it was to be followed, a couple of days later, by a lecture to the biochemistry students at the University at Memphis, in Tennessee. There was no question but that I could renege on my agreement, having an excuse that would be sympathetically accepted, but I decided not to do so. The thought of traveling to a place I had never seen before, and interacting with people who had no previous connection to either Helen or me, gave a distinct lift to my spirits, and presented itself as a possible first step on the road to healing.

It was thus that I found myself, only a couple of weeks after the funeral, laying out my travel clothes and dusting off some of the potentially impressive psychedelic compounds which I had toyed with over the past couple of years, but had not moved up into any reasonably high priority. I planned for myself a program of serious assaying which, in retrospect, might be seen as being somewhat too demanding, considering my emotional fragility. My rationalization of all of this was that, by insuring that my attention would be focused on the drug assays, I would have less time for memories and grief.

I began my tasting program on the following Saturday with a new level of 4-thiomescaline, 40 milligrams, and found it impressively rewarding. The next Wednesday, I was on the red-eye flight to Atlanta, and tried a new level of 2C-B, 16 milligrams, sitting in first class with a totally unresponsive crowd of fellow travelers of the airplane sort, rather than of the psychedelic sort. I learned the hard way that one should never try to evaluate a new level of a drug in the environmentally dull atmosphere of a midnight flight. It was a waste of time and a waste of energy. I squirmed in my seat for hours, feeling utterly stupid, since all I could do was sip orange juice and wish I could find some way to get to sleep.

Two nights later, having explored the city of Birmingham by bus and by foot, I tried to recapture my sense of equilibrium. It kept eluding me. I took 140 milligrams of MDMA, and the only result was that I found myself pacing my motel room, unable to sleep for the rest of the night. I was certainly giving maximum expression to the stimulant component of any drug I tried.

Saturday was my day to meet my hosts, Professor Pelletier and his wife, at the airport in Memphis. Despite a driving rainstorm and broad electrical power failure, they were there to greet me. Off we went to their home, and I settled in for the weekend. I was looking forward to the next day, Sunday, when my assay program dictated the trying of a new level of 2C-E, 20 milligrams. I had no lecture obligations until Monday, so why not? I was staying busy.

Charles Pelletier's home was a comfortable place, large enough to be called a mansion, with a sprawling garden and an atmosphere of relaxed ease. After a good, quiet night in their guest room, I decided to take a walk into the center of Memphis, to see the waterfront and to get the feel of the city. I started off just before noon, and as soon as I was out of sight of the house, I took out of a pocket my assignment for the day, the 20 milligrams of 2C-E, opened the vial and swallowed its contents.

I continued into the center of the city and, as I looked across the Mississippi river, I felt the first tinglings of effect. It seemed very important that I was standing at the interface between two states. I was here, and Arkansas was over there, and between us, surprisingly far below me, flowed the river. Tom Sawyer probably drifted down thataway, and just a few miles to my left he would have found himself in the State of Mississippi. A strange sense of decadence came over me. I realized that I was alerting with the 2C-E, and feeling a hint of discomfort. I turned and walked the mile back to the house, to my nest in the pretty guest room.

When I reached the house, it was the one-hour point after ingestion of the drug, and I was fully aware that the next hour would take me into new territory. Lunch was being served, and my hostess, Marlene, called me into the dining room to join the family in eating. I managed to carry it off reasonably well, despite the growing awareness of visual changes, which were rapidly becoming visual distortions, some of them disturbing, most of them hilariously funny. I knew that I had to get out of there and be by myself; there was no way of guessing where all this would lead. I excused myself with some muttered words about needing to be alone for a while and rest. Everyone knew me to be in mourning, so there were no protests, only understanding murmurs. I began the third hour of the experiment safely in my room.

The hours that followed proved to be a time of concepts, revelations, compelling fantasy and authentic memory that was very frightening and yet, in retrospect, of extraordinary value. What I faced, over those three or four hours, were some impressive angels and demons, and I asked questions and experienced insights that went to the roots of my psyche.

My notes begin with the number of hours since ingestion of the little vial's contents. And my retrospectives follow each of these directly.

[2:45] "Lunch over. Charles' backside! Child's face!"

As I retreated from the company of lunch, I looked about me and saw the backside of Charles, who was at that moment standing at the sideboard, and I was amazed at the fact that a man who was not only the head of the Department of Psychopharmacology, but also a deacon in his local church, could have such a rear end! It appeared to be monstrous. It dominated the room. The word steatopygia reverberated in my mind. And the face of one of his daughters surprised me with its revelation of boredom and chronic resentment underneath what I had previously seen as an expression of good-humored pleasantness.

[3:15] "Completely out of control. About equal to 300 mikes of LSD. I have cracked up. I must control. Am scared shitless. I have made a fool of myself. Am I catalytically fixed? I am counting the minutes — entertainment long gone. I must not try to go to sleep, as I don't dare lose the visual connection to sanity. I see myself dying."

When I lay on my bed, I saw myself as an old, old man, many years in the future. I was appalled to see my forearm as a withered, dry-skinned, almost-bone which could only be that of someone dying. I looked down at the rest of me, and I was thin, emaciated, brittle, shallow. I knew I was alone in this time of my life, this time of my death, because a long time ago, back when my wife had died, I had chosen to be alone. Who was I? I was seeing myself, but why was I seeing me here, now, at this dying stage of life? Was I sharing the experience of dying with Helen; was it some kind of final obligation I had, to share death with her this way?

[3:45] "A nihilist illusion, consummated by a nihilist organism — a nadir of nothingness. If I can conceive of such nonsense, I must be repairing. I hope. I am extremely scared. God help. This is the insanity game."

Within those few minutes, I became a nihilist. (The seeds from which this evolved must have been there for quite a while.) But I thought, if I can recognize this insanity, if I can identify my nothingness, I must be doing it with something that exists. I called to Ursula for help, then realized with a shock that I had a bond to her which could influence my world. Had it influenced those fateful last moments with my dying Helen? Was I my own agent after all? Was there even a "me" there? I was fully aware of the layer upon layer of these thoughts, and strangely enough, these layers gave body and, in some sense, substance to a me that was feeling essentially non-existent.

[3:50] "Okay again? Not okay again. Was the Vermeer scene out of the window real? Still life? What an intellectually shitty way to commit suicide. Why not with a gun like a man?"

I had gotten up and looked at the window, which was the same as looking out of the window. I was looking at a painting of a window, through which there could be seen a girl outside who was holding a watering can full of water, intent on watering some flowers in the garden. But as I looked, I saw that it really was a window and the painting of the watering-can girl was on the outside. How could that be? And when I looked back at the outside painting a moment later, it was still the same artist's style but the girl had been relocated. It was my hostess Marlene with a sprinkling can, watering flowers in the garden below. But she was frozen, from scene to scene, each different, each without life or motion. I could see the brush strokes, and the entire image was done on a flat canvas with cool and friendly colors. A 17th century lady (whose name was Marlene) with a tight-fitting head-scarf was standing over a geranium with a watering pot, obviously watering it, being watched through the window by me, and she and the window were both part of the painting. If things were moving, it was in somebody else's time.

The entire mood was one of death, or dying. I felt that I was avoiding the final act by letting time and nature do everything for me; making the world about me inanimate and letting myself deteriorate. By living, I was somehow escaping the inevitable.

[4:00] "Possibility of repair? No, I have lost it again."
[4:20] "More okay than out, but when out, really out. The window is a sense game. Fine. This is stark insanity. My father, clear, immediate, right there, speaking to me in Russian, reading to me, with his patient voice. I am very little, sitting on his knee. I was not hostile, just arrogant."

I was a two-year-old child on my father's lap, being instructed with love in the Russian words that illustrated the alphabet, from a child's book of Russian letters. I heard my father say the letter, then the word, and I was repeating both while squirming in his lap. I thought, he is surely trying to perpetuate himself through me, and this is not love but, rather, selfishness. But I had it all over him, because I was a strong, determined person who had no intention of learning his mumbo-jumbo.

How can one be so arrogant at the age of two! One certainly can be. I was. Does a state of mind as an infant dictate the final form of the adult? But right now I was the child, not the adult. This was not a memory of being two years old in my father's lap; this was actually *being* two years old in his lap. I was looking out of two-year-old eyes at the pages of the book and I could see the colored letters on the paper, in a room which was extremely high and wide and long.

Why, I thought, did he sometimes threaten me with with his belt? I don't think he ever actually did spank me, but he might as well have; the scars are right there to be seen.

[4:45] "I may have destroyed Helen with my arrogance — must I destroy myself? Yet it is this very arrogance that has made me what I am, that has permitted discovery, invention. I have experienced the birth of that arrogance and the death of it. At the moment, I am recovering the central control of it."

I thought, Helen left us all without a lasting trace, and so shall I. Another generation, and another and another, and I will be, as will she, a nothing bump on a nothing record. Did I bring about her death by my assurance or ignorance? I remember I had been told that the little light on the respirator came on when she made some effort to breathe for herself. And when I was standing beside her in the intensive care unit and the light came on, I sent her silent messages to do more, keep doing more. Or was it that the light came on when the machine did the work of breathing? Could my messages actually have been accepted by her as encouragement to let the machine do the job for her? Did I for some selfish reason work against her survival? Did I need to escape her world?

[5:00] "Recovering control. Know where I'm going. Not hungry."

As I lay on the bed, I realized a decision had been made by some part of me, during the last few hours. I was going to return to the world of meaningful exploration, the world of the MEM's and TM's and especially the 2C-E's. I sent a message: thank you, Helen, if you've helped me in coming to see where I have to go.

Before her death, I had spent several months pedantically making and tasting some 15 to 20 close analogues of MDMA, finding only that the whole family, from MDE to MDOH, were either simply intoxicants much like MDA, or they were not potent enough to bother with. I now understood I'd been wasting valuable time.

[5:15] "Rapid improvement. Better now than when I went to lunch at 2 hours."

The world began to reintegrate. The pictures on the walls of my room became, very gradually, less active and more solid. I began hearing voices downstairs; people were putting dinner together. I inspected my body and I seemed to be all right.

[5:40] "Might almost consider venturing into the kitchen.

Finally, I emerged from my room into a small crowd of guests. I talked casually with my hostess (now without medieval head-cover and watering can) and ended up helping to make an apple pie. Then I got into a lively conversation with the widow of a publisher I had known, and this delightful lady wanted to learn English as keenly as I wanted to learn her native language, French. We got into a marvelous, slightly off-color discussion that brought together the words for the flattening of automobile tires and the passing of gas, and I knew I would be in good shape for tomorrow's seminar.

This was an extraordinary day, with a maximum dosage level and a maximum number of pluses. These notes are personal treasures for me, and even now the experiences at which they hint are vivid in my mind.

They were the stepping stones that led me to a complete conviction as to where I wished to go with my work, and how I intended to get there.

And I had made another decision, perhaps the most important of all. I would not cut myself off from the richest resource I had. I would stay with people, work with people, and learn from people. Mine was a world of exploration of new chemicals, and I could not be the only crucible. I thought, others will see things differently from me, and I must acknowledge their views as being equal in value to my own. I cannot, just by personal experience, satisfactorily define a drug. The definition of a drug's action can only come from a consensus amongst the users of that drug, and the larger the number of people contributing to that definition, the closer it will be to the truth.

Needless to say, there were no more experiments in Tennessee.

Part Two:

Alice's Voice

CHAPTER 16. SPIRAL

When I finally gave it a name, I called it the Spiral.
This is how it was. Lying down for nap time (as a child) or at night for sleep, I would have reached that point of relaxation where one is not very much aware of the body. The small itches and discomforts have subsided, and the mind is beginning to drift. When I sensed it beginning (I never knew when it was going to come), I would immediately snap into alertness, excited and pleased, then I would just lie quietly as it unfolded.
The first thing that happened was a change in my breathing. It became increasingly shallow, to the point where my rib cage was barely moving at all.
If someone came into the room and talked to me, as sometimes happened, I could open my eyes and answer normally; the experience continued uninterrupted inside my head.
Every part of it, every stage, was the same each time. It was always in black and white. There was no color anywhere, and try as I did, especially around the age of fourteen, I could not force color to come onto the screen. And I could never extend it, by so much as a few seconds. When it was finished, it was finished.
First came the image-sensation after which I named the entire experience — the spiral. I felt my entire self drawn rapidly into a tiny point which kept shrinking, until it could shrink no further, at which time the microscopic point became a tunnel in which I continued traveling at great speed, inexpressibly small and implacably diminishing.
Simultaneously, I was expanding. I was expanding to the edges of the universe, at the same tremendous speed as that of the shrinking, and the combination, the contraction-expansion, was not only an image, it was also a sensation the whole of me recognized and welcomed. This experience of myself as microcosm-macrocosm lasted exactly four minutes.
The image of the spiral is found everywhere that the human has left

his mark on earth. It has been cut into rock faces, painted on huts and clay pots, traced on the walls of initiation caves. I'm certain that it has been important to all the races of man because it is a symbol for the experience I'm describing, and for the concept, the understanding that the intellect forms out of what is initially not an intellectual, but a soul experience of the Alpha and Omega.

The next stage came abruptly, as did all the changes. I was looking at standing figures which were vaguely human, dark thin figures being pulled into elongated shapes, like the sculptures of Giacometti. They stretched out, arms and legs like black string, until it seemed they could elongate no further, then the scene changed and I was watching obscenely rounded bodies, Tweedledums and Tweedledees without costumes, their small heads and legs disappearing into their puffed, bloated flesh.

The sensation accompanying this stage was one of discomfort, unpleasantness, a feeling of something grating on my soul. I once timed this part and the one that followed; they lasted a total of six minutes. I disliked them intensely.

Abruptly again, the inner screen became white, a horrible dead-white, nasty and aggressive like the underbelly of a sting-ray. After presenting itself for a few seconds, the flat white began to curdle from the outer edges into black, until finally the screen was totally black. A thick, awful, dead black, a pool of tar in an unlit cave deep underground. After another brief pause, the black began to curdle at its edges into the white again. This process repeated itself once, and the sensation was similar in every way to the previous one: irritating, grating, a feeling of unpleasantness that approached repugnance. I always endured it with a mental gritting of teeth, knowing it had to be gone through because that's the way it always went and it was not to be changed.

And then, finally, I broke out into the last stage, the final part for which I had always been and always would be willing to undergo the middle parts.

Now I was at the edge of an unseen cliff, looking out into a very different blackness, the deep, cradling blackness of the infinite universe, of space which stretched without end. I was completely happy and comfortable in that place, and would have stayed there indefinitely, had I been allowed, breathing in the beautiful darkness and the exquisitely familiar sense of infinity as a living presence, surrounding me, intimate and warm.

After a moment of this pleasure, came the greeting. From the upper left-hand corner of the universe there came a greeting from Something which had known me, and which I had known, since before time and space began. There were no words, but the message was clear and smiling: Hello, dear friend, I salute you with respect-humor-love. It is a pleasure-with-laughter-joy to encounter you again.

That which greeted me was an entity so far removed from anything in human experience that I concluded, when I was an adult, trying to find a way to describe it to myself, that even the word, "entity," could not be applied; a word creates boundaries, it says this is the shape of what you are describing, as different from other shapes which are bounded by other words. It had no shape, no form, no definition, no boundaries. It was. It is. It was my oldest friend and it greeted me as its equal. I always replied to it with a rush of love and delight and my own laughter.

Then it was over.

It had taken exactly twelve minutes.

It was something I'd always experienced, taken for granted, and had given no thought to when I was very young. Not until age fourteen did I take a good look at it and recognize it as unusual, something peculiarly my own, my secret private treasure. I also got very analytical about the whole thing, began my habit of timing it and made the first of my unsuccessful efforts at altering it. But I didn't decide on a name for it until many years later, discarding "Microcosm-macrocosm," as too long and unwieldy, and settling on the simpler "Spiral."

It had probably been going on since I was born. There's no way to be sure, of course, but because it had been part of my life ever since I could remember, I tend to assume it was familiar to me from the very beginning. My mother said something once about having seen a change of some kind coming over me occasionally when I was a baby; she said she didn't worry about it because when it passed, I appeared to be quite normal.

It always (with one single exception) came under the same circumstances, when I had settled down in bed for a nap or for the night's sleep, but well before sleep itself took over.

The one exception happened when I was around fifteen, shortly after my father had been transferred to Santiago de Cuba as American Consul. We were staying in a hotel, while those responsible for helping us find a home were still busy with their search. My father and mother, my brother Boy and I were having lunch in the hotel dining room and my eyes focused on the butter plate on the table. In the exact center of the round plate was a single pat of butter, and somehow the sight triggered the familiar feeling I associated with the beginning of the Spiral. I was surprised and very pleased, because it was a new thing to have it start under such unusual circumstances.

I was also pleased because it was my special thing, and in asking to be excused from the table to go up to my room, I felt a certain sense of importance, which was rare when I was with my family. I said just enough to make it clear that my strange "thing" was beginning, and my parents grudgingly gave permission for me to leave. I reached the room upstairs in time for the completion, the wonderful last few moments. It turned out to be the only time it ever happened that way — when I was out of my bed, involved with ordinary matters of daily living.

I tried to make it come, searching out all sorts of images of round space with dots in the center, but nothing worked. I never found a way to make it happen. It came when it chose to, unexpectedly, once in a while. The times it chose had no apparent connection to anything else that was going on in my life, either generally or in particular. In twenty-five years, believe me, I looked for every possible connection; I found none. When I was very little, I think it might have happened as often as once a week or so, but as I grew older it came less and less often, until around age twenty-five, when it happened only twice in one year, then never again.

The discovery that I was not alone in my journey into the interior cosmos came as a complete surprise. It gave me a great deal of excited pleasure and opened up a whole new series of questions. It happened when I was around twenty two, and — interesting enough in itself — the two proofs came to me within a single four month period.

The incidents were astoundingly similar.

The first one took place one evening when I went to a party given by a friend in San Francisco. I was in the host's kitchen with several of the other guests, doing what people usually do in strange kitchens at informal parties — talking, drinking and munching potato chips and carrot sticks — and after a while one young man named Evan and I found ourselves alone, deeply involved in a conversation about unusual experiences, mostly read about or heard from others, the kind of conversation that seems to come about more easily, somehow, in the midst of a high energy, noisy party than at any other time.

Suddenly Evan was telling me about what he referred to as "a really weird thing," which had been happening to him ever since he was very young. I remember the prickling that spread up my back as he began describing it, and I understood immediately the look that gradually came into his face, a mixture of embarrassment and anxiety (She's going to think I'm crazy; why am I talking about this?). I tried to make it easier for him to continue by nodding encouragingly and once — when he faltered briefly — I volunteered what I knew was going to be the next image, and he looked startled, almost frightened, drank a bit from his glass, muttered, "Yes, exactly," and continued to the end. His end was not mine; his journey came to a close after the black and white curdles. I thought, with a touch of pity, that he seemed to have missed the best part, although he did have the wonderful spiral at the beginning. I was glad I hadn't prompted him further. When he'd finished his story, I told him I'd had every one of the images he had described, and that he was the first person I'd ever met who shared the experience. I said nothing about my own different ending.

He was staring at me, and I wasn't sure he'd really heard what I'd been telling him. Finally, he smiled and said that I was the first person he'd ever told about this private, "crazy thing," and he couldn't believe — it was so extraordinary — that I actually knew what he was talking about. He said that he had always wondered if the experience was a sign of insanity of some kind, and it was such a relief to know that somebody else had had it. Neither of us felt it necessary to add that, in a situation like this, it was also reassuring to see that the person who shares your strangeness appears to be relatively sane and reasonably functional.

I smiled back and said I understood exactly how he felt. We left the kitchen and joined the rest of the party. I never saw him again, and didn't particularly expect or want to. It was enough to have heard one other person repeating what I knew so well, and it was intriguing to know that my journey, or process, had gone farther, longer, than Evan's; after all, although I was more than willing to give up exclusive rights to the whole thing, I didn't mind retaining a little bit of superiority.

The second incident was almost identical to the first, the only difference being that the young man (whose name I forgot almost immediately) was talking to me in somebody's living room, instead of the kitchen, in the middle of another noisy party, when he began describing the "strange vision" that he, too, had had ever since he was a small child. His, also, ended short of where mine did, and he was astounded and obviously very relieved to know that there was somebody else in the world who knew about it.

Both young men seemed quite unremarkable, although pleasant enough and intelligent. I never saw the second one again, either.

I remember wishing briefly that I could put an ad in the Chronicle or Examiner, something along the lines of, "Seek contact with others who have experienced...," and of course, the imaginary ad stalled there.

It happened — my beloved Spiral — for the last time when I was twenty-five. I had no way of knowing, of course, that it would not come again. It may or may not have been a coincidence that, within three weeks of the last time, I had my first encounter with a psychedelic material, the Divine Cactus, peyote.

CHAPTER 17. CACTUS

In the late 1950's, I was working at the University of California Medical Center, which is a large group of buildings dedicated to both medical training and the practice of medicine, on the crest of a hill in San Francisco called Mount Parnassus. This Mount Parnassus, unlike its Greek counterpart, is wrapped in fog most of the year; I lived just two blocks from the medical center and seldom caught a glimpse of the City down below. In May and June, when the radio reported people sweltering in 90-degree-plus heat, across the Bay in Marin and Contra Costa counties, I thought with resentment that six months on Mount Parnassus would surely cure their complaints. (I couldn't afford a car on my salary, and it takes a car to search for apartments for rent in the Bay Area, so I was stuck where I was.)

I was a medical transcriber in the Department of Pathology and, at the end of my working day, I would often have supper in one of the two immense hospital dining rooms, usually finding a seat near the large double windows and reading whatever book I was enjoying at the time. I did a lot of reading in those days, since I was living alone and books were, as they had always been, among my best friends. They kept me company and fed me with richness at a time when the rest of my life was dry, anxious and slightly grey. I was in my mid-twenties.

Since beginning work at the center, I'd dated a few medical residents, then found myself deeply involved for several months with a gentle, thoughtful psychiatrist named Paul. I first became interested in him one evening in the cafeteria when a group of doctors sitting at the far end of my supper table got into an excited, argumentative discussion. Among them was an attractive, pale-haired man with a nice chuckle, who exhibited a character trait which is extremely rare in ordinary people and, among doctors, practically nonexistent: he didn't seem to mind discovering that he had some fact wrong, that he was in error; he appeared to actually welcome having a piece of misinformation corrected.

When he remained at the table after the others had returned to duty, I got up the courage to remark on his lack of defensiveness or resentment when contradicted — I said it carefully, as charmingly as I could — and added that this was a most remarkable thing, in my experience, and much to be admired. He laughed and asked if he might join me, and would I like some more coffee?

By the end of that evening, I had discovered that Paul was intelligent, funny, in the midst of a difficult divorce, and that I liked him. By the end of the following week, we both knew we had found in each other exactly what we needed — someone to have fun with, to make love with, to talk and share with.

A few months later, I discovered I was pregnant.

Paul was caught in a terrible ambivalence, having tried throughout his failed marriage to father a child, finally coming to believe that he could not, and never would. It was the wrong time for him to discover that he wasn't sterile, after all. The bitter divorce battle made it necessary that no one else know I was seeing Paul, much less expecting his child. Another sad fact was that Paul and I were not committed to each other for the future, so that what should have been a joyful surprise was, instead, a more than awkward embarrassment. We had begun to talk about abortion.

Nature doesn't give a damn about embarrassments, but she does have a way, sometimes, of executing judgement on certain defects or insuffi-ciencies, and there must have been something not quite to her liking going on inside me, by the time I was about two months along.

One day, alone in my apartment after work, I began having contrac-tions that felt familiar (I had given birth to my son Christopher during a brief, disastrous marriage at age 20) and made my way to the bathroom. Grunting and moaning with the pain, I squatted on the toilet, gazing blindly through trickles of sweat at the black and white floor tiles, until finally I had birthed the fetus. I looked down only once, to see the tiny shape floating in blood, and sent a sad apology to the soul which had intended to inhabit it, "Sorry; it wasn't the right time, my dear Whoever. Maybe someday — ."

After stripping off my stained clothes, I found a clear plastic tablecloth, folded it a couple of times and put it on my bed, then lowered myself carefully into the middle of it and leaned back on heaped bed pillows, exhausted. When I felt occasional soft clots of blood emerging from my body, I thought they were parts of the afterbirth, and continued to drowse, relieved at the absence of pain. Paul was on duty at the hospital that night, and I had every intention of cleaning up all the mess in time for his return the next morning, but for the moment I could only rest until the bleeding stopped and my strength came back.

It must have been at least a couple of hours before I became vaguely aware of a coldness on my skin and opened my eyes, to find myself sitting in blood clots almost up to my hips. I was very light-headed, and it dawned on me that perhaps there was more blood than there should have been with just the losing of the afterbirth, and that maybe I should try phoning for advice. I couldn't think of whom to call — I certainly wasn't going to disturb Paul while he was on duty — then I remembered the pretty young nurse called Tess who lived in the apartment next door. It seemed a good idea to ask her to take a look at me, just in case I wasn't evaluating the situation as well as I thought I was.

When I tried to move off the bed, a warning voice told me to move very carefully. It said, YOU MUSTN'T FAINT. I wasn't in the least frightened, but thought it might be sensible to avoid standing up because of the light-headedness, so I crawled slowly on all fours toward the living room, pulling my dressing-gown off the end of the bed as I moved past, until I had reached the phone at the far end of the apartment. I lifted it from the coffee table and put it on the floor, surprised at how heavy it was.

Tess was home, and I crawled to the door to unlock it, then returned to my place — now marked by a small puddle of blood — on the floor. When she came in, Tess took one look at me and grabbed for the phone. I heard her saying something about emergency and hemorrhage, then she knelt down and carefully put my dressing gown on me, and when she had tied the belt, she said only, "Don't move, honey; save your strength," while I smiled happily at her, feeling altogether peaceful and good-humored.

When she went to get a towel for me, she stopped at the side of the bed and muttered something that sounded like, "Jesus!"

Having given me the towel to tuck between my legs, Tess picked up my purse, raised me slowly from the floor, and helped me down the outside stairs and into her car. While she was locking my front door, I sat like an obedient child, slipping in and out of consciousness, feeling safe and content. When we arrived at the Emergency entrance to the hospital, Tess went inside to arrange things, and I opened my purse and took out a compact. I giggled at the reflection in the mirror; I'd never seen anyone that color before. Pale grey, with a faint touch of green in the shadows.

Lying on a hospital bed, with several people around me — I had the impression of a couple of doctors and at least one nurse — who were trying to find a vein that wasn't too flat to stick a transfusion needle into, I knew I was going to be all right, and tried to tell all the earnest, bustling figures not to worry, that I wasn't going to die. What I got in response was a curt order to keep quiet; they seemed irritated by my good humor. I felt a bit hurt, then angry at the reprimand. After all, I hadn't done this to myself; nature and the gods had made the decision.

Almost immediately, the hurt and anger drifted away. I was left again in the state of gentle euphoria that the ancient Romans must have known all about, when they chose bleeding to death from opened wrists (while sitting in a bathtub full of warm water) as the preferred form of suicide, at least for the upper classes.

A few days later, someone explained to me that most of the clots had not been pieces of afterbirth, after all. They were the result of bleeding from some little capillary inside the uterus which had failed to close off as it was supposed to, after the expulsion of the fetus. I had lost a bit more than six pints of blood; I forget the exact amount, but I do remember being impressed, having been reminded that women's bodies contain an average of only nine pints.

Paul, when he discovered what had happened, went to my apartment and cleaned up what he half-humorously described as, "The scene of a bloody ax-murder." But he was deeply shaken, and found himself contending with too many conflicting feelings — horror, relief and sorrow. He couldn't forget, he told me later, that I had come so close to dying. It was all too much.

It took me six weeks to recover my strength, and by that time I had become miserably aware of Paul's increasing distance and coldness. So we had the inevitable long talk with tears and pain, finally agreeing to be just good friends. I returned to work and did my best not to let myself feel freshly bruised at each occasional glimpse of him in the corridors of the hospital.

Now, it was an evening in March, and I was sitting over cold coffee in the dining room, reading by the fading light from the big window, when a friend of mine slid his food tray onto the table across from me and sat down. Dr. Samuel Golding was suffering through his internship year, headed for a residency in psychiatry. He was only a few inches taller than I, rather chunky, with a head of wiry black hair, and he was one of the most interesting — and delightfully strange — people I had ever met. While he was assigned to the Pathology Department, we had recognized each other as mavericks, and had begun to talk at lunchtime, and sometimes at supper, if he was on late duty and saw me in the cafeteria.

Sam was absent-minded to the point of near-unconsciousness, at times, possibly as a reaction to the schedule he was obliged to keep and the attention he was expected to pay to things which bored him, all of which he regarded as necessary evils to be endured on the way to the only thing that mattered — becoming a psychiatrist. I was familiar enough by now with the medical world to know that psychiatry was considered an orphan child and its practitioners generally peculiar; at least, that was the standard attitude of the average physician and most particularly of the average medical school professor, so that anyone studying medicine who made it known that his goal was psychiatry was in for more than the usual amount of sarcastic put-downs by the instructors, not to speak of his fellow students.

(It amused me greatly that, while — according to at least one study — 98% of medical doctors were Republicans, every psychiatrist I'd ever come across turned out to be a Democrat. Peculiar, indeed.)

The most hilarious example I'd seen of Sam's absent-mindedness, however, had nothing to do with boredom, but with its opposite — single-mindedness. One evening, sharing supper in the cafeteria, we were in the middle of an intense discussion about the ritual practices of a certain tribe of American Indians, when I told Sam I had to go to the bathroom, but I'd be right back. He rose with me, followed me — still explaining and gesturing with both hands — down the corridor to the door marked WOMEN, where I quite reasonably expected him to wait. As I walked into the stall, I heard Sam coming right through the rest room door behind me — still talking — apparently oblivious of the fact that there was no such thing as a unisex rest room in the medical center. I decided not to risk sending him into some kind of shock by reminding him where he was, but simply sat on the toilet behind the stall door and listened, grunting uh-huh's as seemed appropriate, stifling my laughter and hoping desperately that no other nearby woman would happen to have a full bladder at the moment.

When I was finished (a little more hurriedly than usual), we left. Sam followed me back to the cafeteria, his untied surgical smock trailing in the back as it often did; we resumed our places at the table and continued the conversation. I never told him.

We usually talked about the human mind, about the world in general, and occasionally the cosmos, but inevitably — no matter where our conversations started — we would sooner or later get around to one of two subjects. The first was Indian tribes of North and South America, about which Sam seemed to know everything — customs, traditions, rituals, beliefs — everything; or so it seemed to me. The other was psychedelic drugs, both natural and synthetic. Of course, the two subjects converged easily and often, since every American Indian culture appears to have made use of some kind of consciousness-altering plant, and Sam seemed to know about all of them, too.

I knew only what I had read in books, while Sam had actually lived in the Amazon area for a while among some of the Indians and had personally tasted a lot of different psychedelics, so my role had became primarily that of appreciative listener and learner, which was comfortable for both of us.

With one exception. I had discovered that Sam had a true gift for drawing. He had once handed me a written autopsy report to be typed up, and around the edges of the lined yellow paper there were beautiful little pencil sketches of strange creatures, plants, flowers, trees, and what looked like jewels. When I said, "Good Lord, Dr. Golding, these are incredible!"

he looked at me in honest bewilderment, then leaned over my shoulder to see what I was referring to.

"Those? Oh, I doodle that kind of stuff all the time. What's incredible about them?"

It turned out that, growing up in a family of physicians, he had never heard anyone remark on his ability to draw; no one talked about art of any kind. Apparently his parents were not interested in, nor did they expect their children to have any interest in, anything that did not have an obvious application to medicine. Having drawn and painted all my life, I was outraged at such neglect, and offered to teach him the simple rudiments of painting.

Sam was touched by this unexpected interest, and had agreed to come to my little apartment on Tuesday evenings, unless he was on duty at the hospital, to find out how to use different brushes and watercolors and pastels. I had never properly learned to paint in oils, and couldn't afford to buy a set of them, but I taught him what I could of the other media.

He worked on scenes which he told me were visual images he'd had while using psychedelic drugs, as a member of an ongoing private experimental research group, headed by a friend of his called Shura — a name I promptly forgot — and he talked about these sessions as he painted. He had also been involved with a series of Saturday drug experiments conducted a few months before by an innovative instructor at the psychiatric teaching clinic attached to the main hospital, who believed that anyone planning a career in psychiatry should experience the effects of some of the most widely used drugs, since they would undoubtedly have patients in their future practice who would be influenced by the use and abuse of such chemicals.

This group of experimenters — most of them third-year residents in psychiatry — had made movies of themselves under the influence of heroin, marijuana, LSD and mescaline, one day on each drug, and Sam talked to me for hours in the cafeteria about the sessions and what he had learned, and during our Tuesday evenings he painted some of the images which had appeared in his mind during both the clinic and Shura group experiments, telling me as he worked about the emotions and concepts he had experienced, interrupted only by my occasional demonstration of some useful trick or technique with brush or smearing thumb.

Late one Tuesday evening, while we were putting away the paints and brushes, I had dared ask him if I might possibly take one of these drugs someday, with him as my guide.

"I don't see why not," he said, "Which one do you think you'd like to try?"

Since I'd read Huxley's beautiful account of his mescaline experiment, as well as Andre Michaux's bitter story of his day with mescaline, I told

Sam it seemed to me that the peyote cactus, after all, had been used for centuries by thousands of people, which was a pretty impressive track record, and that I would really love to try it. I added that I wasn't sure what the difference was between mescaline contained in the peyote and mescaline synthesized in a laboratory, but I was ready to take whichever one he could get hold of.

Sam said he would do his best to arrange it, though he couldn't guarantee anything. I thanked him and promised myself not to hope too much, in case it never happened, for whatever reason. Knowing Sam's absent-mindedness, I knew I'd even have to be prepared for the possibility that he might just forget about the whole thing.

That had been two weeks ago.

Now, putting my book down with a paper napkin tucked in it to hold my place, I grinned at my rumpled friend, who was wearing his green surgical smock, untied at the back again.

"How ya doin', Sam?"

"I thought you'd like to know," he said in his usual abrupt way, tearing apart a piece of sourdough bread, "I have come into possession of some peyote buttons, enough for both of us."

I stared at him, my mouth open, "You got some? How wonderful! You really have it?"

Sam swallowed some soup, then asked, "Do you still want to try it?"

My stomach was doing a small up and down dance, but I leaned across the table on my elbows and peered at him, "I really want to do it, Sam. Very much. Just tell me when and where?"

"How about next Sunday?"

I nodded, "That's fine. Next Sunday." I thought frantically, is there anything happening next Sunday that I should remember?

No, Paul isn't with me and it isn't my weekend to be with Christopher.

Once a month, I spent a Sunday with my young son, who was living with his father and his father's new wife in Marin County because she didn't have to work. They didn't want me visiting my boy more frequently than every four weeks because, they said, it was disruptive to him.

Nothing is happening next Sunday.

"Where do we do it, Sam?"

Sam ate more soup, then said, "Where would you be most comfortable — how about your place? We could start there."

"Yes, of course. My apartment." I was in a state of confusion. I'd never taken a psychedelic drug before. I hadn't even smoked pot. Now, all of a sudden, Aldous Huxley's miraculous world was going to open up — or perhaps that of Michaux's demons — and I didn't know what to ask next.

Sam was sopping up the last of his soup with a piece of sourdough, and I hoped he wouldn't sense my brain-fuzz.

He mustn't change his mind, he mustn't!

"What time?"

"What time?" asked Sam, looking up, "Oh, you mean what time on Sunday. Well, how about 9:00 in the morning? Don't want to start too late; it's going to be a long day, remember."

"Yes, of course." I mentally reviewed what he'd already said, and wondered what I should ask next. I felt like an idiot. How do you go about preparing for a day under the influence of something like peyote?

"We won't be spending much time inside," said Sam, "Maybe we can walk down to the park, once you've got your sea-legs. It's always best to be outside, in natural surroundings, during this kind of experience."

Suddenly, Sam was no longer the young man who failed to check whether his socks matched and managed to forget half the conferences he was supposed to attend; he was a knowledgeable person, a teacher.

I nodded.

There must be something else I should be asking. What do I have to know before Sunday?

"Is there anything I should do ahead of time, Sam? I mean, do I have to prepare in some way? Am I supposed to have an empty stomach?"

Sam was rising with his tray, "Ah — glad you reminded me. Yes. Empty stomach on Sunday morning. You can drink all the fluids you want, but no food. You'll probably vomit anyway. People usually do."

He turned to go, then looked back at me, "And don't put cream in your coffee. Nothing with oil or fat. Retards absorption. Oh, yes. Better have some orange juice in your fridge. See you Sunday morning."

I watched him moving between tables and around chairs on his way to the tray disposal, and I thought a jumble of things, a tangle of images, apprehensions and excitements. I wondered for a moment whether I might die during the experience, and was amused to note that the thought didn't scare me at all.

I was up and dressed in blue jeans and a light blue sweater by 8:00 AM on Sunday, an hour when I would normally have been deeply asleep, making up for all the weekday risings at 6:30. I sipped coffee with sugar and no cream and waited at my living room window for Sam. I had an absolute certainty that what would happen this day was going to change my life in ways I couldn't begin to guess at. And I knew that I was ready. It's time, I thought. It's time.

At five minutes past 9:00 he arrived, carrying a large paper bag under one arm. My stomach was growling occasionally with emptiness and anxiety, and I sat down on the couch, arms folded tightly across my chest, smiling weakly, "How do we do this, now?"

"Do you have some orange juice?"

"Sure. Wait a minute." I got the bottle of juice and two tall drinking glasses, carried them to the coffee table and sat down again. Sam was still standing, and while I watched, he opened the paper bag and pulled out a large jar half filled with a thick brownish-black liquid with lumps, and placed it carefully on the table. I muttered, "Good grief, that looks awful. Is it the peyote?"

"Yup, it's mashed peyote buttons. We'll mix it with the orange juice; that may help the taste a bit."

"Does it taste as horrendous as it looks?"

"Oh, much worse," said Sam, cheerfully, sitting down beside me, "It's probably the vilest taste in the whole world!"

I remembered what he'd said in the cafeteria, about vomiting. I felt a sudden shortness of breath, as I stared at the jar.

"Sam, what happens if I do vomit — I mean, will that ruin the whole thing?"

"No," replied Sam, "For some reason, vomiting doesn't seem to have any effect on the experience, as long as you've managed to keep it down for a little while before it comes up again."

My God, this is going to be a lot harder than I realized.

I squinted at the witch's ooze. "How many buttons do you have?"

"I mashed 14 large buttons, so we'll each have seven, if I can measure it out very exactly, which is what I'm going to do right now."

I watched, rocking slightly, while Sam sat beside me and dribbled a little of the thick, dark stuff into first one glass, then the other, and continued the careful, slow process until each was a third full. Then he opened the bottle I'd brought from the kitchen and poured out enough juice to fill the glasses to within an inch of their tops. That done, he leaned back on the couch and expelled a long breath.

I muttered, "Now, we drink, yes?"

"Now we drink."

He stood up. I stood, too, and touched the rim of my glass to his.

He smiled and looked directly into my eyes, which was unusual for Sam; he was, in some ways, quite shy.

"May the Gods bless us," he said. I was both surprised and touched. It was not a typical Sam thing to say.

I took a small amount of the mixture into my mouth and immediately spat it back into the glass. "My God, Sam! That's AWFUL!"

"Yeah, it is, isn't it," he agreed, proudly. I watched him. He kept taking swallows, his face scrunched up, eyes closed, while I looked at the dreadful mixture in my hand and thought, how will I ever get this down?

The taste was not just bitter; the moment it hit the tongue, the gorge rose in response. It was as if the body had decided instantly that this was something not intended for human consumption and was ready to resist its passage down the throat any and every way it could.

I carried my glass through the archway that divided the living room from the bedroom and sat down on the side of my bed, from where I had a direct view of the toilet in the bathroom. I'll be able to make a quick dash to there from here, I thought, then took one swallow, and began concentrating on not thinking about what I was doing.

Half an hour later, I was still sitting on the bed, my glass drained, and Sam was pacing the floor of the living room, drinking the last of his liquid, neither of us having spoken a word to each other since the ordeal began. I didn't want to move, and I didn't want to talk, either. I was going to just sit and be very quiet so that my tummy would continue to occupy its normal place and not go anywhere else.

Suddenly, Sam was coming through the archway, running across the wooden floor. He disappeared into the bathroom. I heard the sounds of vomiting, and stuck fingers into my ears immediately.

Don't let the idea in. Think about the light coming through the windows in the other room; think about lying down on this bed and not moving ever again; think about how nice and peaceful it is in here, how quiet.

When I finally unplugged my ears, the only thing to be heard from the bathroom was the sound of running water. I eased myself very gradually onto the bed, and lay down.

No fast movements. Everything slow-motion.

The bathroom door opened. Sam emerged and stood there, looking faintly embarrassed. I grinned at him, "You okay?"

"Yeah. Always happens to me. How 'bout you?"

"So far, so good. I'm just going to stay very still for a while."

He climbed onto the bed and stretched out beside me, "Good idea. Me, too."

It was very quiet in the room, and there was no tension, no feeling of awkwardness about lying on the bed with Sam next to me. I folded my arms under my head and gazed up at the ceiling for a while, waiting for something to happen, but all I could be sure of was that I was finally comfortable, my stomach was staying in place, and it was so wonderful not to be drinking that terrible stuff any more.

I wondered briefly whether I would ever be able to look at orange juice again without feeling sick, and decided I would, because I liked orange juice. Then I thought about women and vomiting and about whether men had a harder time with nausea because they didn't have to deal with it as often as women did; some women had upset stomachs with their periods, and most women had some morning sickness when they got pregnant. They learned how to move slowly and how to keep the stomach quiet with water and dry crackers and patterns of thought that were smooth and even. Men probably fought nausea like an enemy, I thought, squeezing themselves tight against it, which is no way to calm a queasy stomach.

I turned my head to say something about this to Sam, but stopped with my mouth half open. His eyes were closed, and the soft light coming through the archway from the living room outlined his face. His mouth was that of a serious child, a bit vulnerable and wistful except in the corners, where a firmness was quite apparent.

Firmness. What's the difference between firmness and stubbornness? Of course! When you like the person and agree with him, it's firmness; when you're in opposition to him, he's stubborn.

There was a soft radiance about that grown-up child-face. I had never before spent time searching Sam's face; one didn't, after all, stare curiously at someone who was neither relative nor lover — not in our culture, anyway — and it was remarkable how very much of him was revealed in that mouth, once you took the time to look.

It seemed perfectly natural to be examining him closely.

I broke the silence with something else I was seeing, "I just realized, Sam; you really are the outsider, aren't you? And that's the way you want it; you like being the strange one." I was childishly pleased with myself, for perceiving so much, so well.

Sam's eyes opened; they were brown, and they looked straight at mine, without any shyness at all.

He asked, "What are you seeing?"

"I'm seeing a fascinating combination of things that show especially in your mouth, and it just came to me — I don't know why — that you've chosen to stay outside the usual, you know, medical fraternity. The doctor club. It isn't so much that they don't understand you, make friends with you; you don't *want* to be accepted, because you don't like them. And that means I don't have to worry for you, after all, which is something I tend to do."

I wondered if what I'd said made any sense to him.

He smiled slightly and looked away. After a while, he said, "Take a look around you. See anything interesting?"

I sat up and gazed around. The first thing that occurred to me was that I had moved without thinking about my tummy. I looked down at my body and felt it out; everything seemed all right. No nausea, no more feeling that I'd better stay still. I was free to pay attention to other things.

The surface of the bedroom walls moved with a faint shimmer of light. If I focused deliberately on any single point, the movement in that place stopped, but the rippling continued on the periphery.

There was another difference in the way everything looked, but for a few moments I couldn't pin down exactly what the change was. The bed was still a bed, the lamp was the same old lamp, sitting on the small bedside table which was still a table.

Through the archway, I could see the windows of my living room illuminated by the soft spring light. The furniture looked familiar and friendly. Nothing had turned into anything else. No creatures danced on the floor. There was a feeling inside me that was new, though. I would have to look closer at that. And time was different. It didn't seem to be passing, at least for the moment.

I looked down at Sam, "Everything looks the way it's supposed to. I mean, the chairs haven't become mythical beasts or anything, but something's very different about all of it. The way it feels is very personal, sort of nice and intimate, as if my two little rooms *like* me — I know that's not the most scientific observation you've ever heard, but — well, there's a kind of — a friendly feeling to all of it."

"I didn't ask for a scientific observation," observed Sam mildly.

"And time —," I added, "Time isn't moving in the usual way."

I sat for a while just gazing, then said, "The light in the room out there is simply beautiful. There are little dust motes floating in the air and I think they're singing songs."

Sam said nothing, but the silence in the room was perfectly comfortable. I thought about how comfortable the silence was, and how I wouldn't mind if it went on forever, and that I wouldn't mind if it were broken, either. There simply was no tension anywhere, no anxiety. Just the radiance and utter peacefulness.

I said, "My insides are smiling. And I have the impression that all is well with the world. At least, all's well right here, in this corner of it."

"Good," said Sam briskly, swinging his feet to the floor, " We'll be taking a look at the rest of it pretty soon."

"Oh, Lord. You mean, outside? Do you think it's safe to do that?"

Sam turned around, "Safe? Why wouldn't it be safe?"

He's wondering if maybe I'm not feeling all right.

"I'm fine, Sam, but I just wondered if people outside will notice — I mean, I feel very different, and I don't know how different we're going to seem to other people."

"That reminds me, this is a good time to do something very important," said Sam, "Go take a look at yourself in your bathroom mirror, then come back and tell me what you saw."

"Okay." I stood up, observing that my body felt light and very strong. I was aware of some kind of energy moving through me, without any specific tingling or sensitivity anywhere.

I snapped on the bathroom light and looked in the mirror. The face I saw was myself at 18 or 19, when I had resembled the actress Ingrid

Bergman closely enough to be mistaken for her by strangers, a few times
— to my great delight — and had not yet earned the lines in the forehead
and around the mouth. The eyes were grey-blue, the pupils huge. There
was something really likeable about that face, I decided, and there were no
traces of anger or bitterness, where usually there were faint signs around
mouth and eyes that said, Careful, don't barge in unless invited. Now
there was only kindness and humor and it really was a nice face to look at.

I thought to myself, with a sense of having stumbled onto something
important: this is a good human being; this person I'm looking at is to be
treasured. All her faults and all her failures do not take away from the
warmth and the ability to care and love that's there. I saw the reflected
eyes blur with the start of tears, and felt a burst of amusement at such
sympathy for myself.

I turned off the light and reported to Sam, "I look ten years younger. Is
that usual?"

"That often happens. It must have something to do with the relaxation,
dropping the usual defenses and tensions. Anything else?"

"Yes," I thought about how to say it, "I liked the face I saw. I mean, I
really liked that person in the mirror. I'm not exactly used to that. I
suppose most people aren't."

"My turn." Sam jumped off the bed and went into the bathroom, and
I thought, his tummy is over its problems, obviously. When he emerged, I
looked at him and waited, but he only smiled at me and walked on into the
living room. I followed. He was wearing blue jeans and a toffee brown
sweater, and I realized I hadn't registered details like that earlier; I'd been
too anxious and distracted.

He went over to the bay window and squinted through the blinds.

"Sunlight's fading. Got a raincoat you can take with you? The radio
said chance of rain, so we may as well be prepared."

"Raincoat?" I stood there, trying to make sense out of "raincoat". My
mind was intensely occupied with the glowing immediacy of everything
around me, the sense of light that still suffused the room, even though the
shafts of sunlight had disappeared. The glow was as much *felt* as seen.

"You're okay, aren't you?" asked Sam, "I mean, your stomach's settled
down, hasn't it?"

"Oh, yes, it feels fine."

"Then I think it's time to go exploring. Don't worry about anybody
noticing you. People only see as much as they want to see."

"All right." I went to the closet and took out my blue plastic raincoat.
It was pretty flimsy, but at least it had a hood. I asked Sam, "Do you have
one?"

"In my car. I'll get it on our way."

I remembered to pick up my purse. I pulled the strap over my shoulder and stood there, trying to look intelligent and normal.

"Got your door key?"

I searched inside the purse and found it, "Yeah, it's here."

"Okay, let's go."

Thank heaven I'm with someone who can think of ordinary necessary things like keys. My mind wants to wander all over the place.

Outside, Sam put on his coat and held out one arm, bent for me. I took it and we started down the sidewalk together. He said, "Whenever you want to stop and spend time with something, just tell me. We're not in a hurry."

"Okay, yes. Thanks." I was looking around at the sidewalk, the buildings, the lamp-posts; everything seemed to emit a subtle light. We passed a tiny garden in which the low bushes seemed to present themselves, calling out for attention, for acknowledgement. I smiled at them and said Hi, under my breath.

An elderly man in a worn coat was walking slowly ahead of us. As we moved past him, I glanced at his profile, trying to see inside. I could feel invisible walls and a dull, irritable tiredness, a readiness to be annoyed. I thought, if only it were possible to stop him and say something like, "Dear sir, just open your eyes and look around you; it's an incredible world! Don't close yourself off from all the life and beauty around you!"

I had been basking no longer than a few seconds in my own niceness and wisdom when a piece of information shoved itself at me and I suddenly knew that, first, the man needed his walls just exactly where they were, and didn't want to be rescued from them. Second, that it was not my right, not anyone's right, to tell him that there was another way to live, a better way to be, to urge him to see or hear what he didn't choose to see or hear. It was his choice to live the way he was living, and I must not make the mistake of passing judgment on the conduct of a life I knew nothing about.

Oh, boy. Just got slapped.

I remembered my mother telling me that there is a basic rule in spiritual matters: never offer what the other person hasn't asked for. Her phrase was, "Wait until you get the question before you volunteer the answer."

I thought about all the books — millions of books all over the world — in which human beings in many places and times had written about the human psyche, about life and death and the nature of God, and of how few people read them. I thought, how many people have taken peyote? I've heard lots of people talk about Huxley and his mescaline experience, wishing they could explore the way he did, have that kind of adventure, but how many of them actually go looking for mescaline or peyote to try it themselves? Most people hold onto the familiar. Who wants to actually risk having his universe changed?

I do. Me.

Sam was saying, "How about the park? It's only a few blocks more." "Yes, sure."

We were walking hand in hand, now. Every time I saw someone on the sidewalk or across the street, I would open myself to the feel of that other body's movements, trying to be inside the person, to sense whether there was unhappiness or daydreaming or anticipation and pleasure. I found it easy to pick up the emotional field, and had to remind myself that there was no way to know whether what I believed I was perceiving had any relation to reality — the other's reality.

Doesn't matter; I'm enjoying it.

After a few blocks, I realized I was walking with an easy, rhythmic stride which somehow matched everything around me. I was feeling completely in-tune, and everything I saw — a child running up a short stairway to the door of a house, a woman leaning out of a high window to shake a piece of cloth, a man in a leather jacket digging in the earth around a rose-bush — was music. In being who we were, in feeling what we felt, in moving as we moved, all of us were creating a silent music.

Sam was asking me, "Would you like to sit here for a bit, just to get your bearings?"

We were inside the park, and he was pointing to the base of a big oak tree. I spread my raincoat on the ground and sat with my back against the tree trunk, Sam next to me. We were surrounded by trees — eucalyptus, live-oak, cypress, others I couldn't identify — and by grass growing in at least five shades of green.

Across the path from us was another large oak, and as I looked up at it, I saw — with Van Gogh eyes — energy moving up the trunk, out each branch, bursting into tiny, leaf-shaped explosions; a tree massively still, yet alive with continuous, urgent motion. I knew that what I was looking at was real; I had just forgotten how to see it.

(Years later, at a museum exhibit of Morris Graves' paintings, I would hold my breath for a stunned moment at my first sight of his incredible pine trees. Another one who had remembered how to see!)

It's some kind of life-force; is it what they call the etheric, the life-body? Is there some way I can see that continuous movement all the time, not just when I take a drug?

The answer presented itself instantly, "All you have to do is take the time to pay full attention."

Tracing with my eyes the line of a thick lower branch as it rose, giving birth to increasingly slender extensions, I found that I could also *hear* it as a line of music, a single note branching into an elaboration of harmonizing notes.

I remembered standing outside the walls of the girl's boarding school

I had attended in Canada, when I was 16, looking up at the sky where a bird was riding a high air current, and discovering that I could mentally translate its line of flight into sound.

"Try something, Alice," said Sam. It was funny, hearing him use my name. In fact, now that I thought about it, I couldn't remember his ever having called me Alice before.

My, my! Apparently it takes a courageous leap into the depths of the unknown, or whatever it is I'm doing today, before Doctor Golding is going to rack his brain for whatever the hell my name is!

I giggled, but decided not to share the joke; it was too complicated. Besides, I didn't mind Sam not having used my name until now. It was part of his peculiar brand of shyness.

I smiled at him, "Yes?"

"Hold your hand up in front of you and look at it."

That seemed simple enough. I held up my right hand and froze in astonishment. It was the dear, strong, pianist-square hand I was used to, but the entire surface of it was a mass of infinitely tiny points in incredibly rapid motion. I knew what I was seeing; I didn't have to check it out with anyone else.

"My God! So that's what atoms look like!"

I turned my head and met the biggest Sam grin I had ever seen.

He's so pleased — this must be wonderful for him, too — seeing someone opening up to all this for the first time.

I went back to my hand, watching the extraordinary energies bursting through and around the skin. Then I looked at the big oak tree, at all the other trees and their leaves, at the grass around us; everything, everywhere, was surging with this continuous movement.

Everything is energy, energy which assumes the shapes of grass blades and rabbits and human bodies and rocks, but we move around in a world which we've learned to see as stable, quiet, solid. Wonder at what age we begin to screen out this other reality level? Must be very early.

"Care to share some thoughts?" I realized that Sam was being very considerate, wanting to know what was going on, yet determined not to intrude more than necessary. I felt a rush of warmth for this dear, stubborn, brilliant maverick, this so very odd man out, who had gone to a lot of trouble to open these doors for me.

I looked into his eyes and said, "Thank you, Sam. Thank you very much for giving me this day." He blinked, then rubbed his nose vigorously, mumbling that the day wasn't over yet; there was still a long way to go.

"Sam, there's a thing I've got to tell you before I forget it, because it seems important."

"Okay — say on."

"You know that everything I've been experiencing is new and — well

— every time I turn around, I see something I didn't expect to see — ?"

Sam was sitting beside me, head bent, listening.

"The funny thing is that, despite all the newness, there's something about all of it that feels — well, the only way I can put it is that it's like coming home. As if there's some part of me that already knows — knows this territory, — and it's saying Oh yes, of course! Almost a kind of remembering — !"

Sam was nodding, "That happened to me, too, the first time. A feeling of familiarity. I'm used to it, now. I mean, I'm used to the idea that somewhere in my soul I see this way all the time, but the conscious mind has learned to screen it out. Maybe it hasn't the survival value that the ordinary way of seeing does."

"Why wouldn't it have survival value?"

"Well," said Sam, getting to his feet and reaching down for my raincoat, "If you think about it, in this state a man-eating tiger could very well appear the epitome of beauty and enchantment, and a person might just stand there in awe and appreciation — right? — at the ruby-red tongue and the softly glowing ivory fangs — `Tiger, tiger, burning bright' — and there goes one member of the human race, too busy being full of wonder to notice that he is about to become lunch."

I was hooting with laughter at Sam's tiger image, when something said, "Careful," and I checked myself as a group of four people walked by on the sidewalk; they were wearing tweeds and raincoats and looking over at us. I found myself doing for the first time something that would, many years later, become a habit — scanning my surroundings to pick up, as best I could, the reality level being experienced by others, then moving body and adjusting face to fit in with that level, in order to be not noticed, not demanding of attention. The people who had passed us were conveying a mixture of amusement, disapproval, boredom and curiosity. Nothing troublesome. Just a reminder to keep my laughter and talking at a polite and unobtrusive level.

"Oops," I muttered to Sam, taking my raincoat from him and putting it on. As we moved from under the tree, I felt raindrops on my face, and pulled up the hood. Sam took my hand.

We walked slowly. The tree trunks were black in the rain; there was fresh grass beneath my feet and nobody around. I went ahead, needing to be alone for a few moments. Moving over green-jeweled hillocks, I remembered how tired I always used to feel, as a child, when I was climbing any kind of rise. How tired I was most of the time, as a child.

Here, in this quiet dripping wood, I was stepping with a sure lightness, a lover making herself known to the body of the beloved. I didn't have to think about whether the ground was sloping up or down, or whether there might be stone or stick to avoid; my feet were taking care of all that. They knew how to go and where to go and I was walking in pure pleasure.

A knowing spread from the soles of my feet, up my legs and into the rest of me, that the earth I walked on was indeed a body, a living body, that it was a sentient thing, with a consciousness of a kind I could not yet comprehend, and that it truly was The Mother.

I stopped and waited for Sam to catch up.

We were deep in Golden Gate Park, walking down the side of a road, not talking, just listening to the breathing of wet trees and other growing things, when just ahead of us there was a harsh screeching of car brakes, followed by the terrible, unmistakable sound of an animal injured unto death. We rounded a curve and stopped.

A man in an overcoat, obviously the driver of the braking car, was squatting in the road, one hand on his car bumper, the other hovering helplessly over the body of a panting, squeaking dog which was trying to die, to get past the pain and go, and on the sloping hill to our right, frozen under the dripping trees, were three young women in raincoats. A yellow raincoat uppermost, just below her a red raincoat, and to the side of that one, a white raincoat. They stood like figures in a Greek tragedy, a silent, stricken chorus, hands to their mouths.

While we stood there, waiting for the little dog to be released, I became aware that all living things around us — every tree, bird and insect — had gone quiet, clenching with the struggle of the dog. All of us were trying to push his soul free of the body, free of the pain, and I knew when he'd made it because suddenly I could feel everything relax and let go. One bird chirped, then the woods were filled again with bird sounds and the croaking of tree-frogs.

There arose in me then a certainty that all life on this planet is connected, all the time, at some unconscious level; that whatever is felt by a single living one of us is experienced, in some way I couldn't define, by everything else that lives.

I didn't try at that moment to formulate it, to put the right words to it. I was just aware of being taught something I was meant to learn and remember. I had read it a thousand times in as many places; it was an old, lovely cliche — "No man is an island" — and all that. Now I was being shown the truth behind the cliche, and it went farther than the poet had implied. It wasn't just human life we were connected with; it was everything alive.

There was the sound of a woman's voice, calling out in the woods, not very far away. Calling for her dog, whose still body lay on the road before six people who were standing around in the rain, crying quietly to themselves.

As we walked slowly past the car, past the crouched driver, past the now moving figures on the hill, I realized something else. I told Sam what

I had felt while the dog was dying, the sense of everything around us squeezing tight, holding its breath.

"When the dog died, it was all right again," I told him, "I mean, it isn't death that is the — the terrible thing, the enemy; it's pain. The trees and everything else around me, I could feel them all start breathing again when the pain stopped."

We walked in silence for a few moments, then Sam said, "I remember seeing a dead bird lying in the grass, once, in the middle of a peyote session. I stopped to look at it because I wanted to understand death, to know what it was, what it seemed like when I was seeing differently. I was looking down at the bird and it came to me that all the parts of the body were being dissolved back into the earth, some of them very fast, some of them slowly; it was all going to return, one way or another, to the earth, and that that's the way it's supposed to happen. The life that used to be in the bird belonged somewhere else, and it had gone there, and what was left, the physical part, was going back to where IT belonged. There was a rightness about it. Death was simply a moving from one state to another."

I nodded, remembering some of the phrases I'd read in books and articles about psychedelic experiences, phrases like "Everything's all right just exactly the way it is," and the equally infuriating, "I'm okay, you're okay," which had always sounded unbearably fatuous and self-satisfied. I'd often thought angrily that the writers had conveniently forgotten about the babies in Calcutta garbage cans, sorrow and hurt and loneliness, and the rest of a planetful of miseries. I'd said to myself, here's some whacked-out idiot rhapsodizing about life being all right just the way it is. It had never stopped me from reading about such experiences, but my liberal soul had always ground its teeth at that aspect of the reports.

Now — now I would have to take it all back, all that resentment, because I was beginning to understand. I stopped in the road and looked at Sam and looked past him, and around and up at the grey sky and knew that everything in the world was doing exactly what it was supposed to be doing; that the universe was on course, and that there was a Mind somewhere that knew everything that happened because it *was* everything that happened, and that, whether I understood it with my intellect or not, all was well. I simply knew it and I knew that I would try to figure it out later, but that I had to absorb the truth of it now, standing on a wet road in Golden Gate Park with a patient, quiet friend who was waiting to see if there was anything I wanted to tell him.

I said, "I just understood that it's all going the way it's supposed to be going. Hope that makes sense to you, because it's the only way I can say it, right now."

Sam nodded again.

We walked on until we found ourselves nearing the California Academy of Sciences, a huge stone building which stands on one side of a circle that includes, at its opposite side, the De Young Museum. In between the two, there is a small park, bare of grass, with a band shell and lots of trees with room under them for chairs, where people sit in the spring and summer and listen to music played from the little stage.

"Let's go in," said Sam, pulling me up the steps of the Academy. I trotted obediently after him, practicing normal facial expressions, trying to dull my eyes so that they wouldn't lift an innocent bystander off the floor if I should happen to glance his way.

My God, how do you not broadcast this kind of energy?

We walked through the immense rotunda without attracting any attention, and Sam led me to the aquarium, which was nice and dark, except for the lights in the fish tanks. I stood in front of a window full of tiny, darting fish and became all the little silver bodies at once.

How is it I'm aware of being completely me — I can locate my Self, my center — yet, at the same time, I can scatter my consciousness into hundreds of fishes?

I moved to the next tank, where an immense grouper swam in lonely dignity, and I became the big, ungainly fish, lower jaw protruding. It was a restful place to be, however briefly, because the grouper didn't seem to be particularly involved with anything complicated, like thinking. I looked around for Sam and smiled to see him at another window, as rapt as I had been. I walked over and joined him.

We stood, side by side, gazing into a tank full of tropical fish, trying to assimilate the extraordinary sight. One creature swam by, wearing a canary yellow bib outlined in velvety black, its mouth a prudish pout; behind it came a small gem in bright orange, marked by two broad tapering blue splashes, while above darted several tiny zebra-striped characters. The parade grew more fantastic as we watched: meticulously painted red stripes alternating with black-bordered blue stripes; a pursed blue mouth topped by a fashionable black eye mask, leading a body of blue and yellow stripes, the whole piece of enamelwork finishing in an orange chiffon tail.

Watching all of it — the designs, the brilliant geometric patterns, the funny, pompous little faces — it occurred to me that the creator of these little bits of sea life had a tremendous sense of humor.

(It would be a long time before the rest of that train of thought would present itself: how is it that human beings are equipped to see whimsy, beauty and comedy? What is it in us that makes us respond to the colors in nature with awe and delight, and to some natural designs with laughter? What strange quirk was wired into our genes which causes us to see something as funny? Were we made that way because the God-mind wanted company when it laughed?)

We moved out of the aquarium and spent time looking at the reptiles in their glass cases. All I could feel was pity and the need to send an apology to them; they belonged out in the woods and the desert, not in here.

I leaned over the edge of a deep wet pit in the middle of the reptile room and let myself be captured by the crocodile that lay there, unmoving. The beast seemed to be almost entirely stomach; his soul lived in mouth and gullet and intestine, and I was sinking into a stolid heaviness. I broke the contact, shuddering a little.

Then I found the sea horse tank. I planted myself in front of the delicate grey-brown miniatures and went into a world that tasted of a certain sweetness, then I was feeling the strength, the firmness of the tiny bodies balancing themselves in the water, fins flickering. They seemed to carry small sparks of light inside. I laughed to myself.

Hello, little darlings! Hello, there. My, aren't you just the answer to that ol' heavy in the pit!

I found Sam again and we wandered through the immense rotunda of the building, past people standing in line for the Planetarium show, and into a portion of the museum which presented dioramas behind glass, showing early cave-dwellers, progressing to later cave-dwellers, all the figures life-sized, caught in the act of doing ordinary daily tasks.

There was no one else in the hall.

Around us were low walls of polished stone, topped by the glass exhibit cases; there were metal strips running up the edges of the glass. I was looking at the first exhibit — a stone age man wearing animal skins, apparently trying to light a fire — when I began feeling very odd.

It was as if the center of my body — just above the navel and below the ribcage — was suddenly becoming an empty space, a void. It felt like a rapidly widening hole in me where, seconds before, there had been only humming aliveness. I stepped back from the wall and stood in the middle of the hallway, focusing all my attention on this new sensation.

In front of me there was now a transparent curtain of pale grey, like silent rain falling, and I could feel the magnificent energy draining out of me. I realized I was beginning to come down, losing my place in the peyote-opened world, and I didn't want that to happen. I looked around me, and a suspicion formed in my mind. I said to Sam, "Excuse me for a moment; I have to try something out, but I'll come right back."

He looked at me, puzzled, but said nothing. I went down the corridor to the rotunda and kept going until I had drawn almost level with the Planetarium queue. The hollow in my middle was filling in again. I stopped just a few feet behind the last person in the line, feeling the hunger subside. Something was being replenished.

I looked around me and breathed deeply. The falling grey rain had disappeared. I was a being of energy again, back in the world of the gods.

If I'm right about what made this happen, I can test it pretty easily.
I went back to the hallway where Sam stood waiting for me. I walked slowly past him, continued for a few feet, then turned around again, my question answered. It had taken less than half a minute in this place for the draining sensation to return. I smiled broadly at Sam and said, "I'll explain everything, but I have to get away from here," and took his hand, pulling him out of the corridor and across the rotunda, to where we could lean against a wall while we talked.

As visitors strolled by us, I told Sam what had happened.

"The only explanation that makes sense," I concluded, "Is that there's a basic — that people *need* to be in contact with living things, and when they're surrounded only by stone and metal and glass, something drains out of them. It felt awful, Sam. I was actually coming down, out of the magic, losing everything."

"Why didn't you say something?"

"I wanted to test it out first. That's what I was doing. I thought I'd just see what would happen if I walked over to where there were a lot of living bodies, and I was right! It worked, Sam! As soon as I was within a few feet of the line — those people waiting for the astronomy show — the hole in my center began filling up. I could feel it, like an empty mouth being fed. And I was going up again."

"How are you now?"

"I'm feeling wonderful. Everything's repaired."

I looked around the rotunda, at the little children with their shiny yellow or red Christopher Robin raincoats, at the people leaning over the railing around a huge depression in the floor over which a great pendulum was slowly swinging a large metal ball, at a small child who watched the shining sphere with open mouth; I saw people waiting in a new line for the astronomy show in the Planetarium, some of them reading pocketbooks to pass the time, others talking.

I knew that I could tune in to anyone I could see; all I had to do was reach out in my mind to a particular person and open myself inside, so that what they were and what they felt could reach me. I only had to be open, making no evaluation or judgement, in order to experience anxious tightness, impatience, or contentment.

I examined myself and felt my body humming again and knew that in the middle of my chest there was a radiant center of energy, and another one just above my navel, and that they were probably what the spiritual teachers of India call chakras. I couldn't remember how many there were supposed to be, altogether; five or seven, maybe. I was certainly aware of two of them, anyway.

Sam said, "I don't know if you realize this, but there are some researchers — doctors — who are giving this kind of drug to volunteers, to

PIHKAL — A Chemical Love Story

see what the effects are, and they're doing it the proper scientific way, in clean white hospital rooms, away from trees and flowers and the wind, and they're surprised at how many of the experiments turn sour. They've never taken any sort of psychedelic themselves, needless to say. Their volunteers — they're called `subjects,' of course — are given mescaline or LSD and they're all opened up to their surroundings, very sensitive to color and light and other people's emotions, and what are they given to react to? Metal bed-frames and plaster walls, and an occasional white coat carrying a clipboard. Sterility. Most of them say afterwards that they'll never do it again."

"Jesus! Right now, after what I've just gone through, that sounds worse than awful."

"Not all of the research is being done that way, thank God, but too much of it is."

"What a shame," I said, saddened by the picture, "What a shame!"

"Ready to go exploring again?"

"Sure. Where shall we go?"

"I'd like to see the Japanese Tea Garden, for a start. How about you?"

"Oh, yes," I said, "That's a lovely place. Don't think I've been there for several years."

We stood outside the front door for a moment, looking around. The rain had stopped. Every tree shimmered faintly with the light that permeated all growing things, yet each tiny leaf and twig was outlined sharply in the clean air.

We walked across the road outside and down the steps to the park. On the other side of the great circle, we stopped at the big lotus pool in front of the entrance to the art museum. Leaning over the edge, we looked down into a world of dark green and black water; there were copper reflections here and there from the bottoms of lotus leaves. An occasional blur of orange-gold in the depths reminded us that this was a home to fish. We lost ourselves in the jade and copper world, watching insects and leaves and grasses and jeweled beetles as if they were the inhabitants of a separate planet.

Finally, Sam moved and took my hand, "Let's go," and I walked with him down the road to the Japanese Tea Garden, where we paid the small admission and I practiced ordinary-face until we were past the people at the gate.

It wasn't very crowded, probably because of the rain, but there were some patient, raincoated visitors who were obviously used to this kind of weather and we would have to expect them around every turn, so I kept my mind at least partially on maintaining normal body-language and making sure I did not glance directly at faces coming our way on the narrow paths.

Strolling the gardens, we stopped every few feet as one or the other of us was struck by an outline of rock or an exquisiteness of blossoming color. I had appreciated the garden before, but I understood it, now.

There was a deliberate juxtaposition of shapes and textures which captured not only eyes, but emotions. I could follow the unfolding of an inner experience created by the gardener, as he sculptured with moss-covered stone, fleshy plant leaves, delicate ferns, moving water and subtle gradations of color in the pebbles that drifted across the floors of the various water bodies. All this, I had in earlier visits glanced at; now, I was truly seeing it, giving grateful acknowledgement to the insight of the person who had so lovingly formed all this for others to see and feel. I said to Sam, "What an extraordinary work of art!"

"I had the same reaction, when I first saw it under the influence. Quite an experience, isn't it!"

I nodded, tears in my throat.

"By the way," said Sam, once, when we had been standing for a while, looking across water at a young willow rising from a bed of coral-pink flowers, "Have you noticed how time stops when you really focus your attention on something?"

I hadn't been noticing time. I said, "Give me a second, and I'll see."

He chuckled.

I concentrated on the willow tree poised at the tip of its peninsula of garden, watching its own reflection in the water, and felt the stillness. There was no here-going-to-there, only willow, water, me, in a Now that eternally folded itself into itself.

Time moved again with Sam's hand on my shoulder.

We walked on and came to a low stone wall, where Sam stopped to rest his elbows. "Come and see this," he said, and I looked over the wall, down a slope of grass to a mass of vivid spring flowers. I could feel his eyes on my face as I flinched and stepped back from the impact of red, orange and bright purple. The colors were physically painful to my eyes, unless I squinted.

"I almost can't look at them, Sam."

"They're really quite a shock, aren't they!"

I averted my eyes, then tried looking again, amused and annoyed at the same time. I asked him if he knew why the colors hurt the eyes, and he explained about frequencies and certain parts of the color spectrum, and about the sensitivity of the eye when the pupil was enlarged, and I nodded and said Oh, I see, knowing I wouldn't remember the explanations and that it was all right.

What was important was that I'd been reminded that no matter how strong the spirit or soul, how flexible and complex and magical the mind, there was still a physical body to be considered, and it operated according to laws which were the laws of the physical universe, and I must never allow myself to forget that.

Climbing a small hill behind the tea house, we came across the seated Buddha, the great golden, gently smiling Buddha which watches the upper path, and we stood before it for a long time, in silence.

A little while after leaving the Japanese Tea Garden, we were going single file down a narrow path between trees and Sam was ahead of me, his head bent, hands in his pockets. I slowly became aware of an entirely new change in my body; something was happening, had happened. I walked behind Sam, trying to define it, to understand what it was.

My entire spine had become activated; it was a living channel of energy moving between the crown of my head and the tip of my spine. The intensity of it was just barely tolerable. As I continued down the dirt path, the energy charge in my back seemed to transform somehow, and I realized that I was feeling something throughout my entire body which, if I had been experiencing it in my genitals, would have been recognizable as orgasm. It was not confined to the genitals at all, but it certainly was orgasm and it was all up and down the spine, in the chest and stomach and legs, in head and throat and bladder. I was walking along like any ordinary person, experiencing total orgasm without having to close my eyes, without any loss of control or ability to think. Good grief, I thought. Everloving Pete! How do I ask Sam about this?

Answer: I don't ask Sam about this.

As I looked at his back, a few feet ahead, it occurred to me that I could reach out with my mind and actually touch him, and when I wondered how best to go about doing it, an image came of peeling layers of Sam away — like an onion — until I got to the core of him, and I would be able to touch that directly. I simply knew I could do it, and the idea seemed delightful and very funny.

I began mentally peeling Sam's layers, one by one, gently, as I followed him. After a while, I sensed a shining thing that had no shape, in the middle of his body, and I reached out with the will to touch, and poked it at the shining. Sam jumped in mid- step and turned, both hands spread against his back. He looked at me standing there, grinning, and said, "What the hell..?"

I apologized, not meaning it, and told him what I'd discovered I could do. I was very pleased with myself. It was like being a kid with a very powerful, brand new toy, I thought, and the message came that I should be careful and responsible, even though it was an awful lot of fun to play with.

Sam's face was rather thoughtful, and when he asked me politely to walk beside him from now on, I laughed and promised to behave.

The orgasmic energy continued to flood me, body and mind. I noted that I was in complete control of what I said, what I did, and I couldn't remember any time in my life when my thought processes had been sharper or clearer. I had absolute trust in my own judgement.

We walked on together, talking now and then, most of the time absorbed in our own thoughts, until we found ourselves emerging from the woods into a field which sloped up gently on three sides, forming a shallow bowl of wet grass and red-brown earth.

We stopped and looked around us at the earth, the sky and each other, then I saw something forming in the air, slightly above the level of my head. I thought that it was perhaps a few feet from me, then realized I couldn't actually locate it in space at all. It was a moving spiral opening, up there in the cool air, and I knew it was a doorway to the other side of existence, that I could step through it if I wished to be finished with this particular life I was living, and that there was nothing threatening or menacing about it; in fact, it was completely friendly. I also knew that I had no intention of stepping through it because there was still a great deal I wanted to do in my life, and I intended to live long enough to get it all done. The lovely spiral door didn't beckon; it was just matter-of-factly there.

Any fear I might have had of death, of the actual crossing of the border, was left behind at that moment. I was seeing the way through, and there was nothing to be frightened of. As I gazed up at the energy-charged patch of sky, I was again aware of being unsurprised, because some part of me remembered this.

(I still have the fear of dying before I have done all I want to, but I have no fear of the journey itself, nor of what lies on the other side of that opening. I know that when I get there, I will recognize the territory very well indeed, and that it will be truly a returning home.)

Sam had been silent during the few minutes it took for me to undergo the experience. When I put my hand on his arm and told him about the gently revolving doorway, he listened, then said that he had seen the death place himself, once, during an experiment with Shura Borodin's group, but that, for him, it had taken the form of a short passageway which turned a blind corner, appearing just a bit ahead of where he was walking in a meadow.

"I had the same impression; it was friendly, and there wasn't anything dramatic or threatening about it at all. It was just letting me know it was there. I could go around that corner any time I really was finished with this act of the play. And I said Thank you for showing me, but I still have a lot of things I want to do, so it'll be some time yet."

I smiled at him, nodding.

We left the quiet hollow and moved on for a while in silence until suddenly we were on the edge of the highway. Standing on the sidewalk, we watched cars moving at a speed which was not ours, in a space-time that was not the one we were in, knowing that if we wanted to cross the street, we would have to tune ourselves into that other space and time and act within it, remembering what red lights and green lights meant, and what the rules of crossing roads were.

Sam smiled, "I'm getting hungry; how about you?"

"Now that you mention it, I think I'm ravenous."

"There's a pizza place across the street. Want to give it a try?"

"Let me have a moment to tune into this — this aspect of the world again."

"I'm used to it. Just hold onto me."

I grasped his hand and kept an eye on the stoplights, and when the light ahead of us turned green, I checked and double-checked to make sure that the light that was to our right was red, and that meant the cars would stop and we could walk in front of them without danger. I muttered, hearing myself with some amusement, "Green ahead of us means okay to move across the street. Red means stop and green means go. That's right, isn't it?"

"Yeah," said Sam, hurrying me across the wet pavement, "That's exactly right, by George! Couldn't have said it better myself."

The orgasmic state was mellowing out, very gradually, to a level of energy flow less pressing, less intense than it had been before. I existed and moved in a field of light, and there was a steady flow, like a continuing note of music, underneath, that could only be called bliss — a connection with that aspect of the Great Mind, the Great Spirit, which was love and joy and laughing affirmation.

In the small restaurant, we were careful to squint so that our eyes would not startle anyone, and a waitress led us to a table with a red and white checked tablecloth and the obligatory candle stuck in a raffia-wrapped wine bottle. It was a nice place and we were not going to disturb anyone. The menu was immense, and I suppressed a strong desire to giggle at the endless listing of pizza names and hamburger titles and salad possibilities. I was concentrating deeply on a paragraph that described a particularly well-endowed pizza, when the laminated paper in front of me burst into searing golden light, so bright that I jumped and held the menu at arm's length. I looked up to tell Sam about this unexpected event, and saw him grinning wickedly at me over the top of his menu.

What do you know! He's found out how to do it!

We sat and laughed out loud, and I said Congratulations! and he said Thank You, then we became aware of the waitress standing over us and we both knew that she was very uneasy and didn't know why she was feeling that way. We sobered fast and gave our orders in voices that were as monotone and mechanical as we could make them, trying to remember what it was like to talk in the ordinary world, trying to dim the light, the energy, so it wouldn't infringe on her, doing our best to wall ourselves off from everyone else in the room, to tone down our broadcasting. I thought to myself, Boy, there's an awful lot to learn awfully fast.

Later, back in my apartment, Sam and I made love very simply and silently, for the first and last time.

At the door, I said, "Thank you for this day," and he said, "It was a privilege, my friend," and kissed me softly on the cheek.

I locked the door behind him and sat on my bed and cried. I thought, everything I've gone through, all the pain and grieving, all the loneliness and the dark places — they were all balanced, paid for, answered, by this one extraordinary, blessed day.

I went to my bookcase, found Huxley's The Doors of Perception and, in the intimate silence of the very early morning hours, re-read it and cried again, sending love and gratitude to the author for having found the words. Then I turned off the bedside lamp and looked through the darkness to wherever that beautiful, funny, tremendously loving part of God was, thanked it with all of my being, and fell asleep.

CHAPTER 18. THE BEGINNING

Shura and I met on a Thursday evening in the fall of 1978. It was the first meeting of a new weekly discussion group; at least, that's what my friend Kelly expected it to become. I was sitting cross-legged on the living room floor of an old house on Adler Street, in Berkeley, wondering how many of the 30 or so invited people would turn up. I had promised Kelly I would come to this first gathering, adding that I couldn't commit myself beyond that, and he'd said okay, he understood.

Actually, at that point, I no longer thought of Kelly Toll as a friend at all; he was a recent, brief involvement which I was doing my best to end — as smoothly and quietly as possible.

He was an intense man with a striking, angular face, in his late thirties, who had met me at a Mensa gathering four months earlier. The next day, he came to my house and asked me to marry him. He explained, much later, that of course he knew I would refuse — had counted on it, in fact — but that he had often found proposing marriage to be an effective way of getting a woman's attention.

There was no denying it had done just that.

I was 48 and newly divorced, my ego as fragile as a piece of hundred year-old burlap. Being pursued by a youngster in his thirties gave me something I hadn't had in years: the feeling that I was still an attractive woman, not just a middle-aged parent.

Kelly's passions in life were computers, good-looking older women and the creation of new IQ tests. I also discovered that he had a generalized contempt for humanity, referring to most people as "turkeys," and a tendency to uncontrolled explosions of rage, which often resulted in his having to apologize later for damage done to someone else's furniture or a relationship — usually both.

He explained about his painful illnesses in childhood and his demanding, punitive father, and asked me to be understanding and patient.

It worked for a while (I've always had a soft spot for intelligent neurotics), but after one memorable day when he smashed some of my records in front of the children, screaming at me for coming home ten minutes late from work and keeping him waiting, I told him if he didn't go into therapy, I was through.

Kelly's answer was, "I've never met a psychiatrist I couldn't out-think and out-reason; I'm not about to waste my time or my money on one of those cretins!"

This Thursday gathering in Berkeley was an effort on Kelly's part to bring together people he considered intelligent enough to, as he put it, appreciate what he could teach them about using their minds effectively. I hoped it would all work out the way he wanted, but if it didn't, it wasn't going to be my problem.

I was sitting close to the fireplace so I could blow my cigarette smoke in the general direction of the chimney and avoid offending non-smokers. These were the early days of the anti-smoking campaign and Berkeley, as usual, was ahead of everywhere else in making it a cause. You could still expect to find ashtrays in most homes in San Francisco and Marin County, but in Berkeley, you apologized for needing to smoke and let yourself out into the back yard until you'd done your little addiction thing and were ready to rejoin the free souls inside.

By 8:00 PM, there were only four of us in the room: Kelly, myself and the person who lived in the house — a short, black-haired man in his early 40's with a seductive, lopsided grin, who translated ancient Chinese medical texts into English for the love of it, and was at the moment unemployed. The fourth was a very pretty woman, an attorney, who had been telling us wearily how it had recently come to her that she detested everything about the law, but that she couldn't decide what else to do with her life.

By 8:15, two more people had arrived; a short blonde woman with a pale face and hesitant smile, and a man with angry eyes who was introduced as a psychologist. Then the door opened and in came a slender, very tall man whose hair was a thick Old Testament mane of silver, matched by a trim beard which had streaks of blond hair mixed in with the white. He was wearing brown corduroy pants and a worn corduroy jacket, and Kelly yelled out his name, "Doctor Alexander Borodin, people, known to his friends as Shura!"

I must have been staring at the newcomer rather intently, because, as we were introduced, he met my gaze and lifted one large white eyebrow fractionally. Then he smiled as I patted the floor beside me. I'd heard just enough from Kelly about the man called Shura to be extremely curious. He'd said once, "Shura's the only person I've ever met — with the exception of Doctor Needleman — that I respect. He's a true, honest-to-God genius. He may even have a higher IQ than mine." He'd chuckled, and so had I. We both knew that Kelly found it hard to really believe in any IQ higher than his own, which was in the 170's. I had been intrigued by the admittedly faint possibility that a person who inspired respect in my difficult friend might actually turn up at the meeting. And anyone who rated equal seating, in Kelly's eyes, with the philosopher Jacob Needleman must be pretty remarkable, I thought.

I watched the man with the gorgeous hair as he took off his jacket and sat down on the floor to my left. He hooked his arms around his knees and said, "Hello," his eyes clear blue and interested. I said in a low voice, "I'm honored to finally meet one of the two people in the world to whom Kelly does not apply the word, 'turkey'!"

"Oh, really?" Shura looked sharply at me, then glanced over to where his host was animatedly talking to the blonde woman. "I suppose I should be flattered, but I hardly know him. Only met him a couple of times, at the Berkeley Brain Center. Don't know where he developed such regard for me." I grinned at the mention of what was usually referred to as the BBC, a very large and successful lecture and discussion group Kelly had taken me to a few times. Berkeley, like most university towns, was full of discussion groups continually being born and dying, and the BBC had lasted longer than most.

I asked him, "What made you decide to come tonight, if you don't know Our Leader all that well?"

"Oh, I had a free evening after my class on the U.C. campus, and thought I might stop in here instead of going straight home. Just curiosity. And I suppose I wasn't looking forward to home that much. Since my wife died, the evenings have sometimes been a bit too quiet."

I said, "Oh, dear, how long ago did she die?" He said about a year ago, and I made a small sympathetic sound, thinking, I wonder if it was a happy marriage. I changed the subject and asked if the class he referred to was one he was teaching, or was he a student? He said it was a class in Forensic Toxicology, and that he taught it every fall at the university.

He's forgotten to ask who the other non-turkey is. Should I tell him?

"Since you didn't ask," I said, "Kelly's only other hero is Jacob Needleman. You're in pretty good company."

"Is that so?" He didn't have to say it; he wasn't familiar with the name.

I chuckled, "That's okay. I don't know anything about him either, except that he's a philosopher and he's written some excellent books which I haven't read yet."

During the break in the meeting, Shura and I took our cigarettes and coffee outside to the front porch and talked. I found out that he was a chemist and specialized in something called psychopharmacology, and that we knew a lot of the same people. He, too, had been to Esalen. He told me a story about a certain rather stolid psychiatrist whom I had also met, doing a handstand, stark naked, in one of Esalen's famous hot tubs, with an audience of the great and near-great, also naked but less ambitious, doing their best to avoid being swamped by the tidal wave. He said it was his favorite memory of Esalen. When I stopped laughing, I promised him an equally hilarious anecdote of my own about the hot tubs, at some future time. I was already looking forward to a future time. I liked this man, despite Kelly's approval of him.

Somewhere along the way, I managed to make it clear to Shura that I had known Kelly for several months and that I was in the process of bringing closure, as gently as I could, to the relationship. It wasn't the right moment for details, and I didn't offer any.

Shura said he had been married for 30 years and that his wife, Helen, had died of a stroke last year. When I asked him if he had children, he said there was one son, Theo, who was grown and living on his own, not far from the family home in the East Bay.

I wonder what age range is "grown?" I can't tell how old this man is. The white hair says one thing, but the face and the way the body moves say something entirely different.

When he asked, "How about you? Do you have children?" I took a deep breath and began, talking fast because Kelly was calling everyone back to the hard work of learning to think properly. "I'm divorced from a psychiatrist and I have four children, but the oldest, from my first marriage (I thought of adding that I was very young at the time — around five or so — but resisted the temptation) is living up north. He's a very good teacher in a private school and he has his own family."

The word, "family," implies children, which means I'm a grandmother. So, okay. I'm a grandmother.

I stubbed out my cigarette, "I live with my three teenagers in Marin County and we have a house across the street from my ex, so the kids just climb up the hill to their father's house on weekends and spend the time with him, and come back at the end of Sunday. It's a very civilized arrangement and I'm glad I managed to do it that way, because it's paid off for everybody. I mean, my children haven't really had too bad a time with the divorce."

I finished up at supersonic speed, "I work in a hospital as a medical transcriber and I hate the job but it's a living." I expelled a long breath, and Shura grinned. We returned to the living room.

I'm glad I'm still reasonably attractive and I have lovely long hair, and thank God I lost weight last year and I'm a size 9. I want this man to be interested. No — make that fascinated.

I liked him. I liked his face and the long, lean body; I liked the husky tenor voice and the way his eyes observed and the impression he gave of an open directness overlying something very inward, very private.

When the meeting was over, we walked out of the house together and stopped on the sidewalk beside my old Volkswagon bus. I asked him if he planned to be at the next meeting, and it was then that I learned the rest of what I had to know.

He said, "No, I'm afraid I'm going to have to leave it at this one time, because I'm starting lessons in French next Thursday."

"For any specific reason, or just to learn French?"

"Well, I've always intended to learn French anyway, but right now there's a reason for trying to learn as much as I can in a very short time."

He leaned back against my car, his arms folded, and the street light gave him a corona of orange-gold. His face was in shadow.

"For the past year or so," he said, "I've been in a — a strange sort of relationship with a woman named Ursula, who lives in Germany. She was over here with her husband to study psychology and I fell in love with her, which was a bit inconvenient, since her husband is a person I like very much and consider a good friend, but it happened. It happened to both of us. I don't know how it's going to work out, but I'm going to meet her in Paris for a few days around Christmas, and we're going to try to figure out what to do. The French is because she speaks it fluently and I have a smattering of it and it's easier for me to improve what I have than to try learning German."

I said the only thing I could, "Oh, I see." The Observer — my name for the part of me that keeps track of everything — noted with interest that there was suddenly a hollow feeling just below my rib cage. I smiled pleasantly at the shadowed face and said, "I hope it works out the way you want it to," not meaning a word of it.

Just before I got into my car, I turned to him and put out a tendril, just in case.

"When you get back," I said, "I'd love to know how it all turned out."

I dug in my purse for the pen and small notebook I always carried, wrote my name and phone number and handed it to him. He took a large, worn wallet from the front pocket of his pants and carefully tucked the piece of paper into it.

From the driver's window, I looked at the tall, brown-jacketed figure and said, "I'm very glad to have finally met you and I hope we meet again," speaking the ordinary, standard phrase slowly, with emphasis, as if it were the Open Sesame to treasure.

Shura Borodin braced his hands on the edge of the car window, brought his head down to where he could look directly into my eyes, and said one quiet word, "Yes."

A small shock went up my spine. I drove home, smiling for a long time.

I didn't see him again for over two months. During that time, Kelly reluctantly packed up the assortment of things he'd kept at my house and, to my considerable surprise, said goodbye with a shy kiss on my forehead and an almost apologetic shrug, as if he realized that, this time, his usual tantrums would gain him nothing at all. I was touched and relieved and had all the locks changed the next morning.

Then there was Christmas and everything that meant to me as a mother. Ann, Wendy and Brian were not only my children; they were also my only close friends. The divorce had made painfully clear that most of the people Walter and I had known during our marriage were going to remain attached to the partner with the medical degree and the social standing; apparently, it had not occurred to them to continue being friends with both of us.

I had to work for a living; Walter's support payments were all he could afford, and they were not quite enough to cover the needs of three teenagers and the monthly bills as well.

Ann, the older of my two girls, was — at age 17 — enjoying her new shapely figure, after years of misery with baby-fat. Wendy, one year younger, had also fought the bulge battle and won. The three of us had dieted together the year before until, finally, the day came for all of us to drive to the big shopping center up Highway 101, and walk together into a shop where they sold only blue jeans. While Brian sat waiting, the girls and I pulled on pants in sizes we had only dreamt of eight months earlier, and I bought a new pair for each of us, giggling at Brian's exaggerated look of boredom (he never had weight problems). Celebration day.

So for Christmas, with the seductive credit cards I knew I should be avoiding, I bought some pretty, sexy clothes for my daughters. For Brian, my gentle, observant young son, I found an expensive sweater with an understated brown and blue pattern. Brian might be the youngest at 14, but he was no longer the baby; there was actually a shadow on his upper lip, which his sisters occasionally commented on, and he had a very definite taste in clothes, tending toward the simple and conservative. Suffering from a mild dyslexia, he had learned, when very young, to avoid the taunts and jeers of school bullies by being as quiet and unobtrusive as possible, and I suspected that this was at least part of the reason for such understatement in his choice of what to wear.

Ann and Wendy were bright, lovely-looking girls; each had thick blonde hair that fell in a straight, shining river to her buttocks. They had always complained bitterly when they were younger about the fact that Brian's darker hair had all the curls, but in high school their own falls of gold had earned them so much attention, they gradually lost the habit of curl-envy. I felt vindicated in having threatened them with banishment, execution or worse, if they so much as thought of cutting anything more than a split-end.

They were kind, thoughtful people, my children, sensitive to the feelings of others, and patient with me as I struggled, not very efficiently, to keep both job and home going. I had always been a poor housekeeper, and suffered bouts of guilt when I realized how often the kids picked up after me. The only trouble they gave me was in a tendency to silly arguments with each other, like most siblings. They were just starting to outgrow this particular form of fun and games, to my great relief.

I adored them, not just because they were my own, but because they were good human beings, people of integrity.

On New Year's Eve, when the children had gone up the hill to be with their father, I went to a Mensa party in San Francisco, but returned home relatively early, wanting to face the first hours of the new year away from the noise and lurching of people who had drunk too much. I stood outside on the deck, in darkness, looking up at the star-frosted sky, letting myself feel without censoring the ache and hope that belonged to that night, and I sent out a prayer for connection with someone who would be — finally — the person I'd needed to be with all my life, someone who would have gone through his own changes and wars of the spirit and emerged a true adult. A grown-up man. Who wouldn't mind my being a grandmother, for Pete's sake. A man somewhat like Shura Borodin — or what Shura seemed to be.

I cried a bit because the wanting was so very intense and the clear night sky so very indifferent, and everything I was in body and soul might yet grow old without a lover and friend who could be to me what I was capable of being to him. I toasted myself, hope, the new year and the magnificent cold stars with a bit of wine, then went to bed.

Toward the end of January, I received a phone call from a woman I'd met several times at the BBC discussion group meetings, a sweet, flittering, childlike woman of 60-odd, who reminded me of a Hungarian countess my parents had known in Italy, when I was a child. Hilda even wore jewelry the same way the countess had, thin bird fingers glittering with rings, neck hung with numerous chains and pendants. She was the president of a psychology foundation whose name I could never quite remember, and she constantly fretted about the book for which she seemed to be forever gathering material.

She was phoning to invite me to an evening at her home with her new discovery, " — an extraordinary spiritual teacher from India; you *must* meet him, my dear!" She urged me not to miss the performance of Indian music she had arranged for, and the company of what she assured me were, "The most wonderfully interesting people, very special people, darling!" I said to myself, Oh, why not, and to her, "Thank you, Hilda, it sounds absolutely irresistible."

It was a Saturday night. When I entered Hilda's large living room, the first thing I saw was a magnificent dark red Persian rug and the second thing was Shura Borodin. He was standing at a large fireplace, resting one arm easily on the mantel, talking to three people whose backs were to me, two men and a woman. After the first shock of seeing him again, I found myself wondering where the German Ursula person was, not knowing what to look for — brown, black or blonde hair, although presumably it would be blonde — and I noted without amusement that my pulse rate had gone up considerably within the past few seconds.

I searched around for other familiar faces to focus on; I didn't want to be caught looking at him. I thought, he might even have gotten married, then remembered he had told me Ursula was already married to a good friend (or former good friend), so that idea could be ditched.

Maybe he's engaged. To hell with it. He never did call me, so Paris must have worked out the way he wanted, and if she's here, I'll find out soon enough.

Hilda called the room to order, and invited her 25 or so guests to please form a half-circle, sitting on the pillows scattered around the floor. I sat down on a dark brown velvet pillow close to an archway, arranging my long skirt gracefully on the carpet, and reminded myself that, when I looked around to identify Shura and his German lady, I should do so very casually.

Suddenly there was a body unfolding itself onto a large pillow next to me. It smelled warm and male and unaccountably familiar, and it was Shura. I smiled at him and said, "How good to see you again! Did you bring your German lady with you?"

"No, I'm afraid it wasn't possible, this time."

Oh hell, I meant to the party, not from Europe. Does he mean the same thing? Does he mean she's here in California, but didn't come to the party? Or that he couldn't bring her home with him from Paris?

I tried again, "When did you get back?"

"From France? Oh, about two weeks ago."

"And it went well for you?"

He didn't answer right away. I saw his profile, with its fine-bridged nose, as he squinted at the room. I waited, all my antennae on alert. After what seemed a very long time and was quite probably all of four seconds, he answered, "I really don't know."

I kept looking at him and said nothing.

"I've never had a relationship anything like this," he said, "And sometimes I wonder if I've convinced myself of something that isn't really there at all."

He sat, hunched over his knees, his voice subdued, "Yet, I'm sure of what's been said and I remember what was done, and I know that some part of it's quite real. And I suspect that some part of it isn't." He turned to me and shrugged, "My problem is, how to find out which is which."

Well, well, he doesn't waste time with small-talk answers, bless him.

I met his eyes and openly read them. There was inwardness, and pain at the corners, and something else right in the center, and that something else had to do with me, not with anybody named Ursula. I thought, he really is seeing me; I'm not just a couple of sympathetic ears. That's good. Just as long as he doesn't suspect how very much I detest beautiful (I assumed she was beautiful) German women, specially those called Ursula. After all, we've only met once before. I couldn't possibly be as interesting to him as he is to me. No, I thought, that isn't true. I didn't believe that part, and my Observer was pleased to note that I didn't.

Hilda was asking for everyone's attention.

But I couldn't very well be as fascinating to him as Ursula, because he's in love with her. On the other hand, people have been known to recover from being in love. Especially if things don't go well and there's another nice, warm, caring person around to pick up the pieces.

I got a sudden image of my usually cool Observer holding its head in despair. Okay, okay, I thought, I'll go easy. We don't even know whether Ursula is in California, do we?

When the turbaned Indian person was well launched into his presentation, I put my mouth up to Shura's right ear and whispered, "Does that mean Ursula didn't come back with you?"

He inclined his head and nodded a confirmation. All right. Maybe she was arriving next week or something, but at least she wasn't with him right now. I kept my face impassive, thanking the gods that most of us humans were not competently telepathic, most of the time. It would have been hard to explain the fierce little thrust of exhilaration I felt. It was hard enough to explain it to myself, considering.

At the end of the talk, before the music was to start, there was an intermission. The guests helped themselves to wine or coffee at Hilda's table; Shura and I went outside onto the wide deck, to smoke our cigarettes. He held a plastic cup of wine in one hand and perched on the wide wooden railing. I suddenly remembered a question I had forgotten to ask the first time we'd met.

"By the way," I said, "I'm sure you must have answered this a thousand times, but — are you related in any way to the composer Borodin, the Prince Igor Borodin?"

"Only very distantly, I'm afraid. Not enough to boast about."

"Okay, now that's out of the way, tell me what you're going to do about your German lady. Did the two of you make any kind of decision about where to go from here? Or there?"

Shura tapped ash off the end of his cigarette, "Yes, I suppose you could say we made some kind of decision. She's going to begin proceedings for a divorce, start packing her things, and before long — whatever that means — she'll join me here."

I thought about the curious flatness of his voice, and decided to take a chance.

"That all sounds very hopeful; why are you not sounding — well, your tone of voice doesn't match what you're saying, if you'll forgive my ...." I made an apologetic gesture.

He shifted his weight on the railing and glanced toward the glass doors and the lights of the living room, taking his time with the answer, "Yes, I suppose I don't sound that full of excitement, and it's probably because there've been an awful lot of false starts in this thing. It isn't the first time she's told me she would be moving out here, but somehow there never seems to be a definite date."

He looked around for an ashtray and I offered him a small cracked blue saucer I'd found on the deck floor — probably the cat's dish.

"When she does come for a visit," he continued, "She lets me know her plans a very short time in advance, and she never stays long. Yet while she's here, she talks as though she really does intend to move in; you know, things like wanting to change this or that in the house, sounding as if she can't wait to be settled in, to be staying with me forever. Yet, she always goes home, after a couple of weeks, and it's always, 'Just a few more months, please be patient just a few more months.'"

I asked, "What is the husband doing, in the meantime?"

Shura looked directly at me, the furrow between his eyebrows deepening in the reflected light, and he said, "You know, that's probably the strangest part of this whole very strange business; Ursula has told me, over and over, that Dolph is very upset and angry about all this, even on the verge of violence of some kind — which would not be totally unexpected, after all — and yet, he's answered the phone a few times, when I've called Germany to ask Ursula something that couldn't wait for a letter, and he always talks to me as if I am still his friend and nothing has changed, nothing is going on. I don't know what to think."

"Maybe he's just being stiff-upper-lip?"

"No, I don't think so. There's always some strain in the voice when a person's doing that — you can pick it up pretty easily — and there's absolutely no strain in Dolph's voice, no hint of anything underneath. He sounds as if he honestly enjoys hearing from me and still likes me, unbelievable as that sounds. He rattles on about articles in journals, stuff like that, and we talk just as we used to when he was visiting here. Then he says goodbye very affectionately and turns the phone over to his wife."

"Good Lord," I said, genuinely surprised, "That doesn't make sense at all, does it? You'd expect some explosion or accusations — or at least some sadness, wouldn't you?"

"Yes," said Shura, "I would think so."

Hilda appeared at the glass doors and motioned us in. As I headed toward my corner, I thought about what Shura had been telling me.

He's wondering if his lady is playing games of some kind; he's sensing something out of kilter, but doesn't know what it is or where to look for it.

We settled down on our pillows, and after the music — played by three men dressed, Indian fashion, in white tunics with broad red sashes around the waist — had been going on for about ten minutes, Shura rose very quietly. When I looked up, he grasped my hand, pulled me to my feet and led me through the open archway into Hilda's darkened hall. As he urged me along, I giggled at the suspicions tumbling through my mind, and Shura turned around, finger to lips, pantomiming Silence.

I followed him into a small room at the end of the hall, where I could make out a large desk and piles of books and magazines on the floor, and two chairs. Shura left the door open for what there was of available light, and settled himself in an old-fashioned captain's chair with wheels. I sat, knee to knee with him, in the other chair.

I smiled at him and said, "Oh?"

He grinned back, "I decided talking to you was more important than listening to the music, beautiful as it is, and fond of it as I am. Do you mind?"

"Terribly."

"Okay. What I want to talk to you about is the work I do."

This is getting wilder and wonderfuler all the time. He drags me into a little darkened room to tell me about his work. I am intrigued. I think I adore this marvelous character and I hope Germany sinks into the sea.

I said, "I would love to hear about your work."

He began, "Do you know what psychopharmacology is?"

"Not really."

"I think I told you, the last time we talked, that I am a chemist and a psychopharmacologist. Actually, what I do is somewhat different than what is done by most of the other people who call themselves psychopharmacologists. Everyone in this particular discipline studies the effects of drugs on the central nervous system, which is what I also do. But most of them study those effects in animals, and I study them in humans. I don't investigate all kinds of drugs, just a certain kind in particular."

"What certain kind in particular?"

"The drugs I work with are called psychedelics or psychotomimetics. I assume you've heard something about them?"

"You mean, things like mescaline and LSD?"

"Exactly"

"Well, I've never had LSD, but one of the most extraordinary and important days of my life was the day I took peyote."

Shura leaned forward, "Really! When was that?"

"Oh, good grief, I think it was — I have to count backwards for a moment — I think about 15 — no, more than that — maybe 20 years ago. A very interesting man who has since become a psychiatrist took me on the journey; his name is Sam Golding. Do you know him?"

Shura laughed, "Yes, I know Sam very well. We did a lot of work together in the 60's; in fact, he co-authored a couple of papers with me. That was a long time ago, though. I haven't seen him for at least a year."

"Sam's an unusual man, and he was a good guide for me. I haven't seen him in years, either. Anyway — go on."

"About 20 years ago, I left a very good job with a large company I'm sure you've heard of, Dole Chemical?"

I nodded.

"I went back to school, to learn everything I could about the central nervous system. It was a somewhat risky thing to do, since I had a wife and child to support, but Helen went to work as a librarian at the university, without even a hint of protest — she was totally supportive, bless her — then, after I'd done two years of medical school, I set to work creating a private laboratory in a large room about a hundred yards behind my house. It had been the basement of my family's first home on the property. The house burned down one summer and everything was lost except that perfectly good basement. Then I went through the long process of finding out how to deal with the red tape and the authorities, in order to get the kind of license I needed for what I wanted to do, which is an interesting story for another time. And I became a consultant."

I was still tasting the promising words, "... an interesting story for another time," and had to replay the mental voice tape quickly to catch up.

"What kind of consultant?"

"In the field of the effects of psychoactive drugs on the human sensorium, particularly those kinds called psychedelic. I began publishing everything I was doing and discovering. And I continued to find new ones — new drugs."

I shifted in my chair, my knee bumping his, not sure I understood. "You found new psychedelics?"

"I invented new ones. I still invent them. I try each new drug out on myself, starting at extremely low levels and gradually increasing the amount until I get activity. It saves a lot of mice and dogs, believe me. If I like what I'm seeing with the new compound, I run it through my research group. After that, I write up the results and publish them in a journal, usually a very respected one called the Journal of Medicinal Chemistry."

Jesus Aitch! I can't believe this! He INVENTS psychedelics!

I realized I was staring at him with my mouth open. I said, "It sounds like the most exciting work in the universe, or am I mistaken?"

"No, you're absolutely right. At least, in my eyes, it is. Most people who call themselves psychopharmacologists, however, would assume I'm out of my mind."

"Why?"

"Because trying new compounds out in your own body has gone out of fashion. It used to be the only responsible way for a person who called himself a scientist to evaluate a drug which was intended for human consumption, particularly if the drug was his own creation. Now, scientists shudder at the idea of anything but animal work, and when you argue that a mouse or a dog can't possibly tell you how a drug is changing their perceptions or their feelings, it falls on deaf ears. They're entirely comfortable with their way of doing things, and my old-fashioned approach strikes them as very strange and dangerous."

"What drugs have you invented? Would I know any of the names?"

"Well, the most notorious one was developed while I was still at Dole Chemical, and the fact that my name was connected to it has made certain people very distrustful of me, even though I was in no way responsible for the mess it caused. Have you ever heard of DOM?"

"No, I'm afraid not."

"That's all right. Most people haven't heard of it under that name. It got onto the street as STP."

"Oh, yes, I've heard of that. I don't remember any details, though. I have a vague impression that there was something called STP around and people were having problems with it, but it was a long time ago, when the papers were full of all sorts of hysteria about drugs in the Haight-Ashbury."

Shura leaned back, his chair creaking, "Well, while I was still working for Dole, I was invited to give a lecture at Johns Hopkins in Baltimore and I talked about several compounds, including DOM and — this is entirely speculation, but it's the most logical explanation I can come up with — someone in that audience must have decided to run with it, go into business for himself with a brand new turn-on, because within a few months there were reports of a new menace on the streets of San Francisco, with people piling into the Haight-Ashbury Clinic, totally out of control, sure they were dying."

"Good grief!"

"What happened, apparently, was that our unknown entrepreneur had put the stuff out in capsules of 20 milligrams each, and it's fully effective — I mean, *fully* — at a third of that amount. I didn't know any of this at the time, of course, because I had no reason to associate anything I'd made with this STP thing I was hearing about. And, as if the overdose weren't enough — DOM is a very, very powerful psychedelic — the people getting it weren't told that it takes two to three hours before the full effects are realized. So some of them were swallowing their pill and when nothing much happened after 40 or 50 minutes, they'd take another one."

"Oh, boy."

"When the effects caught up with them, they panicked and rushed into emergency clinics because they couldn't handle it. I don't think *anyone* could handle 20 milligrams — much less twice that — of DOM!"

"How did you find out that it was your DOM?"

"It took quite a while. I kept getting bits of information from various sources; I heard it was a long-lasting drug, over 24 hours' duration — at that dosage level, anyway — that it took a long time to come on, and that STP stood for Serenity, Tranquility and Peace."

I nodded, "Ah, that does sound familiar."

"I also heard that, according to the Berkeley police, STP stood for Too Stupid To Puke."

I laughed, repeated the words to myself and laughed all over again.

Shura continued, "Eventually, word filtered down to me from a friend that the FDA — the Food and Drug Administration — had tracked the stuff down to a patent held by Dole Chemical, and that Dole had identified it as one of the drugs I'd developed while I was working for them. I sent to the FDA for the information I assumed they had, but never got a reply. Finally, a chemist I knew got hold of a sample and analyzed it, and that was that; it was my old friend, DOM."

He crossed one leg over the other and I saw that he was wearing sandals. I remembered he'd had on sandals the first night I'd met him. *Maybe he always wears sandals. Have to ask him sometime.*

"How many psychedelic drugs have you invented, so far?"

"Oh," he sighed, "Somewhere over a hundred — hundred and fifty or so. Some of them aren't worth pursuing, others are."

It caught up with me, all of a sudden. Here was a man I had liked from my first sight of him, was liking more and more — in fact, I was absolutely captivated, by now — and he had just told me that he'd invented about a hundred and fifty psychedelic drugs. I was assuming that they worked like mescaline — at least, some of them did — opening up the soul's eyes to other realities, and here I was, sitting in Hilda's little study, touching knees with a person who didn't just possess and try out these extraordinary treasures; he created them — doorways to a world in which plants emit light and God holds your hand.

I was aware of silence, and felt Shura's eyes on me. I looked at the bearded face and realized that, despite the appearance of casualness in his half-smile and the sprawl of his body in the chair, he was watching me intently.

I smiled fully at him, feeling excitement in my throat like the pressure of laughter. I sat straight and opened my hands to help me speak, "I don't know quite how to say this, but I have to try. For years and years, I've been fascinated by this whole area of — of experience, exploration — and I've read Huxley and Michaux and anybody else I could find who seemed to know anything about it."

Shura nodded.

I continued, "I even had a secret dream about setting up, or at least being part of, some sort of research project for testing ESP before, during and after the taking of a psychedelic, and although nothing ever came of it, the idea still appeals to me."

The shadowed figure was still, listening.

"It's hard to believe that I've finally met somebody who's doing all these things, exploring this world, and isn't afraid of what he'll discover. It's incredible!" I laughed, holding out my hands in mock helplessness.

Shura smiled, then reached over and took my left hand. He held it as he talked. "There are a lot of people doing the kind of research I do, but at the moment, I'm the only one I know of anywhere who publishes on the effects of these materials in human beings."

"Why aren't the others publishing?"

"Mostly because chemists want to make enough money to support families and house payments, and buy the usual nice things, so they hire themselves out to large companies, or they work for universities, and one of the things you depend on in a university is government funds. When you're dependent on funding from the government, or in a business which has contracts from the government, you play the game according to government rules. And since the government decided that psychedelic drugs are too dangerous for anybody but the Pentagon and the CIA to play around with, they've refused to fund anything but animal research, and most of that animal research is directed toward reinforcing the idea that psychedelic drugs are dangerous in man."

"Well," I countered, "They are, aren't they, if they're not used the right way?"

Shura was quiet for a moment, then said, "Well, yes, of course they are. But just what is the right way? Use them with care, and use them with respect as to the transformations they can achieve, and you have an extraordinary research tool. Go banging about with a psychedelic drug for a Saturday night turn-on, and you can get into a really bad place, psychologically. Know what you're using, decide just why you're using it, and you can have a rich experience. They are not addictive, and they're certainly not escapist, either, but they're exceptionally valuable tools for understanding the human mind, and how it works."

"A lot more than just the mind," I muttered, remembering my day in Golden Gate Park with Sam.

"Well, one of the problems in talking about this kind of exploration," said Shura, "Is vocabulary. There simply aren't the right words available

— words everybody can agree on — to do a good job of defining a lot of this territory. The word, 'mind,' for instance, can mean only the thinking function, or it can stand for everything that isn't purely physical, the whole psyche. You get used to being very exact in the way you use words, after a while, when you're trying to communicate with someone about this area of experience."

I kept gazing at him, trying not to let my happiness show. It was a rare thing for me to be feeling so happy. Of course, there was still the wonderful, lovely, young, intelligent Ursula — it was best to assume she was all of those things — but he wasn't, at the moment, holding anyone's hand but mine.

From down the hall came the sounds of applause. I thought, we don't have much time before somebody's going to come looking for us, and I have to make it possible for us to continue this.

"Shura, before they hunt us down, could you write a date in your appointment book, if you have one?"

He let go of my hand and reached for his wallet. Out of it he produced a small notebook, and from a pocket of his jacket came a pen. He sat, poised to write.

"In February, I'm giving a Valentine's Day party at my home, and I want you to come." I gave him the date and time, my address and instructions on how to find it; I couldn't remember whether I had given him anything more than my phone number the first time we'd met.

"I would be happy to come," he said, writing in the little book, "I don't see any conflict that day."

"It'll be mostly Mensa people," (for once, I didn't feel it necessary to explain that Mensa was an international society for people whose IQ's tested out over 132, or play apologetic games about being a member) "And some other friends, including my kids — at least, the three I'm living with — and please try to get there; I want to continue this conversation," I concluded, "I have an awful lot of questions to ask you."

My God! Do I have QUESTIONS!

"I'll do my best to be there," he said, standing and taking my hand again to help me up. We started out of the study just as Hilda turned on the lights in the hallway and cried, "Oh, *here* you are!"

Back in the living room, we were separated immediately by other guests, and I decided to leave the party without saying goodbye to him. It wasn't necessary. If he was going to see me again, it would be within two weeks. He had the address, the phone number and the date, and he'd said yes. Now we'd see whether he meant it. There was no reason for me to hang around him, acting like a moonstruck idiot. I kissed Hilda, said, "Thank you, it was wonderful," speaking the absolute truth, then got my coat and quietly let myself out.

CHAPTER 19. SEDUCTION

On the night of the party, I dressed in black ballet tights and black dancer's top with low-cut neck and long sleeves. Around my waist I tied a long wraparound skirt with a paisley design in dark red, and hung tiny red balls from my ears.

Checking my reflection, I felt a quick surge of pleasure; when you're only 5 feet, 4 inches tall, every excess pound shows, and the body in the long bathroom mirror had a clean outline, with no bulges to apologize for. Small breasts. Brown hair falling in thick waves to a few inches below the shoulders, glinting reddish blonde where the light caught it. My face no longer reminded me of the young Ingrid Bergman, but then, neither did Ingrid Bergman's. At least, the lines were mostly what people call laugh lines, in the usual places around mouth and eyes. During the past year or so, the children had made me smile just enough to keep my face from beginning to sour, as can happen all too easily when you're over forty and your marriage has taken a long, bitter time to end.

I bared my teeth in a final grin at the mirror and snapped off the bathroom light. Against the dark I saw again the image of the tall man with the observing eyes and reminded myself, not for the first time that day, to try — to do my very best — not to look for Shura. He might not come. I wanted to believe that he would have phoned if he couldn't make it, but I didn't know him well enough to be sure. Perhaps he said yes to too many people and ran into conflicts, or maybe he just hadn't remembered to look at his appointment book; perhaps he'd heard from Ursula and she was arriving to stay forever and he'd forgotten that I existed.

My first guest turned out to be the one member of Mensa who would inevitably feel uneasy at finding himself the early bird. Stanley was one of two people in the local Mensa society who could be described as idiot savants; he was awkward, socially inept, a 26 year old man with the general intelligence of a 12 year old child, except for one thing: the ability to do mathematics, all kinds of mathematics, with the speed and accuracy of a computer. One of the two intelligence tests given by Mensa to prospective members was loaded in the math direction — or so it had seemed to me. I had done miserably on that one and made it into membership on the basis of my score on the second test, which contained almost no math. Stan had done the same thing, in reverse.

I took my shy guest's hand and led him with his wine bottle into the kitchen, where I gave him a plastic cup and said, "Pour yourself whatever you want, and since you're here first, you get the good seat by the fire." He smiled and filled his cup, then let me guide him to the long couch, which I had moved near the big fireplace.

From the outside, this was an impressive-looking A-frame house. It had three storeys — four if you counted the little room at the very top, under the peak of the roof, which was Brian's. I rented out the small apartment on the first floor to a young couple, and the children and I lived in the rest of the house.

The place was dominated by its three-storey living room and an impressive fireplace, built out of polished dark stone and volcanic rock. There were immense windows which allowed a view of trees and a small river which flowed past us, down below. For parties, it was wonderful; for daily living, less wonderful. There was no insulation anywhere; the windows and doors leaked cold air, and every winter there was a new drip of water from yet another hole in the aging roof. Sometimes, if we were lucky, the new hole would seal itself up as the wood expanded with the rain, but that still left a couple of old friends which kept us busy laying out pots and pans on the floor.

Thank heaven, I thought, no rain tonight. I put on a record, hoping it would reassure Stan that there actually was going to be a party here.

More guests arrived, and within an hour there were over forty of them, with drinks in their hands, talking and laughing; several were taking over the choosing of records, reading the jackets of my albums and arguing about what should go on next. I had made sure there would be music playing all evening, laying out a selection of jazz, Simon and Garfunkel, the Beatles and — for the later and mellower hours — some of my classical albums, Copeland and de Falla, and a few others that had rhythm and sensuality and lightness of heart.

Kelly arrived with his new girlfriend and I gave him a heartfelt hug, glad we were now, finally, friends. He hugged me back, taking a few seconds longer than his lady fully appreciated; I saw her mouth tighten and moved quickly to hug her, too, before she could step back from me.

Don't worry, sweetheart; he's all yours!

The front door kept opening, and the light from clusters of candles throughout the room flickered softly on brown silk, red wool and the occasional blue denim. I paused, finally, listening to the noise level, and knew I could relax. The party was underway.

For a while, I was in the small kitchen, which was divided from the living room by a long tiled bench at table height, which the children and I used for our meals. The room was crowded, and I was perching on the edge of the bench, laughing with two women about the New Year's party we had attended, at which one of Mensa's less introverted bachelors had appeared in a costume consisting of one large red satin bow tied around his penis and absolutely nothing else, when suddenly, in the archway dividing kitchen from hall, I saw Shura. A wave of goose-bumps went up my back.

He came! He really came!

I stood on tiptoe and called out, "Hello, Shura! Bring your bottle over here!" He made his way toward me, his head easily visible above everyone else's, and when he arrived, I took his bottle of red wine out of its paper bag, placed it on the tiles and gave him a plastic glass and a cork-puller. When he had poured out his drink, I took his hand and led him through the sardine pack, out to the big room.

We found a piece of unoccupied space against one side wall, and I said, "Let me tell you a bit about the people — a few of them, at least," and proceeded to give him rapid-fire descriptions of some of Mensa's main attractions, as they stood talking or moved past us. In my best museum-guide manner, I told him, addressing his right ear closely because of the noise in the room, "You see that man there, the tall one with the red vest? He created the SIG — Special Interest Group — which is known as the Orgy SIG; I forget his official title for it, something like Sexual Freedom SIG, but everyone refers to it by the other name. I've never been to a meeting, but I hear they're a lot of fun for those who go in for that sort of ..." I waved my hand vaguely in the air to complete the picture.

Okay, I'm obviously trying to be amusing and maybe even shock him a bit, but now he can assume I'm not a swinger.

I continued, "That woman over there in the purple dress, the one standing in a straight line between us and the candles," I glanced at him and he nodded, "That's Candice. She's a very good-hearted, motherish person who gives the Mensa tests in this area, and for a while her little boy, Robin, was the youngest member of Mensa in the country. He's around ten now, and no longer the youngest."

I pointed across the room, "Now, the small-boned man with the bow tie, standing at the end of the couch; he's the best chess-player in the Northern Californian Mensa. I've only managed to beat him once, but that once fed my ego for a long, long time. He's a dear; a very funny, kind person who never seems to find it necessary to say anything nasty about anybody. His name is Jack, and I like him very much."

Shura said, raising his voice over the noise, "I like chess, but I haven't played it for years, now. It would be fun to try it again."

I looked up at him and smiled, showing all my teeth, "I learned long ago that the most dangerous opponent is the one who tells you he hasn't been near the game in years. He's the one who'll wipe the board with you, while apologizing for being so terribly rusty."

Shura laughed.

"And now," I continued, "That tall man with the black beard, standing near the door — he's got a big house in Black Mountain, which is a nice, wealthy little neighborhood a bit north of here, and he gives a lot of Mensa parties and his swimming pool is usually full of naked people — I almost said naked members — and one of my finest moments was during a party last summer, when I wore the black dancer's outfit I'm wearing tonight and toward the end of the evening I decided to be really daring, and I took off the skirt and plunged into the pool fully dressed in the top and tights. You never saw a woman get so much attention! Every naked male in that pool wanted to know my name and asked where I'd been hiding myself; I was the belle of the pool! I guess they were tired of so much bare pinkness and I was a vision of temptation in all those clothes."

I had him laughing again.

I told him about the mathematical computer which inhabited the sometimes bewildered soul of the young man on the couch, and he said he was very interested in that kind of mind, and would go over and talk with him later on. I said I had hoped he would want to do that, because few people paid any attention to the boy, and he was very sweet.

I asked Shura's ear, "Why haven't you joined Mensa, by the way? It's a good way to meet interesting people, especially when you've been divorced or — or widowed."

"Well," shouted Shura, "To tell you the truth, I never thought of applying, probably because you have to take an IQ test, and I will not take an IQ test."

"Why, in heaven's name?"

I could sense hesitation, and waited for him to decide whether to explain or not. Finally, he turned toward me and said, "I feel total, complete disgust for all tests of intelligence, and only limited patience with the people who give them. When I was in the third grade or thereabouts, I was given a so-called IQ test, a Binet-something-something —"

I said, "Stanford-Binet."

" — and I made an honest and diligent effort to complete it. There were angular objects, and number games, and if-this-then-what types of questions, and the strategies needed for getting to most of the answers were pretty obvious."

"You did well?"

"Of course I did, and that's where I really tangled with the school principal. He accused me of having cheated, since no one could get the results I had gotten without cheating, and so I was in essence thrown out of the testing group, and was pretty much humiliated. They obviously wanted scores that fit on a kind of distribution curve about some sort of a norm. Mine was a bit too far to the right of the curve. My mother was furious with the principal; she pulled me into his office and confronted him and lectured him about my integrity, which made me want to run and hide even worse than before. I swore then that I'd never take another IQ test, and I never will."

I nodded in sympathy, "Of course, of course."

Then the front door opened and I caught sight of my former husband, Walter Parr, respected psychiatrist and author, adoring father and compulsively unfaithful mate. The children were with him. I took Shura's hand and said, "I want you to meet these ones. Walter is my ex, and he's truly a very good man and a fascinating person to talk to, and I'm not saying that just to give you the impression that I'm a noble and forgiving woman, which of course I am."

I forgot; I haven't told him anything about the marriage yet, so he won't know what exactly I'm being noble and forgiving about. Okay, okay.

As we squeezed past warm bodies, I continued shouting over the voices and music, "The children are Ann, Wendy and Brian; they are absolutely the world's most wonderful people, and that is a completely objective, dispassionate, clinical observation."

When we reached Walter, I introduced him to Shura and added, "Dr. Walter Parr is a very good Jungian analyst and he's written two books about the myth-making aspects of the human psyche, and they are genuinely worth reading, and I did some superb line drawings for one of them," then I pointed at Shura's chest and told Walter, my mouth close to his ear because of the din, "Shura is *the* expert on psychoactive drugs and their effects in humans, and he invents new ones and publishes all the information in big, important chemistry journals!" Then I pantomimed loss of voice due to strain, while the men said hello and shook hands.

The children were already drifting away, so I pulled Shura by the sleeve and caught up with each one in turn and yelled the name to him, and he shouted hello and when that was done, I gestured that I had to go in the direction of the kitchen, patted his sleeve and left him standing there, holding his wine glass, with a bemused expression on his face, hemmed in by strangers.

I tried not to look for the big gleaming head, during the next 15 or 20 minutes, while I checked supplies in the kitchen and said hello to as many people as I could, making sure they had everything they needed and knew where the bathroom was. I caught sight of Shura often enough to reassure myself that he hadn't left the party. When I had done everything I had to do as a good hostess, I began pushing through the people-clusters toward where I'd last seen him.

A few brave souls were trying to dance and the idea showed signs of spreading; I called out encouragement, since it was my belief that dancing could make the difference between a nice party and a great one. I eased past warm shoulders and backs, sweat trickling between my breasts.

I know what it would take to make this a truly great party: if I could convince the Big Man to stay after everybody else has gone home. Wonder whether he would? How to invite him without making it hard for him to say no? Mustn't put him on the spot.

I made my way to a little antique desk sitting against the far wall and searched through its drawers until I found some small pastel-colored note cards with envelopes, and a pen. I leaned down and carefully wrote my message on a small pink card: "Dear Dr. Borodin, I would be most appreciative and grateful if you found it possible to remain for a while after the other guests have left? Would like to have a chance to talk."

I wondered if it was a bit too forward; after all, it could be exactly what it seemed to be, an invitation to continue our conversation of the other evening. I actually had no plan. I just wanted to have a chance to really talk, to really get to know him, to hear about some of his adventures, some of what he had learned. If it led to something beyond holding hands, well, all right. I'd tackle that when and if the time came. I considered adding something about gracefully accepting a refusal, promising to ask for his exclusive company again, at a later time, if he should have to decline tonight. I decided against it. In for a penny, in for a pound. Let it stand as it was. I printed his name on the front of the envelope, then eased through the crowd toward the white head which I'd spotted near one of the wooden walls.

Most of the guests were dancing now, and when I reached Shura, he was engaged in what looked like an animated conversation with Walter. I handed him the note, saying only, "I believe this is for you," and brushed past, hearing the two men resume their discussion behind me, aware of feeling a mixture of triumph and terror.

I could very well have just given that man a solid and final reason to get out of my life and stay out, considering the fact that he's in love with a lady named Ursula and apparently committed to making a future life with her. What the hell am I doing, anyway, involving myself in this situation?

I'd never been part of a triangle in my life; I'd been too proud, perhaps too arrogant — or maybe too unbelieving in myself — to even momentarily consider the possibility of competing with another woman for a man I liked. It just wasn't my kind of scene. So why, *why*, was I doing this?

I poured myself a drink of vodka in cranberry juice, then went down the hall to the bathroom and locked myself inside for a moment of quietness. In the mirror I saw flushed cheeks and very bright eyes. Finally, I said to the face, "All right. We'll see. Good luck, friend."

By midnight, the crowd had thinned a bit and those who were left were either dancing vigorously, sweat shining on their faces, or sitting in small clusters, talking with the open, expansive, whole-body gestures that emerge when people have had quite a lot to drink and have forgotten to be self-conscious. Shura was sitting with Stan, hands clasped over his knees, listening intently to the young math genius, who looked animated and happy. I left them alone. I checked the record stack and added some more dance music to the top of the pile. The fire was still burning and crackling, the way a good fire should.

He's had plenty of time to tell me he can't stay. Enough time to get cold feet and leave. He's still here. Still here.

It wasn't until quarter to two in the morning that the last of the guests, fortified with hot coffee, said goodnight and left me alone with Shura and the spitting fire and one of my favorite records playing — Concerto de Aranguez, by Rodrigo — which I had put on to gently discourage further dancing, while maintaining the mellow, pleasurable mood of the evening.

I turned from locking my front door and said to Shura, who was sitting on the couch, watching me, "I need your help in putting a couple of things back where they belong."

We pushed the couch into its usual mid-room place, then I went to the under-stair closet and hauled out a thick foam mat which, I explained to him, belonged in front of the fireplace except when there was a party. We placed the mat a few feet back from the hearth because the fire was still throwing off occasional sparks, and I covered it with a double-bed-sized Indian cotton spread with the classic Tree of Life pattern in blue, green and yellow.

Moving quickly around the big room, I rescued all my floor cushions, big and small, and scattered them around the edges of the mat, then said to Shura, "Help yourself to anything you want in the kitchen. I'm going to change and I'll be back in a moment."

He was moving toward the tiled bench as I went upstairs to the bedroom and grabbed my best form-fitting blue jeans and a crisp white blouse with a softly ruffled V-neck. I ripped off my black stockings and black top and changed out of my black panties, putting on plain white cotton briefs and a white bra. In the bathroom, I squirted a small spray of musk cologne on my shoulders, considered spraying elsewhere, then decided to powder instead with baby powder, for a warm, innocent, friendly smell. A few minutes later, I was ready. I walked down the stairs, into the living room.

Shura was seated cross-legged on the mat. In front of the fireplace, sitting on the polished hearthstones, was a bottle of red wine and another, half-full, of white. He had found two of my wine-glasses and put them on the dark, gleaming surface, where they sparkled in the firelight.

As I eased myself onto the mat, Shura rose to his knees and poured red wine into one of the glasses, then asked, "Which would you like?" I said white, thank you, and took my drink from him.

We sat cross-legged, our profiles to the fire. I smiled at him apologetically and said what I needed to say, "I hope you'll forgive the presumption — that note — but I very much wanted to have a chance to continue our conversation, at least for a few moments, you know, without hordes of people around ..." I waggled my hand helplessly and shrugged, feeling apprehensive and a bit silly. He was looking at me, smiling slightly.

"I thank you for the invitation. It was an excellent idea, and if you hadn't come up with it, I'm sure I would have found a way to suggest it myself." It was a slightly formal, gallant gentleman thing to say.

Well, maybe he would have and maybe he wouldn't, but he doesn't look as if he's here under protest; he looks comfortable and at ease, so no more apologies.

The fire spat orange, then settled into a comfortable crackling.

I wonder if he remembers our conversation at Hilda's place. Don't know how many conversations this man has with interesting people maybe every day; he may not remember that evening, although I can't believe he would completely forget holding my hand.

I took a sip of wine and plunged, "I have so much to ask you, I don't know where to begin. I'll just have to dive in and bombard you with questions, if you can stand it?" I looked at him, suddenly anxious. Maybe he didn't want to answer questions right now?

"Go right ahead. Ask."

"Let me try to lay out what I think I understand of your life, so far. You teach some kind of chemistry at University of California, on the Berkeley campus, yes?" He nodded. I hurried on, "And you have a private laboratory behind your house, and you have official licenses to do the work you're doing, and you are an expert — a consultant — on the effects of psychedelic drugs in human beings, right?"

"Yes."

"Who asks you about those effects; I mean, what kind of people consult you?"

"Well, let's see," Shura said thoughtfully, "I've been consulted by NIDA — that's the National Institute on Drug Abuse — and NIMH, which stands for the National Institute of Mental Health —"

I nodded my familiarity with the names as he continued, "I was a consultant to NASA for a while, which is an interesting story I'll tell you some day, and I'm occasionally an expert witness in court cases involving so-called illegal drugs and what the police insist on calling illegal labs, although there's no such thing as an illegal lab, because it isn't against the law to have a lab; it's only the activity inside it that can be termed illegal."

He was wearing dark blue corduroy slacks and a cream-colored, silky shirt. I could see his nipples through the fabric.

I nodded, smiling, "I see. All right."

"Also, there are people in the DEA — the Drug Enforcement Administration — who consult with me and sometimes refer people in other government agencies to me when they've got an unusual problem they think I might be of help with. And local county labs. And private individuals with questions. I think that's about all I can think of at the moment," he concluded and drank from his glass.

He's a bit of a ham, too. Not one for false modesty and aw-shucks.

I laughed and said, "NASA, huh? I want to hear about that! But first, another question, okay?"

Shura poured himself more wine, then held out his hand for my glass and replaced the little I had drunk.

"You told me that you invent new psychedelics and that you have a group of people who try them out after you've made sure they're safe and ..."

He interrupted, "Not safe. There is no such thing as safety. Not with drugs and not with anything else. You can only presume relative safety. Too much of anything is unsafe. Too much food, too much drink, too much aspirin, too much anything you can name, is likely to be unsafe."

He was looking very intent, almost scowling.

Boy, I guess we hit a button, we did.

"The most I can ever do in regard to a drug," he continued, a shade more gently, "Is establish what appears to be a relatively safe level for myself, for my own body and mind, and invite my fellow researchers to sample the same material at what we decide is a relatively safe level for their particular bodies and nervous systems."

He paused, glancing at my eyes, "Sorry to pounce on you, but I feel it's an important point to make."

"Absolutely," I reassured him, "Pounce all you like. It's all new learning for me."

I had a flash of amusement, realizing that the invitation to pounce could be taken more than one way.

I sipped some wine and continued, "So you check the new inventions out with your group, then you publish articles telling all about them, how to make them in the lab and what their effects are on people?"

He nodded.

"And do all the government people who consult you for drug information — do all of them know that you're doing this, that you're creating new ones and publishing everything about them? I mean, don't they ever get uncomfortable or try to stop you doing it?"

"Well, as to the first part of the question, a lot of them have some idea, I suppose, if they've done their homework, but most people don't really read much, especially in the scientific literature. Second part: no. They've never tried to get in the way. They may be a bit uncomfortable about what they think I'm doing, some of them, but they have no reason to stop me. I'm not doing anything that's in any way against the law —"

I nodded quickly, hoping I hadn't sounded naive. Well, I *was* naive about this kind of thing.

Shura was saying, " — and I'm a quiet person; I don't make a lot of noise in public; I'm not leading any new social movements. I don't sell drugs. I have done work, under contract to the government, which involved making reference samples for them, and I bill them for my time, but it's a matter of principle for me, not to exchange drugs for money in any way. It keeps life a lot simpler. In the meantime, there are probably a lot of people in the government who are very interested indeed in what I publish. I have no doubt whatsoever that the CIA and probably the Defense Department take a close look at some or all of the compounds I write up; they probably feel I'm doing a lot of their work for them, as a matter of fact."

"You mean, testing them for use in war — biological warfare sort of stuff?"

Shura shrugged, "Or possibly for crowd control, or prisoner-of-war interrogation, or maybe helping drive an unfriendly head of state into some kind of befuddlement — who knows? Their objectives are not my objectives."

I leaned forward and asked softly, "What is your goal, then — discovering how the mind works, or the psyche, just the pure excitement of finding out everything you can?"

Shura drank from his glass and brushed moisture off his mustache before answering, "Isn't that sufficient reason?"

There's a faint touch of tease here, but he also wants to know how I'm relating to all this.

I said, "Sure, that's a perfectly respectable objective. But there's another one, isn't there?"

If he's the kind that gets irritated easily, I'll probably find out now.

"All right," he said, showing no signs of irritation, "But let me turn that question back to you and ask what other goal you feel there could be, or should be?"

Each of us is determined to find out as fast as possible what the other one's philosophy and ways of thinking are. And, for that matter, whether or not the other is basically sane and rational. Okay. Here goes.

I sat staring at my knees for a moment as I tried to put broad, wide images into small, tidy words, "Well, my day with peyote helped me clarify a lot of things I had thought and felt all my life, but not pinned down, not really sorted out. It was — I think it really was the most extraordinary day of my life. It was such a treasure of an experience, I remember thinking just before I went to sleep that if I should wake up dead, it would have been worth it. I've done a lot of thinking about what I learned that day — years of thinking. And I understand more and more, all the time, about that one experience. The understanding keeps unfolding, bit by bit."

I looked up at Shura, who was leaning back on one elbow, his face attentive.

I went on, "It seems to me that the magic plants — and the psychedelic drugs — are there to be used because the human race needs some way of finding out what it is, some way of remembering things we've usually forgotten by the time we're grown up. I also think that the whole 1960's eruption — all that psychedelic experimenting and exploring — was due to some very strong instinct — maybe on the collective unconscious level, if you want to use Jung's term — an instinct that's telling us if we don't hurry up and find out why we are the way we are, and why we do the things we do, as a species, we could very soon wipe ourselves out completely."

"Which is," said Shura, "The very reason I publish."

"Aaah," I said, and paused for a moment, "So it doesn't matter if the CIA people or whoever are interested in your drugs for their own reasons —"

He completed it for me, "I'm still putting the information out, broadcasting as widely as I can, in as quiet a way as I can, and perhaps among the readers will be a few souls who have the same concerns I do, and will put them to the right use."

"Yes, I see."

"That's the hope. There's no avoiding the fact that a lot of idiots who don't know diddley-squat about chemistry are going to go to work to make some of those drugs — the easier ones — for sale on the street. And people are going to take them at parties and use them in stupid, irresponsible ways, the same way they use alcohol. All kinds of people read the journals I publish in. At least, psychedelics are not physically addictive and most people find them anything *but* psychologically addictive. My hope is that, here and there, someone with a good mind — and heart — uses one of these tools and perhaps begins to understand something he didn't understand before. And that there may be a few with the courage and ability to write about what they've learned, so that others can read and begin to think. And so on and so on."

"Like Huxley."

"Yes. Unfortunately, there aren't many Huxleys around, ever. But each voice counts. All I can hope for is that there'll be enough voices and enough time."

I said, "Well, the world seems to be full of people trying all kinds of ways to change consciousness; I mean, there are lots of meditation teachings, and hypnotic trance, and breathing techniques —"

Shura replied, "Of course, there are many ways to alter your consciousness and your perceptions; there always have been, and new ways will keep being developed. Drugs are only one way, but I feel they're the way that brings about the changes most rapidly, and — in some ways — most dependably. Which makes them very valuable when the person using them knows what he's doing."

He paused to drink from his glass, then continued, "I thought for a while that I could use music to accomplish what I wanted to do, because music can be a very powerful consciousness changer, but when I discovered that I had a certain knack for chemistry, I made a decision to go that way, to concentrate on developing these tools. Mostly, I suppose, because these particular drugs, these materials, *are* a way to bring about new insights and perceptions quickly, and — well, I just don't know if we have much time. Sometimes I suspect it may be too late already."

I sat there, thinking Oh, dear. Shura's eyes were for a moment unfocused, and I knew he was in private territory, with images I had no way of sharing. I kept silent for a few moments, in deference to the possibly imminent end of the human race.

Finally, I shrugged. "I tend to be something of an incurable optimist; I figure we've *got* to have enough time, so we *will* have enough time."

Shura's eyes focused again, and he grinned at me, "You may be right, but I have no intention of getting lazy, and there's nothing better than a suspicion that time's running out, to keep you working hard."

I drank the last of my wine and decided to head into different and more dangerous territory. "Tell me about Ursula. Does she experiment with you — I mean, does she take your potions with you?"

"Yes, she enjoys them tremendously and she uses them well. I suppose that's been one of the strongest elements in our closeness. And it's one of the reasons I find it hard to understand some things about our relationship, because it's almost impossible to get away with lying about your feelings when you're sharing an altered state. She's a very intelligent woman; she's had difficult and complex insights and she's shared them with me, as I've shared mine. I know how she feels about me."

He hesitated, then said, "I should amend that. To be exact, I know how she feels about me when we're alone together. When she goes back to her home and her husband, though, she — it's as if she's disappeared into another world; I can't quite reach her there. I don't really know what to think, and I'm beginning to wonder how long we can keep things going this way, with nothing resolved and no way of being sure it ever will be."

"Has she begun divorce proceedings yet?"

"No. She says she'll have to make the final break with Dolph at just the right moment, when he's calmer, when there's less risk of his exploding into some kind of suicidal violence, or something of that sort. And it always seems that the right moment hasn't arrived yet."

"Yet, she leaves him to be with you for a couple of weeks or so — how often?"

"She's been here twice and gone back."

"And with all this, her husband is still friendly to you on the phone?"

Shura looked at me, frowning, "Sounds bizarre, doesn't it?"

I said carefully, "Well, it sounds like a rather unusual sort of marriage."

His face had saddened and there was anxiety in the air between us, and I thought, time to change subjects again. I got to my knees, leaning forward to touch the bottle of white wine, knowing that my body was outlined by the firelight, and that he could be expected to notice. He stirred and came to my rescue, lifting the bottle and pouring my glass full.

When I returned to the pad this time, I lay lengthwise, supporting my head on one hand, holding the wine glass steady with the other.

The atmosphere had begun to change in a subtle way. I knew that his focus had shifted and that he wasn't remembering Ursula, just at the moment. I spoke, almost apologetically, not wanting to say something that would drive him back to sadness, "Please tell me if you'd rather not talk about it right now, but I'd like very much to know what your marriage was like. What kind of person was your wife — Helen?"

I caught what looked like a flicker of amusement in his eyes as he replied, "Yes, Helen. No, I don't mind talking about her. I think I told you we were married for 30 years. She was a good person. Very bright, interested in a lot of different things. She was always completely supportive of me, even when I wanted to make a break with my perfectly good job at Dole — I mentioned that to you before — to start doing something I believed in. When I told her I needed to study two years of medicine, she went to work in the University library, to help pay the bills. She enjoyed getting back into the Berkeley activity, actually. She didn't really like the Farm that much — "

I interrupted, "The farm?"

"We live — I live — on a 20-acre farm. At least, it used to be a farm, with cows and goats and a horse. There still is a vegetable garden, when somebody attends to it. Helen wanted to like the Farm, but she missed the stimulation of Berkeley, her friends, all the things you find in a university town. So I think going back to work was very satisfying for her. Our son was growing up, so she didn't have to be a full-time mother, and — although I had a good scholarship to pay my way — it was a help to have that extra money coming in while I studied."

"Did she take the psychedelics with you?"

"No. She couldn't — didn't have enough trust in herself; she was afraid of losing control, and self-control was a religion with her. I didn't try to persuade her, because that's one thing that must never be done — ever. It's not a decision that can be made by one person for another. But during her last year, for some reason, she got up the courage to try. One day, she came to me and said she'd like to take mescaline. She'd done quite a bit of reading about it, and finally she'd made up her mind that it would be all right to take it because it was one material that had a long, respected history.

"So, one Sunday we gathered together with some of our closest friends and all of us — except the person who was doing the driving — took mescaline, then we piled our picnic and blankets into the car and went up to a place that has a tremendous view of the whole Bay, and settled down on the hillside for the afternoon. Helen had a wonderful experience, a really beautiful experience. And now, looking back, I wonder if — whether she might have had some intuition, some feeling about the future — but, anyway, I'm very glad she made the decision."

"And that she didn't have to regret it."

"Yes. It was a wise choice, I think. But, then, I have great faith in mescaline, since it was my own introduction to the whole world of consciousness expansion. It's a true ally, for me. And I'm very grateful that it turned out to be an ally for Helen."

I remembered Castaneda's teacher, Don Juan, referring to his "little ally," but I couldn't recall exactly which plant it was. It was a pleasing word, for some reason, stronger than "friend," as if there were a suggestion of weapons at the ready, to help defend you against dangers. A friend with strength to back up his loyalty. Ally.

I glanced at Shura's face and saw him far away again, so I told him what I'd been thinking. He smiled, "Yes. It's a good word. I'm not sure about weapons at the ready, but yes, it has a strength to it and that's the way certain psychedelics strike me — as friends and allies." He thought for a moment, then added, "Or, at least, they put you in touch with some part of yourself which serves you as friend and ally."

By now, the wine had relaxed me completely. I felt comfortable, warm, at ease with either words or silence. I focused my eyes on the fire, letting images and thoughts drift. Shura put his glass down on the floor and got up to add more logs; when he sat down again, it was in a different place, closer to me. I found myself smiling again at the pleasure I felt, being with him. Then, on impulse, I rose up on my knees, opposite him. I asked, "Are you getting tired of all these questions?"

"Not at all," he said, and put out a hand to gently trace the outline of my cheek, "I'm a teacher, you know, and teachers love questions. It means somebody's interested."

"Ah, yes," I said, placing my hands on his shoulders, "I am very interested indeed. As you perfectly well know."

He then did something completely unexpected. He placed his right hand behind my shoulder, then the left went between my thighs and up my back, so that he had me sitting on his upper arm, my breasts against his face. Inside the blue jeans, my body responded to the pressure of the arm with a flush of warmth. I was suddenly aware of the center seam of the jeans pressing into me. I pushed back a bit, riding now on his forearm. It was a strange, lovely sensation, having that long muscled arm pressing up into the seam, into the soft flesh inside it. I looked down at his face, my hands still on his shoulders. His eyes were open and he was looking directly into mine, not smiling now. I bent my head down until my forehead touched his. There was a slight sheen of perspiration on him, and I knew my own skin was damp.

His right hand moved to my waist and pulled part of my blouse out, then I felt his fingers on the back fastening of my bra. I thought, Oh, dear, he'll never manage it, and I laughed and said, "You'll have trouble with that. I'd better help a little."

Still riding on the hard, muscled arm, I undid the buttons of my blouse and slowly, feeling very thoughtful, took it off, then threw it up in the air; there was a glimpse of pink firelight on white cotton, then it was gone. I said, "I'm going to get a cover for us, just in case the fire doesn't last forever," and he pulled his forearm slowly from between my thighs and said, "All right. Don't take too long, though. I'd hate to have you forget I'm here, you know?" Fat chance, I thought, grinning down at him.

I was back almost immediately with my old patched eiderdown. It was immense and soft and well-worn and I bunched it up at the end of the pad farthest from the fireplace. Shura was very carefully placing another log on the fire, and by the time he turned around, I had taken off my bra and was rising to my knees to pull the jeans down over my hips. He sat on the pad, cross-legged, with the firelight behind him; it gave him a corona of yellow and orange. He asked, "Would you mind if I took my clothes off? I really would feel much more comfortable. It's rather hot in here, at the moment."

I whooped with laughter. Then I lay on my back and pulled the jeans off my upraised legs, like a child fooling around at bedtime. I hesitated for a moment, weighing modesty and ladylike behavior against the bother of having to think about clothes at all, then realized that both modesty and the lady had vanished in the recent arm-ride, and the panties may as well come off too.

I lay on my tummy, naked as a two-year old in a sunny back yard, and supported my chin on my hands while I watched Shura's slow, dignified performance. Underneath the soft beige shirt he wore nothing. His rib cage was huge, and it presided over a stomach so flat, it looked almost undernourished. There was a scatter of dark hair on his chest, and his nipples shone softly pink. When he had carefully placed his folded shirt on the side hearthstones, away from the fire, he rose to take off his slacks. I peered up at him and thought, my God, he's so damned tall! I said, "I see that you grow dark hair on the other parts of your body. I mean, what I can see so far," and giggled as he stepped out of boxer shorts, "Which is pretty much everything, at this point, I guess."

He eased himself down and lay on his side, facing me, one hand supporting his head, and I observed, "You really don't have much fat on you, do you?"

"I feel much better without it."

I arranged my own body opposite his, about two feet away, and continued with the earlier thought, "Does that mean you were dark-haired before you went all gorgeous silver?"

"No, as a matter of fact, I wasn't. The hair on my head was quite blonde, strangely enough, even though — as you see —" he allowed himself a small twitch of the mouth, "The hair on the body is dark."

I kept my eyes averted from the curly nest below his stomach, and asked him when did his hair turn white, and was it all at once, and what was the drug he was researching at the time?

"It all began turning when I was 30."

"Thirty! Good heavens. Any particular reason — a shock of some kind?"

"No, no shock. And no drug, either. At that time in my life, I was still working for Dole and hadn't really begun doing my own research."

"It's beautiful, as I'm sure you know."

Shura smiled broadly, this time, and said, "I thank you. My hair thanks you. I have only one theory as to why it all went white so early. I suspect I was unconsciously preparing myself to look the part of the harmless old professor, which can be useful at times when you do the kind of work I do. And publish what I publish. Sound reasonable to you?"

"Well, it's a great theory, but I think you goofed. You don't look at all harmless. In fact, you look like the archetypal alchemist or mad scientist. My ever-loving Pete, do you look like the perfect mad scientist!" I was laughing again, and I was thinking, I can't believe how completely happy I am. Naked with this long drink of water with — oh, my — the loveliest slender man legs I've ever seen, and the world's most erotic forearm, and he's in love with a girl in Germany and it doesn't matter.

"Alice," he said.

"Yes, Sir?"

"You're a very beautiful woman."

"You're rather appealing, yourself."

"All I can offer you is truth. I will always tell you the truth — about my feelings, about what I'm thinking — and the rest I have to leave up to you."

I reached up and stroked the side of his cheek and said, "Thank you." There was no doubt in me, no hesitation at all. There was a feeling of complete rightness about everything. A rightness that was almost a sense of inevitability, as if this part of the script had been written long ago, and there was no other way to play it. I had no desire to change anything, right now. Tomorrow did not exist and neither, for the moment, did Ursula.

There were so many reasons for being with him. His sharp, clear mind, the almost palpable lust for ideas, for knowing; the excitement about new experiences and new ways of thinking about things. Beneath the sadness of recent loss and occasional bewilderment about Ursula, there was something else, something inside him which was a laughing, shining thing, eager for life, greedy for living. The dark side of him — that, I hadn't met yet.

Now, I thought, another face of the man would begin to be known. He reached out to finger-trace the line of my hipbone. We were still about a foot apart and each of us was supporting head on hand. There was going to be no hurry. No hurry at all.

The light fingertips moved thoughtfully, up over the top of my shoulder, and paused behind my ear. Then, very gently, he clenched his fingers in my hair and moved his body close to me. His mouth came down on mine, open, his tongue meeting my tongue; I tasted wine and Shura. His mouth holding mine, he took his hand from my hair and I felt the palm, open, exploring the side of one breast, moving down, firmly, over my stomach, like a potter shaping the side of a clay vase.

The hand took charge. It explored and insisted. I suddenly felt vulnerable, because I knew he was aware of the response inside me, that he had tuned in to my longing, was letting himself be open to my pride, my aching for him, and all the questions I had yet to ask. I felt his breath on my nose and mouth.

I opened my eyes to meet his direct, clear gaze and hold it for a moment, then I closed my eyes again.

As my body clenched itself, I could hear his breathing quicken, and when the purple iris flower behind my eyelids opened its petals fully, I heard him cry out with me, then his hand came to rest like a benediction on my pubic bone.

After a moment, I opened my eyes and stroked his head where it lay, covering my tummy, and I said, "You know, that's the first time anyone has ever done that — I mean, that way. What an extraordinary hand you have, Doctor Borodin!"

Shura raised his head and said, "Well, I don't think one should be limited to making love with just one or two parts of the body, do you? And — I have to tell you that, at least for now, the other way — the usual way — well, I feel that I must reserve that for Ursula. I know it seems a bit foolish, but the coming into a woman's body with mine involves a degree of intimacy, for me, that has to belong to her, at least for a while."

"Oh," I said, thinking, what a strange way of staying loyal — if not exactly faithful. "I understand," I said, "I understand."

I sat up, shook out my hair and smiled down at him, then murmured, "With your permission," and moved myself downward.

I spotted one long white hair, curled in his left groin, cried "Ah Ha!" and drew it out to its full length. Shura looked at my fingers, holding up the single hair, and asked what the noise was all about.

"Just look at this! I'll bet you never bother looking down *here* to see if anything is turning silver, do you!"

"Hadn't occurred to me to think about it, I must admit."

I laughed and let the hair spring back to its original place, then leaned down again. I heard a soft gasp, and his head fell back. Once, I opened sweat-blurred eyes to see his hand on the pillow beside him, fingers spread, as if in agony. As I closed my eyes, the hand was grasping the pillow, the knuckles ivory in the flickering light.

When it came, the sound from his throat was strangled, as if he had come to the end of some strange, exhausting battle, and I slowly took my mouth from him. I reached across his body for a corner of the eiderdown, and pulled it over both of us. His voice, in a harsh whisper, said, "It's been so long. So long."

"Me, too," I answered, truthfully. I lay quietly for a while, my head on his shoulder, then knew I was going to have to give words to something which was pushing at me from the inside; it was just the way things had to be.

I said, "I must tell you something. Don't let it frighten you. You've promised to tell me the truth, and I'm going to do the same. Please don't give me an answer, because I know there can't be one, right now."

I looked at the fine line of one nostril, at the profile with its peacefully closed eye, and said, matter-of-factly, "I'm in love with you. It may not be sensible, but that's the way it is. Now, good night, and sleep well." I kissed a hollow in his neck and wiggled contentedly against him, then I became aware of a rich smell — something like carnations and fresh cut grass — coming from his armpit. It wasn't cologne or powder; it was Shura. I thought, he tastes lovely and he even smells wonderful. I've got to tell him what a delicious armpit he has. The words were arranging themselves in my mind as I fell asleep.

CHAPTER 20. DOOR CLOSING

The next morning, while I cooked a breakfast of scrambled eggs and toasted English muffins, Shura played my piano, an old mellow-toned upright which occupied the corner to the right of the big windows. He played a Chopin prelude with a mixture of passion and gentle sweetness, then something fiercely joyful by Beethoven. When he had finished, he sat with head bowed, his hands braced on the edge of the piano. I waited for a moment, until the last ghosts of sound had melted into the slanting wooden walls, before calling out that breakfast was ready. When he sat down, I told him, "That was a pleasure. You're very good. How do you like your coffee and do you play any other instruments?"

"Black, please, and I play some piano, a lot of viola, used to play the clarinet many years ago, and I can switch to the violin pretty easily — most viola players can."

Across the table from him, I looked again at the bearded face and the eyes, which seemed a darker blue than they had the night before. He looked back at me with an expression I was beginning to recognize: direct, thoughtful, a suggestion of amusement at the corners of the eyes. Then he looked down at his eggs and picked up his paper napkin. I realized I was smiling only when he glanced up again and smiled in return.

When the eating was done, we took our coffee cups over to the mat and sat cross-legged, while he told me about growing up on the farm outside the town of Almond, in the East Bay, the cow named Bluebell, who was his favorite, and the three goats. I asked him if he liked farm life with all the animals, and he said that a little cow-milking went a very long way and that, despite his affection for the animals, he was quite happy to live without that kind of responsibility, these days.

I asked, "Do you have any animals around, now?"

He stubbed out his cigarette and lay back on a pillow with his arms folded behind his head. "I have two cats who live outside and hunt gophers and mice. I used to have a wonderful dog named Bruno, and after he died, I didn't have the heart to replace him. Besides," he shrugged, "This way, I can pack up and take off anywhere without worrying about kennels and all that stuff. The cats take good care of themselves. They hunt all day and there's always a bit of running water somewhere on the Farm."

I said I'd never seen the town of Almond, and hardly ever heard it mentioned; it didn't seem to come up in the news much. Shura said, "It's very small and quiet and not too many of its inhabitants go in for murder or armed robbery, but things are growing and expanding pretty rapidly, so all that can be depended upon to change before long; real civilization can't be too far off."

I laughed and said I hoped Almond would stay a quiet, uncivilized backwater for a long, long time.

He said, "We used to own a lot more than the present 20 acres, but a couple of parcels were sold off. Sad to say, the crest of the hill right behind us —," he caught himself, "— behind me, has been built up now with a whole row of apartments. They're just a few feet from my property line. For some reason, I never thought anyone would build up there. It was my skyline, you know; it was supposed to look that way forever. It's a strange feeling to look up the hill, across the grass, and see those buildings staring down, where there used to be nothing but sky and trees." He shrugged, "But that's the way it goes. Nothing in the world stays the same and you learn to roll with the changes. If you don't," he paused to sip coffee, "You waste a lot of energy and a lot of time regretting. Or trying to hold back what isn't going to be held back. I still have a lot of privacy and I keep planting more trees every year to block the view into my place."

I asked about his childhood, and he told me he had been born in Berkeley, and grew up there. I repeated, "Berkeley! You were actually born in Berkeley?"

His eyebrows shot up, "Yes, I actually was. What is it about my being born in Berkeley that strikes you as unlikely?"

"Because you're far too exotic to have been born like an ordinary person in an ordinary place like Berkeley!"

"Oh, I see," he smiled. "Actually, Berkeley isn't that ordinary, you know. Once you get to know it, you find it's full of exotic people."

I chuckled. At least he hadn't denied being one of them.

I lit another cigarette and Shura talked about the changes in the East Bay since the time his parents first moved there, the wild animals and the birds, the snakes and spiders which had lived all around them, and he listed the ones that had gradually disappeared as the roads had come in and more houses were built on the hills. When he mentioned the black widows, I said, "Surely you don't miss *them*?"

"Yes, I do. I'm saddened when any form of life is pushed out by people. It's happening too often and too fast, and it means the natural balance of things is being upset in too many places."

"I understand; I share that concern. It's just that — well, it's hard for me to feel too much sympathy for the black widow."

"You learn to live with dangerous spiders, just as you do with other forms of life. Usually, if you leave them alone they'll do the same to you. By the way," he leaned forward, "Have you ever examined a black widow web?"

"No, I can't remember ever seeing one. Why?"

"They're quite extraordinary. Very, very strong silk. It's so strong, in fact, that it was used in World War II for the cross-hairs in gunsights. Did you know that?"

"No," I said, "I didn't."

I watched him as he talked about how you could tell when it was a black widow web by testing one of the strands with a finger and if it was, the strand would spring back like elastic. His body was relaxed, the long legs sprawled on the mat. I remembered the wonderful smell in the hollow under his arm, a smell of grass and something like carnations.

Maybe marigolds. Not carnations. Marigolds. How many men in the world have armpits that smell like that? There just isn't anything about this beautiful creature that I don't like. Not so far, anyway.

I must have smiled, because he stopped and looked at me, questioningly.

"Sorry," I said, "I was listening to you, but a nice memory rose up suddenly."

I waited for him to ask me what the memory was, but instead he pulled himself up and padded across the floor to the kitchen. I rose and followed him, holding out my cup. He silently poured coffee for us both, and I added sugar to mine. As we returned to our pillow fortress, I felt a change. Something was different.

He said nothing for a moment, apparently concentrating on his coffee. Then he raised his head and looked straight at me, not smiling. I stayed quiet and waited.

"Alice, I have to tell you something. I'd better say it now. Remember, I promised to tell you the truth, no matter how hard it might be. I'm not used to doing that; I haven't made a habit of it in my relationships, perhaps because it usually seemed kinder to other people if I kept my feelings to myself. The negative ones, anyway. I have a tendency to be sharp, I suppose, and people can be hurt. Even my closest friends have said I have a cruel tongue — " He paused.

What in God's name are you going to tell me? I'd better be ready for something bad. Oh, please, don't let it be too bad, please. I love you.

Shura was saying, "Not very long ago, I decided — I made a decision to be who I am and say what I think and feel and those who can't accept that and be equally open and honest with me —" he leaned forward, "I have things I want to do — must do — and I don't know how much time I have, and I don't want to waste any more time or energy than I have to, on people who play games or deal in half-truths. Not at this stage of my life."

There was a faint bitterness in his voice.

Is he talking about Ursula?

I said, softly, "Yes."

Yes to you. Yes to telling truth. Yes to your beautiful big hands and intuitive fingers and all the rest of you. What are you trying to say?

He took a deep breath, then said, "Ursula called me from Germany last night, before I came to the party, and it seems she can — she'll be coming to be with me for while. I'm meeting her plane tomorrow morning."

He looked up at the big windows, then back at me. "I don't know how long she'll stay this time. She never really says anything I can count on; it's usually 'I may be able to stay a week or two,' or she says she doesn't know — that it depends on how Dolph is coming to terms with the situation, or something else equally hard to pin down. She's a wonderfully gentle, kind person and can't bear to cause anyone pain. So I just have to continue being patient and let her work it through her own way."

I drank some coffee because suddenly my mouth was very dry.

"So all I can tell you is that she's coming and she'll be with me a week or a couple of weeks, or maybe she'll actually stay this time. I just don't know."

I'd had many years of practice in keeping both my voice and my face calm under fire. I made a deliberate effort to relax the muscles of my throat before I spoke.

"Thank you for telling me, Shura. I don't know what to say except that I can't wish both of you luck. I wish myself the luck, to be honest, because I would like very much to be with you, as I told you last night."

My actual words had been, "I'm in love with you," but there was no need to repeat them; he would remember if he wanted to.

"Alice, I want you to hear what I say now. I enjoy being with you. Very, very much. Last night — last night was — it was a beautiful gift. I had a great need for what you gave me. You're the last person I want to hurt in any way. I just don't know what's going to happen, and I realize it's all very unfair to you, and there's nothing I can do to make it easier. For myself or for you."

I couldn't let him go any further along that road, so I interrupted, "No, no. Please don't do that. I mean, don't try to avoid hurting me. If I were really that afraid of — of heartache — I wouldn't have asked you to stay last night. Don't push me out of your life until you know you have to, until you know that she's really going to stay. I promise you, if things turn out that way, I'll go quietly. But until then, trust me to survive whatever happens. I'm really a very strong person, you know."

My hand had found its way onto his knee. He covered it with his own.

I continued, "I would appreciate it very much if you could let me know what's going on — as soon as you have some idea, yourself. Could you just give me a quick phone call, perhaps, so I don't have to spend a lot of time wondering? Would you mind doing that?"

Shura met my eyes and his gaze was dark and intense, "I promise you, I'll phone as soon as I have any idea of what the situation is. I certainly won't leave you in the dark."

At the door, he looked down at me, then wrapped his arms around me and lifted me off the floor. His mouth came down on mine, and I lost myself for a moment in the taste of him, the feel of lips that were achingly familiar, by now. Finally, he put me back on my feet and held me at arms' length for a moment, his eyes moving over my face and body, as if memorizing. He whispered, "Thank you, little one."

Then he was gone. I became aware of the faint prickling around my mouth from his mustache and beard. I went to the kitchen, poured myself a fresh cup of coffee and took it back to the mat, where I settled down to do the crying.

CHAPTER 21. DOOR OPENING

I thought of it as The Closing of the Door, complete with capitals. It was the first time I'd cried because of Shura.

I went to work as usual and took care of the children, and the next weekend I attended a Mensa party, carrying my bottle of cranberry juice laced with vodka, and my little folding magnetic chess set. I played a couple of good games, drank enough to make me dangerously sleepy driving back home, and resolved never to risk disaster that way again.

Brian had his eyes checked and we discovered that he needed glasses for reading. We spent a long time fooling around in a store where they sell frames, laughing at how he looked in some of the fancy ones, settling finally for something that looked like him — quiet, a bit serious, not liable to attract attention.

Brian had always been a good-looking boy, with curly brown hair and large, blue-grey eyes. When he was in the second grade — his year of humiliation and terror — his handsomeness gave the young bullies who scapegoated him for his dyslexia that much more reason to tease, poke and kick. Now, at 14, he didn't have to fear the same kind of persecution, and the girls were beginning to notice him. I knew he wasn't the kind to attract the jock-chasers, but the more interesting, thoughtful girls would begin to seek him out. The second grade had taught him to be inconspicuous; I often urged him to ask questions in class, but understood his preference for getting help from teachers only after the rest of the students had filed out the door.

I hadn't hauled Brian out of the second grade because, at the time, I thought the teachers knew more than I did when they told me that my son had to undergo his trial by fire with no help from them, because that's the way things were among small boys, that every year there was one singled out to be the scapegoat, and there was nothing they could do about it. He'll survive it, they said; he'll be all right.

I had long talks with Brian about the psychology of bullying children, but it didn't help much. He would carry the scars from that year for a long time, and when, years later, I understood that the teachers had been wrong, I also understood that I would always carry in myself the bitter knowledge that I could have, and indeed should have, taken him out of his hell and put him in some other school, after confronting both administrators and teachers and demanding that they change their policy of resignation and indifference to the scapegoating. They wouldn't have changed anything, of course, but I should have said it anyway.

There was, however, one positive result of Brian's ordeal; he developed, very early, an ability to empathize with others — usually schoolmates — in trouble, to listen patiently to their tales of sadness and fear. I thought he was showing signs of being the kind of person who becomes a therapist, a healer of emotionally damaged people; he had the heart and clearness of mind for it.

My lovely Ann was discovering that she enjoyed math and science, and that she was good at both of them. Her directness, her habit of saying exactly what she thought, sometimes without sufficient efforts at diplomacy, earned her some enemies and a growing number of good friends. She was beginning to attract boys, of course, and I was trying to be as subtly persuasive as possible about the advantages of playing the field before relinquishing one's virginity. Not certain I could win this particular battle — not even sure I was going to know when the battle began or who the enemy would be, for that matter — I took her to the family doctor to be started on The Pill.

She tried marijuana for the first time, at a high school friend's party, and got very sick on the lawn; that was the end of her experimentation with psychoactive drugs.

Wendy and Brian were as uncomfortable with math as I had been, but both of them were showing unquestionable gifts in art. Brian had recently won a school award for a piece of work he'd done on leather, an engraving of a magnificent dragon, breathing fire in the best dragon tradition. We had it framed and hung on a living room wall.

Wendy had been so sensitive as a child to the slightest sign of parental displeasure, Walter and I had dreaded exposing her to the brutal realities of school, and were surprised — astounded, in fact — at the ease with which she made friends and charmed teachers. Our vulnerable Wendy, it seemed, was a lot tougher than we'd thought, and her social skills had flowered with every passing month. She was now a beautiful girl who — like her siblings — showed a certain gentleness in her face, and had a quick, whimsical sense of humor.

My oldest, my son Christopher, born of a very brief and bitter marriage to a fellow art student when I was 19, was living in a town a couple of hours away by car, to the north. He was teaching in a private school, and had already made me a grandmother twice over with two little boys. I saw him and his wife, Jane, very seldom, because of the distance and my lack of free time, but whenever I visited them, I was aware of feeling great affection for Jane. She was thin, shy and as poor a housekeeper as I, but a very good, caring, attentive mother. Jane had shown an unexpected strength in her determination to keep her marriage intact, which wasn't particularly easy, with a husband who tended to be exacting, and impatient with household disorganization, a legacy of his years with his abusive stepmother, Irene. She had demanded of him a military-school neatness, and struck him for minor infractions of her many rules, telling him constantly how stupid and impossible he was.

I had failed to rescue Christopher, too, many years earlier. After divorcing his father, at age 21, I had lived with my small child in the only place — a housing project apartment — we could afford, on the little money Dick could give us; a young commercial artist couldn't earn very much, unless he somehow managed to get one of the rare jobs available in the advertising department of a large retail store like Macy's or The Emporium.

Christopher and I had lived the kind of life everyone in a housing project used to live, before the age of crack cocaine. There was not as much crime at that time as there was later, but I soon discovered that in places like Sunnydale, those who steal prey on others as deprived as themselves. I learned what it was to be really poor, what it does to the human spirit. I avoided pretty store windows at Christmas time, and told my parents that the baby and I were doing well, but that this wasn't the right moment to visit us, that we would much rather visit them, instead. My father, recovering from a heart attack, had no money to spare, and I knew they would be upset if they saw the place I was living in. So the baby and I went to see them, instead, now and then.

It was in the housing project that I began to experience a dreadful tiredness, an emotional dullness that would not lift. I stopped listening to classical music; it stirred feelings I couldn't trust myself to handle. Beauty hurt me. I didn't know I was suffering from an illness known as depression; I thought that I was, for the first time in my life, seeing the world as it really was, a place of struggle and pain and betrayal, all of it meaningless, a place in which only self-deluded, naive people hoped for things to get better and happier.

Much later, during my marriage to Walter, I read the newspaper accounts and watched the television coverage of the riots in a suburb of Los Angeles called Watts. In a grocery store, one day, I heard two housewives, behind me in the checkout line, expressing indignation at the way some of the poor people in Watts had looted the shops, not for food, but for television sets and other luxuries. I tightened my jaw against a surge of anger and suddenly realized that I knew something these comfortable women had no way of knowing — that food is not enough; that sometimes a person who has been poor for many years is hungrier for some pretty, sparkling, impractical thing than for bread, and that a television set is what everybody else has, a symbol of everything he is denied. It wasn't right or good, but I understood it.

Some evenings, in Sunnydale, I played poker for pennies with the only friends I had there, a black couple with two small sons. Most evenings, I read books from the library. It was only while I was reading that the sad, dry ugliness disappeared and I forgot to be afraid. I took care of my baby, but he must have tuned in to my depression, as babies always share the psychic field of the parent, and the greyness in my soul surely invaded him at the deepest level.

I found work in the pathology department of a San Francisco hospital, typing tissue biopsy reports and autopsies, and I put my little boy in a place which called itself a nursery school and I worried when I picked him up every evening because he didn't laugh or even smile very much. But then, I didn't either, in those days.

So, when Dick told me he was going to marry a wonderful girl who was a graduate of a good college, and argued that Christopher would have a good home with them, I thought about it for a long time, feeling a kind of pain in my chest which I'd never felt before, and finally said yes, as long as I could see him as often as I wanted. When he was gone, I cried in the silence, but told myself I'd done what was best for him. I felt inadequate, and I didn't know how to be otherwise, and my baby deserved a real home with a good, cheerful mother.

After a while, Irene and Dick asked me to limit my visits to twice a month, so that my son could have a chance to fully accept his new life. He was upset, they explained, when I left at the end of my hours with him. I said all right, because I didn't know what else to say, and because the two of them together conveyed a sense of cool authority that made me feel alone and helpless.

I moved out of the Sunnydale housing project, to a small apartment a few blocks below the hospital where I worked, and I saw my little son two weekends a month, traveling by bus to Marin County, until Dick and Irene told me that more often than once a month was disruptive and disturbing to Christopher's security and routine. I felt, again, like an unwashed peasant bargaining with the people who dress in silk, and I acquiesced.

When my boy told me that his stepmother sometimes hit him, I persuaded myself it was childish exaggeration; I held him, kissed him and took him to places where we could have fun.

It wasn't until years later, after he had one step-brother and then a step-sister, that I let myself hear the depression in his voice, but when I screwed up my courage to tell his parents what was disturbing me, I was met with appalling fury, outraged denials of mistreatment, and an increase in the freezing hostility which they had, for some time, made no attempt to hide. I was too unsure, too powerless, to continue asking difficult questions, so I assured myself that at least Christopher was a member of a real family, that he had a stepmother who could stay home and siblings to grow up with, whereas I could give him none of those things.

When Christopher was a grown man, beginning his own family, he finally told me what Irene had done to him, how she had treated him, especially after she had her own children; he recounted the physical blows, the humiliations, the attacks on his self-esteem. I cursed and wanted to kill her. And I hated myself for not finding out, for not having taken him away, not having somehow saved him. We talked and cried and I asked him to forgive me, for having been young and bewildered and blind.

Christopher said that he had managed to become friendly with Irene since she had divorced his father and remarried. He said she treated him well, now that he was an adult — too big to hit or humiliate — and that he had forgiven her, ever since she had made an effort, one day, to apologize for her mistakes, for having made things very hard for him when he was young.

I couldn't forgive her, any more than I could forgive myself.

Christopher was a good father, gradually healing himself by being to his boys what his parents had not been to him. Like most abused children, he could be a difficult and demanding grownup, and I blessed Jane for being patient and determined and loving him enough to stay with him, even though he often showed little tolerance for her inadequacies and mistakes. She, too, had scars from childhood, and sometimes the two of them bruised each other emotionally, but there seemed to be a deep commitment at some level that kept them together.

I once sat in on Christopher's class, and — watching him with the youngsters — felt a bursting pride in having a son who was so excellent a teacher — I consider teaching to be the most important of all the professions. After saying goodbye at the end of my visit, I sat in my car for a while, tears running down my cheeks, aching with the knowledge that Brian, if he'd had teachers like his older brother, would have been spared much of the sorrow and rage and, above all, helplessness, he'd experienced so very young. Christopher did not allow scapegoating in his class.

I was working, now, at a private hospital, transcribing medical reports, typing very fast and very accurately and spelling all the medical words properly. I was one of five women in a small room where a huge tape drum revolved all day long, as doctors inside and outside the hospital phoned in their descriptions of surgical procedures, reports on physical examinations and letters to colleagues, all of it recorded on the tape. We had ten minutes each morning for a coffee break, half an hour for lunch, and ten minutes' break in the afternoon again. We worked all day, eight hours a day, with earphones on our heads; we were transcribing machines, paid the way most non-unionized hospital workers were paid — badly. I had a theory that, long ago, all hospital administrators had caught on to the fact that there are a certain number of people in the world who love medicine, would have become doctors if they'd been able to, and would put up with relatively poor pay and often stressful working conditions, just to be around those who practiced medicine, to feel themselves part of the medical world. I was one of them.

It was a hard job, but I'd never worked at an easy one, and to some extent it helped me to avoid thinking about Shura and Ursula. By the beginning of the second week of the lady's stay, I was getting accustomed to an unsettling sensation, a mixture of hope and dark despair that tended to make itself felt at unexpected moments, somewhere around the area of my diaphragm. I would clamp down on it quickly, telling myself to be patient; I'd know sooner or later and there was nothing to be done in the meantime but work and be mother.

At the end of the second week, Shura phoned. It was a Friday evening, and the children had crossed the street to their father's house. I was cleaning the tiled shelf, stacking papers and a few books to one side, half watching the evening news on television, when the phone rang. With the sound of his soft hello, my automatic pilot switched on and — while the rest of me stood there, frozen in shock — I heard myself saying cheerfully, "How nice to hear from you! I've been wondering how things were going."

"I thought you might want to know," said the tenor voice, "Ursula was here —"

I know, I know.

"— for two weeks, and she's just gone back to Germany. I put her on the plane a couple of hours ago."

"Oh."

"It was a wonderful visit, and she says she's going to take the bull by the horns, so to speak, and tell Dolph that she's going to get a divorce and come and live with me here."

"Ah," I said, feeling absolutely nothing.

"She says that this time she'll really do it and that she's still very worried that Dolph may do something violent, but she's not going to postpone it any longer."

It was like a replay of the night at Hilda's party. I was hearing a cheerful message spoken in a voice that didn't match. I took a deep breath and asked, "Shura, what's wrong? Are you just tired, or is it something else?"

There was a moment of silence. When he spoke again, there was no mistaking the sound of discouragement. "I'm just not sure, that's all. It's so hard to understand exactly what's going on, and I've heard all these promises before. I don't know. I suppose I'm a bit tired, too."

I took a chance, "Would you like to come over and just relax? The kids have left for the weekend, and you can talk all you want or just be quiet and listen to music and have some wine."

Oh Lord — there's no red wine in the house.

There was another pause, then he said, "It wouldn't be fair to you, for me to come over and talk about — about somebody else."

Please, don't back away. I'll take you under any conditions, Beautiful!

"That's nonsense. Of course you need to talk about Ursula, and I'd love to see you. Don't complicate things that are perfectly simple. Just come over."

"I appreciate your offer and I'd like to accept it, if you think you can put up with me —"

"I'll put up. There's one thing you can do for me, though: bring your own red wine. I don't think I've got any here."

"I'll be glad to do that. It'll take me about an hour, all right?"

"Fine. See you when you get here."

When he finally stood in the doorway, I went completely quiet inside. The scurrying around of the previous hour — the choosing of dark green skirt and pale blue blouse and filigree earrings, the stacking of pillows around the mat before the fireplace — all vanished in the rightness of his being here, now, with me. In that instant, everything in the world was where it belonged, and there was all the time we needed.

Shura made a fire and talked as he stacked the wood. I handed him old newspapers to twist for fuses and listened. He told about Ursula going through the house, pulling him by the hand, pointing out what she would want to put here and take away there — little things, homey things, he said — and how he had begun to believe it, believe that she actually would make the break and come to him. And stay.

"It was wonderful, being with her. She's a beautiful woman, kind and intelligent and — and passionate. We share a love for so many things, classical music, art, taking journeys with the materials. And we dislike a good many of the same things," he smiled, "Which can be just as impor-tant."

I sat across from him on the mat with my wine glass half full, waiting, with no feeling of impatience, to discover the reason for the sadness, the discouragement.

"We discussed the possibility of her staying for several months, this time, phoning Dolph from here and telling him what she'd decided to do, so he would have time to get used to it before she went back to see a lawyer and pack up all her things."

I kept my eyes on his face, that young, alive face with the lines and the white hair.

"But she didn't want to do it that way. She said it would be too cold, over the phone; she had to do it in person, looking into his eyes and holding his hands. She explained that she would worry about his doing something terrible to himself, if she didn't go about it the right way. A few days ago she said to me,'I have to go home. I want to get it over with, and I must go home to do it.' So I put her on the plane for Germany, and now it's the waiting game again."

I still couldn't understand the depression. I asked, "What is it that worries you, then? It sounds as if you're going to have everything you want, doesn't it?"

Shura gazed into the fire for a while, then turned to me and said, "This is the third time it's gone this way. She tells me she's going to leave him, she's finally going to come and be with me, and I'm always left waiting for word from Germany, thinking 'This time, it's happening.' Then she writes and explains how disturbed and emotionally fragile Dolph is, and how she'll have to pick the right moment, asking me to just be patient."

"What do you think is going on?"

Shura reached over to his wine bottle and poured his glass full. When he touched the rim of my glass with a finger, I said No thanks, I still had some.

"I don't know," he said, "I don't understand. Sometimes I wonder if she's — if maybe she has a fantasy that she lives when we're together, and that it doesn't — that it loses its reality when she's back home."

"What about Dolph — is that short for Adolph?"

"Yes, yes it is."

"You're sure he knows his wife is with you, when she's away?"

"Oh, there's no question about that; he's made references to her coming here. He knows she's with me. But, as I told you before, whenever I've phoned there and caught him instead of Ursula, he's sounded friendly and spontaneous and warm; not a hint of distress."

"That's weird."

"Completely weird. There are moments when I actually wonder if I'm suffering from some kind of delusion — simply imagining the whole thing. But this time, she will either move on this, very soon, or I'll begin to think I've been made a fool of. But that wouldn't make sense, either. I know what she feels for me; I have no doubt at all that she loves me. You can't be under the influence of psychedelic drugs and play games with the truth — not without the other person sensing it. Not when you're that close, that intimate. If there's a lie, you can hear it in the voice, feel it in your gut. I know she hasn't been lying about her feelings."

I tried to sum it up, "You're wondering, then, whether there's a possibility that she believes it completely when she's saying it? That maybe she's not consciously lying at all, just living a scenario that falls apart when she gets home?"

He didn't answer that directly, nor did he deny it, "Well, I should know before long. By the end of the week, one of us is going to call the other and by then, she should have said what she has to say to Dolph. Something must have happened by then, something clear and understandable to all parties."

This is crazy. It's not like me to be in the middle of a mess like this. Listening to a man I've fallen in love with, a man I want to be with the rest of my life, while he talks about the woman he loves. Reassuring him, being a good friend. Crazy. But I don't have much choice.

I asked, "And if nothing has happened by then?"

Shura shook his head, rubbing his eyes with one hand, "Again, I don't know. I suppose it depends on what she says. Cross that bridge when it looms in front of me."

"Yes, I suppose that's all you can do."

I felt a subtle shift in him. He was letting me come into view, focusing on me.

"You're very good, very generous — listening to all this. I must apologize. It's a ridiculous thing for me to be doing — dumping my problems onto you. Not at all considerate."

I laughed and leaned forward to pat his knee. "No apologies, please. We already went through that on the phone. I care very much about you and the only thing I can do for you right now is to listen and try to help you solve the puzzle."

"Would you like to see the Farm?"

The question took me by surprise. I stared at him, my mouth open, then nodded, "I'd love to see it, yes."

"How about coming out tomorrow? I'll give you a very good set of directions — it can be a bit hard to find without them. I'd like to show you around the house and my funny little lab."

"Yes, please."

I brought him a large pad of paper and a pen. He wrote rapidly for a few minutes, then tore the page off and handed it to me. I said, "What time should I be there?"

"What's best for you? I'm usually up around seven, even on weekends, so any time after that is fine for me."

"I gather it takes about an hour from here? I'll plan on eleven, if that's all right?"

"Eleven it is." He stood and stretched. "Time to get some sleep. It's been a long day." He grasped my hand to pull me up and said, "Again, thank you."

At the door, he placed his hands on my shoulders and turned me around to face him. I looked up at the shadowed eyes and the full, sensual mouth, remembering a night two weeks ago. This time there was no kiss, but he put his arms around me and held me to his chest, rocking very slightly. I closed my eyes until I felt his arms leave me, then he was gone and I was locking the door behind him.

I sat down again on the mat, facing the fire while I finished my wine, reviewing what had been said by both of us. The phrase, "Girding for battle," sprang to mind, and I caught myself smiling.

CHAPTER 22. WINDOW

I missed the road, the first time. It was tucked right behind a blind corner formed by an outcropping of rock and scrub. I swept by and kept going for a few blocks until there was an opportunity to turn around and retrace my way. At the entrance, a small sign nailed to a telephone pole announced "Borodin Road."

I'll have to ask him how he managed that.

I'd built an imaginary Farm in my mind, long ago, ever since Shura had first mentioned it to me. So far, it wasn't at all like my fantasy. To the left of the narrow road, grassy fields sloped gently to a line of trees below. Beyond that stretched a wide valley and on the horizon was what I assumed was Mount Diablo, an immense, mist-softened shape rising from rounded foothills. To the right of the road, which seemed to be mostly clay with occasional patches of ancient concrete, I could see only an uphill sweep of grass and several huge live oaks, magnificent trees with thick, twisting branches, bearing shadowy clusters of mistletoe.

The big wooden farm gate was open, as Shura had promised it would be. I followed the driveway up to a large circular parking area in front of an open garage, and looked down on a single-storey wooden house whose dove-grey paint showed heavy weathering.

As I parked my car, Shura appeared at the top of a stairway leading up from the house. Flanked by two overgrown juniper bushes, he stood on the red bricks, legs apart, hands tucked into the front pockets of his brown corduroy pants. He wore a woolen blue and green plaid sports shirt. His hair stirred in a light breeze and he was smiling broadly.

When we walked into the living room, my chest tightened. I hadn't known what to expect, but had hoped it would be something like this. Books lined one entire wall, and the room was divided into two sections by a center wall of stacked bookshelves that stretched to the ceiling. At the far end of the room, there were big windows through which I could see the mountain, and in one corner sat a grand piano. On the floor were several worn Persian rugs and there was a long blue couch behind a coffee table. Above the small fireplace hung a large framed map, in blue and white. Moving closer, I recognized the outline of the Ile de la Cite from many photographs I'd seen of Paris. The map showed a section of streets and buildings on either side of the Seine. I looked up at Shura and said, "That's wonderful. Do you know Paris very well?"

"Not very well. It would take years to know it very well. But what I have seen of it, I love. You've never been there?"

"No. I grew up in Italy — a good part of my childhood was spent there. My father was American Consul in Trieste, and my brother and I saw Venice and some other places, but I never got to France. Or England. Or most other countries in Europe."

God, would I love to go back! I long to see Europe again, as an adult, this time, knowing what I'm seeing. Wonder if it'll ever happen.

The kitchen was comfortably large, with a linoleum floor so old its original pattern was lost in a general brown-ness. It had been swept clean, but no broom or mop could really rescue it, I decided. Past the far half-wall I could see a small dining room where an oval table, its polished wood shining in the morning light, was sitting on a beige, blue and grey Chinese rug. There was a basket of fresh fruit on the table; I reminded myself that it had probably been here for Ursula.

Shura showed me the bedroom with its oversized bed, long enough for a very tall man. Windows ran the entire length of the room's outer wall, and there was a floor of red-brown tiles.

It's beautiful. He made love with Ursula on this bed. Don't look at it for too long; he'll know damned well what you're thinking.

Across the hall from the bedroom was his study. Ceiling high bookcases thrust out into the room, three rows of them, crammed with books; there were more books piled on the floor between each row. Long shelves high above his desk were filled with magazines, journals and thick catalogues; steel filing cabinets lined the far wall. His big wooden desk had a clear space in the center, but papers were stacked at the sides. I saw what looked like letters and envelopes on one pile, and a magazine with the title, "Journal of Psychoactive Drugs," and I laughed at the wonderful, lived-in mess. A scholar's study.

I was reminded of another study I'd seen years ago, when Walter and I had visited the writer-philosopher Alan Watts on board his houseboat in Sausalito. Alan's living room was decorated and furnished in the style of a Japanese house, immaculate and serene, with wide stretches of polished wood floor and every piece of furniture apparently chosen, not only for comfort, but also for beauty of shape and color. It was a work of art, created for quiet thought and meditation. When he showed us his study, I had been delighted at the contrast. Every inch of wall was covered with notes, photographs and memos, each corner piled high with books and pamphlets. No Japanese clarity and serenity here; it was the study of a busy scholar, a man who read and wrote a great deal. As was this.

"What?" asked Shura, bending his head to look at my face. He meant the laugh.

"Oh, it's just — it's so much what I hoped it would be — "

"Well, wait 'til you see the lab," he said. He led me down the hall and out the back door. We walked along a narrow dirt path, past clumps of early narcissus, under buckeye and pine trees, until we came to a small stone building which had once been painted white. Ivy covered its walls. Pine branches were overhanging the roof and scraping the sides of a small chimney.

Inside, I saw a laboratory which could have been the original inspiration for every mad-scientist movie ever made, with an additional touch of color the movie sets had lacked: small brown piles of dead leaves, swept up against the sides of several oversized glass bottles and metal cans clustered under the work benches. I supposed that the wind blew them in. They gave a certain flavor to the place; so did the spiderwebs, which were definitely out of Dr. Frankenstein's castle.

At the far end of the room was a stone fireplace; firewood was piled to one side and, next to it, some neatly stacked cardboard boxes. On the other side was an old-fashioned, glass-fronted bookcase, filled with labeled bottles of all sizes; high over the fireplace were shelves carrying more bottles, most of them small. Metal pipes, glass beakers and rubber tubing were everywhere.

I laughed again, "Oh, dear ever-loving God!"

"Is this what you expected, too?"

"No," I shook my head, "No — I certainly didn't expect this!"

"It's a working lab," said Shura, "A true working lab should look like an artist's studio, not a sterile room with immaculate benches and wall-to-wall carpeting like they show in television commercials."

There was a hint of defensiveness in his voice.

"I never thought of a chemistry lab as being comparable to an artist's studio; it's an interesting way to look at it. But it does make sense, when you think about it."

"A lot of work gets done here," said Shura, "And a lot of magic has happened in this place, over the years."

He loves it; he really loves this room and what he does in it. I can actually feel it in the air here.

"I think it's wonderful," I said, "Strange and weird and it looks just like a mad scientist's lab in the movies, as I'm sure you realize."

"I never saw a mad scientist movie," said Shura.

"Dr. Jekyll and Mr. Hyde? Frankenstein?"

He shook his head and shrugged, "Just culturally deprived, I guess."

"Oh, my, you certainly are. I'll have to drag you to some of them, if they ever play in a theater again. Maybe you can catch them on television. They usually have old movies on Friday nights, sometimes Saturdays."

"I'm afraid I hardly ever watch television. There's one in the house, but I don't know when I last turned it on."

"Never mind," I smiled, "Never mind. This is better than anything they show in the movies anyway."

There was a sharp knock on the roof, and I looked up, startled.

Shura said, "Probably a pine cone; they're always falling off the big trees."

I asked him, "What's in the big boxes near the fireplace?"

"Oh, those. Mostly evidence from court cases."

"Court cases?"

"I thought I told you that I'm what is known as an expert witness, in cases involving drugs — illegal drugs — and sometimes the police deliver the evidence in boxes like those, and when I'm through analyzing what I'm asked to analyze, I notify them that I'm finished, and they're supposed to pick the stuff up, but sometimes it just sits there and nobody comes for it. Possibly the case got thrown out of court, or something else happened that made everyone lose interest. I never know why, and I don't have the time or inclination to track down the reasons, so the boxes just sit there, year after year."

"I see. And I guess you don't really dare throw that sort of thing out — not for a long time anyway? Just in case?"

"Oh, I don't think anyone's going to pick them up now. To tell the truth, they've been there so long, I don't even notice them anymore. I suppose I really should go through them one of these days and toss out the prehistoric ones."

As we turned to leave I saw, pinned to the wall next to the door, some pieces of paper with official-looking borders. When I reached up to touch one, Shura said, "That's the license which allows me to work with sched-uled drugs; that means drugs listed in the five DEA schedules. Schedule I drugs are the ones like LSD and marijuana and heroin; they're forbidden, illegal, and you can't touch them, even for research, without half a dozen government agencies looking over your shoulder."

To the right of the door was a large cabinet with leaded glass windows, a larger relative of the one near the fireplace. On its shelves I could see more rows of bottles, stacked three deep, some freshly labeled, others with labels so faded, I couldn't make out any writing at all. One of the legible ones said, "Parsley." I went closer to the glass and peered in, seeing "Dill," "Safrole," and a clear glass bottle with "Asarone" scrawled on its side in thick black letters.

I shook my head, not quite believing it all, official licenses, leaves and spiderwebs, the big stone laundry-room sink, the shelves holding clean flasks (one of the shelves curved gently downward in the middle as if it had born years of weight and was finally giving out). It was intimate and personal, a place for alchemy.

Shura said, "Okay? Ready for lights out?" When I nodded, he reached up to the low ceiling and touched a switch, and we went through the door. Outside, pale winter sunlight shone on grass and tree leaves and a narrow brick stairway leading up to a level grassy shelf. We climbed the stair and Shura led me to the end of the green terrace. The hill dropped steeply away beneath us and I could see the valley spread below. Mount Diablo dominated the horizon, lavender blue in the haze from the valley floor. I let out a deep breath. It's so quiet, I thought. Shura named the towns below us and told me that the county seat, Martinez, lay out of sight to the far left. I said, "What an incredible view!"

We stood in silence for a while, gazing out over the nearby sloping fields and the houses far below, listening to the birds, then he put his hand on my arm and led me back down the stairs.

I was thinking, as I followed him back to the house, of how different all this seemed from Marin county, across the Bay. I'd never been to any of the towns in Contra Costa county. I couldn't remember even seeing Mount Diablo before, except on the local television news.

I want to live here. With him.

Shura poured glasses of wine, white for me and red for himself, and I sat down at the dining room table. He seemed to hesitate, then said, "Just a moment — I want to show you something," and went into his study. He returned with a framed photograph which he put in front of me without comment. I was looking at a black and white picture of a young woman in her thirties, leaning back casually on what looked like a wooden bench, outdoors, smiling softly. Next to her was Shura, in a similar pose, obviously relaxed, wearing one of his half-smiles. There was a bank of ivy in the background. I have never studied a photograph more closely in my life.

"Ursula?"

"Yes."

"She's very lovely. She looks sweet and intelligent."

Finally, the enemy has a face.

"She is."

"And you're in love with her, yes."

"I never knew what it meant to be in love, before Ursula. She changed everything about me."

"In what way?"

"I was — my closest friends will tell you, without hesitation — I was a bitter, sarcastic person, very negative, impatient. Often hard to be around. They'll tell you, believe me, that I was not very nice and not particularly kind. In fact, my best friends will say they don't know how they put up with me for the past twenty years or so. And they'll also tell you that I've changed. I'm almost nice, now. At least, I'm a lot nicer than I was. And the reason is that Ursula opened me to feelings I'd never had before. I suppose you could say I learned what it meant to open the heart, being with her."

His face was slightly flushed.

Okay. We all owe Ursula thanks. Thank you, pretty woman who is probably everything I can't be. So what the hell am I doing here? Why has he invited me into his home like this — into his life?

I said, "Thank you for showing me what she looks like. It's hard to deal with just a name."

Shura rose and took the photograph back to the study. When he returned to the table, we clinked our wine glasses and drank from them. He leaned back in his chair and asked me, "Well, what would you like to do with the day? I'm at your disposal. My house, my cats and my weaving spiders are at your disposal."

Thank heaven he hasn't suggested going to bed. Right now it would be unthinkable. Ursula would be in the room with us.

I asked for what I wanted, since there seemed no reason not to, "I wonder, is there any possibility of my — of taking one of your materials? I just thought there might be something not too long-lasting that I could try?"

The word "materials" is so much nicer. It's awful, how "drugs" sounds so — bad, dangerous, irresponsible. I guess I've been programmed pretty thoroughly, just like everyone else.

Shura sat for a moment, looking at his glass. I held my breath. Then he leaned his elbows on the table and said, "Yes, there is something you might find interesting. I'll tell you a bit about it. First of all, it's not one of my materials. It was discovered a long time ago, in 1912, in Germany. Nobody paid any attention to it until a good friend of mine — a delightful, funny, slightly crazy girl who's also a very good chemist — called my attention to an old publication that mentioned several compounds, this one among them, and told me she thought it might be an interesting one to synthesize. It was simply intuition, on her part, some kind of extraordinary intuition —"

"What's the name of it?"

He grinned, his eyes teasing, "Methylenedioxymethamphetamine. MDMA for short."

I repeated the initials under my breath.

He continued, "I suppose I can take credit for step-fathering it, anyway, if not for inventing it. I made it in my lab and nibbled. It gave me a pleasant lightness of spirit. That's all. No psychedelic effects whatsoever. No moving walls or glowing colors; nothing of that sort. Just a distinct lightening of mood. And an inclination to get busy and do things that needed doing. So I concluded that it might be an anti-depressant of some kind, and I took some over to an old friend, Adam Fisher, a psychologist in his late sixties or early seventies who had told me he was getting ready to retire — beginning to phase out his practice. I knew that he was very experienced with psychedelics, had been for years. So I asked him if he'd like to sample this MDMA stuff and tell me what he thought."

I sipped from my glass and realized, with a burst of warmth inside me, that I was very happy. Being here, listening to Shura telling the story, with sunlight glowing on the fruit in the bowl, I was content simply to exist in this moment and let everything else go.

He was saying, "Adam tried it, and the result of that experience was —," he paused, chuckling, "Well, to put it briefly, Dr. Fisher came out of retirement. He changed his practice, and in some ways I suppose you could say MDMA completely altered the course of his life."

"How did he change his practice?"

"Well, since then — that was about seven years ago — he's spent his time training people, mostly therapists, in the use of MDMA. He's introduced probably several thousands of them across the country to this drug, teaching them how to use it properly, for themselves and their patients. At least, for those patients who are considered good candidates for the experience."

"It was an anti-depressive, then, as you thought?"

"Yes and no. It had that effect on me, in a mild sort of way, but it had a very much more important effect on Adam, and I gather on most other people who take it. They say it makes it possible for them to have remarkable insights into the way they're living, what they're doing with their lives. They see how they're making problems for themselves, or wasting what they have, what they are. It's a drug that seems to allow insight, but it lets them see and understand without being afraid. It doesn't threaten them with any loss of control."

"Which is what most people are afraid of —," I nodded.

"Yes. The fear of losing control, being helpless, seems to be almost universal, and it certainly comes up in people who've never taken a psychoactive drug before. MDMA allows you to be totally in control, while getting a really good look at yourself. Adam told me that it does away with what he calls the fear barrier, the fear people have of seeing what's going on inside them, who they are. Most people describe a feeling of acceptance inside which makes it all right to take a good look at themselves. It makes the insight relatively non-threatening."

I asked, "Has anyone had a bad experience with it?"

"Oh, certainly. I've heard of a few really bad trips. In most of the ones I've been told about — by Adam, and by other therapists — the people were reluctant to undergo the whole MDMA thing in the first place; they'd been talked into it by a husband or wife, or the therapist, and they weren't really choosing to do it for their own sake. They went along with it because of pressure from someone else. The results were predictably negative. And the therapists involved learned a hard lesson."

"Do you mean that taking this drug has to be something you really want for yourself, or things go wrong?"

Shura leaned forward, "Not just this one; any psychoactive drug. That's why people almost always have what they call bad trips when some smart-ass has put a psychedelic drug in the punch, or it's been slipped to them in some way without their having been told. That's something I consider truly unforgivable — giving somebody a psychoactive drug of any kind without telling them and getting their consent. Personally, I don't think a doctor should do that even with a prescription drug; it should absolutely never be done with a psychedelic. Or with something like MDMA, which is not a psychedelic, but has a definite effect on a person's state of consciousness."

His eyes had narrowed in anger.

I nodded again and asked, "How long does the experience last?"

His face cleared, and he looked at me, "Are you sure you want to give it a try? Today? Now?"

"If you like the idea — if it's all right with you?"

"The duration," he said, "Is about three hours or so, unless you take a supplement, which is usually about a third of the initial dose. If you take a supplement, at about the hour and a half point, the level of full effect will continue for one more hour before it begins to taper off."

"Would it be possible for us to take it together? Does that appeal to you? Please tell me if you'd rather not — for any reason."

"I would be most honored, as a matter of fact," said Shura.

"Do you always call it MD — whatever it is. Sorry." I did the remorse bit, hitting the side of my head with an open palm.

"MA," finished Shura.

"MDMA. Thank you."

"Methylenedioxymethamphetamine," he reminded me, grinning. I stuck out my tongue.

"Easy for YOU to say!"

He got up from the table, "Wander around, if you'd like. I'll be back in a couple of minutes."

I stayed where I was, looking at the books in the bookcase against one wall, reading the spines. The Art of India, The Lascaux Caves, The Voices of Silence by Malraux, The Law (in two volumes), Boswell in Holland, Chaplin, Bernard Shaw, Limericks and a collection of erotic art (Ah, yes!). I saw Sophie's Choice and a copy of The Wisdom of China and India, by Lin Yutang. I remembered having read a book by Lin Yutang that deeply impressed me, years and years ago, but couldn't recall the title. Two entire shelves were filled with the works of Aldous Huxley, a few of them in duplicate.

Of course, he'd like Huxley.

Shura returned, carrying four small glass vials with white tops. He went into the kitchen and I followed, watching as he opened a cupboard and brought out two wine glasses, which he placed on the tile surface near the sink. The tiles were a pale, faded blue, probably as old as the floor, I thought, but at least you can keep tiles clean. Shura opened two of the vials and emptied one container of white powder into each glass, then added a small amount of hot tap water and swirled the contents gently before handing one to me. He stood straight, almost formally, clinked his glass with mine, and said, "Blessings."

I downed the fluid and immediately clapped a hand to my mouth, almost gagging. The taste was bitter, nasty. I said so.

Shura said, "I believe in knowing what it tastes like, before you find out what it does. I should have warned you; most people don't enjoy the taste, I have to admit. Next time, you can add juice, if you'd like."

Thank you for that "next time," darling man.

I peered at him suspiciously, "Don't tell me you really like that taste!"

He said airily, "I think it's rather nice! A perfectly honest, straightforward taste. A taste with character, I'd say. A taste with personality!"

"You're out of your ever-loving mind!" I opened the refrigerator, found a bottle of grapefruit juice and poured out enough to wash this particular character and personality out of my mouth. Shura chuckled at my grimace, which was only slightly exaggerated.

All right, Ursula, go. This is my day now, and he's mine, for just a little while.

Shura led me out of the kitchen, back into the warm living room. I dropped my purse onto the coffee table and joined him at the large windows. He asked, "Do you know Diablo? Have you ever been on it?"

"I don't think I've ever seen it before, in person. As a matter of fact, I don't think I've been in this county before. I got as far as Berkeley a few times, but never came through the tunnel to this side."

"By the way," said Shura, still gazing at the mountain, "You should know that I gave us each a very low amount of MDMA, 100 milligrams, to be exact. Just enough to let you feel the full effects, but not enough to be overwhelming in any way, this first time. Unless you turn out to be extremely sensitive to the compound, of course. That's always a possibility which has to be taken into account when trying a drug that's new to you."

"How soon should I be feeling something?"

"Oh, probably between 30 and 35 minutes. Usually, people taking it for the first time are aware of a rather strange feeling — a sensation that's unfamiliar to them — in about half an hour. If you can just relax and let it be, the strangeness is over with in about 20 more minutes, then you'll find yourself on the plateau, which is where you'll remain for about an hour. Then, if you like where you are and want to remain there for another hour before you begin dropping, I'll give you a supplement, an additional 40 milligrams."

"And that keeps the plateau going for a while, but doesn't do anything else?"

"That's right. You won't feel any change in intensity; it just lets you stay where you are a bit longer than you would otherwise."

Looking out the window, I remembered the question I wanted to ask him, when I first drove in from the highway. "By the way," I asked, "How did you manage to get the name Borodin on the street where you live?"

"Ah, yes," he chuckled, "It's kind of a neat story. When my parents and I moved out here, there were walnut trees, orchards, everywhere that you now see houses and highways. There was no freeway, only country roads. We lived in the only house on the land, an old abandoned ramshackle place that had belonged to the original owners many years earlier. It actually leaned. I think it was held up by the acacia tree alongside it. There was one central room, surrounded by a verandah which actually sloped downwards, outwards, on all sides.

"My folks and I started to build this house, the one we're in now, about the time of World War Two. And someone from the post office dropped in, and told us that Almond was becoming too civilized to allow anyone to live in a rural route box. People had to live on a street.

"'What's going to be the name of this street?' my father asked.

"'You give it a name,' said the postmaster, or whoever the man was.

"'Borodin Road?'

"'Fine. Why not?' the man said.

"Then, a few years later, there was another administration, another postmaster. He came out and said, 'You can't just live on a road; you've got to live at a number on a road.'

"'How about number one?' said my father, quite reasonably, since we were the only family on Borodin Road.

"Number one apparently wasn't one of the postal department's options. 'Let's make it 1692,' said the postmaster.

"That was okay by my father. 'Why not?' he said, and that was that. Nobody ever discovered the reason for that number being chosen; I suppose nobody ever asked the postmaster, and now it's far too late. It was a mystery then, and it remains a mystery to this day!"

I laughed, "That's a great story. But I remember you saying something once about civilization not having arrived yet in the town of Almond?"

"I meant *real* civilization. The kind that means murders and bank holdups and people who don't know you in the grocery store."

I laughed, "Ah, now I understand!"

Turning from the window, I stopped in surprise. Against this side of the wall that divided the room hung a large portrait in a frame of antique gold. It showed a young boy, dressed in a blue silk tunic with a high neck and embroidery in the Russian style. I knew it was Shura and I went close to it and looked at the face. Blond hair, very blond. A firm chin and lower lip, a determined mouth. The eyes were clear blue and alert.

He spoke from behind me, "I'm not sure exactly what age I was then. Probably around twelve."

"That's a beautiful portrait. I like it."

The child was holding a musical instrument that looked familiar. I asked Shura what it was.

"That's a balalaika. I still have it; as a matter of fact, it's on top of the piano, but it hasn't been tuned in years, I'm sorry to say."

I glanced over at the piano and saw the shape of the instrument, but suddenly decided that closer inspection would have to wait. I was feeling something changing inside me.

I told Shura I was going to sit down. I curled up in a corner of the couch with pillows and concentrated on what was starting to happen. He sat down in a large armchair, facing me, his feet on a hassock which was covered with the same material as the chair. I found myself staring at the pattern, soft blue stripes against a silvery grey background, with a suggestion of tiny flowers. It was old-fashioned, I thought, and comfortable. Like the room.

I looked around, seeing things I hadn't noticed earlier. A large oriental vase on a bookcase shelf, a stack of photograph albums on a shelf below it, a miniature stone owl on the mantel of the fireplace, and next to it a small framed photograph of a woman.

I'd like to see that photograph. Probably his wife. It looks old, sepia tint. Maybe it's his mother. I'm not going to move from here, though, not until I know what's happening inside me. Strange new feeling, he said. Okay. Take a deep breath and relax the body.

"You're aware of something?" asked Shura.

"I'm not sure," I replied, picking up my purse to get my cigarettes. On the coffee table, which was set with small beige tiles, there was a copper ashtray. Next to it sat a round, sand-colored stoneware vase, holding white daisies. A few of them were wilting.

Flowers for Ursula.

Now, there was unmistakably something happening, and it was, indeed, an unfamiliar sensation. It wasn't like what I remembered of the start of the peyote effect; that had begun more as a change in the light, or rather, a change in the way I saw light. Light had seemed almost palpable, I recalled, a living presence in the room.

I sensed that Shura was watching me, but I wasn't about to pay attention to him, right now. The strangeness was quite physical, I decided, mostly in the chest, where it felt like a mixture of fear and excitement.

All right, I thought, it's a new feeling. I mentally surveyed myself, noting that the back of my neck was tingling, and my spine was alert. No surprise there. But the sensation I had at first assigned to my chest was now all throughout my body.

It's like a voice speaking from inside, without words. Not unpleasant at all. Just new.

"There's no need to talk," said Shura, quietly. "You must feel free to do anything you wish. Anything that feels comfortable to you."

"Yes," I said. My head was changing, now. It felt light. Not dizzy, just light. There was something else I was just beginning to be aware of: a feeling of peacefulness taking the place of the strangeness. Simple, overwhelming peacefulness.

"I'm feeling a bit more relaxed, now," I said to Shura.

I forgot — he took it, too. Wonder what he's experiencing. I'm not going to ask him yet. Have to listen to my own innards for a while.

"You're probably at the plateau, or you will be very shortly," Shura said, "And what you're feeling now is pretty much what you'll continue feeling. I mean, the intensity of it. It'll stay the same from now on — for the next hour or so, anyway — and there shouldn't be any further increase."

"I understand. Thank you."

"You're welcome," he replied, softly, not teasing.

He's watching, listening, noting everything. He's relieved that I'm okay. He cares and he wants this to be good for me.

"It's a very lovely feeling, very peaceful and gentle," I said.

"Good. I was hoping it would be like that."

"I think I'll get up and walk around, if that's all right?"

He stood and gave me his hand, pulling me up slowly. Then he put his hands on my arms and looked into my eyes for a moment. His eyes were very blue in the light from the windows, and I looked into them and saw seriousness and unmistakable affection. Caring and watchfulness. I reached up with both hands to hold his face and stood on tiptoe to put my lips on his, very lightly. Then I turned and walked toward the kitchen.

Behind me, Shura asked, "Would you like me to walk with you, or would you prefer to be alone right now?"

I stopped to think and knew immediately that I needed to be alone, to explore by myself for a while, and told him so.

He nodded, "I'll be in my study if you need me. Take your time. You can come for me, or just call out if you want company. I'll hear you calling if you're near the house."

He means if I'm in trouble, but he's not going to say that. He doesn't want to program me to expect anything negative.

"Thank you very much, my dear," I said, and left him. I walked, my body light, moving easily, to the back door. There had been no hesitation in saying, "My dear." I knew his dearness to me, and there had been no need to censor either the feelings or that one small expression of them.

Outside, the dirt path was dappled with sun and leaf shadow. It was cool and I was glad of my cardigan. I sat down on a grassy area to the right of the path, not far from the door, began to reach into the shirt pocket where I'd put my cigarettes, and stopped. The peacefulness had changed. Something I hadn't expected at all was pushing up inside me — a sudden surge of grief so powerful, I braced myself with hands on the ground.

Oh, Lord, no! I don't need this!

It was coming like a wall of water roaring down a dry desert wash. Tears were rising in my throat and I let them come, not even trying to fight what I knew would not be held back. Part of me scolded that this wasn't the way to encourage Shura to give me this stuff again — or any other psychoactive drug, for that matter. But there was a deeper, overriding certainty that this sorrow had been gathering inside me for a long time, for years, and that the pain had to be experienced, had to be released, if I was to become strong and whole.

There was another thing making itself heard, something which went beyond the traumas and sorrows of the past or present, a message with an energy of its own which would not allow it to be lost in the crying.

I am driven by an urge, a need, to find out — to know — what is, how it is, why it is. The truth about myself, other living things, the world, and whatever drives the universe. It's the First Commandment for my life, and although I don't understand why, it must always be the First Commandment: keep wanting to know, trying to know.

The sorrow was pushing through me in waves, as sorrow always does, but my mind continued to function clearly, separate from the tears and the convulsive sobs. I thought of the time I read someone's cynical observation that the desire to understand the What's, How's and Why's of life and the cosmos was an obsession of the young, usually outgrown by the end of the second year of college; thus, concluded the writer, it was appropriate to call them The Great Sophomoric Questions.

So be it. I'm a bloody sophomore.

All right. Today's truth was a simple one: I had found a man unlike any other I had ever known; he was the man I had waited for all my life; the man I wanted to be with, live with, to experience life with, and he was in love with a woman named Ursula. I had made the decision to stay as close to him as he would allow, for as long as possible — win or lose — and I had to acknowledge that I was involved in all this by my own choice. It was my responsibility.

I cried for a long time, huddled with my arms around myself, rocking in place, sobbing on the grass until the torrent began to lessen and I could pay attention again to the Observer, who noted that the peaceful center was still there, and that I should take another look at it.

Underneath the terrible grief, there was a calmness, a serenity, and something that felt, incredibly, like joy.

Don't try to understand. Just know it's there. You're held in God's hand, and that hand cradles you with complete love. All is well, even though that doesn't make any sense right now.

There had been no sound, but suddenly I knew Shura was near. I could feel his presence in the hall, out of my direct sight. I was aware of his concern, and something underneath it which I knew was his own sadness and bewilderment about Ursula, and I found myself crying again, more gently, this time for him.

Finally, it was over.

I waited patiently while my breathing gradually returned to normal, with only an occasional shuddering breath to remind me of what had passed through. I got up from the grass and went into the house.

There was no one in the hall, but I heard papers rustling and knew Shura had returned to his study.

Standing in the doorway, I said, "Thank you for your patience. It seems I had to get something out of my system, and it's all over." I was smiling easily at him, knowing my eyes were red and probably beginning to swell, and that it didn't matter.

Shura came to where I stood and put his arms around me, holding me tightly to his chest. He whispered, "I'm sorry."

I looked up at his face and said, firmly, "No. Sorry is not what I want — in fact, it's the last thing I want from you. I enjoy being with you, and it's not your fault that I love you — it's not even my fault, it's just the way things are — and as long as we are both absolutely honest with each other, it'll be all right. Believe me, whatever happens, it'll be all right."

Don't know where that certainty comes from, but it feels true, so it's okay to say it.

He nodded, "I don't want to cause you pain. I just don't want to hurt you in any way."

I pressed my cheek to his chest, "I know that. But if I have to choose between being with you and having some pain, or — or not being with you just to stay pain-free, you know perfectly well what my choice is. Please let it be that way. I don't believe I'll regret the decision, and I hope you won't either."

We went back to the living room. We talked about me, this time. I told him about growing up in Italy, in a village called Opicina, high on the cliffs behind the city of Trieste, where my father had been Consul for six years before World War II. I told him about my brother, Edward, who was always called by a very English nickname — Boy — until we returned to the United States, when I had to get used to calling him by his chosen grown up name — Ted.

I said, "My father was Jewish, but he had diplomatic immunity, of course. Boy and I knew very little about what was going on, but I remember being told very sternly that whenever our governess took us for our daily walk and we ended up in the village — which wasn't very often, because usually we went into the fields behind our house — but if we did go to the village, and we wanted to say something about the man called Il Duce or the other person we heard mentioned by the grown-ups — Hitler — we were to use the code names, 'Mr. Strong-arm' and 'Mr. Strong-heart.' It was impressed upon both of us that this was not a game and that it could mean serious trouble for our parents — for our entire family — if the wrong passerby heard us using the other names."

"Did you run into trouble in school?"

"No," I replied, "We didn't go to school. They were being run by the Fascists. We were taught at home by whoever happened to be our governess at the time, using the Calvert System. It's based — I imagine it's still in existence — in Baltimore, and Foreign Service families have it sent to them when they're assigned to a place where the available schools are poor, or there's some other reason to keep their kids out of them. It was a superb education, by the way. Greek and Roman mythology along with the usual elementary school stuff, believe it or not!"

I told of the morning when huge red letters were found, scrawled in red paint on the outside of our iron gate, letters Boy and I couldn't understand, but which the maid told us meant "Jew," and of watching the cleaning lady and my father scrubbing the paint off the black iron, while I wondered if I should ask what a Jew was. And of the nice neighbor across the street, an elderly, stooped man whose name I couldn't remember, who disappeared one night and never came back.

I said, "We were told it was because he was Jewish, and Mr. Strong-arm and Mr. Strong-heart were bad men who were very powerful in their countries, and they didn't like Jews or gypsies or anybody who disagreed with them, and sometimes they took them away. They didn't say to where, and we children weren't allowed to ask a lot of questions. I suppose this was around 1939, maybe 1940, and people were beginning to vanish in the middle of the night, though Boy and I were told nothing about any of that."

Shura was listening intently, then — at a pause in my tale — he suddenly jumped from his chair, saying, "Hold it a minute; I've got to check the time," and rushed to the kitchen. When he came back he announced, "It's past the hour and a half point, so I need to ask you if you wish a supplement or not?"

"Oh," I replied, and silently consulted myself, "If I took the supplement, I would simply continue where I am for longer than I would otherwise?"

"Exactly. Approximately an hour longer."

"Then yes, please. I would like very much to have the supplement, if you don't mind.

"No, of course not. I'll join you. Wait just a moment."

When he brought out our wine glasses again, I shuddered at the memory of the taste, and Shura apologized, "I forgot. Let me bring you some juice." From the kitchen, he called out, "As a matter of fact, you should be drinking a lot of fluid, because this drug tends to cause a bit of dehydration."

I excused myself to go to the bathroom. Sitting on the toilet, I looked around at the pale green wall tiles and the old-fashioned sink, and saw that there was one very neat, well-spun spiderweb in a corner of the light blue ceiling. I assumed it had been left there deliberately, because the rest of the bathroom was clean and tidy and dusted.

In the living room, I clinked glasses with Shura and downed the juice without difficulty.

I settled back onto the blue tweed couch, and Shura brought in a pitcher of ice water and an empty plastic tumbler. As he put them on the table in front of me, I smiled. "Thank you. I'll try to remember to keep drinking."

"It's important that you do," he said, seated again in his armchair. I saw a glass of water on the small table by his side.

"Before you continue your story," Shura said, "I'd like you to tell me if you notice any physical effects of any kind, at this point?"

"Physical?" I paid attention and reported, "There's a bit of dryness in the mouth, now that I think of it, and a funny little feeling, a kind of tension, in the jaw hinges; it's not a problem though."

"Notice anything about the eyes?"

I rolled my eyes, looked to right and left and said, "There's a tendency for them to wiggle a bit, when I look to either side; I don't mind it. Actually, it's sort of fun."

"That's called nystagmus. Most people have a touch of it with MDMA, especially the first time they take it."

I practiced the eye-wiggle a few times and laughed at the sensation.

"Are you comfortable with where you are?"

I answered yes, thinking that "comfortable" was not exactly the word I would have chosen. I was seeing my world differently. There was still the peacefulness within me, and a clarity to whatever I looked at, inside myself and outside. I was not afraid; there was no anxiety. Then the realization struck me that I lived most of the time in a state of habitual anxiety. I was so used to it, I had long ago forgotten to notice or wonder at it. Anxiety was my way of life. It was very unusual — and it felt wonderful — to be without it.

That can't change yet. Too many things to be responsible for. The children. My job. Paying bills. Wondering if I'll ever have a true soulmate, like this one, to share life with. So many things to do, to keep in balance. Can't relax and trust the universe yet.

Shura spoke, "Please continue with your story. I don't want you to think I wasn't involved with what you were saying, when I remembered about the supplement."

"Oh, no," I replied, "It isn't that. I just got seduced by some other thoughts. I was realizing how much anxiety I normally live with. I hadn't seen before that a certain level of anxiety is an absolute habit with me. And that's probably been the case for years and years. I'm not sure I can even remember a time when it wasn't there. Except perhaps that day on peyote."

Shura nodded.

"It was an interesting bit of insight. Not that I can do anything about it, at this particular time in my life. But it's important for me to realize it consciously, I think."

I was looking across the space between us at Shura's face in the shadow of the divider wall. I lost myself for a moment in the study of that lion's mane, the deep furrows between nostrils and mustache, the full lips which seemed softer now than they usually did. The MDMA has brought out the warmest part of him, I thought. There was an openness, a vulnerability in his face which I had seen before only on the night we made love.

He's a very controlled person, and he's allowing some of that control to go; he's not guarding as much as usual. His face is very beautiful. I wonder if he looks so to other people.

Shura smiled at me, his eyes glinting in the shadows.

"I was appreciating your face," I said, "You're beautiful, you know."

"So are you, my little friend," he said, then swung his feet off the hassock and leaned forward.

"I'm going to ask you to do something, right now, if you would. Go into the bathroom and look at yourself in the mirror. Don't stay there long; it's easy to hypnotize yourself, when you're in this state. But I want you to look at your face for a moment, then come back and tell me what you've seen."

I remembered Sam making the same request, on the peyote day.

I went to the bathroom and looked into the mirror. The face I saw was radiant, the eyes glowing, pupils large. It looked open and unguarded. There was sadness there, kindness, longing, and a faint touch of hope. I smiled at the reflection.

When I returned to the living room, I said only, "I saw a person I like very much."

Shura said, "I was hoping you would. I like you very much, too. For whatever that's worth to you."

"Thank you. It's worth a great deal."

I would have it love as well as like, but that's something neither of us has control over.

I settled back on the couch and thought about continuing my story, but a question had come to mind.

"Shura, you said that you never had the experience of being in love before Ursula. Weren't you in love with Helen when you married her?"

Shura rubbed his beard, thinking. He sighed, "No. We were comfortable with each other and we enjoyed doing things together, but I suspect we got married more to escape being lonely than because we really loved each other. And to aggravate our parents. Hers had made it clear that, in their opinion, I wasn't quite what they had in mind for their daughter, and mine most definitely felt I could do better. We both thought it was very funny, and we decided to elope, I guess to punish them."

The glow I'd seen in his face a while ago had dimmed. I wondered if it was the remembering.

"We weren't very happy, I regret to say. She was a good person, kind and intelligent, and she brought a much needed order into my life; you know, a clean house, fresh shirts and meals on time, even when she went back to work. It gave me a routine, a structure I could depend on, especially at times when I had doubts about the wisdom of the decisions I'd made — leaving Dole, going back to school. I wasn't always sure I could make a good enough living as a consultant to allow me to follow my peculiar and very different drummer."

"But you weren't happy together?"

"No, not happy. There were several major stones on the path, sorry to say, and neither of us was able to find a satisfactory way around them. For one, Helen was intensely phobic. She was afraid of a lot of things. Her greatest fear, as I said, was of losing control, being vulnerable, and as a result, certain aspects of our relationship suffered."

I poured ice water into the clean glass Shura had put out for me. I was aware of dryness in my mouth and remembered he'd mentioned dehydration.

He took my cue and drank from his glass before continuing. "When she gave birth to Theo, she had a lot of pain, and she told me she didn't want to go through that experience again. She said Theo would have to be an only child, because she couldn't face another childbirth. That saddened me because I'd been an only child and I sometimes thought that it might have been better — many things in my life might have been better — if I'd had siblings. But she felt so strongly about it, I had no choice but to accept her decision."

"You didn't consider adoption?"

"No, I can't remember ever discussing adoption, though I suppose it must have been mentioned, somewhere along the way. We were both probably too elitist to seriously consider it."

"Did she have her tubes tied?"

"No. Nothing like that. She was too afraid of surgery. She couldn't tolerate the pill and — not unreasonably — she didn't trust condoms. What happened was that we gradually — love-making just happened less and less often. We began to withdraw from each other." He frowned, "Are you sure you want to hear all this?"

"As long as you don't mind sharing it, I appreciate your telling me. After all, it was a whole thirty years of your life."

And it means you trust me.

"No, I don't mind talking about it. Matter of fact, it feels good to talk about it. I haven't told anyone about this aspect of the marriage, even Ursula. She and Dolph knew Helen; they genuinely liked each other, and they got on very well. All four of us got on well. We used to go on weekend trips together, in fact, even after I'd realized I was in love with Ursula and she'd said she loved me. Of course, Helen never knew. Thank God, she never knew."

"Did Dolph know?"

"I assumed at the time that he didn't, but at this point, I can't be sure. He gave no indication, then, of feeling differently towards me, but he doesn't now, either — on the phone. And he certainly knows about it now!"

He paused to drink, and I kept quiet.

"We did our best to be good parents, Helen and I. I think we were good parents, in every way but one. Neither of us really gave Theo the depth of acceptance and love that he needed. Helen did better than I, in that respect, but there was something missing for Theo. I wasn't as supportive as I should have been, and I've regretted it deeply without knowing how to remedy it. As I said, I wasn't a very loving human being at that time."

I nodded.

"I suppose I was too critical and judgemental, and I know I was often impatient with poor Theo, and he suffered from it. He could never be sure, really sure, at the deepest level, that he was a worthwhile person and unconditionally loved, and I was more to blame than Helen for that. But, to be fair — to myself — I was gradually becoming emotionally dried up, withdrawing from people more and more."

He lit a cigarette, and so did I.

"I think that, for many years, I was unable to give much love to anyone. Until Ursula happened to me, and I began to thaw out a lot of what had been frozen for so long. I even felt more love for Helen, at that time, than I ever had before. And I actually felt kind, on occasion, and bit my tongue instead of delivering my usual devastatingly clever, cutting comments. I was careful not to overdo it, of course. There wasn't any point in alarming everybody!"

I laughed. I couldn't imagine him as an unkind man with a dry heart. The critical, impatient aspect, I had seen hints of; I could believe in that. But not in lack of kindness.

Is he judging himself too harshly, remembering the past? Or is he warning me — unconsciously, maybe — of some aspects of himself I don't know yet?

"We irritated each other too often, Helen and I. We argued a lot about little things, things not worth arguing about. It was a reflection of the deeper disappointment we both felt about the whole relationship, the way our marriage had turned out."

"But she never tried to stop you from doing your research, you said?"

"No, she wasn't in any way negative about that. She was interested in my descriptions of effects, but she declined to take part in any experiment. Until that one time with mescaline. It must have been very hard for her sometimes, knowing the kind of research I was engaged in; phobic as she was, I'm sure she was often scared of my doing myself some injury, but she kept it to herself, and I bless her for that."

"What kind of phobias did she have?"

"She was afraid of straining her body in any way — thus the withdrawal from sex — and of injury, of course. I always helped with anything in the kitchen that involved the use of a sharp knife, for instance. And of death, which is not unusual, I realize, but there were times when she seemed a bit obsessed with the threat of death. We got a little 20-foot sailboat, and for a while she enjoyed it when we went out as a family, but she was terrified for my safety when I went sailing alone. Eventually, she came to be afraid of sailing altogether."

"Poor soul!"

"When I learned to fly a small plane," said Shura, "She refused to drive down with me to the flying school. If we had to take a regular airline flight to anywhere, I had to give her Miltown before we got on board. None of this, you understand, prevented her from functioning quite normally and efficiently, in most respects. It's just that fear was always part of our life together, and it came between us in a lot of ways."

"She never went into any kind of therapy?"

"Oh, no. Psychotherapy was frightening to her, too. She dismissed any such suggestion out of hand."

"Unfortunately," I said, "that's not unusual. A lot of people think a therapist is going to lay open everything bad and unacceptable in them; they really expect some kind of professional Final Judgement."

Shura nodded, stubbing out his cigarette. "After she had her first minor stroke, several years before her death, we developed a quite different relationship. She allowed herself to trust me, and I was able to help her a great deal. I wanted her to gain independence from her medications as soon as possible, so I introduced her to biofeedback. She learned to regulate her blood pressure, to the point where she could get off both her medications — with the doctor's approval, of course — without any negative consequences."

"That's wonderful!"

"She showed tremendous courage. It touched me very deeply, her courage and her trust in me. And it paid off. She was able to stop thinking of herself as an invalid and go back to the job she loved, in Berkeley."

"You said she didn't enjoy living out here on the Farm?"

"Not really. She wanted to like it, but this kind of life just wasn't her cup of tea. She was a city girl at heart. That's just the way it was. She took care of everything, she was an excellent housekeeper, as I said. I am not a very neat or tidy person, and I left it to her to keep things picked up and running smoothly, and that's what she did, but she was never able to love this place the way I do."

He needs to live with someone organized and tidy, and I'm neither.

I asked him, "Did she have another stroke, or was her death due to something else?"

"She was working in the library — this was about three years after the first stroke — and apparently she complained to a friend that her right arm had suddenly gone dead, then she lost consciousness and — well, she never woke up. Pontine hemorrhage; a massive stroke."

"Oh, dear." I knew there were tears on the shadowed face, and I thought, how very good that he had wanted to tell me all of it. I wondered whether it might be one of the effects of MDMA, this kind of trust and openness.

"Thank you for telling me."

"I suppose I needed to talk about it. Thank you for being interested."

I smiled at him, then focused on taking a drink from my water glass, because I needed the water and because it would give him a chance to wipe his eyes. I heard the sound of a nose being unashamedly blown, and saw a balled up Kleenex drop to the floor.

Shura asked, his voice thickened but cheerful, "How are you feeling right now?"

I told him I suspected the effects might be starting to fade, just a bit, "It's a barely perceptible change. Perhaps I'm just getting used to the state."

"Maybe, but I wouldn't be surprised if you were starting to experience the decline."

"Already?"

Shura was smiling, "Do I detect a bit of disappointment?"

"Oh, of course you detect disappointment. It would be nice to keep going this way for a lot longer."

"I'm glad it's been a good experience. Very glad."

He means it, he really is pleased. I wonder how much of the pleasure is because he cares for me or because he believes this stuff is good and wants it to be good for everyone. Maybe a bit of both. Doesn't matter.

We spent the next hour or so wandering over the Farm. I asked how the MDMA had been for him, and he told me that he'd had a pleasant experience, but that it didn't do the same things for him that it seemed to do for so many other people.

"Just my peculiar body chemistry, I guess," he said, "I don't mind."

"You don't mind?"

"No, I enjoy what it does give me, and since I take it these days only with other people, I also enjoy the experience of seeing them open up and discover themselves. I don't do it often, but every time I have shared it with somebody else, I've felt truly privileged. That's the only way I can put it."

We made our way down an overgrown path behind the garage, and Shura opened the door of a small greenhouse which was missing some sections of its glass. There was a hole in the back wall through which a few ground vines had entered. Patches of yellowing grass were growing on the floor and red pots clustered on an old redwood table. Some of the pots contained unidentifiable green plants and one held a small cactus.

Shura said, regretfully, "Have to get this fixed up and working again."

We walked past a slope of grass where a single grapevine, leafless still, wound itself around a crude wooden frame. Beyond it was a very old, dark barn, where Shura showed me the remnants of a huge wine barrel and a wall of bottles — homemade plum wine — resting on their sides in rows, barely visible in the dark. He said the lights hadn't worked for years and that he fully intended, one of these days, to repair them. In the meantime, he cautioned, I should watch my step, because there were all sorts of things lying around on the floor, waiting to turn ankles.

After the barn we saw more grapevines and a place on the hill where he said there used to be a vegetable garden, and would be again, when he got around to doing some work on it. On our way back, we talked about the satisfaction of growing one's own vegetables, and the virtues of drip irrigation. I told him that it seemed to me the effects of the MDMA were gone, or almost gone.

"How do you feel, now?"

We were standing at the top of the brick stairway in front of the house. I put out a hand to explore the texture of juniper and thought carefully before answering.

"There's still a peacefulness inside. There's a kind of acceptance of things as they are, a feeling that everything is — everything makes some kind of sense. Not to the mind, because intellectually, there's a lot of confusion, but in the heart. And a — what I can only call excitement. Some part of me can't wait to see what life's going to come up with next! Anticipation without the usual anxiety. And underneath it all is the feeling that we both belong here, just as we are, right now."

I think I said that pretty well. I've even impressed myself.

"Do you feel hungry?" asked Shura.

"Hungry?"

What kind of response is that, to my gorgeous speech?

Shura was asking, a tease in his voice, "How does the idea of pork chops and mashed potatoes strike you?"

I thought of pork chops and mashed potatoes, and replied, "Not the most alluring thing in the world, exactly."

He grinned as if I had passed a difficult exam.

"That's the normal response. MDMA is highly anorexic. You probably won't feel like eating for quite a few hours yet."

We returned to the living room and I remarked that, although my appetite was gone, I certainly felt thirsty, and proceeded to drink all the remaining water in my glass.

"Good girl," said Shura, "Keep drinking."

I flashed him a good-girl smile, baring my teeth, then said what I had to say, "I'd better think about getting home, you know."

For just a fraction of a moment, there was a look of confusion on his face, as if my words had surprised him. Then he looked away and said, "Yes, of course. I hadn't thought about you going home, to tell the truth."

Oh, thank you, love.

"I feel perfectly fine, Shura. I wouldn't suggest going home if I had any doubts about driving."

"No, of course not," he said, "But let me give you a quick check, anyway. Go into the bathroom for a moment and I'll get my flashlight."

What in heaven's name is he going to do with a flashlight?

When he joined me in the bathroom, he turned off the light and told me to stand with my back to the window. He said, "Tell me if you see any tracers — you know what I mean by tracers, don't you?"

"The after-impression you get from a moving point of light, if you're under the influence, yes?"

"Right."

He clicked on the flashlight and swept it across my field of vision, then turned it off. I assured him there were no tracers.

"Fine," he said, leading me back to the living room, "But you might still get light flashes at the periphery of your vision. Just be prepared for them, especially when you're facing headlights on the highway. Don't get confused."

I said I was sure I wouldn't get confused, and I hadn't seen any peripheral light flashes yet.

Shura urged, "Promise me, if you feel the slightest unease while you're driving, either turn right around and come back here, or at least get off the highway and wait for a while. All right?"

He was holding my shoulders, looking into my face.

"Of course I will," I promised him, "I have great respect for my own health and safety, believe me. I'll come right back here if there's any question at all."

Shura walked down the driveway while I was starting my engine, to lock up after me. When I reached the gate, I put on the brake and stepped out of the car. I hugged him, my head on his chest, "Thank you for a beautiful day, and for being who you are."

"Whatever that is," he laughed, hugging me back.

"Whatever that is," I agreed.

He bent his head and kissed the tip of my nose.

Driving home, I realized that neither of us had mentioned my coming back to the Farm, or even seeing each other again. And it didn't matter.

We wait. It's in the hands of the gods. He waits for Ursula and I wait for him.

CHAPTER 23. THE GROUP

Late the next morning, Shura called to ask how I was feeling. I said very well, thank you, adding that I was still not hungry, to my great delight, and hoped the anorexia would continue for a long time.

He said he was glad it had been a positive experience.

"I'm very grateful," I said, "It was good of you to do that for me — and with me."

He replied, "It was my pleasure."

Nothing was said about a return engagement.

Wednesday evening, I put on my nightgown and sat down to watch the late news on television. The children were asleep. I was drained from the day's work, but reluctant to go to bed because all I could look forward to after the night's sleep was getting up and going back to the pressure of the Medical Records Department, which — having two transcribers out with flu — was even more frantic than usual.

When the phone rang, my first thought was that, at this late hour, it might be an emergency, and I wasn't in the mood for emergencies. I did not expect Shura's voice, and must have sounded surprised, because he asked me, "Am I calling too late? I didn't mean to wake you up — were you asleep?"

"No, no! Not at all. I was watching the late news, as a matter of fact. How nice to hear from you!"

"I called to tell you I'm having some friends — part of my research group — over next Saturday. Thought you might like to join us, if you don't have other plans?"

The aching tiredness in my shoulders and neck had disappeared.

"I'd love to. What time, and can I bring anything?"

"I'm asking everyone to be here by ten in the morning. Bring whatever kind of juice you like, and — let's see — we could use some fresh fruit. Everything else is taken care of. Oh, by the way, you might want to skip breakfast."

Why? They're probably having a brunch, that's why.

Saturday was cool, the air fresh and clear from the previous day's rain. I had stopped at the market for oranges, apples and bananas and a bottle of my old standby, cranberry juice. Tucked away in the back of the Volkswagon bus was a decorated shopping bag, left over from Christmas, containing my toothbrush, an extra blouse, and my best pale blue silk nightgown.

You never know, as the Boy Scouts say.

As I turned into Borodin Road, I realized I was feeling more than ordinary, everyday anxiety; I was scared to death. In a few minutes, I would be meeting Shura's best friends; they would inevitably compare me with Ursula — the lovely, gentle, young, intelligent Ursula — and probably resent me as a poor substitute. Surely they would wonder at my presence here, today. I was wondering at it, myself.

Okay. Nothing to do but be happy Shura invited me and hope his friends are inclined to mercy and compassion.

The kitchen was noisy with talk, laughter and the sounds of bowls and cutlery being arranged on tile surfaces. Shura turned to see me hesitating in the doorway and called, "Alice! I didn't hear you drive up. Come on in!"

I put my sack of groceries on the counter, while Shura shouted happily that he wanted to introduce a good friend of his, Alice Parr. I flashed a quick grin at the blur of faces, then turned to busy myself with the job of putting the fruit in an empty basket, giving my mouth a chance to relax. I was afraid my old facial tic might return.

For most of my life, whenever I was being introduced to a roomful of people I didn't know, the tiny muscles on either side of my mouth would go into a twitching spasm if I tried to maintain a smile while I was being stared at, the newcomer on display. I had no way of knowing whether or not the tic was visible to anyone else, and had no intention of finding out. Only when one of the strangers made some gesture or spoke to me, would the tension ease, allowing me to smile back in a reasonable imitation of spontaneity. For years, now, I hadn't had trouble with the spasm, but I recognized the familiar feeling of suffocating tightness in my throat, and there was no sense in taking a chance.

When I turned around again, a moment later, I was sure I looked pleasantly expectant, without actually smiling.

I shook hands with five people, trying to register each name while knowing my nervousness would, as usual, make it impossible. I'd grown used to explaining that I found it hard to remember names with the first introduction, having discovered that it was a fault I shared with a large part of the human race.

First, there was Ruth Close, followed by her husband, George. Ruth was a small woman, a few inches shorter than I, with a comfortably rounded body and a face which showed kindness and warmth; a mother-face. Her black hair was cut short and feathery with streaks of grey showing at the temples. Dark eyes, friendly and questioning, looked into mine as she patted my hand.

George, who was only slightly taller than his wife and equally rounded, leaned forward with a wide grin, his eyes squinting behind glasses; he took both my hands in his and pumped them enthusiastically, "Hello, hello! So you're Alice! Welcome to the madhouse!"

My tension evaporated with George's greeting. Suddenly, my smile was back and I knew the tic wouldn't be.

Next came Leah Cantrell, a tall, thin girl-woman with long, dark blond hair fastened against the back of her neck with a blue ribbon. Hazel eyes searched mine, wanting to know everything. I felt an immediate liking for this quietly lovely person with the sensitive face.

Shura introduced her husband as "Doctor Morris Benjamin Cantrell, called Ben."

Ben said, "Welcome, Alice! It's a pleasure to meet you," sounding as if he meant it. His voice was resonant and warm, with an undertone of authority. He was a solidly built man with thinning white hair and an intelligent, powerful face, obviously more than a few years older than his wife. His eyes looked straight into mine, as he smiled.

Last to greet me was John Sellars, a slender man with smooth pink cheeks who, at first glance, seemed no older than forty. It was only upon looking more closely at him, later in the day, that I saw the many fine lines on the forehead and around the eyes, and realized that the straw-colored hair was mostly grey. His face was compelling; a Botticelli angel grown to middle-age, with thoughtful eyes.

While she washed lettuce for a salad, Ruth asked me questions. Where did I live, what kind of work did I do, how did I meet Shura? I answered willingly, aware of the mixture in her voice of empathy and strong curiosity. When, in response to a question, I told her I had four children, she said that she had wanted some of her own but found she couldn't have them. I said I was surprised to hear that, because she had impressed me as the kind of person who would have lots of children, all of them well loved. She chuckled, "Well, I suppose I make up for it by mothering just about everybody else."

Shura called out from the dining room, "All right, people, gather 'round," and the talk hushed. We crowded around the table.

"We're doing a new one, today," said Shura, "And not only is it a new material, it's also one of a new family of compounds. I've named it Aleph-2, and full activity has been established at between 4 and 8 milligrams. As

I think I indicated on the phone, it's relatively long, about eight or nine hours. At least, it was for me. For those of you who are very sensitive, there's always the possibility it might take longer than that to return to baseline, which is why I suggested you bring sleeping bags."

He didn't mention sleeping bags to me. He didn't even tell me there would be an experiment. Maybe he doesn't say things like that over the phone. Oh, of course! That's what he meant when he said to skip breakfast!

Leah's voice said, "Good! It's been a while since we've tried a new one."

George sighed loudly, rolling his eyes, "My oh my, the sacrifices we make for science!"

Ruth said, "Just as long as it isn't anorexic — I've got a gorgeous salad!"

"Then you'll be happy to hear that anorexia is not one of its properties," replied Shura.

"Hooray!" said George.

A discussion began about the level of drug which would be appropriate to each member of the group, and I noted that Ruth and George agreed immediately to Shura's suggestion of four and five milligrams, respectively. I wondered if they were both sensitive to these kinds of drugs, or were being conservative because it was new to them. I was curious to see whether anyone would elect to take the maximum amount Shura had mentioned.

Leah also chose a modest level, four milligrams, but her husband asked for six. John scratched the back of his head thoughtfully, then said he would take a chance with seven.

Shura scribbled on a large piece of paper, then announced, "As for me, I'll go with seven milligrams, this time. I tried eight, and it was a bit strong."

He looked across the table at me. I felt myself flushing, and he smiled reassuringly, "Alice, you're more than welcome to participate if you'd like, or just be with us without taking anything, if you'd prefer." He added, "I'm not sure I even made it clear to you there was going to be an experiment today, did I?"

I shook my head, "No, but that's okay. I'd like very much to join in, if it's all right."

There was a chorus of encouragement from the others.

Shura said, "If you want to give it a try, might I suggest something like four or five milligrams? It's a modest level, but you should get the full effects."

"Five, then, please."

Shura asked Ben to help him, and they left for the lab with seven glasses of assorted sizes and shapes. I sat down in a chair near the sliding glass doors which formed one wall of the dining room.

What the blazes am I doing, taking a new psychedelic drug with a lot of people I've never met before? I'll have to be careful, behave very well. They don't know me. I don't want them to know too much too fast.

Ruth came up to me and asked, "Have you had any experience with psychedelics before, Alice?"

"Well, I took peyote many years ago, and last week I had my first MDMA experience. That's all." Then I remembered, "Oh, I did try marijuana once, but I'm afraid I didn't enjoy it very much."

Ruth put a hand on my shoulder, "Well, don't worry. We're nice people, you know, and you'll be just fine. It's certainly a new and different way to get to know a bunch of strangers, isn't it!" I was surprised to hear a faint note of disapproval in her voice.

I smiled at her and agreed it certainly was that!

She doesn't think Shura should have put me in this position. He gave me a choice, though. He said I was welcome to be here without taking anything. He probably thinks I'm a grownup and can make grownup choices for myself.

Shura and Ben returned and eased the glasses — now marked with initials and covered by neat caps of aluminum foil — onto the dining room table. Ruth brought out several bottles of juice.

There was an instant of silence, as everyone standing around the table looked at what had been placed there, and thought their private thoughts. Then someone sighed audibly and Shura said, "Well, are we ready?"

Leah said, "Ready," and picked up her glass, reading the initials out loud, "L.C., if I'm not mistaken." Shura handed me mine and I saw in it a small amount of white powder. I looked up and met George's eyes. He flashed a grin at me, peered into his own glass and shuddered dramatically, making a sound of strangled horror, then looked back at me and said, very seriously, "I strongly advise you to add juice; Shura's concoctions usually taste absolutely terrible, and I'll bet this one is no exception."

I was still laughing as I poured cranberry juice into my glass.

Shura was protesting, "There's nothing terrible about the taste; it's all part of the personality of the drug, part of its identity, its soul. Think of what you're missing; think of what you'll never know —"

George interrupted him with another shuddering groan. Ruth was chuckling, patting Shura on the back, and Leah said, "We know, Shura, we know all about your beautiful little drug souls, and we have found them wanting in the area of palatability."

We drifted into the kitchen and formed a small circle, holding up our glasses. I stood between Ben and John, looking up at Shura, as was everyone else. He said, "Prosit!" and everyone clinked glasses, saying, "Happy voyage," "Blessings," and to me, "Welcome Alice," then we drank.

It was more than an hour before the first announcement came, and it was from George.

We were gathered outside, wearing sweaters and jackets. Ben and Leah were seated on a weathered redwood bench next to the front door, and Ruth was at the other end of the brick apron that stretched across the front of the house, talking with Shura and John. I was sitting on a large floor pillow somebody had brought out from the living room, and George was nearby on a bank of ivy, leaning against an immense oak tree whose roots were beginning to displace some of the bricks on the walkway around us.

Ben had been telling me about his childhood in Brooklyn, and the ways in which growing up poor — "my early survival training," he called it — had influenced the direction of his later life. I had learned that he was the founder and head of a graduate school of psychology, which he referred to as "the institute," in a town north of the Bay Area. He had a sharp, subtle mind and a sense of humor to match.

I had shared some of my own much briefer experience of poverty, in the housing project with Christopher, and what it had taught me. I didn't mention having discovered, at first hand, the meaning of the term, "chronic depressive state."

Suddenly, from his place underneath the oak, George spoke for the first time since coming outside, "By the way, is anyone else feeling this stuff yet? I must say I am!"

Leah answered, "Yes, so am I. A lot." She put her hand on her husband's thigh, "Are you cold, honey? Do you want a blanket?"

Ben looked thoughtful, as if examining himself for the first time, and said he was feeling fine, not cold at all. Leah rose and went into the house. I paid attention to my own state and concluded I was off baseline, as Shura would say, but only lightly, perhaps one shot of vodka's worth. I called out to George and asked him how he was.

"Oh," he replied, his voice strained, "Hard to say. There's an awful lot of visual stuff; the ivy is wiggling non-stop. I wouldn't mind a five-minute breather from it all, at the moment."

Leah reappeared with a stack of blankets of different sizes and colors, and George said, "Ah, thank you, thank you. I can use a couple or five of those," and grabbed at the one Leah offered him. He wrapped it around himself and lay down, huddled like a child at the base of the tree. I told Leah I was grateful for the offer, but didn't think I needed one yet. She rejoined Ben, her blanket clutched around her, visibly shivering. Her husband put an arm over her shoulders and kissed her cheek.

I asked Ben, "How is your experience?"

"Well, it impresses me as a mellow, pleasant material, so far. It certainly did creep up on me while we were doing all that talking." He chuckled comfortably. I glanced up at George, now invisible under his blanket.

I took the same amount he did, and I'm not feeling much at all. I've been talking a lot, though. Guess that could be counted as an effect.

I pressed Ben, "Are you getting visual things of any kind?"

"Yes, I'd have to say that there's quite a lot of movement, now that I'm paying attention."

I heard the scuffing of Shura's sandals on the bricks behind me. He went over to Ben and Leah and leaned down to peer into their faces, "How's it going? Where are you?"

"Very nice, indeed," said Ben, "It shows potential, Shura. Quite a bit of visual; comfortable body, reasonably strong effect. I'd say it's pushing a plus-three."

"Me, too," said Shura. He put a hand on Leah's blanket covered shoulder, "How about you, kid?"

"A bit intense, at the moment. Also, I'm feeling the cold a lot. I keep shivering, but I'm sure that'll smooth out in a while. I'd say a very strong plus-three, and I hope it softens a bit. In the meantime, I'm just going to go with it and not talk much."

Ruth was standing beside me, holding her sweater tightly around her body, "It's not too strong for me, for a change. Sort of pleasant, though I'm not sure I can tell you exactly what's happening. Just very definitely not baseline," she smiled, then went over to the ivy covered mound and climbed up beside George.

Shura squatted down in front of me. His eyes were dark and liquid, the pupils large, and I realized mine must be also. His face glowed with a look of frank pleasure. I smiled at him; you could only smile at that open face.

I reported, "I'm getting relatively little effect, really. It's a nice, relaxed sort of feeling, but it's only — well — it's like the effect of one cocktail, that's about it."

Shura looked puzzled, "How much did I give you? Five?"

"Yes, it was five."

"John's quite light, so is Ruth; Ben's kind of middling strong, Leah's very intense, and," he glanced up at George, "George is cocooning, I see. George?" He rose and climbed up on the ivy. George mumbled something to him from underneath the blanket. Shura patted him and climbed down, leaving him to Ruth's care.

"Well, this is why we have a research group," Shura said, hands in the pockets of his corduroy jacket, "But I must say, this one is hard to figure out. So far, there seems to be an awfully wide range of responses to the drug."

He stooped down to me again and asked, "Are you content with where you are, or would you like to try a supplement of a couple of milligrams, just to see if it boosts you into more of a real effect?"

I didn't hesitate, "I wouldn't mind a boost, if that's okay."

"I'll measure out two milligrams more. That'll put you at my level — seven — and that certainly should do it."

I followed him into the house. In the kitchen, he paused, my glass in his hand, and asked me, quietly, "How's it going?"

"Very well. Beautifully, in fact. I had a good talk with Ben, and I do like him."

"Yes, we go back a long way, Benjamin and I. It's a sort of brother relationship — the brother neither of us had, I suppose. I'm glad you had a chance to talk to him." He smiled, "I'm going to get your booster. Be back in a moment."

I wandered into the living room, saw two more big pillows on the carpet beside the piano, and dragged them outside. George was still curled up under the tree, and Ruth lay next to him, murmuring gently. I could hear only small sounds from George, and wondered what kind of difficulty he was having.

I don't know him, though; I don't know any of them. Maybe George always curls up in a blanket during experiments. Maybe Leah always feels chilled.

I couldn't understand my own lack of response to the drug, although there was always the possibility that my need to be in control was over-riding everything else. No way to tell. The additional two milligrams might make a change.

Shura brought out my glass, with some juice in it. I said thank you and drank it down. He climbed up on the ivy to sit with George and Ruth.

I found myself in conversation with John Sellars. He asked me friendly, polite questions about myself and told me he was an anthropologist. Then we discovered our mutual love of art, he as — in his words — a lifelong student and critic, I as a person who had drawn and painted all my life. We talked eagerly about the Brundage collection in Golden Gate Park, where the museum had built an entire wing to house some of the greatest masterpieces of Oriental art in the world, and I told him how the sight of the great seated Buddha on the path above the Japanese Tea Garden had pierced my heart, on the peyote day, many years ago. He, in turn, offered his experience in the Oakland museum, under the influence of one of Shura's materials, enchanted by the blue and red horses of Franz Marc.

An introverted man, I thought, slow to trust somebody new. Yet he seemed to appreciate my responses, his brief smile startling in its sweetness.

I finally rose to go to the bathroom, and as I passed by Leah, she reached out a hand and I took it. She looked up at me and smiled with unmistakable warmth. I felt a surge of gratitude so strong, my throat caught on tears. When I squeezed her hand in response, she released me and withdrew again into her blanketed isolation.

A short time later, I was sitting inside by myself, on the couch, still not more than slightly off baseline, despite the supplement, when Ben came in and sat down on the hassock. He leaned forward, hands clasped, his face serious.

"I was hoping to have a chance to talk to you alone," he said, "I thought perhaps you might be interested in hearing somebody else's view of our girl, Ursula?"

"Yes," I said, surprised, "I certainly am."

"I'm going to speak rather bluntly," said Ben. "She's a good-looking young woman, bright, charming, and highly manipulative. She has Shura totally blinded; he can't see what she is, and of course he won't hear anything from anybody who doesn't worship the ground she walks on. It so happens that I've come across her kind before. Shura's had relatively few women in his life, and certainly not this type, and of course he doesn't have the background of experience with different sorts of people that a practicing psychologist does, so there's no reason to expect him to understand what he's up against."

My God, what is this? He doesn't like her! He doesn't like Ursula!

I nodded, my eyes riveted on his face.

"Ursula is — how best to put it — she's a person who, when she's attracted to a man, intuitively senses what's lacking in his emotional life, and she has a compulsion to become whatever that man most needs in a woman. She probably convinces herself each time that she's truly in love, but I doubt she's capable of what most of us would call real loving. The Jungians have a term, 'anima woman.' The anima woman lacks a solid identity; like many great actors, she borrows — she takes on — a sense of wholeness from playing a part. In this case, it's the part of the muse, the inspiration, the adored dream-woman. She fulfills a fantasy, and you can imagine the tremendous emotional rewards there are for her in such a role, as long as the affair lasts. Each affair lasts, of course, only until the next needy attractive man comes along.

"It's all unconscious, by the way; I don't think Ursula has the slightest idea of what she's doing or why she feels compelled to do it. Or, for that matter, why the men she's drawn to always happen to be married. When it's time to move on, she explains — and probably believes — that she's ending the relationship because she couldn't live with the responsibility of having broken up a marriage."

I sat stunned, listening.

"When she first joined the group, we had long talks with each other, under the influence of Shura's materials, and she told me a lot about her involvements with married men; she told me more than she realized or intended to. It was a subtle form of preening, under the guise of telling problems to a wise, sympathetic psychologist, you understand?"

He grinned briefly at me.

"Gradually, I put enough of the pieces together to understand the pattern. By that time," Ben chuckled, "She had stopped telling me personal things about herself and her life, and I sensed that she was feeling uncomfortable around me. Nothing obvious, no overt avoidance, but nonetheless...." He paused, "As I said, she's highly intuitive."

I lit a cigarette, noting a very slight tremor in my body. It felt delicious.

Ben went on, "The dynamics of this kind of psychological compulsion are more than I want to go into right now, but what worries me is that I believe Ursula is simply not capable of true emotional commitment to anyone. She'll play the role for a time, as I said, until somebody else comes along — someone she finds appealing, with an emotional hole that's begging to be filled — and she'll move on to the new challenge.

"That's what's going to happen to Shura. I'm sure of it. I know it! I love him very much — we all do, you know — and sooner or later, he's going to be badly hurt. That's why I'm more pleased than I can say, to see you here. I don't know what your relationship is with Shura, but it's clear that you care for him, and I hope that — umm — I hope you'll stay around. To help cushion the blow, when it comes; to give him something real to hold onto, when the unreal thing begins to unravel. Which I'm sure will happen before long, now that Ursula finds herself involved with a man who has — quite unexpectedly — become free to make an open commitment to her and ask her to do the same. Her bluff is being called."

Oh, you wonderful man! The clouds are beginning to lift. The sun is breaking through. Twenty-thousand tweety-birds are singing their damn-fool heads off!

I said, "As a matter of fact, Ben, Shura has said several times that he's beginning to wonder whether she'll ever ask her husband for a divorce, as she says she intends to do, and he's getting a bit cynical about all the promises she keeps making. He's aware that certain things just don't fit, don't make sense — like her husband's behavior, for instance. He says that whenever he's called Germany and Dolph has answered the phone, it's as if nothing is happening; Dolph still talks as if he and Shura are the best of friends. Not the kind of response you'd expect from a betrayed husband, is it?"

Ben was watching me, occasionally nodding.

I continued, "Maybe Shura's intuition is telling him what he doesn't want to acknowledge consciously. Otherwise, why would he have allowed me into his life, even just the little bit that he has? I keep asking myself why, if he's so much in love with Ursula, he's let himself get more than casually involved with me? He knows that —," I hesitated, not sure I should trust Ben with this one, then realized he'd already detected the signs, " — I'm in love with him. I told him that; I stated it very clearly. Maybe it hasn't scared him off because he already has some inkling —."

Ben said, "I'm relieved to hear that. Thank you for telling me." He shrugged, "I may be wrong, of course; Ursula may yet surprise us both. But I don't think so. I don't think I'm mistaken about her."

He stared at his clasped hands for a minute, then smiled at me, "I wish you luck. I also wish you a great deal of courage. Shura isn't the easiest person to understand and probably not the easiest to live with, either. But he's worth the effort. At least, I think he is. But, then, I'm not a woman who loves him; I'm not vulnerable to the kind of pain you could find yourself facing, in a situation like this."

Ruth came in. I could feel her intense desire to know what was going on, but she only waved to us and walked through, heading for the kitchen.

"Thank you," I said to Ben, who was getting up from his seat, "I'll keep what you've said to myself, of course, but it really helps to hear a different opinion; something besides how wonderful and sensitive and intelligent Ursula is, 'specially because I have no way of evaluating any of it."

"Glad you're here, Alice," said Ben. He pressed my shoulder firmly, and left to rejoin the people outside.

I sat on the couch for a long time, mentally replaying the conversation, word by extraordinary word, smoking absentmindedly.

The whole universe just took a step to one side of where it used to be. Reality shift.

In the early evening, we gathered together for supper. George sat at the table, his blanket still draped around him, making a brave effort to join in with the talking. He smiled shakily at me and said, "I must say, this day has been a surprise, not what I expected. Looks as if I'm a tad more sensitive to Aleph-2 than the rest of you. Happens that way, sometimes."

John seemed to be in a good state of mind and body; he ladled out a bowl of Leah's matzoh ball soup and reminisced with Shura and Ben about past experiments. Ruth and Leah laughed, occasionally adding details the men had forgotten. Now and then, Ruth would glance at George, who had settled down to eating bread and soup. The food was apparently helping him; I thought he was beginning to look more comfortable.

Finally, Shura sat back, burped loudly, and — after the boo's and catcalls had subsided — said, "Summing up time, yes? Ben, why don't you go first?"

"Good day, for me," said Ben, "Good talking. Body felt fine. No hints of trouble that I can recall, physical or mental. Plus-three and generally a positive experience."

Shura was making notes again. He turned to John and pointed.

"I had a good one, too, although it was light. There was a slight body tremor for a while, but it wasn't a problem, just felt like good energy. No dark corners. No particular insights, but I was too busy talking to go inside much. It was a friendly material, for me. What else? Oh, yes. I'd put it down as a plus-two, definitely. And I wouldn't hesitate to take it again."

Leah was next, "I was really cold, most of the time. I'm just beginning to warm up now, in fact. The food probably helped. As for insights, well —" she paused, "I didn't feel like doing much talking, so I reviewed some things that've been happening recently — difficult interactions with a certain professor, a couple of good discussions I've had recently with other people, that kind of thing — and I was able to get a fresh view, see some things I hadn't seen before. So I'd have to say there was insight, yes." She smiled impishly, "Of course, it might not have been the drug. Maybe it was just giving myself a chance to be quiet and think for a while. These days, I'm so damned busy, I forget I should make time to just sit and think about what's going on."

Shura chuckled, "Don't we all, luv, don't we all!"

Leah concluded, "I'd say it was a plus-three, pretty strong, with the only negative being the cold; I was just as cold inside the house as outside. I couldn't seem to get warm anywhere. Otherwise, mainly okay, but I've had a lot more fun with other materials."

"I'll second that," said Ruth, "Okay for me, too, but not much fun, not the kind we've had on other things. Of course, I was a wee bit worried about George, and that probably influenced me. It wasn't more than a two-plus, I'd say, and I'm not sure I'd get too excited at the prospect of taking it again, to tell you the truth."

We laughed.

Shura pointed his pen at me, so I took a deep breath and gave my report, "I was off baseline, but not very much. Even after the supplement, I couldn't feel anything more than a pleasant relaxation, about a single vodka-with-juice's worth."

Shura scribbled and said, "I'll put it down as plus-one."

"I think I talked a lot, though," I added, "And I forgot to be terrified about what Shura's best friends were going to think of me."

There were sympathetic smiles and murmurs of approval around the table. Even George grinned and croaked, "Good for you!"

Not entirely true. I'm still wondering what they think of me. But I'm no longer scared to death, just plain ordinary everyday so-what-else-is-new anxious.

Shura was saying, "I had a fine time. Plus-three, body good, mind brilliant, thoughts incisive, observations profound — as usual, I might add."

Loud hoots and snorts erupted. When the noise had died down, Shura went on, "Don't remember any great insights, but I was too busy exchanging wild tales and fond memories, most of the time, to bother looking for any. I think seven milligrams is about the highest I want to go, though."

He wrote again, then looked over at George. "You got the overload this time, friend. Sorry about that. Plus-three and much too strong in the visuals department?"

"Yes, I'd say that's accurate," said George, his voice sounding stronger, "About as plus-three as you can get, and even with eyes closed, I couldn't escape the movement. You know how I love visuals, usually, but these were so powerful, I was almost seasick!"

"Can't figure it out," muttered Shura, "That wide a range is very unusual; Alice barely plus-one with a total of seven milligrams, and you blasted out of your skull with five. Looks as if I'll have to go carefully with the rest of the Aleph's, in case this turns out to be typical of the whole family."

An hour later, I was getting ready to go home, feeling entirely normal, sober and back to baseline.

Ruth and George had agreed to stay the night on a big mat which Shura had laid out on the floor of the living room.

John was preparing to leave. He said he was feeling quite okay and able to drive, but he kept getting into animated conversations with Shura and the Closes, obviously reluctant to see the day end.

Ben and Leah had already gone. Both of them had hugged me, Leah saying she was sorry she hadn't had a chance to really talk with me, but next time she'd make up for it.

I said my goodbye's. Outside, standing next to my car, I took Shura's face in my hands and kissed him on the forehead, suspecting we were being watched from the house. I said, "Thank you. It was a very good day, even if I didn't get much effect."

Shura hugged me and said he would be in touch soon, adding, "Thanks for being so courageous and going along with things so gracefully."

Driving home, I savored the word, "gracefully," rolling it around in my mind. I decided, finally, that it tasted like a superb caramel custard.

Crossing the San Rafael Bridge, I broadcast a message.

Thank you, Ben, with all my heart. Blessings. Sleep well.

It wasn't until I had reached home and was getting out of my car that I remembered the blue nightgown in the shopping bag, and laughed.

Next time. God and Mercy willing, next time.

CHAPTER 24. 2C-B

The crucial communication which Shura was relying upon to tell him, once and for all, whether Ursula was going to follow through on her promises, turned out to be a letter, and it was less decisive than he had expected, but sufficiently persuasive to renew his hope. He phoned me on Thursday to read me parts of it.

She sounded both eager and sad, assuring him that Dolph knew the marriage was at an end and that she was leaving him soon. However, she cautioned, her husband's emotional and mental state was fragile, and she had moments of fear that he might lose control and "do something terrible," if she did not smooth out the hurts and reassure him of his essential worth. "Before I go," she wrote, "He must know in his heart that I will always care for him and that no part of what has happened is his fault." She pleaded for Shura to believe that it would not take long, concluding that she had to do it her way, the loving way, "Otherwise, our bright future will be clouded with guilt and blaming."

I was beginning to believe her, myself.

"She's a compassionate person," said Shura, "And I can certainly understand why she wants to end it as gently as possible, even if I don't think she's going about it the wisest way."

After the letter-reading was over, he asked me if I would like to come out to the Farm after work on Friday, to stay the weekend. I hesitated for one entire second before saying I would like to very much, thank you.

Friday evening, we took a drug called 2C-B, which Shura described as one of his favorite materials, among his best discoveries. He told me it was a relatively short-acting psychedelic, lasting only about five or six hours.

"Unlike MDMA," he explained, "This one heightens all the senses. You'll enjoy food, smells, colors, and textures. The texture of skin, for instance —" he stared at me, stone-faced, " — and other aspects of eroticism, are thoroughly enjoyable."

I nodded, equally grave.

"Most people can't begin to have an orgasm with MDMA, but 2C-B places no such restrictions on you, as I hope you'll discover." He flashed what was probably meant to be a leer, and I broke into laughter at the ridiculous sight.

"I suggest we try a modest dosage level, this first time," he continued, unabashed, "I think eighteen milligrams should give you a plus-three without bowling you over. I'll take the same."

After he had given me my wine glass with the tiny bit of powder in it, Shura poured a small amount of water onto the white crystals, telling me, "This stuff doesn't dissolve quickly; it takes warm water to get it into solution." He handed me one of the glasses. "Give it a moment." We carefully swirled the liquid until no white flecks were visible in either glass.

Then he said, "I want you to take a small sip of the 2C-B as it is now, before adding juice, just so you'll have the experience of tasting the pure material — even if you only do it once — because the taste is part of its character."

I smiled, remembering Leah teasing him about little drug souls.

I sipped. The taste was completely different from that of MDMA, but fully as horrible, and I said, "Eeeyuck! I'm sorry, but I've got to have juice."

"Sure," replied the Spartan, "There's apple juice in the 'fridge. At least, now you know what you're covering up, before you cover it up!"

"I certainly do," said I, "The memory will linger a long, long time, believe me!"

I put on my dressing gown and sat quietly on the couch through the transition phase — the time between first becoming aware of some change in myself and the plateau. Shura had told me that transition could take anywhere from 45 minutes to over an hour, and that the plateau should last about three hours.

Shura had gone to his study to work, since I had told him I wanted to experience the transition by myself. After half an hour, I got into the bath I'd prepared earlier, and lay down in the warm water, feeling out the nature of the 2C-B, the way it was expressing itself in my body and mind. The first thing I noticed was a slight movement of the hand-towels hanging beside the sink and a faint shimmer of the pale green shower curtain. Visual effects, I thought; wonderful terminology. A few minutes later, I realized that, although my body was all right, the rest of me was not; I seemed to be reviewing my worst faults — untidiness, disorganization, insecurity — as, one after another, they paraded through my mind. I was beginning to feel a rising anger and contempt at the whole miserable mess, when the Observer stepped in with a sharp comment.

Then, of course, we have the baddest fault of all — being judgemental and unforgiving toward yourself. You wouldn't dream of treating a friend that way; what gives you the right to treat yourself with any less patience and compassion than you'd give a friend? Cut it out!

Humor trickled back, slowly.

All right, all right. I'll be good.

Getting out of the bath, I realized I was feeling what I had come to call the energy tremor. It was rather nice.

I put on my beautiful, sexy French nightgown, the pale blue one, and my dressing gown.

In the bedroom, I looked around at the chests of drawers, the curtains, the floor tiles, and was pleased to note that the idea of Ursula having been here before me didn't seem important. That was another reality, and it had nothing to do with this one.

Shura was sprawled on the bed in his robe. He asked me, "How are you feeling?"

"Well, better than I did earlier. I went through a few moments of seeing all my worst faults and being both the prisoner in the dock and the execution squad, but it passed."

He remarked, "You shouldn't be overloaded on eighteen milligrams, unless you're very sensitive to this particular material."

I assured him I felt fine. Not overloaded.

"How's your experience?" I asked.

"Delightful!"

When I took off my robe, he looked at me and asked, "What are you doing in a nightgown?"

"What do you mean, what am I doing in a nightgown? It's my very best, sexiest nightgown, and you're supposed to be impressed!"

He took his own robe off and said, "I don't believe in wearing clothes in bed. How can you feel somebody's skin when you're all bundled up like that? Besides, they always wrap around you in the night."

I sighed and stripped off the pale blue silk and let it fall to the floor.

He turned off the bedside lamp, leaving only the radio dial for light, while I climbed onto the bed and lay on my back to examine the ceiling, which was pale cream. Suddenly, he was climbing over me, and I heard myself gasp as his tongue took me over. My eyes closed and my mouth enfolded him.

Inside my eyelids, I saw a blue sky behind an immense castle wall; there was the knowledge of turrets somewhere to the right, out of my line of vision. I was standing in grass and there were a few small daisies and lots of dandelions around me. The great wall appeared to be built of mossy yellow-brown stones, and I felt quite small, child-sized. There was a sense of familiarity, neither pleasant nor unpleasant; it was my world, where I lived. The part of it that was especially mine, I knew, was the bottom of the castle wall, where it met the high grass. That was where I liked to play, and I moved toward it now, climbing a rise, past the scattered wild flowers.

Then I remembered where I was, in this life, what my tongue and throat were doing, and what a passionate mouth was doing to me. I was on the bed of a man I belonged with and who belonged with me, and we were making love to the humming sound of a little floor heater and the music of Beethoven.

Another image took over, in all possible shades of red — coral and pink, purple and rose — all of it textured like the interior of a body, smooth and slippery and strong. We were The Man and The Woman, Shiva and his bride, engaged in the Great Dance, the coming together and going apart in order to come together again. We were a single knot in a vast mesh which linked us to every other human being making love, everywhere.

We were The Node, that to which all lines of life go, that from which all lines of life come.

There was a sense of gold somewhere in the red. For an eternity, neither of us moved, neither tongue nor lips nor hands. We were. There was no separation between us.

Later, we put on our robes and wandered into the kitchen, where the pot of black bean soup I'd brought from home sat on the stove, waiting for a splash of sherry and a bit of seasoning. I turned the heat on under it and stood, leaning back against the tiled counter, waiting for Shura to return from the bathroom. Now the 2C-B was a gentle pulse of energy inside me, just enough to be noticeable if I paid attention. The legs of the red-painted kitchen table glowed, and the room was alive with soft light.

Suddenly, something was taking shape across the room, next to the table. It was man-sized and dark, black-brown. I couldn't make out features. I was not seeing it as a physical presence, but with the eyes of the mind, and I felt it smiling contemptuously at me, the embodiment of intentional, malicious evil, full of power.

It was Enemy. I stared at it, anger flooding me.

What the hell are you doing here? Get out of this place! You can't touch me! I am filled with goodness and peace and my strength is as the strength of ten, because my heart is pure, as Launcelot said. Or Gawain, or somebody.

The black man-figure lounged there, elaborately casual, enjoying my anger, radiating superiority.

What I did then was informed by a knowledge my conscious mind didn't possess. I became aware that fighting and opposing was a spiritual trap, because in order to destroy this enemy, I would have to use his tools, play his game, step into his battlefield, and that he was much better at that kind of fighting than I, and that, moreover, I didn't want to become good at it.

I did the only thing I could. I closed my eyes and brought my arms up as if holding a baby to my chest. I visualized a child in the circle of my arms — anyone's child. I dismissed the figure in black from my world and focused all my attention on remembering what it was to love, to care, to nurture, to take away hurt and pain. I stood there and let loving take me over. The act of loving was all that existed, and I remained immersed in it.

When I finally opened my eyes, the dark shape had gone.

Shura came out of the bathroom and I poured soup into two bowls and asked him to get a couple of soup spoons. We went into the living room, where I sat him down in a chair and explained that I was going to introduce him to television. Gradually, I said. Nothing too extreme. Something delightful and British called, "Upstairs, Downstairs," which it was absolutely necessary for him to see at least once.

He muttered a skeptical, "Hmmm," but didn't protest. Within a few minutes, he was enraptured, as I had hoped he would be.

I sat in my favorite couch corner and decided to think about the encounter in the kitchen for a while before telling him about it. I had learned something, but it would take some time to figure out exactly what.

Some parts of it are obvious. If you meet evil with hate, you lose. Hate belongs to the dark side. And yes, the temptation to oppose is a powerful force; it's immensely strong. You want to go at him, you want to hit, to strangle, to destroy. And all those emotions are his tools. So maybe the lesson is that if you really want to say No to what he represents, you refuse to enter the ring with him at all. You just become what he is not. Love. You become love. And when you do that, he's not there and he never was.

When Shura and I were in bed later, curling up together for sleep, I said, "Thank you for the 2C-B experience. It was quite extraordinary, and I'll write the whole thing up first thing tomorrow, I promise, and give you a copy for your notebook."

"Good girl," he said. We drifted into sleep with Mozart playing softly on the radio and the chatter of mockingbirds outside the bedroom windows.

CHAPTER 25. DRAGONS

There began a new order of things. Shura would phone during the week, almost every night, just to talk. He talked about trials he had participated in as an expert witness, describing the lawyers and the judges; he told me about university politics, about the heads of departments and the students he taught; he would tell me what he was doing in the lab, using chemical terms freely, knowing that I would get what he called "the music," if nothing else — he was well aware that I understood nothing at all about chemistry — and that I would ask for clarification when I needed it. He would, matter-of-factly, tell me what was going on with Ursula, according to her latest letter.

I would talk about the children, a book I was reading, a little about work — work was too hard, too pressured to talk about lightly, so I avoided saying much about it — and I would listen like an old friend to excerpts from Ursula's letters which detailed her problems and worries, locking myself into Shura's voice, reading the changes, the tension under the casualness. I was careful to say nothing sharp, nothing negative.

Then, close to the weekend, he would ask me if I would like to come out to the Farm when I was through work on Friday, and I would say I'd love to, as if it were a welcome surprise. Never take it for granted, I reminded myself, because it can stop in a moment, and it will, as soon as Miss Germany decides she wants another vacation in sunny California.

I began keeping a daily journal, writing to myself what I could not say to Shura.

On the bookshelf beside Shura's bed there was a stereo set which played radio and cassette tapes. We explored each other to music, usually classical. If we turned the dial and found ourselves in the middle of a piece of music we weren't able to identify immediately, we would compete to see who could correctly name the composer. Shura introduced me to Glenn Gould's recordings of Bach, and I brought him some Prokofiev treasures which he had somehow managed to overlook, and Bartok's "Miraculous Mandarin," which surprised and delighted him.

The long, beautiful legs became familiar to me. The small, rounded buttocks stirred me to admiration, which I expressed freely. His back was my playground, as I showed him what could be done with the tips of fingernails running lightly from thigh to neck; he shivered with pleasure as I smoothed out the gooseflesh with the palm of my hand and began all over again, up and then back down, on the front of his body this time. He did the same to me, expert with the first try, and chuckled as I responded.

Sometimes on a Friday or Saturday evening, we would take one of his psychedelics, then go to bed. He teased me about something I'd said to him a long time ago, to the effect that I couldn't understand how anyone could take a psychedelic drug more often than once every few years, because there was so much to assimilate, to learn, from one good experience. I laughed and reminded him that he was always telling me things change, life is change.

"So," I said, "I'm learning new things!"

"We both are," he replied.

We both were. Perhaps it was the sense that everything could end at any time, be over with; whatever the reason, we shared our experiences, even our sexual fantasies, each of us withholding only a little, feeling out each other's acceptance as we talked.

One Saturday afternoon in late spring, we each took 5 milligrams of Shura's infamous DOM, the drug he had told me about, that night in Hilda's study, which had been nicknamed STP on the street.

He said, "This is a very long-lasting material, babe. You sure you don't mind being in an altered space that long?"

I said no, I didn't mind, and besides, "You told me it can be a wonderful experience, when you take it at the right level, and I assume you'll give us the right level, and how long is 'that long,' anyway?"

"At least 12 hours, and probably more, depending on your chemistry, and you do tend to milk a lot of extra mileage out of these drugs, you know!"

I made a nyah-nyah face at him, "You're just jealous, because you come down before I do. It's one of the few advantages of having a slow metabolism; in fact, I can't really think of any others at all!"

Shura showered while I watched television, then I took my bath, watching the unmistakable undulating of surfaces and rippling of edges develop, keeping an interior eye on the strong energy tremor, observing the first-time anxiety as it mellowed out into trusting acceptance of the state and where it was going.

I rubbed myself dry with a towel and sat down on the toilet, still naked.

Shura had said to me, some time ago, "Don't ever lock a door behind you, please, inside this house. Not even when you're in the bathroom. I have a strong fear of having something happen behind a door that I can't open quickly; it's a left-over from Helen being sick, and I beg you to please observe it."

I had observed it, faithfully.

Now, there were footsteps in the hall and suddenly, the door opened. I gasped, "Hey!"

Shura, wearing his dressing-gown, stood grinning at me. As I frantically grabbed for my towel, he teased, "I thought we were going to have complete honesty in this relationship!"

"There are limits, Shura!"

"Limits? No, no! No limits agreed on," he laughed, kissing me on the mouth and fondling my breast before leaving. He closed the door behind him and I sat there, caught between outrage and amusement. Then, an uncomfortable thought occurred to me.

Is it possible he's one of those people who like to watch things like urination?

When I reached the bedroom, the bedside lamp was lending a soft, butter-yellow glow to the undulating cabbage roses in the ancient wallpaper. I scrambled onto the bed and sat cross-legged in my robe, looking down at Shura, who was stretched naked on the blanket, pink and shining from his shower, smiling at me. I asked him, doing my best to sound casual and light, "Are you one of those bathroom voyeurs, by the way, or are you just a tease?"

His hair and beard were throwing off tiny multi-colored sparks, "No, I'm not. And yes, I'm a terrible tease. I have a whole lot of secret fascinations, but that's not one of them. How about you?" Innocent face, wide blue eyes, looking at me. I assured him that kind of thing wasn't my cup of tea at all.

He asked me, "How is the experience, so far? Comfortable?"

"Yes, considering that it's — as you said — a pretty strong psychedelic and obviously not for naive and innocent people, I'm doing pretty well. Especially considering that I had to go through the shock of being — being *invaded*, you know? While sitting on the potty, yet. By the same trustworthy gentleman who asked me to please not lock any doors, would you believe!"

"I never said I was a gentleman, did I? Did I ever make that claim?"

I admitted he never had.

He fiddled with the radio dial, settling on something by Sibelius. Then he folded his arms behind his head and remarked, off-handedly, "Speaking of strange, dark fascinations — "

Uh-oh — this is going to be important.

He looked at me, "Have you ever, in your numerous experiences, been tied up or tied someone up, just to see what it felt like?"

I replied that I'd never done that, but I'd often had the fantasy.

He raised himself on one elbow, "Then why did you never do it?"

"I suppose probably because it would have to be someone I could be really vulnerable with, and there haven't been too many men I've felt I could trust that much. Besides, nobody I've been really close to ever brought it up, and I wasn't about to shock anyone by suggesting it first, believe me."

"Is it a shocking thing, really?"

He wants to be told it's all right to have that kind of fantasy.

"It isn't shocking to me," I replied, "It's what they call 'bondage,' isn't it? From what I understand, lots of people enjoy that. I read a very interesting article — I think in a psychology journal — that said a large number of the men who enjoy being tied up in love-making tend to be very powerful people with a lot of responsibility in their lives; people like judges and senators and doctors. It explained that they enjoy the feeling of being powerless, you know, with somebody they trust, because their lives are too full of decisions they have to make and be held accountable for, and being tied up allows them to ditch all that, to be able to enjoy the sexual feelings without having to be responsible for them."

Shura was silent for a moment, then said, "I've always wanted to know how it felt."

I thought about it, then said, "I remember seeing a clothesline in back of the house. Do you have any more of it around?"

"Sure, plenty."

"I hope you've got the nylon kind, because cotton clothesline is pretty rough, and I don't want to hurt you." I paused, then I leaned forward and squinted at him, "Or — do you like being hurt?"

"No, I don't."

"Me neither," I said, immensely relieved.

"Wait here," he said, "I'll be right back." He put on his bathrobe and left me in the bedroom with the music playing and the wallpaper roses moving. So far, I thought, this DOM is very nice. I was aware, off and on, of the energy tremor. It was still strong, but I was getting used to it.

Why aren't we always aware of this flow of energy in our bodies? Why does it take a drug like this to make it show itself? Maybe it would serve no purpose for us to be feeling it all the time.

Shura returned, carrying a tangle of white nylon cord. I laughed, "A gen-yu-ine Gordian Knot!" and we set to work to undo the mess.

We cut the cord into various lengths, giggling when we weren't humming along with Beethoven's 3rd Piano Concerto, then Shura proposed that we try it out on me first. I said okay, thinking several things at once. First, that it was going to be hard not to feel silly; second, that it was obvious Shura hadn't done this before, which meant he hadn't done it with Ursula; third, that this was something neither of us would consider doing with a companion we didn't trust absolutely.

If there's some unknown dark thing in either of us, this might well bring it out in the open — at least, we'd get a glimpse of it. It would have to be acknowledged, talked about.

The music had changed to our beloved Prokofiev by the time Shura had finished tying me. I looked up at him and tried to smile, feeling suddenly exposed and painfully shy. His eyes were shining, but his expression was more thoughtful than lustful, searching my face. Then he moved downward, and I closed my eyes.

Inside my head, Prokofiev flared blue-green and gold. I was distantly aware that my body was trembling and that I was being very loud. The world was a tunnel, spiraling down to soft darkness, then there was coming out of that far shadowed place — rising toward me with exquisite slowness — an immensity of petals unfolding, dark purple to blood-red, and as my throat opened in one long, final cry, a sear of light passed through my eyes and out the top of my head.

Shura quietly untied the bonds and lay down beside me, one leg over my thighs, his hand resting on my stomach, while my heartbeat slowed.

When I was breathing evenly again, I turned to him and whispered, "Thank you, love."

"I was with you, little one. I went with you."

After a while, I rose on one elbow and grinned down at him, "Now. Your turn."

Halfway through the business of tying him up, carefully, so that although he was secure, the nylon cord wouldn't bite into his wrists or ankles too much, I glanced at his face and found him watching me, and decided that I would feel a lot less self-conscious if he were blindfolded. I told him to relax, that I had to get something essential, and left the room. I found my shopping bag — the one in which I packed my clothes for the weekend — and took out the long silk scarf which I used to tie around my head after washing my hair. Back in the bedroom, I bound it around Shura's head, covering the eyes but leaving both ears free for the music.

He said, "Ahhh."

Looking down at him, I knew he was immersed in sensations he had only imagined until now. This was something he'd wanted to have, wanted to explore. On his face was the same seriousness, the same concentration you see in a small child when he unwraps the one Christmas present he most hoped for. I felt a surge of tenderness for him, and wondered what I would do when he was completely tied. I had no pattern to go by. I hadn't done much reading in these realms.

So, I'll go with instinct. Just be sure it's graceful.

We now had a Strauss waltz and, as I tied the last knot around the leg of the bed, I muttered my impatience and said I was going to search the radio dial for something else.

"Not the most erotic music in the world, is it?" He was finally smiling.

"Nope. Intolerable." I found another of our favorite stations, KDFC, and breathed, "Hooray!" It was Bach, and deliciously familiar.

"Well, well," I said, turning back to my victim, "The gods are smiling."

"It's one of the Brandenburgs," Shura said, contentedly.

He had told me, the first time we had made love in his bed, that he had very sensitive nipples, and that he loved having them touched. I hadn't asked him if he'd shared that with Ursula; it was reasonable to assume he had. I feather-touched them now, seeing them shrivel in a sea of gooseflesh. I closed my eyes. The Bach was a moving thread of silver against a background of blue and emerald, then I sensed other colors — orange and sun-yellow — pulsing from behind the music, coming swiftly toward me.

Masses of deep orange, edged with red, flooded my mind. I opened my eyes for a second to see Shura's head rising from the pillow as his body strained against the ropes, then Bach was drowned in a roar that echoed off the walls.

All right, this is what I want. It's all worth it — whatever it's going to be like, whatever is going to happen — just for this. Thank you, thank you, thank you.

We lay side by side, the nylon cords abandoned on the floor, with only the light from the radio dial to see by, and we talked about what it felt like, what it meant, to trust somebody that way.

Shura said, "It's an extraordinary thing, knowing that you have complete power over the other person, that you can hurt — misuse that power in some way, any way you want — and that you won't do it, don't choose to do it; that you can trust yourself, even the darkest corners of yourself, not to do something the rest of you doesn't want to do."

"Uh-huh."

"And then it's your turn to experience being helpless, and it's the other person who has to be aware of hidden dark impulses, and make those choices."

I murmured, "And you can only lie there, hoping they know themselves well enough."

"Yes," he said, "Yes. And yet," he paused, "I have to say, I didn't have any fear. I just knew."

That you could trust me. Yes. Of course you knew. Just as you know other things you won't allow yourself to be aware of.

I asked him if he'd ever seen the paintings of the German artist called Sulamith Wolfing. He said the name wasn't familiar.

I explained, "Most people know her work from the yearly calendars she puts out, and her old calendars from years ago are sold at exactly the same price as the current ones, because her fans will do anything to get their hands on her paintings — never mind the year. Her publishers finally put out postcards — in Marin County you can find them in all the bookstores. The picture that I love best, the one that moves me most, shows the head of a big, dark green dragon. Its mouth is open, and curled up on the big red tongue is a tiny baby, sound asleep."

Shura smiled.

"That's what our little experiment reminds me of," I said. "It's like bringing a beautiful fire-breathing dragon out of its cave and making friends with it."

"Walking the dragon," said Shura, "I like the image."

"Me, too."

He rose on his elbow, hair springing in all directions, and looked into my face, "Did you enjoy that as much as I did?"

"You know perfectly well I did."

Closing my eyes, I saw a multi-colored dragon with jeweled scales. Its wings were black, tipped with gold, and around its neck was a long brown dog leash, which — it assured me — it didn't mind at all.

CHAPTER 26. FUNGUS

One Friday, after I had cleared the supper dishes and we were sitting at the table with our wine, Shura told me about the letter from Ursula that had arrived the day before.

"She said she's getting really frightened by the way Dolph is acting; seems there are increasing signs of depression, and a couple of times he's flared up with an intensity she's never seen before. She told me she's had nightmares about Dolph killing them both. He's barely speaking to her now, apparently, except when other people are around, to keep up appearances."

Shura traced around the rim of his glass with a finger, "She said surely I could understand why she has to wait just a little while longer before she sits down and holds his hands and says the final goodbye and all that."

"It sounds bad."

"Yes," said Shura, "Not exactly new, but pretty bad."

I waited, knowing there was more.

"So, I telephoned Germany this morning," he glanced at me, "To urge her to get out of there, to just pack a few things in a bag and get out, not to take the chance of something tragic happening, not now, when she's so close to resolving the whole thing!"

I realized my mouth was gaping, and closed it.

Shura sipped from his glass, then continued, "Dolph answered the phone."

He certainly has an instinct for the dramatic pause, whether he's aware of it or not.

"Oh."

"I don't have to tell you what happened!"

I kept quiet.

Shura leaned back in his chair, throwing his arms wide, "My dear old friend, Dolph, his voice full of sunshine, positively bubbling with delight

that I was calling; how was I and had I seen the latest article on enkepha-
lins in Arzneimittel Forschung? When we'd talked about that for a couple
of minutes, he asked me did I want to speak to Ursula, and I could hear
him calling her to the phone, 'Darling, come quickly, it's Shura!'"

"Methinks I've heard something like this before."

"If he was acting, it was the kind that gets you all sorts of prizes in that
Hollywood operation — what's it called — ?"

I nodded absentmindedly, "Academy Awards — the Oscars."

"Whatever."

What's going on? What's happening in that house in Germany?

Shura's elbows were back on the table, "Then Ursula came to the
phone. She whispered to me that I shouldn't have phoned; things were
very sensitive, very precarious. I just went ahead and said everything I'd
planned to say. Pack your bag. Get out quickly. Get away. She said she
couldn't talk any more on the telephone, but she would tell me everything
in a letter. Then she said — still whispering — that she loved me and now
she must go, and goodbye."

I waited, not moving.

"So, what do we think?" He looked at me, his face expressionless.

I remembered Ben, sitting across from me in the living room, telling
me he thought it wouldn't be long now before Ursula moved to bring
things to some kind of closure. This wasn't any kind of closure; this was
crazy, and it was going on and on.

I replied, "We are reduced to a lot of guessing, as before."

Shura nodded.

*Something's got to be done. He can't keep living in this state of uncertainty
and misery. What's going on, for God's sake?*

After supper, Shura worked in his study. He told me he was completing
the first draft of an article he was going to submit to a new chemical
journal. We went to bed early, both of us tired.

Curled against Shura's back in the dark, I tried to open myself to what
was inside him, as he settled into sleep. Underneath the good humor that
remained from the past couple of hours, I sensed a dark knot of bewilderment and fear.

*What kind of woman is the Lovely Ursula? Is this her way of letting him
down gradually, weaning him from his hopes? Or is Ben wrong, and she's telling
the truth, and really intends to come and live here? Nothing explains the husband
sounding so warm and friendly, though. Unless Shura isn't as good at reading
voices as he believes he is. That's possible. Whatever's happening, it can't go on
this way much longer.*

The next morning, we began the day in Shura's preferred way, reading
the San Francisco Chronicle, in silence, with our coffee. He always began
the paper with the last section, working his way to the front; I read it from

front to back. He read quickly, barely glancing at some parts; I tended to read every word, except for the business and sports sections, which I usually ignored. When we were through, he sat back in his chair as I poured more coffee and said, "How would you like to try one of the great classic psychedelics today?"

"Which particular great classic psychedelic do you have reference to?"

"Ever heard of psilocybin? The magic mushroom?"

"Oh, yes, of course. I remember that wonderful article in Life magazine, years ago. Wasson? Was that his name?"

"Gordon Wasson, yes. You've never tried it, have you?"

"Never. I've been very curious about it."

"So — think you might venture?"

"Absolutely. I'd love to."

"I don't have the mushrooms themselves, but I do have some of the active ingredient, psilocybin," he said, "So you won't have to munch a whole lot of little dried things."

"Does the psilocybin by itself give you the full experience? I mean, the same as you'd get from the mushrooms?"

"Well, I've taken it both ways, in the form of mushrooms and as a white powder, and I find no difference at all in the effects. Although, of course, there are people who will swear that the natural plant gives the only true, genuine experience. I just don't find it so."

Shura remembered that he had to correct student exams, so we decided to postpone the mushroom world until evening, when all his paperwork would be completed. I spent the rest of the day in his living room, writing my own overdue letters on his typewriter.

At 7 o'clock, having bathed and put on our dressing gowns, we each took fifteen milligrams of a sparkling crystalline substance, dissolved in fruit juice, Shura noting the time on a slip of paper, as usual. Then we walked out to the lab, hugging ourselves against the evening chill, so that he could close down a chemical reaction he'd had going all afternoon, and put the lab to sleep for the night.

Inside the laboratory, I leaned against the door and spoke about something he had mentioned that morning.

"You know, I've been thinking over what you said earlier, about people who believe that if there's a psychedelic plant, you should only use the natural growing thing, not a synthetic form of the — what do you call it? — the active ingredient?"

"Yeah," said Shura, fiddling with stopcocks and flasks, "There's a very interesting and quite delightful person I know — you'll have to meet him someday — named Terence McKenna, who writes and lectures about sacred plants; it's his specialty, and he's an absolutely persuasive speaker on the subject."

"The name sounds familiar, though I can't remember where I've come across it."

"Well," continued Shura, "He believes, absolutely believes, that only in the plant itself can you find the particular balance of — well, I suppose you could say spiritual essences or influences — along with the actual chemicals, which go to make up the true experience that the plant — or, in this case, the mushroom — has to offer. He's absolutely adamant about the synthetic chemical not giving you the genuine thing. We've argued about it — in a friendly way, of course — for years."

"Well," I said, hesitatingly, "As a matter of fact, I have a lot of sympathy with that view, and I'd like to explore it a bit."

"Of course," said the alchemist in the brown dressing-gown, taking my arm and turning off the light, "Tell me. After all, how can I convince you of the error of your viewpoint unless I know what that viewpoint is?"

I stopped on the path to aim a symbolic kick at his rear. He ducked and took my arm again.

I said, "I know this sounds absolutely ridiculous to a scientist, but I was brought up believing something which I still believe, and that is that all growing things have some kind of — I don't know exactly what word to use — some form of consciousness attached to them. Not human-type consciousness, but a — a plant-awareness of some kind."

He opened the back door for me, as I continued, "Remember those experiments which proved — well, they seemed to prove — that plants react to human thought?"

"Carrots having nervous breakdowns when someone thought boiling water at them? Yes, I remember."

"Well?"

"Well, what?" Shura was going through the house, locking doors and closing windows, as I followed. "Do I think there's a possibility that plants have some non-physical level of awareness? Well, let me take the so-called scientific experiments first. I don't know the details of how the experiments were done, so I can't say much about them. I think I would have to be there myself, in the lab, before I could accept the findings without question. And even then — frankly, I tend to be skeptical. Scientists can fool themselves just like non-scientists, I'm afraid, especially when they have an emotional investment in a certain outcome."

I nodded. Shura came close to me, "Before we continue with this very interesting subject, I need to check on how you're feeling?"

"There's sort of a chill — kind of a variation on the energy tremor. It comes and goes."

"Any other effects?"

I went inside myself and explored for a moment, then reported, "Yes. I'm definitely off baseline. Gentle, but distinctly something."

Shura grinned.

"How's your level?" I asked him, and saw that his eyes were glowing as they always did when he was on.

"About the same, except that I don't have your little chill."

I smiled at him, "You're radiating, you know."

He laughed and squeezed my arm, "Let me take a moment to finish up the mess in the office — I've got things scattered all over the place. Would you mind if I left you on your own for just a couple of minutes?"

I told him I wouldn't mind at all, "As a matter of fact, I'd rather like to be by myself for a little while and pay attention to what's happening."

I sat comfortably on the couch with a glass of juice in front of me on the tiled table. There was soft light from a lamp on the bookcase to my left, and the sound system had been turned on from the back room so that I could hear the music; it was Brahm's Piano Concerto No. 2, which I knew by heart. Through the windows at the far end of the room I was able to see the two tiny lights, red and white, that marked the top of Mount Diablo, and I felt both peaceful and excited, waiting for the world to change.

I picked up one of the art books I had put out on the table earlier in the day, and settled back to look through it. The book was large and satisfyingly heavy, a collection of Goya's paintings and sketches, and I was aware, holding it on my lap, that I had slipped suddenly into one of those states which are among the most treasured gifts of the psychedelics, a moment which is endless, a sense of being in what has been described most simply and accurately as the Now.

There is no time, there is only the quiet aliveness of existing here, holding this book, sitting cross-legged on this couch, being the person who is myself, with the other person who is Shura — the complex and extraordinary human being to whom I have chosen to be tied, for however long or short a time — a few rooms away, but not separated from me.

I looked up from the book and saw a room totally transformed. I was sitting to the side of two rooms divided by what I knew to be the bookcase, but which now appeared as an ordinary wall separating the two halves of a native hut of some kind. Familiar objects which would identify this place as Shura's living room had been swallowed by the shadows. To the left of the dividing wall there was a chair which I had left there earlier, and thrown across it was a Guatemalan woven scarf, gleaming vividly in the soft light. I stared open-mouthed at the stripes of yellow and pale green, the panels of red and black, and wondered if the scarf had triggered the associations to a native hut in a strange land. I looked around me, locating the Chinese vase on its shelf, almost lost in the dark at the back of the room. I saw the bulk of the piano on the other side of the dividing wall and recognized the bookcases under the windows; everything was there, yet I couldn't shake the impression that I was in a native hut with a dirt floor, somewhere in Central or South America. I half expected to see an iron soup pot suspended over the logs in the little fireplace and strings of peppers drying in the corners of the room.

The world has changed, indeed, oh yes. How extraordinary. Like seeing a completely new dimension of this place.

As I looked around, allowing myself to accept the total strangeness, the shift from familiar to incomprehensibly different, I began to understand part of the change. I was seeing the room as if I had never been in it before, the way it would have appeared if I had just come through the front door for the first time and sat down on the couch in an unfamiliar, darkened place, seeing everything — rugs, fireplace, the beams of the ceiling, the gleam of windows, the chair — thrust into the stranger's perspective that regards every object in a new place as equally important, because there is no way of knowing the relative importance of anything.

Only living with the room will cause the mind to assign unconscious priorities and a resulting new perspective.

With familiarity, I thought, the mind tends to notice only certain pieces of furniture and ignore others. One moves past this or that table or chair without conscious thought — only the absence of a particular thing in the room will make one notice — and the attention is to those parts of the room which involve whatever action or concern one is busy with at the moment.

The little table near the front door is always noted in passing, because Shura and I use its top to stack various things that must be taken out of the house the next time one of us leaves — letters or parcels or books to be returned to the library. The piano and the bookcases don't invite conscious attention. They're simply there, and we ignore them as we pass through.

I decided that my original suspicion about the origin of the native hut association had probably been right; it had been triggered by the woven Guatemalan scarf. My unconscious mind had filled in the rest of the rich image, creating something recognizable out of a place which had unexpectedly presented itself as alien territory.

When Shura appeared in the doorway, I rose and went to him, and began explaining what I had been seeing. We went to the bedroom and Shura closed the door behind us to keep in the warmth.

When I told him I thought the scarf had triggered the native hut vision, he said, "That may be, but keep in mind that you know something about the history of the sacred mushroom, and it's just as likely that the look of the room was due to your associating psilocybin with that part of the world, Mexico or Central America; after all, you've read about Wasson's first experience, and it happened in a place that undoubtedly looked somewhat like what you saw, don't you think?"

I mulled that one over and admitted, "You're probably right."

We lay facing each other on the bed, still in our dressing gowns, and I glanced at the bedside electric clock and saw that not quite 40 minutes had passed since we'd taken the white powder. It seemed like several hours, and I remarked to Shura that there seemed to be a lot of time-slowing with this material.

"Yes, I've noticed that too," he said, then asked, "Are you at peace with it, so far?"

"Oh, my, yes. It's getting quite intense, though. Have we reached the plateau, or will it climb some more?"

"Oh, I don't think we've plateau'd yet. Still a little way to go, another 15 or 20 minutes."

I examined the friendly roses in the wallpaper and saw that they were moving gently. In the bookcase beside the bed, the books were dusty jewel-colored treasures, trying to say something, or perhaps just wanting to be noticed. Across from me, the face of the boy with white hair glowed from inside with life and humor and something close enough to love to fill the space inside me that sometimes ached.

I remembered what we had been talking about before.

"Okay," I said, "Back to natural and synthetic. Even though you might not accept without question any particular experiment with plants, or the conclusions those particular people came to — that plants have some kind of consciousness — is it absolutely inconceivable to you that a plant might have another dimension? Some kind of energy, if you want to call it that?"

"Of course it's not inconceivable," Shura said, "Everything that exists, not just plants, but rocks, animals — everything we see and everything we can't see, for that matter — is a form of energy, and there certainly are interactions of energy fields — but it's a considerable step from that to assigning some kind of personality to a plant, or the ability to pick up thoughts telepathically from humans. There's certainly no scientific basis for assuming anything like that."

I protested, "I didn't say anything about scientific proof; I just wondered if you can allow for the possibility of such a thing as every plant having a distinct, individual energy field of some kind associated with it? Something that might even be seen as a — well, you know how some people see what they call fairies or elves or gnomes — is it possible, in your view, that —" I floundered, not sure exactly what I was asking, then remembered what my original point had been. I waggled a hand in the air to indicate that I was still completing a thought.

Shura stayed quiet, watching me with only a suggestion of amusement in his face.

"All right, let me make this a statement, then," I said, sitting up cross-legged on the bed and trying to ignore the increasing excitement of the wallpaper roses, "I don't know if this is what your friend Terence believes exactly, but I do know that there are a lot of people in the world who believe that every plant has some kind of — I guess you could call it an entity — attached to it. So that, when you eat the plant, you're taking in that thing, the spiritual dimension, if you want, along with the purely physical stuff, and they probably believe that a synthetic drug doesn't have those other energies, dimensions. It's sort of like taking in just the physical part, the purely chemical part, which didn't come from the earth and has no connection to the earth, so it has no spiritual entity attached to it as a plant does. Do you understand what I mean? Those people feel that a synthetic chemical has no soul, I suppose you could say."

Shura lay back on his pillow and gazed up at the ceiling for a while, then raised himself on one elbow again, "Let me tell you something that might interest you," he said.

I nodded, and a roomful of prisms nodded with me.

"I can't speak for other chemists, but I know that when I'm working in the lab, putting together a new compound, I not only see it upside down, inside out and in three dimensions, in my mind, but I also sense other aspects of what is developing. You might say that a personality or, to use your term, an entity, begins to take shape as I work. I try to feel it out, to get a sense of whether it's friendly or not, whether it's liable to open up this area of the mind or that; does it have a dark nature which may mean I'm going to have to watch out for over-stimulation of the nervous system, or some other difficulty I can't anticipate?

"By the time the new compound is completely developed, ready to nibble, it has a personality. Not yet known, because I have to interact with it, my chemistry has to interact with a substance it's never had a relationship with before, but even though I can't define that new personality yet, it's certainly there. By the time I've explored the new compound through its active levels, its nature has become quite clear, and the 'entity' has accepted some of my inputs to its creation and its personality. I can say, without any hesitation at all, that every compound I've discovered and tried has a real character all its own, quite as distinct as anything supposedly attached to a growing plant."

I sat looking at him, astonished, then leaned forward to tell him, "That's the first time I've heard anything like that. I had no idea that sort of thing could happen in a lab. It puts a completely different light on lots of things. Did you ever explain that to your friend Terence?"

"No. I've never told anyone before. It's not the sort of thing one would consider including in a lecture to the New York Academy of Sciences, you know."

I laughed. Then I asked him if he didn't think the wallpaper was getting awfully active, even more than usual.

"I guess it is, now that I look at it, yes. How about you? Still together, body and soul?"

I said I was all right. "It feels very strong, very intense. Maybe I just wasn't keeping track of it while we were talking, but it's certainly catching up with me now!"

"Me, too. It seems to have taken a leap upward, from the last time we noted the effects."

Good Lord, this is really powerful! Everything is moving, waving, broadcasting meaningfulness of some kind.

I let my teeth chatter audibly as a strong shudder traveled through my body, "How about getting under the covers right now, maybe?"

Shura swung his legs off the side of the bed and took off his dressing gown. The skin of his left thigh rippled faintly, as if an electric current were flowing across it. I looked at the long, muscled back and the lovely, small, rounded bottom, but I wasn't quite enough at ease yet to reach out and stroke it. The energy tremor had become impossible to ignore. I dropped my gown on the floor and scrambled under the sheets where I lay, grasping Shura's hand, watching the tiny fans of rainbow color which crowded the ceiling.

I closed my eyes and held my breath in astonishment at the multitude of colored images filling the mental screen. I was standing on the floor of a mosque, looking up at arches painted with gold-edged designs.

I was aware of Shura throwing off the covers.

The two of us were joining in the net of light that covered the earth, adding ourselves, our emotions and thoughts, our experiences of each other's smells and tastes, to flavor the whole. In the slowing of time, each touch of hand and mouth was an act of beauty, an offering of our own livingness and power to affirm. We were saying Yes to ourselves, to each other, to being alive, and Yes was pulsing back to us.

How do we learn to make love? How do we know to trace brocade circles with our fingers on the beloved's skin, to say I Want with a stroke of ankle on thigh, to honor the beauty of curve and bone with hand and mouth. It's a language of body, and it opens with the opening of love in the heart and mind. It can't be explained. It teaches itself as you touch.

When Shura cried out, De Falla's Nights in the Gardens of Spain was playing.

After a while he attended to me. I saw far ahead a clear gemstone — it looked like a pale aquamarine — and, spiraling up from it, blue-white gems which gradually shaded to to mauve, then to violet, as they passed on either side of my head.

I felt the aura of the Grail, then a flood of exquisiteness roared toward me, and I was left floating in a sea of soft blue light.

I whispered, "Thank you," and lay beside him, my eyes still closed, breathing evenly.

Suddenly, I was rising off the bed, Shura beside me. We drifted upwards to the ceiling and passed through it, our heads emerging on the other side. We could move no further. Surrounding us was brown earth, and a few feet away I saw a dirt clearing in front of a small hut; I couldn't be sure whether there was more than one room in the deep shadows beneath the thatched roof. Around us, in what looked like the light of early morning, was an abundance of flowers and leaves. The air was warm. There were large yellow lilies, spotted with brown, and tiny scarlet blossoms on a thick vine that wound through and around a fence climbing the bank behind us. Tall clusters of dark green, broad-leafed plants were visible under overhanging trees and I glimpsed wooden baskets hanging from beneath the roof of the hut, spilling pink and white flowers. There was a smell of rich, moist soil and plants growing.

Shura and I were children, being allowed — for a brief moment — to poke our heads into a place that belonged to the grownups. My eyes were drawn to the left of the thatched roof where I saw an immense dark shape, still as rock, out of which rose the outlines of three great heads, silhouetted against the slowly lightening sky. I knew that I was seeing three massive bodies, seated side by side, watching us. I was filled with awe at the power, the numinous majesty of what was sitting there: I felt again like a child discovered trespassing on forbidden ground.

The Great Ones were looking down on our two heads with what I sensed was a mixture of benign amusement and fond impatience. The message came: that's far enough, little ones, and long enough. Now you will return to where you belong.

I found myself lying in the bed, gripping Shura's hand.

"Did you see it?"

"See what?"

"The three — Buddhas or Gods or whatever they were. You were there with me, you were right beside me."

"Tell me what you saw."

I told him, aware and not caring that my voice was shaking with tears. When I had finished, he pulled me to him and we were silent together until the music changed to something by Wagner; both of us simultaneously cried "Oh, no," and broke into laughter as he reached to change the station.

CHAPTER 27. SIBERIA

Shura and I were coming to know the dark sides of each other.

My problem was one which — I was beginning to realize — troubled a majority of humans on earth: I did not, at the very deepest level, believe in my own worth. There was a place in my soul where something fierce and strong lived, but I was in touch with it only in times of crisis and loss.

One of the few times the strong thing within me had spoken was when I finally discovered, after eight years of marriage, that Walter had a long-standing habit of falling in love with other women — often patients — approximately every six months, and that, moreover, he honestly could not understand or accept my anguished response when I found out. He told me, in all earnestness, "My relationship with (whoever it was at the moment) in no way affects my love for you and my bond with you." I tried a lot of vodka for a while to kill the pain. Then, one day, when we were driving to the market, the hidden lioness opened my mouth, and I heard my voice saying to Walter, firmly and matter-of-factly, that I wanted him to pack and leave the house immediately, and that I was going to file for divorce. He was quiet for a moment, then said — his voice rational and reasonable — that he thought I was being irrational and unreasonable.

But he left.

By that time, my already none too fabulous self-image was — not surprisingly — quite a bit further damaged. After I had spent some time nursing the certainty that I was ugly, in soul if not body, inadequate and generally unlovable (except of course to my children, who didn't know any better, bless them) the lioness thing — or whatever she was — finally roared inside me, one day, furious and passionate, declaring that if that's what I was, so then, that's what I was, and I would just have to get on with my life and make the best of it.

By the time the children and I moved to the A-frame house, across the street from Walter, the divorce was complete and I was able to look at myself in the mirror and believe that on the outside, at least, I was not too bad at all. But the self-image of basic worthlessness and uglitude remained — my sad, nasty little secret.

One of my ways of unconsciously buying favor and approval was to try to do whatever was asked of me by somebody I worked for or liked, whether I really wanted to or not. The inevitable result was often a job done less than enthusiastically, and occasionally badly.

Another way was to feed people. I brought enough food to the Farm every weekend to keep a small army advancing sturdily through a month-long Russian blizzard. Shura began to gain a little weight, and finally said that he liked to be able to feel his backbone through his navel, and would I stop cooking so much for him. I argued that he always finished whatever I put on his plate, and he replied, in exasperation, "I'm as greedy as the next person, and that's why I'd rather have less on my plate to tempt me!"

"Okay," I said, and began explaining, "Half of me is Jewish, remember, and that half is inclined to be a Jewish mother — in the nurturing sense, of course, not the horrid sense —"

Shura interrupted to say, curtly, "I still want less on my plate, please?"

I said, "Okay, sorry," and shut up.

The triangle situation I'd signed on for was ready-made for insecurity and self-doubt, and I often had to remind myself that it was I who had chosen it, that there had been no coercion by Shura, no half-truths, and little if anything withheld. We both knew the situation, and I had urged him to let me take this role, promising I would not cause him to regret it. I was an adult, responsible for my own decisions.

But sometimes it got to me — the knowledge that I was the fill-in, the second-best — and my deeper self, less amenable to clarity of reason and purpose than the rest of me, showed its anger and fear in strange ways, at unexpected moments, despite my determination to avoid any obvious signs of stress.

One evening at the Berkeley Repertory Theater with Ruth and George, during intermission, while everyone was lining up to buy snacks at the counter in the lobby, Shura asked me if I would like coffee, and I found myself in a state of total brain-fuzz; the simple question had splattered in my mind like paint thrown by Jackson Pollock.

I looked up at him and said, "Coffee. I don't know. I'm feeling awfully confused for some reason, out of place here, as if I don't belong."

The look he gave me could only be described as freezing, and he walked away. A few minutes later, he brought me a cup of coffee, black — the way he drank it, not the way I did — and all he said was, "Here," then turned and left me again.

I moved behind a column, embarrassment added to the scatter of other dark and sorrowful things which had chosen that ill-timed moment to surface. Hot liquid spilled on my hand and I felt awkward, clumsy and stupid. All I could think of was that Shura hadn't bothered to remember how I took my coffee; I didn't even mean that much to him. I took a shaky breath and gritted my teeth against the threat of tears, wondering if I was going to unravel completely in some unimaginable and appalling way, right there in front of all the nice theatergoers.

It didn't occur to me that I was undergoing a classic anxiety attack, and it's probable that the realization wouldn't have helped, anyway.

When we resumed our seats for the second act, Shura didn't reach for my hand as he usually did. I sat stiffly beside him, wondering how I was going to recapture my usual calm casualness and sense of humor.

We were both strained and careful for the rest of the evening, and at bedtime, we turned our backs to each other and went to sleep without the customary affectionate words and touches.

Much later, I understood that Shura hadn't been prepared to see me — without warning, in the middle of a pleasant evening at the theater — in such a state of pathetic confusion. I had sworn to him I would not be a victim, that I would not put him in the position of victimizer, if he let me become part of his life at this difficult, anxious time, and there I was, huddled like a lost waif against the lobby wall, looking at him beseechingly, piercing him with guilt. He had frozen and become distant, not knowing what else to do.

There were days when I found myself more than usually vulnerable, more sensitive to the wall inside Shura and the subtle emotional withholding that I understood and accepted intellectually, and feelings of inadequacy would flood me, thickening the air between us. At such times, he gradually withdrew, his face changing from open to defensive, then to hard and cold.

However, these incidents tended to happen at the beginning of the weekend, and after a night's sleep, I usually awoke with my courage and ease restored, and we could relax and laugh with each other for the rest of our hours together, before I had to leave for work early Monday morning.

Shura acknowledged and was critical of his own tendency to a particular kind of quiet arrogance, but I didn't find this aspect of him unappealing. It not only gave him a necessary strength, but was — in my view — the kind of elitism that many children born with very high intelligence learn to carry within them, if they are not to be crushed by the hostility of their peers when their gifts first become apparent in school.

Besides, as I told him, what he called arrogance might just as well be called self-validation, and as long as it never expressed itself in such a way as to make somebody else feel inadequate — and I had never seen that happen — it was a damned good thing to have.

I had come to know enough highly intelligent people in my life to understand what most of them had gone through, when they were too young to realize that the bright one is the enemy to his classmates, unless they had been lucky enough to be placed in a special school with others equally gifted. Most of them hadn't been that lucky. Some of them had been permanently scarred by these early experiences. As adults, they either continued to censor themselves, to speak diffidently, avoiding words or phrases which might reveal intelligence beyond the average, or they became — like Kelly — neurotically aggressive, confrontational, even insulting to many of the people they had to deal with. Either way, they were always aware of a sense of un-belonging, and lived with a deep-seated, ever-present loneliness.

Shura had not fallen into either trap. He had somehow learned or decided, by the time I met him, to be simply what he was, making no effort to hide any aspect of himself. By teaching, year after year, he developed patience, finding ways to make clear to his undergraduate students the concepts he wanted them to master. He told me that he knew it was up to him to find the words and the right way to put them together, and when a student failed to understand, he accepted the responsibility for that failure; it meant he hadn't taught well enough.

But there was a part of him that sometimes got angry and frustrated, and it emerged in a form I had no way of recognizing or preparing for. The first time it happened, it rang no alarm bells at all.

One weekend evening, after seeing a movie, we went to a small cafe and ordered cheeseburgers. While we ate, Shura told me he was seriously considering giving up his Farm and moving to some place in Northern California where nobody knew him and he had no ties to anyone. He explained, between bites, that he was tired of people, tired of everything, and thought it was time to pull up stakes and start a new life, probably keeping to himself for the most part, he added, so that he could avoid getting involved in other people's problems or imposing on them with his own.

I sat there and stared at him, wondering what had triggered such bitterness, hoping I was not included among the people he was tired of, but not daring to ask. I was very disturbed at the thought that he might actually sell his beautiful place and go away, and said so. He shrugged and changed the subject.

When we talked on the phone later in the week, nothing further was said about such a plan or intention, and I eventually dismissed it as a brief mood of sadness and anger which had passed and didn't have to be taken seriously.

The next time it happened, many weeks later, the strangeness lasted three days, and came close to being a disaster.

I arrived at the Farm one Friday, and it was immediately apparent that something was wrong. After an abrupt greeting, Shura turned away, informing me that he had a great deal of work to do at his desk and I would have to take care of myself for a while. I assured him I would be fine, wondering to myself what was wrong.

While I prepared dinner, Shura would occasionally stride through the house, silent, his face grim, as if everything he saw, including me, was somehow wrong, wrong. His few words to me were stilted, excessively polite, and there wasn't a trace of his marvelously wicked sense of humor.

We ate in silence. I sank into a state of profound misery, certain that he was through with me, that my faults had driven him to total exasperation, and that he was about to ask me to get out of his life.

After clearing the table, I said in a soft voice that I was going to wash the dishes and watch television and relax, while he got his work done. He nodded and took his wine into the study.

I didn't question the sudden change of personality; I took for granted that I was the cause of whatever negativity he was feeling. After cleaning up, I sat at the dining room table, hands folded tightly in my lap. When he came out of his office and passed through the room, ignoring me, I said, hesitatingly, to his retreating back, "Have I done something to make you angry, Shura?"

"No," he answered, curtly, and continued on his way.

Of course, I didn't believe him.

More than an hour later, I finally got up the courage to go to his study and face whatever had to be faced. I stood just inside the door, hands clasped before me, humbly waiting.

When he looked up from his desk, it was to speak in a voice tight with anger, "I'm so sick, sick, of being the one who has to solve everything for everybody. I'm sick of being the candy-man, the one who busts his ass in the lab to create new materials, new tools for exploring the human mind and how it works, while everyone around me only wants another trip. Nobody cares one whit about real research, real investigation, real work in this area. Nobody else wants to go to the trouble of writing and publishing what they've discovered through the use of these drugs. They just look to me to turn them on, give them goodies. Not a single one of them cares about me, just me, for my own sake. It's the candy-man they love, not Shura Borodin."

I stood there, stunned. It was the most appalling self-pity, and completely unlike him.

I stammered, "Of course, you have a lot of responsibilities, you do a lot for people, but you must know your friends love you deeply, Shura, candy or no candy! You can't really believe what you're saying, all this —"

"Yes, I do believe it," he shouted, banging his desk with a fist, "I know it!" He lowered his voice and continued, "I fool myself most of the time into thinking there's real love and caring, but it's all a pathetic delusion, and it's time I faced it. It's time I gave all this up and moved to a different place. I'm going to sell this house and move to the north, where nobody knows what I do, and I'll start over, away from all of you. I'm not even going to tell anybody I'm going. I just won't be around, one day, and everyone will have to take responsibility for themselves. I won't be there to solve all their damned problems."

Whose damned problems has he been solving; what's he talking about?

I ventured a bit further into the room, not daring to sit down yet, because I suspected that all this was actually some kind of displacement of anger at me, or anger at himself for having kept me around, for being too weak to wait for Ursula without the distraction and comfort of being with another woman.

I asked again, "Have I made you angry in some way?"

"Well, you haven't been much help," he said, glaring at me, "You leave things all over the house; there's junk everywhere that you never seem to take care of. I know I'm not the neatest person in the world, but when I have to face your mess as well as my own, it's just too much, too much! I need some order in my home, otherwise I simply cannot function. And — while we're on the subject of what's making me angry — you insist on bringing too much food here, no matter how often I ask you not to. I don't usually say anything about any of this, because your insecurity makes me feel I have to treat you with kid gloves, or you'll come apart at the seams."

I stood, turned to stone, looking at the flushed, angry face.

He went on, grimly, "I should never have allowed you to do this to yourself — this ridiculous situation with me and Ursula — and I blame myself for letting it all go on, to the point where it's going to cause a lot of pain all round. Stupid, stupid! It's an impossible situation and I've been stupid to let it happen." He struck his forehead with an open hand, and I turned and left the room, closing the door behind me very quietly, my chest and throat clogged with tears.

We went to bed without speaking to each other. Shura had been drinking a lot of wine, and fell asleep immediately, while I stared into the darkness, crying silently until I was too exhausted to resist the pull of sleep.

The next day, I stayed in the living room, knowing that I should pack my things and leave, even though it was only Saturday. I kept hoping that Shura would come in and say everything was all right, that I could stay, that he wanted me there. He didn't. I could hear him, now and then, slamming out of the back door on his way to the lab, and I huddled on the couch and cried, hope dying, angry at him for his incredible unfairness, hating myself for being at fault, loving him, wondering what to do.

I knew he was right, that I had done so many things to cause him to lose patience. I was disorganized, self-indulgent, essentially lazy, careless, and yes, depressingly insecure. The insecurity was understandable, certainly, but it was a burden he shouldn't have to carry.

Once, when I heard him in the kitchen, opening the refrigerator, I thought of making him lunch, but after what had been said, and what I suspected he had not yet expressed of his resentment, I didn't dare. I tried to read, but couldn't. Everything we had been to each other, with each other, was over. The graceful ending I had planned when Ursula arrived to stay, the dignified, loving closing of the door, the final closing — if it turned out to be final — was never to happen. Instead, it was all ending with me as a swollen-eyed, hurt, bewildered victim who didn't even have the courage to gather her things and go, as he was obviously waiting for me to do.

It was dusk when Shura came in and sat down in the armchair, and tried to tell me what was going on, as best he could.

"I'm sorry, Alice. You've just had your first glimpse of an aspect of my world that I can't explain. It happens sometimes, this strange state of mind, and I don't know what triggers it. It's like a dark thing inside me that takes over. I feel completely alone, and I can't believe in anybody or anything; I lose all feelings of trust. There's only anger, at everybody — myself most of all. Everything I'm doing, everything I plan to do, seems suddenly pointless, meaningless. I hope you'll be able to sit it out and forgive whatever I said that might have hurt you. I do get annoyed at you, sometimes, as I'm sure you do with me, but my intention was not to undermine you, wound you, and I'm very grateful — or I would be if I could feel gratitude — well, some part of me is grateful that you stayed. That's all I can say."

I sat, looking at the blur of his face in the shadows, able to see only the shine of hair and beard. I was in a state of shock, thoughts and emotions tangled in a confusion of fear, grief and shame, still expecting a final dismissal.

Only the Observer was keeping track. It slowly got its message through, informing me that I didn't have to leave, that this morning's explosion had not been ultimate truth-telling, that it was time I stopped crying. Act with dignity, it said; get up and go over to him, but don't touch.

I rose and went to the hassock, where I sat a few inches from his knees and said, "Are you still in this — this darkness — now, or is it over with?"

"No, I'm afraid it isn't over with yet. Bear with me, please. I would appreciate your company, even though I probably won't have much to say, for a while."

His voice had an unfamiliar dullness to it.

This is called depression. This is unquestionably acute depression. But right

now, I keep my mouth shut.
"Would it be all right if I got you something to eat?"
Shura's head thudded against the back of the armchair and he cried, "Oh, for God's sake, I'm not going to bite! You don't have to be so damned tentative; it makes me feel like a monster!"
"Sorry. I'll get you a bit of supper."
I escaped into the kitchen and put a couple of frozen dinners into the oven, then went to the bathroom and combed my hair and put a little lipstick on — Shura didn't like makeup of any kind, so I used just enough to take the pallor out of my mouth. There was nothing I could do about my eyelids or the redness around the eyes. I looked drawn and ugly to myself, pathetic and not in the least appealing.
Dinner was silent again. When I stole a glance at Shura's face, he no longer seemed angry; he looked sad and far away.
He thanked me politely for supper and excused himself to go to his office and finish some letters. I said I would watch television for a bit, or read, and that I would be perfectly fine on my own. We both knew it was best that we continue being apart for a while.
When Shura was in his office, I washed the few dishes and cleaned every surface in sight, moving quietly so that he wouldn't hear sounds and come out to see what was going on; I didn't want him to feel more guilt at having said so much about tidiness.
When the cleaning was finished, I turned on the television and went around the living room picking up my things. I hung my coat properly in the closet behind the front door, gathered my art pad, paints and brushes together, packed them in the shopping bag I'd brought them in, and put the bag next to the couch.
Then I sat and focused my eyes on the television screen. I saw and heard almost nothing, my thoughts scrambling in an effort to organize information. After a while, I noticed that my breathing was uneven and my body tense, almost rigid. I deliberately relaxed my muscles and rotated my head to ease the tightness in neck and back.
When Shura came to call me to bed, I was already in my robe, teeth brushed, hormone pills swallowed, my hair combed again. In bed, there was no attempt at lovemaking. He put his arm around my shoulders and drew my head onto his chest. We fell asleep listening to Stravinsky's sad, wistful Petrouchka on the radio.
By the time I left for work on Monday morning, the worst of it seemed to be over. When he phoned me on Tuesday evening, his voice carried the usual enthusiasm and there was no doubt that his sense of humor had returned in full force.
I eventually gave these eruptions of Shura's dark side my own name: The Siberian Wastelands.

A long time later, I had a talk with Theo, who supplied some of the missing pieces. He told me that these episodes had been going on ever since he was a small boy. They always began the same way, he said. If there were any dishes in the sink which had not been washed, his father would suddenly start washing them. "Usually," said Theo, "Dad left dishes and cleaning to my mother, and when you're around, he leaves all that kind of stuff to you, right?"

"Sure," I said, "He takes care of basic tidying up when he's alone, but when I'm here on weekends, I do it. He certainly doesn't seem compulsive about any of it, normally."

"Exactly," said Theo, "A few dirty mugs and forks don't bother him, except when one of these attacks is starting. I learned very early that, whenever I saw Dad at the sink, washing dishes and scrubbing the counters with that intense look on his face, it was time for me to take to the hills. I just split, went out to the barn or up on the hill, keeping out of his sight until it was supper time and I had to come back in the house." He laughed.

I wondered to myself if Ursula had ever been around when the Wastelands struck.

The next time that Shura went into his attack of depression and anger, many months later, I had an inspiration. I asked him if he would take MDMA with me, and he agreed, while making clear that he thought it a pointless experiment.

Within forty minutes, his tense, angry face had cleared and he was sitting in his armchair, smiling at me. A few minutes later, he held out his arms and demanded that I come over and sit on his lap, right now, pronto, immediately.

Siberia had been defeated.

I knew it was not a resolution of the conflicts his psyche was dealing with, but there was no question that MDMA was effective against this particular form of shark attack from the depths.

Shura still occasionally let loose his dark side when he'd had a large amount of wine, indulging in elaborate sarcasm and sharp-edged teasing, but the Siberian Wastelands never overtook him in the old way again.

Eventually, I discovered — quite by accident — how to defuse the occasional wine-released nastiness. One evening, when he had been honing his verbal fencing skills even more aggressively than usual, at my expense, it struck me suddenly that the whole attack had slipped over the line from clever thrusts to ridiculous overkill — and I started laughing. I laughed until I was doubled over, and when I regained some control and straightened up, a glimpse of Shura's astonished face set me off again. It was a losing battle for him; he sputtered, chuckled a few times, then gave in, howling with laughter, until we were holding onto each other for dear life — weak, gasping and feeling absolutely wonderful.

CHAPTER 28. A WORLD OF LIGHT

It was a Thursday evening in late spring when Shura called to tell me that a long letter from Ursula had come in the mail.

"Ah," said I, settling cross-legged into my armchair. *She Who Listens. She Who Waits.*

He said, "There's the usual stuff about Dolph still being very unstable, and she says she's handling it by being loving and gentle, and she feels he's gradually getting used to the idea of her leaving, and that by the time the day comes, he'll have recovered his self-respect, and his perspective."

I murmured sympathetically, feeling terribly sorry for Dolph.

"In the meantime, she told me that I shouldn't worry, that she knows him very well, and there's no way she would let the situation turn into some sort of tragedy. I guess that's in response to my pleading with her to pack up and get out right away, and all that."

"Yes, of course."

"I'm just giving you the general mood of it, you understand."

"Sure," I replied. "But, you know, I can't help wondering if she isn't running a risk of — uh — isn't there a possibility that Dolph could keep her there indefinitely by continuing to be miserable? I mean, he might do it unconsciously, but if his suffering keeps her there, why would he have any incentive to feel better or get adjusted to anything?"

"I guess that could happen," Shura said, "But at some point, she's going to have to say, 'Okay, this is it; I'm going, I wish you well, I'm sorry, goodbye,' or something along those lines. No matter how lovingly she says it, eventually the words will have to be said."

"I suppose."

"Besides," said Shura, "What it comes down to is that she's the only one who can handle the situation; even if I were there, I couldn't do it for her. So I have to leave it to her instincts and assume she's going about it the right way, unless and until events prove otherwise."

"Yes. That's all you can do."

Shura went on, "I kept the good part for last. Ursula said something that makes me feel a lot more hopeful. She finally got all of her books packed in a big shipping trunk and it had just been sent off by surface, the day before she wrote the letter. There's no way of knowing how long it'll take to get here — it's coming by sea, of course — but at least it's on its way."

I said, "That's good to hear," and made it sound convincing.

Jesu Maria san Roman!

"She said she knew this was the kind of news I'd been waiting to hear," said Shura, "And I have to admit, I'm very relieved. I hadn't been aware, until I read that part, how many little doubts have been accumulating during the past few weeks —"

"Well, you've been getting an awful lot of vague promises up to now; this is a lot more tangible."

There was a cold knot in my gut.

A trunk full of books sailing across the briny deep, bloody damn. She's serious. I've been fooling myself, believing Ben was right. Wanting to believe he was right. But books — books are real. You don't send your books unless you mean business.

Shura was saying something about having the research group at his house again, next Saturday. This time, he said, I would have a chance to meet the two members who lived farthest away, in the Owens Valley area, about two hours' drive from Death Valley. He asked, "Have you ever been to Death Valley?"

Put aside Ursula. Go with what's now.

"No," I replied, "I've wanted to see it for years, but haven't had the chance yet."

"That's a place you absolutely must see! One of the wonders of the world, like the Grand Canyon and the Tower of Babylon."

I grunted, "Babel."

He tsk'd, "You're confusing the Hanging Gardens of Babel with the Leaning Tower of Babylon. It's a common mistake."

Despite the heaviness in my chest, I smiled, "You're right, of course. Silly of me. Always get them mixed up."

"That's all right," Shura said, soothingly, "I've been known to make mistakes, too. Made one in 1947, in fact. Remember it to this day."

I couldn't help it; I laughed.

He's trying to make me feel better. Okay. I'm feeling better.

"Anyway," he continued, briskly, "Dante and Gemina Sandeman live in a little town called Gold Tree. They moved out there several years ago and built a terrific house with the mountains as a backdrop and coyotes howling them to sleep at night — wonderful place. I've known them for a long time and love them both dearly."

"I look forward to meeting them."

This is ridiculous. I'm going to be getting to know new people and I'll probably like them, then Ursula sweeps in and I vanish from the scene. It makes no sense.

"By the way," Shura was saying, "Nobody calls her Gemina. She's known as Ginger, and she has the hair and personality to match."

"You mean, a redhead temper?"

"No, no, I wasn't thinking of temper, although she has a perfectly good one. I meant a sort of energy and — ah — spunk, I guess you'd call it. She's quite a gal. Dante — well, when you get out here on Friday, I'll fill you in."

"Okay," I said, "Dante and Ginger. Those names, even I can't forget!"

I went to my job at the hospital and did what had to be done at home. I was in a state of mental suspension, freezing out as best I could all speculation, hope or fear. I hugged the children and remembered to smile, but occasionally caught them looking at me curiously, as if sensing something wrong.

Friday evening, having seen them off to their father's house, I packed my car with the makings of a big salad, as requested by Ruth, who was in charge of organizing the food for the day. There were hard-boiled eggs, tomatoes, avocadoes, small green onions, three kinds of lettuce and, just in case, two bottles of salad dressing: Thousand Island, which Shura liked, and a good Italian. This time, I didn't have to worry about bringing too much, since there were going to be lots of people.

Shura greeted me with a bear-hug and kissed me on the mouth. He was obviously feeling fine. I resolved to ignore the trunk of books sitting at the bottom of my stomach, and act as if only the present were real, and only this weekend mattered.

When I made a remark, during the evening, about nine people coming the next day, Shura said, "Actually, there'll be ten. You've heard me mention David Ladder, the young chemist who comes out here once a week to work with me in the lab? We've done a great deal of publishing together, and I consider him to be as good a chemist as anyone I know, a lot better than I am in many respects."

"The name's familiar, yes. Is he coming tomorrow?"

Shura nodded cheerfully, "He's been busy with grant-writing for the past few weeks, trying to keep his laboratory funded, and he's finally got it all done. That means we're actually going to have the full contingent, the whole research group. The only time that happens is when the Sandemans make the trip back here to see relatives or the latest grandchild or whatever."

"Tell me about David."

"Sure," replied Shura, "I've known him for years. He's in his late thirties, though he looks barely drinking age, except for the grey in his hair. Father's a psychiatrist — Freudian trained, to anticipate your next question — a good-humored, rumpled, friendly man. It's a large family. His sister, Joanna, plays cello professionally; wonderful cellist, truly a joy to hear. Two brothers, both mathematicians. David's the only chemist in the bunch. What else do you want to know?"

"How does he get on with his family?"

"As a matter of fact, they all seem to genuinely like each other, from what I've seen over the years. They're pretty close-knit, do a lot of things together. David seems to enjoy the family stuff; he thrives on visits from baby nephews and birthday celebrations — all that kind of mess."

I put supper on the table and sat down.

Shura continued, "David's a quiet person, somewhat introverted — I suspect he inherited some shyness genes from his mother. But there's nothing shy about him in the lab. He loves chemistry, even more than I do. I can get pretty enthusiastic about other things — I can see myself having become a writer or musician — but I really don't know what David would do without a lab somewhere. It's a major part of his world, his vehicle for self-expression. Of course, music's part of his world, too. But chemistry is his true and abiding love."

"Is he married?"

"No," Shura sighed, "He lived with a girl for a couple of years, but it went sour. She probably got tired of playing second fiddle to chemistry journals! We don't talk about it. He's a very private person, and when he comes over here after work — usually Wednesdays — we just dive into our world of weird nytrostyrenes and strange sulfur perfumes and we talk mostly about what we're doing and how we're going to write it up — and nasty gossip about other chemists, of course."

Sounds like a father-son relationship. Whatever it is, it's important.

"David's one of the world's few totally honest people," continued Shura, "He has complete integrity in the scientific area, and I can't say that about many of the scientists I know. It's not that there's intentional dishonesty or fudging of data or picking and choosing what's to be presented; there are very few who actually cheat in the lab. It's more a matter of judicious compromise, with far too many of them, especially those funded by the government. Sad to say, there's almost nobody working in the academic area these days who *isn't* funded by the government, directly or indirectly!"

I asked, "What kind of compromise, and why?"

He said, "The problems that you look at, the questions you try to answer, are the ones presented by your source of funds, and the answers you give back are often phrased in a way best calculated to keep that source happy with you."

"You mean, there are lots of scientists who'll only present results that are pleasing to their — their money source?"

"Not lots, no," Shura waved his hand, "And there are many shades of grey. There are a few who will only report what is wanted by their bosses, and there are a few who report exactly what they see, even if it conflicts with currently accepted social philosophies. The remaining 99% are scattered in between. David is at the extreme that represents complete integrity."

I hope David likes me.

When we'd finished eating, I poured Shura a glass of red wine and myself some white. I asked, "By the way, what are you planning to give us tomorrow? We are taking something, aren't we?"

"Well, whenever Dante and Ginger are here, we like to celebrate by doing something special."

"Ah-ha!"

"And it occurred to me that we might try a real challenge, if everyone feels comfortable with the idea. They've all had mescaline in the past — that is, all except David — and I'm going to propose that we try it at a higher level than any of us has had before, with five hundred milligrams as the upper limit. That'll be for the hard-heads, of course."

In bed, after a couple of half-hearted attempts at love-making, we acknowledged it was a lost cause, curled up together and went to sleep.

The next morning, over our coffee, Shura told me more about Dante Sandeman. "He retired from a job in broadcasting, a few years ago. You'd think that sort of background would produce a certain amount of street-smarts, maybe even cynicism, but not in his case, it didn't. He's one of the world's most trusting souls; he tends to have faith in people, believe what they tell him. Most of us who've managed to live beyond 25 or 30 have got some cautionary little voice that says, 'Hold it, watch it. Is this person genuine; is he really what he seems to be?' Right?"

"Uh-huh."

"Not our Dante." Shura paused, sipped coffee, then amended, "I don't mean to exaggerate the innocence aspect. He's a very astute guy, intelligent, observant; it's just that he's inclined to take people at their word. Needless to say, he's been burned a few times."

I said, "He sounds like a basically good man, your Dante."

Shura settled back in his chair, "There was a notorious figure in the '60's, a wild character, complex, very shrewd, and totally without conscience, called Bill Proctor — William Shelley Proctor — who regarded himself as the Johnny Appleseed of LSD. He loved to turn people on, and he turned a *lot* of people on, in his time. Despite everything else you could say about him, I have to allow him one thing: he was the first person, as far as I know, to recognize the value of LSD as a spiritual opener, and he was adamant and vocal about his belief that everybody — or almost everybody — should have the experience. And he certainly did his level best to contribute to that goal, believe me."

"How did he talk them into it?"

"Bill Proctor's approach was to challenge somebody he thought would be a good candidate, really bully him into going into the desert — he believed that the desert was the best place for a first time — and he'd hit the guy with about four hundred mikes.

"You haven't had LSD, I know, but you can take my word for it: four hundred micrograms is one hell of a way to be introduced to altered states of consciousness. Anyway, he managed to get away with it, because apparently everyone he turned on found it an immensely rewarding experience. Nobody ever sued him or arrested him or took a gun and plugged him. Of course," Shura chuckled, "Some of us did occasionally tease him — you know, 'Hey, Bill, what did you do with the bad trips, huh? How many bodies are out there in the sand dunes, Bill?' But the truth is, I think he actually managed to initiate a lot of people very successfully."

"But he wasn't a good person? You said he was —"

"Good? He was a con artist! He was always coming up with some scheme or other to get money out of people, and he persuaded Dante to invest a lot of money in some kind of scam, and then — well, suddenly the whatever-it-was had fallen through for all kinds of elaborate reasons, and Bill was riding off into the sunset, presumably with his loot intact, leaving Dante — like many before him — wondering what the hell had hit him. The full story is more involved than that, of course, but that's essentially what happened.

"He was one of a kind; he'd turn up at parties in a policeman's uniform — God knows what part of his past that belonged to, if any — and he'd strut around with a gun in his belt, playing the role to the hilt. He was an amazing character. It was fun just to watch him operate, if you knew what he was. Not much fun if you got conned. Dante still doesn't like to talk about it."

"How he could be a good user of LSD," I asked, "And know about the spiritual dimension — all that sort of thing — and still be a crook? I don't understand."

"Then it's time you did. Psychedelic drugs don't change you — they don't change your character — unless you want to be changed. They enable change; they can't impose it. Proctor liked being just what he was. He enjoyed himself immensely. He loved being the big honcho spiritual guide with his LSD initiations, and he certainly enjoyed the admiration and gratitude of the people he took through those trips. I have to assume that some other side of him — a side the rest of us never saw — came into play during those desert sessions, because the people who went through them with Bill Proctor really worshipped the guy.

"LSD couldn't give him a conscience, because he had no use for a conscience, and it didn't make him humble or truthful, for that matter, because he didn't need humility in his life, and truth was a very flexible commodity, to be used only when it was in his own best interests to do so. No, Proctor was perfectly content being just the way he was. However, he did get a bit of a comeuppance, finally, in a very funny way."

"What happened?"

"He became very paranoid, sometime in the '70's, and got it into his head that somebody was going to bust down his door and confiscate his stash of LSD, which was a considerable stash, believe me. So he went out to Death Valley, which was his favorite place for LSD trips, and he buried the bulk of his supply at the base of a specific fence post, out there in the desert, in some godforsaken corner where the tourists don't wander. Then he went home.

"Anyway, he finally got over his paranoid fit and returned to the desert, about a year later, to dig it all up. And couldn't find the fence. Of course, it might have been buried by blowing sand; in Death Valley, a lot of things disappear that way. Anyway, he searched and dug and kept searching and digging, off and on for weeks. He never found his LSD cache again. So somewhere — somewhere out there in the shifting sands of Death Valley — is a king's ransom — or what used to be a king's ransom — in the form of LSD. Probably never be found!" Shura chuckled, adding, "By this time, it's probably worthless anyway. LSD is very sensitive to heat and light, and Death Valley is one of the hottest places on the planet!"

I laughed, "Wonderful, wonderful. Has anyone else tried to find it, do you know?"

"Never heard of anyone making the attempt. Not too many people knew the story. Have to give him credit, though — he told that one on himself. He died a few years ago, and the world has been marginally safer since. An interesting person. And part of Dante's past which he's not yet come to terms with. It still hurts him, to think that he was taken in so badly, that he mis-read another human being so completely. Even the fact that he was far from the only victim of our Bill doesn't help too much."

So what do you have to do, to avoid being taken in or conned? You have to be very experienced. You have to trust your own intuition. And you can still get fooled.

About Ginger, Shura said, "She's got marvelous energy; she's down to earth, warm, generous. She puts up with Dante's — I don't know what you'd call them — times when he gets depressed and uptight and finds fault with everything, with her and most of all with himself, and I think they've weathered some bad times in the marriage because they've learned to use the psychedelics to help them talk things out honestly with each other and to get some insight into their own emotional baggage, or whatever has been making things bumpy between them. They're both good hearts, good souls. After all, it takes an essentially honest and good man to believe in others as much as Dante does — or used to."

"Yeah," I said, "I was just thinking that people who trust are usually trustworthy, and they tend to project that quality onto others. Better to be that way, I think, than the opposite, even if it means getting hurt at times. Too many cynical, suspicious people in the world, as it is."

"Well," said Shura, "Dante's less of an unquestioning believer now than he used to be, but he's still the kind of person you'd trust with your life. I would, anyway."

I smiled.

He went on, "Ginger is a superb painter, by the way. She began painting only a few years ago — watercolors. They live in the high desert — beautiful country — and she paints what she sees around her."

Maybe I'll get back to my own painting someday. Not enough time or energy, right now. No. That's an excuse. If I cared enough, I'd find a way to do it.

Shura said, "They're both seasoned travelers, Dante from way back. He was one of the founders of a place called The Institute for Consciousness Exploration, or something like that, way back in the '50's, in Berkeley, when LSD was still legal — or at least not illegal. Ever hear of it?"

"I remember hearing about a clinic where anyone could go and spend a day under LSD, for $25, I think it was, and somebody who knew the territory would sit with them and take care of them through the experience. It was in Berkeley."

"That's the one," Shura said, "They did some groundbreaking work there, especially with alcoholics, and they were starting to get a good deal of attention in the medical community, when the law was passed making any research with LSD illegal unless controlled by the government. Of course, if anyone applied to the government, they found it next to impossible to actually get permission to do anything, any real research in humans, any kind of therapy. In the meantime, as we all know," Shura's voice had an edge to it, "LSD went underground and hit the street, and it was available to every hippie and college student who wanted to take it. Of course, everybody did want to take it, because — as they all said — if this stuff was banned by the government, it had to be worth trying; it *had* to be good!"

I nodded, "I wondered what happened to that place, the institute. I knew someone who worked there a few times, a woman psychiatrist who did volunteer work as one of the guides, and she told me a fascinating story about something that happened to her. Maybe I can share it when

Dante is here. He must have known her."

By 10 o'clock, Ruth and George had arrived. The sky, which had been clouded the night before, showed clear and blue. It was a good day for an experiment, I thought. It was going to be warm outside.

Next through the door was John Sellars, and a few minutes later, Ben and Leah Cantrell came in with two people I assumed were the Sandemans.

I smiled at the sight and sound of Shura being his extrovert-self. He always greeted his close friends with a shouted "Ho!" hugging hard and lifting the women off the floor. In a public place, he would sometimes omit the lifting part.

Dante was not a tall man, but he was muscular, built like a boxer, and I was to discover that he kept himself in shape by hiking with Ginger, several times a week, often up the slopes of Mount Whitney, which was near their home. The balding top of his head was tanned and freckled, but the sides showed plentiful grey hair. His triangular face was lined deeply between nose and mouth, the effect being one of great good humor mixed with traces of pain. His smile was wide and open, while his eyes, under bushy, sand-colored brows, held an expression more anxious than curious. He shook my hand firmly and said in a voice that cracked a little at the edges, "I've heard so much about you, Alice! What a pleasure to finally meet you!"

Who told them about me? Shura, or someone else in the group? Wish I knew what they said. Wish I knew what all of them feel about me. Never mind. Never mind. Insecurity rears its bloody head. Just be who I am, let the rest go.

Ginger gripped my hand in both of hers and said, "Hello! It's about time we got to see the real thing!" She was almost as as tall as her husband, with red hair cut in a short, feathery style. One eye was blue and the other green. With a mouth fractionally too wide for prettiness, her face was attractive in its strength and aliveness. She looked ready to enjoy, to laugh. She had a superb figure, lean and athletic, with voluptuous breasts.

No-nonsense type lady. Forties? Fifties? Hint of unsureness underneath. Fighter. Survivor. She's had pain in her life, too. I like them both, so far. Silly — don't know them yet. But they feel good. Nice warm energy.

David Ladder was the last to arrive. I realized, now that I thought about it, that I'd heard his name mentioned often by Shura, particularly when he was talking about difficulties in the synthesis of a drug, or some article which they had co-authored. He was a remarkably young-looking man. As Shura had said, only the grey in his blond hair would lead one to suspect that he was over thirty. He was tall, with a boyishly slim body. He shook hands with me quickly, barely glancing at my face before ducking his head a little to the side, as if afraid of being somehow intrusive.

Shy, indeed. Nice face, kind. Vulnerable. Intelligent, probably very intuitive.

We all congregated in the kitchen, where the various food contributions were laid out on every available surface. Ginger squinted at the top of one window and remarked cheerfully to me, "I see Shura is still keeping faith with his little spiders! I suppose he's warned you on pain of banishment not to deprive the poor things of their sense of security!"

I laughed, "Well, we've compromised on a few token webs in each room, and I get to remove the ordinary overnight types without applying for a special permit."

There was a light touch on my shoulder and when I turned around, Leah greeted me with a kiss on my cheek, "Hello, Alice. Glad to see you again."

I looked into the open, thoughtful eyes and hugged the thin body, "Me, too."

John Sellars gave me his slightly conspiratorial angel smile as he passed through the kitchen.

Finally, Shura shouted to gather 'round, and we went into the dining room. When there was quiet, he made his proposal for the day.

"I thought — in celebration of the Sandeman's all-too-infrequent presence — that we might try something a bit daring, this time, something that will appeal to the hard-head, macho types especially — and there is certainly no dearth of them in this little group —"

There was a scatter of applause and laughter around the table, George adding his loud groan.

Shura continued, "I propose — subject to your approval — a higher dosage than any of us have taken previously of mescaline, with the cut-off point at five hundred milligrams." He beamed at us, leaning forward, fingers splayed on the table.

Dante looked immensely pleased at Shura's suggestion, then frowned and began speculating out loud about exactly how high a dosage he dared take. George sputtered comfortably about five hundred milligrams being a bit rich for him, and Ruth nodded in vehement agreement. Ben, his face thoughtful, said he might consider four hundred, but didn't think he should try higher than that.

Shura called out, "Hold it! First of all, is the idea appealing to everyone? Anybody not happy with it?"

There was a general nodding of heads and assurances that it was, indeed, a great idea. Dante spread his arms wide and cried, "I can't imagine a more spectacular way of being welcomed to the beautiful Bay Area and the beloved Farm and all our friends!"

Shura sat down with a lined pad and began listing names and dosage levels. He turned to Ben first, "You're sure about four hundred?"

"Yes," replied Ben, arms folded, "That's higher than I've taken before, and I expect it'll keep me busy enough."

Shura turned to Leah, "How about it, love? A bit lower?"

Leah looked pensive, her slim fingers tapping silently on the table, then said, "I think I'll go for two hundred, and see what happens. I can supplement later, can't I, if it's too low?"

Shura said, "Yes, certainly, supplements should be effective for probably as long as a couple of hours into it."

He called out, "Everybody, attention for a moment! If any of you wish to be on the conservative side to start with, you can always take more later." He added, "I'm going to measure out an extra couple of hundreds and a couple of fifties, in case someone needs a booster. I'm going to do it ahead of time because I frankly don't know if five hundred milligrams will allow for precision in much of anything, later on, never having taken mescaline at this level before."

Ruth said, "I thought you'd taken everything at every level imaginable, Shura!"

"Almost, almost," said the wizard modestly.

John, his young-old, pink-cheeked face showing only a slight smile, said he would try five hundred milligrams. "Should be interesting," he added, eyes squinting in amusement at the exclamations and hoots from the others.

"John, five hundred," said Shura, busy writing.

Dante was next, frowning again, "Well, since we can take a supplement later, if we need to, I think I'll match Ben's four hundred to begin with and see how it goes."

Ginger said, "Three hundred is as fur as Ah'm a'gonna go, at least to start with, Shura."

I looked at Ginger, and took a moment to appreciate the beauty of the hand-made Mexican smock she was wearing, its white cotton shining against her tanned arms. There were large red and pink roses embroidered around the neckline.

Looks Mexican. I want to go to Mexico someday and get some dresses like that. Delicious roses.

George had decided that three hundred milligrams was high enough for him, and Ruth said she would take a bit lower, how about two hundred, to which Shura replied, "Sounds good to me," and scribbled on his paper.

David cleared his throat and said, "I'm going to be a bit cautious and take two hundred and fifty, because this is my first mescaline."

Shura nodded silently, writing, then looked at me. I said, "I'd like to join you in five hundred milligrams, if that's all right?"

Nobody hooted or teased, this time.

"Alice, five hundred milligrams," Shura wrote. Finally, he took a deep breath and reviewed the list out loud, then asked, "Have I got them right? Any revisions before I go to the lab?"

When nobody spoke up, Shura rose and asked David to come with him to help carry the glasses.

Noise erupted around the table, as Dante and Ginger talked, laughed and answered questions. Names of people and places I didn't recognize were flying everywhere, while I listened, smiling at all the high energy.

When Shura and David returned with the glasses, various fruit juices were poured out according to individual tastes, then we trooped into the kitchen to form the circle.

Shura said, "I've discovered a way to avoid the nausea, you'll be glad to hear. If you sip your drink over half an hour, instead of taking it all down at once, the nausea doesn't present a problem. So take your time, sip it slowly, and the inevitable doesn't have to be inevitable, after all!"

Does that mean synthetic mescaline causes nausea like the natural peyote? Thought that happened only with the plant. Must ask him.

When the toasts to the Sandemans and ourselves and the clinking of glasses was over, the various group members drifted out of the kitchen, sipping cautiously at their drinks.

I asked Shura my question, and he nodded, "Yes, that's a very interesting fact about mescaline; it doesn't matter what form you take it in, the nausea seems to be part and parcel of the experience. If you take it fast, that is. I finally thought of trying it this other way, just to see if it made a difference. This method does, in fact, more nearly parallel the way the Southwest Indians eat Peyote, you know, and I'm happy to say it worked for me. Hope it works for everyone else. If it does, well — next stop, the Nobel Prize! For starters, that is!"

I chuckled and patted his fanny.

Thirty minutes later, Shura was being assured that he had, indeed, made an immensely important contribution to the welfare of the species. No one felt nauseated, although several in the group had decided to walk around outside for a while, finding themselves too attentive to their stomachs inside the confines of the house.

I decided I wanted to be alone for a few minutes and went into the dining room, from where I could see the outside world in two directions, through the big window to the mountain and through the sliding glass doors to the patio and the front stairs. I sat at the table, intending to stay still and quiet until I could be sure my insides could be trusted. I felt no nausea, not even pre-nausea, but wasn't about to tempt fate.

My hope, of course, was for an experience comparable to my first, years ago, the peyote journey with Sam Golding. Shura had warned me not to expect that, because, as he said, "Remember the famous quote, to the effect that you can never step twice in the same river."

The onset of the change, this time, was subtle. I was aware of a sense of something familiar, but couldn't be absolutely sure that what I was feeling was peculiar to mescaline, or simply typical of the transition to an altered state. I noted a mild, rather pleasant tingling in the neck and down my back.

I looked across the table at the daisies I had bought the day before, on my way to the Farm. They were shining softly in their simple glass vase, on top of the bookcase. Each white and yellow blossom seemed to tremble faintly in the light from the big window, as if grateful for the warmth.

Their roots are gone, but they're still alive. They exist fully, in this moment, and somewhere in the universe there's a place where this instant is forever, full of daisies and soft green stems and sunlight.

I had heard and read of the Akashic Records, a name originating in India, as a level of reality where everything that has ever existed in the universe is recorded, and from which a spiritual initiate can retrieve information — the sights, sounds and sensations of any instant in time — if he knows how to do it.

How does one learn to do such a thing? And how is an event recorded — from whose viewpoint, through whose eyes and ears? Whose feelings and sensations become part of that eternal record? The daisies' or the observer's? What if there is no observer; is there still a record of the daisies, and from what perspective?

I smiled at the flowers, sent them my love and respect, and rose from my chair. My tummy was going to be okay.

I wandered into the kitchen, where a big soup pot sat waiting on the stove. On the tile counter were green lettuces and bright-red tomatoes heaped in a woven basket, alongside loaves of bread — one satin brown, another a braid of creamy beige, sprinkled with poppy seeds.

Basic, basic. All us humans connect with each other by giving and sharing food, no matter where in the world. Other animals do that, too. And birds. Food shared is life shared. Eating with others is a way of connecting our livingness with theirs. All of us — humans and animals — take what the earth sends up out of her body, and give back what comes out of ours. Life-system. We are part and parcel of each other — us and our earth.

I saw, as I had seen years before on the peyote day — but in different images this time — the planet itself as a living entity with a consciousness not comprehensible to the thinking mind of the human, since it is of a kind, of an order, entirely different from anything in ordinary human experience. I saw that there is a part of the human psyche which is aware of the planet as a living being, and seeks to interact with it, to stay in relationship to it, as the child of a nurturing mother reaches for her hand, feeling with pleasure the texture of the skin and the solid bones of the fingers.

So humans touch the earth skin, planting and harvesting, and so they touch the planet's bones, hiking mountains and climbing rocks. We used to make our homes inside her, in the caves, like other animals. Then we ventured outside and learned to create our own peculiarly human dwellings. But we still anchor them, whenever we can, in the hard bones of the Mother.

I glimpsed people in steel and concrete cities, shut away from the feel of the earth, unable to touch more than an occasional tree growing out of a hole in the pavement, losing connection with the mother-body, some part of themselves gradually paling, drying to deadness.

I returned to myself, standing in the middle of the kitchen. The images and feelings that accompanied them had taken probably no more than a minute, I realized, but I had experienced that minute as a long, flowing piece of time.

Funny, I'd forgotten that what comes to you when you take a psychedelic is not always a revelation of something new and startling; you're more liable to find yourself reminded of simple things you know and forgot you knew — seeing them freshly — old, basic truths that long ago became cliches, so you stopped paying attention to them.

I left the kitchen, a moving body of streaming energy. I felt as if I were emitting light. Smiling to myself at the thought, I ducked into the bathroom to see my reflection in the mirror, just in case it should actually be so. I saw a soft glow around my head, but it was due to light coming through the thick glass bricks of the window behind me. But what radiated from the wide blue-grey eyes with their enlarged black centers was not reflected light; it was what always showed in the eyes of anyone whose mind had changed its way of seeing and being aware.

I waved to the friend in the mirror and left.

In the living room, I was greeted by Ruth, who said, "Hello, hello! How are *you* doing, or need I ask? No, I needn't ask!" She smiled and patted my arm, "I think everyone's coming back into the house. They all decided it was just a mite too warm for comfort."

I asked her how she was feeling, and she replied, "I think I took just the right amount. I certainly wouldn't want to go higher than this, though. It's just about all I can handle, as a matter of fact, pretty intense. But it's okay; I think it's going to be all right." Her arms were folded, fingers making small, absent-minded stroking movements on the blue silk of her sleeves

She's on the edge of being overwhelmed, but she heard herself say it'll be all right, and she'll believe that, make it true.

I asked how her husband was feeling, remembering the last time he had done an experiment at the Farm; I'd heard from Shura later that it had taken George almost three days to fully return to baseline, which had never happened before on any material. Shura said that George had sworn to be more conservative from then on — whatever that meant — particularly with new drugs.

Ruth said, "George took three hundred milligrams, fifty more than I did, and he seems to be doing fine, no problems this time. So far, that is," she added with a chuckle.

John came through the door, his fine-boned face shining from inside. His blue eyes were piercing, unreadable, and I knew he was focused on whatever was happening within, and content with where he was. He went over to the pile of thin blankets I had folded and placed next to the piano, and when he had wrapped one around himself, he sat down on the big foam pad Shura and I had laid out in the middle of the floor that morning. After rocking gently for a few minutes, he lay back on the pad and closed his eyes.

Dante was saying to Shura, "Just fifty more should do it," as they walked past me into the kitchen. I assumed he was asking for a supplement. I wondered what time it was and looked at my watch. The hands were pointing in interesting directions, but I couldn't make sense out of what they were doing. I tried to recall what Shura had said when we'd been in the circle, and remembered the words, "Eleven, almost on the dot." That was a start. Now, to figure out what it meant. The whole concept of clock time was un-graspable. It didn't seem to apply; it had no relationship to anything that was going on.

I giggled and sat down, trying to understand what my watch was showing me.

I can't remember why I looked at my watch in the first place. What was the question? Why did I want to know the time?

I laughed to myself, trying to keep from disturbing others in the room; the whole thing was ridiculous and hilariously funny.

Shura came into the room, trailed by Dante and Leah. He looked over at me and raised an eyebrow, "What's going on?"

I said, "I'm feeling like a complete idiot; I can't make sense out of my watch! I wanted to know what the time was, and now I can't even remember why!"

Shura smiled and ducked into the kitchen to look at the big electric clock. He reported back that it was twenty minutes to one o'clock in the afternoon and it was still the month of May.

I said thank you and suddenly remembered the question, "Oh, yes! I've got it back! I was wondering how long it's been since we took the mescaline — whether we've plateau'd or not yet — that's why I was looking at my watch in the first place."

Shura said, "It's about one and a half hours, and we've still got a bit of climbing to do before we level out. Are you comfortable so far? Is every-thing okay?"

I said I was fine, except for my problems with clocks and watches.

Leah said to me, "I was a bit light — Dante was, too — so Shura gave us a supplement. It's probably my imagination, but I could swear I'm already feeling it!"

I thought about Ruth and hoped she could tolerate a bit more of a climb, if that's what we had ahead of us. She was seated on the couch, her face showing only a suggestion of anxiety.

Wonder how much farther one can go? I feel engorged with energy-light already.

I rose and walked toward the front door. There was only the slightest sense of physical weight, and every motion, every gesture of the body was graceful.

I walk in grace. I move in grace. I live in Grace.

Outside was the green world. The big pine across the brick path from the front door was an old friend, its branches always busy with birds and squirrels, and of course the insects which sapped a little more of its strength each year, as its natural life came to a close.

I looked down at the uneven bricks in the path, some of them jutting several inches out of the ground, where the pine's roots were pushing them. I smiled, thinking about the tree, whose needs had created a rather unusual entranceway; Shura always warned newcomers that they'd have to watch their step, and probably a lot of them wondered privately why the path to the front door was allowed to remain that way, every second or third brick displaced. Shura had explained to me that any effort to cut the pushing roots under the path would hasten the death of the great pine, and he wanted it to live out its full life-span, so visitors would just have to step carefully.

Hearing laughter from the living room, I postponed further exploration and went back inside.

For the first time since the circle in the kitchen, we were all gathered in one room. John was still stretched out on his back, blanket-wrapped, eyes closed, his face serene. Ruth was on the couch next to George, one hand resting on his thigh. George's face wore a slight, contented smile. Leah was in a chair, looking through one of Shura's big art books, turning the pages very slowly. Ben was seated in the armchair next to her, his head back, eyes closed. Dante was sitting on the edge of the mattress pad, near John, muscular arms folded around his raised knees. He was rocking himself gently.

Ginger was at the big window, arms raised to her sides. Her feet were still, but the rest of her body moved as if she were rehearsing a dance to music only she could hear, while she gazed out at Mount Diablo and the valley below it.

Shura was seated on the piano bench, talking with David, who stood at the back of the grand piano, leaning on its closed black top.

There's nothing to drink out here. I'm hostess. Go to the kitchen, bring out water and juice and glasses. Don't get distracted until that's finished.

Opening kitchen cupboards and gathering together what I needed, I noted my thoughts drifting, and realized I would have to focus deliberately and continuously on each specific task, if anything was to get done. I talked myself through the counting of glasses, persuaded the ice-cubes out of their trays and into a pitcher of water, spoke encouragement to the different juices as I poured them into other various containers, and by using the sound of my own voice as an anchor, managed to keep track of what I was supposed to be doing. I heard myself chuckling, now and then, at being so stoned.

When I had put everything out on the coffee table, I gave myself permission to be not responsible for a while, and sat down cross-legged on the floor near the room-dividing bookcase. My Observer noted, simply as a matter of interest, that I was choosing a place symbolic of where I liked to be in any group, a location which allowed me to see all the others in the room, to keep track of what was going on. I was part of the group, but also subtly detached.

The Watcher. The Outsider. Or is it The Writer? Same thing. This is the perch of a person who doesn't want to be truly part of any gathering, who wants to keep some aspect of herself separate, not absorbed by whatever is going on. Good or bad? Neither. Just the way it is. The way I am. That's why I can identify with Shura's lone-hermit side, the part of him that sometimes wants to be away, off to the mountain. Each of us has a large part that loves connection and sharing, the sense of community, but only for a while. Then we need to be alone again, to draw the energy back inside ourselves.

Ruth was saying, "— colors are really vivid; they seem to jump out at me, you know — a little red Hello here and a blue Hello there — and everything I look at seems to be moving a bit."

George whooped, "Moving! Boy oh boy, is it moving!"

Shura leaned forward to ask, "George, is it all right for you, is it okay?"

"Yup," said George agreeably, "It's quite a bit to handle, but I don't think it's too much. I'm feeling pretty good, so far, to tell the truth."

"Well," said Shura, "Where you are is where you're probably going to stay, at this point. We've been on for about two hours, and I think it's safe to say we're at the plateau."

I remembered Shura telling me that the climb to the plateau could take sometimes as long as two and a half hours, so he must have said that, I thought, to reassure both George and Ruth that they didn't have to be on guard against further intensification.

Since they had told themselves they were able to manage whatever they were already feeling, they would dismiss a slight increase — if there were going to be any — as just more of the same safe, tolerable plateau.

Pretty good thinking, for five hundred milligrams, if that's what he's doing. And I'm not doing too badly, either, considering the fact that I'm sitting here like a lady Buddha made of extremely active light-molecules, not sure I have a body at all.

George said, "I'm relieved to hear it. There's no friend like a good plateau!"

Ruth patted him, smiling in agreement.

Glancing up, I saw Shura's eyes on me, warm and questioning; I responded with a full smile, letting him know I was all right.

He got up and left the room. In a minute, the sound of music came through the speakers from the back room. Gregorian chants. Everyone was silent, listening to the exquisite singing with their eyes closed. Ginger was still standing at the window, but she had turned to face the room. Now, eyes shut, arms lowered, she moved slowly to the music, her face intent.

I closed my own eyes, finally, and found myself inside the top of a cathedral, a golden cupola flooded with light, floating upwards past a stained glass window whose colors were a blur of star brilliance, drifting close to the point where the lines of the roof converged. I could feel something compelling beyond it, urging me to go out through that point to the other side.

The Observer cut in to say that I was quite probably going out of body, and that it might not be the most appropriate thing to do under these particular circumstances, especially since I didn't know how to manage it or what would happen to the part of me I would leave behind. Indulging in such an adventure, it warned, could result in anxiety and even alarm among the others in the group, especially if my body flopped down like a rag doll. I might be thought inconsiderate and attention-hogging or something like that.

I opened my eyes and blew air through pursed lips, looking for some way of staying firmly grounded, still feeling the pull of that place of convergence, the longing to go through that center to whatever was out there beyond it.

It occurred to me that all I had to do was keep my eyes open; there were bodies and faces to look at, to focus on, and in paying attention to them, I would be able to keep from drifting too far out.

Ben rose from his armchair, heading toward the bathroom. He moved somewhat slowly, but seemed steady on his feet. Leah had laid the art book on the floor and was sitting with hands clasped in her lap, head down. I knew she was in a meditative state — relaxed but aware — and that she was intensely involved in an experience of joy; I could feel it in her, from across the room.

George had opened his eyes and was looking around as if checking out the tendency of different things in the room to move and flow. His face was child-open and the only remaining sign of anxiety was in one hand which opened and closed against his sweater, the short fingers extending spasmodically to rub the wool, then folding again.

Ruth's face was set in concentration on whatever she was seeing behind closed eyelids. Both hands lay loosely at her sides.

When Ben returned, he said to the room at large, "That's quite an experience, trying to make sense of the different parts of the toilet and the different parts of myself, all at once! Not to speak of getting them to relate to each other in the appropriate way!"

Eyes snapped open and and comments rose from all quarters, "All you have to remember is lid *up*, stream *down*," and, "I'm next. If I'm not back in half an hour, send out the big wooly dog with the thing around its neck," from David, while John groaned, "Oh, Lord, save me from a full bladder for a while yet."

Sometime during the next hour, Shura got up, flashed a smile at me, and quietly left the room. A moment later, the music was turned off. He returned and tiptoed back to his piano bench.

I was looking through a book of fairy stories with illustrations by the great enchanter, Arthur Rackham, and everyone around me had been silent for a long time, absorbed in their various interior worlds, when suddenly the room was jarred by a single, forceful note struck on the piano. On the pad, John's body jerked in shock. He yelled, "Owww!" and sat straight up, then turned around to glare at Shura, who was grinning broadly behind him, the guilty finger still on the key.

John sputtered, "What do you think you're *doing!*" in such outrage that the rest of us, who had also been jolted by the unexpected hammer-blow of sound, dissolved in laughter. Shura lifted his eyebrows and struck another note, equally loud, watching us intently. John jumped again, as if kicked in the spine. This time, he managed a weak smile as he protested, "Don't DO that, I *beg* you!"

A third ringing note pulsed through all of us, and we watched John, empathizing with him as he huddled in his blanket, now laughing helplessly at his own vulnerability, crying, "Stop, stop, stop, Shura! No more, please!"

"Really remarkable, isn't it," observed Shura, smiling with satisfaction, "How exquisitely sensitive the nervous system can become, under the influence."

Small boy puts tack on chair, rewarded by yelp, now explaining it was scientific experiment.

"That was pretty powerful," said Dante.

"Nobody went through the ceiling, though, except poor John," said Ginger.

"Poor John, indeed," muttered that person, "It was actually painful — I mean, like a physical blow to the body. And will you do me the kindness of warning me if you're going to do it again, so I can leave the room? I really don't want any more surprises of that kind, Shura."

He means it. No more Mister Nice Guy.

Shura had the grace to look faintly embarrassed, "Okay, you can trust me. I won't startle you again. I just had to try it, to see how much increased nervous system sensitivity there might be. I hadn't expected quite that much, John! You certainly are the star lab rat!"

John glowered at him, "Thanks a whole big lot!" then joined in the laughter. But he didn't lie down again, and from where he sat, he could keep an eye on the piano keyboard.

Ginger was sitting against a wall, ankles crossed. She hummed comfortably and said, "Well, I like where I am. I think I could get used to this level, with a little practice."

David picked up a floor cushion and put it down next to the coffee table, where he sat and carefully poured out a glassful of juice. He looked around and asked, "Does anybody else want some of this?"

Shura called out, "By the way, everybody, remember to drink your fluids. There's plenty on the table. Don't let yourselves get dehydrated."

We obediently got up to fill glasses and tumblers, then returned to our chosen places. Again there was stillness, the only sounds being an occasional deep breath expelled inside the room, and bird chatter outside. I looked around at the closed eyes, and gratefully closed my own.

I was aware, first of all, of the enormous energy in my body, and inside my head the entire field of vision was suffused with light. There was a sudden feeling of certainty that if I focused my mind in a particular way — I wasn't sure what that way was, but I knew it existed — I would be able to see through my closed eyelids. I just didn't know how exactly to make it happen.

The waves of microscopic bubbles or light particles, or whatever it was that kept sweeping through me, were intensifying, and I felt close again to going out into another place or dimension, and I wanted to go.

I opened my eyes and looked over at Shura, who was sitting on his bench with closed eyes. I said, as casually as I could, "Shura, could I ask you to come over here for a moment?"

He was by my side immediately, and I whispered, "This may sound melodramatic, but I keep feeling as if I'm going out of body, and I think I shouldn't, considering the circumstances. It would be sort of bad manners. What should I do? It's very strong — the pull to keep going up and out — and I'm not sure how to stay down in here," I pointed to my chest and smiled, because Shura's eyes were huge and glowing, and his hair stood out from his head like white flames.

He stood up and said loudly to the group, "I would like to invite you all to please get up and form a circle, holding hands, for a couple of minutes. It may help anchor anybody who thinks he's floating a bit too much, okay?"

Everyone rose, chairs were pushed back out of the way, and we gathered in a circle, holding hands. I looked around and saw that the faces directly across from me — Dante, Ruth and George — shared a common look of inwardness, and their eyes were closed. I sighed deeply and closed my own. The feeling of wanting to rise through the top of my head was still there, but so was the sturdy presence of the palms and fingers of the people on either side of me, David to my right, Ginger on my left.

I felt myself a complete individual, separate and distinct from everyone else, and simultaneously, a participant with others, a member of a family, which was the entire species. I was aware, as I had been on the peyote day, so long ago, of a level of reality in which every human being was connected with every other, and that the connectedness was not of mind or personality, but of something far more basic; it was a spiritual or psychic touching which was blocked from consciousness most of the time, but which existed nonetheless, from birth to death. We were all woven into one tapestry, and at some deep, unconscious level of ourselves, we each shared everything known and felt by every other living person on the planet.

Why must we be unaware of this, except for times when some of us might experience a revelation, a sudden state of grace, or when others of us might decide to open ourselves with meditation or a psychedelic drug? Why the shutting off of this awareness? Maybe because our assignment is to live our individual lives, our own singular stories, and we can't do that if we're open to everyone else's emotional and spiritual happenings.

We wouldn't be able to focus, to evolve as distinct and different entities, if we could feel everything that was going on in everyone else all the time. We would be a group consciousness, as the rest of the life forms on earth seem to be. And humans are meant to develop single identities, while still participating in their basic connectedness. Why? Because that's what the universal Mind intends as the next step in the adventure, the next chapter in the tale. Whose adventure is it? Whose tale?

Into my mind came the memory of the spiral, my microcosm-macrocosm experience, and the un-nameable Friend-Companion who had greeted me each time, with laughter and love, at the end. It's the Friend's journey, I thought.

And therefore it's also mine. My incomprehensible Friend is what I am also, and our purposes are the same, even though I can't be allowed to remember what they are while I'm living my physical life. And every human being on the planet is what I am — we are all different, one-of-a-kind forms of the Friend.

I opened my eyes. The Observer scanned the passage of time since the circle formed, and said it had only been one or two minutes in the clock world. Shura was looking at me questioningly. I smiled and nodded at him to indicate that I was all right, and that I wasn't having any more trouble staying put in my body.

George muttered, "Phew!" and opened his eyes. David chuckled, "I think being in the circle makes it even more intense, not less!"

Ginger squeezed my hand and gently bumped the side of her head against mine, then said, "This is the damndest level of anything I've ever taken. Did I say that right? What I *mean* is, I don't remember ever being quite so — ah — "

"The word is 'high,' love," laughed Shura, and the circle broke up in giggles and remarks about appropriate words for certain mental states, Ben suggesting "Zonkered," David throwing in, "Clobbered," and Ruth asking, "How about just plain ole 'stoned'?"

"Anybody having problems?" asked Shura, his voice suddenly serious, as he looked at each of our faces.

"Pretty intense, but okay," reported George, adding, "I don't think I'd want to try any higher though. At least, not until I'd had a chance to get used to this. And getting used to this could take a long, long time!"

Leah, her eyes soft, said, "This is beautiful, Shura. I know what you mean about being anchored, though. I keep feeling I could drift out into space — or somewhere — quite easily, if I didn't hold onto my bod."

"Well, let yourself go, if that's what you want to do," replied Shura, "We'll call you back for soup and bread, when it's time to eat."

John reported that he was feeling fine, had never felt better, "As long as you stay off the piano keys, that is."

"Promise," laughed Shura, "But you'll have to admit, those notes had an interesting effect, didn't they?"

"Very interesting effect, yes," said John, smiling despite his effort to sound sarcastic, "Memorably interesting effect, as a matter of fact, and one I would just as soon forego during the rest of the day, if you would be so kind!"

Some of the group decided to try the outside again. George expressed an interest in checking the soup, now that he had been reminded of it by Shura's remark to Leah, and Ruth went with him to the kitchen, holding his arm.

Shura put a hand against my back and gently pushed me through the kitchen, down the hallway, and out the back door.

I stood next to him in the open air, looking around. Every tree, every bush radiated light. I remembered my peyote experience, when I'd had to squint against the pulsing colors of the flowers. Now, the nasturtiums clustered on the bank to the right of the path were glowing rich yellow and an orange-red which I could feel in my stomach, while the grass sang life in the key of green.

Shura put a hand on my shoulder and said, "I wanted to bring you out here to tell you something I've always kept to myself before. You already know my other secrets, and I suppose this is the last one I have."

I looked at him and waited.

"The first time I took mescaline," he said, "I was astonished to discover that the world I found myself in — this world — was what I had been surrounded by, as a child. I spent my childhood in a reality that looked and felt like this. Of course I thought everyone else saw and felt things the same way I did, until it gradually dawned on me that maybe it wasn't the same for other people. Other boys my age didn't seem to want to spend time looking closely into flowers or merging with beetles, as I loved doing when I was alone. Eventually, I began getting the idea that I was different in some way, and I learned not to talk about that kind of thing, and to imitate the behavior of the other boys at the school, so I wouldn't draw attention —"

Shura leaned against the wall of the house, his eyes off in the distance.

"— because I knew instinctively that if others my age sensed any kind of difference, they would attack. So I behaved like everyone else until school was over and I could go home and have a couple of hours by myself doing what I liked to do.

"Just a few minutes ago, I was looking out of the front window in the living room and there were two dogs in the field, down below the house. They were in their world, in their reality, and knew nothing of me, in mine. I was simply an interested observer, so I observed them, and I saw that, although they were following one-another, they weren't moving."

"Not moving?"

"Of course they were moving — intellectually I know that — but the magic of a material like this, mescaline or any other effective psychedelic, is that it lets you put aside the intellectual overlay for a while and just have an immediate, direct experience of something. When I had my first mescaline experience the memory came back of seeing little bugs on the honeysuckle vines that grew over a fence behind my home — when I was very young — and I remembered that the bugs didn't really move; they simply changed their location in my reality, from time to time. Like the dogs in the field today. They weren't moving; there was just a change in where they were, now and then. At least, from the point of view of the reality I was in while I watched. I can't speak for what the dogs were experiencing, of course."

"You know, sweetie," I said, slowly, "I suspect that all children see the world this way at a certain time, very early in their lives. It sounds to me as if your only difference was in maintaining that state, that vision, longer than most others manage to."

Shura glanced at me thoughtfully, then looked away again, "You're probably right. When you're little, you live in what we would call a psychedelic world, surrounded by it."

I said, "I remember, with the peyote, I had the same feeling of familiarity about the world I was seeing. The territory wasn't strange at all; I had just forgotten it."

"Exactly. I can only say, for myself, that with that first opening experience with mescaline, I was in a completely friendly environment and I'd recovered the ability to do things that had once been simple, which had been lost in all the years since then. I was home again." His voice with thick. After a while, he groped in a pocket and blew his nose on a rumpled handkerchief.

"Did your parents know any of this? I mean, that you were still seeing your world differently than most kids your age?"

"I think my mother knew some of it, at least had some suspicion. I knew that she worried sometimes; she probably worried about my ability to get along in the world that everyone else shared, but she never said anything directly to me about it. I suppose the fact that I did well in school helped allay some of her fears."

"What a difficult childhood that must have been!"

Shura turned and smiled, "Actually, I had a wonderful time, especially when I could be by myself. I remember when I was about six or seven, I think, I could travel all the way across the park near my house, without touching the ground — just traveling in the interlocking tree branches! It was great!"

I laughed with him. "Well, that certainly sounds like normal boy-stuff!"

He went on. "There was a certain amount of strain, I suppose, in trying not to be singled out, when I was in school, acting like other boys — but I got pretty good at it."

"When did you lose the — that kind of vision, do you remember?"

"I can't recall any particular time; it just gradually faded, like I guess it does with everybody else. I eventually forgot how it had been. Until the mescaline. Then it all came back; I remembered seeing the world this way before, and I began recapturing the memories."

I said, "I wonder why some people find a mescaline experience frightening?"

"Maybe their childhood world was frightening, or damaging in some way; maybe a lot of it has simply been pushed out of memory by the need to deny and repress the bad memories. And then, to have something reawaken that past, and in an authentic way such as this — it could be terrifying. It could be a dreadful experience, having all of it open up again."

"Yes, yes — I hadn't thought of that."

I looked again at the trees, at the grass, at the flowers, and felt the radiance moving in my own body as it was in their's. We were creatures of light, Shura and I, standing in a little piece of the universe that was showing us, reminding us, how things really were.

This interweaving, this shared energy; it exists between all living things. My Beloved Friend of the spiral is living the story of all things alive, everywhere.
Shura had taken my arm and was leading me up the path to the lab. We walked slowly, in silence, stopping every few steps to look at an exquisite line or flare of color. Every turn of branch, every curve of flower stalk was a word of language, a communication from the particular shape taken by the energy that flowed around us.

I again remembered when I was sixteen, at boarding school, making the great discovery that line could be translated in my mind to sound. It had first happened when I went walking alone and looked up to see a bird moving silently, very high up against the clear sky, and the single pure moving line became a single pure curving note of sound. I began experimenting, after that, looking at the back of an antique chair, the outline of a vase sitting on a table, and confirmed that any line, moving or not, could make a sound in my mind. I shared the discovery, of course, with no one.

I talked to Shura about this kind of association, which I now knew had a name: synesthesia. I went on to tell him the story of how I came to love the music of Bach.

The first man in my life, the first love, was a young Russian of considerable brilliance. We had fallen in love during our senior year of high school. After years of separation, he came back into my life just after my divorce from Christopher's father, while I was living in the housing project with my baby. His name was Vadim Michel Ivanoff, and he loved Bach. When he found out that I couldn't understand the music of his favorite composer, he informed me that he was going to teach me to hear it as it should be heard.

One evening in my apartment, when my small son was asleep upstairs, he ordered me to sit on the old couch in the living room, and not talk. He then brought out a box of twenty household candles — the cheap, plain white kind — lit one, then turned out the lights. While I watched in obedient silence, he fastened the rest of the candles in place with the hot wax and lit them. They stood in a line that went from the concrete floor up the side of the white-painted concrete stairwell, until the small room was blazing with candlelight.

Then he took a record and put it on my record player, and the music of Bach (I didn't know which piece it was and he gave it no name) filled the air around me. I lay down on the couch and closed my eyes and caught my breath in surprise. Before me had appeared a crystal mountain which was being built by the music, and as I watched, the music showed me blue-shadowed crevasses, shelves and peaks and a beauty that belonged to another world. That night, I fell in love with J.S. Bach, as Vadim had intended.

"I'll always be grateful to him," I concluded, "For two things: teaching me how to make Russian hamburgers and how to hear the music of Bach. The rest of my relationship with him was mostly pain and grief, but those two gifts deserve acknowledgement."

Shura was smiling, "I don't know what Russian hamburgers taste like, but certainly, being able to appreciate Bach is one of the things I consider essential to a fully lived life!"

I laughed, "So do I — now."

Shura took my hand and it was like being grasped by my own skin. I found myself thinking how marvelous it would be to make love right now. I didn't share the thought; it would be ungracious of us to leave the group for so long. We were the hosts. Perhaps later.

As we walked back toward the house, Shura said, "I want to remind you, before we rejoin the others, that I've never told anyone else what I just shared with you about my childhood. You may be right, that the only real difference between me and others of my age was in the fact that I continued moving around in that world a lot longer than most children do. But at the time, it was one hell of a difference, believe me!"

"It'll remain between us. But why did you never tell Ursula?"

I'm assuming he didn't.

"Because I've been used to keeping a lot of things to myself most of my life, especially things that I grew up thinking would make people regard me as an oddball. As it was, I was considered an oddball anyway, but it wasn't for lack of discretion about my interior workings. It's only been with you, for God knows what reason," he smiled down at me, "That I made the decision to be truthful and open about who I am and what goes on inside me."

I said, "Thank you."

If I have to go on without you for the rest of my life, I'll have that as my treasure — being the first person you ever trusted so completely. No use telling you that this great secret of yours would be understood by more people than you think.

In the kitchen, Ruth and Leah were laughing uproariously. Leah tried to explain to us, "It's the stove! You see, it's really much more complicated than you realize, understanding what 'front right' and 'rear left' mean — what they *really* mean — and what they have to do with heating up a pot of soup. You think it's simple, I know! I always thought it was simple, myself. Little did I realize the elaborate connections that have to be made by the mind, between those silly little words on the dials and —" she doubled over again, holding her stomach.

Ruth had tears running from her eyes as she joined Leah, crying, "*You* try counting soup bowls, Shura! Just see how far you get before you lose track! I've tried and tried, and it keeps slipping away after three or four bowls. How many people are we, anyway?"

We joined in the laughter and Shura took over the counting of soup bowls. He had no trouble at all, which for some reason sent the two women into further paroxysms until they were both gasping for air. Then Ruth reached out to the wall rack over the stove and held up a soup ladle as if it were an unrecognizable object lifted out of an archaeological dig, and we left the kitchen to the sounds of renewed gasps and croaks.

Ben grumbled from his armchair, "What in heaven's name is going on in the kitchen? I haven't the slightest desire to move, at the moment, so you'll have to tell us the whole thing."

Shura simply shook his head, "Ya hadda bin there."

David was on the floor pad, a few inches from John. Both of them were lying on their backs, eyes closed. David was smiling, I guessed in response to the sounds in the kitchen.

George spoke from the couch, "I must say, Shura, this is quite an experience!" From George, those words could mean one of several things, but his face showed no anxiety and his smile was full, so I assumed they meant that he was enjoying himself. Since Shura did not ask him any questions, I supposed he must have read George's face and reached the same conclusion.

I sat down on a floor cushion and watched Shura quietly move through the room, looking intently at faces, checking for any signs of distress. What he saw apparently contented him, because he slipped off his sandals and sat down in the chair next to Ben, leaning his head back and closing his eyes.

For a long time there was complete silence in the room.

I gave thought, finally, to the matter of Ursula. Ursula and her trunk full of books.

There's no feeling of reality about Ursula coming and staying. It's as if that whole scenario is only one of several possible outcomes of this story, this particular script, and not the one that's going to be the final choice, in the end. But then, I'm not the playwright. Who does make those choices, in this play?

By the time my watch and the kitchen clock agreed on 6:30, we were all seated at the table and the previously incomprehensible ladle had been put to its proper use. We were eating, tearing bread with enthusiasm and refilling our bowls, talking about the day's experience and comparing it with others. There was a telling of stories — remember when Dante got stuck in his guilt and self-negation and Shura and Ben played verbal torture games with him until he finally rebelled and decided that being victim wasn't all it was cracked up to be?

Dante bent over the table, flushed from laughing. I hadn't had a chance to talk with him yet, but I was already in love with his face, with its marvelous mixture of expressions — extroverted warmth and inward searching.

"Remember," someone said, "When Helen finally took the plunge with mescaline and couldn't bring herself to step out of the car, up in Tilden Park, because the gravel looked like the jeweled back of a huge snake and she didn't want to put a dirty shoe on such a beautiful thing?"

I asked if Helen had been afraid of the snake. Shura said, "No, she wasn't afraid of it — she knew what she was seeing was really just the side of a road — but she couldn't bring herself to disturb the pattern of jewels. The rest of us had to spend time persuading her that she wouldn't injure it, that it would still be there if she placed her feet on that scintillating back. She finally dared, but it took a while, believe me!"

No one mentioned Ursula.

George and Ruth stayed the night on the pad in the living room, because George could not trust himself to drive safely. He was still having visuals.

Shura and I made love slowly, holding on to the mescaline effects as long as we could, neither of us able to reach orgasm, laughing at our own futile efforts to focus minds and bodies in the way necessary for such a result. We settled for pleasure and the melting of boundaries, the my-skin-is-your-skin, the light glowing behind our eyelids, the sense of being children playing in the fields of the Lord.

Finally, we curled together spoon-style, my stomach to his back, and fell asleep in the middle of something sweetly familiar by Schubert which neither of us could name.

CHAPTER 29. THE LETTER

Shura often gave me Ursula's letters to read. He knew that seeing her writing for myself gave me an independent, if limited, view of the person which I could get no other way. Sometimes he used me as a reality check. Feeling too close to her, too deeply involved to trust his own judgement, he might hand me a letter and ask what I thought of this or that. I would read carefully and reply with scrupulous objectivity, heart turned off and only head operating.

Ursula's letters were always passionate — not in the erotic sense, but spiritually and emotionally. She never referred to love-making, except by delicate implication, but she often referred to the soul. When she spoke about her future joining with Shura, it was always in terms of the spiritual, the cosmic. She wrote well, sometimes beautifully, considering the fact that her native tongue was German. The occasional temptation to elaborateness and honey-sweetness had to be understood as the efforts of a woman in love trying to convey the urgency of her feelings in a language not her own. My preferred self-image of a fair and honest witness demanded that I keep all that in mind.

I didn't dare question the authenticity of the emotions being expressed. I could question their durability all I wanted, but what I was reading in Ursula's letters often had an intensity and unmistakable yearning that seared the page — and me.

Then came the letter that changed everything.

It was a Saturday afternoon. Shura came into the living room where I was curled up on the couch with a book, and silently handed me a letter which had just arrived. Glancing up, I saw his face clouded. I turned my attention to Ursula's spiky German public school handwriting, which was still hard for me to decipher.

After addressing Shura as her love, her soul-mate and other variations on the theme, she described in detail a trip to the ancient city of Nuremberg, with Dolph and two close friends. They had gone there for the four days of Richard Wagner's Ring Cycle, and there was no mistaking the excitement and delight she had felt during the experience.

I thought it was one of her most enjoyable letters. She told about the dress she wore on opening night, "As I stood before the mirror, I could feel you, my darling, watching me and smiling. I heard your voice telling me I was beautiful in the flowing white silk, the silver shoes and handbag, the embroidered scarf. You were so proud of me, my beloved!"

She went on to convey the magnificence of the theater, the deep blue of the velvet curtains, the superb stage lighting and scenery. She spoke of herself, in her red plush seat, creating in her imagination the figure of Shura sitting next to her, his hand enfolding hers as the magnificent music of Wagner carried their souls upward together.

She either doesn't know or she's forgotten how much he loathes Wagner.

There followed descriptions of some others in the audience, delightfully catty examinations of bad taste as expressed in various hair arrangements, jewelry and clothes.

The only mention of Dolph was in relation to one of the singers, "Dolph and our friend Rudi agreed that this man's voice did not meet the expectations raised by the rest of the divine company. Surely, they will not give to him such an important role next year!"

Then she spoke of the strain she felt, trying to maintain the necessary lightness of conversation with her companions, while thinking privately of what was to come: "Oh, soon now, very soon, my twin, my other Self, we will be together and none shall part us. Thank you for being so patient, for giving me the time I must have to calm the storms within the heart of poor Dolph, so that I can break free, soaring like the music, to join you forever."

Shura was sitting in the armchair, waiting for me to finish the letter. When I put it down, he asked, "Well, what do you think?"

What, exactly, has made him so angry?

"You have to remember," I said, cautiously, "I don't read these things with your eyes. What are you reacting to?"

"Doesn't it strike you," he said, voice tight, "That she has given a great description of a delightful trip, an interlude of several days with Dolph and friends, to see the Ring Cycle, and that not a word of this sounds like a woman agonizing over her husband's suicidal or other-cidal depressions? I don't see anything in that letter to indicate that Dolph wasn't having a fine time, along with the rest of them, do you?"

"Well, she wasn't going into details about Dolph, honey. It was a letter about the trip and the theater —"

He interrupted, hitting the arm of the chair with his fist, "Am I going mad, or is this what you would do if you were trying to wean your husband away from you, trying to get him to accept the end of the marriage? She sends her books across the ocean, then she takes off with the husband she's about to leave at any moment, and a couple of friends, and they all go to see the bloody Ring Cycle in old Nuremberg!"

I'm missing something. It didn't seem that strange to me.

"Oh, I don't know, I don't know!" Shura pounded his forehead, "It just seemed so — so crazy, all of a sudden. All that fun and games at the opera, while Dolph is supposedly suffering the pangs of betrayal and Ursula is nursing him, easing him into accepting her imminent departure — all that tension and misery — then this! It just struck such an incredibly wrong note!"

I thought for a moment, remembering the combination of obvious delight with the sad, wistful longing to have Shura beside her.

Be as objective as you can.

I spoke slowly, carefully, "Well, it seems quite possible to me that she might simply be keeping peace this way, and perhaps things were getting too — well, you know — too closed in, too tense at home. Maybe she thought it would lighten everyone's mood if they just took off and went to the Ring Cycle. She talks of missing you, wishing you were there."

"Yes," Shura nodded, "Almost as if she were remembering every now and then to say the sweet words, to make sure I don't think she's really enjoying herself. But she *was* enjoying herself. I can read it in every line. It's just not — I can't fit it into the picture. Nothing fits the picture properly. None of it makes sense."

Ursula goofed. What now?

An idea came to mind as I looked at Shura's lion head, bent onto his hands. I tuned into his hollow fear that this state of affairs would go on forever, that there would never be a true resolution, and the deeper suspicion that he was being played like a puppet, for unknown and unknowable reasons.

I said, "I just thought of something I might do, my love. I think it's time you jolted the lovely lady a little, and I have an idea of how to do it. I'm going to write a letter to her."

"What?" Shura looked up at me, his face totally uncomprehending.

"Let me work on it, okay? I'll give it to you, of course, and it'll be entirely up to you whether it gets mailed or not. But if it is sent, it must seem as if I'm doing it entirely on my own. You don't want her to suspect that you have any knowledge of it at all, otherwise it'll look like exactly what it is: a ploy. A prod. Just wait and see what I come up with."

Shura shrugged, "I don't know. If you want to try it, I can't stop you, but — what the hell would you say?"

"I'll put it in your hot liddle hands when it's done. No use rehearsing it now. It'll take me a couple of days, then let's see what you think."

It was the strangest letter I'd ever written. The words were from my
heart and gut, and by the time I'd reworked it four times, I was able to call
it a masterpiece (at least to myself), even though I knew that Shura — if he
decided it could be sent — would be using it only to make the woman he
loved jealous and insecure and perhaps inclined to move a bit faster in
tying up her loose ends

My reason for writing it was not complicated. In case Ben was right, .
after all, this might well give her the excuse she needed to break things off
with Shura. It would, in other words, take her off the hook. If, on the other
hand, she really wanted him, wanted to come and stay happily forever
after on the Farm but was dragging her feet for innumerable reasons, this
would almost certainly give her a kick where she needed it. Even if she
were to find out, later, that it wasn't going to be forever after, things would
have been moved along a bit toward whatever the conclusion was going to
be. At this point, I thought, anything that speeds this whole business up is
all to the good; Shura is getting too depressed. It has to be resolved.

Ursula,

I am taking the liberty of writing to you directly, without the
knowledge of Shura, because I think you should know what the
situation is and because he is suffering greatly from what he reads
in your letters — or, rather, what he does not read.

I have been in love with Shura since the Fall of last year, when
I first met him. We allowed ourselves to become involved during
the past many months, because of our mutual loneliness and need
for companionship of a kind that is hard to find for intelligent
people with unusual interests such as ours.

He has told me from the first time we met of his love for you.
He has never failed to mention you, to talk of you, as the woman
he loves and wishes to live with for the rest of his life, and it was in
full knowledge of all this that I decided to continue my relationship
with him, a relationship which must end, of course, when you
finally come to be with him, to live with him and make this place
your home.

What I am attempting to do, in writing this, is to tell you that I
believe this man is worth the pain I feel in knowing that I cannot
have his heart, and the pain it will be for me to relinquish the
closeness and the extraordinary communication of ideas and concepts. I could have saved myself all this pain, both past and
future, if I had decided not to become involved in his life. But I
decided otherwise. For the first time in my life (and most certainly
the last), I let myself be part of a triangle — I allowed myself to

love a man who loves someone else. I am older than you, Ursula, but I am still a woman of some attractiveness and certainly of great pride, so this was not an easy decision.

I wish you to know that I can see him go to you without jealousy or hostility, when you come to join him, because I love him enough to want to see him fulfilled. He believes — and since he does, I must — that you are the one person in the world who can make him truly and deeply happy. Since this is so, I can only hope and pray that your love for him is, and will continue to be, the equal of his for you. If it is, I will be — in time — content and even satisfied.

Please know that he is suffering right now from many doubts and a lot of emotional distress. You might perhaps realize that he needs to have some definite encouragement from you as to the fact that things really are moving and evolving in your effort to leave your marriage and your country. He is becoming deeply discouraged, and I write to you asking you to please do or say something which will be reassuring to him at this time.

I believe it was inevitable that you would learn of my relationship with Shura, since he will want to tell you the truth. We have established our strange, difficult and caring relationship on the basis of absolute truth-telling, playing no games of half-truths with each other, and I know that he will insist on total honesty and openness in his future life with you. I feel that, once you have recovered from the surprise and shock of discovering that someone else shares many of the same feelings about Shura and has had some closeness to him, you will welcome what I have to say: he is in love only with you.

It is one thing to hear from Shura that he made at all times clear to me that you are his one and true and only love; it is even better to hear it from the "other woman." And from me you have heard it. He is yours, lady, his heart and soul belong to you. All I ask is that you treasure them as I would if they had been given to me.

There is no need for a reply. I hope to someday be your friend, but that will be entirely up to you.

Blessings,
Alice Parr

I wrote my return address clearly on the envelope, addressed it by hand, and brought it with me the next Friday evening when I drove to the Farm.

I sat in Shura's office on a stool while he read the letter, and in my mind I reworded the message it contained.

All right, you who are loved by the man I want to be with for the rest of my life; if you truly are what he sees and believes you to be, you deserve to be the uncontested owner of the territory, and I'll have to resign myself to being Graceful Loser. But if by any chance you're playing some kind of game, Pretty-pie, I'll be around to pick up the pieces. Not only that; if you do stay here and I have reason to believe you don't really love him, I'll do everything I can to fight you for him!

When Shura had finished reading, I said, "I'm just going to leave the whole thing in your hands. You mail it or not, as you wish. It's got to be your decision, because there's no way to know how she'll react to something like this, and if it backfires, I have no intention of being held responsible."

He nodded and folded the letter into its envelope.

He's been forced to look at what I feel for him on paper, look it full in the face. No hiding from those words. Doesn't hurt to remind him, yes.

The next morning, Shura said, "There's a new family of compounds David and I have developed, called the 2C-T's. So far, we've completed the synthesis of 2C-T-2, 2C-T-4 and 2C-T-7, and I've taken the "T-2" up to active level."

I murmured, "Uh-huh — ?"

"Quite interesting. Thought you might like to try it with me today?"

"I'd love to," I grinned.

"Just to make sure you're fully informed and will identify the drug properly in your notes," he glared meaningfully at me, as I nodded very hard to indicate that I would, absolutely, write a report, "Its full name is two five dimethoxy, four ethylthiophenethylamine hydrochloride."

"Thanks. I needed that. What level?"

"Well, I took it up to fifteen milligrams and got a plus-two, so I thought we might venture another step, to 18, and see if we can get a plus-three out of it."

The telephone rang. It was an attorney who wanted him to testify in court as an expert witness for the defense in a case involving *Psilocybe* mushrooms. Then there was another call, a reporter in San Jose, who needed information about MDA. Shura went through his usual, "I'll be glad to give you any and all information I have available, but not for attribution. I don't want my name mentioned in the paper," and I sat there, chuckling at his silent pantomime of the usual protests and arguments from the other end of the phone.

Shura had explained to me that he preferred to keep what he called a low profile, that there was no benefit to him in having his name casually publicized, and that if the reporters or journalists were sincere about wanting information, they would accept his condition. They always argued, he said, but in the end they usually agreed to do it his way.

I filled the bathtub and took my bath. When I emerged, Shura was on the phone again, winding up another conversation as I entered his office. He said, "That was an old friend, Terry Major. He used to be part of my experimental group way back in the days when Sam Golding was involved. Terry and Paula — that's his wife — were with Helen and me and the Closes the day Helen took the plunge into mescaline."

"Oh, yes," I said, "The jeweled snakeskin."

"They're among my oldest friends, and we used to do a lot of exploring together. Not as much, the last few years. Terry's a psychologist at the university, and the rest of the time, he and Paula raise mushrooms — the eat-with-your-steak kind, non-psychedelic — and write books about their care and feeding. Good people. You'll meet them someday. Dolph and Ursula became good friends with them, when they were over here from Germany."

Got to get his mind off Ursula and Dolph and Germany.

I sat down and informed him, "I'm ready for the whatsis."

"2C-T-2. That's the 2-carbon analogue, the phenethylamine analogue, of Aleph-2. The T stands for thio, which is a chemist's way of saying you've replaced an oxygen atom with a sulfur atom."

"Oh," I said, "And what's the two for?"

"Which two?"

How many blasted two's are there? Oh, yes.

"The second two."

"It's there because Aleph-2 is the second Aleph compound I made."

"Oh. That explains it," I said brightly, "Thank you very much."

Shura gave me his smart-ass grin and got up. "I'll weigh it out, then."

"I've had my bath, so you can use the water for your shower."

"Let's take our Experimental Substance first. It takes between one and two hours to plateau, so there'll be plenty of time for a shower."

"How long does the whole thing last?"

"Between six to eight hours, if you're me. Going by past experience, you'll probably make it last ten or twelve!"

I laughed. "Okay," I said, "Ingestion of Experimental Substance first, then."

As we clinked our glasses in the kitchen, Shura looked at the clock above the sink and noted, "Two o'clock, give or take," and we drank, toasting ourselves and the lovely warm Saturday.

I curled up on the blue couch and looked through some art books I had stacked on the coffee table earlier. The paintings involved me sufficiently so that I forgot about having taken the 2C-T-2 until reminded by my own alert — a flush of goose bumps up my spine. My watch said 2:35 PM.

I got up and turned on the television. The Discovery channel, one of my favorites, was showing a documentary on Nepal. I watched it with deepening interest until its conclusion. It was 3:00 o'clock and I was definitely plus-one and climbing. I sat down at Shura's typewriter, which I had borrowed again, near the big windows, and began my report with dosage level, date, time of ingestion, and the remark that so far, at over a plus-one, it seemed okay.

Shura came in and asked how I was doing. I said fine, that I was climbing slowly, and asked him, "Where are you?"

He said, "A pretty firm plus-two. You?"

"Not quite a two."

"You want to be alone for a while yet?"

I said yes, thank you, and told him I was writing my report like a good girl. He said, "Will wonders never cease!" and left.

During the next half hour, I became aware of a slight body-load, a sense of strong energy beginning to be felt; at first it was only around the shoulder-blades, but soon spread throughout the rest of me. My tummy asked questions, but there was no nausea, only alertness. Feeling slightly restless, I went outside and turned on the hose to water Shura's new rose bushes, which had been planted by Theo in the early spring. The two cats — Male and Ms — ran up to me and nuzzled my legs passionately. They were usually friendly, but a human in an altered state affected them like catnip. I bent down and stroked them.

A little while later, Shura and I closed the bedroom door to keep out the sound of the telephone, and sat on the bed, cross-legged, facing each other.

"How is it for you, so far?"

"So far, it's fine," I said, "During the transition part, I had a few moments of wondering if my stomach was going to be all right, but that smoothed out. The energy tremor is very strong, but I'm getting used to it, and I think I'm going to like your Two-something."

"What level would you say, at this point?"

"Oh, plus-three, absolutely."

"Me, too." Shura glowed at me, eyes and mouth smiling, as he took off his robe.

There was elegant and stately music playing on KKHI which, we told each other, could only be by Handel.

Shura turned out the bedside light.

At the bottom of my tongue there is a deep black sky with stars in it. There's a different kind of magic down there. Wonder how it feels to him.

I saw a small river flowing between low banks and, on either side of it, carefully tended green lawns sweeping up to mansions separated by flower gardens; there were glimpses of rose trees, marigolds, clusters of blue and violet lobelia, an impression of Greek columns at the front of one great house.

The land of the aristocracy. Absolutely Handel. Serene, measured, then the delicate, playful notes of the flowers. Lovely, lovely.
Sweat trickled across my face. A great ball of scarlet, like a miniature sun, was coming up the river toward me, and I knew what it was. I heard the choking sound in his throat and its explosion into the long, long roar of completion.

I stayed there for a moment, my head on his thigh, sharing the remnants of the beauty.

After a while, I got under the covers to lie beside him, and he rose on one elbow, to look down on me. I closed my eyes.

How easy orgasm used to be, when I was younger. Now, it's a search for the center of my Self; it's hard work, it's a battle to get to an inexplicable thing I can't even name. The threads have to be pulled together by the soul, before the body can release it.

Rachmaninoff's music was forming huge petals of sensuous violet and pink, with a stamen of glowing yellow. Georgia O'Keefe, without question. Suddenly, a tiny fire caught somewhere, far away. The flame spread slowly, and with it rose an almost unbearable sweetness that flooded everywhere as it drove the line of fire toward me, through me.

Shura turned out to be right; I milked the 2C-T-2 for over ten hours. Around 8:00 PM, I finished typing my report on the experiment and went to the Master's study to hand it over. He clapped one hand to his cheek and sputtered disbelief at actually getting my notes without the usual wait of several weeks. I gave him a full Brooklyn raspberry and flounced out, very pleased with myself.

We had some of the soup I had cooked at home, a thick Dutch split pea soup with bits of ham in it, and we sat down to eat in the living room. I turned on the television and found Peter Falk in a rerun of one of his old Colombo murder stories, and for the next hour and a half we both sat hypnotized, moving from our places only during commercials, to go to the bathroom or to pour out more soup.

The carpets and walls were quieter, now, and the energy charge in my body had long since gentled to a comfortable humming.

Just before drifting into sleep, my body fitted to Shura's back, I remembered the letter to Ursula, and knew with complete certainty that he would send it.

CHAPTER 30. ENDING

It took two weeks for Ursula's reply to arrive. She wrote two pages and enclosed my letter, demanding an explanation. Anger, hurt, betrayal, outrage, shock, sorrow; they were all there.

Shura was visibly relieved, smiling broadly as he handed the letter over to me. I read it through and realized that, as far as he was concerned, jealousy and upset were at least consistent with her really loving him.

I reserved comment.

It was interesting, I thought, that she had managed to overlook completely — at least, she made no mention of it — the main and certainly positive message. I tried to put myself in her place, as well as I could, and concluded that — eventually at least — I would have felt some kind of empathy, some degree of compassion for the person who had written that letter, for any woman who had been driven to say to her rival: you've won, and I've lost; be happy and make him happy and bless you. In her place, in fact, I would have written at least a thank you note back to the loser. Eventually.

Everything she'd written added up to a case of hurt pride, which was certainly understandable, but there was no response to my mention of Shura's anxiety and pain. She hadn't even gotten angry at him for doubting her, which I certainly would have.

But, then, I wasn't Ursula and I didn't have enough information to enable me to understand her life, her surroundings or her way of thinking. I had only Shura's view of her, Ben's analysis, and what I could piece together from her letters, and I was still left peering through a very shadowy glass.

Wonder why she didn't phone him, as soon as she got my letter? You'd think that would be the first thing she'd do, with all that surprise and outrage and betrayal and so on. Funny.

One week later, on a Thursday evening, Shura phoned me and said,

"Well, I guess this is it!"

"What is it?" Sinking stomach.

"She's coming. She's leaving there next Wednesday and arriving here a week from today, this time to stay. She phoned me and said that getting your letter made her realize she couldn't keep postponing having it out with Dolph, so it's done — she's said goodbye, and asked her closest friends to keep an eye on him when she's gone — and —," his voice trailed into huskiness for a moment, then he regained his courage, "Thank you, Alice. Thank you for the letter. That was above and beyond, you know."

"I know," I said, not letting myself feel anything yet. Not until the phone call was over.

"Could you possibly come out here for just one last weekend, so we can talk? Is it all right to ask that?" He sounded anxious.

I have to get my things out of there, whatever I've left around. It's going to be hard — everything will be happening for the last time. Maybe.

"Yes, of course it's all right for you to ask it, and I have to pick up my things, so I'll be out — when? Friday evening as usual, or should I come Saturday?"

There was a moment's hesitation, then he said, "Oh, come out like any other weekend, Alice. I know it isn't, and I realize you'll be going through a hard time, but so will I, you know. It's not going to be easy for me, either, this part of it. But if you — if you can see your way clear — Friday would be great. I need to be with you, talk with you."

"Okay. Friday it is."

After I put the phone down, I sat quietly with my cigarette, my Observer frantically active. It was telling me to lay out in my mind everything I knew about the situation, to look at it calmly, review all of it, and to try to postpone grieving because there was still a weekend ahead with Shura.

All right. How do I put off the pain, huh? Part of me is beginning to mourn as I sit here. No way to stop it. And it doesn't matter whether I think she's going to stay forever or not. I still have to go through the closing of the door, as if it were permanent. Because no matter what happens in the future, everything will be changed. Must be changed.

What do I think is going to happen — what does my intuition tell me she'll do? I think she's going to leave him again. Maybe she'll last six weeks. Maybe even six months. But I don't think she'll stay.

Why do I think she won't stay? Because Ben believes it and I want to believe it. No, no — it's more than that. There are too many strange things about this girl's behavior that don't make rock-bottom sense. Anima woman, Ben said, and Ben's pretty shrewd. I hope to God Ben's pretty shrewd!

I got ready for bed with my interior world split into two levels: one was preparing for the grief-anger-pain, and the other was quietly antici-pating the weekend, planning a fast, unemotional gathering up of my various things around the Farm — combs and hairpins and the odd sweater — speculating on whether or not Shura and I would feel like making love. Seeing in my mind the final goodbye, dignified and graceful. Afterwards — afterwards would take care of itself.

Whatever happens in the long run, I'm going to have to shut off this relationship once more and go through the grieving. For the last time. Never again. No matter what, I'll never go through anything like this again, for Shura or anybody else. Never!

That Friday, I was greeted by a long, tight hug. Looking into Shura's eyes, I saw that what he'd said on the phone was true: this part wasn't easy for him. He was going to miss me, and he was already realizing it.

I went around the house, carefully looking for signs of my own presence and removing whatever I found. I was going to play this one clean, with complete integrity. No little mementos lying around. I didn't want her resenting me any more than she already did; there would be no purpose served by hurting her.

Boy, what a good girl am I! Well, that's okay. I have some extraordinary memories and my self-respect, and that's not too shabby.

Friday night, we held each other tightly, without trying to say anything, before turning over to go to sleep.

The next morning, over our coffee, Shura looked at me with a mixture of feelings in his face — happiness, misery, wistfulness — and asked, "How would you feel about having one last experiment with me?"

I replied that, as a matter of fact, it might be very good for both of us.

It's either that, or saying goodbye before the weekend is over, because the ache is getting strong. Tummy and chest. A good psychedelic might help me assimilate some of the pain. Even if it doesn't, it'll still keep us occupied for a while and postpone the goodbye.

"I'd like to share with you one of the old great ones," said Shura, "It's called DOB."

"Uh-huh."

"You should know, it's very long-lasting — between 20 and 24 hours — and it's pretty powerful. I'd like you to know it. That is, if you feel okay about giving it a try?"

"Thank you, yes."

"I was considering a pretty hefty dose, three milligrams. It's fully active as low as two milligrams, but I think you're enough of a hard-head to tolerate three, if you're game?"

I was smiling genuinely for the first time since hearing that Ursula was coming.

"It takes between one and a half to maybe two and a half hours to come on fully, so there's plenty of time to adjust to it," Shura said, and got up to do the weighing out.

We toasted each other silently, this time. The clock over the sink said 10:53. Saturday morning of the last weekend. Maybe.

He's hoping all will go well with Ursula and that I won't hurt too much; I'm hoping all will go badly with Ursula and that I won't hurt too much.

After my bath, I went to the friendly blue couch, and sat curled up in one corner to track the effects. It was a summer day and warm. I was wearing a loose cotton shift, blue with wide stripes of soft yellow, brown and rose. It was years old, worn and comfortable.

Images and phrases drifted through me as I waited.

I remembered Shura telling me, one night, that Ursula had never been able to have an orgasm, and my shock at hearing it. I had wondered if he had enough psychological smarts to know what that might imply, and being unashamedly pleased to have that bit of information. It was, I had thought at the time, another flaw in the beautiful, bright, wonderful Ursula.

Now, gazing out at the great mountain shimmering in the haze, I reviewed what I knew, or thought I knew, about women who could not achieve orgasm — healthy, normal women — and realized I wasn't that sure. Supposedly, they were emotionally immature, or couldn't relinquish control, or were in some way psychologically less well integrated — whatever that meant — than women who didn't have that problem.

And those diagnoses are usually made by men, aren't they? Which should make them slightly suspect. After all, Walter told me early in our relationship that the only mature kind of orgasm was the vaginal; that needing to stroke the clitoris was childish and regressive, or something like that. Which is why I faked orgasm all the years of our marriage, and waited until I was alone to give myself the real thing; I didn't want him to think me immature. I took for granted that, since he was a psychiatrist, he knew whereof he spoke. Until Women's Lib came along, and articles were written about a lot of things people hadn't written about before, and I finally realized that Walter didn't know a damned thing about women's sexuality.

I checked on myself. It was the one-hour point, and I was about a plus-one.

Ursula may well confound all of us. She may turn out to be faithful, constant, deeply loving, all those good things. She may even learn to let go enough to have a full sexual response. With a man like Shura, spending hours and hours making love, it's possible.

I smiled, thinking back. Early in our relationship, Shura had remarked on the strange habit American women had of shaving their underarms and legs, and told me he liked the way European women let body hair grow naturally. Hair, he'd said, was one of the most erotic things about a woman, and he couldn't understand the desire to remove it from any part of the body. I had joked that it was probably some deep-seated streak of pedophilia in the American psyche, adding that I rather liked body hair, myself, that Sophia Loren certainly looked gorgeous enough without shaving, in her early movies, and that if I ever ended up living with him forever after, I would happily forego the use of a razor for the rest of my days.

Suddenly, I was aware of a shift inside, and noted that I'd jumped up to a plus-two within the past 15 minutes. There was a distinct awareness of a change of state, but there weren't any strong visuals yet. Nothing rippled or wiggled. There was an increased feeling of intensity, as if the world was collecting itself to convey a message, but that was usually part of the transition experience with any psychedelic.

Time to ask some serious questions and see what comes up in answer to them. After all, it may be my last psychedelic experience in a long time. Let's start with a simple one: what is the meaning and purpose of life?

The answer slipped in almost casually: "The meaning and purpose of life is life."

Okay. Glad we've cleared that one up.

There was more, apparently.

"All existence is an expression of the One Mind. Allah, The Ground of Being, The I Am, God, are some of the names for that which forms itself, loves itself, hates itself, teaches and learns from itself, gives birth and nourishes itself, kills and devours itself, forever and ever without end."

I sat rock still, then took a deep breath and let it out.

Sweet Jesus! Try cuddling up with THAT in front of the home fire!

I was feeling cold. Transition chill, I thought, and went and got a light cotton blanket to wrap around myself.

When I was settled back on the couch corner, I tried again.

What is love?

"Love is yea-saying with the heart."

Now for the nasty one, I thought, the one that always lurks around the corner.

What about the part of the — God, the It, whatever — that kills and destroys?

"It's there in the service of life, to keep the cycle going. On the God-level, destruction and death are part of the yea-saying to life."

I couldn't stop the process, now. The questions were asking themselves, and the answers were pushing into me instantly, implacably.

That doesn't explain loneliness, pain, sadism, torture, all the cruelty and suffering! Why does the dark side have to be so dark, so evil, so terrible?

"For there to be life, there must be duality — yes-no, positive-negative, male-female. For there to be life, the One must become two halves, Yin and Yang, each half defining itself in opposition — light does not know it is light until it meets darkness — and without this duality, there would be only The Seed, and no flowering. Darkness is. Light is. Each grows, changes and elaborates, shaping itself in new ways, expressing itself in

new forms, destroying itself and renewing itself eternally."
There was a grey, iron weight on my soul.
I'm stoned out of my gourd. No fun, no fun. Wonder if there's going to be a glimmer of hope anywhere in this.
"Within the Yin is an island of Yang and within the Yang is an island of Yin."
Where does THAT leave me, for Pete's sake?
"Right back where you started."
A surge of despair threatened to take over; I shoved against it.
Great. Thanks a lot. Where do you look for compassion, for caring, then, when you need it? Where do you look for love in this Godawful overwhelming universe?
"You look to where compassion and caring are, in the part of the One that loves, the Christ and Buddha, the Great Mother, the Kwan Yin, the countless forms of love and loving everywhere around you, all of them alive within your Self, as are their opposites. You look to your own heart."
The image I'm getting is of an awful cosmic indifference.
"Since we are all forms of the One, there can be no indifference as long as there is a single entity which feels pleasure, sorrow, pain or hope. Whatever a living thing feels, the One feels. Whatever a living thing experiences, the One experiences. The One is each of us; the One is all of us."
I can't accept the idea that half of the One includes so much of evil — what I consider to be evil.
"Yin and Yang are the law of life and do not need your acceptance. Only you need it, and your need is of your own choosing."
I wanted to say, Fuck You! but there wasn't any point in being angry and, besides, I knew it would be ignored.
Is there any other way for me to see all this? Any way to make it easier?
"Life is the One telling stories about itself to itself. It is all story-telling."
I couldn't see how that was supposed to make me feel a whole lot better.
What part do I play in this bloody universe? I mean, of what importance am I in the scheme of things, if any at all?
"With your birth, the universe changed. With the opening of your eyes, the God-mind saw itself as never before. In your ears, all sound was re-created. With you, the One unfolds a new story."
And this happens with the birth of everything alive, am I right?
"Yes."
I remembered the book, Voyage to Arcturus, by David Lindsay, who was one of Tolkien's group of fellow-writers in Oxford. A strange, dark and wrenching story. It wasn't the best writing, but it had a great power.

I'd read it long ago, and was aware at the time that my conscious mind didn't understand what I was reading, but some other part of me did; it took the images, fought them, couldn't let them go, even when I'd finished the book and gone on to other reading.

One scene in particular stayed with me. The hero had wandered into a valley where he saw, all around him, plants thrusting up by the tens of thousands, each individual plant totally unlike any other, some exquisitely beautiful, others grotesque and misshapen; he saw each plant blossoming, withering, then falling lifeless, within moments of its birth. The hero looked on in growing horror until, unable to stand the sight any longer, he ran out of the valley.

I remembering shuddering at what was obviously a portrayal of human existence, each new person emerging with a completely distinctive, never-to-be-repeated set of genes, fingerprints and psychic structure, billions of such one-of-a-kind entities continually being born and dying, all over the earth. The picture was one of terrible waste, of vast indifference on the part of the producing force, and one could only feel a profound horror and, like the book's hero, try to run away.

I had thought at the time, and I thought again now: what was the use of all the suffering, all the joy, all the searches for meaning, if this obscene birthing and dying, this implacable thrusting into blooming life and disintegration back into the dirt was all that was really happening? And why, for God's sake — if God was anything other, anything more than just the unthinking, unstoppable Begetter-Destroyer force — *why* was it happening?

Against that mindless natural machine, that frantic, never-ending life-making and life-taking, there stands what? Only an instinctive knowledge that it is indeed part of the truth of what is, but only part; it is not the whole. I know it's not the whole.

I knew it, because I had met the answer in my spiral experience, week after week, year after year, throughout half of my life. Hello, my dear friend, it said, I greet you with respect, love and laughter. It is joy to meet with you again, it said.

That was the Whole.

Shura came in. He was in his dressing gown and his feet were bare. His hair stood out from his head as it always did when he was in an altered state. He looked at me, wondering how I was, and I smiled at him in reply.

"How's it going?" he asked, leaning down to look into my face.

"I haven't been paying attention to the effects, actually, because I've been too busy with concepts and thoughts and all that there kind of stuff."

"Well, that there kind of stuff *is* part of the effects. What level would you say?"

"Now that I take a look at it, a very much plus-three. How about you?"

"Pounding along nicely. Plus-three, no question. I'll leave you in peace with your thoughts, then. You know where to find me. We haven't plateau'd yet, but it won't be long."

"Yes," I replied, reaching up to take his hand, "I think I'll be with you pretty soon. Just a couple of loose ends to clear up."

He kissed the top of my head and left.

I returned to stalking the wild universe.

Final question, if you please. How do I stop being afraid?

"Know that there is no safety anywhere. There never was and there never will be. Stop looking for it. Live with a fierce intent to waste nothing of yourself or life."

There was one final message.

"Turn fear around. Its other face is excitement."

Shura said that to Dante, during the mescaline day. Can't remember in what context, but I do remember those words.

I took another deep, slow breath and came back to my comfortable old couch. Everything around me was dancing a little at the edges and flowing in the center, and I was reminded of the beloved wallpaper roses in the bedroom. It was time to join Shura.

To the potty, first.

While my body did its usual self-cleansing, the rest of me floated in the soft pulsing of no-time, at peace after battle.

On the bed, we became totally absorbed in the world created by our mouths, our skin, our tangled legs and salty sweat. At one point, lying beneath Shura, I realized I was feeling no sorrow at all, no sense of imminent loss. The coming of Ursula had no reality. What we were doing and feeling now was the only thing that mattered, and there was a moment of knowing that our alliance, the bond between us, would not be broken. The knowledge stood by itself, not susceptible to analysis or cautionary reshaping by the mind.

There was only the two of us, breathing each other's smells, tasting each other's familiar flavors, confusing each other's skin and hair with our own.

The Gods are pleased. We express them well. They like the way we do it.

Shostakovich, Bartok and the delicious Hummel kept us company.

Afterwards, I sat up and said to Shura, "You remember I told you there was a fascinating episode I heard about, from someone who used to volunteer at Dante's institute in Berkeley — you know, the clinic where they allowed people to take LSD trips — and that I was going to tell the group about it, that day on the mescaline?"

Shura nodded.

"Well, I forgot to tell it, obviously. Now that I've thought of it again,

I'll tell you and you can pass it on to Dante."

"Good," said Shura, "But before you begin, I need to empty a bladder."

"Okay, me too," I replied, standing up to put on my shift, "Why don't I heat the soup on the stove, and I can talk while we put some yummies in our tummies."

"Sounds good to me!"

At the table, I began. "I'll tell you what I can remember. One evening, at a party somewhere, Walter and I got into a discussion with a small group of people about psychedelics, particularly LSD, and the conversation got pretty intense. There were several therapists there, and one of them was this sweet, pretty lady with a round face and blonde hair, called Eve, and she told us she'd been a volunteer for a while at the Berkeley place — Dante's clinic — and that it was one of the most fascinating chapters of her life, sitting with people while they went on the LSD journey."

Shura ate slowly, listening.

"I remember telling her that I'd never taken LSD, but that I'd had an extraordinary day on peyote, and I'd had an encounter with what I called the death door, and that it was beautiful and friendly, but I wasn't tempted to go through it because I knew it wasn't time and there was still a lot I wanted to do. I said I'd wondered ever since what might happen to someone who saw that way out of life and *was* tempted; what would happen if he actually went through, or tried to go through?"

I ate some soup, then continued.

"She stared at me and said that, as a matter of fact, she had an answer — at least, she could tell me what happened to one of her clients at the clinic who did just that. She was sitting beside his cot when, apparently, he saw the exit and decided to go through it. What *she* saw was a young guy lying there, who had stopped breathing. She called out to him, and when he didn't respond, she tried to find his pulse and there wasn't any. He was in clinical death, she said. She dashed out to get help. By the time the staff people got back to him with the injection and whatever to kick his heart back to life, he'd been dead for just under three minutes.

"Eve said that, as they rushed through the door, he opened his eyes. He was back. After all the panic had died down, he told her that he'd seen that opening and wanted to go through it, and did, and he got to a place where an entity of some sort told him very firmly, but kindly, that he wasn't allowed to stay because it wasn't his time to die, and he was going to have to go back and stick around until it was the proper time. Then — Zap! — he was waking up on the cot with people running into the room, brandishing hypodermics and stuff.

"He also told her he would never again consider cutting his life short, and that he certainly wouldn't have any fear of death, when it was time to go. One of the things Eve concluded was that there must be some kind of

— ah — Overseer part of us that keeps an eye on things, so to speak. She said she'd never talked about the incident outside of the clinic before, especially not to other psychiatrists, needless to say!"

Shura's eyes squinted at me thoughtfully, and he nodded. After a moment, he said, "Thank you. I'll tell Dante, if he doesn't already know about it. That's quite a story."

When we'd finished eating, we went into the living room, where I curled up in my usual place and Shura pulled the ottoman closer and sat on the edge, leaning forward. He smiled at me, "Did I ever explain my twosies-threesies theory to you?"

I shook my head.

"Didn't think so. Now is as good a time as any to tell it, while we're still blasted out of our skulls. Ready?"

I grinned, "Sure! What's a two-Zee, three-Zee?"

"Well, you know those great old — what's your name for them? Sophomoric Questions? — in particular, the one that goes, 'How did life start on earth?'"

I protested, "Hey, it was someone else who called them that name. Don't lay that one on me!"

"All right, but anyway, this has to do with the question of where we — meaning mankind — originated; on this planet or elsewhere. Okay?"

"Sure. One of my favorite questions, as a matter of fact."

"Let me lay the groundwork for a minute. A living animal, plant, bug or virus can be defined absolutely by a connected series of molecules. These molecules are called nucleotides."

I nodded, hoping I would be able to keep track of details, but sure I'd at least get the music, as Shura would say.

"At the far left of this series is the first nucleotide, and at the far right of the series is the billionth nucleotide. This series, taken as a unit which is called the chromosome, completely defines that animal or plant or bug or virus. Not only does it define the structure and how it will look, it also defines every instinct and how it will behave. All of the shapes and all of the behavior patterns are incorporated in that one series of nucleotides, and in no two individuals is that nucleotide series the same."

So far, so good; I haven't got lost yet. He's so full of energy, talking like this. Beautiful man. He makes ideas as sexy as love-making.

"A small percent of this long series, when the individual molecules are taken three at a time, represent a code for amino acids, and thus represent a code for protein structure. The vast remainder of this series of nucleotides makes no known sense at the moment. But then, again," he gestured at me, "We don't know yet how instincts and memories are encoded, right?"

"Yeah."

"The code is one of triplets, and since one has a choice from among four nucleotides for each position of the triplet, there is clearly the potential for 64 amino acids. Well, 62, anyway, because one code has to say START and one has to say STOP. But there are only about 20 amino acids, so there is a great deal of redundancy in the system. With several of the amino acids, the first two nucleotides define the amino acid, regardless of which nucleotide occupies the third position. You with me so far?"

"So far."

I sort of lost something around the 64 amino acids, but it's basically clear.

"Well," said Shura, rocking a little, "It has always seemed to me a very appealing thought that this triplet system — I call it 'Threesies' — evolved from a simpler, two-nucleotide system, a 'Twosie.'"

I grinned and corrected my mental spelling.

"I enjoy giving my class a theoretical problem, to wit: if you were given physical and chemical hands of infinite skill, could you design a duplication of a living organism, based upon a 'Foursies?' In other words, it would be a task of stretching out an entire chromosome, that which represents a living individual, and introducing a fourth nucleotide after every triplet. It would be a task of designing a ribosome that would require a Foursie to define an amino acid, but the fourth position should be indifferent — meaning that it can be any nucleotide. It would require going at every single aspect of the entire genetic structure, expanding the three's to four's, and then not using the fourth. Then, if this chromosome could be inserted into a living cell, it would produce the same individual, with the same appearance and instincts as when he was a Threesie."

I wonder if this would be easier to pin down and remember if I weren't stoned. Probably not.

"Now, look at the fantastic room that's been made available for evolution! With time, that fourth position may no longer be indifferent, but can be used for survival, adaptation, development, in ways which would be totally unforeseeable. An interesting experiment," he cocked his head at me, "And I think potentially do-able."

I nodded, trying to look keenly intelligent.

"And I believe that that's exactly the way the Threesies evolved from the Twosies!" Shura smiled at me, obviously hoping for a look of startled fascination or, even better, astonished disbelief. Instead, I leaned forward and gave him earnest anticipation. It was the least I could do.

He continued, "Long, long ago, in a place far away, there lived an intelligent species that had its RNA and DNA put together in the form of a binary genetic code. This may have originally limited their proteins to 16 amino acids, or I should really say 14, because one code says START and one says STOP —"

I laughed.

"— but they evolved beyond this limitation and generated complex genetic machinery to create new amino acids. Just as we — we Threesies — require amino acids that don't lie within our chromosomes.

"And so, a professor in this faraway place, long, long ago, proposed to his students: do you think you can design a system in which all the two-unit pairs in our chromosomes incorporate a third unit and become a triplet system? Of course, he said, you're going to have to redesign ribosomes to accept a triplet system and ignore the identity of the third component — as was the case earlier, where the fourth position was to be indifferent, remember? — held in reserve, if you will, for later use.

"And I believe this is what actually occurred. I think spores of this triplet system were scattered to the universe. Some fell into blazing suns and most are, without doubt, still adrift. But at least one fell onto our planet Earth, where it produced a living organism that was, by appearance, related to our Twosies in a faraway place, in a time long ago, but carried within it that third nucleotide potential which allowed, over the intervening billion years, the development of the human!"

I stared at him, mouth open. He was perfectly serious. It was a wonderful theory — what I understood of it — and I believed it.

"Do you think," I asked tentatively, "That it will ever be possible to discover where, exactly, we started from? I mean, where — what planet or what system the professor was in?"

Shura replied, "I'm certain that the star map of our parents lies within the structure of the ribosome they created, but — as they say — that's another story."

Meaning he hasn't figured that one out yet.

"Now, for a flight of fancy," said Shura, and I knew him well enough to assume that he was proposing something he considered a real possibility, but wanted to leave open an escape hatch in case he needed to revise something, "If this Threesies from Twosies is reasonable, then one cannot avoid the question of how did the Twosies evolve from Onesies? It seems inescapable that, on a place even far, farther away, long, longer ago, some professor type was carrying about him chromosomes of our famous four nucleotides, but where each nucleotide represented an amino acid — well, not really four amino acids, because one has to say START and the other, STOP — anyway, this teacher, who was a Onesie and who was composed of protein made largely of two amino acids, was instructing his students to construct a Twosie.

"Now, you get to the real heart of it. This reduces the question of the origin of life to something that could very well be rationalized in light of some recent research on the development of complex molecules by chance. They would have needed only to bring together a few nucleotides which would determine a protein of a few amino acids which, somehow, reinforced the ordering of the nucleotides; namely, the system represented a transform between nucleotides and amino acids that, after many failed trials, stumbled upon one which was self-reinforcing. The time requirement for this having occurred would be unbelievably long, but clearly it did happen. There was not anywhere near the time needed, on this earth of only four billion years' age — a major portion of which was taken up with surface conditions which were intolerant of life — for that to have taken place on this planet."

He spread his arms wide and let them drop again, smiling to indicate that he was finished. I said, "I believe it absolutely. Every fantastic word of it. Have you considered publishing it?"

Shura shook his head, "Not really. No, it's just for my own enjoyment, right now. Every time I propose it to my class, I think of something else to work into it. I guess you could say it's still evolving."

When we went to bed, both of us were still feeling the effects of the DOB. Shura was down to a plus-one; I had descended to a soft plus-two. We weren't sure sleep was going to be possible, but somewhere in the middle of Beethoven's Ninth it must have caught up with us, because we weren't around for the ending.

The next day was Sunday, the day I had decided I should leave, to give each of us one day alone before the work-week began. I knew I would need crying time, and that Shura would have a thousand things to change, to fix, to make ready for his love's arrival on Thursday.

In the intimate warmth of the bed, holding me for what he believed was the last time, and what I hoped would not be, but had to allow might be after all, he said something which was intended as a wistful half-joke, "You know, you and Dolph should get together; if only you were friends, you could keep each other company, help each other through this, you know? Perfect solution!"

I held my breath for a moment, not trusting myself to speak, wondering if I had misunderstood, knowing I hadn't. How could he be so wise, so extraordinarily understanding about so many things, yet say a profoundly stupid thing like that!

I rolled out of his arms, and sat on the edge of the bed to put on my gown. My back to him, I said, "You mean, us poor sad little cast-offs; wouldn't it be nice if we could cheer each other up, so our misery wouldn't cast a pall on the happiness of the Prince and Princess? I must say it isn't one of your more brilliant scenarios, my dear."

There was silence behind me. I could hear him getting out of the bed, and as I walked from the room, I heard a quiet, "I'm very sorry. That was pretty dumb."

Yes, I thought, it damned well was.

How could either of us have expected to get through this weekend without

something hurtful being said, something awkward? It just wasn't possible. Okay.
Drop it now. Don't want my last sight of him to be through a cloud of anger.

At the gate, Shura dropped his head down and into the car window to kiss me, very gently, on each eyelid. I said, noting with pride that my voice sounded even, pleasant, affectionate, "Try to let me know what's going on, when you can. I'll always be a friend to you, my love, and I hope to be a friend to Ursula too."

He said nothing, but there were tear tracks on his cheeks, and it was time to leave.

On the way home, I was surprised to note that I felt no grief yet, only a kind of high-energy state, and thought I was probably maintaining myself in some sort of suspension of emotion —

State of suspended an-emotion. Not bad, for a shattered psyche. Not bad at all.

— some kind of semi-shock state, so that I could drive home with maximum safety. I reminded myself to be extremely attentive to driving details, and not to fall into the trap of getting distracted by thoughts. I kept my adrenalin up by telling myself to be careful, careful, until I had been on the freeways for a good half hour, and decided I was going to be all right. Until I got home, of course. Just keep your attention where it belongs until you get home, I crooned to myself. At home, you can let loose.

Inside my house, I began the grieving. Again. All of it again. And for the last time, I said over and over to myself. No more Mistress Yo-Yo. It had all been my decision, to do what I'd done, but Jesus Aitch Christ, enough is enough is enough. Even the most extraordinary man in the world isn't worth more than — what was it? — two closings of the door and willingness to return. Three? Basta, as the Italians say.

Finally, the angry inner voice subsided and the tears came. My Observer sighed with relief, knowing that the sobs and aching ribs meant that the beginning of healing wasn't too far off.

CHAPTER 31. VOLCANO

When the children came home from their weekend with Walter, I told them, "I've got some grieving to do. The German lady Ursula is coming to stay, and I personally don't believe it's going to last, but I have to act as if it will, because I don't know. No matter what happens in the future, I have to close the door again on my relationship with Shura. You know how I feel about him —," which they did; I'd been open about it all along, " — so it's hard. I have to go through the ending of this, because everything will be changed in the future, no matter how it comes out. So please be patient with me for the next few days. And don't worry. I'll be okay after a while, I promise."

They nodded, their faces shy, and hugged me hard before going off to bed.

On Monday, I phoned the hospital and said that a family emergency made it necessary for me to take the day off. I spent hours writing in my notebook, which helped me ignore the almost constant stream of wetness flowing down either side of my nose. When I went to the bathroom I avoided the mirror. I opened a can of soup and forgot to put it in a pot until two hours later, and remained generally unaware of the details of what I was doing. Everything was on automatic while I wrote out my feelings and let the waves of pain wash through, my Observer keeping watch like the family doctor. I wrote:

"Surges of grief, stomach tightened and churning. Head tension gradually forcing headache. Like childbirth in reverse - - the more you cry, the longer the intervals between waves of pain, and the shorter the wave.

"As soon as Ursula is near, he's ready to give me away. He said Dolph and I should get together; it was a joke, but the truth is, he'd be happy to see me with someone else, with another lover. It would give him only relief, because it would lift his feelings of responsibility. The ultimate rejection is having the person you love hope (and say) that you'll meet someone else and be loved by someone else.

"What did he say in his letter to Ursula? Loss of faith. I'm feeling loss of belief in the validity of what he felt for me. I'm seeing the total absence of love and deep caring, now.

"This is a death I'm grieving for. The death of what has been; of both the good and the not good in our relationship. No matter what Ursula does, he and I will never be the same. I will not have it the same. Because he was so much hers, he was never able to give himself fully to me, and I'll never accept anything like that again. No more triangle, no more half-love, no more withholding. So, either way, the past is past, and dead."

It helped, writing it out.

"Why did I allow this to happen? Because I love him. And it was worth it — worth all the pain and anger. Even three times in one year, which must be a record. And I had love back. Not the words, but very much else. Enough to be unbelievably happy for a while. I have that, and my dignity and pride."

Later in the day, I wrote:

"No appetite. Underneath the pain, I found a knowledge of the rightness of what's happening, and — unexpectedly — a sense of joy! Don't know why, but it's quietly there. Something very far inside me knows all is well, although the rest of me continues to tear itself into bloody strips."

The kids came home from school, glanced at my pink, swollen face and made understanding grimaces. They did their homework quietly and pitched in as usual to set the table for dinner on the long tiled bench. I asked them questions about their school and managed to keep my voice level and my mind reasonably well focused on their answers. They were tuned in to me, I knew, and any effort to pretend what I didn't feel would be detected immediately, so I remained honest in what I said and what I showed in my face, and left it up to them to deal with it as best they could.

Wendy was, as usual, Earth-mother, stroking my head as she passed by, hugging me tightly when it was time for bed. Ann, who usually talked her way through difficult situations, relying on humor and lightness of spirit — or the appearance of lightness — to carry her over the bumps, fell into an irresistible sadness, her empathy with my pain overwhelming her. At one point, I put my hands on her shoulders and said, in as down-to-earth a voice as possible, "Don't let yourself tune into my feelings, honey. It'll really be all right in a day or two, believe me. Sorrow doesn't kill, and the wound does heal. It's going to be okay."

Brian, aware at some level that too much closeness to me could disable him, glanced at me now and then with helpless compassion when he had to be near, and for the most part kept himself separate in his room, concentrating on homework.

I went to the hospital Tuesday and told the people in Medical Records a short story about a favorite relative dying unexpectedly of a heart attack. They were sympathetic and left me alone. I made it through the day, escaping from memories and grief for minutes at a time in the need to concentrate on the flood of medical reports pounding into my ears, hour after hour. I typed at full speed and left at 5 o'clock, relieved at having managed to stifle the tears all day, at not having forced my fellow transcribers to pay more than the slightest attention. They were nice women, all of them, but they weren't close friends, and disturbing them would have been unfair and of no help to me at all.

It wasn't until I was on my way out of the hospital, at a few minutes after 5:00 PM, that the full force of the anger hit.

I stopped in mid-stride on the grey pavement, my car in sight across the parking lot, immobilized by the deep red fury which had suddenly taken over. It was appalling in its intensity. My Observer said, half-humorously, "Uh-oh," and shrugged, knowing that this moment had been inevitable. Then it spoke loudly, reminding me that this kind of anger could get me — or somebody else — killed on the highway, and that I'd better put it under wraps, any way I could manage it, until I got home.

I drove very carefully, paying attention to every move of my own and every other driver around me, as if I were quite drunk and unable to trust my reflexes or my concentration.

At home, I said hello to the children through gritted teeth, aware that I was going to start shaking, and asked them if they would please take care of their own supper, explaining, "I've just gotten hit by lot of anger, all of a sudden — which is a perfectly healthy thing to have happen, by the way — and I need to be by myself for a couple of hours, if that's all right."

They said yes and sure and okay, we'll take care of ourselves, don't worry.

I went to the kitchen and got a glass and a bottle of cranberry juice and took them up to my bedroom. I opened the drawer where I kept the

MDMA that Shura had given me for my own use, many months ago, and took out a little envelope marked 120 milligrams and another one marked 50 milligrams, in case a supplement should seem like a good idea. I swallowed the first dose in some juice and lay down on my bed.

The fury was hot and terrible, deep inside my stomach, where I'd held it during the drive home. I gave it permission to come to the surface. The top of the volcano opened, just above my navel, and a flow of searing, murderous hatred spurted upward like lava. I lay on my back, hands clenched, body trembling, and reminded myself not to scream out loud, because of the children. I was a bit frightened by the rage, by the horrible force of it. It was one thing to know intellectually that it would mellow out to anger, and that the anger, in turn, would soften to acceptance, and that it was all part of the healing process; it was quite another to feel it shaking my body, to realize that it was this kind of sharp, thrusting fury that caused some people to kill other people, just to rid themselves of the ugly pain by putting it into someone else.

I remembered, all over again, the remark about Dolph and me getting together — the insulting pity, the arrogant selfishness of those words — as lava flowed down the sides of the fire mountain, burning trees and fields and Shura and Ursula and everything else in sight, devouring the land to the horizon.

My Observer volunteered a small, tentative thought that the poor guy could be excused, considering the circumstances, for failing to fully appreciate anybody's grief. Come on, for Pete's sake, it said, don't distort your perceptions or your ways of thinking, even though you're feeling murderous. You don't have to justify the rage; it has a right to be there. Just experience it. Let it go through you. You'll stay sane. You'll come out in one piece.

An impulse struck me. I thought of the notebook I'd been writing in since I left him for the last time. I thought of the raw pain, the fresh blood that lay on the most recent pages.

I decided to rip those pages out of the notebook. I imagined putting them into a manila envelope, licking the envelope closed, and addressing it to Dr. Alexander Borodin, and I saw Shura opening it and reading what I had written, and I knew that it was the perfect answer to that last careless, stupid insult. He would never forget what he would read. I knew it wasn't something that could be forgotten. He would carry the gut knowledge of my agony with him for the rest of his life, as I would.

Yes, of course it was my decision to risk all this; of course it was up to me and I said yes and I knew it would mean hurt when it ended. That still doesn't forgive that unconscious message to please take my pain away so his happiness wouldn't be tainted. It doesn't forgive ruining what should have been a loving, graceful goodbye.

I was beginning to feel the first effects of the MDMA. There was a corner of quietness inside, just a hint of a pale, cool, dove-grey feeling at the edge of the searing fire.

I was crying again, hard. My body was still trembling. *The tremor's probably the way the body is handling the too much energy of the anger. It's all right. In fact, it feels good.*

I closed my eyes and felt the looming, blistering shapes of the emotions churning inside me; there was the rage, the wracking sorrow and loss, there was an element of self-destruction, and something howling for help, for an end to the pain, all mixed together. I relaxed into what I expected would be a good long, thoroughly wrenching experience which should leave me — I hoped — very much cleansed and maybe hurting a bit less.

The voice came abruptly, without warning. It snapped open my eyes and jolted me upright on the bed. It spoke without sound and its words were absolutely clear in my head. It was a voice of absolute authority, and it most certainly was not my Observer.

It said, "Stop this *now*! Know your anger, get it out, and be rid of it. Forget about sending notebook pages in envelopes. Put aside being sorry for yourself. Shura is about to undergo a heartbreaking. He will need you and everything loving you can possibly be to him, not six months from now, but within a very short time. You must remain his refuge. Be ready. He'll be in touch with you soon and he'll need you."

It was gone. I was left with a serene, gentle, rather strange feeling of something easing out of me. The strangeness, I thought, was perhaps a different dimension of the grief and struggle. There was still the heaviness in the center of my chest, but it had softened.

I had never before had such an experience.

The message didn't make sense, either, I thought. Ursula was coming in on a plane on Thursday, just a couple of days from now. She was coming. What did the voice mean when it said, Shura would have heartbreak — pain — immediately? Ursula's plane lost in a crash? I didn't want that, I didn't want harm to her. That would be no answer for us. He would be in love with her memory, then. Better an outgrowing, a long-term outgrowing of each other, than something like that.

It mustn't be a tragedy, whatever was going to happen. Could it be that she would not be coming, after all? That simply wasn't believable. She had never, as far as I knew the history of their affair, told Shura she was flying in and failed to arrive when expected.

Sitting on the bed, wondering what the hell that message meant, slightly awed by having had such a thing happen at all, I realized suddenly that there was no anger anywhere. It had vanished. All it left behind was a sob-jump in the throat now and then as I forgot to breathe evenly. There was a sense of utter calm, like a meadow after a violent storm has passed,

everything crystal clear and quiet in my chest and stomach, where the fury
had boiled a few minutes before.

I was even able to laugh at myself.

*Well, whatever that visitation was, it sure cured you for the moment, hey?
What're you going to do now?*

Go downstairs, I decided.

The children were seated in different parts of the living room. Wendy
and Brian were scrunched over homework. Ann was watching television
with the sound turned way down, so I assumed she'd finished hers. I sat
down on the couch and grinned at all three of them in turn and said, "Well,
a funny thing happened on the way to my screaming anger fit. I'll interrupt
you only long enough to tell you about it, and then I'll shut up. By the
way, I'm feeling very all right."

I told them about taking MDMA (they had already heard me talk
about my experiences with that particular drug) and the voice like a river
of cold water on the hot coals I was clutching to my insides, and what the
voice had said. Ann's eyes were round and she laughed with relief. She
was obviously picking up my matter-of-fact pleasantness and the absence
of the pain which had filled the house for days now. Wendy said, very
softly, "Wow!" Brian smiled widely and said, "Boy, I can't wait to see if it
turns out to be true!"

"Well," I said, "Even if it all ends up being imagination and nothing to
do with reality, I must admit that the MDMA has given me a great feeling
of having gone through the worst of all this and coming out the other side.
Maybe it won't last, but I really do feel some healing, some sort of — well,
as if the bleeding has stopped, so to speak. And, by the way, thanks to all
of you for having been so helpful while I was in this state. I'm very
grateful to you and love you very much. End of speech. Continue with
homework."

When I had seen them into bed, having hugged each of them with a
very good hug, so that they could feel with their body antennae the absence
of hurting in me, it was around 10:00 PM.

I looked at the phone and it was clear that I was supposed to pick it up
and call Shura and tell him what had happened.

The Observer said, Hey, hold it! Why don't you just keep this one to
yourself, for the moment?

I knew it would be sensible and reasonable to do just that; in fact, it
made no sense at all to tell him. I would sound like a fool and, moreover,
I would probably appear to be trying to ruin his anticipation and joy. But
the impulse to share it with him was strong enough to be considered
another order from Whomever.

Shura's voice, when he answered, had a hopeful, anxious eagerness
that told me he was waiting to hear from Ursula. I let him down as gently

as I could.

"Hello, my friend, I felt I had to call you tonight. Do you mind?"

"Of course I don't mind, Sweet Alice. In fact, I can't tell you how good it is to hear your voice."

He sounds as if he really means it, bless his heart. I know he was hoping for Ursula, but he did make that sound like genuine pleasure.

I suddenly knew with absolute sureness that Ursula hadn't phoned since I'd left. It was ridiculous to think such a thing, but I knew it was so. Just to be polite, I asked if he had heard from his lady recently, and did he know what plane to meet?

"No, not yet, but I expect to at any moment."

"Okay," I said, "I feel rather weird about telling you what just happened to me, but for some reason I'm sure I'm supposed to."

I told him the little story about taking the MDMA, leaving out the worst of the rage and saying nothing about manila envelopes and notebooks and revenge. I told him about the voice, remarking that this kind of thing had simply never happened to me before, and I didn't expect it to happen again in the future, and I hadn't the slightest idea what it meant, but it was a powerful experience, and I was deeply impressed.

Shura didn't comment on what I gave him of the voice's message, but after a moment's silence he said, very quietly, "Thank you for telling me about it. I can't offer any explanations, of course, any more than you can. We'll just have to wait and see."

I said, "I'm of course taking into account all the usual causes of such an experience, like stress and escape from this and that, et cetera, but there it is. As you say, the rest is waiting to see whether it turns out to be what it seemed or not."

"What it seemed?" Shura sounded confused.

"Oh, you know — like an ESP thing; something like that. Voice from the future or from the cosmos — *whatever*" I ended up with a raspy impatience, and told him to go to sleep and forget all about it. I'd had a compulsion to tell him, I had given in to it, and that was that, so "Goodnight and sleep tight and make sure all those various whatchamacallits don't bite."

He chuckled and wished me good dreams, then he thanked me again.

When I'd put the phone down, my Observer shook its head disapprovingly, but I knew I'd done what I was supposed to do and there was no point in questioning it.

During the night, I dreamed I was housekeeping a mountain highway, cliffs on one side of me and a sheer drop on the other. It was my job to fit a wide red carpet exactly and properly to the road so that trucks coming around the blind corner wouldn't skid or be off balance. I felt very cheerful.

CHAPTER 32. TRANSITION

It was Thursday evening when Shura phoned me. His voice was strained. He told me that the night before, not having heard from Ursula about what plane she was going to be on, or what time she would arrive, he had phoned Germany.

"What happened?"

"Dolph answered the phone," said Shura, "Nice and friendly, as usual. He told me that Ursula left a message for me. The message was that she had gone to a retreat of some kind to think out some conflicts, and that she would be in touch with me when she returned."

"Oh, Lord," I breathed. No plane. No suitcases. Not this Thursday, anyway.

"I asked Dolph if he had any idea when she would be returning, and he said — very sympathetically — that he didn't think she'd be away for more than a few days, although he couldn't be absolutely sure, of course."

"Oh, boy."

"Yeah. Oh boy."

"But she sent her books, Shura!"

He said, deadly quiet, "Did she?"

"Oh — I see what you mean. We only have her word for that. No trunk has actually arrived yet."

"Precisely."

I thought back to the Voice of Authority that had broken up my rage-fest, two nights earlier.

Thank you for that message, that warning, thank you, Whoever you are. Thanks for making me wait. If I'd gone with my anger and sent those notes, I'd be strangling myself right now. Probably would have lost him.

I asked, "Is there anything I can do to help?"

Shura sighed, then after a little silence he said, "It's just good knowing you're there. Thank you for being there for me to talk to, my friend. I simply don't know what's going on, what's going to happen next; I don't know what she intends, what she wants, and why did she just leave me dangling all these days, waiting? Why couldn't she have phoned me herself? Leaving me in silence, waiting for word, waiting to find out which plane — I don't understand somebody doing that to the person they love."

"Neither do I," I said, but softly. I didn't want to put him in the position of having to defend Ursula.

"You see," he said, "With that silence just at the time I should have been hearing from her about travel details, you can imagine what I thought must have happened!"

"Oh, of course," I said, suddenly remembering, "You thought maybe murder and suicide."

"I was beginning to be really terrified; I was talking myself into all sorts of ghastly scenarios. I was so convinced that something was horribly wrong, I couldn't believe I was hearing Dolph's voice on the phone for the first second. I mean, he was not only alive and answering the phone, he was sounding perfectly normal. I just couldn't take it in for a moment, then I felt this tremendous relief, because I knew he couldn't sound that way if there had been some kind of — you know — and then I had one of those milliseconds of wondering if — if I was completely crazy and I'd imagined this entire love affair, the whole thing. Utter disorientation."

"Yes. I know what you mean. Reality gone up-side-down."

"And now," he said, his voice sounding less strained, "I think I'm going to have the rest of my bottle of Burgundy and go to bed as bombed as I can manage, and get some sleep."

"This all happened last night?"

"Yes, last night. I've been trying to come to grips with it all day. Didn't sleep much after the call. Have to catch up tonight."

"My dear Shura," I said softly, "I'm with you, I'm here for you in whatever way you need me; you know that. Sleep as well as you can and let me know what's happening when you find out."

"Thank you, Alice," he said, his voice coming a bit more to life, "I'll let you know everything I know as soon as I know it. You deserve that."

"Yes," I agreed, "I bloody well do."

"Oh, by the way," he said, "Just a closing thought I'll share with you. I can't help feeling that Ursula was there all the time, listening to Dolph telling me she'd gone to think things over in a monastery. Just standing quietly there, you know?"

"That's a rather grim thought," I said, thinking that he'd probably hit the nail on the head.

"Yes, it is, rather."

I murmured, "Get some sleep, honey."

I put the phone down and sat there, trying to think, but all that came to mind was a profoundly silly question that skittered through my head and out the other side.

He said a monastery. Do monasteries take ladies? Or does it have to be a nunnery? Never mind. Never mind.

Shura called me every evening while he waited for further word from Ursula, reporting in, his voice flat, depressed. I gave out as much warmth as I could over the phone, knowing that he was going into a grieving state and that he wouldn't register much of what I said, only the tone of voice.

I said nothing about coming out to the Farm. I realized that the last thing I should do now was push myself on him. I was not a substitute for Ursula, didn't intend to be a fill-in for Ursula, and whatever place I was to have in his life — if at all — it would have to be a completely different one than it had been. And it might not turn out that way at all. Ursula could phone at any moment and say that she was coming, she was over her cold feet, she was ready and she would be on plane this and flight that. It could still happen.

But the Tuesday Night Voice didn't say, "temporary discomfort." It said Shura would be in pain and in need of me. So far, it's been right.

I sat down at my typewriter on Sunday night after the children had gone to bed, and wrote my second and final letter to the German Lady.

This one, she won't send back to Shura.

Ursula:

This will be the last time I write to you, and I do so more as an exercise in futile anger than in the hope that it will accomplish anything worthwhile, because you seem to live in a world that is not understandable to me, and I cannot identify with what you feel and do, although I have tried to do just that for more than six months.

You have been portrayed to me by Shura as a highly intelligent, sensitive, deeply feeling and responsible woman; a woman who opened the long-closed doors inside him and showed him how to experience emotions he had buried for most of his adult life. You were the magic, beautiful and loving person who was his refuge, his other self, his future.

For a long time I believed this to be the true picture, even allowing for his obvious tendency to see everything about you through the well known rose-colored glasses. I did have a hint of something else, from someone close to Shura who loves him dearly and wants to see him happy — a perceptive and wise person who said, with what now appears to be extraordinary insight, "Ursula needs to be wanted and adored, but she needs this from more than one man. She is compelled to fulfill a man's fantasy, to become his ideal, his inspiration. She is a classic anima woman, using Jung's term, and completely unconscious of her own drives and motivations. I believe she is not capable of really giving herself — neither to her husband, nor to anyone else. She cannot commit herself emotionally. And I'm very much afraid of what she will do to Shura — perhaps in a week, perhaps in a year. She will not stay with him, after the first excitement wears off. And he will be desperately hurt."

The friend had not said this to Shura, since he knew it would not be believed, and it could put a strain on a friendship that means a great deal to him. But he did say it to me.

Yet, through Shura I learned a little of your search for yourself, your deep need not to hurt, your apparent determination to bring the relationship with your husband to a graceful close, with kindness and caring, so that you would leave no emotional loose ends. I learned of your great love for Shura, your longing to be with him. I believed it for a long time.

I understood your apparent struggle to find a good way to resolve your question of what to do about these two men in your life. That struggle, that search, obviously had to have an end, a final answer.

The only answer you seemed to come up with was the temporary (and obviously exciting) one of visits across the ocean to the adoring White Knight in California — for a week or so — until the pull of the adoring husband took you back to Germany. Not long enough for the honeymoon to be over, for the reality of septic tanks and dry yellow hills and ironic, angry moods and impatience and head colds and being too tired to make love — not long enough for any of that to assert itself and have to be lived with and dealt with. Just long enough to confirm the adoration and the yearning, to warm yourself in the sexual fire and the open loving made even more open and spiritual by the chemicals. A good vacation for your body and soul.

He was yours, all yours, and he would wait. You knew he loved deeply and would not easily be turned from you. You knew your own beauty and intelligence and ability to make contact with that soul-love — you knew it well enough to assume that he would stay yours until you chose to come for longer, if you wanted to.

And there, in your home, was the other man who yearned and wanted and needed. An embarrassment of riches for any woman.

It becomes even more tempting as one approaches 40, to exercise that kind of power, to know that one can attract, hold, and keep an interesting and desirable man. It's a temptation that one learns — or should learn — to relinquish. That power to seduce carries with it a great deal of excitement. A woman with intelligence and insight feels out the power and recognizes it as a potential danger to herself and to the men who fall in love with her. She learns to be careful of opening up what she will not assuredly nurture. The Buddhists say that, if you save a human being from death, you are forever responsible for the rest of that person's life. That doesn't mean you shouldn't save someone from death; it does mean that you should be aware of your actions and their consequences. In opening up a person's soul, you have the same obligation to be aware of what you're doing, to be careful, and to accept responsibility.

Seeing Shura's love and need and anxiety, I sent you, some time ago, a letter which was very hard to write. There have been many aspects of my love for Shura about which I had no choice — I could not choose to have him love differently; I could not decide how his relationship with you would go. I did, however, have a choice about that letter. And, to ease your mind and heart, I gave you the kind of assurance that every woman truly in love wants and certainly never — almost never — gets from her rival. I told you that the man I love loves you. Who could have asked for more, Ursula?

What you have done since, and most especially what you have done during the past two weeks, has made it impossible for me to see you through Shura's eyes any longer. I believe in your intelligence; I do not believe in your insight. I believe in your need for love; I do not believe in your capacity for real and deep, lifelong loving. I can believe in your agony and conflict in making these choices about your husband and your lover, but I'm no longer sure that it is much more than a need for drama — emotional drama — in your life. It keeps things exciting, and when you can live the fantasy through letters and phone calls, the drama and sparkle of your life is maintained. It continues to feed you. And, most important of all, Ursula is kept assured of her own desirability.

As I write this, you may indeed be on your way to Shura. Your motives may or may not be what I think they are — most probably you are quite unconscious of them yourself — but I have no faith that you come to him with the kind of changes inside you that he has hoped for, and is still hoping for. I do not think you are capable of those changes or that kind of maturing. And I can do nothing about it — I can only wish that you might be able to understand and acknowledge your deepest needs as they really are and — understanding them — free Shura.

I wish you well, Ursula. But I love the man who loves you. And I wish to see him loved as he is capable of loving, for the rest of his life.

Goodbye.
Alice Parr

I wouldn't tell Shura about the letter, I thought. Perhaps some day, but not yet. It would serve no purpose. I mailed it the next morning, on my way to work.

I didn't ask to see him the next weekend, either, and he didn't invite me to come out to the Farm. It was his dark night of the soul, and he was going to go through it by himself, as I would have, in his place.

Sunday, on the phone, he let the bitterness come through. He said, "I don't think I'm going to allow that kind of thing to happen to me again. I'm never going to let myself be that vulnerable again. Nothing is worth this degree of pain. Nothing and no one."

I scanned my innards for the right words and the right tone. What rose up inside me came out of my mouth immediately, "Don't be silly, Shura. That's just the pain talking, and you know damned well you're not going to wall yourself off from life because of this one betrayal. It hurts and it doesn't help to be mad at yourself for having trusted, but it's not as if you've committed a crime; you fell in love, and trust is one of the things that goes along with falling in love, if you're a healthy human being."

"I don't know. I keep wondering how a person of my supposed intelligence could have failed to see — "

"Shura," I said urgently, softly, "You're human. You were in love. It's a strange sickness, and it alters perceptions a lot more effectively than psychedelics. It just hadn't happened to you before, from what you've told me. It's happened to most people at least once — being in love and a bit blinded — and they all tend to make the same mistakes. It's got nothing to do with logic or intelligence."

"You're probably right, but at the moment I seem to be catching up with everything I failed to look at before. I'm seeing all the messages she kept sending and I kept overlooking. I was like a young boy, fixated, able to see and hear only what I wanted to. What idiocy!"

For the first time it occurred to me that he'd probably had quite a bit of

wine already this evening; I had just noticed a hint of slurring in his voice.
Oh, hell. I should be there.
I said softly, "Wish I were with you, dear. It's up to you, of course,
when I come out there. But please feel my warmth around you. You're
not alone in this, remember."

"Thank you, my little friend. I've got to get through this mourning
period by myself, first. Before I ask you to come out here again."

"After all, Shura," I said, reluctantly, "There's a real possibility that
she actually is working through some very hard problems and that she
still could be coming out to be with you, isn't there?"

"No," he said, his voice suddenly harsh, "No, there is no such possibility. It's been quite clear to me for several days now that it's over. She
simply didn't know how to bring it to the right sort of happy-ever-after
conclusion. I think she got herself stuck and had to ask Dolph to help her
get out of the trap she'd woven for herself. She plays fantasy games, Alice.
I think she truly believes them herself, for a while, at least. I believe she
and I could have gone on forever with what she essentially saw as a
spiritual love-affair, if only Helen hadn't died. That made it a different
ball-game, and she just didn't know how to enjoy all the goodies she could
have with me without getting deeper and deeper into a commitment she
had no desire for. She never intended to leave Dolph. It's a strange
marriage; about that, I was right. About all the rest, I was one more blind,
love-sick fool."

*Oh, Jesus Aitch. That's maybe being a bit too hard on the girl. I wonder,
though. Didn't Ben say something about her having let slip to him, when she was
on the psychedelics, that she'd had problems in other affairs with married men?*

"Shura," I asked, "This is just an off-the-wall question, but do you
have any way of knowing whether she's ever done this with anyone else
— I mean, has she ever had an affair before you — during her marriage —
that you know of?"

"Oh, yes," he said, "She made no secret of it. There were other involvements; there was another professor, in Germany, just before she met
me. She described it as a very brief episode, which she brought to an end
because he was married and she didn't want to be responsible for damaging
a marriage. But all I know is her version of events, of course. I don't know
details; I didn't ask for any. She swore to me she had never been in love
before the way she was — ," I heard a sharp intake of breath, and said
nothing. After a moment, he continued, his voice under control, "So the
answer to your question is yes. I was not the first. I suspect I will not be
the last."

When he'd said goodnight, I sat by the phone, thinking intently. It
was, in a way, like discovering I'd been holding my breath for days without knowing it. I had been supposing that Ursula could well change her

mind and decide to come to California — for whatever period of time — and that Shura would not be able to resist one more meeting. I hadn't expected the brutally realistic view he'd presented. It meant that he really was through, that she could not manipulate him any further. It meant a lot of things.

The following evening, Shura phoned me and his voice was cool. He said, "I hope you'll understand, I have a lot of thinking to do. I might not be in touch as much as I have been, for a while. Please be patient. I'll get back to you and tell you what decisions I've come to, if I come to any at all. But for a while, I'm probably going to have to isolate myself until I work things through."

It was like a ball of ice hitting the inside of my stomach, and my guard clanged up, loudly and hard. I said, "I understand very well, my dear. If you and I have any future together, it's going to have to be on a completely different basis, needless to say, and that means thinking a lot of things through, for both of us."

So, nyah to you too, kid! I'm not going to beg, you know. Not any more. No more Mrs. Goody-goody for this baby. You either need me and really love me, or at least see the possibility of having those feelings for me, or I'm lost to you. No more second-best, ever, ever. That would be worse than never seeing you again. My gut doesn't believe that, but it's true.

It was the beginning of a different kind of agony, and it lasted every inch of three weeks.

Shura didn't phone at all, the first week. I went to work and told my children what was going on — once — then didn't refer to it again, because there was nothing to say until the man I loved made up his mind what he was going to do with his life and with me.

In the early part of the second week, he phoned to share the letter he'd just received from Ursula. He sounded fond and warm, with only the slightest hint of withholding, all of which I read as meaning he hadn't decided whatever he had to decide yet.

He read the letter perfectly straight, from beginning to end, without comment..

Dearest, dearest Shura,

A window has widely opened to you, a soul-window, a love-window, of graceful being — being together. A common space of breathing, of light touch, of inner smile. I could let these hours pass without telling you, and then you would never know what I am feeling — you would have only your own experience.

Or I could share this with you.

That is what I am doing.

A space we are in, you and I, a space beyond geographical location, beyond events, developments, desires, longings, doubts, griefs, it is a space of love. Love and the melting frontiers of self-protection. A touch of each others hands, eyes — a common aura that surrounds us.

Yes, I feel it again, this aura. A total yes to whatever is and will be.

I feel light in this benign space. I have let go of what we were, you and I, and I have experienced, over and over again, what we truly *are*, forever and ever.

I do not always succeed in letting go, and my heavy dreams of the last weeks and nights are revealing to me how much I am still attached — to your personality, to our plans, to the farm. That specific place on this globe must have penetrated into deep levels in me; I am bound to each hill, tree, grass, to each corner in the rooms, each view, to everything existing there. It is all strongly integrated into my awareness and memory. I have lived there and, at least in extensive dreams, I am still there. I have visions of the changes made around you, in materialistic things as well as in spirits. I see it for hours and hours. If only I could paint well enough, I could show you what I see!

Your lab especially appears very often, but now so sterile! Everything stored away, well ordered, no flair anymore. This certainly cannot be true. Ah, the strange realms of the mind!

Let me tell you openly what I had only wanted to tell you in a very private moment. This moment is private enough and it flows out of me:

In a past life, about 2,000 years ago, you took a long knife and cut my throat, took my life, murdered me, in the desert! You were the chief of our tribe, and I was a young girl, and you killed me! The why's are irrelevant. I have seen this over and over, and others who lived with us in that time have come to me in this life and warned me to be aware of this old karmic connection.

We were, I think, of a nomad people, in North Afrika, when this happened so long ago.

Search into our individual past is only meaningful because it brings light into our present problems, constellations, traumas, etc. I do not see any merit to dig deeper. Either it reveals by itself, or it does not. Therefore, my only reason for mentioning these "shadows of the past" to you is to help us understand the present situation.

In this moment of open love, you might be able to believe what I say to you, that I do not have *any* misgiving or second thoughts about emotional involvements with you because of this vision of what happened so long ago.

No, my only concern is, and this is very real to me, to free myself and to give you the possibility of freeing yourself, from these old, old bonds of emotional slavery which must not be repeated in this life. In this life, through our deep love, we have the real chance of changing this by bringing it out into the open. We have broken a karmic consequence and do no longer have to blindly bear the burdens of the past life and tragedy.

I am leaving Dolph and I will go to a place to begin a new life with myself. I do not think I will marry again. I must seek alone my true path of the soul.

I love you very deeply and I go to live my own life, of which you are a wonderful spiritual part. Maybe it will come that you will be a material part as well. But now you must live the present as completely as you can.

Shura, my dearest one, I want you to be free as a bird. Unfold your wings and leave all pain behind you, all possible accumulated guilt, all disquietness, all sorrows. Be free, and newly born, and walk into sunrise!!!!

Fly and be!
Ursula

Shura added, "By the way, in the margin was a little note in red ink which said 'Please read only when you are alone!'"

I laughed and laughed and kept on laughing. It was so good, that tumbling release of pent-up feelings; I hadn't laughed like that in a long time. For the moment, I didn't care whether Shura liked it or not, I just let it take me. When I had control again, I said weakly into the phone, "I'm sorry. That may not have been the most appropriate response, but it was genuine. I hope I didn't hurt your feelings."

"Noooo," came his voice, elaborately sarcastic, "Do go ahead, don't mind me. Feel free to *express* yourself!"

I burst into laughter again, and my ear, squeezed to the phone, picked up what might have been an aborted chuckle.

"Okay, okay. I'll behave," I said, finally.

"I just thought you'd want to know," said Shura, "As soon as I heard from the lady."

"Yes, thank you very much, very much."

"How are you?" The tone was not as warm as I might have wished; he was still withdrawn.

"I'm fine, thank you. As fine as can be expected, considering all the strange things that are going on in my life, like waiting to hear what Dr. Alexander Borodin has decided he's going to do with his future, if that's what you're busy deciding, and trying to take care of my wonderful children — who most of the time are probably taking better care of me than I am of them — and keeping my mind on medical reports eight hours a day; you know — all that sort of thing."

"How are the children?"

"They're fine, except for Brian, who's still getting over a nasty head-cold."

"Please say hello to them from me?" A shade more warmth, this time.

I replied that I certainly would, and we said goodnight.

All right. He had already closed off Ursula; he's been going through separation and grieving, and now this letter from her completes it. She loves him in spirit and will always love him in spirit — that's her message. The old murder in the desert may be a genuine memory of a past life — who knows? — I don't think she could have written all that, the way she did, unless she were convinced it was true. And now, when she's faced with having to make a final decision, that so-called memory becomes the basis of the resolve to stay apart from him, in body, while still, of course, being tied to him on the soul level. If it weren't so ironic, so hilariously funny, it would be — what? — almost sweet, like a child creating her own fairy tale to help explain to herself what's going on and what she should do.

Shura guessed, and he's probably right, that she completely believes what she says when she says it; she probably believed, when she was with him on the Farm, that she was his true love and he was hers, and that she was really going to leave Dolph and come to live here happily ever after. Then, when she got home, she was back to the other reality of being Dolph's wife, and the Farm and Shura faded, became unreal. What incredible unconsciousness! And what damage a person like that can do without ever intending it.

I remembered the remark about Shura's laboratory — her vision of it being orderly, neat, all sterile. What had she said? "No flair anymore?" Of course. She meant, "Without my presence, there will be no magic in your life. Whoever this other woman is, she will undoubtedly bring organization and neatness, and she will suppress your genius, your sparkle, your imagination, your sense of excitement and wonder. Only in your thoughts of me, only in your soul-tie to me, will you keep your sense of the fantastic."

I laughed again, thinking of the lab under the trees, old leaves and spiderwebs rampant within its walls, the very air full of energy. Magic in every dusty corner.

No, lady. If he asks me to come back into his life, it certainly won't be because I bring order and neatness. It'll be because I bring love — the kind that stays and puts down roots — and because I share the adventuring and the excitement.

I remembered the words about her soul being connected to everything, every little place, on the Farm. What she was saying, of course, was, "I will always be there, I will always be with you. No other woman can take my place."

I told the kids about Ursula's letter. Ann said, "Well, I guess your Voice from Outer Space knew what it was talking about!"

I said, "Yeah, certainly looks that way! But it doesn't change the fact that Shura's still got a decision to make about the rest of his life, right now, and there's no guarantee that he'll want to be with me."

Their faces showed confusion and something like embarrassment. I realized they didn't know how to deal with the possibility that their mother might be unwanted or rejected by a person she loved, now that the rival had withdrawn from the field.

I tried to put it in perspective, "Sometimes when you go through a miserable thing like this, you can sort of get allergic to everyone connected with it; you don't want to be around people who remind you of what you went through — at least for a while. Besides, as I told you, Shura and I can't go back to the way things were before, and I don't know how it's going to come out. It's up to him. I can't do anything but wait 'til he works it through. But," I concluded with a grin for all of them, "At least The Lady from Germany is out of the picture, thank heaven!"

They cheered and Wendy danced around the couch to celebrate.

Ursula — as we all discovered much later — had not gone into either a monastery or a nunnery, and she didn't leave Dolph. Shura received a happy announcement, about a year later, of the birth of their first child, a girl, who weighed exactly seven pounds and looked just like her mother.

CHAPTER 33. RESOLUTION

By the end of the second week, Shura hadn't called and I was feeling grim. I kept my emotions repressed, on hold, but underneath I was sometimes aware of terror, a certainty that I was not worthy, not good enough, not sufficient in this or adequate in that. It was my old program, and the silence from Shura triggered the worst of the familiar recording, and it played quietly underneath everything I consciously felt and thought. And, to make matters worse, in response to the negativity, some part of me that was concerned only with my own survival was getting seriously angry. When I took a chance and looked deep inside, I saw a dark canvas like a Clyfford Still painting, split halfway down from the top by a thin sliver of red hate. I recognized the feelings and the images as defensive and self-protective and maintained my silence and my dignity.

I took the children to a movie once, and talked to them in the evenings about what was happening at school, spending more time on details than I usually did, immersing myself in what they could tell me of their worlds. They were kind to me and cooperated, telling me stories and describing incidents.

When they went across the street for the weekend, I dressed up and packed my portable magnetic chessboard and went to a Mensa party, intending to get reasonably potted on my own vodka in cranberry juice, but couldn't bring myself to drink very much. After listening for an hour to a long story of misery from a recently divorced man, I managed to get a chess game going, but my opponent was too drunk to keep his mind on the game. Finally, I gave up and drove home, too tired to think or care about anything but sleep.

At work, I typed automatically and began to seriously consider looking for another job, because I knew that if I had to face life and work without Shura — if that's the way things were going to turn out — I had better find a job which threatened me with a somewhat less early death than this one did.

By the time the phone call came, on Thursday of the third week, I had stopped letting myself feel very much at all. I could be affectionate with the children, and only my interactions with them convinced me that I hadn't completely turned to granite. I had become very silent at work, keeping to myself at coffee-breaks and lunch because I couldn't find the energy necessary to maintain the appearance of ease and normalcy.

Underneath, the anger was no longer in hiding. It was an old friend, by now, a quiet bed of hot coals waiting beneath the dark crust of numbness and non-responsiveness that had formed during the past weeks.

Now, on the phone, Shura's voice was carefully casual as he asked me how I would feel about coming out the following weekend.

I cleared my throat against a choking mass of conflicting feelings and thoughts, and said, "That's a nice idea. When would be a good time for me to be there?"

"Oh, how about Friday after work? Would that be all right for you?"

"Fine," I said, aware that my voice was a bit dull and not knowing how to bring life into it without letting the furies break through; dull it would have to stay, for the moment.

"I need to ask you," I said, carefully, "How long are you inviting me for? Since this is a new chapter, I gather, one doesn't want to — ah — take anything for granted." It was meant to be funny, but somehow it didn't sound funny at all. What I heard in my own voice, with a tinge of helpless fear, was sarcasm. I desperately hoped Shura wouldn't catch it.

"How about staying through Sunday? Does that appeal to you?"

This time I forced lightness, "It does, indeed, thank you. I'll see you Friday evening."

When I had hung up the phone, I sat and cried, grateful that the children were already in bed. I cried rage and love and relief and fear and murder and love again. Then I went to bed.

It was during the drive out to the Farm, Friday evening, that I began to understand the possible reason for the silence, the coolness, all the signs of distancing, which had resulted in the flaring hurt and humiliation I'd been suppressing during the past endless days.

He's being a bastard, putting me through a mini-version of what Ursula put him through, all the lack of contact, dangling me on a string, and it's all because he believes — whether he's aware of it or not — that being with me is inevitable. He's feeling trapped in the inevitability of it, at this point, instead of taking pleasure in what it could mean. That's why the silence, letting me wonder if he considers me worth any more of his bloody time. He's feeling he really has no choice, and he's angry. Maybe it's a kind of "Either I replace Ursula with Alice, or I go the hermit route and shut out everyone." Is that what he's fighting? And if it is, what the hell can I do about it? I'm through being the blasted saint and martyr. I'm not going to make it easy for him.

I was still numb, and my Observer said that was okay. Numbness is quite understandable at the moment, it said, and probably safer than the alternatives.

Shura met me at my car, as he usually did. He stood there, as I got out with my shopping bag full of clothes and other things I needed for a weekend. Neither of us made much of an attempt to smile, and when he greeted me it was without the usual enveloping hug and kiss on the mouth. His hands went to my face and he touched his forehead to mine, and I thought briefly that the gesture was more one of commiseration than anything else, and that it seemed quite appropriate.

When I was inside and had dumped my bag on the floor next to the couch, I looked around at the familiar books and fireplace and the hazy bulk of Diablo through the windows. It was all so much a part of me, by now — this room, this whole house — so permeated with memories of the two of us; yet, in that moment, it looked alien, strange. It took me a few minutes to realize that the strangeness was my own fear reflected back to me from everything I looked at. As I was maintaining distance from my own emotions, so I perceived myself as distant from the piano, the rugs, the couch, all the old friends — or what had been old friends. I was keeping locked up the pain, the bewilderment, the profound anger, and while all of it was wrapped safely and stored deep inside, I could not touch anything with my feelings.

Everything I saw around me spoke of memories, of the past, and I was stuck now in a place which was not the past, and not anywhere else either. I could not believe in a future with Shura, I dared not believe in it because such a belief would make me vulnerable to a degree I just couldn't risk. So I must not believe in a future with his house, his furniture, his cactus plants, or anything else I saw here. All of it might have to belong only to my past, and I dared not expect it to be otherwise.

He had invited me here, this weekend, and that could mean he wanted us to continue, but it could perfectly well be that his idea of the conditions under which we could continue — well, they might be conditions I could not agree to, conditions which would break what was left of my spirit and heart and belief in myself.

If you won't put up with second-best, you may have to put up with nuthin' at all, kid, because he may not have anything but second-best to give you.

We sat at the dining room table, looking at each other without letting ourselves see deeper than the surface. I could sense his wall as I knew my own.

This is going to be one fun weekend, yeah.

"I would like to make a suggestion which might help both of us," he said, leaning back in his chair, focusing his gaze on the edge of the carpet,

"If you're willing to go along with it, I'd like to do something with you that we haven't done before; I'd like to share with you about 100 micrograms of LSD. Most people have a lot of anxiety about LSD because of all the wild stuff in the papers they read in the '60's, and all the negative propaganda since then. I thought you might want to explore it yourself and make up your own mind. Unless you'd rather postpone it, which I would certainly understand?"

I looked at him and wondered for a moment if he had the slightest idea what kind of state I was in, and what a cauldron was simmering close to the surface. I looked at his body, leaning casually in the chair, and saw that the casualness was not real. When I let myself pick up his feelings, I knew that he too was tightened up and afraid, and that he didn't know how to let anything out without risking saying something wrong, or in the wrong way.

"Okay," I said, "How long does it last? I mean, will we be up most of the night?"

"Yes, probably," he said, and I caught a glimpse of blue eyes actually daring to look at me, "Is that all right? I don't have any plans for tomorrow morning, myself, and we can sleep in."

"Well, I'm willing to experience LSD, in fact I'm very pleased with the idea of finally meeting the dangerous enemy face to face, if you think it's a good idea — I mean, considering the fact that we're both in a strange sort of — well, state of mind, to say the least?"

That's not the clearest sentence ever spoken.

"As a matter of fact," he said, "I thought it might help us break through our various — whatever you'd call 'em — walls, barriers. I'm feeling very stuck right now, and I don't really know how to get unstuck, and it just could be a help. I thought perhaps you might be having the same kind of trouble, and if so, this might be an interesting way to loosen ourselves, help us say what we need to say."

He's almost as anxious as I am. Why? It's all up to him; it's not up to me. He's the one who can decide everything. Maybe he just isn't certain of what he feels.

"Sure," I said, "At least, it's not liable to be a dull evening."

"That," — he said directly to me with his first grin — "Is for sure."

As I took a bath, my thoughts were a confused mess. One thing returned to my mind several times, and that was the fact that Shura was proposing a new experience tonight, which meant that he was still teaching me, introducing me to something new, and that wasn't the kind of thing one did to a person one was intending to part company with.

All right. That's not the worry. Of course he wants me around, if for nothing more than great love-making. But what if he decides to be a hermit, after all, except for an occasional weekend with me — or with some other woman, for that matter — what do I say? I want to be part of his life forever, and I want to live with him the rest of his life and mine, and I don't want to be short-changed any more. And he may not feel he can give me anything close to what I want from him, and if he makes that clear — if that's what he tells me this weekend — what do I do? That's the Goddamned problem.

In the kitchen, we stood facing each other, wearing our dressing gowns, as Shura explained, "The duration of this material is about six hours, give or take, depending on your sensitivity. The one thing really different from other psychedelics is the rapidity of the onset. Instead of waiting for 30 minutes or an hour, you'll find yourself feeling the effects very fast — usually within about 15 minutes. LSD is known as a 'pushy' material — you've probably heard me refer to that particular quality — and it's one of the complaints people have about it, even the people who love it; they say it tends to take over, to push you. In the higher dosage ranges, people who aren't used to it sometimes feel they have less control than they would like. It simply has to be learned, like all psychedelics. Once you're familiar with the quickness of it and realize you can control it whenever you decide you want to, there's no reason for anxiety. The scare stories have been mostly from naive people who took too high a dose the first time — "

"I've heard some pretty wild stories about first times, yes."

" — and the rest were cases of people who were fragile emotionally or mentally. If you're fragile, or ready to tip over, then anything can send you off center; LSD or falling in love or losing someone or having a big fight with your father."

"I suppose there's a hidden compliment in there somewhere," I said, smiling faintly, "At least I'll take it as such. You're assuming I'm not mentally fragile, right?"

"Oh," said Shura, his eyebrows shooting up, "Absolutely, absolutely. I mean, absolutely not! Certainly not! Rock solid, you are. Emotionally, of course, you're a quivering mess — "

I gasped, caught between shocked anger and a sudden desire to explode with laughter. Two months ago, I would have aimed a kick at his balls, but this was not two months ago. I returned my face to impassive as he continued, " — but your sanity is, without question, unshakeable."

I realized that he knew I was controlling myself, and I knew what he might not be that sure of, which was that I had excellent control and would not lose it easily, with or without LSD. Not unless I wanted to, and right now, I didn't want to.

After we drank the colorless liquid, which consisted mainly of distilled water with the tiny amount of LSD in it (Shura had explained that tap water contained chlorine which would kill LSD immediately, as would strong light), we sat in the living room, I on the couch as usual and he in his big armchair, and I listened to him talk about the past week.

"I told Ruth and George about Ursula's letter, and they asked me over there to dinner so we could discuss it. I read it to them, and they were completely bewildered. They didn't see the humor of it as you did, and they didn't try to dissect her motives. On the other hand, I think their real concern was to help me feel better, and I think they knew that attacking Ursula — blaming her for what she'd done — wasn't what I needed at that point."

"No, of course not."

"They just became family. Let me talk myself out and tucked me into bed when I'd drunk too much wine, and gave me a wonderful breakfast in the morning. I left there feeling a lot more solid. It was a great help."

I nodded, then raised my hand in the air, "Could I be feeling something already?"

Shura got up from his chair and went into the kitchen to look at the clock. He returned and said, "You certainly could."

"Well, I think I'm beginning to."

"How does it feel to you?"

I paid attention and chose my words carefully, "As if the cells of my body are trying to re-align themselves in a different way than usual."

"Comfortable or not comfortable?"

"Comfortable's the wrong word. Intriguing is the right word."

Shura laughed softly, "Sounds all right. Just let it happen; you'll get the hang of it in a while."

I looked around at the room and said, "There's a lot of color. It's more noticeable than usual — I mean, there are little prisms, rainbows, everywhere."

Shura nodded silently.

I looked out the windows at the twilight and continued, "I see what you mean by saying it's pushy. It does sort of press on you a bit. Maybe it's because the transition begins so soon. But it also gets very intense quickly, doesn't it? I mean, there's a certain sense of being on a roller-coaster ride."

Shura nodded again.

"Aside from that, it's pretty much familiar territory. So far."

"Would you like to repair to the warm bedroom with the music, or is it better for you to stay here?"

Oh, my, how very carefully he said that!

In answer, I rose and led the way through kitchen and dining room and down the hallway to the bedroom, the place of love and music. When I moved, I felt solidly connected with the physical world, yet there was still that feeling of being more a body of energy particles than of flesh and bone. It was quite pleasant, when I allowed myself to feel pleasantness, and the thought occurred to me as I pushed open the bedroom door that it was time to stop worrying about keeping control or appearing in this light or that; it was time to just be who I was and let myself feel the emotions, including laughter, because to do otherwise was to be untrue to myself, manipulative of Shura, and wasteful of a possibly great experience.

We lay beside each other on the bed, Shura naked and I still in my dressing gown. When I closed my eyes, the inner world erupted into detailed imagery. Shura went up the radio dial and found Chopin, and when he turned back to me, I sat up and took off my gown. I saw behind closed eyelids a lovely scene. We — Shura and I — were looking down from an open balcony into a central courtyard. We were in a place that appeared to consist of balconies hung with baskets of flowers, storey upon storey, surrounding the courtyard below. Ivy plants rose from the edges of the garden and crept up the walls and columns. Looking down into the center of the round garden space, I saw a tiled platform and on it, a grand piano which was being played — Chopin's music, of course — by a young man in a tuxedo. I could see only the top of his brown hair and his moving hands.

When I heard Shura's gasp and the start of the shaking cry, I had a moment of startled anxiety, realizing that what we were doing, he and I, must be completely visible to anyone who might be standing on a balcony above ours, and that we could very well be in serious trouble if we made too much noise. The pianist might stop, and look to see what was happening up there above him. I thought of warning Shura not to yell, as he usually did, but before I could say the words, I realized that we were perfectly safe on the big bed, and that I had been letting the line between reality and fantasy blur. Shura howled, sitting up in bed, one hand clenched in my hair.

The pianist played on, undeterred, and in my place on the floor of the balcony, I giggled into Shura's belly and stroked his hip.

"For a moment there," I murmured, "I really did think we were going to frighten the horses."

"Horses?"

I reminded him of the famous saying of Mrs. Patrick Campbell, friend of George Bernard Shaw, who said that she didn't care what people did in making love just as long as they didn't do it in the street and frighten the horses.

"Oh."

I told him about my vision and he laughed, still a bit out of breath.

"Did you go with me on that one?" he asked, as he usually did.

I sat up and folded my legs, "To tell you the truth, I lost track because of my fascination with the fuzzing of lines between realities. I was think-ing about how easy it is to get caught in that inner picture, and what fun it is, but how frightening it could be to somebody who'd never had a psychedelic drug before and didn't know how to get back in touch with his normal, ordinary reality because he couldn't tell which one it was."

He said, "But you didn't stay fooled, did you? I mean, even a very naive person, if he finds himself seeing places and things with his eyes closed, knows at some level that he can open his eyes. Unless he's taken a real overdose, of course. To make sense of things with a heavy overdose, you have to have a good deal of experience, and even then it can be pretty hairy for a while."

I moved up and lay beside him. The long fingers began lightly stroking, and as I looked past the big head to the ceiling, I saw against the shadowed surface a multitude of tiny kaleidoscopes, moving, bumping into each other the way blood cells do under a microscope. I smiled, and when Shura's hand paused for a moment and his eyes opened wider in question, I explained what was happening all over the ceiling. He looked up, "Yes, it's pretty active, isn't it!"

The hand was exploring again. I thought of how well he knew my body, and then I heard him say, sounding slightly amused, "You know, I made a little experiment that might interest you. I asked Ruth and George this last week the same thing I'd asked the others in the group, over the past week or so, everyone except David. I asked them what they thought of my settling down to live with you. Every one of them, believe it or not, said something along the same lines: no, don't do it, beware of rebounds, I don't think she's the right woman for you, Shura. I can't remember one person saying anything positive about the idea; isn't that interesting, considering?"

I had gone rigid. My Observer commented that most people would respond negatively just because the question had been asked in the first place; if you have to ask, the answer is no.

I opened my mouth to say just that to him, reasonably, to explain quietly and rationally why all his friends had come up with negative responses, but suddenly — without any warning at all — something shattered and the red coals were on their way up the funnel. I was trying to focus through hot tears which were welling up and over and down and dripping off my chin. With no awareness of having moved, I found myself sitting upright on the bed, my hands clenching the blanket in front of me. My entire world had shrunk, within the space of a few seconds, to a dark purple-red tunnel which contained only pain. I was sobbing, shuddering with the force of the grief that was pulsing up from the bottom of the tunnel and scalding my eyes, then I felt bright orange knifing into the scene — anger — and the flow of energy changed. The sobs felt now as if they were grunting their way out, and I was dimly aware that my jaw hinge was tight. I lost sight and I could hear nothing but the sound of my own explosion. I seemed to be screaming through clenched teeth, and it was all making a lot of noise.

The Observer, almost lost in the chaos, wondered with a touch of amusement whether the dear man had by any chance let loose a somewhat larger tiger than he'd expected to have to deal with.

Shura waited quietly until the storm had begun to subside. I was on my stomach, at that point, vaguely aware of having spit out words like "cruel," "sadistic," and "insufferable;" there was an echo of "appalling," and even "stupid." I lay face down on a wet pillow and felt the tide slowing. The color of it was no longer purple-red or orange or yellow or black; the only colors I could feel were gentle blue and violet, with a edging of rose. I was washed clean of emotions, peaceful.

I lifted myself up and turned around, slowly, until I was lying on my back again. I stared up at the ceiling, knowing that a glass wall was between me and Shura, and that the wall was my friend and would stay there unless he came up with an awfully good reason for it to come down. The best thing was, I realized with a feeling that was almost pleasure, that I wasn't hurting any more. For the moment, at least, I didn't care. In the center of my chest there was a pond of blue water, and I could float contentedly in it for a long, long time, until everything healed.

Shura's voice came in quietly from my right, from the other side of the glass wall, "I guess I didn't say what I meant to say, or I said it in the wrong sequence, or something like that. You see, as I told you, it was a sort of experiment, asking them. I'll admit it wasn't the nicest thing to try with old friends, but I made a bet with myself, a while ago, that everyone in that group — again, I didn't ask David the idiotic question, but he was the only exception — I made a bet that they would all warn me against deciding to throw my lot, as the saying goes, in with you. I made the bet because I was pretty sure I knew why they'd give me negative responses, and I thought, when I told you, that you'd understand immediately, too. It was a stupid, bitter sort of joke and it was made by the less admirable side of myself — you know, the part of me that rather enjoys seeing the worst expectations come true?"

I heard him, but nothing inside me was touched. I had no reason to speak.

Shura continued, "I was certain that every one I asked would have some degree of worry about a woman — even one they knew and liked — becoming so close to me that she might influence my relationships with them. I knew that they'd always been afraid Ursula would do that, you know, but I never asked them what they thought about her; I never gave them a chance to say no, and they knew better than to try to influence me against her. They were always uneasy about her. I knew that. So this time, just for the fun of proving myself right, I thought I'd give them a chance to have some sort of input. I asked them, individually, what they thought of my settling down with you.

"I guessed that they'd all say don't do it, because every one of them is afraid you'd change things in some way they couldn't foresee. They don't want me to need them less, to spend less time with them. It was a stupid experiment, and all it did was confirm what I already suspected."

I looked at him and spoke in what sounded to my Observer like a steady, reasonable voice, "Didn't it occur to you that the very fact that you asked them meant that the answer had to be no? I would have said no, myself. The rule with loving somebody is: if you have to ask your friends, you're not sure, and if you're not sure, it isn't real love. Or something like that."

"Yes," he said, "I suppose that's true. I think it's also true that they're jealous of anyone who gets closer to me than they are."

"Okay. Maybe so. It was a cruel experiment, as you admit yourself. And what did you expect me to do when you told me — laugh?"

"I thought you might see the humor of it, yes."

"Uh-uh, no humor. Not funny."

"So I have learned. I'm sorry, Alice."

He held my head to his chest, and then he said, "Look, there's no use apologizing, is there? I don't want to waste time doing that. So why don't I just ask you: what do you think of the idea of quitting your job and moving out here with me?"

"Jesus!" I muttered.

"You called?" he replied.

I laughed despite myself, and muttered into his ribs, "You idiot!"

"Well, how about it?"

In reply, I put my arms around his neck and watched the glass wall quietly crumble into diamond dust.

"Are you sure?" I whispered.

"Waddya mean, am I sure! I'm not sure of anything! I'm probably a complete and utter fool and this is probably the path to total disaster! Of course, I'm not sure! But I want you to live with me, because this weekend off and on stuff is ridiculous, and besides, you're not a bad kid, everything considered, and I probably could do a lot worse!"

I hit his chest with my fists and he grabbed my wrists and, when I started crying again, he hissed, "Stop that or I'll throw ya across the room!"

I laughed and sobbed, and he repeated the threat in what was probably meant to be a Chicago gangster accent, until I finally lay back on my pillow, face wet, gasping with laughter, and yelled, "All right, all right, all right!"

Suddenly I thought of something — something too important to leave for later. I had to have the answer immediately, if I was to believe all this. I sat up, looked intently at Shura, and asked him, "Does this mean we can do it in the missionary position, now?"

He stared at me, "*Now*? I'm afraid I might not be up to it, right now. Could you possibly consider waiting until tomorrow morning? I'm not 18 any more, you know; it takes me a few hours to recover!"

I shoved him back onto the bed, sputtering, "I meant from now *on*, you louse! Not now immediately!"

He grinned, and I realized he'd understood all along.

"Sure," he said, "If you *insist*."

"Just occasionally," I said, "Just to make sure we don't forget how to do it the classic, old-fashioned way."

"I'm trying to remember," grunted Shura, "But I think it goes something like this, right?" He made a circle with his left hand and poked in and out of it with the right index finger, in the gesture understood around the world.

I nodded vehemently, giggling, "Uh-huh, that's it!"

Nothing reserved any more for Ursula. Thank you, thank you.

I hiccuped and laughed, and hiccuped again. The hiccups were silver-colored spikes against the rainbowed ceiling.

CHAPTER 34. THE FOURTH

On the 4th of July, 1981, in response to approximately 80 invitations to a picnic at the Farm, 67 people arrived. They brought their own meat for the barbecue and several of them brought portable barbecues and some extra bags of charcoal. They came in short pants and slacks and halter tops, carrying hot dogs, hamburger meat, chicken, potato salad, green salad, raw vegetables, cake and jello and ice cream.

It was a hot day and there were people everywhere I looked. I knew there had never before been a gathering this large on the Farm. Most of them knew each other, but there was an occasional one who had to be introduced, someone who was from outside what we called the network; these included a few old friends of mine and two women from the hospital where I had worked the year before.

Walter had been invited, along with the children, who now lived with him. During the past year, Shura and Walter had become comfortable with each other, and all of us got together for a pot-luck dinner with friends every couple of weeks, at Walter's house in Marin, as a way of keeping family ties strong.

Ruth remarked to me, in some surprise, when we found ourselves occupying the same corner of the living room for a moment, "I can't believe Shura actually invited such a crowd! I've never known him to have more than twelve people at a time out here!"

I told her that it was my idea, and he'd gone along with it just this once. "I thought it would be really fun to ask all our friends to a barbecue picnic, you know? He said okay, as long as it was a one-time-only experiment."

Ruth laughed, "Amazing! Never thought I'd see the day," she beamed at me, "And wasn't it wonderful that Dante and Ginger happened to be out here just for these few days!"

Dante and Ginger had called Ruth and George a couple of weeks ago and asked if they could stay with them, explaining that they were visiting relatives in the area and had heard that we were giving a picnic, so why didn't they all go to the Farm together? Ruth and George were delighted and offered their spare bedroom.

Of all the research group, only these two — Dante and Ginger — knew our plans. Because they lived so far from us, they could not have been persuaded to make the journey just for a 4th of July barbecue, and we realized we'd have to tell them, swearing them to secrecy.

The only others who knew what was going on were Shura's son Theo, my four children, and a very good friend of Shura's, Paul Freye, of the Federal Narcotics Lab, who was going to act today in his capacity as a minister of the Eternal Life Church.

I had come to feel strong affection for Paul. He was highly intelligent, thoughtful, and had an appallingly unsubtle sense of humor which Shura happily shared, usually over a bottle of red wine on occasional Sundays.

In the back of the house there was a grassy area below the level of the path. It measured about 20 feet at its widest, and it gradually narrowed to five feet across. !t was shaded by trees and relatively cool in the summer. We had laid out old Persian rugs and some big floor pillows, and when people asked what all that was for, we explained that later in the afternoon there would be chamber music. Everyone was very polite, said How nice! and turned back to their conversations.

At 2:00 o'clock in the afternoon, I gathered my children and gave them their orders, and while they scattered over the Farm, rounding up the guests for a special program to be presented in back of the house — in some cases meeting with blank stares and in others, frank resistance, which had been anticipated — Shura and I locked ourselves into our bedroom and changed our clothes.

I put on a filmy Indian print dress of rose, gold and brown, made of sheer cotton over a pink slip, floor length; there were dusty pink dance slippers on my feet. Shura wore sandy brown slacks and a new tweed jacket and a tie. We laughed at ourselves in the mirror, at the sweat trickling down our faces, then kissed quickly and left the bedroom.

We waited at the back door until Brian ran up the stone steps from the place where the murmuring crowd of curious, half-annoyed guests had been politely bullied into sitting down. At his wave, we emerged and walked down the steps, hand in hand. To our right, under the trees, stood Paul, who now rang a big brass bell — a relic of Shura's days in the Navy — which had been hung from a sturdy tree branch.

There was a shocked silence as we walked in front of the guests, and turned to the rug-covered area in front of Paul Freye. He had in his hand the paper on which we had written the words of our wedding ceremony, and in the stunned quiet, his voice, shaking very slightly, said the opening words, familiar and beautiful. I looked to my right and exchanged smiles with my son, Christopher, who was my ring-bearer, and to Shura's left, where Theo stood as best man, his camera on the rug near his feet.

"Dearly Beloved: we are gathered together to join this man and this woman in holy matrimony."

Inserted into the ceremony were words of a benediction borrowed from the Apache Indians.

"That, clasping one another's hands,
Holding one another fast,
You may fulfill your roads together."

After Shura had put the ring on my finger, Paul continued, gradually losing his fight against the tears in his throat:

"Now you will feel no rain,
For each of you will be shelter to the other.
Now you will feel no cold,
For each of you will be warmth to the other.
Now there is no more loneliness for you.
Now you are two bodies,
But there is only one life before you.

"Go now to your dwelling place,
To enter into the days of your togetherness.
And may your days be good
And long upon the earth!"

His cheeks wet, our dear Paul concluded:

"I join you to one another and to all of us who love you. I now pronounce you man and wife."

Later, in the kitchen, when Ruth had stopped crying and Leah's nose was losing its pinkness, I explained why we'd done it this way, "Shura said he didn't mind getting married as long as we could do it in such a way that there wouldn't be any big present-giving mess, because he hates that kind of thing, and as far as he was concerned, we didn't need wedding presents and he wanted to keep things simple.

"So I said why not invite everybody to a picnic and surprise them, and that was the beginning of the plan. We decided nobody except our children would know what was going on — we needed their help, and it would be fun having them in charge of a secret like that. Of course," I grinned at Ruth, "Ginger and Dante had to know why they were being asked to come all that way, and Paul had to be ready to be our minister!"

"I don't know when I've been so completely taken by surprise," said Ruth, beginning to sob again. I put my arms around her and hugged, then I leaned back against the sink, folded my arms, and said to them, "I want you both to know — and everyone else in the group, of course — that this marriage won't cause anything to change in your friendship, your relationship with Shura. That's the last thing I would want to see happen. I know that you all love him, and I have no desire to squirrel him away from his friends. That's just not the way I am. I think you had fears of that happening with Ursula, but I'm not Ursula — "

Leah made an exaggerated gesture of relief, wiping her forehead with the back of a limp hand, as Ruth laughed.

" — and I don't have to have him all to myself and not share. The more extended family, the better, as far as I'm concerned. He needs all of you, and I want to thank you for being his friends. And mine."

Horribly sentimental. But they need to hear it. Now get a Kleenex and blow your blasted nose and get out of here so they can talk to each other.

Ann, Wendy and Brian cornered me and reported with obvious relish that they had watched their father to see his reaction, when Shura and I stopped in front of Paul and it became clear what was about to happen.

"His mouth opened," said Brian, "And it just stayed that way."

Wendy illustrated, crossing her eyes over her hanging jaw.

"You never saw anyone so absolutely dumbfounded in your life," laughed Ann, holding her stomach, "It was wonderful, Mom. I wouldn't have missed that sight for anything in the world!"

"Boy," I said, "You guys have a *weird* sense of humor, you know?"

I hugged each of them and said many thanks for having done their part so beautifully.

"Well," Ann remarked, as they turned to go back to the party, "At least you'll never be able to forget the date of your anniversary, right?"

"Not easily, sweetheart."

July Fourth. Celebration of freedom. The freedom of being tied forever to the man I want to be tied to forever. Thank you, God and all the Little Gods. I send you my joy and gratitude. Bless us and keep us, amen.

Part Three:

Both Voices

CHAPTER 35. AACHEN

(Alice's voice)

A few weeks after the wedding, Shura was given the opportunity to attend a nuclear medicine conference in the city of Aachen, Germany, and we decided to make the trip together, as part of a honeymoon which would include my first visits to London and Paris.

I hadn't seen Europe since leaving it as a child, in 1940, on the last refugee ship out of Trieste, Italy, where my father had been American consul. The idea that I was actually going to see any part of Europe again seemed almost too wonderful to be true; I had dreamt of such a return for years with increasing disbelief in the possibility of it ever really happening.

I was going to cross the Atlantic once more, this time by plane instead of ocean liner, and I was about to see England and France and Germany, all for the first time. I felt a mixture of reluctance and excitement about the Germany part of it; reluctance because throughout most of my life, the name, "Germany" had usually been tied to the word "Nazi," but there was also the excitement of seeing a country I hadn't seen before, a country out of which had come some of the greatest musicians, artists and thinkers of all time. The Germany of castles and rivers and Black Forest elves. The land of Bach and Mozart.

Shura had told me that we were going to travel his preferred way, with backpacks and no other luggage. That way, he said, we wouldn't be held up in airports, waiting for suitcases, and we wouldn't be frustrated by constantly having to watch baggage. Everything we needed would be on our backs.

I was known in my family for packing enough stuff to last about a month, every time I planned for a weekend trip, but I was willing to try the backpack method, and there was something really challenging about the idea. It made sense, after all. Nobody wants to baby-sit a suitcase. And learning experiences are learning experiences.

The backpacks we bought were large and dark-colored with no metal frames, just lots of compartments. Shura had packed an extra pair of his dark blue corduroy slacks and I put in jeans, a denim skirt and several blouses. I was going to live in denim — skirt and pants — since it was the one material that wouldn't show dirt easily and, of course, it would wear like iron.

As Shura reminded me, while we folded things into our backpacks, "We aren't planning to attend any formal concerts or go to expensive night-clubs, so our wardrobes can be practical and relatively dull." He added, "No matter what clothes we take, we'll be sick of the sight of them in a couple of weeks, anyway," to which I had to agree.

My camera, an old Yashica, was going to be used for documentary purposes, mainly, and to keep track for me when my eyes and mind might be too tired to register important details, as tends to happen on long adventures in strange places. Shura's camera was coming too, in its soft leather carrying case. He would take the more deliberate and careful shots.

A very long plane ride later, leaning out the window of a hotel on Piccadilly Square, I breathed in the smell of London — sharp, sooty and wet from recent rain. This was the city of my childhood nursery rhymes, and I was on my way to seeing the places I'd heard about from the time I could talk ("They're changing the guard at Buckingham Palace, Christopher Robin went down with Alice,") and to fall completely in love with the British Museum, just as Shura had predicted I would.

After a few days, we were on our way to Aachen, by plane and then train, and I was finally in Germany.

Aachen is a very, very ancient city known by different names in several different languages because it is situated at the point where Germany, Belgium and Holland meet. Its other most familiar name is Aix-la-Chapelle. Apparently its history as a city began when the Romans discovered hot springs in the area and built watering-places and bath-houses around and over what they believed were healing waters. Some of the graceful columns left over from that time are still standing throughout the city, surrounded now by shops, cafes, tiled piazzas and, of course, boxes full of geraniums. (During the long time since I had left Europe as a young girl, whenever I heard or read the word, "Europe," I always saw in my mind red and pink geraniums clustering in a window box, and heard the echoing of church bells.)

We first saw Aachen early on a Sunday morning. Having just gotten off the train, very tired and grimy and wanting baths, we were interested only in finding a hotel as fast as possible. We looked for anyone who might point us in the right direction, but there were few people to be seen at that hour, as we walked into the town. We both assumed that we would be able to find somebody who spoke English, because everyone back home who knew anything about Europe had said, "Practically all Germans speak English."

After several encounters with smiling, pleasant-faced citizens, out early, walking their dogs or picking up newspapers, it became painfully apparent that we had landed in the one single exception to the rule. Nobody in this particular place in Germany appeared to speak any English — or French, for that matter — and absolutely no one understood what I had always believed was a universal word, "hotel." The people we came across all gave the impression of being friendly and eager to help, but there was no sign of even the slightest comprehension of anything we said in either of our two available languages.

Finally, walking down yet one more cobbled street, we saw the sign of a hotel, three stars, which we would ordinarily have considered a bit rich for our blood, but we were too weary to search further, and told each other it probably wouldn't be *that* much extra. Inside, we found that the young, pretty lady behind the counter spoke heavily accented English and the price was manageable. We sighed thankfully and smiled all over her and took the keys to a room on the second floor with gratitude and relief.

After showers and a few hours' nap, we unpacked and put on fresh clothes. It was time to explore. We walked some of the city streets, had beer and coffee in an outdoor cafe, and marveled at the huge, old cathedral called the Dom (we also discovered that "Dom" means "cathedral" in German). We went inside for a few minutes, long enough to see the famous chandelier and the little statue of the Madonna in her hand-embroidered gown. It seems that there are certain women in the city of Aachen who commit themselves to sewing magnificent brocaded dresses for the statue, and the Madonna wears a new one every week. The custom is centuries old, and the honor is, when possible, passed down from mother to daughter. This day, the Madonna was wearing a gold-embroidered pink dress with a white and gold cloak.

The Dom was built in the 8th Century AD, and inside its great walls, there was a many-layered quietness. Soft candlelight reflected deep orange on the polished tops of the pews facing the Madonna. Above the huge pillars loomed comfortable darkness, and we could make out against the shadows the immense circle which formed the chandelier presented to the Dom by Frederick Barbarossa — Red-Beard the Great. Not for the first time and far from the last, I found myself wishing I had read more and could remember more of what I had read, about people like Barbarossa. I had heard the name from when I was a child, and there was a vague mental picture of a big man with red hair who was an important, powerful German chieftain of some kind. Or was he an Emperor? In the Middle

Ages — or was it the Dark Ages — ?

The discomfort of realizing how little I knew, and how much I might miss because of my failure to read more, before the trip, gradually gave way to a delicious feeling of awe. Here we stood, Shura and I, looking up at something which a man of power in a time long, long past, had given to this very building. My back prickled at the thought of that much human time, represented by the simple circle of bronze.

(A couple of days later, along with the nuclear medicine group, we were given a private tour of the cathedral's less accessible corners, and found ourselves standing before a marble seat, cut plain, without embellishment of any kind, which had been the coronation throne of the emperor Charlemagne, and we stood with the rest of those who had chosen to go exploring, in silence. It was like facing a closed doorway into another world; a seat shaped simply, its lack of adornment stating, as nothing else could have, the emperor's sureness of his own absolute power.)

But now, having been in Aachen for only a few hours, we decided to put off a really detailed exploration of the Dom until later; these first hours would be a tasting of the different flavors of the city, a tentative smelling and feeling out of its nature. As we strolled, there seemed to be friendliness and ease in all the faces on the street, and courtesy and smiles whenever we went into a cafe for Shura's lager and my coffee. There still didn't seem to be any English spoken anywhere, though, outside the hotels.

It would not be until the following day, when I went exploring by myself while Shura was busy delivering his lecture at the nuclear medicine complex (security rules forbade my admission) — not until I was a single foreign woman asking for a pack of cigarettes in a kiosk or for a cup of coffee in a cafe — that I would discover that the friendliness and courtesy were totally absent as soon as I had no man at my side. By myself, I was ignored, pointedly overlooked and, in one case, openly sneered at. Interesting.

But this aspect of Aachen — in fact, of many parts of Germany — we did not know on that Sunday. We were discovering a series of wonderful cobblestoned and tiled streets, some of them old and narrow, others broad and obviously modern. Aachen had been bombed during World War II and the ruined parts of the city had been rebuilt with imagination and, in some respects, a whimsical sense of humor.

There were fountains everywhere in this new Aachen, fountains more complex, playful and beautiful than any others we had seen, anywhere. Walking down one street, we stopped at the entrance to a park, seeing in the middle of it a 15-foot fountain shaped like a lotus-flower, covered with reflecting metal squares which shone like silver. As we watched, the petals of the lotus closed slowly until they formed a bud-shape, then slowly and silently opened again to full flower, spouting a delicate spray of water from the center.

A few blocks away, in a busy little square, we found a small, child-sized fountain, a metal well sprouting bronze doll-figures with movable heads, arms and legs. On the top of a pole emerging from the center of the well was a small bronze soldier on a horse. An excited little girl called to her parents to watch as she bent and straightened the arms of a bronze peasant woman. I looked up at Shura; he grinned and gestured at my camera. He had left his at the hotel.

We found another fountain, near the train station, honoring the needle boys of Aachen, adolescent boys who had worked in the needle factories of the city before World War II. Three lean bronze figures held their right arms raised, each hand showing a long little finger distinctly crooked because (we were told later) they had been trained to use their little fingers to sort good needles from bad.

At one point in our explorations, Shura said to me, "Have you noticed, no matter where we walk, all we have to do is look up, and there's the top of the Dom. Anytime you think you're lost, just look for it and head back in that direction." I hadn't consciously noted it, but he was right. The great grey cathedral dominated the center of the city visible above the rooftops, sitting there, quiet and solid like a venerable grandmother keeping an eye on the young ones.

We bought some bread, fruit and cheese, a big bottle of orange soda for me and a beer for Shura, and took it all back to our hotel. We discovered the strangely made-up beds (the pillows were rolled like bolsters and the sheets were folded like apple-pie beds or what Shura called short-sheeting; you were supposed to undo all of it before you got in). I sat at the little desk in front of the windows and looked out at what I could see of the city, and thought about the faintly hollow sensation in the general region of my tummy.

I said, "You know, I'm just beginning to feel a little bit of weirdness for the first time since we left home. Don't know why I didn't feel it before this — I mean, realizing that I'm actually in a foreign country, and it isn't home, and I don't really belong here — maybe it's not knowing the language. I certainly didn't feel this way in England. I guess it must be the language. Not being able to understand anything people say and knowing they don't understand what I'm saying. It really makes a difference."

Shura agreed, "It does, yes. At least we'll never tell anybody not to worry about traveling in Germany because practically everybody speaks English!"

I laughed and groaned at the memory of the early morning search for a hotel.

Looking at the little pile of food we'd put on the desk, I made a decision.

"Shura?"

"Alicia?"

"A thought occurs to me. Maybe this would be a good time for the 2C-I; what do you think? Maybe it would let me get a bit of a handle on this displaced feeling? It's just an idea. Say no if you're too tired, or think we shouldn't for any reason."

We had brought with us four doses of MDMA and two of 2C-I, just in case. I thought to myself that perhaps it would turn out to be a waste of a good, lusty psychedelic, if we were too tired to make love, but the prospect of integrating with the 2C-I, and whatever fooling around we might manage, was pretty tempting.

"Fine with me," said Shura, "But if we're going to do it, we should start pretty soon. I've got a really full day tomorrow at the nuclear thing."

I stretched and yawned, "Right now's okay with me. We shouldn't be up too late if we take it now."

Shura unpacked his set of vials and held up two of them, each marked 2C-I, 16 mgs. We dribbled a bit of tap water into each vial and shook them carefully. Then we clicked vials. Shura said, "To us," and I said, "To adventure," and we swallowed it. The taste wasn't any better than usual. I said "Bleah," and Shura showed off, smacking his lips and murmuring an appreciative "Yummm," which I ignored. I opened the bottle of orange soda and poured some of it into a bathroom drinking glass, remarking to him that — since he enjoyed the taste of 2C-I so much — I wouldn't offer him soda to help wash it down. He said he'd have some anyway, just to keep me company.

While Shura was taking his turn in the bathroom, I figured out the sheets and the quilts and checked the window-blinds, after pausing a moment to look out again on the quiet street below. When he came back into the room, we pushed the two beds together, speculating — between grunts — about the sex lives of Germans. We had asked for a double bed, and they'd given us two narrow singles.

Then, naked under the big downy quilts, we explored each other's skin with gentle fingers and shared our impressions of what we had seen that day. We were feeling the first effects of the 2C-I, when I took a moment to look around at the room, softly lit by the one bedside lamp. The wallpaper was a Victorian floral pattern in blue-grey and white, and the desk across the room was made of polished, dark wood. The carpet was red and there were cocoa colored drapes over the windows. I decided I liked the room, specially the wallpaper. Everything was moving a bit, shimmering slightly, which meant the 2C-I effect was by now at least plus-two.

I turned back to Shura. Our heads were a few inches apart as we talked. Suddenly, I was aware of something right outside our window. It was immense and powerful and I wondered for a frightened moment if it was trying to get in. I sat up quickly and Shura said, "What's wrong?"

I told him, "I just got hit by an extraordinary feeling that there's some kind of thing — a presence — outside the window. I don't know what it is, but boy, is it strong!"

"Do you want me to take a look?"

"I don't think there's anything to actually see, honey. It's just a — something tremendously big like a mountain, and very powerful. Feels sort of dark grey. Frankly, it's a bit scary. What the hell could it be? I've never felt anything like it before."

"Well, I'll look anyway," Shura said. He climbed out of his bed and lifted the blinds. "Nope, all clear." He got back on the bed and sat cross-legged, watching me.

"This is very strange," I said, hugging my knees and trying to figure out what could possibly be out there, pushing to be acknowledged. I bent my head down and closed my eyes, keeping myself as open as possible to the presence.

"It feels like — well, if I were to give it a shape — it's hard to get any kind of shape in my mind, but maybe like a pyramid, sort of. I don't even know whether it's good or evil; it's just huge and strong. That's the closest I can get to it. Like a pyramid, awfully old and absolutely immense. It doesn't feel like anything human, really."

Shura asked, "If it doesn't feel human, what does it remind you of?"

"I can't think of anything it reminds me of. It's a completely new experience." I kept trying to touch the thing with my mind, like a blind person feeling out a piece of sculpture with insistent hands.

After a few minutes, I told him, "I'm not sure about the non-human part, now. Maybe it has something to do with humans, but it's not like a person. It's part of the human world, in some way, I think, but it's too immense to be any single human being." I took Shura's hand, "I know I'm not making any sense, but I'm working as hard as I can to understand what it is. My main reaction is wanting to push it away, but maybe that's just because it's so strange, and I can't figure it out."

Shura asked, "Does it frighten you?"

I thought about that for a moment, then told him, "No, not really. It's just surprising to get hit by something so intense, all of a sudden like that."

"Why don't you lie back and close your eyes," suggested Shura, "Just let the impressions come to you. Don't try to push at it. Let it tell you what it is in its own way."

I said I'd give it a try.

As we lay next to each other, I speculated out loud about what the thing might be. Maybe the cathedral, just a few blocks away? That didn't make sense; the cathedral had been full of warmth and peace. Could it be some kind of memory of the Nazi time here? That didn't fit, either. There wasn't a feeling of evil about the thing.

"I think it's somehow beyond good and evil," I said, still probing with my mind, with every antenna I had, "Or maybe it includes them."

The answer came as such answers always do — like a confirmation of what some part of me already knew. It was clear and certain and Of Course.

I turned to Shura and said, "I know what it is! It's the city. Aachen! It's the whole city, the whole of everything that Aachen has ever been, thousands of years of this place. I'm feeling the city, the total of all the lives and deaths and everything that's happened here!"

Shura nodded.

I sat upright again, "That's it, honey, that's it! My God, what an experience! I've never felt a city before, not that way. It's like a — it's not like a person, but it's got an identity, almost a personality; it really does have a kind of pyramid shape to it, like a mountain, and it's so incredibly *strong*!"

"Now that you've figured it out, does it feel friendly or unfriendly?" asked Shura.

"Neither. It's just there. It exists. It's good and evil and everything in between that human life is. Wow! How fantastic!"

"Well," said Shura, pulling me down beside him, "Now that we've got that figured out, how about some very personal contributions of our own, to the City of Aachen, huh?"

We made love, then. The pressure was still there at the window, but it no longer demanded attention, and I knew it would slowly fade, now that I'd identified and acknowledged it.

Later, as we lay quietly on Shura's bed, my leg folded around his, our sweat pooling in the center of his chest, a new image began forming behind my closed eyes. I said to him, "I'm seeing something very interesting inside my head, and I'll try to tell you as it develops, okay?" He grunted, and I described the pictures as they unfolded.

There was a large grassy clearing in a forest, perhaps a hundred feet across. The trees around it were thick and tall, and there was sunlight on the grass. Around the edge of the sunlit oval, between the trees, were people, some standing, some sitting. Small children ran, shrieking and laughing, around the perimeter of the circle, darting in and out of the trees and bushes, but they didn't venture into the clearing. The adults were quiet, all of them looking toward the center of the grass, where the sunlight seemed to be gathered most intensely.

I knew that the people were worshipping and that the way they did it was to gather around a place like this, where the life energy was strongly present, even if only for a short while, and simply allow themselves to become part of it, greeting it and letting it greet them, feeding their bodies and their souls.

I said to Shura, "They know that the energy, the life-force, whatever you call it, is everywhere, that they can choose to contact it, immerse themselves in it, anywhere at all. This just happens to be one of their favorite places, when the sun is shining on the grass."

Then, the scene changed and I was watching a man, driven and single-minded, obsessed with what he believed to be his life's purpose, gathering stones to make a wall around another clearing much like the one I'd seen earlier. He was directing other people to lift and place the stones, and they were obeying his instructions, some good-naturedly, some with resentment. They all thought of him as not quite sane — out-of-balance, out-of-harmony in some way — but they were doing as he wished because of the force of his desire, his urgency. These people had not developed psychic or emotional boundaries, I realized.

The man was building a worship-place by putting stones around the grass circle, closing it in. I saw that he didn't know and couldn't understand, as the others did, that the singing life-energy was everywhere and could not be contained within walls.

The man believed that he had been singled out by some kind of Great Being to build a place for it to live in, a wall of stones which he, himself, would control, because he had built it. He would make the rules about it, because it was of his making, and because he was the appointed instrument of the God-thing which had ordered that this be done.

I felt the pity that some of his tribe had for him, and the irritation and impatience that others were beginning to feel; I saw that, before long, they would leave him alone in his circle and go to some other place together, because there was no point in being around a soul so dark and sad and unable to hear anything they said.

"He was pretty sick, I suppose," I murmured to Shura, "But I wonder if it's a picture of the beginning of a new development in humans; I mean, maybe he was a mutation, you know?"

"A mutation?"

"Well, maybe it was the beginning of individuality. A mutation who was one of the first individuals. What humans eventually had to become — closed-off individual egos. They couldn't do that if they stayed telepathic, without psychic boundaries. It meant giving up some of that interconnectedness, in order to develop the single, separate Self — for whatever that's worth! It certainly isn't a particularly happy picture, I must admit; in fact, it's very sad — that disconnected, power-hungry little mutant."

"Well," said Shura, putting his arm around my shoulders, "The whole history of the human race is somewhat sad, wouldn't you say, if you look at it in a certain way? But then, if you squint a bit differently, it isn't sad at all. Just extraordinary."

When the pictures faded, I respectfully saluted the City of Aachen, which still leaned against the window, and silently thanked it for the experience. I murmured a thank you to Shura and he kissed my nose and turned over with his back to me, and I fitted myself against him and we went to sleep.

CHAPTER 36. 5-TOM

(Alice's voice)

Sometime in the early '80's, David and Shura developed a new drug, to which they gave the charmingly odd nickname, 5-TOM. Shura began running it up (as he calls the early nibbling of a new material) in the fall of 1983, with my infrequent help. Between the two of us, threshold activity was eventually established at around twelve milligrams, and the nature of the effect at higher levels — between 35 and 50 milligrams — was reported in our notebooks as benign, de-stressing, and enabling fantasy and visual interpretation, though without much in the way of conceptualization.

In April of 1984, we decided to get together for Shura's 59th birthday, (we always celebrated group members' birthdays with an experiment, followed by soup, bread and cheese, a cake with candles and small token presents), and — although Dante and Ginger wouldn't be able to attend this time, Theo and his girlfriend, Emma, said they would be coming.

Theo had become part of the research group several years earlier. He had met the tiny, exquisite Emma at a poetry reading and, six weeks later, moved into her house. Within a few months — after the usual consultation with all the permanent members — she was invited to join the group. The young couple didn't participate in our experiments very often, because they worked during the week and, like most people in their thirties, they had a lot to do on weekends.

Emma was less than five feet tall, with a lovely figure and a fine-boned, delicately sensual face. I never tired of looking at her. As befitted a poet, she tended to introversion and occasional dark moods, but when she was having a good time, her brown eyes crinkled with humor and she laughed a low, velvety laugh. When Theo visited the Farm on Sunday afternoons for a few hours, Emma usually accompanied him, settling gracefully into the role of appreciative audience for Shura's ebullient ham-

and-nonsense.

I hadn't kept up as much as I should have with modern poetry, but it seemed to me that the poems both of them wrote, although quite different in style and content, were extraordinarily good, and I was always surprised at how demanding they were of themselves as poets, and how critical of their own beautiful pieces. They both used psychedelics or MDMA a couple of times a month, as writing tools, and brought Shura and me copies of the poems which had first taken shape under the influence. Emma also brought delicate watercolor paintings of flower-forms and mandalas, which she had created while using certain of the 2C-T compounds, her favorites being 2C-T-2 and 2C-T-8.

I was delighted to hear that they would be coming to the birthday celebration, and told them we would be trying out a new material with the funny name of 5-TOM.

So, at 10:00 AM on a Saturday in April, we gathered at the Close's house in Berkeley. Ben and Leah, Ruth and George, John Sellars and David, Shura, myself, and Theo with his lovely Emma, greeted each other in the high-ceilinged living room, with its view (when the fog was absent) of the Golden Gate Bridge and some of downtown San Francisco.

The house was the Close's treasure, and although I had never seen it otherwise than immaculately clean, it managed to be completely comfortable; couches and low tables were expected to support feet, and spills on the Persian rugs were taken care of with paper towel or sponge, and without fuss. The house was like its owners: neat, organized, and warmly welcoming.

While Shura weighed out the various dosages of the material of the day in the kitchen, Leah was in the dining room with David, Theo and me, telling us that she had finally completed her Ph.D. thesis, after grueling years of work. She said, "I can't believe it's over! It's going to be hard, you know, learning how to relax again — maybe even waste a few minutes, now and then — after all that pressure. Of course, I've still got a lot of stuff ahead of me, before I'm a proper psychologist-with-shingle, but the worst of it's done, *done!*"

We cheered and David reminisced, "I'll never forget the day I finished my thesis! There's no feeling like it, when you look at that stack of paper and realize you don't have to re-read or re-write or even re-think anything, any more! Far as I was concerned, getting the official document was an anticlimax."

Ben called us into the kitchen, where Shura was leaning against the sink, arms folded, ready to tell all of us about the drug we would be taking. Behind him, lined up in a neat row on the counter, were ten kitchen glasses of varying sizes and shapes.

"This," he said, "Is one of the sulfur analogues of DOM and DOET that

David and I have been sweating over for months now. Its full name is 2-methoxy-4-methyl-5-methylthioamphetamine, but you can call it 5-TOM. We refer to the family as the TOMS and TWATS." He waited until the groans had quieted down, and explained, "That last one is spelled T-O-E-T, of course, being the sulfur analogue of DOET, and there's obviously only one way to pronounce it, which is TWAT. At least, that's how David and I see it."

David laughed, "Last week, we were having lunch with a bunch of very dignified chemists, visiting from the East Coast, and one of them asked the usual polite question, 'What are you two working on these days?' and when Shura told him — you know, very casually and completely straight-faced — about the TOMs and TWATs, there was this dead silence, then one guy broke up, and the others choked on their sandwiches, and — well, it was sort of downhill all the way from there, you might say!"

"Anyway," said Shura, when quiet was restored, "Alice and I have taken this up to fifty milligrams, and I'm willing to try that again — ," he glanced at me, and I nodded, " — but some of you may want to go a bit lower, since it's a new one."

George nodded vigorously, as did Ruth. I was sure John would match Shura's and my fifty; he usually took the maximum level offered. Ben wasn't predictable; sometimes he matched Shura, but at others he seemed cautious, probably because of a recent rise in his blood pressure which — he'd told us — was slight but nonetheless worrisome, at his age.

Shura continued, "There seems to be some time distortion, a lot of eyes-closed fantasy, and Alice found it very interesting to look at paintings in art books. It takes anywhere from forty-five minutes to something over an hour to plateau, and the drop-off begins around the fourth or fifth hour.

"It's a long one; between eight and twelve hours before you can sleep, depending on the dosage. I was energetic the next day, but Alice said she was pretty flaked out, so you may or may not need Sunday to recoup."

Ruth spoke up, "We've got mats and covers for everyone, in case anybody wants to spend the night. And lots of eggs and bacon for breakfast!"

"How is this stuff on the body?" asked Theo.

"For me, fine. Alice had some heaviness, one time, but it was okay the next, so no predictions on that. Neither of us found any neurological threat anywhere."

After the usual discussion, Ruth decided to be modest, at 35 milligrams, while George said he'd try 40; Emma, who was usually pretty venturesome — she described herself proudly as a China Doll with an iron head — said she'd take 45. Ben, Theo and David said 45 sounded reasonable. John, as I'd expected, voted for the same dosage as the Borodins: 50 milligrams.

After clinking glasses in the traditional circle and swallowing our 5-

TOM, we dispersed in various directions. I went out the back door of the kitchen to the patio, where I could sit at the round white-painted outdoor table and smoke, under a magnificent kiwi vine the Closes had lovingly tended for years. It was carried around one entire side of the patio area by a wooden trellis, and every fall gave them baskets full of kiwis, which they shared with everyone they knew who liked the delicate, translucent green fruit.

I returned to the kitchen for a glass of ice-water, and met Ruth, who smiled at me, "How are you doing?"

"Okay, so far. I felt an alert a while ago, and I guess it's developing. What about you?"

She pulled her sweater around her in a familiar gesture, "I don't know. A teeny bit sluggish, I think. Not bad, but not much fun, yet. Guess I'll just stay with the others in the living room and listen to Shura and Ben competing with each other; that'll keep me distracted until I plateau."

I returned to the patio, with its soft sunlight, and stayed for a while, smoking, enjoying the isolation, while keeping track of the effects. I become increasingly aware of a certain discomfort of my own, and recalled Ruth's word, "sluggish." There was also a vague ache across the back of my shoulders, and my mood was anything but light-hearted. In fact, I was feeling slightly depressed.

May as well join the rest of the guinea pigs. Transition is often a drag for me. Nothing new in that.

In the living room, I found Theo lying on his back on one of the rugs, near the big fireplace. At the other end of the long room, David lay curled up on another rug, with John a few feet away. Ben and Shura were seated on the couch, exchanging atrocious puns, while Emma sat curled up in an armchair, laughing. She seemed to be feeling fine.

Ruth was sitting in another chair and she seemed a bit restless; her bare feet twisted and rubbed against each other and her hands were either stroking her skirt or fingering the agate stones of her necklace.

George was very still in his chair, only the tips of his fingers moving on the armrests. As I watched, he suddenly shuddered and got up, announcing in an unusually flat voice that he was going upstairs. "I've got to get under the electric blanket, because I'm very cold. If you will please excuse me?"

Ruth went upstairs with him, while Ben and Shura watched from the couch, their banter forgotten. I saw them exchange speculative looks, then Shura asked the rest of us, "Anyone else feeling chilled?"

Nobody replied.

"How's the body, for the rest of you? Any problems?"

Theo spoke up, his arms folded behind his head, "I'd say it's not the kindest material I've ever tried. I've got a bit of stomach cramping, and I can't seem to get really comfortable, no matter how I shift my different parts around."

I glanced over at him from my own place on the floor, a few feet away, and agreed, "Yeah, I'm with you. Not the stomach problem, but it makes me feel sort of heavy; it reminds me a little of the MDA cloak, in fact. Not one of my favorite sensations."

John spoke up from his corner near the big window, "What's the MDA cloak?"

"It's the reason I don't take MDA. I get a sensation around the upper back and shoulders that feels as if I'm wearing a leaden cloak. I can't shake it off, and it's all I can think about. MDA is a total waste of time for me, because I don't experience anything else. No insights, no nice visual stuff, no images or fantasies; just the ache in my back and wishing I were out of it."

"Oh dear," said John, "And is that what you're feeling now, with the 5-TOM?"

"Not quite that badly, but almost, and nothing's happening inside that's interesting enough to make up for the body discomfort, up to now."

Emma stretched and yawned, then reported, "Well, it's been great for me, so far. It's a wonderful de-stressor. I've been talking a blue streak and having a great time, but I see what Alice means, about there not being much going on. Colors are bright and friendly, and the leaves of that plant on the mantelpiece are moving nicely, but otherwise — well, I have the impression that I wouldn't get much done if I tried writing on this."

"All right," said Shura. He turned to Ben, "You, Benjamino?"

"I second that — about the de-stressing quality — and for the rest, I'll have to admit I've been too busy having fun with puns to pay attention. I haven't been aware of any physical problems at all. Quite comfortable, in fact. I'll focus on the psychological aspects for a while and see what turns up."

In response to Shura's questioning look, Leah, seated on the floor with her elbows on the coffee table, smiled and said, "I'm seeing some lovely visuals and I feel fine, very relaxed. I suppose it isn't specially insightful, but that's okay with me, right now. It's the relaxation I need. It's nice, Shura."

Shura's voice rose slightly, "David, how about you?"

His long, thin body unfolding with obvious reluctance, David slowly pulled himself into sitting position, arms hugging his denim knees, and cleared his throat. He said, "It's been mostly a lot of — uh — kind of depressing stuff, so far. Reviewing some disappointments and frustrations. And a lot of loneliness. I tried switching to another channel, but it didn't work. The same record seems to want to keep on playing. Not a very positive report, I'm afraid."

I wished fervently, not for the first time, that someone could find exactly the right girl for David. She would have to either adore chemistry, herself, and be as excited by it as he was, or else love and admire him enough to be content with the knowledge that chemistry was his first love, his life-blood, and that she would always come second to it — even if only fractionally second — in his heart.

At least, she wouldn't have to worry about competing with another woman; only with methyl groups and sexy things on the four-position!

Shura got up, "I'm going to check on George. Be back in a minute."

Theo said, "I think I'm going to try sitting up at the table and see if I can do a bit of writing, maybe start my report on the 5-TOM. I suspect lying around on the floor like this, doing nothing, makes me pay too much attention to small twips and twirps in the body."

I watched him ease himself onto his feet and wished him luck. He was a good-looking young man, with a dark beard and full head of hair. Although the light blue of his eyes was inherited from Shura, his mother's genes had shaped the rest of his face. He called me his "wicked stepmother," and we had become very good friends.

Emma was sharing her impressions of a recent exhibit at the Oakland Art Museum with Leah, when Shura came down the stairs. He went over to Ben and murmured, "Come up to the bedroom, for a sec. Take a look at George. I need your professional expertise." I saw him slip his feet back into the sandals he'd thrown off, hours earlier.

Ben put on his glasses.

Shura had said to me with some amusement long ago, that you could always tell when there was trouble during an experiment, because he would put on his sandals, and Ben would put on his glasses. "For no logical reason," he'd said, "We each react in those particular ways when there's a problem. It's the first instinctive step in gearing ourselves up — getting into focus — to deal with something that's not as it should be."

I went into the dining room, where Theo was writing in his notebook, and sat across the table from him. I said, "Your father just took Ben upstairs to look at George. Something must be going on."

Theo looked up, "What do you think? Has Ruth come down?"

"Nope. I think I'm going to tiptoe up there and find out what's happening. By the way, how're you feeling now? Still not too comfortable?"

"I've been happier," he admitted, "I've been making some notes, but it feels like work, not inspiration. This is going to be a definite no-repeat, for me."

"Me, too," I said, "I keep trying to shake off the discomfort, but it doesn't shake, and there's nothing much else to concentrate on. No concepts, no cosmic revelations, no nuthin'. In fact, if I weren't so annoyed, I'd be just plain bored!"

We both laughed.

"Can I see what you've written, so far? Would you mind?"

"Go ahead." He turned the notebook around and pushed it over to me.

The body of the notes began with the number, [1:25], which meant one hour and twenty-five minutes into the experiment.

"Probably +2. Somewhat visual, particularly in light/shadow texture. Colors tend to run into each other. No problem writing. Some slight stomach cramps, muscle fatigue. Something on the edges disturbing. Distinct time distortion, but time not much concern. Peripheral vision very active. Felt as toxic to the body, not intellectual. 'No Exit' feeling. Motion and depth somewhat disfigured. Wanting to do something, and yet — what?

"Hard time making up mind. Is it a toxic response or just the effect of this chemical? Non-productivity."

I nodded and thanked him, sliding the notebook back across the table. When I went past the living room, Emma and Leah were still talking animatedly about the museum. I climbed the carpeted stairway to the second floor. Shura and Ben were on either side of George, holding him under his arms and urging him to walk. Ruth was standing by the bed, her face set and anxious. Shura glanced at me and said, carefully casual, "A few odd little neurological signs that bear watching. Ben thinks as I do, that the heat from the electric blanket is probably intensifying the effects — he had it up to the highest setting, by the way — and we're trying to persuade him to go downstairs, where we can keep an eye on him."

George had a calm, pleasant look on his face, but he said nothing. I tried to look into his eyes, to make contact of some kind, and it was clear that he didn't see me.

"There are coordination problems with the eyes," said Shura.

"He's certainly conscious," Ben remarked, "But there's no response to external stimuli, and he certainly isn't communicating from the inside."

"Looks like nothing in, nothing out," summarized Shura, "And motor coordination is shot."

They continued to move him forward, through the door and onto the landing, and his steps were shuffling, almost robotic.

"Here we are, George," said Ben, speaking as if to a small child, "Now let's go down the stairs, slowly. We're holding you, so you can't fall."

Shura, on the other side, said, "Come on, George. It's just a few steps. You're absolutely safe."

George had come to a stop within a few inches of the stairway. He still made no sound, but the body language was clear. He wasn't going any further.

Ruth was pleading, "Honey, you'll be all right. We just want to get you to the living room, please? I'm right here with you. You won't fall, sweetheart! Just take one step at a time," with no results. After a few more tries, Shura speculated that George might be more easily persuaded if Ruth took his place, that maybe the physical contact with his wife would get through to him.

She tried for a while, but George wasn't budging.

Finally, when Ruth said she would have to take a moment out to go to the bathroom, I volunteered to take her place, holding George under the armpit and urging him, softly and continuously, "Come on, George, lift the foot and put it down. We're holding you. Come on, dear, move your foot!"

When Ben and I shifted our hold on him, placing our arms across his back, George's left hand found the curve of my breast and the fingers pressed in and out of the softness spastically, the way a newborn infant's hand kneads the mother's breast while nursing.

I remarked to Shura that some part of him seemed to recognize a female breast, anyway, but that I didn't think he was going to be persuaded to go downstairs by anyone, at least not right now.

Shura and Ben decided to lead George away from the stair and into his study, where he could sit down on the little couch and be at peace until he repaired.

None of us said out loud what we were all thinking: that whatever had happened might never repair, that there was at least a tiny, very frightening possibility that George would remain catatonic, his face permanently open and unguarded, eyes unseeing, unable to remember speech.

When they turned him in the new direction, he moved willingly again, though his steps were still awkward. I had no doubt that if his supports were taken away, he would fall to the floor in a heap.

We took turns sitting with him in the study. Now and then, a soft explosion of sound came up his throat and out of his mouth. There was an urgency to the eruption, a forcefulness, but I detected no sense of fear or anxiety. I had the impression he was communicating, and I wondered, for an instant, how long it would take for any of us to begin understanding his language, if it turned out to be necessary to do so.

I talked to him, slowly and affectionately, about the photographs he had fastened to the wall above his desk, about his friends downstairs, about how we loved him and everything was going to be all right. I talked about anything that came to mind.

When Shura relieved me, I went downstairs and found Ruth in the kitchen, keeping herself busy, preparing food for the table. She seemed very calm, and when I remarked on the amazing absence of panic or anger — either or both of which would have been justified, under the circumstances — she said, "Well, you know, I keep having this feeling that he's going to be all right. Maybe it's the effect of the 5-TOM, but every time I start wondering what I'm going to do if he doesn't come out of this, a little voice inside tells me not to worry. It says just be patient, he'll be good as new very soon. So I've decided to believe that, and in the meantime, some nice food on the table might make everybody feel better. And as soon as George starts coming out of wherever he is, he's going to feel hungry, right?"

"That much, we *can* be sure of!"

I went outside with my cigarettes and glass of water, after telling her I'd be under the kiwi for a while, in case she needed me for anything.

An hour later, Leah was babysitting George upstairs and the rest of us were seated around the dining table, savoring tastes and smells, grateful for good food and good friends, mentally pulling at George to come back.

We had progressed to dessert, and Ruth's legendary poppy seed cake was being cut when David, who had been taking his turn in the study, came hurrying downstairs and told us, "I have a feeling George is getting better. I'm pretty sure there's some kind of change. His eyes are beginning to focus more, and I think maybe he recognizes me. Why don't we try him on the stair again and see what happens?"

Fifteen minutes later, George had made it down the stairs and was seated in his favorite armchair in the living room, beginning to remember English. Leah brought him a piece of fresh buttered sourdough bread with a slice of cheese, and Ruth sat beside him, spooning soup into his mouth. His face was happy and his eyes seemed to be functioning normally. I had the impression that some corner of his soul was still attached to wherever it was he'd been, but the tie was weakening. He was definitely coming back.

His first full sentence was, "Good grief! Why am I being fed like a baby?"

Ruth handed him the spoon, chuckling, and he finished the bowl of soup on his own. Then he sat back in his chair, burped appreciatively, and looked around the room at the faces intently watching his every move. We were all smiling at him, and he smiled back.

"It's fading," he complained, "I was in the most amazing place, and lots of things were going on, but I'm losing it now. I don't want to forget it. Have to tell you as much as I can remember, before it all goes."

We clustered around him, in chairs and on the floor, while he spoke, slowly, trying to hold on to the images, "I remember the sea. I was on a long, curving beach and the sky was deep blue. Beautiful. At one point, I remember seeing what looked like the bands of a spectrum, and for a while I thought they were some kind of expression of my energy levels, but now I think maybe the horizontal lines were just my mind's way of trying to make something familiar and recognizable out of whatever was going on.

"Eventually, I could see real images, but they were tremendously distorted, like Cubism paintings by Picasso, with intense and very strange colorations. There were colors I've never seen before, but it's getting hard to remember them, now. Why am I losing them so fast?"

We urged him to tell us as much as he could before the amnesia curtain came completely down, and he said, "I know I wasn't afraid at any time. Everything was benign. As I began coming down, I realized I'd had an extraordinary experience, but I wasn't prepared for it to start slipping away like this!"

Shura asked, "Would you be willing to take this material again?"

George didn't hesitate. "Yes, I'd certainly take it again, but at a way smaller dose, next time."

We all joined in the laughter.

"I asked that question when I did," said Shura, "Because it was important to get your spontaneous reaction to the idea of a repeat, while you were still in the after-glow, so to speak."

"Sure," beamed George, "That was one singular, unique, fantastic experience, and I can assure you I'm going to get homesick for that beach. It was the loveliest, most satisfying place I've ever been in my life, though I can't even begin to tell you why."

Later we all grouped around the table again, to sing Happy Birthday and watch the Birthday Boy open cards and small nonsensical gifts. Then Shura went around the circle and asked for summaries.

Theo said, "It's a no-win, for me, I regret to say. The food helped my stomach, but even now, I'm not really comfortable. If there had been something spectacular going on mentally to compensate for the physical, it would have been a different story, but there wasn't."

I repeated what I'd said earlier about the cloak made of lead, and said that I, too, regretted having to conclude it was not my cup of tea. I added that I would probably pass on any future tries of the material, although I still loved its name.

Emma said, "I'm feeling almost guilty, at this point, for having had such a good time, but I did! I liked it!"

We said things like, That's okay, and Don't apologize, David adding, "After all, *somebody* had to enjoy the poor thing!"

Emma added, "I do agree with one thing Theo and Alice said, though. There wasn't much content, when you get down to it. Very relaxing and I felt terrifically good-humored, but there wasn't much else going on inside. It hasn't the richness of my favorite ones."

Ruth, her chair pulled as close to her husband's as it could go, said, "There's one very positive thing I've got to say about my experience. All the time George was upstairs, going through his troubles — I gather he didn't think he was in trouble, but the rest of us sure did! — anyway, all that time, I wasn't really frightened. I knew I should be, but I just had a strong feeling, as I told Alice, that everything was going to turn out all right. A little voice told me not to worry, so I just kept busy and stopped worrying, believe it or not!"

Shura said, softly, reaching over to grasp her hand, "I was prepared for you to be pretty angry with me, kiddo. I'm very relieved to hear you didn't feel that way, what with your man suddenly wandering around in outer space, and one of my drugs the apparent cause. It would have been understandable, at least for a while there, if you'd damned me and all my works to bloody perdition!"

He was smiling, but his eyes were moist.

Ruth shrugged, "Well, I probably have to give credit to the 5-TOM for keeping me from panicking, because I couldn't help having the thought that maybe he wouldn't ever come out of it, you know — "

"That did cross my mind, too, at one point," admitted Ben, and Shura grimaced in agreement.

She went on, " — and that's when I got the message it was really okay. As for the rest of my experience, aside from the worry over George —"

David interrupted, grinning, with the old joke, "Aside from that, Mrs. Lincoln, how did you enjoy the play?"

Ruth chuckled, "Yes, right. Well, actually, the rest of the play wasn't bad, although I didn't really keep track of things after George went upstairs. I think the first hour I was quite restless; it felt sort of bumpy — that's the only way I can describe it — but nothing else of great interest to report."

Shura was making notes. "Would you take it again?"

Ruth said, "Nope."

The summaries continued. Ben said, "I had no difficulty at all, body or mind. It was thoroughly enjoyable, in fact, with a great deal of fancy footwork in the pun area with you, before George went and captured our undivided attention!"

George laughed with the rest of us.

Leah said she'd had a nice experience, but that she couldn't see any reason to take 5-TOM again. She explained, "There are a lot of other materials which give more than just relaxation and a general feeling of pleasantness. This one doesn't appear to have much depth or richness, as Emma said. Not enough to justify spending the time to explore it further, especially considering the cloud there is over it, now."

John was thoughtful, choosing his words carefully, "I had a restless feeling, too, during the early part, and I'll go along with the others, when they say it lacks depth. I couldn't work with it, there was no insightful thinking, and my general impression was that it's a stoning material, and not much else. And no," he added, anticipating Shura's question, "I don't think I'd go out of my way to take it a second time."

David reported, "Not too good for me. My body was okay, but I guess I'll always associate 5-TOM with getting into a loop of sad and very lonely thoughts that I couldn't get away from. Maybe it wouldn't do the same thing to me another time, but I'm not eager to find out, to tell you the truth."

Finally, George spoke up, "I had the best experience of all, it seems! I don't know where I went, but I do know it was truly fantastic! I wouldn't mind taking it again, maybe at something like 5 milligrams, just to see what happens."

There was a medley of amused responses around the table, Ruth's being the last, clearest and most appreciated, "You and I are going to have a little heart-to-heart talk, sweetheart!"

When we'd settled down again, Shura folded the paper on which he'd been making notes. He leaned back in his chair and said, "Well, it is something of a mixed bag. Some of us seemed to be in a pretty much okay place, but several had a rough time of it."

He looked over at George, "And I suspect that you have a strange and wonderfully idiosyncratic sensitivity to 5-TOM which there was no way of predicting."

"Well, I have been pretty sensitive to other sulfur things," George observed.

"Yes, a little. But nothing like this. As I recall, you always tended to cocoon with the Alephs, but today was more than the usual cocooning; this time, you went full pupa!"

John went into one of his helpless fits of laughter, holding his sides, and the rest of us, watching him, slowly dissolved into giggles and croaks. John's fits were always catching.

When calm was restored, George asked, "Do you think there's something about sulfur that my body doesn't like?"

"I don't know," responded Shura, "But I doubt it, somehow. Your responses to the other 2C-T compounds have generally been okay, remember — in fact, you've had a great time with them, on the whole — and they all have a sulfur somewhere on the ring."

"So it's probably just this one particular compound, then, that I'm super-sensitive to? Just the 5-TOM?"

Shura nodded, "That's what I suspect. But we could test it out, just to be certain."

He turned to David, "How about putting together a sulfur thing that's inactive — totally inactive — and give it to George to see if, by any chance, he just might metabolize sulfur differently in some way, compared with the rest of us?"

David leaned forward eagerly, "Hey, good idea! Why don't we give it to the whole group and collect urines all round and do a real study! If George turns up with something really unusual, it might just be publishable in some journal!"

Theo laughed, "You could title it, `The George Effect; A Hitherto Unknown Response to Sulfur in the Five Position.'"

"Or maybe, A Close Call with a Sulfur Atom," Shura added. The puns had started again.

I thought of the laughter, how heartfelt it was, and how deep the relief underlying it.

Later, hugging Ruth and George goodbye, Shura said, "Well, I guess this has been one more reminder of our favorite maxim: 'There is no casual experiment.'"

Ruth agreed, "I suppose it's good to keep in mind that if you're going to do this kind of research, you have to expect to be surprised, every once in a while!"

5-TOM was never taken again.

CHAPTER 37. FUGUE

(Shura's voice)

The word "fugue" has always had a most pleasant sound for me. It is a French word meaning flight, or escapade. Some adventurous event that lasts only a short while. *"On fait une fugue,"* is an idiom that means he ran away from home, but only for a few days.

Musically, a fugue is the spinning of a phrase against itself. It is the flow of a line of music followed, after a few moments' delay, with the same line of music played again, totally locked in pace. The line may be identical, it may be harmonically offset, it may be inverted, but it is clearly recognizable. Yet, the two substantially identical lines, with just a displacement in time, can make a two-voice melody which paints a picture that is quite new and different from the original. There is the feeling of the original theme chasing itself, and you are never quite sure how it could ever end, if it cannot catch up with itself. How can two children chasing one another ever have a winner? Bach was the master of this idiom.

In the world of psychology, a fugue is — as I understand it — a state of mind involving amnesia, and a loss of connection with oneself for a period of time. It is brought about by extreme stress. It is not organic, not a seizure; it is purely psychological.

Three times, I have experienced something I call a fugue, although I probably shouldn't call it that, because I can recall what happened, I can describe every detail, and the only thing I can't do is make any sense out of it. But I love the word, so that's the word I'm going to use. It's my story, after all.

My three experiences were essentially the same; they differed only in duration. There was a separation of about ten years between each of them.

Let me try to reconstruct the first, and longest lived, of these events. It happened one day somewhere in the mid-1970's. I got up, put on my clothes, started down the road to get the morning paper, and became aware that everything about me had been rotated ninety degrees. I was in completely familiar surroundings, where I knew that north was straight ahead of me, east to the right, and so on. But it was as if I had been lifted up, given a quarter turn, and put back down, so that when I again faced the direction that I knew was north, it seemed to be west. Everything was somehow wrong, all around the compass.

Probably everyone has had some encounter with this sort of location-vertigo. Maybe you were once at a convention being held in a giant box-like hotel in a strange city. You park outside, and go in by the closest of the four entries on the four bordering streets. Inside, there are halls that make right and left turns, meeting rooms off these hallways, and alternate exits from the rooms to other halls.

After a full day, with no attention having been paid to the tally of right and left turns, something somewhere slips a cog and, upon exiting by what you thought was your original door, you find yourself on an unfamiliar street. Which way is the car? You know you're in the wrong place, but you can't be sure why or how it's wrong, and there's no way to intellectually straighten it out. However, in this case, you have only to walk around the hotel to put your surroundings in proper perspective, and free yourself from confusion.

On the other hand, in my fugue state, even though the landscape in all directions was completely familiar, the sense of rotation persisted. There seemed no way of making myself right, again. I was going to have to live with it, and there was no telling for how long.

Back in the house, I discovered another strangeness, a disquieting uncertainty involving the meaning of certain words. It was at this point that I began making the notes which I completed the next day.

"Any words that have concrete meanings are fine and completely friendly. That thing outside the window is a tree. The soft whatsis underfoot is a rug. That is a photograph, over there on the book-case. I am at peace with these representational names, the tree, the rug, the photo, the bookcase. People's names are OK too, I guess because they represent things. That photo there is of Manuel. Because Manuel is a concrete thing, I recognize his face. So, the representation can lean a little bit towards the symbolic, and pro-portionally away from the actual tangible reality. The photograph of a person is equivalent to the person.

"But words which are meaningful only in their immediate context come at me as total strangers. The photograph of the face of Manuel makes sense, but reading the time from the face of the clock does not. There is no face, there. Manuel is a face, but there is no such thing on the clock. The time displayed on the front of the clock is a little too abstract. The meaning is not apparent from looking at the individual numbers and letters, or trying to analyze these components."

I remember a psychological test for certain forms of mental disturbance that asks the patient to explain the meanings of idiomatic phrases. The rolling stone gathers no moss. A stitch in time saves nine. I am sure that, during my fugue, I would have been able to deal only with the literal meanings of each of these expressions, and so have failed the test hands down. I would even have had trouble with the phrase, "hands down." It would have been fascinating to have challenged myself with a familiar foreign language.

Early in the fugue experience, I didn't think of using the radio as a source of spoken language, to test my comprehension. I rather suspect that the sound of speech would have been all right, but that, if I'd had to read a written text corresponding to what I was hearing, I would have found it quite a bit more troublesome.

The best way of making clear the nature of this fugue state is in the use of numbers. Each of the three times it happened to me, I found that the careful, structured use of numbers was an excellent way of defining and describing the actual experience.

"Numbers are straightforward. I can add them, manipulate them, count backwards by sevens from a hundred, or by 27's from 275, and I still can mentally extract square roots. But — as with words — when numbers are presented in a form that requires context, everything falls apart. Telephone numbers have no logical connection with people. I can come up with all sorts of telephone numbers from memory, but the dialing of them has no meaning. Intellectually, I know that if I push the buttons, someone's voice will materialize in the ear piece. But I can't really understand what the pushing of a series of phone buttons has to do with talking to anybody!

"A street address is just as nonsensical. Let's say, I live at 3038 Birch Terrace. Birch, okay; terrace, nearly okay, but the 3038 thing makes no sense, in that context.

"The numbers on the digital clock are equally worthless. They can give me absolutely no insight as to what time it is at the moment. Sure, it is 10:40, but where and what is a 10:40?

"The date is equally mysterious. It is June 19, 1978. What is a 1978? It adds up to the sum 24, and the reduced integer is 6, but I can't see any apparent relevance to anything else, including the birth of Christ.

"I remember having looked at the morning Chronicle a half dozen times to make some connection between the printed date and the assignment page in my appointment book. The paper says today is June the 16th. It is a Monday, and my little book says that, at 2:30, I have to be in Federal Court as an expert witness for the defense in a criminal case. I must be in a courtroom on the 17th floor.

"The digital clock on my desk has a 10:40 on it. How does that come together with a 2:30? And what is the meaning of 17th floor?

"The day of the week is certain from the morning paper, and from the calendar on the wall, but it has no absolute position in the flow of time as I am experiencing it. Can I find boundaries to contain the phenomenon, then shrink these limits sufficiently to pin-point the Now, with complete certainty?

"Perhaps I am maybe just the slightest bit light-headed. I can hear it now — 'He clearly was suffering one of the most notorious evils associated with consciousness-expanding drugs, a flashback,'which this decidedly is not."

Are there such things as flashbacks? Yes, but they are pretty rare, and there is always some uncertainty involved in connecting them to the action of a drug. There have been proposed both chemical and psychological mechanisms. The chemical argument — the unexpected re-activation of a lingering molecule — is without merit. If 100 micrograms of LSD was effective today, and if the blood level dropped with a half-life of a couple of hours, then in a few days there will be an undetectable amount of the drug present in the body. If such a vanishingly small quantity of any drug were to be active, it would mean that that drug would have an over-whelmingly high potency. No such compound is known to exist.

So it is not a physical thing. Can it be psychological? Absolutely. But I would give good odds that any flashback will turn out to be related in some measure to a traumatic experience. Say, for instance, you had a bad driving accident, several months ago, in which you swerved your car to avoid hitting a pedestrian in a red shirt who had suddenly appeared in front of you, and you crashed into a large beer truck. You broke your right leg and had over $2,000 worth of medical bills which your insurance never covered. I'll wager that the appearance of a red shirt in the pedestrian crosswalk, in front of your car — months later — might well produce a sharp pain in your leg. Your right leg, specifically. That is the mechanism of a flashback, whether drug-related or not. It's a conditioned response.

If you'd had a drug experience that was memorably traumatic, then the flashback could well be your way of reliving it. All you need is the catalyst, the red shirt, and the scene could pop up from your unconscious to replay itself, in living Technicolor, not to speak of sound effects and emotions, as well.

But my fugues have no apparent relation to past trauma of any kind.

I decided, on that day, to look closely at blood pressure, and at the possible need of my brain for sugar. Knowing that I had to be in court in the afternoon, I had no choice but to extricate myself from this strange situation.

I had to put on San Francisco clothes (a white shirt, a non-outrageous tie, a jacket, and clean socks). Brute subtraction (present time from target time) told me that I had to be in court in less than four hours. To start with, I was going to have to come to grips with the meaning of the concept, "four hours," pretty damned fast.

A frightful thought hit me. What if I found myself on the witness stand, still in this peculiar state of dissociation? Would I be able to understand the questions I might be asked? Would the very concept of question and answer be meaningful? Could I simply grit my teeth, and carry it all off without anyone being the wiser?

I thought, let's see if I can answer that by turning on the radio; maybe that will help define the geometry of my strange altered place.

The radio gave me a late Mozart piano concerto, coming across with complete integrity. A stellar thing of beauty without any trace of disconnection or disjointedness. Fine, I thought, let's turn to a news station and get words.

I was hit with the time, the weather, an advertisement for a travel service, and a stock market report, all within the first minute of listening. It felt as if I had just been dealt a poker hand in which every card carried a different suite, and each card had a different number. Nothing made sense.

I did not look forward to a spirited cross examination on the witness stand. Maybe this was all due to some unprecedented drop in my blood sugar level. I voraciously ate a couple of oranges, and began getting ready for my trip to the City. I showered (everything went well), I searched for a suitable shirt (that was not as easy), and I found reasonably polished sandals.

Can I drive? I will certainly find out.

As it turned out, my driving was flawless. It was quite another matter to unravel the intricacies of underground parking, there under the Civic Center, but I was able to call up the correct procedure from some emergency memory bank, and all went smoothly.

Still wondering if my blood sugar was involved, I sat down at a lunch counter and ordered a tall glass of orange juice.

Gradually, imperceptibly, things began slipping into their normal place. My body was slowly rotating back into its proper north-south orientation. It became more and more comprehensible that today was Monday, June the 19th, because yesterday had been Sunday. Tomorrow, of course, would be Tuesday.

By 1:00 PM everything was pretty much normal. Normal? Yes, normal. My appearance on the witness stand, I felt, would be under control. And so it was.

In retrospect, what was that all about? I had drifted, like a wide-winged bird, over many things that were without meaning, yet my mind was clicking away quite properly on other levels. The elapsed time of this event, this fugue, was around five hours.

Twice, since then, basically identical experiences have occurred, but in shorter time. The most recent lasted only twenty minutes.

Somebody will undoubtedly say, "Maybe certain of his brain cells got burned out as a result of too many exploratory drug assays!"

But that theory isn't logical, because, if such had been the case, how could they have repaired themselves in a two to three hour period? The professional neurochemists tell us that these cells never repair themselves.

The flashback, as I said, is not a good explanation as there is no obvious trauma being relived. The fugue event has properties quite removed from any drug experience I have ever had.

Might it have been hypoglycemia? I don't think so. My two later fugue experiences simply dissolved and disappeared without my paying any attention to sugar at all.

I think that fugues such as this might be part and parcel of normal brain function. Perhaps they are ascribed, by whoever becomes aware of such an oddness, to stress or lack of sleep or too much drinking the night before. The obvious response is to phone the boss and tell him you're sick, and go to bed until it passes.

Maybe there is a man in the backwoods of Idaho who is walking through the trees on his land, one day, and suddenly realizes that the familiar surroundings have become alien territory; he is a stranger in a forest that belongs to someone or something else. The back of his neck prickles as hair rises, and he turns around and heads for home.

I am convinced that this phenomenon, the fugue, is part of the heritage of the human animal.

And I have come to appreciate, at a very deep level, the possibility that this state (blessedly transient with me), might be the day-to-day reality of some guy out there on the street.

It's a thought that gives rise to immense compassion.

I look forward to my fourth occurrence. If the apparent pattern is maintained, the next episode should take place in another five years, and may last only a few minutes. That is an extremely short period of time in which to run experiments in word association and counting numbers backwards, but I will try to do both. I am most curious.

CHAPTER 38. CRISIS

(Alice's voice)

SUNDAY

This is the story of a major alteration of consciousness which occurred because, apparently, it was time for it to happen.

It began on a Sunday afternoon one November in the mid-'80's. Shura was working in his office and I was in the bedroom, beginning to sort out what I thought of as my shit pile, a collection of such things as clothes, belts, stockings, photographs, and old magazines, all waiting to be put where they belonged. The pile was a symbol, a reminder to me of a side of myself I detested — scattered, disorganized, and procrastinating. I wasn't sure which was worse, looking at that mound of stuff or fighting the sluggishness that always crept over me when I began trying to organize a personal mess of this kind.

I understood the depression; I had long ago figured out the conflicts involved in trying to clear up any accumulation of objects that represented some part of myself — *especially* if it was an unwanted part — but understanding hadn't resolved the problem.

I started in, lifting boxes onto the bed and folding clothes into drawers, feeling slow and dull.

So when Shura called out to me from his office, "Hey, how would you like to help push back the foreskin of science while you're working?" I shouted back that I couldn't imagine anything more appealing, and what did he have in mind?

He crossed the hall and leaned against the door frame, "There's this new thing I've taken up to thirty milligrams. I haven't spotted any activity yet, and I thought you might want to take it one more step up — maybe forty milligrams? You almost certainly won't get any effects, but I would

appreciate having one more level out of the way, if you feel like volunteering?"

"Sure," I smiled, "What is it?"

"It's 3,5-dimethoxy-4-methylphenethylamine. DESOXY, for short."

"Okay, I volunteer," I said, suddenly not tired any more. Even if there
wasn't liable to be activity at forty milligrams, I thought, it would help my
morale to know I was trying out the next level of a new drug, to have the
self-image of Alice the Useful to help counteract that of Alice the Messy.

Shura went to the lab and came back with a glass containing a bit of
white powder and beckoned me to follow him to the kitchen. I asked if he
was taking anything himself, and he said, "Nope. I had an inactive level of
something else yesterday and I need to stay clean today."

I poured out a bit of pink lemonade onto the powder. Shura clinked
his coffee mug against my glass, "To science." I replied, "I'll drink to
that," and did. Then I said, "Bleah," and poured out more lemonade to
wash the taste away.

I hugged him, "Thanks, honeybun! I feel useful and virtuous and
important!"

"Well," he cautioned, "As I told you, I don't honestly expect we'll get
any activity, but you never know. You could have a threshold, if we're
lucky. But I wouldn't count on it."

On our way out of the kitchen, I asked, "What makes you so sure I
won't get activity?"

He explained that, if he hadn't detected any effects at thirty milligrams,
a mere ten milligrams more couldn't be expected to present anything but a
threshold, at the most. "All drugs," he said, "Have what is called a dose-
response curve; with more material you get more effect. But most things
like these phenethylamines show a pretty shallow slope. If you get nothing at one level, there's rarely much to be seen at even twice that level."

I paused at the door of the bedroom, "Okay. But you don't usually
double the dose of a new compound, do you, in the first stages of trying it
out?"

Shura shook his head, "Not when it might be getting into the area of
activity, but, yes, I might in the earlier stages. Anyway, with this DESOXY
stuff, we're not doubling, just going up by one third again. Normally, I
jump by half again with each new trial, so this is a pretty modest increase."

I went back to work, making neat stacks of letters and catalogs which
had inserted themselves between ancient copies of The Saturday Review
and Newsweek, and listened to talk radio to keep my mind from turning
to mush.

About forty minutes had passed before it dawned on me that something
had changed. I couldn't define it at all; I just knew I was off baseline. I
went into the office and told Shura that things were going on, though I

couldn't tell exactly what, and he said, "That's great! I didn't really expect you'd get anything. Think it's distinct enough to be counted as a definite threshold?"

"It feels more like a plus-one, actually," I said, "But let's wait and see."

"Well, keep me informed."

"You'd better believe it!"

I stooped and lifted and grumbled, threw crumpled clothes into the ironing basket, examined photographs and stacked them carefully in a shoe box on the bed, feeling increasingly strange and not entirely comfortable. There was no apparent body load; it was just a general uneasiness, and I couldn't really pin it down.

By the time an hour had gone by since ingestion of the drug, I had come to the conclusion that this was more than a plus-one, and that I didn't give a damn about organizing things any more. I wanted to lie down, so I shoved boxes around to give myself space on the bed. I still couldn't define the discomfort.

There was no apparent visual activity of the kind that we look for when there's more than a plus-one effect; nothing was moving on the walls or ceilings; there was no rippling of curtain edges. But when I looked through the window at Mount Diablo and its foothills, they had taken on a disturbing aspect.

I love Diablo; I've seen many sunrises over it, often standing with Shura's arms around me at the tail end of a good experiment. The distinctive shape is part of us, part of our home, one of the first things our eyes go to when we return from being away. I had never before seen it present itself the way it did now — hard, unfriendly, almost hostile.

I looked away from the window.

Feeling cold, I got an old, soft, taffy-brown sweater out of the closet and put it on before lying down again. It seemed best to stay quiet for a while longer, because movement of any kind caused a chill to go through me, and there was a hint of nausea.

Lying on my back, hands clasped behind my head, I examined the room. There was an ordinariness to it; it was just a room, not the treasured place where Shura and I made love and heard music. It was merely walls and furniture and a mound of stuff against the far wall and a big bed piled with dusty cardboard boxes. I felt no attachment to any of it.

In fact, I realized, I felt no emotions at all, just a faint distaste.

When Shura came in and asked how things were going, I said, "It's really weird. I don't think I like it much."

He sat on the bed and asked me what level of activity I thought it was, and I said, "Close to a plus-two, I think."

His eyebrows shot up, then he frowned, "Maybe you're very sensitive to it; I can't understand how you could be getting a plus-two at just ten milligrams more than I took."

I said I couldn't understand it either, but it definitely was not going to be one of my favorite materials at *any* level; of that, I was certain. At least, not from what I'd seen of it so far.

He asked about body or nervous system load and I said, "All that seems okay; it's just a mental uncomfortableness."

He stroked my leg thoughtfully, then made a suggestion, "Why don't you go outside and see if that improves things?"

I said, "All right, I'll give it a try," feeling no enthusiasm for the idea. I got up and walked down the hall to the back door. Shura called out after me, "Do you want company?"

"No, thanks, let me try it by myself, at least to start with."

I walked slowly down the path, past the lab and up the short brick stairway. My arms were folded against the cold, and I felt slightly irritable. I wandered to the edge of the grassy shelf. We often sit there when the weather is good, in canvas patio chairs which wobble on the uneven ground, and look out over the valley.

I turned my eyes to the mountain in the east and then north to where the county seat, the old town of Martinez, was hidden under a thin layer of white fog. Aside from the faint irritability, I felt nothing. There was no excitement, no depression, no fear; no real emotion at all. The valley and the mountain were very much present, but I could see neither beauty nor ugliness anywhere, and I felt no personal connection to any of it.

Everything I saw seemed to very intensely exist, but not in relation to me.

It all looks cold, clear, distant, and there's no response inside me. No caring of any kind. For anything. Which means this damned drug will go no further than Shura and me. Well, well, waddya know! "Damned drug" implies some feeling, after all. Some part of me is angry! That's interesting.

As I stood there watching the fog layer at the end of the valley, it began to take on a new aspect; it seemed alive — a cold, white, alien entity. It was, I thought grimly, like an externalized form of my own state of mind.

Am I feeling this way because I'm seeing nature as it really is, without the sentimental overlay that humans put on it? People always think, "I care about this tree, that river; I love the mountain, the hills. Therefore they care about me, they love me, too." Without being aware of it, we project onto the natural world entirely human feelings which it doesn't share and has no concern with. Is that it? I'm feeling no emotion because I'm tuning into what's around me and seeing the way it really is; a physical landscape in which emotions don't exist at all. Only animals and humans have emotions. The rest of nature has none.

My tummy was still not sure of itself, so I went back to the house and stopped at Shura's office door to tell him maybe I'd try putting a bit of food into the bod.

He asked, "How was the outside world?"

"Couldn't appreciate it, I'm afraid. Everything is very strange and distant and not particularly friendly, so I thought I'd come back and heat up some soup. Do you want some?"

"Sure, sounds good. Do you need help fixing it?"

"Good heavens, no, thanks. I'm okay."

At the table, Shura reached for my hand and held it for a moment. The hot cream of tomato soup and sourdough bread was making me feel a little better.

When we'd finished eating, he sat back in his chair and looked at me, smiling slightly, and said, "Well, I guess we'd have to call it a surprising experiment, to say the least!"

"Yup, I'd say so. Not entirely a pleasant one, either. It pretty much flattens out my emotions, which is something I just do...not...like. It's really strange; I'm aware that some part of myself is angry at this whole thing, but I can't connect with the anger. I know I'll be able to experience it tomorrow, when I'm back to normal, but now, I don't seem to be able to feel it; I just know it's there."

He nodded. "Where are you now, plus-wise?"

"Oh, I think it's easing off. I'm on the down slope, thank heaven. About a plus one, I'd guess."

"Good. I'm going to go very carefully with this one, from here on. That is, if it seems worth taking any farther, and there's some doubt about that, from what you've said. It certainly looks like an extremely steep response curve."

"Uh-huh, it sure does."

"You going to be all right?"

"Oh, yes. I'll do the dishes, then just relax and watch TV for a while and keep myself distracted until I'm back to normal."

He came over to me and held my head against his stomach. He stroked my hair, then bent down and kissed my forehead. I hugged him and got up to clear the table.

By 9:00 P.M., I was pretty much baseline. There was still a sense of emotional flatness and the remnants of disconnection from my surroundings, but I kept myself occupied with television, until an attack of yawning signaled bedtime.

Curled up back to back with Shura, I discovered that my nervous system was not, after all, completely at peace. Once, I jumped — what Shura called "darting" — startling myself out of an uneasy drift into sleep, and a few minutes later my right ear was attacked by a viciously aggressive buzzing which came diving straight into it. I knew it was only a phantom wasp, having experienced it before, but a feeling of vulnerability remained for some time. I made a mental note to tell Shura that the body's wiring was a bit sensitive to this stuff.

MONDAY

It was a good sleep. When I woke, I looked at the the sunlight streaming in across the ceiling and thought, Oh boy, that was awful yesterday. That was awful! I sat up and put my feet on the floor, aware of a full bladder, and looked around me again and knew, in an instant of shock, that I was still in it. It wasn't over.

For the first time, I felt fear.

I went down the hall to the bathroom, thinking furiously.

What is this? I thought I was baseline last night; I'm sure I was. How could Shura have had no activity at all at thirty milligrams and I not only had a resounding plus-two, at just a little bit more, but it's lasting into the next day? Is it possible that something in my psyche opened and got stuck open?

I sat on the toilet, staring at the floor, trying to figure it out.

I don't want to be here like this. What is it I'm locked into? There's a sense of some kind of intelligence; I can feel it, like a cold, observing Mind. It's everywhere, watching everything. It sees me. What feelings does it have about me? Probe. No feelings. I can't pick up any kind of feelings. Just awareness. I don't want to be anywhere near it. I want to be back to my old self and my familiar old world.

There was one distinct difference from the day before: I had emotions this morning. Mostly despair. And anger.

After I'd dressed in my jeans and sweater, I made the coffee and scrambled some eggs, then sat at the table with Shura, picking at food I had no appetite for. I waited until he had finished reading the Chronicle before I told him, "I'm still on, honey."

He frowned, "What do you mean? You're still feeling something from yesterday?"

"I know I was baseline, last night. There was some residue, because I darted while I was going to sleep, but I was definitely down. This morning, I woke up and found myself right back on again. About a plus two, in fact."

Shura's eyes searched me, then he reached over and cradled my face in his hands, "I don't know what to say, Buns. This just doesn't make sense."

"I know it doesn't."

"Is there anything I can do for you?"

"Nothing at all, honey. You don't have to stay home or anything. I'm okay by myself, believe me. If I feel weird or out of control or really worried, I'll phone you at work and tell you so, I promise."

The truth is, I am feeling weird and I certainly don't have an ounce of control over this, and the word "worried" doesn't even begin to describe it. But I've got to work it through myself.

Shura got up and began gathering his papers from the end of the bookcase.

"Are you sure you don't need me here with you? I can call in —"

"No, I mean it. I only told you because you had to know there's a continuation of the drug effect. I don't understand how, considering everything, but what else could it be?"

"Don't be silly! Of course you had to tell me! Don't ever withhold something like that, sweetie! You would expect me to tell you, wouldn't you, if our positions were reversed?"

"Yes."

When Shura was dressed for the outside world (he worked with David, twice a week, in a research laboratory in San Francisco), I stood in the kitchen and looked at him, at the blue eyes shadowed by concern, and asked, "What if this state turned out to be permanent, honey? I know that's not very likely, but what if it were?"

He looked into my eyes and took a deep breath, "Well, if it did turn out to be permanent, we'd find out how you can adapt to living at a plus-two. You would have no choice but to learn to adjust to it as your normal state. And you would, you know, just as I would if it happened to me."

I grinned weakly, "Yeah, I suppose that's exactly what I'd have to do."

That was a scared-child question. He's answering me as if I'm a grown-up, bless him.

"I really don't think that's going to happen, Alice," he said, putting down his ancient briefcase and hugging me hard.

Jesus, I can't cry now! I've got to hold on until he's out the door. There's nothing he can do, and he'd just worry.

I squeezed him back and said, my voice as down-to-earth as I could manage, "I know it isn't, Luv. Just a wild thought. I'll be all right. You know I can take good care of myself. If I had any doubts at all, I wouldn't let you go to work — you should know by now I'm not the martyr type."

I sounded completely convincing to my own ears, and he kissed me, said he'd phone during the day, and turned to go. At the door, he hesitated, then muttered, "I don't understand all this. It doesn't make sense — or have I said that before?"

I said, "I already came to the same conclusion. It doesn't compute. But, in the meantime, I'm going to be pretty busy trying to work my way out of it."

I kissed him goodbye again, and watched his dusty little green car drive off.

As I turned to go back to the kitchen, I remembered an incident Shura had told me about, a long time ago. He had wakened one morning, having done no drug experiments for several days before, and found himself in a totally altered state of consciousness. He had set to work trying out various things to bring himself back to normal, including eating oranges for the sugar, which had no effect either. I recalled his telling me that, by the middle of the afternoon, the strange experience had apparently run its course, and when he woke up the next morning, he was okay. He'd never figured out the what or why of it, he'd said, and probably never would.

Perhaps this was my equivalent, I thought, and maybe it would be over with by the time he came home.

I started washing the few dishes in the sink, watching myself adjusting the temperature of the tap water, scrubbing forks, rinsing, as if I were a movie camera recording A Day in the Life Of. In the bedroom, I observed myself pulling the fitted bottom sheet on the bed to smooth out the wrinkles, noting the efficiency with which I made the ordinary, familiar moves, and tried to remember the correct psychological term for this kind of detachment. The only word that came to mind was "discombobulation," which was certainly appropriate, but not what I was searching for. (Much later the word came back; it was, of course, "dissociation.")

All the while, I kept a determined wall between myself and the Thing, to which I had decided to give the temporary name, White Mind — white, as in fog. And ice. I knew I would have to deal with it sooner or later, but at least I had enough control over the situation — so far — to be able to decide when, and that would be after doing what had to be done in the house.

I didn't bother looking out the window because I already knew what I'd see.

Finally, after sitting for a few minutes with a cup of coffee, I unlocked the back door and went outside. It wasn't that the White Mind was located there; it was more a matter of my having chosen to do my battling of it out where there were trees and grass and sky, where I could move, walk, have space.

A few feet from the house, I paused and looked over the valley and, this time, I was not sensing the cold, dispassionate consciousness only in my immediate surroundings; I stood, arms folded in the instinctive body language of self-protection, next to a patch of bare ground where we had planted spring bulbs — hyacinths and daffodils — and knew that I was tuning in to a pure consciousness of unlimited intelligence and absolute clarity; there was a crystal awareness, everywhere, that watched everything, having neither liking nor disliking nor any other feelings for anything it saw. It observed love and hate and recorded, it observed atoms and elephants and recorded, it observed agony and orgasm and recorded. And it learned from everything; it learned all the time.

Suddenly, I was remembering Carlos Castenada's spokesman, Don Juan, describing what he called the Eagle — an immense, implacable, emotionless spiritual force which lived for only one thing: awareness. I had read about the Eagle with revulsion, a long time ago; I could still recall my resistance to the idea of such an entity existing on any level of reality.

I went back into the house and found the passage in Castaneda's book, The Eagle's Gift:

"The power that governs the destiny of all living beings is called the Eagle ... because it appears to the seer as an immeasurable jet-black eagle ... its height reaching to infinity.

"The Eagle is devouring the awareness of all the creatures that, alive on earth a moment before and now dead, have floated to the Eagle's beak, like a ceaseless swarm of fireflies, to meet their owner, their reason for having had life. The Eagle consumes them; for awareness is the Eagle's food."

Shaken by a burst of intense anger, I returned the book to the shelf and went back outside.

I will not call it the Eagle. That's Castaneda's image, his world, his universe. I will not name this — whatever it is — after somebody else's lousy, godforsaken bird!

I was being pressed down upon by its presence.

Why am I so angry? It's more than anger; it's closer to fury. There's something about this Thing I'm tuned into which pushes all my buttons, and I've got to figure out why. Okay, it's because there's nothing more dreadful to me than impersonal intelligence, thought unattached to feeling. Why is it so terrible? Because it is inhuman — unhuman. What's bad about a mind being non-human? I'm not hostile to the idea of non-human beings living on other planets, and perhaps visiting earth, am I? Why not? Because I believe — I prefer to believe — that non-humans would have feelings, that's why.

For the first time that day, I smiled. Why did I assume that aliens from other parts of the galaxy would inevitably have feelings of some kind?

Probably because the fact that they were visiting us would mean they were curious and wanted to find out, wouldn't it? Curiosity is most definitely a feeling, as well as an intellectual function. Rocks aren't curious, rivers and trees aren't curious. Only the animal world has curiosity. So I figure that visiting non-humans would be feeling something we could understand: wanting to know. And if they can experience one emotion, they must have the capacity for others — or so the reasoning goes. And we can make contact, touch, communicate with feelings, even when we can't speak the other's language.

I looked up at the hazy November sky, and wondered if this crystal-cold awareness was the Mind of the Creator.

Whatever it is, I loathe it.

I remembered another time, years before, when I had learned that God is everything that exists, good and bad, and that it experiences every emotion and sensation felt by every one of its parts. *Okay, this is not the Mind of God. On the other hand, what if the answer I got before was wrong, and this is the true nature of the consciousness that runs the cosmos? If it isn't, then why do I sense it to be universal; why has it taken over everywhere, so I can't tune in to anything else? And what am I supposed to do with it?*

I flashed undiluted hatred at the Thing, the White Mind that watched and recorded, knowing that neither my hatred, nor the fact that I was deliberately communicating it, mattered in the least to it. It would continue to observe and register and learn without prejudice, bias or emotion.

I walked down the little path, brushing past the new grass which had sprung up with the first fall rains. The tawny yellow edges of California's summer-dried hills were starting to blur into long-forgotten green. I saw nothing of the growing things on either side of me as I walked the dirt trail, barely dry from the last rain; I was making a decision.

I refuse it. I will not accept it as the force that runs my universe. I will not assent to a spiritual intelligence that has no feelings, no caring.

I found myself outside the dear old scarred, dirty laboratory door. I put a hand out and touched one of the glass panes; they had been painted white on the inside long, long ago, to prevent the uninvited from seeing in.

Shura. Beautiful, incredible man of mine. How could we have actually managed to find each other? How is it that he has the heart and the patience to put up with me?

I turned around and began slowly walking back in the direction of the house, my head down, aware of nothing but the streams of thoughts flowing through me.

What happens to us when we die? Do we get absorbed by this clear, unfluctuating awareness, this inhuman, uncaring Recorder? Does all human experience mean only more material for a cosmic information-bank?

It didn't feel true. I was missing something.

How could an Overmind which has no feelings create living things which feel all the time?

Time had stopped moving. I sensed that I was on the edge of discovering something, at least a piece of the answer; I could feel it, just around a corner.

I knew the Enemy was observing my sequence of thoughts and questions, feeding itself with what was going on inside me, along with everything else going on everywhere else.

I can't live with this Thinking Machine. I will not accept it as the final truth of the nature of God. I do not accept!

I stopped next to an oak sapling and looked up at the clouds which were beginning to gather overhead.

Anger swept over me again, and it was edged with hate.

Do you hear me, you damned monstrous son-of-a-bitch? I say NO to you! I DENY YOU!

I realized that tears had been flowing down my cheeks for some time; I just hadn't noticed before. They would have to be ignored; I was too busy right now. I had just informed what might well be the Creator that I wasn't going to play in its lousy sandbox. Now what?

Why am I feeling no fear? Because this is too important for me to waste time being afraid. Besides, what is there left to be afraid of? The worst possible thing which any cosmic Mind could do to a little human one has already been done: it has revealed its own nature, and in doing so, it has managed to effectively strip my world of all meaning, all purpose. I'd rather confront an eight-armed demon with razor fangs! You can battle with a demon, you can embrace a demon; what the hell can you do with a fucking spiritual computer?

I folded my fingers around a handful of cedar bush, needing the touch of something friendly.

I have to solve a rather serious question, and soon. The question is: if I refuse to live in a universe run by this — this Thing, and if I have no intention of committing suicide, then what kind of universe will I consent to live in? And how do I go about creating it?

An interesting observation drifted quietly in.

If I can experience the White Mind and reject it, that means I have a choice, because I have made that choice. And I obviously have the right to say no, because I have just said it.

I sat down on a grassy slope next to the brown path, and rocked myself back and forth to help the thinking.

If the essential core of all life in the universe, including the human, is in truth this Mind that only thinks and learns and does not feel, then my alternative is a universe run by a consciousness that feels. A Mind that is capable of love. Does that mean it has to be capable of hate? We've had that one already in good old Jehovah. No. Yes. You can't have just the good half; it's all or nothing, my friend. If my acceptable God-mind loves, it also hates. If it feels any emotion, it feels all emotions. Jesus. Start again.

One of the cats had discovered me. I knew she wouldn't leave, so I would either have to put her in my lap and try to ignore the passionate clawing which would accompany the purrs, or get up and go inside. For the moment, I decided to turn my lap over to the cat, because I wanted to keep searching for some kind of answer here, outside, under the sky.

I kept working, trying to find out what it would take to create another universe and another God — one I could assent to — and what the rules would have to be. I already knew that there had to be positive and nega-tive, male and female, Yin and Yang. For there to be life, there had to be death. I understood that much. There had to be pain as a sign of imbalance, of something needing to be fixed. If there was connection with another living being, one would experience loss when that other was taken away; if you open yourself to love, you open also to sorrow.

I shook my head sharply to clear it, wiping off tears with a furiously impatient hand. The sound of purring continued, and I resumed my rocking.

All those thousands and thousands of years of human beings trying to survive, everywhere on the planet, scrambling to get food and build shelters, finding a bit of joy in loving and working and singing together, and all of them desperate to discover what the meaning of existence is — all the suffering and pain, all the beauty — trying to understand because they've been created with the kind of mind that is compelled to try to understand. It's been built into us, that urge to figure it out.

Images paraded through me: abandoned old people dying alone in dirty rooms, children crying because their parents hurt them, young soldiers losing arms and legs and their manhood; eons of pain and anguish, fear and loss of hope.

My God and all the little gods! Is all of it just food for some sort of horrendous Watcher-Recorder-Computer?

I cried for a while, real crying, for all the innocent, injured, rejected, helpless people and other living things, all over the world. There was a racking pain in my chest, and I remembered having been in this place of sorrow before, one evening, years ago, after taking one of Shura's compounds. I remembered calling it the Sorrow Place, and the Valley of the Shadow of Death, finally realizing that it was a bottomless pit and asking Shura what I should do with it.

He had answered, "Step out. Now that you've learned what it is, decide you've been there long enough, and simply step out. Get back to the world of life and love and humor, which exists right alongside it, and is just as valid."

I had asked how he would get himself out, if this were happening to him, and he'd said, "When I get stuck in a difficult place, I go to the lab and wash glassware, until the difficulty resolves itself, or transforms into something else. Sooner or later, it always does. But, since washing glassware's not your thing, why don't you sit down at your typewriter and put it on paper? You could make it one of your great reports to Dante and Ginger!"

I did exactly that until, very gradually, I began to glimpse images of the Smiling Buddha and then, many small children playing on a field of grass, and I found myself coming out of that place of pain and sorrow.

It was time to step out again, I thought. If I could. That still left me with my number-one problem, though.

Since I will not assent to this White Mind being the ruling intelligence of my universe, I'm going to have to construct a God-Mind I can accept.

I sat on the grass, rocking, absently stroking the cat.

And obviously, the only way I can conceive of another kind of God-Mind is to form it out of myself, my own mind and soul.

Comprehension began trickling in.

Is that what I am? A piece of the God-Mind trying to give itself a new definition? Or am I going to make a full circle and end up re-affirming what already exists?

The ringing of a telephone reached me through the back door. I spilled the cat off my lap and went inside to the office, hoping it would not be a complicated call, but as my hand touched the top of the phone, I knew it was Shura.

He asked, "How are you, Buns?"

"I'm okay, honey. Struggling with the cosmos, but okay."

"Anything changed for the better?"

"I really don't know. I mean, it's hard to look at it all objectively enough to say whether something's better or not. I'm just awfully busy trying to figure things out."

"Not coming down yet?"

"I don't think so, Luv, but I know in my heart of hearts that it won't be permanent, so I'll just keep on doing what I have to do and wait until it's run its course."

That's interesting. I didn't know I was going to say that. The words came out of some part of me that DOES know it won't be permanent, that it will pass.

Shura said he loved me and would be home soon, and I told him there was no need to worry, repeating that I was basically okay, in some peculiar sort of way, and that I loved him very much.

As I hung up, a face appeared in my mind, the face of the psychologist, Adam Fisher, our favorite grandfather figure and wise-man. I went to the living room, where I could sit on the couch and use the ashtray, and dialed his number.

"Adam," I said, "This is Alice." He said Hi, in his warm, smiling voice. I told him, "I'm in trouble, and I need help."

I could feel him snapping into focus on the other end of the phone, "Tell me."

I told him, pausing every now and then to gulp down the tears that kept rising in my throat.

I summarized, "I'm living in a universe that is full of some kind of cold intelligence that watches and records everything and has no feelings at all, and it may very well be the truth of what God is, although I don't really think so, but I don't know what else it could be, because it's everywhere and I can't get away from it. I've decided I'm not going to accept it. I know that sounds ridiculous, but that's the way I feel."

I clenched my teeth to stop the tears from choking me, and plunged on, "All I seem to be able to do is think a flood of thoughts and cry continual stupid tears and inside I'm screaming NO, NO! at something that couldn't care less, and I want to get the hell out." I stopped for a moment, coughing to clear my thickened throat.

I heard him say, his voice sharp and emphatic, "First, you haven't discovered anything about the cosmos at all. Whatever you're facing is not out there, it's inside you. It's you, not God and not the universe. Start dealing with it as an aspect of yourself."

I said Oh.

"Next thing," continued Adam, "What you're going through is a process. You don't have any way of understanding what it is or why it's happening; don't try to understand, right now. You're just going to have to accept the fact that some kind of process is taking place which needs to take place and there's only one thing you can do, *must* do, and that is: don't get in its way."

"Jesus, Adam," I said, "Am I going to be stuck here forever?"

"No," said Adam, the sharpness gone, "You're not going to be stuck there forever. In fact, I can assure you that you'll be out of it by the end of the week."

I understood, with a brief flash of amusement and admiration, that he was programming me — my unconscious, anyway — for recovery by the weekend, and I felt a surge of gratitude. I mentally dug an elbow into my own ribs and flashed the thought, "Listen, you, hear what he said? Out by the end of the week!"

"Thank you so very much, Adam. Listen, if I get to where I can trust myself to drive safely, can I come over and talk to you for a while? Will you be home the next couple of days, in case I can manage the car and everything?"

His voice was gentle and I realized he was speaking more distinctly and a bit slower than usual, so that I would hear him through tangle and confusion, "You call me any time of the day or night, and if I'm not here, leave a message on my answering machine and I'll get back to you as soon as I'm home. And when you can drive safely, you come over here and spend all the time you want. I'm here for you," he said, intently, "I'm here for you any time, just as you would be for me."

I thanked him again and hung up. Then I put my head in my hands and cried, hard, for a long time.

When Shura got home, he kissed me and held me to him, then searched my face and hugged me again. I knew he was concerned, and that it couldn't be helped — so was I. But whatever this was, it had to be lived through. I told him that the streams of thought were very intense and that

I couldn't shut them off, so I would either talk to him or write them out, although the images and the concepts had become so continuous and so complex, it was hard to focus on any of them long enough to write them down. I said I seemed to be reviewing all aspects of human life and experience, but that I was tuned in, most of all, to the painful, sad, tragic aspects, and it was getting to be a drag.

I followed him into the dining room, where he always put down his work papers and the mail. I suggested he go ahead and read his letters while I attended to dinner, which was going to be a matter of taking a frozen meal out of the refrigerator and putting it in the oven. Nothing more complicated than that, I said, which I was sure he'd understand, considering.

He told me he was perfectly willing to go out and get a cheeseburger, if I preferred to leave kitchen stuff alone right now. I assured him I could manage a frozen dinner without any problems at all, and heard myself actually chuckling. It was a nice, normal sound.

When he had finished with letters and bills, I sat down at the table and gave him a shortened version of the day's struggles, and described the call to Adam.

I concluded, "He said everything I'm going through is inside me, that what I'm facing is an aspect of myself. He said it's a process of some kind that has to happen, otherwise it wouldn't be happening, and that all I should do is not get in its way."

Shura half-smiled and nodded, "Sounds reasonable to me."

I smiled back, "And he told me I'd be out of it, all through and back to normal — whatever the hell *that* is! — by the weekend. Isn't that great?"

We both laughed.

When I put his meal on the table, Shura tried to persuade me to eat something, but I said I had no appetite — which was perfectly fine with me, considering my eternal weight problem — and would he mind eating alone while I went and sat down at my typewriter and made notes on all this crazy business? He said he wouldn't mind at all, and to call him if I needed anything, including just plain loving. I kissed him, and turned away so he wouldn't see the tears rolling again.

At the door of the kitchen, I looked back and decided to tell him about the watering eyes, instead of trying to hide them, because that would eventually become impossible.

"Shura?"

He looked up quickly, his face anxious, "Uh-huh?"

"I think I should explain that part of this — whatever is happening — seems to be an almost continual dripping of tears. Sometimes it is actual crying, but most of the time they just flow down my face for no particular emotional reason, you know; they're just there. It seems to come with the territory, and I haven't the slightest idea why. So you don't need to pay attention to them, okay? Tears don't mean what they usually do, while this stuff is going on."

He smiled at me, "All right; I'll ignore your tears unless you tell me I shouldn't."

"Good," I grinned, wiping away the latest example.

I sat at my desk and turned on the electric typewriter. It was time to start writing an account of this whole very strange business.

"DESOXY, 40 mgs.," the report began, "This is the oddest experience I've ever had. I've taken drugs before which were threatening, but the problems were entirely neurological. The difficulty this time is not physical, but psychic."

I wrote a brief summary of the previous day's experience, for the record, then continued:

"Adam said it's all myself. That means I've been projecting onto the world around me some part of my psyche that observes and registers everything and learns. That is its function."

I remembered the pressure of that unseen awareness, an almost physical sense of being pushed at, as I stood outside the back door.

On the other hand, that old phrase, "As above, so below," could also mean, "As inside, so also outside." The universe outside me mirrors the one inside me, and visa versa; of that, I am sure.

I was suddenly recalling, vividly, a painting I'd seen in a book on the mythology of the East, of an Indian god surrounded on all sides by huge pearls which reflected his face and body. And I remembered its name: the Net of Indra. A net of pearls which is the cosmos; a cosmos which mirrors the God.

So whatever I've been projecting onto the world outside is within me, but it's also an archetype of some kind in whatever surrounds me. Out there. Whatever "out there" means. Okay.

My notes went on:

"It is entirely possible, and at this moment I think probable," I wrote, "That whatever the God-Mind is, my human psyche reflects it, and that means I've been confronting not only my own Fact-Recorder, but the cosmic one, as well. I got into trouble because I was afraid that it was the Whole Truth about God, and it isn't."

It isn't? Of course, it isn't. I know that. I've known it all the time, somewhere within me. Just forgot because that crystal intelligence took over the whole field and didn't seem to be leaving room for anything else. But it's only a part of the God-awareness, as it's only part of mine.

As I sat there, reading what I had just typed, a series of concepts formed in my mind, and I started writing again.

"We are indeed being true to this aspect of ourselves — what I was calling the White Mind — in our creation of thinking machines which function without emotions. Computers, for instance. Strange (and funny, in a way) how we've given birth to the computer — a really helpful, power-giving tool — out of those very elements of ourselves which are farthest from what we usually think of as human."

Another thought was forming, and I typed as it took shape.

"What about the part of us — the human species — which showed itself in the so-called 'scientific experiments,' done on the inmates of the Nazi concentration camps? There were people, including doctors, who were able to turn off all empathy, all connectedness, and just watch. They watched pain, fear and horror, and made notes, feeling nothing but intellectual interest. What was that, if not the Fact-Recorder, put to use by the side of us that loves to dominate and control, and wants to devour another's power and freedom?

"The White Mind is, I suppose, pure intellect. It is morally neutral. It serves our survival — individually and as a species — and it functions effectively because it is untouched by the world of feeling.

"An integrated, complete human being, of course, uses all of himself — emotional, intellectual and spiritual — and does not fail to exercise any one part, in favor of another.

"Isn't that what some people are doing when they conduct animal experiments which cause pain to the animals? 'It's necessary to do this; it's in a good cause,' a scientist reasons, 'Therefore compassion cannot be allowed to enter into it.' He's afraid that empathy might interfere with the gathering of factual information for a scientific paper which, he hopes, will earn him the respect of his peers and the continuation of his grants."

After I'd re-read the words, I added,

"Of course, there are many scientists and laboratory workers who love animals and don't cut themselves off from caring and sympathy, but there are too many of the others, and there should be none. In my opinion, that is. There ought to be a law that only people who love animals are to be allowed to do experiments on animals."

I smiled. Fat chance. If you could legislate love and empathy, the world would have been cured of its ills long ago.

When Shura came in to see how I was getting along, I was writing hard, ignoring the tears, which were dripping off my chin.

"How about a good night's sleep, Babe?" he suggested.

"Now that you mention it, I guess I'm ready for exactly that."

When we were under the covers, Shura held me and stroked me gently, watching my face in the dim light from the radio. I closed my eyes and felt the firm, skillful hand on my body for a few moments, then looked up at him and apologized, "Honey, I know it sounds ridiculous, but I'm feeling practically anesthetized down there; it's like a piece of wood. I can't remember this ever happening before!"

Shura said, "Well, it's certainly an unusual development —"

"You mean, `A reeVOLTIN' deeVELupmint,' don't you," I said in my best Durante.

He was continuing, " — but if lust isn't on the agenda, at least for the moment, its absence will only serve to sharpen our anticipation of its return," his fingers prodded, "To whet our —"

I made a grab at his ribs and he arched backwards, then caught my wrists and pinned them to the bed. He had me laughing again, and it felt wonderful.

We were both hoping a little bit of playing around might help me get back to some kind of normal. Never expected the whole region to go dead like that. What the hell could be making that happen?

When we had settled down under the covers, I kissed him and said, "Thank you for being so patient, my love. This is all very peculiar and I don't seem to have much control over any of it, so I just have to wait until it resolves. One way or another. The worst of it is the self-centeredness, you know, all the obsessive involvement with my own inner workings, but I guess that's what I'm stuck with, for the moment."

Shura hugged me to his chest, "You do what you have to, Buns, and I'll do whatever I can to help you. If nothing else, I'm here to love you, all right?"

I nodded silently, knowing that he would feel the heat of tears on his skin, hoping he would ignore them. He did.

I lay on my back, staring at the ceiling, as Shura settled into sleep, his hand occasionally twitching slightly, in mine.

So the White Mind is just one component of my own consciousness, an essential part which observes, records and learns. That's all.

I thought of my own, very personal Observer, which I had always considered a friend, not a disinterested machine; it was able to keep track of events, precisely because it wasn't influenced by emotions, yet I had always regarded it as a caring, concerned interior ally, with a great capacity for humor.

Perhaps my Observer is the Alice version of this same archetype. I've dressed it up in nice things like caring and humor, but its essence is exactly what I projected onto the world around me and fought as an enemy, today, because I didn't understand what it was. It's not an enemy at all; it's a necessary part of me.

I wondered if I would be able to sleep. It was the last waking thought I had.

I had vivid dreams, but was able to recall only one of them later. It involved a long adventure with some friends, and I was aware of the White Mind overseeing the whole thing, but this time with fondness, and unmistakable amusement.

All the dreams had a feeling of peacefulness underlying them, as if my soul understood perfectly well what was going on and was satisfied with the way it was all progressing.

TUESDAY

Before opening my eyes, I checked out the world and myself, feeling around with mental antennae like a nervous cockroach, and knew I wasn't out of my private little hell yet.

This time, getting dressed in the bathroom, I felt grim. We are not amused, I thought, brushing my teeth. When I had washed my face, I picked up a comb and set to work on my sleep-tangled hair, examining my reflection in the mirror with great care. My eyes had a familiar look; they appeared liquid and soft, and the pupils were enlarged, as if I were under the influence of a psychedelic.

Not young any more, that face. But it actually looks quite beautiful. Eyes swollen, but still — not bad to look at. Ah, well; for small favors, we are grateful.

Shura taught his toxicology class in the fall, on Tuesdays and Thursdays, and he would not have to leave for the University until noon. He was reading the morning paper and I planted a kiss on his neck before sitting down at the table with my coffee.

I decided to find out how much I could understand of the news — to see if I could focus on anything in print — before giving him an update. I felt him glance at me a few times, but there was no need to hurry, I thought; let the poor man have at least a few minutes of good coffee and Chronicle time, to begin his day.

After a while, I realized I was re-reading everything two or three times. My mind was Grand Central Station, and no more than a few printed phrases penetrated the steady rush-hour foot traffic, the comings and goings of thought after thought, idea after idea. I was busy.

When we had disposed of the paper, I filled him in on the latest developments, and we talked.

I said, "Whatever this damned thing is, there's no question that any standard-issue psychiatrist in the world would label it psychosis, right?"

Shura shrugged, "Probably, for whatever that's worth, and we both know it isn't worth much!"

I smiled in agreement. Most of our friends — those who weren't chemists or writers — were psychologists and psychiatrists, or did therapy of some kind, and we both knew how little any of them really understood about the nature of either mental health or mental disorder. But the term "psychosis" seemed a reasonably good starting place in attempting to define this experience.

"Okay," I said, getting up to sponge off the plastic tablecloth, "Everything about this — the streams of thought, the continual imagery and the intensity of the concepts, ideas falling over each other, there's so many of them; all the crying, the fact that I know I couldn't possibly drive a car, because of the distraction of what's going on inside — it's all the kind of thing you'd label psychotic, if you were an ordinary, unimaginative psychiatrist, right?"

"Well, now, I'm not so sure," replied Shura, "There are a lot of things about this that just don't fit with that diagnosis."

I considered for a moment, reviewing. "Yes, I see what you mean. I haven't lost my center, my sense of Self."

"And your grasp of reality is pretty much intact."

"Like, I notice when the stove is on and remember to feed the cats and make the bed and stuff?"

"Uh-huh. And you don't expect me to share your world; you aren't expecting me to see what you're seeing and feel what you're feeling. You're able to accept that I'm living in what might be called everyday, consensual reality, while you're not."

"Ah! And a psychotic wouldn't be able to maintain that kind of perspective?"

"Something like that, yes."

I leaned back against the kitchen sink. "You know, it's occurred to me several times, how much worse this whole business might have been, if I hadn't had experience with psychedelics? I mean, I'm used to altered states, and I don't panic. I sure don't like what's happening, but I haven't felt frightened more than a couple of times, and the fear didn't last — probably because I was so involved in being angry."

Lost the original train of thought. Oh, yes! Got it again.

"As I said before," I continued, "I haven't lost my core, my sense of being me. In fact, in a funny kind of way, I don't think I've ever felt more centered in my life! Can you imagine what it might have been like to go through this if I'd never had any kind of experience with consciousness-changing?"

Shura poured himself another cup of coffee and asked if I was ready for a refill. I said, "No, thanks. I just need to explore things a bit more with you".

When I focus like this, talking with him, there's less noise from the thought-parade.

I asked him, "Can you think of any possible explanation for what's been happening, on the purely chemical and physical level?"

He said, "I'm sure I could come up with a couple of plausible-sounding theories, but we both know you can't get any real answers in this area by isolating just the chemical and physical factors."

"All right, but speaking just of the chemistry, anyway, could this possibly be the result of taking forty milligrams of the DESOXY? Two whole days ago?"

"I'm less and less convinced that it has anything to do with the material you took on Sunday," he replied, "But we can't be sure until I've tried it again myself, at the same level. And, eventually, you should take it once more — at a much lower level, of course, just to see if by any chance you're extraordinarily sensitive to it. If you can bring yourself to do it. I mean, when all this is over, when you've recovered."

He's thinking he shouldn't have said that, right now, about my taking it again. He's anxious.

I smiled, to reassure him, "Sure. Maybe try two or three milligrams, and if there's any effect at all, we'll have our answer, but it won't be strong enough to cause a repeat performance."

He nodded, obviously relieved.

"I must admit," I said, "I can't wait to see what happens when you take it, though my instinct tells me you're right; it probably won't have any effect at all. I certainly hope you don't have anything like this happen to you, Beautiful. Ever. This is hell, you know!"

I realized, with a tiny flash of amusement, that my voice had sounded quite cheerful.

I suppose there actually can be a bit of perverted satisfaction in going through such a strange, dramatic process as this; it is pretty exotic, for all of the misery. Besides, may as well get all the little satisfactions I can — of any kind — since I don't have much choice about being here.

Shura asked, "Do you think you can detect any kind of change from the first two days, anything you can pin down?"

"Oh, yes. There's a lot of change, but it's not easy to define. The White Mind is still around, but it doesn't dominate the field anymore. I guess my recognition of what it is, and realizing it isn't the Whole Truth and Nothing But the Truth, cosmically speaking, helped it to fade into the background. It isn't pushing at me, now. The streams of thought are going great guns, though."

"What kind of content? Can you describe any of it at all?"

I sighed, knowing that the tears would start flowing again as soon as I started telling him, but needing to share it anyway.

"Well, there are often several levels going on at the same time. Right now, on one level, there seems to be a sort of compulsive surveying of human history, images of people from prehistoric times up through the present, creating cities, books, paintings, religions, political systems, wars, making the same damned mistakes, over and over, and every generation asking the same basic questions and having to figure out their own versions of the answers.

"It's hard not to feel a dreadful despair about the whole picture. I mean, why don't we get wiser, as a species? Why can't one generation pass on what it's learned in such a way as to save its children from falling into the old stupid traps?"

I shrugged, spreading my hands, "Then, on another level, I'm seeing that if the elders of each generation were capable of really instilling chunks of wisdom into their children, they would also be able to instill other things. Along with the good stuff, you'd also get all the misconceptions, prejudices, traditional tribal hatreds — all that sort of thing would be absorbed and perpetuated too — and that would mean no new perspectives, no moving forward at all. If there's to be growth, evolution, the children have to shape their world differently, taking some of the good and some of the bad from parents and ancestors, but basically remodeling it, putting their own stamp on it."

Shura was listening intently.

"There's another level where I'm seeing the rise of all the great spiritual teachers, the ones who change the way people think about life — Christ, Buddha, Mohammed, thousands of others we have no record of — and how their teachings are always used, sooner or later, as just another excuse for persecuting other people, taking power over them, making them do as you do, and going to war, killing and destroying in the name of God and Allah and Whomever. You know, the endless perverting of original good into a new form of evil. The old story."

Shura nodded.

"But, alongside that, goes the realization that even such an horrendous power structure as the medieval Church made it possible for a lot of creativity to be expressed, and a lot of beautiful things to come into existence. There's an image of a black field, stretching to the horizon, an awful, smothering blanket which represents all the arrogance and cruelty and persecution that goes along with religious power —"

Shura was nodding again; this was a subject we'd often discussed. In fact, it was he who had told me that, in the Middle Ages, unauthorized possession of a copy of the Bible was grounds for execution by those who enforced the power of the Church. Only royalty and the clergy were allowed to read the Holy Word or dare to interpret it. Ordinary peasants were to believe what they were told and live as they were ordered — by the priests — and were not to ask questions.

" — but out of that black landscape," I went on, "There are little green plants growing, here and there, representing the music and paintings and other forms of art which that same Church encouraged and made possible. Their motives weren't, of course, to encourage individual expression, but to add more glory to the good old Church. Nonetheless, those beautiful things came into being, to a great extent, because of the support of one of the most repressive dictatorships in history! Good out of evil, to balance the evil created out of original good.

"That's just one example of the kind of thing that's working itself out in my head, all the time," I said, "History on parade, sort of, with examples — illustrations — and continual images.

"The hard part," I paused, swallowing, "Is that I'm being bombarded mostly with the sadness, the suffering, the loss of meaning that human beings have gone through during their lives, century after century — and it's still going on that way, of course, all over the world. So much misery and gross stupidity, and I'm really getting sick of it. I'd much rather be in Philadelphia, to quote Whatsisname. I just want it to turn off!"

Shura moved quickly. He held me as I sobbed against his chest. I didn't have to tell him that it was real crying, this time.

After a few minutes, I got my control back and apologized, "Sorry 'bout that! Didn't intend to drag you into it that way. I don't want you to tune into me, honey. You have to keep your psychic boundaries, because it won't help either of us if you lose them. I need you to stay strong and sane in all this mess."

"Don't worry about me, Luv," he said, his voice firm, "I'm not being sucked in and I'm not really worried. I don't like seeing you in pain of any kind, of course, but I know you'll come through this and out the other side with something you didn't have before. This whole experience will turn out to be of great value to you, in some way neither of us can foresee at the moment."

I looked up at him and saw that his eyes were wet, but there was a grin on his face that seemed genuine.

I felt better; relieved and almost peaceful.

Needed to let it out. It helped to dump on him a little, even though I shouldn't do it. Just makes it harder for him. He's feeling helpless enough already. But I do feel lighter, for the moment.

I smiled and gave him the only positive thing I had to offer, "I have one very nice and rather odd bit of information for you. My dreams, these last two nights, have had a general feeling of contentedness about them, a sense of everything being in balance and even funny, now and then. As if my unconscious knows exactly what's going on and isn't disturbed or anxious at all. Believe it or not!"

Shura pulled me to him again, murmuring, "That's good. Trust your unconscious, sez I!"

I said I did, as a matter of fact, adding, "I know, underneath the confusion, that whatever this process is, it's going to take a certain amount of time and it's going to proceed in its own way, with or without my consent, but that, eventually, it's going to work itself through, and I'll be back to some version of normal."

I squeezed his waist and told him I was now going to wash the dishes from yesterday, and thanks for letting me unload on him.

He said, "Any time, Luv. I'll get to work at my desk, if that's all right with you. Call if you need me."

When I had finished the few dishes, I spent time scrubbing at the refrigerator, the stove, then the cupboard doors, grateful for the simplicity, the uncomplicatedness of cleaning.

It was while I was keeping busy in this way, that I gradually became aware of the hurting. Everything — thoughts, images, motions of the body — was being experienced through a faint haze of pain. I realized I'd been subconsciously aware of it for a long time, but — because of the intensity of the thought-flow — hadn't fully acknowledged it before.

Pain is a sign of imbalance, yes? Or a result of some kind of transition. Transition from one state to another usually carries with it some sort of irritation, grating. Snakes are known to feel miserable when their skins loosen, aren't they? Does a butterfly struggling out of its cocoon get cross and resentful? Probably. It's not physical at all, the pain, when I take a good look at it. It's the soul that hurts. Why? What message am I supposed to get? What am I supposed to be doing that I'm not doing? Or is it just another part of the process I have to live with?

It was really quite subtle, I thought; not intrusive, just continuously there, like a dull psychic toothache.

When Shura had left for his class, with my assurance that I would be safe and all right alone, I sat for a while on the couch, staring out the window at what had been my mountain, but wasn't any more.

I'm beginning to get really tired.

My Observer said, No, you're not tired. You think you ought to be, you're trying to persuade yourself you are, but it's just one more way of trying to escape. Take another look. You're full of energy; you're a living body of energy!

All right, all right, I'm not physically tired, but I don't want this any more. I need time off.

I thought again about yesterday, about the pressure, the insistent, inescapable pushing, of the Watcher-Recorder. And how it wasn't doing that to me, today.

It receded as soon as I really worked on it and began to understand what it was. Now, it's just one more thing humming away beneath all the other stuff. Why did it take over like that? Why did it come at me as if it was everything, as if it really was the mind of God, the only essential Truth, instead of letting me know it was just one of many important parts of the Whole? How was I supposed to know it wasn't the only thing that had any reality in the universe?

I sat, smoking my cigarette, as the outlines of an answer formed.

The unconscious psyche doesn't have a way of distinguishing between Whole Pizza and One Slice of Pizza — there's just Pizza.

That part of me which wants to bring something to conscious attention doesn't evaluate as to size or importance. On the level where I was operating, yesterday, there are no gradations, no comparisons, to help the conscious mind get some perspective on what's happening. Whatever is active at the moment — whatever is being brought up to be confronted and processed — fills the screen completely, so that, for a while, it seems to be all there is.

Why can't the damned psyche label things better than that? It makes everything so much harder than need be. Not to speak of bloody inefficient, for that matter! A lot of time got wasted yesterday in fear and loathing which could have been used for figuring it out and understanding it sooner. Stupid!

My coffee was cold. I got a fresh cup and returned to the couch.

How is one supposed to know what the rules are, about going through something like this, if there's nobody around to tell you? What would have happened if there hadn't been an Adam for me to call on, someone who knew exactly what to tell me?

The Observer answered immediately. There *was* an Adam, it said. He was there, you called him, you got help. What-if's are pointless speculation.

I wandered into the dining room, wondering what else might be inside me that I was going to have to confront and acknowledge consciously, before this grinding so-called process would consent to leave me in peace.

Any more surprises waiting to pounce, huh? Am I going to have to look my deficiencies in the face, maybe? My inadequacies, my failures? I'm already miserably aware of most of them, aren't I?

I was standing beside the table, looking at the basket of winter oranges in its center, when I felt something coming at me from behind. I became very still, my back crawling. It was hate I was sensing; the most utterly virulent hatred I had ever met in my life. A murderous, contemptuous hatred so intense, my mouth opened in shock. It was directed at me, at everything I was. Something wanted me gone, destroyed, eliminated, never to have existed.

Oh, my God! Where did THAT come from! What could hate me so much! Has this been living inside me all my life?

I took a deep breath and groped my way back to the living room and the shelter of the couch, trying to stay open to what was coming through. I sat down and closed my eyes.

I was in a forest, standing at the side of an old, abandoned well. I leaned on the stones and looked over the edge, peering into the darkness of the well's floor.

I see me — a sort of twisted, squashed version of me — it's hard to see what its shape is — have to focus. Yes. Oh, Christ. Looks like a slimy little pink maggot. Dirty. Disgusting. The maggot feels the hate-contempt and knows it deserves it. Why? Because it's a maggot, and it's filthy and intolerable.

My hands were locked together in my lap. I opened my eyes to look around and saw the room in a blue half-light. I knew I had to go back to the well.

I have to connect with the maggot, with that — that terrible self-image — with the feelings it has. I have to do it. If I don't, it'll come back later. All right. Have to go inside it.

I took a moment to reconnect with my body, to shift to a more comfortable sitting position, legs folded, with cushions at my back. Then I closed my eyes, and was instantly back in the forest, peering into the well.

The maggot is a part of myself which believes it is the only real me, the essence of what I am. It knows it is unbearable, impossible to love. It identifies itself as a monster, a nauseating little piece of shit — Jesus Aitch! Is this what Jung means by the Shadow? Is this my Shadow?

I connected with the maggot and felt the wrenching awfulness, the screaming humiliation of being uncovered, revealed, examined.

The phone rang. It was Wendy, asking what time I was expecting to be over in Marin County. I realized numbly that this was my day to drive to Marin for an afternoon with Wendy and Brian (Ann was away at college), and heard my voice, husky and dulled, telling her why I would have to change my plans, "I woke up with the world's worst sinus attack, honey. I'm totally immobilized! Haven't had one this bad in years!"

"Oh, Mom, you poor thing! Don't worry about it. I'll tell Brian, and you just take care of yourself. We'll see you next week, when you're okay."

"Thanks, Sweetheart. I'm getting a prescription filled and I should be fine in a day or two. I'll give you a call when it's all cleared up. Sorry I didn't phone you right away, baby. I couldn't think of anything but my throbbing head!"

"You go rest," she said, "Take care of yourself. Talk to you later when you feel better."

When I'd hung up, I lit a cigarette. I thought about my children, about the almost painful pride I had in them.

I've been a good mother. For all my faults and mistakes, I've been a damned good mother.

There were hot tears on my cheeks.

How does that fit with the pathetic little maggot image? Or is this slimy, dirty thing lying in the dark of the well — is it left over from childhood? Has it lived down there, trying to stay hidden, since I was a child?

The answer was Yes.

And the hate? The killing hatred — has that been there from childhood, too? Is it me hating myself? Where did I learn it?

There was a memory of myself as a child, hearing a voice telling me that my clothes always had an unpleasant smell.

Someone said that to me, when I was little. The child knows intuitively what that means. Your smell is yourself; everyone smells of themselves. The message is, I am someone whose soul smells bad. Who I am smells bad to others. Who I am is a bad smell.

A governess? We'd had some good, affectionate ones, but there had been two who weren't. One was a tight-lipped German woman who resented us — we felt it, we knew it, Boy and I — but she hadn't stayed long. We weren't told until much later that she was an admirer of a very bad man called Hitler.

Was she with us long enough to cause this? A sour Nazi woman, taking care of the children of a Jew?

My mother and I had come to be at peace with each other, during the past decade; I loved her and knew that she loved me, but I had always believed that she hadn't really loved me when I was a child. She wasn't happy with my father in those days, and I heard the same feelings in her voice when she talked to me that I heard when she spoke to him: impatience, annoyance, and exasperation. I knew, from looking at old photographs, that she had held and cuddled me when I was a baby, but I could not remember her touching me with affection, or hugging me, at any time during the later years, while Boy and I were growing up in Italy.

My brother had been the favorite, and knew it. Incredibly, he took no advantage of his position; instead, he became my ally. I could remember one time when he actually took the blame for something I had done wrong. He knew as well as I did that she never got really angry with him.

My poor mother! Did I absorb her occasional feelings of impatience and disappointment and create a monster out of them? Did the German governess just add to what was already shaping itself in my unconscious as a self-image of something wrong-smelling and awful?

The hatred, I thought. Where did I get that from?

If you suspected you were a disgusting piece of filth in your soul, what would you want to do with yourself? Negate, of course. Kill, wipe out. The part of you that identified with the powerful grownups, and what you perceived as their negative feelings toward you, would become a hanging judge, an executioner.

My father had always shown love, warmth and caring. And my brother. Why, I wondered, hadn't I modeled my self-image on their feelings toward me?

Another part of you did, or you would have destroyed yourself long ago.

I opened my eyes and got up. In the kitchen, I made myself a cup of hot tea.

Enough. I've done enough for today. No more, right now. Time for a break.

A sharp stabbing pain hit me on the surface of my left shoulder-blade, and vanished. I held my breath. It meant: you must continue. No break. Not yet. The stab was also a symbolic illustration of what can happen in the body when the needs of the psyche are ignored.

Okay, I get it. But I want to have an intermission. I really am getting tired. Sufficient unto the day, for Pete's sake!

The needle stab came again, this time in my upper arm. And I understood, with a sense of astonishment, why those particular physical locations had been chosen. Neither the shoulder blade nor the upper arm were places where a quick pain-strike would cause me to suspect injury or illness.

All right, all right. Back to work.

I returned to the couch and took two long sips of tea, then folded my legs under me again and closed my eyes.

What am I supposed to do with my maggot-self? How do I heal this sick little piece of shit?

Love it, came the answer.

I gazed down at the cringing thing in the well and suddenly knew what had to come next. I could see, now, that the maggot was contained in an old, worn basket, and that the basket was connected to a rope which came up the length of the well and wound around some kind of crank with a handle which was within reach. I began winding the rope, very slowly, so that nothing would break or fall.

As the smudged pink shape came closer, I saw that it was not a maggot after all; it was a baby. It was emaciated, with skin more grey than pink, lying in its own mess. The baby was dying.

When I lifted it out of the basket, my first thought was that it needed cleaning up, and all I had handy was a bunch of leaves.

Not an It; a She. Of course. And there's no time to worry about dirt. She's failing. What do I do now?

As I stood by the well, the tiny shivering child in my hands, a door opened in my stomach.

Ah, I see. All right. Inside me she goes. Door is shutting. I am to be its mother, its nurturer, until it can make it on its own. Until it — she — is healthy and full of life again. When she's ready to emerge from my body, she'll be beautiful and strong and proud of herself. That's what has to happen.

I opened my eyes and drank the rest of the tea, then went inside again.

What about the other thing, the hanging judge, I thought? What was I supposed to do with that implacable, searing hatred?

Inform it that it's no longer welcome. It has no home here. It will have to transform into tolerance and compassion, because I will harbor it no more as Destroyer.

I sighed. This time, when I looked around the room, the blue shadows had gone, and I knew my work — at least, this particular piece of it — was done.

An idea came to me, of a possible way out of this whole business. I deserved to have a breather, I thought. If not an end, at least a breather!

I held my breath for a moment, waiting for another stab, but none came.

At the back of the house, I measured out a hundred and twenty milligrams of MDMA, the amount known among therapists as the customary therapeutic dose. This was the drug that always restored my balance, my sense of humor and objectivity. It was an old, beloved friend.

Maybe it'll get me back to normal — out of all this. If it doesn't work, it certainly won't do me harm. The worst it can do is intensify what's already going on. If that happens, I'll just grit my teeth for an hour and a half, until the effect begins to drop off. I'll be okay. It's worth a try, anyway.

An hour later, my cheeks were wet again, but this time with tears of relief. The world, inside and outside, was settling into a relaxed, friendly, even humorous normalcy. I could still feel the remnants of what I'd been dealing with, but they were subsiding now, fading from awareness. For the first time in three very long days, I could stand at the window and look out at the mountain, watch its top being folded into rain clouds, and feel my soul at peace.

Thank God — whoever and whatever You are, Thank you. Thank you.

When Shura came home, I told him what the MDMA had done. I didn't tell him about the maggot at the bottom of the well and the Judge-Executioner. That could wait for another time. He ate the simple dinner I had prepared for him, listening to me and reaching for my hand between forkfuls, while I apologized again for having been so self-centered during the past few days.

"I know you understand, and it's not the kind of thing I usually do — all that self-involvement, to the exclusion of everything else — but I wasn't able to stop it. I feel better if I can apologize and thank you for being so good and so patient."

"Sure," Shura said, "As I said before, it doesn't seem to me you had much choice, but I know you're a guilt-addict, so apologize all you want! Whatever makes you happy!"

He shifted his ankle out of range just in time.

We went to bed early.

A brief experiment established the fact that my body hadn't yet returned to its normal responsiveness, but we both knew that the apparent anesthesia might be attributable to the MDMA. It was widely recognized as a material which, while enabling one to feel empathy and love, was — for most people — *not* an aphrodisiac.

That night, I had my first experience of lucid dreaming. I was conscious, my ego intact, aware that I was asleep and dreaming, aware also that I was meant to learn something of importance. I knew I would remember what I was being shown, and what its meaning was, when I woke up.

In front of me was the upper portion of a great stained glass window. Its simple, petal-shaped design was divided into an upper section and a lower one. There were two colors of glass, blue and green. At first, the green was on the top and, across the dark line of leading, the lower petals glowed blue.

As I watched, the blue and green quietly seeped through the leading until, finally, they had changed places. I remained there, observing, while the exchange happened again, slowly, silently, each color diffusing through the dividing line until it had taken the other's place.

I knew what it meant. The blue and green represented the dual nature of the living universe, and of the human soul. Plus and minus, male and female, Yin and Yang. The colors had been chosen deliberately to avoid any possible inclination to ascribe positive or negative qualities to either. The ancient symbol of Yin and Yang is traditionally portrayed in black and red, colors which would have tempted me to say yes to one and no to the other. Blue and green were morally and spiritually neutral.

The lesson was clear: each is equal to the other and each, in time, transforms into the other. Accept the two aspects, do not reject or shut out either one; let both the blue and the green teach you. Prefer one, ally yourself with one if you must, but live at peace with both.

It was a simple statement of truth about all existence, conscious and unconscious, inside the soul and outside it, and the necessity of learning acceptance.

I said it was going to be difficult for me, but I would try to find a way to do it. I added that I would appreciate any help I could get, from anywhere.

I remained conscious, watching the beautiful green and blue and their continuous, gentle exchange, until it was time to wake up.

I opened my eyes, for the first time in four days, with a feeling of pleasure. I told Shura that I had just had my first lucid dream, and that it had been an extraordinary experience, which I would explain over breakfast.

I was really quite proud of myself.

WEDNESDAY

Except for an energy level somewhat higher than usual, I felt entirely normal. I got into my car and decided I wasn't really baseline, but close enough to it so that I could risk driving, at least as far as the shopping center a few blocks down the road.

There were no problems that day. I was delighted with my freedom, and with my body's sense of well-being.

At night, Shura and I made love. It was reassuring to both of us. I begged off trying for my own climax because I was too tired to bother, and insisted that his own had given me all the pleasure I needed, thank you. I didn't see any point in telling him that I was still feeling nothing in my genitals. I persuaded myself that I had detected a faint response, the beginning of recovery, and left it at that.

THURSDAY

I woke up with the sunlight streaming through curtains which were completely inadequate for room-darkening purposes, and my first thought was that I would have to replace them with honest-to-God drapes, and soon. I sat up and searched for the electric blanket on/off switch with my left big toe. As I pulled on my robe, I remembered that there had been something happy, and much laughter, going on in my dreams, although I couldn't recall any details.

I had reached the bedroom door before it dawned on me that the almost-normalcy of the day before had disappeared and that I was, in fact, right back at a plus-two.

Yesterday was just a day off. A 24-hour vacation. What was it I asked for — a breather? That's exactly what I got. Shit — SHIT!

I dressed and brushed my teeth and washed my face in hot water. Comb in hand, I turned to the mirror and saw in it a woman with thick, wavy hair whose face was a study in dull resentment.

I decided not to complain to Shura, at least for a while. While cutting a grapefruit in half for breakfast, I glanced over at him as he sat, sipping coffee and reading the paper, and realized I was open to his state of mind and feelings. I was picking up very clearly a level of intense thinking (he always read the paper quickly, with absolute concentration) and an underlying current of something else I couldn't immediately identify. It took me a minute to realize what it was: a quiet, steady flow of impatience.

I wondered why he was feeling impatient, then understood that this was his normal state in the morning; I had simply become aware of it, for the first time.

I took the grapefruit to the table and waited until we had finished eating before I told him, casually, "By the way, I seem to be a wee bit telepathic, this morning, and if I describe what I've been picking up, would you please tell me whether or not it's an accurate reading?"

He said, "Sure! Let's hear it."

When I'd told him what I'd been getting over the airwaves, he thought for a moment, then said, "Yes, that sounds pretty much like what's going on while I'm reading the paper: focused thinking and a chronic impatience underlying it. I'd have to say you're right on the button!"

I asked, "What are you chronically impatient about?"

There was another brief silence, then he replied, "Myself, mostly. All the things I want to get done and am not getting done." He shrugged, "You know, the usual."

I smiled, thinking perhaps it was just as well I wasn't that good a receiver, under normal conditions.

Shura's expression told me he was waiting for an explanation.

I said only, "Seems I'm back on again. Yesterday was a little intermission, I guess. I'm beginning to feel like an old hand at this, by now."

Today, so far, there were no tears flowing, to my relief. I also noted that my earlier feelings of betrayal had gone, and in their place was a dry kind of almost-humor.

Thursday was another teaching day for Shura, and he had the Owl Club in the evening. He played viola in the club orchestra, and I approved of the weekly ritual, if for no other reason than that it kept his skill with one musical instrument reasonably well-honed; his piano playing had gradually come to a stop over the years, to my regret, because — as he always said, when I asked him about it — there were so many other things to do. However, while he remained a member of the Owl Club, his viola playing would not be allowed to get rusty.

When it came time for him to leave, he asked, "Are you going to be okay, or would you be more comfortable if I skipped the club and came home right after work?"

I repeated that I was getting used to it, and it would be fine for him to go to the club. We agreed that he would phone after his class, before he left for San Francisco, just to make sure I didn't need him.

After he had gone, class papers in one hand and the viola case in the other, I poured myself a fresh cup of coffee and sat down on the couch with my cigarettes.

The phone rang. It was Ruth, and I said I was having a very bad sinus attack and would she forgive me for not talking at all today. I promised I would get back to her soon, maybe tomorrow, when the worst of the pain was gone. She was immediately sympathetic; I could feel her concern, her empathy over the wires and knew it was completely genuine, an intrinsic part of her nature. I hung up the phone with a feeling of intense love for her, and gratitude for her ability to accept me, even when — as sometimes happened — she found me not entirely understandable.

The streams of thought were back, but I could keep track of them more easily than before; they seemed to have slowed down a bit.

Somebody said that the function of the conscious mind — or one of its major functions — is to suppress the barrage, the noise, of everything that's continually going on in the unconscious; that what we call consciousness functions as a filter, in order to avoid exactly what I'm experiencing: an overwhelming flood of activity in mind and soul. It certainly makes it hard to go about your daily life, when the input to the conscious mind is this overwhelming.

I wondered if it would be possible for me to drive to Berkeley.

I phoned Adam and, when he said he was free after noon, I said, "I'm going to try to get to your place. If I don't feel safe on the road, I'll come back here and phone, to let you know."

He said, "Take care."

Driving slowly down Borodin Road, on my way to the highway, I kept watch for anything that might make driving my little Volkswagon car difficult or dangerous. The actions necessary to shift gears, engage the clutch or use the brakes were still automatic; there seemed to be no interference with that kind of function. But my mind continued to pour thoughts, and the change of scenery served to stimulate yet more observations, more images, all moving through me with extraordinary rapidity.

Halfway down the road, I looked at the hill across the highway where rows of beehives were sitting beneath our neighbors' fruit trees, and found myself thinking of the ancient mythical relationship of bees to the archetypal Earth Goddess. I saw the figures of men and women, throughout the millennia, making their pacts with the bees — thus with the Goddess — setting out homes for the swarms, moving the hives as necessary to keep the bees comfortable as the seasons changed, and harvesting, in return, the golden treasure, whose name defined sweetness.

Then I was picturing the open spaces between the wooden beams that supported our dining room floor, spaces where generations of 'possums (which I loved) were born and sometimes died. There were images of the small rooms under the house, called Basements One, Two, and Three, respectively, where our two independent cats held their territory against curious raccoons. I was seeing the hollow wooden supports extending outside from Basement One which swarms of honeybees, year after year, returned to claim as their home. They built their honeycombs inside the sturdy walls and, after a couple of futile attempts involving friends, protective clothing and smoke — together with a lot of nervous laughter — we'd given up trying to discourage them. I remembered the day when our bees had swarmed; they rose in a cloud over the roof, and I sang the single note they were humming and ran into the house to find the note on the piano. It was A. So bees swarm in the key of A, I told Shura that night. At least, I amended, our bees did.

As I came in sight of the mailbox at the end of our road, I was busy with the realization that Shura and I stayed in harmony with the Earth Goddess, by allowing the downstairs animals and insects to go about their business without interference. And with the necessary acceptance of occasional deaths among these creatures, we kept in touch with — and came to accept — the destruction and death aspect of the Great Mother, whether we realized it consciously or not.

And there's no mistaking, in our house, when a death has occurred downstairs, especially in summer! The awful smell stays around for weeks. Shura says, "Well, look at it this way; it's a reminder not to get all romantic and sentimental about Nature, right?

Borodin Road was short — a half-minute drive at the most — and I had reached the entrance. Examining my mental state carefully, I concluded that it would be possible to drive to Berkeley only if I stayed aware of everything I was doing and everything all the other cars were doing. I sent a telegram to whatever might pass for a guardian angel, "Please keep me safe," and edged out into the traffic.

On the highway, I focused on what I knew was an absolute necessity for survival: driving carefully and paying attention. The stream of ideas and concepts were continuing, but muted now, like music playing on the radio with the volume turned down.

I noted, without surprise, that I seemed to be able to pick up the general mind-state of any driver in my vicinity. I was getting brief exposures to a succession of emotions: impatience, resignation, irritability and, in one case, an almost delirious happiness.

It occurred to me that I might be broadcasting my own psychic state quite strongly, and that it would be a good idea to practice some kind of shutting-down, if I could figure out how to do it. After a while, I knew there wasn't going to be a problem; other drivers were occupied with their own thoughts, and no disturbed or curious glances were being directed at me. I began to feel less anxious, and finally concluded that, if I stopped extending my antennae to discover other people's feelings, and instead kept the focus on myself, my car and the road ahead, I would be minimizing my risks, both real and imagined.

I felt fear only once. Driving off the connecting ramp onto Shoreline highway, I saw in my rearview mirror a man at the wheel of a heavy, silver-colored American car in the lane to my left. He was driving fast, and his face wore an expression that was truly startling, a mixture of exaltation and malevolence. He was grinning to himself. As he passed me, I caught the impact of a shark-mind, strong and predatory. I glanced quickly at his profile, and away.

Keep castle walls strong and the drawbridge up. Don't make mental contact. That one's dangerous. Slow down a bit and let him get well ahead of you.

When he was finally out of sight, I became aware that I'd been holding my breath. I let it out slowly,

Oh, baby! What kind of human being is THAT?

It took me a while to shake off the clinging remnants of darkness which the silver car had left in its wake.

Twenty minutes later, I was knocking on the door of Adam's little house. He showed me in, and held me in the hug for which he was famous in our circle of friends, and undoubtedly well beyond it, a hug which always communicated energy and strength and a deep level of acceptance. I often told him that his was the most seductive hug in North America; it took all one's will-power to leave those encircling arms. He would chuckle and pat my cheek. Once, he said, "Well, I claim a good hug as one of my few remaining sensual privileges!"

I knew that, in truth, Adam used his hug the same way I used mine — not only to welcome, but to make contact with the core of the other person, to feel out the state of a friend's emotional and spiritual health. The information doesn't come through the arms; it is transmitted from one solar plexus to another, and a hug is the only socially acceptable way of coming that close to the body of someone who is not a lover.

I sat on his old brown leather couch and stayed silent while he did things to his tape-recorder on the low table in front of me. "All right," he said, finally, sitting back in his chair, "The tape's started. I'll give it to you when you leave. Now, tell me what's going on."

I started talking.

As I gave the highlights of the past few days' experiences, the tears welled up again. I apologized and explained that this went on all the time, and asked him not to pay attention. He said, "All right, I won't."

Once, he interrupted me to say, "You know, there's no use your trying to make sense out of what you're experiencing, because any conclusions you come to will probably be wrong. Stop wasting time with theories.

Just describe it."

"Okay," I answered, bewildered, because I didn't see how I could divorce myself from efforts to explain, comprehend, and give some kind of structure to all I'd been going through. Then I understood; he didn't want me using my intellect to control whatever turmoil I was feeling, thus risking repression of emotions which needed to be experienced and released.

Adam sat across the table from me, watching and listening.

I concluded, "A lot of the stuff that's been happening has been really extraordinary — like the lucid dream, for instance — and if they were coming at me during a psychedelic experiment, I'd be fascinated and grateful, you know? But there's too much of the sad, painful aspects of existence running through my mind, and worst of all, moments of feeling that it's all meaningless. Maybe I'm just tuning in to the sense of meaninglessness that most human beings suffer at least once in their lives, and the despair that goes along with it. That's the worst of all."

He was nodding his head.

"And it makes no sense for me to be feeling that way, because if there's anything I'm certain of, Adam, it's what the psychedelics taught me: that everything — every damned thing — in the universe is *intensely* meaningful!"

I told him about Shura, "He's always there for me, giving me love and being supportive and reassuring, but I worry about his tuning in too much, hurting for me —"

"You can't change that," said Adam, firmly, "It isn't possible to love someone without sharing some grief, now and then; you have to stop trying to protect everybody else. People who love you will try to help — and they can't — and they'll hurt for you, just as you would for them. And you wouldn't want it any other way, you know! But you can remind Shura of something that'll help him keep his boundaries, and that's the same thing you told me: that somewhere in your soul, you know everything's all right."

"Yes, I have told him that. I guess I can repeat it, now and then, to remind him."

"Good."

"Why does this kind of process have to be so hard, Adam? Everything hurts a little bit, all the time."

He replied, "I don't know why it hurts, but I know it does."

"What I need help with is — well, I don't know what to do with all this, where to go with it. What am I supposed to be *doing*?"

"I told you on the phone," he said, "That this is a process, and the only thing you can do is not get in its way — don't try to direct it, don't try to explain it — just let it be, and learn as much as you can."

I heard the sound of breath whistling out from between my teeth.

"Whatever is happening," he continued, "Has to happen, and right now all you can do is experience it. Understanding is for later. Maybe. It's possible you may never completely understand it, but believe me when I tell you that whatever is going on is necessary — necessary to who you're going to be — otherwise it wouldn't be happening. Don't censor it. You'll do your darnedest to get away from it —"

"Like the MDMA experiment. It worked, for a while."

"Yes. For a while. One day's vacation, you called it. By now, I think you realize that this process is going to do its thing, whatever that is, and you may as well go with it and stop wasting energy fighting it."

I was silent for a moment, thinking. Then I sighed and asked him, "Is there a name for this —? Aside from 'psychosis,' that is?"

"Sure — lots of names. Psychosis is not among them, by the way. Names don't matter."

"But it helps, Adam, it helps to give it a name — any name! Not the wrong one, of course," I added quickly, "But it would be something to hold onto; it would give me some of my power back, to be able to name it."

"Okay. If it helps you, fine. Just don't take names seriously, don't let them limit your experience. So let's give it a name. The right one. It's called a spiritual crisis."

I burst out laughing, "But *everything's* a spiritual crisis, Adam! *Life's* a spiritual crisis!"

He smiled, "Nonetheless, that's what it's called, and it's hell. It's one of the toughest things anyone can go through, but someday you'll be grateful for it. You'll be glad it happened. Believe me. I know."

I blew my nose. Then his words registered, and I looked up, "Did you ever go through anything like this, yourself?"

He sat back in his chair and took a moment before answering, "I lived through something very similar for two whole years."

"Oh, Lord, no! Two years of *this*? When?"

"Oh, about twenty years ago. I was around fifty-something, I think."

"What happened? How did you get out of it?"

"I guess you could say I just outlived it. But there was at least one time when, if I'd had a gun, I would probably have used it on myself. The pain was that bad. Everything hurt, all the time."

I nodded in recognition. I asked, "Did you have anyone to go to, to help you get through it?"

"No one. I tried to sign myself into mental hospital, at one point. I had to drive one of my patients up to a hospital in Sonoma and after he was taken care of, I looked around and figured I needed to be in there as much as he did, so I asked if I could sign myself in for a couple of days. They said no. Wouldn't take me."

I grimaced in sympathy. "I found myself thinking just that, today — how nice it would be to tuck myself into a safe quiet room in a hospital or a retreat, some place where I wouldn't have to deal with anybody else, or worry about affecting anyone else, until this was all over with."

Adam nodded, "As a matter of fact, that's what I finally did. I drove to a monastery in the hills, a Catholic monastery, and told them I was a Jew who was having some kind of trouble in his soul, and just needed isolation until what I was going through was resolved, and would they let me stay there for a while. They took me in and gave me a clean, quiet little room and plain good meals and left me alone. I suppose they were keeping an eye on me, but they didn't intrude; they just gave me what I asked for. It saved my life."

"How long did you stay there?"

"About a month, I think. I lost track of time. Which was part of what I needed to do, probably. I stayed until I knew that whatever had been crippling me was finally beginning to heal; the psychic noise was calming down, and I was able to function without feeling as if I was bleeding from every pore."

"How terrible that you didn't have an Adam Fisher to help you, as I do!"

"Funny thing is, I was in analysis at the time, with Phil Wilkerson —"

I smiled. Dr. Wilkerson was a friend of my ex-husband, a fellow Jungian analyst.

"— and I stopped by the side of the road on my way back from getting chucked out of the hospital in Sonoma, and phoned him. He didn't have Idea One about what to do." He chuckled, "Well, the truth is, no one can do much for you while it's happening. It's a solitary journey, like being born and dying."

I protested, "But you've helped me immensely — just the few words you said that day on the phone were exactly the right words, and it means more to me than I can tell you, to be able to talk to somebody who knows the territory."

"That's exactly it. Only someone who's been there and come through it can help, just a little. Poor Phil had never been there. I suppose that's why I've spent a lot of my life since then doing what I do — being here for people who are making this kind of journey, letting them know they're not completely alone. And that they aren't in the least crazy."

Before I left his little apartment, with its photographs of children and friends crowding the mantel of the small fireplace, and shelves of books and manuscripts lining the walls, Adam took the tape out of the recorder and handed it to me, saying, "Phone me any time and come over whenever you need to. I'll be here."

We hugged each other silently.

Driving home on the highway was not frightening and didn't feel dangerous. In the middle of the usual rush-hour slowdown on the western side of the Caldicott Tunnel, an interesting thought came to me that, if I tried, I could almost get a glimpse of what it would be like to be a whole, integrated human being. For a moment, as my car edged along at two miles an hour with the rest of the rats, I moved into a state of being at peace, strongly centered, and accepting of everything around and inside me. There was, for that brief time, a sense of having immense, singing energy, and something that felt like light, radiating from a place just above my navel.

My Observer reminded me not to stay distracted for too long, since I was still behind the wheel of a car.

Late that night, when Shura came home from the club, I told him that I'd actually managed to drive to Berkeley and see Adam, and that I would tell him all about it, but not until tomorrow.

In bed, I finally admitted that I was still made of wood where it counted, and he said that if this did turn out to be a permanent new state of consciousness, we would have to work at redirecting some of the energy back into this place and that, and he illustrated with fingertips, in case I had forgotten. I laughed and kissed him goodnight.

As we settled on our pillows, I let myself become open, as before, to the different layers of feeling inside Shura. On top, there was a quiet concern; underneath that, I felt a place in him that was picking up the ever-present hurting, the chafed-raw feeling, the urgent tumbling of ideas and emotions, and knew that he was trying not to be too receptive to all of it, for the sake of both of us. Beneath all the rest was a layer of serenity, a certainty that everything was all right, that whatever I was going through was meant to happen and would resolve itself. I fell asleep locked into that part of him, at one with it.

During the early morning hours, I found myself conscious again in my sleep, aware that I was dreaming and being shown what had to be learned. What I saw this time were two doors, side by side in a high wall. One was painted red, the other yellow. The lesson was the same as that of the first lucid dream. The doors were the Great Duality in yet another form. The red color on the left slowly changed places with the yellow on the right, and changed back, over and over again, until I became impatient, standing there watching, and finally said, "I already know this one, if you don't mind. It's beginning to get boring."

The doors continued their slow exchange of colors.

I sighed, and addressed whoever might be directing this repetitive scenario. I admitted that I didn't yet know how I was going to come to terms with what I was being shown, but did believe it was a truth I had to accept and assimilate. I promised I would not try to postpone or escape dealing with it, and I suggested — this time with respect, with humbleness — that it had gone on long enough, already, and could we maybe have another slide, please?

I was ignored. The teaching continued until I woke up.

FRIDAY

Shura got ready to leave for work, promising to come home as early as he could manage. I said I would be fine, that things were feeling a mite better, inside, less bumpy, less frantic, maybe starting to mellow out a bit. I added, "I hope you've noticed that my cheeks are dry, today?"

"Well, that's fine, but I love you either way — wet or dry!"

I grinned and we kissed goodbye.

I spent most of the day writing. The pain-haze had faded, and the intensity of the thought-streams seemed to gentle and stay subdued, as long as I kept typing. I was determined to put down every detail I could recall of the week's experiences, and I broke stride only for the time it took to fix myself a tomato sandwich for lunch.

I wrote:

"I have been shown, twice now in lucid dreams, that my resistance to the destructive, killer aspect of the Great Duality must change. I don't know yet if that means an acceptance of only the archetype, the primal energy or force, or whether I must learn to accept all its manifestations, including the evil and repugnant ones.

"Is it simply a matter of understanding and assenting to the basic rule of opposition as a necessity for life — water crashing against shore, the continual reshaping of the skin of the planet by earth-quakes, the body fighting for survival against bacteria and viruses — and recognizing that, for life to continue on all levels — animal, human and vegetable — adaptation is vital, and adaptation requires change, which comes about as a response to challenge?

"I can accept, in the deepest part of myself, the existence of aggres-sive power and destruction as a necessary force in the service of life, but some of its manifestations — especially in the human world — still seem to me evil, wrong, and unacceptable. That's where I run into serious trouble, because my human instincts say *no*, and I keep being in opposition, heart and soul, to the dark and terrible elaborations on the theme that the human race seems to be constantly creating.

"I can continue to love my cat, even when I see, over and over, the game it plays with the mouse — and since our cats are outside cats and excellent hunters, I've seen it often, because they bring their mice to the patio outside the dining room for the final stages — and Shura's explanation of how the teasing is part of a cat's honing of its hunting skills makes sense.

"The cat has been programmed to exercise her power this way, and it may well be that Nature has made the game satisfying on the emotional level, too — in other words, she enjoys the feeling of power and the mouse's fear — because if it were not satisfying emotionally, the cat would not pursue the activity, and the result might well be that her skills would lose their edge, thus potentially threatening her survival.

"But I have trouble with human cruelty, the enjoyment of another person's pain and fear. I have a hard time believing that it serves human life, as it does the animal's. Besides, it seems to me that human cruelty does not arise from natural survival programming, but is the result of having experienced powerlessness — having been victimized by the cruelty of others, as a child — and having had available as models only the kinds of grownups who take power away from others, people who have never developed their capacity for caring and empathy.

"The whole terrible business of victimized child growing into victimizing adult is, to me, a tragic, twisted, stunted perversion of what should have been. And what should have been, of course, was a free, validated flowering of the child into a fully integrated member of the human family. I see such a taking away of another's power to self-affirm as an evil thing, and I believe in my heart and soul that, while I am incarnated as a human being, I am supposed to make choices — the right ones — between that dark element in my own soul and the loving, yea-saying part of myself. The making of those choices, consciously and unconsciously, over and over again — in small daily matters as well as in important, big ones — is what gives me my individual shape, what makes me the person I am, and eventually — I hope — the person I want to become.

"Am I supposed to continue making choices, but without rejecting or trying to fight that dark side of the human soul?

"I will have to work this out, on all levels of my psyche. I am supposed to learn a truth, as my inner Self has made abundantly clear in the dreams, but first, I will have to discover exactly what it is — the archetype alone, or the archetype *and* all its manifestations — that I'm being urged to make peace with."

In the afternoon, I sat down at the dining room table with a cup of tea, and my attention fastened on the spine of a tall book. It was an old friend from childhood, a collection of fairy tales, most of its pages loosened from the cracked binding. I took it out of the bookcase and leafed through it until I found "Beauty and the Beast."

I read the ancient story through, as if for the first time.

The Beast is a beast until he is loved and accepted, green scales, fangs and all; then, and only then, is he transformed into the prince. My maggot, and all such buried dark images of the Self, are the Beast. They must be uncovered, brought up into the light of conscious awareness, and they must be given compassion and love, as Beauty came to love and care for her Beast. Then — not suddenly, as in the fairy story, but gradually — the reshaping will begin to take place, and the Beast will become — what? — a survivor, a guardian, a strong part of oneself that does not fear. An ally.

Do all the old fairy stories have the same essential meaning? Are they tales of the journey of the human soul to completion, the struggle to achieve wholeness? Did they all originate as spiritual teaching stories, like the Sufi tales of the East?

I spent the next few hours reading fairy stories, understanding them in the light of my own experience of the Shadow, and feeling a growing admiration for the people of courage, the wise teachers who had first created them. They had disguised spiritual truths as tales for children, probably because the all-powerful Church of that time reserved for itself the right to instruct in matters of the soul, and enforced its rules with torture and death.

That evening, the final lesson came.

After supper, when Shura went to his office to find out how his new IBM computer worked, I turned on the television. There was a documentary on Channel 9. It had been created by an extraordinary husband and wife team living in Kenya, Allan and Joan Root. Two years of work had gone into their portrayal of the mating and family-raising of a pair of hook-billed birds. The wisdom that revealed itself in the instinctual activities of the pair and, later, their babies, struck me with unusual force. There was a strong, almost palpable, impression of a vast intelligence that lay behind the pattern of behavior being followed by these beautiful birds.

I gradually became aware of something else: an immeasurable love permeating all that was taking place. Not the kind of love familiar to us as humans, but love as affirmation of both life and death, without sentimentality or regret. Love as YES, to everything that is.

My tears started again, this time in response to the presence of a mystery, and to the intense joy that I sensed running like a silent stream within it.

The documentary continued with the yearly migration of the big brown creatures called wildebeest. Thousands of animals were shown by the camera, pouring across the yellow African plains, struggling through the swift waters of a wide river — with the loss of hundreds of them to drowning or exhaustion — on the way to their other home.

I watched the screen, hypnotized, as the wildebeest raced over the dry grass, thundering towards the river, the immense herd photographed from a small plane flying above. Against the yellow background, the running animals took the form of a great brown tree with three branches, and suddenly I knew this was an entity, a single entity composed of thousands of wildebeest. I was seeing a group-soul. I felt, again, a form of consciousness that has no counterpart in the human world. It was immensely powerful, implacably driving all its component parts in the direction it had to go. It was not a comfortable thing to see. I could feel no love for it, only a profound respect and awe.

When the camera returned to the ground, following the wildebeest into and across the river, the Roots took time to record the dying of a large group of animals which had collapsed from exhaustion on the riverbank, half in the water, their heads hanging, legs tangled. Allan Root waded out to the pile of dead and dying wildebeest and struggled to disengage one young male, urging him to continue his journey across the river. The animal was having none of it; he was clearly sinking without fear into death, and didn't want to be pulled back out.

I was being shown the attraction, the seduction of that state of giving in, not fighting any more, dissolving into peace.

Somewhere within my own psyche there is that same death-pull, that potential for giving up, relinquishing the effort that life entails. I'm seeing the death-drive, there on a riverbank in Africa. All living things eventually come to it, that wanting to cease, to stop trying, to give over and float gently into a final sleep. It's there in potential, in each of us, and one has to push against it, not let it take over, if one wants to continue living. And, for humans as well as animals, that can sometimes be hard to do, if suffering has been going on too long, and exhaustion has drained the will.

The wildebeest entity I was watching did not concern itself with the death of some of its cells. The loss was an intrinsic part of the necessary movement of itself from one place to another, and served to winnow out weakness. The whole would survive.

After the documentary was over, I was sitting curled up on the couch, thinking about what I had seen, when Shura came into the room and sat down in the big armchair.

"How are you feeling, Buns?" he asked, and I said things were changing continually, and I'd just been through a rather extraordinary experience, watching something absolutely awesome on television.

He said, "I have an idea I'd like to run by you. Tell me what you think."

I smiled at him, "Okay, what is it?"

"You know how good old 2C-B always connects you with your body, how it integrates the mental world with the physical?"

I nodded.

"It's taking a chance," he said, "But it seems to me that if you opened up the possibility of reminding your body of how it normally feels, maybe it would help you bring everything back into some kind of balance, get the scattered parts of you together again. Work through the body, as well as the mind. And 2C-B is familiar to you, after all; it's an old friend. What do you think of giving it a try, just to see what happens? Of course," he added quickly, "It goes without saying that the slightest feeling of hesitation or uneasiness on your part must be respected. Go with your instincts."

I smiled. "It sounds like a perfectly fine idea. I can't see how it could hurt. At worst, it'll have no particular effect, and everything will just keep going on as before. If it does work, well, I must say I'm more than ready to get back to normal, and is *that* the understatement of the century!"

We each took twenty-five milligrams of 2C-B, and lay on our big double bed side by side. Shura found Leonard Bernstein's music on the radio, and we began to touch each other.

Two hours later, we were still making love, sweating in the warm air, and I was crying again, now with gratitude for the familiar sensations of arousal and response in my body. We loved and we talked, for four hours, getting up for occasional pee-breaks and some fresh oranges. I felt whole and full of joy, and told Shura that he was, indeed, a man of wisdom, and said thank you, lovely person, thank you.

SATURDAY

When I woke up, I was myself. I was at baseline and I knew I would stay that way. The process, as Adam had promised, had completed itself by the end of the week. I phoned to tell him it had gone just the way he had predicted, and thanked him again. He laughed and said that, of course, he would be happy to take credit for anything that turned out well, whether he deserved it or not. He said, "*Vaya con Dios*, my dear."

I walked outside and saw that Mount Diablo was part of what was, part of the natural world of which we humans are also a part, and that it was all right to love it, even though it couldn't love back in quite the same way.

Shura took me out to dinner at our favorite Mexican restaurant to celebrate. We toasted the Mysteries of The Human Mind, Life Its Own Self, and the Wonderful World of The Normal and Ordinary.

It was inexpressibly good to be back.

SUNDAY

Shura took the DESOXY at the same level, forty milligrams, that he had given me on the previous Sunday. It was, he reported, completely inactive.

SIX MONTHS LATER.

One fine Sunday morning, I persuaded Shura to give me the full forty milligrams of DESOXY again, telling him I was certain that — this time — I, too, would find no activity.

I was right. There were no effects at all.

CHAPTER 39. DANTE AND GINGER AND GOD

(Alice's voice)

Of all the research group, Dante wrote the best reports. They were long, detailed, and unreservedly honest. Ginger often sent us her own separate account, folded alongside Dante's in the same envelope, and they always sounded like her — enthusiastic, breezy and down to earth — but when she was involved with family matters or house-guests, she confined herself to scrawling brief post-scripts to Dante's typed descriptions. We told her we were grateful for whatever she wrote, long or short, considering how hard it was to pull anything out of the rest of the group; at least it had been until George got his own MacIntosh computer and discovered how much fun it was to write up experiments, especially now that he could illustrate them with little pictures and appropriate symbols!

Dante and Ginger had their private supply of psychedelic drugs, out there in the high desert country, halfway between the town of Gold Tree and their favorite hiking place, Mount Whitney. Over the years, they had gradually developed their own group of fellow travelers, many of whom lived in Los Angeles and would come to stay for an entire weekend, making it hard for Ginger to get to her painting as often as she would have liked.

Finally, she put her foot down and got Dante to agree to no more than one group experiment a month, max. He later admitted to us that it was a decision they should have made long ago, because he had begun feeling quite tired, and Ginger certainly needed fewer hours in the kitchen and more in her studio. After all, he said proudly, her incredible watercolor landscapes were beginning to attract attention in the outside world!

Many times, their experiments with visiting friends turned into therapy sessions, and both of them were becoming increasingly skillful at handling the occasional psychological breakthrough and the inevitable — and often challenging — surprises.

Shura and I took a trip to Gold Tree once or twice a year, usually with David and the Closes. The Sandeman's lovely big ranch house had sleeping space for five or six guests, if you counted the living room floor and the summer favorite, the outside deck. When the moon was full, and the coyotes at howl in the foothills, the deck became a place of dark-shadowed enchantment; the only difficulty we had, when we spent the night out there, was in closing our eyes and settling down to sleep.

One May, in the 1980's, Dante wrote an account of a complex and quite extraordinary experience with a drug he and Ginger had found very friendly and insightful in several earlier trials. Its name is 2C-T-7. I include the account in this book because it moved me deeply when I first read it and it moves me still. I would call this a plus-four.

It is a beautiful May afternoon. I am sitting in the park in downtown Gold Tree. I've come to my favorite place, a park bench under a huge cottonwood. Nearby a stream is flowing, and I delight in its continual murmuring as it makes its way over the rocks in the stream bed. There is something magical about the breeze rustling through the trees. It is still early enough in the year for the air to be comfortable, and the breeze is fresh and caressing. The expanse of green grass and the shimmering leaves vibrating in the sunlight make this a wonderful place to sit and contemplate.

And contemplate I must, about the intense activities of last weekend. I don't know if it's possible to adequately describe all of it, the arguments and discussions, the searching thinking, the sadness and depression over apparently irreconcilable points of view, and what remains afterwards.

How to describe what remains? This wonderful glow inside my being, the remembrance of having been touched by the most exquisite Feminine Presence imaginable, touched in such a way that goodness, beauty, tenderness and love are reflected all around me, in everything I see. And the wonder and majesty of the Mystery that created this universe, endowing it with the miracle of its Presence.

How long will this last, this delicious feeling of being alive, of having penetrated the veil which hides beauty and the wonders of celestial vistas? It doesn't matter, as there can be nothing but gratitude for even a glimpse of what exists for those who can become open to it.

Here is what happened. Charles [*a friend of the Sandemans who was a student of Asian history and had written several books on the subject*] and Glenn [*an engineer*] arrived on Friday. We hadn't seen each other for many months, and there was much to share, the recent activities of mutual friends, and our growing understanding of what we ourselves are about.

Our continual discussion was augmented by three bracing excursions into the mountains. We enjoyed the stretching of our bodies, and thrilled to the grandeur of the high granite faces of the Sierras. It is especially satisfying to enjoy the beauty of the high country in the company of good friends and stimulating conversation.

We all consider ourselves seekers of God, yet have quite different views of what God-realization is and how it is to be accomplished. Glenn sees God so far away that direct contact is impossible. Only by leaving this corrupt and pain-engrossed world, he says, can one hope to breathe the atmosphere of the Divine.

Charles holds the view that the evil and corruption of the world are far too great to be the result of our own doing. Instead, he views the dark forces as a result of demigods, or the demiurge, an arrogant and power-hungry creator who imposes the darkness on humanity. Thus we do not have to feel guilty for the troubles of the world, as they are not our fault. He says that recognizing who we truly are, and drawing upon divine assistance, we can become free of the works of the demiurge and the archons that assist him.

My own experience is that God is everywhere, the essence of everything that exists, "As near as hand and feet," waiting to join us as soon as invited. For He will not violate His established law of free will. Our role is to grow in consciousness, in awareness, and to so open ourselves that we may be joined with the Divine, that we may become partners, channels, for bringing the Divine into the world. Until ultimately there is complete union, as the great mystics have taught, with no separation between God and man.

I find Carl Jung to hold the most accurate view of the psyche. What stands in the way of integrating with our Inner Self, apart from our reluctance, for whatever reason, to discover who we really are, is the Shadow. As a simplified approximation, the Shadow is composed of all the material that we keep repressed from our conscious awareness. Most of us are not at all pleased with the prospect of encountering much of this material, and in fact usually strenuously avoid it. This readily accounts, in my mind, for most of the difficulties in the world.

In my personal experience, encountering and reconciling

Shadow material results in leaps in growth, brings understanding, freedom from unconscious forces, and also releases for our use the energy that was formerly tied up in the repressed material. And with this freeing comes a heightening of all of our functions.

My dear friend Glenn holds it entirely unnecessary to pursue the Shadow material and the psychological understanding that comes with that pursuit. He says that it is only necessary to hold fast to our sense of the Divine, and all will be well.

While he agrees with Charles as to the horrible state of the world and the hopelessness of saving it, he is not sure that Charles is entirely right about everything else.

We sat down that evening to a delightful dinner which Glenn had prepared for us. We were soon into a hot and heavy discussion, which lasted right up until bedtime.

I argued eloquently for my position, bringing up my personal experiences and evidence that supports it. Glenn was equally eloquent, and stood firmly in his position. God was far too far away to have any direct contact with humans, and we would only find the Divine by freeing ourselves of the bloody mess of this world.

Much to my surprise, Charles came forcefully to Glenn's side, thoroughly supporting him in all of his views, and castigating me for the errors of mine, and for my love and faith in the world.

I went to bed quite saddened. Our differences were so great and seemed so unreconcilable that I wondered about spending the next day together under the influence of a powerful chemical agent.

I had a horrible nightmare that night, far more intense and real than any dream I've had for years. I was at a hotel, and all of my belongings were in my room. Guests of the hotel were being entertained by what seemed like a group of friendly, outgoing men and women, putting on skits and performing for their benefit. I returned to my room, and found that all of my possessions had been taken by the performers. I wanted to raise an alarm, but they immediately surrounded me, and physically restrained me. I was told that if I didn't do exactly what they said, I would receive severe physical punishment. I felt I had no choice but to comply. I was outraged, and continually racked my brain for ways to get free and report them. But no matter what I came up with, they countered and defeated me. I was helpless. I would have to spend the rest of my life in their grasp, doing their will.

I awoke strongly affected, and in a deep, deep depression. I thought to myself, I can never have a psychedelic experience in this state. I shall have to call off my participation in the session. The only way I could participate is if I could re-establish my contact with God, and get back into a good frame of mind.

It was about 4:00 AM, at that point, and I lay back, holding my mind still, inviting God to enter. It took a long time, but after a while the familiar Presence began to make itself felt. With great relief, I maintained the contact, and was lifted higher and higher, out of my depression. It became clear to me that I could participate in the planned journey by doing exactly as I was now doing: keeping my attention completely focused on God, and ignoring the others and what was happening with them.

I arose about 6:30 AM, half an hour earlier than planned, feeling refreshed and clear. I avoided conversation with anybody else, and completed my preparations for the day.

We all convened at 9:00 AM and the feeling tone of the group was excellent. Ginger and I took twenty milligrams of the 2C-T-7, or T-7, as we call it; the others took only fifteen milligrams each, since it was their first time with this material.

About half an hour or so later, we are all feeling it. By one hour, it is getting intense. I sit on the deck, and it feels very good to close my eyes and go inside. I hold still, and it feels as though this contributes to the mounting of the energy. I refrain from thinking, and the energy grows. This feels like a marvelous procedure, with wonderful, undefined energy swelling inside. I look at the sky, at its utter blueness, and am filled with wonder.

Charles is off by himself. He has been feeling nauseous, and suddenly throws up. This relieves him somewhat.

Glenn is in a struggle. He reports that he is having to eat his words of the night before. He is torn between what he sees as Charles' way and mine. He had felt, before, that I have been seduced and caught by the beauty of the world, and that this has held me off the true path. Now, he himself is seeing incredible beauty in nature, and is not so sure any more that it is a distraction.

Ginger comes outside and announces that she has given birth to the universe. The T-7 is a fantastic material for her, and she is feeling marvelous. After giving birth, she says, she dismissed the universe and told it that it was on its own.

This is my very best entry into an experience. I am enjoying myself immensely, being filled with joy and great love. I put on a recording of Gounod's St. Cecelia Mass, and the music soon carries me away. I begin to reach new heights of experience, touched with beauty, love and understanding, and frequently cry deeply. It is ecstatic to release so completely to such exquisite feelings.

I feel myself being drawn back in time — far, far back — to the Beginning. I do not see clearly, but I am suddenly aware that the whole thing started in Love. A love so great, so tremendously charged that it was like a huge fiery furnace, brighter than any sun.

Suddenly I am completely pierced, down to the core of my being, by what feels like the penetration of the Finger of God. It seems to be a female source that reaches me and touches. I am totally undone by this deep touching, and sob uncontrollably for several minutes, crying out all my pain and fears, and feeling sheer ecstasy. As I feel gratitude for the beauty, I am pierced again and again, and continue to sob.

What has happened is a once-in-a-liftime event, a touch of God that is worth dying for. It seems as though it will stand forever and ever. I feel totally changed.

I ask to see this essence in my surroundings, and everything around me immediately lights up with unspeakable beauty and love. I enjoy this for a while, then go to find Ginger. We sit alone together on the deck, and I ask to see the Feminine Presence in her. I then begin to see incredible beauty in Ginger, she is astonishing, and I am overcome with love. It's impossible to describe the satisfaction and fulfillment.

Charles is feeling better, and we all take a walk over to my favorite rock formation. We sit and drink in the surroundings. Ginger shares the way she is perceiving the landscape, and everywhere I feel the wonderful Feminine Presence, and am filled with utter gratitude that it stays with me.

I see clearly that everyone has as much God as he or she wishes. One need only ask. I have never before experienced more profoundly the intimacy of God, how close He is, how close He wishes to be, waiting only for our invitation.

My previous experiences with Shura's compounds are richly confirmed. While there may be other truths, I see very clearly that this is my role, to deeply explore the intimate relation of man and God. Others can and will specialize in other things, but I am so filled, and find this path so ecstatic, that I see no need to consider other paths, at least for as long as I can now foresee. And the Presence I am experiencing continues to burn as a flame within me, for which I am utterly grateful. (Writing this, five days later, I still feel it strongly inside, and hope that it never goes away.)

For the first time, on my rock, I don't feel like talking about what I am feeling, but am content to address myself to fully living it. The afternoon and evening clouds are immensely beautiful, with intricate lacy patterns, and the outstanding lenticulars that often form on the leeward side of the mountains. The closeness and energy among us have grown to powerful proportions, and we are all intensely enjoying the experience.

Charles is feeling better physically than when he arrived. It will be very interesting to see how this session sits with him. All agree that there is great promise in this substance, 2C-T-7, and that more explorations should be carried out.

For myself, I feel more deeply in touch than ever before with another whole level, which seems to pour much more freely into my life. My previous experiences and the value systems I have developed from them have been abundantly confirmed. I feel much more confident with them, their logical consistency has grown, and I feel much less likely to be swayed by other thought systems.

A fierce sense of independence wells up, and I remember that the basis of Gnosticism is each individual's right, if not duty, to develop his own unique path to the realization of God. And to develop his own unique talents. I look at my activities and am pleased with what I am doing.

I feel I can abandon that self-judgment which automatically assumes that I am wrong and the other person is right, and which produces a sinking feeling that blanks out clear thinking and evaluation. I am overjoyed with this deepening of contact, and will keep it as alive as possible.

I have been in a remarkable place since that day. There was a relapse the second day after the T-7, and I felt tired again, but it is my view that, following a profound experience, there are many by-products released in the body which were correlates of the psychic armor and take a few days to dissipate. In fact, I have often found a welling up of deep Shadow material a few days after a good, positive experiment.

For the couple of days following that, I was most pleased with my state of being, with the clarity, ability to think clearly, and the high energy.

Today, five days after the session, I am in such a different state than I have been following previous experiences that I want to document some of the changes I am aware of:

1.   My psyche feels clearer and freer than ever before. I am much more able to concentrate on the task at hand, and enter it wholeheartedly. I am enjoying household chores as I never could before, because I usually had a sense of being driven by time, and the need to be doing something more important. I am very aware

of how the degree of intention mobilizes the energy to complete the task.

2.   My body feels clearer and more free, too. Much of the stiffness has gone, and the occasional arthritic sensations have diminished. Walking outdoors is extremely enjoyable.

3.   My impotence has disappeared. This had grown to quite a factor, and I later realized that loss of sexual ability was a source of some of my very deep anger. I wasn't sure whether the cause was old age, the result of my prostate surgery several months ago, or dissatisfaction with my partner. This T-7 experience has resolved the situation. I have dropped my concerns about aging, and the flow of love between Ginger and me has never been better.

4.   I feel in a more elevated state, the way I feel during the good part (usually the descent) of a psychedelic experiment. This is a real shift in consciousness. It feels almost as though I am carrying my head higher, above the concerns that used to distract me, and in contact with higher energies. Occasionally, an unexpected euphoria sweeps over me, a most wonderful feeling. Sometimes I remember pleasant things from childhood which I had completely forgotten. In time, I will work out the connection between a current event, or thought, and the sweep of good feeling, but right now the connection escapes me, and it doesn't matter.

5.   My energy is being sustained at a much higher continuous level than ever before. I love it.

6.   I am amazed at how quickly I can change my feeling state. Sometimes, especially when first arising in the morning, the old feelings of tiredness and sludginess come over me. I used to think these were heavy burdens that would take a great deal of time to work out of. Now I know that they are only feelings, and that by simply changing the focus of my attention, I can drop them and move into my new state. Hallelujah!

7.   When I take the time to be still, I quickly move into a transcendental space of great beauty and realization. I could amuse myself for hours at a time, if I simply wished to sit and look at my surroundings with an open heart. However, I don't intend to over-indulge. There are things I have to accomplish.

Thank you, Shura, for these materials, and for the privilege of working and growing with them.

Ginger had written a separate note. It read:

Had a great time with our delightful guests. This was one of the most pleasant, joyful, high experiences of my life. Visually tremendous — colors, shapes, smells heightened. At one time, around 3 or 4 hours into it, we all walked to the rocks and zoom-zowie, there it was! The most phenomenal, radiant scene I've ever looked at. The ground was alive with energy, the trees thrust out of the ground with life-force that was visible. The cattle were grazing over yonder on our neighbor's ranch, and it was a picture of true peace — totally pastoral — just exquisite. Charles couldn't believe it was real, and Glenn was amazed at it, too. Our eyes were able to see this new dimension of the universe because they were wide open. I was aware of the great love that permeates the planet — at least as we, or I, see it. From here, it looks wonderful!

I feel blessed, feel such a grace has been bestowed upon me. Gratitude continues.

Am still in a peaceful state after five days. All I have to do to remind myself is look out the window and see the glory.

Love to you both, and thank you — Ginger.

I asked Dante, after reading his letter and Ginger's note, what changes — if any — he had observed in Charles and Glenn, as a result of their 2C-T-7 experience. He replied that he is looking forward to another visit from each of them, on separate weekends, during the next couple of months, and will let me know what he finds out.

CHAPTER 40. MORTALITY

(Shura's voice)

I have already briefly described the Owl Club, a collection of many different sorts of gentlemen who meet once a week in downtown San Francisco at what is called the City Club. For over a hundred years, the Owlers have had an annual encampment in a large, privately owned forest, several hours' drive from the Bay Area. This takes place each summer and lasts for two full weeks.

When someone asks me just what one does in the encampment that justifies spending such a length of time, I can honestly tell them that a person may do as much or as little as he wishes. He may interact and socialize. He may retreat and meditate. Many members come only on the week-ends when there is a great deal of planned activity, ranging from concerts and stage plays to interminable cocktail parties and gourmet dining. Others spend the during-the-week time there, appreciating the fact that they can be free from exactly such planned activity.

For me, this time of luxurious self-indulgence has become an effective period of rejuvenation in the middle of a frantic year of getting and spending. I have never lacked for activities that make demands on my time, but almost all of them can be classified as "have-to's." However, with this annual retreat to the forest, I can select from a menu of Schubert quartets, Rex Stout mysteries, and miles of back-country hiking. Technically, rejuvenation means to make young again, but a reversal of the living process is not in the cards and I am content to accept a simple undoing process, where I might be able to repair some of the wear and tear that has accumulated during the rest of the year. Just holding even is all I ever ask for.

There is an interesting concept tucked away in that phrase, "just holding even." Each of us knows his biological age — he was born in such-and-such a year, thus he is exactly so many years old. But that is not our age according to our own self- image. Ask someone how old he is, and you get the biological age. Then ask him how old he sees himself to be, as defined by his life-style, his activities, his opinions. You will almost always get a candid answer. It may be five years younger; it could be twenty years younger.

Another thing that goes along with the "self-image age" is the observation that it does not change with time. With each birthday, the body is biologically one year older, but the self-image remains the same. If you see yourself as twenty-eight when you are thirty-five, you will probably still see yourself as twenty-eight when you are forty.

Each of us has suffered the parental put-down, usually in the form of spoken words, although it might be nothing more than a look of disapproval, "Why don't you act your age?" This has probably never changed anyone's behavior, but it is said in an effort to move the child's self-image into consistency with his biological real-world. "You're a grown-up boy now," or, "Can't you be a bit more mature?" Such rebukes always demand a change of behavior in the direction of greater age. I have rarely been urged to, "Act like a kid, again," or told, "Why don't you just let yourself be a little less responsible!"

I am, of course, fully aware, intellectually, that I am in my sixties. But I have always acted out of an internal, unspoken certainty that I was really in my late forties. Maybe 46, maybe 48. I look out at the world with eyes that cannot see themselves, and thus cannot see me. Both the eyes that are doing the seeing and the world that is being seen are strangely programmed to respond to me as they did at some earlier time. Catching a reflection of myself in a store window, I note the immediate denial that the person being reflected is really me. I'm not *really* that old, wrinkled, gray person with the protruding belly. Yes, of course I know it's myself I see in the mirror, but when you get to know me as well as I know me, I'm not *really* the way I appear.

The many miles of trails in the Owl Club forest preserve have always provided me with a unique opportunity. The privacy and safety of walking in the back woods offer perfect conditions for exploring a psychedelic drug. I have occasionally taken long walks with this or that friend who has chosen to set aside a few hours for talking and exchanging ideas, with the aid of a magic elixir. Sometimes, the purpose of the experience has been the resolving of a problem, an effort to change perspective and thus, it is hoped, to get unstuck; sometimes, it has been a simple matter of opening and deepening communication.

A couple of years ago, a good friend and occasional fellow traveler, Luke, expressed a desire to walk and talk. Well, I thought, this may be an excellent time for him to bring up some aspects of a medical problem that I knew had been bothering him. He had recently undergone elbow surgery which had been botched by haste and carelessness, and had refused to entertain the possibility of legal redress. Further, he had been dragging his feet in even getting help for the resulting disability. I suggested 15 milligrams of 2C-E, and, being familiar with the material, he agreed, saying he thought that would be an excellent level.

The next morning we skipped breakfast, except for coffee, and at ten o'clock, we took the chemical.

The walk along the valley floor was quiet and peaceful. There were sounds of music from various camps, as we passed; a Rachmaninoff etude from the right, then — a bit further along — a small Dixieland group on the left. There was the ever-present clicking of domino tiles, interspersed with an occasional burst of tipsy laughter (some leaders of the nation start relaxing quite early in the day). In a few minutes, we were at one of the trail heads; we left the merriment behind us and headed for the quiet of the outback.

I found the walking progressively more difficult as we ascended the first steep climb out of the valley. The effects of the 2C-E were unmistakably coming on for both of us, but — despite being well rested and in good physical shape — I found myself breathing heavily. In another hour, we were walking along one of the deserted fire-trails at over a thousand feet, and were probably a full two miles from the populated valley floor. The drug was in full bloom now, at the end of the second hour, and for me, things were getting increasingly grim and morbid. The hiking was becoming harder and harder, with each step having to be calculated before execution. Finally, I said to Luke, "I need to sit down and go inwards for a while."

My hiking companion was holding forth about the unbelievable colors of the trees, mosses, clouds and sky, grasses, everything. There was a continuous palate of greens and blues and browns that co-existed side by side, he observed, without ever quite blending into one another. He talked about what he called, "living toothpicks," trees around sixty to eighty feet tall that have been dedicated to the giving of young limbs for spreading on the ground around campfires. Some bear a greenish fuzz like caterpillar-fur, a few feet in diameter, made up of hundreds of fine branchlets which have grown straight out from the main trunk. Others stand as bare poles, having been recently harvested by a stripping of all this new growth from top to bottom. In a couple of years they will have grown a new crop of fur. A strange blend of mutilation and conservation.

The road was very dusty, but my dear friend Luke saw the dust as a magical sheen which had settled on the leaves and dead limbs lying on every side of us. He pointed out the red-neck hawks circling in the distance, in search of lunch. Everything was completely enchanting and he was enjoying himself immensely.

And where was I? I found myself seeing only the negative: my unexpected physical inadequacy for the climb; the dead limbs covered with brown dust, the mutilated trees and the ugly fate of whomever the hawks would choose for lunch.

I looked down to find myself sitting on an old, dead log which was undergoing a crumbling transition back to the earth. I realized I had no choice but to try to sort out the difficult thoughts that were running my show at the moment. I seemed to be reviewing my actions of the last few years through a very dark glass. Looking to the future, I could anticipate nothing there that seemed any happier. I clearly saw myself for what I really was, an old man who had a physical and emotional age that was no longer in the forties, but, rather, in the all too real and brutal sixties. How the hell did I get here? I hadn't asked for such sudden maturity! I was overwhelmed by this stark and un-looked-for truth, and I could not remember having been aware of any of the subtle steps and stages by which the maturing process must have actually occurred.

Hold on, I thought, just whom am I kidding? This is not maturity. This is simply Old. It's been developing at a steady pace all along, but I chose to look the other way. It isn't maturity, and it hasn't been sneaking up on me. It's the dying process, and I have been moving steadily towards that final moment at a crashing pace. I've simply been fooling myself by all of these game-playing deceptions. I am an old man, and my death is a certainty. Who knows when? Maybe right now. Is this the time and place to close it all off? The Ponce de Leon search for youth was absurd when it took place in the Everglades of Florida, and it is equally absurd when trying to act the young fool with a consciousness-changing psychedelic drug. Dammit it — grow up and act your age! You are a dying old man who cannot face the fact of your own mortality.

I was feeling too exposed and too ponderous, sitting way up there on my log. My instincts said to me, get closer to the earth. I slid forward and down, off my dead log and onto the ground, where the log became my back-rest. I declined Luke's offer to talk, so he wandered off to see more of the marvelous things that surrounded him. I just wanted to dwell in my own thoughts.

I wondered, is the German word that would describe my state of mind, "Weltschmerz?" I was indeed sick of the world, in spades. I reviewed my continuing burden of trying to stay active, to maintain a high volume of productivity in writing, and to keep trying to make this and that in the laboratory for everybody under the sun. It was all such an obvious waste of effort. Everything would slowly close down about me, with nothing completed and all communication forever closed off, and it really would make no difference at all. On the previous evening, Luke and I had talked about death and transition, and the state I found myself in right now could well be reflecting that conversation. It was not a good place to be.

I once heard a terrible joke about a man who had a trained mule. It would sit when told to, it would lie down, beg or fetch. It would follow any verbal order it was given. But whenever the owner was asked to put on a demonstration, and before he gave the mule his first command, he would pick up a piece of two-by-four and hit the animal over the head with it. His explanation was simple, "First, you have to get his attention." Old mule Shura had been hit over the head with a chemical two-by-four. Something, somewhere, was trying to get my attention.

My buddy bounced up to me again, and this time succeeded in breaking through my funk. He told me he had observed that, "If you look at distant scenery, and there's something located at arm's length that you can focus on, and you do focus on it, then the thing close to you can be seen in full detail, but the backdrop suddenly looks like it's made of cardboard!" He was insistent.

I struggled down a few feet to the right, from where my back-rest log disappeared into the weeds, and found a spider suspended on its web. I sat down and focused on it, somewhat resentfully, (how could Luke have been so selfish as to have wrested me from my rich self-pity?), and indeed, Wow! The distant trees and landscapes were flat and unnatural. They looked like a badly painted back-drop. I moved my gaze to the left. No spider, no illusion. Back to the right; the spider was clear and, again, the distance became artificial.

I was reminded of another experience with 2C-E many years ago in Tennessee, when I had looked through a closed window to see what appeared to be a painting of a medieval lady watering her plants in the back yard. This vivid memory had been with me for a long time and it was just now that I realized it might have been the panes of window glass that had become the focus of my eyes, serving as the counterpart of the spider web. A nifty parallel, I thought, although by no means an explanation.

The memory of that garden illusion caught me up again in turmoil, because there was another resemblance between this 2C-E experience and that dramatic one I had weathered in Tennessee over a decade ago. There had been a death thing there, as well, another playing of the role of the tired old man. But there, I had seen myself externally as wizened, with wasted, wrinkled arms and sunken face. Here, this time, it was a viewing of my inner self. I thought, I am seeing myself as an old person, a tired person, someone saddened by the knowledge that he cannot possibly complete everything he wants to complete. Hell, most of what I want to do, I haven't even started yet! So here I sit, wallowing in self-pity, bemoaning the fact that my most important work is not done and never will be done.

The query came from somewhere inside me, quite gracefully. Are you interested in walking, by any chance? I chuckled, realizing that the spiral down into the world of despair was an endless one, and I must try to step out of it. Tired, tired, tired. The best way to combat tiredness is to walk it off. I turned my body around in order to push myself up from my strange position on the ground, feeling extremely awkward, and was finally able to get on my feet. I dusted debris off my behind, and moved on again with Luke. The pace started slowly at first, but began picking up as I got out of myself and into the visual pleasures of my surroundings. We were soon at the far-point of the trail where it branched, and had to choose whether to continue on around the outer trail (some three hours of hiking still ahead of us) or whether to cut back onto the middle road. Our canteen was more than half empty, and the 2C-E had given us dry mouths. We agreed to take the shorter route.

We tried and failed to analyze the spiderweb painted-backdrop illusion, and I was just starting to share the dark, dark places where I had so recently been, when, Whammo! There was the two-by-four again. I had a sudden, very strange sensation in my groin. It was on my right side, and I knew that something had happened to me; something was very wrong. It was not really painful, but it felt as if the right testicle had gone back up inside my body. I had an overpowering urge to push it out again.

I stepped to the side of the road (we were still far from home base, both drug-wise and trail-wise) and lowered my pants. I stuck my hand inside my shorts, and discovered that when I put the edge of my right index finger against the cleft between my genitals and right thigh, and firmly pushed inward, I felt okay. When I took my finger away, it felt all wrong again. Oh for Heaven's sakes, please, I thought, not a hernia!

I had had some such thing when I was 10 years old, but couldn't remember how it came to be. There was a vague impression of sliding down a banister in the Spruce Street house, but I have been told that you have to lift something too heavy in order to separate the tissue. Certainly, just getting up from a ground-level sitting position to a vertical hiking stance could not have been such a strain. I could recall with total clarity my wheeling myself to surgery during the childhood event, and the friendly smell of ether. And, since they removed my appendix for good luck at the same time, that hernia had also, probably, been on my right side.

Must I undergo some stupid surgery, now, at my present age, just because something-or-other is trying to get my attention? And just exactly what is my present age, anyway?

With great reluctance I proposed to Luke that we abort our hike, and seek out some competent and unstoned medical opinion as to the status of my body. We walked very slowly back to the valley floor; I with my hand down inside my pants, underneath a loosened belt, and my friend with a benign look of amusement on his face.

Once back, we boarded one of the mini-buses that patrol the Grove roads all day long, and I requested that the driver take me directly to the Owl camp hospital. In the lobby, I found four men sitting in what struck me as ridiculously puffy easy chairs. I asked — a rather silly question, in retrospect — if anyone there was a physician. "Yes," said a voice, "We all are."

"Well," I said, somewhat sheepishly, "I think I may have hurt myself." One of the young men, a cardiologist as it later turned out, glanced at the others (who nodded at him), and got to his feet. He led the way to a private examination room, donned obstetric gloves, and asked me to drop my pants. Push your finger in there and cough, he ordered, then said something about feeling a bit too much tissue here, and suggested that I go to the nearby town and get a truss (inguinal, medium size, right hand side), to give me support until I could get to my own physician. At least my intestines were not hanging out of my body, he added pleasantly.

I thanked him, ran the gauntlet of quietly smiling professionals in the front room, and rejoined my friend, Luke, who had been contentedly waiting for me on a shaded redwood bench.

For me, the entire experience had been completely bizarre and excruciatingly embarrassing. Upon entering the hospital, I had become somewhat paranoid, seeing the incident from the point of view of a very sober emergency physician, hired to be in attendance at an encampment of 2000 titans of industry — or, to be more exact, 1,900 titans and a scatter of musicians, actors and artists — having been told to expect at least three heart attacks and two accidental ice-pick punctures.

And — so went my uncomfortable fantasy — suddenly there appears a disheveled and uncoordinated grey-hair of sixty-something, with his finger in his crotch, mumbling vaguely about having hurt himself, hiking on the trails. Is it possible, thinks the physician, that at one of the camps a bet had been made that they could get a young emergency MD to jiggle the balls of a titan? How would they do it? Have him stagger into the hospital with some cock and bull story about a maybe hernia, that's how. After all, if such a bet had been made by bored, drunken men with nothing else to do — so reasons the physician residing in my suspicious mind — he, as a doctor, has no choice but to put on his gloves and inspect the presented balls and inguinal canal.

No matter that the examination had been conducted with complete professionalism and no hint of disbelief in either face or voice. I was sure I was suspected, perhaps by all four of the doctors, of playing some part in an elaborate, puerile joke. I felt I had been placed in a situation that was neither of my own making nor under my control, and I was miserable.

Luke and I walked away from the hospital, moving slowly. We would find a cold glass of soda water somewhere, and try to avoid running into anyone we knew. He was still bouncing happily about with the 2C-E, but I had ended up with a pretty heavy load of stuff for consideration.

I decided, as the effects of the material slowly declined, that I had been whacked yet a third time by the nasty piece of lumber, with the hospital experience and my disturbingly paranoid fantasies of how I was being perceived by the physicians.

Dammit, I said to myself. Enough. I get the message. I'm no longer in my forties, and when I go hiking on the Owl trails, I must pay attention to my body and remember, like it or not, that it's been around for sixty-something years and can no longer be relied upon to have the resiliency of forty-something.

I survived, but the darkness of the imagery was not easily dispelled. It was all of four days before I was able to get completely out of the dying mode, and realize that the instinct for life was still predominant. But I could not effectively reset my self-image clock back to my forties. I was now a much older person than I had been. I had aged twenty years in three hours.

I spent those four days looking about me and observing closely my friends in the Owl Club world — musicians, business men, teachers, retired this and that — who were also in the sixty to seventy year old age slot. How were they conducting themselves? My God. Two of them had walking problems, in one case due to hip trouble and, in the other, a bad knee. One friend had lost his voice box to cancer. Most of them had hypertension, and were being medicated for it. Prostate surgery everywhere. Impotence, incipient senility, and a pandemic narrowing of political tolerance, along with a decreasing curiosity about new things. Several had recently gone to the extreme of dying. But, there was a spark of hope. There were a few, sadly only a very few, but a few nonetheless, who were up there in the eighty to ninety year old slot, but acted and carried themselves as if they were still in their sixties. Might there also be hope for me?

A dozen questions had to be addressed. Was this new, old-man self-image the truth of what I really was? How might my relationships with others change, now that my warts and blemishes had suddenly become apparent to me? Since I had suddenly leapt into a new age bracket, must I conduct myself in some new way? Could I manage to recover that fortyish self-image, or was I destined to be sixtyish from here on? For that matter, did I even have the choice of surviving a little longer from here on? Was the deterioration that comes with aging never to be invisible to me again? Did I want it to be? Might I see myself, when I am eighty, as a person of sixty-five? Or is that remarkable age displacement unique for this particular time in life?

I have been unable to recover the innocence of my earlier age-gap. Some of it, maybe, but by no means all. I find myself now, from time to time, weighing the virtues of being an antique, in that, for instance, there are some audiences in my world who will not give serious attention to a person who is only in his forties.

I feel that my mind, while it is now housed in a container which is beginning to look like an elder statesman of some sort, still — most of the time — has the bounce and wit of age forty; in fact, I sometimes suspect, with pleasure, that it never left the twenties.

Be that as it may, no matter what my apparent age or appearance, I remain capable of acting on my beliefs, and my beliefs are strong.

I have no intention of softening my insistence on the preservation, at any cost, of the human freedoms and liberties that we still have; I cannot anticipate yielding on the demand that we must recover, again at any cost, the freedoms and liberties which have already disappeared from our society.

I intend to persist in being curious about the unknown. It is in the urge to learn, and in the drive to understand, that youth is to be found.

I will continue to honor the values of all the religions of man, as I believe they were originally conceived and taught, not as they are presently practiced. I intend to remain open to new forms of expression taken by the human spirit, wherever I shall find them.

And finally, I must admit that I now look forward with total fascination to discovering the shape — and age — of my self-image, when the calendar tells me I have turned eighty-five!

CHAPTER 41. 2C-T-4

(Shura's voice)

A few years ago, I was again graced with a Plus-Four. The following are my notes, written during the experiment and completed a few days later.

_____

9:00 AM is (0:00) of the experiment. April 3, 1985, on the Farm. 12 mg 2C-T-4 in water. Trivial taste.

(:50)   Aware.

(1:20)   To a plus one.

(1:30)   To a one-and-a-half plus.

(2:00)   A full plus two and climbing. Alice ready to leave about here, and I fibbed and told her I was at a plus-one only. If I had said plus-two and climbing, she would have been interested/concerned, and would be trying to reach me by telephone and — maybe not getting me — might have worried. Forgive me the small white lie, my love.

(2:30)   Greater than plus two.

(3:00)   To a plus three. This is not an out-in-public drug. One would be compelled to be guarded, to tone things down, to continuously monitor one's interactions. Very erotic. Obsession with things physical, sexual. Once past this, one can allow the richer aspects to be manifest.

(3:15)   There is some visual brightening — not quite that of 2C-T-2 but the potential is there. This seems excellent for thinking about relationships.

(3:40)   This is a very profound plus three. And I will try to compose notes for the first time on the computer, rather than trust to handwriting.

This is so long, so profound and implacable, that an unhappy person would have nowhere to go to get away from it. It would follow him everywhere he went, into the bathroom, into a book, into his memories. For the last hour I stayed out of the house, in part because I felt blackmailed by the telephone. I was afraid it would ring, and I simply did not want to interact with anyone in that world, not for the moment. So I stayed in the lab and started a reflux on the steam-bath. Then I went up behind the lab and sat a while with my thoughts. These became bittersweet memories, strongly encouraged by the magic place I was in; it was warm and I was almost completely hidden. But not totally, so there remained a connection with the outside world. I thought that to avoid the house was giving in to blackmail. Then — so simple — it came to me that I would not answer the phone. Rather, I decided, I will count the times it rings and try to deduce, with some humor, who it is. Or, rather, who it might have been, that was so insistent on demanding a response. So, freed from blackmail, I am here and have started my report on a remarkable substance.

A completely remarkable substance. It is as if I had just rediscovered the Alephs — a plus 1 at one hour, then plus 2 at two hours, and not a full plus 3 until the third hour.

What a marvelous way to express oneself, writing on the computer! Not looking at what is being written, and certainly not correcting trivial mistakes at the moment; simply letting things run on without either barriers or editing.

I have been spending some time trying to deduce where in the brain this is operating. What is it that has disconnected me from the known behavior patterns that would allow me to go out into the world and drive and talk to someone and protect myself from somebody else? At the moment, none of these interactions would seem possible. Perhaps I could screw something-or-other together and interact with an attorney about a court case (assuming he was reasonably un-perceptive) and maybe carry it off. I am glad that I need not do so.

But what has opened up with 2C-T-4? I feel in a simultaneous connection with everything outside of myself, in one moment of time that keeps going on and on, and this is a form of universal knowing.

The music playing in the next room is sadly artificial. It has been played and played a million times to the same tired ears, and has assumed the criminal status of background. Something to fill the cavities for the moment, to perhaps stop the incessant internal dialog. I wish to stop the music. Much better. I want the dialog, the monolog, to go on, and to tell me things about myself that only I can know, and that only I should hear.

It is said that with psychedelics one can gain communication from the unconscious. That's only partly right. We have continuous access to these deep, primitive things within us, the survival and instinctual things, with psychedelics or without. It is only a self-inflicted pattern of thought and behavior that keeps us from living all parts of ourselves continuously.

We are taught, really driven, to believe that whatever is in our depths must be kept bound and in its place, in our interactions with ourselves and others, else we are naught but animals.

But we are animals in our exterior, and in every way in our interior. We are continuously in communication with our unconscious; this is the heritage of every cell in the body. So 2C-T-4 does not do anything unexpected or new; it simply reminds us of this continuing interaction.

I want this monolog to continue, as I feel that it can bring up to my conscious mind treasures that are buried within me — knowledge that cannot be articulated — genetic histories that are only read, otherwise, as the silly DNA that means proteins to scientists, separated by miles of what they so charmingly call "nonsense." That our heritage is 5% protein and enzyme, and 95% nonsense, is an incredibly foolish idea. We have evolved for millennia to become what we are today, and we cannot decipher 95% of our heritage just because we have only this scientific certainty that DNA stands for protein and nothing else.

I may be playing with a plus four. There is a simultaneous union with everything around me, and thus with everything within me too. A complete identification with my environment. And a sense of being at total peace with it, as well. If this is me, then I thank the dear Lord for a wonderful awareness, at least for a short time, of the fact that we can be so rich and beautiful. The mind flows and with it the soul, and no matter what words I put down in an effort to catch the wondrous monolog, I can do it little justice.

But then, as once before (and I was fooled then), I wonder what if this were not the moment, and me, and an extraordinary experience of an extraordinary day, but a property of 2C-T-4?

I have been fooled, again and again, into thinking that the magic of the unified reality was in the drug, and not in the person. Of course it is in the person — and only in the person — but if a drug could be found that would consistently catalyze this, then it would be one of the most powerful and awesome drugs that could be conceived of by man. If it were this material, 2C-T-4, it would have to be held apart with a reverence that would be impossible to describe or explain in a patent application!!

I am going to tour the farm for a minute to check on things.

All is serene. Not so serene — the telephone just rang, with a shrillness completely unexpected. I allowed it to ring itself out, eleven rings, each dutifully counted. Now, silence again.

(4:30)   It is now 1:30 p.m.and this is an amazing experience. I'm excited at the thought of having Alice share this with me, and we will allow ourselves a full day, with the freedom not to answer the phone.

The full plus-four is still upon me, a tinge of omnipotence blended with a modest amount of omniscience. I forget what the third omni is, but it's present also.

How can one describe a bliss state, except to say that it is a state that we are all in, whether in pleasure or in pain, awake or asleep, alone or in crowds, and that we are simply too hurried to be aware of it. Or, as said earlier, we've been taught to believe that it is not part of a productive reality, or a "proper" reality, and must not be allowed to intervene in our day-to-day commerce. More than having been taught to disavow, we have come to actually believe as fact, as gospel, that this bliss-interaction-union state is at best drug-induced, at worst a result of chemical imbalance, and should be left to hippies and other ne'er-do-wells who are naught but cancers on the body social.

But this state is with us at all times. We have sadly learned to tune it out. If this drug can bring this state of unity again in me — and through some miracle in another person — and if this is indeed a property contained in its makeup, then this is truly the most powerful and saintly piece of scripture that could ever be written.

A tour of the body this time. There seems to be no threat from any corner; a good, benign at-peaceness. Pulse 88 and blood pressure 145/95 with good-health sounds. Weight a perennial 200 lbs. and blood alcohol averaging a perennial 0.05 gram percent. I can't afford either one any more.

On the piano I played a Bach two-part quite well without looking once at my hands! Couldn't do that straight! And I have just helped a wasp escape from the kitchen.

A brisk walk to the road entrance, for the mail. Mind still going a mile a minute, thoughts such as: I hope I don't run into anyone on the walk. Not paranoid so much as not wanting to have my internal flow interrupted. A very significant cattapiuller — how do you spell that monster? — was moving across the road at the last turn. When I came back, I saw that there were dozens of caterpillars [*I looked it up*] all over the road, and I felt a gladness that we had not gone after the tent moth nests in the moribund almond tree. In the balance and flow of things, the tree supported the moth-nests (the tent-caterpillar), who in turn mature to moths, who then do something else somewhere else, which in turn helps another almond tree to replace this one. Don't muck with nature. It had eons to establish a working balance before man and his intelligence appeared on the scene to improve things.

Hearing is more acute. I heard children's voices, and checked the perimeter of the Farm again. Turned out they were way down below the hill.

(5:30)   I feel that there has been an astounding amount of integration, and — as with my previous plus-four — a sadness to see things coming together in a way that is socially acceptable again, but there is a sense of indescribable personal wealth that has resulted from the integration of all that internal talk. It is time to start re-shielding myself for eventual public interactions. Tonight is the get-together in Marin County at Walter's house, with Alice's children and our friends, which takes place every two weeks.

In the mail there was a strange and beautiful letter from a young alive chemist in Germany who has found that an antitussive, a cough suppressant called "Isoaminile," at 300 mg has hallucinogenic properties. And since this can be warped into an indole ring that looks like DMT, he wants to make the alpha-methyl analogue, and the psilocybin analog, and thus discover a "new" class of psychotomimetic substances. Of course. This is also a caterpillar. Leave it alone. I will encourage him, but never direct his way of looking. Somewhere in the balance of things his role, although not yet defined, will be played out.

Coffee tastes terrible to drink, but what else can you do with it?

Back to the letter from Germany. What a strange sort of omen, that out of the occupied country of our victory in World War II, appear what seem to be the seeds of a renaissance in awareness, and a naive openness in studying altered states, something quite disallowed in our own FDA-dictated society. Professor S.'s work is continuing, and now this young one.

It is now 3:00 p.m., exactly six hours into the experiment. I am obliged to leave the house in three hours, so I will institute an unwanted but necessary program for reintegration. No, wrong word — I am integrated as never before. My program is for re-installing the social interfacing skills needed for dealing with others.

(7:00)   Back to an honest plus three.

(8:00)   Still pretty much plus three.

(9:00)   Ah, repair occurring for the re-exposure to the outside world; now simply a plus two.

(9:20)   Have showered, changed clothes and am heading, with great care and love for myself as well as Alice, to pick up David at the hospital for the Marin dinner.

(10:00)   At the hospital, still quite aware, though hard to tell the plusness. There was no difficulty driving, but maybe still a 1-1/2 plus.

(15:00)   Still residual awareness. Have consumed no alcohol whatsoever, and am quite alert and substantially baseline.

(17:00)   Went to sleep without much difficulty.

Next evening, at (36:00) tried a challenge with 30 milligrams of 2C-B, and had only a modest response. Definitely some loss of sensitivity.

An extraordinary and never to be forgotten day.

Final note. Alice took 2C-T-4 with me, at the same dosage level, a few weeks later. We both had a very satisfying plus-3 experience. The plus-4 was not repeated.

CHAPTER 42. LECTURE AT THE UNIVERSITY

(Shura's voice)

For a goodly number of years I have been teaching a class in the Fall, at the University of California, in Berkeley. It is, officially, a toxicology course with both lecture and laboratory, dealing with the analysis of drugs in body fluids with an eye to the preparation of evidence for the courts of law. But some years ago I made a point of writing out all of my lectures, so that they could be read by my students before class, and the actual lecture time could be used in offering additional explanations, or answering questions.

If there were no questions, then the two-hour slot became a rich opportunity to explore any topic I wished to. The consistent underlying theme of these lectures was the excitement of science and of learning. I had been shocked, year after year, by the total distaste that my students had for organic chemistry, which was one of the prerequisites for my class. It apparently had been taught along the lines of, "For next Monday read from pages 134 to 198 in the text and we will have a quiz on the material." They memorized reactions and mechanisms, struggled through the exams, promptly forgot everything that had been memorized, and never took the second year course. They hated it.

So I would try to present chemistry as an art form, rather than as a science. Why are sugars usually white? Why don't food additives ever have smells? Make a guess as to how some interesting drug might change in the body? How would you explain chromatography to a jury with no scientific background?

And sometimes I would be on a particular kick, and the whole time would be devoted to a single subject that I felt deserved emphasis. Recently just such an occasion arose, and I presented the following lecture to my fifteen or so undergraduate students.

I know that I have been scheduled to use this time to build up a picture of the how's and where's of drug action in the brain. It has been listed as a lecture on the pharmacokinetics and pharmacodynamics of centrally active compounds. But I am going to exercise one of the precious freedoms allowed me as a professor — I am going to change the topic, and make it a lecture on politics and government.

In fact, I am going to talk to you about our freedoms in general, and about the loss of certain of these freedoms under the shameful excuse of waging a war on drugs.

Our form of government is known as a constitutional republic. The federal structure was established by the signing of the Constitution, some ten years following our Declaration of Independence from England, and many of our present inalienable freedoms were explicitly guaranteed by the passage of the first ten amendments to our Constitution, the Bill of Rights, some four years later. These freedoms — of speech, of the press, and of the practice of religion, our protection against unreasonable searches and seizures, the rights of anyone accused of a crime to know the nature of the accusation and to be judged by an impartial jury — these are the bedrock of our nation and are integral to our national way of life.

This Bill of Rights is continuously being challenged, largely through the enactment of laws by Congress which have been written without sufficient thought as to whether they might endanger or restrict basic freedoms. The function of the Supreme Court has always been to serve as a safeguard against the enforcement of laws which do not respect the Constitution, but it has become increasingly clear that we can no longer rely on this protection.

There are other freedoms that we retained from England, even when declaring our independence from her. England has never had a written constitution; rather, there has been a structure based largely on a few remarkable acts of reform such as the Magna Carta. From these collective acts came our concepts of habeas corpus (of what am I accused) and of trial by jury (by whom shall I be judged), both now embodied in the sixth amendment to the Constitution.

There are three most important freedoms that are part of this heritage which were never included in our Constitution, but which have nevertheless been a foundation of our national self-image. These are the presumption of innocence, the right to privacy, and freedom of inquiry. These are being rapidly eroded. Also, one hears more and more voices declaring that the relinquishing of these traditional rights is of little importance, as long as the national purpose is thereby achieved. The stated national purpose, at the moment, is the winning of the so-called War on Drugs. In the future, it may take the form of a war against some other threat to our national security — that phrase has worked before, and it can be counted on to work again — and the restoration of the lost rights and freedoms will simply not take place; at least, not in our time, nor in the time of our children or grandchildren.

We must act by ourselves — those of us who are aware of what is happening — either as individuals or collectively, to demand restoration of what has been taken away, and to prevent further losses.

Laws are born as concepts, but must be recorded as the written word when finally put into effect. And the exact interpretation of some of those words depends to a considerable extent upon current popular usage and understanding of their meanings. Since there cannot be complete consensus as to some definitions, there will remain a certain degree of ambiguity. I will examine a few examples of recent shifts in the manner in which such ambiguities are being handled, if not exactly resolved.

Consider the basis for the determination of innocence or guilt of a person who, as a potential defendant, has fallen under official scrutiny because of some accusation. In the past, the accusation had to be stated as a formal complaint, an arrest had to be made, and the task of providing evidence to support the charge was the province of the plaintiff, usually the people.

In a case where the crime is a felony (one which can be punished by a stay in a Federal prison), guilt must be proven beyond a reasonable doubt. Doubts are obviously challenges to presented evidence, but for heaven's sake, what is meant by "reasonable?" It has evolved in legal practice that what this means is that a jury unanimously agrees that no doubt remains in their minds as to an accused person's guilt. This is the criterion that must be met to convict someone of such a crime.

However, in the current madness involving drugs and violation of drug laws, it is no longer necessary to convene a jury or — for that matter — to even bring a charge, in order to hurt and punish someone suspected of having been involved in drug-related activity. Only the thinnest of evidence, far short in quantity or quality of what would be necessary to obtain a verdict of "guilty, beyond a reasonable doubt" in a courtroom is now regularly used to "get" the suspected wrongdoer.

If you are a person in authority, you now don't have to confront the suspected wrongdoer; you confront his possessions, instead. Accuse his bank account of being the result of illegal activity, and seize it. Accuse his truck of having transported illegal drugs, and confiscate it. Accuse his house of having been bought with cocaine dollars, and take it from him. This is a move from criminal procedures to civil procedures. Such a person, invested with the power of the law, can decide that your car, your boat, your lower twenty acres of pasture land, have been associated with the commission of a drug-related crime. He can and will seize this car (boat, land), invoking the mechanisms of civil forfeiture, and you can't do a thing about it. By association with a crime, it is meant that the seized item was used in the commission of a criminal act, or that it was obtained as the result of a criminal act.

All of the above acts on the part of the authorities are possible without any jury findings whatsoever; in fact, without a trial of any kind having been held.

Our protection against civil forfeiture was also part of our British heritage of common law, and it had been steadfastly respected here in the United States since the time of the founding fathers. But it was dissolved in 1978 by Congress, with the passage of the Psychotropic Substances Act. That law must be withdrawn.

These acts of confiscation follow the criterion of "a preponderance of evidence."

Consider that phrase, "preponderance of evidence." The first thought that comes to mind is that the word, "preponderance," suggests an excess or a superiority of evidence. That is what the dictionary says, but that is not its common usage in the courts. In legal usage, a relationship (say, between your car and illegal drugs) is established as being valid by a preponderance of evidence if it is deemed more likely, on the basis of the available evidence, to be valid than not valid. In other words, the connection is at least 51% valid. The decision that no additional evidence need be sought, can be made by one person, by one judge, even by one single policeman. Thus, the quality of proof can be miniscule.

Keep in mind that the obtaining of additional information will sometimes show a presumed fact to be fiction; additional evidence might well establish innocence.

If you are reentering the country from abroad and the stub of a marijuana joint is found in your coat pocket, the immigration authorities can seize your passport. If I, as a person with sufficient authority, discover that you have a $23,000 savings account in the local Wells Fargo Bank, and I think the money came from drug transactions, I can and will seize this money. I no longer have to file a criminal charge or even a criminal complaint, and I certainly don't have to wait until you are convicted of an unlawful act in a court of law. I merely have to state that, in my opinion, there is a preponderance of evidence that you have been naughty.

The frightening extension of this is that someone who feels that you are doing things he doesn't approve of, can effectively take from you your ability to travel abroad, or can seize the assets that might have allowed you to establish your innocence with the help of good legal counsel, if and when charges against you are finally brought.

Very recently, the courts have decided that, after a conviction of a drug-related crime (using the "beyond reasonable doubt" criterion), the sentencing phase — which must follow the sentencing guideline standards — can be made more severe with the presentation of additional facts that need only meet the "preponderance of evidence" requirement.

As an example of how these distinctions can be blurred, consider a person who was arrested with a given quantity of ephedrine in his bedroom (ephedrine is a listed precursor to methamphetamine, but not illegal to possess). He might be charged with the intent to manufacture the drug, based on the possession of a precursor, and these days he will probably be found guilty. But, in the invocation of the sentencing guidelines, the quantity of the (legal) precursor that was under the bed can be used for determining the severity of his sentence.

Next, consider the fact that, in this country, there has been a long-standing prohibition of any involvement of the military forces in civil law enforcement (the *Posse Comitatus* statute) unless specifically authorized by the Constitution or by Congress. This, too, Congress changed with the 1981 passage of the Department of Defense Authorization Act. This specified in detail the nature of assistance and support that the military will now provide civilian law enforcement personnel involved in the war against illegal drugs.

In 1982 the military provided its initial help in the President's Task Force, in South Florida, with aviation and radar surveillance, and logistic and vessel support. From then on up to the present, with the phasing out of communism as a military target, the drug war has received continuously increasing military attention, as an acceptable justification for continued funding by Congress. The Pentagon has now been given the lead responsibility to serve as the intelligence and communications hub linking the anti-drug efforts of all U.S. agencies. This does not sit well with competing agencies such as the DEA, FBI and CIA, each of which has its own intelligence structure. Recent military involvement with the local government police against the well armed guerrilla groups in central Peru may be laying the foundation for an actual shooting war. And recently, the National Guard was directed to make their personnel available as customs inspectors, to swell the manpower at ports of entry.

The IRS, too, got into the act in 1982. Tax information is now available to law-enforcement agencies, on request, to facilitate their prosecution of drug-related criminal cases.

Now, consider the term, "a reasonable suspicion." This is a still more nebulous measure of guilt. Yet it is one that has been used in the drug area with appalling effectiveness. A Coast Guard boat has always been able to come up to your sailing boat to look for a violation of safety rules, but now the skipper of the Coast Guard vessel can, by simply stating that something looks odd to him and he has a reasonable suspicion that there might be drugs aboard, search your boat for drugs. What if they find nothing? They may still seize your boat, secure it for hours or days, remove chunks of it as they choose, until they either succeed in discovering something illegal, or give up in their search.

All that is needed is a reasonable suspicion.

Let us turn our attention to the phrase, "in good faith." We are getting further yet from hard evidence, and much closer to an undocumentable whim. Here anything goes, because to prove that a man (or woman) of authority acted in bad faith you must show that he or she acted recklessly, or lied. And that is pretty heavy duty proving. "I smelled methyl amine, and this has always meant to me a methamphetamine lab, and I got a warrant based on this statement. So it turned out to be an LSD lab and there was no methyl amine present. That's okay, since I acted in good faith." The warrant stands.

"My cannabis-trained dog told me ,'there is pot in there.' It turned out that there were psilocybin-containing mushrooms, yes, but no marijuana. That's all right, because I acted in good faith, on the basis of my dog's response." The warrant stands.

An extension of this is the use of profiles, and the stopping and searching of people who are judged — again in good faith — to meet the composite picture of a person who is involved in drugs. The exact make-up of a profile is kept secret by the authorities, but in airports it involves such factors as the color of the skin, being in a hurry, having bought a one-way ticket, and having bought it with cash. If the profile is that of a courier, he can be detained, questioned, and searched as intimately as is wanted by the person in authority. If the profile is one of a swallower (one who swallows pouches of drug, to be recovered later) he can also be X-rayed without his consent and, if desired, held until the body contents are expelled naturally.

On the highways, the profile includes not only the driver's appearance, but the quality and make of his car and, believe it or not, the extent of his adherence to the local speed limits (so as not to attract attention). "He had a Florida license plate, and an expensive-looking car, and was traveling at exactly the speed limit. In my opinion, he fit the profile of a drug courier. I pulled him over and found almost $5000 dollars in cash in his glove compartment. This money showed a detectable presence of cocaine. I seized the money, but I did not charge him with any crime."

The seizure stands, because it was done in good faith, and it can be argued that cocaine on the money suggested that some drug-related criminal act had been committed.

However, government forensic chemists have demonstrated that randomly selected samples of paper money in the United States are presently contaminated with a detectable quantity of cocaine. We have instruments now that are so sensitive, they can potentially document a trace of cocaine on any piece of paper money of any denomination, in anyone's wallet.

Even though the Supreme Court last year endorsed the use of profiles with airline passengers, I still feel that this form of interception and interrogation can too easily be abused by the authorities, and it is neither needed nor should it be wanted in this country.

Yet further down this graded scale of decreasing quality of proof of guilt, there is a level where no guilt need even be implied by a person in authority against an individual. This is a rapidly expanding area of drug-related police-state activity that simply denies the person any presumption of innocence, and as he is no longer presumed to be innocent he is, by default, guilty. It rests with the accused to prove that he is not committing a felony. I am speaking of the random urine test.

What follows is a pretty harsh statement, but I mean it with total sincerity, from my heart:

There is no justification, at any time, at any place, in my country, for a urine test to be made on any individual, unless there is a reason stated for supposing that there has been a crime committed.

Let me state that again, in different words. To demand that a person pee in a cup whenever you wish him to, without a documented reason to suspect that he has been using an illegal drug, is intolerable in our republic. You are saying to him, "I wonder if you are not behaving in a way that I approve of. Convince me that you indeed are."

Outrageous.

Intolerable.

I don't care if the man is the pilot of Air Force One with the President on board, or the trigger man on a nuclear submarine with 24 Trident II D-5 missiles at his disposal; it is unthinkable that there could ever be a urine test demanded of a person, unless there were reason to suspect him of being impaired. Yes, it is possible that we might lose a plane here, or a skirmish there, but such would be a minor price for us to pay for having a nation that respects the privacy of the individual and the presumption of his innocence.

The pilot/trigger man could be in a bad state of mind for many reasons (argument with a lover, burnt toast for breakfast), so our efforts must be directed to an evaluation of his behavior, his capabilities, and the intactness of his skills; there can be testing of his reflexes and coordination, in order to give evidence of impairment. If he is not considered completely competent to do his job, then — and only then — can a search into his urine be justified.

In any case, a blind search for drugs in a pilot's urine can provide only miniscule protection against aberrant behavior, since he will fly his plane today, and the urine test results won't be available until next week. There is no protection provided under these conditions.

I believe that a major reason for the wide promotion of urine testing is that, as a new, rapidly growing industry, it is an extraordinary money-maker.

There are other actions of the authorities that illustrate this "assume them guilty and let them prove otherwise" attitude. Last year the DEA contacted all the advertisers in the counter-culture magazine High Times who were offering hydroponic horticultural supplies for sale. Their customer lists were confiscated, and all those who had made purchases of any kind were visited by representatives of the DEA, on the assumption that they were growing marijuana. After a number of innocent orchid growers had been raided, the authorities' enthusiasm died down. But the heavy-handedness of this undertaking does present a frightening picture of our law enforcement authorities in action.

As a way of exacting revenge at the legislative level, and also proving to the electorate that each and every congressman is doing everything necessary to win the war on drugs, there is a continuous demand for increasingly harsh penalties associated with drug-related convictions.

There have now been established inflexible prison terms and fine schedules that must be invoked for doing such-and-such with specifically designated quantities of certain illegal drugs. Your minimum time in prison is predicated on how much drug is involved, whether you have some special skills, whether you have been arrested before, and whether there was a gun involved. Here is a very important thing to remember. If there is any detectable amount of an illegal drug present in a seized mess, the entire weight of the mess will be considered as being the weight of the drug. If you are a boat captain, or a lawyer, or have some advanced education, you have a special skill, and you can be given an increased penalty. You might have a gun in a drawer in your bedroom at home, nowhere near the scene of the alleged crime. These particulars can all contribute to an increased and inflexible minimum sentence in prison, with times ranging from months to years to life, and with penalties climbing up there into the millions of dollars.

If you are a major drug dealer (whatever that means), under certain of the above circumstances, several laws that are now being proposed can demand that you receive a death sentence. A recently proposed law, just passed by the Senate, says that all you have to do is deal in such-and-such a quantity of a given drug, and that quantity alone will qualify you as a "major" dealer. And if you are found guilty, you will be executed. Capital punishment as a mandatory price to pay for possession of more than XYZ grams of dope. Where in the world, but here in the United States, and in Iran, and maybe in Malaysia? The unauthorized possession of an atomic bomb, by the way, is worth a maximum of 12 years.

I am confident that this bill presently being prepared for introduction into Congress (by Senator Gramm and Representative Gingrich) will never be signed into law, but the very fact that it is being seriously proposed is chilling. It introduces a whole new generation of penalties related to drug offenses (in addition to the mandatory execution of a person possessing more than an arbitrarily specified amount). These penalties include the denial of early release from prison until at least five years has been served; it demands that the state be required to conduct urine tests on anyone arrested, jailed, released or paroled (as a condition of the state continuing to receive Federal funds); it mandates that anyone convicted of use or possession of a drug will have to pay the cost of his trial and will also be fined 10% of his annual income; it says that there will be explicit permission given to states, counties, cities, school systems and private entities to engage in periodic and random drug testing.

A much more subtle and insidious form of freedom loss can be seen in our schools. There is *de facto* censorship being implemented within the colleges and universities by the Government, in the way it funds research and thus controls its direction. There is an outright propaganda campaign being presented through the informational media, and there is no challenge being brought by those who know the facts and should be insisting on adherence to truth. Let me touch on these one at a time, as each of them is directed at a different population target.

In the public schools, the efforts are being directed at the student. The message is, "Just Say No." There is no effort to inform, to educate, to provide the complex body of information that will allow the exercise of judgment. Rather, there is given the simple message that drugs kill. This is your brain. This is your brain on drugs. Sizzle, sizzle, sizzle, and the egg is suddenly fried. Your sweet, virginal daughter was killed because she didn't learn about drugs. She should have learned to, "Just Say No." None of this can be called education. It is an effort to influence behavior patterns by repeating the same message over and over again. It is propaganda.

All kinds of drugs are deeply, permanently, infused into our culture, into our way of life. Their values and their risks must be taught to our children, and this teaching must be done with honesty and integrity.

And what is the status of research in the medical schools, and the universities, and the industrial laboratories across the nation? I can assure you that since psychedelic drugs are not officially acknowledged as a valid area for human research, there is no money being made available in any university or medical school for the exploration and study of their actions and effects in humans.

It is a fact of life that all research today, at the academic level, is supported almost exclusively by federal funds, and if a grant application does not meet the wishes or needs of the granting agency, the research will remain unfunded, thus it will not be done. In the controls which have been put into place over the pharmaceutical industries, there is another effective mechanism of prohibition of inquiry. Research on drugs can only be approved for eventual medical use if the drugs involved have accepted medical utility. And there is an official statement that there are no drugs, not one single drug, in the fascinating area of the psychedelics, that has an accepted medical use. They are all, you understand, Schedule I things, and — by definition — neither they, nor any of their analogues, have any medical utility.

As for the messages being pushed in the media? All too often, a lurid story is presented, and a later retraction is ignored. A couple of examples can illustrate this.

Consider the phrases, "Even the first time can kill," and "Even pure material can kill," as applied to cocaine use. Both were promoted as statements of fact, as outgrowth of the tragic death of a sports figure named Mr. Len Bias, who died from an overdose of cocaine. This happened at a critical time, just weeks before the biannual drug bill was to be voted on.

According to the newspapers, the autopsy report stated that the young man was a first time user, and that he had used pure cocaine. This is patent nonsense. Neither the purity of a drug, nor the frequency of its use in the past, can be gleaned from an analysis of the body's tissues after death. When the final autopsy report was released, it was published in the Journal of the American Medical Association, and it seemed apparent to the scientists involved that Mr. Bias had been given a large quantity of cocaine by mouth (in a soft drink, perhaps, as there was no alcohol in him) and the suggestion was advanced that it might not have been self-inflicted. Translated, that means there was a possibility that he had been murdered.

This latter view was not advertised, and the two catchy phrases are still used for their "educational" value. Even the first time can kill. Even pure stuff can kill.

The anti-drug bill, needless to say, passed by an impressive margin.

Then, there was a train crash outside the city of Baltimore, in early 1987, that killed 16 people and injured 170 others. The newspapers trumpeted the discovery that the engineer responsible for the accident was found to have tested positive for the presence of marijuana in his body. This has been one of the major driving forces in focusing the public's attention on the need for urine testing as a necessary aspect of public safety, especially in the transportation area.

Six months later, a review of the evidence in this case resulted in the appearance of a report which showed that the supervisor of the testing laboratory which had presented the marijuana findings (the FAA lab in

Oklahoma City) had been fabricating drug test results for months. Results were being reported from tests that had never been performed, because there had been no one in the laboratory who knew how to run the sophisticated instruments.

When an effort was made to challenge the specific findings in the case of this engineer, the original computer data had apparently been lost. And there was none of the original blood sample left for a re-analysis. It will never be known if that engineer had indeed been impaired by marijuana, but political and emotional capital is still being made from the original story.

The constant repetition by the press of the very term, "Drug War," has an insidious influence on public opinion. It evokes an image of our side, as opposed to their side, and the existence of a struggle for victory. Not to be victorious is not to survive as a nation, we keep hearing. There is a continuing message being advanced, that most of our nation's troubles — poverty, increasing unemployment, homelessness, our monstrous crime statistics, rising infant mortality and health problems, even dangers to our national security involving terrorism and foreign agents — are the direct results of illegal drug use, and all of these problems would neatly disappear if we would simply find an effective solution to this one terrible scourge.

Do you remember hearing the word, *Krystalnacht*, from the history of the rise of the Nazis to power in Germany, in the late 1930's? This was the night of broken crystal, when there was a sweep of the state-empowered police and young Nazis through the Jewish sections of the German cities, when every pane of glass that was in any way related to the Jewish culture — be it the window of a store, a synagogue, or a private home — was shattered. "If we rid ourselves of the scum known as Jews," the authorities said, "We will have solved the social problems of the nation."

I see a comparable move here, with merely a few changes in the words. "If we rid ourselves of the drug scum of our society, if we deprive them of their homes, their property, their crack houses, we will have solved the social troubles of the nation."

In Germany the Jewish population was attacked and beaten, some of them to death, in a successful effort to focus all frustrations and resentments on one race of people as the cause of the nation's difficulties. It forged a national mood of unity and single-mindedness, and it allowed the formation of a viciously powerful fascist state. The persecution of the Jews, needless to say, failed to solve the social problems of Germany.

In our present-day America, the drug-using population is being used as the scapegoat in a similar way, and I fear that the end point might well be a similar state of national consensus, without our traditional freedoms and safeguards of individual rights, and still lacking resolution of our serious social troubles.

How severe is the illegal drug problem, really? If you go down through the generalized statistics, and search out the hard facts, it is not very large. From the point of view of public health, it is vanishingly small.

Just the two major legal drugs, tobacco and alcohol, are together directly responsible for over 500,000 deaths a year in this country. Deaths associated with prescription drugs are an additional 100,000 a year. The combined deaths associated with all the illegal drugs, including heroin, cocaine, marijuana, methamphetamine, and PCP, may increase this total by another 5,000. In other words, if all illegal drug use were to be curtailed by some stroke of a magic wand, the drug-related deaths in the country would decrease by 1 percent. The remaining 99% remain just as dead, but dead by legal, and thus socially acceptable means.

What about the highly touted $60 billion cost to business resulting from lost productivity in the work place? This number came from a single study which contained a number of assumptions that the National Institute of Drug Abuse admits were not valid. In this study done by Research Triangle Park, nearly 4000 households were surveyed, and the average incomes were correlated with the admission that someone who lived there had used marijuana regularly. These families had a lower income, and that decreased monthly pay-check was stated to be due to the fact that there had been marijuana use. When this was extrapolated to the population as a whole, the calculations gave a figure of $28 billion. Then there were added the costs of drug-related crime, of health problems and accidents, and the number swelled to $47 billion. Adjustment for inflation and population increase increased it further up to the often quoted $60 billion. This shameful study is a major basis for our crusade against the use of illicit drugs in industry.

This is the only study of its kind that has been made, and in this study, questions had been asked concerning other illegal drug use. Had the correlations used the findings that were made with cocaine or heroin use, rather than marijuana use, there would have been no lower average income at all. The only conclusion that could have been made (with cocaine or heroin, rather than with marijuana) was that there was no cost to business whatsoever, from drug abuse. The drug that had been used in the calculation was the only one that could have provided the numbers that were needed to fuel the drug war.

The drug problem may not be the size we are being told it is, but it is large enough for concern. What are some of its causes? There is a feeling of helplessness in much of our poor population, particularly among young Black and Hispanic males. There is a total absence of any sense of self-worth in most of the residents of our inner cities. There is extensive homelessness, and an increasing state of alienation between the middle-to-upper and the lowest classes. On one side, there is a growing attitude of, "I've got mine, and the hell with you," and on the other, "I've got nothing to lose, so screw you."

There is a shameful public health problem of massive proportions (AIDS, teen-age pregnancies, rising infant mortality and the abandonment of any serious effort to help those with debilitating mental illnesses). There are children who have no families, no food, no education, and no hope. There is near anarchy in the streets of our big cities, matched by a loss of community integrity in the rural areas. All of this is blamed on the "drug problem," although the use of drugs has nothing to do with it. Drug use is not the cause of any of these terrible problems. It may certainly be one of the results, but it is not the cause. Nonetheless, a major national effort is being made to convince the American people that winning the "War on Drugs" will indeed cure us of all ailments, if we would but relinquish a few more individual rights in the pursuit of victory.

This war cannot be won. And we will only lose more and more of our freedoms in a futile effort to win it. Our efforts must be directed towards the causes, not just the consequences of drug mis-use. But, in the meantime, things are going downhill at a rapid rate. People tell me that I am a defeatist to suggest the obvious answer, which is to legalize the use of drugs by adults who choose to use them.

I have been accused of giving the message that drug use is okay. Remove the laws, they say, and the nation will be plunged overnight into an orgy of unbridled drug use. I answer that we are already awash in illegal drugs, available to anyone who is able to pay, and their illegality has spawned a rash of criminal organizations and territorial blood-lettings, the likes of which have not been seen since the glory days of Prohibition.

Yes, it's possible that with the removal of drug laws a few timid Presbyterians will venture a snort of cocaine, but in the main, drug abuse will be no worse than it is now, and — after some initial experimentation — things will return to a natural balance. There is no "Middle America" sitting out there, ready to go Whoopie! with the repeal of the drug laws. The majority of the population will, however, benefit from the return of the criminal justice system's attention to theft, rape, and murder, the crimes against society for which we need prisons. Pot smoking, remember, is not intrinsically antisocial.

Let me ask each of you this simple question. What indicators would you accept as a definition of a police state, if it were to quietly materialize about you? I mean, a state that you could not tolerate. A state in which there is a decrease in drug use, but in which your behavior was increasingly being dictated by those in power?

Each of you, personally and privately, please draw an imaginary line in front of you, a line that indicates: up to here, okay, but beyond here, no way!

Let me suggest some thoughts to use as guides. What about a requirement for an observed urination into a plastic cup for drug analysis before getting a welfare check, or to qualify for or maintain a job at the local MacDonalds, or to allow your child enrollment in the public schools? Would any one of these convince you that our nation was in trouble?

More and more companies are requiring pre-employment urine testing, and insisting upon random analyses during working hours. Not just bus drivers and policemen, but furniture salesmen and grocery store clerks. Some local school districts are requiring random urine tests on 7th graders, but as of the present time they are still requesting the parent's permission. Recipients of public housing, of university loans, or of academic grants must give assurance that they will maintain a drug-free environment. Today, verbal assurance is acceptable, but what about tomorrow?

What about the daily shaving of the head and body so that no hair sample can be seized to provide evidence against you of past drug-use? There are increasingly strong moves to seize and assay hair samples in connection with legitimate arrests, as a potential source of incriminating evidence of past illegal drug use.

What if you had to make a formal request to the government, and get written permission, to take more than $300 out of the country for a week's vacation in Holland? Or $200? There used to be no limit, then the limit dropped to the current level of $10,000, but this number will certainly continue to drop as legislation becomes more severe with regard to the laundering of drug money.

A lot of what I have been talking about has to do with the "other guy," not you. It is your drug-using neighbor who will have to live in fear, not you. It is easy to dismiss these invasions of personal rights when they don't affect you directly. But let me ask you a not-quite-so-simple question, the answer to which is very important to you, indeed: where are your own personal limits?

To what extent do you feel that it is justifiable for someone else to control your personal behavior, if it contributes to the public's benefit? Let me presume that the idea of urine tests for cocaine use is okay with you. You probably don't use cocaine. Would you allow demands upon you for random urine tests for tobacco use? What about for alcohol use? The use of coffee?

To what extent would you allow the authorities into your private life? Let us presume that, having committed no crime, you would permit a policeman, who is visiting you officially, into your home without a warrant. But what about officials entering your home in your absence? Would you still proclaim, "I don't mind; I've got nothing to hide!"

I doubt that there are many of you who feel disturbed about the existence of a national computerized fingerprint file. But how about a national genetic marker file? What about police cards for domestic travel? How would you react to a law that says you must provide hair samples upon re-entering the country from abroad? How would you feel about the automatic opening and reading of first class mail? Any and all of these things could be rationalized as being effective tools in the war against drugs. Where would you personally draw the line?

Each of us must carefully draw that line for himself or herself. It is an exquisitely personal decision, just where your stick is to enter the ground to mark that boundary. This far, and no further.

There is a second and equally important decision to be made.

Let's ease into it by recapitulation. The first requirement is to establish a line, up to which you will allow the erosions of liberties and freedoms, all in the good cause of winning the drug war.

The second requirement is to decide, ahead of time, exactly what you will do, if and when your personal line has been breached. The point at which you say, "This has gone too far. It is time for me to do such-and-such."

Decide what such-and-such really is. You must figure it out well beforehand. And beware. It is so easy to say, "Well, my line has been exceeded, but everything else seems benign and non-threatening, so perhaps I will relocate my line from right here to over there." This is the seductive rationalizing that cost millions of innocent people their lives under the Nazi occupation in Europe.

If you can move your line, then your line was not honestly positioned in the first place. *Where is your line?* And if your limits are exceeded, *What will you do?*

Stay continuously aware of where things are, politically, and in what direction they seem to be heading. Think your plans out ahead of time, while doing everything in your power to prevent further dismantling of what rights and freedoms are left the citizens of your country.

Do not give away your rights simply to make the police enforcement of criminal law easier. Yes, easier enforcement will catch more criminals, but it will become an increasing threat to you, as well. The policeman's task should not be easy; the founders of this country made that clear. A policeman's task is always difficult in a free country.

A society of free people will always have crime, violence and social disruption. It will never be completely safe. The alternative is a police state. A police state can give you safe streets, but only at the price of your human spirit.

In summary, remember that the accused must always be assumed innocent, and allowed his day in court. The curious citizen must always have open access to information about anything he wants, and should be able to learn whatever interests him, without having some other person's ideology superimposed on him during the course of his learning. The maverick must be allowed to retreat to his private domain and live in any manner he finds rewarding, whether his neighbors would find it so or not. He should be free to sit and watch television all day long, if that's what he chooses to do. Or carry on interminable conversations with his cats. Or use a drug, if he chooses to do that. As long as he does not interfere with the freedom or well-being of any other person, he should be allowed to live as he wishes, and be left alone.

I believe that the phasing out of laws regarding drug use by adults, and an increase in the dissemination of truth about the nature and effects — positive and negative — of different drugs, the doing away with random urine testing and the perversion of justice that is its consequence, will certainly lead to smaller prison populations, and to the opportunity to use the "drug-war" funds for desperately needed social improvements and public health matters, such as homelessness, drug dependency and mental illness. And the energies of law-enforcement professionals can once again be directed towards crimes that deserve their skill and attention.

Our country might possibly become a more insecure place in some ways, but it will also be a healthier place, in body and spirit, with no further profit to be made on drugs by young men with guns on the streets of our cities. Those who abuse drugs will be able to find immediate help, instead of waiting for six months or more, in confusion and helplessness. And research in the area of drug effects and possible therapeutic use will come alive again in our centers of learning.

And we will once again be the free citizens of a free country, a model for the rest of the world.

Finally, I want to read an excerpt from a letter I received only yesterday, a letter sent by a young man who has found the psychedelics to be of great value to him in his growth as a writer:

Is it any wonder that laws prohibiting the use of psychoactive drugs have been traditionally ignored? The monstrous ego (or stupidity!) of a person or group of persons, to believe that they or anyone else have the right, or the jurisdiction, to police the *inside* of *my body*, or *my mind*!

It is, in fact, so monstrous a wrong that, were it not so sad — indeed, tragic! — it might be humorous.

All societies must, it seems, have a structure of laws, of orderly rules and regulations. Only the most hard-core, fanatical anarchist would argue that point. But I, as a responsible, adult human being, will *never* concede the power, to *anyone*, to regulate *my* choice of what I put into my body, or where I go with my mind. From the skin inward is *my* jurisdiction, is it not? I choose what may or may not cross that border. Here I am the Customs Agent. I am the Coast Guard. I am the sole legal and spiritual Government of this territory, and only the laws I choose to enact within myself are applicable!!!

Now, were I to be guilty of invading or sabotaging that same territory in *others*, then the external law of the Nation has every right — indeed, the responsibility — to prosecute me in the agreed-upon manner.

But what I think? Where I focus my awareness? What bio-chemical reactions I choose to cause within the territorial boundaries of my own skin are *not* subject to the beliefs, morals, laws or preferences of *any* other person!

I am a sovereign state, and I feel that my borders are far more sacred than the politically drawn boundaries of any country.

To which I can only say amen. That's it. See you next week.

BOOK II

THE
CHEMICAL
STORY

Penalties against possession of a drug should not be more
damaging to an individual than the use of the drug itself.

President Jimmy Carter, October 2, 1977

A SHORT INDEX TO THE PHENETHYLAMINES

This short index to the phenethylamines lists the 179 entries that follow in alphebetical order. The abbreviation PEA is for phenethylamine, and A is for amphetamine. The long index includes all synonyms and is in Appendix A.

	Code	Compact chemical name	
1	AEM	α-Ethyl-3,4,5-trimethoxy-PEA	458
2	AL	4-Allyloxy-3,5-dimethoxy-PEA	460
3	ALEPH	4-Methylthio-2,5-dimethoxy-A	462
4	ALEPH-2	4-Ethylthio-2,5-dimethoxy-A	464
5	ALEPH-4	4-Isopropylthio-2,5-dimethoxy-A	468
6	ALEPH-6	4-Phenylthio-2,5-dimethoxy-A	469
7	ALEPH-7	4-Propylthio-2,5-dimethoxy-A	472
8	ARIADNE	2,5-Dimethoxy-α-ethyl-4-methyl-PEA	475
9	ASB	3,4-Diethoxy-5-methoxy-PEA	480
10	B	4-Butoxy-3,5-dimethoxy-PEA	484
11	BEATRICE	2,5-Dimethoxy-4,N-dimethyl-A	486
12	BIS-TOM	2,5-Bismethylthio-4-methyl-A	487
13	BOB	4-Bromo-2,5,ß-trimethoxy-PEA	490
14	BOD	2,5,ß-Trimethoxy-4-methyl-PEA	492
15	BOH	ß-Methoxy-3,4-methylenedioxy-PEA	496
16	BOHD	2,5-Dimethoxy-ß-hydroxy-4-methyl-PEA	498
17	BOM	3,4,5,ß-Tetramethoxy-PEA	500
18	4-Br-3,5-DMA	4-Bromo-3,5-dimethoxy-A	501
19	2-Br-4,5-MDA	2-Bromo-4,5-methylenedioxy-A	502
20	2C-B	4-Bromo-2,5-dimethoxy-PEA	503
21	3C-BZ	4-Benzyloxy-3,5-dimethoxy-A	507
22	2C-C	4-Chloro-2,5-dimethoxy-PEA	509

148	5-TASB	3,4-Diethoxy-5-methylthio-PEA	832
149	TB	4-Butylthio- 3,5-dimethoxy-PEA	834
150	3-TE	4-Ethoxy-5-methoxy-3-methylthio-PEA	837
151	4-TE	3,5-Dimethoxy-4-ethylthio-PEA	840
152	2-TIM	2-Methylthio-3,4-dimethoxy-PEA	843
153	3-TIM	3-Methylthio-2,4-dimethoxy-PEA	846
154	4-TIM	4-Methylthio-2,3-dimethoxy-PEA	848
155	3-TM	3-Methylthio-4,5-dimethoxy-PEA	849
156	4-TM	4-Methylthio-3,5-dimethoxy-PEA	852
157	TMA	3,4,5-Trimethoxy-A	857
158	TMA-2	2,4,5-Trimethoxy-A	864
159	TMA-3	2,3,4-Trimethoxy-A	868
160	TMA-4	2,3,5-Trimethoxy-A	869
161	TMA-5	2,3,6-Trimethoxy-A	873
162	TMA-6	2,4,6-Trimethoxy-A	876
163	3-TME	4,5-Dimethoxy-3-ethylthio-PEA	880
164	4-TME	3-Ethoxy-5-methoxy-4-methylthio-PEA	882
165	5-TME	3-Ethoxy-4-methoxy-5-methylthio-PEA	884
166	2T-MMDA-3a	2-Methylthio-3,4-methylenedioxy-A	886
167	4T-MMDA-2	4,5-Thiomethyleneoxy-2-methoxy-A	888
168	TMPEA	2,4,5-Trimethoxy-PEA	891
169	2-TOET	4-Ethyl-5-methoxy-2-methylthio-A	893
170	5-TOET	4-Ethyl-2-methoxy-5-methylthio-A	896
171	2-TOM	5-Methoxy-4-methyl-2-methylthio-A	900
172	5-TOM	2-Methoxy-4-methyl-5-methylthio-A	904
173	TOMSO	2-Methoxy-4-methyl-5-methylsulfinyl-A	907
174	TP	4-Propylthio-3,5-dimethoxy-PEA	909
175	TRIS	3,4,5-Triethoxy-PEA	912
176	3-TSB	3-Ethoxy-5-ethylthio-4-methoxy-PEA	913
177	4-TSB	3,5-Diethoxy-4-methylthio-PEA	916
178	3-T-TRIS	4,5-Diethoxy-3-ethylthio-PEA	918
179	4-T-TRIS	3,5-Diethoxy-4-ethylthio-PEA	921

PHENETHYLAMINES

#1 AEM; α-ETHYLMESCALINE; 2-AMINO-1-(3,4,5-TRIMETHOXYPHENYL)BUTANE; 1-(3,4,5-TRIMETHOXY-PHENYL)-2-AMINOBUTANE

SYNTHESIS: To a solution of 45 g 3,4,5-trimethoxybenzaldehyde in 1.2 L IPA, there was added 125 g nitropropane and 67.5 g t-butylammonium acetate and the reaction mixture was held at reflux for 16 h. This was poured into 6 L H_2O, and extracted with 2x250 mL hexane. The pooled extracts were stripped of solvent under vacuum giving a residue that slowly set to a crystalline mass. On filtering, there was obtained 9.4 g of a crude yellow product which, on recrystallization from hexane provided 8.7 g of slightly sticky bright yellow crystals of 2-nitro-1-(3,4,5-trimethoxyphenyl)butene-1, with a mp of 71-73 °C. A second recrystallization from hexane gave fine yellow crystals with a mp of 72-73 °C. Attempts at the preparation of this nitrostyrene by the more conventional methods with ammonium acetate in acetic acid led either to the formation of a white product $C_{23}H_{30}N_2O_8$ which was composed of a molecule of the nitrostyrene, one of the benzaldehyde itself, and a molecule of ammonia, or to 3,4,5-trimethoxybenzonitrile, from reaction with the decomposition products of nitropropane.

A stirred suspension of 5.9 g LAH in 310 mL anhydrous Et_2O was held at a gentle reflux in an inert atmosphere. A solution of 8.5 g 2-nitro-1-(3,4,5-trimethoxyphenyl)butene-1 in 125 mL Et_2O is added drop-wise over the course of 0.5 h. The reaction was maintained at reflux for 6 h, then cooled, and the excess hydride destroyed by the cautious addition of 300 mL 1.8 N H_2SO_4. The phases were separated, and the aqueous phase brought to a pH of 6 by the addition of a saturated Na_2CO_3 solution. The neutral solution was brought to a boil, and clarified by filtration through paper. To the hot filtrate there was added a solution of 8.9 g picric acid in 100 mL boiling EtOH. The mixture was stirred and cooled, with the formation of a heavy yellow crystalline mass. After standing in the ice tub for several hours the mixture was filtered, providing 8.0 g of the picrate salt with a mp of 176-181 °C from H_2O. A solution of this salt in 300 mL boiling H_2O was treated with 60 mL concentrated HCl. On cooling, there was a deposition of picric acid, which was removed by filtration. The aqueous filtrate was washed with 3x50 mL nitrobenzene, then with 3x50 mL Et_2O. The pH was brought above 9 by the addition of aqueous NaOH, and the filtrate was extracted with 3x100 mL CH_2Cl_2. Removal of the solvent from the pooled extracts gave a nearly colorless oil, which was dissolved in 300 mL anhydrous Et_2O and saturated with hydrogen chloride gas. The white crystals of 2-amino-1-(3,4,5-trimethoxyphenyl)butane hydrochloride (AEM) were removed by filtration, Et_2O washed, and air dried. They weighed 4.72 g.

DOSAGE: greater than 220 mg.

DURATION: unknown.

EXTENSIONS AND COMMENTARY: The extension of the two-carbon chain of mescaline by alpha-methylation to the three carbon chain of TMA approximately doubled the potency of the compound. And it was felt to be a completely logical possibility that, by extending it one more carbon atom, to the four carbon chain of alpha-ethyl-mescaline, it might double again. And following that logical progression, the doubling of potency with each additional carbon atom, the factor would be 2 to the 7th power by the alpha-octyl (or 256x that of mescaline, or a milligram as active dose) and with a side chain of a 70-carbon alkyl group (alpha-heptacontylmescaline) it would take just a single molecule to be intoxicating. This was rich fantasy stuff. As an active compound, just where would it go in the brain? With an 80-carbon side-chain, would one-thousandth of a single molecule be enough for a person? Or might a single molecule intoxicate a thousand people? And how long a chain on the alpha-position might be sufficient that, by merely writing down the structure on a piece of paper, you would get high? Maybe just conceiving the structure in your mind would do it. That is, after all, the way of homeopathy.

Maybe it was just as well that this added two-carbon side-chain with lowered activity was already enough to disprove the doubling pattern. But by the time this non-activity had been learned, the alpha series had already been pushed out quite aways. The machinery of making the appropriate nitroalkane was straightforward, by reaction of the alkyl halide with nitrous acid, and separating the unwanted nitrite ester from the wanted nitroalkane by fractional distillation. The nitrostyrenes all formed reasonably although often in terrible yields, and reduced reasonably, and all formed crystalline picrates for isolation and crystalline hydrochloride salts for pharmacological manipulation. But since the first of these, AEM, was not active, there was no enthusiasm for tasting anything higher. This family was never published; why publish presumably inactive and thus uninteresting material? The Table presents the properties of the precursor nitrostyrenes, and the product picrate and hydrochloride salts, at least whatever information I can still find after thirty years:

TABLE. Physical Properties of the α-Alkylmescaline Homologues and their Precursor Nitrostyrenes

Code	Name	NS mp °C	picrate mp °C	HCl mp °C
APM	Alpha-propylmescaline	82-83		214-218
ABM	Alpha-butylmescaline	73-74	169-174	182-184
AAM	Alpha-amylmescaline	54-55	162-163	155-158
AHM	Alpha-hexylmescaline	51-52		
ASM*	Alpha-heptylmescaline	43-44		
AOM	Alpha-octylmescaline	**		
ANM	Alpha-nonylmescaline	46-47	***	
AUM	Alpha-undecylmescaline		***	

* S is for septyl, to distinguish heptyl from hexyl. **Never made, as no nonylbromide could be located to make the needed nitrononane. ***The synthesis got as far as the nitrostyrene stage when the inactivity of AEM was determined, and the project was dropped.

#2   AL;   4-ALLYLOXY-3,5-DIMETHOXYPHENETHYLAMINE; 3,5-DIMETHOXY-4-ALLYLOXYPHENETHYLAMINE

SYNTHESIS: A solution of 5.8 g of homosyringonitrile (see under E for its preparation), 100 mg decyltriethylammonium iodide, and 13.6 g allyl iodide in 50 mL anhydrous acetone was treated with 6.9 g finely powdered anhydrous K_2CO_3 and held at reflux for 16 h. The color changed from a near-black to a light yellow. The mixture was filtered, the solids washed with acetone, and the solvent from the combined filtrate and washes removed under vacuum. The residue was suspended in acidified H_2O, and extracted with 3x100 mL CH_2Cl_2. The pooled extracts were washed with 2x50 mL 5% NaOH, once with dilute HCl (which lightened the color of the extract) and then stripped of solvent under vacuum giving 12.4 g of an amber-colored oil. This was distilled at 125-137 °C at 0.1 mm/Hg to yield 5.7 g of 3,5-dimethoxy-4-allyloxyphenylacetonitrile as a yellow oil. Anal. $(C_{13}H_{15}NO_3S)$ C,H.
     A suspension of 4.0 g LAH in 150 mL anhydrous THF under N_2 was cooled to 0 °C and vigorously stirred. There was added, dropwise, 2.8 mL 100% H_2SO_4, followed by 5.5 g 3,5-dimethoxy-4-allyloxyphenylacetonitrile in 10 mL anhydrous THF. The reaction mixture was stirred at 0 °C for a few min, then brought to a reflux on the steam bath for 30 min. After cooling back to room temperature, there was added sufficient IPA to destroy the excess hydride, followed by sufficient 10%

NaOH to form granular solids. These were removed by filtration, and washed with 20 mL IPA. The filtrate and washes were stripped of solvent under vacuum and the residue added to 100 mL dilute H_2SO_4. This was washed with 2x50 mL CH_2Cl_2, made basic with aqueous NaOH, and extracted with 2x75 mL CH_2Cl_2. These extracts were pooled, the solvent removed under vacuum, and the residue distilled at 110-120 °C at 0.4 mm/Hg to give 4.9 g of a colorless oil. This was dissolved in 15 mL IPA, neutralized with concentrated HCl (55 drops required), and diluted with 50 mL Et_2O. The product was removed by filtration, washed with Et_2O, and air dried to give 4.9 g of 3,5-dimethoxy-4-allyloxyphenethylamine hydrochloride (AL) as white crystals.

DOSAGE: 20 - 35 mg.

DURATION: 8 - 12 h.

QUALITATIVE COMMENTS: (with 24 mg) "I first became aware of something in about 10 minutes, a pleasant increase in energy. By 20 minutes it was getting pronounced and was a nice, smooth development. During the next hour positive and negative feelings developed simultaneously. Following a suggestion, I ate a bit of food even though I had not been hungry, and to my surprise all the negative feelings dropped away. I felt free to join the others wherever they were at. I moved into the creative, free-flowing kind of repertoire which I dearly love, and found everything enormously funny. Much of the laughter was so deep that I felt it working through buried depressions inside me and freeing me. From this point on, the experience was most enjoyable. The experience was characterized by clear-headedness and an abundance of energy which kept on throughout the day and evening. At one point I went out back and strolled along to find a place to worship. I had a profound sense of the Presence and great love and gratitude for the place, the people, and the activities taking place. The come-down from the experience was very gradual and smooth. Food tasted wonderful. I went to bed late, and quite ready for bed, although the energy was still running. However, sleep was not long in coming."

(with 24 mg) "The onset was extremely gradual and graceful, with the first alert that one could really sense at about 50 minutes. This was succeeded by a slow gentle climb to the peak at one hour and fifteen minutes. The experience itself left all of the sensory modalities functional; speech was cogent and rather fluid. In fact, there was an unusual ease of free association. All throughout the session, the talk was high in spirits and somehow indicative of an inner excitement. Affect was entirely pleasant, but not exalting nor conducive to insight or to problem solving. There were no requirements for withdrawal into the self. The material seemed wholly social in nature. No visual, auditory or olfactory sharpening was in evidence. The plateau for this material seemed unusually long. I was unable to sleep for several hours, and took 25 mg Librium before sleep arrived. The next day was a lethargic and slow one, with the inner feeling that the effects had not worn off until the middle of the day following ingestion."

(with 35 mg) "I was a distinct +1 in 35 minutes and a +2 by the end of the hour. My head congestion in no way cleared up, absolving the material from having that particular virtue. The entire experience was somewhat dissociated — I could not connect with my feelings. Although my mind remained clear, there was a hangover feeling at the end of the experiment."

EXTENSIONS AND COMMENTARY: This compound was first explored in Prague by Leminger. He provided only the synthetic details and the statement that it was the most active compound that he had studied, with activity at 20 milligrams, with perceptual changes, color enhancement, and difficult dreams during sleep that night. Some effects persisted for more than 12 hours. Dosages above 35 milligrams remain unexplored.

As AL is one of the most potent 3,4,5-trisubstituted phenethylamines yet described, and since the corresponding amphetamines are of yet greater potency, it would be a good guess that 4-allyloxy-3,5-dimethoxyamphetamine (3C-AL) would be an interesting compound to explore. It could be made from syringaldehyde in reaction with allyl iodide, followed by the formation of a nitrostyrene with nitroethane, followed by reduction with aluminum hydride. It is, as of the present time, both unsynthesized and unexplored.

#3   ALEPH;   DOT;   PARA-DOT;   DMMTA;   2,5-DIMETHOXY-4-METHYLTHIOAMPHETAMINE

SYNTHESIS: A solution of 2.3 g 2,5-dimethoxy-4-(methylthio)benzaldehyde (see under 2C-T for its synthesis) in 7.5 mL nitroethane was treated with 0.45 g anhydrous ammonium acetate and heated on the steam bath for 6 h. The excess solvent/reagent was removed under vacuum leaving a mass of orange crystals as residue. These were ground up under 10 mL MeOH, collected by filtration, washed with a little MeOH, and air dried to provide 2.6 g crude 1-(2,5-dimethoxy-4-methylthiophenyl)-2-nitropropene. After recrystallization from 140 mL boiling MeOH, filtering and drying there was in hand 1.8 g of bright orange crystals with a mp of 137-138 °C. Anal. (C$_{12}$H$_{15}$NO$_4$S) C,H,N,S.

A suspension of 1.4 g LAH in 10 mL anhydrous Et$_2$O and 40 mL anhydrous THF was put under an inert atmosphere and, with good stirring, brought up to a gentle reflux. A solution of 1.8 g 1-(2,5-dimethoxy-4-methylthiophenyl)-2-nitropropene in 30 mL anhydrous THF was added dropwise at a rate that maintained the reflux. Heating and stirring were maintained for an additional 7 h, then the reaction mixture was allowed to return to room temperature. There was added 1.6 mL H_2O (dissolved in a little THF), followed by 1.6 mL 15% NaOH, and finally another 4.8 mL H_2O. Stirring was continued until all the curdy solids had turned white. The reaction mixture was filtered, and the filter cake washed with THF. The filtrate and the washings were combined, and the solvent removed under vacuum. The residue was 1.3 g of a colorless oil that solidified. Its mp of 90-93 °C was improved slightly to 91-93 °C with recrystallization from hexane. The product was dissolved in 25 mL warm IPA, neutralized with concentrated HCl (0.57 mL required) and then diluted with 100 mL anhydrous Et_2O. After a moment's delay, the white crystalline product appeared. It was removed by filtration, washed with Et_2O, and air dried to provide 1.2 g 2,5-dimethoxy-4-methylthioamphetamine hydrochloride (ALEPH) with a mp of 200-201 °C. Recrystallization from IPA gave an analytical sample with a mp of 204-205 °C. Anal. $(C_{12}H_{20}ClNO_2S)$ C,H; N: calcd, 5.04; found, 5.52.

DOSAGE: 5 - 10 mg.

DURATION: 6 - 8 h.

QUALITATIVE COMMENTS: (with 5 mg) "The initial hints of action were physical — warming of first the legs, and then a comfortable warmth spread over the entire body. Intense intellectual stimulation, one that inspired the scribbling of some 14 pages of handwritten notes. Which is a pretty good record for an experience that is almost entirely non-verbal. The afterglow was benign and rich in empathy for everything. And by the sixth hour I was quite hungry."

(with 10 mg) "There was a rapid shift of frame of reference that made simple tasks such as reading and tuning the radio quite alien. I happened to catch the eyes of Pretty Baby, the cat, at the same moment she looked at me, and she turned and fled. I am able to interact with people on the telephone quite well but mechanical things, such as arranging flowers or alphabetizing names, are beyond me. Driving would be impossible."

EXTENSIONS AND COMMENTARY: This specific compound is probably the first sulfur-containing phenethylamine to have been evaluated as a potentially active CNS stimulant or psychedelic. It was a complete, total, absolute unknown. The first trials were made at the sub-microgram level, specifically at 0.25 micrograms, at 11:30 AM on September 3, 1975. Part of this extreme precaution was due to the uniqueness of a new heteroatom in a phenethylamine system. But part was due to the strange manic excitement that occurred at the time of the isolation and characterizing of the final product in the laboratory. Although it was certainly all placebo response, I was jumpy and unable to stay in the lab for more than a few minutes at a time. Maybe dust in the air? Maybe some skin contact with the free base? Now, I know there was nothing, but the possibility of extraordinary potency was real, and I did indeed wash everything down anyway. In fact, it took a total of 18 trials to work the experimental dosage up to as much as a single milligram. In retrospect, overly cautious. But retrospection, as they say, is cheap.

The 5 milligram experiment, briefly quoted from above, is the stuff of Chapter 14 of this book, important in that it gives an interesting example of some thought processes associated with psychedelic intoxication, ego-inflation, and what might be thought of as bits of mania. As is always the case with peak experiences that happen to be catalyzed by drugs, this extraordinary event could not be duplicated. At 7 milligrams there was an uneventful +1, and some 10 milligrams was needed to generate a full +3 experience. The first clue of the erratic nature of the Aleph family came from an independent assay by a colleague of mine, one who was very familiar with such states of consciousness, but for whom this was not a time for peak experiences. At 10 milligrams he told me that he had had only mild effects which he found relatively uninteresting.

As it stands, ALEPH remains relatively unexplored. Its two positional isomers are entered here as ORTHO-DOT and META-DOT. Three higher homologues have been more thoroughly looked at, and the generic name ALEPH (the first letter of the Hebrew alphabet) was given this group on the basis that they might have extraordinary properties in common. But the real treasure came in the exploring of the 2-carbon homologues, the compounds that make up the 2C-T family. Here, there proved to be much less uncertainty as to reasonable dosages, and much more richness in the subjective nature of the experience.

#4   ALEPH-2;   2,5-DIMETHOXY-4-ETHYLTHIOAMPHETAMINE

SYNTHESIS: A solution of 2.0 g 2,5-dimethoxy-4-(ethylthio)benzaldehyde (see under 2C-T-2 for its synthesis) in 12 mL nitroethane was treated with 0.4 g anhydrous ammonium acetate and heated on the steam bath for 3 h. All volatiles were removed under vacuum, leaving a residue that set up as brilliant red crystals. These were mechanically removed from the evaporation flask, blown free of nitroethane vapor, and recrystallized from boiling EtOH, producing 1.8 g pale orange crystals, with a mp of 110-112 °C. Recrystallization from 20 mL boiling IPA gave, after filtering and air drying, 1.70 g light orange crystals of 1-(2,5-dimethoxy-4-ethylthiophenyl)-2-nitropropene with a mp of 112-113 °C.

A suspension of 1.2 g LAH in 75 mL anhydrous THF was put under an inert atmosphere and, with good stirring, brought up to a gentle reflux. A solution of 1.5 g 1-(2,5-dimethoxy-4-ethylthiophenyl)-2-nitropropene in 20 mL anhydrous THF was added dropwise. Heating and stirring were maintained for an additional 24 h, and then the reaction mixture was allowed to come back to room temperature with stirring. There was added 1.4 mL H_2O (dissolved in a little THF), followed by 1.4 mL 15% NaOH and finally another 4.2 mL H_2O. Stirring was continued until all the curdy solids had turned white. The reaction mixture was filtered, and the filter cake washed with THF. The filtrate and the washings were combined, and the solvent removed under vacuum. The residue was 1.1 g of a pale amber oil. This was dissolved in 6 mL IPA, neutralized with concentrated HCl (about 8 drops were required) and then diluted with 150 mL anhydrous Et_2O. The slightly cloudy solution was stirred for a couple of min, then there was the formation of a heavy white crystalline mass. This was removed by filtration, washed with Et_2O, and air dried to provide 1.1 g 2,5-dimethoxy-4-ethylthioamphetamine hydrochloride (ALEPH-2) with a mp of 128-130 °C with decomposition.

DOSAGE: 4 - 8 mg

DURATION: 8 - 16 h.

QUALITATIVE COMMENTS: (with 4 mg) "There was a warm feeling in the total body and a light pressure in the head that changed with time into the feeling of a balloon without any anatomical definition. The usual color perception was not very much increased, and my vision was not sharpened as it was with DOM. Rather, I noticed waves of movement, very smooth and not too busy. Both my tactile perception and auditory acuity were enhanced. The main effect for me was, paradoxically, an easier handling of the outer world. None of the jitters of amphetamine. The body feeling is good, healthy, and I am at peace with the body-mind dualism. These are pretty much personal comments — I will write up the pharmacological points later."

(with 5 mg) "This turned out to be a day of extraordinary visuals and interpretations. About two hours into it, I felt that the effects were still climbing, but there was a marvelous onset of visual distortions and illusions, right at the edge of hallucination. The logs in the fireplace were in continuous motion. The notepaper I was writing on seemed to scrunch and deform under the pressure of the pen. Nothing would stay still; everything was always moving. There was a phase of unabated inflation. The intensity was noticeably dropping at the five hour point and I observed considerable residual shakes and a muscular tremor. Even towards midnight there was some tooth-rubbiness, but I was able to get a somewhat fretful though adequate sleep."

(with 5 mg) "I was exposed to a number of new environments and it was difficult to completely separate the experience into what was seen differently and what was seen for the first time. The Santa Cruz Mystery Spot should have been bizarre but it was simply hokey. And yet the boardwalk that should have been depressing was totally magical. The day was unworldly and I ended up with considerable muscular weakness. All in all, I handled it well, but I probably won't do it again."

(with 7 mg) "An amazing unification of visual hallucination seen only in the very fine detail of something, and what must be considered retinal hallucination. There is no one-to-one correspondence between the many retinal cells of the high-resolution part of the eye. Thus, the mind can pick and choose, sometimes from the right eye, and sometimes from the left. And so a small curve or bump can become whatever you wish. For a moment. And then it chooses again, but differently. Is all of our perceived world as subjective as this?"

(with 8 mg) "Extreme intoxication, but almost no visual phenomena. Even well into the evening, I know I absolutely could not drive. Why? I don't know, since this experiment, at least, seemed to be quite free of strange colors and wiggly lines and streaks of light. It's that I don't trust that the reality I see is the same reality that the other driver might see. I am very much the center of the world about me, and I don't think I could trust anyone else to fully respect my reality."

EXTENSIONS AND COMMENTARY: As with ALEPH itself, and in most ways with the entire ALEPH family, there is no predictability of the dose/response relationship. One person had expressed his psychic isolation by taking and maintaining a fetal position in relative hibernation for several hours and with substantial amnesia; this at a four milligram dose. Yet another person, at fully twice this amount, was aware of a slight light-headedness that could in no way be measured as more than a bare threshold. But by the time this erratic nature had become apparent, the ALEPHS had been assigned and made, up to and including ALEPH-7.

ALEPH-3 was intended to be the methallylthio compound, 2,5-dimethoxy-4-(ß-methallylthio)amphetamine. The thioether (2,5-dimethoxyphenyl ß-methallyl sulfide) was easily made from 2,5-dimethoxythiophenol (see 2C-T-2 for its preparation) with 3.4 g dissolved in a solution of 1.7 g KOH in 25 mL boiling EtOH, and 2.72 g methallyl chloride, heated 1 h on the steam bath, poured into 250 mL H_2O, extracted with 3x100 mL CH_2Cl_2, and solvent removal yielding 4.4 g of the sulfide as an amber oil. An effort to convert this to 2,5-dimethoxy-4-(ß-methallylthio)-benzaldehyde (7.2 g $POCl_3$, 6.7 g N-methylformanilide, 4.2 g of the crude sulfide from above, 15 min heating on the steam bath, H_2O hydrolysis, hexane extraction of the residues from a CH_2Cl_2 extraction) produced 3.1 g of a peppermint-smelling oil that distilled at 140-160 °C at 0.3 mm/Hg and which did indeed have an aldehyde group present (by proton NMR) but the rest of the spectrum was a mess, and the project was abandoned.

Several years later, this entire project was reinitiated, and the aldehyde was obtained as a yellow crystal, but again it was not pursued. At that time, the earlier try had been totally forgotten, and a brand new ALEPH- (or 2C-T-) number had been assigned; i.e., 20. Thus, the corresponding phenethylamine (2,5-dimethoxy-4-(ß-methallylthio)phenethylamine), had it ever been made, which it was not, would have been called either 2C-T-3 or 2C-T-20, and the amphetamine homologue would probably have been ALEPH-20.

A closely related 2C-T-X compound was also started quite a while later — this was the allylthio homologue of the methallyl material 2C-T-3 or 2C-T-20. Its place in the flow of things is evident from its numbering, 2C-T-16. A mixture of 2,5-dimethoxythiophenol and KOH and allyl chloride in MeOH gave 2,5-dimethoxyphenyl allyl sulfide as a white oil which boiled at 110-125 °C at 0.25 mm/Hg. This, with $POCl_3$ and N-methylformanilide provided 2,5-dimethoxy-4-(allylthio)benzaldehyde which distilled at 140-160 °C at 0.4 mm/Hg and could be recrystallized from MeOH as a pale yellow solid. Reaction of this aldehyde in nitroethane in the presence of ammonium acetate (steam bath for 2.5 h) provided 2,5-dimethoxy-4-allylthio-ß-nitrostyrene as red crystals from acetonitrile. Its mp was 114-115 °C. Anal. ($C_{13}H_{15}NO_4S$) C,H. This has not yet been reduced to the final amine, 2,5-dimethoxy-4-allylthiophenethylamine, 2C-T-16. The corresponding amphetamine would be, of course, ALEPH-16.

ALEPH-5 was to be the cyclohexylthio analogue (2,5-dimethoxy-4-cyclohexylthioamphetamine). The thioether (2,5-dimethoxyphenyl cyclohexyl sulfide) was successfully made from 1.7 g 85% KOH pellets in 25 mL hot EtOH, 3.4 g 2,5-dimethoxythiophenol (again, see under 2C-T-2 for its preparation), and 4.9 g cyclohexyl bromide, 3 h on the steam bath, into 500 mL H_2O, extraction with 3x100 mL CH_2Cl_2, washing the extracts with 5% NaOH, and evaporation to yield 5.2 g of an amber oil. The aldehyde, (made from 6.1 g $POCl_3$ and 5.4 g N-methylformanilide, heated until claret colored, then treated with 5.0 g of the above crude thioether, heating for 20 min on the steam bath, into 300 mL H_2O, and over-night stirring) was obtained as 3.1 g of a flesh-colored solid that was clearly neither pure nor completely correct. Repeated partitioning with organic solvents and cooling and scratching the residues finally provided a pale orange crystal (1.3 g, mp 88-93 °C) which, after twice recrystallizing from MeOH, gave 0.4 g of pale yellow crystals with a mp 95-96 °C and a textbook perfect NMR in $CDCl_3$ (CHO, 1H (s) 10.41; ArH 2H (s) 6.93, 7.31; OCH_3, 6H, (2s) at 3.88 and 3.92; CH, 1H br. at 3.34; and $(CH_2)_5$ 10H br. at 1.20-2.34). The nitrostyrene was prepared from 200 mg of the above aldehyde in 1.2 mL nitroethane and 0.1 g ammonium acetate overnight on the steam bath, the solvent removed to give an orange oil that spontaneously crystallized after a few months' standing. This was never characterized, but sits there on the shelf to be reduced to ALEPH-5 some inspired day. The two-carbon homo-logue of this (2,5-dimethoxy-4-cyclohexylthiophenethylamine) will some-day be called 2C-T-5 (if it is ever made).

The remaining members of this family, ALEPH-4, ALEPH-6, and ALEPH-7 have actually been prepared and they have all been entered here in Book II, under their own names.

#5   ALEPH-4;   2,5-DIMETHOXY-4-(i)-PROPYLTHIOAMPHETAMINE

SYNTHESIS: A solution of 2.0 g 2,5-dimethoxy-4-((i)-propylthio)benzaldehyde (see under 2C-T-4 for its synthesis) in 12 mL nitroethane was treated with 0.4 g anhydrous ammonium acetate and heated on the steam bath for 12 h, then allowed to stir for another 12 h at room temperature. The excess solvent/reagent was removed under vacuum leaving a residue as a heavy deep orange two-phase oily mass. This was brought into one phase with 2 mL MeOH and then, with continued stirring, everything spontaneously crystallized. This product was removed by filtration and, after washing sparingly with cold MeOH and air drying, yielded 2.0 g of 1-(2,5-dimethoxy-4-(i)-propylthiophenyl)-2-nitropropene as orange crystals with a mp of 96-98 °C. After recrystallization from 15 mL boiling 95% EtOH, filtering and air drying to constant weight, there was obtained 1.6 g of orange crystals with a mp of 99-100 °C.

A suspension of 1.0 g LAH in 100 mL warm THF was stirred under a N_2 atmosphere and heated to a gentle reflux. To this there was added, dropwise, a solution of 1.2 g 1-(2,5-dimethoxy-4-(i)-propylthiophenyl)-2-nitropropene in 20 mL anhydrous THF. This mixture was held at reflux for 1 day, then stirred at room temperature for 2 days. There was then added, slowly and with caution, 1 mL of H_2O, followed by 1 mL of 15% NaOH, and finally by another 3 mL of H_2O. Stirring was continued until the reaction mixture became white and granular, then all solids were removed by filtration and the filter cake was washed with additional THF. The filtrate and washings were combined, and the solvent removed under vacuum to give 1.1 g of residue which was an almost white oil. This was dissolved in 6 mL IPA, neutralized with concentrated HCl (10 drops were required) and then diluted with 200 mL anhydrous Et_2O. The resulting slightly turbid solution was clarified by filtration through a sintered glass filter, and the clear and slightly yellow filtrate was allowed to stand. A fine white crystalline product slowly separated over the next few h. This product, 2,5-dimethoxy-4-(i)-propylthioamphetamine hydrochloride (ALEPH-4) was removed by filtration, and after washing with Et_2O and air drying, weighed 0.5 g and had a mp of 146-147 °C, with prior sintering at 144 °C.

DOSAGE: 7 - 12 mg.

DURATION: 12 - 20 h

QUALITATIVE COMMENTS: (with 7 mg) "Things started off going downhill, initially negative with tension and depression, but as the momentum developed, so did the positive effect. My discomfort continued to develop, but I was struck by the visual beauty of the trees and the small stream that flowed off the mountain. My experience continued to grow, simultaneously, in both the negative and the positive direction. Physically I was uncomfortable and found my breathing difficult, but I acknowledged a rapture in the very act of breathing. All moved over to the plus side with time, and the evening was gorgeous. I have never seen the sky so beautiful. The only flaw was when I choked on some lemonade and it seemed to me I almost drowned. I have been extremely conscious of eating, drinking and swallowing ever since. I barely slept the whole night and awoke extremely tired. I felt that the experience continued for many days, and I feel that it is one of the most profound and deep learning experiences I have had. I will try it again, but will block out more time for it."

(with 8 mg) "There was without question a plus two, but none of the edges of unreality that are part of LSD. The sounds that are just outside of my hearing are intriguing, and distract me from the eyes-closed imagery that is just barely possible with music while lying down. But, going outside, there were no obvious sources of the sounds that I heard. Could I drive? I suspect so. I took a shower and did just that — I drove to San Francisco without incident, and walked amongst the many strange faces on the downtown streets."

(with 12 mg) "The experience was very intense but completely under control except for a twenty minute period right in the middle of it. I had to get away from everything, from everyone. There was a sense of being surrounded and moved in upon that was suffocating. I was weighed down with everything — physical, psychic, emotional. My clothes had to come off, my hair had to be released, my shoes went, I needed to move away from where I was, to somewhere else, to some new place, any new place, with the hope that my other old place wouldn't follow me. Pretty soon I found I was myself, I could breathe again, and I was OK. Rather sheepishly, I dressed and rejoined the group. The rest of the day was spectacular, but those few minutes were scary. What if I couldn't have escaped?"

EXTENSIONS AND COMMENTARY: Again, there are hints and suggestions of complexities. These, and several other reports, suggest some sensory confusion, and interpretive aspects that are to some extent threatening. There is an underlying suggestion of body toxicity. I know of no experiment that exceeded 12 milligrams and I would not be able to predict what might come forth at higher dosages. I personally choose not to try them.

#6 ALEPH-6 2,5-DIMETHOXY-4-PHENYLTHIOAMPHETAMINE

SYNTHESIS: To a 300 mL three-neck round-bottom flask set up with a magnetic stirrer and protected with a N_2 atmosphere, there was added 75 mL hexane, 3.5 g tetramethylethylenediamine, and 4.2 g p-dimethoxybenzene. The reaction mixture was cooled to 0 °C with an external ice bath, and there was then added 19 mL of 1.6 M butyllithium in hexane. With stirring, the reaction was brought up to room temperature, and there were produced loose, creamy solids. There was then added, as a solid and portionwise, 6.6 g diphenyldisulfide which resulted in an exothermic reaction and the production of a nearly clear solution. After stirring an additional 10 min, the reaction was quenched in 500 mL of dilute NaOH. The hexane phase was separated, and the aqueous phase extracted with 4x100 mL CH_2Cl_2 The organic extracts were combined, washed with dilute HCl and the solvents were removed under vacuum to provide 6.0 g of 2,5-dimethoxyphenyl phenyl sulfide as an impure amber oil. A small sample was saved for microanalysis and NMR, and the remainder converted to the corresponding benzaldehyde.

A mixture of 6.1 g $POCl_3$ and 5.4 g N-methylformanilide was heated for 3 min on the steam bath, and then added to the remainder of the above-described 2,5-dimethoxyphenyl phenyl sulfide. The reaction became immediately a deep red and, after heating on the steam bath for 0.5 h, was dumped into a large quantity of H_2O, producing a granular brown solid. This was removed by filtration, and washed sparingly with cold MeOH (the washes were saved). The resulting pale yellow solids were recrystallized from 20 mL boiling absolute EtOH providing, after cooling, filtration and air drying, 4.4 g of extremely pale yellow crystals of 2,5-dimethoxy-4-(phenylthio)benzaldehyde. This had a mp of 119-119.5 °C. All washes and mother liquors were combined, flooded with H_2O and extracted with CH_2Cl_2. This solvent was removed under vacuum, and the residue (a viscous oil) was dissolved in a little EtOH which, on cooling in dry ice, gave 1.2 g of a second crop of the aldehyde, mp 117-119 °C. Recrystallization from 5 mL 95% EtOH gave an additional 0.4 g product with a mp of 118-119 °C. This mp was not improved by recrystallization from cyclohexane. The NMR specrum was excellent, with OCH_3 singlets (3H) at 3.45 and 3.80 ppm; ArH singlets at 6.28 and 7.26 ppm, the C_6H_5 as a broad peak centered at 7.50, and the CHO proton at 10.37 ppm.

A solution of 4.4 g 2,5-dimethoxy-4-(phenylthio)benzaldehyde in 32 mL nitroethane was treated with 0.8 g anhydrous ammonium acetate and heated on the steam bath for 21 h. The excess solvent/reagent was removed under vacuum, leaving a dark red oil as residue. After much diddling and fiddling around, this set up as a crystalline mass. These solids were ground under 20 mL cold MeOH and filtered, providing 5.3 g of the crude nitrostyrene as an orange crystalline residue product after air-drying. This was ground up under 10 mL MeOH, the insolubles collected by filtration, washed with a little MeOH, and air dried to provide 5.3 g crude 1-(2,5-dimethoxy-4-phenylthiophenyl)-2-nitropropene as yellow crystals, with a mp of 100-102 °C (with prior sintering at about 98 °C). This was recrystallized from 50 mL boiling 95% EtOH. After cooling in an ice bath, it was filtered, washed with EtOH, and air drying provided gold-yellow crystals with a mp of 105-106 °C. The proton NMR was excellent (in $CDCl_3$).

A suspension of 2.0 g LAH in 100 mL refluxing THF, under an inert atmosphere and with good stirring, was treated with a solution of 3.5 g 1-(2,5-

dimethoxy-4-phenylthiophenyl)-2-nitropropene in 20 mL anhydrous THF added dropwise at a rate that maintained the reflux. Heating and stirring were maintained for an additional 36 h, and then the reaction mixture was stirred at room temperature for an additional 24 h. There was added 2.0 mL H_2O (dissolved in a little THF), followed by 2.0 mL 15% NaOH, and finally another 6.0 mL H_2O. Stirring was continued until all formed solids had turned white. The reaction mixture was filtered, and the filter cake washed with THF. The filtrate and the washings were combined and the solvent removed under vacuum. The residue was 2.8 g of an oil that quite obviously contained some H_2O. This was dissolved in 400 mL CH_2Cl_2, washed first with dilute NaOH and then with 4x150 mL 1N HCl. The organic phase was stripped of solvent under vacuum, yielding a pale amber oil that crystallized. This was ground first under Et_2O, giving 3.4 g of a yellow solid. This was then ground under 10 mL of acetone, yielding 2.4 g of a white crystalline solid that darkened at 170 °C, sintered at 187 °C and had a mp of 191-193 °C. This was dissolved in 20 mL hot 95% EtOH, and diluted with 40 mL Et_2O to provide a clear solution which, after a minute's scratching with a glass rod, deposited 2,5-dimethoxy-4-phenylthioamphetamine hydrochloride (ALEPH-6) as white solids. After filtration and air drying, the weight was 1.8 g, with a mp of 194-195 °C. The dilute HCl washes, after being made basic with aqueous NaOH and extraction with CH_2Cl_2 gave a trivial quantity of additional product.

DOSAGE: greater than 40 mg.

DURATION: probably long.

QUALITATIVE COMMENTS: (with 30 mg) "I had an alert at the one hour point, and in another hour there was a clear 1+. There was a not well defined, gentle un-worldliness. And it was still there quite unchanged twelve hours later. In a group I find that all voices about me are of equal intensity and equal importance. But this is not at all distracting. This will be a long lived thing for sure."

(with 40 mg) "I am into a subtle but real effect, no more than one plus, but real. I feel primed, but nothing more. It is not interfering with work, maybe even helping with it. After another hour of static one-plusness I decided to use it as a primer to LSD, using the usual 60 microgram quantity that is standard for primer studies. The combination showed definite synergism, with a rapid show of the LSD effects (within fifteen minutes) and an almost three plus effect. This is most unusual for the usual 60 microgram challenge amount. An absolutely delightful intoxication that had sufficiently descended towards baseline that I accepted a ride to a party that evening in Marin County to attend a poetry reading. There I felt myself at baseline and accepted (unusual for me) a little marijuana. And with the utmost quiet and delicacy, a rather incredible change of state took place. The most memorable event was the awareness of a clarinet playing somewhere, and the sneaky sounds from it actually coming along the carpet out of the dining room and into the hallway and through the door and into the room where I was, and all of them gathering at my feet like docile kittens waiting for me to acknowledge them. I did, non-verbally, and I was amazed at the many additional follow-up sounds that came from the same clarinet along the same twisty path along the floor and through the door and into my space, over what seemed to be the next million hours. I ended up with a marvelous collection of notes and phrases at my feet, and I felt somehow honored. My speech sounded OK to me, but I knew that it would be odd to the ears of others, so I kept quiet. A final measure of the weirdness of the ALEPH-6/LSD/Pot combination was the viewing of the Larkspur ferry at its dock, abandoned for the evening and with no one aboard it, and with all that clean, dry sleeping space going to waste with so many people sleeping on the streets these days. Once home, I slept soundly and for a long while. Incredible experience."

EXTENSIONS AND COMMENTARY: In a sense, this compound was a disappointment. The beauty of putting a whole new ring into an active structure is that it provides a marvelous vehicle for introducing new substituents in new arrangements. Had Aleph-6 been a cleanly active and potent compound, then the new phenyl group could have been made electronegative to varying degrees (with methoxy substitution for example) or electropositive to varying degrees (with trifluoromethyls or nitros) and this fine-tuning could have been extremely rewarding.

But this material had the earmarks of one of those forever threshold things. The 40 milligram experiment was hopelessly compromised, and nothing higher was ever scheduled or tried. The two-carbon homologue, 2,5-dimethoxy-4-phenyl-thiophenethylamine, or 2C-T-6, has never even been synthesized, let alone assayed.

#7 ALEPH-7; 2,5-DIMETHOXY-4-(n)-PROPYLTHIOAMPHETAMINE

SYNTHESIS: A solution of 2.6 g 2,5-dimethoxy-4-((n)-propylthio)benzaldehyde (see under 2C-T-7 for its synthesis) in 20 mL nitroethane and 0.5 g anhydrous ammonium acetate was heated on the steam bath overnight. The excess solvent/ reagent was removed under vacuum leaving an orange oil as a residue that crystallized spontaneously. This crude product was recrystallized from 20 mL boiling MeOH to give, after cooling, filtering, and air drying, 2.4 g of 1-(2,5-dimethoxy-4-(n)-propylthiophenyl)-2-nitropropene as orange crystals. Its mp was 83-84 °C with prior sintering at 81 °C.

A suspension of 1.5 g LAH in 150 mL of warm anhydrous THF was stirred under an inert atmosphere and brought up to a gentle reflux. A solution of 2.3 g 1-(2,5-dimethoxy-4-(n)-propylthiophenyl)-2-nitropropene in 25 mL anhydrous THF was added dropwise at a rate that maintained the reflux. Heating and stirring were continued for 2 days, and then the reaction mixture was allowed to stir at room temperature for an additional 2 days. There was added 1.5 mL H_2O (dissolved in

10 mL THF), followed by 1.5 mL 15% NaOH, and finally another 4.5 mL H$_2$O. Stirring was continued until all the curdy solids had turned white. The reaction mixture was filtered, and the filter cake washed with slightly wet THF. The filtrate and the washings were combined, and the solvent removed under vacuum. The residue was about 2 mL of an amber colored oil that was dissolved in 200 mL CH$_2$Cl$_2$. This solution was washed with first dilute NaOH, and then with saturated brine. Removal of the solvent gave a pale amber oil that was dissolved in 10 mL IPA, neutralized with about 14 drops of con-centrated HCl, and diluted with 200 mL anhydrous Et$_2$O. The clear solution was decanted from a little gritty material, and then set aside to allow the formation of 2,5-dimethoxy-4-(n)-propylthioamphetamine hydrochloride (ALEPH-7) as fine white crystals. After filtration and air drying, there was obtained 1.8 g of an off-white powder.

DOSAGE: 4 - 7 mg.

DURATION: 15 - 30 h.

QUALITATIVE COMMENTS: (with 4 mg) "At the second hour I had a paraesthetic twinge or two (all pins and needles), and then felt quite relaxed, quite willing to let this play itself out. In the evening my ears still feel 'popped' and there is a little bit of physical awareness. There is not much fun with this. The night following, I was unable to sleep and only dozed slightly, but I seemed to be OK the next day."

(with 6 mg) "The alert was felt within a half hour, and then nothing more. Then, over the next two hours, there was the evolution of an extremely neutral state. I danced wildly to a record of Keith Jarrett, but somehow didn't care for his style. I fell apart emotionally, with tears and a feeling of total loss of everything. Everything was visible to me only in some strange wide-angle lens viewing. I went for a walk, a waste of time. I tried classical music, but only jazz was acceptable. It was a couple of days before I lost the residual strangeness feeling. Never again."

(with 7 mg) "I did this alone, and in retrospect I wish I had not. Somewhere between the hours 2 and 3, I got to a full +++, and I was concerned that I saw the effects still developing. Where would it go now? There was no reality loss as with LSD, no shakes or shimmers, but an intense and profound +++ of something characterized only by the absence of extremes. And I am frightened because this is still deepening. A couple of calls to friends were not successful, but I found an ally in the Palo Alto area, and I told him I was coming to visit. My greater than one hour drive there was okay only because I had programmed every move ahead of time. In retrospect, to drive was completely stupid, and I certainly will never do it again, under any circumstances. But, there I was. I knew which lane I would be on, on the

S.F. Bay Bridge, at every moment of my travels. The middle lane through the tunnel. The second from the left when descending into San Francisco. The white lane-marker stripes were zipping up past my lateral field of vision as I drove, those that were to my right zipped past my right eye, those to the left past my left eye. Like disturbed fruit flies leaving an over-ripe peach. But, as everything had been preprogrammed, there were no surprises. I made it successfully, and my baby-sitting friend probed, with a blend of curiosity, love, and envy, my uncaring state. And in the course of the next couple of hours, this state evolved into a friendly, familiar place. I was still fully +++, but now for the first time I was at peace with it. A fruit salad tasted heavenly. By midnight I was able to doze lightly, and the next day I was sure that there were some residual effects. The second evening's sleep repaired everything. The neutralness was something new to me. I don't like not caring. Was this the "Beth" state of the strange twenty minutes seen by SL in the ALEPH-4 experience?"

(with 7 mg) "Strange, pleasant, unexciting, long-lasting. The induced state was characterized by: clear unintoxicated central field of vision, concentration but with the periphery sensed as being filled with a kind of strangeness, and also something sensed inside, at the back of the head. A feeling of something waiting to erupt, which never does. I had a faint touch of amusement, yet no part of the experience had the depth or richness of other compounds. No tremors. Slight visuals, but only when looked for. Hunger not present, but food tasted fine when eaten. Mildly pleasant but one would not take it again unless bored stiff."

EXTENSIONS AND COMMENTARY: This drug was the first definition of the term, Beth state.

There is something of the Fournier Transform in any and all drug experiments. A psychedelic drug experience is a complex combination of many signals going all at the same time. Something like the sound of an oboe playing the notes of the A-major scale. There are events that occur in sequence, such as the initial A, followed by B, followed by C-sharp and on and on. That is the chronology of the experience, and it can be written down as a series of perceived phenomena. The notes of the scale. Black quarter notes, with flags at the tops of their staffs, going up the page of music.

But within each of these single events, during the sounding of the note "A," for example, there is a complex combination of harmonics being produced at the same time, including all components from the fundamental oscillation on up through all harmonics into the inaudible. This mixture defines the played instrument as being an oboe. Each component may be shared by many instruments, but the particular combination is the unique signature of the oboe.

This analogy applies precisely to the study of psychedelic drugs and their actions. Each drug has a chronology of effect, like the notes of the A-major scale. But there are many components of a drug's action, like the harmonics from the fundamental to the inaudible which, taken in concert, defines the drug. With musical instruments, these components can be shown as sine waves on an oscillo-scope. One component, 22%, was a sine wave at a frequency of 1205 cycles, and a phase angle of +55°. But in psychopharmacology? There is no psychic oscillo-scope. There are no easily defined and measured harmonics or phase angles. Certainly, any eventual definition of a drug will require some such dissection into components each of which makes some contribution to the complex whole. The mental process may some day be defined by a particular combination of these components. And one of them is this Beth state. It is a state of uncaring, of anhe-donia, and of emotionlessness.

Many drugs have a touch of this Beth state, ALEPH-7 more than most. If a sufficient alphabet of effects (I am using the Alephs, Beths, Gimels, and Daleths of the Hebrew as token starters only) were to be accumulated and defined, the actions of new materials might someday be more exactly documented. Could depression, euphoria, and disinhibition for example, all be eventually seen as being made up of their component parts, each contributing in some measured way to the sum, to the human experience? The psychologists of the world would be ecstatic. And drugs such as ALEPH-7 might be useful in helping to define one of these parts.

#8   ARIADNE;   4C-DOM;   BL-3912;   DIMOXAMINE;   1-(2,5-DIMETHOXY-4-METHYLPHENYL)-2-AMINOBUTANE;   2,5-DIMETHOXY-α-ETHYL-4-METHYLPHENETHYLAMINE

SYNTHESIS: In 50 mL of benzene there was dissolved 31.6 g 2,5-dimethoxy-4-methylbenzaldehyde (see recipe for 2C-D for its preparation), 20.2 mL 1-nitropropane, and 6 mL cyclohexylamine. This solution was held at reflux in a Dean Stark apparatus for 24 h, effectively removing the water of reaction. Upon cooling, there was deposited 19.6 g of 1-(2,5-dimethoxy-4-methylphenyl)-2-nitro-1-butene as brilliant orange crystals. The mp, after recrystallization from MeOH, was 114-115 °C and a second recrystallization increased the mp another 2 °C. Anal. $(C_{13}H_{17}NO_4)$ C,H,N.

A suspension of 12.5 g LAH in 600 mL anhydrous THF was stirred magnetically, and brought up to a reflux. To this there was added, dropwise, 15.0 g 1-(2,5-dimethoxy-4-methylphenyl)-2-nitro-1-butene dissolved in 150 mL THF. Refluxing was continued for 15 h and, after cooling, the excess hydride was decomposed by the addition of 12.5 mL H_2O. The inorganic salts were made loose and granular by the addition of 12.5 mL 15% NaOH followed by an additional 37.5 mL H_2O. These solids were removed by filtration, and the filter cake was washed with THF. The combined filtrate and washings were stripped of solvent under vacuum. The residue was dissolved in anhydrous Et_2O, and treated with hydrogen chloride gas, yielding 1-(2,5-dimethoxy-4-methylphenyl)-2-aminobutane hydrochloride (ARIADNE) as white crystals which, after recrystallization from IPA, weighed 11.4 g and had a mp of 232.5-234.5 °C. Anal. $(C_{13}H_{22}ClNO_2)$ C,H,N,Cl. The racemic mixture was resolved into its optical isomers by the formation of salts with (+)-2'-nitrotartranilic acid (to give the "S" isomer) or with (+)-2'-chlorotartranilic acid (to give the "R" isomer). The "R" isomer can also be prepared by the reductive amination of 1-(2,5-dimethoxy-4-methylphenyl)-2-butanone (from the above nitrostyrene and elemental iron) with (+)-α-methyl benzylamine followed by the hydrogenolysis of the benzyl group.

DOSAGE: as psychedelic, unknown.

DURATION: short.

QUALITATIVE COMMENTS: (with 12 mg) "I believe that my mood has distinctly improved, and my sleep that evening was excellent. This is physically benign."

(with 32 mg) "There was some sort of threshold that lasted for a couple of hours."

(with 25 mg of the "R" isomer) "There is the alert of a psychedelic, with none of the rest of the package. Perhaps a bit of paranoia. And by the fifth hour everything is largely gone."

EXTENSIONS AND COMMENTARY: How does one discover a new drug for a malady that does not exist in experimental animals? Drugs that interfere with sleep, or with appetite, or with some infecting bacterium, are naturals for animal screening, in that animals sleep, eat, and can be easily infected. But there are lots of syndromes that involve a state of mind, and these are uniquely human. Many of the psychopharmacological anti-this or anti-that agents address ailments such as anxiety, psychosis, paranoia, or depression, which are only known in man. So how does one discover a new drug in areas such as these? If one has in hand a drug that is known to be effective in one of these human ailments, an animal assay can be set up to give some measurable response to that specific drug, or a biochemical property can be rationalized as being related to a mechanism of action. And with the known drug as a calibration, and restricting your search to structurally related compounds, you can find structural relatives that give the same responses.

But how does one find a new class? One way is to kind of stumble into it as a side-line of human experimentation with new psychedelics. But it is really difficult to pick up the clues as to what will be a good anti-depressant if you are not depressed. This compound, to which I had given the name of ARIADNE as the first of my ten "classic ladies" (I'll say more about them later), was not really a stimulant of any kind, certainly it was not a psychedelic, and yet there was something there. It had been explored rather extensively as a potential psychotherapeutic ally by a friend of mine. He said that there seemed to be some value in a few of his patients who had some underlying depression, but not much of anything with the others. So, I decided to call it an anti-depressant. I had mentioned some of this history one time when I was giving an address at a conference on the East Coast, and my host (who happened to be the research director at a large pharmaceutical house) asked if I would send him a sample. His company did many animal tests, one of which showed that it was not hallucinogenic (a cat whose tail erected dramatically with DOM did nothing with ARIADNE) and another that showed re-motivation (some old maze-running monkeys who had decided not to run any more mazes changed their minds with ARIADNE).

So patents were obtained for the "R" isomer, the more effective isomer, covering its use for such things as the restoring of motivation in senile geriatric patients. And a tradename of Dimoxamine was assigned it, despite several voices that held out for Ariadnamine. But it didn't have what was needed to make it all the way to the commercial market

Many, many analogues of ARIADNE have been made, and for a variety of reasons. In the industrial world there is research backup carried out, not only for the discovery of new things, but also for patent protection of old things. Several dozen analogues of ARIADNE have been made and pharmacologically evaluated, and some of them have been put into the published literature. The major points of variation have been two: keep the 4-position methyl group intact, and make the variations on the alpha-carbon (propyl, butyl, dimethyl, phenyl, benzyl, phenethyl, etc. — an extensive etc.) or: keep the alpha-position ethyl group intact and make the variations on the 4-position (chloro, iodo, methylthio, carboxy, etc. — again, an extensive etc.).

Some of these analogues I had made, and sent in for animal screening. The high potency of DOB suggested the bromo-counterpart of ARIADNE. The making of this entailed the proteo counterpart, 1-(2,5-dimethoxyphenyl)-2-aminobutane. Reaction of 2,5-dimethoxybenzaldehyde with nitropropane in benzene in a Dean Stark apparatus with cyclohexylamine as a catalyst produced 1-(2,5-dimeth-oxyphenyl)-2-nitrobutene, which crystallized as orange crystals from MeOH with a mp of 47-47.5 °C. Anal. $(C_{12}H_{15}NO_4)$ C,H,N. This was reduced to the amine 1-(2,5-dimethoxyphenyl)-2-aminobutane with LAH in ether, and this gave a hydro-chloride salt with a mp of 172-174 °C after recrystallization from acetonitrile. The free base of this compound was brominated in acetic acid to give 1-(2,5-dimethoxy-4-bromophenyl)-2-aminobutane which yielded a white hydrochloride salt with a mp of 204-206 °C following recrystallization from IPA. The isomeric non-brominated analogue, 1-(3,4-dimethoxyphenyl)-2-aminobutane was made and explored by the Chemical Warfare group at Edgewood Arsenal; its code number is EA-1322.

Several of the alpha-ethyl analogues of ARIADNE were N,N-dialkylated, and were target compounds for halogenation with radio-iodine or radio-fluorine, for evaluation as potential brain blood-flow indicators. In these studies. all examples followed a common flow diagram. The reaction of the appropriate benzaldehyde and nitropropane, using N,N-dimethylethylenediamine as a catalyst and following recrystallization from MeOH, gave the corresponding 1-aromatic-2-nitro-1-butene (the nitrostyrene) which, by reduction with elemental iron, gave the corresponding 2-butanone (which was distilled at about 0.3 mm/Hg). This led, by reductive amination with dimethylamine hydrochloride and sodium cyanoborohydride, to the corresponding N,N-dimethyl product which was distilled at about 0.3 mm/Hg and which, in no case, either formed a solid HCl salt or reacted with carbon dioxide from the air. From 2,4-dimethoxybenzaldehyde, the nitrostyrene appeared as yellow crystals, the ketone as a white oil, and the product N,N-dimethyl-1-(2,4-dimethoxy-phenyl)-2-aminobutane as a white oil. From 2,5-dimethoxybenzaldehyde, the nitrostyrene formed bright yellow crystal, the ketone was an off-white oil, and the product N,N-dimethyl-1-(2,5-dimethoxyphenyl)-2-aminobutane was a white oil. From 3,5-dimethoxybenzaldehyde, the nitrostyrene formed pale yellow crystals that discolored on exposure to the light, the ketone was an off-white clear oil, and the product N,N-dimethyl-1-(3,5-dimethoxyphenyl)-2-aminobutane was a white oil. From 2,6-dimethoxybenzaldehyde, the nitrostyrene was obtained as orange crystals, and was not pursued further.

A number of ARIADNE analogues have been made, or at least started, purely to serve as probes into whatever new areas of psychopharmacological activity might be uncovered. One of these is a HOT compound, and one is a TOM compound, and a couple of them are the pseudo (or near-pseudo) orientations. The HOT analogue was made from the nitrostyrene precursor to ARIADNE itself, reduced not with LAH or AH (which would give the primary amine), but rather with sodium borohydride and borane dimethylsulfide. The product, 1-(2,5-dimethoxy-4-methylphenyl)-N-hydroxy-2-aminobutane hydrochloride, was a white crystalline material. The 5-TOM analogue got as far as the nitrostyrene. This was made from 2-methoxy-4-methyl-5-(methylthio)benzaldehyde (see under the 5-TOM recipe for its preparation) and nitropropane in acetic acid, and gave bright yellow crystals. The true pseudo-analogue is the 2,4,6-trimethoxy material based on TMA-6, which is the "real" pseudo-TMA-2. The nitrostyrene from 2,4,6-trimethoxybenzaldehyde and nitropropane crystallized from MeOH/CH₃CN as fine yellow crystals, and this was reduced with AH in cold THF to 1-(2,4,6-trimethoxyphenyl)-2-aminobutane which was a bright, white powder.

And the near-pseudo analogue?

First, what is near-pseudo? I have explained already that the "normal" world of substitution patterns is the 2,4,5. Everyone knows that that is the most potent pattern. But, the 2,4,6 is in many ways equipotent, and has been named the pseudo-stuff. The "real," or "true" pseudo-stuff. So what is the "near" pseudo-stuff? I am willing to bet that the rather easily obtained 2,3,6-trisubstitution pattern, and the much more difficult to obtain 2,3,5-substitution pattern, will produce treasures every bit as unexpected and remarkable as either the 2,4,5- or the 2,4,6-counterparts. These are neither "real" nor "pseudo," but something else, and I will find a name for them when the time comes, something weird from the Greek alphabet. And this will double again the range of possible exploration. The TMA-5 analogue mentioned came from 2,3,6-trimethoxybenzaldehyde and nitropropane using cyclohexylamine as a catalyst (yellow-orange solids) which was reduced to the amine with AH. This hydrochloride salt is an air-stable white powder. All of these materials remain unexplored.

Somewhere in the wealth of compounds implicit in the many structural variables possible (the normal versus the pseudo versus the near-pseudo patterns, coupled with the wide variety of promising substituents that can be placed on the 4-position, together with the availability of the the unexplored members of the Ten Classic Ladies harem), it would seem inescapable that interesting compounds will emerge.

Just what is this all about the ten "Classic Ladies?" In the chemical structure of DOM, there is a total of nineteen hydrogen atoms. Some of these are indistinguishable from others, such as the three hydrogen atoms on a methyl group. But there are exactly ten "types" of hydrogen atoms present. And, not having much, if any, intuition as to just why DOM was so powerful a psychedelic, I decided to systematically replace each of the ten unique hydrogens, one at a time of course, with a methyl group. And I planned to give the resulting materials the names of famous ladies, alphabetically, as you walk around the molecule.

ARIADNE was the first of these, the methyl for a hydrogen atom on the methyl group of the amphetamine chain. It was Ariadne who gave the long piece of thread to Theseus to guide him through the mazes of the Labyrinth so he could escape after killing the Minotaur. The record is fuzzy as to whether, after the successful killing, she went with him, or let him go on alone. A methyl group on the nitrogen atom produced BEATRICE. There is the legendary Beatrijs of the Dutch religious literature of the 14th century, and there is the Beatrice from *Beatrice and Benedict* (of Berlioz fame). But the one I had in mind was the lady from Florence whom Dante immortalized in the *Divina Commedia,* and she is entered under her own name in this footnote. Replacing the alpha-hydrogen of DOM with a methyl group would give the phentermine analogue which is named CHARMIAN. You may be thinking of Cleopatra's favorite attendant, but I was thinking of the sweet wife of a very dear friend of mine, a lady who has been in a state of gentle schizophrenia for some forty years now. The MDA analogue of CHARMIAN has been described in this foornote under the code name of MDPH. CHARMIAN, herself, has been synthesized and is of very much reduced potency in animals, as compared to DOM. It has not been tried in man as far as I know.

The two beta-hydrogen atoms of DOM are distinct in that, upon being replaced with methyl groups, one would produce a threo-isomer, and the other an erythro-isomer. I have named them DAPHNE (who escaped from Apollo by becoming a laurel tree which was, incidentally, named for her) and ELVIRA (who might not be too well known classically, but whose name has been attached to Mozart's 21st piano concerto as its slow movement was used as theme music for the movie *Elvira Madigan*). I don't know if either of this pair has been made — I started and got as far as the cis-trans mixture of adducts betweeen nitroethane and 2,5-dimethoxy-4-methylacetophenone. Whoever finally makes them gets to assign the names. I had made and tested the corresponding homologues of DMMDA that correspond to these two ladies.

And there are five positions (2,3,4,5 and 6) around the aromatic ring, each of which either carries a hydrogen atom or a methyl group that has a hydrogen atom. There is the 2-methoxy group which can become a 2-ethoxy group to produce a compound called FLORENCE. Her name is the English translation of the Italian Firenze, a city that, although having a female name, has always seemed thoroughly masculine to me. There is the 3-hydrogen atom which can become a 3-methyl group to produce a compound called GANESHA. This is a fine elephant-headed Indian God who is the symbol of worldly wisdom and also has been seen as the creator of obstacles. Here I really blew it; the Classic Lady turned out to be a Classic Gentleman; not even the name is feminine. There is the 4-methyl group which can become a 4-ethyl group to produce a compound called HECATE who presided over magic arts and spells. There is the 5-methoxy group which can become a 5-ethoxy group to produce a compound called IRIS, who is the Goddess of the rainbow. And there is the 6-hydrogen atom which can become a 6-methyl group to produce a compound called JUNO, who is pretty much a lady's lady, or should I say a woman's woman.

GANESHA, 2,5-dimethoxy-3,4-dimethylamphetamine has been made, and has proven to be an extraordinary starting point for a large series of potent phenethylamines and amphetamines which are described in this book. HECATE was given a synonym early in this process, and is now known as DOET (2,5-dimethoxy-4-ethylamphetamine). IRIS has also been entered under her name, and the other ethoxy homologue, FLORENCE, would be easily made based on the preparation of the phenethylamine analogue, 2CD-2ETO. Perhaps it has already been made somehow, somewhere, as I have noted that I have claimed its citrate salt as a new compound in a British patent. And, finally, JUNO (3,6-dimethoxy-2,4-dimethylamphetamine) has been made (from 2,5-dimethoxy-m-xylene, which was reacted with $POCl_3$ and N-methylformanilide to the benzaldehyde, mp 53-54 °C, and to the nitrostyrene with nitroethane, mp 73-74 °C from cyclohexane, and to the final amine hydrochloride with LAH in THF). Rather amazingly, I have had JUNO on the shelf for almost 14 years and have not yet gotten around to tasting it.

#9   ASB;   ASYMBESCALINE;   3,4-DIETHOXY-5-METHOXY-PHENETHYLAMINE

SYNTHESIS: To a solution of 32 g of 5-bromobourbonal in 150 mL DMF there was added 31 g ethyl iodide and 32 g of finely ground 85% KOH pellets. There was the formation of a purple color and a heavy precipitate. On gradual heating to reflux, the color faded to a pale yellow and the precipitate dissolved over the course of 1

h. The heating was continued for an additional 1 h. The reaction mixture was added to 1 L H_2O, and extracted with 2x150 mL of petroleum ether. The extracts were pooled, washed with 2x200 mL 5% NaOH and finally with H_2O. After drying over anhydrous K_2CO_3 the solvents were removed under vacuum to yield 36 g of crude 3-bromo-4,5-diethoxybenzaldehyde as an amber liquid. This was used without purification for the following step. Distillation at 105-115 °C at 0.3 mm/Hg provided a white sample which did not crystallize. Anal. $(C_{11}H_{13}BrO_3)$ C,H.

A mixture of 36 g 3-bromo-4,5-diethoxybenzaldehyde and 17 mL cyclohexylamine was heated with an open flame until it appeared to be free of H_2O. The residue was put under a vacuum (0.4 mm/Hg) and distilled at 135-145 °C, yielding 42 g 3-bromo-N-cyclohexyl-4,5-diethoxybenzylidenimine as a viscous light greenish oil. This slowly set to a crystalline glass with a mp of 60-61 °C. Recrystallization from hexane gave a white crystalline product without any improvement in the mp. Anal. $(C_{17}H_{24}BrNO_2)$ C,H. This is a chemical intermediate to a number of active bases, taking advantage of the available bromine atom. This can be exchanged with a sulfur atom (leading to 5-TASB and 3-T-TRIS) or with an oxygen atom as described below.

A solution of 18 g 3-bromo-N-cyclohexyl-4,5-diethoxybenzylidenimine in 250 mL anhydrous Et_2O was placed in an atmosphere of He, stirred magnetically, and cooled with an external dry ice/acetone bath. Then 36 mL of a 1.5 M solution of butyllithium in hexane was added over 2 min, producing a clear yellow solution. This was stirred for 10 min. There was then added 30 mL of butyl borate at one time, the stirring continued for 5 min. The stirred solution was allowed to return to room temperature. There was added 150 mL of saturated aqueous ammonium sulfate. The Et_2O layer was separated, and the aqueous phase extracted with another 75 mL Et_2O. The combined organic phases were evaporated under vacuum. The residue was dissolved in 100 mL MeOH, diluted with 20 mL H_2O, and then treated with 15 mL 35% H_2O_2 added over the course of 2 min. This mildly exothermic reaction was allowed to stir for 15 min, then added to 500 mL H_2O. This was extracted with 2x100 mL CH_2Cl_2 and the solvent removed under vacuum. The residue was suspended in 150 mL dilute HCl and heated on the steam bath for 0.5 h. Stirring was continued until the reaction was again at room temperature, then it was extracted with 2x75 mL CH_2Cl_2. These extracts were pooled and extracted with 3x100 mL dilute aqueous KOH. The aqueous extracts were washed with CH_2Cl_2, reacidified with HCl, and reextracted with 2x75 mL CH_2Cl_2. These extracts were pooled, and the solvent removed under vacuum to yield a brown residue. This was distilled at 107-127 °C at 0.4 mm/Hg to yield 8.3 g of 3,4-diethoxy-5-hydroxybenzaldehyde as an oil that set to a tan solid. Recrystallization from cyclohexane gave a white product with a mp of 70.5-71.5 °C. Anal. $(C_{11}H_{14}O_4)$ C,H.

A solution of 8.3 g of 3,4-diethoxy-5-hydroxybenzaldehyde and 3.0 g

KOH in 75 mL EtOH was treated with 5 mL methyl iodide and stirred at room temperature for 5 days. The reaction mixture was added to 400 mL H_2O and extracted with 2x50 mL CH_2Cl_2. The extracts were pooled, washed with 2x150 mL dilute NaOH, and the solvent removed under vacuum. The residual oil was distilled at 95-110 °C at 0.3 mm/Hg to yield 8.2 g of 3,4-diethoxy-5-methoxybenzaldehyde as a pale yellow liquid. This product was a crystalline solid below 20 °C but melted upon coming to room temperature. It was analyzed, and used in further reactions as an oil. Anal. $(C_{12}H_{16}O_4)$ C,H.

To a solution of 6.4 g 3,4-diethoxy-5-methoxybenzaldehyde in 40 mL nitromethane there was added about 0.5 g anhydrous ammonium acetate, and this was held at reflux for 1 h. The excess solvent/reagent was removed under vacuum, producing a red oil which set up to crystals. These were recrystallized from 40 mL boiling MeOH to yield 3.0 g of 3,4-diethoxy-5-methoxy-ß-nitrostyrene as yellow plates, with a mp of 89-90 °C. Anal. $(C_{13}H_{17}NO_5)$ C,H.

A solution of 3.0 g LAH in 150 mL anhydrous THF under He was cooled to 0 °C and vigorously stirred. There was added, dropwise, 2.1 mL of 100% H_2SO_4, followed by the dropwise addition of a solution of 3.5 g 3,4-diethoxy-5-methoxy-ß-nitrostyrene in 30 mL anhydrous THF, over the course of 10 min. The addition was exothermic. The mixture was held at reflux on the steam bath for 30 min. After cooling again, the excess hydride was destroyed with IPA, followed by the addition of 10% NaOH sufficient to covert the aluminum oxide to a white, granular form. This was removed by filtration, the filter cake washed with IPA, the mother liquor and filtrates combined, and the solvents removed under vacuum to provide a yellow oil. This residue was added to 100 mL dilute H_2SO_4 producing a cloudy suspension and some yellow insoluble gum. This was washed with 2x75 mL CH_2Cl_2. The aqueous phase was made basic with 25% NaOH, and extracted with 2x75 mL CH_2Cl_2. The solvent was removed from these pooled extracts and the residue distilled at 110-135 °C at 0.4 mm/Hg to provide 2.0 g of a colorless liquid. This was dissolved in 7 mL IPA, neutralized with about 40 drops of concentrated HCl, followed by 50 mL anhydrous Et_2O with stirring. The initially clear solution spontaneously deposited a white crystalline solid. This was diluted with an additional 30 mL Et_2O, let stand for 1 h, and the solids removed by filtration. After Et_2O washing, the product was air-dried to yield 1.25 g of 3,4-diethoxy-5-methoxyphenethylamine hydrochloride (ASB) with a mp of 142-143 °C. Anal. $(C_{13}H_{22}ClNO_3)$ C,H.

DOSAGE: 200 - 280 mg.

DURATION: 10 - 15 h.

QUALITATIVE COMMENTS: (with 240 mg) "There was a pleasant and easy flow of day-dreaming thoughts, quite friendly and somewhat erotic. There was a gentle down-drift to my starting baseline mental status by about midnight (I started at 9:00 AM). I never quite made it to a +++, and rather regretted it."

(with 280 mg) "The plateau of effect was evident by hour two, but I found the experience lacking the visual and interpretive richness that I had hoped for. Sleep was very fitful after the effects had largely dropped — it was hard to simply lie back and relax my guard — and even while being up and about the next day I felt a residual plus one. Over all, there were few if any of the open interactions of 2C-B or LSD. Some negative side seemed to be present."

(with 280 mg) "The entire session was, in a sort of way, like being in a corridor outside the lighted halls where a beautiful mescaline experience is taking place, sensing the light from behind a grey door, and not being able to find my way in from the dusky underside passageways. This is sort of a gentle sister of mescaline, but with a tendency to emphasize (for me, at this time) the negative, the sad, the struggling. Sleep was impossible before the fifteenth hour. When I tried, I got visions of moonlight in the desert, with figures around me which were the vampire-werewolf aspect of the soul, green colored and evil. I had to sit quietly in the living room and wait patiently until they settled back to wherever they belonged and stopped trying to take over the scene. During the peak of the experience, my pulse was thready, somewhat slowed, and uneven. There was a faint feeling of physical weirdness."

EXTENSIONS AND COMMENTARY: This specific amine was a target for a single study in cats many years ago, in Holland, using material obtained from Hoffman La Roche in Basel. Their findings are hard to evaluate, in that 200 milligrams was injected into a 3.75 kilogram cat (53 mg/Kg), or about twice the dosage that they used in their studies with metaescaline. Within 5 minutes there were indications of catatonia, and within a half hour the animal was unable to walk. This condition persisted for two days, at which time the animal died. Although this dose was many times that used in man, perhaps hints of the physical unease and long action are there to be gleaned. The consensus from over a half dozen experiments is that there is not enough value to be had to offset the body load experienced.

A comment is needed on the strange name asymbescaline! In the marvelous world of chemical nomenclature, bi- (or di-) usually means two of something, and tri- and tetra- quite reasonably mean three and four of something. But occasionally there can be an ambiguity with bi (or tri or tetra) in that bi some-thing-or-other might be two something-or-others hooked together or it might be two things hooked onto a something-or-other. So, the former is called bi- and the latter is called bis-. This compound is not two escalines hooked together (bi-escaline) but is only one of them with two ethyl groups attached (bis-escaline or bescaline). And since there are two ways that this can be done (either symmetrically or asymmetrically) the symmetric one is called symbescaline (or SB for short) and this one is called asymbescaline (or ASB for short). To complete the terminology lecture, the term tri- becomes tris- (the name given for the drug with all three ethoxy groups present in place of the methoxys of mescaline) and the term tetra- mutates into the rather incredible tetrakis-!

#10   B;   BUSCALINE;   4-(n)-BUTOXY-3,5-DIMETHOXY-
PHENETHYLAMINE

SYNTHESIS: A solution of 5.8 g of homosyringonitrile (see under E for preparation), 100 mg decyltriethylammonium iodide, and 11 g n-butyl bromide in 50 mL
anhydrous acetone was treated with 6.9 g finely powdered anhydrous K_2CO_3 and
held at reflux for 10 h. An additional 6 g of n-butyl bromide was added to the
mixture, and the refluxing continued for another 48 h. The mixture was filtered, the
solids washed with acetone, and the solvent from the combined filtrate and washes
removed under vacuum. The residue was suspended in acidified H_2O, and extracted
with 3x175 mL CH_2Cl_2. The pooled extracts were washed with 2x50 mL 5% NaOH,
once with dilute HCl, and then stripped
of solvent under vacuum giving 13.2 g
of a deep yellow oil. This was distilled
at 132-145 °C at 0.2 mm/Hg to yield
5.0 g of 4-(n)-butyloxy-3,5-dimeth-
oxyphenylacetonitrile as a pale yellow
oil which set up to crystals spontaneously. The mp was 42-43 °C. Anal. ($C_{14}H_{19}NO_3$)
C H N.
        A solution of AH was prepared by the cautious addition of 0.67 mL of
100% H_2SO_4 to 25 mL of 1.0 M LAH in THF, which was being vigorously stirred
under He at ice bath temperature. A total of 4.9 g of 4-(n)-butyloxy-3,5-dimethoxy-
phenylacetonitrile was added as a solid over the course of 10 min. Stirring was
continued for another 5 min, then the reaction mixture was brought to reflux on the
steam bath for another 45 min. After cooling again to room temperature, IPA was
added to destroy the excess hydride (about 5 mL) followed by 10 mL of 15% NaOH
which was sufficient to make the aluminum salts loose, white, and filterable. The
reaction mixture was filtered, the filter cake washed with IPA, and the mother liquor
and washes combined and the solvent removed under vacuum to yield an amber oil.
This residue was treated with dilute H_2SO_4 which generated copious solids. Heating
this suspension effected solution, and after cooling, all was washed with 3x50 mL
CH_2Cl_2. The aqueous phase was made basic with aqueous NaOH, and the product
extracted with 2x100 mL CH_2Cl_2. The extracts were evaporated to a residue under
vacuum, and this was distilled at 128-138 °C at 0.5 mm/Hg yielding 3.8 g of a
colorless oil. This was dissolved in 40 mL IPA, neutralized with concentrated HCl
(about 55 drops required) and, with vigorous stirring, 80 mL of anhydrous Et_2O was
added which produced fine white plates. After standing for several h, the product
was filtered, washed with 20% IPA in Et_2O, and finally with Et_2O. Air drying
yielded 3.9 g of 4-(n)-butyloxy-3,5-dimethoxyphenethylamine hydrochloride (B)
with a mp of 152-153 °C. An analytical sample melted at 155-157 °C. Anal.
($C_{14}H_{24}ClNO_3$) C,H,N.

DOSAGE: greater than 150 mg.

DURATION: several hours.

QUALITATIVE COMMENTS: (with 120 mg) "There is a strange taste, not really bitter, it does not linger. The slight change of baseline has certainly disappeared by the eighth hour. No noticeable changes in either the visual or the auditory area.

(with 150 mg) "Throughout the experiment it was my impression that whatever effects were being felt, they were more in body than mind. The body load never mellowed out, as it would have with mescaline, after the first hour or two. Mental effects didn't develop in any interesting way. I was aware of brief heart arrhythmia. Tummy was uncomfortable, off and on, and there was light diarrhea. Even as late as the fifth hour, my feet were cold, and the whole thing left me with a slightly uncomfortable, 'Why did I bother?' feeling."

EXTENSIONS AND COMMENTARY: There is a jingle heard occasionally in chemical circles, concerning the homologues of methyl. It goes, "There's ethyl and propyl, but butyl is futile." And to a large measure this is true with the 4-position homologues of mescaline. This butyl compound, B or Buscaline, had originally been patented in England in 1930 without any physical or pharmacological description, and the few physical studies that had involved it (lipophilic this and serotonin that) suggested that it was less active than mescaline.

In principle, the 5-, the 6-, the 7- and the on-up homologues might be called amylescaline (possibly pentescaline?), hexescaline, heptescaline (possibly septescaline), and God-knows-what-scaline. They would certainly be easily makeable, but there would be little value that could be anticipated from nibbling them. In keeping with the name B (for butoxy), these would be known as A (for amyloxy, as the use of a P could confuse pentoxy with propoxy), as H (for hexyloxy, but careful; this letter has been used occasionally for DMPEA, which is Homopiperonylamine), and as S (the H for heptyloxy has been consumed by the hexyloxy, so let's shift from the Greek *hepta* to the Latin *septum* for the number seven). It seems most likely that the toxic symptoms that might well come along with these phenethylamines would discourage the use of the dosage needed to affect the higher centers of the brain. The same generally negative feeling applies to the amphetamine counterparts 3C-B, 3C-A, 3C-H and 3C-S.

A brief reiteration of the 2C-3C nomenclature, to avoid a possible misunderstanding. The drug 2C-B is so named in that it is the two-carbon chain analogue of the three-carbon chain compound DOB. The drug 3C-B is so named because it is the three-carbon chain analogue of the two-carbon chain compound Buscaline, or more simply, B. There is no logical connection whatsoever, either structural or pharmacological, between 2C-B and 3C-B.

#11   BEATRICE;   N-METHYL-DOM;   2,5-DIMETHOXY-4,N-DIMETHYLAMPHETAMINE

SYNTHESIS: A fused sample of 5.0 g of white, crystalline free base 2,5-dimethoxy-4-methylamphetamine, DOM, was treated with 10 mL ethyl formate, and held at reflux on the steam bath for several h. Removal of the solvent gave 5.5 g of a white solid, which could be recrystallized from 15 mL MeOH to give 3.8 g of fine white crystals of 2,5-dimethoxy-N-formyl-4-methylamphetamine. An analytical sample from ethyl formate gave granular white crystals.

To a stirred suspension of 4.0 g LAH in 250 mL anhydrous Et_2O at reflux and under an inert atmosphere, there was added, by the shunted Soxhlet technique, 4.2 g of 2,5-dimethoxy-N-formyl-4-methylamphetamine as rapidly as its solubility in hot Et_2O would allow. The mixture was held at reflux for 24 h and then stirred at room temperature for several additional days. The excess hydride was destroyed with the addition of dilute H_2SO_4 (20 g in 500 mL water) followed by the additional dilute H_2SO_4 needed to effect a clear solution. The Et_2O was separated, and the aqueous phase extracted with 100 mL Et_2O and then with 2x250 mL CH_2Cl_2. Following the addition of 100 g potassium sodium tartrate, the mixture was made basic with 25% NaOH. The clear aqueous phase was extracted with 3x250 mL CH_2Cl_2 These extracts were pooled, and the solvent removed under vacuum. The residual amber oil was dissolved in 400 mL anhydrous Et_2O, and saturated with hydrogen chloride gas. The white crystals that formed were removed by filtration, washed with Et_2O, and air dried to constant weight. There was obtained 4.2 g of product with a mp of 131.5-133.5 °C. This product was recrystallized from 175 mL boiling ethyl acetate to give 3.5 g 2,5-dimethoxy-4,N-dimethylamphetamine hydrochloride (BEATRICE) as pale pink crystals with a mp of 136-137 °C. A sample obtained from a preparation that employed the methyl sulfate methylation of the benzaldehyde adduct of DOM had a mp of 125-126 °C and presented a different infra-red spectrum. It was, following recrystallization from ethyl acetate, identical to the higher melting form in all respects.

DOSAGE: above 30 mg.

DURATION: 6 - 10 h.

QUALITATIVE COMMENTS: (with 20 mg) "There was a gentle and demanding rise from the one to the three hour point that put me into an extremely open, erotic, and responsive place. I had to find a familiar spot to orient myself, and the kitchen served that need. As the experience went on, it showed more and more of a stimulant response, with tremor, restlessness, and a bit of trouble sleeping. But there was no anorexia! An OK experience."

(with 30 mg) "There is a real physical aspect to this, and I am not completely happy with it. There is diarrhea, and I am restless, and continuously aware of the fact that my body has had an impact from something. The last few hours were spent in talking, and I found myself still awake some 24 hours after the start of the experiment. The mental was not up there to a +++, and yet the physical disruption was all that I might care to weather, and exceeds any mental reward. When I did sleep, my dreams were OK, but not rich. Why go higher?"

EXTENSIONS AND COMMENTARY: This is another example of the N-methyl homologues of the psychedelics. None of them seem to produce stuff of elegance. It is clear that the adding of an N-methyl group onto DOM certainly cuts down the activity by a factor of ten-fold, and even then results in something that is not completely good. Three milligrams of DOM is a winner, but even ten times this, thirty milligrams of N-methyl-DOM, is somewhat fuzzy. In the rabbit hyperthermia studies, this compound was some 25 times less active than DOM, so even animal tests say this is way down there in value. This particular measure suggests that the active level in man might be 75 milligrams. Well, maybe, but I am not at all comfortable in trying it at that level. In fact I do not intend to explore this any further whatsoever, unless there is a compelling reason, and I see no such reason. For the moment, let us leave this one to others, who might be more adventurous but less discriminating.

In browsing through my notes I discovered that I had made another N-substitution product of DOM. Efforts to fuse free-base DOM with the ethyl cyclopropane carboxylate failed, but the reaction between it and the acid chloride in pyridine gave the corresponding amide, with a mp of 156-157 °C from MeOH. Anal. $(C_{16}H_{23}NO_3)$ C,H,N. This reduced smoothly to the corresponding amine, N-cyclopropyl-2,5-dimethoxy-4-methylamphetamine which formed a hydrochloride salt melting at 153-156 °C. I can't remember the reasoning that led to this line of synthesis, but it must not have been too exciting, as I never tasted the stuff.

#12   BIS-TOM;   4-METHYL-2,5-bis-(METHYLTHIO)-AMPHETAMINE

SYNTHESIS: A solution of 9.0 g 2,5-dibromotoluene in 50 mL petroleum ether was magnetically stirred under a He atmosphere. To this there was added 50 mL of a 1.6 M hexane solution of butyllithium, and the exothermic reaction, which produced a granular precipitate, was allowed to stir for 12 h. The mixture was cooled to 0 °C and there was then added 7.5 g dimethyldisulfide. There was a heavy precipitate formed, which tended to become lighter as the addition of the disulfide neared completion. After 20 min additional stirring, the reaction mixture was poured into H_2O that contained some HCl. The phases were separated and the aqueous phase extracted with 50 mL Et_2O. The organic phase and extract were combined, washed with dilute NaOH, and then with H_2O. After drying over anhydrous K_2CO_3, the solvent was removed under vacuum and the residue distilled to give a fraction that boiled at 75-85 °C at 0.3 mm/Hg and weighed 5.3 g. This was about 80% pure 2,5-bis-(methylthio)toluene, with the remainder appearing to be the monothiomethyl analogues. A completely pure product was best obtained by a different, but considerably longer, procedure. This is given here only in outline. The phenolic OH group of 3-methyl-4-(methylthio)phenol was converted to an SH group by the thermal rearrangement of the N,N-dimethylthioncarbamate. The impure thiophenol was liberated from the product N,N-dimethylthiolcarbamate with NaOH treatment. The separation of the phenol/thiophenol mixture was achieved by a H_2O_2 oxidation to produce the intermediate 3-methyl-4-methyl-thiophenyldisulfide. This was isolated as a white crystalline solid from MeOH, with a mp of 78-79 °C. Anal. $(C_{16}H_{18}S_4)$ C,H. It was reduced with zinc in acetic acid, and the resulting thiophenol (a water-white liquid which was both spectroscopically and microanalytically correct) was methylated with methyl iodide and KOH in MeOH to give the desired product, 2,5-bis-(methylthio)toluene, free of any contaminating mono-sulfur analogues.

A solution of 3.9 g of 2,5-bis-(methylthio)toluene in 20 mL acetic acid was treated with a crystal of iodine followed by the addition of 3.5 g elemental bromine. This mixture was heated on the steam bath for 1 h, which largely discharged the color and produced a copious evolution of HBr. Cooling in an ice bath produced solids that were removed by filtration. Recrystallization from IPA gave 1.9 g of 2,5-bis-(methylthio)-4-bromotoluene as a white crystalline solid with a mp of 133-134 °C. Anal. $(C_9H_{11}BrS_2)$ C,H. An alternate synthesis of this intermediate was achieved from 1,4-dibromobenzene which was converted to the 1,4-bis-(methylthio)benzene (white crystals with a mp of 83.5-84.5 °C) with sodium methylmercaptide in hexamethylphosphoramide. This was dibrominated to 2,5-dibromo-1,4-bis-(methylthio)benzene in acetic acid (white platelets from hexane melting at 195-199 °C). This, in Et_2O solution, reacted with BuLi to replace one of the bromine atoms with lithium, and subsequent treatment with methyl iodide gave 2,5-bis-(methylthio)-4-bromotoluene as an off-white solid identical to the above material (by TLC and IR) but with a broader mp range.

A solution of 2.4 g 2,5-bis-(methylthio)-4-bromotoluene in 100 mL anhydrous Et_2O, stirred magnetically and under a He atmosphere, was treated with 10 mL of a 1.6 M solution of butyllithium in hexane. After stirring for 10 min there was added 2.5 mL N-methylformanilide which led to an exothermic reaction. After another 10 min stirring, the reaction mixture was added to 100 mL dilute HCl, the phases were separated, and the aqueous phase extracted with 2x50 mL Et_2O. The combined organic phase and extracts were dried over anhydrous K_2CO_3, and the solvent removed under vacuum. The partially solid residue was distilled at 140-150 °C at 0.2 mm/Hg to give a crystalline fraction that, after recrystallization from 15 mL boiling IPA gave 2,5-bis-(methylthio)-4-methylbenzaldehyde as a yellow-brown solid which weighed 1.1 g and had a mp of 107-109 °C. An analytical sample from MeOH melted at 110-111 °C with an excellent IR and NMR. Anal. ($C_{10}H_{12}OS_2$) C,H. An alternate synthesis of this aldehyde employs the 2,5-bis-(methylthio)toluene described above. A CH_2Cl_2 solution of this substituted toluene containing dichloromethyl methyl ether was treated with anhydrous $AlCl_3$, and the usual workup gave a distilled fraction that spontaneously crystallized to the desired aldehyde but in an overall yield of only 11% of theory.

To a solution of 0.5 g 2,5-bis-(methylthio)-4-methylbenzaldehyde in 15 mL nitroethane there was added 0.15 g anhydrous ammonium acetate and the mixture was heated on the steam bath for 1 h. The excess solvent was removed under vacuum and the residue was dissolved in 10 mL boiling MeOH. This solution was decanted from a little insoluble residue, and allowed to cool to ice bath temperature yielding, after filtering and drying to constant weight, 0.55 g of 1-[2,5-bis-(thiomethyl)-4-methylphenyl]-2-nitropropene as pumpkin-colored crystals with a mp of 90-91 °C. This was not improved by recrystallization from EtOH. Anal. ($C_{12}H_{15}NO_2S_2$) C,H.

A cooled, stirred solution of 0.5 g LAH in 40 mL THF was put under an inert atmosphere, cooled to 0 °C with an external ice bath, and treated with 0.42 mL 100% H_2SO_4, added dropwise. A solution of 0.5 g 1-[2,5-bis-(thiomethyl)-4-methylphenyl]-2-nitropropene in 20 mL anhydrous THF was added over the course of 5 min, and the reaction mixture held at reflux for 30 min on the steam bath. After cooling again to ice temperature, the excess hydride was destroyed by the addition of IPA and the inorganics were converted to a loose, white filterable form by the addition of 1.5 mL 5% NaOH. These solids were removed by filtration and the filter cake was washed with 2x50 mL IPA. The combined filtrate and washings were stripped of solvent under vacuum to give a residue that was a flocculant solid. This was suspended in dilute H_2SO_4 and extracted with 2x50 mL CH_2Cl_2, and the combined organics extracted with 2x50 mL dilute H_3PO_4. The aqueous extracts were made basic, and the product removed by extraction with 2x75 mL CH_2Cl_2. After removal of the solvent under vacuum, the residue was distilled at 126-142 °C at 0.2 mm/Hg to give 0.2 g of product which crystallized in the receiver. This was dissolved in 1.5 mL hot IPA, neutralized with 4 drops of concentrated HCl, and diluted with 3 mL anhydrous Et_2O to give, after filtering and air drying, 0.2 g. of 2,5-bis-(methylthio)-4-methylamphetamine hydrochloride (BIS-TOM) as white crystals with a mp of 228-229 °C. Anal. ($C_{12}H_{20}ClNS_2$) C,H.

DOSAGE: greater than 160 mg.

DURATION: unknown.

QUALITATIVE COMMENTS: (with 160 mg) "I was vaguely aware of something in the latter part of the afternoon. A suggestion of darting, physically (when going to sleep), but nothing at the mental level. This is as high as I will go."

EXTENSIONS AND COMMENTARY: It is reasonable, in retrospect, to accept that BIS-TOM is not an active compound. The replacement of the 2-position oxygen of DOM with a sulfur atom (to give 2-TOM) dropped the potency by a factor of 15x, and the replacement of the 5-position oxygen with a sulfur atom (to give 5-TOM) dropped the potency by a factor of about 10x. It would be a logical calculation that the replacement of both oxygen atoms with sulfur might drop the potency by a factor of 150x. So, with DOM being active at maybe 5 milligrams, a logical prediction of the active level of BIS-TOM would be 750 milligrams. And maybe this would be the right level, but with the hints of neurological disturbance that seemed to be there at 160 mg, there was no desire to go up by a factor of five again. The rewards would simply not be worth the risks.

The 2-carbon analogue, 2C-BIS-TOM, was prepared from the intermediate aldehyde above, first by reaction with nitromethane to give the nitrostyrene as tomato-colored crystals from EtOAc, mp 145-146 °C. Anal. ($C_{11}H_{13}NO_2S_2$) C,H. This was reduced with AH to give 2,5-bis-(methylthio)-4-methylphenethylamine hydrochloride as ivory-colored crystals with a mp of 273-277 °C.

Although there are many interesting psychedelic drugs with sulfur atoms in them (the TOM's, the TOET's, the ALEPH's and all of the 2C-T's), there just aren't many that contain two sulfur atoms. BIS-TOM bombed out, and 2C-BIS-TOM remains untried, but will probably also fail, as the phenethylamines are rarely more potent than the corresponding amphetamines. This leaves 2C-T-14 as the remaining hope, and its synthesis is still underway.

#13   BOB;   ß-METHOXY-2C-B;   4-BROMO-2,5-ß-TRIMETHOXY-PHENETHYLAMINE

SYNTHESIS: To a vigorously stirred suspension of 2.1 g 4-bromo-2,5-dimethoxy-ß-nitrostyrene [from 4-bromo-2,5-dimethoxybenzaldehyde and nitromethane in acetic acid with ammonium acetate as a catalyst, mp 157-158 °C, anal. ($C_{10}H_{10}BrNO_4$) C,H] in 20 mL anhydrous MeOH, there was added a solution of sodium methoxide in MeOH (generated from 0.5 g metallic sodium in 20 mL anhydrous MeOH). After a few min there was added 10 mL acetic acid (no solids formed) followed by the slow addition of 50 mL of H_2O. A cream-colored solid was produced, which was removed by filtration and washed well with H_2O. After air drying the product, 1-(4-bromo-2,5-dimethoxyphenyl)-1-methoxy-2-nitroethane, weighed 2.0 g. An analytical sample from MeOH was off-white in color and had a mp of 119-120 °C. Anal. ($C_{11}H_{14}BrNO_5$) C,H.

A solution of LAH (15 mL of 1 M solution in THF) was diluted with an equal volume of anhydrous THF, and cooled (under He) to 0 °C with an external ice bath. With good stirring there was added 0.38 mL 100% H_2SO_4 dropwise, to minimize charring. This was followed by the addition of 1.0 g 1-(4-bromo-2,5-dimethoxyphenyl)-1-methoxy-2-nitroethane as a solid over the course of 5 min. After an hour of stirring at 0 °C, the temperature was brought up to a gentle reflux on the steam bath for 30 min. There was no vigorous exothermic reaction seen, unlike that with the syntheses of BOD, BOH and BOM. The reaction mixture was cooled again to 0 °C, and the excess hydride was destroyed by the cautious addition of IPA. This was followed by suffecient dilute aqueous NaOH to give a white granular character to the oxides, and to assure that the reaction mixture was basic. The reaction mixture was filtered, and the filter cake washed first with THF followed by IPA. The combined filtrate and washings were stripped of solvent under vacuum and dissolved in dilute H_2SO_4, with the apparent generation of yellow solids. This was washed with 2x50 mL CH_2Cl_2, and the aqueous phase made basic with NaOH. This was extracted with 2x50 mL CH_2Cl_2, and the pooled extracts were stripped of solvent under vacuum. The residue was distilled at 130-150 °C at 0.2 mm/Hg to give 0.2 g of product as a clear white oil. This fraction was dissolved in 10 mL IPA, and neutralized with 4 drops concentrated HCl. The addition of 30 mL anhydrous Et_2O allowed the formation of 4-bromo-2,5,ß-trimethoxyphenethylamine hydrochloride (BOB) as a fine white crystalline product. This was removed by filtration, washed with Et_2O, and air dried. There was obtained 0.1 g white crystals with a mp of 187-188 °C. Anal. ($C_{11}H_{17}BrClNO_3$) C,H.

DOSAGE: 10 - 20 mg.

DURATION: 10 - 20 h.

QUALITATIVE COMMENTS: (with 10 mg) "I don't know if it was me this day, or if it was the chemical, but I got into a granddaddy of a paranoid, sociopathic snit, without feeling and without emotion. I was indifferent to everything. Later on, there was some improvement, with body tingling (good, I'm pretty sure) and a sense of awareness (good, I guess) but I still canceled my evening dinner company. All in all, pretty negative."

(with 10 mg) "I had to get away and into myself, so I weeded in the vegetable garden for almost an hour. Then I lay down in the bedroom, and enjoyed a magnificent vegetable garden, in Southern France, in my mind's eye. An extraordinary zucchini. And the weeds had all been magically pulled. In another couple of hours a neurological over-stimulation became apparent, and I spent the rest of the day defending myself. In the evening, I took 100 milligrams phenobarbital which seemed to smooth things just enough. Too bad. Nice material, otherwise."

(with 15 mg) "The erotic was lustful, but at the critical moment of orgasm, the question of neurological stability became quite apparent. Does one really let go? Everything seemed a bit irritable. The tinnitus was quite bad, but the excitement of the rich altered place I was in was certainly worth it all. Through the rest of the day, I became aware of how tired I was, and how much I wanted to sleep, and yet how scared I was to give myself over to sleep. Could I trust the body to its own devices without me as an overseeing caretaker? Let's risk it. I slept. The next day there was a memory of this turmoil. Clearly the first part of the experience might have been hard to define, but it was quite positive. But the last part makes it not really worth while."

EXTENSIONS AND COMMENTARY: This compound, BOB, is the most potent of the BOX series. And yet, as with all of the members of this family, there are overtones of physical concern, and of some worry as to the integrity of the body. There may well be a separation of activity with the two optical isomers, but there is not a tremendous push to explore this particular family much further. They can't all be winners, I guess. What would be the activities of compounds with a sulfur instead of an oxygen at the beta-oxygen position? What would be the nature of action if there were an alpha-methyl group, making all of these into amphetamine derivatives? Or what about both a sulfur and a methyl group? And what about the isomers that are intrinsic to all of this, the threo- and the erythro- and the "D's" and the "L's"? All this is *terra incognita*, and must someday be looked into. It is chemically simple, and pharmacologically provocative. Someone, somewhere, someday, answer these questions!

#14   BOD;   ß-METHOXY-2C-D;   4-METHYL-2,5,ß-TRIMETHOXYPHENETHYLAMINE

SYNTHESIS: A solution of 39.6 g 1-(2,5-dimethoxy-4-methylphenyl)-2-nitrostyrene (see recipe for 2C-D for its preparation) in 300 mL warm MeOH was prepared. Separately, a solution of 9 g elemental sodium in 150 mL MeOH was also prepared. This sodium methoxide solution was added to the well-stirred nitrostyrene solution, which resulted in a dramatic loss of color. There was then added 75 mL acetic acid, and all was poured into 2 L H_2O. This was extracted with 3x100 mL CH_2Cl_2. The pooled extracts were stripped of solvent, and the 35 g of residue was treated with 5 mL MeOH, allowed to stand for a short while, decanted from some insoluble residue, and the separated clear solution kept at 0 °C overnight. There was the deposition of a yellow crystalline product which, after removal by filtration and air drying, weighed 9.7 g. Recrystallization from 25 mL MeOH gave, after filtering and drying, 8.4 g of canary-yellow crystals of 1-(2,5-dimethoxy-4-methylphenyl)-1-methoxy-2-nitroethane with a mp of 78-79 °C. Evaporation of the mother liquors from the filtration of the first crop yielded 3.8 g of additional product which, upon recrystallization from 11 mL MeOH, provided another 2.7 g with a mp of 77-78 °C. Further workup of the mother liquors yielded only impure starting nitrostyrene.

A solution of LAH (96 mL of 1 M solution in THF) was cooled, under He, to 0 °C with an external ice bath. With good stirring there was added 2.4 mL 100% H_2SO_4 dropwise, to minimize charring. This was followed by the addition of 10.8 g 1-(2,5-dimethoxy-4-methylphenyl)-1-methoxy-2-nitroethane. There was immediate discoloration. After the addition was complete, the reaction mixture was held at reflux on the steam bath for 2 h. After cooling again, the excess hydride was destroyed with 4 mL IPA and the reaction mixture made basic with 15% NaOH. The insoluble inorganic salts were removed by filtration, and the filter cake was washed first with THF, and then with IPA. The bright yellow filtrate and washes were pooled and stripped of solvent under vacuum, yielding 14 g of a yellow oil. This was suspended in 1 L dilute H_2SO_4 to give

an ugly, cloudy, yellow-orange mess. Extraction with 3x75 mL CH_2Cl_2 removed much of the color, and the remaining aqueous phase was made basic with 25% NaOH, and extracted with 3x75 mL CH_2Cl_2. Evaporation of the solvent under vacuum gave 9 g of a pale amber oil which was distilled at 115-130 °C at 0.4 mm/ Hg. The water-white distillate was dissolved in 15 mL IPA, neutralized with concentrated HCl, and then diluted with 70 mL anhydrous Et_2O. After a few min, white crystals formed, and these were removed by filtration and Et_2O washed. When air-dried to constant weight, 4.49 g brilliant white crystals of 4-methyl-2,5,ß-trimethoxyphenethylamine hydrochloride (BOD) with a mp of 171-172 °C with decomposition, were obtained. The mother liquors on standing deposited 0.66 g additional crystals which were impure and were discarded. Anal. $(C_{12}H_{20}ClNO_3)$ C,H.

DOSAGE: 15 - 25 mg.

DURATION: 8 - 16 h.

QUALITATIVE COMMENTS: (with 20 mg) "There were some very pleasant visuals starting at 2-2.5 hours and continuing to 4-5 hours after the beginning of the experiment. Open eye visuals seem to come on after staring at particular areas, such as the living room ceiling or at trees. The surroundings tended to move slightly. There was no flowing of the images at all. When looking at the pine trees, the needles appeared crystal clear and sharply defined, with strong contrasts. Though the mental effect is difficult to define, I am not sure it was all that great. I did become tired of the effect (along with the confusion) after 8 hours, and was quite happy to note that it did taper off in the early evening. I am not particularly sure I would want to try this material again."

(with 20 mg) "For the first three or so hours, the beauty of the experience was marred by a strange discomfort. There was some queasiness, and I felt a sluggishness of mind. Then I began moving in and out of a pleasant place, and finally the discomfort completely dissolved and the experience turned full on. Height of beauty, visual perception. Lights below are amazing. Outside, marvelous sense of Presence. There is not an elation, as often with other materials, but a strong, even powerful sense of goodness, inner strength, solidity."

(with 25 mg) "This was quite quick. The onset of the experience was apparent within a half hour, and we were both at +++ within the hour. Body load minimal. There was very little visual, compared with some materials. Very interesting eyes-closed, but not continually — just now and then an intense vision might flash. Very benign and friendly and pleasant and good-humored feeling. Superb for conversation and conceptualization."

(with 25 mg) "The body load was quite noticeable for everyone. But the general state of mind was excellent; everyone was extremely relaxed and funny. Puns, insults, delightful amusement. Not very much insight work possible. Juices were needed and tolerated well, but no one was particularly hungry. Sleep was difficult for most people, not deep and not too refreshing. Excellent material, but body price a bit too much for the mental effects. Pleasant, and I wouldn't hesitate to take it again, but nothing very memorable except the tremendous humor and laughter, which was truly delightful."

EXTENSIONS AND COMMENTARY: This compound, BOD, was the first exploratory member of a new family of phenethylamines. This family is called the BOX series because an oxygen atom has been put on the benzylic carbon (the "benzyl-oxy" or "BO") of each of several well studied drugs with recognized substituent patterns on the aromatic ring. The "X" would be "D," as used here with BOD, making reference to 2C-D, it would be a "B" in BOB making reference to 2C-B, etc. Actually the original thought was to make the "O" into an "OM" for methoxy, as this would allow more versatility in the naming of things such as ethoxys ("OE") or hydroxys ("OH"), but the methoxylated 2C-B analogue would have come out as BOMB, so the idea was dropped.

Actually, the concept of naming of drugs with some acronym that is pronounceable has led into some interesting byways. Some examples have been unintended. I have heard DOM pronounced "dome" and DOET pronounced as "do it." And elsewhere I have mentioned the embarrassing occasions where the TOM and TOET families were pronounced "the toms and twats." Some examples have had names that have been contractions of popular names, such as XTC for ecstasy. And there are instances where a name might be proposed simply to irritate the newspaper people. An early street suggestion for PCP was FUK, and a current name for free-base methamphetamine is SNOT. And marijuana is fondly called SHIT by its aficionados. The final "A" on government groups such as the CIA or the DEA or the FDA is strongly reminscent of the final "A" which stands for amphetamine in things such as TMA and MDMA. Might there someday be a drug such as 4-cyclopropylmethyl-N-isopropylamphetamine (CIA), or 3,5-dimethoxy-4-

ethylamphetamine (DEA)? It has just occurred to me that there is already a 4-fluoro-2,5-dimethoxyamphetamine (FDA), but I have already named it DOF. If all drugs were known only by publicly embarrassing names, there might be less publicity given them by the press.

Back to the commentary on BOD. The rationale for this inclusion of a beta-oxygen atom into the structure of a phenethylamine is based directly on the chemistry that occurs naturally in the brain. The phenethylamine neurotransmitter, dopamine, is converted both in the brain and in the body to the equally important transmitter norepinephrine by just this sort of transformation. There is the enzymatic addition of an oxygen atom to the "benzylic" position of dopamine. And identical chemistry goes on with tyramine in a number of plants and animals, with a similar addition of oxygen to form octopamine, so-named for its discovered presence in the salivary glands of *Octopus vulgaris*. In the first explorations in the BOX series, this oxygen was intentionally blocked with a methyl group, to ease its entry into the brain, and increase the possibilities of its being active as a psychedelic. As mentioned above, the "D" in BOD follows from its ring orientation pattern being the same as that of 2C-D (and this, originally from the mimicking of the pattern of DOM). All of these D- compounds have the 2,5-dimethoxy-4-methyl ring-substitution pattern.

An interesting complication is also part of this structure package. The added methoxy group (or hydroxy group, see recipe for BOHD) also adds a new asymmetric center, allowing for the eventual separation of the material into two optical isomers. And at such time as the corresponding amphetamine homologues might be made and studied, the presence of yet another chiral center (under the alpha-methyl group) will demand that there be actually two racemic compounds synthesized, and a total of four isomers to contend with, if really careful and thorough work is to be done.

A parallel chemistry to all of this follows the addition of sodium ethoxide (rather than sodium methoxide) to the nitrostyrene. The final product, then, is the ethoxy homologue 2,5-dimethoxy-ß-ethoxy-4-methylphenethylamine, or BOED. It is down in human potency by a factor of three, with a normal dosage being 70-75 milligrams. It has a ten hour duration, and is both anorexic and diuretic. There have been no visual effects or insights reported, but rather simply a highly intoxicated state.

Two synonyms, two definitions, and an expression of admiration. The word norepinephrine is synonymous with noradrenalin, and the word epinephrine is synonymous with adrenalin. The distinctions are that the first in each case is American and the second British. And the term "chiral" indicates a potential asymmetry in a molecule that would allow eventual separation into two optical isomers. The term "racemic" refers to a mixture of these two isomers which has not yet been separated into the individual components. A racemic mixture is called a racemate and, from the point of view of the human animal (which is completely asymmetric), must be considered as a mixture of two structurally identical but optically mirror-image isomers, which can be potentially separated and which will certainly have different pharmacologies. And the admiration? This is directed to the explorer who ventured close enough to an octopus to locate its salivary glands and to discover a phenethylamine there!

#15   BOH;   ß-METHOXY-3,4-METHYLENEDIOXY-PHENETHYLAMINE

SYNTHESIS: To a solution of 30 g piperonal in 100 mL acetic acid there was added 20 mL nitromethane and 10 mL cyclohexylamine. After heating on the steam bath for 1.5 h, the reaction mixture started to crystallize. The mixture was cooled in an ice bath, and the heavy mass of deposited crystals removed by filtration and washed with 20 mL acetic acid. All was supended in 100 mL warm MeOH, cooled again, and filtered to give 24.5 g of 3,4-methylenedioxy-ß-nitrostyrene as canary-yellow crystals, with a mp of 158-160 °C. Reduction of this compound with LAH gives rise to MDPEA, which is a separate entry with a recipe of its own.

To a vigorously stirred suspension of 20 g 3,4-methylenedioxy-ß-nitro - styrene in 100 mL anhydrous MeOH there was added a freshly prepared solution of 5.5 g elemental sodium in 100 mL MeOH. The nitrostyrene goes into solution over the course of 5 min. There was then added, first, 50 ml acetic acid with the stirring continued for an additional 1 min. There was then added 300 mL H_2O. An oil separated and was extracted into 200 mL CH_2Cl_2. The organic extract was washed with 500 mL dilute aqueous $NaHCO_3$, followed by 500 mL H_2O. Removal of the solvent gave a residue that was distilled at 128-145 °C at 0.4 mm/Hg, providing 16.6 g of a yellow viscous liquid which slowly crystallized. An analytical sample was recrystallized from four volumes of MeOH to give 1-methoxy-1-(3,4-methylenedioxyphenyl)-2-nitroethane as bright yellow crystals with a mp of 58-59 °C. Anal. ($C_{10}H_{11}NO_5$) C,H.

A solution of LAH (100 mL of 1 M solution in THF) was cooled, under He, to 0 °C with an external ice bath. With good stirring there was added 2.5 mL 100% H_2SO_4 dropwise, to minimize charring. This was followed by the addition of 12 g 1-methoxy-1-(3,4-methylenedioxyphenyl)-2-nitroethane over the course of 2 min. There was an immediate loss of color. After a few minutes further stirring, the temperature was brought up to a reflux with a heating mantle. There was a gentle gas evolution for a few min, followed by an exothermic reaction that exceeded the capacity of the condenser. Once the reaction had subsided, the unreacted hydride was destroyed with a minimum of IPA, and 15% NaOH was added to convert the inorganics to a loose white filterable mass. The reaction mixture was filtered, and the filter cake washed thoroughly with THF. The combined filtrate and washes were stripped of solvent under vacuum, providing an orange oil. This was dissolved in 400 mL dilute H_2SO_4, which was washed with 3x75 mL CH_2Cl_2. After making the aqueous phase basic, it was extracted with 2x100 mL CH_2Cl_2. The pooled extracts were stripped of solvent under vacuum, and the residue distilled at 103-112 °C at 0.5 mm/Hg. There was obtained 2.5 g of a colorless, viscous oil which was dissolved in 25 mL IPA, neutralized with 45 drops of concentrated HCl, and finally diluted with 30 mL anhydrous Et_2O. There was thus formed ß-methoxy-3,4-methylenedioxyphenethylamine hydrochloride (BOH) as a fine white crystalline product. The mp was 105-106.5 °C, with bubbling and darkening. The mp properties proved to be inconsistent, as the salt was a hydrate. Recrystallization from CH_3CN, or simply heating to 100 °C in toluene, converted the salt to an anhydrous form, with mp of 152-153 °C. Anal. ($C_{10}H_{14}ClNO_3$) C,H.

DOSAGE: 80 - 120 mg.

DURATION: 6 - 8 h.

QUALITATIVE COMMENTS: (with 90 mg) "Distinct body awareness in an hour. The threshold is mostly physical. Faint sense of inside warmth, skin prickling, cold feet, loose bowels, anorexia. By the fifth hour, I was on the downslope, and in retrospect I found it good humored but not insightful."

(with 100 mg) "There was a vague nausea, and a chilling of the feet. It reached a real plus two, with dilated pupils and quite a thirst. How can one describe the state? There were no visuals, and I was not even stoned. I was just very turned on. And I was completely back to baseline by hour number six."

EXTENSIONS AND COMMENTARY: There are several reports of a nice, mild mood enhancement in the 20-40 milligram dosage area, but searches for psyche-delic effects at higher levels gave a strange mix of some sort of an altered state along with bodily discomfort. The BOH name for this member of the BOX family follows the convention discussed in the BOD recipe — with "H" for homopiperonylamine, the simplest of the muni-metro family, q.v. The demethylated homologue of BOH is BOHH, and is the methylenedioxy analogue of norepinephrine. It might well hydrolytically open up in the body to provide this neurotransmitter, and serve as some sort of transmitter in its own right. It is discussed under DME.

Maybe there is something to the concept that when you imitate a neuro-transmitter too closely, you get a hybrid *gemisch* of activity. The term "pro-drug" is used to identify a compound that may not be intrinsically active, but one which metabolizes in the body to provide an active drug. I feel the term should have been pre-drug, but pro-drug was the word that caught on. BOH may well act in the body as a pro-drug to norepinephrine, but with the temporary blocking of the polar functions with ether groups, it can gain access to the brain. And once there, it can be stripped of these shields and play a direct neurological role. I uncovered a very similar analogy in the tryptamine world some years ago. Just as norepinephrine is a neurotransmitter, so is serotonin. And I found that by putting an O-ether on the indolic phenol (to hide its polarity) and an alpha-methyl group next to the primary amine (to protect it from metabolic deaminase), it became an extremely potent, and most complex, psychedelic. This was the compound alpha,O-dimethylserotonin, or α,O-DMS. There is an uncanny analogy between this tryptamine and the phenethylamine BOH.

Somehow the quiet voice deep inside me says, don't use too much, too quickly. Maybe one of the optical isomers is the body thing, and the other isomer is the mind thing. So far, only the racemic mixture has been tasted, to the best of my knowledge.

#16   BOHD;   2,5-DIMETHOXY-ß-HYDROXY-4-METHYL-PHENETHYLAMINE

SYNTHESIS: A solution of 0.4 g 1-(2,5-dimethoxy-4-methylphenyl)-1-methoxy-2-nitroethane (see preparation in the recipe for BOD) in 3.0 mL acetic acid was heated to 100 °C on a steam bath. There was added 1.0 g powdered zinc, followed by additional acetic acid as needed to maintain smooth stirring. After 0.5 h there was added 1.0 mL concentrated HCl and, following an additional few minutes heating, the reaction mixture was poured into 300 mL H_2O. After washing the aqueous phase with 3x75 mL CH_2Cl_2, the mixture was made basic with 25% NaOH, and extracted with 3x50 mL CH_2Cl_2. Removal of the solvent and distillation of the residue at 130-140 °C 0.25 mm/Hg gave an oil that, on dissolving in IPA, neutralization with concentrated HCl, and the addition of anhydrous Et_2O, gave beautiful white crystals of 2,5-dimethoxy-ß-hydroxy-4-methylphenethylamine hydrochloride (BOHD). The yield was 0.2 g, and the mp was 180-181 °C. The infrared spectrum was that of an amine salt with a strong OH group present. Anal. ($C_{11}H_{18}ClNO_3$) C,H.

DOSAGE: greater than 50 mg.

DURATION: unknown.

QUALITATIVE COMMENTS: (with 50 mg) "At about the two hour point, there was a precipitous drop of blood pressure (from 120/72 to 84/68) although the pulse stayed steady at 60. This trend had been apparent in earlier trials, and was being watched carefully. No further tests are planned."

EXTENSIONS AND COMMENTARY: The usual method of making beta-ethanolamine such as this is through the reduction of the cyanohydrin of the corresponding benzaldehyde and, in fact, that method is described in the recipe for DME. This above procedure was actually part of an exploration of different agents that might be used in the reduction of the intermediate nitroalkane. This product was the unexpected result of trying zinc.

Why the potent cardiovascular effect seen by this compound? There are a couple of points that might argue for some adrenolytic toxicity. This material is a beta-ethanolamine and, with maybe one or two exceptions, clinically used beta-receptor blockers are beta-ethanolamines. In fact, a few of these so-called beta-blockers actually have two methoxy groups on the aromatic rings, also a property of BOHD. The antidiabetic drug Butaxamine (BW 64-9 in the code of Burroughs Wellcome) is identical to BOHD except that the 4-methyl group is on the alpha-carbon instead, and there is a tertiary butyl group on the nitrogen atom. Another point involves the proximity of the beta-hydroxy group and the methoxyl oxygen atom in the 2-position of the ring. There is going to be a strong hydrogen-bonding with this orientation, with the formation of a stable six-membered ring. This might help obscure the hydrophilic nature of the free hydroxyl group and allow the compound to pass into the brain easily. If this group is masked by an easily removed group such as an acetate ester, one gets the compound beta-acetoxy-3,4-dimethoxy-4-methylphenethylamine (BOAD) which is similar to BOHD as a hypotensive.

The code-naming procedure used here (and elsewhere here in Book II) is: (1) to use "BO" as the alert to there being an oxygen on the benzyl carbon of a phenethylamine (it is a benzyl alcohol); (2) if there is just one more letter (a third and last letter) it will identify the 2C-X parent from which it has been derived ["B" comes from 2C-B, "D" comes from 2C-D, "H" comes from homopiperonylamine (MDPEA) rather than from 2C-H, "M" comes from mescaline, and in every case the beta-substituent is a methoxy group]; and (3) if there are four letters, then the fourth letter is as above, and the third letter (the next to last letter) is the substituent on that benzylic oxygen. With a three letter code, the substituent is a methyl group, an "H" for a third letter of four makes it a hydroxyl group, and an "A" for the third letter is an acetyl group, and an "E" is for an ethyl group. A similar sort of cryptographic music was composed by Du Pont in their three-number codes for the Freons. The first number was one less than the number of carbons in the molecule, the second number was one more than the number of hydrogens in the molecule, the third number was the exact number of fluorines in the molecule, and the rest of the bonds were filled with chlorines, Thus Freon 11 (really Freon 011) was trichlorofluoro-methane and Freon 116 was hexafluoroethane.

Complex, yes. But both systems are completely straightforward, and flexible for future creations. A few additional examples of similar beta-ethanolamines are scattered throughout Book II and they have, in general, proved to be uninterest-ing, at least as potential psychedelic compounds.

#17   BOM;   ß-METHOXYMESCALINE;   3,4,5,ß-TETRA-
METHOXYPHENETHYLAMINE

SYNTHESIS: To a vigorously stirred suspension of 9.0 g ß-nitro-3,4,5-
trimethoxystyrene (see under the recipe for M for the preparation of this intermediate) in 50 mL anhydrous MeOH there was added a solution obtained from the
addition of 2.0 g metallic sodium to 50 mL anhydrous MeOH. The bright orange
color faded to a light cream as the nitrostyrene went into solution. After 3 min there
was added 30 mL acetic acid, which produced white solids, and this was followed
by further dilution with 150 mL H_2O. The formed solids were removed by filtration,
washed well with H_2O, and recrystallized from 150 mL boiling MeOH. After
removal of the product by filtration and air drying to constant weight, there was
obtained 6.9 g of 1-methoxy-2-nitro-1-(3,4,5-
trimethoxyphenyl)ethane as fine, cream-colored
crystals. The mp was 143-144 °C, and the Rf by
TLC (silica-gel plates and CH_2Cl_2 as moving
phase) was identical to that of the starting aldehyde. Anal. ($C_{12}H_{17}NO_6$) C,H.

A solution of LAH (50 mL of 1 M solution in THF) was cooled, under He,
to 0 °C with an external ice bath. With good stirring there was added 1.25 mL 100%
H_2SO_4 dropwise, to minimize charring. This was followed by the addition of 6 g of
solid 1-methoxy-2-nitro-1-(3,4,5-trimethoxyphenyl)ethane over the course of 2
min. There was some gas evolution. After 5 min additional stirring, the temperature
was brought up to a reflux with a heating mantle. There was a gentle gas evolution
for a few minutes, followed by an exothermic reaction with vigorous gas evolution.
Once everything had settled down, the reaction mixture was held at reflux temperature for an additional 2 h. The excess hydride was destroyed by the addition of IPA
and 15% NaOH was added to convert the inorganic salts to a loose white filterable
mass. The reaction mixture was filtered, and the filter cake washed thoroughly with
THF. The combined filtrate and washes were stripped of solvent under vacuum
which provided a red-brown liquid. This was dissolved in dilute H_2SO_4 and washed
with 3x75 mL CH_2Cl_2. After making the aqueous phase basic with NaOH, it was
extracted with 2x100 mL CH_2Cl_2. The pooled extracts were stripped of solvent
under vacuum, and the colorless residue distilled at 120-150 °C at 0.3 mm/Hg.
There was obtained 2.8 g of a colorless oil which was dissolved in 30 mL IPA and
neutralized with concentrated HCl, allowing the spontaneous formation of the
hydrochloride salt. This was diluted with 75 mL anhydrous Et_2O, yielding 2.8 g
3,4,5,ß-tetramethoxyphenethylamine hydrochloride (BOM) as a white crystalline
product. This had a mp of 198.5-199.5 °C. Anal. ($C_{12}H_{20}ClNO_4$) C,H.

DOSAGE: greater than 200 mg.

DURATION: unknown.

EXTENSIONS AND COMMENTARY: There are some indicators of central activity with assays involving both the 120 milligram and the 180 milligram levels, but nothing that can be rated as over a plus one. It can be seen with the two active members of the BOX series (BOD and BOB) that the potency is about equal to, or a little more (up to a factor of maybe x2), than the analogue without the methoxyl group on the aliphatic chain. If this formula were to hold in the relationship between mescaline and BOM, the active level might well be in the 200-400 milligram range. But at the moment, it remains unknown.

Again, the name of the compound (BOM) is from the "BO-" prefix of this family (from benzyl + oxy), plus the "M" of mescaline (which has provided the ring substitution pattern).

#18   4-BR-3,5-DMA;   3,5-DIMETHOXY-4-BROMOAMPHETAMINE

SYNTHESIS: The starting material 3,5-dimethoxy-4-bromobenzoic acid (made from the commercially available resorcinol by the action of methyl sulfate) was a white crystalline solid from aqueous EtOH with a mp of 248-250 °C. Reaction with thionyl chloride produced 3,5-dimethoxy-4-bromobenzoyl chloride which was used as the crude solid product, mp 124-128 °C. This was reduced with tri-O-(t)-butoxy lithium aluminum hydride to produce 3,5-dimethoxy-4-bromobenzaldehyde which was recrystallized from aqueous MeOH and had a mp of 112-114 °C. Anal. ($C_9H_9BrO_3$) C,H. This aldehyde, with nitroethane and anhydrous ammonium acetate in acetic acid, was converted to the nitrostyrene 1-(3,5-dimethoxy-4-bromophenyl)-2-nitropropene, with a mp of 121-121.5 °C. Anal. ($C_{11}H_{12}BrNO_4$) C,H,N. This was reduced at low temperature with just one equivalent of LAH, to minimize reductive removal of the bromine atom. The product 3,5-dimethoxy-4-bromoamphetamine hydrochloride (4-BR-3,5-DMA) was isolated in a 37% yield and had a mp of 221-222 °C. Anal. ($C_{11}H_{17}BrClNO_2$) C,H,N.

DOSAGE: 4 - 10 mg.

DURATION: 8 - 12 h.

QUALITATIVE COMMENTS: (with 3 mg) "This is certainly no placebo. At about 2 hours I felt some analgesia and numbing in my extremities, but if there were any sensory distortions, they were barely perceptible."

(with 6 mg) "There is a very shallow threshold, no more."

(with 10 mg) "I can certainly confirm the indications of anesthesia that were hinted at. It was for me central in nature, however. I could (this at three hours) pierce a skin pinch on my left arm with no bother except for the emerging of the needle due to skin resistance. There was little bleeding. And multiple needle prickings into the thumb abductor were not felt. A quick plunge of the tip of my little finger into boiling water elicited reflex response, but no residual pain. Judgment was OK, so I stayed out of physical trouble, luckily! The perhaps ++ was dropping in the fourth or fifth hour, and by the tenth hour there were few effects still noted, except for some teeth-rubbiness and a burning irritation at the pin-prick area, so feeling is back. No sleep problems at just past midnight."

EXTENSIONS AND COMMENTARY: Here is a complex and, at the moment, totally undefined drug. There were two independent reports of analgesia, yet a thorough screen in experimental animals, conducted by a major pharmaceutical house, failed to confirm any of it. A ++ report does not necessarily reflect a psychedelic effect, since this quantitative measure of the level of activity represents the extent of impairment of function, regardless of the nature of the drug producing it. In other words, if you were experiencing the effects of a drug that would in your judgment interfere with safe and good driving, this would be a ++ whether your performance was being limited by a psychedelic, a stimulant, a hypnotic or a narcotic. None of the quantitative reports ever mentioned any sensory distortion (analgesia is a loss, not a distortion) or visual effect. Perhaps 4-BR-3,5-DMA showed its ++ as a narcotic. But then, the rats had said no.

#19   2-BR-4,5-MDA;   6-BR-MDA;   2-BROMO-4,5-METHYLENEDIOXYAMPHETAMINE

SYNTHESIS: A solution of 3,4-methylenedioxyamphetamine (MDA) in acetic acid was treated with elemental bromine, generating the hydrobromide salt of 2-bromo-4,5-methylenedioxyamphetamine in a yield of 61% of theory. The mp was 221-222 °C. Anal. $(C_{10}H_{13}Br_2NO_2)$ C,H,Br.

DOSAGE: 350 mg.

DURATION: unknown.

EXTENSIONS AND COMMENTARY: Both the synthetic and the pharmacological details for this compound are sparse. There has been only a single report of the human activity of this drug in the literature, and the statement has been offered that the effects are amphetamine-like. No other qualitative comments have been made available, and neither I nor anyone in my circle has tried it, personally. Someday, perhaps. But at that high level, perhaps not.

#20   2C-B;   4-BROMO-2,5-DIMETHOXYPHENETHYLAMINE

SYNTHESIS: A solution of 100 g of 2,5-dimethoxybenzaldehyde in 220 g nitromethane was treated with 10 g anhydrous ammonium acetate, and heated on a steam bath for 2.5 h with occasional swirling. The deep-red reaction mixture was stripped of the excess nitromethane under vacuum, and the residue crystallized spontaneously. This crude nitrostyrene was purified by grinding under IPA, filtering, and air-drying, to yield 85 g of 2,5-dimethoxy-ß-nitrostyrene as a yellow-orange product of adequate purity for the next step. Further purification can be achieved by recrystallization from boiling IPA.

In a round-bottomed 2 L flask equipped with a magnetic stirrer and placed under an inert atmosphere, there was added 750 mL anhydrous THF, containing 30 g LAH. There was then added, in THF solution, 60 g 2,5-dimethoxy-ß-nitrostyrene. The final solution was a dirty yellow-brown color, and it was kept at reflux temperature for 24 h. After cooling, the excess hydride was destroyed by the dropwise addition of IPA. Then 30 mL 15% NaOH was added to convert the inorganic solids to a filterable mass. The reaction mixture was filtered and the filter cake washed first with THF and then with MeOH. The combined mother liquors and washings were freed of solvent under vacuum and the residue suspended in 1.5 L H_2O. This was acidified with HCl, washed with with 3x100 mL CH_2Cl_2, made strongly basic with 25% NaOH, and reextracted with 4x100 mL CH_2Cl_2. The pooled extracts were stripped of solvent under vacuum, yielding 26 g of oily residue, which was distilled at 120-130 °C at 0.5 mm/Hg to give 21 g of a white oil, 2,5-dimethoxy-phenethylamine (2C-H) which picks up carbon dioxide from the air very quickly.

To a well-stirred solution of 24.8 g 2,5-dimethoxyphenethylamine in 40 mL glacial acetic acid, there was added 22 g elemental bromine dissolved in 40 mL acetic acid. After a couple of min, there was the formation of solids and the simultaneous evolution of considerable heat. The reaction mixture was allowed to return to room temperature, filtered, and the solids washed sparingly with cold acetic acid. This was the hydrobromide salt. There are many complicated salt forms, both polymorphs and hydrates, that can make the isolation and characterization of 2C-B treacherous. The happiest route is to form the insoluble hydrochloride salt by way of the free base. The entire mass of acetic acid-wet salt was dissolved in warm H_2O, made basic to at least pH 11 with 25% NaOH, and extracted with 3x100 mL CH_2Cl_2. Removal of the solvent gave 33.7 g of residue which was distilled at 115-130 °C at 0.4 mm/Hg. The white oil, 27.6 g, was dissolved in 50 mL H_2O containing 7.0 g acetic acid. This clear solution was vigorous stirred, and treated with 20 mL concentrated HCl. There was an immediate formation of the anhydrous salt of 2,5-dimethoxy-4-bromophenethylamine hydrochloride (2C-B). This mass of crystals was removed by filtration (it can be loosened considerably by the addition of another 60 mL H_2O), washed with a little H_2O, and then with several 50 mL portions of Et_2O. When completely air-dry, there was obtained 31.05 g of fine white needles, with a mp of 237-239 °C with decomposition. When there is too much H_2O present at the time of adding the final concentrated HCl, a hydrated form of 2C-B is obtained. The hydrobromide salt melts at 214.5-215 °C. The acetate salt was reported to have a mp of 208-209 °C.

DOSAGE: 12 - 24 mg.

DURATION: 4 - 8 h.

QUALITATIVE COMMENTS: (with 16 mg) "A day at the Stanford museum. Things were visually rich, yet I felt that I was reasonably inconspicuous. The Rodin sculptures were very personal and not terribly subtle. I saw Escher things in the ceiling design, when I decided to sit in a foyer somewhere and simply pretend to rest. Walking back, the displays seen in the bark of the eucalyptus trees, and the torment and fear (of others? of themselves?) in the faces of those who were walking towards us, were as dramatic as anything I had seen in the art galleries. Our appetites were enormous, and we went to a smorgasbord that evening. A rich experience in every possible way."

(with 20 mg) "The drug effect first became known to me as a shift of colors toward golden and rose tones. Pigments in the room became intensified. Shapes became rounder, more organic. A sensation of lightness and rivulets of warmth began seeping through my body. Bright lights began pulsing and flashing behind my closed lids. I began to perceive waves of energy flowing through all of us in unison. I saw all of us as a gridwork of electrical energy beings, nodes on a bright, pulsating network of light. Then the interior landscape shifted into broader scenes. Daliesque vistas were patterned with eyes of Horus, brocades of geometric design began shifting and changing through radiant patterns of light. It was an artist's paradise — representing virtually the full pantheon of the history of art."

(with 20 mg) "The room was cool, and for the first hour I felt cold and chilled. That was the only mildly unpleasant part. We had been hanging crystals earlier that day, and the visions I had were dominated by prismatic light patterns. It was almost as if I became the light. I saw kaleidoscopic forms — similar to, but less intense than, when on acid — and organic forms like Georgia O'Keefe flowers, blossoming and undulating. My body was flooded with orgasms — practically from just breathing. The lovemaking was phenomenal, passionate, ecstatic, lyric, animal, loving, tender, sublime. The music was voluptuous, almost three-dimensional. Sometimes the sound seemed distorted to me, underwater like. This was especially so for the less good recordings — but I could choose to concentrate on the beauty of the music or the inadequacy of the sound's quality, and mostly chose to concentrate on the beauty."

(with 24 mg) "I am totally into my body. I am aware of every muscle and nerve in my body. The night is extraordinary — moon full. Unbelievably erotic, quiet and exquisite, almost unbearable. I cannot begin to unravel the imagery that imposes itself during the finding of an orgasm. Trying to understand physical/ spiritual merging in nature — ."

EXTENSIONS AND COMMENTARY: Four quotations were chosen arbitrarily from literally hundreds that have worked their ways into the files. The vast majority are positive, ranging from the colorful to the ecstatic. But not all are. There are people who choose not to go into the corporeal but, rather, prefer the out-of-body experience. They express discomfort with 2C-B, and seem to lean more to the Ketamine form of altered state, one which dissociates body from mind.

There have been reports of several overdoses that prove the intrinsic safety of this compound. Prove is used here in the classic British sense; i.e., to challenge. "The proof of the pudding is in the eating," is not a verification of quality, but an inquiry into the quality itself. (The French simplify all this by using two separate verbs for prove.) One overdose was intentional, the other accidental.

(with 64 mg) "I found only mild visual and emotional effects at the 20 milligram dose, so I took the remaining 44 milligrams. I was propelled into something not of my choosing. Everything that was alive was completely fearsome. I could look at a picture of a bush, and it was just that, a picture, and it posed no threat to me. Then my gaze moved to the right, and caught a bush growing outside the window, and I was petrified. A life-form I could not understand, and thus could not control. And I felt that my own life-form was not a bit more controllable." This was from the comments of a physician who assured me that he saw no neurological concerns during this dramatic and frightening experience.

(with 100 mg) "I had weighed correctly. I had simply picked up the wrong vial. And my death was to be a consequence of a totally stupid mistake. I wanted to walk outside, but there was a swimming pool there and I didn't dare fall into it. A person may believe that he has prepared himself for his own death, but when the moment comes, he is completely alone, and totally unprepared. Why now? Why me? Two hours later, I knew that I would live after all, and the experience became really marvelous. But the moment of facing death is a unique experience. In my case, I will some day meet it again, and I fear that I will be no more comfortable with it then than I was just now." This was from the comments of a psychologist who will, without doubt, use psychedelics again in the future, as a probe into the unknown.

Many of the reports that have come in over the years have mentioned the combination of MDMA and 2C-B. The most successful reports have followed a program in which the two drugs are not used at the same time, nor even too closely spaced. It appears that the optimum time for the 2C-B is at, or just before, the final baseline recovery of the MDMA. It is as if the mental and emotional discoveries can be mobilized, and something done about them. This combination has several enthusiastic advocates in the psychotherapy world, and should be the basis of careful research when these materials become legal, and accepted by the medical community.

A generalized spectrum of 2C-B action can be gleaned from the many reports that have been written describing its effects. (1) There is a steep dose response curve. Over the 12 to 24 milligram range, every 2 milligrams can make a profound increase or change of response. Initially, one should go lightly, and increase the dosage in subsequent trials by small increments. A commonly used term for a level that produces a just perceptible effect is "museum level." This is a slightly-over-threshold level which allows public activities (such as viewing paintings in a museum or scenery watching as a passenger in a car) to be entered into without attracting attention. There can be considerable discomfort associated with being in the public eye, with higher doses. (2) The 2C-B experience is one of the shortest of any major psychedelic drug. Wherever you might be, hang on. In an hour or so you will be approaching familiar territory again. (3) If there is anything ever found to be an effective aphrodisiac, it will probably be patterned after 2C-B in structure.

There are two "Tweetios" known that are related to 2C-B. (See recipe #23 for the origin of this phrase.) The 2-EtO- homologue of 2C-B is 4-bromo-2-ethoxy-5-methoxyphenethylamine, or 2CB-2ETO. The unbrominated benzaldehyde (2-ethoxy-5-methoxybenzaldehyde) had a melting point of 47.5-48.5 °C, the unbrominated nitrostyrene intermediate a melting point of 76-77 °C, and the final hydrochloride a melting point of 185-186 °C. The hydrobromide salt had a melting point of 168.5-169.5 °C. It seems that one gets about as much effect as can be had, with a dosage of about 15 milligrams, and increases above this, to 30 and to 50 milligrams merely prolong the activity (from about 3 hours to perhaps 6 hours). At no dose was there an intensity that in any way resembled that of 2C-B.

The 2,5-DiEtO- homologue of 2C-B is 4-bromo-2,5-diethoxyphenethylamine, or 2CB-2,5-DIETO. The unbrominated impure benzaldehyde (2,5-diethoxybenzaldehyde) had a melting point of about 57 °C, the unbrominated impure nitrostyrene intermediate a melting point of about 60 °C, and the final hydrochloride a melting point of 230-231 °C. The hydrobromide salt had a melting point of 192-193 °C. At levels of 55 milligrams, there was only a restless sleep, and strange dreams. The active level is not yet known.

I have been told of some studies that have involved a positional rearrangement analogue of 2C-B. This is 2-bromo-4,5-dimethoxyphenethylamine (or 6-BR-DMPEA). This would be the product of the elemental bromination of DMPEA, and it has been assayed as the hydrobromide salt. Apparently, the intravenous injection of 60 milligrams gave a rapid rush, with intense visual effects reported, largely yellow and black. Orally, there may be some activity at the 400 to 500 milligram area, but the reports described mainly sleep disturbance. This would suggest a stimulant component. The N-methyl homologue of this rearranged compound was even less active.

#21   3C-BZ;   4-BENZYLOXY-3,5-DIMETHOXYAMPHETAMINE

SYNTHESIS: A solution of 268 g 2,6-dimethoxyphenol and 212 g allyl bromide in 700 mL dry acetone was treated with 315 g anhydrous K_2CO_3 and held at reflux for 16 h. The solvent was removed under vacuum, and the residue dissolved in H_2O and extracted with 3x100 mL CH_2Cl_2. The pooled extracts were washed with 5% NaOH, then with H_2O, and the solvent removed under vacuum. The residue, which weighed 245 g, was stirred and heated in an oil bath to 230 °C at which point an exothermic reaction set in. The heating was maintained at 230 °C for 0.5 h, and then the reaction mixture distilled. There was obtained a total of 127 g of 5-allyl-1,3-dimethoxy-2-hydroxybenzene as a colorless distillate, that was identical in all respects to natural 5-methoxyeugenol obtained from Oil of Nutmeg.

A solution containing 40.4 g 5-methoxyeugenol and 26.6 g benzyl chloride in 65 mL EtOH was added, all at once, to a hot and well stirred solution of 11.7 g KOH in 500 mL EtOH. The potassium salt of the phenol crystallized out immediately. By maintaining reflux conditions, this slowly redissolved, and was replaced by the steady deposition of KCl. After 6 h, the reaction mixture was cooled, and the solids removed by filtration. The filtrate was stripped of solvent under vacuum to give 57 g of crude 5-allyl-2-benzyloxy-1,3-dimethoxybenzene. This was dissolved in a solution of 60 g KOH in 80 mL EtOH and heated on the steam bath for 16 h. The reaction mixture was quenched in 500 mL H_2O, and extracted with 2x200 mL CH_2Cl_2. Removal of the solvent under vacuum gave 35.6 g of crude 2-benzyloxy-1,3-dimethoxy-5-propenylbenzene.

To a stirred, ice-cold solution of 33.6 g of the above impure 2-benzyloxy-1,3-dimethoxy-5-propenylbenzene and 13.6 g pyridine in 142 mL acetone, there was added 24.6 g tetranitromethane. After stirring for 3 min, there was added a solution of 7.9 g KOH in 132 mL H_2O, followed by additional H_2O. The oily phase that remained was H_2O washed, and then diluted with an equal volume of MeOH. This slowly set up to yellow crystals, which were removed by filtration and washed sparingly with MeOH. There was obtained 9.2 g 1-(4-benzyloxy-3,5-dimethoxy-phenyl)-2-nitropropene with a mp of 84-85 °C. An analytical sample, from EtOH, had a mp of 86-87 °C.

To a refluxing suspension of 5.5 g LAH in 360 mL anhydrous Et_2O under an inert atmosphere, there was added 8.6 g 1-(4-benzyloxy-3,5-dimethoxyphenyl)-2-nitropropene by letting the condensing Et_2O leach out a saturated solution from a modified Soxhlet condenser. The addition took 1.5 h and the refluxing was maintained for an additional 4 h. After cooling, the excess hydride was destroyed by the cautious addition of 330 mL of 1.5 N H_2SO_4. The aqueous phase was heated up to 80 °C, filtered through paper to remove a small amount of insoluble material, and treated with a solution of 8 g picric acid in 150 mL boiling EtOH. Cooling in the ice chest overnight gave globs of the amine picrate, but no clear signs of crystallization. These were washed with cold H_2O, then dissolved in 5% NaOH to give a bright yellow solution. This was extracted with 3x150 mL CH_2Cl_2, the solvent removed under vacuum, the residue dissolved in 300 mL anhydrous Et_2O, freed from a little particulate material by filtration through paper, and then saturated with hydrogen chloride gas. There was thus obtained, after filtering, Et_2O washing and air drying, 2.5 g 4-benzyloxy-3,5-dimethoxyamphetamine hydrochloride (3C-BZ) as a white solid with a mp of 161-164 °C.

DOSAGE: 25 - 200 mg.

DURATION: 18 - 24 h.

QUANTITATIVE COMMENTS: (with 25 mg) "I went into an emotionally brittle place, and for a while I was uncomfortable with childhood reminiscences. The seeing of my family's Christmas tree in my mind was almost too much. I cried."

(with 50 mg) "The action is distinct — wakeful — alerting and wound up. Hypnogogic imagery, and I could not sleep at night with my mind doing many uncontrolled, tangential, busy things. I had fleeting nausea early in the process."

(with 100 mg) "I took this in two portions. Following 50 milligrams I was aware of a slight light-headedness at a half-hour, but there was little else. At 1 1/2 hours, I took the second 50 milligrams and the augmentation of effects was noted in another half hour. The experience quietly built up to about the fifth hour, with some erotic fantasy and suggestions of changes in the visual field. I could not sleep until the twelfth hour, and my dreams were wild and not too friendly. There was no body threat from this, but I was not completely baseline until the next day. I am not too keen to do this again — it lasts too long."

(with 100 mg) "No effects."

(with 150 mg) "This is in every way identical to 100 micrograms of LSD."

(with 180 mg) "I can compare this directly to TMA which was the material I took last week. Many similarities, but this is unquestionably more intense than the TMA was at 200 milligrams. It is hard to separate the degree of impact that this drug has, from the simple fact that it lasts forever, and I was getting physically tired but I couldn't sleep. There is some amphetamine-like component, more than with TMA."

EXTENSIONS AND COMMENTARY: Two points are worthy of commentary; the potency and the promise of 3C-BZ.

As to potency, there is such uncertainty as to the effective dose, that it is for all intents and purposes impossible to predict just what dose should be considered for a person's first time with this. The choice of quotations was made with the intention of giving a picture of this scatter. A total of ten subjects have explored this compound, and the very broad range given above, 25 to 200 milligrams, reflects the degree of variation that has been encountered. Which is a shame, because the concept of a new ring such as is found here on the 4-position would have allowed an extremely wide array of substituents. Electron-rich things, electron-poor things, heavy things, light things, and on and on. This could have been a location of much variation, but it is a possibility that the uncertainties of dosage might extrapolate to these novel ring substitutions as well. Only a single variation was made, the 4-fluorobenzyl analogue. This was prepared following exactly the procedure given here for 3C-BZ, except for the replacement of benzyl chloride with 4-fluorobenzyl chloride. The allyl intermediate was an oil, but the propenyl isomer gave solids with a melting point of 59-60 °C from hexane. The nitrostyrene was a yellow crystalline solid from methanol with a melting point of 98-99 °C. The end product, 3,5-dimethoxy-4-(4-fluorobenzyloxy)amphetamine hydrochloride (3C-FBZ) was a white solid with a melting point of 149-150 °C. It has been assayed only up to 4 milligrams and there was absolutely no activity of any kind observed at that level.

#22   2C-C;   2,5-DIMETHOXY-4-CHLOROPHENETHYLAMINE

SYNTHESIS: (from 2C-H) The free base of 2,5-dimethoxyphenethylamine was generated from its salt (see recipe for 2C-H for the preparation of this compound) by treating a solution of 16.2 g of the hydrochloride salt in 300 mL H_2O with aqueous NaOH, extraction with 3x75 mL CH_2Cl_2, and removal of the solvent from the pooled extracts under vacuum. The colorless residue was dissolved in 75 mL glacial acetic acid (the solids that initially formed redissolved completely) and this was cooled to 0 °C with an external ice bath. With vigorous stirring, there was added 4.0 mL of liquid chlorine, a little bit at a time with a Pasteur pipette. The theoretical volume was 3.4 mL, but some was lost in pipetting, some on contact with the 0 °C acetic acid, and some was lost by chlorination of the acetic acid. The reaction turned a dark amber color, was allowed to stir for an additional 10 min, then quenched with 400 mL H_2O. This was washed with 3x100 mL CH_2Cl_2 (which removed some of the color) then brought to neutrality with dilute aqueous NaOH and treated with a small amount of sodium dithionite which discharged most of the color (from deep brown to pale yellow). The reaction was made strongly basic with aqueous KOH, and extracted with 3x75 mL CH_2Cl_2. The pooled extracts were washed once with H_2O and the solvent was removed under vacuum leaving about 10 mL of a deep amber oil as residue. This was dissolved in 75 mL IPA and neutralized with concentrated HCl which allowed spontaneous crystallization. These crystals were removed by filtration, washed with an additional 20 mL IPA, and air-dried to constant weight. There was thus obtained 4.2 g 2,5-dimethoxy-4-chlorophen-ethylamine hydrochloride (2C-C) with a mp of 218-221 °C. Recrystallization from

IPA increased this to 220-222 °C. The position of chlorination on the aromatic ring was verified by the presence of two para-protons in the NMR, at 7.12 and 7.20 ppm from external TMS, in a D_2O solution of the hydrochloride salt.

Synthesis from 2C-B. To a solution of 7.24 g 2,5-dimethoxy-4-bromophenethylamine (2C-B) and 4.5 g phthalic anhydride in 100 mL anhydrous DMF there was added molecular sieves. After 16 h reflux, the reaction mixture was cooled and the sieves removed by filtration. The addition of a little CH_2Cl_2 prompted the deposition of yellow crystals which were recrystallized from EtOH. The resulting 1-(2,5-dimethoxy-4-bromophenyl)-2-(phthalimido)ethane weighed 7.57 g and had a mp of 141-142 °C. Anal. ($C_{18}H_{16}BrNO_4$) C,H,N,Br.

A solution of 14.94 g of 1-(2,5-dimethoxy-4-bromophenyl)-2-(phthalimido)ethane and 4.5 g cuprous chloride in 300 mL anhydrous DMF was heated for 5 h at reflux. The cooled mixture was poured into 20 mL H_2O that contained 13 g hydrated ferric chloride and 3 mL concentrated HCl. The mixture was maintained at about 70 °C for 20 min, and then extracted with CH_2Cl_2. After washing the pooled organic extracts with dilute HCl and drying with anhydrous $MgSO_4$, the volatiles were removed under vacuum to provide a solid residue. This was recrystallized from EtOH to provide 12.18 g of 1-(2,5-dimethoxy-4-chlorophenyl)-2-(phthalimido)ethane as yellow needles that had a mp of 138-140 °C. Anal. ($C_{18}H_{16}ClNO_4$) C,H,N,Cl.

To 60 mL absolute EtOH there was added 12.2 g 1-(2,5-dimethoxy-4-chlorophenyl)-2-(phthalimido)ethane and 2.9 mL of 100% hydrazine. The solution was held at reflux for 15 min. After cooling, the cyclic hydrazone by-product was removed by filtration, and the alcoholic mother liquors taken to dryness under vacuum. The residue was distilled at 145-155 °C at 0.05 mm/Hg to give 5.16 g of a clear, colorless oil. This was dissolved in anhydrous Et_2O and treated with hydrogen chloride gas, producing 2,5-dimethoxy-4-chlorophenethylamine hydrochloride (2C-C) as white crystals with a mp of 220-221 °C. Anal. ($C_{10}H_{15}Cl_2NO_2$) C,H,N.

DOSAGE: 20 - 40 mg.

DURATION: 4 - 8 h.

QUALITATIVE COMMENTS: (with 20 mg) "This is longer lived than 2C-B, and there is a longer latency in coming on. It took an hour and a half, or even two hours to get there. It had a slight metallic overtone."

(with 24 mg) "I was at a moderately high and thoroughly favorable place, for several hours. It seemed to be a very sensual place, but without too much in the way of visual distraction.

(with 40 mg) "There were a lot of visuals — something that I had noted at lower levels. There seems to be less stimulation than with 2C-B, and in some ways it is actually sedating. And yet I was up all night. It was like a very intense form of relaxation."

EXTENSIONS AND COMMENTARY: Other reports mention usage of up to 50 milligrams which seems to increase yet further the intensity and the duration. I have one report of an intravenous administration of 20 milligrams, and the response was described as overwhelming. The effects peaked at about 5 minutes and lasted for perhaps 15 minutes.

The halogens represent a small group of atoms that are unique for a couple of reasons. They are all located in a single column of the periodic table, being monovalent and negative. That means that they can be reasonably stable things when attached to an aromatic nucleus. But, being monovalent, they cannot be modified or extended in any way. Thus, they are kind of a dead end, at least as far as the 2C-X series is considered. The heaviest, iodine, was explored as the phenethylamine, as 2C-I, and as the amphetamine as DOI. These are the most potent. The next lighter is bromine, where the phenethylamine is 2C-B and the amphetamine is DOB. These two are a bit less potent, and are by far the most broadly explored of all the halides. Here, in the above recipe, we have the chlorine counterpart, 2C-C. There is also the corresponding amphetamine DOC. These are less potent still, and much less explored. Why? Perhaps because chlorine is a gas and troublesome to handle (bromine is a liquid, and iodine is a solid). The fluorine analogue is yet harder to make, and requires procedures that are indirect, because fluorine (the lightest of all the halides) is not only a gas, but is dangerous to handle and does not react in the usual halogen way. There will be mention made of 2C-F, but DOF is still unexplored.

The treatment of the 2C-B phthalimide described above, with cuprous cyanide rather than cuprous chloride, gave rise to the cyano analog which, on hydrolysis with hydrazine, yielded 2,5-dimethoxy-4-cyanophenethylamine (2C-CN). Hydrolysis of this with hot, strong base gave the corresponding acid, 2,5-dimethoxy-4-carboxyphenethylamine, 2C-COOH. No evaluation of either of these compounds has been made in the human animal, as far as I know.

#23 2C-D; LE-25; 2,5-DIMETHOXY-4-METHYL-PHENETHYLAMINE

SYNTHESIS: Into 1 L H_2O that was being stirred magnetically, there was added, in sequence, 62 g toluhydroquinone, 160 mL 25% NaOH, and 126 g dimethyl sulfate. After about 2 h, the reaction mixture was no longer basic, and another 40 mL of the 25% NaOH was added. Even with stirring for a few additional days, the reaction mixture remained basic. It was quenched in 2.5 L H_2O, extracted with 3x100 mL CH_2Cl_2 and the pooled extracts stripped of solvent under vacuum. The remaining 56.4 g of amber oil was distilled at about 70 °C at 0.5 mm/Hg to yield 49.0 g of 2,5-dimethoxytoluene as a white liquid. The aqueous residues, on acidification, provided a phenolic fraction that distilled at 75-100 °C at 0.4 mm/Hg to give 5.8 g of a pale yellow distillate that partially crystallized. These solids (with mp of 54-62 °C) were removed by filtration, and yielded 3.1 g of a solid which was recrystallized from 50 mL hexane containing 5 mL toluene. This gave 2.53 g of a white crystalline product with a mp of 66-68 °C. A second recrystallization (from hexane) raised this mp to 71-72 °C. The literature value given for the mp of 2-methyl-4-methoxyphenol is 70-71 °C. The literature value given for the mp of the isomeric 3-methyl-4-methoxyphenol is 44-46 °C. This phenol, on ethylation, gives 2-ethoxy-5-methoxytoluene, which leads directly to the 2-carbon 2CD-5ETO (one of the Tweetios) and the 3-carbon Classic Lady IRIS.

A mixture of 34.5 g $POCl_3$ and 31.1 g N-methylformanilide was heated for 10 min on the steam bath, and then there was added 30.4 g of 2,5-dimethoxytoluene. Heating was continued for 2.5 h, and the viscous, black, ugly mess was poured into 600 mL of warm H_2O and stirred overnight. The resulting rubbery miniature-rabbit-droppings product was removed by filtration and sucked as free of H_2O as possible. The 37.2 g of wet product was extracted on the steam-bath with 4x100 mL portions of boiling hexane which, after decantation and cooling, yielded a total of 15.3 g of yellow crystalline product. This, upon recrystallization from 150 mL boiling hexane, gave pale yellow crystals which, when air dried to constant weight, represented 8.7 g of 2,5-dimethoxy-4-methylbenzaldehyde, and had a mp of 83-84 °C. Anal. ($C_8H_{12}O_3$) C,H,N. The Gattermann aldehyde synthesis gave a better yield (60% of theory) but required the use of hydrogen cyanide gas. The malononitrile derivative, from 5.7 g of the aldehyde and 2.3 g malononitrile in absolute EtOH, treated with a drop of triethylamine, was an orange crystalline product. A sample recrystallized from EtOH gave a mp of 138.5-139 °C.

A solution of 8.65 g 2,5-dimethoxy-4-methylbenzaldehyde in 30 g nitromethane was treated with 1.1 g anhydrous ammonium acetate and heated for 50 min on the steam bath. Stripping off the excess nitromethane under vacuum yielded orange crystals which weighed 12.2 g. These were recrystallized from 100 mL IPA providing yellow crystals of 2,5-dimethoxy-4-methyl-ß-nitrostyrene which weighed, when dry, 7.70 g. The mp was 117-118 °C, and this was increased to 118-119 °C upon recrystallization from benzene/heptane 1:2.

To a well stirred suspension of 7.0 g LAH in 300 mL of warm THF under an inert atmosphere, there was added 7.7 g 2,5-dimethoxy-4-methyl-ß-nitrostyrene in 35 mL THF over the course of 0.5 h. This reaction mixture was held at reflux for 24 h, cooled to room temperature, and the excess hydride destroyed with 25 mL IPA. There was then added 7 mL 15% NaOH, followed by 21 mL H_2O. The granular gray mass was filtered, and the filter cake washed with 2x50 mL THF. The combined filtrate and washes were stripped of their volatiles under vacuum to give a residue weighing 7.7 g which was distilled at 90-115 °C at 0.3 mm/Hg to provide 4.90 g of a clear, white oil, which crystallized in the receiver. This was dissolved in 25 mL IPA, and neutralized with concentrated HCl which produced immediate crystals of the salt. These were dispersed with 80 mL anhydrous Et_2O, filtered, and washed with Et_2O to give, after air drying to constant weight, 4.9 g of fluffy white crystals of 2,5-dimethoxy-4-methylphenethylamine hydrochloride (2C-D). The mp was 213-214 °C which was not improved by recrystallization from CH_3CN/IPA mixture, or from EtOH. The hydrobromide salt had a mp of 183-184 °C. The acetamide, from the free base in pyridine treated with acetic anhydride, was a white crystalline solid which, when recrystallized from aqueous MeOH, had a mp of 116-117 °C.

DOSAGE: 20 - 60 mg.

DURATION: 4 - 6 h.

QUALITATIVE COMMENTS: (with 10 mg) "There is something going on, but it is subtle. I find that I can just slightly redirect my attention so that it applies more exactly to what I am doing. I feel that I can learn faster. This is a 'smart' pill!"

(with 20 mg) "Butterflies in stomach whole time. OK. This is about the right level. In retrospect, not too interesting. Primarily a stimulant, not entirely physically pleasant. The visual is not too exciting. I am easily distracted. One line of thought to another. I feel that more would be too stimulating."

(with 30 mg) "I was into it quite quickly (not much over three-quarters of an hour) and got up to a ++ by the end of an hour. There is something unsatisfactory about trying to classify this level. I had said that I was willing to increase the dose to a higher level, to break out of this not-quite-defined level into something psychedelic. But I may not want to go higher. Under different circumstances I would not mind trying it at a considerably lower dosage, perhaps at the 10 or 15 milligrams. I do not have a comfortable label on this material, yet."

(with 45 mg) "There was a rocket from the half-hour to the one and a half hour, from nothing up to a +++. Somehow the intimacy and the erotic never quite knit, and I feel that I am always waiting for the experience to come home. Talking is extremely easy, but something is missing. Appetite is good. I am down by the fifth hour, and sleep is comfortable. This compound will take some learning."

(with 75 mg) "This is a +++, but the emphasis is on talking, not on personal interacting. I am putting out, but my boundaries are intact. I was able to sleep at the sixth hour. Communication was excellent. This is fast on, but not too long lived. Maybe a therapy tool?"

(with 150 mg) "A truly remarkable psychedelic, one which could compare favorably with 2C-B. There are intense colors, and I feel that more would be too much."

EXTENSIONS AND COMMENTARY: Wow! This particular compound is what I call a pharmacological tofu. It doesn't seem to do too much by itself, always teasing, until you get to heroic levels. But a goodly number of experimental therapists have said that it is excellent in extending the action of some other materials. It seems to boost the waning action of another drug, without adding its own color to the experience. Yet, the comment above, on the high level of 150 milligrams, is a direct quote from the use of this compound in Germany (where it is called LE-25) in therapeutic research.

This is probably the most dramatic example of the loss of potency from an amphetamine (DOM, active at maybe 3 milligrams) to a phenethylamine (only one tenth as active). It is so often the case that the first of a series is not the most interesting nor the most potent member. As intriguing and as difficult-to-define as the 2C-D story might be, the next higher homologue of this set, 2C-E, is maximally active at the 15 to 20 milligram level, and is, without any question, a complete psychedelic.

The N-monomethyl and the N,N-dimethyl homologues of 2C-D have been synthesized from 2C-D. The N-monomethyl compound was obtained by the quaternization of the Schiff's base formed between 2C-D and benzaldehyde with methyl sulfate, followed by hydrolysis; the hydrochloride salt had a melting point of 150-151 °C, from EtOH. The N,N-dimethyl compound resulted from the action of formaldehyde-formic acid on 2C-D; the hydrochloride salt had a melting point of 168-169 °C from EtOH/ether. These two compounds were some ten times less effective in interfering with conditioned responses in experimental rats. There is no report of their having been explored in man.

I have learned of an extensive study of ethoxy homologues of a number of the phenethylamines in the 2C-X series; they have been collectively called the "Tweetios." This Sylvester and Tweety-bird allusion came directly from the compulsive habit of trying to alleviate the boredom of driving long distances (not under the influence of anything) by the attempt to pronounce the license plates of cars as they passed. The first of this series of compounds had a name that indicated that there was an ethoxy group at the 2-position, or 2-EtO, or Tweetio, and the rest is history. In every compound to be found in the 2C-X family, there are two methoxy groups, one at the 2-position and one at the 5-position. There are thus three possible tweetio compounds, a 2-EtO-, a 5-EtO- and a 2,5-di-EtO-. Those that have been evaluated in man are included after each of the 2C-X's that has served as the prototype. In general, the 2-EtO- compounds have a shorter duration and a lower potency, the 5-EtO- compounds have a relatively unchanged potency and a longer time duration; the 2,5-di-EtO- homologues are very weak, if active at all.

The 2-EtO-homologue of 2C-D is 2-ethoxy-5-methoxy-4-methylphen-ethylamine, or 2CD-2ETO. The benzaldehyde (2-ethoxy-5-methoxy-4-tolu-aldehyde) had a melting point of 60.5-61 °C, the nitrostyrene intermediate a melting point of 110.5-111.5 °C, and the final hydrochloride a melting point of 207-208 °C. The hydrobromide salt had a melting point of 171-173 °C. At levels of 60 milli-grams, there was the feeling of closeness between couples, without an appreciable state of intoxication. The duration was about 4 hours.

The 5-EtO- homologue of 2C-D is 5-ethoxy-2-methoxy-4-methylphen-ethylamine, or 2CD-5ETO. The benzaldehyde (5-ethoxy-2-ethoxy-4-tolualdehyde) had a melting point of 81-82 °C, and the details of this synthesis are given in the recipe for IRIS. The nitrostyrene intermediate had a melting point of 112.5-113.5 °C and the final hydrochloride salt had a melting point of 197-198 °C. The hydrobromide salt had a melting point of 158-159 °C. At dosage levels of 40 to 50 milligrams, there was a slow, gradual climb to the full effects that were noted in about 2 hours. The experience was largely free from excitement, but with a friendly openness and outgoingness that allowed easy talk, interaction, humor, and a healthy appetite. The duration of effects was 12 hours.

The 2,5-di-EtO- homologue of 2C-D is 2,5-diethoxy-4-methylphen-ethylamine, or 2CD-2,5-DIETO. The benzaldehyde (2,5-diethoxy-4-tolualdehyde) had a melting point of 102-103 °C, the nitrostyrene intermediate a melting point of 108-109 °C, and the final hydrochloride salt a melting point of 251-252 °C. At a level of 55 milligrams, a plus one was reached, and what effects there were, were gone after four hours.

#24   2C-E;   2,5-DIMETHOXY-4-ETHYLPHENETHYLAMINE

SYNTHESIS: A suspension of 140 g anhydrous $AlCl_3$ in 400 mL CH_2Cl_2 was treated with 100 g acetyl chloride. This slurry was added to a vigorously stirred solution of 110 g p-dimethoxybenzene in 300 mL CH_2Cl_2. Stirring was continued at ambient temperature for an additional 40 min, then all was poured into 1 L water and the phases separated. The aqueous phase was extracted with 2x100 mL CH_2Cl_2 and the combined organic phases washed with 3x150 mL 5% NaOH. These washes, after combination and acidification, were extracted with 3x75 mL CH_2Cl_2 and the extracts washed once with saturated $NaHCO_3$. Removal of the solvent under vacuum provided 28.3 g of 2-hydroxy-5-methoxyaceto-phenone as yellow crystals which, on recrystallization from 2 volumes of boiling MeOH and air drying, provided 21.3 g of product with a mp of 49-49.5 °C. Ethylation of this material serves as the starting point for the synthesis of 2CE-5ETO. The CH_2Cl_2 fraction from the base wash, above, was stripped of solvent on the rotary evaporator to give a residual oil that, on distillation at 147-150 °C at the water pump, provided 111.6 g of 2,5-dimethoxyacetophenone as an almost white oil.

In a round bottom flask equipped with a reflux condenser, a take-off adapter, an immersion thermometer, and a magnetic stirrer, there was placed 100 g 2,5-dimethoxyacetophenone, 71 g 85% KOH pellets, 500 mL of triethylene glycol, and 125 mL 65% hydrazine. The mixture was brought up to a boil by heating with an electric mantle, and the distillate was removed, allowing the temperature of the pot contents to continuously increase. When the pot temperature had reached 210

°C, reflux was established and maintained for an additional 3 h. After cooling, the reaction mixture and the distillate were combined, poured into 3 L water, and extracted with 3x100 mL hexane. After washing the pooled extracts with water, the solvent was removed yielding 22.0 g of a pale straw-colored liquid that was free of both hydroxy and carbonyl groups by infrared. This was distilled at 120-140 °C at the water pump to give 2,5-dimethoxy-1-ethylbenzene as a white fluid product. Acidification of the spent aqueous phase with concentrated HCl produced a heavy black oil which was extracted with 3x100 mL CH_2Cl_2. Removal of the solvent on the rotary evaporator yielded 78 g.of a black residue that was distilled at 90-105 °C at 0.5 mm/Hg to provide 67.4 g of an orange-amber oil that was largely 2-ethyl-4-methoxyphenol. This material could eventually be used as a starting material for ethoxy homologues. However, remethylation (with CH_3I and KOH in methanol) provided some 28 g additional 2,5-dimethoxyethylbenzene.

A solution of 8.16 g of 2,5-dimethoxy-1-ethylbenzene in 30 mL CH_2Cl_2 was cooled to 0 °C with good stirring and under an inert atmosphere of He. There was then added 11.7 mL anhydrous stannic chloride, followed by 3.95 mL dichloromethyl methyl ether dropwise over the course of 0.5 h. The stirred reaction mixture was allowed to come up to room temperature, then held on the steam bath for 1 h. The reaction mixture was poured into 1 L water, extracted with 3x75 mL CH_2Cl_2, and the pooled extracts washed with dilute HCl. The organic phase was stripped under vacuum yielding 10.8 g of a dark viscous oil. This was distilled at 90-110 °C at 0.2 mm/Hg to yield a colorless oil that, on cooling, set to white crystals. The yield of 2,5-dimethoxy-4-ethylbenzaldehyde was 5.9 g of material that had a mp of 46-47 °C. After purification through the bisulfite complex, the mp increased to 47-48 °C. The use of the Vilsmeier aldehyde synthesis (with $POCl_3$ and N-methylformanilide) gave results that were totally unpredictable. The malononitrile derivative (from 0.3 g of this aldehyde and 0.3 g malononitrile in 5 mL EtOH and a drop of triethylamine) formed red crystals which, on recrystallization from toluene, had a mp of 123-124 °C.

A solution of 21.0 g of the unrecrystallized 2,5-dimethoxy-4-ethyl-benzaldehyde in 75 g nitromethane was treated with 4 g of anhydrous ammonium acetate and heated on the steam bath for about 2 h. The progress of the reaction was best followed by TLC analysis of the crude reaction mixture on silica gel plates with CH_2Cl_2 as the developing solvent. The excess solvent/reagent was removed under vacuum yielding granular orange solids that were recrystallized from seven volumes of boiling MeOH. After cooling in external ice-water for 1 h, the yellow crystalline product was removed by filtration, washed with cold MeOH and air dried to give 13.4 g of 2,5-dimethoxy-4-ethyl-ß-nitrostyrene. The mp was 96-98 °C which improved to 99-100 °C after a second recrystallization from MeOH.

A total of 120 mL of 1.0 M solution of LAH in THF (120 mL of 1.0 M) was transferred to a 3 neck 500 mL flask, under an inert atmosphere with good magnetic stirring. This solution was cooled to 0 °C with an external ice-water bath, and there was then added 3.0 mL of 100% H_2SO_4 over the course of 0.5 h. This was followed by a solution of 5.85 g of 2,5-dimethoxy-4-ethyl-ß-nitrostyrene, in 40 mL of warm THF. The reaction mixture was stirred for 0.5 h, brought to room temperature, heated on the steam bath for 0.5 h, and then returned to room temperature. The addition of IPA dropwise destroyed the excess hydride, and some 4.5 mL of 5% NaOH produce a white cottage cheese, in a basic organic medium. This mixture was filtered, washed with THF, and the filtrate evaporated to produce 2.8 g of an almost white oil. The filter cake was resuspended in THF, made more basic with additional 15 mL of 5% NaOH, again filtered, and the filtrate removed to provide an additional 2.8 g of crude product. These residues were combined and distilled at 90-100 °C at 0.25 mm/Hg to give a colorless oil. This was dissolved in 30 mL IPA, neutralized with concentrated HCl, and diluted with 50 mL anhydrous Et_2O to provide, after spontaneous crystallization, filtration, washing with Et_2O, and air drying, 3.87 g of 2,5-dimethoxy-4-ethylphenethylamine hydrochloride (2C-E) as magnificent white crystals. A similar yield can be obtained from the reduction of the nitrostyrene in a suspension of LAH in THF, without the use of H_2SO_4. With 11.3 g of LAH in 300 mL dry THF, there was added, dropwise, a solution of 13.4 g of 2,5-dimethoxy-4-ethyl-ß-nitrostyrene in 75 mL THF over the course of 2 h. The mixture was kept at reflux for an additional 8 h, and killed by the careful addition of 11 mL H_2O, followed with 11 mL 15% NaOH, and finally another 33 mL of H_2O. This mass was filtered, washed with THF, and the combined filtrates and washes evaporated to a residue under vacuum The approximately 15 mL of residue was dissolved in 300 mL CH_2Cl_2 and treated with 200 mL H_2O containing 20 mL concentrated HCl. On shaking the mixture, there was deposited a mass of the hydrochloride salt which was diluted with a quantity of additional H_2O. The organic phase was extracted with additional dilute HCL, and these aqueous phases were combined. After being made basic with 25% NaOH, this phase was again extracted with 3x75 mL CH_2Cl_2 and after the removal of the solvent, yielded 12.6 g of a colorless oil. This was dissolved in 75 mL of IPA and neutralized with concentrated HCl. The solidified mass that formed was loosened with another 50 mL IPA, and then filtered. After Et_2O washing and air drying there was obtained 7.7 g of 2,5-dimethoxy-4-ethylphenethylamine hydrochloride (2C-E) as lustrous white crystals. Anal. ($C_{12}H_{20}ClNO_2$) C,H.

DOSAGE: 10 - 25 mg.

DURATION: 8 - 12 h.

QUALITATIVE COMMENTS: (with 16 mg) "There was a strange devil-angel pairing. As I was being told of the ecstatic white-light ascent of my partner into the God-space of an out-of-body experience, I was fighting my way out of a brown ooze. She saw the young Jesus at the bottom of a ladder drifting upwards step by step to some taking-off place, and I saw all the funny gargoyles around the base of the ladder surrounded by picnic bunting. For me it was the 4th of July, rather than Easter!"

(with 20 mg) "The view out of the window was unreal. The garden was painted on the window, and every petal of flower and tuft of grass and leaf of tree was carefully sculptured in fine strokes of oil paint on the surface of the glass. It was not out there; it was right here in front of me. The woman who was watering the plants was completely frozen, immobilized by Vermeer. And when I looked again, she was in a different place, but again frozen. I was destined to become the eternal museum viewer."

(with 25 mg) "I have a picture in my living room that is a stylized German scene with a man on horseback riding through the woods, and a young girl coming out to meet him from the nearby trees. But she was not just 'coming out.' He was not just riding through the woods. The wind was blowing, and his horse was at full gallop, and his cape was flapping in the storm, and she was bearing down upon him at full bore. The action never ceased. I became exhausted."

(with 25 mg) "Within minutes I was anxious and sweaty. Each person has his own brand of toxic psychosis — mine always starts with the voices in my head talking to me, about all my worst fears, a jumble of warnings and deep fears spinning faster. Twenty minutes later this complex chaos passed as quickly as it had come. At lower dosages 2C-E has been a truly enjoyable esthetic enhancer. But it really has a steep dose/response curve."

EXTENSIONS AND COMMENTARY: Here is another of the magical half-dozen. The range is purposefully broad. At 10 milligrams there have been some pretty rich +++ experiences, and yet I have had the report from one young lady of a 30 milligram trial that was very frightening. My first experience with 2C-E was really profound, and it is the substance of a chapter within the story. The amphet-amine homologue is DOET, which is not only much longer in action, but consid-erably more potent. Several people have said, about 2C-E, "I don't think I like it, since it isn't that much fun. But I intend to explore it again." There is something here that will reward the experimenter. Someday, the full character of 2C-E will be understood, but for the moment, let it rest as being a difficult and worth-while material. A very much worth-while material. One Tweetio of 2C-E is known. The 5-EtO-homologue of 2C-E is 5-ethoxy-4-ethyl-2-methoxyphenethylamine, or 2CE-5ETO. The nitrostyrene intermediate had a melting point of 110-110.5 °C, and the final hydrochloride a melting point of 184-185 °C. The effective level of 2CE-5ETO is in the 10 to 15 milligram range. It is gentle, forgiving, and extremely long lived. Some 3 to 4 hours were needed to achieve plateau, and on occasion experi-ments were interrupted with Valium or Halcion at the 16 hour point. After a night's sleep, there were still some effects evident the next day. Thus, the dose is comparable to the parent compound 2C-E, but the duration is 2 to 3 times longer. It was given the nickname "Eternity" by one subject.

#25   3C-E;   3,5-DIMETHOXY-4-ETHOXYAMPHETAMINE

SYNTHESIS: A solution of 3.6 g syringaldehyde (3,5-dimethoxy-4-hydroxybenzaldehyde) in 50 mL MeOH was combined with a solution of 3.7 g 85% KOH in 75 mL warm MeOH. This clear solution suddenly set up to crystals of the potassium salt, too thick to stir satisfactorily. To this suspension there was added 7.4 g ethyl iodide (a large excess) and the mixture was held at reflux temperature with a heating mantle. The solids eventually loosened and redissolved, giving a clear amber-colored smooth-boiling solution. Refluxing was maintained for 2 days, then all volatiles were removed under vacuum. The residue was dissolved in 400 mL H$_2$O, made strongly basic with 25% NaOH, and extracted with 4x100 mL CH$_2$Cl$_2$. The pooled extracts were washed with saturated brine, and the solvent removed under vacuum to give 3.3 g of a pale amber oil which set up as crystals of 3,5-dimethoxy-4-ethoxybenzaldehyde with a mp of 47-48 °C. A small sample recrystallized from methanol had a mp of 48-49 °C.

A solution of 3.3 g 3,5-dimethoxy-4-ethoxybenzaldehyde in 25 mL nitroethane was treated with 0.5 g anhydrous ammonium acetate and heated on the steam bath for 36 h. The solvent/reagent was removed under vacuum giving a thick yellow-orange oil that was dissolved in two volumes hot MeOH. As this cooled, crystals appeared spontaneously, and after cooling in ice for a short time, these were removed by filtration and washed sparingly with cold MeOH, Air drying to constant weight provided 2.2 g 1-(3,5-dimethoxy-4-ethoxyphenyl)-2-nitropropene with a mp of 84-85 °C. The mother liquors, on standing overnight, deposited large chunks of crystalline material which was isolated by decantation, ground up under a small amount of methanol, then recrystallized from 60% EtOH. A second crop of 0.7 g of the nitrostyrene was thus obtained, as canary-yellow crystals with a mp of 83-85 °C.

A solution of 2.7 g 1-(3,5-dimethoxy-4-ethoxyphenyl)-2-nitropropene in 20 mL anhydrous THF was added to a suspension of 2.0 g LAH in 150 mL warm THF. The mixture was held at reflux for 48 h. After stirring at room temperature for another 48 h, the excess hydride was destroyed by the addition of 2.0 mL H$_2$O in 10 mL THF, followed by 2.0 mL 15% NaOH and then an additional 6.0 mL H$_2$O. The inorganic salts were removed by filtration, and the filter cake washed with THF. The combined mother liquor and washings were stripped of solvent under vacuum leaving a yellow oil with some inorganic salts still in it. This was dissolved in 300 mL CH$_2$Cl$_2$, washed with dilute NaOH, and extracted with 3x150 mL 1 N HCl. The pooled extracts were washed once with CH$_2$Cl$_2$ made basic with 25% NaOH, and extracted with 3x100 mL CH$_2$Cl$_2$. The combined organics were washed with saturated brine, and the solvent removed under vacuum to yield about 2 mL of a colorless oil. This was dissolved in 10 mL IPA, neutralized with concentrated HCl (10 drops were required), and diluted with 125 mL anhydrous Et$_2$O. The slight cloudiness gradually became the formation of fine white crystals. After standing at room temperature for 2 h, these were removed, Et_2O washed, and air dried. There was thus obtained 1.9 g of 3,5-dimethoxy-4-ethoxyamphetamine hydrochloride (3C-E) as brilliant white crystals.

DOSAGE: 30 - 60 mg.

DURATION: 8 - 12 h.

QUALITATIVE COMMENTS: (with 40 mg) "It developed into a strange and indefinable something. It is unworldly. I am very much in control, but with an undertone of unreality that is a little reminiscent of high doses of LSD. If there were a great deal of sensory input, I might not see it. And if I were in complete sensory quiet I would miss it, too. But just where I am, I can see it. Eerie state of awareness. And by the 8th hour I am sober, with no residue except for some slight teeth clenching, and pretty much disbelieving the whole thing."

(with 60 mg) "Visuals very strong, insistent. Body discomfort remained very heavy for first hour. Sense of implacable imposition of something toxic for a while. I felt at the mercy of uncomfortable physical effects — faint or pre-nausea, heavy feeling of tremor (although tremor actually relatively light) and general dis-ease, un-ease, non-ease. Kept lying down so as to be as comfortable as possible. Fantasy began to be quite strong. At first, no eyes closed images, and certainly anti-erotic. 2nd hour on, bright colors, distinct shapes — jewel-like — with eyes closed. Suddenly it became clearly not anti-erotic. That was the end of my bad place, and I shot immediately up to a +++. Complex fantasy which takes over — hard to know what is real, what is fantasy. Continual erotic. Image of glass-walled apartment building in mid-desert. Exquisite sensitivity. Down by ? midnight. Next morning, faint flickering lights on looking out windows."

EXTENSIONS AND COMMENTARY: This is an interesting closing of the circle. Although mescaline launched the entire show, the first half could be called the amphetamine period, with variations made on all aspects of the molecule except for that three-carbon chain. And it was found that the 4-substitution position was of paramount importance in both the potency and the quality of action of a compound. Then, looking at the long-ignored chain, lengthening it by the addition of a carbon atom eliminated all psychedelic effects and gave materials with reduced action. The action present was that of an antidepressant. But removing a carbon atom? This returned the search to the world of mescaline, but with the knowledge of the strong influence of the 4-position substituent. The two-carbon side-chain world was rediscovered, principally with 2C-B and 2C-D, and the 4-ethoxy-analogue of mescaline, E. This second half of the show could be called the phenethylamine period. And with compounds such as 3C-E which is, quite simply, Escaline (or E) reextended again to a 3-carbon chain amphetamine, there is a kind of satisfying closure. A fascinating compound, but for most subjects a little too heavy on the body.

#26   2C-F;   2,5-DIMETHOXY-4-FLUOROPHENETHYLAMINE

SYNTHESIS: A solution of 76.6 g 2,5-dimethoxyaniline in 210 mL H_2O containing 205 mL fluoroboric acid was cooled to 0 °C. with an external ice bath. There was then added, slowly, a solution of 35 g sodium nitrite in 70 mL H_2O. After an additional 0.5 h stirring, the precipitated solids were removed by filtration, washed first with cold H_2O, then with MeOH and finally Et_2O. Air drying yielded about 100 g of the fluoroborate salt of the aniline as dark purple-brown solids. This salt was pyrolyzed with the cautious application of a flame, with the needed attention paid to both an explosion risk, and the evolution of the very corrosive boron trifluoride. The liquid that accumulated in the receiver was distilled at about 120 °C at 20 mm/ Hg, and was subsequently washed with dilute NaOH to remove dissolved boron trifluoride. The product, 2,5-dimethoxyfluorobenzene, was a fluid, straw-colored oil that weighed 7.0 g.

To a vigorously stirred solution of 40.7 g 2,5-dimethoxyfluorobenzene in 215 mL CH_2Cl_2 cooled with an external ice bath, there was added 135 g of anhydrous stannic chloride. There was then added, dropwise, 26 g of dichloromethyl methyl ether at a rate that precluded excessive heating. The reaction mixture was allowed to come to room temperature over the course of 0.5 h, and then quenched by dumping into 500 g shaved ice containing 75 mL concentrated HCl. This mixture was stirred for an additional 1.5 h. The separated organic layer was washed with 2x100 mL dilute HCl, then with dilute NaOH, then with H_2O and finally with saturated brine. Removal of the solvent under vacuum yielded a solid residue that was recrystallized from aqueous EtOH yielding 41.8 g 2,5-dimethoxy-4-fluorobenzaldehyde with a mp of 99-100 °C.

A solution of 2.5 g 2,5-dimethoxy-4-fluorobenzaldehyde in 15 mL acetic acid containing 1 g nitromethane was treated with 0.2 g anhydrous ammonium acetate, and heated on the steam bath for 4 h. After cooling, and following the judicious addition of H_2O, crystals separated, and additional H_2O was added with good stirring until the first signs of oiling out appeared. The solids were removed by filtration, and recrystallized from acetone to give 2.0 g of 2,5-dimethoxy-4-fluoro-ß-nitrostyrene with a mp of 159-162 °C.

To a suspension of 2.0 g LAH in 200 mL cool anhydrous Et_2O under an inert atmosphere, there was added a THF solution of 2.0 g 2,5-dimethoxy-4-fluoro-ß-nitrostyrene. The reaction mixture was stirred at room temperature for 2 h and then heated briefly at reflux. After cooling, the excess hydride was destroyed by the cautious addition of H_2O, and when the reaction was finally quiet, there was added 2 mL of 15% NaOH, followed by another 6 mL of H_2O. The basic insolubles were removed by filtration, and washed with THF. The combined filtrate and washes were stripped of solvent, yielding a residual oil that was taken up in 10 mL of IPA, neutralized with concentrated HCl, and the generated solids diluted with anhydrous Et_2O. The white crystalline 2,5-dimethoxy-4-fluorophenethylamine hydrochloride (2C-F) was recrystallized from IPA to give an air-dried product of 0.5 g with a mp of 182-185 °C.

DOSAGE: greater than 250 mg.

DURATION: unknown

QUALITATIVE COMMENTS: (with 250 mg) "Even at 250 milligrams, the effects were slight and uncertain. There may have been some eyes-closed imagery above normal, but certainly not profound. At several hours there was a pleasant lethargy; sleep was completely normal that night."

EXTENSIONS AND COMMENTARY: A number of graded acute dosages were tried, and it was only with amounts in excess of 100 milligrams that there were any baseline disturbances at all. And at no dose that was tried was there any convincing indication of believable central effects.

The three-carbon amphetamine analogue of 2C-F would quite logically be called DOF (2,5-dimethoxy-4-fluoroamphetamine). It has been prepared by reaction of the above benzaldehyde with nitroethane (giving 1-(2,5-dimethoxy-4-fluorophenyl)-2-nitropropene, with a melting point of 128-129 °C from ethanol) followed by LAH reduction to DOF (the hydrochloride salt has a melting point of 166-167 °C, after recrystallization from ether/ethyl acetate/ethanol). Animal studies that have compared DOF to the highly potent DOI and DOB imply that the human activity will be some four to six times less than these two heavier halide analogues. As of the present time, no human trials of DOF have been made.

#27   2C-G;   2,5-DIMETHOXY-3,4-DIMETHYLPHENETHYLAMINE

SYNTHESIS: To a clear solution of 40.4 g flake KOH in 400 mL warm EtOH there was added 86.5 g 2,3-xylenol followed by 51.4 g methyl iodide. This mixture was held at reflux for 2 days, stripped of volatiles under vacuum, the residues dissolved in 1 L of H_2O, and extracted with 4x200 mL CH_2Cl_2. The pooled extracts were washed with 5% NaOH until the washes remained basic. Following a single washing with dilute HCl, the solvent was removed under vacuum, and the residue, 41.5 g of a pungent smelling amber oil, spontaneously crystallized. The mp of 2,3-dimethylanisole was 25-26 °C and it was used without further purification in the next step. From the aqueous basic washes, following acidification, extraction, and solvent removal, there was obtained 46.5 g crude unreacted xylenol which could be recycled.

A mixture of 205 g $POCl_3$ and 228 g N-methylformanilide was allowed to incubate at room temperature until there was the development of a deep claret color with some spontaneous heating. To this, there was added 70.8 g 2,3-dimethylanisole, and the dark reaction mixture heated on the steam bath for 2.5 h. The product was then poured into 1.7 L H_2O, and stirred until there was a spontaneous crystallization. These solids were removed by filtration, H_2O washed and air dried to give 77.7 g of crude benzaldehyde as brown crystals. This was distilled at 70-90 °C at 0.4 mm/Hg to give 64.8 g of 2,3-dimethyl-4-methoxybenzaldehyde as a white crystalline product with a mp of 51-52 °C. Recrystallization from MeOH produced an analytical sample with a mp of 55-55.5 °C. Anal. ($C_{10}H_{12}O_2$) C,H. The malononitrile derivative (from the aldehyde and malononitrile in EtOH with a drop of triethylamine) had a mp of 133-133.5 °C from EtOH. Anal. ($C_{13}H_{12}N_2O$) C,H,N. Recently, this aldehyde has become commercially available.

A solution of 32.4 g 2,3-dimethyl-4-methoxybenzaldehyde in 800 mL CH_2Cl_2 was treated with 58.6 g 85% m-chloroperoxybenzoic acid and held at reflux for 3 days. After cooling to room temperature, the white solids (m-chlorobenzoic acid) were removed by filtration (about 40 g when dry). The filtrate was extracted with several portions of saturated $NaHCO_3$ (on acidification, this aqueous wash yielded additional m-chlorobenzoic acid) and the organic solvent removed under vacuum. The crystalline residue (weighing 32 g and deeply colored) was dissolved in 150 mL boiling MeOH to which there was added 18 g of solid NaOH and the solution heated on the steam bath for a few min. The mixture was added to 800 mL H_2O, and a little surface scum mechanically removed with a piece of filter paper. The solution was acidified with concentrated HCl, depositing 30.9 g of a tan solid. Recrystallization from H_2O gave 2,3-dimethyl-4-methoxyphenol as white needles, with a mp of 95-96 °C. Anal. ($C_9H_{12}O_2$) H; C: calcd, 71.06; found 70.20. The N-methyl carbamate was made by the treatment of a solution of the phenol (1 g in 75 mL hexane with 5 mL CH_2Cl_2 added) with 2 g methyl isocyanate and a few drops of triethyl amine. The pale pink solids that separated were recrystallized from MeOH to give a product that had a mp of 141-142 °C. Anal. ($C_{11}H_{15}NO_3$) C,H,N.

To a solution of 23.1 g flake KOH in 250 mL hot EtOH there was added 61.8 g 2,3-dimethyl-4-methoxyphenol followed by 60 g methyl iodide. This was held under reflux for 12 h, then stripped of solvent under vacuum. The residue was dissolved in 1.2 L H_2O, acidified with HCl, and extracted with 3x200 mL CH_2Cl_2. The combined extracts were washed with 3x100 mL 5% NaOH, and the solvent was removed under vacuum. The residue set up as an off-white mass of leaflets weighing 37.7 g after filtering and air drying. Recrystallization from MeOH gave 2,3-dimethyl-1,4-dimethoxybenzene as white solids, with a mp of 78-79 °C. Anal.

($C_{10}H_{14}O_2$) C,H. An alternate route leading from 2,3-xylenol to this diether via nitrogen-containing intermediates was explored. The sequence involved the reaction of 2,3-xylenol with nitrous acid (4-nitroso product, mp 184 °C dec.), reduction with sodium dithionite (4-amino product, mp about 175 °C), oxidation with nitric acid (benzoquinone, mp 58 °C), reduction with sodium dithionite (hydroquinone) and final methylation with methyl iodide. The yields were inferior with this process.

A mixture of 88 g $POCl_3$ and 99 g N-methylformanilide was allowed to incubate until a deep claret color had formed, then it was treated with 36.5 g 2,3-dimethyl-1,4-dimethoxybenzene and heated on the steam bath for 3 h. It was then poured into 1 L H_2O, and stirred until the formation of a loose, crumbly, dark crystalline mass was complete. This was removed by filtration, and dissolved in 300 mL CH_2Cl_2. After washing first with H_2O, then with 5% NaOH, and finally with dilute HCl, the solvent was removed under vacuum yielding 39.5 g of a black oil that solidified. This was extracted with 2x300 mL boiling hexane, the extracts were pooled, and the solvent removed under vacuum. The yellowish residue crystallized to give 32.7 g 2,5-dimethoxy-3,4-dimethylbenzaldehyde with a mp of 46-47 °C. Repeated recrystallization from MeOH raised the mp to 59-60 °C. The malononitrile derivative was prepared (aldehyde and malononitrile in EtOH with a few drops triethyl amine) as yellow crystals from EtOH, with a mp of 190-191 °C. Anal. ($C_{14}H_{14}N_2O_2$) C,H; N: calcd, 11.56; found, 11.06, 11.04.

To a solution of 16.3 g 2,5-dimethoxy-3,4-dimethylbenzaldehyde in 50 mL nitromethane there was added 3.0 g anhydrous ammonium acetate, and the mixture was heated on the steam bath overnight. There was then added an equal volume of MeOH, and with cooling there was obtained a fine crop of yellow crystals. These were removed by filtration, washed with MeOH, and air dried to provide 4.4 g of 2,5-dimethoxy-3,4-dimethyl-ß-nitrostyrene with a mp of 120-121 °C which was not improved by recrystallization from MeOH (50 mL/g). The mother liquors of the above filtration were diluted with H_2O to the point of permanent turbidity, then set aside in a cold box. There was a chunky, granular, tomato-red crystal deposited which weighed 2.5 g when dry. It had a mp of 118-119.5 °C, which was undepressed in mixed mp with the yellow sample. Both forms had identical NMR spectra (2.20, 2.25 CH_3; 3.72, 3.84 OCH_3; 6.80 ArH; 7.76, 8.28 CH=CH, with 14 cycle splitting), infrared spectra, ultra violet spectra (max. 324 nm with shoulder at 366 nm in EtOH, two peaks at 309 and 355 nm in hexane), and microanalyses. Anal. ($C_{12}H_{15}NO_4$) C,H,N.

A solution of LAH (56 mL of a 1 M solution in THF) was cooled, under He, to 0 °C with an external ice bath. With good stirring there was added 1.52 mL 100% H_2SO_4 dropwise, to minimize charring. This was followed by the addition of 3.63 g 2,5-dimethoxy-3,4-dimethyl-ß-nitrostyrene in 36 mL anhydrous THF over the course of 1 h. After a few minutes further stirring, the temperature was brought up to a gentle reflux on the steam bath for about 5 min, then all was cooled again to 0 °C. The excess hydride was destroyed by the cautious addition of 9 mL IPA followed by 2.5 mL 15% NaOH and finally 7.5 mL H_2O. The reaction mixture was filtered, and the filter cake washed first with THF and then with IPA. The filtrate was stripped of solvent under vacuum and the residue was distilled at 110-120 °C at 0.2 mm/Hg to give 2.07 g of 2,5-dimethoxy-3,4-dimethylphenethylamine as a clear white oil. This was dissolved in 10 mL IPA, neutralized with concentrated HCl, and then diluted with 25 mL anhydrous Et_2O. The crystals that formed were filtered, Et_2O washed, and air dried to constant weight. There was obtained 2.13 g of beautiful white crystals of 2,5-dimethoxy-3,4-dimethylphenethylamine hydrochloride (2C-G) with a mp of 232-233 °C. Anal. ($C_{12}H_{20}ClNO_2$) C,H.

DOSAGE: 20 - 35 mg.

DURATION: 18 - 30 h.

QUALITATIVE COMMENTS: (with 22 mg) "I am completely functional, with writing and answering the telephone, but the coffee really tastes most strange. While the mental effects (to a ++ only) were dispersing, the body still had quite a bit of memory of the day. Sleep was fine, and desirable, in the early evening."

(with 32 mg) "Superb material, to be classified as a 'true psychedelic' unless one is publishing, in which case it could be best described as an 'insight-enhancer' and obviously of potential value in psychotherapy (if one would wish to spend 30 hours in a therapy session!). I suppose it would be best to simply stick with the insight-enhancing and skip the psychotherapy. Just too, too long. There was not any particular visual impact, at least for me. The non-sexual and the anorexic aspects might indeed change, with increasing familiarity. Remains to be seen. The length of the experience is against its frequent use, of course, which is a pity, since this one is well worth investigating as often as possible."

(with 32 mg) "There was, at the very beginning, a certain feeling of non-physical heat in the upper back which reminded me of the onset of various indoles, which this ain't. The energy tremor was quite strong throughout, but somehow the body was generally at ease."

(with 32 mg) "At a plateau at two hours, with just a bit of tummy queasi-ness. And I am still at the plateau several hours later. Sleep finally at the 18th hour, but even after getting up and doing all kinds of things the next day, I was not completely baseline until that evening. And a couple of days more for what is certainly complete repair. That is a lot of mileage for a small amount of material."

EXTENSIONS AND COMMENTARY: Here is the first example, ever, of a phen-ethylamine that is of about the same potency as the related three-carbon amphet-amine. At first approximation, one is hard put to distinguish, from the recorded notes, any major differences either in potency, in duration, or in the nature of activity, between 2C-G and GANESHA itself.

I had always thought of the phenethylamines as being somewhat weaker than the corresponding amphetamines. Sometimes a little weaker and sometimes a lot weaker. But that is a totally prejudiced point of view, an outgrowth of my earliest comparisons of mescaline and TMA. That's the kind of thing that can color one's thinking and obscure what may be valuable observations. It is equally valid to think of the phenethylamines as the prototypes, and that the amphetamines are somewhat stronger than the corresponding phenethylamines. Sometimes a little stronger and sometimes a lot stronger. Then the question suddenly shifts from asking what is different about the phenethylamines, to what is different about the amphetamines? It is simply a historic fact, that in most of my exploring, the amphetamine was made and evaluated first, and so tended to slip into the role of the prototype. In any case, here the two potencies converge.

#28   2C-G-3;   2,5-DIMETHOXY-3,4-(TRIMETHYLENE)- PHENETHYLAMINE;   5-(2-AMINOETHYL)-4,7- DIMETHOXYINDANE)

SYNTHESIS: To a solution of 22 g of KOH in 250 mL of hot EtOH, there was added 50 g of 4-indanol and 75 g methyl iodide. The mixture was held at reflux for 12 h. There was then added an additional 22 g KOH followed by an additional 50 g of methyl iodide. Refluxing was continued for an additional 12 h. The mixture was poured into 1 L H_2O, acidified with HCl, and extracted with 3x75 mL CH_2Cl_2. The pooled extracts were washed with 5% NaOH, then with dilute HCl, and the solvent was removed under vacuum. The residue of crude 2,3-(trimethylene)anisole weighed 56.5 g and was used without further purification in the following reaction.

A mixture of 327 g N-methylformanilide and 295 g $POCl_3$ was allowed to incubate until a deep claret color had formed. To this there was then added 110 g of crude 2,3-(trimethylene)anisole, and the mixture heated on the steam bath. There was a vigorous evolution of gases, which largely quieted down after some 4 h of heating. The reaction mixture was added to 4 L H_2O and stirred overnight. The oily aqueous phase was extracted with 3x200 mL CH_2Cl_2, and after combining the extracts and removal of the solvent there was obtained 147 g of a black, sweet-smelling oil. This was distilled at 182-194 °C at the water pump to yield 109.1 g of a pale yellow oil. At low temperature, this crystallized, but the solids melted again at room temperature. Gas chromatography of this product on OV-17 at 185 °C showed detectable starting anisole and N-methylformanilide (combined, perhaps 5% of the product) and a small but real isomeric peak, (about 5%, slightly faster moving than the title aldehyde, again about 5% of the product) of what was tentatively identified as the ortho-aldehyde (2-methoxy-3,4-(trimethylene)-benz-aldehyde). The bulk of this crude product (74 g) was redistilled at 110-130 °C at 0.3 mm/Hg to give 66 g of 4-methoxy-2,3-(trimethylene)benzaldehyde as a nearly colorless oil which set up as a crystalline solid. A portion on porous plate showed a mp of 28-29 C. A gram of this aldehyde and a gram of malononitrile in 25 mL of

EtOH was treated with a few drops of triethylamine and gave pale yellow crystals of the malononitrile derivative. This, upon recrystallization from 50 mL boiling EtOH, had a mp of 176-176.5 °C. Anal. ($C_{14}H_{12}N_2O$) C,H,N. A side path, other than towards the intended targets 2C-G-3 and G-3, was explored. Reaction with nitroethane and anhydrous ammonium acetate gave the 2-nitropropene analogue which was obtained in a pure state (mp 74-75 °C from MeOH) only after repeated extraction of the crude isolate with boiling hexane. Reduction with elemental iron gave the phenylacetone analogue which was reductively aminated with dimethylamine and sodium cyanoborohydride to give N,N-dimethyl-4-methoxy-2,3-(trimethylene)amphetamine. This was designed for brain blood-flow volume studies after iodination at the 5-position, a concept that has been discussed under IDNNA. It has never been tasted by anyone. The corresponding primary amine, 4-methoxy-2,3-(trimethylene)amphetamine has not yet even been synthesized.

A solution of 34.8 g 4-methoxy-2,3-(trimethylene)benzaldehyde in 800 mL CH_2Cl_2 was treated with 58.6 g of 85% m-chloroperoxybenzoic acid and held at reflux for 3 days. After cooling and standing for a few days, the solids were removed by filtration and washed sparingly with CH_2Cl_2. The combined filtrate and washings were washed with 200 mL saturated $NaHCO_3$, and the solvent removed, yielding 43.5 g of a deeply colored oil. This was dissolved in 150 mL MeOH to which was added 9 g NaOH and all heated to reflux on the steam bath. After 1 h, a solution of 9 g NaOH in 20 mL H_2O was added, heated further, then followed by yet another treatment with 9 g NaOH in 20 mL H_2O followed by additional heating. All was added to 800 mL H_2O, washed once with CH_2Cl_2 (which removed a trivial amount of material) and then acidified with HCl. The dark crystals that were generated were filtered and air dried to constant weight, yielding 27.5 g dark but nice-looking crystals with a mp of 89-91 °C. By all counts, this should have been the product phenol, 4-methoxy-2,3-(trimethylene)phenol, but the microanalysis indicated that the formate ester was still there. Anal. ($C_{10}H_{12}O_2$) requires C = 73.08, H = 7.37. ($C_{11}H_{12}O_3$) requires C = 68.73, H = 6.29. Found: C = 69.04, 68.84; H = 6.64, 6.58. Whatever the exact chemical status of the phenolic hydroxyl group might have been, it reacted successfully in the following methylation step.

To a solution of 10 g KOH in 100 g EtOH (containing 5% IPA) there was added 27.5 g of the above 89-91 °C melting material, followed by 25 g methyl iodide. The mixture was held at reflux overnight. All was added to 800 mL H_2O, acidified with HCl, and extracted with 3x100 mL CH_2Cl_2. The combined extracts were washed with 3x100 mL 5% NaOH, then once with dilute HCl, and the solvent removed under vacuum yielding 20.4 g of a fragrant crystalline residue. This was recrystallized from 60 mL boiling MeOH to give, after filtering and air drying, 16.0 g of 1,4-dimethoxy-2,3-(trimethylene)benzene (4,7-dimethoxyindane) with a mp of 86-88 °C. Anal. ($C_{11}H_{14}O_2$) C,H.

To a mixture of 39.0 g of N-methylformanilide and 35.9 g POCl$_3$ that had been allowed to stand at ambient temperature until deeply claret (about 45 min) there was added 15.8 g of 1,4-dimethoxy-2,3-(trimethylene)benzene. The mixture was heated on the steam bath for 4 h and then poured into 600 mL H$_2$O. After stirring overnight there was produced a heavy crystalline mass. This was removed by filtration and, after air drying, was extracted with 3x100 mL boiling hexane. Pooling and cooling these extracts yielded 9.7 g of salmon-colored crystals with a mp of 67-68 °C. This was recrystallized from 25 mL boiling EtOH to give, after filtration, EtOH washing, and air drying to constant weight, 7.4 g of 2,5-dimethoxy-3,4-(trimethylene)benzaldehyde, with a mp of 71-72 °C. The mother liquors on cautious treatment with H$_2$O, yielded, after EtOH recrystallization, 1 g additional product. Anal. (C$_{12}$H$_{14}$O$_3$) C,H. A solution of 150 mg aldehyde and an equal weight of malononitrile in 2.3 mL EtOH treated with 3 drops triethylamine gave immediate yellow crystals of the malononitrile derivative, with a mp of 161-162 °C. Anal. (C$_{15}$H$_{14}$N$_2$O$_2$) C,H,N.

A solution 3.7 g 2,5-dimethoxy-3,4-(trimethylene)benzaldehyde in 15 g nitromethane was treated with 0.7 g anhydrous ammonium acetate and heated on the steam bath for 14 h. The volatiles were removed under vacuum, and the residue set up to 3.5 g dark crystals, which melted broadly between 126-138 °C. Recrystallization of the entire mass from 70 mL boiling EtOH gave 3.2 g burnished gold crystals with a mp of 129-137 °C. A further recrystallization of an analytical sample from MeOH gave 2,5-dimethoxy-3,4-(trimethylene)-ß-nitrostyrene as yellow crystals with a mp of 146-147 °C. Anal. (C$_{13}$H$_{15}$NO$_4$) C,H.

To a cold solution of LAH in THF (40 mL of a 1 M solution) well stirred and under an inert atmosphere, there was added dropwise 1.05 mL freshly prepared 100% H$_2$SO$_4$. There was then added, dropwise, a solution of 2.39 g 2,5-dimethoxy-3,4-(trimethylene)-ß-nitrostyrene in 25 mL THF. The bright yellow color was discharged immediately. After the addition was complete, stirring was continued for an additional 20 min, and the reaction mixture brought to a reflux on the steam bath for another 0.5 h. After cooling, the excess hydride was destroyed with IPA (8 mL required) followed by sufficient 15% NaOH to convert the inorganics into a loose, filterable mass. This was removed by filtration, and the filter cake washed with THF. The combined filtrate and washes were stripped of solvent under vacuum, and the residue dissolved in dilute H$_2$SO$_4$ After washing with CH$_2$Cl$_2$, the aqueous phase was made basic with 25% NaOH and extracted with 3x75 mL CH$_2$Cl$_2$. After removal of the solvent under vacuum, the residue was distilled at 125-160 °C at 0.45 mm/Hg to yield 0.80 g of a white oil. This was dissolved in 8 mL IPA, neutralized with 20 drops of concentrated HCl (the salt crystals started to form before this was completed) followed with the addition of 65 mL anhydrous Et$_2$O. The white crystalline mass was filtered, washed with Et$_2$O, and air dried to provide 1.16 g of 2,5-dimethoxy-3,4-(trimethylene)phenethylamine hydrochloride (2C-G-3) with a mp of 214-216 °C with decomposition. Anal. (C$_{13}$H$_{20}$ClNO$_2$) C,H.

DOSAGE: 16 - 25 mg.

DURATION: 12 - 24 h.

QUALITATIVE COMMENTS: (with 16 mg) "It came on in little leaps and bounds. All settled, and then it would take another little jump upwards. I am totally centered, and writing is easy. My appetite is modest. Would I drive to town to return a book to the library? No ever-loving way! I am very content to be right here where I am safe, and stay with the writing. It does take so much time to say what wants to be said, but there is no quick way. A word at a time."

(with 22 mg) "I walked out for the mail at just about twilight. That was the most courageous thing that I could possibly have done, just for one lousy postcard and a journal. What if I had met someone who had wanted to talk? Towards evening I got a call from Peg who said her bean soup was bubbling in a scary way and what should she do, and I said maybe better make soap. It was that kind of an experience! Way up there, lots of LSD-like sparkles, and nothing quite really making sense. Marvelous."

(with 25 mg) "There was easy talking, and no hint of any body concern. Sleep that evening was easy, and the next day was with good energy."

EXTENSIONS AND COMMENTARY: The positives of a completely intriguing altered state free from apparent physical threats, are here coupled with the negative of having to invest such a long period of time. There is a merry nuttiness which can give a joyous intoxication, but with the underlying paranoia of how it looks to others. There is an ease of communication, but only within surroundings that are well-known and friendly. This might be a truly frightening experience if it were in an unfamiliar or unstructured environment.

The numbering of this compound, and all the extensions of GANESHA, have been made on the basis of the nature of the stuff at the 3,4-position. Here there are three atoms (the trimethylene bridge) and so 2C-G-3 seems reasonable. With this logic, the dimethylene bridge would be 2C-G-2 (and the corresponding amphetamine would be G-2, of course). But these compounds call upon a common intermediate which is a benzocyclobutene, OK in principle but not yet OK in practice. The right benzyne reaction will be there someday, and the dimethylene analogues will be made and assayed. But, in the meantime, at least the names have been assigned.

#29   2C-G-4;   2,5-DIMETHOXY-3,4-(TETRAMETHYLENE)-PHENETHYLAMINE;   6-(2-AMINOETHYL)-5,8-DIMETHOXY-TETRALIN

SYNTHESIS: To a solution of 49.2 g 5,6,7,8-tetrahydronaphthol (5-hydroxy-tetralin) in 100 mL MeOH, there was added 56 g methyl iodide followed by a solution of 24.8 g KOH pellets (85% purity) in 100 mL boiling MeOH. The mixture was heated in a 55 °C bath for 3 h (the first white solids of potassium iodide appeared in about 10 min). The solvent was stripped under vacuum, and the residues dissolved in 2 L H_2O. This was acidified with HCl, and extracted with 4x75 mL CH_2Cl_2. After washing the organic phase with 3x75 mL 5% NaOH, the solvent was removed under vacuum to give 48.2 g of a black residue. This was distilled at 80-100 °C at 0.25 mm/Hg to provide 33.9 g 5-methoxy-1,2,3,4-tetrahydronaphthalene as a white oil. The NaOH washes, upon acidification and extraction with CH_2Cl_2 gave, after removal of the solvent under vacuum and distillation of the residue at 0.35 mm/Hg, 11.4 g of recovered starting phenol.

A mixture of 61.7 g $POCl_3$ and 54.3 g N-methylformanilide was heated on the steam bath for 15 min which produced a deep red color. This was added to 54.3 g of 5-methoxy-1,2,3,4-tetrahydronaphthalene, and the mixture was heated on the steam bath for 2 h. The reaction mixture was quenched in 1.2 L H_2O with very good stirring. The oils generated quickly turned to brown granular solids, which were removed by filtration. The 79 g of wet product was finely triturated under an equal weight of MeOH, filtered, washed with 20 mL ice-cold MeOH, and air dried to yield 32.0 g of 4-methoxy-5,6,7,8-tetrahydronaphthaldehyde as an ivory-colored solid. The filtrate, on standing, depos-ited another 4.5 g of product which was added to the above first crop. An analytical sample was obtained by recrystallization from EtOH, and had a mp of 57-58 °C. Anal. ($C_{12}H_{14}O_2$) C,H.

To a solution of 25.1 g 4-methoxy-5,6,7,8-tetrahydronaphthaldehyde in 300 mL CH_2Cl_2 there was added 25 g 85% m-chloroperoxybenzoic acid at a rate that was commensurate with the exothermic reaction. Solids were apparent within a few min. The stirred reaction mixture was heated at reflux for 8 h. After cooling to room temperature, the solids were removed by filtration and washed lightly with CH_2Cl_2. The pooled filtrate and washes were stripped of solvent under vacuum and the residue dissolved in 100 mL MeOH and treated with 40 mL 25% NaOH. This was heated on the steam bath for an hour, added to 1 L H_2O, and acidified with HCl, producing a heavy crystalline mass. This was removed by filtration, air dried, and distilled at up to 170 °C at 0.2 mm/Hg. There was thus obtained 21.4 g of 4-methoxy-5,6,7,8-tetrahydronaphthol as an off-white solid with a mp of 107-114 °C. An analytical sample was obtained by recrystallization from 70% EtOH, and melted at 119-120 °C. Hexane is also an excellent recrystallization solvent. Anal. ($C_{11}H_{14}O_2$) C,H. As an alternate method, the oxidation of the naphthaldehyde to the naphthol can be achieved through heating the aldehyde in acetic acid solution containing hydrogen peroxide. The yields using this route are consistently less than 40% of theory.

A solution of 21.0 g of 4-methoxy-5,6,7,8-tetrahydronaphthol in 100 mL acetone in a 1 L round-bottomed flask, was treated with 25 g finely ground anhydrous K_2CO_3 and 26 g methyl iodide. The mixture was held at reflux on the steam bath for 2 h, cooled, and quenched in 1 L H_2O. Trial extraction evaluations have shown that the starting phenol, as well as the product ether, are extractable into CH_2Cl_2 from aqueous base. The aqueous reaction mixture was extracted with 3x60 mL CH_2Cl_2, the solvent removed under vacuum, and the residue (19.6 g) was distilled at 90-130 °C at 0.3 mm/Hg to give 14.1 g of an oily white solid mixture of starting material and product. This was finely ground under an equal weight of hexane, and the residual crystalline solids removed by filtration. These proved to be quite rich in the desired ether. This was dissolved in a hexane/CH_2Cl_2 mixture (3:1 by volume) and chromatographed on a silica gel preparative column, with the eluent continuously monitored by TLC (with this solvent system, the Rf of the ether product was 0.5, of the starting phenol 0.1). The fractions containing the desired ether were pooled, the solvent removed under vacuum and the residue, which weighed 3.86 g, was dissolved in 1.0 mL hexane and cooled with dry ice. Glistening white crystals were obtained by filtration at low temperature. The weight of 5,8-dimethoxytetralin isolated was 2.40 g and the mp was 44-45 °C. GCMS analysis showed it to be largely one product (m/s 192 parent peak and major peak), but the underivitized starting phenol has abysmal GC properties and TLC remains the best measure of chemical purity.

A well-stirred solution of 3.69 g 5,8-dimethoxytetralin in 35 mL CH_2Cl_2 was placed in an inert atmosphere and cooled to 0 °C with an external ice bath. There was then added, at a slow rate, 4.5 mL anhydrous stannic chloride, which produced a transient color that quickly faded to a residual yellow. There was then added 2.0 mL dichloromethyl methyl ether, which caused immediate darkening. After a few min stirring, the reaction mixture was allowed to come to room temperature, and finally to a gentle reflux on the steam bath. The evolution of HCl was continuous. The reaction was then poured into 200 mL H_2O, the phases separated, and the aqueous phase extracted with 2x50 mL CH_2Cl_2. The organic phase and extracts were pooled, washed with 3x50 mL 5% NaOH, and the solvent removed under vacuum. The residue was distilled at 120-140 °C at 0.3 mm/Hg to give 3.19 g of a white oil that spontaneously crystallized. The crude mp of 1,4-dimethoxy-5,6,7,8-tetrahydro-2-naphthaldehyde was 70-72 °C. An analytical sample from hexane had the mp 74-75 °C. The GCMS analysis showed only a single material (m/s 220, 100%) with no apparent starting dimethoxytetralin present. Attempts to synthesize this aldehyde by the Vilsmeier procedure ($POCl_3$ and N-methylformanilide) gave complex mixtures of products. Synthetic efforts employing butyllithium and DMF gave only recovered starting material.

To a solution of 1.5 g 1,4-dimethoxy-5,6,7,8-tetrahydro-2-naphthaldehyde in 20 g nitromethane there was added 0.14 g anhydrous ammonium acetate and the mixture heated on the steam bath for 50 min. The rate of the reaction was determined by TLC monitoring, on silica gel with CH_2Cl_2 as the moving solvent; the Rf of the aldehyde was 0.70, and of the product nitrostyrene, 0.95. Removal of the volatiles under vacuum gave a residue that spontaneously crystallized. The fine yellow crystals that were obtained were suspended in 1.0 mL of MeOH, filtered, and air dried to yield 1.67 g 2,5-dimethoxy-ß-nitro-3,4-(tetramethylene)styrene with a mp of 151.5-152.5 °C. Anal. $(C_{14}H_{17}NO_4)$ C,H.

DOSAGE: unknown.

DURATION: unknown

EXTENSIONS AND COMMENTARY: The road getting to this final product reminded me of the reasons why, during the first few billion years of the universe following the big bang, there was only hydrogen and helium. Nothing heavier. When everything had expanded enough to cool things sufficiently for the first actual matter to form, all was simply very energetic protons and neutrons. These were banging into one-another, making deuterium nuclei, and some of these got banged up even all the way to helium, but every time a helium nucleus collided with a particle of mass one, to try for something with mass five, the products simply couldn't exist. Both Lithium-5 and Helium-5 have the impossible half-lives of 10 to the minus 21 seconds. Hence, in the primordial soup, the only way to get into something heavier than helium was to have a collision between a couple of the relatively scarcer heavy nuclei, or to have a three body collision. Both of these would be extremely rare events, statistically. And if a few got through, there was another forbidden barrier at mass 8, since Beryllium-8 has a half life of 10 to the minus 16 seconds. So everything had to wait for a few suns to burn down so that they could process enough helium into heavy atoms, to achieve some nuclear chemistry that was not allowed in the early history of the universe.

    And in the same way, there were two nearly insurmountable barriers encountered in getting to 2C-G-4 and G-4. The simple act of methylating an aromatic hydroxyl group provided mixtures that could only be resolved into components by some pretty intricate maneuvers. And when that product was indeed gotten, the conversion of it into a simple aromatic aldehyde resisted the classic procedures completely, either giving complex messes, or nothing. And even now, with these two hurdles successfully passed, the presumed simple last step has not yet been done. The product 2C-G-4 lies just one synthetic step (the LAH reduction) away from completion, and the equally fascinating G-4 also that one last reduction step from being completed. Having gotten through the worst of the swamp, let's get into the lab and finish up this challenge. They will both be active compounds.

#30   2C-G-5;   3,6-DIMETHOXY-4-(2-AMINOETHYL)-
BENZONORBORNANE

SYNTHESIS: To a stirred solution of 25 g 3,6-dihydroxybenzonorbornane (from Eastman Kodak Company) in 200 mL acetone there was added 200 mg decyltriethylammonium iodide, 40 g of powdered anhydrous K_2CO_3, and 55 g methyl iodide. The mixture was held at reflux with a heating mantle overnight. After removal of the solvent under vacuum, the residue was added to 2 L of H_2O, acidified with concentrated HCl, and extracted with 3x100 mL CH_2Cl_2. The pooled extracts were washed with 2x150 mL 5% NaOH and once with dilute HCl, and the solvent was removed under vacuum to give 19.0 g of a black oil as a residue. This was distilled at 90-115 °C at 0.3 mm/Hg to yield 15.5 g of an orange oil which set up as a crystalline solid. The product, 3,6-dimethoxybenzonorbornane, had a mp of 35-37 °C from hexane or 40-41 °C from MeOH. Anal. $(C_{13}H_{16}O_2)$ C,H.

A solution of 4.6 g $POCl_3$ and 4.6 g N-methylformanilide was heated briefly on the steam-bath until the color had become deep claret. There was then added 3.05 g of 3,6-dimethoxybenzonorbornane and the solution was heated on the steam bath for 12 h. The black, tarry reaction mixture was poured into H_2O, and after hydrolysis, the H_2O was decanted and the insoluble residues were washed alternately with H_2O and with CH_2Cl_2. The combined washes were separated, and the aqueous phase extracted with 2x50 mL CH_2Cl_2. The combined organic fractions were washed with 5% NaOH, and the solvent removed under vacuum. The fluid, black residue was distilled at 130-140 °C at 0.3 mm/Hg to give 1.17 g of an almost white oil. This was dissolved in 1 mL MeOH, and cooled to -50 °C to give a white crystalline solid that was removed by filtration and washed sparingly with -50 °C MeOH and air dried. There was obtained 0.83 g 3,6-dimethoxy-4-formylbenzonorbornane with a mp of 37-40 °C which could be increased, by wasteful recrystallization from MeOH, to 53-54 °C. An intimate mixture of this product with the starting diether (mp 40-41 °C) was a liquid at room temperature. Anal. $(C_{14}H_{16}O_3)$ C,H.

To a solution of 3.70 g 3,6-dimethoxy-4-formylbenzonorbornane in 20 g nitromethane, there was added 1.3 g anhydrous ammonium acetate and the mixture was heated on the steam bath for 45 min. The excess reagent/solvent was removed under vacuum, and the residue was dissolved in 20 mL boiling MeOH. A speck of seed crystal started a heavy crystallization of orange crystals which were removed by filtration and washed with

MeOH. After drying, the product 3,6-dimethoxy-4-(2-nitrovinyl)benzonorbornane was yellow, weighed 3.47 g, and had a mp of 88-89 °C. Recrystallization of an analytical sample from MeOH did not improve this mp. Anal. $(C_{15}H_{17}NO_4)$ C,H.

A solution of LAH (46 mL of a 1 M solution in THF) was cooled, under He, to 0 °C with an external ice bath. With good stirring there was added 1.25 mL 100% H_2SO_4 dropwise, to minimize charring. This was followed by the addition of 3.4 g 3,6-dimethoxy-4-(2-nitrovinyl)benzonorbornane in 30 mL anhydrous THF. After a few min further stirring, the temperature was brought up to a gentle reflux on the steam bath for 10 min, and then all was cooled again to 0 °C. The excess hydride was destroyed by the cautious addition of 7 mL IPA, followed by 2 mL 15% NaOH and 5 mL H_2O, which gave an easily filtered white granular solid. This was removed by filtration, and the filter cake was washed with THF. The combined filtrate and washes were stripped of solvent under vacuum providing a pale amber oil which was distilled at 150-160 °C at 0.3 mm/Hg to give 1.45 g of a white oil. This was dissolved in 7 mL IPA, and neutralized with 15 drops of concentrated HCl. There was then added 25 mL anhydrous Et_2O and, after a short delay, white crystals formed spontaneously. These were removed by filtration, Et_2O washed, and air dried to constant weight, yielding 1.13 g of 3,6-dimethoxy-4-(2-aminoethyl)-benzonorbornane hydrochloride (2C-G-5). The mp was 199-200 °C. Anal. $(C_{15}H_{22}ClNO_2)$ C,H.

DOSAGE: 10 - 16 mg.

DURATION: 32 - 48 h.

QUALITATIVE COMMENTS: (with 14 mg) "I was well aware of things at the end of two hours, and I was totally unwilling to drive, or even go out of the house. I was reminded continuously of 2C-B with its erotic push, and the benign interplay of colors and other visual effects. But it is so much longer lived. I am a full +++, very stoned, and there is no believable sign of dropping for another several hours. There is a good appetite (again, 2C-B like), and I managed to sleep for a few hours, and all the next day I was spacey and probably still a plus one. The day yet following, I was finally at a believable baseline. Both of these days were filled with what might be called micro doze-offs, almost like narcolepsy. Maybe I am just sleep deprived."

(with 16 mg) "The first effects were felt within one hour, and full effects between 2 1/2 and 3 hours. Tremendous clarity of thought, cosmic but grounded, as it were. This is not at all like LSD, and is a lot mellower than the 2C-T family. For the next few hours it was delightful and fun and I felt safe and good-humored. I got to sleep without much difficulty while still at a plus three, and my dreams were positive and balanced, but I awoke irritable and emotionally flattened. I did not want to interact with anyone. The first 16 hours of this stuff were great, and the second 16 hours were a bit of a drag. Just twice as long as it ought to be."

(with 16 mg) "I was at full sparkle within three hours, and I continued to sparkle for the longest time. The tiredness that comes after a while probably reflects the inadequacy of sleep. I was aware of something still going on some two days later."

EXTENSIONS AND COMMENTARY: In the eventual potency assessment of a drug, there must be some consideration of not only the dosage needed, but the duration of effects. The area under the curve, so to speak. By these measures, this phenethylamine is a record breaker, in that it is not only amongst the most potent, but it goes on and on and on.

There are a couple of chemical commentaries. One, the miserable phenol-to-ether-to-aldehyde series of steps, so maddeningly unsatisfactory in the 2C-G-4 process, was completely comfortable here. The reactions rolled, and the yields were most satisfactory. Secondly, this is one of the few phenethylamines that is a racemate. The strange geometry of the norbornane ring carries within it a chiral character, so this compound is potentially resolvable into two optically active forms. That might be quite a task, but it would have the value of providing for the first time a pair of isomers that were asymmetric in the 3,4-aliphatic part of the molecule. To the extent that some insight into the geometry of the receptor site can be gleaned from the absolute configurations of active agonists, here is a compound where the subtle variations are over there at the ring substitution area of the structure, rather than at the well-explored alpha-carbon atom. Some day I might try to resolve this drug into its optical isomers. But I suspect that it might be quite difficult.

A number of chemical variations of 2C-G-5 are obvious. The dihydroxy-benzonorbornane compound that was the starting point of all this was certainly the adduct of cyclopentadiene and benzoquinone, with the double bond reduced. The same chemistry with 1,3-cyclohexadiene would give a two-carbon bridge instead of the one-carbon bridge of norbornane and, after hydrogenation, would provide a non-chiral analog with two ethylene bridges between the 3- and 4-position carbons. This is a cyclohexane ring connected, by its 1- and 4-positions, to the two methyl groups of 2C-G. With six carbons in this aliphatic mess, the compound is probably best called 2C-G-6. It should be easily made, and it is certain to be very potent. And there are potentially several other Diels Alder dienes that might serve with benzoquinone as the dieneophile. There are aliphatic things such as hexa-2,4-diene and 2,3-dimethylbutadiene. The textbooks are filled with dozens of diene candidates, and benzquinone will always provide the two oxygens needed for the eventual 2,5-dimethoxy groups of the phenethylamine.

#31   2C-G-N;   1,4-DIMETHOXYNAPHTHYL-2-ETHYLAMINE

SYNTHESIS: A solution of 17.5 g 1,4-naphthaquinone in 200 mL MeOH was heated to the boiling point, and treated with 28.5 g stannous chloride at a rate that maintained a continuous rolling boil. At the completion of the addition, the reaction mixture was saturated with anhydrous hydrogen chloride, and held at reflux on the steam bath for 2 h. The reaction mixture was poured into 700 mL H_2O and treated with aqueous NaOH. During the addition there was transient development of a curdy white solid which redissolved when the system became strongly basic. This was extracted with 3x200 mL CH_2Cl_2 and the pooled extracts were washed first with H_2O, then with dilute HCl, and finally again with H_2O. Removal of the solvent under vacuum yielded 15.75 g of a low melting black flaky crystalline material which was distilled at 160-180 °C at 0.05 mm/Hg to give 14.5 g of an amber, solid mass with a mp of 78-86 °C. Recrystallization from 75 mL boiling MeOH provided 1,4-

dimethoxynaphthalene as white crystals melting at 87-88 °C.

A mixture of 20.0 g POCl$_3$ and 22.5 g N-methylformanilide was allowed to stand at room temperature for 0.5 h which produced a deep claret color. To this there was added 9.4 g 1,4-dimethoxynaphthalene and the mixture was heated on the steam bath. The reaction mixture quickly became progressively darker and thicker. After 20 min it was poured into 250 mL H$_2$O and stirred for several h. The solids were removed by filtration, and washed well with H$_2$O. The wet crude product (a dull yellow-orange color) was dissolved in 125 mL boiling EtOH to give a deep red solution. On cooling, this deposited a heavy crop of crystals that was removed by filtration, and washed with cold EtOH. There was obtained, after air-drying to constant weight, 7.9 g 1,4-dimethoxy-2-naphthaldehyde as white crystals with a mp of 119-121 °C. This was not improved by further recrystallization. The malononitrile derivative, from the aldehyde and malononitrile in EtOH with a drop of triethylamine, had a mp of 187-188 °C.

A solution of 3.9 g 1,4-dimethoxy-2-naphthaldehyde in 13.5 g nitromethane was treated with 0.7 g anhydrous ammonium acetate, and heated on the steam bath for 1 h. The excess reagent/solvent was removed under vacuum giving a residue that spontaneously crystallized. This crude product was removed with the aid of a few mL MeOH, and pressed on a sintered funnel with modest MeOH washing. There was obtained 3.6 g (when dry) of old-gold colored crystals with a mp of 146-148 °C. Recrystallization from 140 mL boiling EtOH gave 3.0 g 1,4-dimethoxy-2-(2-nitro-vinyl)naphthalene as deep gold-colored crystals with a mp of 146-147 °C. A small sample, upon recrystalization from MeOH, melted at 143-144 °C. Anal. (C$_{14}$H$_{13}$NO$_4$) C,H.

A solution of LAH (50 mL of a 1 M solution in THF) was cooled, under He, to 0 °C with an external ice bath. With good stirring there was added 1.32 mL 100% H$_2$SO$_4$ dropwise, to minimize charring. This was followed by the addition of 2.80 g 1,4-dimethoxy-2-(2-nitrovinyl)naphthalene in 40 mL anhydrous THF. There was an immediate loss of color. After 1 h stirring at 0 °C, the temperature was brought up to a gentle reflux on the steam bath for 20 min, then all was cooled again to 0 °C. The excess hydride was destroyed by the cautious addition of 7 mL IPA followed by 5.5 mL 5% NaOH. The reaction mixture was filtered, and the filter cake washed with several portions of THF. The combined filtrate and washings were stripped of solvent under vacuum providing 3.6 g of a pale amber oil that was distilled at 145-160 °C at 0.2 mm/Hg to give 1.25 g of product as an absolutely white oil. This was dissolved in 7 mL IPA, and neutralized with concentrated HCl forming immediate crystals of the hydrochloride salt in the alcohol solvent. Thirty mL of anhydrous Et$_2$O was added, and after complete grinding and mixing, the hydrochloride salt was removed by filtration, Et$_2$O washed, and air dried to constant weight. The spectacular white crystals of 1,4-dimethoxynaphthyl-2-ethylamine hydrochloride (2C-G-N) weighed 1.23 g and had melting properties of darkening at 190 °C, and decomposing in the 235-245 °C area. Anal. $(C_{14}H_{18}ClNO_2)$ C,H.

DOSAGE: 20 - 40 mg.

DURATION: 20 - 30 h.

QUALITATIVE COMMENTS: (with 24 mg) "The effects were interestingly colored by the reading of Alan Watts' Joyous Cosmology during the coming-on period. The only body negatives were some urinary retention and a feeling of a shallow but continuing amphetamine stimulation. But not enough to be actually jingly, nor to interfere with sleep that evening. There is not much psychedelic here, but there is something really going on anyway. This has some similarities to the antidepressant world."

(with 35 mg) "Much writing, much talking, and there was considerable residual awareness the next day. Somehow this material is not as friendly as the other 2C-G's."

(with 35 mg) "Thinking is clear. No fuzziness, no feeling of being pushed. None of the walking on the fine middle line between light and dark that is the excitement and the threat of LSD. This is just a friend, an ally, which invites you to do anything you wish to." [comment added two days later] "My sleep was not deep enough, but it was pleasant and relatively resting. The whole next day I was feeling happy, but with an overlay of irritability. Strange mixture. By bedtime the irritability had become a mild depression. I feel that there might have been a threshold continuing for a couple of days. The character of my dreaming had the stamp of drug on it. This compound, in retrospect, presents some problems that cause a faint unease."

EXTENSIONS AND COMMENTARY: There is always a wish in the design of new compounds to find something that is of interesting activity, with an aromatic ring at some location pretty much away from the site of activity. This would then allow some subtle fine-tuning of the nature of the action by putting any of a wide range of electron pushing or electron pulling groups on that ring. But here, with 2C-G-N, by the time the ring got put into place, the activity was already on the wane, and the action was too long, and there are indicators of some not completely friendly effects. Ah well, some other molecule, some other time.

#32   2C-H;   2,5-DIMETHOXYPHENETHYLAMINE

SYNTHESIS: A solution of 50 g 2,5-dimethoxybenzaldehyde in 100 g nitromethane was treated with 5 g of anhydrous ammonium acetate, and heated on the steam bath for 4 h. The solution was decanted from a little insoluble material, and the solvent removed under vacuum. The clear oily residue was dissolved in 100 mL boiling IPA which, after standing a moment, set up as dense crystals. After returning to room temperature, these were removed by filtration, the product was washed with IPA and air dried, yielding 56.9 g 2,5-dimethoxy-ß-nitrostyrene as spectacular yum-yum orange crystals with a mp of 119-120 °C. An analytical sample, from ethyl acetate, melted at 120-121 °C.

A suspension of 60 g LAH in 500 mL anhydrous THF was placed under an inert atmosphere, stirred magnetically, and brought up to reflux temperature. There was added, dropwise, 56 g of 2,5-dimethoxy-ß-nitrostyrene dissolved in THF, and the reaction mixture was maintained at reflux for 36 h. After being brought to room temperature, the excess hydride was destroyed with 40 mL IPA, followed by 50 mL of 15% NaOH. An additional 100 mL THF was required for easy stirring, and an additional 150 mL H$_2$O was needed for complete conversion of the aluminum salts to a loose, white, filterable consistency. This solid was removed by filtration, and the filter cake washed with additional THF. The combined filtrate and washes were stripped of solvent under vacuum, and the residue dissolved in dilute H$_2$SO$_4$. Washing with 3x75 mL CH$_2$Cl$_2$ removed most of the color, and the aqueous phase was made basic with aqueous NaOH and reextracted with 3x100 mL CH$_2$Cl$_2$. Removal of the solvent yielded 39.2 g of a pale amber oil that was distilled. The fraction boiling at 80-100 °C at 0.4 mm/Hg weighed 24.8 g and was water-white product amine. As the free base, it was suitable for most of the further synthetic steps that might be wanted, but in this form it picked up carbon dioxide rapidly when exposed to the air. It was readily converted to the hydrochloride salt by dissolution in 6 volumes of IPA, neutralization with concentrated HCl, and addition of sufficient anhydrous Et$_2$O to produce a permanent turbidity. Crystals of 2,5-dimethoxyphenethylamine hydrochloride (2C-H) spontaneously formed and were removed by filtration, washed with Et$_2$O, and air dried. The mp was 138-139 °C.

DOSAGE: unknown.

DURATION: unknown.

EXTENSIONS AND COMMENTARY: I know of no record of 2C-H ever having been tried by man. It has been assumed by everyone (and probably correctly so) that this amine, being an excellent substrate for the amino oxidase systems in man, will be completely destroyed by the body as soon as it gets into it, and thus be without action. In virtually all animal assays where it has been compared with known psychoactive drugs, it remains at the "less-active" end of the ranking.

It is, however, one of the most magnificent launching pads for a number of rather unusual and, in a couple of cases, extraordinary drugs. In the lingo of the chemist, it is amenable to "electrophilic attack at the 4-position." And, in the lingo of the psychopharmacologist, the "4-position is where the action is." From this (presumably) inactive thing have evolved end products such as 2C-B, 2C-I, 2C-C, and 2C-N. And in the future, many possible things as might come from a carbinol group, an amine function, or anything that can stem from a lithium atom.

#33   2C-I;   2,5-DIMETHOXY-4-IODOPHENETHYLAMINE

SYNTHESIS: A mixture of 7.4 g phthalic anhydride and 9.05 g of 2,5-dimethoxy-phenethylamine (see the recipe for 2C-H for its preparation) was heated with an open flame. A single clear phase was formed with the loss of H_2O. After the hot melt remained quiet for a few moments, it was poured out into a crystallizing dish yielding 14.8 g of a crude solid product. This was recrystallized from 20 mL CH_3CN, with care taken for an endothermic dissolution, and an exothermic crystallization. Both transitions must be done without haste. After filtration, the solids were washed with 2x20 mL hexane and air dried to constant weight. A yield of 12.93 g of N-(2-(2,5-dimethoxyphenyl)ethyl)phthalimide was obtained as electrostatic yellow crystals, with a mp of 109-111 °C. A sample recrystallized from IPA was white, with a mp of 110-111 °C. Anal. ($C_{18}H_{17}NO_4$) C,H,N.

To a solution of 12.9 g N-(2-(2,5-dimethoxyphenyl)ethyl)phthalimide in 130 mL warm (35 °C) acetic acid which was being vigorously stirred, there was added a solution of 10 g iodine monochloride in 40 mL acetic acid. This was stirred for 1 h, while being held at about 30 °C. The reaction mixture was poured into 1500 mL H_2O and extracted with 4x75 mL CH_2Cl_2. The extracts were pooled, washed once with 150 mL H_2O containing 2.0 g sodium dithionite, and the solvent removed under vacuum to give 16.2 g of N-(2-(2,5-dimethoxy-4-iodophenyl)-ethyl)phthalimide as yellow amber solids with a mp of 133-141 °C. This mp was improved by recrystallization from 75 mL CH_3CN, yielding 12.2 g of a pale yellow solid with mp 149-151 °C. A small sample from a large quantity of IPA gives a white product melting at 155.5-157 °C.

A solution of 12.2 g N-(2-(2,5-dimethoxy-4-iodophenyl)ethyl)phthalimide in 150 mL hot IPA was treated with 6.0 mL of hydrazine hydrate, and the clear solution was heated on the steam bath. After a few minutes there was the generation of a white cottage cheese-like solid (1,4-dihydroxyphthalizine). The heating was continued for several additional h, the reaction mixture cooled, and the solids removed by filtration. These were washed with 2x10 mL EtOH, and the pooled filtrate and washes stripped of solvent under vacuum giving a residue which, when treated with aqueous hydrochloric acid, gave 3.43 g of voluminous white crystals. This, after recrystallization from 2 weights of H_2O, filtering, washing first with IPA and then with Et_2O, and air drying, gave 2.16 g 2,5-dimethoxy-4-iodophenethylamine hydrochloride (2C-I) as a white microcrystalline solid, with a mp of 246-247 °C. Anal. $(C_{10}H_{15}ClINO_2)$ C,H,N.

DOSAGE: 14 - 22 mg.

DURATION: 6 - 10 h.

QUALITATIVE COMMENTS (with 0 mg) "I was present at a group meeting, but was only an observer. With zero milligrams of 2C-I, I was able to get to a delightful plus 2.5 in about five minutes after I arrived at your place, and absorbed the ambience of the folks who had actually imbibed the material. My level lasted about four hours and came down at about the same time as did the others. There were no after-effects experienced except for a pleasant languor."

(with 15 mg) "Comfortable onset. Most notable are the visuals, patterning like 2C-B (Persian carpet type), very colorful and active. Much more balanced emotional character, but still no feeling of insight, revelation, or progress toward the true meaning of the universe. And at 5 1/2 hours drop-off very abrupt, then gentle decline. I would like to investigate museum levels."

(with 16 mg) "There was an immediate alert within minutes. As usual, it was only an awareness, then nothing happened for a while. In retrospect, I see some type of activity or awareness within 40 minutes, which then builds up over time. The peak was at 2 hours and seemed to maintain itself for a while. Near the peak, there was some hallucinogenic activity, though not a lot. The pictures in the dining room had color and pattern movement that was fairly detailed. Focusing on other areas, such as walls or the outside of the house, produced little activity, though I tried. There was certainly a lot of color enhancement. There was also that peculiar aspect of the visual field having darkened or shadowed areas. These darker areas seemed to shift around to some degree. That aspect seems to be similar to 2C-B. I don't think I was more than +2.5 at the peak. Coming down was uneventful. I was down within 6 hours. I had no problems driving home, nor were there any difficulties with sleep. There were no body problems with this material. I ate like a horse."

(with 16 mg) "The 16 was a bit much, I realized, because my body was not sure of what to do with all the *energy*. Next time I'll try 14 or 15. However, my conversations were extremely clear and insightful. The degree of honesty was incredible. I was not afraid to say anything to anyone. Felt really good about myself. Very centered, in fact. A bit tired at day's end. Early bedtime."

(with 20 mg) "I think there is slightly less than full immersion in the sensual, with this material, compared with 2C-B, but I suspect it's more a matter of getting used to the language of 2C-I and the feelings — getting tuned to a slightly different frequency, really — rather than that the material is less sensual or less easy to use sensually. Just different frequency, and we are very, very used to 2C-B. Good on the body. Transition, for me, not as strongly dark as 2C-B. But it could certainly take a lot more exploring, if we were able to give the time (about 9 hours) to it. Next day: sleep excellent. Energy next day unusually good. Quite tired by evening."

EXTENSIONS AND COMMENTARY: The frequent comparisons between 2C-I and 2C-B stem, without doubt, from a bit of chemical suggestion. The two compounds have structures that are truly analogous, in technical terms. In one, there is a strategically located iodine atom, and in the other, an identically placed bromine atom. These are directly above and below one-another in the periodic table. And what is particularly maddening to the synthetic diddler, is that they cannot be lengthened, or shortened, or squooshed around in any way. You can't make a longer and narrower version of a bromine atom, as you can do with, say, a butyl group. You've got what you've got, like it or not. No subtle variations.

But, on the brighter side of the picture, you have a heavy atom here, and this atom is intrinsic to the central activity of the compound. So, these materials are naturals for radio-labelling experiments. 2C-I has been made radioactive with radio-iodine, but the most impressive findings have been made with the 3-carbon analog, DOI.

One quotation from an observer of a group experiment is enclosed; an experiment with zero milligrams being taken. This is a instructive observation of what has been called a "contact high."

There is one Iodotweetio known. In Scrabble, would you challenge a word that had seven of its eleven letters as vowels? Especially if the vowels were, specifically, iooeeio? It sounds just a little like the noise coming out of Old McDonald's farm. But a Tweetio there is, namely, the 2-EtO-homologue of 2C-I. This is 2-ethoxy-4-iodo-5-methoxyphenethylamine, or 2CI-2ETO. The hydrochloride salt was a white, crystalline product with a melting point of 175-175.5 °C. The threshold level of activity was seen at an oral dose of 5 milligrams, and the generated effects were completely dispersed in a couple of hours. Most interestingly, larger doses, of up to 50 milligrams orally, seem to produce no more intense an effect, but simply to stretch out this threshold for an additional couple of hours. At no level that has been tried, has 2CI-2EtO produced even a plus-two response.

Where else can one go, from 2C-I? The iodine is the fourth, and the last of the so-called halogens, at the bottom of the classical periodic table. But, thanks to the miracles that have accompanied us into the nuclear age, there is a fifth halide now known, Astatine. All of its isotopes are radioactive, however, and it seems unlikely that there will ever be an entry (other than this one) for 2,5-dimethoxy-4-astatophenethylamine. What might be speculated as to its activity? Probably similar in potency to 2C-I, requiring maybe 10 or 20 milligrams. The duration would be dicey to measure, since the isotope with the longest known half-life is half decayed in about 8 hours, and the longest lived natural isotope (for those who insist on natural rather than man-made things) is half decayed in less than a minute. Two predictions would be pretty solid. You might have quite a job accumulating your 10 milligrams of Astatine, as the most that has so far been made at one time is only about 0.05 micrograms, approximately a millionth of the amount needed. And the second prediction? You would not survive the screaming radiation that would bombard you if you could get the needed 5 or 10 milligrams of radio-astatine onto that magic 4-position, and the resulting 2C-A into your tummy!

#34   2C-N;   2,5-DIMETHOXY-4-NITROPHENETHYLAMINE

SYNTHESIS: A cooled, stirred solution of 1.0 g 2,5-dimethoxyphenethylamine (see the recipe for 2C-H for its preparation) in 20 mL glacial acetic acid was treated with 3.3 mL 70% HNO_3 in small portions, with the reaction temperature kept down with periodic cooling. After the addition was completed, the stirring was continued until there was the spontaneous separation of a yellow solid. This was 2,5-dimethoxy-4-nitrophenethylamine nitrate (2C-N) which was obtained after removal by filtration, washing with Et_2O and air drying, as a fluffy yellow solid. This weighed 1.04 g and melted, with decomposition, in the area of 170-180 °C, depending on the rate of heating. A solution of 0.8 g of this nitrate salt in 50 mL H_2O was made basic with aqueous NaOH. Extraction with 3x50 mL CH_2Cl_2, and removal of the solvent under vacuum gave the free base as a residue. This was distilled at 130-150 °C at 0.35 mm/Hg to give an orange-red oil that weighed 0.5 g and set up as crystals. This was dissolved in 3 mL IPA, neutralized with 7 drops of concentrated HCl (the color lightened considerably at the titration end point) and diluted with 5 mL anhydrous Et_2O. There was the formation of the hydrochloride salt which was a pumpkin-colored crystalline mass. After removal by filtration, Et_2O washing and air drying, these crystals weighed 0.44 g. The mp, 193-195 °C, was not improved by recrystallization from any of several solvents (MeOH, IPA, CH_3CN). The perchlorate salt was a yellow solid from MeOH, with a mp of 211 °C, with decomposition. Nitration of 2C-H in a mixture of acetic acid and acetic anhydride produced the acetamide derivative of 2C-N as yellow crystals with a mp 142.5-143 °C. For the nitrate salt: Anal. $(C_{10}H_{15}N_3O_7)$ C,H. This was the form used for all human titrations.

DOSAGE: 100 - 150 mg.

DURATION: 4 - 6 h.

QUALITATIVE COMMENTS: (with 120 mg) "This came on very fast — I was aware of it within a half hour, and it got as far as it would go by an hour. There are similarities to MDMA, but missing is the benign anti-stress component. I am light-headed, and there just might be a little eye wiggling. And then it dropped right off to nothing within a couple of hours."

(with 150 mg) "There may have been some visual changes, I'm not sure. But the talking was extremely easy. If there were no other things to use, this would be excellent, but there are other compounds available. This doesn't have too high a priority."

(with 150 mg) "Am I enjoying it? Not exactly, but I am in a good mood. There is not the light-filled energy that some other materials can provide. By six hours, pretty much baseline. Strange material, but okay. Final score: body +3, mind +2, barely."

EXTENSIONS AND COMMENTARY: A most consistent feature with 2C-N was the fact that in every report, somewhere, there is the note that it somehow came up just a little short of expectations. From the esthetic point of view, the pure salt is yellow rather than the usual white color, so the solutions that are to be consumed are by definition also yellow colored. From the structural point of view, the 4-nitro group, like the 4-bromo group of 2C-B, is a dead-end. It cannot be stretched or compressed or lengthened or shortened. This unique aspect demands that you have to live with what you have, as there are no subtle ways of modifying the molecule. With 2C-B, the end product was a total winner; there was no wish to modify it. With 2C-N the end product is something a little less, and there is no way to modify it.

#35   2C-O-4;   2,5-DIMETHOXY-4-(i)-PROPOXYPHENETHYLAMINE

SYNTHESIS: To a solution of 3.10 g 85% KOH pellets in 30 mL warm MeOH there was added 6.16 g 2,5-dimethoxyphenol (there was immediate darkening) followed by 8.5 g isopropyl iodide. The reaction mixture was heated on the steam bath for 3.5 h. White crystals of KI appeared at the end of the first h. The mixture was poured into 800 mL H_2O (it was still basic) and acidified with HCl. This was extracted with 3x100 mL CH_2Cl_2, and the combined extracts washed with 2x100 mL 5% NaOH. The organic phase was stripped of solvent under vacuum, and the residual dark amber oil (6.4 g) distilled at 110-130 °C at 0.7 mm/Hg. There was obtained 5.7 g of 1,4-dimethoxy-2-(i)-propoxy-benzene as a white oil.

A mixture of 10 g N-methylformanilide and 10 g $POCl_3$ was heated on the steam bath for 10 min producing a deep claret color. To this there was added 5.1 g of 1,4-dimethoxy-2-(i)-propoxybenzene, and the immediately exothermic reaction mixture was heated on the steam bath for 45 min. It was then poured into 800 mL H_2O which was stirred until the dark oil changed into loose, light-colored solids. These were removed by filtration giving 5.7 g of an amber crystalline product with a mp of 76-78 °C. This was dissolved in an equal weight of MeOH, and heated to a solution which was clear at the boiling point. This was brought to 0 °C and held there for several hours, yielding 2,5-dimethoxy-4-(i)-propoxybenzaldehyde as a fine, off-white crystalline product which, after filtering and air drying, weighed 4.03 g. The mp was 79-80 °C with prior shrinking at 71 °C. Anal. $(C_{12}H_{16}O_4)$ C,H.

A solution of 3.9 g 2,5-dimethoxy-4-(i)-propoxybenzaldehyde in 20 g nitromethane was treated with 0.17 g anhydrous ammonium acetate and heated on the steam bath for 1.25 h. The progress of the condensation was readily followed by a TLC analysis of the reaction mixture. With silica gel plates, the starting aldehyde and the product nitrostyrene had Rf's of 0.16 and 0.50 resp., using CH_2Cl_2 as a developing solvent. The excess solvent was removed under vacuum to give a red residue that was dissolved in 10 mL boiling MeOH. The solution spontaneously crystallized giving, after filteration and air drying, 4.1 g of orange crystals of 2,5-dimethoxy-ß-nitro-4-(i)-propoxystyrene.

A solution of LAH (60 mL of a 1 M solution in THF) was cooled, under He, to 0 °C with an external ice bath. With good stirring there was added 1.60 mL 100% H_2SO_4 dropwise, to minimize charring. This was followed by the addition of 4.0 g 2,5-dimethoxy-ß-nitro-4-(i)-propoxystyrene as a solid, perhaps 200 mg at a time. There was an immediate loss of color after each addition. The final pale salmon-colored solution was stirred for 2 h as it returned to room temperature. The excess hydride was destroyed by the cautious addition of 8 mL IPA, which was followed by 5 mL 15% NaOH followed, in turn, by sufficient additional THF to make the suspension of inorganic salts loose and filterable. The reaction mixture was filtered, and the filter cake washed with additional THF. The filtrate and washings were combined and stripped of solvent under vacuum providing 4.6 g of a pale amber oil. This was dissolved in dilute H_2SO_4, washed with 2x50 mL CH_2Cl_2, made basic with aqueous NaOH, and extracted with 3x50 mL CH_2Cl_2. Removal of the solvent under vacuum yielded 2.3 g of residue which was distilled at 115-125 °C at 0.3 mm/Hg to give 0.94 g of a clear white oil. This was dissolved in 5 mL IPA, neutralized with 12 drops of concentrated HCl, and diluted with 10 mL anhydrous Et_2O. White crystals of 2,5-dimethoxy-4-(i)-propoxyphenethylamine hydrochloride (2C-O-4) separated, and were removed by filtration, Et_2O washed, and air dried. The final weight was 0.58 g.

DOSAGE: greater than 60 mg.

DURATION: unknown

QUALITATIVE COMMENTS: (with 60 mg) "I became aware of something in the front part of my head, and there was a lot of yawning. The body was aware of the experiment. But also there was a general exhilaration and excitement, which lasted for a few hours. At best, I am at a plus one."

EXTENSIONS AND COMMENTARY: The full activity of 2C-O-4 is yet to be discovered. It represents an interesting hybrid lying in between several fascinating compounds.

First and foremost, all these carry the 2,4,5-trisubstitution which has consistently proven to be the most interesting and the most active of the phenethylamines. And with very few exceptions, the 2- and the 5- are methoxyl groups.

The sulfur analogues in this area, compounds with an alkylthio group at the 4-position of the 2,5-dimethoxyphenethylamine backbone, are the 2C-T things. The replacement of a sulfur with an oxygen, quite rightly, should give rise to the 2C-O counterparts. And they have been given the same numbering system that was bestowed upon the "T" series. 2C-T-4 was the 4-isopropylthio compound and one of the most interesting of this family. And so, quite reasonably, the oxygen counterpart should be the 2C-O-4 analogue, and should be one of the first explored.

The extension of the 4-alkoxy-group led to the discovery of the TMA-2 — MEM — MIPM — MPM — MBM series of amphetamine analogues. The 2-carbon counterparts of these would be a fascinating series to explore, I thought, if there was some encouragement to be had from a preliminary try in this field.

This was a first shot in the dark, the actual trial example, and it certainly didn't provide much encouragement. The three-carbon analogue, MIPM, was made (q.v.) but not explored, following the disappointing trials of MPM. If this area is ever re-opened, the numbering should reasonably follow the sulfur materials. The 4-ethoxy material would be 2C-O-2, the 4-(n)-propoxy compound 2C-O-7, and the 4-(n)-butoxy compound 2C-O-19. These are the exact analogues of 2C-T-2, 2C-T-7, and 2C-T-19, resp., and the 2-carbon homologues of MEM, MPM, and MBM. The simplest member of this series, the methyl counterpart, is 2C-O, and it is the obvious analogue of 2C-T. This is also called 2,4,5-TMPEA, and its story is presented elsewhere.

But, with the probable low eventual potency of 2C-O-4, I feel that the 2C-O series will not be an exciting one.

#36 2C-P; 2,5-DIMETHOXY-4-(n)-PROPYLPHENETHYLAMINE

SYNTHESIS: To a stirred solution of 138 g p-dimethoxybenzene in 400 mL CH_2Cl_2 there was added a suspension of 172 g anhydrous $AlCl_3$ in 500 mL CH_2Cl_2 which contained 92.5 g propionyl chloride. After stirring for 1.5 h the reaction mixture was poured into 2 L H_2O containing ice. The phases were separated, and the aqueous fraction was extracted with 2x100 mL CH_2Cl_2. The organic phase and the extracts were pooled, washed once with H_2O, and then with 2x100 mL 5% NaOH. The solvent from the organic phase was removed under vacuum, yielding a deeply colored residue. This was distilled at 150-165 °C at 20 mm/Hg yielding 170 g of 2,5-dimethoxypropiophenone as a pale amber-colored oil. Acidification of the sodium hydroxide extract, extraction with CH_2Cl_2, and evaporation of the solvent, yielded 3 g of an oil that slowly crystallized. These solids, on recrystallization from MeOH, provided 1.0 g of 2-hydroxy-5-methoxypropiophenone with a mp of 47-48 °C. The same Friedel Crafts reaction, conducted on the same scale in CS_2 rather than in CH_2Cl_2, required reduced temperature (5 °C) and a 24 h reaction period. This solvent variation, with the same workup and isolation, gave 76 g of 2,5-dimethoxy-propiophenone as a pale amber oil boiling at 130-137 °C at 4 mm/Hg.

A total of 150 g mossy zinc was amalgamated by treatment with a solution of 15 g mercuric chloride in 1 L H_2O. After swirling for 0.5 h, the H_2O phase was removed by decantation and the zinc added to a 1 L three neck flask. To this there was added 20 mL H_2O and 20 mL concentrated HCl, followed by 20 g of 2,5-dimethoxypropiophenone dissolved in 50 mL EtOH. This mixture was held at reflux with a heating mantle overnight, with the occasional addition of HCl as needed to maintain acidic conditions. After cooling to room temperature, the residual solids were removed by filtration, and the filtrate extracted once with 100 mL CH_2Cl_2 (this was the upper phase). Sufficient H_2O was then added to allow extraction with 2x100 mL additional CH_2Cl_2 with the organic solvent being the lower phase. The combined organic extracts were washed twice with 5% NaOH, followed by one washing with dilute acid. Removal of the solvent under vacuum yielded 18 g of a dark brown oil that was distilled at the water pump to yield 7.2 g of 2,5-dimethoxypropylbenzene as a light yellow oil boiling at 90-130 °C.

A mixture of 22 g 2,5-dimethoxypropylbenzene, 23 g $POCl_3$ and 22 g N-methylformanilide was heated on the steam bath for 1.5 h. The hot, dark reaction mass was poured into 1 L H_2O, which allowed the eventual separation of 2,5-dimethoxy-4-(n)-propylbenzaldehyde as a clear yellow oil weighting 14 g. Although the homologous 4-ethyl and 4-butyl benzaldehydes were clean crystalline solids, this propyl homologue remained an oil. Gas chromatographic analysis showed it to be about 90% pure, and it was used as obtained in the nitrostyrene steps with either nitromethane (here) or nitroethane (under DOPR).

To a solution of 13 g 2,5-dimethoxy-4-(n)-propylbenzaldehyde in 100 mL nitromethane, there was added 1.3 g anhydrous ammonium acetate and the mixture held at reflux for 1 h. Removal of the solvent/reactant under vacuum yielded a spontaneously crystallizing mass of orange solids that was removed with the help of a little MeOH. After filtering and air drying there was obtained 7.5 g 2,5-dimethoxy-ß-nitro-4-(n)-propylstyrene with a mp of 118-122 °C. Recrystallization from CH_3CN gave an analytical sample with a mp 123-124 °C. Anal. ($C_{13}H_{17}NO_4$) N.

In a 1 L round bottomed flask with a magnetic stirrer under a He atmosphere there was added 120 mL 1 M LAH in tetrahydrofuran. This stirred solution was cooled with an external ice bath, and there was added, dropwise, 3.2 mL of 100% H_2SO_4, freshly made by the addition of 13.5 g 20% fuming H_2SO_4 to

15.0 g of ordinary 96% concentrated H_2SO_4. When the addition was complete, a total of 7.2 g of dry 2,5-dimethoxy-ß-nitro-4-(n)-propylstyrene was introduced as solids in several batches, against a flow of He, over the course of 20 min. The reaction mixture was allowed to come to room temperature, and stirred for an additional 0.5 h, then brought to reflux for 10 min on the steam bath. The excess hydride was destroyed with 18 mL IPA, and then sufficient 15% NaOH was added which made the aluminum oxides distinctly basic and of a filterable texture. The inorganics were removed by filtration, and the filter cake washed with additional THF. The combined filrate and washes were stripped of solvent, yielding several g of a pale yellow oil that was suspended in a large quantity of dilute H_2SO_4. The aqueous phase was filtered free of insolubles, washed with a little CH_2Cl_2, and made basic with aqueous NaOH. This was extracted with 3x40 mL CH_2Cl_2 and, after the removal of the solvent under vacuum, the residual 2 g of off-white oil was distilled. A fraction that distilled at 100-110 °C at 0.3 mm/Hg was water white, weighed 1.59 g and spontaneously crystallized. This fraction was dissolved in 7.5 mL warm IPA and neutralized with 0.6 mL concentrated HCl. The spontaneous crystals of 2,5-di-methoxy-4-(n)-propylphenethylamine hydrochloride (2C-P) were suspended in 20 mL anhydrous Et_2O, filtered, Et_2O washed, and air dried. The weight was 1.65 g and the mp was 207-209 °C with prior sintering at 183 °C., Anal. ($C_{13}H_{22}ClNO_2$) N.

DOSAGE: 6 - 10 mg.

DURATION: 10 - 16 h.

QUALITATIVE COMMENTS: (with 6 mg) "I was not feeling so good. Hangover, I guess. The material was so gentle in coming on, and soon my body became jangled. Thinking was easy. Verbalizing was easy. Being comfortable with my body was not. My back hurt and then my legs hurt. My lower back was in spasm. At first I did not particularly like what this drug was doing to my body, but took a good look at it and decided that I was the culprit. Took a good look at my drinking so much, and decided that I didn't need it. So much energy was going through me I didn't know what to do with it. The whole day was spent in physical discomfort. Food tasted good, and we nibbled all day. My stomach was bloated. Next day I was more or less like a zombie. I was wiped out."

(with 8 mg) "Comes on slowly, not feeling intently until into 2nd hour. I feel slight discomfort but override it responding to music. I take in air, directing it inside to heal uncomfortable places, open up my clogged sinuses. Wonderful experience of clean, fresh, healing air. Find that discomfort zone is places where I think there is something wrong with me. I dissolve these places with the feeling I'm OK. Like myself better and better, and find more reasons to enjoy and appreciate myself. I find this material powerful, and an excellent working material. Under other circumstances, would probably spend more time working alone inside, where there were great openings, and some of the most beautiful visuals I have seen for a long time. Usually I do not get visuals. I like the long action. I feel that this material worked for a good week after the experience, with internal processes taking place, many insights, and energy running. At times the energy was a little uncomfortable, but could always be quelled by taking a moment for deep relaxation or looking directly at the internal process. I feel that much good internal work has been done, a lot of it unconscious."

(with 9 mg) "At the one hour point, I am barely off of baseline. It is not until almost the third hour that the experience is fully developed, and once there it is maintained for another four hours. I was well grounded but rather diffuse. I explored writing (which went quite well), interpretation (pictures and reading both OK) and talking (very good). This is an excellent level, and probably near the max."

(with 12 mg) "Slow and even rise. At five minutes to seven (suddenly the clock time makes no sense at all) I am at a 3+ and feel that I have not yet plateau'd. Erotic was excellent. Music good. Eyes-closed imagery very different place than usual experiences. Slow, calm, strong images from an area that has no apparent connection with usual waking world, yet underlies all of it. A cool, wise place which has its own rules. All emotions and feeling available, but there is a cool perspective which informs all thinking. Talking superb and fun, and it was possible to feel our bodies healthy and full of determination to remain so, despite obvious faults and self-indulgences. Could do a lot of learning with this material, but probably not a group thing. It would lend itself too easily to hypnotic power-games, and it would be too easy to open up the shared consciousness level, which would be frightening to a lot of people and bring about necessary escapes such as sickness. Excellent feeling the next day."

EXTENSIONS AND COMMENTARY: There is certainly a broad mixture of experiences with 2C-P but, on the whole, probably more favorable than not. There was one report of an experience in which a single dosage of 16 mg was clearly an overdose, with the entire experiment labeled a physical disaster, not to be repeated. A consistent observation is that there may not be too much latitude in dosage between that which would be modest, or adequate, and that which would be excessive. The need for individual titration would be most important with this compound.

#37   CPM;   CYCLOPROPYLMESCALINE;   4-CYCLOPROPYLMETHOXY-3,5-DIMETHOXYPHENETHYLAMINE

SYNTHESIS: To a solution of 2.8 g homosyringonitrile (see under E for synthesis) in 20 ml acetone containing about 50 mg decyltriethylammonium iodide, there was added 3.0 g cyclopropylmethyl chloride and 5.0 g NaI. Stirring was continued during a color change from pale yellow to blue. There was then added 2.9 g of finely powdered anhydrous K_2CO_3, resulting in a beautiful turquoise color. The mixture was held at reflux on the steam bath for 3 h, which discharged all color. The solvent was removed under vacuum, and the residues were added to 100 mL H_2O. This solution was extracted with 3x75 mL CH_2Cl_2, the extracts were pooled, washed with 2x50 mL 5% NaOH, and the organic solvent removed under vacuum. The residual oil weighed 4.2 g, and was distilled at 140-155 °C at 0.4 mm/Hg to yield 4-cyclopropylmethoxy-3,5-dimethoxyphenylacetonitrile as a colorless oil weighing 2.8 g which spontaneously crystal-lized. Its mp was 44-44.5 °C after recrystallization from MeOH/H_2O. Anal. ($C_{14}H_{17}NO_3$) C,H.

A suspension of 1.3 g LAH in 65 mL anhydrous THF under He was cooled to 0 °C with stirring, and 0.85 mL of 100% H_2SO_4 was slowly added. Then, with continued stirring, a THF solution of 2.7 g of 4-cyclopropylmethoxy-3,5-dimethoxyphenylacetonitrile in 50 mL THF was added dropwise. After the addition was complete, the mixture was brought to a boil briefly on the steam bath, cooled, and treated with sufficient IPA to destroy the excess hydride. Then there was added an amount of 15% NaOH sufficient to produce a loose filterable solid form of aluminum oxide. This was removed by filtration, and the filter cake washed with THF. The pooled filtrate and washes were stripped of solvent, and the residue was dissolved in dilute H_2SO_4, washed with 2x50 mL CH_2Cl_2, made basic with aqueous NaOH, and then extracted with 2x50 mL of CH_2Cl_2. After removal of the solvent, the residue was distilled at 128-140 °C at 0.4 mm/Hg to yield 2.5 g of a white oil. This was dissolved in 10 mL IPA, and treated with 30 drops of concentrated HCl which was just sufficient to demonstrate acidity as judged by external dampened pH paper. The addition of 25 mL anhydrous Et_2O to the stirred solution allowed, in a few minutes, the product 4-cyclopropylmethoxy-3,5-dimethoxyphenethylamine hydrochloride (CPM) to spontaneously crystallize as a fine white solid. The yield was 1.8 g, and a second crop of 0.8 g was obtained from the IPA/Et_2O mother liquors. The mp was 172-173 °C. Anal. ($C_{14}H_{22}ClNO_3$) C,H.

DOSAGE: 60 - 80 mg.

DURATION: 12 - 18 h.

QUALITATIVE COMMENTS: (with 70 mg) "I was surprised at the fast development of this drug, with the knowledge that it was a long-laster. Twenty minutes into it I was aware of some changes, and by the end of one and a half hours there was a complete plus three. The most remarkable property is the eyes-closed imagery. No, not just imagery but fantasy. It is not completely benign, but it locks into music with an extraordinary fit. I was at one moment keenly aware of my body touching the rug, the tactile aspects of my surroundings, and then I would find that my world was simply my personal sphere of reality that kept engulfing everything about me, all completely augmented by the music. Constructed by the music. I hoped that I wouldn't offend anyone else around me with this growing world of mine. Eyes open, there was not that much of note. Not much insight. Not much in the way of visuals. By the eighth hour an effort to sleep showed me how exposed and vunerable I was, and when I closed my eyes I needed my guards against this fantasy world. Even at the twelfth hour there was no easy way to relax and sleep. Use higher dosages with caution."

(with 70 mg) "There is a goodly amount of eyes-closed patterning but I found external sounds to be irritating. Voices, and even music, seemed to be intrusive. I didn't want to share my space with anyone. I was reminded of mescaline, in that I kept losing the awareness of the drug's role in my experience. Visual exaggerations are probably right around the corner. The residual effects were too much to ignore, but 100 milligrams of phenobarb at about the twelfth hour allowed me to lie down quietly."

(with 80 mg) "A wild day of profound philosophy, with discussions of the art of molecules, the origins of the universe, and similar weighty trivia. Much day-dreaming in erotic areas, but by and large, it went on a bit too long. I was tired."

EXTENSIONS AND COMMENTARY: In the literary world, the guy who is on your side, your leader, your champion, is the protagonist and the guy he battles, your enemy, is the antagonist. These same roles are played in the world of pharmacology, but the names are slightly changed. A drug which does the needed or expected thing is called the agonist rather than protagonist, but the drug that gets in its way is still called the antagonist.

The cyclopropylmethyl group plays an interesting role in the world of narcotics. There are numerous examples of opiates with a methyl group attached to a nitrogen atom which are famous for being valuable in producing analgesia and sedation. These run the gamut from natural alkaloids such as morphine and codeine, to synthetic variants such as Dilaudid and Percodan. And yet, with most of these narcotics, when the methyl on the nitrogen is removed, and a cyclopropylmethyl group put into its place, the agonist becomes an antagonist. Oxycodone (the active narcotic thing in Percodan) becomes Naltrexone, a drug that will immediately snap a heroin victim out of his overdose.

Cyclopropylmescaline (CPM) is a molecule that is very simply mescaline itself, with a methyl group removed from an oxygen atom and a cyclopropylmethyl group put on instead. Might CPM be not only inactive, but actually block the action of mescaline? Interesting concept. But it turned out to be entirely wrong.

The amphetamine analog of CPM should be easily made from the alkyl-ation of syringaldehyde with cyclopropyl chloride, followed by conventional reaction of the resulting aldehyde with nitroethane, and finally a reduction step. There is no reason to believe that the resulting compound 3,5-dimethoxy-4-cyclo-propyloxyamphetamine (3C-CPM) would be any shorter acting than CPM.

#38   2C-SE;   2,5-DIMETHOXY-4-METHYLSELENEO-PHENETHYLAMINE

SYNTHESIS: A suspension of 5.65 g 1,4-dimethoxybenzene in 100 mL petroleum ether containing 6.5 mL N,N,N',N'-tetramethylethylenediamine was magnetically stirred, placed in an inert atmosphere, and cooled to 0 °C with an external ice bath. There was then added 27 mL of 1.6 M butyllithium in hexane. The solids present went into solution, and after a few min continued stirring, a fine precipitate appeared. The reaction was allowed to stir while coming up to room temperature. There was then added 4.8 g dimethyl diselenide which led to an exothermic reaction, bringing the petroleum ether up to a reflux and showing a color change from white to yellow, to light green, to an eventual brown, all over the course of 30 min. After 2 h additional stirring, the reaction was quenched by pouring into dilute NaOH. The organic phase was separated, and the aqueous phase extracted with 2x75 mL Et$_2$O. The pooled organics were washed first with dilute NaOH, then with dilute HCl, and then the solvent was removed under vacuum. Distillation of the residue at 0.4 mm/ Hg gave an early fraction (75-100 °C) that solidified in the receiver and was largely unreacted dimethoxybenzene. A pale yellow oil distilled from 100 to 120 °C which proved to be largely 2,5-dimethoxyphenyl methyl selenide. Microanalysis gave C = 49.86, 49.69; H = 5.32, 5.47. As C$_9$H$_{12}$SeO$_2$ requires C = 46.76, H = 5.23, there is approximately 13% dimethoxybenzene present (C$_8$H$_{10}$O$_2$ requires C = 69.54, H = 7.29). This mixture was used as such, without further purification.

A mixture of 1.25 g POCl$_3$ and 1.1 g N-methylformanilide was warmed on the steam bath for several min until the color had become a deep claret. There was then added 1.5 g of the 87% pure 2,5-dimethoxyphenyl methyl selenide and the steam bath heating continued for an additional 25 min. The very tarry reaction mixture was poured into 100 mL H$_2$O, producing fine yellow solids almost immediately. These were removed by filtration and distilled at 0.2 mm/Hg. A first fraction distilling up to 100 °C was a mixture of unreacted ethers and what appeared to be 2,5-dimethoxybenzaldehyde. A second cut distilled at 140-150 °C, solidified to a yellow solid in the receiver, and weighed 1.2 g. A small amount of this product (with mp 91-96 °C) was recrystallized from MeOH to give an analytic sample of 2,5-dimethoxy-4-(methylseleneo)benzaldehyde with a mp 88-92 °C. All efforts to achieve a tighter melting range were unsuccessful. Anal. (C$_{10}$H$_{12}$O$_3$ Se) C,H. Although this benzaldehyde migrates normally on a silica gel TLC plate (Rf of 0.4 employing CH$_2$Cl$_2$ as a solvent) when it is once completely dried on the plate, there seems to be some irreversible reaction with the silica, and the spot will no longer move at all.

To a solution of 0.85 g 2,5-dimethoxy-4-(methylseleneo)benzaldehyde in 10 mL nitromethane there was added 150 mg anhydrous ammonium acetate, and the solution was heated for 35 min on the steam bath. Removal of the volatiles under vacuum yielded brick-red solids (1.1 g) which were ground under a small amount of MeOH, filtered, and air dried. This yielded 0.88 g of solid 2,5-dimethoxy-4-methylseleneo-ß-nitrostyrene with a mp of 170.5-171.5 °C. Recrystallization from IPA or from toluene gave no improvement of mp. Anal. ($C_{11}H_{13}NO_4Se$) C,H.

A solution of LAH (20 mL of a 1 M solution in THF) was cooled, under He, to 0 °C with an external ice bath. With good stirring there was added 0.53 mL 100% H_2SO_4 dropwise, to minimize charring. This was followed by the addition of 0.85 g 2,5-dimethoxy-4-methylseleneo-ß-nitrostyrene in 20 mL hot anhydrous THF. There was an immediate discoloring. After a few minutes further stirring, the temperature was brought up to a gentle reflux on the steam bath for 0.5 h, then all was cooled again to 0 °C. The excess hydride was destroyed by the cautious addition of IPA and, when there was no further activity, the reaction mixture was poured into 500 mL dilute H_2SO_4. This was washed with 2x100 mL CH_2Cl_2, and then made basic with 5% NaOH. The milky aqueous phase was extracted with 2x100 mL CH_2Cl_2, and extensive centrifuging was required to obtain a clear organic phase. Evaporation of the pooled extracts gave 1.6 g of an oil that crystallized. This was distilled at 130-140 °C at 0.15 mm/Hg providing 0.6 g of a white oil that set to a crystalline solid melting at 87-89 °C. This was dissolved in 4 mL boiling IPA, neutralized with 8 drops of concentrated HCl and the formed solids further diluted with IPA with a little anhydrous Et_2O. This crystalline product was removed by filtration, washed with Et_2O, and air dried to constant weight, yielding 2,5-dimethoxy-4-methylseleneophenethylamine hydrochloride (2C-SE) with a mp of 240-241 °C.

DOSAGE: perhaps 100 mg.

DURATION: 6 - 8 h.

QUALITATIVE COMMENTS: (with 50 mg) "My tongue feels as if I had eaten hot food. Overall I got up to a plus 1, and found the effects to be completely benign. I wandered about within the Graves exhibit at the Oakland Museum but there seemed to be only minor enhancement of the visual input."

(with 70 mg) "The water solution of this material has an unspeakable smell. But there is no lasting taste, thank heaven. This is up to a 1.5 + and probably half again would be an effective dose. The first awareness was at 45 minutes, and the plateau lasted from 1.5 hours to about the fourth hour. I was at certain baseline at 8 hours."

EXTENSIONS AND COMMENTARY: With an entirely new hetero atom in the molecule (the selenium), and with clear indications that large dosages would be needed (100 milligrams. or more), some discretion was felt desirable. There was certainly an odd taste and an odd smell. I remember some early biochemical work where selenium replaced sulfur in some amino acid chemistry, and things got pretty toxic. It might be appropriate to get some general animal toxicity data before exploring those dosages that might get to a +++.

What doors are opened by the observation that the selenium analog of 2C-T is an active compound? The potency appears to be in the same ball park, whether there is a sulfur atom or a selenium atom there.

From the point of view of the thing that is hung onto the hetero-atom, the selenium, the most active (and as first approximation the most safe) analogue would be the same ones that are the most potent with sulfur. These would probably be the Se-ethyl, the Se-propyl, or the Se-isopropyl, the analogs of S-ethyl, S-propyl, and S-isopropyl. If one were to be systematic, these would be called 2C-SE-2, 2C-SE-4, and 2C-SE-7. And a very special place might be held for 2C-SE-21, the analogue of 2C-T-21. Not only is this of high potential potency, but it would certainly be the first time that both fluorine and selenium are in the same centrally active drug. In fact, might not this compound, 2C-SE, be the first compound active within the human CNS with a selenium atom in it? It is certainly the first psychedelic with this atom in it!

From the point of view of the hetero-atom itself, there are two more known below selenium in the Periodic Table. Each deserves some special comment. The next atom, directly below selenium, is tellurium. It is more metallic, and its compounds have a worse smell yet. I heard a story about a German chemist, many years ago, who was carrying a vial of dibutyl telluride in his pocket in a passenger coach from here to there in Germany, back at about the turn of the century. It fell to the floor and broke. No one could remain in the car, and no amount of decontamination could effectively make the smell tolerable. Scratch one railway coach. But the compound, 2C-TE, would be readily makeable. Dimethyl ditelluride is a known thing.

However, the atom below tellurium (and at the bottom of that particular column of the Periodic Table) is the element polonium. Here one must deal in terms of theory, as far as human activity goes, since there are no non-radioactive isotopes of polonium. The only readily available isotope is that with mass 210, which is also called Radium F, and is an alpha-particle emitter. If this were ever to be put into a living organism, and if it were to seek out and hang around some particular site of action, that area would be thoroughly and completely cooked by alpha-particle emission. It would be a fun academic exercise to make 2C-PO (2,5-dimethoxy-4-methylpoloneophenethylamine), but in no way could it ever go into anyone. I knew an eminent physiologist named Dr. Hardin Jones (now dead) who always argued that the continuing use of drugs would burn out the pleasure center of the brain. It is a certainty that 2C-PO would, quite literally, do this. If I ever made it, I would call it HARDINAMINE in his honor.

There was an interesting observation associated with the making of 2C-SE. In the synthesis of many of the sulfur compounds (of the 2C-T family) is was quite common to find, when there was a quantity of some organic sulfide let go as a by-product of a reaction on a warm summer night, a number of flies coming into the lab to pay a visit. On the first synthesis of the starting material for 2C-SE, a quantity of CH₃SeH was let go into the environment. Within minutes, there were two beautiful dragonflies in the lab. A coincidence certainly, but somehow, it was a nice message to receive.

#39   2C-T ;   2,5-DIMETHOXY-4-METHYLTHIO-PHENETHYLAMINE

SYNTHESIS: A solution of 149 g sodium thiosulfate in 300 mL H_2O was vigorously stirred. To this there was added, over the course of 10 min, a solution of 43.2 g benzoquinone in 200 mL acetic acid. After an additional 1 h stirring at room temperature, all volatiles were removed under vacuum. The residual syrup slowly set up as crystals which, after grinding under brine, were removed by filtration and washed with additional brine. These were dissolved in MeOH, clarified by filtration through a Celite bed, and the clear filtrate stripped of solvent under vacuum. The yellow, powdery sodium 2,5-hydroxyphenylthiosulfate weighed 67 g when dry. This intermediate was dissolved in aqueous HCl (50 g in 200 mL H_2O containing 400 mL concentrated HCl), cooled with an external ice bath, and treated with 250 g zinc dust added at a rate that kept the temperature below 60 °C. About 1.5 h were required, and caution must be taken concerning the poisonous hydrogen sulfide that evolves. An additional 50 mL concentrated HCl was added, and the aqueous phase decanted from the unreacted zinc metal. This was extracted with 6x100 mL Et₂O, and these extracts were pooled, washed with brine, and the solvent removed under vacuum to yield 33.1 g of 2,5-dihydroxythiophenol as pale yellow needles with a mp of 118-119 °C.

A solution of 118.6 g KOH pellets in 200 mL H_2O was placed under N₂, and to it was added 24.0 g 2,5-dihydroxythiophenol. With vigorous stirring, there was then added 160 g methyl sulfate at a rate that maintained the temperature at about 60 °C. This took about 2 h. After the addition was complete, the mixture was held at reflux for 3 h, and allowed to stir at ambient temperature overnight. It was then filtered, and the filtrate extracted with 6x100 mL Et₂O, the extracts pooled, washed with 2x50 mL brine, dried over anhydrous Na₂SO₄, and the solvent removed under vacuum. The residue was distilled at 86-88 °C at 0.04 mm/Hg to provide 25.9 g of 2,5-dimethoxythioanisole as a white oil that crystallized on standing. Its mp was 33-34 °C. An alternate preparation of this compound follows the direct methylation of 2,5-dimethoxythiophenol (see under 2C-T-2 for the preparation of this common intermediate) with methyl iodide.

To 40 mL dry CH₂Cl₂ there was added 6.07 g 2,5-dimethoxythioanisole, and this was cooled to 0 °C under N₂. To this well stirred solution there was added 13.02 g stannic chloride over the course of 2 min. This was followed by the dropwise addition of dichloromethyl methyl ether over 5 min, and the reaction mixture allowed to stir for an additional 15 min. After returning to room temperature, it was stirred for an additional 1 h. The reaction mixture was poured over 15 g ice, and the organic phase separated, washed with 3x25 mL 3 N HCl, with 3x50 mL brine and, after drying over anhydrous Na_2SO_4 the solvent was removed under vacuum. The residue was a solid and, after recrystallization from $MeOH/H_2O$, gave 5.86 g 2,5-dimethoxy-4-(methylthio)benzaldehyde with a mp of 95-97 °C. Purification via the bisulfite complex provided an analytical sample with mp of 99-100 C. Anal. $(C_{10}H_{12}O_3S)$ C,H,S. The malononitrile derivative (from equal weights of the aldehyde and malononitrile in EtOH with a drop of triethylamine as catalyst) was recrystallized from an equal volume of EtOH to give orange crystals with a mp of 185-186 °C. Anal. $(C_{13}H_{12}N_2O_2S)$ C,H,N,S.

A solution of 2.1 g 2,5-dimethoxy-4-(methylthio)benzaldehyde in 7.5 mL nitromethane was treated with 0.45 g anhydrous ammonium acetate and held at steam bath temperature for 6 h. The deep red solution was stripped of solvent to give a residue that spontaneously crystallized. This was ground up under 12 mL MeOH, filtered, and washed with MeOH to yield, after air-drying, 1.7 g of 2,5-dimethoxy-4-methylthio-ß-nitrostyrene as orange solids. Recrystallization from EtOH provided rust-orange colored crystals with a mp of 165.5-166 °C. Anal. $(C_{11}H_{13}NO_4S)$ C,H,N; S: calcd, 12.56; found, 11.96.

To a gently refluxing mixture of 1.4 g LAH in 40 mL anhydrous THF under an inert atmosphere there was added, dropwise, 1.7 g 2,5-dimethoxy-4-methylthio-ß-nitrostyrene in 25 mL THF. The refluxing was continued for 18 h, and the stirring continued for another day at room temperature. There was then added 1.5 mL H_2O (diluted with a little THF), 1.5 mL 15% NaOH, and finally 4.5 mL H_2O. The white aluminum oxide salts were removed by filtration, and the filter cake washed with THF. The filtrate and washings were combined and stripped of solvent under vacuum yielding a straw-colored residue that crystallized (mp 81-92 °C without purification). This residue was dissolved in 25 mL IPA and neutralized with concentrated HCl. The slightly pink solution spontaneously crystallized. There was added 100 mL anhydrous Et_2O, and the white crystalline mass of 2,5-dimethoxy-4-methylthiophenethylamine hydrochloride (2C-T) was removed by filtration, washed with Et_2O, and air dried. The final weight was 1.0 g, and had a mp of 232-237 °C. Recrystallization from EtOH provided an analytical sample with mp 240-241 °C. IPA was not a good recrystallization solvent. Anal. $(C_{11}H_{18}ClNO_2S)$ C,H,N,S.

DOSAGE: 60 - 100 mg.

DURATION: 3 - 5 h.

QUALITATIVE COMMENTS: (with 60 mg) "Poetry was an easy and natural thing. Both the reading of it and the writing of it. This is a potential MDMA substitute since it opens things up but it doesn't do anything to get in the way."
(with 75 mg) "I am already aware at a quarter of an hour into it! It develops

very quickly but very quietly. There are no visuals at all but, rather, a tactile sensitivity, with warm close feelings. This could be very erotic. There is some fantasy to music, but nothing very demanding. The viewing of pictures doesn't do much either. The drop-off was extremely relaxed, with a good body feeling. At the fifth hour I was able to drift into an excellent, deep sleep with busy dreams. In the morning I felt refreshed and active, without apparent deficit."

(with 75 mg) "I got up to a thin and fragile plus two, but there was a continuing feeling of a hooded cloak brought down over my head. Nothing obvious — it is transparent — but it somehow separated me from everything around me. I do not think the overall experiment was worth it."

(with 100 mg) "Material all right, but a little bit along the lines of a 'generic' psychedelic effect. Sharper edges than 2C-B. The one true negative, which has been pretty consistent with this drug, is that there is a certain emotional removal. One teeny step removed. One is connected with feelings, certainly, but there is a tendency for the intellect to be more evident, in me, than the heart. All this is moderately so. Nothing extreme. Pretty good material, but there are more interesting ones. However, if you are looking for a really short one, this is one of the answers. For most people. For me, it's still around 5 to 6 hours long. I wish we had more shorties, indeed."

(with 125 mg) "There was some physical tummy uncertainty, but once that was past, talking was extremely easy. This is probably really psychedelic, but I am not really sure why, as there is not much in the way of visuals. Dropping was noted just after hour number three, and I was at baseline three hours later."

EXTENSIONS AND COMMENTARY: The earliest work with the sulfur atom was with the three-carbon chain materials, the ALEPHs. It was only after a considerable time of working with them, and trying to come to peace with their property of being so different from person to person as to potency, that the two-carbon homologues were looked at. Although the first of these (this compound, called 2C-T) was prepared at the same time as ALEPH-1, there was a lapse of about four years between their trials. The relatively low potency of 2C-T was a bit discouraging. But the methodical pursuit of the higher 2C-T's (to parallel the higher ALEPHs) proved to be a treasure house, and they have been explored much further than any of the ALEPHs.

A note on the "T" in 2C-T. Many, in fact most, of the 2C's have their name based on the last letter of the amphetamine prototype. 2C-B from DOB, 2C-C from DOC, 2C-I from DOI, 2C-N from DON, etc. And since the original name for ALEPH-1 was DOT (the desoxy- and a thiomethyl group at the 4-position), the 2C-T naming followed this general pattern. And as a note on the subsequent numbering, they (both the ALEPHs and the 2C-T's) are assigned numbers as they are thought up. There is no structural significance in the number but they have been, like the houses on the streets in residential Tokyo, assigned numbers in strict historical order, documenting the sequence of construction rather than the relative position down the side of the street.

Both of the homologous mono-ethoxy Tweetios of 2C-T have been synthesized and evaluated. The 2-EtO-homologue of 2C-T is 2-ethoxy-5-methoxy-4-methylthiophenethylamine, or 2CT-2ETO. The benzaldehyde (2-ethoxy-5-methoxy-4-(methylthio)benzaldehyde) was an oil, the nitrostyrene intermediate had a melting point of 137-138 °C, and the final hydrochloride a melting point of 215-216 °C. The effects were felt very quickly, and there was a blurring of vision. However, the highest dose tried, 50 milligrams, was not able to produce a greater-than-plus one state, and what did occur, lasted for only 4 hours.

The 5-EtO-homologue of 2C-T is 5-ethoxy-2-methoxy-4-methylthio-phenethylamine, or 2CT-5ETO. The benzaldehyde (5-ethoxy-2-methoxy-4-(methyl-thio)benzaldehyde) was impure, and had a melting point of about 66 °C, the nitrostyrene intermediate a melting point of 133-134 °C, and the final hydrochloride a melting point of 184-185 °C. There was a body awareness and modest eyes-closed visuals following the use of 30 milligrams of 2CT-5ETO. The experience was quiet, peaceful, contemplative, and insightful. The duration was perhaps 15 hours and Halcion was needed to allow sleep. There were a lot of dreams, and the next day was restful.

#40   2C-T-2;   2,5-DIMETHOXY-4-ETHYLTHIOPHENETHYLAMINE

SYNTHESIS: To a solution of 165 g 1,4-dimethoxybenzene in 1 L of CH_2Cl_2, in a well ventilated place and well stirred, there was cautiously added 300 mL chlorosulfonic acid. With about half the acid chloride added, there was a vigorous evolution of HCl gas and the generation of a lot of solids. As the addition was continued, these redissolved to form a clear, dark green solution. Towards the end of the addition, some solids were again formed. When everything was stable, there was added 2 L H_2O, a few mL at a time, commensurate with the vigor of the reaction. The two phases were separated, and the aqueous phase extracted with 2x75 mL CH_2Cl_2. The original organic phase and the extracts were combined and the solvent removed under vacuum. The residue weighed 162 g and was quite pure 2,5-dimethoxybenzenesulfonyl chloride, a yellow crystalline solid with a mp of 115-117 °C. It need not be further purified for the next step, and it appears to be stable on storage. The sulfonamide, from this acid chloride and ammonium hydroxide, gave white crystals from EtOH, with a mp of 147.5-148.5 °C.

The following reaction is also a very vigorous one and must be performed in a well ventilated place. To a solution of 400 mL 25% H_2SO_4 (V/V) in a beaker at least 2 L in size, there was added 54 g of 2,5-dimethoxybenzenesulfonyl chloride, and the mixture was heated on a steam bath. The yellow crystals of the acid chloride floated on the surface of the aqueous layer. There should be 80 g of zinc dust at hand. A small amount of Zn dust was placed at one spot on the surface of this chapeau. With occasional stirring with a glass rod, the temperature was allowed to rise. At about 60 or 70 °C an exothermic reaction took place at the spot where the zinc was placed. Additional dollups of zinc were added, and each small exothermic reaction site was spread about with the glass stirring rod. Finally, the reaction spread to the entire solid surface layer, with a melting of the acid chloride and an apparent boiling at the H_2O surface. The remainder of the 80 g of zinc dust was added as fast as the size of the reaction container would allow. After things subsided again, the heating was continued for 1 h on the steam bath. After the reaction mixture had cooled to room temperature, it was filtered through paper in a Buchner funnel, and the residual metal washed with 100 mL CH_2Cl_2. The two-phase filtrate was separated, and the lower, aqueous phase was extracted with 2x75 mL CH_2Cl_2. The addition of 2 L H_2O to the aqueous phase now made it the upper phase in extraction, and this was again extracted with 2x75 mL CH_2Cl_2. The organic extracts were pooled (H_2O washing is more trouble than it is worth) and the solvent removed under vacuum. The light amber residue (30.0 g) was distilled at 70-80 °C at 0.3 mm/Hg to yield 25.3 g 2,5-dimethoxythiophenol as a white oil. This chemical is certainly not centrally active, but it is a most valuable precursor to all members of the 2C-T family.

To a solution of 3.4 g of KOH pellets in 75 mL boiling EtOH, there was added a solution of 10.0 g 2,5-dimethoxythiophenol in 60 mL EtOH followed by 10.9 g ethyl bromide. The reaction was exothermic with the immediate deposition of white solids. This was heated on the steam bath for 1.5 h, added to 1 L H_2O, acidified with HCl, and extracted with 3x100 mL CH_2Cl_2. The pooled extracts were washed with 100 mL of 5% NaOH, and the solvent removed under vacuum. The residue was 2,5-dimethoxyphenyl ethyl sulfide which was a pale amber oil, weighed about 10 g and which was sufficiently pure for use in the next reaction without a distillation step.

A mixture of 19.2 $POCl_3$ and 18.0 g N-methylformanilide was heated briefly on the steam bath. To this claret-colored solution there was added the above 2,5-dimethoxyphenyl ethyl sulfide, and the mixture heated an additional 20 min on the steam bath. This was then added to 500 mL of well-stirred warm H_2O (pre-heated to 55 °C) and the stirring continued for 1.5 h by which time the oily phase had completely solidified to a brown sugar-like consistency. The solids were removed by filtration, and washed with additional H_2O. After being sucked as dry as possible, these solids were dissolved in 50 mL boiling MeOH which, after cooling in an ice-bath, deposited almost-white crystals of 2,5-dimethoxy-4-(ethylthio)-benzaldehyde. After filtration, modest washing with cold MeOH, and air drying to constant weight, there was obtained 11.0 g of product with a mp of 86-88 °C. Recrystallization of a small sample again from MeOH provided an analytical sample with mp 87-88 °C. Anal. ($C_{11}H_{14}O_3S$) C,H.

To a solution of 11.0 g 2,5-dimethoxy-4-(ethylthio)benzaldehyde in 100 g of nitromethane there was added 0.5 g of anhydrous ammonium acetate, and the mixture was heated on the steam bath for 80 min (this reaction progress must be monitored by TLC, to determine the point at which the starting aldehyde has been consumed). The excess nitromethane was removed under vacuum leaving a residue that spontaneously set to orange-red crystals. These were scraped out to provide 12.9 g crude 2,5-dimethoxy-4-ethylthio-ß-nitrostyrene with a mp of 152-154 °C. A sample recrystallized from toluene was pumpkin colored and had a mp of 148-149 °C. Another sample from acetone melted at 149 °C sharp, and was light orange. From IPA came spectacular fluorescent orange crystals, with a mp 151-152 °C. Anal. ($C_{12}H_{15}NO_4S$) C,H.

A suspension of 12.4 g LAH in 500 mL anhydrous THF was stirred under He. To this there was added 12.4 g 2,5-dimethoxy-4-ethylthio-ß-nitrostyrene in a little THF, and the mixture was held at reflux for 24 h. After the reaction mixture had returned to room temperature, the excess hydride was destroyed by the cautious addition of 60 mL IPA, followed by 20 mL of 5% NaOH followed, in turn, by sufficient H_2O to give a white granular character to the oxides. The reaction mixture was filtered, and the filter cake washed first with THF and then with MeOH. Removing the solvents from the combined filtrate and washings under vacuum provided 9.5 g of a yellow oil. This was added to 1 L dilute HCl and washed with 2x100 mL CH_2Cl_2 which removed all color. After making the aqueous phase basic with 25% NaOH, it was extracted with 3x100 mL CH_2Cl_2, the extracts pooled, and the solvent removed under vacuum to provide 7.3 g of a pale amber oil. Distillation at 120-130 °C at 0.3 mm/Hg gave 6.17 g of a clear white oil. This was dissolved in 80 mL IPA and neutralized with concentrated HCl, forming immediate crystals of 2,5-dimethoxy-4-ethylthiophenethylamine hydrochloride (2C-T-2). An equal volume of anhydrous Et_2O was added and, after complete grinding and mixing, the salt was removed by filtration, washed with Et_2O, and air dried to constant weight. The resulting white crystals weighed 6.2 g.

DOSAGE: 12 - 25 mg.

DURATION: 6 - 8 h.

QUALITATIVE COMMENTS: (with 12 mg) "I don't feel this for fully an hour, but when I do it is quite a weight. It feels good to work it through. It is OK to be with pain. You can't eliminate it. And it is OK to contact your deep pools of anger. And all of it stems from the lack of acknowledgment. All the macho carrying on, the fights, the wars, are ways of demanding attention, and getting even for not having had it in one's life. I am experiencing more deeply than ever before the importance of acknowledging and deeply honoring each human being. And I was able to go through and resolve some judgments with particular persons."

(with 20 mg) "I chose 2C-T-2 at this dose level because the lateness of getting started, and I wanted a shorter experience with my daughter and her family around. I feel, however, that I have somewhat less of a body load with 2C-T-7. Today I was badly in need of the help that might possibly come from this material, and today it was my ally. I sorely needed the type of help that it afforded. The result was to work off the heavy feeling of tiredness and lack of motivation that had been hounding me. The next day I felt that I had dropped my burden."

(with 20 mg) "There is a neutralness to this. I am at the maximum, and I am asking myself, 'Am I enjoying this?' And the answer is, 'No, I am experiencing it.' Enjoyment seems beside the point. It is a rather intensely matter-of-fact +3. Is it interesting? Yes, but mostly in expectation of further developments. Is it inspiring? No. Is it negative? No. Am I glad I took it? Yes. Not glad. Satisfied and contented. This is a controlled +3. No threat. The body is all right. Not superbly healthy — but OK. Of no interest, either way. If I were to define the body's state, I would have to define it in image. The image is of a not comfortable state of being clenched. Clenched? Well, carefully bound in control."

(with 22 mg) "A slow onset. It took an hour for a plus one, and almost another two hours to get to a +++. Very vivid fantasy images, eyes closed, but no blurring of lines between "reality" and fantasy. Some yellow-grey patterns a la psilocybin. Acute diarrhea at about the fourth hour but no other obvious physical problems. Erotic lovely. Good material for unknown number of possible uses. Can explore for a long time. Better try 20 milligrams next time."

(with 25 mg) "I was at a +++ in an hour! It is most difficult to do even ordinary things. I took notes but now I can't find them. This is much too high for anything creative, such as looking at pictures or trying to read. Talking is OK. And to my surprise I was able to get to sleep, and a good sleep, at the seven hour point."

EXTENSIONS AND COMMENTARY: There is a considerable parallel between 2C-T-2 and 2C-T-7, and both have proven to be excellent tools for introspection. The differences are largely physical. With 2C-T-2, there is more of a tendency to have physical disturbances such as nausea and diarrhea. And the experience is distinctly shorter. With 2C-T-7, physical disturbances are less common, but you are into the effects for almost twice as long. Both have been frequently used in therapy as follow-ups to MDMA.

A point of potential misidentification should be mentioned here. 2C-T-2 has occasionally been called, simply, T-2. This abbreviated nickname has also been used for T-2 Toxin, a mycotoxin of the Tricothecene group, formed mainly by the *Fusarium* spp. This is the infamous "warfare agent" in Southeast Asia, which was finally identified as bee feces rather than a Soviet military adventure. T-2 and 2C-T-2 are radically different compounds.

All three Tweetios of 2C-T-2 have been made and looked at through human eyes. The 2-EtO-homologue of 2C-T-2 is 2-ethoxy-4-ethylthio-5-methoxyphenethylamine, or 2CT2-2ETO. The benzaldehyde (2-ethoxy-4-ethylthio-5-methoxybenzaldehyde) had a melting point of 73-75 °C, the nitrostyrene intermediate a melting point of 122-123 °C, and the final hydrochloride a melting point of 202-204 °C. Fifty milligrams was a completely effective level. The effects were felt very quickly. Vision was blurred, and there were intense eyes-closed visuals and the generation of a pleasant, contemplative mood. Baseline was re-established in five or six hours, but sleep was restless, with weird dreams. Nasal administration showed considerable variation between individuals, but a typical dose was 10 milligrams.

The 5-EtO-homologue of 2C-T-2 is 5-ethoxy-4-ethylthio-2-methoxy-phenethylamine, or 2CT2-5ETO. The benzaldehyde (5-ethoxy-4-ethylthio-2-methoxybenzaldehyde) had a melting point of 49 °C, but it was impure. The nitrostyrene intermediate melted at 107-108 °C, and the final hydrochloride had a melting point of 180 °C. At levels of 20 milligrams, there was a slow, gentle climb to a full effect at the third or fourth hour. The flooding of thoughts and easy conversation lasted for many hours, and on some occasion a sedative was needed at the 16 hour point. There was a feeling of being drained for the following day or two. Some intoxication was still noted in the second day. Again it is true here, as had been stated as a generality, that the 5-Tweetio analogues have potencies similar to that of the parent compound, but show a much longer duration. The nickname of "forever yours" had been applied. There may indeed be insight, but 24 hours' worth is an awful lot of insight.

The 2,5-DiEtO-homologue of 2C-T-2 is 2,5-diethoxy-4-ethylthiophen-ethylamine, or 2CT2-2,5DIETO. The benzaldehyde, 2,5-diethoxy-4-(ethylthio)-benzaldehyde, had a melting point of 84-85 °C, the nitrostyrene intermediate a melting point of 123-124 °C, and the final hydrochloride a melting point of 220-221 °C. Levels that were evaluated from 10 to 50 milligrams were not particularly different in intensity, but were progressively longer in duration. At 50 milligrams there was a nervousness and edginess during the early part of the experience, but for the next several hours there was evident both energy and high attentiveness. There were few if any sensory alterations. There were no negatives on the following day. The duration was perhaps nine hours.

#41   2C-T-4;   2,5-DIMETHOXY-4-(i)-PROPYLTHIO-PHENETHYLAMINE

SYNTHESIS: To a solution of 2.5 g of KOH pellets in 40 mL hot EtOH, there was added 5.4 g 2,5-dimethoxythiophenol (see under 2C-T-2 for its preparation) and 8.7 g isopropyliodide. White solids appeared in a few min, and the reaction mixture was heated on the steam bath overnight. This mixture was added to 200 mL H_2O followed by additional aqueous NaOH to raise the pH to a deep purple-blue on universal pH paper. This was extracted with 3x75 mL CH_2Cl_2. The pooled extracts were stripped of solvent under vacuum, and the residue distilled at 100-110 °C at 0.2 mm/Hg to yield 6.9 g of 2,5-dimethoxyphenyl isopropyl sulfide as a pale yellow oil. It has a very light, pleasant smell of apples.

A mixture of 4.8 g $POCl_3$ and 4.5 g N-methylformanilide was stirred and allowed to stand at room temperature for 1 h To this claret-colored solution was added 3.0 g of 2,5-dimethoxyphenyl isopropyl sulfide, producing an exothermic reaction and immediate reddening. This was heated for 0.5 h on the steam bath, then quenched in 200 mL of warm H_2O producing immediate crystals. Stirring was continued for a few min, and then the solids were removed by filtration, washed with H_2O and sucked as dry as possible. When they were ground up under an equal weight of cold MeOH, refiltered and air dried, they gave 2.35 g of 2,5-dimethoxy-4-(i-propylthio)benzaldehyde as pale yellow solids (in some runs this was a pale lime-green color) with a mp of 89-90 °C. A wasteful recrystallization from MeOH gave pale yellow crystals with a mp of 90 °C sharp.

To a solution of 6.7 g 2,5-dimethoxy-(i-propylthio)benzaldehyde in 40 g of nitromethane there was added 0.10 g of anhydrous ammonium acetate, and the mixture was heated on the steam bath for 2 h. The excess reagent/solvent was removed under vacuum yielding 8.9 g of orange solids. This was recrystallized from 200 mL boiling MeOH providing 6.2 g of 2,5-dimethoxy-ß-nitro-4-(i-propylthio)styrene as lustrous golden orange platelets.

A solution of LAH (80 mL of a 1 M solution in THF) was cooled, under He, to 0 °C with an external ice bath. With good stirring there was added 2.1 mL 100% H_2SO_4 dropwise, to minimize charring. This was followed by the addition of 5.74 g 2,5-dimethoxy-ß-nitro-4-(i-propyl-thio)styrene as a solid, a bit at a time. After 15 min further stirring, the temperature was brought up to a gentle reflux on the steam bath for another 15 min, then allowed to stand at room temperature overnight. After cooling again to 0 °C, the excess hydride was destroyed by the addition of 7 mL IPA followed by 6 mL 15% NaOH which was sufficent to give a white granular character. The reaction mixture was filtered and the filter cake washed with THF. The filtrate and washings were pooled, stripped of solvent under vacuum providing 3.9 g of a pale amber oil which was dissolved in 250 mL dilute H_2SO_4. This was washed with 3x75 mL CH_2Cl_2 which removed the residual yellow color. After making basic with 25% NaOH, the product was extracted with 3x75 mL CH_2Cl_2 and the solvent removed under vacuum to give 2.72 g of a residue which was distilled at 140-145 °C at 0.2 mm/Hg to give 2.42 g of a clear white oil. This was dissolved in 25 mL IPA, and neutralized with concentrated HCl. This gave a clear solution which, with good stirring, was diluted with 100 anhydrous Et_2O to provide 2.40 g 2,5-dimethoxy-4-(i)-propyl-thiophenethylamine hydrochloride (2C-T-4) as white crystals.

DOSAGE: 8 - 20 mg.

DURATION: 12 - 18 h.

QUALITATIVE COMMENTS: (with 8 mg) "Visual effects set in at about two hours. There was much color enhancement, particularly of green, and some flowing of colors. The bright impressionistic picture of the little girl, in the bathroom, was particularly good for the visuals to take over, especially when I was concentrating on urinating. The shadows in the large picture above the fireplace would change constantly. I could not either control or turn off these effects during the middle period (3-6 hours). From the physical point of view, something early in the experience simply didn't feel right. Both my lower legs tended to fall asleep, and this seemed to spread to my hands and lower arms. It was uncomfortable and although I was apprehensive at first it didn't get any worse with time so I ignored it. This is not one my favorite materials, and it takes too long to wear off. If I were to do it again I would settle for 4 or 5 milligrams. It may well cut out the extremity problem amd still allow for a pleasant experience."

(with 9 mg) "An important characteristic of this experience was the sense of letting go and flowing with it. Just follow where it leads. This seemed to lead to a growing euphoria, a feeling of clearing out of body residues, and the handling of very impressive insights. My thinking continued to grow in clarity, visual perception was crystal clear, and it was a joy to simply look over the scenery, enjoy the beauty, enjoy the companionship, and ponder whatever came to mind. This clarity of body and mind lasted the rest of the evening with a wonderful feeling of peace and centeredness. I still felt a lot of push from the chemical at bed time, causing some tiredness, and allowing very little sleep. I kept working at what had taken place, all night, just to release the experience."

(with 14 mg) "Very rational, benign, and good humored. The insight and calm common to the 2C-T's are present, with less of the push of body-energy which makes 2C-T-2 difficult for some people. There are no particular visuals, but then I tend to screen them out consistently, except in cases of mescaline and LSD and psilocybin, so I can't judge what others would experience in the visual area. The eyes-closed imagery is very good without being compelling. The decline is as gradual and gentle as the onset. I am fully capable of making phone calls and other normal stuff. Music is marvelous, and the body feels comfortable throughout."

(with 14 mg) "Persistent cold feet, and an uncertain stomach when moving around. Brilliant color trails reminiscent of 2C-B. But a change is occurring and I can't talk myself out of it. There are dark corners. If I were with other people, this would bring out the worst in me, which can be pretty bad."

(with 19 mg) "I was caught by the TV. Leonard Bernstein conducting West Side Story. I think I know every note. This was a 1985 rehearsal with the goofs and the sweat. And now Peter, Paul and Mary, grown older along with the songs we all sang. *Where Have All the Flowers Gone* — and an audience of grown-older people singing *Puff the Magic Dragon* like earnest children and probably crying along with me. It is good to have lived through the 60's and not to be in them now. Now there's a new song about El Salvador and it's the battle all over again on a different field, but it will always be so, until and unless. Now, in the 80's, I don't get really angry anymore. I am more warrior than angry protester, and that's a much better way to be. In fact, I am quite happy to be where I am. I know a lot more about the game, and what it is, and why it is played, and I have a good idea about my part in it, and I like the part I've chosen."

(with 22 mg) "The transition took place over three hours, an alert in 30 minutes followed by a slow and gentle climb. I found it difficult, not physically but mentally since I was for a while locked into the illogical and disconnected aspects of human experiences and expressions, particularly laws and pronouncements and unseeing prejudices, most of which I was picking up from reading the Sunday paper book reviews. As time went on, things became less pushy and I came to be at ease with very positive feelings about everything going on. No self-rejecting aspect at all. Sleep was excellent, but the next day things went slowly and I had to nap a bit. Next time, maybe 18 milligrams."

EXTENSIONS AND COMMENTARY: There are shades of the variability of the Alephs. Some observers are overwhelmed with colors and visual activity; others volunteer their absence. And a very wide range of dosages represented, from an estimated 4 or so milligrams for full effects, to something over 20 milligrams without any loss of control. That is an unusually wide lattitude of activity. And a rich variety of effects that might be experienced. The same wide range of effective dosages was also observed with the corresponding Tweetio. The 2-EtO-homologue of 2C-T-4 is 2-ethoxy-5-methoxy-4-(i)-propylthiophenethylamine, or 2CT4-2ETO. The benzaldehyde (2-ethoxy-5-methoxy-4-(i-propylthio)benzaldehyde had a melting point of 43-44 °C, the nitrostyrene intermediate a melting point of 77-79 °C, and the final hydrochloride a melting point of 153.5-154 °C. There were practically no differences between trials at 5 milligram increments within the 10 and 25 milligram range. Each produced a gentle plus two level of effect which lasted for some 10 hours. A code name of "tenderness" was felt to be appropriate, as there was a peaceful meditative inner receptiveness and clarity noted, with an honest connection felt with those who were present during the experience. Sleep was not comfortable.

I have heard 2C-T-4 referred to as T-4. There is a potent explosive used by terrorists called cyclotrimethylenetrinitramine, known by the code name RDX, or T-4. There is also a T-4 term that refers to thyroxine, an amino acid in the body. The drug 2C-T-4 is neither an explosive nor an amino acid, I am happy to say.

#42   Ψ-2C-T-4;   2,6-DIMETHOXY-4-(i)-PROPYLTHIO-
PHENETHYLAMINE)

SYNTHESIS: A stirred solution of 8.3 g 3,5-dimethoxy-1-chlorobenzene and 7.2 g isopropylsulfide in 100 mL anhydrous Et_2O was cooled with an external ice bath, and then treated with 67 mL 1.5 M lithium diisopropylamide in hexane which was added over the course of 10 min. The reaction mixture was allowed to return to room temperature and the stirring was continued for 0.5 h. The mixture was poured into dilute H_2SO_4, the organic layer was separated, and the aqueous phase extracted with 3x75 mL EtOAc. The organic phases were combined, dried over anhydrous K_2CO_3, and the solvent removed under vacuum. The resulting 4.54 g of almost colorless oil was distilled at 85-95 °C at 0.1 mm/Hg to give 4.2 g of 3,5-dimethoxyphenyl isopropyl sulfide as a colorless oil, showing a single spot on TLC with no indication of starting chlorobenzene. The product formed a picrate salt, but this had an unsatisfactory mp character (partly melting at 45-47 °C, and then completely at about 80-90 °C). The microanalysis for this picrate was low in the carbon value, although the hydrogen and nitrogen were excellent. Anal. $(C_{17}H_{19}N_3O_9S)$ H,N; C: calcd, 46.25; found, 44.58, 44.45.

　　To a well-stirred solution of 4.1 g 3,5-dimethoxyphenyl isopropyl sulfide and 3.5 mL N,N,N',N'-tetramethylethylenediamine in 25 mL anhydrous Et_2O that had been cooled to -78 °C with a dry-ice/acetone bath, there was added 10 mL 2.5 M hexane solution of butyllithium. The mixture was allowed to return to room temperature, and there was added 3.5 mL DMF which caused the yellow color to progressively darken. The reaction mixture was poured into dilute H_2SO_4, the Et_2O layer was separated, and the aqueous phase extracted with 3x75 mL EtOAc. The solvent was removed from the combined organic phases, and the residue distilled at 0.15 mm/Hg to give two fractions. One, boiling at 120-140 °C, was 0.98 g of a pale yellow mobile liquid, which was part starting sulfide and part product aldehyde by TLC. The second cut, boiling at 160-180 °C, was a viscous liquid, weighed 1.66 g, and was largely 2,6-dimethoxy-4-(i-propylthio)benzaldehyde. This formed a crystalline anil with 4-methoxyaniline (by fusing equimolar amounts of the two with a flame) which, after recrystallization from MeOH, gave fine yellow crystals with a mp of 87.5-89 °C. Anal. $(C_{19}H_{23}NO_3S)$ C,H.

　　A solution of 0.8 g 2,6-dimethoxy-4-(i-propylthio)benzaldehde in 10 mL nitromethane was treated with 0.2 g anhydrous ammonium acetate and heated on the steam bath for 1 h. The excess reagent/solvent was removed under vacuum, and the residue spontaneously solidified. This was recrystallized from 5 mL MeOH to give 0.70 g 2,6-dimethoxy-ß-nitro-4-(i)-propylthiostyrene as a pale yellow fluffy solid, with a mp of 83-84.5 °C. Anal. $(C_{13}H_{17}NO_4S)$ C,H.

　　A solution of LAH (20 mL of a 1 M solution in THF) was cooled, under He to 0 °C with an external ice bath. With good stirring there was added 0.54 mL 100% H_2SO_4 dropwise, to minimize charring. This was followed by the addition of 0.54 g 2,6-dimethoxy-ß-nitro-4-(i)-propylthiostyrene in a small volume of anhydrous THF. The color was discharged immediately. After a few minutes further stirring, the temperature was brought up to a gentle reflux on the steam bath for about 10 min, and then all was cooled again to 0 °C. The excess hydride was destroyed by the cautious addition of IPA followed by sufficent 15% NaOH to give a white granular character to the oxides, and to assure that the reaction mixture was basic. The reaction mixture was filtered, and the filter cake washed well with THF. The filtrate was stripped of solvent under vacuum and the residue dissolved in 100 mL of dilute H_2SO_4. This was washed with 2x50 mL CH_2Cl_2 (the washes were saved, see below), made basic with aqueous NaOH, and then extracted with 2x50 mL CH_2Cl_2. The residue remaining after the removal of the solvent was distilled at 130-140 °C at 0.05 mm/Hg to give 0.11 g of a white oil. This was dissolved in 10 mL IPA, neutralized with 5 drops of concentrated HCl and diluted with 50 mL anhydrous Et_2O. After filtration of the formed crystals, Et_2O washing, and air drying, there was obtained 80 mg of 2,6-dimethoxy-4-(i)-propylthiophenethylamine hydrochloride (ψ-2C-T-4) as fine white crystals. The removal of the solvent from the CH_2Cl_2 washes of the dilute H_2SO_4 solution gave a H_2O-soluble white solid that proved to be the sulfate salt of the product. This provided, after making the H_2O solution basic, extraction with CH_2Cl_2, and solvent removal, the free base that was converted, as described above, to a second crop of the hydrochloride salt.

DOSAGE: above 12 mg.

DURATION: probably short.

QUALITATIVE COMMENTS: (with 8 mg) "I might actually be up to a plus 1, and with a very good feeling. But I cannot say how long it lasted, and it was probably pretty short. It just sort of faded away."

(with 12 mg) "At the 25 minute point I am reminded of the experiment, and in another quarter hour I am into something. Will this be another forever threshold? I feel very good, but there is no sparkle."

EXTENSIONS AND COMMENTARY: Here is another example of the presentation of a compound for which there has not yet been an effective level determined. Why? For a very good reason. This is an example of a whole class of compounds that I have called the pseudos, or the ψ-compounds. Pseudo- as a prefix in the literary world generally stands for "false." A pseudopod is a thing that looks like a foot, but isn't one. A pseudonym is a fictitious name. But in chemistry, it has quite a different meaning. If something has a common name, and there is a second form (or isomer, or shape, or orientation) that is possible and it doesn't have a common name, it can be given the name of the first form with a "pseudo-" attached. Ephedrine is the erythro-isomer of N-methyl-ß-hydroxyamphetamine. There is a second stereoisomer, the threo- isomer, but it has no trivial name. So it is called pseudoephedrine, or the "Sudafed" of sinus decongestant fame.

The pseudo-psychedelics are the 2,4,6-trisubstituted counterparts of the 2,4,5-trisubstituted psychedelics. Almost all of the 2,5-dimethoxy-4-something-or-other compounds are active and interesting whether they be phenethylamines or amphetamines, and it is an exciting fact that the 2,6-dimethoxy-4-something-or-other compounds are going to be just as active and just as interesting. A number of examples have already been mentioned. TMA-2 is 2,4,5-trimethoxyamphetamine (a 2,5-dimethoxy-substituted compound with a methoxyl at the 4-position). The pseudo- analogue is TMA-6 (2,4,6-trimethoxyamphetamine) and it is every bit as potent and fascinating. Z-7 could be called pseudo-DOM, and although it is quite a bit down in potency, it is an active drug and will both demand and receive much more clinical study some day.

Will the other 2,4,5-things spawn 2,4,6-things that are active? Without a shadow of a doubt. Chemically, they are much more difficult to synthesize. The 2,5-dimethoxy orientation made the 4-position a natural and easy target. The 2,6-dimethoxy orientation pushes for 3-substitution, and the 4-position is completely unnatural. Tricks are needed, but tricks have now been found. The above synthesis of pseudo-2C-T-4 shows one such trick. This is, in my opinion, the exciting chemistry and psychopharmacology of the next decade. Well over half of all the psychedelic drugs mentioned in Book II are 2,4,5-trisubstituted compounds, and every one of them has a (potentially active) 2,4,6-pseudo-counterpart.

It goes yet further. The antidepressant series of "Ariadne" compounds are 1-phenyl-2-aminobutanes. But the 1-phenyl is again a 2,4,5-trisubstituted compound. The 2,4,6-isomer will give rise to a pseudo-Ariadne family, and I will bet that they too will be antidepressants. The 1-phenyl-2-aminobutane analog of ψ-2C-T-4 is the 2,4,6-analogue and it has been prepared as far as the nitrostyrene. It has not yet been reduced, so it is not yet been evaluated, but it could be a most remarkable psychopharmacological probe.

And it goes yet yet further. Think back to the six possible TMA's. TMA and TMA-3 were relatively inactive. And TMA-2 and TMA-6 were the interesting ones. The first gave rise to the last twenty years of psychedelic chemistry, and the other (as speculated upon above) will give rise to the forthcoming ten years. But what of TMA-4 and TMA-5? Both showed activity that was more than TMA but less than that of the -2 or -6 isomers. Could they, some day, provoke yet other families of psychedelics? Maybe the 3-position of these two might be focal points of leverage as to psychological activity. What are the letters that follow ψ in the Greek alphabet? If I remember correctly, the next letter is the last letter, omega. So, I guess that Nature is trying to tell us something, that the -4 and -5 isomers will not engender interesting families. What a pity. The chemistry is so unthinkably difficult that it would have been a true challenge. My next incarnation, maybe?

#43 2C-T-7; 2,5-DIMETHOXY-4-(n)-PROPYLTHIO-PHENETHYLAMINE

SYNTHESIS: To a solution of 3.4 g of KOH pellets in 50 mL hot MeOH, there was added a mixture of 6.8 g 2,5-dimethoxythiophenol (see under the recipe for 2C-T-

2 for its preparation) and 7.4 g (n)-propylbromide dissolved in 20 mL MeOH. The reaction was exothermic, with the deposition of white solids. This was heated on the steam bath for 0.5 h, added to 800 mL H$_2$O, additional aqueous NaOH added until the pH was basic, and extracted with 3x75 mL CH$_2$Cl$_2$. The pooled extracts were washed with dilute NaOH, and the solvent removed under vacuum. The residue was 2,5-dimethoxyphenyl (n)-propyl sulfide which was obtained as a pale yellow oil, and which weighed 8.9 g. It had a light pleasant fruity smell, and was sufficiently pure for use in the next reaction without distillation.

A mixture of 14.4 g POCl$_3$ and 13.4 g N-methylformanilide was heated for 10 min on the steam bath. To this claret-colored solution was added 8.9 g of 2,5-dimethoxyphenyl (n)-propyl sulfide, and the mixture heated an additional 25 min on the steam bath. This was then added to 800 mL of well-stirred warm H$_2$O (pre-heated to 55 °C) and the stirring continued until the oily phase had completely solidified (about 15 minutes). The resulting brown sugar-like solids were removed by filtration, and washed with additional H$_2$O. After sucking as dry as possible, they were dissolved in an equal weight of boiling MeOH which, after cooling in an ice-bath, deposited pale ivory colored crystals. After filtration, modest washing with cold MeOH, and air drying to constant weight, there was obtained 8.3 g of 2,5-dimethoxy-4-(n-propyl-thio)benzaldehyde with a mp of 73-76 °C. Recrystallization from 2.5 volumes of MeOH provided a white analytical sample with mp 76-77 °C. The NMR spectrum in CDCl$_3$ was textbook perfect, with the two aromatic protons showing singlet signals at 6.81 and 7.27 ppm, giving assurance that the assigned location of the introduced aldehyde group was correct.

To a solution of 4.0 g 2,5-dimethoxy-(n-propylthio)benzaldehyde in 20 g of nitromethane there was added 0.23 g of anhydrous ammonium acetate, and the mixture was heated on the steam bath for 1 h. The clear orange solution was decanted from some insoluble material and the excess nitromethane removed under vacuum. The orange-yellow crystalline material that remained was crystallized from 70 mL boiling IPA which, on slow cooling, deposited 2,5-dimethoxy-ß-nitro-4-(n)-propylthiostyrene as orange crystals. After their removal by filtration and air-drying to constant weight, they weighed 3.6 g, and had a mp of 120-121 °C. Anal. (C$_{13}$H$_{17}$NO$_4$S) C,H.

A solution of LAH (132 mL of a 1 M solution in THF) was cooled, under He, to 0 °C with an external ice bath. With good stirring there was added 3.5 mL 100% H$_2$SO$_4$ dropwise, to minimize charring. This was followed by the addition of 8.4 g 2,5-dimethoxy-ß-nitro-4-(n)-propylthiostyrene in 50 mL anhydrous THF. There was an immediate loss of color. After a few min further stirring, the temperature was brought up to a gentle reflux on the steam bath, then all was cooled again to 0 °C. The excess hydride was destroyed by the cautious addition of IPA (21 mL required) followed by sufficent 5% NaOH to give a white granular character to the oxides, and to assure that the reaction mixture was basic (15 mL was used). The reaction mixture was filtered and the filter cake washed first with THF and then with IPA. The filtrate and washes were combined and stripped of solvent under vacuum providing about 6 g of a pale amber oil. Without any further purification, this was distilled at 140-150 °C at 0.25 mm/Hg to give 4.8 g of product as a clear white oil. This was dissolved in 25 mL IPA, and neutralized with concentrated HCl forming immediate crystals of the hydrochloride salt in the alcohol solvent. An equal volume of anhydrous Et_2O was added, and after complete grinding and mixing, 2,5-dimethoxy-4-(n)-propylthiophenethylamine hydrochloride (2C-T-7) was removed by filtration, Et_2O washed, and air dried to constant weight. The resulting spectacular white crystals weighed 5.2 g.

DOSAGE: 10 - 30 mg.

DURATION: 8 - 15 h.

QUALITATIVE COMMENTS (with 20 mg) "A wonderful day of integration and work. Took about 2 hours for the onset. Some nausea on and off — that seemed to cycle periodically throughout the day. Visuals were great, much like mescaline but less sparkly. Lots of movement and aliveness — velvety appearance and increased depth perception. Neck and shoulder tension throughout the day along with legs. I would periodically notice extreme tightness of muscles, and then relax. Working was very integrative. Back and forth constantly between wonderful God-space — similar to MDMA but more grounded — then always back to sadness. I felt that it really showed me where I was unfinished, but with self-loving and tolerance. Tremendous processing and letting go. Seeing things very clearly and also able to laugh at my trips. Lots of singing. In spite of shoulder tension, vocal freedom and facility were very high. I felt my voice integrated and dropped in a way it never had before, and that remained for several days. Able to merge body, voice, psyche and emotions with music and then let go of it as a role. I also realized and gave myself permission to do whatever it takes to get free. I let go of Dad with tragic arias. The next day I let go of Mom by singing Kaddish for her, and merging with it."

(with 20 mg) "I lay down with music, and become engrossed with being as still as possible. I feel that if I can be totally, completely still, I will hear the inner voice of the universe. As I do this, the music becomes incredibly beautiful. I see the extraordinary importance of simply listening, listening to everything, to people and to nature, with wide open receptivity. Something very, very special happens at the still point, so I keep working on it. When I become totally still, a huge burst of energy is released. And it explodes so that it takes enormous effort to quiet it all down in order to be still again. Great fun."

(with 25 mg) "This was a marvelous and strange evening. This 2C-T-7 is good and friendly and wonderful as I remember it. I think it is going to take the place of 2C-T-2 in my heart. It is a truly good material. I got involved with a documentary on television. It was about certain people of Bolivia, people living in the high mountains and about a small village which — perhaps alone among all the places in the country — maintains the old Inca ways, the old traditions, the old language. Which is, I gather, against the law in Bolivia. It showed a yearly meeting of shamans and it was quite clear that hallucinogens played a major part in this meeting. The shaman faces, male and female, were startling in their intensity and earthy depth. The Virgin Mary is worshipped as another version of the ancient Pacha Mama, the Earth Mother. Wonderful dark, vivid look at places and people who are not usually to be seen or even known about."

(with 30 mg) "The visuals have an adaptable character to them. I can use them to recreate any hallucinogenic substance I have known and loved. With open eyes, I can go easily into LSD flowing visuals, or into the warm earth world of Peyote, or I can stop them altogether. With closed eyes, there are Escher-like graphics with a lot of chiaroscuro, geometric patterns with oppositional play of sculptured light and dark values. Green light."

EXTENSIONS AND COMMENTARY: If all the phenethylamines were to be ranked as to their acceptability and their intrinsic richness, 2C-T-7 would be right up there near the top, along with 2C-T-2, 2C-B, mescaline and 2C-E. The range is intentionally extended on the lower side to include 10 milligrams, as there have been numerous people who have found 10 or so milligrams to be quite adequate for their tastes.

One Tweetio related to 2C-T-7 has been made and evaluated. This is the 2-EtO-homologue of 2C-T-7, 2-ethoxy-5-methoxy-4-(n)-propylthiophenethyl-amine, or 2CT7-2ETO. The benzaldehyde (2-ethoxy-5-methoxy-4-(n-propyl-thio)benzaldehyde had a melting point of 69-71 °C, the nitrostyrene intermediate a melting point of 106-106.5 °C, and the final hydrochloride a melting point of 187-189 C°. At the 20 milligram level, the effects were felt quickly, and the eyes-closed visuals were modest but real. It was very short-lived, with baseline recovery at about the fifth hour. The next day there was an uncomfortable headache which seemed on an intuitive level to be an after-effect of the compound.

The unusual properties of a number of N-methyl-N-(i)-propyltryptamines suggested the possibility of something like a similar set of N-methyl-N-(i)-propylphenethylamines. Why not try one from 2C-T-7? The thought was, maybe N-methylate this compound, then put on an isopropyl group with reductive alkylation, using acetone as the carbon source and sodium cyanoborohydride. Towards this end, the free base of 2C-T-7 (from one gram of the hydrochloride) was refluxed for 2 h in 1.3 g butyl formate, and on removing the solvent/reactant the residue spontaneously crystallized. This formamide (0.7 g) was reduced with lithium hydride in cold THF to provide 2,5-dimethoxy-4-(n)-propyl-N-methyl-phenethylamine, METHYL-2C-T-7, which distilled at 150-170 °C at 0.4 mm/Hg. A very small amount of the hydrochloride salt was obtained (65 milligrams) and it had a brown color. Too small an amount of an impure product; the entire project was dropped.

#44   2C-T-8;   2,5-DIMETHOXY-4-CYCLOPROPYLMETHYLTHIOPHENETHYLAMINE

SYNTHESIS: To a solution of 2.8 g of KOH pellets in 25 mL hot MeOH, there was added a mixture of 5.9 g 2,5-dimethoxythiophenol (see under 2C-T-2 for its preparation) and 5.0 g of cyclopropylmethyl bromide. There was an immediate exothermic reaction with spontaneous boiling and the formation of white crystals. This was heated on the steam bath for 4 h, and then added to 400 mL of H_2O. After extraction with 3x75 mL CH_2Cl_2, the pooled extracts were washed first with dilute NaOH, then with saturated brine, then the solvent was removed under vacuum. The residue, 8.45 g of crude 2,5-dimethoxyphenyl cyclopropyl methyl sulfide, was distilled at 120-140 °C at 0.3 mm/Hg to give a white oil weighing 7.5 g.

A mixture of 13.5 g $POCl_3$ and 13.5 g N-methylformanilide was heated for 10 min on the steam bath. To this claret-colored solution was added 7.28 g of 2,5-dimethoxyphenyl cyclopropylmethyl sulfide, and the spontaneously exothermic mixture was heated for an additional 10 min on the steam bath, and then quenched in 400 mL of 55 °C H_2O with good stirring. After a few

minutes a reddish solid phase separated. This was removed by filtration, and washed with additional H_2O. After sucking as dry as possible, this 8.75 g of ochre-colored solid was dissolved in 14 mL of boiling MeOH, and after cooling, filtering, washing sparsely with MeOH, and air drying, gave 7.27 g of white solid crystals of 2,5-dimethoxy-4-(cyclopropylmethylthio)benzaldehyde. The proton NMR spectrum was impeccable; CHO 9.38, ArH 7.27, 6.81 2 s., OCH_3 3.93, 3.90 2 s., SCH_2 t. 2.96, CH_2, m. 1.72, and CH_2, t. 1.11.

To a solution of 6.6 g 2,5-dimethoxy-4-(cyclopropylthio)benzaldehyde in 82 g of nitromethane there was added 0.12 g of anhydrous ammonium acetate, and the mixture was heated on the steam bath for 6 h. The reaction mixture was allowed to stand overnight producing a heavy crystallization crop. Filtration, washing lightly with MeOH, and air drying gave 4.72 g of orange crystals of 2,5-dimethoxy-4-cyclopropylmethylthio-ß-nitrostyrene as yellow crystals. The evaporation of the mother liquors and grinding of the resulting solids with MeOH provided another 2.0 g of the product.

A solution LAH (40 mL of a 1 M solution in THF) was cooled, under He, to 0 °C with an external ice bath. With good stirring there was added 1.05 mL 100% H_2SO_4 dropwise over 10 min, to minimize charring. This was followed by the addition of 2.95 g 2,5-dimethoxy-4-cyclopropylmethylthio-ß-nitrostyrene as a solid, over the course of 10 min. After a few min further stirring, the temperature was brought up to a gentle reflux on the steam bath, then all was cooled again to 0 °C. The excess hydride was destroyed by the cautious addition of 6 mL IPA followed by 3 mL 15% NaOH which gave the aluminum oxide as a curdy white solid. The reaction mixture was filtered, and the filter cake washed with additional THF. The filtrate and washes were stripped of solvent under vacuum providing about 1.8 g of a colorless oil. The addition of dilute H_2SO_4 produced a thick mass of white solids. This was washed with CH_2Cl_2, and the remaining aqueous phase, still containing solids, was made basic with 25% NaOH. The aqueous phase was extracted with 3x75 mL CH_2Cl_2, and the combined extracts stripped of solvent under vacuum. The result was 1.4 g of colorless oil. This was distilled at 150-165 °C at 0.2 mm/Hg to give 1.2 g of a white oil. This was dissolved in 6 mL IPA, neutralized with 0.6 mL concentrated HCl producing spontaneous white crystals. These were diluted with 8 mL additional IPA, and suspended under 60 mL anhydrous Et_2O to provide, after filtering and air drying, 1.13 g of 2,5-dimethoxy-4-cyclo-propylmethylthiophenethylamine hydrochloride (2C-T-8) as white crystals.

DOSAGE: 30 - 50 mg.

DURATION: 10 - 15 h.

QUALITATIVE COMMENTS: (with 30 mg) "Bad taste, worse smell. But I like it. I can paint easily, and wouldn't hesitate to take a little more next time, but this is enough with no one to talk to. Manual dexterity good. Body rather warm. Wouldn't mind fooling around. In retrospect, it has a smooth onset, and is not too stimulating. This is a good one."

(with 40 mg) "This is beginning to develop at one and a half hours into it. High energy, good feeling. I have had a heavy, dense feeling between me and my work for several days now, but this is rapidly dissolving, and with this loss, the day continues into one of the most remarkable experiences I have ever had. Excellent feelings, tremendous opening of insight and understanding, a real awakening as if I had never used these materials effectively before. For the next several hours it was an internal journey for me; I wished to interact with myself. I cannot recall all the details, but I did review many aspects of myself and my personal relations. I know that I am the better for all of this."

(with 40 mg) "I first noted the effects at three quarters of an hour, and at two hours I have pain in my sinuses. My head is split in two — this is not being two or three different people — this is one person with a head living in two different universes at the same time. Not a crisis experience, but one of extreme and prolonged discomfort. Hypersensitivity to light, noise, motion, with the belief that it would not go away when the chemical wore off. My visual and spatial perceptions were divided in two along a vertical axis, with both halves moving in uncoordinated ways. A feeling that the eyes were working independently of each other. Nausea without vomiting, even when I tried to. Vertigo became intolerable if I closed my eyes or lay down, so I felt that I would never lie down or close my eyes again. Problems with 'boundaries.' The outside environment seemed to be getting inside my head. The parts of myself seemed to either separate uncontrollably or run together into someone I didn't know. A late movie, and Tranxene, and a little sleep all helped me out of this. However, a buzzing in the head, an uncertain balance, and an out-of-it feeling lasted for 3 days, and was still faintly present after a week."

(with 43 mg) "For the first two hours I rocked in place and felt quite happy not trying to 'do' anything useful or expected, but watched some excellent programs on TV. Later I sat at the typewriter and felt the energy and the opening of the particular kind of thinking-connection that I associate with 2C-T-2. I felt this very strongly; I was fully into my own energy and capable of being aggressive if I decided to. I was very good humored and completely anchored to the earth. In the late evening I went to bed and felt that I would not allow myself to sleep, since the tendency to go completely out of conscious body was quite strong. However, before I could get up and continue happily writing, as I intended, I fell asleep. I slept thoroughly, well, and woke up the next day with good energy and a willingness to get on with the day."

(with 50 mg) "The whole experience was somewhat negative, self-doubting, paranoid. Basically, I am not in a good place. No constructive values ever knit, and although there was a lot of talking, nothing positive developed. I was glad of sleep at about twelve hours into it, and this aspect of it was completely friendly. Next day, no deficit. Strange. Maybe too much."

EXTENSIONS AND COMMENTARY: With 2C-T-8, there are as many negatives as there are positives, and the particular substitution pattern is not one to set the world on fire. The first step was made towards the synthesis of the 3-carbon counterpart, 2,5-dimethoxy-4-cyclopropylmethylthioamphetamine, ALEPH-8. The above benzaldehyde (2.2 g) was cooked overnight on the steam bath in nitroethane (20 mL) containing ammonium acetate (0.4 g) and when the solvent was removed, the residue was converted to orange crystals by the addition of a little MeOH. This was not pursued further. Although the cyclopropylmethyl group was quite something on the mescaline oxygen atom, it is less appealing on the 2C-T-X sulfur atom, and there is even less enthusiasm to put it into an ALEPH. That's the way it is, and who could have guessed!

#45   2C-T-9;   2,5-DIMETHOXY-4-(t)-BUTYLTHIO-PHENETHYLAMINE

SYNTHESIS: To a well-stirred ice-cold suspension of 2.8 g p-dimethoxybenzene and 3.2 mL N,N,N',N'-tetramethylethylenediamine in 100 mL petroleum ether under an inert atmosphere of He, there was added 13 mL of a 1.6 N solution of butyllithium in hexane. The suspended dimethoxybenzene became opaque and there was a pale yellow color generated. The reaction mixture was warmed to room temperature which converted it to light white solids. After an additional 0.5 h stirring, there was added, slowly, 3.6 g of di-(t)-butyldisulfide. The yellow color deepened, the solids dissolved and, after 1 h, the color was a clear deep brown. This solution was poured into 100 mL dilute HCl and the organic phase was separated. The aqueous fraction was extracted with 3x75 mL CH_2Cl_2. The combined organic phases were washed with dilute aqueous NaOH, with H_2O, and then stripped of solvents under vacuum. The residue was distilled at 95-105 °C at 0.5 mm/Hg to provide 3.7 g of 2,5-dimethoxyphenyl (t)-butyl sulfide as a white, mobile liquid. Anal. $(C_{12}H_{18}O_2S)$ C,H. A solid derivative was found in the nitration product, 2,5-dimethoxy-4-(t)-butylthio-1-nitrobenzene, which came from the addition of 0.11 mL of concentrated HNO_3 to a solution of 0.23 g of the above sulfide in 5 mL ice cold acetic acid. Dilution with H_2O provided yellow solids which, on recrystallization from MeOH, had a mp of 92-93 °C. Anal. $(C_{12}H_{17}NO_4S)$ C,H. Attempts to make either the picrate salt or the sulfonamide derivative were not satisfactory.

A mixture of 72 g $POCl_3$ and 67 g N-methylformanilide was heated for 10 min on the steam bath. To this claret-colored solution was added 28 g of 2,5-dimethoxyphenyl (t)-butyl sulfide, and the mixture heated for 10 min on the steam bath. This was then added to 1 L of H_2O and stirred overnight. The residual brown oil was separated from the water mechanically, and treated with 150 mL boiling hexane. The hexane solution was decanted from some insoluble tars, and on cooling deposited a dark oil which did not crystallize. The remaining hexane was removed under vacuum and the residue combined with the above hexane-insoluble dark oil, and all distilled at 0.2 mm/Hg. An early fraction (70-110 °C) was largely N-methylformanilide and was discarded. Crude 2,5-dimethoxy-4-(t-butylthio)benzaldehyde came over at 120-130 °C and weighed 12.0 g. This was never satisfactorily crystallized despite the successful formation of seed. It was a complex mixture by TLC, containing several components. It was used for the next step as the crude distilled fraction.

To a solution of 10 g impure 2,5-dimethoxy-(t-butylthio)benzaldehyde in 75 mL of nitromethane there was added 1.0 g of anhydrous ammonium acetate, and the mixture was heated on the steam bath 1.5 h. Removal of the excess solvent/ reagent under vacuum produced an orange oil that was (not surprisingly) complex by TLC and which would not crystallize. A hot hexane solution of this oil was allowed to slowly cool and stand at room temperature for several days, yielding a mixture of yellow crystals and a brown viscous syrup. The solids were separated and recrystallized from 40 mL MeOH to give 3.7 g 2,5-dimethoxy-4-(t)-butylthio-ß-nitrostyrene as fine lemon-yellow crystals, with a mp of 93-94 °C. A second crop of 1.4 g had a mp of 91-92 °C. Anal. $(C_{14}H_{19}NO_4S)$ C,H.

A solution of LAH (70 mL of a 1 M solution in THF) was cooled, under He, to 0 °C with an external ice bath. With good stirring there was added 2.1 mL 100% H_2SO_4 dropwise, over the course of 20 min. This was followed by the addition of 4.7 g 2,5-dimethoxy-4-(t)-butylthio-ß-nitrostyrene in 20 mL anhydrous THF. There was an immediate loss of color. After a few min further stirring, the mixture was allowed to come to room temperature, and the stirring was continued for 5 h. The excess hydride was destroyed by the cautious addition of 10 mL IPA followed by 6 mL 15% NaOH and finally 6 mL H_2O. The loose white solids were removed by filtration, and the filter cake washed with THF. The filtrate and washes were combined and, after stripping off the solvent under vacuum, there was obtained 4.66 g of a pale yellow oil. Without any further purification, this was distilled at 0.2 mm/ Hg. A first fraction came over at up to 120 °C and was a light colorless oil that was not identified. The correct product distilled at 130-160 °C as a pale yellow viscous oil that weighed 1.66 g. This was dissolved in 10 mL IPA, neutralized with 20 drops of concentrated HCl and diluted with 80 mL anhydrous Et_2O. After standing a few min there was the spontaneous generation of white crystals of 2,5-dimethoxy-4-(t)-butylthiophenethylamine hydrochloride (2C-T-9) which were removed by filtration, and air dried. The weight was 1.10 g.

DOSAGE: 60 - 100 mg.

DURATION: 12 - 18 h.

QUALITATIVE COMMENTS: (with 90 mg) "2C-T-9 tastes the way that old crank-case motor oil smells. I was up to something above a plus two at the third hour. Although there were no visuals noted, I certainly would not choose to drive. Somehow this does more to the body than to the head. I feel that the effects are waning at maybe the sixth hour, but there is a very strong body memory that makes sleeping difficult. Finally, at sometime after midnight and with the help of a glass of wine, some sleep."

(with 125 mg) "There was a steady climb to a +++ over the first couple of hours. So far, the body has been quite peaceful without any strong energy push or stomach problems, although my tummy insists on being treated with quiet respect, perhaps out of habit, perhaps not. At the fifth hour, the body energy is quite strong, and I have the choice of focusing it into some activity, such as love-making or writing, or having to deal with tapping toes and floor-pacing. For a novice this would be a murderously difficult experience. Too much energy, too long a time. I suppose I could get used to it, but let me judge by when I get to sleep, and just what kind of sleep it is. It turned out that sleep was OK, but for the next couple of days there was a continuing awareness of some residue in the body — some kind of low-level poisoning. I feel in general that there is not the excitement or creativity to connect with, certainly not enough to justify the cost to the body."

EXTENSIONS AND COMMENTARY: The three-carbon analog of 2C-T-9 (this would be one of the ALEPH series) has never been made and, for that matter, none of the higher numbered 2C-T's have had the amphetamine counterparts synthesized. They are, as of the present time, unknown compounds. This nifty reaction with di-(t)-butyl disulfide worked so well, that three additional disulfides that were at hand were immediately thrown into the chemical program, with the quick assignment of the names 2C-T-10, 2C-T-11, and 2C-T-12.

The lithiated dimethoxybenzene reaction with 2,2-dipyridyl disulfide produced 2,5-dimethoxyphenyl 2-pyridyl sulfide which distilled at 135-150 °C at 0.4 mm/Hg and could be recrystallized from cyclohexane containing 2% EtOH to give a product that melted at 66-67.5 °C. Anal. ($C_{13}H_{13}NO_2S$) C,H. This would have produced 2,5-dimethoxy-4-(2-pyridylthio)phenethylamine (2C-T-10) but it was never pursued.

The same reaction with di-(4-bromophenyl) disulfide produced 2,5-dimethoxyphenyl 4-bromophenyl sulfide which distilled at 150-170 °C at 0.5 mm/Hg and could be recrystallized from MeOH to give a product that melted at 72-73 °C. Anal. ($C_{14}H_{13}BrO_2S$) C,H. This was being directed towards 2,5-dimethoxy-4-(4-bromophenylthio)phenethylamine (2C-T-11) but it also was abandoned.

The same reaction with N,N-dimorpholinyl disulfide produced virtually no product at all, completely defusing any plans for the synthesis of a novel sulfur-nitrogen bonded base 2,5-dimethoxy-4-(1-morpholinothio)phenethylamine (2C-T-12). One additional effort was made to prepare a 2C-T-X thing with a sulfur-nitrogen bond. The acid chloride intermediate in the preparation of 2,5-dimethoxy-thiophenol (as described in the recipe for 2C-T-2) is 2,5-dimethoxybenzenesulfonyl chloride. It reacted smoothly with an excess of diethylamine to produce 2,5-dimethoxy-N,N-diethylbenzenesulfonamide which distilled at 155 °C at 0.13 mm/Hg and which could be recrystallized from a 4:1 mixture of cyclohexane/benzene to give a product with a melting point of 41-42 °C and an excellent proton NMR. This amide proved totally refractory to all efforts at reduction, so the target compound, 2,5-dimethoxy-4-diethylaminothiophenethylamine, has not been made. It has not even been given a 2C-T-X number.

#46   2C-T-13;   2,5-DIMETHOXY-4-(2-METHOXYETHYLTHIO)PHENETHYLAMINE

SYNTHESIS: To a solution of 3.25 g of KOH pellets in 25 mL hot MeOH, there was added 6.8 g of 2,5-dimethoxythiophenol (see under 2C-T-2 for its preparation) followed by 4.73 g of 2-methoxyethylchloride. This mixture was heated on the steam bath for 0.5 h, then added to 500 mL H_2O. This very basic aqueous phase was extracted with 3x100 mL CH_2Cl_2, the extracts pooled, and back-washed with 5% NaOH. The solvent was removed under vacuum to give 8.82 g of a white oil. Distillation gave 2,5-dimethoxyphenyl 2-methoxyethyl sulfide with a bp 115-125

°C at 0.3 mm/Hg, and a weight of 6.65 g.

A mixture of 10 g $POCl_3$ and 10 g N-methylformanilide was heated for 10 min on the steam bath. To this claret-colored solution was added 6.16 g of 2,5-dimethoxyphenyl 2-methoxyethyl sulfide. There was an immediate exothermic reaction and gas evolution. The mixture was heated for 15 min on the steam bath, at which time there was no starting sulfide present by TLC. This was then added to 500 mL of well-stirred warm H_2O (pre-heated to 55 °C) and the stirring continued until only a thin oily phase remained. This was extracted with CH_2Cl_2, the extracts were combined, and the solvent removed under vacuum. The residue was extracted with 5 sequential 20 mL

portions of boiling hexane which deposited crystals on cooling. Filtering gave a total of 4.12 g crystalline solids. Recrystallization from MeOH gave a poor yield of a cream-colored crystal with a mp of 68-69 °C. A more efficient purification was achieved by distillation (155-168 °C at 0.3 mm/Hg) yielding 3.50 g of 2,5-dimethoxy-4-(2-methoxyethylthio)benzaldehyde as a pale yellow solid, with a mp of 67-68 °C. A faster moving (by TLC) trace component with an intense fluorescence persisted throughout the entire purification scheme, and was still present in the analytical sample. Anal. ($C_{12}H_{16}O_4S$) C,H.

To a solution of 3.41 g 2,5-dimethoxy-4-(2-methoxyethylthio)benz-aldehyde in 50 g of nitromethane there was added 0.11 g of anhydrous ammonium acetate, and the mixture was heated on the steam bath for 2 h, at which time the starting aldehyde had largely disappeared by TLC (silica gel plates with CH_2Cl_2 as the developing solvent) and a faster moving nitrostyrene product was clearly visible. The clear orange solution was stripped of the excess nitromethane under vacuum producing a yellow oil that crystallized yielding 3.97 g of a yellow solid with a mp of 99-104 °C. Recrystallization of a small sample from MeOH produced (when dry) yellow electrostatic crystals of 2,5-dimethoxy-4-(2-methoxyethylthio)-ß-nitrostyrene with a mp of 107 °C sharp. From IPA the product is a burnished gold color with the mp 106-107 °C. Anal. ($C_{13}H_{17}NO_5S$) C,H.

A solution of LAH (40 mL of a 1 M solution in THF) was cooled, under He, to 0 °C with an external ice bath. With good stirring there was added 1.05 mL 100% H_2SO_4 dropwise, to minimize charring. This was followed by the addition of 3.07 g 2,5-dimethoxy-4-(2-methoxyethylthio)-ß-nitrostyrene in small portions, as a solid, over the course of 10 min. There was a considerable amount of gas evolved, and a little bit of charring. After a few min further stirring, the temperature was brought up to a gentle reflux on the steam bath, and then all was cooled again to 0 °C. The excess hydride was destroyed by the cautious addition of 8 mL IPA followed by 3 mL 15% NaOH which gave the reaction mixture a curdy white granular character. The reaction mixture was filtered, the filter cake washed with THF, and filtrate and washes were stripped of solvent under vacuum providing about 3 g of a pale amber oil. This was dissolved in about 40 mL CH_2Cl_2 and extracted with 200 mL dilute H_2SO_4 in three portions. All of the color remained in the organic phase. The pooled aqueous extracts were washed with CH_2Cl_2, then made basic with 25% NaOH, extracted with 3x75 mL CH_2Cl_2, and the combined extracts pooled and stripped of solvent under vacuum. The 2 g pale yellow oily residue was distilled at 155-165 °C at 0.2 mm/Hg to give 1.23 g of a clear white oil. This was dissolved in IPA, neutralized with concentrated HCl, and diluted with anhydrous Et_2O to produce crystals of 2,5-dimethoxy-4-(2-methoxyethylthio)phenethylamine hydrochloride (2C-T-13). After filtration, washing with Et_2O, and air drying, this white crystalline product weighed 0.89 g.

DOSAGE: 25 - 40 mg.

DURATION: 6 - 8 h.

QUALITATIVE COMMENTS: (with 25 mg) "I felt it was somewhat noisy as we went into the experience. This noisiness lasted only about an hour, then stopped. At the peak, which seemed to be at about 1 to maybe 1.5 hours, some eyes-closed visuals appeared. There was a white field with colored visuals, at times geometric in shape. These eye-closed images were pleasant and I enjoyed them when I did not concern myself with, or listen to, the conversation. There was an eyes-open change in color, the ivy became a little lighter or maybe a little stronger in color. I'm not sure which. I felt there was a gradual diminishing of activity (whatever that undefined activity was) starting at 2 to 2.5 hours, and coming close to baseline at 6 PM. The descent was pleasant and I would say pleasurable. The experience did not lead to any confusion which I sometimes notice in other experiences. There was no problem with anorexia. We ate constantly during the experience. The grapes and other fruit were lovely. This is one of the few times I would say that I would try a higher dose. Maybe 30 or 33 milligrams. I suspect the experience would be similar, with just a heightened peak at 1 hour and perhaps a little more body effect. It may well be one to try with one's wife."

(with 28 mg) "There was a strange, disturbing twinge exactly eight minutes after starting this, that asked me, 'Should I have done this?' I answered, 'Yes' and the twinge disappeared. And then there was nothing until the expected time of development, at a half hour when I felt a light head and slight dizziness. There was a solid plus two for a couple of hours. I paid careful attention for auditory oddities that I had noted before, but they were not there. In an earlier trial (with 20 milligrams) the radio had the sound of being located in the outdoors with the sounds coming through the wall and into the room where I was. I was at a neutral baseline at about seven hours."

(with 35 mg) "There was a quiet climb, but it was marred with some tummy unquiet, and an annoying persistence of diarrhea. I was very impressed with eyes-closed patterning, which seemed to do its own thing independently of the music. I was clearly up to a +++, but there was a feeling that as soon as it got there it started to go away again. There was no there, there. Yet there were a couple of touches of introspection, of seriousness which I had to respect."

(with 40 mg) "There were four of us, and the entry was individual for each of us. Two of us were nauseous. One volunteered a statement, almost a confession, of too much food and drink in the immediate past. One of us needed his cigarette right now, and then he saw that he was killing himself, and he swore off. Don't know if it will last, however. At the two and a half hour point there is a consensus that this has gone its route and will lose its impact, so three of us decided to supplement on 2C-T-2. Six milligrams proves to be a little light so, some four hours later, we each took another six milligrams. Excellent. In a while we discoved that we were very hungry, and food tasted marvelous. Headaches acknowledged in the early evening, but the extension from T-13 to T-2 seemed to be absolutely correct. And as of the next day, the non-smoker was still a non-smoker.

EXTENSIONS AND COMMENTARY: Most of the synthetic adventures of putting a basic something away out from the benzene ring, at the four-position, have involved subtle things such as unsaturated bonds or three-membered rings. This was the first try with the actual use of a different atom (an oxygen). What about other heteroatoms such as sulfur or nitrogen or silicon or phosphorus, or some-such? The sulfur counterpart of 2C-T-13 was named 2C-T-14, and was immediately launched. The reaction of 2,5-dimethoxythiophenol and KOH with 2-methylthioethyl chloride in hot MeOH gave 2,5-dimethoxyphenyl 2-methylthioethyl sulfide as a white oil (boiling point of 140-160 °C at 0.3 mm/Hg). This underwent a normal Vilsmeier reaction (phosphorous oxychloride and N-methylformanilide) to give 2,5-dimethoxy-4-(2-methylthioethylthio)benzaldehyde with a melting point of 64-64.5 °C from MeOH. This, in nitromethane containing a little ammonium acetate, was heated on the steam bath for 10 hours and worked up to give an excellent yield of 2,5-dimethoxy-4-(2-methylthioethylthio))-ß-nitrostyrene as garish orange-red "Las Vegas" colored crystals from acetonitrile, with a melting point of 126-127 °C. And as of the moment, this is sitting on the shelf waiting to be reduced to the target compound 2,5-dimethoxy-4-(2-methylthioethylthio)phenethylamine hydrochloride, or 2C-T-14. Will it be active? I rather suspect that it will be, and I'll bet it will be longer-lived than the oxygen model, 2C-T-13.

#47 2C-T-15; SESQUI; 2,5-DIMETHOXY-4-CYCLOPROPYLTHIOPHENETHYLAMINE

SYNTHESIS: To a solution of 3.3 g of KOH pellets in 150 mL hot MeOH, there was added 10 g 2,5-dimethoxythiophenol (see recipe for 2C-T-2 for its preparation) followed by 10 g 1-bromo-3-chloropropane. The reaction was exothermic, and immediately deposited white solids of KCl. The reaction mixture was warmed for a few min on the steam bath, and then quenched in H_2O. The basic reaction mixture was extracted with 3x75 mL CH_2Cl_2. The pooled extracts were stripped of solvent under vacuum. The residual oil was distilled at 145-155 °C at 0.2 mm/Hg to give 16.5 g of 2,5-dimethoxyphenyl 3-chloropropyl sulfide as a clear, colorless oil.

A solution of the lithium amide of 2,2,6,6-tetramethylpiperidine was prepared by the addition of 20 mL of 2.6 M butyllithium in hexane to a well stirred hexane solution of the piperidine in 100 mL hexane, under an atmosphere of He. The reaction was exothermic, formed a white solid precipitate, and was allowed to continue stirring for a few min. There was then added 6.5 g 2,5-dimethoxphenyl 3-chloropropyl sulfide, and a strongly exothermic reaction ensued. This was stirred for 30 min and then poured into dilute H_2SO_4 (the progress of the reaction must be followed by TLC, silica gel plates, CH_2Cl_2:petroleum ether 50:50 to determine when it is done; in one run over 2 h were required for completion of the reaction). The organic phase was separated, and the aqueous phase extracted with 3x75 mL EtOAc. The combined organic phases were washed first with dilute NaOH, then with dilute HCl, then the solvents were removed under vacuum. The residue was distilled to provide 2,5-dimethoxyphenyl cyclopropyl sulfide as a pale yellow liquid that boiled at 100-115 °C at 0.1 mm/Hg. The use of other bases to achieve this cyclization were less successful. Incomplete cyclization resulted from the use of lithium diisopropyl amide and, if the conditions were made more vigorous, there was dehydrohalogenation to the allyl sulfide. An unexpected difficulty was that the allyl sulfide (from elimination) and the 3-chloropropyl sulfide (starting material) behaved in an identical manner on TLC analysis. They were easily separated, however, by GC analysis.

A completely different approach to the synthesis of this sulfide was explored through the reaction of cyclopropyllithium with an aromatic disulfide, thus avoiding the base-promoted cyclization step. A solution of 2.6 g di-(2,5-dimethoxyphenyl)disulfide (from 2,5-dimethoxythiophenol and hydrogen peroxide, bp 220-230 °C at 0.3 mm/Hg) was made in anhydrous Et_2O, and well stirred. In a separate flask, under an atmosphere of He, 4 mL of 2.6 M butyllithium was added to a solution of 1.2 g cyclopropyl bromide in 20 mL anhydrous Et_2O. This mildly exothermic combination turned a bit cloudy, was stirred for 1 h, then transferred with an air-tight syringe to the above-described Et_2O solution of the aromatic disulfide. A heavy precipitate formed, and stirring was continued for an additional 0.5 h. The reaction mixture was then poured into H_2O, the layers separated, and the aqueous phase extracted with CH_2Cl_2. The extracts were pooled, washed with dilute aqueous KOH, and the solvents removed under vacuum. Distillation gave 0.7 g of 2,5-dimethoxyphenyl cyclopropyl sulfide with identical gas chromatographic behavior to the sample prepared by the cyclization of the chloropropylthio compound.

A mixture of 7.2 g $POCl_3$ and 6.7 g N-methylformanilide was heated on the steam bath until it was claret red. To this there was added 4.5 g of 2,5-dimethoxyphenyl cyclopropyl sulfide, and the exothermic combination heated on the steam bath for about 5 min. The deep red, bubbling reaction mixture was added to 150 mL H_2O and stirred until all oils had been converted into loose solids. These were then removed by filtration, washed with H_2O, and sucked as dry as possible. They were dissolved in boiling MeOH which, after cooling in an ice-bath, deposited yellow crystals of 2,5-dimethoxy-4-(cyclopropylthio)benzaldehyde that weighed 3.43 g after air drying, and had a mp of 97-99 °C. Anal. ($C_{12}H_{14}O_3S$) C,H.

To a solution of 3.0 g 2,5-dimethoxy-4-(cyclopropylthio)benzaldehyde in 40 g of nitromethane there was added 0.2 g of anhydrous ammonium acetate, and the mixture was heated on the steam bath for 3 h. The excess nitromethane was removed under vacuum yielding 3.4 g orange crystals. These were recrystallized from 150 mL boiling IPA containing a little toluene. After cooling, filtering, and air drying there were obtained 2.75 g of 2,5-dimethoxy-4-cyclopropylthio-ß-nitrostyrene as pumpkin-colored crystals with a mp of 159-160 °C. Anal. ($C_{13}H_{15}NO_4S$) C,H.

A solution of LAH (40 mL of a 1 M. solution in THF) was cooled, under He, to 0 °C with an external ice bath. With good stirring there was added 1.05 mL 100% H_2SO_4 dropwise, to minimize charring. This was followed by the addition of 2.5 g 2,5-dimethoxy-4-cyclopropylthio-ß-nitrostyrene in 40 mL anhydrous THF over the course of 15 min. There was an immediate loss of color. After a few min further stirring, the temperature was brought up to a gentle reflux on the steam bath and held there for 2 h. After recooling, there was added IPA (to destroy the excess hydride) followed by sufficent 15% NaOH to give a white granular character to the oxides, and to assure that the reaction mixture was basic. The reaction mixture was filtered, and the filter cake washed with THF. The filtrate and washes were stripped of solvent under vacuum providing a yellow oil that was treated with dilute H_2SO_4. This produced a flocculant white solid, apparently the sulfate salt of the product. This was washed with 4x75 mL CH_2Cl_2 which removed most of the yellow color. The aqueous phase was made basic with aqueous NaOH and extracted with 3x75 mL CH_2Cl_2. Removal of the solvent under vacuum gave a light yellow colored oil that was distilled at 0.3 mm/Hg. The fraction boiling at 140-150 °C was a colorless, viscous oil that weighed 1.97 g. This was dissolved in a few mL IPA, and neutralized with concentrated HCl forming immediate cottage cheese-like crystals of the hydrochloride salt. This was diluted by suspension in anhydrous Et_2O, removed by filtration, and air dried to give 1.94 g of 2,5-dimethoxy-4-cyclopropylthio-phenethylamine hydrochloride (2C- T-15) that had a mp of 203-5-204.5 °C. Anal. ($C_{13}H_{20}ClNO_2S$) C,H.

DOSAGE: greater than 30 mg.

DURATION: several hours.

QUALITATIVE COMMENTS: (at 30 mg) "I was somewhere between a threshold and a plus one for several hours, and appeared to be quite talkative in the evening."

EXTENSIONS AND COMMENTARY: The commonly used name for 2C-T-15, during its synthesis, was SESQUI. The general name for a 15-carbon terpene is sesquiterpene, from the Latin prefix for one and a half. The active level of 2C-T-15 is not known. The highest level yet tried was 30 milligrams orally, and there had been threshold reports pretty regularly all the way up from 6 milligrams. But no definite activity yet. This compound is isosteric with the isopropyl group as seen in the analogous compound 2C-T-4 (the three carbons are in exactly the same positions, only the electrons are located differently) and it is a little surprising that the potency appears to be considerably less. Just over 20 milligrams of the latter compound was overwhelmingly psychedelic.

The entire mini-project of hanging cyclic things onto the sulfur atom was an interesting problem. This is the three carbon ring. The six carbon ring (the cyclohexyl homologue) was discussed as 2C-T-5 in the recipe for of ALEPH-2. The cyclobutyl and cyclopentyl homologs were assigned the names of 2C-T-18 and 2C-T-23, respectively, and their preparations taken as far as the nitrostyrene and the aldehyde stages, respectively, before the project ran out of steam.

Towards the cyclobutyl homologue, a solution of 2,5-dimethoxythiophenol and cyclobutyl bromide in DMSO containing anhydrous potassium carbonate was stirred for several hours at room temperature and yielded 2,5-dimethoxyphenyl cyclobutyl sulfide as a white oil that boiled at 135-140 °C at 0.3 mm/Hg. Anal. ($C_{12}H_{16}O_2S$) C,H. This was brought to react with a mixture of phosphorus oxychloride and N-methylformanilide producing 2,5-dimethoxy-4-(cyclobutylthio)-benzaldehyde that had a melting point of 108-109.5 °C from MeOH. Anal. ($C_{13}H_{16}O_3S$) C,H. Coupling with nitromethane in the presence of ammonium acetate produced 2,5-dimethoxy-4-cyclobutylthio-ß-nitrostyrene as lustrous orange crystals from boiling acetonitrile, melting point 160-161 °C. Anal, ($C_{14}H_{17}NO_4S$) C,H. This will some day be reduced to 2,5-dimethoxy-4-cyclobutylthiophenethylamine hydrochloride, 2C-T-18.

Towards the cyclopentyl homologue, a solution of 2,5-dimethoxythiophenol and cyclopentyl bromide in DMSO containing anhydrous potassium carbonate was stirred for several hours at room temperature and yielded 2,5-dimethoxyphenyl cyclopentyl sulfide as a white oil that boiled at 135-145 °C at 0.3 mm/Hg. This was brought to react with a mixture of phosphorus oxychloride and N-methylformanilide producing 2,5-dimethoxy-4-(cyclopentylthio)benzaldehyde as yellow crystals from MeOH. This will some day be converted to the nitrostyrene and then reduced to 2,5-dimethoxy-4-cyclopentylthiophenethylamine hydrochloride, 2C-T-23.

**#48   2C-T-17;   NIMITZ;   2,5-DIMETHOXY-4-(s)-BUTYLTHIO-
PHENETHYLAMINE**

SYNTHESIS: To a solution of 2.6 g of KOH pellets in 50 mL hot MeOH, there was added a mixture of 6.8 g 2,5-dimethoxythiophenol (see under 2C-T-2 for its preparation) and 5.8 g (s)-butyl bromide. The reaction was exothermic, with the deposition of white solids. This was heated on the steam bath for a few h, the solvent removed under vacuum, and the resulting solids dissolved in 250 mL H$_2$O. Additional aqueous NaOH was added to bring universal pH paper to a full blue color. This was extracted with 3x40 mL CH$_2$Cl$_2$, the extracts pooled, and the solvent removed under vacuum. The residue was 2,5-dimethoxyphenyl (s)-butyl sulfide which was a pale yellow oil, weighing 10.12 g. It was sufficiently pure for use in the next reaction without a distillation step.

A mixture of 15.1 g POCl$_3$ and 14.1 g N-methylformanilide was heated for 10 min on the steam bath. To this claret-colored solution was added 9.4 g of 2,5-dimethoxyphenyl (s)-butyl sulfide, and the mixture heated for 35 min on the steam bath. This was then added to 200 mL of well-stirred warm H$_2$O (pre-heated to 55 °C) and the stirring continued until the oily phase had completely solidified (about 15 min). These light brown solids were removed by filtration, and washed with additional H$_2$O. After sucking as dry as possible, these solids (12.14 g wet) were ground under an equal weight of MeOH which produced a yellowish crystalline solid with a mp of 76-81 °C. Recrystallization of a 0.4 g sample from an equal weight of boiling MeOH provided 0.27 g of 2,5-dimethoxy-4-(s-butylthio)benz-aldehyde as a pale cream-colored crystalline material with a mp of 86-87 °C.

To a solution of 8.0 g of the crude 2,5-dimethoxy-4-(s-butylthio)benz-aldehyde in 40 g of nitromethane there was added 0.38 g of anhydrous ammonium acetate, and the mixture was heated on the steam bath for 1 h. The reddish colored solution was decanted from some insoluble tan material and the excess nitromethane removed under vacuum. The heavy red oil that remained was diluted with an equal volume of boiling MeOH, and allowed to return to room temperature. The orange-colored crystals that slowly formed were removed by filtration and, after air drying, weighted 6.24 g. This was again recrystallized from an equal volume of MeOH, yielding 2,5-dimethoxy-4-(s-butylthio)-ß-nitrostyrene as yellow, somewhat beady crystals that weighed (when dry) 3.50 g and which had a mp of 62-65 °C. A small portion of this fraction was crystallized yet again from MeOH to provide an analytical sample that was yellow-orange in color, and had an mp of 68-69 °C. Anal. (C$_{13}$H$_{17}$NO$_4$S) C,H.

A solution of LAH (120 mL of a 1 M solution in THF) was cooled, under He, to 0 °C with an external ice bath. With good stirring there was added 3.3 mL 100% H$_2$SO$_4$ dropwise, to minimize charring. This was followed by the addition of

8.83 g 2,5-dimethoxy-4-(s-butylthio)-ß-nitrostyrene in 80 mL anhydrous THF dropwise over the course of 2 h. After a few min further stirring, the temperature was brought up to a gentle reflux on the steam bath, and then all was cooled again to 0 °C. The excess hydride was destroyed by the cautious addition of 18 mL IPA followed first by 5 mL of 15% NaOH and then by 15 mL of H_2O. The reaction mixture was filtered, and the filter cake washed with THF. The filtrate and washing were combined and stripped of solvent under vacuum providing about 8.5 g of a pale amber oil. Without any further purification, this was distilled at 135-150 °C at 0.4 mm/Hg to give 6.12 g of a clear white oil. This was dissolved in 30 mL IPA, and neutralized with 2.1 mL of concentrated HCl forming crystals immediately. Another 10 mL of IPA was added to allow the solids to be finely dispersed, and then about 100 mL of anhydrous Et_2O were added. The solids were removed by filtration, Et_2O washed, and air dried to constant weight. The product, 2,5-dimethoxy-4-(s)-butylthiophenethylamine hydrochloride (2C-T-17) was obtained as spectacular white crystals, weighing 5.67 g.

DOSAGE: 60 - 100 mg.

DURATION: 10 - 15 h.

QUALITATIVE COMMENTS: (with 60 mg) "This material took fully three hours to get into its maximum effect. I never was at a +++, quite, and I am not sure why it is really active, but I know it is. There does not seem to be any interference with my concentration or mental coordination, but I wouldn't want to drive right now. Good appetite in the evening, for a Chicago-style pizza, and there was no Tomso effects (the rekindling of a psychedelic effect with alcohol) with a glass of wine. An over-all good and instructive ++, no visuals, totally benign. There is no hesitation in doing it again some day."

(with 100 mg) "A small fragment hadn't dissolved when I drank the solution, and it must have stuck to the back of my mouth, because it made a searing spot that burned for 5 minutes. The first central effects were noted at an hour. The plateau stretched from the 3rd to the 7th hour, then tapered off quite quickly. My sleep was fitful, with some hints of nervous sensitivity. I felt that there were some residuals even into the next morning. A truly heavy psychedelic, but with very few explicit sensual changes or unusual perceptions to justify that comment. Why is it heavy? It just is. This dosage is high enough."

EXTENSIONS AND COMMENTARY: An interesting, and quite logical, habit that seems to always pop up when a lot of talk and energy become directed at a specific compound, is the habit of using a nickname for it. The Tweetios are an example, and in the 2C-T-X family I had mentioned the term SESQUI. Here, this compound was called NIMITZ, for the obvious reason that the major freeway from Oakland to San Jose, the Nimitz freeway, was also called State Highway 17. Its name has been changed to Interstate 880, and I guess it could now only be used as a reference point if efforts were being made for a 2C-T-880.

The reason that 2C-T-17 is of special theoretic interest is that it is one of the very first of the active psychedelic compounds (along with 2C-G-5) to have a potential optically active center on the side of the ring away from the nitrogen atom. One of the oldest and best studied variants of the phenethylamine chain are the alpha-methyl homologues, the substituted amphetamines. Here there is an asymmetric carbon atom right next to the amine group, allowing the molecule to be prepared in either a right-hand way or a left-hand way. The "R" or the "S" isomer. And in the several studies that have looked at such isomers separately, it has always been the "R" isomer that has carried the psychedelic effects. This probably says something about the nitrogen end, the metabolic end, the "north" end of the receptor site that recognizes these compounds, and suggests that there is some intrinsic asymmetry in the area that binds near to the basic nitrogen atom.

But very little is known of the receptor's "south" end, so to speak, the geometry of the area where the opposite end of the molecule has to fit. Here, with 2-C-17, there is a secondary butyl group, and this contains an asymmetric carbon atom. But now this center of asymmetry is clear across the benzene ring from the nitrogen, and should certainly be in some entirely new part of the receptor site. Why not make this compound with the "R" and the "S" forms in this new and unusual location? Why not, indeed! Why not call them the right-lane and the left lane of the Nimitz? Fortunately, both "R" and "S" secondary butyl alcohols were easily obtained, and the synthesis given above for the racemic compound was paralleled for each of these isomers, separately. Is there any chemistry that is different with the specific optical isomers from that which has been reported with the racemic? There certainly is for the first step, since the butyl alcohols rather than the butyl bromides must be used, and this first step must go by inversion, and it cannot be allowed any racemization (loss of the optical purity of the chiral center).

The synthesis of 2C-T-17 "R" required starting with the "S" isomer of secondary butanol. The "S" 2-butanol in petroleum ether gave the lithium salt with butyllithium which was treated with tosyl chloride (freshly crystallized from naphtha, hexane washed, used in toluene solution) and the solvent was removed. The addition of 2,5-dimethoxythiophenol, anhydrous potassium carbonate, and DMF produced "S" 2,5-dimethoxyphenyl s-butyl sulfide. The conversion to "R" 2,5-dimethoxy-4-(s-butyl-thio)benzaldehyde (which melted at 78-79 °C compared to 86-87 °C for the racemic counterpart) and its conversion in turn to the nitrostyrene, "S"-2,5-dimethoxy-4-(s)-butylthio-ß-nitrostyrene which melted at 70-71 °C compared to 68-69 °C for the racemic counterpart, followed the specific recipes above. The preparation of the intermediates to 2C-T-17 "S" follows the above precisely, but starting with "R" 2-butanol instead. And it is at these nitrostyrene stages that this project stands at the moment.

It would be fascinating if one of the two optically active 2C-T-17's carried all of the central activity, and the other, none of it. What is more likely is that the spectrum of effects will be teased apart, with one isomer responsible for some of them and the other isomer responsible for the others. Then, again, maybe the south end of the receptor site in the brain is totally symmetric, and the two optical antipodes will be indistinguishable.

An incidental bit of trivia — yet another bit of evidence that we are all totally asymmetric in our personal body chemistry. "R" and "S" secondary butanols smell different. The "R" has a subtle smell, which is rather fragrant . The "S" is stronger, hits the nasal passages harder, and reminds one of isopropanol more than does the "S" isomer.

#49   2C-T-21;   2,5-DIMETHOXY-4-(2-FLUOROETHYLTHIO)PHENETHYLAMINE

SYNTHESIS: To a solution of 6.9 g of KOH pellets in 100 mL hot MeOH, there was added 13.0 g 2,5-dimethoxythiophenol (see under 2C-T-2 for its preparation) followed by 9.6 g 2-fluoroethyl bromide. The reaction was exothermic, with the immediate deposition of white solids. This was allowed to stand for 2 h, added to 1 L H_2O, and extracted with 3x75 mL CH_2Cl_2. The extracts were pooled and the solvent removed under vacuum. The residue was 2,5-dimethoxyphenyl 2-fluoroethyl sulfide which was a colorless oil and weighed 17.2 g. It was sufficiently pure for use in the next reaction without a distillation step.

A mixture of 26.8 g $POCl_3$ and 24.8 g N-methylformanilide was heated for 10 min on the steam bath. To this claret-colored solution was added 17.0 g of 2,5-dimethoxyphenyl 2-fluoroethyl sulfide, and the mixture heated an additional 25 min on the steam bath. This was then added to 1.5 L of well-stirred warm H_2O (pre-heated to 55 °C) and the oily phase that formed solidified almost immediately. This brown sugar-like product was removed by filtration, and washed with additional H_2O. After sucking as dry as possible, the residual solids (weighing 19.0 g wet) were dissolved in an equal weight of boiling MeOH which, after cooling in an ice-bath, deposited pale ivory colored crystals of 2,5-dimethoxy-4-(2-fluoroethylthio)benzaldehyde. This was air dried to constant weight, which was 15.1 g.

To a solution of 15.0 g 2,5-dimethoxy-(2-fluoroethylthio)benzaldehyde in 75 mL nitromethane there was added 1.35 g of anhydrous ammonium acetate, and the mixture was heated on the steam bath for 70 min (the progress of the reaction must be followed by continuous TLC monitoring). The clear deeply-colored solution was decanted from some insoluble material and the excess nitromethane removed under vacuum. There resulted 17.78 g of almost dry brick-red crystals which were dissolved in 110 mL boiling EtOAc. After cooling overnight in the refrigerator, the crystalline product was removed, washed with EtOAc, and air dried. There was obtained 14.33 g of 2,5-dimethoxy-4-(2-fluoroethylthio)-ß-nitro-styrene as bright orange crystals.

A solution of LAH (140 mL of a 1 M solution in THF) was cooled, under He, to 0 °C with an external ice bath. With good stirring there was added 3.7 mL 100% H_2SO_4 dropwise, to minimize charring. This was followed by the addition of 8.9 g 2,5-dimethoxy-4-(2-fluoroethylthio)-ß-nitrostyrene in 40 mL of hot anhydrous THF (a heat lamp was needed to keep the nitrostyrene in solution). As the nitrostyrene entered the hydride solution, there was an immediate loss of color. After 1 h stirring at room temperature, the temperature was brought up to a gentle reflux on the steam bath, then all was cooled again to 0 °C. The excess hydride was destroyed by the cautious addition of 15 mL IPA and the inorganic solids were made white and filterable by the addition of 15 ml 15% NaOH. The loose cottage-cheesy solids were removed by filtration, and washed with additional THF. The filtrate and washes were pooled and stripped of solvent under vacuum providing 7.39 g of a pale amber oil. This was dissolved in 600 mL dilute H_2SO_4, and washed with 3x50 mL CH_2Cl_2 (which removed the light yellow color). The aqueous phase was made strongly basic with 25% NaOH, extracted with 3x75 mL CH_2Cl_2 and, after pooling, the solvent was removed under vacuum leaving 4.91 g of product as an oil. This was distilled at 145-160 °C at 0.4 mm/Hg giving 3.91 g of a white oil. This was dissolved in 40 mL IPA and neutralized with 35 drops of concentrated HCl. The beautiful white solids that formed were removed by filtration, and washed with IPA. All were suspended in, and ground under, 40 mL anhydrous Et_2O, refiltered and air dried. The final weight of 2,5-dimethoxy-4-(2-fluoroethylthio)phenethylamine hydro-chloride (2C-T-21) was 4.07 g of glistening white crystals.

DOSAGE   8 - 12 mg.

DURATION: 7 - 10 h.

QUALITATIVE COMMENTS: (with 6 mg) "I noticed something undefined within five minutes which went away. Within 15 minutes I noticed a definite awareness of activity. There was a progressive increase in awareness of something happening over the next two hours with a plateau of perhaps an hour then occurring. The nature of the happening, as usual, was not clear. During the experience I was more talkative than I usually am. I seemed to be interacting with all others. There was no euphoria but, then, there was no body load or nausea, nor was there any nystagmus. I found a little mental confusion at the peak and there was some searching in my memory bank for the right chips at times. I lost the entire line of one of my conversations at one point during the plateau and had to ask what I was talking about. I tested my visual field on a painting and with sufficient concentration I could get the center part to wiggle a little. I didn't try to observe anything with my eyes closed. I feel that there was something physical about the eyes. In the evening, after-images were quite intense, and the next day my eyes seemed tired or bothered. What can I say? The material was pleasant and I certainly got the feeling of being high but not getting too much out of it. There were no insights or "ah-hahs." I wonder if periodic and frequent use (say twice a day) at the one or two milligram level would be a positive mood enhancer?"

(with 8 mg) "Comes on very gradually and slowly. Takes about an hour to feel. Reasonably intense in two hours, ++. Very pleasant material, enhancing communication, clear thinking, good feeling. There is a feeling of closeness; the bondedness with the group grows steadily during the day, reaching a highly rewarding level. For me a couple of firsts regarding food. I was hungry only two hours into it. I usually don't want food 'til well down as I usually feel that it interferes with the experience. And, also, I nibbled constantly as I felt that there was nothing in my body. And I enjoyed it thoroughly, feeling only the warmth and energy, with no contrary developments. There was a nice feeling of inner strength and peace."

(with 8 mg) "It was very difficult to fix the times of ascent or descent. Some chilling during onset but not later. And there was some yawning and ear-popping. It is easy on the body, in no way threatening. This time I am very relaxed and somewhat lethargic; the visuals are not too pronounced. Excellent sleep."

(with 10 mg) "I find I can use it if I set my energy in a direction I really want to go in. Otherwise I can just be stoned and self-indulgent. Not out-of-body cosmic at all. But it's good material, an ally, not presenting hidden negatives."

(with 12 mg) "Well ... 12 milligrams is quite enough for a +3, which was established within the first hour and plateau'd by the end of the second. Body felt quite safe, again, but there was considerable push of energy. I did not feel particularly interested in doing anything like writing and in fact preferred to watch television while rocking a bit on the couch, to ease the push. Mood was faintly grim, but not more than faintly. I noted something that I hadn't seen before with this material: time slowing. The first two hours seemed to last a very long time. There was no anorexia. It wasn't until 10 PM [fifth hour] that the idea of writing had any appeal at all. By then, I was still +3 but a lot more at ease. I wrote two letters and enjoyed the process. Sleep was fine. My mood next day was slightly introverted, not very spontaneous for a while. Late in the afternoon, it was a lot better."

EXTENSIONS AND COMMENTARY: This is about as potent a phenethylamine as they come. There are a couple in the 2C-G family that are similar in potency, but they are much longer lived. The motivation for the use of the beta-fluoroethyl group can be seen under the discussion of DOEF, where there was an amalgamation of two lines of reasoning: the imitation of potent serotonin agonists with a need of including an atom (the fluorine) that is potentially labelable with a positron emitter. And the mass-18 isotope of fluorine, with a half-life of just under 2 hours, is ideal for many biological studies. In fact, much of the research work being carried out by the Nuclear Medicine group in Berkeley is based on the analogy between a halogen atom and a beta-fluoroethyl group. There are some similarities in pharmacology so that if there is a bromine or an iodo atom present in a drug, it is a fair guess that the corresponding beta-fluoroethyl would also be active. In a sense, the cute (and chemically impossible) idea of putting a bromo atom on the sulfur of the 2C-T family is nicely satisfied by using the beta-fluoroethyl group instead (which is chemically completely possible).

A logical extension of 2C-T-21 is the three carbon amphetamine analogue which should be, by comparing structures and activities, a very potent and interesting material in its own rights. This would be 2,5-dimethoxy-4-(2-fluoroethylthio)amphetamine or, following the nomenclature used with the earlier members of this series, ALEPH-21. A solution of 2,5-dimethoxy-4-(2-fluoroethylthio)-benzaldehyde (see earlier in this recipe) in nitroethane with ammonium acetate gave 1-(2,5-dimethoxy-4-(2-fluoroethylthio)phenyl)-2-nitropropene as yellow-orange crystals from MeOH with a melting point of 102-104 °C. And that is where the project now stands. It has not yet been reduced to the amine.

This phenethylamine, 2C-T-21, was the last of the 2C-T's to be completed. A couple of other sulfur analogues have been given numbers, and have been started, but the syntheses are still at some intermediate state.

The (n)-butyl compound, named 2C-T-19, has been taken to the nitrostyrene stage. Reaction between 2,5-dimethoxythiophenol and (n)-butylbromide with KOH gave 2,5-dimethoxyphenyl (n)-butyl sulfide as a colorless oil. This, with phosphorus oxychloride and N-methylformanilide, provided 2,5-dimethoxy-4-(n-butylthio)benzaldehyde as pale orange solids from MeOH, with a melting point of 78-79 °C. This, with nitromethane and ammonium acetate, gave 2,5-dimethoxy-4-(n-butylthio)-ß-nitrostyrene, with a melting point of 133-134 °C from either IPA or acetonitrile.

The 2,2,2-trifluoroethyl compound, which I have named 2C-T-22, has been taken to the benzaldehyde stage. Reaction between 2,5-dimethoxythiophenol and 2,2,2-trifluoroethyliodide with KOH gives 2,5-dimethoxyphenyl 2,2,2-trifluoroethyl sulfide as a very pale amber oil. This, with phosphorus oxychloride and N-methylformanilide provided 2,5-dimethoxy-4-(2,2,2-trifluoroethyl)-benzaldehyde as crystals that proved to be exceedingly difficult to purify. Yellow solids can be obtained from several solvents, and they melt in the 70 °C area. The initially isolated fraction melted at 69-72 °C and showed three major spots by both TLC and GCMS. The largest GC peak was the correct product with a parent peak of 280 m/e, and cracking fragments at 154 and 234 m/e. A small sample was finally obtained from hexane with a melting point of 78-79 °C but I am not sure that even it is particularly pure. Not surprisingly, the reaction of this crude benz-aldehyde with nitromethane and ammonium acetate gave a nitrostyrene product that was a complex mixture. And there that project also rests.

A couple of additional efforts warrant comment. The reaction between trifluoromethyliodide and 2,5-dimethoxythiophenol should have produced 2,5-dimethoxyphenyl trifluoromethyl sulfide, but it didn't produce anything. And one more. What about a bare thio group at the 4-position in this 2C-T-family? Maybe this can be protected through everything as the disulfide, and be reduced at the last step! The disulfide, 2,5-dimethoxyphenyl disulfide (see under 2C-T-15) was aimed towards the needed bis-aldehyde with phosphorus oxychloride and N-methylformanilide, but all that came out of this were black oils and tars. This has also been abandoned for now.

And it has just occurred to me that there is yet another effort that is certainly worth making, inspired by the observation that 2,2-difluoroethyl iodide is commercially available and not prohibitively expensive. It, with 2,5-dimethoxy-thiophenol, and following the obvious steps to the aldehyde, the nitrostyrene, and the final amine, would produce 2,5-dimethoxy-4-(2,2-difluoroethylthio)-phenethylamine hydrochloride. It lies exactly half way between the highly potent 2C-T-21 (the mono-fluoro), and the yet to be finished 2C-T-22 (the trifluoro). Let's be weird, and call it 2C-T-21.5. I will wager *mucho* that it will be very potent.

#50   4-D;   3,5-DIMETHOXY-4-TRIDEUTEROMETHOXY-PHENETHYLAMINE

SYNTHESIS: To a solution of 34.0 g homosyringonitrile (3,5-dimethoxy-4-hydroxyphenylacetonitrile, see under ESCALINE for its preparation) in 350 mL acetone containing 0.5 g decyltriethylammonium iodide, there was added 25 g trideuteromethyl iodide followed by 50 g of finely powdered anhydrous K_2CO_3. This mixture was held at reflux on a steam bath for 12 h, added to 2 L of dilute HCl, and extracted with 3x100 mL of CH_2Cl_2. The extracts were washed with 5% NaOH, and

the solvent removed under vacuum, yielding 28.0 g yellow solids. These were distilled at 135-150 °C at 0.5 mm/Hg providing 19.4 g 3,5-dimethoxy-4-trideuteromethoxyphenyl-acetonitrile which melted at 76.5-77.5 °C after crystallization from toluene, or 77-78 °C from methylcyclohexane/CHCl$_3$ 3:1. The mp of the proteo-reference compound, from toluene, was 77-78.5 °C. The OCD$_3$ stretch in the infra-red occured at 2072 cm^{-1}.

A solution of 275 mL of 1.0 M LAH in THF was cooled under He to 0 °C and treated with 7.25 mL 100% H_2SO_4 added very slowly with vigorous stirring. A solution of 19.3 g 3,5-dimethoxy-4-trideuteromethoxyphenylacetonitrile in 200 mL anhydrous THF was added slowly, and following the addition stirring was continued for 20 min. The reaction mixture was brought to a reflux for 30 min on a steam bath, cooled again to 0 °C, and the excess hydride destroyed with 25 mL IPA. About 15 mL of 15% NaOH was required to convert the solids to a filterable white consistency. These were removed by filtration, the cake washed with IPA, the filtrates and washes were combined, and the solvent removed under vacuum leaving a white oil as residue. This was dissolved in 1.5 L dilute H_2SO_4, washed with

3x75 mL CH_2Cl_2, made basic with aqueous NaOH, and then extracted with 3x75 mL CH_2Cl_2. Removal of the solvent from these extracts under vacuum yielded 18.5 g of a colorless oil which was distilled at 120-150 °C at 0.5 mm/Hg to provide 13.5 g of a white oil. This was dissolved in 70 ml IPA and neutralized with concentrated HCl, producing spontaneous crystals. These were removed by filtration, washed first with IPA then with anhydrous Et_2O. After air drying, the final yield of 3,5-dimethoxy-4-trideuteromethoxyphenethylamine hydrochloride (4-D) was 13.50 g.

DOSAGE: 200 - 400 mg (as the sulfate salt); 178 - 356 mg (as the hydrochloride salt).

DURATION: 12 h.

QUALITATIVE COMMENTS: (with 275 mg) "The onset was smooth and gradual. Within the hour, the slight queasiness I experienced (not as much as with mescaline) completely disappeared. Some visual enhancement, good energy, good communication. It was a very special day for me as I was in a good place pretty much the whole day, and able to communicate clearly without deeper feelings getting in the way. While most enjoyable, and at times remarkable fun, I did not experience the intensity I am familiar with, with mescaline."

(with 300 mg) "The taste was bitter to a moderate degree but faded fast. About 40 minutes later the first stirrings of pleasurable experience came on. It was very mild. Twenty minutes after that an unease of the stomach was apparent, and it stayed with me until I ate some crackers an hour or so later. I got no sharpened visual reactions and no physical instability at any time. I did feel a quickening of thought and verbal flow; again, this was mild and unlike my earlier mescaline patter."

(with 350 mg) "A rapid onset — alert in 20 minutes. Climbed to a plus two in about one hour and stayed there. During the first two hours had a slight queasiness or pre-nausea, and cold hands and feet, but this all disappeared completely and I became very hungry during the whole latter half of the experience. I did not eat much at any one time, but did a lot of snacking and everything tasted good. Very pleasant after the plateau was reached. Pretty good visuals with eyes closed, but not as bright as 2C-B. Very little visuals with eyes open — some movement and flow of objects — pupils dilated. Spent most of the day lying down — had no aversion to conversation but it felt good just to be still. I was in a funny place I can't quite describe — I was in an 'alert lassitude,' a state of 'interested detachment,' or a place of 'vibrating equanimity' or whatever. While trying to recapture the day, it seemed to me that it was a good day, but that nothing much had really transpired. However, upon reflection, I am startled to find that several important shifts took place. It was a day that allowed some peaceful gear-shifting in the mind."

(with 400 mg) "Not a great taste. Some type of awareness at approx. 20

minutes. Considerable nausea peaking at about 1 hr. Some nausea continued through the experience but became quite low. I enjoyed the color show considerably. Trees outside would change color in a wave-like manner. The book-covers upstairs would also change colors and become distorted. Brightly lighted items would undergo the same thing. Believed I could suppress the vision, but concentrating on something would cause it to easily undergo the color and visual changes. Evidently I had little problem following the conversation downstairs, but I remained somewhat quiet. Had an element of confusion that seemed to last for some 4 or 5 hours. Had no problems dropping off to sleep that evening."

EXTENSIONS AND COMMENTARY: The effects of 4-D and ß-D are similar to one-another, both as to dosage and effect. And with both, there is a close parallel to those reported from mescaline. It is reasonable to assume that the human body handles these materials in the same manner, although no metabolic studies have ever been published.

A similar deuterium substitution pattern is of course completely feasible with TMA and related 3,4,5-trimethoxy-substituted analogues. Some studies have supported the idea that the ability to remove methyl groups from such aromatic ethers might be correlated to endogenous schizophrenia. It is possible to imagine that, in such individuals, the effects of substituting trideuteromethyl groups for normal methyl groups might result in psychopharmacological differences of action. Two reports exist that describe metabolic products of mescaline that have lost this methyl group on the 4-position oxygen. It is possible that these might be produced in abnormal quantities in mentally ill subjects. There are also similar reports of the 3-methoxyl group being demethylated in man. Here, studies with 3,5-D (3,5-bis-trideuteromethoxy-4-methoxyphenethylamine) might reveal some differences in quantitative responses in man. These are extremely minor metabolites, however. I suspect that more extensive studies will establish that 4-D, 3,5-D and ß-D all have properties indistinguishable from one-another, at least in healthy subjects.

#51   ß-D;   3,4,5-TRIMETHOXY-ß,ß-DIDEUTERO-
PHENETHYLAMINE

SYNTHESIS: To a solution of 13.6 g homosyringonitrile (see under ESCALINE for its preparation) in 150 mL acetone containing 200 mg decyltriethylammonium iodide and 30 g of finely powdered anhydrous K_2CO_3, there was added 20 g methyl iodide. The mixture was held at reflux for 18 h in a heating mantle with effective stirring. This was added to 1 L H_2O, acidified with concentrated HCl, and extracted with 3x75 mL CH_2Cl_2. The extracts were pooled, washed with 2x100 mL 5% NaOH, once with dilute HCl, once with saturated brine, and the solvent was removed under vacuum. The pale yellow residue was distilled at 130-150 °C at 0.3 mm/Hg to yield 12.9 g of 3,4,5-trimethoxyphenylacetonitrile as an off-white solid. Upon crystallization from methylcyclohexane/CHCl₃ it was white and had a mp of 77-78 °C. Attempts to prepare this compound by the theoretically appealing route from 3,4,5-trimethoxybenzaldehyde to N,N-dimethyl-3,4,5-tri-methoxy-benzylamine (reductive amination with dimethylamine), to 3,4,5-trimethoxy-N,N,N-trimethylbenzylammonium iodide (methylation with methyl iodide), and then to 3,4,5- trimethoxyphenylacetonitrile (with some source of cyanide ion) gave excellent yields in the first two steps, and no product at all in the last step.

A solution of 20.6 g of 3,4,5-trimethoxphenylacetonitrile in 70 g pyridine was treated with 15 mL 99+% D₂O and held at reflux for 24 h. All volatiles were stripped first under vacuum and finally with a hard vacuum at room temperature in a Kugelrohr apparatus. The dark residue was treated again with another 30 mL pyridine and another 15 mL 99+% D₂O. The flask was protected with a drying tube and held at reflux for another 24 h. Again, all volatiles were stripped, and the residue distilled at 110-130 °C at 0.25 mm/Hg to yield 16.77 g of an almost white solid. The GCMS verified this chemical to be 3,4,5-trimethoxy-ß,ß-dideuterophenylacetonitrile, with a parent peak at m/e 209 and no visible peak at m/e 207.

A solution of 250 mL of 1 M LAH in THF was cooled under He to 0 °C and treated with 6.8 mL 100% H₂SO₄ added very slowly with vigorous stirring. A solution of 18.23 g 3,4,5-trimethoxy-ß,ß-dideuterophenyl-acetonitrile in 200 mL anhydrous THF was added slowly, and following the addition stirring was continued for 20 min. The reaction mixture was brought to a reflux for 30 min on a steam bath, cooled again to 0 °C, and the excess hydride destroyed with 15 mL IPA. About 10 mL of 15% NaOH was required to convert the solids to a filterable white consistency. These were removed by filtration, the cake washed with IPA, the filtrates and washes were combined, and the solvent removed under vacuum leaving 17 g of a white oil as residue. This was dissolved in 2 L dilute H₂SO₄, washed with 3x75 mL CH₂Cl₂, made basic with aqueous NaOH, and then extracted with 3x75 mL CH₂Cl₂. Removal of the solvent from these extracts under vacuum yielded 10.3 g of a colorless oil which was distilled at 120-130 °C at 0.3 mm/Hg to provide 9.2 g of a white oil. This was dissolved in 50 ml IPA and neutralized with concentrated HCl, producing spontaneous crystals. These were diluted with 50 mL anhydrous Et₂O, removed by filtration, washed first with Et₂O/IPA, and then with anhydrous Et₂O. After air drying, the final yield of 3,4,5-trimethoxy-ß,ß-dideuterophenethylamine hydrochloride (ß-D) was 10.0 g of white needles.

DOSAGE: 200 - 400 mg (as the sulfate salt); 178 - 356 mg (as the hydrochloride salt).

DURATION: 12 h.

QUALITATIVE COMMENTS: (with 200 mg) "The onset was very gradual and very gentle. At about an hour and a half I was rather out of my body (at least I wasn't aware of my body, it felt so light). I was listening to Berlioz Requiem, and it took me to the highest realm. I was totally caught up in the magnificence of the music, of the genius it took to compose it, the love it took to complete it, and the devotion of the composer. I felt as though this music had been written for me. What came next is hard to remember because I was so taken with this experience which came only 1 1/2 hours after ingestion. I wondered what time it was and how come I was having a peak experience so soon, because this material was supposed to reach its peak after two hours. Well, now we can revise the records, heh? Incidentally this material is really good for interior work. It was a magnificent experience — one of the best."

(with 275 mg) "I begin to feel it in 15 minutes, stomach getting squeamish. Looking up into the clouds, becoming absorbed in them, watching light grow in intensity, stomach feelings disappeared. Became totally absorbed by the music. Listening to Boito's Prologue to Mephistopheles — exquisitely beautiful, dramatic. Lying on the couch, the music continuing, I was suddenly filled with enormous power. I realized that raw, male power was pouring through me as I had never before experienced it. I was wild, totally self satisfied, and completely oblivious of others and their needs. I wanted to strike out, to win, to conquer. I felt what conquerers have felt in the past, the unbridled passion to vanquish everything. I could see how such misguided power could lead nations to war. Wanting still more power, I was about to find out if God would grant me the power to destroy the world if I wished it, when I felt a gentle kiss on my brow. My wife had leaned over just in time to save the world."

(with 275 mg) "Never had I had such a magnificent appreciation of God. It was clear that if I minded my business and turned to Him to learn as I had been doing today, then I could continue to grow and learn in a most wonderful way. It became crystal clear to me that I didn't have to help anybody or heal anybody, as everyone can turn directly to the source for their needs. An earth-shaking experience."

(with 300 mg) "I had extreme nausea, and vomited. This had a very hard impact on me, and I had to retreat with a paranoia that swept over me without warning. I lay down and let it sweep on, and through this came several very important insights. At least they were important to me. It was about the fourth hour before I could emerge from my retreat, and at that time I knew that I had answered some troublesome personal problems. It was a satisfactory day, but I probably shall not repeat it."

(with 350 mg) "Strong body awareness started within 15 minutes. Visual activity started within half an hour. Visuals were typical kinds, but seemed to arrive earlier. A strong experience of pleasantness started and continued throughout the experience. I tended to internalize to some extent. Ended on a water bed at maybe an hour and a half, pulled covers over me, and went inward with considerable visuals but not much insight. I felt good about where I was. I would not mind being there again, so something was going well. I am not sure how long this continued. The visuals decreased somewhere around the 5th or 6th hour. After 8 or 9 hours, activity considerably decreased. I felt quite clear and reasonably centered. Would I do this again? The answer is yes."

(with 500 mg) "I consumed the material over a period of twenty minutes, and at the 1 hour 45 minute point, haven't had any nausea, but I am still careful not to bounce around. Am absolutely grounded even though I am completely into the experience. No more that state in which it is possible to seriously consider trying to rise two inches above the floor and skim, as I do so expertly in dreams. As a matter of fact I haven't had those dreams for some time now. This material doesn't allow the straddling of realities as does ordinary mescaline. I know where my realities are, and reality is, basically, where my center is. Thus I am grounded in the physical reality even when the doors are open to non-physical levels."

EXTENSIONS AND COMMENTARY: The 4-D and the ß-D are two of five obvious deuterium isomer derivatives of mescaline. The three remaining are: (1) 3,5-D (4-methoxy-3,5-bis-trideuteromethoxyphenethylamine); (2) 2,6-D (2,6-di-deutero-3,4,5-trimethoxyphenethylamine); and (3) α–D (α.α-dideutero-3,4,5-tri-methoxyphenethylamine). I fully expect both 3,5-D and 2,6-D to be indistinguish-able from mescaline in effect, since it is known that not much metabolism takes place in man at these locations of the molecule.

The last compound, α-D, could be quite a different matter. The principal metabolite of mescaline is 3,4,5-trimethoxyphenylacetic acid, and this product requires enzymatic attack at the exact position where the deuteriums will be located. To the extent that they are harder to remove (come off more slowly or to a lesser degree), to that extent the molecule will be more potent in man, and the dosage required for effects will be less. The compound will be easily made by the reduction of 3,4,5-trimethoxyphenylacetonitrile with lithium aluminum deuteride. And if there is a believable difference between α-D and mescaline, it will be necessary to synthesize each of the two optically active α-mono-deutero analogs. That will be quite a challenge.

Some years ago I performed a fascinating series of experiments with another isotopically labeled mescaline derivative. This was ß-^{14}C labeled material, which I self-administered on three occasions, at three different levels. One dosage was with 350 milligrams, a second a few weeks later was with 4 milligrams, and a third was a few weeks later yet, with about 60 micrograms. In each case, exactly the same absolute quantity of radioactivity was administered, so the metabolic distribution was equally visible. Only the weight dosage was different. Urinary analysis was run for each experiment for the presence of unchanged mescaline, and for the primary metabolite, 3,4,5-trimethoxyphenylacetic acid. The smaller the dosage, the proportionately larger amount of mescaline was oxidized to the inactive acetic acid, and the smaller amount was excreted in an unchanged state. It seemed to me that there might be a finite capacity of the body to oxidatively deaminate mescaline, and at larger and larger dosages, this capacity became increasingly depleted. Perhaps this is why mescaline requires such a large dosage to be effective in man.

#52   DESOXY;   3,5-DIMETHOXY-4-METHYLPHENETHYLAMINE

SYNTHESIS: To a well-stirred solution of 31 g 2,6-dimethoxytoluene in 200 mL CH_2Cl_2 there was added 11 mL elemental bromine, a portion at a time. There was a copious evolution of HBr and the color gradually faded from deep red to straw. The reaction mixture was poured into 500 mL H_2O, and the organic layer separated, washed first with dillute NaOH and finally with dilute HCl. The solvent was removed under vacuum, and the residue distilled at 85-90 °C at 0.4 mm/Hg to provide 44 g of 3-bromo-2,6-dimethoxytoluene as a white oil.

A well-stirred solution of 42 mL diisopropylamine in 100 mL petroleum ether was placed in a He atmosphere and cooled to 0 °C with an external ice-water bath. There was then added 120 mL of a 2.5 M solution of n-butyllithium in hexane, producing a clear but viscous solution of the lithium amide. Maintaining this temperature, there was added 100 mL of anhydrous THF, followed by 10 mL dry CH_3CN, which produced an immediate white precipitate. A solution of 23 g of 3-bromo-2,6-dimethoxytoluene in 75 mL anhydrous THF was then added which produced a light red color. The reaction mixture was allowed to come to room temperature. The color became progressively darkened, eventually becoming a deep red-brown. After 0.5 h, the reaction mixture was poured into 500 mL of dilute H_2SO_4, the layers were separated, and the aqueous layer extracted with 2x75 mL CH_2Cl_2. The organics were combined, the solvent removed under vacuum, and the residue distilled. Discarding a first fraction, the cut boiling at 125-165 °C at 0.3 mm/Hg was collected. This light yellow fraction spontaneously crystallized and weighed 11.0 g. Trituration under 20 mL petroleum ether provided 1.72 g of 3,5-dimethoxy-4-methylphenylaceto-nitrile as a yellowish solid.

A solution of LAH in anhydrous THF under nitrogen (20 mL of a 1.0 M solution) was cooled to 0 °C and vigorously stirred. There was added, dropwise, 0.54 mL 100% H_2SO_4, followed by 1.5 g 3,5-dimethoxy-4-methylphenylacetonitrile as a solid. The reaction mixture was stirred at 0 °C for a few min, then brought to room temperature for 1 h, and finally to a reflux on the steam bath for 30 min. After cooling back to 0 °C there was added IPA until no more hydrogen was evolved, followed by sufficient 15% NaOH to produce a granular texture. The white solids were removed by filtration, and washed with THF. The filtrate and washes were stripped of solvent under vacuum, the residue added to 150 mL dilute H_2SO_4 and washed with 2x50 mL CH_2Cl_2. The aqueous phase was made basic with 25% NaOH, and extracted with 3x100 mL CH_2Cl_2. These extracts were pooled, the solvent removed under vacuum, and the residue distilled at 110-120 °C at 0.45 mm/Hg to give a colorless viscous oil. This was dissolved in 10 mL of IPA, neutralized with 10 drops of concentrated HCl and diluted with 20 mL anhydrous Et_2O. The product was removed by filtration, washed with Et_2O, and air dried to give 0.55 g 3,5-dimethoxy-4-methylphenethylamine (DESOXY) as white crystals.

DOSAGE: 40 - 120 mg.

DURATION: 6 - 8 h.

QUALITATIVE COMMENTS: (with 40 mg) "Initially I felt very chilled, so I lay down under a blanket. Eyes-closed imagery became very dream-like and my general state was felt as having lost my center. Also, not much in touch with feelings, sense of strangeness, almost alien view of the world. Not through recognizable eyes. Neither pleasant nor unpleasant, just strange. Was able to drift into sleep very easily, or sleep-like trance state, with disconnected, far-out imagery. After 3 hours the nausea was gone, I was able to get up and explore. A little food went down well. No drive, no strong focus in any direction. Feel this was a quite fascinating experience. Completely down by six hours. Would go a bit slowly because of slight hints of neurological sensitivity — the instant chilling and a tendency to dart on going to sleep. The nervous system does not feel over-exposed, but all of a sudden there will be a millisecond of auditory hallucination, or an out-of-the-blue startle. So take it easy going up." [Some 24 hours after this experiment had been completed, and a normal baseline re-established, a complex and psychologically disruptive syndrome occurred, that lasted for the better part of a week. The temporal juxtaposition between the use of desoxy and the subsequent "spiritual crisis" initially suggested some possible connection, but in retrospect the events seem to be unrelated].

(with 40 mg) "I have offered to be a control on an experiment where there had been a close relationship between a trial with desoxy and what might have been a psychotic break, or some kind of so-called spiritual emergency. These two events lay within a day of one another. I was aware of my 40 milligram dosage at about three-quarters of an hour into the experiment, and felt that there was no more intensification at the two-hour point. At that time I felt distinctly spaced but with a very good feeling, and I could see no reason not to increase the dosage at some future time. There was a good and mellow mood, and enjoyment in escapist reading. The only physical oddity that I noted was that there had been no urge to urinate, and only a small amount of quite concentrated urine was passed rather late in the experiment. I was at baseline at the fifth hour, and there was nothing unusual at any time during

the following week."
    (with 100 mg) "The stuff has a sweet taste! There was a slight heart-push in the early awareness period, with a pulse up to 100 and a feeling of pressure in the chest. There were no apparent visual enhancements, but the eyes-closed imagery to music was noteworthy. Thinking skills and conversation seemed to be fully under control, if not enhanced. There was none of the colorful psychedelic world of mescaline, but this might be just around the corner; perhaps with a larger dose. This is a comfortable in-between level. Sleep was not possible at the sixth hour, but two hours later, it was easy and very restful. There was no negative price to pay the next day."

EXTENSIONS AND COMMENTARY: All substituents that are involved with the several drugs being discussed in this writing are really things that are stuck like warts on the benzene ring that is central to every phenethylamine. Some of these warts are things attached with a oxygen atom; there are some of these in every single compound in this story. No oxygen atom, no psychedelic effect. Without them, one has stimulants or, more frequently, no effects at all.
    But the removal of an oxygen atom (in those cases where there is more than one) can radically change the nature of the effects seen. This is the exact meaning of the term "desoxy." "Des", without, and "oxy", the oxygen. Since this drug is simply the structure of mescaline with the oxygen at the 4-position plucked out of the picture, the first impulse was to abbreviate this compound as DOM for desoxymescaline. However, a long, long time ago, in a universe far, far away, a compound was synthesized that had a methoxy group replaced by a methyl, and it was already named DOM. This was the first of the STP analogs, and the initials stood for desoxy (DO, losing an oxygen) and methyl (M, having it replaced with a methyl group). These are two different worlds. One M stands for Mescaline, and the other M stands for Methyl. Let's call it 4-desoxymescaline, or simply DESOXY, and be exact.
    This drug is a prime example of a pharmacological challenge directed to the metabolic attack at the 4-position as a mechanism for the expression of biological activity. A methoxy group there would allow easy removal of the methyl group from the oxygen by some demethylation process, but a bare methyl group there cannot be removed by any simple process. It must be removed by a very difficult oxidation.
    This is not the first time that oxygen atoms have been removed from the mescaline molecule. Both the 3,5-dideoxymescaline (3,5-dimethyl-4-methoxyphenethylamine) and 3,4,5-trideoxymescaline (also called desoxymescaline in the literature, but really tri-desoxymescaline or 3,4,5-trimethylphenethylamine) have been studied in the cat, and have shown extraordinary pharmacological profiles of CNS action. The trimethyl compound showed behavior that was interpreted as being intense mental turmoil, accompanied by a startling rise in body temperature. The significance is hard to determine, in that LSD gave similar

responses in the cat, but mescaline was without effects at all. No human studies have been made on these compounds, just animal studies. But they might prove upon trial in man to be most revealing. They would have to be performed with exceptional care.

The 3-carbon chain amphetamines that correspond to these mescaline look-alikes with one or more methoxy groups replaced with methyl groups, are largely untested and would require independent and novel syntheses. The 3,4,5-trimethylamphetamine is known, and is known to be very hard on experimental cats.

A mescaline analogue with a bromo atom in place of the 4-methoxyl group is an analogue of mescaline in exactly the same way that DOB (a very potent amphetamine) is an analog of TMA-2 (the original trisubstituted amphetamine). This analogue, 3,5-dimethoxy-4-bromoamphetamine, has been found to be a most effective serotonin agonist, and it is a possibility that it could be a most potent phenethylamine. But, as of the present time, it has never been assayed in man.

#53   2,4-DMA;   2,4-DIMETHOXYAMPHETAMINE

SYNTHESIS: To a solution of 10 g 2,4-dimethoxybenzaldehyde in 50 mL nitroethane there was added 0.5 g anhydrous ammonium acetate, and the mixture was heated on the steam bath for 2 h. The excess solvent/reagent was removed under vacuum, and the residue oil dissolved in 25 mL boiling MeOH. On cooling, this deposited yellow crystals of 1-(2,4-dimethoxyphenyl)-2-nitropropene that, after filtering, MeOH washing, and air drying, weighed 10.2 g and had a mp of 78-79 °C.

A magnetically stirred suspension of 6.0 g LAH in 300 mL anhydrous Et_2O was brought up to a gentle reflux under a He atmosphere. A total of 8.5 g 1-(2,4-dimethoxyphenyl)-2-nitropropene was introduced into the reaction mixture by allowing the condensed Et_2O to leach it from a modified Soxhlet condenser. After the addition was complete, the reaction was held at reflux for an additional 24 h. After cooling with an external ice bath, the excess hydride was destroyed by the cautious addition of H_2O. When the exothermic reaction had subsided, there was added 500 mL H_2O, 150 g potassium sodium tartrate, and sufficient base to bring the pH above 9. The phases were separated, the organic phase dried over anhydrous $MgSO_4$, the drying agent removed by filtration, and the clear filtrate then saturated with anhydrous HCl gas to produce white crystals of 2,4-dimethoxyamphetamine hydrochloride (2,4-DMA) with a mp of 146-147 °C.

DOSAGE: greater than 60 mg.

DURATION: short.

QUALITATIVE COMMENTS: (with 60 mg) "This is definitely threshold, or even a bit more. There is a lot of amphetamine-like component, and a certain blush of euphoria. There is also a diffusion of association, so it's more than just amphetamine, no question about it. At the three-hour point, it is definitely quieting down."

EXTENSIONS AND COMMENTARY: What can one say as to the active dosage of 2,4-DMA? Nothing. What can one say as to the duration? Probably short. The 60 milligram report given above is the highest level that I personally know of having been tried in man, and there is no hint as to what might be found at a fully active dose, or just where that dose might be. It might be fully speedy. It might be fully psychedelic. It might give a cardiovascular push that would be scary. Studies of 2,4-DMA on vascular strips (associated with serotonin action) were not impressive in comparison with structurally related psychedelics, and it seems as if its action might involve norepinephrine release. It is a reasonable guess that there would be cardiovascular activity at higher levels. But it will only be with human trials, someday, that the answer will be known for sure.

The meta-orientation of the two methoxyl groups does, however, greatly increase the susceptibility of the aromatic ring to electrophilic attack. This is one of the three possible meta-dimethoxy substituted amphetamines, and it is the best studied one in the pursuit of potential radio-halogen substituted brain blood-flow agents. This strategy is discussed under IDNNA; the other two meta-compounds are discussed under 3,4-DMA.

The homologues of 2,4-DMA that were iodinated (or occasionally fluorinated) were mono- or di-alkylated on the nitrogen, and the precursor that was common to all was the corresponding acetone. The above nitrostyrene, 1-(2,4-dimethoxyphenyl)-2-nitropropene, was reduced in acetic acid with elemental iron, and the base-washed extracts stripped of solvent and distilled (125-145 °C at 0.5 mm/Hg) to give 2,4-dimethoxyphenylacetone as a water-white oil. The principal reductive amination product of this, the one that was most thoroughly explored with various halogenation schemes, was obtained by the reaction of 2,4-dimethoxyphenylacetone with dimethylamine and sodium cyanoborohydride. This product, 2,4-dimethoxy-N,N-dimethylamphetamine or 2,4-DNNA, distilled at 105-115 °C at 0.4 mm/Hg and formed a perchlorate salt that melted at 98-98.5 °C. This could be iodinated with the radio-iodide anion, when oxidized with chloramine-T in buffered sulfuric acid, to give the iodinated analogue (2,4-dimethoxy-N,N-dimethyl-5-iodoamphetamine) in an excellent yield. Radio-fluorination with acetyl hypofluorite gave the 5-fluoroanalogue (2,4-dimethoxy-N,N-dimethyl-5-fluoroamphetamine) in an acceptable yield. Both compounds went into a rat's brain to a pretty good extent, but both of them washed out too rapidly to be clinically interesting.

A large family of other N-substituted homologues of 2,4-DMA were similarly prepared from the above ketone and sodium cyanoborohydride. Methylamine, ethylamine, propylamine, isopropylamine and hexylamine gave the corresponding N-alkyl homologues. The N,N-diethyl homologue was made from the primary amine, 2,4-DMA itself, with acetaldehyde and sodium cyanoborohydride but the product, N,N-diethyl-2,4-dimethoxyamphetamine, could not be converted into a crystalline hydrochloride salt.

Yet another variation on these structures was launched, again with the design of making radio-iodination targets which are not psychedelic and thus might be useful clinically. In this variation, the nitrogen atom substitution pattern was held constant, with two methyl groups, as were the ring locations of the two oxygen atoms. But the identities of the alkyl groups on these oxygen atoms were varied. The synthetic procedure followed was to make the appropriate 2,4-dialkoxybenzaldehyde, convert it to the nitrostyrene with nitroethane, reduce this to the phenylacetone with elemental iron, and then reductively aminate this ketone with dimethylamine. Following this reaction scheme, five amphetamine homologues of 2,4-DMA were made, three with the 4-methoxy group maintained but the 2-position extended, and two with both groups extended symmetrically. These are: (1) N,N-dimethyl-2-ethoxy-4-methoxyamphetamine; (2) 2-(n)-butyloxy-N,N-dimethyl-4-methoxy-amphetamine; (3) 2-(n)-decyloxy-N,N-dimethylamphetamine; (4) 2,4-diethoxy-N,N-dimethylamphetamine; and (5) N,N-dimethyl-2,4-di-(i)-propoxyamphetamine. I believe that most of these have been iodinated and assayed in rats, and several of them appear quite promising. But none of them have been assayed in man, yet. The bromination product of 2,4-DMA (5-bromo-2,4-dimethoxyamphetamine, 5-Br-2,4-DMA) is way down in activity (see its recipe, separately). Since all iodo analogues are of about the same potency as the bromo counterparts, and since the addition of two methyl groups on the nitrogen does not appear to enhance central activity, I feel the iodination products of these N,N-dialkyl-dialkoxyamphetamines would not have any interesting psychopharmacology.

There is something vaguely counterproductive, in my evaluation of things, when the goal of a research project is to avoid activity rather than to create it. Although this chemistry was completely fascinating and could have produced the world's best positron-emitting, brain-scanning diagnostic compound, I feel it quite unlikely that it would have produced the world's best insight-revealing, empathy-enhancing psychedelic, so this research direction never totally caught my fancy. I went on to other things.

#54 2,5-DMA; DMA; 2,5-DIMETHOXYAMPHETAMINE

SYNTHESIS: A solution of 10.0 g 2,5-dimethoxybenzaldehyde in 50 mL glacial acetic acid was treated with 6.8 g of nitroethane and 4.0 g of anhydrous ammonium acetate. This mixture was heated on the steam bath for 3 h and then the reagent/solvent was removed under vacuum. The residue was suspended in H_2O and extracted with $CHCl_3$. Removal of the solvent from the pooled extracts yielded 11.2 g of an impure 1-(2,5-dimethoxyphenyl)-2-nitropropene which, on recrystallization from 75 mL boiling MeOH, gave 6.7 g of product with a mp of 73-75 °C. Anal. $(C_{11}H_{13}NO_4)$ C,H,N. This nitrostyrene has been periodically available commercially from a number of sources.

A solution of 17.0 g of 1-(2,5-dimethoxyphenyl)-2-nitropropene was prepared in 500 mL anhydrous Et_2O. This solution was added slowly to a well-stirred suspension of 12.0 g LAH in 700 mL anhydrous Et_2O. The mixture was then brought up to a reflux and maintained there for 20 h, cooled with an external ice bath, and the excess hydride destroyed by the cautious addition of H_2O. Finally, a total of 500 mL H_2O was added, followed by the addition of 300 g potassium sodium tartrate, and sufficient aqueous NaOH to bring the pH above 9. The two phases were separated, and the ether phase dried by the addition of anhydrous $MgSO_4$. The drying agent was removed by filtration, and the clear filtrate saturated with a stream of anhydrous HCl gas. The formed crystals of 2,5-dimethoxyamphetamine hydrochloride (2,5-DMA) were removed by filtration, washed with anhydrous Et_2O, and dried to constant weight of 16.3 g. Recrystallization from EtOH gave an analytical sample with a mp of 114-116 °C. The hydrobromide salt is reported to melt at 129-131 °C.

DOSAGE: 80 - 160 mg.

DURATION: 6 - 8 h.

EXTENSIONS AND COMMENTARY: The qualitative information on 2,5-DMA is very sparse. I was up to a 1+ with 80 milligrams of the hydrochloride, and since it appeared to be totally a physical trip with tremors and some cardiovascular push and nothing of a sensory nature, I chose to explore it no further. A report from South America found the intoxication to be largely pleasant (this, at 75 milligrams), with an enhanced interest in one's surroundings, but no perceptual changes, no overt stimulation, and no gross physiological effects other than a slight mydriasis (dilation of the pupils). I have also been told of a single trial of 250 milligrams of the tartrate (this is equivalent to somewhere in the 150-200 milligram range of the hydrochloride salt, depending upon the acid/base ratio of the tartrate salt) with some "speedy" effects but still no sensory changes. A seizure of capsules reported by the drug law enforcement authorities some 20 years ago found that each contained some 200 milligrams of the hydrobromide salt. This is equivalent to 170 milligrams of the hydrochloride salt, and suggests that level may be an effective dosage.

An intriguing, but little studied, analogue of 2,5-DMA is the compound with methyls in place of the methoxyls. 2,5-Dimethylamphetamine has been looked at, in man, as a potential anorexic, but there is little effect even at 150 milligrams. The 3,4-isomer, 3,4-dimethylamphetamine or xylopropamine, is an adrenergic agent and it has been found to be an analgesic in man at as little as 10 milligrams.

This was assayed, rather remarkably, by attaching electrodes to the tooth fillings of the experimental subjects. But with this base, cardiovascular effects were not observed until doses of about 100 milligrams were administered, and toxic effects (nausea and vomiting) were reported at 150 milligrams. There was no suggestion of anything psychedelic.

All three isomers of monomethylamphetamine have also been looked at in man. The ortho- and meta-isomers, 2-methyl- (and 3-methyl-) amphetamine are weak anorexics. At doses of up to 150 milligrams orally, there were signs of stimulation noted — talkativeness and loss of appetite. The para-isomer, 4-methyl-amphetamine or Aptrol, is more potent. At 75 milligrams (orally, in man) there is clear adrenergic stimulation, and at twice this dosage there are signs of mild toxicity such as salivation, coughing and vomiting.

There is a mystery, at least to me, concerning the commercial production of 2,5-DMA. At regular intervals, there is a public announcement of the production quotas that are requested or allowed by the Drug Enforcement Administration, for drugs that have been placed in Schedules I or II. In the Schedule I category there are usually listed amounts such as a gram of this, and a few grams of that. These are probably for analytical purposes, since there are no medical uses, by definition, for drugs in this Schedule. But there is a staggering quantity of 2,5-DMA requested, regularly. Quantities in the many tens of millions of grams, quantities that vie with medical mainstays such as codeine and morphine. I have heard that this material is used in the photographic industry, but I have no facts. Somewhere I am sure that there is someone who has to keep a lot of very careful books!

In the area of psychedelic drugs, the value of 2,5-DMA is mainly in its role as a precursor to the preparation of materials that can come from a direct electrophilic attack on the activated 4-position. These uses can be found under things such as DOB and DOI and DON. The radio-halogenation of N-substituted homologues of 2,5-DMA with hypoiodite or hypofluorite is part of an extensive study underway in the search for radio-labeled brain blood flow agents. The rationale for this work is to be found in the commentary under IDNNA. In essence it has been found that the N-substitution or N,N-disubstitution of 2,5-DMA where the 4-position is unsubstituted and thus available for the introduction of a radioactive nucleus can give rise to potentially useful drugs. Most of these 2,5-dimethoxy exploratory compounds were made by the reductive alkylation of 2,5-dimethoxy-4-(radio)-iodophenylacetone, using various mono or dialkyl amines. This, too, is described under IDNNA.

However, the study of various direct iodinations and fluoridations that would have the N,N-dimethyl substitution on the amphetamine nitrogen atom, would require the 4-proteo- analogue, and this was made from the above nitrostyrene. A solution of the above nitrostyrene, 22.3 g 1-(2,5-dimethoxyphenyl)-2-nitropropene in 100 mL acetic acid was added to a suspension of elemental iron in acetic acid (45 g in 250 mL) and worked up with water and base washing to give, after distillation at 92-106 °C at 0.35 mm/Hg, 13.8 g 2,5-dimethoxyphenylacetone as a pale yellow oil. This underwent reductive amination with dimethylamine hydrochloride in MeOH solution, using sodium cyanoborohydride, to give the target compound 2,5-dimethoxy-N,N-dimethylamphetamine oxalate with a melting point of 133-134 °C (4.6 g ketone gave 1.38 g of salt). Anal. ($C_{15}H_{23}NO_6$) C,H. It has also been prepared by the N,N-dimethylation of 2,5-DMA directly, with formaldehyde and formic acid. This has been called 2,5-DNNA, or IDNNA without the "I." This intermediate, 2,5-DNNA, underwent direct radioiodination with labeled iodine monochloride in the presence of perchloric acid to give IDNNA with a 40% incorporation of isotope. Reaction with labeled acetyl hypofluorite, on the other hand, gave only a 2% in-corporation of the radio-isotope. This latter compound is, chemically, 4-fluoro-2,5-dimethoxy-N,N-dimethylamphetamine and, using the reasoning suggested above and with IDNNA, might best be encoded FDNNA.

The 2,5-dimethylamphetamine analogue mentioned above was also explored in this IDNNA concept. The commercially available 2,5-dimethylbenzaldehyde was converted to the nitrostyrene with nitroethane (1-(2,5-dimethylphenyl)-2-nitropropene, yellow crystals with a melting point of 24.5-25.5 °C) which reacted with elemental iron in acetic acid to give the ketone 2,5-dimethylphenylacetone (boiling at 140-150 °C at 0.4 mm/Hg). Reductive amination with dimethylamine and sodium cyanoborohydride gave 2,5-DMNNA (2,5,N,N-tetramethylamphetamine) as a clear oil with a boiling point of 115-125 °C at 0.35 mm/Hg. It gave poor yields of the 4-fluoro analogue with acetyl hypofluorite.

All of these latter materials remain unevaluated in man.

#55   3,4-DMA;   3,4-DIMETHOXYAMPHETAMINE

SYNTHESIS: A solution of 33.2 g of veratraldehyde in 15.0 g nitroethane was treated with 0.9 g of n-amylamine and placed in a dark place at room temperature. In a day or so, separated H_2O was apparent and, after a couple of weeks, the mixture completely solidified. The addition of 50 mL EtOH and heating effected complete solution and, on cooling, this provided 1-(3,4-dimethoxyphenyl)-2-nitropropene as yellow crystals, 29.0 g, with mp of 70-71 °C. The more conventional reaction scheme, 6 h heating of a solution of the aldehyde and nitroethane in acetic acid with ammonium acetate as catalyst, gave a much inferior yield of product (33.2 g gave 14.8 g) of the same purity. Recrystallization from MeOH increased the mp to 72-73 °C.

To a refluxing suspension of 7 g LAH in 600 mL anhydrous Et_2O, stirred and under an inert atmosphere, there was added 7.5 g 1-(3,4-dimethoxyphenyl)-2-nitropropene by allowing the returning condensed ether to leach out the material as a warm solution from a Soxhlet thimble. Following the completion of the addition of the nitrostyrene, refluxing was maintained for 24 h, and the reaction mixture allowed to stand several days at room temperature. The excess hydride was destroyed by the cautious addition of 500 mL H_2O containing 40 g H_2SO_4, and the phases were separated. The aqueous phase was washed with both Et_2O and CH_2Cl_2. There was then added 200 g potassium sodium tartrate, and the pH brought above 9 by the addition of aqueous NaOH. This clear solution was extracted with 3x150 mL CH_2Cl_2, the extracts were pooled, and the solvent removed under vacuum to give a residual oil. This was dissolved in Et_2O, saturated with anhydrous HCl gas, and the resulting solids removed by filtration. Recrystallization from 10 mL acetone gave 1.35 g 3,4-dimethoxyamphetamine hydrochloride (3,4-DMA) as beautiful white crystals with a mp of 144-145 °C.

DOSAGE: a few hundred milligrams.

DURATION: unknown.

QUALITATIVE COMMENTS: (with 70 mg i.v.) [One patient received 0.004 mM/Kg of the hydrochloride salt intravenously and exhibited only slight increase in psychiatric symptoms; a comparable dosage in a second individual also elicited only insignificant changes.]

(with 700 mg i.v.) [When one of these patients was reinjected at a later date with approximately 0.04 mM/Kg of 3,4-DMA a definite 'mescaline-like' state was induced. The symptoms included colored hallucinations of geometric figures and occasional structured forms. The other individual experienced visual distortions, notable after-imagery, feelings of unreality, and paranoid ideas. Marked mydriasis and gross body tremors also occurred but apparently no hallucinations were experienced.]

EXTENSIONS AND COMMENTARY: These "Qualitative Comments" are not explicit quotations from people who had taken 3,4-DMA. They are written descriptions by the observers who had given 3,4-DMA to psychiatric patients. This is one of the most outrageous chapters in the books on military medicine. The chemical warfare group within the U.S. Army explored many potential psychedelics by administering them to innocent patients with not even a thought of obtaining informed consent. These experiments took place at the New York State Psychiatric Institute (amongst other places) in the early 1960's. The Edgewood Arsenal code name for 3,4-DMA was EA-1316. A few non-military studies have indicated that 3,4-DMA is orally active at 160 milligrams, and so probably its potency by this more conventional route would fall midway between that of mescaline and of MDA. The 3-methoxy-4-other-than-methoxy things (such as hydroxy, ethoxy, allyloxy and methyl) are mentioned in the recipe for MEPEA. The alpha-ethyl homologue of 3,4-DMA, 2-amino-1-(3,4-dimethoxyphenyl)butane, and of other DMA's are discussed under the recipe for ARIADNE.

There are a total of six possible amphetamine molecules with two methoxyl groups attached. The 3,4-orientation has always been the most appealing to the life scientists as this is the positional substitution pattern found in the natural neuro-chemicals dopamine, norepinephrine and epinephrine. These latter two are called noradrenalin and adrenalin in England. Two adjacent hydroxy groups represent the catechol in the well known word catecholamines. You might read in a textbook, "This is where nature placed the groups when she put the compounds in our brains. So that is where the groups might be the most interesting in a psychedelic." Why? I have never understood this kind of reasoning. If a possible psychedelic has just the exact oxygen positioning of a neurotransmitter, then, voila, that's why it is active. And if a possible psychedelic has some positioning of these oxygen atoms that is different than that of a neurotransmitter? Then voila again. That's why it is active. Both sound equally reasonable to me, and neither one even begins to address the fundamental question, how do the psychedelic drugs do what they do? A study in the human animal of the intimate effects of one of these neurotransmitter analogues might bring us a little bit closer to answering this fundamental question. But maybe it wouldn't, after all. Nothing has made much sense so far! Anyway, 3,4-DMA is one of the ten essential amphetamines that can, in theory, arise from the ten essential oils of the spice and herb trade. In this case, the origins are methyl eugenol and methyl isoeugenol.

Two of these "different" isomers, 2,4-DMA and 2,5-DMA, have already been discussed in their own separate recipes. And the remaining three of the six possible DMA's that are "different" have been made and studied pharmacologically in animals but not in man. These are the 2,3-DMA, 2,6-DMA and the 3,5-DMA isomers. The products of their reaction with elemental bromine are discussed under META-DOB.

Both the 2,6- and the 3,5-isomers, as the N,N-dimethyl homologues, have been looked at as potential radio-halogen recipients in the search for positron-emitting brain blood-flow indicators, as discussed in the recipe for IDNNA. Both were made from the appropriate nitrostyrene via the corresponding phenylacetone.

The 2,6-isomer was derived from 2,6-dimethoxybenzaldehyde. This, in nitroethane and ammonium acetate, gave the nitrostyrene as canary-yellow crystals from MeOH that melted at 101.5-102.5 °C. Elemental iron in acetic acid converted this nitrostyrene to 2,6-dimethoxyphenylacetone (a water-white oil with boiling point of 95-105 °C at 0.4 mm/Hg. Anal. ($C_{11}H_{14}O_3$) C,H) and reductive amination with dimethylamine and sodium cyanoborohydride gave 2,6-dimethoxy-N,N-di-methylamphetamine perchlorate (2,6-DNNA) with a melting point of 109-110 °C. This base was readily fluorinated with ^{18}F acetylhypofluorite and iodinated with chloramine-T-oxidized [122]I iodide ion. It was also halogenated with (non-radioac-tive) bromine and iodine monochloride to give the corresponding 3-bromo-(and 3-iodo)-2,6-dimethoxy-N,N-dimethylamphetamines but these, in turn, did not react with radioactive acetyl hypofluorite.

The 3,5-isomer followed precisely the same flow sheet. 3,5-Dimethoxybenzaldehyde gave the nitrostyrene (with a melting point of 87-88 °C), the phenylacetone (with a boiling point of 110-130 °C at 0.3 mm/Hg) and the product 3,5-dimethoxy-N,N-dimethylamphetamine perchlorate (3,5-DNNA) with a melting point of 100-101 °C. This also reacted readily with ^{18}F acetylhypofluorite and [122]I-hypoiodite. Several alpha-ethyl homologues of these compounds have also been discussed in the recipe for ARIADNE.

#56   DMCPA;   2-(2,5-DIMETHOXY-4-METHYLPHENYL)CYCLO-PROPYLAMINE

SYNTHESIS: To a solution of 25 g 2,5-dimethoxy-4-methylbenzaldehyde (see the recipe for 2C-D for the preparation) and 29.2 g malonic acid in 50 mL anhydrous pyridine, there was added 2 mL piperidine and this was heated on the steam bath for several h. The mixture was added to a solution of 125 mL concentrated HCl in 500 mL H_2O at 0 °C, and the solid product that was formed was removed by filtration, and washed with H_2O. Recrystallization from aqueous EtOH yielded 31 g 2,5-dimethoxy-4-methylcinnamic acid with a mp of 163-166 °C. Anal. $(C_{12}H_{14}O_4)$ C,H.

In a cooled high-pressure reaction vessel there was placed a suspension of 30 g 2,5-dimethoxy-4-methylcinnamic acid in 150 mL liquid isobutene. This was treated dropwise with 0.6 mL concentrated H_2SO_4, then sealed and brought to room temperature. After 48 h shaking, the vessel was cooled again to -10 °C, opened, and poured into 200 mL of 10% Na_2CO_3. This was extracted with hexane, the pooled extracts washed with H_2O, and the solvent removed to yield 17.0 g of (t)-butyl 2,5-dimethoxy-4-methylcinnamate as an amber oil. Anal. $(C_{16}H_{22}O_4)$ C,H.

The cyclopropane ester was prepared by the reaction between 16 g (t)-butyl 2,5-dimethoxy-4-methylcinnamate and dimethylsulfoxonium methylide, prepared as described in the Kaiser reference in the acknowledgements. Hydrolysis of this ester gave 53% trans-2-(2,5-dimethoxy-4-methylphenyl)cyclopropanecarboxylic acid which, after recrystallization from a MeOH/ H_2O mixture, had a mp of 136 °C. Anal. $(C_{13}H_{16}O_4)$ C,H.

A suspension of 4 g of trans-2-(2,5-dimethoxy-4-methylphenyl)-cyclopropanecarboxylic acid in an equal volume of H_2O, was treated with sufficient acetone to effect complete solution. This was cooled to 0 °C and there was added, first, 2.0 g triethylamine in 35 mL acetone, followed by the slow addition of 2.5 g ethyl chloroformate in 10 mL acetone. This was stirred for 0.5 h, and then there was added a solution of 1.7 g NaN_3 in 6 mL H_2O, dropwise. After 1 h stirring at 0 °C, the mixture was quenched by pouring into H_2O at 0 °C. The separated oil was extracted with Et_2O, and extracts dried with anhydrous $MgSO_4$. Removal of the solvent under vacuum gave a residue of the azide, which was dissolved in 10 mL anhydrous toluene. This solution was heated on the steam bath until the nitrogen evolution was complete, and the removal of the solvent under vacuum gave a residue of crude isocyanate as an amber oil. This intermediate isocyanate was dissolved in 5.4 g benzyl alcohol and the reaction mixture was heated on the steam bath for 6 h. The excess benzyl alcohol was removed by distillation, yielding trans-2-(2,5-dimethoxy-4-methylphenyl)carbobenzoxyamidocyclopropane as a crystal-line residue. This was recrystallized from an EtOAc/hexane mixture to give 6.13 g of a crystalline product with a mp of 107-108 °C. Anal. $(C_{20}H_{23}NO_4)$ C,H,N.

A solution of 1.5 g trans-2-(2,5-dimethoxy-4-methylphenyl)carbo-benzoxyamidocyclopropane in 120 mL MeOH containing 200 mg 10% Pd/C was shaken under hydrogen gas at 35 psig for 45 min. The solution was filtered through celite, and a sufficient amount of a solution of 5% HCl in EtOH was added to the filtrate to make it acidic. Removal of all volatiles under vacuum gave a solid residue that was recrystallized from an EtOH/ether mixture to give 0.98 g of trans-2-(2,5-dimethoxy-4-methylphenyl)cyclopropylamine hydrochloride (DMCPA) as white crystals with a mp of 210-211 °C.

DOSAGE: 15 - 20 mg.

DURATION: 4 - 8 h.

QUALITATIVE COMMENTS: (with 10 mg) "The effects were quite real at an hour, but very hard to define. Nothing left at four hours, but my sleep was filled with bizarre and colorful dreams. Something was still working somewhere, at some level."

(with 20 mg) "I found myself lightheaded, and the thinness seemed to be, rather remarkably, on the left side of my brain. The experience was flighty. I was reminded of the aura that has been described preceding a convulsion. I was decoupled from my experience and from my environment. Not all of the control is there, and I am uncomfortable. But in an hour, there is complete control again, and I can relax my conscious guard which allows an easy plus three. With this, there was easy fantasy, erotic, quite a bit of movement in the visual field, and mild anorexia. The residual hyperreflexive thinness is largely gone, and not at all worrisome. This stuff is complicated, with a little too much of the physical. The next day was without any residues at all."

EXTENSIONS AND COMMENTARY: Most of the human trials took place in the fifteen to twenty milligram range. Several reports describe some muscular tremor, especially in the earliest part of the experience, but this never seemed to be a concern. The efforts to lock imagery to music were not too successful. All of these clinical studies were conducted on the trans-compound, but on the racemic mixture. This has been resolved into the two optical isomers, but they have not been compared in man. The cis-mixture is unknown.

This material is intimately related to tranylcypromine, a clinically proven antidepressant. This drug is a known monoamine oxidase inhibitor, and it is certainly possible that some of this pharmacological property might be found in

DMCPA if it were to be looked for. The hints of physical toxicity at the higher doses assayed might suggest some such activity.

This compound, DMCPA, was modeled directly after the structure of DOM, with the 2,5-dimethoxy-4-methyl substitution pattern. Another analogue of tranylcypromine, similarly modeled, is 3,4,5-trimethoxytranylcypromine, or trans-2-(3,4,5-trimethoxyphenyl)cyclopropylamine (TMT). It has been evaluated at levels of only 13 milligrams orally, and at this dose there were no hints of central activity.

#57   DME;   3,4-DIMETHOXY-ß-HYDROXYPHENETHYLAMINE

SYNTHESIS: To a solution of 10.2 g 3,4-dimethoxybenzaldehyde in 10 mL EtOH, cooled to 0 °C, there was added a solution of 4.2 g KCN in 40 mL H_2O. With good stirring, there was slowly added 10 mL concentrated HCl (caution: HCN is evolved) and the two-phase reaction mixture was allowed to continue stirring until there was the spontaneous formation of crystals. After a few days standing, these were removed by filtration and well washed with H_2O. All was recrystallized from 75 mL of 50% MeOH and air dried to provide 6.95 g of the cyanohydrin 3,4-dimethoxy-α-hydroxyphenylacetonitrile. The mp was 104-106 °C, which can be increased to 109 °C by recrystallization from benzene.

A well-stirred suspension of 4.7 g LAH in 500 mL anhydrous Et_2O was brought up to a gentle reflux, and 4.7 g 3,4-dimethoxy-α-hydroxyphenylacetonitrile was leached in from a Soxhlet thimble, over the course of 3 h. The color of the ether solution progressed from yellow to green, to an eventual blue. The reflux was maintained for 16 h. After cooling again, there was added (carefully) a solution of 27 g H_2SO_4 in 500 mL H_2O. The completely clear two-phase mixture was separated, and the aqueous phase treated with 87 g potassium sodium tartrate. The addition of 25% NaOH brought the pH >9, and this phase was extracted with 4x100 mL CH_2Cl_2. Removal of all the organic solvents under vacuum gave a residue that was part oil and part solid. This was extracted with 4x50 mL boiling Et_2O, the extracts pooled, and saturated with anhydrous HCl gas. The 0.95 g of pale-yellow crystals that formed were removed by filtration, and finely ground under 5 mL CH_3CN. There remained, after refiltration and air drying, 0.85 g of 3,4-dimethoxy-ß-hydroxyphenethylamine hydrochloride, DME, with a mp of 170-172 °C.

DOSAGE: greater than 115 mg.

DURATION: unknown.

QUALITATIVE COMMENTS: (with 115 mg) "I was faintly nauseous about an hour after taking the compound, and perhaps I was more alert than usual in the evening. Substantially no effects."

EXTENSIONS AND COMMENTARY: The rationale for exploring the beta-hydroxylated phenethylamines, especially those with oxygens at the biologically important 3- and 4-positions, has already been presented. Norepinephrine is a ß-hydroxylated phenethylamine with oxygens at these two ring positions. With DME, these are masked as two methyl ethers, and the initials DME stand for 3,4-dimethoxyphenyl-ß-ethanolamine. This is an alternate name for 3,4-dimethoxy-ß-hydroxyphenethylamine.

An exactly analogous compound is 3,4-methylenedioxy-ß-ethanolamine, where the masking is done with the biologically more fragile methylenedioxy ether. Originally I had called this compound MDE (methylenedioxyethanolamine) but that code has been, since 1975, used exclusively for 3,4-methylenedioxy-N-ethylamphetamine, which is a recipe all by itself. Under the discussion of members of the BOX series, there is a methylenedioxyphenethylamine with a methoxyl group at the ß-position, and it is called BOH (q.v.). There, a reasonable code name for this specific compound is given, namely BOHH. "BO" stands for the beta-oxygen function on a phenethylamine; this is the heart of the BOX family. The "H" which is the third letter of BOHH stands for the free hydroxyl group. And the final "H" is for homopiperonylamine (which is the trivial name for the compound without the hydroxyl group). BOHH, or 3,4-methylenedioxy-ß-hydroxyphenethylamine, or 3,4-methylenedioxy-ß-ethanolamine, has also be assayed in man at up to 100 milligrams without any effects, and must be considered, as of now, to be inactive centrally. The possible toxic roles of ß-ethanolamines as potential adrenolytic agents, have been discussed in the BOHD recipe. And beware of the use of the code name MDE in the very old literature. It might be this BOHH compound.

#58   DMMDA;   2,5-DIMETHOXY-3,4-METHYLENEDIOXY-AMPHETAMINE

SYNTHESIS: Apiole, as the crystalline essential oil 1-allyl-2,5-dimethoxy-3,4-methylenedioxybenzene, is isolated directly from commercial Oil of Parsley, by careful fractional distillation. It is the fraction that boils at 165-167 °C at 27 mm/Hg. A solution of 19.8 g apiole in a mixture of 43 g KOH and 60 mL hot EtOH was heated in the steam bath for 24 h. With vigorous stirring, it was diluted with H_2O, at a rate which the crystals that formed spontaneously could accumulate from the turbidity that was generated. When no more H_2O could be added (there was persistent oiling out of material) the reaction

mixture was filtered to give 12.1 g of an amber solid material. This was recrystallized from 20 mL boiling hexane, which was filtered while hot to remove insolubles.
From the cooled filtrate, there was obtained 9.3 g of 2,5-dimethoxy-3,4-methylene-
dioxy-1-propenylbenzene, isoapiole, as pale cream-colored solids.

A stirred solution of 8.8 g 2,5-dimethoxy-3,4-methylenedioxy-1-
propenylbenzene and 3.9 g pyridine in 45 mL acetone was cooled to ice-bath
temperatures, and treated with 7.9 g tetranitromethane. This extremely dark reaction was stirred at 0 °C for 5 min, then quenched with a solution of 2.6 g KOH in
45 mL H_2O. With continued stirring, there appeared yellow crystals of 1-(2,5-
dimethoxy-3,4-methylenedioxyphenyl)-2-nitropropene which, after filtering,
washing with 50% acetone and air drying, weighed 8.0 g and had a mp of 110-111
°C.

To a well-stirred and gently refluxing suspension of 6.3 g LAH in 500 mL
anhydrous Et_2O, under an inert atmosphere, there was added 7.5 g 1-(2,5-dimethoxy-
3,4-methylenedioxyphenyl)-2-nitropropene by leaching out the nitrostyrene from
a thimble in a modified Soxhlet condenser apparatus. The addition took 1.5 h, and
the refluxing was maintained for an additional 3 h. After cooling, the excess hydride
was destroyed by the cautious addition of 300 mL of 1.5 N H_2SO_4. The aqueous
phase was brought to a pH of 6 with Na_2CO_3. This was heated to 80 °C and clarified
by filtration though paper. The addition of a stochiometric amount of picric acid in
boiling EtOH gave rise to precipitation of the product picrate as globs that did not
crystallize. These were washed with cold H_2O, then dissolved in 30 mL 5% NaOH.
Extraction with 2x75 mL Et_2O, and the stripping of the solvent from the pooled
extracts, gave 3.1 g of an oily residue which, upon dissolving in 250 mL Et_2O and
saturation with anhydrous HCl gas, gave white crystals. These were removed by
filtration, Et_2O-washed, and air dried, to give 2.9 g of 2,5-dimethoxy-3,4-methyl-
enedioxyamphetamine hydrochloride (DMMDA) that melted in the 165-175 °C
range.

DOSAGE: 30 - 75 mg.

DURATION: 6 - 8 h.

QUALITATIVE COMMENTS: (with 25 mg) "The intoxication was there at an
hour and a quarter, and I was hit with nausea with no particular warning. I am shaky,
a little dilated in the eyes, and there is a modest depersonalization (reminding me
of LSD). Time might be slightly slowed, and there is a mild ataxia in the legs. A
couple of hours later, all effects are going away fast. I ate an apple, but maybe my
mouth didn't work quite right. The apple was incredibly noisy."

(with 32 mg) "I am up to a 2 1/2 plus at something after two hours, with
no apparent visuals, no push, no erotic. And a few hours later it is quietly slipping
away. It felt completely safe, and without any conspicuous psychedelic action, at
least at this level."

(with 50 mg) "I took graded doses of 10 milligrams every thirty minutes for a total of 50 milligrams, and there were no effects at all."

(with 50 mg) "In the middle of this all, I found myself getting into abstract thinking, and maybe some imagery as well. The effects were disappointingly light."

(with 75 mg) "This was equal to somewhere between 75 and 100 micrograms of LSD. I was caught up with the imagery, and there was an overriding religious aspect to the day. The experience had an esthetic value. I liked it."

EXTENSIONS AND COMMENTARY: DMMDA was the first of the tetraoxygenated amphetamine derivatives that was ever explored in man, back in 1962. And it is not easy to find an acceptable single phrase to describe its action or an acceptable number to describe its potency. I have put the value of 10 mescaline units (M.U.) into the literature and this would imply that maybe 30 milligrams was an active dose. This is probably too low, and some day I would like to run an experiment with the entire research group with this compound to see just what it really does.

The essential oil that corresponds to DMMDA is, of course, apiole from the Oil of Parsley, which again ties together the spice world and the amphetamine world. And there is isoapiole, also a natural thing. This pair represents the ring-substitution pattern of one of the ten essential oils and DMMDA is one of the ten essential amphetamines.

Several people have asked me what I thought about the potential activity of a compound with a methyl group added to DMMDA. One of these possibilities would be the N-methylated derivative, 2,5-dimethoxy-N-methyl-3,4-methylenedioxyamphetamine, or METHYL-DMMDA (or DMMDMA for the dimethoxy-methylenedioxy-methamphetamine nomenclature). It is a MDMA analogue, and is described in the recipe for METHYL-MMDA-2.

The placement of an added methyl group onto the ß-position of DMMDA, rather than on the nitrogen atom, produces a pair of stereoisomeric homologues. These are the threo- (or-trans-) and erythro- (or cis)-2,5-dimethoxy-ß-methyl-3,4-methylenedioxyamphetamines. They have never been assigned trivial names (my original codes for them were S-1495 and S-1496 which is not too intuitively informative). Their chemically proper names would have the 2-amino-3-substituted phenylbutane form. The synthesis of these DMMDA homologues started with the reduction of the nitrosyrene to the ketone (see under METHYL-MMDA-2 for this preparation), followed by methylation with fresh sodium isopropoxide and methyl iodide, to give the beta-methyl product. This formed the two possible oximes, one with a mp of 120 °C, and the other from MeOH with a mp of 146 °C. The 120 °C oxime, with fresh sodium ethoxide gave threo-2-amino-3-(2,5-dimethoxy-3,4-methylenedioxyphenyl)butane hydrochloride. This salt had a mp of 247-249 °C. The 146 °C oxime gave erythro-2-amino-3-(2,5-dimethoxy-3,4-methylenedioxyphenyl)butane hydrochloride with a mp of 188-189 °C. The threo-isomer showed a possible threshold effect at 80 milligrams, with hyperventilation and perhaps some mental muddiness. The erythro-isomer showed no effects, but it had been taken up only to 10 milligrams.

The only other ß-methyl homologue of an active material that was explored chemically, was related to MDA. The ketone (3,4-piperonylacetone, see under MDMA) was methylated with sodium isopropoxide and methyl iodide, and a crystalline oxime was obtained. Reduction with Zn dust gave what appeared to be 2-amino-3-(3,4-methylenedioxyphenyl)butane hydrochloride, but there were sufficient uncertainties (possible dimethylation, only one oxime isolated, the need of strong reducing conditions) that the entire project was placed in, and still is in, an indefinite holding pattern. The similar analogues for DOM are the two Classic Ladies, DAPHNE and ELVIRA, and they, too, are for some time in the future.

#59 DMMDA-2; 2,3-DIMETHOXY-4,5-METHYLENEDIOXY-AMPHETAMINE

DOSAGE: about 50 mg.

DURATION: unknown.

QUALITATIVE COMMENTS: (with 50 mg) "I am into it; it is much like MDA."

EXTENSIONS AND COMMENTARY: This is pretty sparse information upon which to build a picture of biological activity. First, the synthesis was done by someone else and, as I have not been able to find where the notes are, this will be the one recipe in the footnote without explicit directions incorporated. The procedure used was exactly the same as that described for DMMDA, except that the starting material was dillapiole rather than apiole. The dillapiole was obtained by the careful fractionation of Oil of Dill (as opposed to the isolation of apiole from the careful fractionation of Oil of Parsley). Isomerization to isodillapiole, nitration with tetra-nitromethane to give 1-(2,3-dimethoxy-4,5-methylenedioxyphenyl)-2-nitropropene, and its reduction with LAH in ether to give 2,3-dimethoxy-4,5-methylenedioxyamphetamine hydrochloride (DMMDA-2) proceeded in a precisely analogous manner to the preparation of DMMDA.

And the pharmacological part is rather thin as well. I was not the taster, and can only quote what I had been given. This same observer found a threshold at 28 milligrams. Under other circumstances, this comment on DMMDA-2 would have been tucked into the commentary on DMMDA where it belongs, but the activity level was called for in a large review article, and on the basis of the above, both its initials and the value of 5x the potency of mescaline were permanently enshrined in the published literature. What is it really like? I don't know. Its structure is an appealing amalgamation of that of MMDA and MMDA-2, and it might be quite a winner if the dosage and the duration were known. It is, after all, one of the ten essential amphetamines, since dillapiole is one of the ten essential oils.

At the time that DMMDA and DMMDA-2 were synthesized, I had visions of doing the same thorough study with these as I had set up with the TMA's (six possible, six done) and the MMDA's (six possible, five done). Here, too, with a pair of methoxy groups on an amphetamine skeleton, with a methylenedioxy ring thrown in, six isomers are possible but only these two have been prepared. The unknown ones will certainly be called DMMDA-3, -4, -5 and -6, but the assignments of code to structure haven't even been thought out yet. The remarkable and totally unexpected activity of DOM was discovered at about this time and it was a much more tempting direction to follow. The remaining four possible DMMDA's have been left to that famous time, a future "rainy day."

#60 DMPEA; 3,4-DIMETHOXYPHENETHYLAMINE

SYNTHESIS: A solution of 33 g 3,4-dimethoxybenzaldehyde in 140 mL acetic acid was treated with 23 mL nitromethane and 12.5 g anhydrous ammonium acetate, and heated on the steam bath for 45 min. To this there was slowly added, with good stirring, 300 mL H_2O, and the resulting solids were removed by filtration. The product was finely ground under a small amount of MeOH, filtered again, and air dried to give 13.5 g 3,4-dimethoxy-ß-nitrostyrene with a mp of 142-143 °C.

To a stirred suspension of 12.0 g LAH in 500 mL anhydrous Et_2O that was at a gentle reflux and under an inert atmosphere, there was added 11.45 g 3,4-dimethoxy-ß-nitrostyrene by leaching it from a thimble in a modified Soxhlet

condenser. The addition took 2 h and the reflux-ing was maintained for another 16 h. After cool-ing to room temperature, the excess hydride was destroyed by the cautious addition of 500 mL 1.5 N H_2SO_4. The phases were separated, and to the aqueous phase there was added 250 g potassium sodium tartrate. The pH was brought to >9, and the clear solution was extracted with 3x100 mL CH_2Cl_2. Remo-val of the solvent from the combined extracts under vacuum gave 5.2 g of a pale yellow oil. This was dissolved in 300 mL anhydrous Et_2O and saturated with an-hydrous HCl gas, giving 5.0 g of a slightly sticky off-white solid. This was recrystallized from 75 mL of boiling CH_3CN to give 3.3 g 3,4-dimethoxyphen-ethylamine hydrochloride (DMPEA) as beautiful white crystals.

DOSAGE: greater than 1000 mg.

DURATION: unknown.

QUALITATIVE COMMENTS: (with 500 mg) "Nothing."
(with 1000 mg) "Nothing."
(with 10 mg i.v.) "Nothing."
(with 1000 mg of 3,4-dimethoxyphenylacetic acid, a major human metabolite of DMPEA) "Nothing."
(with 500 mg of N-acetyl-3,4-dimethoxyphenethylamine, a major human metabolite of DMPEA) "Nothing."

EXTENSIONS AND COMMENTARY: Why all the interest? Why keep pursuing a compound that is so obviously without activity? Or a metabolite that is also without activity? The answer is that these are totally fascinating compounds *just because* they have no activity! By the way, in this instance, I actually made up most of the quotations. I am not sure that the subjects actually said, "Nothing," but they did report that there were no effects. In my own experiments, my notes record the phrase, "No effects whatsoever."

A little background: one of the transmitter heavyweights in the brain is dopamine. Dopamine is called dopamine because it is an amine that comes from an amino acid that is 3,4-dihydroxyphenylalanine and this, in German, is Di-Oxo-Phenyl-Alanine, or DOPA. The levo-optical (or L-) isomer of DOPA has rather cutely been called the punch-drunk Spanish matador, or El Dopa. But that is not part of the story.

The story is really about the "Pink Spot of Schizophrenia." Many years ago, an observation was made in a biochemical laboratory on the East Coast that stirred up a rolling controversy. It had been found that if the urines of schizophrenic patients (sloppily called "schizophrenic urines") were extracted in such and such a way, and the extracts chromatographed, a pink spot would develop at a particular place on the chromatogram. Well, if this proved to be true with urines of a sick population, and were this proved to be different from the urines of a healthy population, it would constitute an objective diagnosis of schizophrenia. A simple chemical test to confirm a pathology that had defied all efforts to achieve consensus amongst the psychiatrists of the world.

The literature was suddenly filled with dozens of papers. Researcher A confirmed that the pink spot was found with schizophrenics, and not with normal controls. Researcher B found the pink spot in all urines, regardless of pathology. Researcher C found it in no urines at all. Researcher D argued that it was a factor from the hospital diet. Researcher E found that the pink spot reflected the time of day that the urine sample was collected. Researcher F drew a conclusion about where truth might lie by tallying the number of papers that supported argument A, B, C, D, or E.

The only confirmable fact that endured was that the pink spot was due to DMPEA. So a bright spotlight was directed towards its possible role in mental illness. And this expressed itself in the simple question: would it produce schizophrenia in a normal subject? No. And in a way I am comforted that that did not evolve into a simple litmus test for a schizophrenic diagnosis. There are so many cultural, political, and social factors that come to bear on the assignment of a diagnosis of mental illness, that I would have been forever skeptical of a neat biochemical marker.

A chemical modification of DMPEA that has been explored in this question of pink spots, mental pathology, and diagnostic markers, is the corresponding acetamide. One of the metabolites of DMPEA was found to be the N-acetyl derivative, N-acetyl-3,4- dimethoxyphenethylamine. It was found to be demethylated in man, and to have pharmacological activity in animals. Maybe this was the active compound that could be involved in the schizophrenic process. But human trials with it, as with the principal metabolite 3,4-dimethoxyphenylacetic acid, showed nothing at all in man.

Another chemical modification is the beta-hydroxy analogue of DMPEA. It has been explored separately, and is the subject of its own recipe, in its own rights. See DME.

Pink was not the only colorful spot associated with schizophrenia. Somewhere at about this same time, a research paper from Canada reported the observation of a mauve spot in the chromatographic analysis of urines of schizophrenic patients. This had nothing to do with DMPEA. I was working closely with a researcher at the psychiatric institute and we were fascinated by, again, a possible diagnostic marker. We assayed the urines of the next 10 patients being admitted as acute schizophrenics. No trace of mauve. We wrote to Canada, and verified the analytical procedure. We were told that the whatzis should have been added after, rather than before, the whosey, and that we should have heated for 30, not 10 minutes. Okay. We assayed the urines of the next 10 patients being admitted using these new directions. No trace of mauve. Another call to Canada, and we were informed that we still weren't doing it right. They were consistently batting a 100% positive correlation between mauve spots and schizophrenics, and 0% with healthy controls. In fact, they actually gave this positive test the name of a disease, Malvaria.

Then, that little burst of insight! Aha! What if, just what if, they had been seeing something given to their schizophrenics? Chlorpromazine was the popular treatment of the day. We took a whopping dose of chlorpromazine, and over the next couple of days did manage (barely) to collect our urine samples. Both of us were positive Malvarians! And three days later, we were again negative. We were most likely seeing a metabolite of chlorpromazine. One last call to Canada with the ultimate question — had you given any medication to your schizophrenics before your urine analysis? Of course (came the answer) — it would not be ethical to leave them untreated. Another color down the drain, and still no objective measure for mental illness.

By the way, I cannot say I like the chlorpromazine trip. There is no real communication either with others or with yourself, with that stuff. You are a zombie, but if you are both schizophrenic and a zombie, you cannot possibly be troublesome for anybody in the emergency room.

#61 DOAM; 2,5-DIMETHOXY-4-(n)-AMYLAMPHETAMINE

SYNTHESIS: A solution of 110 g p-dimethoxybenzene and 102 g valeric acid in 168 g polyphosphoric acid was heated on the steam bath for 3 h, giving a deep red homogeneous solution. This was poured into 1 L H_2O with good stirring. The strongly acidic, cloudy suspension was extracted with 3x200 mL CH_2Cl_2, the extracts pooled, washed with 4x150 mL 5% NaOH, and finally once with dilute HCl. The solvent was removed under vacuum, and the residual amber oil cooled overnight at 0 °C. Some 30 g of crystalline, unreacted dimethoxybenzene were removed by filtration, and the 85 g of residual oil distilled at the water pump. Another 15 g of di-methoxybenzene came over as an early cut, but the fraction boil-ing at 184-192 °C (mostly 188-192 °C) weighed 53.0 g and was reasonably pure 2,5-dimethoxyamylophenone. The reaction of the acid chloride of valeric acid with p-dimethoxybenzene and anhydrous $AlCl_3$ in CH_2Cl_2 (parallel to the preparation of the butyrophenone analog, see DOBU) gave an inferior yield (23.2 g from 92 g dimethoxybenzene), but did provide a sizeable sample (12.2 g) of 2-hydroxy-5-methoxyamylophenone from the basic washes of the crude reaction mixture. This pale yellow solid, after recrystallization from MeOH, had a mp of 62-62.5 °C. Anal. ($C_{12}H_{16}O_3$) C,H.

To 360 g mossy zinc there was added a solution of 7.2 g mercuric chloride in 200 mL warm H_2O, and this was swirled periodically for 2 h. The H_2O was drained off, and the amalgamated zinc added to a 2 L three-neck round-bottomed flask, treated with 200 mL concentrated HCl, and heated with an electric mantle. A solution of 53.0 g of 2,5-dimethoxyamylophenone in 107 mL EtOH containing 30 mL concentrated HCl was added drop-wise over the course of 4 h accompanied by 330 mL of concentrated HCl added batchwise over this same period. The mixture was held at reflux overnight and, after cooling, diluted with sufficient H_2O to al-lowed CH_2Cl_2 to be the lower phase. The phases were separated, and the aqueous phase was extracted with 2x200 mL additional CH_2Cl_2. These organic phases were combined, washed first with 5% NaOH and then with H_2O, and the solvent removed under vacuum. Distillation at the water pump yielded two fractions. The first distilled from about 100-130 °C, weighed 8.8 g, had a faint smell of apples and fennel, and was free of a carbonyl group in the infra-red. It proved to be only 50% pure by GC, however, and was discarded. The major fraction was a pale amber oil distilling between 152-170 °C and was substantially free of smell. It weighed 18.9 g, and was (by GC) 90% pure 2,5-dimethoxy-(n)-amylbenzene.

A mixture of 36.3 g $POCl_3$ and 40.9 g N-methylformanilide was allowed to incubate for 0.5 h. To this there was then added 18.5 g of 2,5-dimethoxy-(n)-amylbenzene and the mixture heated on the steam bath for 2 h. This mixture was poured into a large quantity of H_2O and stirred overnight. The black oily product was extracted with 3x100 mL CH_2Cl_2, and the extracts combined and stripped of solvent under vacuum. The black residue was distilled at 180-205 °C at 20 mm/Hg to give 12.5 g of a pale amber oil that slowly set up to a crystalline mass. An analytical sample was recrystallized from MeOH to provide 2,5-dimethoxy-4-(n)-amylbenzaldehyde with a mp of 25-26 °C. Anal. $(C_{14}H_{20}O_3)$ H; C: calcd, 71.16: found, 71.92, 71.74.

A solution of 12.3 g 2,5-dimethoxy-4-(n)-amylbenzaldehyde in 50 mL acetic acid was treated with 4.0 g anhydrous ammonium acetate and 12 mL nitroethane. This mixture was heated on the steam bath for 4 h, then poured into a large quantity of H_2O. This was extracted with 3x200 mL CH_2Cl_2, the extracts washed with H_2O, and the solvent removed to give a deep red oil that, on standing in the refrigerator, slowly set to a crystalline mass weighing 13.5 g. An analytical sample was recrystallized from MeOH to provide 1-(2,5-dimethoxy-4-(n)-amylphenyl)-2-nitropropene as fine yellow microcrystals with a mp of 44 °C sharp. Anal. $(C_{16}H_{23}NO_4)$ C,H,N.

To a gently refluxing suspension of 10 g LAH in 500 mL anhydrous Et_2O under a He atmosphere, there was added by 13.2 g 1-(2,5-dimethoxy-4-(n)-butyl-phenyl)-2-nitropropene by allowing the condensing ether drip into a Soxhlet thimble containing the nitrostyrene which effectively added a warm saturated solution of it dropwise to the reaction mixture. Refluxing was maintained for 18 h, and the cooled reaction flask stirred for several additional days. The excess hydride was destroyed by the cautious addition of 1 L 8% H_2SO_4. When the aqueous and Et_2O layers were finally clear, they were separated, and the aqueous layer was washed with an additional 2x100 mL Et_2O. Removal of the solvent from the organic phase and washings provided 4.7 g of a thick red oil that was discarded. The aqueous phase was then extracted with 2x200 mL CH_2Cl_2 which actually removed the product as the sulfate salt. This organic phase was washed with 2x100 mL 5% K_2CO_3 (removing the H_2SO_4) and with the evaporation of the solvent there was obtained 6.2 g of an oily amber residue. This was dissolved in 200 mL Et_2O and saturated with anhydrous HCl gas. Fine white crystals of 2,5-dimethoxy-4-(n)-amylamphetamine hydrochloride (DOAM) separated, were removed by filtration, Et_2O-washed and air dried, and weighed 5.2 g. The mp of 136-139 °C was increased to 145-146 °C by recrystallization from CH_3CN. Anal. $(C_{16}H_{28}ClNO_2)$ C,H,N.

DOSAGE: greater than 10 mg.

DURATION: unknown.

QUALITATIVE COMMENTS: (with 10 mg) "There was a clear threshold that in no way interfered with my day's activities. I was quite gay and voluble at lunch and bubbled on into the afternoon with puns and high spirits. There may have been a little motor incoordination as noted in handwriting, and there was a strange tenseness during driving. There were no sequelae, there was no trouble sleeping, and with this potency way down from the lower homologues, I have no pressing desire to take this compound to a higher dose."

EXTENSIONS AND COMMENTARY: The actual procedure that was published for the isolation of this final amine was a different one, one that would certainly work, but which was based on the procedures tried and proven with the lower homologues. The process described above is just a bit bizarre (a sulfate salt extracting into methylene chloride) but it was the actual thing that was done. The work was started towards two additional compounds but these never got past the first "ketone and phenol" stage. p-Dimethoxybenzene was brought into reaction with n-caproic acid with polyphosphoric acid (aiming towards 2,5-dimethoxy-4-(n)-hexylamphetamine, DOHE) but this was dropped when DOAM proved to be down in potency. And the reaction between p-dimethoxybenzene and benzoyl chloride with anh. aluminum chloride went well (aiming towards 2,5-dimethoxy-4-benzylamphetamine, DOBZ). A goodly amount of the phenol (2-hydroxy-5-methoxybenzophenone) was obtained as fine yellow crystals, but this line of inquiry was also dropped.

The preparation of DOAM was, as a matter of fact, the last of the homologous series of compounds actually completed, which stemmed from the original discovery of DOM. The "Ten Classic Ladies" concept was mentioned under ARIADNE, and the adding of a methyl group in the place of a hydrogen atom at the 4-position-methyl led to the synthesis of Ms. HECATE and gave rise to DOET. The whole series of methyl-ethyl-propyl-butyl-amyl compounds was appealing to me, in that the potency seemed to increase initially as the chain got longer, and then it abruptly dropped off. Wouldn't it be nice, I thought, if I could interest some pharmacologist in looking at this tight set of drugs with some animal model, to see if there is some neurotransmitter activity that would show a parallel action.

I learned of a curious young researcher in Washington who had an elegant procedure for measuring serotonin agonist action using the (otherwise) discarded sheep umbilical artery strips. These become available each year at lambing time, do not cost the life of anything, and require very little compound. He assayed my compounds and, lo and behold, the serotonin activity also went through a maximum in the middle of this series. We published a short paper to this effect, which served as a excellent vehicle to get the cogent human data into the scientific literature.

I have never understood the reasons that there might be connection between the twitching of a umbilical artery in a sheep and the appearance of an insight in the mind of man. And, I have never personally met this pharmacologist. Some day, I hope to do both.

#62   DOB;   2,5-DIMETHOXY-4-BROMOAMPHETAMINE

SYNTHESIS: To a well-stirred solution of 1.95 g of the free base of 2,5-dimethoxyamphetamine (2,5-DMA) in 12 mL glacial acetic acid, there was added 1.8 g elemental bromine dissolved in 4 mL acetic acid over the course of 5 min. The slightly exothermic reaction was allowed to stir for 3 h, and then added to about 200 mL H_2O. The cloudy solution was washed with 2x100 Et_2O, made basic with aqueous NaOH, and extracted with 3x100 mL CH_2Cl_2. Evaporation of the solvent from the pooled extracts gave about 3 mL of a pale amber oil which was dissolved in 250 mL anhydrous Et_2O and saturated with anhydrous HCl gas. The fine white crystals of 2,5-dimethoxy-4-bromoamphetamine hydrochloride, DOB, were removed by filtration, Et_2O washed, and air dried. These weighed 1.7 g and had a mp of 195-196 °C. Recrystallization from IPA brought this up to 207-208 °C. Proton NMR spectroscopy of the hydrochloride salt in D_2O gave confidence that the bromine atom had uniquely entered the 4-position, in that there were only two unsplit aromatic hydrogen atoms present, at 6.97 and at 7.20 ppm downfield from external TMS.

DOSAGE: 1.0 - 3.0 mg.

DURATION: 18 - 30 h.

QUALITATIVE COMMENTS: (with 0.4 mg) "There was a distinct enhancement of visual perception, and some strengthening of colors. A clean, cold feeling of wind on the skin. I felt an enriched emotional affect, a comfortable and good feeling, and easy sleeping with colorful and important dreams."

(with 2.0 mg) "There was a continuous tremor at the physical level, and an incredible Moebius strip representation of reality at the intellectual level. I was able to enter into personal problems easily, and get out again when I chose to. During the next day, there were brief lapses of attention, or little fugue states, and it was not until the following evening that I was completely myself again."

(with 2.8 mg) "About three hours into this I had a severe cramp, and had a near fainting response to the pain, and yet there was no pain! I felt that I was very near a loss of consciousness, and this was most disturbing. There were flashes of depersonalization. I saw rings around the moon with prismatic colors, and there were long-lasting "after-images" following any viewings of points of light. I was still a good plus 1 at 14 hours, but did manage to sleep. It was the next day before I was again at baseline."

(with 3.0 mg) "This was a complex, but a very good day. It involved making a large pot of chicken-vegetable soup, and listening to H.L., my favorite Saturday morning fundamentalist Christian radio preacher, bless 'im. The Democrats are not exactly all anti-American dupes of Moscow (or the Devil), but to H.L., they are practically, almost, next-door to it. The Rapture is supposed to happen tomorrow according to a certain book, newly published (just in time, looks like) and he is busy softening the possible disappointment of those who may find themselves unchanged Monday morning. Wunnerful. It's been one heck of a good experiment, and I can't understand why we waited nine years to try this gorgeous stuff. Without going into the cosmic and delicious details, let's just say it's a great material and a good level."

(with 0.5 mg of the "R" isomer) "I am underway, and this is a smooth intoxication. I am completely functional, but still really a plus two. I would not choose to drive a car. Not very far. I felt a rather quick dropping to a plus-one at the fifth hour, but there is a residual stimulation still the following morning."

(with 1.0 mg of the "R" isomer) "By the fourth hour I am absolutely a +++ and am searching the kitchen for food. But what I eat is only so-so. There is not the introspection or intensity of 2.0 milligrams of the racemate material, but this is a rewarding place nonethless. At the 18th hour, there was some fitful sleep, with bizarre dreams. The next day I was still hungry for altered spaces, and successfully challenged the residual plus one with LSD and, as is usually the case, acid cut right through the detritus and allowed a direct shot up to a +++ again."

(with 1.5 mg of the "R" isomer) "This is a +++ but it is vaguely irrational. I feel a heavy body load, but then the temperature outside is over a hundred degrees and I may not be in the best of all physical environments. I would not wish any higher dosage. There were cat-naps at the twelfth hour, but most symptoms were still there at the 18th hour. A good experience. It would be interesting to compare this, some day, with 3.0 milligrams of the racemate."

(with 0.5 mg of the "S" isomer) "There are no effects at all."

(with 1.0 mg of the "S" isomer) "There is something warm and nice at a couple of hours into this, but I am no more than threshold, and the effects are very slight. By the fifth hour there are no longer any effects."

EXTENSIONS AND COMMENTARY: The stars had clearly lined up in favor of making DOB and exploring its biological activity. This preparation had been completed in 1967 and the report of this compound and its unprecedently high potency published in 1971. And very shortly, two additional papers appeared completely independently. One described DOB made via a different route, and describing high activity in rats. The other described DOB and a couple of closely related brominated amphetamines and their action in man.

This is one of the last of the experimental compounds within the phenethylamine family on which any animal toxicity studies were performed by me prior to human studies. A mouse injected with 50 mg/Kg (ip) showed considerable twitching and was irritable. Another, at 100 mg/Kg (ip), had overt shaking at 20 minutes, which evolved into persistent hyperactivity that lasted several hours. Yet another, at 125 mg/Kg (ip), lost much of her righting reflex within 15 minutes, entered into convulsions at 50 minutes, and was dead a half hour later. A fourth mouse, at 150 mg/Kg (ip), entered into spontaneous convulsions within 10 minutes, and expired in what looked like an uncomfortable death at 22 minutes following injection. What was learned? That the LD/50 was somewhere between 100 and 125 mg/Kg for the mouse. And an effective dose in man of maybe 2 mg (for an 80 Kg man) is equivalent to 25 ug/Kg. Therefore the index of safety (the therapeutic index, the lethal dose divided by the effective dose) is well over a thousand. I feel that two mice were killed without anything of value having been received in return.

Actually, it is very likely that the damaging, if not lethal, level of DOB in man is a lot lower than this ratio would imply. There was a report of a death of a young lady following the snorting of an amount of DOB so massive, there was the actual recovery of over nine milligrams of the drug from her body tissues in the post-mortem examination. It was said that she and her companion had thought that the drug they were using was MDA and, taking a dosage appropriate for this, effectively overdosed themselves. He survived, following convulsions and an extended period (several weeks) of being in a comatose state. Tragic examples have been reported that involve arterial vascular spasm. But in most overdose cases ascribed to DOB, the identity of the drug has remained unestablished.

As with DOI, the presence of a heavy atom, the bromine atom, in DOB makes the radioactive isotope labelled material a powerful research tool. Studies with DOB labelled with either ^{82}Br or ^{77}Br have been used in human subjects to follow the distribution of the drug. The use of a whole body scanner permits the imaging of the intact body, with the travelings of the radioactivity easily followed from outside. A fascinating finding is that DOB goes first and foremost to the human lung where it accumulates for a couple of hours. It is only afterwards that the brain level builds up. There is a strong implication that some metabolic conversion occurs in the lung, and it is only after this that the truly active metabolite is available for central action. This is consistent with the relatively slow onset of effect, and the very long duration of action.

As with all the other psychedelics which can and have been studied as their optical isomers, it is the "R" isomer of DOB that is the more active than the racemic mixture, and the "S" is certainly much less active, but it has never been run up to fully active levels. The alpha-ethyl homologue of DOB is mentioned under ARIADNE. The positionally rearranged isomers of DOB are discussed under META-DOB.

#63   DOBU;   2,5-DIMETHOXY-4-(n)-BUTYLAMPHETAMINE

SYNTHESIS: A well stirred suspension of 140 g anhydrous AlCl$_3$ in 400 mL CH$_2$Cl$_2$ was treated with 102 g butyryl chloride. This mixture was added in small portions, over the course of 20 min, to a well-stirred solution of 110.4 g p-dimethoxybenzene in 300 mL CH$_2$Cl$_2$. After an additional 1 h stirring, the mixture was poured into 1

L H_2O, and the two phases separated. The aqueous phase was extracted with 2x100 mL CH_2Cl_2, and the organic fractions pooled. These were washed with 4x125 mL 5% NaOH which removed both unreacted butyric acid as well as a small amount of 2-hydroxy-4-methoxybutyrophenone. Removal of the CH_2Cl_2 under vacuum gave 156.7 g of a residue that was distilled at 170-178 °C at the water pump. The isolated 2,5-dimethoxybutyrophenone was a pale yellow oil that weighed 146 g and was about 85% pure by GC analysis. The principal impurity was unreacted dimethoxybenzene. The identical preparation with CS_2 as a solvent, rather than CH_2Cl_2 gave a somewhat smaller yield of product.

To 150 g mossy zinc there was added a solution of 3 g mercuric chloride in 60 mL H_2O, and this was swirled periodically for 2 h. The H_2O was drained off, and the amalgamated zinc added to a 1 L three-neck round-bottomed flask, treated with 80 mL concentrated HCl, and heated on the steam bath. A solution of 20.8 g of 2,5-dimethoxybutyrophenone in 45 mL EtOH containing 10 mL concentrated HCl was added in increments over a 4 h period. During this period an additional 140 mL of concentrated HCl was added periodically to the ketone solution. Heating was maintained for an additional 4 h. After cooling, the aqueous filtrate was extracted with

3x100 mL CH_2Cl_2 and these pooled extracts washed with 2x200 mL 5% NaOH to remove a small amount of phenolic impurity. After removal of the solvent under vacuum, the residual 16.1 g of clear oil was distilled over the 100-160 °C range (largely at 141-145 °C) at the water pump to give 10 g of 2,5-dimethoxy-(n)-butylbenzene as a white oil. This was about 90% pure by GC analysis, and was used without further purification in the next step.

A mixture of 98 mL $POCl_3$ and 108 mL N-methylformanilide was allowed to incubate for 0.5 h. To this there was then added 47.3 g of 2,5-dimethoxy-(n)-butylbenzene and the mixture heated on the steam bath for 1.5 h. This mixture was poured into 1 L H_2O and stirred overnight. The H_2O was drained from the extremely gooey black crystals that were formed, and extracted with 2x100 mL portions of hexane. The black residue was diluted with these extracts and, on slow evaporation there was deposited 26.4 g of oily amber crystals. Filtering these through a medium porous funnel and sucking the oily phase away from the solids yielded 14.8 g of yellow crystals that could be recrystallized from 50 mL MeOH to give, after filtration and air drying to constant weight, 6.4 g of 2,5-dimethoxy-4-(n)-butylbenzaldehyde as pale yellow crystals with a mp of 47-48 °C. The recovery of all organic soluble things from the above process gave, after removal of the extraction solvents and making boiling hexane extractions of the residues, a second crop of aldehyde of equal weight and of identical mp. An analytical sample, from hexane, had the same mp. Anal. ($C_{13}H_{18}O_3$) C,H.

A solution of 13.2 g 2,5-dimethoxy-4-(n)-butylbenzaldehyde in 50 mL acetic acid was treated with 4.0 g anhydrous ammonium acetate and 10 mL nitroethane. This mixture was heated on the steam bath for 4 h, then poured into a large quantity of H_2O. This was extracted with 2x200 mL CH_2Cl_2, the extracts washed with H_2O, and the solvent removed to give 19 g of a deep red oil. This was dissolved in 35 mL hot MeOH and slowly cooled, depositing yellow-orange crystals. These were removed by filtration, washed with cold MeOH, and air-dried to constant weight. Thus there was obtained 11.8 g of 1-(2,5-dimethoxy-4-(n)-butylphenyl)-2-nitropropene with a mp of 54-56 °C. Recrystallization of an analytical sample from MeOH tightened the mp to 55-56 °C. Anal. ($C_{15}H_{21}NO_4$) C,H,N.

To a gently refluxing suspension of 8.5 g LAH in 300 mL anhydrous Et_2O under a He atmosphere, there was added 11.0 g 1-(2,5-dimethoxy-4-(n)-butylphenyl)-2-nitropropene by allowing the condensing ether to drip into a Soxhlet thimble containing the nitrostyrene, thus effectively adding a warm saturated solution of it dropwise. Refluxing was maintained overnight, and the cooled reaction flask stirred for several additional days. The excess hydride was destroyed by the cautious addition of 600 mL H_2O containing 55 g H_2SO_4. When the aqueous and Et_2O layers were finally clear, they were separated, and 250 g of potassium sodium tartrate was dissolved in the aqueous fraction. Aqueous NaOH was then added until the pH was above 9, and this was then extracted with 3x200 mL CH_2Cl_2. Evaporation of the solvent produced 12 g of an amber oil that gelatinized to a waxy, amorphous mass. This was leached as thoroughly as possible with anhydrous Et_2O which was clarified by filtration, then saturated with anhydrous HCl gas. After a few minutes delay, there commenced the separation of fine white crystals of 2,5-dimethoxy-4-(n)-butylamphetamine hydrochloride (DOBU). These weighed, after filtration, Et_2O washing, and air drying to constant weight, 5.8 g. Recrystallization from boiling CH_3CN (this is an unusually exothermic crystallization) yielded 5.4 g of a fluffy white product with mp 151-152 °C. Anal. ($C_{15}H_{26}ClNO_2$) C,H,N.

DOSAGE: uncertain.

DURATION: very long.

QUALITATIVE COMMENTS: (with 2.2 mg) "It was almost the fourth hour before I noticed something. Then I felt an increasing manic intoxication, winding up tighter and tighter. Sleep was impossible until some 18 hours after the start of the trial. There was some paresthesia, but no mydriasis. This might be a stimulant, but it is not a psychedelic, at least at this level. Go up slowly."

(with 2.8 mg) "Nothing for over seven hours. Then there was what seemed to be an irritability and shortness of temper. Mentally I am completely clear, but no more alert than usual. There was no sleep that evening, and the next day there was a feeling of overall depression. Perhaps that was due to the lack of sleep, but there were no signs of residual sleepiness."

EXTENSIONS AND COMMENTARY: It is not possible to give a dosage range for DOBU. There is no question but that whatever is occurring is slow of onset, and very long lived. In general, the effects resemble stimulation more that anything else.

A butyl group has four carbons, and they can be interconnected in four ways (as long as you don't connect them in rings). If all four of them are in a straight chain, you have the so-called normal butyl (or n-butyl) group, and this is the exact arrangement that is found in the DOBU. The atoms can be numbered #1 through #4, going outwards from the point of attachment. The chain can, however, be only three carbons long, and the fourth or extra carbon attached on the #2 carbon atom; this is called the iso-butyl (or i-butyl) group. Or the extra left-over carbon can be attached to the #1 carbon atom; this is called the secondary butyl (or sec-butyl or s-butyl) group. Or lastly, the atoms can be all scrunched up, with the chain only two carbons long, and the other two left-over methyl carbons attached to the #1 carbon atom. This isomer is called the tertiary butyl (or tert-butyl or t-butyl) group. In animal studies, and in preliminary human studies, the activity of these compounds drops as the butyl group gets more and more scrunched.

The isomer with the iso-butyl group has been synthesized by the Friedel-Crafts reaction of isobutyryl chloride with p-dimethoxybenzene, followed by reduction of the ketone to an alcohol, dehydration to a dimethylstyrene, and final hydrogenation to a hydrocarbon. The formation of the benzaldehyde, reaction with nitroethane, and final lithium aluminum hydride reduction to 2,5-dimethoxy-4-(2-methylpropyl)-amphetamine hydrochloride (DOIB, mp 164-166 °C) were completely conventional. In drug discrimination studies in rats, DOIB was only a third as active as DOM, and in humans the activity falls in the 10 to 15 milligram area. The isomer with the sec-butyl group was made in a somewhat similar manner, from 2,5-dimethoxyacetophenone. The addition of ethyl magnesium bromide gave an alcohol which with dehydration yielded a pair of dimethylstyrenes isomeric to the compound mentioned above. From there an identical sequence of steps (hydrogenation, benzaldehyde synthesis, nitrostyrene, and lithium aluminum hydride reduction) produced 2,5-dimethoxy-4-(1-methylpropyl)amphetamine hydrochloride (DOSB, mp 168-170 °C.). In the rat studies it was only a twelfth the potency of DOM, and in man the active dose is in the 25 to 30 milligram area. As with the normal butyl compound, there is a strong stimulation factor, with real and long-lasting sleep disturbance.

The last of the butyl isomers, the tert-butyl compound, was made from a much more obvious starting material. This is the commercially available tert-butyl hydroquinone. It was methylated in sodium hydroxide with methyl iodide, and then carried through the above sequence (benzaldehyde. mp 124 °C from cyclohexane, nitrostyrene, yellow crystals from methanol, mp 95-96.5 °C, and lithium aluminum hydride reduction) to give 2,5-dimethoxy-4-(1,1-dimethylethyl)amphetamine hydrochloride (DOTB, mp 168 °C). Rats trained in a process called the Sidman Avoidance Schedule gave behavior that suggested that DOTB had no activity at all, and in human trials, doses of up to 25 milligrams were totally without effect.

An effort was made to prepare a butyl analogue containing a ring, but it was never completed. This was the cyclopropylmethyl isomer, 2,5-dimethoxy-4-cyclo-propylmethylamphetamine hydrochloride, DOCPM. Only the first step of its synthesis was complete (the reaction of cyclopropylcarboxylic acid chloride with p-dimethoxybenzene) and even it went badly. The desired ketone (2,5-dimethoxyphenyl cyclopropyl ketone) was most difficult to separate from the recovered starting ether. A promising approach would be the isolation of the phenol (2-hydroxy-5-methoxyphenyl cyclopropyl ketone) which is a beautiful yellow solid with a melting point of 99-100 °C from methanol. Anal. ($C_{11}H_{12}O_3$) C,H. It then could be methylated to the wanted intermediate. It is the major product when the reaction is conducted with anhydrous aluminum chloride in methylene chloride.

The 2-carbon phenethylamine homologues of these compounds could all, in principle be easily made by using nitromethane instead of nitroethane with the intermediary benzaldehydes. But, as of the present time, none of them have been made, so their pharmacology remains completely unknown.

#64   DOC;   2,5-DIMETHOXY-4-CHLOROAMPHETAMINE

SYNTHESIS: A solution of 6.96 g 2,5-dimethoxyamphetamine hydrochloride (2,5-DMA) in 250 mL H_2O was made basic with aqueous NaOH and extracted with 3x75 mL CH_2Cl_2. After removal of the solvent from the pooled extracts under vacuum, the residual free base was dissolved in 36 g glacial acetic acid and, with good stirring, cooled to 0 °C with an external ice bath. There was then added, with a Pasteur pipette, 3 mL of liquid chlorine. The generation of HCl was evident, and the reaction was allowed to stir for an additional 3 h. The mixture was then poured into 300 mL H_2O and washed with 3x100 mL Et_2O. The aqueous phase was made basic with NaOH and extracted with 3x150 mL CH_2Cl_2. After removal of the solvent from the pooled extracts, the residue was dissolved in Et_2O and saturated with anhydrous HCl gas. There was the formation of a heavy oily precipitate. The ether supernatent was decanted, and the residue was intimately mixed with 200 mL of fresh anhydrous Et_2O. Everything set up as an off-white crystalline mass weighing 2.3 g. This was dissolved in 12 mL of boiling MeOH and diluted with 230 mL boiling Et_2O. The clear solution was quickly filtered to give a clear, pale amber mother liquor, which soon started depositing lustrous white crystals. After filtering, Et_2O washing, and air drying to constant weight, there was obtained 1.4 g of 2,5-dimethoxy-4-chloroamphetamine hydrochloride (DOC) From the mother liquors (from the original HCl saturation) an equal amount of product could be obtained by exploiting the acetone insolubility of the hydrochloride salt of the product. The published mp of this salt, from acetone/EtOH, is 187-188 °C. A sample of this hydrochloride salt, prepared from the amino analogue via diazotization and eventual hydrolysis of an acetylated precursor, was recrystallized from EtOH/ether and had a mp of 193-194.5 °C.

DOSAGE: 1.5 - 3.0 mg.

DURATION: 12 - 24 h.

QUALITATIVE COMMENTS: (with 1.6 mg) "I was hit with a slightly light head; the effects were quite real. I was disconnected, and somehow spacey, but this was a favorable spacey which was kind of fun. Somewhere at about the sixth hour I realized that I was beginning to drop off a bit, but six hours later yet, there was still a lot of memory. This is a long thing."

(with 2.4 mg) "This is what I might call an archetypical psychedelic. Everything is there in spades, with few if any of the subtle graces, the 'gentle images' and 'gentle fantasies' of the 2-carbon phenethylamines. This is the works. There are visuals, and there are interpretive problems with knowing just where you really are. The place where nothing makes sense, and yet everything makes sense. I have just slept for a few hours, and now I am awake and it has been eighteen hours, and there is a lot still going on, although I have a relaxed, good feeling. Anyone who uses this had better have 24 hours at their disposal."

(with 2.4 mg) "Here I am at the sixth hour, and I am still roaring along at a full plus three. I have established that this material is neither anti-erotic nor anorexic. The body is very comfortable, and so is the mind. There is an interesting aspect, perhaps peculiar only to this experiment and under these conditions. With my eyes closed the fantasy is a completely dark screen, lovely and seductive, subtle, and yet light must be deliberately brought in. This is not in any way negative for being in the dark, but is just unusual. I will have to try this in the daylight next time, to see what the eyes-closed brings to the mind-screen. At 24 hours, I have found that my sleep was not too great. My dreams were tight, and I kept defending against trouble; the nervous system was too alert. I was in a good humor, though, and I still am. This is excellent stuff, but start early in the day."

EXTENSIONS AND COMMENTARY: It is clear that the three halo-amphetamine derivatives, DOI, DOB and DOC, are all pretty much of the same potency. And all of them very long lived. The difference between the various halogen atoms was brought up under the 2C-C discussion. DOC is clearly a long-lasting, dyed-in-the-wool psychedelic.

In the making of this, by the procedures that have been followed in Canada, there are two chemical intermediates which might, some day, be looked at as potential psychedelics under their own colors. Reduction of the compound that is called DON in this Book II (2,5-dimethoxy-4-nitroamphetamine hydrochloride) with Pd/charcoal and hydrogen, gives the 4-amino derivative. This is 2,5-dimethoxy-4-aminoamphetamine dihydrochloride, DOA, which melts at 248-250

°C. And the reduction of an oxime intermediate gives rise to the acetamido analogue, 2,5-dimethoxy-4-acetamidoamphetamine hydrochloride, DOAA, with a mp of 249-250 °C. Neither compound has been tasted, but someday this omission will be corrected. DOA and DOAA have a sinister ring to them, however, and some changes of terminology might be needed. DOA, in the coroner's vocabulary, means Dead-On-Arrival. But then, AMA (the American Medical Association) just happens to also mean (in the jargon of emergency medicine) Against-Medical-Advice. Everything averages out, somehow. Remember that the amyl homolog (amyl at the 4-position) follows the 4-letter convention of all of the DOM homologues, and has the code name of DOAM. Thus, DOA, amino; DOAA, acetamido, and DOAM, amyl.

One must learn to keep one's sense of humor. The immortal humorist Wavy Gravy once said, "If you can't laugh at life, it just isn't funny anymore." The code name of this compound, 2,5-dimethoxy-4-chloroamphetamine is, after, all, DOC. This should certainly appeal to some physicians.

#65   DOEF;   2,5-DIMETHOXY-4-(2-FLUOROETHYL)-AMPHETAMINE

SYNTHESIS: A well-stirred solution of 0.45 g free base DOB in 2 mL CH_2Cl_2 was treated with 0.37 g triethylamine, cooled to 0 °C, and there was then added a solution of 0.39 g 1,1,4,4-tetramethyl-1,4-dichlorodisilylethylene in 2 mL CH_2Cl_2 The reaction mixture was allowed to return to room temperature, with stirring continued for 2 h. The solvent was removed under vacuum, the residue suspended in hexane, and the insoluble by-products removed by filtration through celite. Removal of the solvent under vacuum gave 0.60 g 1-(4-bromo-2,5-dimethoxyphenyl)-2-(1-aza-2,5-disila-2,2,5,5-tetramethylcyclopentyl)propane as a gold-colored impure semi-solid mass which was used without further purification.

To a solution of 0.60 g 1-(4-bromo-2,5-dimethoxyphenyl)-2-(1-aza-2,5-disila-2,2,5,5-tetramethylcyclopentyl)propane in 10 mL anhydrous Et_2O under an inert atmosphere and cooled to -78 °C there was added 1.8 mL of a 1.7 M solution of t-butyl lithium in hexane. The resulting yellow solution was stirred for 20 min, and then treated with 1.65 mL of a 1.4 M solution of ethylene oxide in Et_2O, the stirring was continued for 40 min, then the reaction mixture allowed to come to room temperature over an additional 40 min. There was added 20 mL hexane, and the temperature increased to 50 °C for an additional 2 h. The reaction mixture was treated with 3 mL H_2O and diluted with 60 mL Et_2O. The organic phase was washed with saturated NH_4Cl, dried over anhydrous $MgSO_4$, and after filtering off the inorganic drying agent, the organic solvents were removed under vacuum. The gold-colored residual oil was dissolved in 10 mL MeOH and treated with a 10% KOH. This mixture was heated for 30 min on the steam bath, returned to room temperature, and the volatiles removed under vacuum. The residue was dissolved in 3% H_2SO_4, washed twice with CH_2Cl_2, brought to pH 12 with 25% NaOH, and extracted with 3x50 mL CH_2Cl_2. The pooled extracts were combined, dried with anhydrous Na_2SO_4, and the solvent removed under vacuum to give 0.24 g of 2,5-dimethoxy-4-(2-hydroxyethyl)amphetamine (DOEH) as a white solid with a mp of 102-104 °C.

To a suspension of 0.94 g DOEH in ice-cold anhydrous Et_2O containing 1.4 g triethylamine, there was added 2.4 g trifluoroacetic anhydride dropwise over the course of 10 min. The reaction mixture was brought to reflux temperature, and held there with stirring for 1 h. After cooling, 60 mL of CH_2Cl_2 was added, and the organic phase washed with saturated $NaHCO_3$. The solvent was removed under vacuum, providing a gold-colored solid as a residue. This was dissolved in 50 mL MeOH, diluted with 30 mL H_2O and, following the addition of 0.76 g solid $NaHCO_3$ the reaction mixture was stirred at room temperature for 3 h. The excess MeOH was removed under vacuum, and the remaining solids were suspended in CH_2Cl_2 and washed with H_2O. After drying the organic phase with anhydrous Na_2SO_4 and removal of the solvent under vacuum, there was obtained 1.34 g 1-(2,5-dimethoxy-4-(2-hydroxyethyl)phenyl)-2-(2,2,2-trifluoroacetamido)propane as white solid with a mp of 129-131 °C. Anal. ($C_{15}H_{20}F_3NO_4$) C,H.

A well-stirred solution of 0.09 g 1-(2,5-dimethoxy-4-(2-hydroxy-ethyl)phenyl)-2-(2,2,2-trifluoroacetamido)propane in 15 mL CH_2Cl_2 was cooled to -78 °C and treated with 0.05 g diethylaminosulfur trifluoride (DAST) added dropwise. The pale yellow reaction solution was stirred an additional 5 min and then brought up to room temperature and stirred for 1 h. There was then added (cautiously) 3 mL H_2O followed by additional CH_2Cl_2. The phases were separated, the organic phase washed with H_2O, dried with anhydrous Na_2SO_4 and, after filtering off the drying agent, stripped of solvent under vacuum. There was thus obtained 0.088 g of 1-[2,5-dimethoxy-4-(2-fluoroethyl)phenyl]-2-(2,2,2-trifluoroacetamido)propane as a white solid with a mp of 102-104 °C.

A solution of 0.12 g 1-[2,5-dimethoxy-4-(2-hydroxyethyl)phenyl]-2-(2,2,2-trifluoroacetamido)propane in a mixture of 5 mL CH_2Cl_2 and 5 mL IPA was treated with 0.2 mL 2 N KOH, heated on the steam bath for 30 min, and then stripped of solvents under vacuum. The residue was suspended in CH_2Cl_2 and washed with 20% NaOH. The organic phase was dried with anhydrous Na_2SO_4 which was removed by filtration, and the combined filtrate and washings stripped of solvent under vacuum. The residual glass (0.08 g) was dissolved in IPA, neutralized with concentrated HCl and diluted with anhydrous Et_2O to provide 2,5-dimethoxy-4-(2-fluoroethyl)amphetamine hydrochloride (DOEF) as a white crystalline solid with a mp of 205-208 °C. Anal. ($C_{13}H_{21}ClFNO_2$) C,H.

DOSAGE: 2 - 3.5 mg.

DURATION: 12 - 16 h.

QUALITATIVE COMMENTS: (with 2.2 mg) "Somewhere between the first and second hour, I grew into a world that was slightly unworldly. Why? That is hard to say, as there was no appreciable visual component. I just knew that the place I was in was not completely familiar, and it was not necessarily friendly. But it was fascinating, and the music around me was magical. Time was moving slowly. I had to drive across the bay at about ten hours into this, and I was comfortable. That evening I slept well, but my dreams were pointless."

(with 3.0 mg) "It took almost three hours to full activity. The first signs of effects were felt within a half hour, but from then on the progress was slow and easy, without any discernible jumps. There was absolutely no body discomfort at all. Completely comfortable. There was a general humorousness about my state of mind which is always a good sign. We went to the bedroom at the two and a half hour point, and proceeded to establish that the material is far from anti-erotic. Beautiful response, without a mention of any feeling of risk at orgasm. I myself was not able to reach orgasm until about 5th to 6th hour, and then it was full and exceptionally delicious. So was the second one, a couple of hours later, if I remember correctly. All systems intact, body, mind and emotion. Gentle. Good for writing. No dark corners apparent at all. For me, not highly visual. Would take again, higher."

(with 3.0 mg) "There was no body threat at any time — very comfortable. Good eyes closed, with complex imagery to music, but not too much with eyes-open. My attention span is relatively short, and easily diverted into new directions — all quite reminiscent of DOI both as to dosage and effect. At 13 hours, I am still too alert to sleep, but a couple of hours later, OK. In the morning there is still a trace of something going on. This was a valid +++."

EXTENSIONS AND COMMENTARY: I was asked by a student of mine a while ago, when I told him of this material, just why would anyone just happen to place a fluorine atom at the end of the 4-ethyl group of DOET? It wasn't the sort of thing that someone would just happen to do. If there were a rationale, then that's fine. But by capricious impulse, no. But there is a rationale of sorts, which I just hinted at in the discussion under 2C-T-21.

This argument of reason goes as follows. Assume that I would like to put a fluorine atom into a drug that does not normally have one. Why would I want to? Because I want to have the molecule carry a radioactive fluorine atom into some inner recess of the brain. Why? Because by using a positron-emitting fluorine I could possibly visualize the area of the brain that the drug went to. And if it went there in some abnormal way, the exact measure of that abnormality might give some clue as to potential brain misfunctioning.

But, if you put a fluorine atom on a drug, it becomes a totally new drug and, quite reasonably, a pharmacologically different drug. However, a body of evidence is being accumulated that if a halogen, such as a bromine or an iodine atom, is replaced by a beta-fluoroethyl group, the electronic and polar properties of the drug can be pretty much the same. So, what psychedelics have a bromo or an iodo group? Obviously, DOB and DOI. Thus, DOEF is a natural candidate for fluorine-18 positron emission tomography, and also a natural candidate for clinical trials. And, voila, it is an active material.

And I'll bet you dollars to doughnuts, that if one were to make the two-carbon analog 2,5-dimethoxy-4-(2-fluoroethyl)-phenethylamine, it would be every bit as much a treasure and ally as is 2C-B or 2C-I. In fact, I am sure enough about this prediction that I am willing to name the stuff 2C-EF. It will be easily made from 2C-B by the same reaction scheme that was used above for DOEF. And I will even guess that its activity level will be in the 20-30 milligram area.

#66   DOET;   HECATE;   2,5-DIMETHOXY-4-ETHYL-AMPHETAMINE

SYNTHESIS: To a solution of 19.7 g 2,5-dimethoxy-4-ethylbenzaldehyde (see the recipe for 2C-E for its preparation) in 72 g glacial acetic acid there was added 6.5 g anhydrous ammonium acetate and 10.2 g nitroethane. After heating for 1.75 h on the steam bath, the reaction mixture was cooled in a wet ice bath, diluted with 10 mL H_2O, and seeded with a small crystal of product. The yellow crystals were removed by filtration (7.6 g wet with acetic acid) and another 2.25 g was obtained from the mother liquors with additional H_2O. The combined fractions were recrystallized from 25 mL boiling MeOH, to give 6.5 g fine yellow crystals of 1-(2,5-dimethoxy-4-ethyl)-2-nitropropene, with a mp of 67.5-68.5 °C. Anal. $(C_{13}H_{17}NO_4)$ C,H,N.

A suspension of 6.5 g LAH in 500 mL well stirred anhydrous Et_2O was held at reflux under an inert atmosphere, with the return of the condensed solvent passing through a Soxhlet thimble containing 6.5 g 1-(2,5-dimethoxy-4-ethylphenyl)-2-nitropropene. After the addition of the nitrostyrene was complete, the stirred suspension was maintained at reflux for an additional 18 h, then cooled to room temperature. The excess hydride was destroyed with 500 mL 8% H_2SO_4, added cautiously until the hydrogen evolution ceased, then at a speed that allowed the formed solids to disperse. The phases were separated, the aqueous phase washed once with Et_2O, treated with 150 g potassium sodium tartrate, and finally made basic (pH >9) with 5% NaOH. This was extracted with 3x100 mL CH_2Cl_2, the extracts pooled, and the solvent removed under vacuum. The residue, 7.9 g of a clear oil, was dissolved in 100 mL anhydrous Et_2O and saturated with anhydrous HCl gas. After standing at room temperature for 2 h, the crystalline 2,5-dimethoxy-4-

ethylamphetamine hydrochloride (DOET) was removed by filtration, washed with Et_2O, and air dried to constant weight. There was obtained 5.9 g of lustrous white crystal with a mp of 190-191 °C. Recrystallization from CH_3CN or EtOAc increased the mp to 194-195 °C. Anal. $(C_{13}H_{22}ClNO_2)$ C,H,N.

DOSAGE: 2 - 6 mg.

DURATION: 14 - 20 h.

QUALITATIVE COMMENTS: (with 1.0 mg) "This was a very gentle, relaxing level, but there were no psychedelic effects that were apparent. Easy, and relaxed, and I am in no way intoxicated or turned on. But I was in the throes of my menstrual period, and the cramps (and the accompanying irritability) were completely knocked out. Perhaps this is why I felt so relaxed and at peace."

(with 2.5 mg) "There is much, too much, movement with my eyes closed. And an awful lot there with my eyes open. The movement on the concrete floor in the basement when I went downstairs for wood for the fireplace, was too much. I felt almost sea-sick. And I am having reality problems — I cannot seem to find my centering point of reference. There has to be a place to pin myself down to, and it is not findable anywhere I look. And my legs are twitching, and feeling as if they are falling asleep, and I had a crawling sensation on my body, so the body is not at peace either. In the morning I was still ++, but there is a clear indication that I am repairing. Anyway, I survived the experience. This is definitely not my thing."

(with 4 mg) "Just after an hour into the experiment, I was surprised by the awareness of some effects — I had forgotten that I had taken something. At the second hour, it was real, but subtle. As a psychotomimetic or STP-like thing, there is very little there. But as a mood energizer, it is really a ++ or more. The clinical literature is right — none of the hallucinogenic effects, but one brings into play whatever one wants to. Worked at cleaning up the office until 11 PM. I slept well. This has none of the LSD or STP seriousness."

(with 6 mg) "The onset was slow, and subtle. But the effects are fully there in about three or so hours. Everything I smelled was vivid, as are all the colors and shapes; they are clean, beautiful, serenely self-contained. No visual movement. The eyes-closed fantasy images tend to take off on their own, however, and they are extremely rich. I don't see any dark corners. I believe it might well be possible to be creative with this, and there is no suggestion of body depletion, of body load."

(with 7 mg) "A hot day. Unbelievably lovely erotic-to-divine, deep loving, open, not much visual, eyes-closed form-image-symbol. Sleep attempts very shallow, slight 'thinness', with an anticipation of darts. Intellect and feeling-emotion area intact and functioning at all times. Next morning still at a plus one. Incredible material. Perhaps best at 6 to 7 milligrams, no higher due to body load."

EXTENSIONS AND COMMENTARY: The original code for this compound was

DOE, which was completely logical based on DOM being the methyl member of this series (DO for the removal of the oxygen, desoxy, and M for putting a methyl in its place). And the putting of the ethyl thence should be DOE. This was fine until it was pointed out to me by a close colleague that DOE was a classic abbreviation for desoxyephedrine, a synonym for methamphetamine. The pressure to add the "T" of the "ET" of the ethyl was heightened by looking ahead to other members of the series. DOA became DOAM, DOE became DOET, but DOM was already too firmly set in popular usage. And, anyway, DOME really looked strange.

The original publications of the action of DOM clearly documented the compound as being a psychedelic and one with a sizeable measure of potential abuse. And, it is not a surprise that it was quickly shuffled into a legal classification that effectively precluded any further study of it. So, when this immediate homologue of DOM was studied and discussed in the literature, all reported dosages were those that were at the lowest levels, and no disturbing hints of abusability were mentioned. And this particular homologue has so far escaped the attention and restrictive action of the drug enforcement agencies, although the specific wording of the Controlled Substance Analogue Enforcement Act of 1986 might make this point moot, at least as far as human trials are concerned. At modest levels, DOET has the reputation of being a cognitive enhancer and is largely free of those sensory distortions that would catch the attention of the authorities who cannot tolerate drugs that distort the senses. The higher levels mentioned here have never been put into the published literature. It must be noted that there is a considerable variation of individual responses to this material and some people have had very negative experiences with as little as five milligrams. Some people are quite sensitive. Our Classic Lady HECATE can be quite capricious.

The young experimental subject who had the dramatic relief from menstrual cramps at the one milligram dose tried the compound again the following month, and again had complete relief. But another volunteer, also plagued with severe cramping at that particular time of month, found no relief at all. A 50% success rate. No one else has, to my knowledge, explored this particular property.

#67 DOI; 2,5-DIMETHOXY-4-IODOAMPHETAMINE

SYNTHESIS: A mixture of 14.8 g phthalic anhydride and 19.5 g of 2,5-dimethoxyamphetamine (2,5-DMA) as the free base was heated gradually to about 150 °C with an open flame. A single clear phase was formed with the loss of H_2O. After the hot melt remained quiet for a few moments, it was allowed to cool to about 50 °C and then diluted with 100 mL of hot MeOH. The solution was stirred until homogenous, seeded with product, and then cooled in an ice bath to complete the crystallization. After removal of the product by filtration, washing sparingly with MeOH, and air drying, there was obtained 24.6 g of N-(1-(2,5-dimethoxyphenyl)-

2-propyl)phthalimide as off-white crystals, with a mp of 105-106 °C. Anal. $(C_{19}H_{19}NO_4)$ C,H,N.

To a solution of 2.0 g N-(1-(2,5-dimethoxyphenyl)-2-propyl)phthalimide in 15 mL warm acetic acid which was being vigorously stirred, there was added a solution of 1.2 g iodine monochloride in 3 mL acetic acid. This was stirred for 2 h at about 40 °C during which time there was a definite lightening of color, but no solids formed. The reaction mixture was poured into 600 mL H_2O which produced a reddish glob floating in a yellow-orange opaque aqueous phase. The glob was physically removed, dissolved in 30 mL boiling MeOH which, on cooling in an ice bath, deposited off-white crystals. These were removed by filtration, washed with MeOH, and air dried to give 1.5 g of N-[1-(2,5-dimethoxy-4-iodophenyl)-2-propyl]phthalimide as fine white crystals with a slight purple cast. The mp was 103-105.5 °C and the mixed mp with the starting non-iodinated phthalimide (mp 105-106 °C) was depressed (85-98 °C). Extraction of the aqueous phase, after alkalinification, provided an additional 0.15 g product. Anal. $(C_{19}H_{18}NO_4)$ C,H,N.

A solution of 0.75 g N-(1-(2,5-dimethoxy-4-iodophenyl)-2-propyl)-phthalimide in 10 mL EtOH was treated with 0.3 mL of hydrazine hydrate, and the clear solution was held at reflux on the steam bath overnight. After cooling, there was a crystallization of 1,4-dihydroxyphthalizine that started as small beads but finally became extensive and quite curdy. These solids were removed by filtration and had a mp of about 340 °C (reference samples melted over a five to ten degree range in the area of 335-350 °C). The filtrate was dissolved in 100 mL CH_2Cl_2 and extracted with 2x150 mL 0.1 N HCl. The aqueous extracts were washed once with CH_2Cl_2, made basic with 5% NaOH, and extracted with 3x100 mL CH_2Cl_2. Removal of the solvent under vacuum gave 0.5 g of a colorless oil which was dissolved in 300 mL anhydrous Et_2O and saturated with anhydrous HCl gas. There was obtained, after filtration, and air drying, 0.35 g of 2,5-dimethoxy-4-iodoamphetamine hydrochloride (DOI) as white crystals that melted at 200.5-201.5 °C. This value did not improved with recrystallization. Anal. $(C_{11}H_{17}ClINO_2)$ C,H,N.

DOSAGE: 1.5 - 3.0 mg.

DURATION: 16 - 30 h.

QUALITATIVE COMMENTS: (with 0.6 mg) "There was a nice spacey light-headedness for a few hours, and time seemed to move quite slowly. Then a generic sadness came over me, as I reminisced about earlier days (recalling pleasures now gone) and wondered if I would be allowed to be here on the Farm when I am old and not important. There is so much to be done, and I cannot do it all, and no one else cares. My mood became present-day and healthy by about the seventh hour."

(with 1.6 mg) "The general nature of the experience was depressing, with a sad view of life. There was no way I could connect with my emotions. Even my sadness was vague. At about the ninth hour I decided that enough was enough, and this strangely disappointing about-plus-two was aborted with 125 micrograms of LSD. The emotions became present and living within a half hour. I was greatly relieved. The erotic was not a mechanical attempt but a deeply involved feeling with an archetype of orgasm easily available. It was shaped like a flower, richly colored, with an unusual "S" shape to it. This was a lovely end to a difficult day."

(with 3.0 mg) "This is a clear, clean psychedelic. The eyes-closed imagery is excellent, with clearly delineated patterns, pictures, and colors. Perfect for an artist, and next time I'll devote some time to painting. Total ease for the body, but no help for my smoking problem. I still want to smoke. And at sixteen hours into this I am still at 1.5+ but I'll try to go to bed anyway, and sleep."

(with 3.5 mg) "I was at a full crashing +++ for about three or four hours. There was none of the LSD sparkle, but there were moments of 'light-headedness' where one could move sideways with reality. I could leave where I was right over there, and come over here and get a strange but authentic view of where the 'there' was that I had left. It would be out-of-body, except that the body came over here with me rather than staying there. This doesn't make sense now, but it sure did then. There was no trace of body impact, and I slept late that evening, but with some guardedness due to the intense imagery. This was no more intense than with 3.0 milligrams, but it was a little bit more to the unreal side."

(with 1.0 mg of the "R" isomer) "There was a clear ++ from the second to the eighth hour, but somehow there was not quite the elegance or the push of the racemate. I was sensible, and managed to do several technical chores in a reasonable way. Easy sleep at 15 hours into it."

(with 2.3 mg of the "R" isomer) "The water solution of the hydrochloride salt has a slightly sweetish taste! I was at a +++ without question, but there was a slight down mood towards the end. And it lasted a really long time; I was distinctly aware of residual stuff going on, well into the next day."

(with 6.3 mg of the "S" isomer) "I was at a benign one-and-a-half plus at about two hours, and finally flattened out at a ++. Would I double this dose? Probably not, but half again (to 9 or 10 milligrams) would feel safe for a plus 3. By evening I was near enough baseline to drive into town for a social obligation, but even when trying to sleep later that night there was some residue of imagery; remarkably, it was all in slow motion. The fantasies were slow-paced and sluggish. It would have been interesting to have explored eyes-closed during the day."

EXTENSIONS AND COMMENTARY: Again, as with every other psychedelic amphetamine analogue which has a chiral center and has been explored as the individual optical isomers, it is the "R" isomer that is the more potent. And again, the other isomer, the "S" isomer, still shows some activity. The same was true with DOB, and DOM, and MDA. The only exception was MDMA, but then that is more of a stimulant, and there is virtually no psychedelic component to its action. Rat studies, where there is a measure of the discrimination of a test compound from saline, have shown the "R" isomer to have about twice the potency of the "S" isomer. That the "R" is more potent is certain, but the above reports would suggest that the factor would be closer to times-four rather than times-two.

A number of studies with DOI in animal models have shown it to have an extremely high binding capacity to what are called the 5-HT$_2$ receptors. Serotonin is a vital neurotransmitter in the brain, and is strongly implicated in the action of all of the phenethylamine psychedelics. The place where it acts, at the molecular level, is called its receptor site. As an outgrowth of the cooperative studies of the medicinal chemists working closely with the neuropharmacologists, a number of compounds have emerged that interact with these sites. But this one interacts with these sites and not those, and that one interacts with those sites and not these. So, there has developed a collection of sub-divisions and sub-subdivisions of receptor sites, all related to serotonin, but each defined by the particular compound that interacts most tightly with it.

Thus, there were serotonin "1" receptors, and then there were "1" and "2" receptors, and then "1a and "1b" and "2a" and "2b" receptors, and on and on. These are called 5-HT receptors, since the chemical name for serotonin is 5-hydroxytryptamine, and the scientist would never want to let the layman know just what he is talking about. DOI has been synthesized with a variety of radioactive iodine isotopes in it, and these tools have been of considerable value in mapping out its brain distribution. And by extrapolation, the possible localization of other psychedelic compounds that cannot be so easily labelled. A small neurochemical research company on the East Coast picked up on these properties of DOI, and offered it as a commercial item for research experiments. But I doubt that they are completely innocent of the fact that DOI is an extremely potent psychedelic and that it is still unrecognized by the Federal drug laws since, in their most recent catalog, the price had almost doubled and a note had been added to the effect that telephone orders cannot be accepted for this compound.

The four-carbon butylamine homologue (the ARIADNE analogue) of DOI has been synthesized. A mixture of the free base of 1-(2,5-dimethoxyphenyl)-2-aminobutane (see preparation under DOB) and phthalic anhydride was fused, cooled, and recrystallized from either methanol or cyclohexane to give crystals of N-[1-(2,5-dimethoxyphenyl)-2-butyl]phthalimide with a melting point of 76-77 °C and an analysis ($C_{20}H_{21}NO_4$) C,H,N. This was iodinated with iodine monochloride in acetic acid to give N-[1-(2,5-dimethoxy-4-iodophenyl)-2-butyl]phthalimide which was chromatographically distinct from the uniodinated starting material (silica gel, CH_2Cl_2), but which did not crystallize. This was treated with hydrazine hydrate in ethanol to provide 1-(2,5-dimethoxy-4-iodophenyl)-2-aminobutane hydrochloride which was crystallized from $CH_3CN/EtOH$ to give white crystals with a mp of 217-218.5 °C and an analysis ($C_{12}H_{19}CINO_2$) C,H,N. This butyl homolog of DOI has been assayed at up to four milligrams, and is without any central effects whatsoever. An experiment with 12.4 microcuries of ^{131}I labelled material with the whole body scanner showed most of it accumulating in the gut and liver, with almost none to the brain.

For those who find such statistics interesting, the parent compound DOI vies with DOB as probably the most potent of the phenethylamine psychedelics as of the moment, and certainly one of the most long lived.

A very important, centrally pivotal, and completely paradoxical compound in this area, is the N,N-dimethyl homologue of DOI, or 2,5-dimethoxy-N,N-dimethyl-4-iodoamphetamine (IDNNA). This compound was the starting point of the study of a large number of homologues and it deserves, and has received, a separate recipe.

#68   DOM;   STP;   2,5-DIMETHOXY-4-METHYLAMPHETAMINE

SYNTHESIS: To a solution of 54.9 g 2,5-dimethoxy-4-methylbenzaldehyde (see the recipe for 2C-D for its preparation) in 215 g glacial acetic acid there was added 19.5 g anhydrous ammonium acetate and 30.6 g nitroethane. This mixture was heated for 3 h on the steam bath, the reaction mixture was cooled in a wet ice bath, allowing the spontaneous formation of yellow crystals. As much H_2O as possible was added (just short of a persistant cloudy oily character) and after a few additional h standing, the crystalline 1-(2,5-dimethoxy-4-methylphenyl)-2-nitropropene was removed by filtration and recrystallized from boiling acetic acid. The yield, after drying to constant weight, was 28.3 g and the mp was 87-88 °C. Anal. ($C_{12}H_{15}NO_4$) C,H,N.

A suspension of 9.5 g LAH in 750 mL well stirred anhydrous Et_2O was held at reflux under an inert atmosphere, with the return of the condensed solvent passing through a Soxhlet thimble containing 9.5 g 1-(2,5-dimethoxy-4-methylphenyl)-2-nitropropene. After the addition of the nitrostyrene was complete, the stirred suspension was maintained at reflux for an additional 4 h, then cooled to room temperature and allowed to continue stirring overnight. The excess hydride was destroyed by the addition of 750 mL 8% H_2SO_4, cautiously, until the hydrogen evolution ceased, then at a speed that allowed the formed solids to disperse. The phases were separated, the aqueous phase washed once with Et_2O, treated with 225 g potassium sodium tartrate, and finally made basic (pH >9) with 5% NaOH. This was extracted with 3x150 mL CH_2Cl_2, the extracts pooled, and the solvent removed under vacuum. The residue was 9.6 g of a clear oil which spontaneously formed crystals with a mp of 60.5-61 °C from hexane. These solids were dissolved in 150 mL anhydrous Et_2O, and saturated with anhydrous HCl gas. After standing at room temperature for 2 h, the crystalline 2,5-dimethoxy-4-methylamphetamine hydrochloride (DOM) was removed by filtration, washed with Et$_2$O, and air dried to constant weight. There was obtained 8.25 g of glistening white crystals that had a mp of 190.5-191.5 °C. The sulfate had a mp of 131 °C. Anal. (C$_{12}$H$_{20}$ClNO$_2$) C,H,N. The above nitrostyrene may also be converted to the final amine product through the intermediary of the corresponding phenylacetone. To a well stirred suspension of 10.4 g powdered iron in 20 mL glacial acetic acid held at reflux temperature, there was added 4.9 g 1-(2,5-dimethoxy-4-methylphenyl)-2-nitropropene as a solid. Refluxing was continued for 2 h and then all was filtered through wet Celite. After washing with 300 mL H$_2$O followed by 300 mL Et$_2$O, the combined filtrate and washes were separated, and the aqueous phase extracted with 2x100 mL Et$_2$O. The organic phase and extracts were combined and washed with 2x100 mL saturated K$_2$CO$_3$ and the solvent was removed under vacuum yielding a reddish oil weighing 3.3 g. This was distilled at 111-115 °C at 0.5 mm/Hg to give a pale green solid. After recrystallization from benzene, there was obtained 2.8 g 1-(2,5-dimethoxy-4-methylphenyl)-2-propanone as white crystals with a mp of 57-59 °C. This ketone has also been described as a pale-yellow oil with a bp of 115-118 °C at 0.4 mm/Hg. A solution of 0.7 g 1-(2,5-dimethoxyphenyl-4-methyl)-2-propanone in 20 mL MeOH was treated with 6.0 g ammonium acetate, 0.3 g sodium cyanoborohydride, and 3 g Linde 3 A molecular sieves. The mixture was stirred overnight, the solids removed by filtration, and the filtrate dissolved in 100 mL H$_2$O. The solution was acidified with dilute H$_2$SO$_4$, and washed with 2x25 mL CH$_2$Cl$_2$. The aqueous phase was made basic with aqueous NaOH, and the product extracted with 2x25 mL CH$_2$Cl$_2$. The solvent was removed under vacuum, and the residue distilled (at 160 °C at 0.2 mm/Hg) to give colorless product which was dissolved in 3 mL IPA, neutralized with concentrated HCl, and diluted with 50 mL anhydrous Et$_2$O. There was obtained 0.18 g of 2,5-dimethoxy-4-methylamphetamine hydrochloride (DOM) as a white solid with a mp of 187-188 °C.

The optical isomers of DOM have been prepared in two ways. The racemic base has been resolved as the ortho-nitrotartranilic acid salt by recrystallization from EtOH. The (+) acid provides the (+) or "S" isomer of DOM preferentially. Also, the above-mentioned 1-(2,5-dimethoxy-4-methylphenyl)-2-propanone can be reductively aminated with optically active alpha-methyl benzylamine with Raney Nickel. This amine is isolated and purified by recrystallization of the hydrochloride salt. When optically pure, the benzyl group was removed by hydrogenolysis with palladium on carbon. The mp of either of the optical isomers, as the hydrochloride salts, was 204-205 °C.

DOSAGE: 3 - 10 mg.

DURATION: 14 - 20 h.

QUALITATIVE COMMENTS: (with 1.0 mg) "There is almost certainly an effect. Physically there is a slight dryness in the mouth, and my eyes are noticeably dilated.

There is an eerie feeling overall."

(with 2.3 mg) "Mood elevation at 2-3 hrs. After 3 hours, emotional effects become more pronounced, enhancement of color also. Very little distortion of perception, no disorientation, no creeping or flowing, but color enhancement considerable. The emotional content and empathy for others was closer to mescaline than to amphetamine, a welcome change. No suggestion of nausea at any time. Unable to sleep at ten hours, so I took 3/4 grain Seconal. Headache and listlessness next morning, probably due to the Seconal."

(with 3 mg) "In the middle of the experience I found that I was able to separate components of complex things so as to evaluate them separately. There is no need to respect their normal purpose. The sharpness of observation is enhanced, but one can focus at every different depth of a thing or a concept. Colors are not just brighter; there are more of them. There is a profoundness of meaning inherent in anything that moves. A line of thought or a bit of personal history ties the thinker to the objects that had been thought of, or once experienced. It is this relationship that will prove productive. Not like in a movie which is circular in its totalness, but as in true life where the future is the result of your own involvement with everything about you."

(with 4 mg) "The first four hours were largely directed to the body. There was a shuddering, and a tight jaw, and I am not particularly motivated to talk to anyone. It is more arousing (like amphetamine) than depressing (like phenobarb). I am feeling just a little sick at the three hour point, but a bit of regurgitation clears this up. Then at the fourth hour, it went totally outside of me. I saw the clouds towards the west. THE CLOUDS!!! No visual experience has ever been like this. The meaning of color has just changed completely, there are pulsations, and pastels are extremely pastel. And now the oranges are coming into play. It is a beautiful experience. Of all past joys, LSD, mescaline, cannabis, peyote, this ranks number one. Normally I have no color effects with mescaline. A dynamic experience. Feels good, too."

(with 5 mg) "There was the magnification of light, color and odors. It was all very pleasant and beautiful, except that I had an overwhelmingly negative feeling. This at times grew to considerable intensity, and I feel it was clearly due to anger. At times the negativity disappeared completely, and I broke into the most enjoyable, even hilarious experiences. I alternated about 50-50 between joy and discomfort. As the evening drew on, I became withdrawn and pensive. It seemed clear that I had made all the wrong decisions — choice of partner, place to live, isolation, no meaningful activity. The greatest shocker was that my practice of meditation, which is one of my central focuses, and which I thought had brought me much peace and understanding, seemed to be a delusional solution to my unhappiness and isolation. The experience continued unabated throughout the night with much tension and discomfort. I was unable to get any sleep. I hallucinated quite freely during the night, but could stop them at will. While I never felt threatened, I felt I knew what it was like to look across the brink to insanity."

(with 8 mg) "The very quiet development picks up speed betweeen the first and second hour. There is a rich curly-imaged eyes-closed show that interlocks closely with music. It is occasionally an off-beat fantasy and not directly knit together, and even occasionally unenjoyable. But always intense and completely appropriate to the music. There is a continuous thirst, and little urine. Napping seems OK at 16 hours, but real sleep must wait until the 20 hour point. Overall a rolling +++, and I am looking forward to a repeat some day."

(with 10 mg) "If on this page I shall have expressed it to you then it is true that DOM has the glory and the doom sealed up in it. All that's needed to unseal it is to surround it with a warm living human for a few hours. For that human for those hours all the dark things are made clear."

(with 12 mg) "The first awareness was at 30 minutes and it was in the tummy. The development was extremely rapid, something more like LSD than previously remembered. The body tremor feels like poisoning, there is no escaping the feeling of being disabilitated, but at least there is no nausea. This transition ended and the trauma cleared completely at about the second hour. The music was exceptional, the erotic was exceptional, the fantasy was exceptional. Listz's "A Christmas Cantata #1," part 1, with eyes closed was an experience without precedent. There were some residual effects still noted the next day. This may be a bit much for me."

(with 0.3 mg of the "R" isomer) "Maybe slightly wiry? No effects."

(with 0.5 mg of the "R" isomer) "There is a real effect, and it is significant that the first effects of the racemate were noted at 1.0 milligram. There is a trace of time slowing and in general a pretty full manic state. There is some mydriasis. Everything had pretty much cleared up by evening."

(with 2.0 mg of the"S" isomer) "No effects. There was an unexpected slight tachycardia at the two hour point, but nothing suggesting psychotropic action."

(with 2.6 mg of the "S" isomer) "There are signs of both pulse increase and blood pressure increase. There is some teeth-rubbiness, but still no psychological turn on at all."

EXTENSIONS AND COMMENTARY: The rationale for the design and making of DOM has already been discussed. One could predict that it could have been, theoretically, a totally inactive compound and maybe an effective blocker for whatever receptor sites are being occupied by other psychoactive drugs and even for strange things that some unbalanced people might actually make within their bodies, using their own personal chemistry. On the other hand, it could have been a potent psychedelic in its own rights, and if so, probably long lived. The latter "could have been" proved to be so.

The very modest amount of study of the individual optical isomers clearly indicates that the "R" isomer is the more active. The sparse comments suggest that some of the heavier physical aspects of the racemate might be due to contributions from the "inactive" "S" isomer. It is, after all, the "S" isomer of amphetamine that carries the major punch of that stimulant. Maybe if that isomer were removed, and one were to explore the pure "R" isomer of DOM, the dramatic visual aspects of the larger dosages might not be complicated with a troublesome physical component.

This compound, unbeknownst to me, was scattered widely and plentifully in the heyday of the Haight-Ashbury in San Francisco, in mid-1967. It was distributed under the name STP, which was said to stand for Serenity, Tranquility, and Peace. It was also claimed to represent Super Terrific Psychedelic, or Stop The Police. The police called it: Too Stupid to Puke. Actually, the name was taken from the initials of a motor additive which was completely unrelated chemically. Incredibly, and sadly, one of the avowed experts in the area of the "sensuous drugs" actually stated that STP, the motor oil additive, was really one and the same as STP, the highly dangerous psychedelic. The motor oil additive, he wrote in a book of his, had properties somewhat related to those of LSD, mescaline, and the amphetamines. How fortunate that the love children of the time didn't do much reading, for they might have gotten into yet deeper pharmacological troubles with drug raids on the local gasoline stations.

Two complications became apparent during this first appearance and they led to serious difficulties. One, there was no equation made between STP and DOM. No one knew what this drug was which had been distributed in a cavalier way throughout the city. There could be no educated guess as to the best treatment of overdose emergencies. And secondly, the initial tablets that had been distributed apparently contained 20 milligrams of DOM per tablet; later, it was dropped to 10 milligrams. Either of these, in retrospect, is now known to be a thoroughly whopping dose. The overdose situation was aggravated by the slow onset of DOM. The user may be aware of some initial effects at the half-hour point, there will be what might be called a + or ++ at the end of the first hour, and the full impact of the drug is not appreciated until some two hours have elapsed. But many of the recipients of the free handouts of DOM were familiar with LSD which can show its alert in 15 to 20 minutes, or even sooner with a large dose, and there is already a deep and compelling intoxication felt at the half-hour point. They, quite reasonably, expected this familiar activity pattern with STP and assumed, when there was little if any activity noted at the half-hour point, that the potency was less than expected. They took one or even two additional dosage units. Thus, some of the overdose victims of that period may well have taken as much as 30 mg of DOM. The slow onset of action, coupled with the remarkably long duration, caught many innocent users unprepared.

Clinical studies have documented the rapid tolerance development from repeated exposures to DOM. Five volunteers were given 6 milligrams daily for three days. Objectively, psychological tests showed a decrease in responses. Subjectively, all found extremely intense effects on the first day, and all but one found it unpleasant. By the third exposure on the third day, all had diminished responses, ranging from only "moderately strong" to "felt absolutely nothing." One actually slept during the experience on the third day.

The hexadeutero-analogue (deuterium atoms on the two methoxyl groups) has been prepared as an internal standard for analytical work, but there are no reports of its human pharmacology. A study with this sort of derivative would be a fine companion to the studies already underway with the mescaline analogues that are similarly substituted. A difference exists, however. With mescaline, it is believed that the loss of a methoxyl group is a step towards the inactivation of the compound, whereas with DOM this loss may be associated with the formation of an active metabolite. The several fascinating questions raised by possible differences in both the rates and the degree of demethylation of these two compounds are well worth trying to answer.

A number of compounds related to DOM had been synthesized and studied at the University of California at San Francisco, at about this time. Two of these were simply the juggling of the two methoxyl groups and the methyl group on the ring, still maintaining the 2,4,5-ness relative to the amphetamine chain. These are 2,4-dimethoxy-5-methylamphetamine and 4,5-dimethoxy-2-methylamphetamine. Since the slang name for DOM in and about the medical center was STP, and since STP was the name of a motor oil additive, it is not unreasonable that the first of these to be synthesized, the 2,4-dimethoxy-5-methyl isomer, was referred to by the name of another motor oil additive popular at that time, F-310. The Vilsmeier reaction between 2,4-dimethoxytoluene and the Vilsmeier complex of $POCl_3$ and N-methylformanilide gave the benzaldehyde (mp 117-118 °C) with a yellow malononitrile derivative from EtOH with a mp of 193-194 °C. The nitrostyrene from this and nitroethane formed yellow crystals from CH_3CN, with a mp 138-139 °C. The amine formed easily with LAH in ether, and the product F-310 (or 5-DOM) gave white crystals from CH_3CN with a mp of 182-183 °C.

And the other isomer, the 4,5-dimethoxy-2-methyl counterpart, became known familiarly as F-320, or sometimes simply 2-DOM. Its preparation followed an identical procedure, starting from 3,4-dimethoxytoluene. I have been told that F-310 is not active even at 20 milligrams in man, which would make it several times less potent than DOM (STP). I know of no trials with F-320. The use of the letter "F" does not imply any relationship between these two compounds and the series described elsewhere with the "F" code followed by other numbers, such as F-2 and F-22. These latter are F's because they are furans, not motor oil additives. And yet another oil additive, well known at the time as Z-7, became associated with the synthesis of the DOM (STP) isomer with its groups in the 2,4,6-positions. This is entered separately under ψ-DOM.

#69   Ψ-DOM;   Z-7;   2,6-DIMETHOXY-4-METHYLAMPHETAMINE

SYNTHESIS: To a solution of 2,6-dimethoxy-4-methylbenzaldehyde (mp 92-93 °C from the lithiation of 3,5-dimethoxytoluene followed by reaction with N-methylformanilide) in 10 mL nitroethane, there was added 0.1 g anhydrous ammonium acetate and the mixture was heated on the steam bath for 16 h. Removal of the solvent under vacuum gave a slightly oily red-orange crystalline mass which was finely ground under 1 mL of MeOH. Filtration and a sparing wash with MeOH gave, after air drying, 0.8 g of a light yellow crystalline solid with a mp of 121-122.5 °C. Recrystallization from 4 mL boiling absolute EtOH gave 0.6 g of 1-(2,6-dimethoxy-4-methylphenyl)-2-nitropropene as very light yellow platelets, which melted at 123-124 °C.

To a solution of 0.25 g LAH in 25 mL refluxing THF, well stirred and under He, there was added a solution of 0.3 g 1-(2,6-dimethoxy-4-methylphenyl)-2-nitropropene in 5 mL dry THF. Upon the completion of the addition, the reaction mixture was held at reflux for 48 h. After cooling with an external ice bath there was added, in sequence, 0.5 mL H_2O, 0.5 mL 15% NaOH, and finally 1.5 mL H_2O. The inorganic solids were removed by filtration, and the filter cake washed with THF. The solvent from the combined filtrate and washings was removed under vacuum, and the residue (0.3 g) was a crystal clear colorless oil with a high refractive index. This was dissolved in 2 mL IPA, neutralized with concentrated HCl, and diluted with 35 mL of anhydrous Et_2O. After a minute's standing, the solution became turbid, followed by the slow deposition of very fine white crystals. After standing 1 h at room temperature, these were removed by filtration, Et_2O washed, and air dried to constant weight. There was thus obtained 0.3 g 2,6-dimethoxy-4-methylamphetamine hydrochloride (ψ-DOM) with a mp of 203 °C. sharp.

DOSAGE: 15 - 25 mg.

DURATION: 6 - 8 h.

QUALITATIVE COMMENTS: (with 14 mg) "I am really quite spacey. I can go from a train of thought straight up into thin air. Then, to get to another one there must be a careful choice of words. Logic has nothing to do with any of it. There is no trace of the MDMA-like magic. This is an interpretive drug, not simply an ASC [*altered state of consciousness*] opening."

(with 18 mg) "There is a light-headedness, and a somewhat starry-eyed stoned state. Nothing visual, and no body concern except for what seems to be a very fine inner tremor. I think that with a little more, things might very well begin to move in the visual field. But I have no feeling of great concern about taking a somewhat higher dosage."

(with 25 mg) "I was at a +++ for about three hours, and it was a very weird place. There were some visuals, but they were not at all commensurate with the degree to which I was simply stoned. The erotic does not knit, and it's hard to get involved with music. It is as if you were going down some totally unknown street in a completely familiar city. You know the territory, but yet it is strangely all new. Eyes closed fantasy and shaped imagery was quite remarkable. But some heart arrhythmias and a pretty constant diarrhea made the experience less than totally ideal. My sleep was good and with good dreams."

EXTENSIONS AND COMMENTARY: I can't remember the exact names of the companies that went with the oil additives. STP was, I believe, it's own thing, and originally stood for Scientifically Treated Petroleum. And F-310 was, I believe, a Chevron Oil product. F-320 was, of course, the product of the wild and happy chemists at the Pharmaceutical Chemistry Department at the University of California in San Francisco, playing with what they fondly called "funny drugs." And when the 2,4,6-orientation became an obvious positional isomer, the Pennzoil Oil Company's additive, Z-7, was a natural to have its name volunteered to the cause. There was one additional isomer possible, with the methyl in the 2-position and the methoxyl groups at the 4- and 6-positions. This followed the more conventional aldehyde made from 3,5-dimethoxytoluene via the Vilsmeier process, with $POCl_3$ and N-methylformanilide. This material (2,4-dimethoxy-6-methylbenzaldehyde with mp 64-65 °C from cyclohexane or from MeOH) is completely distinct from the isomer used above (2,6-dimethoxy-4-methylbenzaldehyde with a mp of 92-93 °C from MeOH). The amphetamine from this isomer is 2,4-dimethoxy-6-methylamphetamine, and had been christened by the chemistry crowd as Z-7.1.

Much effort had been put forth in research by this medical school group of graduate students and graduate advisors, to try to explain the biological activity of the 2,4,5-things such as TMA-2 and DOM (STP). And a considerable investment had been made in the attempt to tie together the amphetamine world of psychedelics with the indole world of psychedelics. The convenience of having two methoxy groups para to one another was a clear invitation to speculate upon the formation of a benzoquinone intermediate of some kind, and this would require the loss of the methyl groups which were already known to be metabolically labile. This "quinone-like" intermediate was the cornerstone of a "hydroquinone hypothesis," as it allowed further condensation within the molecule itself involving the primary amine group, to form something called an indolene which, with some arcane electron pushing and removal, could eventually become an indole. There. We now have a tie-in to the tryptamine world, and to serotonin, and that entire neurotransmitter magic.

There was only one small fly in the ointment. No matter how the 2,4,5-things were explained, none of the proposed mechanisms could allow for the 2,4,6-things to also be active.

How can one accommodate such blasphemy? The first and obvious approach was the simplest. Denial. The 2,4,6-things aren't really active at all. Placebo stuff. There is a commonly used phrase, "bad science" which is an infamous term used to belittle findings that do not fit with one's theories or purposes. But that simply didn't wash, because I knew, as did a few others who chose not to identify themselves too publicly, that TMA-2 and TMA-6 were both fully active in the 40 to 50 milligram area. And although not as potent as DOM, the compound of this recipe, ψ-DOM or Z-7, was certainly an active one. So, since approach number one didn't work, try approach number two. Make the shoe fit the wearer, without respect to the size of his foot. One single size shoe fits all. One single mechanistic hypothesis explains all. It was obvious that for the "hydroquinone" hypothesis to survive, Z-7 would have to undergo some metabolic oxidation — phenol formation — in the 3-position.

And guess who was actually euchred into embarking onto the synthesis of this hypothetical metabolic Lucy [that's the anthropological-type, not the LSD-type Lucy]? Moi! On to a new methoxylated amphetamine which would be called Z-7.2. Oxidation of the above 2,4-dimethoxy-6-methylbenzaldehyde with meta-chloroperoxybenzoic acid gave 2,4-dimethoxy-6-methylphenol which smoothly methylated (KOH, CH_3I) to give 2,3,5-trimethoxytoluene as a white oil, bp 59-62 °C at 0.1 mm/Hg. This formed the anion between the meta-methoxy groups with butyllithium, and N-methylformanilide gave the new compound 2,3,6-trimethoxy-4-methylbenzaldehyde, also an oil (bp 130-140 °C at 0.7 mm/Hg) with an excellent NMR spectrum. This formed the 3-carbon nitrostyrene with nitroethane, as bright yellow crystals from methanol with a mp 67-68.5 °C (and excellent NMR and microanalysis, C,H,N). Lithium aluminum hydride reduction gave rise to what I was assuming would be the target amphetamine, 4-methyl-2,3,6-trimethoxy-amphetamine or Z-7.2. This formed a hydrochloride salt which, although analytically excellent, insisted in remaining as an ether and chloroform-soluble oil which had an excellent NMR spectrum. This was certainly MY target compound, but it was not THEIR target compound. The upper echelons who were running the show were serious about this hydroquinone thing. Therefore, this product Z-7.2, that should have been entered into human evaluation, was instead processed further by the substitution of a t-BOC on the amine group, oxidation to the quinone with ceric ammonium nitrate, reduction to the hydroquinone with dithionite, and finally deprotection of the blocking t-BOC group by hydrochloric acid. The final product, 2,5-dihydroxy-6-methoxy-4-methylamphetamine hydrochloride, was an extremely light-sensitive solid which was looked at by NMR (excellent spectrum in D_2O) and by cyclic voltimetry (destructive and uninformative) but which would have been totally worthless to have tasted.

In fact, the whole 2,4,6 substitution concept is just now beginning to explode. Fully half of the drugs described in this Book II are of the classical 2,4,5-trisubstitution pattern, and it is becoming evident that every one of them will have a 2,4,6-trisubstituted counterpart that bids fair to be an active psychedelic. Diligence could thus easily double the number of known psychedelics. The nickname "pseudo" is really the Greek letter "psi" which looks like a candelabrum standing on the table holding up three candles. If I can find the type in some font, I will simply precede each known drug with this letter, to indicate that the 2,4,5-ness has become a 2,4,6-ness. Therefore, Z-7 is also pseudo-DOM.

Z-7.2 might have been an interesting compound to taste. But the academic climate was not appropriate at that time (early 1977) for such honesty. The "hydroquinone hypothesis" is now not much more than a minor bit of history. And anyhow, it was just about this time that I had uncovered a slick way of getting a sulfur atom into the amphetamine molecule. I quickly lost interest in the pursuit of other people's hypotheses that didn't seem to lead anywhere. Maybe, someday, some single earth-shaking mechanism will emerge to explain everything. But in the meantime, the best contribution I can make to this "grand unified theory of psychedelic activity" is to continue to make new and unexpected things which, if they are active, will effectively destroy any hypothesis that just happens to be popular at the moment. It is a lot more exciting, too.

#70   DON;   2,5-DIMETHOXY-4-NITROAMPHETAMINE

SYNTHESIS: A solution of 8.4 g 2,5-dimethoxyamphetamine base in 40 mL acetic acid was added dropwise over the course of 0.5 h to 43 mL of 50% nitric acid which was well stirred and cooled with an external ice bath. The resulting solution was quenched with ice water, made basic with aqueous NaOH, and extracted with a benzene-ether mixture. The residue that remained after the removal of the solvent was dissolved in dilute HCl which, upon evaporation of the H_2O, yielded a nearly colorless residue. Recrystallization from an ethanol/ether mixture gave, after drying, 10.5 g of 2,5-dimethoxy-4-nitroamphetamine hydrochloride (DON) with a mp of 206-207 °C. The acetamide derivative melted at 166-168 °C. The formamide derivative was easily hydrolyzed with 3N HCl. And the R-isomer of DON hydrochloride had a mp of 231-232 °C.

DOSAGE: 3.0 - 4.5 mg.

DURATION: 8 - 15 h.

QUALITATIVE COMMENTS: (with 3.0 mg) "There was an amphetamine-like stimulation that was apparent an hour into it, and considerable anxiety. I had stomach cramps, but there were indications that there might be something hallucinogenic at a higher dose."

(with 4.5 mg) "An enhancement of color perception, and some auditory distortion, that was still noticeable some eight hours into the experience. The visual changes were intense. I felt I was running a slight fever, and was restless, but there was almost no physical malaise. I was still somewhat wound up even at the 14th hour."

EXTENSIONS AND COMMENTARY: These qualitative comments are not true quotations, but have been reconstructed from the published summaries of the human trials reported by several South American researchers. I have personally never tasted DON and have only these fragments from which to create a portrait of activity. A brief quotation, from a note published by these researchers in a bulletin that is restricted to forensic scientists serving law enforcement agencies, is certainly subject to a number of interpretations. It reads as follows: "This action [a strong stimulant action reminiscent of amphetamine] seems to reduce the incidence of insightful, and therefore potentially unpleasant experiences, and thus [DON seems likely] to appear on the market as an illicit recreational drug." I must admit that I have tried, and I am still not able, to interpret this quotation.

#71 DOPR; 2,5-DIMETHOXY-4-(n)-PROPYLAMPHETAMINE

SYNTHESIS: A suspension of 285 g mossy zinc in 285 mL H_2O containing 5.7 g mercuric chloride was treated with 285 mL concentrated HCl and shaken as needed to effect amalgamation. The H_2O was then drained off, the zinc washed with fresh water and drained again. There was added a solution of 74 g 2,5-dimethoxypropiophenone (from the reaction of propionic acid and p-dimethoxybenzene in the presence of polyphosphoric acid, see under DOAM for an effective general procedure) in 140 g EtOH. The reaction mixture was held at reflux for 24 h with the periodic addition of concentrated HCl. It was then cooled, diluted with H_2O and CH_2Cl_2, and the organic phase separated. The aqueous phase was extracted with 2x100 mL additional CH_2Cl_2. The combined organic phases were washed with 5% NaOH until the washes remained basic, once with H_2O, and then the solvent was removed under vacuum. The residue was distilled at the water pump, giving an early fraction quite rich in starting p-dimethoxybenzene, and a second fraction (61 g, bp 140-160 °C) which was free of carbonyl group by infra-red, and which was largely 2,5-dimethoxypropylbenzene. It was used without further purification in the following aldehyde synthetic step.

A mixture of 124 g N-methylformanilide and 140 g $POCl_3$ was allowed to stand until there was the development of a strong red color. There was then added 60 g of the above 2,5-dimethoxypropylbenzene and the mixture was held on the steam bath for 2 h. The mixture was added to 2 L H_2O and stirred until the excess acid chloride had completely decomposed. The mixture was extracted with 3x100 mL CH_2Cl_2 and, after the removal of the solvent from the combined extracts, the residue was extracted with 3x100 mL boiling hexane. Removal of the solvent gave the product 2,5-dimethoxy-4-propylbenzaldehyde as an oil, 23 g, which was characterized as its malononitrile derivative. Equal weights of the product and malononitrile in EtOH with a catalytic amount of triethylamine gave yellow crystals which, on recrystallization from toluene, had a mp of 113-114 °C.

A solution of 21.5 g of the above crude 2,5-dimethoxy-4-propylbenz-aldehyde in 75 g acetic acid, was treated with 10.4 g nitroethane and 6.6 g anhydrous ammonium acetate. This was heated on the steam bath for 1.75 h, then cooled and diluted with H_2O to the point of turbidity. With long standing and scratching, there finally was the deposition of crystals which were removed by filtration and sucked as dry as possible. This 23 g of crude product cake was triturated under MeOH, filtered again, and air dried to give 11 g of dull orange crystals. Recrystallization from boiling MeOH gave 1-(2,5-dimethoxy-4-(n)-propylphenyl)-2-nitropropene as fine orange crystals which weighed, after filtering, washing, and drying, 7.4 g, and which had a mp of 94-96 °C.

To a suspension of 6.0 g LAH in 500 mL anhydrous Et_2O, which was being stirred and also held at a gentle reflux, there was added a saturated solution of the above (2,5-dimethoxy-4-(n)-propylphenyl)-2-nitropropene in warm THF. The reaction mixture was held at reflux for 24 h, then cooled to room temperature. The excess hydride was destroyed by the cautious addition of 500 mL dilute H_2SO_4. The phases were separated, and the aqueous phase washed with additional Et_2O. There was then added 150 g potassium sodium tartrate, and the pH was brought to >9 with aqueous NaOH. The product was extracted with Et_2O and, after removal of the solvent, the residue was dissolved in 200 mL anhydrous Et_2O and saturated with anhydrous HCl gas. The solids that formed were removed by filtration, giving 6.15 g 2,5-dimethoxy-4-(n)-propylamphetamine hydrochloride (DOPR) as an electrostatic, white crystalline powder, with a mp of 182.5-183 °C. This was not improved by recrystallization from either IPA or CH_3CN.

DOSAGE: 2.5 - 5.0 mg.

DURATION: 20 - 30 h.

QUALITATIVE COMMENTS: (with 2.0 mg) "The onset is slower than any other thing I can think of. There was nothing at all at the end of an hour, and only a threshold a half hour later. By the middle of the third hour, I was up to 1+, and that seemed to be about as high as it intended to take me. Attempts to sleep at the ninth hour were not successful, as there were strange patterns of not-quite logical thinking going on. Stuff like: 'The block events (like a baby's rectangular building blocks) that were gotten, along with other things, from the full octaves of the left hand in

Listz's Hungarian Rhapsody, events that allowed an easy recognition of the odds of achieving successful re-entry from any of several erotic codes.' Clearly this was not a baseline state. After six hours of successful sleep, I was still off-baseline , and on into the following day. Go on up with curiosity but with caution."

(with 3.6 mg) "Imagery that was constructed in response to the music turned out to be necessary to organize and contain it. The trio is the nucleus that transforms the written to the heard, but it has created its own bubble without connections to the real world, and must play on and on and on to keep itself afloat and never touching the stage again."

(with 5.0 mg) "I am now at midnight, and still strongly +++. This is certainly maximum dosage, at least for a long time. There are faint intimations of nervous system scrungies. You know, the kind of thing that makes you figure it's going to be a while before you'll try to relax into sleep. This material, like all the other DO's, is a heavy duty psychedelic, the kind that says to you, 'Forget all that stuff about screening out visuals,' and then proceeds to prove it. Sort of indole-like in that way. Your body as well as your mind tells you you're into it, baby, and better relax and enjoy the trip, because you've left the shore way behind. When it was time for bed, I got to sleep with surprising ease, and slept for only about six hours. My dreams were excellent, balancing, and good humored. But the next day I realized I was still carrying the DOPR in me, and that baseline was definitely not there. But it was OK. No problems except for sleepiness. The next evening I went to bed at unheard-of hour of 9 PM and slept for 13 hours, give or take. Fascinating compound, but I won't go out of my way to take it again soon."

EXTENSIONS AND COMMENTARY: There is a thread of disconnection and of inconsistent reference that pervades most of the reports that I have received concerning the use of DOPR. The word that comes to mind is hypnogogic. There is a drifting into that place that lies between a not-quite-awake and a not-quite-asleep state seems to characterize this compound. There is no question but that it is very potent, and that it is very long-lived. But there is a nagging suggestion of the out-of-body, out-of-center character that is the hallmark of the anesthetic and delusional drugs such as scopolamine or ketamine. With them, the psychedelic effects become clouded with touches of amnesia. If DOPR shows this with it's three carbon alkyl group, there is every reason to pay close attention as the chain becomes longer.

There had been quite a bit of speculation in the literature that the metabolic attack on DOM was at the 4-position, and this was an oxidation process. In a moment of inspiration, I decided to explore a similar oxidation step in DOPR, since it is probably the most potent of the DO-series. Why not make the compound which would be the first step in this oxidation, the 1-hydroxypropyl analogue? This I did, by using the phthalimide derivative of 2,5-dimethoxyamphetamine (described in the synthesis of DOI) and making the propiophenone using propionic acid as both reagent and solvent, and polyphosphoric acid as the condensing agent. The ketone product (a white crystalline solid from methanol) was dissolved in warm methanol and reduced to the alcohol with sodium borohydride. This product, also a white crystalline solid, was stripped of the phthalimide blocking group with overnight refluxing with hydrazine in ethanol. The product, 2,5-dimethoxy-4-(1-hydroxy-propyl)-amphetamine (hydroxy-DOPR) had a mp of 148-150 °C from IPA. Its activity is not yet known, but there were no effects at all at trials, orally, of up to 200 micrograms.

But this is all with the normal-propyl compound. There is a rich collection of misinformation and potential discovery that is associated with the isopropyl isomer. This structural isomer, 2,5-dimethoxyl-4-(i)-propylamphetamine is properly called DOIP for des-oxy-iso-propyl. It has been synthesized and explored in animals and, to a modest extent, in man. The synthesis has proceeded from 2,5-dimethoxyacetophenone by the addition of a methyl group to the carbonyl followed by reduction to the hydrocarbon. Aldehyde formation, nitropropene synthesis with nitroethane, and lithium aluminum hydride reduction are uneventful, providing the hydrochloride salt DOIP, which has a mp of 183-184 °C as an analytical sample. Animal tests (such as rabbit hyperthermia assays), have indicated that the isopropyl compound DOIP is less potent than the propyl prototype, DOPR, by between one and two orders of magnitude. In man, a dose of four milligrams, a rousing dose of DOPR, is without any effects. At 10 milligrams, there is some disturbance but substantially no effects. I have been told that with doses in the 20 to 30 milligram range there are valid changes in mental state, but I have not been told the nature of these changes.

A fascinating red herring had been drawn across all of these exacting lines by a strange visitor to this research project. An olive-faced M.D., Ph.D., passed through this confusing scene briefly, and when he left, a small supply of DOPR left with him. He promptly published in an obscure journal some animal behavioral responses which he ascribed to the isopropyl analogue, DOIP. But what he had studied could only have been DOPR since DOIP, at that time, had not yet been synthesized either by me, or by either of the other two active synthesists of that moment. It was not yet a known material. We all made it some time later, but by that time our olive-face had disappeared. There is a magnificent French phrase that applies here as nowhere else; *Il a foutu le camp*. Its idiomatic meaning is equivalent to our, "He took off," or "He split the scene," but the literal translation is, "He fucked the camp."

#72 E; ESCALINE; 3,5-DIMETHOXY-4-ETHOXYPHENETHYLAMINE

SYNTHESIS: To a solution of 72.3 g 2,6-dimethoxyphenol in 400 mL MeOH, there was added 53.3 g of a 40% solution of aqueous dimethylamine folowed by 40 g of a 40% aqueous solution of formaldehyde. The dark solution was heated under reflux for 1.5 h on a steambath. The volatiles were then removed under vacuum yielding a dark oily residue of 2,6-dimethoxy-4-dimethylaminomethylphenol. This residue was dissolved in 400 mL of IPA, to which there was added 50 mL of methyl iodide. The spontaneously exothermic reaction deposited crystals within 3 min, and was allowed to return to room temperature and occasionally stirred over the course of 4 h. The solids were removed by filtration, washed with cold IPA, and allowed to air dry yielding 160 g of the methiodide of 2,6-dimethoxy-4-dimethylamino-methylphenol as a cream-colored crystalline solid.

A suspension of 155 g of the above methiodide of 2,6-dimethoxy-4-dimethylaminophenol in 600 mL H_2O was treated with a solution of 130 g KCN in 300 mL H_2O. The reaction mixture was heated on a steam bath for 6 h during which time there was a complete dissolving, the development of a brownish color with a bright blue film on the surface and the walls of the flask, and the gentle evolution of fine gas bubbles. The hot reaction mixture was poured into 1.2 L H_2O and acidified with concentrated HCl (careful, HCN evolution). The aqueous solution was extracted with 3x150 mL CH_2Cl_2, the extracts pooled, washed with saturated $NaHCO_3$ which removed much of the color. The solvent was removed under vacuum yielding about 70 g of a viscous black oil. This was distilled at 0.4 mm/Hg at 150-160 °C to provide 52.4 g of homosyringonitrile (3,5-dimethoxy-4-hydroxyphenylacetonitrile) as a white oil that spontaneously crystallized to lustrous white crystals that melted at 57-58 °C.

A solution of 5.75 g of homosyringonitrile and 12.1 g ethyl iodide in 50 mL dry acetone was treated with 6.9 g finely powdered anhydrous K_2CO_3 and held at reflux for 18 h. The mixture was diluted with 100 mL Et_2O, filtered, and the filtrate solvent removed under vacuum The residue was recrystallized from Et_2O/hexane to yield 5.7 g 3,5-dimethoxy-4-ethoxyphenylacetonitrile with a mp 57-58 °C. Anal. ($C_{12}H_{15}NO_3$) C,H,N.

A solution of 2.21 g 3,5-dimethoxy-4-ethoxyphenylacetonitrile in 25 mL EtOH containing 2.5 mL concentrated HCl and 400 mg 10% palladium on charcoal, was shaken in a 50 lb/sq.in. atmosphere of hydrogen for 24 h. Celite was added to the reaction suspension and, following filtration, the solvents were removed under vacuum. The residue was recrystallized from IPA/Et_2O to yield 2.14 g 3,5-dimethoxy-4-ethoxyphenethylamine hydrochloride (E) with a mp of 166-167 °C.

Synthesis from syringaldehyde: A well-stirred suspension of 21.9 g syringaldehyde in 45 mL H_2O was heated to reflux in a heating mantle. There was then added a solution of 15 g NaOH in 60 mL H_2O. The heating and stirring was continued until the generated solids redissolved. Over a period of 10 min, there was added 23 g diethyl sulfate, then refluxing was continued for 1 h. Four additional portions each of 5 g diethyl sulfate and of 6 mL 20% NaOH were alternately added to the boiling solution over the course of 2 h. The cooled reaction mixture was extracted with Et_2O, the extracts pooled and dried over anhydrous $MgSO_4$, decolorized with Norite, and stripped of solvent. The crude 3,5-dimethoxy-4-ethoxy-benzaldehyde weighed 21.8 g and melted at 51-52 °C.

A solution of 14.7 g 3,5-dimethoxy-4-ethoxybenzaldehyde and 7.2 mL nitromethane in 50 mL glacial acetic acid was treated with 4.4 g anhydrous ammonium acetate and held at reflux for 30 min. Cooling the reaction allowed the formation of yellow crystals which were removed by filtration and washed sparingly with cold acetic acid. The dried 3,5-dimethoxy-4-ethoxy-ß-nitrostyrene weighed 11.5 g and melted at 108-109 °C after recrystallization from EtOH Anal. $(C_{12}H_{15}NO_5)$ C,H. Alternately, this product may be prepared from 3.9 g. 3,5-dimethoxy-4-ethoxybenzaldehyde in 60 mL nitromethane containing 0.7 g ammonium acetate and heated on a steam bath for 1 h. The solvent was removed under vacuum, and the residue dissolved in a minimum of hot MeOH. Cooling provided, after filtration and air drying, 2.3 g of bright yellow crystals of 3,5-dimethoxy-4-ethoxy-ß-nitrostyrene, with a mp of 105-107 °C.

A solution of 2.25 g LAH in 45 mL anhydrous THF was vigorously stirred and cooled to 0 °C under He. There was added 1.5 mL 100% H_2SO_4 dropwise, followed by 2.3 g 3,5-dimethoxy-4-ethoxy-ß-nitrostyrene in anhydrous THF. After the addition was complete, the mixture was allowed to stir for 30 min, and then brought to room temperature. The unreacted hydride was decomposed with 2.3 mL H_2O in THF, followed by the addition of 9.2 mL of 15% NaOH. The white suspension was filtered, the filter cake was washed with THF, the filtrate and washings combined, and the solvent removed under vacuum. The residue was dissolved in 300 mL dilute H_2SO_4, washed with 2x75 mL CH_2Cl_2, made basic with 25% NaOH, and the product extracted with 3x75 mL CH_2Cl_2. After removal of the solvent, the residue was distilled at 110-120 °C at 0.3 mm/Hg yielding 1.4 g of a colorless oil. A solution of this oil in 20 mL IPA was neutralized with 17 drops of concentrated HCl and diluted with 100 mL anhydrous Et_2O. After a few minutes there was the spontaneous formation of white crystals of 3,5-dimethoxy-4-ethoxyphenethylamine hydrochloride (E) which was recrystallized from 40 mL boiling EtOAc containing 1 mL MeOH. The mp was 165-166 °C.

DOSAGE: 40 - 60 mg.

DURATION: 8 - 12 h.

QUALITATIVE COMMENTS: (with 40 mg) "This is a powerful and complex intoxicant — I could not have coordinated any rational muscular activity. I could not walk; I could not tie my shoe-laces. There is analgesia and an incoordination that I cannot shake. My menstrual flow started a bit ahead of time, but it was light."

(with 50 mg) "I felt that the body tensions outweighed the psychological and sensory rewards, in that I had a lot of dehydration and my sleep had a nightmare quality. This pretty much offset the few virtues that I felt I had obtained."

(with 60 mg) "There is a quality of rational analysis and insight that is totally impressive. Many subtle factors in my life can be viewed with insight, and usefully dissected. I got into a deep discussion, but I was not argumentative or even defensive and I remained detached and kept a tone of cool impersonality. I had a good appetite. But I also had some tachycardia and muscular tension. There was unquestionable sensory enhancement, but without an intellectual component. Overall it was most pleasant."

EXTENSIONS AND COMMENTARY: In an isolated situation, there is easy fantasy, but little synthesis of external sensory inputs such as music or visual stimulae. A gradual decline brings the subject back to a restful baseline somewhere before the 12th hour. The following day is often seen as one of tiredness and low energy. An anonymous flyer appeared in the California drug community in 1984 stating an effective range to be 50 to 100 milligrams, but it described the drug as the sulfate. The above data all pertain to the hydrochloride salt.

The replacement of that one methyl group with an ethyl group leads to a nice *jeu de mots*. The play on words depends on a remarkable coincidence. The name of the alkaloid mescaline stems from an ancient Nahuatl word for a drink (Mexcalli) which also provided the source of the term Mescal (an Agave of entirely different pharmacology). The prefix for the simplest, the one carbon organic radical, is methyl. This is from the Greek word "methy" and represents wine from wood. Such is, indeed, methyl alcohol, or methanol, or wood alcohol, the simplest one-carbon drink and a rather dangerous one for the human animal. And this is the group that is on the central oxygen of mescaline.

It is customary to refer to homologs (bigger-by-one) of methanol by their classical chemical names, so the natural extension of methyl is ethyl, and that of mescaline would be escaline. One carbon-chain on the 4-position oxygen becoming a two-carbon chain. This is all entymologically appealing, but there is no botanical support for any of it. The ethyl group is much more rare in nature. It is just a happy coincidence that mescaline (the plant), and methyl (the alkyl group involved), and methoxy (the group on the 4-position of the aromatic ring) all happen to start with the letter "M".

Very few of the homomescaline phenethylamines have been synthesized as their three-carbon chain counterparts, the corresponding analogues of amphetamine. And only three of them have been explored in man (four, if you count the amphetamine analogue of mescaline itself, TMA). The obvious names for these compounds have, unfortunately, already been used. It would be logical to use the letter M for a methoxy, and the letter E for ethoxy, etc. and simply read the groups from around the ring. But this is the naming system for the 2,4,5-trisubstituted amphetamines. MEM is, for example, 2,5-dimethoxy-4-ethoxyamphetamine (in sequence, methoxy, ethoxy, methoxy reading around the ring, and a fascinating compound talked about at length in this book), so this term cannot represent 3,5-dimethoxy-4-ethoxyamphetamine.

A truly simple code employs the length of the carbon chain. The phenethylamine chain is two carbons long, and the amphetamine chain is three carbons long.

If a drug has been initially developed (and initially named) as an amphetamine derivative (three carbon chain) then the two-carbon chain analogue will use the original name (or a symbolic part of it) with the term 2C ahead of it. The two-carbon analogue of DOB (a three-carbon chain compound) will become 2C-B. DOI becomes 2C-I, DON becomes 2C-N, and DOET becomes 2C-E. Each of these is a substituted amphetamine derivative lacking one carbon atom, thus becoming a phenethylamine derivative. Most of these have 2,4,5-substitution patterns.

And if a drug has been initially developed (and initially named) as a phenethylamine derivative (two carbon chain) then the three-carbon chain analogue will use the original name with the term 3C ahead of it. The three carbon analogue of E (escaline, a two-carbon chain compound) will become 3C-E. P becomes 3C-P and CPM becomes 3C-CPM. Most of these have 3,4,5-substitution patterns.

Thus, "2-C" implies that a known amphetamine drug has been shortened to a phenethylamine, and "3-C" inplies that a known phenethylamine has been lengthened to an amphetamine. A great number of the former have been made and have proven to be most rewarding. Only a few of the latter are known, but most of them will eventually prove to be potent psychedelics.

#73   EEE;   2,4,5-TRIETHOXYAMPHETAMINE

SYNTHESIS: A solution of 13.3 g 3,4-diethoxyphenol (see the recipe for MEE for its preparation) in 20 mL MeOH, and a solution of 4.8 g KOH in 100 mL hot MeOH were combined. There was added 8.2 g ethyl bromide and the mixture was held at reflux on the steam bath for 2 h. The reaction was quenched by the addition of three volumes H_2O, made strongly basic by the addition of 10% NaOH, and extracted with 3x150 mL CH_2Cl_2. The solvent was removed from the pooled extracts under vacuum giving a residue of 9.1 g 1,2,4-triethoxybenzene that solidified to a crystalline mass. The mp was 28.5-29.5 °C, but the infra-red analysis showed the presence of unreacted phenol. The CH_2Cl_2 solution was again washed thoroughly with 10% NaOH and, after removal of the solvent, the solidified residue weighed 6.0 g and appeared free of impurities. The mp of this sample was 33-34 °C.

To a mixture of 10.5 g N-methyl formanilide and 11.9 g $POCl_3$ that had incubated at room temperature for 0.5 h (it had become quite red in color) there was added 6.4 g of the solid ether, 1,2,4-triethoxybenzene. The mixture was heated on the steam bath for 2.5 h, then poured into 500 mL of shaved ice. After a few minutes stirring, crystals appeared. The reaction was allowed to stand for a few h, then filtered and sucked as dry as possible. The damp 14.4 g of slate-green crude solids were dissolved in 30 mL boiling MeOH, and allowed to cool to room temperature overnight. Filtration of the cream-colored product, and air drying, gave 6.1 g of 2,4,5-triethoxybenzaldehyde with a mp of 94-95 °C. A solution containing 0.5 g of this aldehyde and 0.4 g malononitrile in 7 mL absolute EtOH was treated with three drops of triethylamine. There was an immediate formation of granular yellow crystals of 2,4,5-triethoxybenzalmalononitrile which, on filtering and air drying, weighed 0.4 g and had a mp of 169-170 °C.

A solution of 5.0 g 2,4,5-triethoxybenzaldehyde and 2.6 g nitroethane in 14.8 g glacial acetic acid was treated with 1.6 g anhydrous ammonium acetate and heated on the steam bath for 2 h. The addition of an equal volume of H_2O gave a slightly turbid solution which, upon the administration of a small amount of externally developed seed, smoothly set up as orange crystals as the reaction mix returned to room temperature. The product was removed by filtration, washed with a little 50% acetic acid, and allowed to air dry to constant weight. There was thus obtained 2.5 g of fluffy yellow-orange (almost yellow) crystals of 2-nitro-1-(2,4,5-triethoxyphenyl)propene with a mp of 91-92.5 °C. Anal. ($C_{15}H_{21}NO_5$) C,H.

To a gently refluxing suspension of 1.7 g LAH in 200 mL anhydrous Et_2O under a He atmosphere, there was added 2.5 g 2-nitro-1-(2,4,5-triethoxyphenyl)-propene by allowing the condensing Et_2O to drip into a shunted Soxhlet thimble containing the nitrostyrene, thus effectively adding a warm saturated solution of the nitrostyrene dropwise. Refluxing was maintained for 5 h, and then the reaction mixture was cooled with an external ice bath. The excess hydride was destroyed by the cautious addition of 300 mL 1.5 N H_2SO_4. When the aqueous and Et_2O layers were finally clear, they were separated, and 50 g of potassium sodium tartrate were dissolved in the aqueous fraction. Aqueous NaOH was then added until the pH was above 9, and this was extracted with 3x200 mL CH_2Cl_2. Removal of the solvent under vacuum produced an amber oil that was dissolved in anhydrous Et_2O and saturated with anhydrous HCl gas. After a few min delay, there com-menced the separation of fine white crystals of 2,4,5-triethoxyamphetamine hydro-chloride, (EEE). These weighed, after filtration, Et_2O washing, and air drying to constant weight, 1.75 g and had a mp of 167-168 °C, with prior softening at 162 °C. Anal. ($C_{15}H_{26}ClNO_3$) C,H,N.

DOSAGE: unknown.

DURATION: unknown.

EXTENSIONS AND COMMENTARY: This amphetamine, the final item on the ethoxy homologue of TMA-2 project, has never been tried in man. I do not know how it tastes, but I suspect that it is probably bitter. An interesting sidelight concerning this project, and one which can serve as a measure of the enthusiasm that went into it, is that (except for the 2-ethoxy homologue EMM) all of the possible ethoxy homologues of TMA-2, including MEM, MME, EEM, EME, MEE and EEE, their precursor nitrostyrenes, the precursor aldehydes (and their malononitrile derivatives), the precursor ethers, and the precursor phenols, for a total of 33 compounds, were all synthesized, purified, and characterized within a period of just over three weeks. Actually it was 23 days, and that was a magically exciting time. And there were two true treasures that came out of it all. The compound MEM, and the knowledge that the 4-position was where the action is.

#74   EEM;   2,4-DIETHOXY-5-METHOXYAMPHETAMINE

SYNTHESIS: To a solution of 12.3 g 3-ethoxy-4-methoxyphenol (see recipe for MEM for the preparation of this phenol) in 20 mL MeOH, there was added a warm solution of 4.8 g KOH in 100 mL MeOH. There was then added 8.2 g ethyl bromide, and the mixture held at reflux on the steam bath. Within 0.5 h, severe bumping ensued. An additional 3 g ethyl bromide were added, refluxing continued for another 0.5 h, then the reaction mixture was allowed to come to room temperature and to stand overnight. It was poured into 3 volumes H_2O which produced crystals spontaneously. There was added additional base, and the mixture was extracted with 3x150 mL CH_2Cl_2. Removal of the solvent from the pooled extracts under vacuum gave 6.4 g of 2,4-diethoxyanisole as tan crystals with a mp of 48-48.5 °C.

A mixture of 10.9 g N-methylformanilide and 12.3 g $POCl_3$ was allowed to stand at room temperature for 0.5 h producing a deep red claret color. There was then added 6.2 g 2,4-diethoxyanisole and the mixture was heated on the steam bath for 2 h. All was poured into 200 g chipped ice, and stirred mechanically. The dark viscous gummy oil gradually became increasingly granular and finally appeared as jade-green solids. These were removed by filtration and washed with H_2O, giving a wet cake weighing 18 g and having a mp (from a porous plate) of 95.5-96.5 °C. The entire crop was recrystallized from 75 mL boiling MeOH which gave, after filtering, washing lightly with cold MeOH, and air drying, 5.4 g of 2,4-diethoxy-5-methoxybenzaldehyde with a mp of 98-99 °C. A solution of 0.2 g of this aldehyde, and 0.3 g malononitrile in 2.0 mL warm EtOH was treated with a drop of triethylamine. There was an immediate generation of crystals which were removed by filtration, EtOH-washed, and dried to constant weight. The bright yellow needles of 2,4-diethoxy-5-methoxybenzalmalononitrile weighed 0.15 g and had a mp of 172-172.5 °C.

A solution of 5.0 g 2,4-diethoxy-5-methoxybenzaldehyde in 16 g glacial acetic acid was treated with 2.7 g nitroethane followed by 1.7 g anhydrous ammonium acetate. The mixture was heated for 2.5 h on the steam bath, then removed and diluted with a equal volume of H_2O. With cooling there was the generation of a heavy crop of orange crystals which was removed, washed with 50% acetic acid, and sucked as dry as possible. The product had a mp of 97-104 °C, and there was spectrographic evidence of some unreacted starting aldehyde. A small sample was recrystallized from boiling MeOH, with considerable loss, to give an analytical sample of 1-(2,4-diethoxy-5-methoxyphenyl)-2-nitropropene as orange-yellow crystals with a mp of 112-113 °C. Anal. $(C_{14}H_{19}NO_5)$ C,H. The unpurified first crop was employed in the following synthesis of the corresponding amphet-amine.

To a gently refluxing suspension of 2.9 g LAH in 400 mL anhydrous Et_2O under a He atmosphere, there was added 4.0 g of impure 1-(2,4-diethoxy-5-methoxyphenyl)-2-nitropropene by allowing the condensing ether to drip into a shunted Soxhlet thimble apparatus containing the nitrostyrene. This effectively added a warm saturated solution of the nitrostyrene dropwise over the course of 1 h. Refluxing was maintained for 5 h and the reaction mixture was cooled with an external ice bath with the stirring continued. The excess hydride was destroyed by the cautious addition of 400 mL of 1.5 N H_2SO_4. When the aqueous and Et_2O layers were finally clear, they were separated, and 100 g of potassium sodium tartrate was dissolved in the aqueous fraction. Aqueous NaOH was then added until the pH was above 9, and this was then extracted with 3x150 mL CH_2Cl_2. Removal of the solvent under vacuum produced 2.7 g of a pale amber oil that was dissolved in 300 mL anhydrous Et_2O and saturated with anhydrous HCl gas. After a few minutes delay, there commenced the separation of fine white crystals of 2,4-diethoxy-5-methoxyamphetamine hydrochloride (EEM). After the crystallization was complete, these were removed by filtration, washed with Et_2O and air dried, providing 2.55 g of a fine white crystalline solid with mp 158-159 °C. Anal. $(C_{14}H_{24}ClNO_3)$ C,H,N.

DOSAGE: unknown.

DURATION: unknown.

EXTENSIONS AND COMMENTARY: This particular identity and arrangement of the alkoxy groups on the amphetamine molecule, EEM, is a totally unexplored molecule. It is reasonable to assume that it would be way down in potency, but there is no way of guessing what the nature of its activity might be at the dosage that would be active.

#75   EME;   2,5-DIETHOXY-4-METHOXYAMPHETAMINE

SYNTHESIS: To a solution of 14.0 g 4-ethoxy-3-methoxyphenol (see the recipe for MME for the preparation of this starting material) in an equal volume of EtOH, there was added a solution of 5.3 g KOH in 100 mL hot MeOH. This was followed with 9.1 g ethyl bromide, and the mixture was held at reflux for 2 h. The first deposition of KBr was apparent in 5 min, and there was rather severe bumping by the end of the reaction. The mixture was diluted with 3 volumes H_2O and 1 volume 5% NaOH, and extracted with 2x200 mL Et_2O. The extracts were pooled, and the solvent removed under vacuum, yielding 14.3 g of a pale amber oil that set to crystals of 2,5-diethoxyanisole with a mp of 44-45 °C. The compound had been reported in the literature from the action of diethyl sulfate on methoxyhydroquinone.

To a mixture of 24.1 g N-methylformanilide and 27.3 g $POCl_3$ that had been allowed to stand at room temperature until strongly red-colored (about 0.5 h) there was added 13.8 g solid 2,5-diethoxyanisole and the mixture was heated on the steam bath for 2 h. The black, thick reaction product was poured over chipped ice

and, with continuous stirring, the color lightened and there was the formation of a yellowish powder. After a few h standing, this was removed by filtration and sucked as dry as possible. The 32 g of damp product showed the presence of isomeric contaminatiion by GC, and the aqueous mother liquor, upon extraction with CH_2Cl_2 and concentration, showed yet more aldehyde-like impurities. The isolated solids were recrystallized from 125 mL boiling MeOH giving 15.8 g yellowish crystals (wet weight) that still showed detectable impurities by GC. A second recrystallization from 100 mL boiling MeOH gave off-white fluffy crystals of 2,5-diethoxy-4-methoxybenzaldehyde which weighed, after air drying, 8.5 g. The mp was 109-110 °C. The combined mother liquors from the two MeOH crystallizations were stripped of solvent, and the resulting solid mass crystallized again from MeOH to give a second crop of aldehyde, 5.7 g, with a mp of 110-111 °C. A solution of 1.0 g of this aldehyde and 0.7 g malononitrile in 40 mL warm absolute EtOH was treated with a few drops of triethylamine. In a minute or so, there was the formation of crystals. These were removed by filtration, washed with EtOH, and air dried, giving 0.6 g of 2,5-diethoxy-4-methoxybenzalmalononitrile as brilliant yellow crystals with a mp of 156.5-158 °C.

A solution of 6.7 g 2,5-diethoxy-4-methoxybenzaldehyde in 21 g glacial acetic acid was treated with 3.1 g nitroethane and 1.93 g anhydrous ammonium acetate, and heated on the steam bath for 2.5 h. The addition of a small amount of H_2O to the hot reaction mixture instituted crystallization of an orange product which, after the mixture had come to room temperature and stood for several h, was removed by filtration, H_2O washed, and air dried. The product, 1-(2,5-diethoxy-4-methoxyphenyl)-2-nitropropene, was dull orange in color, weighed 3.0 g and had a mp of 84-86 °C. An analytical sample from toluene had a mp of 85-86 °C. Anal. ($C_{14}H_{19}NO_5$) C,H.

To a gently refluxing suspension of 2.0 g LAH in 250 mL anhydrous Et_2O under a He atmosphere, there was added 2.8 g 1-(2,5-diethoxy-4-methoxyphenyl)-2-nitropropene by allowing the condensing Et_2O to drip into a shunted Soxhlet thimble containing the nitrostyrene. This effectively added a warm saturated solution of the nitrostyrene dropwise. The addition took 1 h and the refluxing was continued for an additional 6 h. The reaction mixture was brought down to ice-bath temperature, and the excess hydride was destroyed by the cautious addition of 150 mL 1.5 N H_2SO_4. When the aqueous and Et_2O layers were finally clear, they were separated and 50 g of potassium sodium tartrate were dissolved in the aqueous fraction. Aqueous NaOH was then added until the pH was >9, and this was then extracted with 3x150 mL CH_2Cl_2. Removal of the solvent under vacuum produced 2.3 g of a clear white oil that was dissolved in 300 mL anhydrous Et_2O and saturated with anhydrous HCl gas. At first the solution remained completely clear, and finally there was the start of the formation of fine white crystals. When the crystallization was complete, these solids were removed by filtration, Et_2O washed, and air dried. There was thus obtained 2.2 g of 2,5-diethoxy-4-methoxyamphetamine hydrochloride (EME) with a mp of 162-164 °C with prior softening at 154 °C. Anal. ($C_{14}H_{24}ClNO_3$) C,H,N.

DOSAGE: unknown.

DURATION: unknown.

EXTENSIONS AND COMMENTARY: This is another of the collection of all possible ethoxy homologues of TMA-2. The latter and heavier members of this series were synthesized and completed before the directions of biological activity had become evident from the earlier ones. This compound has never been assayed, and it is a reasonable guess that it will have a very low potency, with hints of toxicity at higher dose levels. I suspect that it will never be assayed, certainly not by me.

#76 EMM; 4,5-DIMETHOXY-2-ETHOXYAMPHETAMINE

SYNTHESIS: A solution of 166 g 3,4-dimethoxybenzaldehyde in 600 mL acetic acid was well stirred, and brought up to an internal temperature of exactly 25 °C. There was added, in very small portions, a 40% solution of peracetic acid in acetic acid. The evolved heat was removed with an external ice bath, and the rate of addition was dictated by the requirement that the internal temperature should not exceed 25 °C. A total of 210 g of the 40% peracetic acid was used. The reaction mixture was poured into 3 L H_2O, and the acetic acid neutralized by the addition of solid K_2CO_3. The neutral aqueous phase was extracted with 5x150 mL Et_2O, and the solvent from the pooled extracts was removed under vacuum. To the red-colored residue there was added 300 mL 10% NaOH, and the mixture was heated for 1 h on the steam bath. This was cooled, washed once with CH_2Cl_2, acidified with HCl, and extracted with 5x150 mL Et_2O. The pooled extracts were washed once with saturated $NaHCO_3$ (which removed most of the color) and the removal of the solvent under vacuum gave 105 g of 3,4-dimethoxyphenol as an amber oil that slowly set up to crystals.

The above crude 3,4-dimethoxyphenol was dissolved in 200 mL EtOH, and treated with a solution of 38.1 g KOH in 300 mL hot EtOH. The clear solution of the potassium salt was a deep red color, and was promptly treated with 94.3 g allyl bromide, at a rate commensurate with the exothermic reaction. The mixture was held at reflux for 2 h. This was then added to 1 L H_2O and extracted with 5x100 mL Et_2O. The extracts were pooled, and removal of the solvent under vacuum gave a residue of 98 g of a black oil. This was distilled at 104-108 °C at 0.7-1.0 mm/ Hg to give 59.3 g 1-allyloxy-3,4-dimethoxybenzene as a pale yellow oil with a greenish cast.

A total of 59 g of the neat 1-allyloxy-3,4-dimethoxybenzene was provided with an internal thermometer, and heated with an open flame. The color quickly became purple, then lightened to a red at 70 °C, and finally to a pale pink by 210 °C. At 240 °C an exothermic reaction set in with the temperature going up to almost 290 °C. It was held in the 270-280 °C range for several min, then allowed to return to room temperature. GC analysis showed two peaks, the second and major one being the desired 1,2,4,5-isomer. A small sample was caught by prep-GC, and it successfully seeded the crude Claisen rearrangement product. The isolated 2-allyl-4,5-dimethoxyphenol, pressed on a porous plate, had a mp of 39.5-40.5 °C which was improved to 41.5-42 °C by recrystallization from hexane.

To a solution of 9.7 g 2-allyl-4,5-dimethoxyphenol in a few mL EtOH, there was added a solution of 2.8 g KOH in 25 mL boiling EtOH followed by 5.5 g ethyl bromide. The mixture was held at reflux for 3.5 h and then poured into 200 mL H_2O and extracted with 3x100 mL CH_2Cl_2. Pooling the extracts and removal of the solvent under vacuum gave a residue of 10.4 g of 4,5-dimethoxy-2-ethoxy-1-allylbenzene as a clear, mobile oil. It was substantially a single component by GC and was used in the following isomerization step without further purification.

A solution of 9.4 g 4,5-dimethoxy-2-ethoxy-1-allylbenzene in 10 mL EtOH was treated with 20 g flaked KOH, and heated on the steam bath. The progress of the isomerization was followed by the assay of isolates by GC. After 5 h, the reaction mixture was poured into 250 mL H_2O which immediately generated a pasty solid. This was sucked free of solvent and other liquids on a sintered funnel, giving 5.5 g of trans-4,5-dimethoxy-2-ethoxy-1-propenylbenzene as an amber solid with a mp of 65-67 °C. A small analytical sample from hexane had a mp of 68 °C.

A solution of 5.0 g trans-4,5-dimethoxy-2-ethoxy-1-propenylbenzene in

27 g acetone that contained 2.2 g pyridine was magnetically stirred and cooled to 0 °C. There was then added 4.5 g tetranitromethane and, after 2 minutes stirring at this temperature, the reaction mixture was quenched with a solution of 1.5 g KOH in 26 mL H_2O. The reaction mixture remained a clear deep orange color, and additional H_2O was required to institute crystallization. There was the slow deposition of bright yellow crystals of 1-(4,5-dimethoxy-2-ethoxyphenyl)-2-nitro-propene which weighed, after EtOH washing and air drying to constant weight of 4.4 g. The mp was 75-76 °C.

To a gently refluxing suspension of 3.5 g LAH in 250 mL anhydrous Et_2O under a He atmosphere, there was added 3.9 g 1-(4,5-dimethoxy-2-ethoxyphenyl)-2-nitropropene by allowing the condensing Et_2O to drip into a shunted Soxhlet apparatus with the thimble containing the nitrostyrene. This effectively added a warm saturated solution of the nitrostyrene dropwise; the nitrostyrene was very soluble in Et_2O. Refluxing was maintained for 2.5 h and the reaction continued to stir at room temperature for an additional 3.5 h. The excess hydride was destroyed by the cautious addition of 225 mL 1.5 N H_2SO_4. When the aqeous and Et_2O layers were finally clear, they were separated, and 75 g of potassium sodium tartrate was dissolved in the aqueous fraction. Aqueous NaOH was then added until the pH was >9, and this was then extracted with 3x100 mL CH_2Cl_2. Evaporation of the solvent under vacuum produced 2.8 g of a clear, almost colorless oil that was dissolved in anhydrous Et_2O and saturated with anhydrous HCl gas. This initially generated a solid that then oiled out. After a few minutes stirring, this began to solidify again and it finally transformed into a loose fine white solid. This was recrystallized by dissolution in 50 mL warm IPA followed by dilution with 300 mL Et_2O. After a few minutes, crystals of 4,5-dimethoxy-2-ethoxyamphetamine hydrochloride (EMM) formed which were removed by filtration, Et_2O washed, and air dried. These weighed 2.7 g and had a mp of 171-172 °C. Anal. $(C_{13}H_{22}ClNO_3)$ C,H,N.

DOSAGE: greater than 50 mg.

DURATION: unknown.

QUALITATIVE COMMENTS: (with 50 mg) "There were no effects."

EXTENSIONS AND COMMENTARY: This was the first of the ethoxy homo-logues of TMA-2, and it was immediately (well, within a couple of months) run up from an initial dab to 25 milligrams. This was in early 1963, and the lack of activity of EMM was keenly disappointing. This was a level at which the prototype, TMA-2, was very active, and the conclusion was that maybe any change on the molecule would result in a loss of activity. So this approach was shelved for a while, and all efforts were directed into the relocation, rather than the elongation, of the methoxy groups. A few months later, the ethoxy question was addressed again, and the discovery of MEM rekindled full interest in this ethoxy question.

#77   ETHYL-J;   2-ETHYLAMINO-1-(3,4-METHYLENEDIOXYPHENYL)BUTANE; N-ETHYL-1-(1,3-BENZODIOXOL-5-YL)-2-BUTANAMINE

SYNTHESIS: A stirred solution of 9.0 g 1-(3,4-methylenedioxyphenyl)-2-butanone (see the recipe for J for its preparation) in 150 mL MeOH was treated with 9.0 g ethylamine hydrochloride, 4.0 g anhydrous NaOAc, and 3.0 g sodium cyanoborohydride. The pH was maintained between 6 and 7 by the periodic addition of HCl. After the base formation had stabilized, there was added an additional 9.0 g ethylamine hydrochloride, 9.0 g NaOAc and 2.0 g sodium cyanoborohydride. With continuous stirring, there was HCl added over the course of 1 h until the final pH was approximately 2. The reaction mixture was poured into 700 mL dilute NaOH, and extracted with 3x75 mL CH_2Cl_2. These extracts were pooled, and back-extracted with dilute H_2SO_4. This was washed with 2x50 mL CH_2Cl_2, then made basic with dilute NaOH and extracted with 2x75 mL CH_2Cl_2. Removal of the solvent under vacuum gave a 0.81 g residue which was dissolved in 10 mL IPA. Neutralization with concntrated HCl formed white crystals spontaneously. These were diluted with Et_2O, filtered, Et_2O washed and air dried to provide 0.85 g 2-ethylamino-1-(3,4-methylenedioxyphenyl)butane hydrochloride (ETHYL-J), with mp of 176-177 °C. Anal. ($C_{13}H_{20}ClNO_2$) C,H. The neutral fraction that remained in the organic phase following the dilute sulfuric acid extraction, was recovered by removal of the solvent under vacuum. There was obtained about 5 g of an amber liquid that was largely 2-hydroxy-1-(3,4-methylenedioxyphenyl)butane.

DOSAGE: greater than 90 mg.

DURATION: probably short.

QUALITATIVE COMMENTS: (with 65 mg) "Perhaps aware at 20 minutes. Definitely aware at 45 minutes. Diffusing to nothing at 3-4 hours."
        (with 90 mg) "I am somewhere between ± and +. And everything became lost in the evening with a couple of glasses of wine and talk that went on to 3 AM."

EXTENSIONS AND COMMENTARY: And nothing higher has ever been looked at. If the analogy with the amphetamine counterparts (J with MDA, METHYL-J with MDMA, and this, with MDE) were to hold up (a drop of about a third in potency with the lengthening of the chain by a carbon atom), one might guess that this compound would be an interesting intoxicant, but probably not until you got up into the area at or above a 200 milligram dose. And that is a lot of chemical for the body to have to handle. Some day, maybe.

#78 ETHYL-K; 2-ETHYLAMINO-1-(3,4-METHYLENEDIOXYPHENYL)PENTANE; N-ETHYL-1-(1,3-BENZODIOXOL-5-YL)-2-PENTYLAMINE

SYNTHESIS: A solution of 120 mg mercuric chloride in 160 mL H_2O was poured over 4.7 g aluminum foil (Reynolds Wrap, regular weight, cut into 1 inch squares) and allowed to stand until the amalgamation was well underway (about 30 min). The H_2O was then drained and the foil washed with 2x200 mL H_2O with thorough draining. There was then added, in sequence and with good swirling and agitation between each addition, 8.5 g ethylamine hydrochloride dissolved in 7 mL H_2O, 21 mL IPA, 17 mL 25% NaOH, 7.1 g 1-(3,4-methylenedioxyphenyl)-2-pentanone (see the recipe for METHYL-K for its preparation), and finally 40 mL IPA. The reaction mixture was periodically heated on the steam bath to keep the reaction moving and active. After all the metal had been consumed, the mixture was filtered, and the filter cake washed with MeOH. The solvent was removed from the combined filtrate and washings, and the residue suspended in 800 mL dilute HCl. This was washed with 3x100 mL Et_2O, made basic with 25% NaOH, and extracted with 3x100 mL CH_2Cl_2. The pooled extracts were stripped of solvent under vacuum yielding a residue of 6.3 g of an amber oil. This was distilled at 115-125 °C at 0.4 mm/Hg to give 5.61 g of an almost white liquid which was dissolved in 28 mL IPA, neutralized with concentrated HCl, and diluted with 100 mL anhydrous Et_2O. The resulting clear solution became cloudy, then set up in a cottage cheese texture, and then all broke up to a beautiful loose solid. This was filtered, Et_2O washed and air dried to give 5.99 g 2-ethylamino-1-(3,4-methylenedioxyphenyl)pentane hydrochloride (ETHYL-K) with a mp of 157-158 °C. Anal. ($C_{14}H_{22}ClNO_2$) C,H.

DOSAGE: (greater than 40 mg).

DURATION: unknown.

QUALITATIVE COMMENTS: (with 40 mg) "There was a paresthetic twinge in my shoulder area at about an hour — other than that, absolutely nothing."

EXTENSIONS AND COMMENTARY: And that is as high a dose as has apparently ever been tried with ETHYL-K. The compounds with the hexane chain (L-series) rather than the pentane chain of the K-series have been made, but they have been spun into the recipe for METHYL-K.

#79   F-2;   2-M;   6-(2-AMINOPROPYL)-5-METHOXY-2-METHYL-2,3-DIHYDROBENZOFURAN

SYNTHESIS: To a solution of 43.2 g KOH pellets in 250 boiling EtOH there was added 96 g 4-methoxyphenol followed by the slow addition of 131.2 g allyl bromide, and the mixture was held under refluxing conditions for 16 h. After cooling, the reaction was added to 1.6 L H_2O, and made strongly basic with 25% NaOH. This was extracted with 3x100 mL CH_2Cl_2, the extracts pooled, washed once with dilute NaOH and then once with dilute HCl. Removal of the solvent under vacuum gave 93.8 g of 4-allyloxyanisole as a pale amber oil, which was used in the following reaction without further purification.

A round-bottomed flask containing 93 g crude 4-allyloxyanisole was equipped with an immersed thermometer and heated with an external flame until an exothermic reaction set in at 230 °C. The temperature rose to 270 °C and it was maintained there with the flame for five minutes. After cooling to room temperature, the reaction mix was poured into 2 L H_2O and made strongly basic with the addition of 25% NaOH. This dark aqueous phase was washed with 2x200 mL CH_2Cl_2, and then acidified with HCl. This was then extracted with 2x200 mL CH_2Cl_2, and the pooled extracts washed first with saturated $NaHCO_3$ and then with H_2O. Removal of the solvent under vacuum gave 65.6 g of 2-allyl-4-methoxyphenol as a clear, amber oil. To a solution of 1.66 g of this crude phenol in 5 mL hexane with just enough CH_2Cl_2 added to effect a clear solution, there was added 1.3 g phenyl isocyanate followed with three drops of triethylamine. An exothermic reaction ensued which spontaneously deposited white crystals. These was removed and hexane washed to give 2-allyl-4-methoxy-phenyl N-phenyl carbamate, with a mp of 88-89 °C. The acetate ester, from the phenol and acetic anhydride in pyridine, did not crystallize.

To a solution of 37.7 g 2-allyl-4-methoxyphenol in 125 mL glacial acetic acid there was added 19 g zinc chloride followed with 63 mL concentrated HCl. The mixture was held at reflux temperature for 40 min, then cooled to room temperature, diluted with 300 mL H_2O, and extracted with 2x200 mL CH_2Cl_2. The pooled extracts were washed repeatedly with 8% NaOH until the washings remained basic. Removal of the solvent under vacuum gave a clear pale yellow oil that was distilled at the water pump. A fraction boiling at 150-165 °C was 5-methoxy-2-methyl-2,3-dihydrobenzofuran which weighed 25 g and which was a highly refractive colorless oil. The infra-red spectrum indicated that some small amount of hydroxy group was present, but the NMR spectrum was in complete accord with the benzofuran structure. A higher cut in this distillation gave 4.5 g of a phenolic product tentatively assigned the structure of 4-methoxy-2-propenylphenol. The target dihydrobenzo-furan has also been synthesized from the open-ring o-allyl phenol in acetic acid solution with the addition of a catalytic amount of concentrated H_2SO_4.

To a half-hour pre-incubated mixture of 69 g POCl$_3$ and 60 g N-methyl-formanilide there was added 29.0 g 5-methoxy-2-methyl-2,3-dihydrobenzofuran and the mixture was heated on the steam bath for 2 h. The reaction mixture was poured into 1 L H$_2$O, and allowed to stir overnight. The brown gummy solids were removed by filtration, and air dried as completely as possible. These weighed 32 g and were shown by GC on OV-17 to consist of two benzaldehyde isomers in a ratio of 7:2. This was triturated under 18 mL MeOH, and the undissolved solids removed by filtration and washed with 6 mL additional MeOH. The mother liquor and washings were saved. The 17.8 g of dull yellow solids that were obtained were repeatedly extracted with 75 mL portions of boiling hexane (4 extracts were required) and each extract, on cooling, deposited yellow crystals of the major aldehyde. The dried crystals of 6-formyl-5-methoxy-2-methyl-2,3-dihydro-benzofuran were combined (9.5 g) and had a mp of 80-82 °C. The methanol washes saved from above were stripped of solvent, and the sticky, orange solids that remained were enriched in the minor aldehyde isomer (3:2 ratio). Several injections of this crude material into a preparative GC OV-17 column gave sufficient quantities of the "wrong" isomer for NMR characterization. The 2-methyl group was intact (eliminating the possibility of a dihydrobenzopyran isomer) and the ring meta-proton splitting required that the formyl group be in the benzofuran 7-position. This crystalline solid was, therefore, 7-formyl-5-methoxy-2-methyl-2,3-dihydro-benzofuran.

A solution of 9 g of 6-formyl-5-methoxy-2-methyl-2,3-dihydrobenzo-furan in 35 mL glacial acetic acid was treated with 6 mL of nitroethane followed with 3.1 g anhydrous ammonium acetate. This mixture was heated on the steam bath for 4 h, diluted with half its volume with warm H$_2$O, and seeded with a bit of product that had been obtained separately. The slightly turbid solution slowly crystallized as it cooled, and was finally held at 0 °C for several h. The deep orange product was removed by filtration, washed with 50% acetic acid, and air dried to constant weight. There was thus obtained 7.0 g 5-methoxy-2-methyl-6-(2-nitro-1-propenyl)-2,3-dihydrobenzofuran with a mp of 89-90 °C from MeOH.

A suspension of 5.0 g LAH in 500 mL of well stirred anhydrous Et$_2$O at a gentle reflux, was treated with a warm, saturated solution of 7.0 g 5-methoxy-2-methyl-6-(2-nitro-1-propenyl)-2,3-dihydrobenzofuran in Et$_2$O added dropwise. The mixture was kept at reflux temperature for 36 h, allowed to stand 2 days, and then the excess hydride destroyed by the cautious addition of 500 mL 6% H$_2$SO$_4$. The phases were separated, and the aqueous phase washed with 2x200 mL CH$_2$Cl$_2$. A total of 125 g potassium sodium tartrate was added to the aqueous phase, and sufficient 25% NaOH added to bring the pH to about 10. This phase was extracted with 3x150 mL CH$_2$Cl$_2$, and the pooled extracts were stripped of solvent under vacuum. The residual oil (4.8 g, amber in color) was dissolved in 300 mL anhydrous Et$_2$O which, upon saturation with anhydrous HCl gas gave a clear solution that suddenly deposited white crystals. The hydrochloride salt of 6-(2-aminopropyl)-5-methoxy-2-methyl-2,3-dihydrobenzofuran weighed 2.3 g and was not satisfactory as a solid derivative, but it appears that the oxalate salt is both nonhygroscopic and quite stable. It (F-2) had a mp of 216-218 °C and it displayed a textbook NMR.

DOSAGE: greater than 15 mg.

DURATION: unknown.

EXTENSIONS AND COMMENTARY: This material, which is certainly a mixture of two diastereoisomeric pairs of racemates since there are two chiral centers present, showed no effects at levels of up to 15 milligrams orally. Doses of 100 mg/Kg were without effects in mice following i.p. injections, although half again this amount proved to be lethal. In rats trained to discriminate LSD from saline, F-2 proved to be about 40 times less potent than the reference compound DOM, requiring some 5 mg/Kg for positive responses. But the human trials were only up to about 0.2 mg/Kg.

This was the prototype compound that was originally put together to justify giving a paper at a marijuana conference in Sweden, in 1968. Although I had never done much with marijuana or with its principal ingredients, I thought maybe I could bend the topic a bit to embrace some potentially active phenethylamines. There is a story of an international conference held in Geneva a few years earlier to discuss the worrisome decrease in the elephant population. A German zoologist invested a full eight-hour day in a summary of his 21 volume treatise on the anatomy and the physiology of the elephant. A French sociologist presented a lively slide show on the mating rituals and rutting behavior of the elephant. And a rabbi from Tel Aviv entitled his talk: "Elephants and the Jewish Problem." My Swedish talk should have been named "Marijuana and the Psychedelic Amphetamines." The memorable story of meeting the chief of the Swedish equivalent of the Bureau of Narcotics, and ending up playing Mozart sonatas in the attic of his home, has been spun out elsewhere in the book.

The original concept was a grand plan to imitate two of the three rings of tetrahydrocannabinol. There is an aromatic ring (with an alkyl group and two oxygens on it) and it is fused to a pyran ring with a couple of methyl groups on it. So, if one were to tie the methyl group at the 4-position of DOM around with a short carbon chain into the oxygen atom at the five position, one could squint and say that the resulting amphetamine was kinda something like an analogue of THC. Thus, the resulting six-membered ring (a pyran) or five-membered ring (a furan) could be peppered with methyl groups at different locations (and up to two per location). If the ring was a five-membered structure, then the parent system would be a benzofuran, and the location of methyl groups on the ring would be indicated by the appropriate numbers following the letter "F" which would stand for "furan". And if it were to be a six-membered ring, the resulting benzopyran would be indicated with a "P" for pyran, and again the methyl group or groups would be indicated by the substitution position. This code would cover all polymethylated homologues with codes that would look like F-22 and P-2234. If any of them showed up with fascinating activities, I would extend methyls to ethyls, and work out some whole new naming code at some future time. An early system, naming this compound 2-M for a methyl group on the 2-position of the furan ring, was abandoned when it became apparent that the pyran world would screw everything up.

The isolation of characterizable quantities of 7-formyl-5-methoxy-2-methyl-2,3-dihydrobenzofuran from the benzaldehyde recipe above gave a fleeting fantasy of a whole new direction that this little project might go. If this unexpected benzaldehyde were to be converted to the corresponding amphetamine, one would have 7-(2-aminopropyl)-5-methoxy-2-methyl-2,3-dihydrobenzofuran. Suddenly here would be a 2,3,5-trisubstituted thing with a ring at the 2,3-position, similar to the still unmade MMDA-4. The temptation to be diverted in this way lasted, fortunately, only a few minutes, and the project was shelved. Someday, when there are buckets of spare time or hosts of eager graduate students, some fascinating chemistry might lie this way, and maybe some fascinating pharmacology, even.

The plain furan analogue, without any methyl groups on it, has been made. Five-methoxybenzofuran formed the 6-formyl derivative (the aldehyde) with a mp of 79-80 °C and from it the nitrostyrene (orange needles, mp 89-91 °C) and the final amphetamine (white solids, as the methane sulfonate, mp 141-144 °C) were prepared in a manner similar to the preparation of F-2 above. In the rat studies, it was three times more potent than F-2, but still some 15 times less potent than DOM. And in initial human trials (of up to 30 milligrams) there were again no effects noted. Naming of this material is easy chemically (6-(2-aminopropyl)-5-methoxy-2,3-dihydrobenzofuran) but tricky as to code. If the numbers that follow the "F" give the location of the methyl groups, then this material, without any such groups, can have no numbers following, and should properly be simply "F." OK, it is "F." The preparation or the attempted preparations of other homologues such as F-23 and F-233 are outlined under the recipe for F-22.

#80   F-22;   6-(2-AMINOPROPYL)-2,2-DIMETHYL-5-METHOXY-2,3-DIHYDROBENZOFURAN

SYNTHESIS: To a solution of 43.2 g flaked KOH in 250 mL hot EtOH there was added 96 g 4-methoxyphenol followed by 90 g 2-methylallyl chloride over the course of 2 h. The mixture was held at reflux for 24 h, then added to 1.6 L H_2O. There was sufficient 25% NaOH added to make the phase strongly basic, and this was then extracted with 3x200 mL CH_2Cl_2. The pooled extracts were washed with H_2O, and the solvent removed under vacuum. The residue, 125 g of a pale amber oil, was crude 4-(2-methylallyloxy)anisole and was used without further purification in the following reaction.

In a round-bottomed flask containing an internal thermometer, there was

placed 125 g of unpurified 4-(2-methylallyloxy)anisole, and this was heated with
an open flame. At an internal temperature of 190 °C an exothermic reaction set in,
raising the temperature to 250 °C, where it was held for an additional 2 min. After
the reaction mixture had cooled to room temperature, it was poured into 500 mL
H_2O, made strongly basic with 25% NaOH, and extracted repeatedly with 100 mL
portions of CH_2Cl_2 until the extracts were essentially colorless. These extracts were
pooled and the solvent removed to provide 80.0 g of a deeply colored oil that proved
to be largely the appropriately substituted dihydrobenzofuran. The aqueous residue
from above was acidified with concentrated HCl, and again extracted with CH_2Cl_2.
Removal of the solvent gave 17.7 g of 4-methoxy-2-(2-methylallyl)phenol as an
amber oil which eventually set down as white crystals with a mp of 52.5-54 °C.

A solution of 17 g of 4-methoxy-2-(2-methylallyl)phenol in 56 g acetic
acid was treated with 8.4 g zinc chloride followed with 28 mL concentrated HCl.
This mixture was heated at reflux temperature with a mantle for 1 h. After cooling,
this was poured into H_2O and extracted with 2x150 mL CH_2Cl_2. The pooled extracts

were washed with several portions of 8%
NaOH, until the extracts were colorless.
The organic fraction was then washed
with H_2O, and the solvent removed to
yield 5.8 g of 2,2-dimethyl-5-methoxy-
2,3-dihydrobenzofuran as a pale amber oil with a pungent smell. This was purified
by distillation, giving a fraction of an off-white oil with a bp of 136-138 °C at 33 mm/
Hg.

To a mixture of 8.0 g N-methylformanilide and 9.2 g $POCl_3$ which had
been allowed to stand for 0.5 h, there was added 4.0 g 2,2-dimethyl-5-methoxy-2,3-
dihydrobenzofuran, and the mixture held at the steam bath temperature for 2.5 h.
This was then poured into 200 mL H_2O which produced a black oily phase that gave
no hint of crystallization. This mixture was extracted with 3x150 mL CH_2Cl_2 and
the solvent was removed from the pooled extracts under vacuum. The residual oil
(which was shown by GC to contain approximately equal quantities of two isomeric
benzaldehydes A and B) was extracted with three 75 mL portions of boiling hexane,
each of which on cooling deposited a reddish oil that partially crystallized. A fourth
hexane extract gave nothing more. The solvent was decanted from these three
extracts, and the semi-solid residues were ground under 3.0 mL MeOH giving 1.4
g of pale yellow crystals of 2,2-dimethyl-6-formyl-5-methoxy-2,3-dihydrobenzo-
furan, isomer "B". After recrystallization from MeOH, the color was almost white,
and the mp was 79.5-80.5 °C. The combined mother liquors were enriched in isomer
"A" which proved, following preparative GC separation and NMR analysis, to be
the 7-formyl isomer. The 80 g of impure dihydrobenzofuran isolated from the
Claisen rearrangement above was distilled and a fraction (43.8 g) that boiled from
138-153 °C at 30 mm/Hg was processed as described here to the aldehyde mixture.
Following similar hexane extractions, a yield of 4.0 g of a 95% pure isomer "B" was
finally obtained. The remaining components of this fraction were not determined,

but it is possible that there were some that contained the six-membered benzopyran ring system.

To a solution of 5.2 g of 2,2-dimethyl-6-formyl-5-methoxy-2,3-dihydro-benzofuran in 20 mL glacial acetic acid there was added 3 mL nitroethane followed by 1.6 g anhydrous ammonium acetate. This mixture was heated for 4 h on the steam bath, and then a small amount of H_2O was added to the hot solution. This instigated the formation of a copious deposition of brick-red crystals which were, after cooling, removed by filtration, and recrystallized from 50 mL boiling MeOH. After air drying there was thus obtained 2.7 g of day-glo yum-yum orange crystals of 2,2-dimethyl-5-methoxy-6-(2-nitro-1-propenyl)-2,3-dihydrobenzofuran. An additional 0.6 g of product was obtained by working the mother liquors.

A suspension of 2.5 g LAH in 300 mL refluxing anhydrous Et_2O was treated with a solution of 3.1 g 2,2-dimethyl-5-methoxy-6-(2-nitro-1-propenyl)-2,3-dihydrobenzofuran in Et_2O. The mixture was held at reflux temperature for 18 h. After cooling, the excess hydride was destroyed by the cautious addition of 400 mL H_2O which contained 15 g H_2SO_4. The aqueous phase was separated, washed once with Et_2O, and then once with CH_2Cl_2. There was then added 60 g potassium sodium tartrate, and the pH was brought to above 10 by the addition of 25% NaOH. This was extracted with 3x250 mL CH_2Cl_2, the extracts pooled, and the solvent removed under vacuum. There remained 2.8 g of an amber oil with an ammoniacal smell. This was dissolved in 200 mL anhydrous Et_2O, and saturated with anhydrous HCl gas. There was the immediate formation of an oil, from which the supernatent Et_2O was decanted. The residual oil was resuspended in a second 200 mL anhydrous Et_2O, again decanted, and finally a third 200 mL Et_2O effected the dissolving of the remaining oil to give a clear solution. All three solutions became gelatinous over the following few h, and each deposited a crop of white crystals over the following few days. From the first there was obtained 1.4 g of product with a mp of 153-154 °C; from the second, 0.2 g with a mp of 153-154 °C; and from the third, 1.2 g with a mp of 155-156 °C. These crops were combined, and recrystallized from 10 mL of boiling CH_3CN to give 1.7 g 6-(2-aminopropyl)-2,2-dimethyl-5-methoxy-2,3-dihydrobenzofuran hydrochloride (F-22) as a white crystalline solid which had a mp of 154-155 °C. This material, even when dry, showed a tendency to discolor with time.

DOSAGE: greater than 15 mg.

DURATION: unknown.

EXTENSIONS AND COMMENTARY: And here is yet another dihydrobenzofuran which is not of a very high potency if, indeed, it is active at all. This particular dihydrobenzofuran analogue, F-22, had sort of tickled my fancy as being an especially good candidate for activity. It had a certain swing to it. F-22, like LSD-25. And here it was finished, just five days before I had to deliver a paper concerning the syntheses (and activities!) of all these dihydrobenzofurans to the marijuana congress. Could this possibly be another LSD? I was sufficiently convinced that the possibility was real, that I actually started the screening process at a most unusually low level of 10 micrograms. Two days later, I upped this to a dose of 25 micrograms (no activity again) and three days after that, at 1 AM on the polar flight to Copenhagen, I swallowed the "monstrous" dose of 50 micrograms. Shoot the works. If I were to blossom all over the tourist section of the SAS plane, well, it would be quite a paper to give. If not, I could always say something like, "The active level has not yet been found." No activity. Another Walter Mitty fantasy down the tubes.

And, as it turned out, the entire project pretty much ran out of steam. A number of clever analogs had been started, and would have been pursued if there had been any activity promised of any kind with any of these dihydrobenzofurans. The "other" benzaldehyde described above, could have been run in a manner parallel to that proposed for the counterpart with F-2, to make the eventual amphetamine, 7-(2-aminopropyl)-2,2-dimethyl-5-methoxy-2,3-dihydrobenzofuran. Great strides had been made towards F-233 (I have discussed the naming system under F-2, with the F standing for the furan of benzofuran and the 2 and 3 and 3 being the positions of the methyl groups on it). The reaction of 4-methoxyphenol with 1-chloro-3-methyl-2-butene gave the ether which underwent the thermal Claisen rearrangement to 2-(1,1-dimethylallyl)-4-methoxyphenol with a bp of 148-157 °C at 30 mm/Hg. This was cyclized to the intermediate cycle 2,3,3-trimethyl-2,3-dihydrobenzofuran which, after distillation, was shown to be only 80% pure by GC analysis. This was, nonetheless, (and with the hope that is in the very fiber of a young innocent chemist), pushed on to the benzaldehyde stage (and there were a not-too-surprising four benzaldehydes to be found in the oil that was produced, which refused to crystallize). And then (when sheer desperation replaced hope) these were condensed with nitroethane to form an even worse mixture. Maybe something might crystallize from it? Nothing ever did. Junk. Everything was simply put on the shelf where it still rests today, and F-233, 6-(2-aminopropyl)-5-methoxy-2,3,3-trimethyl-2,3-dihydrobenzofuran, remains the stuff of speculation.

And a start towards F-23, 6-(2-aminopropyl)-2,3-dimethyl-5-methoxy-2,3-dihydrobenzofuran, got just as far as the starting ether, when it occurred to me that the final product would have an unprecedented three chiral centers, and so a total of four racemic pairs of diastereoisomers. And then I discovered that the starting allyl halide, crotyl chloride, was only 80% pure, with the remaining 20% being 3-chloro-1-butene. This would have eventually produced a 2-ethyl-analogue, 6-(2-aminopropyl)-2-ethyl-5-methoxy-2,3-dihydrobenzofuran, with its two chiral centers and two more pairs of stereoisomers (not to speak of the need to devise an entirely new coding system). Unless something were to fall into my lap as a crystalline intermediate, the final mess could have had at least six discreet compounds in it, not even considering optical isomers. And I haven't even begun to think of making the six-membered dihydrobenzopyrans which were the THC analogues that presented the rationale that started the whole project in the first place. A recent issue of the Journal of Medicinal Chemistry has just presented an article describing the reaction of 6-methoxytetrahydrobenzopyran with dichloromethyl methyl ether, and approximately equal amounts of all three of the possible isomers were obtained. That would have been the first step towards making the prototypic compound 7-(2-aminopropyl) 6-methoxy-1,2,3,4-tetrahydrobenzopyran. Just as the benzofurans were all named as F-compounds, this, as a benzopyran, would have been a P compound, but P also is used for proscaline, and there would have been some repair-work needed for these codes.

Time to abandon ship. The fact that I had just synthesized and discovered the strange activity of ARIADNE at about this time, made the ship abandonment quite a bit easier to accept.

#81 FLEA; N-HYDROXY-N-METHYL-3,4-METHYLENEDIOXYAMPHETAMINE

SYNTHESIS: (from 3,4-methylenedioxyphenylacetone) A solution of 2.1 g N-methylhydroxylamine hydrochloride and 4.4 g 3,4-methylenedioxyphenylacetone in 5.5 mL MeOH was added to a suspension of 4.5 g NaHCO$_3$ in 30 mL boiling MeOH. There was added about 5 mL H$_2$O (which gave a clear solution) followed by another 50 mL H$_2$O which produced a pale yellow color. To this solution of the unisolated nitrone there was added 1.7 g sodium cyanoborohydride, which generated a goodly amount of foaming. There was HCl added as needed to maintain the pH at about neutrality. The reaction appeared to have stopped after a day or two, so all was poured into 500 mL H$_2$O, acidified with HCl, and washed with 2x75 mL CH$_2$Cl$_2$. The addition of base brought the pH >9, and this was then extracted with 3x75 mL CH$_2$Cl$_2$. Removal of the solvent from the pooled extracts gave a residue of 1.65 g of crude N-hydroxy-N-methyl-3,4-methylenedioxyamphetamine. Efforts to obtain solid seed samples of the salts with hydrochloric acid, perchloric acid, sulfuric acid, phosphoric acid, and with a number of organic acids, all failed. The salt formation from this free-base will be discussed below.

(from MDOH) A solution of 0.75 g crystalline free-base MDOH in a few mL MeOH was treated with a solution of 0.4 g sodium cyanoborohydride in 10 mL MeOH, and there was then added 2 mL of 35% formaldehyde. The stirred reaction mixture was kept at a neutral pH with the occasional addition of HCl. After several days (when additional acid was no longer required) the excess solvent was removed under vacuum, and the residue poured into dilute H$_2$SO$_4$. This was washed with 2x75 mL CH$_2$Cl$_2$ and then, following the addition of base, this was extracted with

3x75 mL CH_2Cl_2. Removal of the solvent from the pooled extracts gave a viscous oil residue of 0.53 g. The free-base product from these preparations was distilled at 110-120 °C at 0.2 mm/Hg to give the N-hydroxy-N-methyl product as a white oil. An alternate methylation procedure used a solution of MDOH in a 4:1 MeOH/acetic acid solution containing formaldehyde which was reduced with sodium borohydride at dry ice temperatures. Its work-up is identical to that involving sodium cyanoborohydride.

The distilled product was dissolved in an equal volume of MeOH, and treated with a half-equivalent of oxalic acid dihydrate, dissolved in 10 volumes of MeOH. This combination gave the slow deposition of crystals of the full oxalate salt (one acid, two bases) as a white crystalline product. The mp of the crude salt was in the 130-150 °C range, and after recrystallization from CH_3CN, N-hydroxy-N-methyl-3,4-methylenedioxyamphetamine oxalate (FLEA) had a mp of 146-147 °C.

DOSAGE: 100 - 160 mg.

DURATION: 4 - 8 h.

QUALITATIVE COMMENTS: (with 90 mg) "The material tastes terrible, like grapefruit juice that has stayed in the can too long. There was no nausea, no feeling of difficulty in swallowing at any time during the day. I felt a dry mouth and was thirsty — sipped water throughout the day. At the beginning of the experiment, there was a glimmer of the MDMA warmth, but later I felt separated and a bit isolated. I was just floating around, seeing the beauty of colors and objects in the house and outdoors and listening first to this conversation, then to that one. All senses seemed enhanced. I found the material pleasant. I was happy with the amount I took but would not be afraid to take more or to take a supplement. I found it similar to, but not the same as, MDMA."

(with 110 mg) "We found this very similar to MDMA, but perhaps slightly slower. I plateau'd at 2:30 hours and had a very gradual descent. My friend had a marvelous and private 'cone of silence' that was to him unique to MDMA or to 2C-T-8. Teeth problems were minor, and the descent from the top of the experience showed less interactive, and more contemplative action, than with MDMA. Very similar to MDMA, but with its own character."

(with 110 mg) "The onset was at about a half-hour. The come-on was more gradual and much easier than with MDMA, and it seemed to be more head than body oriented. I had about two hours of very complex and personal self-evaluation, and I am not at peace in putting all of it down here in writing. Overall I like it, and I would be interested to see if there's a difference in conjunction with MDMA. Thanks very much."

(with 110 mg + 35 mg) "I saw my onset at 20 minutes, and it was subtle, and very pleasant, and had a mild amphetamine-like elevation for me (body lightness, cognitive functions seemed clear and clean, heightened visual awareness and with some enhancement of color). It seemed as if I were on the fringe of LSD-like visual changes, but that never materialized. The affect was very good, communicative, friendly, accepting, but without the profound emotional bonding of MDMA. The following day felt very much like a post-LSD day; we felt great. The body was light, energy good, emotions high, several insights throughout the day, interactions clear and open — a magnificent gift of a day. I started a menstrual period the day of the experience and it lasted 6 to 7 days; all of this was a couple of weeks early. I have a very favorable impression of FLEA although the body penalty seems high."

EXTENSIONS AND COMMENTARY: Most people who were involved with the evaluation of FLEA quite logically compared it with MDMA, as it was presented as being a very close analogue which might share some of the latter's properties. And to a large measure, the comparison was favorable. The dosages are almost identical, the chronological course of action is almost identical, and there are distinct similarities in the effects that are produced. If there is a consensus of similarities and differences it would be that it is not quite as enabling in allowing a closeness to be established with others. And perhaps there is more of a move towards introspection. And perhaps a slightly increased degree of discoordination in the thought processes. But also, part of this same consensus was that, were MDMA unknown, this material would have played its role completely.

And from the scientific point of view, it lends more weight to a hypothesis that just might be a tremendous research tool in pharmacology. I first observed the intimate connection between an amine and a hydroxylamine with the discovery that N-hydroxy-MDA (MDOH) was equipotent and of virtually identical activity to the non-hydroxylated counterpart (MDA). And I have speculated in the recipe for MDOH about the possible biological interconversions of these kinds of compounds. And here, the simple addition of a hydroxyl group to the amine nitrogen atom of MDMA produces a new drug that is in most of its properties identical to MDMA. The concept has been extended to 2C-T-2, 2C-T-7, and 2C-T-17, where each of these three active compounds was structurally modified in exactly this way, by the addition of a hydroxyl group to the amine nitrogen atom. The results, HOT-2, HOT-7 and HOT-17 were themselves all active, and compared very closely with their non-hydroxylated prototypes.

Just how general might this concept be, that an N-hydroxyl analog of an active amine shall be of similar action and duration as the parent drug? What if it really were a generality! What havoc it would wreak in the pharmaceutical industry! If I could patent the concept, then I would be able to make parallel best sellers to all of the primary and secondary amines out there in the industry. Perhaps 90% of all the commercially available drugs that are concerned with the human mental state are amines. And a goodly number of these are primary or secondary amines. And each and every one of these could be converted to its N-hydroxyl analogue, effectively by-passing the patent protection that the originating corporation so carefully crafted. An example, just for fun. A run-away best seller right now is an antidepressant called fluoxetine, with the trade name Prozac. I will make a small wager that if I were to synthesize and taste N-hydroxy-N-methyl-3-phenyl-3-((α,α,α-trifluoro-p-tolyl)oxy)propylamine, I would find it to be an active antidepressant. Remember, Mr. Eli Lilly and Company; you read about it first, right here!

Of course, I was asked, why call it FLEA? The origin was in a classic bit of poetry. A commonly used code name for MDMA was ADAM, and I had tried making several modest modifications of the MDMA structure in the search for another compound that would maintain its particular music without the annoying tooth-grinding and occasional nystagmus, or eye-wiggle, that some users have mentioned. One of these was the 6-methyl homologue which was, with some perverse logic, called MADAM. And, following this pattern, the 6-fluoroanalogue was to be FLADAM. So, with the N-hydroxy analogue, what about HADAM? Which brought to mind the classic description of Adam's earliest complaint, an infestation of fleas. The poem was short and direct. "Adam had 'em." So, in place of HAD 'EM, the term FLEA jumped into being.

#82   G-3;   2,5-DIMETHOXY-3,4-(TRIMETHYLENE)AMPHETAMINE; 5-(2-AMINOPROPYL)-4,7-DIMETHOXYINDANE

SYNTHESIS: A solution of 3.7 g of 2,5-dimethoxy-3,4-(trimethylene)benzaldehyde (see preparation under 2C-G-3) in 15 mL nitroethane was treated with 0.7 g anhydrous ammonium acetate and heated on the steam bath for 2.5 h. The excess solvent was removed under vacuum leaving some 5 mL of a deep orange-red oil which on cooling, spontaneously crystallized. This was finely ground under 10 mL Meoh, filtered, washed sparingly with MeOH, and air dried to give 3.6 g of orange crystals with a strong smell of old acetamide. The mp was 92-93 °C. All was recrystallized from 30 mL boiling MeOH to give, after filtering and drying, 2.9 g of 1-(2,5-dimethoxy-3,4-(trimethylene)-phenyl)-2-nitropropene as yellow crystals with a mp of 93-94 °C. Anal. (C$_{14}$H$_{17}$NO$_4$) C,H,N.

Fifty milliliters of 1 M LAH in THF was placed in an inert atmosphere, well stirred, and cooled to 0 °C with an external ice-bath. There was added, dropwise, 1.35 mL of 100% H$_2$SO$_4$ at a rate slow enough to minimize charring. There was then added, dropwise, 2.8 g 1-(2,5-dimethoxy-3,4-(trimethylene)phenyl)-2-nitropropene in 15 mL THF. At the end of the addition, the stirring was continued for an additional 0.5 h, and then the reaction mixture was held at reflux on the steam bath for another 0.5 h. After cooling again to ice-bath temperature, the excess hydride was destroyed with the addition of 11 mL IPA, followed by 5.5 mL 5% NaOH which converted the inorganic mass through a cottage cheese stage into a loose, filterable texture. The solids were removed by filtration, washed with additional THF, and the combined filtrates and washes stripped of solvent under vacuum. There was obtained 2.51 g of a white oil that was distilled at 115-135 °C at 0.2 mm/Hg to give 1.83 g of a clear colorless oil. This was dissolved in 8 mL IPA, neutralized with 28 drops of concentrated HCl, and diluted with 140 mL anhydrous Et_2O. In about 0.5 h there started a slow snowfall of fine fluffy white crystals which was allowed to continue until no additional crystals appeared. After filtering, Et_2O washing and air drying, there was obtained 1.81 g of 2,5-dimethoxy-3,4-(tri-methylene)amphetamine hydrochloride (G-3) with a mp of 157-159 °C. Anal. ($C_{14}H_{22}ClNO_2$) C,H.

DOSAGE: 12 - 18 mg.

DURATION: 8 - 12 h.

QUALITATIVE COMMENTS: (with 12 mg) "There was a warmth, a mellowness, as things developed. No body disturbance at all, but then there were no visuals either which, for me on this particular occasion, was disappointing. The day was consumed in reading, and I identified completely with the character of my fictional hero. It was a different form of fantasy. I think I prefer music as a structural basis for fantasy."

(with 18 mg) "I am at a plus three, but I am not at all sure of why it is a plus three. With my eyes closed, there are puffy clouds, but no drama at all. Music was not exciting. There could well have been easy eroticism, but there was no push in that direction. No great amount of appetite. Not much of anything, and still a plus three. Simply lying still and surveying the body rather than the visual scene gave some suggestions of neurological sensitivity, but with getting up and moving about and doing things, all was fine. The next morning I was perhaps moving a bit more slowly than usual. I am not sure that there would be reward in going higher."

EXTENSIONS AND COMMENTARY: In a comparison between the 2-carbon compound (2C-G-3) and the 3-carbon compound (G-3) the vote goes towards the phenethylamine (the 2-carbon compound). With the first member of this series (2C-G versus GANESHA) this was a stand-off, both as to quantitative effects (potency) and qualitative effects (nature of activity). Here, with the somewhat bulkier group located at the definitive 3,4-positions, the nod is to the shorter chain, for the first time ever. The potency differences are small, and maybe the amphetamine is still a bit more potent. But there are hints of discomfort with this latter compound that seem to be absent with the phenethylamine. The more highly substituted compounds (q.v.) more clearly define these differences.

#83   G-4;   2,5-DIMETHOXY-3,4-(TETRAMETHYLENE)-AMPHETAMINE;   6-(2-AMINOPROPYL)-5,8-DIMETHOXY-TETRALIN

SYNTHESIS: A solution of 1,4-dimethoxy-5,6,7,8-tetrahydro-ß-naphthaldehyde (see preparation under 2C-G-4) in 20 mL nitroethane was treated with 0.13 g anhydrous ammonium acetate and heated on the steam bath overnight. The volatiles were removed under vacuum and the residue, on cooling, spontaneously crystallized. This crude rust-colored product (1.98 g) was recrystallized from 15 mL boiling MeOH yielding, after filtering and air drying to constant weight, 1.33 g of 1-(2,5-dimethoxy-3,4-(tetramethylene)phenyl)-2-nitropropene as dull gold-colored crystals. The mp was 94-94.5 °C. Anal. ($C_{15}H_{19}NO_4$) C,H.

DOSAGE: unknown.

DURATION: unknown.

EXTENSIONS AND COMMENTARY: The discussion that appeared in the commentary section under 2C-G-4 applies here as well. The major struggles were in the preparation of the aldehyde itself. And although the final product has not yet been made, this last synthetic step should be, as Bobby Fischer once said in his analysis of a master's chess game following a blunder by his opponent, simply a matter of technique.

As with the phenethylamine counterpart, G-4 has a structure that lies intermediate between G-3 and G-5, both potent compounds. It is axiomatic that it too will be a potent thing, and all that now needs be done is to complete its synthesis and taste it.

#84   G-5;   3,6-DIMETHOXY-4-(2-AMINOPROPYL)BENZONORBORNANE

SYNTHESIS: A solution of 3.70 g 3,6-dimethoxy-4-formylbenzonorbornane (see under 2C-G-5 for its preparation) in 20 g nitroethane was treated with 0.88 g anhydrous ammonium acetate and held at steam bath temperature overnight. The excess solvent and reagent was removed under vacuum to yield a residual yellow oil. This was allowed to stand at ambient temperature for a period of time (about 3 years) by which time there was a spontaneous crystallization. The dull yellow crystals were removed by filtration and, after air drying, weighed 4.28 g. A small sample was recrystallized repeatedly from MeOH to provide a pale yellow analytical sample of 3,6-dimethoxy-4-(2-nitropropenyl)benzonorbornane with a mp of 90-91 °C. Anal. $(C_{16}H_{19}NO_4)$ C,H.

A solution of LAH (50 mL of 1 M solution in THF) was cooled, under He, to 0 °C with an external ice bath. With good stirring there was added 1.32 mL 100% H_2SO_4 dropwise, to minimize charring. This was followed by the addition of 4.1 g 3,6-dimethoxy-4-(2-nitropropenyl)benzonorbornane in 20 mL anhydrous THF over the course of 10 min. The reaction mixture was stirred and brought to room temperature over the course of 1 h. This was then brought to a gentle reflux on the steam bath for 0.5 h, and then all was cooled again to 0 °C. The excess hydride was destroyed by the cautious addition of 10 mL IPA followed by 5 mL 5% NaOH and sufficient H_2O to give a white granular character to the oxides. The reaction mixture was filtered, and the filter cake washed with THF. The filtrate was stripped of solvent under vacuum providing a pale amber oil that was distilled at 125-140 °C at 0.2 mm/Hg to give 2.5 g of an almost white oil. This was dissolved in 10 mL IPA, neutralized with 25 drops of concentrated HCl, and then diluted with 140 mL anhydrous Et_2O. There appeared, after about two minutes, white crystals of 3,6-dimethoxy-4-(2-aminopropyl)benzonorbornane hydrochloride (G-5) which, after filtration and air drying, weighed 2.47 g.

DOSAGE: 14 - 20 mg.

DURATION: 16 - 30 h.

QUALITATIVE COMMENTS: (with 15 mg) "As part of the audience at the San Francisco conference, Angels, Aliens and Archtypes, I could simply listen and observe without having to participate. Each speaker stood in a cone of light that was beautifully bright and colorful, casting everything else on the stage into obscurity. Maybe angels really are illuminated from above, and the aliens lurk out of sight until it is their turn. Where does one look for the archetypes? A half of a cream cheese sandwich was all I could eat, and even at dinner that evening I was not hungry. Sleep that evening was difficult."

(with 20 mg) "Very slow to come on, but then it was up there all of a sudden. There is an unexpected absence of visual activity despite being at a full +++. The mental activity is excellent, with easy writing and a positive flow of ideas. But an absence of the bells and whistles that are expected with a psychedelic in full bloom. There is a real drop by the 16th hour and the next day was free of effect except for occasional cat-naps."

(with 20 mg) "The transition period, which usually lasts for most compounds for the first hour or two, with this seems to be much longer. This presages a long-acting material, as usually the slow-in slow-out rule applies. But there are exceptions. There is an indifference towards the erotic, but no separation at all from personal interactions and emotions. I believe in integration, not separation of all parts of ourselves, distrusting any drug states (particularly those that have the reputation of being strongly 'cosmic)' which divorce the consciousness from the body. And with this material there is no separation from feelings, only from my particular color language."

EXTENSIONS AND COMMENTARY: This is as potent as any of the three-carbon Ganesha compounds, but it somehow lacks a little something that would have made it a completely favorite winner. Perhaps it is the generally commented upon absence of visual and related sensory entertainment. There seems to be no bodily threat to discourage further exploration, but there simply was not the drive to explore it much. The comments concerning the enlargement of the ring system (mentioned under 2C-G-5) are equally valid here. The "shrubbery" that is the hallmark of the Ganesha family is, with G-5, about as bulky as has ever been put onto a centrally active molecule. The norbornane group has a one carbon bridge and a two carbon bridge sticking out of it at odd angles. The replacement of the one-carbon bridge with a second two-carbon bridge would make the compound G-6. It would be makeable, but is there really a driving reason to do so? There is a simplification intrinsic in this, in that G-5 actually has two centers of asymmetry (the α-carbon atom on the amphetamine chain, and the norbornyl area itself) and so it is really a mixture of two racemic diastereoisomers. G-6 would still be a racemate, but it would be only a single compound, as are all the other substituted amphetamine derivatives.

Someday I may try making G-6, but it's not a high priority right now.

#85   GANESHA;   G;   2,5-DIMETHOXY-3,4-DIMETHYLAMPHETAMINE

SYNTHESIS: A solution of 15.4 g 2,5-dimethoxy-3,4-dimethylbenzaldehyde (see under 2C-G for the preparation) in 50 mL nitroethane was treated with 3 g anhydrous ammonium acetate and heated on the steam bath for 12 h. The excess nitroethane was removed under vacuum, and the residual oil was diluted with a equal volume of MeOH. There was the slow generation of deep red cottage-cheese-like crystals which were removed by filtration and air-dried to constant weight (9.3 g) with a mp 71-74 °C. Recrystallization from MeOH (10 ml/g) gave an analytical sample of 1-(2,5-dimethoxy-3,4-dimethylphenyl)-2-nitropropene with a mp of 82 °C sharp. Anal. $(C_{13}H_{17}NO_4)$ C,H,N.

The NMR spectra (in $CDCl_3$) and CI mass spectrograph (MH+ = 252) were proper.

To a suspension of 3.3 g LAH in 200 mL refluxing THF, well stirred and maintained under an inert atmosphere, there was added 4.2 g 1-(2,5-dimethoxy-3,4-dimethylphenyl)-2-nitropropene in 25 mL THF. The mixture was held at reflux for 48 h. After cooling, 3.3 mL H_2O was added cautiously to decompose the excess hydride, followed by 3.3 mL 15% NaOH and finally another 10 mL H_2O. The inorganic solids were removed by filtration, and washed with additional THF. The combined filtrate and washes were stripped of solvent under vacuum, and the residue (4.7 g of a deep amber oil) dissolved in dilute HCl. This was washed with CH_2Cl_2 (3x75 mL), then made basic with 5% NaOH and extracted with CH_2Cl_2. Removal of the solvent under vacuum yielded an amber oil that was distilled (105-115 °C at 0.4 mm/Hg) to give 1.2 g of a white oil. This was dissolved in 8 mL IPA, neutralized with 15 drops of concentrated HCl, and diluted with 250 mL anhydrous Et_2O. After a period of time, there was a spontaneous appearance of white crystals which were removed by filtration, Et_2O washed, and air dried. Thus was obtained 1.0 g of 2,5-dimethoxy-3,4-dimethylamphetamine hydrochloride (GANESHA) with a mp of 168-169 °C. This was not improved by recrystallization from either EtOAc or nitroethane. Anal. $(C_{13}H_{22}ClNO_2)$ N.

DOSAGE: 20 - 32 mg.

DURATION: 18 - 24 h.

QUALITATIVE COMMENTS: (with 24 mg) "There was a slow buildup to a ++ or more over the course of about three hours. Extremely tranquil, and no hint of any body toxicity whatsoever. More than tranquil, I was completely at peace, in a beautiful, benign, and placid place. There was something residual that extended into the sleep period, and was possibly still there in the morning. Probably I was simply tired from an inadequate sleep."

(with 32 mg) "A rapid and full development. Lying down with music, the eyes-closed visuals were quite something. There was sudden awareness of a potential toe cramp which I possibly exaggerated, but it kept spinning itself into my awareness, and somehow locked in with my visual imagery. It was not easy to keep the visual/somatic/ cognitive worlds in their proper places. The almost-cramp went away and I forgot about it. There was a back spasm somewhere in this drama, and it really didn't matter either. This dosage may be a bit much for good housekeeping, though! Towards the end of the experiment, I looked at a collection of photos from a recent trip to Europe, and the visual enhancement was wonderful. A rolling +++."

EXTENSIONS AND COMMENTARY: This compound was the seventh of the ten possible Classic Ladies. I have mentioned the concept already under the discussions on ARIADNE. This is the teutonic replacement of each of the distinguishable hydrogen atoms of DOM with a methyl group. The findings with GANESHA were a total surprise. The extension of a hydrogen in the 3-position of DOM with a methyl group should have a minor influence on its steric association with whatever receptor site might be involved. A much greater impact might come not from the size of the group but from its location. This, coupled with a full order of magnitude of *decrease* in potency, seemed to call for an involvement of that particular position as being one that is affected by metabolism. And since the activity is decreased, the obvious role is in the blocking of the metabolic promotion of DOM-like things to active intermediates.

The remarkable point being emphasized here is that the placement of a dull methyl group at a dull position of the DOM molecule actually inactivated (for all intents and purposes) the activity of DOM. It is not the presence of the methyl that has decimated the potency, but the removal of the hydrogen atom.

How can such a hypothesis be explored? A historic premise of the medicinal chemist is that if a structure gives an unusual response in a receptor, vary it slightly and see how the response varies. This is exactly the principle that led to the ten Classic Ladies, and with this particular Lady (who actually turned out to be a gentleman), the same concept should hold. There are two involved methyl groups in GANESHA, one at the 3-position and one at the 4-position. Why not homologate each to an ethyl group, and as a wrap up make both of them into ethyl groups. Look at the differences along two lines of variation; the effects of the homologation of the 3- and 4-positions, coupled with the effects of the homologation intrinsic in the comparison of the two-carbon chain of the phenethylamine with the three-carbon chain of the amphetamine.

There are thus six compounds involved in such a study. And they have been named (as have all the other GANESHA analogues) in accordance with the collective carbon inventory in and about these two ring positions. The first two compounds are related to DOET and to 2C-E. Maintain the methyl group at the 3-position but homologate the 4-position to an ethyl. The ring pattern would become 2,5-dimethoxy-4-ethyl-3-methyl, and the phenethylamine and amphetamine would be called 2C-G-12 and G-12 respectively (a one carbon thing, the methyl, at position-3 and a two carbon thing, an ethyl, at position-4). Reversal of these groups, the 3-ethyl homologues of 2C-D and DOM would thus become 2C-G-21 and G-21. And, finally, the diethyl homologues would be 2C-G-22 and G-22. In each of these cases, the paired numbers give the lengths of the chains at the two positions, the 3- and the 4-positions that are part of the GANESHA concept. And this code is easily expandable to longer things such as 2C-G-31 and 2C-G-41, which would be the 3-propyl-4-methyl, and the 3-butyl-4-methyl homologues, resp.

Unfortunately, these six initially proposed compounds have so far resisted all logical approaches to synthesis, and are at present still unknown. What has been successfully achieved, the building up of a big bulky hydrocarbon glob at these positions, has rather unexpectedly led to a remarkable enhancement of potency. As with all true exploration into areas of the unknown, the deeper you get, the less you understand.

#86 G-N; 1,4-DIMETHOXYNAPHTHYL-2-ISOPROPYLAMINE

SYNTHESIS: To a solution of 3.9 g 1,4-dimethoxy-2-naphthaldehyde (see under 2C-G-N for the preparation) in 13.5 mL nitroethane there was added 0.7 g anhydrous ammonium acetate, and the mixture heated on the steam bath for 5 h. The deep orange reaction mixture was stripped of excess solvent under vacuum. The residue was a red oil that, upon dilution with two volumes MeOH, immediately set to orange crystals. This crude product (mp 115-118 °C) was recrystallized from 70 mL EtOH to yield, after filtering and air drying, 3.3 g of 1-(1,4-dimethoxy-2-naphthyl)-2-nitropropene as gold-orange crystals, with a mp of 121-123 °C. Recrystallization from MeOH gave a gold-colored product with a mp of 119-120 °C. Anal. ($C_{15}H_{15}NO_4$) C,H,N.

A solution of LAH (50 mL of 1 M solution in THF) was cooled, under He, to 0 °C with an external ice-bath. With good stirring there was added 1.32 mL 100% H_2SO_4 dropwise, to minimize charring. This was followed by the addition of 3.12 g 1-(1,4-dimethoxy-2-naphthyl)-2-nitropropene in 40 mL anhydrous THF. After stirring for 1 h, the temperature was brought up to a gentle reflux on the steam bath for 0.5 h, and then all was cooled again to 0 °C. The excess hydride was destroyed by the cautious addition of 16 mL IPA followed by 6 mL 5% NaOH to give a white, filterable, granular character to the oxides, and to assure that the reaction mixture was basic. The reaction mixture was filtered, and the filter cake washed with additional THF. The combined filtrate and washes were stripped of solvent under vacuum providing 3.17 g of a deep amber oil. Without any further purification, this was distilled at 140-160 °C at 0.3 mm/Hg to give 1.25 g of a pale yellow oil. This was dissolved in 8 mL IPA, neutralized with 20 drops of concentrated HCl, and diluted with 60 mL anhydrous Et_2O which was the point at which the solution became slightly turbid. After a few min, fine white crystals began to form, and these were eventually removed, washed with Et_2O, and air dried to provide 1.28 g 1,4-dimethoxynaphthyl-2-isopropylamine hydrochloride (G-N) as the monohydrate salt. The mp was 205-206 °C. Even after 24 h drying at 100 °C under vacuum, the hydrate salt remained intact. Anal. ($C_{15}H_{20}ClNO_2·H_2O$) C,H.

DOSAGE: unknown.

DURATION: unknown,

EXTENTIONS AND COMMENTARY: The evaluation of this compound is not yet complete. An initial trial at the 2 milligram level showed neither central action, nor toxicity. It could be guessed from the activity of the two-carbon counterpart, that an active level will be found in the tens of milligrams area. But, as of the moment, this level is not known to anyone, anywhere, because no one has yet defined it. And when the potency is finally found out, the nature of the activity will also have been found out, all the result of a magical interaction of a virgin compound with a virgin psyche. At the immediate moment, the nature of G-N is not only unknown, it has not yet even been sculpted. There can be no more exciting area of research than this, anywhere in the sentient world.

#87   HOT-2;   2,5-DIMETHOXY-4-ETHYLTHIO-N-HYDROXYPHENETHYLAMINE

SYNTHESIS: A solution of 5.50 g 2,5-dimethoxy-4-ethylthio-ß-nitrostyrene (see under 2C-T-2 for its preparation) was made in 80 mL boiling anhydrous THF. On cooling, there was some separation of a fine crystalline phase, which was kept dispersed by continuous stirring. Under an inert atmosphere there was added 3.5 mL of a 10 M borane dimethylsulfide complex, followed by 0.5 g sodium borohydride as a solid. There was a slight exothermic response, and the color slowly faded. Stirring was continued for a week. There was then added 40 mL H_2O and 20 mL concentrated HCl, and the reaction mixture heated on the steam bath for 15 minutes, with the THF at reflux. After cooling again to room temperature, all was poured into 1 L H_2O and washed with 3x75 mL CH_2Cl_2, which removed all of the color but little of the product. The aqueous phase was made basic with 25% NaOH, and extracted with 3x75 mL CH_2Cl_2. The extracts were pooled and the solvent removed under vacuum to give a residue of 3.88 g of an amber oil. This was dissolved in 30 mL IPA, acidified with concentrated HCL to a bright red on universal pH paper, and then diluted with 200 mL anhydrous Et_2O. After a short period of time, crystals started to form. These were removed by filtration, washed with Et_2O, and air dried to constant weight. Thus was obtained 2.86 g 2,5-dimethoxy-4-ethylthio-N-hydroxyphenethylamine hydrochloride (HOT-2) as off-white crystals, with a melting point of 122 °C with decomposition. Anal. ($C_{12}H_{20}ClNO_3$ S) H; C: calcd, 49.05; found, 50.15, 49.90.

DOSAGE: 10 - 18 mg.

DURATION: 6 - 10 h.

QUALITATIVE COMMENTS: (with 12 mg) "Tastes OK. Some activity noticed in 30 minutes. Very smooth rise with no body load for next two hours. At that time I noted some visuals. Very pleasant. The bright spots in the painting over the fireplace seemed to be moving backwards (as if the clouds were moving in the painting). Upon concentrating on any item, there was perceptual movement with a little flowing aspect. The visuals were never all that strong, but could not be turned off during the peak. At hour three there was still some shimmering, and it was hard to focus when reading. Additionally, there was difficulty concentrating (some mental confusion). The material seemed to allow erotic actions; there was no problem about obtaining an erection. I ate very well, some crazy dips, as well as a fabulous cake. A very gentle down trend and I became close to baseline by 6 or 7 PM. I had no trouble driving. The dosage was good for me. I did not want more or less."

(with 12 mg) "Comes on smoothly, nicely. In 40 minutes I feel nice euphoria, feel home again. Then I begin to get uncomfortable feelings. Gets more and more uncomfortable, feel I am sitting on a big problem. Blood pressure, pulse, go up considerably. Have hard time communicating, lie down for a while, get insight that most important thing for me to do is learn to listen, pay attention to what is going on. I do this the rest of the day, at first with considerable difficulty, then easier and easier. Discomfort stays with me for several hours, and although I get more comfortable towards the end of the day, I am never animated or euphoric. I feel very humbled, that I have a great deal to work out in my life. The next day I find myself very strong and empowered. I see that all I have to do is let things be as they are! This feels marvelous, and a whole new way to be — much more relaxed, accepting, being in the moment. No more axes to grind. I can be free."

(with 18 mg) "I found myself with complete energy. I was completely centered with an absolute minimum of the dark edges that so often appear as components of these experiences. The ease of talking was remarkable. There was some blood-pressure run-up in the early part of the day, but that quickly returned to normal. I would repeat without hesitation."

EXTENSIONS AND COMMENTARY: Again, a case of where the potency range of the "hot," or hydroxylated compound (HOT-2, 10 to 18 milligrams) is very similar to that of the non-hydroxylated prototype (2C-T-2, 12-25 milligrams). It seems to be a well tolerated, and generally pleasant material, with a mixture of sensory as well as insightful aspects. Something for everyone.

#88 HOT-7; 2,5-DIMETHOXY-N-HYDROXY-4-(n)-PROPYLTHIOPHENETHYLAMINE

SYNTHESIS: A well-stirred solution of 1.77 g 2,5-dimethoxy-ß-nitro-4-(n-propylthio)styrene (see under 2C-T-7 for its preparation) in 20 mL anhydrous THF was placed in an He atmosphere and treated with 1.5 mL of 10 M borane-dimethyl sulfide complex. This was followed by the addition of 0.2 g sodium borohydride, and the stirring was continued at room temperature for a week. The volatiles were removed under vacuum, and the residue was treated with 20 mL dilute HCl and heated on the steam bath for 30 min. The cooled yellow solution set up as solids. The addition of H_2O was followed by sufficient K_2CO_3 to make the aqueous phase basic. All efforts to work with an acidified aqueous phase resulted in terrible emulsions. The basic phase was extracted with 3x75 mL CH_2Cl_2, and the pooled extracts washed with H_2O, then stripped of solvent under vacuum. The residual yellow oil was dissolved in 20 mL IPA, neutralized with 15 drops of concentrated HCl, and then diluted with 50 mL anhydrous Et_2O. After a few minutes stirring, a white crystalline solid separated. This was removed by filtration, washed with Et_2O, and air dried to constant weight to provide 0.83 g of 2,5-dimethoxy-N-hydroxy-4-(n)-propylthiophenethylamine hydrochloride (HOT-7).

DOSAGE: 15 - 25 mg.

DURATION: 6 - 8 h.

QUALITATIVE COMMENTS: (with 15 mg) "I am lightheaded, and maybe a little tipsy. I am well centered, but I don't want to go outside and meet people. Shades of alcohol woozy. The effects were going already by the fifth hour and were gone by the seventh hour. I would call it smoothly stoning."

(with 22 mg) "The transition into the effects was a bit difficult, with a faint awareness in the tummy. But by the second hour it was quite psychedelic, and the body was not thought of again, except in terms of sexual fooling around. Very rich in eyes-closed imagery, and very good for interpretive and conceptual thinking. But the eyes-open visuals were not as much as they might have been. At the seventh hour, drifted into an easy sleep."

(with 22 mg) "The experience was very positive, but at each turn there seemed to be a bit of sadness. Was it a complete plus three experience? Not quite. But it didn't miss by much. The erotic explorations somehow just failed to knit by the thinnest of margins. It was a truly almost-magnificent experience."

EXTENSIONS AND COMMENTARY: There is a working hypothesis that has been growing in substance over the last few years in this strange and marvelous area of psychedelic drugs. It all was an outgrowth of the rather remarkable coincidence that I had mentioned in the discussion that followed MDOH. There, an assay of what was thought to be MDOH gave a measure of activity that was substantially identical to MDA, and it was later found out that the material had decomposed to form MDA. So, MDA was in essence rediscovered. But when the true, valid, and undecomposed sample of MDOH was actually in hand, and assayed in its own rights, it was found to have a potency that really was the same as MDA. So, the working hypothesis goes something like this:

AN N-HYDROXY AMINE HAS APPROXIMATELY THE SAME POTENCY AND THE SAME ACTION AS ITS N-HYDROGEN COUNTER-PART.

Maybe the N-hydroxy compound reduces to the N-H material in the body, and the latter is the intrinsically active agent. Maybe the N-H material oxidizes to the N-hydroxy material in the body, and the latter is the intrinsically active agent. Either direction is reasonable, and there is precedent for each. The equivalence of MDA and MDOH was the first suggestion of this. And I have made a number of NH vs. NOH challenges of this hypothesis. The interesting 2C-T-X series has provided a number of amines that are amenable to N-hydroxylation, and this is the first of them. And, after all, if you put a hydroxy (HO) group on a thio material (T), you have a HOT compound.

So, as far as nomenclature is concerned, the family of N-hydroxy analogues of N-H amines is known as the HOT family.

How does HOT-7 compare with 2C-T-7? They are almost identical. The same range of dose (centering on 20 milligrams) and if anything, perhaps slightly less long lived. Lets try some other N-hydroxys!

#89   HOT-17;   2,5-DIMETHOXY-4-(s)-BUTYLTHIO-N-HYDROXYPHENETHYLAMINE

SYNTHESIS: To a well-stirred solution of 6.08 g 2,5-dimethoxy-4-(s)-butylthio-ß-nitrostyrene (see under 2C-T-17 for its preparation) in 80 mL anhydrous THF under a He atmosphere, there was added 3.5 mL 10 M borane dimethylsulfide complex, followed by 0.5 g of sodium borohydride. As the stirring continued, the slightly exothermic reaction slowly faded from bright yellow to pale yellow, and eventually (after three days stirring) it was substantially colorless. There was then added 80 mL of 3 N HCl and the mixture heated on the steam bath for 1 h, and then allowed to return to room temperature. An additional 600 mL H_2O was added

(there was a combination of crystals and globby chunks in the aqueous phase) and this was then extracted with 3x75 mL CH_2Cl_2. The color went completely into the organic phase. This was washed with 2x50 mL aqueous K_2CO_3, yielding a rusty-red colored CH_2Cl_2 solution, which on removal of the solvent, yielded 4.5 g of a red oil. A side effort to make the sulfate salt at this stage with H_2O and a little H_2SO_4, indeed gave solids, but all of the color remained in the sulfate salt. The red oil was dissolved in 45 mL IPA and neutralized with concentrated HCl to bright red, not yellow, on universal pH paper. The addition of 350 mL anhydrous Et_2O instituted the slow precipitation of white crystals. After filtering and air drying, there was obtained 1.32 g 2,5-dimethoxy-4-(s)-butylthio-N-hydroxyphenethylamine hydro-chloride (HOT-17). The aqueous phase from above was just neutralized with 25% NaOH (cloudy, slightly pink color) and then made basic with K_2CO_3 (the color becomes green). This was extracted with 3x75 mL CH_2Cl_2, the extracts pooled, and the solvent removed to yield 0.5 g of a white oil. This was dissolved in 5 mL IPA, neutralized with concentrated HCl, and diluted with a equal volume of Et_2O. An additional 0.36 g of product was thus obtained.

DOSAGE: 70 - 120 mg.

DURATION : 12 - 18 h.

QUALITATIVE COMMENTS: (with 70 mg) "There was a light feeling, a little off-the-ground feeling, which made walking about a most pleasant experience. No distortion of the senses. And there was no sense of the beginning of a drop of any kind until about the eighth hour. Sleeping was a bit tricky but it worked out OK (at the twelfth hour of the experience). A completely valid ++."

(with 120 mg) "HOT-17 has an unbelievably GRIM taste — not bitter, but simply evil. There is a steady and inexorable climb for three hours to a sound and rolling plus three. There was absolutely no body difficulty, but there was still something going on upstairs well into the next day. Writing was surprisingly easy; I was completely content with the day, and would be interested in exploring it under a variety of circumstances."

(with 120 mg) "This is my first time with this material. It is 4:45 PM. Small nudge at 30 minutes, but not too real. At one hour, threshold, quite real. 6:15 to a +1. By 7:25, +3 about. 7:45, no doubt +3. Possibly still climbing; I hope so. No body discomfort at all, no apparent body push. This aspect of it is similar to the easy body of the HOT-2. However, it's at times like these that I reflect on just exactly how hard-headed we two are. I mean, +3 is no longer the out-of-body, nearly loss of center state it used to be, four years ago. The question intrudes: would a novice experience this as a very scary, ego-disintegrating kind of experiment, or not? Silly question which answers itself. Yes, of course. At 3 hours, aware of some mild time-distortion. More a tendency to not think in terms of clock-time, than actual distortion. The mind lazy when attempting to keep track of clock time. Feel it would be quite easy and pleasant to continue writing. The energy could very well go in that direction. However, the idea of the erotic is also quite agreeable. This is, so far, a good-humored Buddha area of the self."

EXTENSIONS AND COMMENTARY: Two virtues sought by some users of psychedelic drugs are high intensity and brief action. They want a quicky. Something that is really effective for a short period of time, then lets you quickly return to baseline, and presumably back to the real world out there.

Intensity is often (but not always) regulated by dose. The pharmacological property of dose-dependency applies to many of these drugs, in that the more you take, the more you get. If you want more intensity, take a second pill. And often, you get a longer duration as an added property. But it is instructive to inquire into the rationale that promotes brevity as a virtue. I believe that it says something concerning the reasons for using a psychedelic drug. A trade off between learning and entertainment. Or between the achieving of something and the appearance of achieving something. Or, in the concepts of the classics, between substance and image.

In a word, many people truly believe that they cannot afford the time or energy required for a deep search into themselves. One has to make a living, one has to maintain a social life, one has a multitude of obligations that truly consume the oh-so-few hours in the day. I simply cannot afford to take a day off just to indulge myself in such-and-such (choose one: digging to the bottom of a complex concept, giving my energies to those whom I can help, to search out my inner strengths and weaknesses) so instead I shall simply do such-and-such (choose one: read the book review, go to church on Sunday morning, use a short-acting psychedelic). The world is too much with us. This may be a bit harsh, but there is some merit to it.

HOT-17 is by no means a particularly potent compound. The hundred milligram area actually has been the kiss of death to several materials, as it is often at these levels that some physical concerns become evident. And it certainly is not a short lived compound. But, as has been so often the case, the long lived materials have proven to be the most memorable, in that once the entertainment aspect of the experience is past you, there is time for dipping deeply into the rich areas of the thought process, and the working through of ideas and concepts that are easily available. And when this access is coupled to the capability of talking and writing, then a rewarding experience is often the result.

As with the parent compound, 2C-T-17 itself, the presence of an asymmetric carbon atom out there on the (s)-butyl side chain will allow the separation of HOT-17 into two components which will be different and distinct in their actions. The activity of the racemic mixture often is an amalgamation of both sets of properties, and the separate assay of each component can often result in a fascinating and unexpected fractionation of these properties.

#90   IDNNA;   2,5-DIMETHOXY-N,N-DIMETHYL-4-IODOAMPHETAMINE

SYNTHESIS: To a stirred solution of 0.4 g 2,5-dimethoxy-4-iodoamphetamine hydrochloride (DOI) in 12 mL MeOH containing 4 mL of a 40% formaldehyde solution there was added 1 g sodium cyanoborohydride. The pH was kept at about 6 by the occasional addition of HCl. When the pH was stable (about 48 h) the reaction mixture was poured into 250 mL H_2O and made strongly basic by the addition of aqueous NaOH. This was extracted with 3x75 mL CH_2Cl_2, the extracts pooled, and extracted with 2x75 mL dilute H_2SO_4, and the pooled acidic extracts again made basic and again extracted with CH_2Cl_2. The solvent was removed under vacuum to give 0.38 g of a colorless oil. This was dissolved in 2 mL IPA and treated with a solution of 0.13 g oxalic acid dihydrate in 1.5 mL warm IPA, and then anhydrous Et_2O was added dropwise until a turbidity persisted. Slowly a granular white solid appeared, which was filtered off, Et_2O washed, and air dried to give 0.38 g of 2,5-dimethoxy-N,N-dimethyl-4-iodoamphetamine oxalate (IDNNA) with a mp of 145-146 °C. Anal. $(C_{15}H_{22}INO_6)$ C,H. The hydrochloride salt of this base proved to be hygroscopic.

DOSAGE: greater than 2.6 mg.

DURATION: unknown.

EXTENSIONS AND COMMENTARY: This base, if it were given a code name based upon its substituents arranged in their proper alphabetical order, would have to be called something like DNDIA, which is quite unpronounceable. But by a rearrangement of these terms, one can achieve IDNNA (Iodo-Dimethoxy-N,N-dimethyl-Amphetamine) which has a nice lilt to it.

One of the major goals of research in nuclear medicine is a drug that can be used to demonstrate the brain blood flow pattern. To do this job, a drug should demonstrate four properties. First, it must carry a radioactive isotope that is a positron emitter (best, a fluorine or an iodine atom, for use with the positron camera) that can be put onto the molecule quickly, synthetically, and which will stay on the molecule, metabolically. Second, as to brain entry, the drug should be rapidly and extensively taken up by brain tissue, without being selectively absorbed or concentrated at any specific sites. In other words, it should go where the blood goes. Thirdly, the absorption should be strong enough that it will stay in the brain, and not be washed out quickly. This allows time to both locate and count the radioactivity that was carried in there. And lastly, the drug must be without pharmacological action.

IDNNA looked like a promising candidate when tried with a radioactive iodine label, and there was quite a flurry of interest in using it both as an experimental drug, and as a prototype material for the synthesis of structural variants. It went in quickly, extensively and quite diffusely, and it stayed in for a long time.

But was it pharmacologically active? Here one finds a tricky road to walk. The animal toxicity and behavioral properties can be determined in a straightforward manner. Inject increasing amounts into an experimental animal and observe him closely. IDNNA was quite inert. But, it is a very close analogue to the extremely potent psychedelic DOI, and it is widely admitted that animal assays are of no use in trying to determine this specific pharmacological property. So, a quiet human assay was called for. Since it did indeed go into the brain of experimental animals, it could quite likely go into the brain of man. In fact, that would be a needed property if the drug were to ever become useful as a diagnostic tool.

It was assayed up to levels where DOI would have been active, and no activity was found. So one could state that it had none of the psychedelic properties of DOI at levels where DOI would be active (this, at 2.6 milligrams orally). But you don't assay much higher, because sooner or later, something might indeed show up. So it can be honestly said, IDNNA is less active than DOI itself, in man. Let's wave our hands a bit, and make our statement with aggressive confidence. IDNNA has shown no activity in the human CNS at any level that has been evaluated. This sounds pretty good. Just don't go too far up there, and don't look too carefully. This is not as unscrupulous as it might sound since, in practical terms, the extremely high specific activities of the radioactive ^{122}I that would be used, would dictate that only an extremely small amount of the drug would be required. One would be dealing, not with milligram quantities, but with microgram quantities, or less.

Some fifteen close analogues of IDNNA were prepared, to see if any had a better balance of biological properties. A valuable intermediate was an iodinated ketone that could be used either to synthesize IDNNA itself or, if it were to be made radio-labelled, it would allow the preparation of any desired radioactive analogue in a single synthetic step. The iodination of p-dimethoxybenzene with iodine monochloride in acetic acid gave 2,5-diiodo-1,4-dimethoxybenzene as white crystals from acetonitrile, with a mp of 167-168 °C. Anal. $(C_8H_8I_2O_2)$ C,H. Treatment of this with an equivalent of butyllithium in ether, followed with N-methyl formanilide, gave 2,5-dimethoxy-4-iodobenzaldehyde as pale yellow crystals from ethanol, with a mp of 136-137 °C. Anal. $(C_9H_9IO_3)$ C,H. This, in solution in nitroethane with a small amount of anhydrous ammonium acetate, gave the nitrostyrene 1-(2,5-dimethoxy-4-iodophenyl)-2-nitropropene as gold-colored crystals from methanol, mp 119-120 °C. Anal. $(C_{11}H_{12}INO_4)$ C,H. This was smoothly reduced with elemental iron in acetic acid to give 2,5-dimethoxy-4-iodophenylacetone as white crystals from methylcyclopentane. These melted at 62-63 °C and were both spectroscopically and analytically correct. Anal. $(C_{11}H_{13}IO_3)$ C,H.

This intermediate, when reductively aminated with dimethylamine, gives IDNNA identical in all respects to the product from the dimethylation of DOI above. But it has also been reacted with ^{131}I NaI in acetic acid at 140 °C for 10 min, giving the radioactive compound by exchange, and this was reductively aminated with over a dozen amines to give radioactive products for animal assay. There was produced in this way, 2,5-dimethoxy-4-iodo-N-alkyl-amphetamine where the alkyl group was methyl, isopropyl, cyclopropylmethyl, hexyl, dodecyl, benzyl, cyanomethyl, and 3-(dimethylaminopropyl). Several dialkyl homologue were made, with the alkyl groups being dimethyl (IDNNA itself), diethyl, isopropyl-methyl, and benzyl-methyl. These specific homologues and analogues are tallied in the index, but a number of other things, such as hydrazine or hydroxylamine derivatives, were either too impure or made in amounts too small to be valid, and they are ignored.

The diethyl compound without the iodine is 2,5-dimethoxy-N,N-diethylamphetamine, which was prepared by the reductive alkylation of DMA with acetaldehyde and sodium cyanoborohydride. This product, DEDMA, was a clear white oil, bp 82-92 °C at 0.15 mm/Hg which did not form a crystalline hydrochloride. An interesting measure of just how different these N,N-dialkylated homologues can be from the psychedelic primary amines, pharmacologically, can be seen in the published report that the beta-hydroxy derivative of DEDMA is an antitussive, with a potency the same as codeine.

None of these many iodinated IDNNA analogues showed themselves to be superior to IDNNA itself, in the rat model, and none of them have been tasted for their psychedelic potential in man.

#91   IM;   ISOMESCALINE;   2,3,4-TRIMETHOXY-PHENETHYLAMINE

SYNTHESIS: A solution of 8.0 g 2,3,4-trimethoxybenzaldehyde in 125 mL nitromethane containing 1.4 g anhydrous ammonium acetate was held at reflux for 1.5 h. The conversion of the aldehyde to the nitrostyrene was optimum at this time, with a minimum development of a slow-moving spot as seen by thin layer chromatography on silica gel plates using $CHCl_3$ as a developing solvent; the Rf of the aldehyde was 0.31 and the Rf of the nitrostyrene was 0.61. The excess nitromethane was removed under vacuum, and the residue was dissolved in 20 mL hot MeOH. On cooling, the yellow crystals that formed were removed by filtration, washed with cold MeOH and air dried yielding 4.7 g yellow crystals of 2,3,4-trimethoxy-ß-nitrostyrene, with a mp of 73-74 °C. From the mother liquors, a second crop of 1.2 g was obtained.

A solution of 4.0 g LAH in 80 mL THF under He was cooled to 0 °C and vigorously stirred. There was added, dropwise, 2.7 mL of 100% H_2SO_4, followed by a solution of 4.7 g 2,3,4-trimethoxy-ß-nitrostyrene in 40 mL anhydrous THF. The mixture was stirred at 0 °C for 1 h, at room temperature for 1 h, and then brought briefly to a reflux on the steam bath. After cooling again, the excess hydride was destroyed with 4.7 mL H_2O in THF, followed by the addition of 18.8 mL 15% NaOH which was sufficient to convert the solids to a white and granular form. These were removed by filtration, the filter cake washed with THF, the mother liquor and filtrates combined, and the solvent removed under vacuum. The residue was added to dilute H_2SO_4, and washed with 2x75 mL CH_2Cl_2. The aqueous phase was made basic with 25% NaOH, and extracted with 2x50 mL CH_2Cl_2. The solvent was removed from these pooled extracts and the amber-colored residue distilled at 95-100 °C at 0.3 mm/Hg to provide 2.8 g of 2,3,4-trimethoxyphenethylamine as a white oil. This was dissolved in 20 mL IPA, neutralized with about 1 mL concentrated HCl, and diluted with 60 mL anhydrous Et_2O. After filtering, Et_2O-washing, and air drying, there was obtained 3.2 g of 2,3,4-trimethoxyphenethylamine hydrochloride (IM) as a white crystalline product.

DOSAGE: greater than 400 mg.

DURATION: unknown.

QUALITATIVE COMMENTS: (with 300 mg) "No effects whatsoever."
(with 400 mg) "Maybe a slight tingle at the hour-and-a-half point. Maybe not. Certainly nothing an hour later. Put this down as being without action."

EXTENSIONS AND COMMENTARY: Some fifty years ago this material was given the name "reciprocal mescaline" in that it was believed to exacerbate the clinical symptoms in schizophrenic patients. In the original report, one finds: "Thus we have discovered an extremely remarkable dependency of the intoxicating action upon the position of the three methoxy groups. Mescaline, the 3,4,5-trimethoxy-ß-phenethylamine, produces in the normal subject a much stronger over-all intoxication than in the schizophrenic patient, whereas 2,3,4-trimethoxy-ß-phenethylamine has quite the opposite effect. It has little action in healthy individuals, being almost without intoxicating properties, but it is very potent in the schizophrenic. The metabolic conversion products of the "reciprocal" mescaline will be further studied as soon as the study of the metabolism of the proper mescaline is complete."
    This is a pretty rich offering, and one that the present medical community has no qualms about discarding. At the bookkeeping level, the promised further studies have never appeared, so all may be forgotten as far as potential new discoveries might be concerned.
    One recent related study has been reported, tying together isomescaline and schizophrenia. Through the use of radioactive labelling, the extent of demethylation (the metabolic removal of the methyl groups from the methoxyls) was determined in both schizophrenic patients and normal subjects. When there was a loading of the person with methionine (an amino acid that is the principal source of the body's methyl groups), the schizophrenics appeared to show a lesser amount of demethylation.
    But might either of these two observations lead to a diagnostic test for schizophrenia? At the present time, the conventional thinking is that this probably cannot be. The illness has such social and genetic contributions, that no simple measure of a response to an almost-psychedelic, or minor shift of some urinary metabolite pattern could possibly be believed. No independent confirmation of

these properties has been reported. But maybe these findings are valid. A major problem in following these leads does not involve any complex research protocols. What must be addressed are the present regulatory restrictions and the Federal law structure. And these are formidable obstacles.

#92   IP;   ISOPROSCALINE;   3,5-DIMETHOXY-4-(i)-PROPOXY-PHENETHYLAMINE

SYNTHESIS: A solution of 5.8 g of homosyringonitrile (see under ESCALINE for its preparation) and 13.6 g isopropyl iodide in 50 mL dry acetone was treated with 6.9 g finely powdered anhydrous K_2CO_3 and held at reflux on the steam bath. After 6 h another 5 mL of isopropyl iodide was added, and refluxing continued for an additional 12 h. The mixture was filtered and the solids washed with acetone. The mother liquor and washes were stripped of solvent under vacuum, The residue was taken up in dilute HCl, and extracted with 3x100 mL CH_2Cl_2. The pooled extracts (they were quite deeply yellow colored) were washed with 2x75 mL 5% NaOH, and finally once with dilute HCl. Removal of the solvent under vacuum yielded 9.8 g of an amber oil, which on distillation at 125-135 °C at 0.3 mm/Hg provided 6.0 g of 3,5-dimethoxy-4-(i)-propoxyphenylacetonitrile as a pale yellow oil. A pure reference sample is a white solid with a mp of 33-34 °C. Anal. ($C_{13}H_{17}NO_3$) C,H,N.

A solution of AH was prepared by the cautious addition of 0.84 mL of 100% H_2SO_4 to 32 mL of 1.0 M LAH in THF, which was being vigorously stirred under He at ice-bath temperature. A solution of 5.93 g of 3,5-dimethoxy-4-(i)-propoxyphenylacetonitrile in 10 mL anhydrous THF was added dropwise. Stirring was continued for 30 min, then the reaction mixture was brought up to reflux on the steam bath for another 30 min. After cooling again to room temperature, 5 mL IPA was added to destroy the excess hydride, followed by about 10 mL of 15% NaOH, sufficient to make the aluminum salts loose, white, and filterable. The reaction mixture was filtered, the filter cake washed with IPA, the mother liquor and washes combined, and the solvent removed under vacuum. The residue (7.0 g of an amber oil) was dissolved in dilute H_2SO_4 and washed with 3x75 mL CH_2Cl_2. The aqueous phase was made basic with aqueous NaOH, and the product extracted with 3x75 mL CH_2Cl_2. The extracts were evaporated to a residue under vacuum, and this was distilled at 125-140 °C at 0.3 mm/Hg yielding 3.7 g of a colorless oil. This was dissolved in 15 mL IPA, neutralized with 50 drops of concentrated HCl which allowed the deposition of a white crystalline product. Dilution with anhydrous Et_2O and filtration gave 3.7 g. of 3,5-dimethoxy-4-(i)-propoxyphenethylamine hydrochloride (IP) with a mp of 163-164 °C. Anal. ($C_{13}H_{22}ClNO_3$) C,H,N. The catalytic hydrogenation process for reducing the nitrile that gives rise to escaline, also works with this material.

DOSAGE: 40 - 80 mg.

DURATION: 10 - 16 h.

QUALITATIVE COMMENTS: (with 75 mg) "Starts slowly. I develop some queasiness, turning into nausea. Feels good to lie down and let go, but the uneasiness remains. Just beginning to break through in 2 hours. But the occasional sense of relief, the breaking into the open, were transient as new sources of discomfort were always being dredged up. Then for some reason I chose to dance. Letting go to dancing, a marvelous ecstatic experience, flowing with and being the energy, body feeling completely free. Noticing how this letting go got one completely out of the feeling of unease, as though attention simply needs to be put elsewhere. Comedown was very slow, gentle, euphoric; a very signicant experience. Sleep that night was impossible, but felt good to simply release to the feelings. Keeping mind still, no thinking, just allowing feelings to go where they wished, became more and more ecstatic. Tremendous feeling of confidence in life and the life process. Complete sense of resolution."

(with 80 mg) "It took about two hours for the body to settle down. Emotions were true and well felt, a fact that is an all-important thing to me as it probably is to everyone else I know in this kind of exploration. Any sense that there is a dulling of the feeling and emotional area of the self is a negative, to be watched and noted as are other things such as disturbed sleep, unpleasant dreams, or irritability or depression the next day. I was interacting with others with a great deal of intensity. People found themselves wandering inside and out, listening to music, stirring soup, eating a bit and enjoying eating, talking, laughing a great deal, and being silent in great contentment. It's not a very silent material, though. Talking is too enjoyable. There was a slight descent noted at 6-7 hours, but very gentle and smooth. Slow and pleasant descent until about 12th hour, when sleep was attempted. Next day, everyone slightly irritable but good mood anyway. The next night I slept deeply and well, and awoke whole and in excellent mood."

EXTENSIONS AND COMMENTARY: These two excerpts give the color and complexity of IP. It has proven to be a completely fascinating phenethylamine. And, as with all the phenethylamines, there is an amphetamine that corresponds to it. This would be 3,5-dimethoxy-4-isopropoxyamphetamine, or 3C-IP. The preparation of it would require access through the O-isopropoxylation product with syringaldehyde, followed by nitrostyrene formation with nitroethane, followed by reduction probably with lithium aluminum hydride. It has not been synthesized, as far as I know, and so it has probably not been evaluated in man. What would be the active level? It would probably be more potent than IP, but I would guess not by much. Maybe in the 30 milligram area.

A moment's aside for a couple of the words that are so much a part of the chemist's jargon. Room temperature, as used above, means the natural temperature that something comes to if it is put on the table and is neither heated nor cooled. The phrase, I discovered during my year at Gif, is completely un-understandable in French. A room has no temperature. Only things in rooms have temperatures. Their expression is more exact. The object achieves, in the French terminology, a *temperature normale d'interieur*, or about 15 to 16 °C. But in common laboratory parlance it has become the *temperature d'ambiance*.

And one finds the prefix "iso" used everywhere. Considerable care should be taken in the two different uses of the prefix "iso" in the nomenclature with the mescaline analogues. In general, the term "iso" means the other one of two possibilities. If you are allowed to paint a house only with green paint or red paint, and green is the color you actually use, then red could be called iso-green. With isoproscaline (here) there is a rearranging of the propyl group on the 4-oxygen of mescaline. It has been replaced with its branched analogue, the other of two possibilities, the isopropyl group. Everything is still with the 3,4,5-orientation on the benzene ring. However, with IM (isomescaline) there is a rearrangement of substitution pattern on the benzene ring, with the repositioning of the trimethoxyl substitution pattern from the 3,4,5- arrangement to the 2,3,4- arrangement. It has been the side-chain that has taken the other of two possible positions. The term "iso" must always be interpreted in precise context.

#93   IRIS;   5-ETHOXY-2-METHOXY-4-METHYLAMPHETAMINE

SYNTHESIS: To a solution of 9.5 g flaked KOH (10% excess) in 500 mL 95% EtOH there was added 20.4 g 4-methoxy-2-methylphenol (see under 2C-D for its preparation). This was followed with 23.5 g ethyl iodide, and the mixture was held

at reflux overnight. The solvent was removed under vacuum and the residue suspended in 250 mL H_2O. This was made strongly basic with NaOH and extracted with 3x50 mL CH_2Cl_2. Removal of the solvent gave 15.75 g of 2-ethoxy-5-methoxytoluene as an amber oil, which was used in the following step without further purification. Acidification of the aqueous phase followed by CH_2Cl_2 extraction gave, after removal of the solvent, crude recovered starting phenol as a dark brown crystalline solid. The reasonably pure phenol was best isolated by sequential extractions with portions of 80 °C H_2O which, on cooling, deposited the phenol as white crystals.

A mixture of 38 mL $POCl_3$ and 43 mL N-methylformanilide was allowed to incubate for 1 h and then there was added to it 15.7 g 2-ethoxy-5-methoxytoluene.

This was heated in the steam bath for 2 h, then poured into 1 L H_2O and allowed to stir overnight. The solids that formed were removed by filtration and H_2O washed, giving 20.7 g of a crude, amber product. This was extracted with 2x150 mL boiling hexane which gave crystals on cooling. These were filtered and hexane washed, giving 12.85 g of 5-ethoxy-2-methoxy-4-methylbenzaldehyde as pale cream-colored solids with a mp of 75-76 °C. Recrystallization of an analytical sample from EtOH two times gave a product with a white color, and a mp of 81-82 °C.

To a solution of 11.35 g 5-ethoxy-2-methoxy-4-methylbenzaldehyde in 48 mL glacial acetic acid containing 4 g anhydrous ammonium acetate there was added 10 mL nitroethane, and the mixture heated on the steam bath for 2 h. Standing at room temperature overnight allowed a heavy crop of brilliant crystals to deposit. These were removed by filtration, washed cautiously with acetic acid, and air dried to give 8.6 g 1-(5-ethoxy-2-methoxy-4-methylphenyl)-2-nitropropene with a mp of 118-120 °C. Recrystallization of all from 200 mL boiling MeOH gave 8.3 g of lustrous crystals with a mp of 121-122 °C.

To a gently refluxing suspension of 6.4 g LAH in 500 mL anhydrous Et_2O under a He atmosphere, there was added 8.1 g 1-(5-ethoxy-2-methoxy-4-methyl-phenyl)-2-nitropropene by allowing the condensing ether to drip into a shunted Soxhlet thimble containing the nitrostyrene. This effectively added a warm saturated solution of the nitrostyrene dropwise. Refluxing was maintained over-night, and the cooled reaction flask stirred for several additional days. The excess hydride was destroyed by the cautious addition of 400 mL H_2O containing 40 g H_2SO_4. When the aqueous and Et_2O layers were finally clear, they were separated, and 160 g of potassium sodium tartrate was dissolved in the aqueous fraction. Aqueous NaOH was then added until the pH was >9, and this was then extracted with 3x50 mL CH_2Cl_2. Evaporation of the solvent under vacuum produced an oil that was dissolved in anhydrous Et_2O and saturated with anhydrous HCl gas. There appeared 5-ethoxy-2-methoxy-4-methylamphetamine hydrochloride (IRIS) as fine white crystals. These weighed, after filtration, Et_2O washing, and air drying to constant weight, 5.3 g and had a mp of 192-193 °C. Recrystallization of an analytical sample from boiling CH_3CN gave lustrous crystals with a mp of 196-197 °C with decomposition.

DOSAGE: greater than 9 mg.

DURATION: unknown.

QUALITATIVE COMMENTS: (with 7.5 mg) "At about three hours I felt that I was at threshold, but an hour later there was nothing."
(with 9 mg) "Maybe a little light headed? Maybe not. Little effect if any."

EXTENSIONS AND COMMENTARY: This is one of the ten Classic Ladies, the ten possible homologues of DOM, which I had discussed under ARIADNE (the first of the Ladies). The active level is unknown, but it is higher than 9 milligrams (the highest dose tried) and since DOM itself would have been smashingly active at this level, it is obvious that IRIS is a homologue with decreased potency.

This lack of activity brings up a fascinating point. I have referred to a drug's action on the mind, quite frequently in these notes, with the phrase "reasonably complex." By that, I do not mean that a drug's action simply shows many facets, and if these were to be tallied, the drug-mind interaction would become clear. There is quite a bit of importance intrinsically implied by the term, complex. Simple things, as we have come to appreciate and depend upon them in our day-to-day living, can have simple explanations. By this, I mean explanations that are both completely satisfactory and satisfactorily complete. Answers that have all the earmarks of being correct. What is the sum of two plus three, you ask? Let's try five. And for most of our needs, five is both factual and complete.

But some years ago, a mathematician named Gödel devised a proof for a theorem that anything that is reasonably complex cannot enjoy this luxury (I believe he used the word "interesting" rather than reasonably complex). If your collection of information is factual, it cannot be entirely complete. And if it is complete, it cannot be entirely factual. In short, we will never know, we cannot ever know, every fact that constitutes an explanation of something. A complete book of knowledge must contain errors, and an error-free book of knowledge must be incomplete.

There is a small warning light deep inside me that starts flashing any time I hear someone begin to advance an explanation of some reasonably complex phenomenon with an air of confidence that implies, "Here is how it works." What the speaker usually has is an intense familiarity with one particular discipline or specialty and the phenomenon is viewed through those eyes, often with the assurance that looking at it that way, intently enough and long enough, will reveal the complete explanation. And be attentive to the phrase, "We are not yet completely sure of exactly how it works." What is really meant is, "We haven't the slightest idea of how it really works."

I must admit to some guilt in this matter, certainly as much as the next person. I am a chemist and I suspect that the way that the psychedelic drugs do their thing can eventually be understood through a comparison of the structures of the molecules that are active and those that are inactive. I put those that have methoxyl groups in pigeon hole #1, and those that are bicyclic into pigeon hole #2. And then, if pigeon hole #2 becomes more and more cluttered, I will subdivide the contents into pigeon hole #2$_A$ for bicyclics with heteroatoms and pigeon hole #2$_B$ for bicyclics without heteroatoms. The more information I can accumulate, the more pigeon holes I need.

But in the adjoining lab, there is a molecular biologist who feels that the eventual explanation for the action of the psychedelic drug will come from the analysis and understanding of the intimate geometry of the places in the brain where they act. These classification pigeon holes are called receptor sites. But they, too, can become more and more subdivided as they become cluttered. One reads of a new sub-sub type quite regularly in the literature. The favorite neurotransmitter of the moment, as far as the current thinking of how these marvelous drugs work, is serotonin, or 5-HT (for 5-hydroxytryptamine). There are 5-HT$_1$ and 5-HT$_{2A}$ and 5-HT$_{2B}$ and (for all I know right now) 5-HT$_{2C}$ and 5-HT$_{2D}$ receptors, and I don't really think that either he or I have come much closer to understanding the mechanism of action.

And, since the mind is a reasonably complex system, Gödel has already informed us both that neither of us will be completely successful. Sometimes I feel that the pigeon hole approach to the classification of knowledge might actually limit our views of the problem. A Harvard Professor of Medicine recently noted: "We must recognize for what it is, man's predilection for dividing things into tidy categories, irrespective of whether clarity is gained or lost thereby."

No. No one will ever have it all together. It is like sitting down in front of a jigsaw with a zillion zillion pieces spread all over the kitchen table. With diligent searching you will occasionally find a piece that matches another, but it rarely provides any insight into the final picture. That will remain a mystery, unless you had the chance to see the cover of the box in some other incarnation. But Oh my, what fun it is, whenever you do happen to find a new piece that fits!

This harangue is really a lengthy prelude to the story of putting an ethoxy group in place of a methoxy on the 2,5-dimethoxy skeleton of these psychedelic families. The making of IRIS was the first move in this direction, done back in 1976. One can have a pigeon hole that is named "Ethoxy In Place of Methoxy" and toss in there the names of perhaps twenty pairs of compounds, which differ from one another by just this feature. Yet when they are looked at from the potency point of view, there are some which show a decrease in potency (which is the case with IRIS and most of the Tweetios) and there are some which seem to maintain their potency (such as the TMA-2/MEM pair) and there are some where there is a distinct potency increase (the mescaline/escaline pair, for example).

What does one do to clarify the contents of this particular pigeon hole? The current fad would be to subdivide it into three subdivisions, maybe something like "Ethoxy in Place of Methoxy if 2- or 5-located" and "Ethoxy in Place of Methoxy if 4-located and other things 2,5" and "Ethoxy in Place of Methoxy if 4-located, and other things 3,5." The end point that soon becomes apparent, down the line, will be to have as many pigeon holes as compounds! And at the moment, this particular piece of the jigsaw puzzle doesn't seem to fit anywhere at all.

Perhaps both my neighboring molecular biologist and I are asking the wrong questions. I am looking at the molecules and asking, "What are they?" And he is following them and asking, "Where do they go?" And neither of us is fully attentive to the question, "What do they do?" It is so easy to replace the word "mind," in our inquiries, with the word "brain."

Yup. The operation of the mind can certainly be classified as a "reasonably complex" phenomenon. I prefer Gödel's term. The mind is without question an "interesting" phenomenon.

#94   J;   BDB;   2-AMINO-1-(3,4-METHYLENEDIOXYPHENYL)-
BUTANE;   1-(1,3-BENZODIOXOL-5-YL)-2-BUTANAMINE

SYNTHESIS: The Grignard reagent of propyl bromide was made by the dropwise addition of 52 g 1-bromopropane to a stirred suspension of 14 g magnesium turnings in 50 mL anhydrous Et_2O. After the addition, stirring was continued for 10 min, and then a solution of 50 g piperonal in 200 mL anhydrous Et_2O was added over the course of 30 min. The reaction mixture was heated at reflux for 8 h, then cooled with an external ice bath. It was quenched with the addition of a solution of 75 mL cold, saturated aqueous ammonium chloride. The formed solids were removed by filtration, and the two-phase filtrate separated. The organic phase was washed with 3x200 mL dilute HCl, dried over anhydrous $MgSO_4$, and the solvent removed under vacuum. The crude 62.2 g of 1-(3,4-methylenedioxy-phenyl)-2-butanol, which contained a small amount of the olefin that formed by dehydration, was distilled at 98 °C at 0.07 mm/Hg to give an analytical sample, but the crude isolate served well in the next reaction. Anal. $(C_{11}H_{14}O_3)$ C,H.

A mixture of 65 g crude 1-(3,4-methylenedioxyphenyl)-2-butanol and 1 g finely powdered potassium bisulfate was heated with a soft flame until the internal temperature reached 170 °C and H_2O was no longer evolved. The entire reaction mixture was then distilled at 100-110 °C at 0.8 mm/Hg to give 55 g of 1-(3,4-methylenedioxyphenyl)-1-butene as a colorless oil. Anal. $(C_{11}H_{12}O_2)$ C,H.

To 240 mL of stirred and cooled formic acid there was added 30 mL H_2O followed, slowly, by 45 mL of 35% hydrogen peroxide. There was then added a solution of 48 g 1-(3,4-methylenedioxyphenyl)-1-butene in 240 mL acetone at a rate that maintained the internal temperature at less than 40 °C. After the addition, the reaction mixture was allowed to stand and stir for several additional days. The excess volatiles were removed under vacuum with the temperature never allowed to exceed 40 °C. The residue was dissolved in 90 mL MeOH and diluted with 450 mL 15% H_2SO_4. This mixture was heated on the steam bath for 2.5 h, cooled, and then extracted with 3x100 mL Et_2O. The extracts were pooled, washed with 2x200 mL H_2O, 2x200 mL 5% NaOH, 2x200 mL brine, and then dried over anhydrous $MgSO_4$. After removal of the solvent under vacuum, the residue was distilled at 105-135 °C at 0.3 mm/Hg to give 28.2 g 1-(3,4-methylenedioxyphenyl)-2-butanone as an amber oil. Redistillation gave a colorless oil, with a bp of 98 °C at 0.11 mm/Hg. Anal. $(C_{11}H_{12}O_3)$ C,H. This intermediate ketone could be prepared by the Wittig reaction between piperonal and the derivative of triphenylphosphonium propyl bromide and dibutyldisulfide, followed by hydrolysis in a HCl/acetic acid mixture, but the yields were no better, Efforts to prepare this ketone by the iron and acid reduction of the appropriate nitrostyrene (1-(3,4-methylenedioxyphenyl)-2-nitro-1-butene, mp 64-65 °C) were thwarted by the consistently unsatisfactory yield of the precursor from the reaction between piperonal and 1-nitropropane.

A stirred solution of 20 g anhydrous ammonium acetate and 4.6 g 1-(3,4-methylenedioxyphenyl)-2-butanone in 50 mL MeOH was treated with 1.57 g sodium cyanoborohydride. Droplets of HCl were added as needed to maintain the pH at approximately 6. The reaction mixture was made basic with the addition of 250 mL dilute NaOH and extracted with 3x100 mL CH_2Cl_2. The pooled organic extracts were extracted with 2x100 mL dilute H_2SO_4, the pooled aqueous extracts made basic again, and extracted again with 2x100 mL CH_2Cl_2. Removal of the solvent gave a residue which was distilled to give 2.6 g of a colorless oil which was dissolved in 15 mL IPA, neutralized with concentrated HCl, and diluted with an equal volume of anhydrous Et_2O. Crystals of 2-amino-1-(3,4-methylenedioxy-phenyl)butane hydrochloride (J) separated slowly. After filtering, Et_2O washing, and air drying there was obtained 2.8 g of white crystals that melted at 159-161 °C. Anal. ($C_{11}H_{16}ClNO_2$) C,H,N.

DOSAGE: 150 - 230 mg.

DURATION: 4 - 8 h.

QUALITATIVE COMMENTS: (with 175 mg) "The first stirrings were evident in a half hour, pleasant feelings, and without any untoward body effects. Within another half hour I was at a plus 2 and there it leveled off. I would be reluctant to drive a car, but I could were it necessary. There were no visual distortions, no giddiness, no introspective urges, and no rise to a psychedelic intoxication of any significance. After about an hour and a half at this level, I gradually dropped back over another two hours. Afterwards I was quite fatigued and languorous."

(with 200 mg and a 75 mg supplement) "A very strong climb, and a very good, interior feeling. It has some of the MDMA properties, but it is difficult to concentrate on any one point. There is a tendency to slide off. Excellent emotional affect; music is fine but not gripping. Someone had used the phrase, mental nystagmus, and there is something valid there. The supplement was taken at the 2 hour point when I was already aware of some dropping, and its action was noticed in about a half hour."

(with 230 mg) "Physically, there was a bit of dry mouth but no teeth clenching, some nystagmus, maybe the slightest bit of dizziness, very anorexic, and it is not a decongestant. Mentally, it is extremely benign and pleasant, funny and good-humored. No visuals. Peaceful. Easy silences, easy talking. More stoning than MDMA."

EXTENSIONS AND COMMENTARY: In general, all subjects who have explored J have accepted it and commented favorably. Perhaps those who have used supplements (in an imitation of the common MDMA procedure) achieved an additional period of effect, but also tended to drop to baseline afterwards more rapidly. The physical side effects, such as teeth clench and nystagmus, were infrequent. The consensus is that J is a bit more "stoning" than MDMA, more like MDA, but with a chronology that is very much the same.

Two nomenclature problems have to be faced in the naming of these compounds. One deals with the Chemical Abstracts terminology as contrasted with the logical and intuitive terminology. The other invokes the concept of the Muni-Metro, delightfully simple, but neither Chemical Abstracts-approved nor intuitive in form. The first problem is addressed here; the second is discussed where it better belongs, under the N-methyl homologue of J (see under METHYL-J).

In short, the two-ring system of J, or of any of the MDA-MDMA family of drugs, can be named as one ring being attached to the other, or by a single term that encompasses both. The first procedure, an old friend with chemists and the one that had been used for years in the abstracting services, calls the combination methylenedioxybenzene and, as a prefix, it becomes methylenedioxyphenyl-something. The benzene or the phenyl-something is the foundation of the name, and there happens to be a methylenedioxy-ring attached to it. On this basis, this compound J should be named as if it had no methylenedioxy ring anywhere, and then simply attach the new ring as an afterthought. So, the one-ring parent of J is 1-phenyl-2-aminobutane, and J is 1-(3,4-methylenedioxyphenyl)-2-aminobutane (or, to be a purist, the amino should alphabetically come first, to give 2-amino-1-(3,4-methylene-dioxyphenyl)butane). The synthesis of the chemical intermediates given above uses this old-fashioned nomenclature.

But the name currently in vogue for this two-ring system is 1,3-benzodioxole. As a prefix it becomes 1,3-benzodioxol-5-yl-something, and so J would be called 1-(1,3-benzodioxol-5-yl)-2-aminobutane. This is the source of the code name BDB. And the N-methyl homologue, the alpha-ethyl analogue of MDMA, is named MBDB, or METHYL-J, and is with its own separate entry in this footnote.

There is a psychological nuance to this new nomenclature. The virtues and potential medical value of MDMA lie in its most remarkable property of facilitating communication and introspective states without an overlay of psychedelic action. This property has prompted the coining of a new pharmacological class name, Entactogen, which comes from the Greek roots for "touching within." But MDMA has been badly smeared in both the public and the scientific view, by its wide popular misuse, its precipitous placement into a Schedule I category of the Federal Drug Law, and a flood of negative neurotoxicological findings in animal studies. There are some properties of both this compound and its methyl-homologue that suggest this "entactogen" world, so why not avoid the "MD" prefix that, in many eyes, is pejorative? Stick with the totally obscure chemical names, and call them BDB and MBDB. Or, even more simply, J and METHYL-J.

#95   LOPHOPHINE;   3-METHOXY-4,5-METHYLENEDIOXY-
PHENETHYLAMINE

SYNTHESIS: A solution of 50 g myristicinaldehyde (3-methoxy-4,5-
methylenedioxybenzaldehyde, see under MMDA for its preparation) in 200 mL
acetic acid was treated with 33 mL nitromethane and 17.4 g anhydrous ammonium
acetate and held on the steam bath for 5 h. The reaction mixture was diluted with
a little H$_2$O and cooled in an external ice-acetone bath. A heavy crop of yellow
crystals formed, which were removed by filtration, washed with cold acetic acid,
and dried to constant weight. There was thus
obtained 19.3 g 3-methoxy-4,5-methylene-
dioxy-ß-nitrostyrene with a mp of 210-212 °C.
The mother liquors were diluted with H$_2$O, and
extracted with 3x100 mL CH$_2$Cl$_2$. The pooled
extracts were washed with 5% NaOH, and the
solvent removed under vacuum yielding 34 g of a dark residue that was largely
unreacted aldehyde. This residue was reprocessed in acetic acid with nitromethane
and ammonium acetate, as described above, and provided an additional 8.1 g of the
nitrostyrene with the same mp.

        A suspension of 25 g LAH in 1.5 L anhydrous Et$_2$O in an inert atmosphere
was stirred magnetically, and brought up to a gentle reflux. Through a Soxhlet
condenser modified to allow Et$_2$O to return continuously to the reaction mixture,
there was added 27.0 g of 3-methoxy-4,5-methylenedioxy-ß-nitrostyrene. The
addition require many h, and when it was completed, the reaction was held at reflux
for an additional 9 days. After cooling the reaction mixture in an external ice bath,
the excess hydride was destroyed by the cautious addition of dilute H$_2$SO$_4$. The final
amount used was 1800 mL H$_2$O containing 133 g H$_2$SO$_4$. The phases were separated, and the aqueous phase was washed with 2x100 mL Et$_2$O. To it was then added
625 g potassium sodium tartrate, and sufficient base to bring the pH to >9. This was
extracted with 3x250 mL CH$_2$Cl$_2$, and the pooled extracts stripped of solvent under
vacuum. The residue was dissolved in anhydrous Et$_2$O and saturated with anhydrous HCl gas, giving a heavy crystallization of salts. These were removed by
filtration, Et$_2$O washed, and air dried, to give 17.7 g 3-methoxy-4,5-methylene-
dioxyphenethylamine (LOPHOPHINE) as an off-white solid with a mp of 160-161
°C. This was dissolved in CH$_3$CN containing 5% EtOH, decolorized with activated
charcoal, filtered, and the removed charcoal washed with boiling CH$_3$CN. Slow
cooling of the solution provided 11.7 g of a white product which melted at 164-164.5
°C.

DOSAGE: greater than 200 mg.

DURATION: unknown.

QUALITATIVE COMMENTS: (with 150 mg) "Between two and five hours, very peaceful and euphoric mood elevation, similar to mescaline, but without any visual distortion. Mild enhancement of color perception, possibly a function of mood elevation. There was no nausea, no eyes-closed vision. Slept easily that evening." (with 250 mg) "Possibly something of a threshold effect from 2:30 to 4:30 of the experiment. Intangible, and certainly there is nothing an hour later."

EXTENSIONS AND COMMENTARY: It looks as if this compound is not active. There is an excellent argument as to why it really should be, and the fact that it is not active is completely unexpected. Let me try to explain.

Quite simply, mescaline is a major component and a centrally active alkaloid of the Peyote plant. It is a phenethylamine, which can undergo a cyclization within the plant to produce a pile of derivatives (tetrahydroisoquinolines) such as anhalonine and O-methylanhalonidine that are marvelously complex alkaloids, all natural components of this magical cactus. But there is another pile of derivatives (tetrahydroisoquinolines) such as anhalonine, and lophophorine, and peyophorine which are the logical cyclization products of another phenethylamine which does not exist in the cactus. It should be there, but it is not. If it were there it would be the natural precursor to a host of bicyclic alkaloids, but it is absent. This is 3-methoxy-4,5-methylenedioxyphenethylamine. I feel that some day it will be discovered as a plant component, and when it is it can be given a name that reflects the generic binomial of the plant. And since the plant has been known as *Lophophora williamsii*, why not give a name to this compound (which should be in the plant), one derived from the Latin name, but one that has never before been used? What about LOPHOPHINE? And so, I have named it, but I have not found it, nor has anyone else. Yet.

It is inevitable that this simple and most appealing precursor will be found to be present in the cactus, at some future time when we will have tools of sufficient sensitivity to detect it. And certainly, it would be reasonable to expect it to be an active psychedelic, and to be as interesting in man as its close cousin, mescaline. But, at the present time, LOPHOPHINE is not known to be present in the plant, and it is not known to be active in man. I am confident that both statuses will change in the future.

#96   M;   MESCALINE;   3,4,5-TRIMETHOXYPHENETHYLAMINE

SYNTHESIS: A solution of 20 g 3,4,5-trimethoxybenzaldehyde, 40 mL nitromethane, and 20 mL cyclohexylamine in 200 mL of acetic acid was heated on the steam bath for 1 h. The reaction mixture was then diluted slowly and with good stirring, with 400 mL H_2O, which allowed the formation of a heavy yellow crystalline mass. This was removed by filtration, washed with H_2O, and sucked as dry as possible. Recrystallization from boiling MeOH (15 mL/g) yielded, after filtration and air drying, ß-nitro-3,4,5-trimethoxystyrene as bright yellow crystals weighing 18.5 g. An alternate synthesis was effective, using an excess of nitromethane as solvent as well as reagent, if the amount of ammonium acetate catalysis was kept small. A solution of 20 g 3,4,5-trimethoxybenzaldehyde in 40 mL nitromethane containing 1 g anhydrous ammonium acetate was heated on the steam bath for 4 h. The solvent was stripped under vacuum and the residual yellow oil was dissolved in two volumes of hot MeOH, decanted from some insolubles, and allowed to cool. The crystals formed are removed by filtration, washed with MeOH and air dried yielding 14.2 g. of bright yellow crystals of ß-nitro-3,4,5-trimethoxy-styrene. The use of these proportions but with 3.5 g ammonium acetate gave extensive side-reaction products even when worked up after only 1.5 h heating. The yield of nitrostyrene was, in this latter case, unsatisfactory.

To a gently refluxing suspension of 2 g LAH in 200 mL Et_2O, there was added 2.4 g ß-nitro-3,4,5-trimethoxystyrene as a saturated Et_2O solution by use of a Soxhlet extraction condenser modified to allow the continuous return of condensed solvent through the thimble. After the addition was complete, the refluxing conditions were maintained for another 48 h. After cooling the reaction mixture, a total of 150 mL of 1.5 N H_2SO_4 was cautiously added, destroying the excess hydride and untimately providing two clear phases. These were separated, and the aqueous phase was washed once with 50 mL Et_2O. There was then added 50 g potassium sodium tartrate, followed by sufficient NaOH to bring the pH >9. This was then extracted with 3x75 mL CH_2Cl_2, and the solvent from the pooled extracts was removed under vacuum. The residue was distilled at 120-130 °C at 0.3 mm/Hg giving a white oil that was dissolved in 10 mL IPA and neutralized with concentrated HCl. The white crystals that formed were diluted with 25 mL Et_2O, removed by filtration, and air dried to provide 2.1 g 3,4,5-trimethoxyphenethylamine hydrochloride (M) as glistening white crystals. The sulfate salt formed spectacular crystals from water, but had a broad and uncharacteristic mp. An alternate synthesis can employ 3,4,5-trimethoxyphenyl-acetonitrile, as described under ß-D.

DOSAGE: 200-400 mg (as the sulfate salt), 178-356 mg (as the hydrochloride salt).

DURATION: 10-12 h

QUALITATIVE COMMENTS: (with 300 mg) "I would have liked to, and was expecting to, have an exciting visual day, but I seemed to be unable to escape self-analysis. At the peak of the experience I was quite intoxicated and hyper with energy, so that it was not hard to move around. I was quite restless. But I spent most of the day in considerable agony, attempting to break through without success. I learned a great deal about myself and my inner workings. Everything almost was, but in the final analysis, wasn't. I began to become aware of a point, a brilliant white light, that seemed to be where God was entering, and it was inconceivably wonderful to perceive it and to be close to it. One wished for it to approach with all one's heart. I could see that people would sit and meditate for hours on end just in the hope that this little bit of light would contact them. I begged for it to continue and come closer but it did not. It faded away not to return in that particular guise the rest of the day. Listening to Mozart's Requiem, there were magnificent heights of beauty and glory. The world was so far away from God, and nothing was more important than getting back in touch with Him. But I saw how we created the nuclear fiasco to threaten the existence of the planet, as if it would be only through the threat of complete annihilation that people might wake up and begin to become concerned about each other. And so also with the famines in Africa. Many similar scenes of joy and despair kept me in balance. I ended up the experience in a very peaceful space, feeling that though I had been through a lot, I had accomplished a great deal. I felt wonderful, free, and clear."

(with 350 mg) "Once I got through the nausea stage, I ventured out-of-doors and I was aware of an intensification of color and a considerable change in the texture of the cloth of my skirt and in the concrete of the sidewalk, and in the flowers and leaves that were handed me by an observer. I experienced the desire to laugh hysterically at what I could only describe as the completely ridiculous state of the entire world. Although I was afraid of motion, I was persuaded to take a ride in a car. The driver turned on the radio and suddenly the music 'The March of the Siamese Children' from 'The King and I' became the most perfect background music for the parody of real life which was indeed the normal activity of Telegraph Avenue on any Saturday morning. The perfectly ordinary people on their perfectly ordinary errands were clearly the most cleverly contrived set of characters all performing all manners of eccentric activities for our particular hilarity and enjoyment. I felt that I was at the same time both observing and performing in an outrageous moving picture. I experienced one moment of transcendant happiness when, while passing Epworth Hall, I looked out of the window of the car and up at the building and I was suddenly in Italy looking up at a gay apartment building with its shutters flung open in sunshine, and with its window boxes with flowers. We stopped at a spot overlooking the bay, but I found the view uninteresting and the sun uncomfortable. I sat there on the seat of the car looking down at the ground, and the earth became a mosaic of beautiful stones which had been placed in an intricate design which soon all began to move in a serpentine manner. Then I became aware that I was looking at the skin of a beautiful snake — all the ground around me was this same huge creature and we were all standing on the back of this gigantic and beautiful reptile. The experience was very pleasing and I felt no revulsion. Just then, another automobile stopped to look at the view and I experienced my first real feeling of persecution and I wanted very much to leave."

(with 400 mg) "During the initial phase of the intoxication (between 2 and

3 hours) everything seemed to have a humorous interpretation. People's faces are in caricature, small cars seem to be chasing big cars, and all cars coming towards me seem to have faces. This one is a duchess moving in regal pomp, that one is a wizened old man running away from someone. A remarkable effect of this drug is the extreme empathy felt for all small things; a stone, a flower, an insect. I believe that it would be impossible to harm anything — to commit an overt harmful or painful act on anyone or anything is beyond one's capabilities. One cannot pluck a flower — and even to walk upon a gravel path requires one to pick his footing carefully, to avoid hurting or disturbing the stones. I found the color perception to be the most striking aspect of the experience. The slightest difference of shade could be amplified to extreme contrast. Many subtle hues became phosphorescent in intensity. Saturated colors were often unchanged, but they were surrounded by cascades of new colors tumbling over the edges."

(with 400 mg) "It took a long time to come on and I was afraid that I had done it wrong but my concerns were soon ended. The world soon became transformed where objects glowed as if from an inner illumination and my body sprang to life. The sense of my body, being alive in my muscles and sinews, filled me with enormous joy. I watched Ermina fill to brimming with animal spirit, her features tranformed, her body cat-like in her graceful natural movement. I was stopped in my tracks. The world seemed to hold its breath as the cat changed again into the Goddess. As she shed her clothes, she shed her ego and when the dance began, Ermina was no more. There was only the dance without the slightest self-consconciousness. How can anything so beautiful be chained and changed by other's expectations? I became aware of myself in her and as we looked deeply into one another my boundaries disappeared and I became her looking at me."

EXTENSIONS AND COMMENTARY: Mescaline is one of the oldest psychedelics known to man. It is the major active component of the small dumpling cactus known as Peyote. It grows wild in the Southwestern United States and in Northern Mexico, and has been used as an intimate component of a number of religious traditions amongst the native Indians of these areas. The cactus has the botanical name of *Lophophora williamsii* or *Anhalonium lewinii* and is immediately recognizable by its small round shape and the appearance of tufts of soft fuzz in place of the more conventional spines. The dried plant material has been classically used with anywhere from a few to a couple of dozen of the hard tops, called buttons, being consumed in the course of a ceremony.

Throughout the more recently published record of clinical human studies with mescaline, it has been used in the form of the synthetic material, and has usually been administered as the sulfate salt. Although this form has a miserable melting point (it contains water of crystallization, and the exact melting point depends on the rate of heating of the sample) it nonetheless forms magnificent crystals from water. Long, glistening needles that are, in a sense, its signature and its mark of purity. The dosages associated with the above "qualitative comments" are given as if measured as the sulfate, although the actual form used was usually the hydrochloride salt. The conversion factor is given under "dosage" above.

Mescaline has always been the central standard against which all other compounds are viewed. Even the United States Chemical Warfare group, in their human studies of a number of substituted phenethylamines, used mescaline as the reference material for both quantitative and qualitative comparisons. The Edgewood Arsenal code number for it was EA-1306. All psychedelics are given properties that are something like "twice the potency of mescaline" or "twice as long-lived as mescaline." This simple drug is truly the central prototype against which everything else is measured. The earliest studies with the "psychotomimetic amphetamines" had quantitative psychological numbers attached that read as "mescaline units." Mescaline was cast in concrete as being active at the 3.75 mg/kg level. That means for a 80 kilogram person (a 170 pound person) a dose of 300 milligrams. If a new compound proved to be active at 30 milligrams, there was a M.U. level of 10 put into the published literature. The behavioral biologists were happy, because now they had numbers to represent psychological properties. But in truth, none of this represented the magic of this material, the nature of the experience itself. That is why, in this Book II, there is only one line given to "dosage," but a full page given to "qualitative comments."

Four simple N-modified mescaline analogues are of interest in that they are natural and have been explored in man.

The N-acetyl analogue has been found in the peyote plant, and it is also a major metabolite of mescaline in man. It is made by the gentle reaction of mescaline with acetic anhydride (a bit too much heat, and the product N-acetyl mescaline will cyclize to a dihydroisoquinoline, itself a fine white crystalline solid, mp 160-161 °C) and can be recrystallized from boiling toluene. A number of human trials with this amide at levels in the 300 to 750 milligrams range have shown it to be with very little activity. At the highest levels there have been suggestions of drowsiness. Certainly there were none of the classic mescaline psychedelic effects.

If free base mescaline is brought into reaction with ethyl formate (to produce the amide, N-formylmescaline) and subsequently reduced (with lithium aluminum hydride) it is converted to the N-methyl homologue. This base has also been found as a trace component in the Peyote cactus. And the effects of N-methylation of other psychedelic drugs have been commented upon elsewhere in these recipes, all with consistently negative results (with the noteworthy exception of the conversion of MDA to MDMA). Here, too, there is no obvious activity in man, although the levels assayed were only up to 25 milligrams.

N,N-Dimethylmescaline has been given the trivial name of Trichocerine as it has been found as a natural product in several cacti of the *Trichocereus* Genus but, interestingly, never in any Peyote variant. It also has proven inactive in man in dosages in excess of 500 milligrams, administered parenterally This observation, the absence of activity of a simple tertiary amine, has been exploited in the development of several iodinated radiopharmaceuticals that are mentioned elsewhere in this book.

The fourth modification is the compound with the nitrogen atom oxidatively removed from the scene. This is the mescaline metabolite, 3,4,5-trimethoxyphenylacetic acid, or TMPEA. Human dosages up to 750 milligrams orally failed to produce either physiological or psychological changes.

One additional manipulation with some of these structures has been made and should be mentioned. These are the analogues with an oxygen atom inserted between the aromatic ring and the aliphatic chain. They are, in essence, aminoethyl phenyl ethers. The first is related to mescaline itself, 2-(3,4,5-trimethoxyphenoxy)ethylamine. Human trials were conducted over the dose range of 10 to 300 milligrams and there were no effects observed. The second is related to trichocerine, N,N-dimethyl-2-(3,4,5-trimethoxyphenoxy)ethylamine. It was inactive in man over the range of 10 to 400 milligrams. Mescaline, at a dose of 420 milligrams, served as the control in these studies.

#97   4-MA;   PMA;   4-METHOXYAMPHETAMINE

SYNTHESIS: A solution of 27.2 g anisaldehyde and 18.0 g nitroethane in 300 mL benzene was treated with 2.0 mL cyclohexane and refluxed using a Dean Stark trap until H_2O ceased to accumulate. A total of 3.8 mL was generated over about 5 days. After the removal of the solvent under vacuum, the viscous red oily residue was cooled and it spontaneously crystallized. This was ground under an equal volume of MeOH, producing lemon-yellow crystals of 1-(4-methoxyphenyl)-2-nitropropene. The final yield was 27.4 g of product with a mp of 45-46 °C. Recrystallization from 4 volumes MeOH did not improve the mp. An excellent alternate synthesis with a comparable yield involved letting a solution of equimolar amounts of the aldehyde and nitroethane and a tenth mole of n-amylamine stand in the dark at room temperature for a couple of weeks. The product spontaneously crystallized, and could be recrystallized from MeOH. The more conventional synthesis involving acetic acid as a solvent and ammonium acetate as a catalyst, produced a poor yield of the nitrostyrene and it was difficult to separate from the white diacetate of the starting anisaldehyde, mp 59-60 °C.

A suspension of 32 g LAH in 1 L anhydrous Et_2O was well stirred and 32.6 g 1-(4-methoxyphenyl)-2-nitropropene in Et_2O was added at a rate that maintained a reflux. After the addition was complete, reflux was continued for 48 h. The reaction mixture was cooled, and the excess hydride was destroyed by the cautious addition of dilute H_2SO_4. The Et_2O was separated, and extracted with additional aqueous H_2SO_4. A solution of 700 g potassium sodium tartrate in 600 mL H_2O was added, and the pH brought to >9 with 25% NaOH. This aqueous phase was extracted with 3x200 mL CH_2Cl_2 which provided, after removal of the solvent, 32.5 g of a clear amber oil. This was dissolved in 100 mL IPA, neutralized with concentrated HCl, and then diluted with 300 mL anhydrous Et_2O. There was obtained white crystals of 4-methoxyamphetamine hydrochloride (4-MA) that weighed, after filtering, Et_2O washing and air drying, 22.2 g and had a mp of 208-209 °C. The amphetamine metabolite, 4-hydroxyamphetamine hydrochloride (4-HA), was prepared by heating 5.0 g 4-MA in 20 mL concentrated HCl at 15 lbs/in. After recrystallization from aqueous EtOH, the product weighed 3.8 g and had a mp of 171-172 °C.

DOSAGE: 50 - 80 mg.

DURATION: short.

QUALITATIVE COMMENTS: (with 60 mg) "At just over an hour, there was a sudden blood pressure rise, with the systolic going up 55 mm. This was maintained for another hour. I found the effects reminiscent of DET, distinct after-images, and some parasthesia. I was without any residue by early evening (after 5 hours)."

(with 70 mg) "It hit quite suddenly. I had a feeling of druggedness, almost an alcohol-like intoxication, and I never was really high in the psychedelic sense."

EXTENSIONS AND COMMENTARY: This is another of the essential amphetamines, because of the appearance of the 4-methoxy group in two most important essential oils. These are the allylbenzene (estragole or esdragol) and the propenyl isomer (anethole). Their natural sources have been discussed under TMA.

Two comments are warranted concerning 4-MA, one of scientific interest, and the other about a social tragedy.

A major metabolites of amphetamine is 4-hydroxyamphetamine, from oxidation at the 4-position. It has been long known that with chronic amphetamine usage there is the generation of tolerance, which encourages ever-increasing doses to be used. When the daily load gets up around one or two hundred milligrams, the subject can become quite psychotic. The question was asked: might the chronic amphetamine user be methylating his endogenously produced 4-hydroxyamphetamine to produce 4-methoxyamphetamine (4-MA), and maybe this is the agent that promotes the psychosis? To address this question, several studies were done with normal subjects, about 20 years ago, to see if 4-MA might produce a psychotic state (it didn't at the highest levels tried, 75 milligrams) and to see if it was excreted to some extent unchanged in the urines of these normal subjects (it was seen even at the lowest dosage tried, 10 milligrams). It produced excitation and other central effects, it produced adrenergic pressor effects, and it consistently produced measurable quantities of 4-MA in the urine, but it produced no amphetamine-like crazies. And since the administration of up to 600 milligrams of amphetamine produced no detectable 4-MA in the urine, this theory of psychotomimesis is not valid.

On the tragic side, a few years later, 4-MA became widely distributed in both the US (as the sulfate salt) and in Canada (as the hydrochloride), perhaps inspired by some studies in rats that had reported that it was second only to LSD in potency as a hallucinogen. The several deaths that occurred probably followed overdose, and it was clear that 4-MA was involved as it had been isolated from both urine and tissue during post mortems. It had been sold under the names of Chicken Power and Chicken Yellow, and was promoted as being MDA. I could find no record of a typical street dosage, but comments collected in association with the deaths implied that the ingested quantites were in the hundreds of milligrams. Recently, the ethoxy homologue, 4-EA, appeared on the streets of Canada. The dosage, again, was not reported. It was promptly illegalized there.

The two positional analogues of 4-MA are known; vis., 2-MA and 3-MA. Their synthesis is straightforward, in imitation of that for 4-MA above. The meta-compound, 3-MA, has been metabolically explored in man, but no central effects were noted at a 50 milligram dose (2x25 milligrams, separated by three hours). There appears to be no report of any human trial of 2-MA. The N-methyl homologue of 2-MA is a commercial adrenergic bronchodilator called Methoxyphenamine, or Orthoxine. It has been used in the prevention of acute asthma attacks in doses of up to 200 milligrams, with only slight central stimulation. The N-methyl homologues of 3-MA and 4-MA are known, and the latter compound is the stuff of a separate entry in this book.

#98   MADAM-6;   2,N-DIMETHYL-4,5-METHYLENEDIOXY-AMPHETAMINE

SYNTHESIS: A mixture of 102 g $POCl_3$ and 115 g N-methylformanilide was allowed to stand for 0.5 h at room temperature during which time it turned a deep claret color. To this there was added 45 g 3,4-methylenedioxytoluene and the mixture was held on the steam bath for 3 h. It was then added to 3 L H_2O. Stirring was continued until the oil which had separated had become quite firm. This was removed by filtration to give a greenish, somewhat gummy, crystalline solid, which was finely ground under 40 mL MeOH and again filtered giving, when air dried, 25 g of an almost white solid. Recrystallization of a small sample from methylcyclopentane gave ivory-colored glistening crystals of 2-methyl-4,5-methylenedioxybenzaldehyde with a mp of 88.5-89.5 °C. In the infra-red, the carbonyl was identical to that of the starting piperonal (1690 cm⁻¹) but the fingerprint was different and unique, with bands at 868, 929, 1040 and 1052 cm⁻¹.

A solution of 23 g 2-methyl-4,5-methylenedioxybenzaldehyde in 150 mL nitroethane was treated with 2.0 g anhydrous ammonium acetate and heated on the steam bath for 9 h. The excess solvent was removed under vacuum to give a dark yellow oil which was dissolved in 40 mL hot MeOH and allowed to crystallize. The solids were removed by filtration, washed modestly with MeOH and air dried, to give 21.2 g of 1-(2-methyl-4,5-methylenedioxyphenyl)-2-nitropropene as beautiful yellow crystals with a mp of 116-118 °C. Recrystallization of an analytical sample from MeOH gave lustrous bright yellow crystals with a mp of 120-121 °C. Anal. $(C_{11}H_{11}NO_4)$ C,H,N.

A suspension of 54 g electrolytic elemental iron in 240 g glacial acetic acid was warmed on the steam bath, with frequent stirring. When the reaction between them started, there was added, a portion at a time, a solution of 18.2 g 1-(2-methyl-4,5-methylenedioxyphenyl)-2-nitropropene in 125 mL warm acetic acid. The orange color of the nitrostyrene solution became quite reddish, white solids of iron acetate appeared, and a dark tomato-colored crust formed which was continuously broken back into the reaction mixture. Heating was continued for 1.5 h, and then all was poured into 2 L H_2O. All the insolubles were removed by filtration, and these were washed well with CH_2Cl_2. The filtrate and washes were combined, the phases separated, and the aqueous phase extracted with 2x100 mL additional CH_2Cl_2. The combined organics were washed with 5% NaOH, and the solvent removed under vacuum. The residue weighed 15.9 g, and was distilled at 90-110 °C at 0.4 mm/Hg to give 13.9 g of 2-methyl-4,5-methylenedioxyphenylacetone that spontaneously crystallized. A small sample from methylcyclopentane had a mp of 52-53 °C, another from hexane a mp of 53-54 °C, and another from MeOH a mp of 54-55 °C. Anal. $(C_{11}H_{12}O_3)$ H; C calcd, 68.73; found 67.87, 67.84.

To a stirred solution of 30 g methylamine hydrochloride in 200 mL warm MeOH there was added 13.5 g 2-methyl-4,5-methylenedioxyphenylacetone followed, after returning to room temperature, by 7 g sodium cyanoborohydride. There was added HCl as needed to maintain the pH at approximately orange on external damp universal pH paper. After a few days, the reaction ceased generating base, and all was poured into 2 L dilute H_2SO_4 (caution, HCN evolved). This was washed with 3x75 mL CH_2Cl_2, made basic with 25% NaOH, and the resulting mixture extracted with 3x100 CH_2Cl_2. The pooled extracts were stripped of solvent under vacuum and the residue, 15 g of a pale amber oil, was distilled at 95-110 °C at 0.4 mm/Hg. There was obtained 12.3 g of a white oil that was dissolved in 60 mL IPA, neutralized with approximately 5.5 mL concentrated HCl, and crystals of the salt formed spontaneously. These were loosened with the addition of another 10 mL IPA, and then all was diluted by the addition of an equal volume of anhydrous Et_2O. The white crystals were separated by filtration, Et_2O washed, and air dried to give 14.1 g of 2,N-dimethyl-4,5-methylenedioxyamphetamine hydrochloride (MADAM-6) as a brilliant white powder with a mp of 206-207 °C. Anal. $(C_{12}H_{18}ClNO_2)$ C,H.

DOSAGE: greater than 280 mg.

DURATION: unknown.

QUALITATIVE COMMENTS: (with 180 mg) "There is a hint of good things there, but nothing more than a hint. At four hours, there is no longer even a hint."
  (with 280 mg) "I took 150 milligrams, waited an hour for results, which was niente, nada, nothing. Took supplements of 65 milligrams twice, an hour apart. No effect. Yes, we giveth up."

EXTENSIONS AND COMMENTARY: The structure of MADAM-6 was designed to be that of MDMA, with a methyl group attached at what should be a reasonably indifferent position. In fact, that is the genesis of the name. MDMA has been called ADAM, and with a methyl group in the 6-position, MADAM-6 is quite understandable. And the other ortho-position is, using this nomenclature, the 2-position, and with a methyl group there, one would have MADAM-2. I should make a small apology for the choice of numbers. MDMA is a 3,4-methylenedioxy compound, and the least ambiguous numbering scheme would be to lock the methylenedioxy group inescapably at the 3,4-place, letting the other ring position numbers fall where they may. The rules of chemistry ask that if something is really a 3,4,6-orientation it should be renumbered as a 2,4,5-orientation. Let's quietly ignore that request here.

  How fascinating it is, that a small methyl group, something that is little more than one more minor bump on the surface of a molecule that is lumpy and bumpy anyway, can so effectively change the action of a compound. A big activity change from a small structure change usually implies that the bump is at a vital point, such as a target of metabolism or a point of critical fit in some receptor site. And since 6-MADAM can be looked upon as 6-bump-MDMA, and since it is at least 3x less potent than MDMA, the implication is that the action of MDMA requires some unbumpiness at this position for its particular action. There are suggestions that the body may want to put a hydroxyl group right there (a 6-hydroxy-dopamine act), and it couldn't if there was a methyl group right there. The isopropylamine side chain may want a certain degree of swing-around freedom, and this would be restricted by a methyl bump right next to it. And there are all kinds of other speculations possible as to why that position should be open.

  Anyway, MADAM-6 is not active. And the equally intriguing positional isomer, the easily made MADAM-2, will certainly contribute to these speculations. A quiz for the reader! Will 2,N-dimethyl-3,4-methylenedioxyamphetamine (MADAM-2) be: (1) Of much reduced activity, akin to MADAM-6, or (2) Of potency and action similar to that of MDMA, or (3) Something unexpected and unanticipated? I know only one way of finding out. Make the Schiffs' base between piperonal and cyclohexylamine, treat this with butyl lithium in hexane with some TMEDA present, add some N-methylformanilide, convert the formed benzaldehyde to a nitrostyrene with nitroethane, reduce this with elemental iron to the phenylacetone, reduce this in the presence of methylamine with sodium cyanoborohydride, then taste the result.

#99   MAL;   METHALLYLESCALINE;   3,5-DIMETHOXY-4-
METHALLYLOXYPHENETHYLAMINE)

SYNTHESIS: To a solution of 5.8 g of homosyringonitrile (see under ESCALINE
for its preparation) in 50 mL of acetone containing 100 mg of decyltriethylammonium
iodide there was added 7.8 mL methallyl chloride followed by 6.9 g of finely
powdered anhydrous K_2CO_3. The suspension was kept at reflux by a heating mantle,
with effective stirring. After 6 h an additional 4.0 mL of methallyl chloride was
added, and the refluxing was continued for an additional 36 h. The solvent and
excess methallyl chloride was re-
moved under vacuum and the residue was added to 400 mL H_2O. This
solution was extracted with 3x75
mL CH_2Cl_2. The extracts were
pooled, washed with 2x50 mL 5%
Naoh, and the solvent removed to provide a dark brown oil. This was distilled at
120-130 °C at 0.4 mm/Hg to provide 6.1 g of 3,5-dimethoxy-4-methyallyloxy-
phenylacetonitrile as a lemon-colored viscous oil. Anal. $(C_{14}H_{17}NO_3)$ C,H.
    A suspension of 4.2 g LAH in 160 mL anhydrous THF under He was
stirred, cooled to 0 °C, and treated with 2.95 ml of 100% H_2SO_4 added dropwise.
This was followed by the addition of 6.0 g of 3,5-dimethoxy-4-methallyloxy-
phenylacetonitrile dissolved in 10 mL anhydrous THF, at a slow rate with vigorous
stirring. The reaction mixture was held at reflux on the steam bath for 0.5 h, brought
back to room temperature, and the excess hydride destroyed with IPA. Sufficient
15% NaOH was added to convert the formed solids to a loose, granular texture, and
the entire mixture filtered and washed with THF. The filtrate and washings were
pooled, the solvent removed under vacuum, and the residue added to 500 mL dilute
HCl. This solution was washed with 2x50 mL CH_2Cl_2, made basic with aqueous
NaOH, and extracted with 3x75 mL CH_2Cl_2. The extracts were pooled, the solvent
removed under vacuum, and the residual pale amber oil distilled at 120-130 °C at
0.3 mm/Hg to provide 1.5 g of a white oil. This was dissolved in 8.0 mL of IPA and
neutralized with 25 drops of concentrated HCl. The addition of 40 ml of anhydrous
Et_2O with stirring produced, after a few moments delay, a spontaneous crystallization
of 3,5-dimethoxy-4-methallyloxyphenethylamine hydrochloride (MAL) as fine
white needles. After standing overnight these were removed by filtration, washed
with an IPA/Et_2O mixture, then with Et_2O, and allowed to air dry to constant weight.
The product weighed 1.1 g, and had a mp of 153-154 °C. Anal. $(C_{14}H_{22}ClNO_3)$ C,H.

DOSAGE: 40 - 65 mg.

DURATION: 12 - 16 h.

QUALITATIVE COMMENTS: (with 45 mg) "Too much overload. I am surrounded with unreality. I do not choose to repeat the experiment."

(with 45 mg) "I am basically favorably impressed. I believe the initial discomfort would be alleviated by taking two 30 milligram doses separated by an hour."

(with 45 mg) "Much too much too much. There are shades of what might become amnesia. I am losing immediate contact. I will not repeat."

(with 50 mg) "A good level. I found myself totally caught up in the visual theater. Although I had trouble sleeping, I would willingly repeat the experiment at the same level."

(with 60 mg) "Extremely restless. Am very impressed with all the activity. But if I repeated it would be at a lower dose."

(with 60 mg) "Friendly territory. There is much kaleidoscopic 'neon' colors. Eyes closed very active. Eyes open there is considerable visual distortions seen in melted wax. Faces are distorted (friendly) but the sinister is not far away."

(with 65 mg) "Completely involved — good psychedelic state — visual entertainment with alternation (i.e., depth and movement) at the retinal level — detail in watercolors. Later in the experience (the 8 hour point) easy childhood memory recall."

(with 65 mg) "Beautiful. To a +2 by the 1st hr and continued climbing. Intense +3 within 2 hrs. Quite strong body. Diuretic. Fantasy, imagery, erotic. Way up, good connections between parts of self. Slight slowing of pulse in 7th to 8th hour. Excellent solid sleep with strong, clear, balancing dreams. But not until after 12 hrs."

EXTENSIONS AND COMMENTARY: This testimony can be accurately described as a mixed bag!

This base, MAL, lies as a hybrid of two other compounds, AL and CPM. It is an olefin (as is AL) which means that it has a place of unsaturation in its structure. And it is an isostere of CPM which means that the carbon atoms are all in the same location, but just the connecting electrons (called the chemical bonds) are in different places. Actually there is yet a third compound in this same picture, called PROPYNYL. And yet, although all of them have extremely close structural similarities, there are such great differences in action that one does not dare to generalize. CPM leads largely to fantasy, MAL largely to visual imagery, AL is twice as potent as either of these but it doesn't show either effect, and PROPYNYL is almost without any action at all.

Speaking of generalization, I am glad that there are always exceptions. Some years ago, I had a most difficult experience with a strain of marijuana that was known by the name of DRED. The only word that I can use to describe my response to it is to say that I felt I had been poisoned. From this I warned myself to beware (and to believe in) whatever common name a drug might have been given. Fortunately, MAL did not live up to its name (at least for me), although some of the experimental subjects might disagree!

One additional compound was suggested by these parallels. Each of these three drugs can be viewed as having a negative something hanging out a-ways from the molecular center. With AL and MAL, this is the olefin double bond. With CPM this is a very strained three-member ring. What about an oxygen? The reaction between homosyringonitrile and methoxyethyl chloride produced the precursor to such a product (3,5-dimethoxy-4-(2-methoxyethoxy)-phenethylamine) but the yield was so bad that the project was abandoned. This same grouping has successfully been put into the 4-position of the sulfur-containing analog, and the result (2C-T-13) has proved to be quite a potent and interesting material. Maybe someday hang a sulfur atom out there at the end of that chain.

The name methallylescaline actually is completely unsound. There is no union of a methallyl with an escaline. What is really there is not an escaline at all, but rather a mescaline with a 2-propene attached to the methyl of the methoxy on the 4-position. There is no way of naming the thing in that manner, so the only logical solution is to take off the methyl entirely, and then put the methallyl on in its place. The name of this would then be 4-methylallyldesmethylmescaline. That would have received the abbreviation MAD which would have been even more difficult to deal with. MAL is preferable.

#100   MDA;   3,4-METHYLENEDIOXYAMPHETAMINE

SYNTHESIS: (from piperonal) To a solution of 15.0 g piperonal in 80 mL glacial acetic acid there was added 15 mL nitroethane followed by 10 g cyclohexylamine. The mixture was held at steam-bath temperature for 6 h, diluted with 10 mL H_2O, seeded with a crystal of product, and cooled overnight at 10 °C. The bright yellow crystals were removed by filtration, and air dried to yield 10.7 g of 1-(3,4-methylene-dioxyphenyl)-2-nitropropene with a mp of 93-94 °C. This was raised to 97-98 °C by recrystallization from acetic acid. The more conventional efforts of nitrostyrene synthesis using an excess of nitroethane as a solvent and anhydrous ammonium acetate as the base, gives impure product in very poor yields. The nitrostyrene has been successfully made from the components in cold MeOH, with aqueous NaOH as the base.

A suspension of 20 g LAH in 250 mL anhydrous THF was placed under an inert atmosphere and stirred magnetically. There was added, dropwise, 18 g of 1-(3,4-methylenedioxyphenyl)-2-nitropropene in solution in THF and the reaction mixture was maintained at reflux for 36 h. After being brought back to room temperature, the excess hydride was destroyed with 15 mL IPA, followed by 15 mL of 15% NaOH. An additional 50 mL H_2O was added to complete the conversion of the aluminum salts to a loose, white, easily filtered solid. This was removed by filtration, and the filter cake washed with additional THF. The combined filtrate and washes were stripped of solvent under vacuum, and the residue dissolved in dilute H_2SO_4. Washing with 3x75 mL CH_2Cl_2 removed much of the color, and the aqueous phase was made basic and reextracted with 3x100 mL CH_2Cl_2. Removal of the solvent yielded 13.0 g of a yellow-colored oil that was distilled. The fraction boiling at 80-90 °C at 0.2 mm weighed 10.2 g and was water-white. It was dissolved in 60 mL of IPA, neutralization with concentrated HCl, and diluted with 120 mL of anhydrous Et_2O which produced a lasting turbidity. Crystals formed spontaneously which were removed by filtration, washed with Et_2O, and air dried to provide 10.4 g of 3,4-methylenedioxyamphetamine hydrochloride (MDA) with a mp of 187-188 °C.

(from 3,4-methylenedioxyphenylacetone) To a solution of 32.5 g anhydrous ammonium acetate in 120 mL MeOH, there was added 7.12 g 3,4-methylenedioxyphenylacetone (see under MDMA for its preparation) followed by 2.0 g sodium cyanoborohydride. The resulting yellow solution was vigorously stirred, and concentrated HCl was added periodically to keep the pH of the reaction mixture between 6 and 7 as determined by external damp universal pH paper. After several days, undissolved solids remained in the reaction mixture and no more acid was required. The reaction mixture was added to 600 mL of dilute HCl, and this was washed with 3x100 mL CH_2Cl_2. The combined washes were back-extracted with a small amount of dilute HCl, the aqueous phases combined, and made basic with 25% NaOH. This was then extracted with 3x100 mL CH_2Cl_2, these extracts combined, and the solvent removed under vacuum to provide 3.8 g of a red-colored residue. This was distilled at 80-90 °C at 0.2 mm/Hg to provide 2.2 g of an absolutely water-white oil. There was no obvious formation of a carbonate salt when exposed to air. This was dissolved in 15 mL IPA, neutralized with 25 drops of concentrated HCl, and diluted with 30 mL anhydrous Et_2O. Slowly there was the deposition of white crystals of 3,4-methylenedioxyamphetamine hydrochloride (MDA) which weighed 2.2 g and had a mp of 187-188 °C. The preparation of the formamide (a precursor to MDMA) and the acetamide (a precursor to MDE) are described under those entries.

DOSAGE: 80 - 160 mg.

DURATION: 8 - 12 h.

QUALITATIVE COMMENTS: (with 100 mg) "The coming on was gradual and pleasant, taking from an hour to an hour and one half to do so. The trip was euphoric and intense despite my having been naturally depleted from a working day and having started so late. One thing that impressed itself upon me was the feeling I got of seeing the play of events, of what I thought to be the significance of certain people coming into my life, and why my 'dance', like everyone else's, is unique. I saw that every encounter or event is a potential for growth, and an opportunity for me to realize my completeness at where I am, here and now, not at some future where I must lug the pieces of the past for a final assemblage 'there.' I was reminded of living the moment to its fullest and I felt that seeing this was indicative that I was on the right track."

(with 128 mg) "Forty-five minutes after the second dosage, when I was seated in a room by myself, not smoking, and where there was no possible source of smoke rings, an abundance of curling gray smoke rings was readily observed in the environment whenever a relaxed approach to subjective observation was used. Visually these had complete reality and it seemed quite unneccessary to test their properties because it was surely known and fully appreciated that the source of the visual phenomena could not be external to the body. When I concentrated my attention on the details of the curling gray forms by trying to note how they would be affected by passing a finger through their apparent field, they melted away. Then, when I relaxed again, the smoke rings were there. I was as certain that they were really there as I am now sure that my head is on top of my body."

(with 140 mg) "I vomited quite abruptly, and then everything was OK. I had been drinking probably excessively the last two days, and maybe the body needed to unpoison itself. The tactile sense is beautiful, but there seems to be some numbness as well, and I feel that nothing erotic would be do-able. Intimacy, yes, but no performance I'm pretty sure. I saw the experience start drifting away only four hours into it, and I was sad to see it go. It was an all around delightful day."

(with 200 mg, 2x100 mg spaced 1 h) "The first portion was apparent at one-half hour. There was microscopic nausea shortly after the second portion was taken, and in an hour there was a complete +++ developed. The relaxation was extreme. And there seemed to be time distortion, in that time seemed to pass slowly. There was a occasional LSD-like moment of profoundness, but by and large it was a simple intoxication with most things seeming quite hilarious. The intoxication was also quite extreme. Some food was tried later in the experiment, and it tasted good, but there was absolutely no appetite. None at all."

(with 60 mg of the "R" isomer) "There was a light and not too gentle development of a somewhat brittle wound-up state, a + or even a ++. Chills, and I had to get under an electric blanket to be comfortable. The effects smoothed out at the fourth hour, when things started to return to baseline. Not too entertaining."

(with 100 mg of the "R" isomer) "Rapid development from the 40 minute point to an hour and a quarter; largely a pleasant intoxication, but there is something serious there too. No great insights, and not too much interference with the day's goings-on. Completely clear at the 8 hour point."

(with 120 mg of the "R" isomer) "This is a stoning intoxicant. I would not choose to drive, because of possible judgement problems, but my handwriting seems to be clear and normal. The mental excitement dropped rapidly but I was aware of physical residues for several additional hours."

(with 80 mg of the "S" isomer) "A very thin, light threshold, which is quite delightful. I am quite willing to push this a bit higher."

(with 120 mg of the "S" isomer) "Perhaps to a one +. Very light, and very much like MDMA, but perhaps shorter lived. I am pretty much baseline in three hours."

(with 160 mg of the "S" isomer) "The development is very rapid, and there is both muscular tremor and some nausea. The physicals are quite bothersome. With eyes closed, there are no effects noticeable, but with eyes open, things are quite bright and sparkling. The muscular spasms persist, and there is considerable teeth clenching. I feel that the mental is not worth the physical."

EXTENSIONS AND COMMENTARY: There are about twenty different synthetic routes in the literature for the preparation of MDA. Many start with piperonal, and employ it to make methylenedioxyphenylacetone or a methylenedioxydihydro-cinnamic acid amide instead of the nitrostyrene. The phenylacetone can be reduced in several ways other than the cyanoborohydride method mentioned here, and the amide can be rearranged directly to MDA. And there are additional methods for the reduction of the nitrostyrene that use no lithium aluminum hydride. Also there are procedures that have safrole or isosafrole as starting points. There is even one in the underground literature that starts with sassafras root bark. In fact, it is because safrole is one of the ten essential oils that MDA can humorously be referred to as one of the Ten Essential Amphetamines. See the comments under TMA.

There is a broad and checkered history concerning the use and abuse of MDA, and it is not the case that all the use was medical and all the abuse was social. One of the compulsive drives of both the military and the intelligence groups, just after World War II, was to discover and develop chemical agents which might serve as "truth serums" or as incapacitating agents. These government agencies considered the area of the psychedelics to be a fertile field for searching. The giving of relatively unexplored drugs in a cavalier manner to knowing and unknowing subjects was commonplace. There was one case in 1953, involving MDA and a psychiatric patient named Howard Blauer that proved fatal. The army had contracted with several physicians at the New York State Psychiatric Institute to explore new chemicals from the Edgewood Arsenal and one of these, with a chemical warfare code number of EA-1298, was MDA. The last and lethal injection into Blauer was an intravenous dose of 500 milligrams.

There have been a number of medical explorations. Under the code SKF-5 (and trade name of Amphedoxamine) it was explored as an anorexic agent. It has been found promising in the treatment of psychoneurotic depression. There are several medical reports, and one book (Claudio Naranjo's *The Healing Journey*), that describe its values in psychotherapy.

MDA was also one of the major drugs that was being popularly used in the late 1960's when the psychedelic concept exploded on the public scene. MDA was called the "hug-drug" and was said to stand for Mellow Drug of America. There was no difficulty in obtaining unending quantities of it, as it was available as a research chemical from several scientific supply houses (as were mescaline and LSD) and was sold inexpensively under its chemical name.

A few experimental trials with the pure optical isomers show a consistency with all the other psychedelic compounds that have been studied in their separated forms, the higher potency with the "R" isomer. The less potent "S" isomer seemed to be more peaceful and MDMA-like at lower doses, but there were worrisome toxic signs at higher levels.

The structure of MDA can be viewed as an aromatic ring (the 3,4-methylenedioxyphenyl ring) with a three carbon chain sticking out from it. The amine group is on the second of the three carbon atoms. The isomers, with the amine function moved to the first of these carbons atoms (a benzylamine) and with the amine function moved to the third (furthest out atom) of these carbon atoms (a (n)-propylamine), are known and both have been assayed.

The benzylamine counterpart (as if one were to move the amine function from the beta-carbon to the alpha-carbon of the three carbon chain of the amphetamine molecule) is alpha-ethyl-3,4-methylenedioxybenzylamine or 1-amino-1-(3,4-methylenedioxyphenyl)propane, ALPHA. The hydrochloride salt has a mp of 199-201 °C. At low threshold levels (10 milligram area) there were eyes-closed "dreams" with some body tingling. The compound was not anorexic at any dose (up to 140 milligrams) and was reported to produce a pleasant, positive feeling. It is very short-lived (about 3 hours). The N-methyl homologue is alpha-ethyl-N-methyl-3,4-methylenedioxybenzylamine or 1-methylamino-1-(3,4-methylenedioxy-phenyl)propane, M-ALPHA. It is similar in action, but is perhaps twice as potent (a plus one or plus two dose is 60 milligrams) and of twice the duration.

The (n)-propylamine counterpart (as if one were to move the amine function the other direction, from the beta-carbon to the gamma-carbon of the three carbon chain of the amphetamine molecule) is gamma-3,4-methylenedioxy-phenylpropylamine or 1-amino-3-(3,4-methylenedioxyphenyl)propane, GAMMA. The hydrochloride salt has a mp of 204-205 °C. At oral levels of 200 milligrams there was some physical ill-at-ease, possible time distortion, and a feeling of being keenly aware of one's surroundings. The duration of effects was 4 hrs.

The phenethylamine that corresponds to MDA (removing the alpha-methyl group) is 3,4-methylenedioxyphenethylamine, or homopiperonylamine, or MDPEA, or simply H in the vocabulary of the Muni-Metro world. This compound is an entry in its own rights. The adding of another carbon atom to the alpha-methyl group of MDA gives compound J, and leads to the rest of the Muni-Metro series (K, L etc). All of this is explained under METHYL-J. The bending of this alpha-methyl group back to the aromatic ring gives an aminoindane, and with J one gets an aminotetralin. Both compounds react in animal discrimination studies identically to MDMA, and they appear to be free of neurochemical toxicity.

The two possible homologues, with either one or two methyl groups on the methylene carbon of the methylenedioxy group of MDA, are also known. The ethylidene compound (the acetaldehyde addition to the catechol group) has been encoded as EDA, and the acetone (isopropylidine addition to the catechol group) is called IDA. In animal discrimination studies, and in *in vitro* neurotransmitter studies, they both seem to be of decreased potency. EDA is down two to three-fold from MDA, and IDA is down by a factor of two to three-fold again. Human trials of up to 150 milligrams of the hydrochloride salt of EDA producd at best a threshold light-headedness. IDA remains untested as of the present time. The homologue of MDA (actually of MDMA) with the added carbon atom in, rather than on, the methylenedioxy ring, is a separate entry; see MDMC.

A final isomer to be mentioned is a positional isomer. The 3,4-methylene-dioxy group could be at the 2,3-position of the amphetamine skeleton, giving 2,3-methylenedioxyamphetamine, or ORTHO-MDA. It appears to be a stimulant rather than another MDA. At 50 milligrams, one person was awake and alert all night, but reported no MDA-like effects.

#101   MDAL;   N-ALLYL-MDA;   3,4-METHYLENEDIOXY-N-ALLYLAMPHETAMINE

SYNTHESIS: A total of about 20 mL allylamine was introduced under the surface of 20 mL concentrated HCl, and the mixture stripped of volatiles under vacuum The resulting 24 g of wet material did not yield any crystals with either acetone or Et_2O. This was dissolved in 75 mL MeOH, treated with 4.45 g 3,4-methylenedioxy-phenylacetone (see under MDMA for its preparation), and finally with 1.1 g sodium cyanoborohydride. Concentrated HCl was added as needed over the course of 5 days to keep the pH constant at about 6. The reaction mixture was then added to a large

amount of H_2O, acidified with HCl, and extracted with 3x100 mL CH_2Cl_2. The aqueous phase was made basic with 25% NaOH, and extracted with 3x100 mL CH_2Cl_2. Evaporation of the solvent from these extracts yielded 3.6 g of an amber oil which, on distillation at 90-95 °C at 0.2 mm/Hg, yielded 2.6 g of an off-white oil. This was dissolved in 10 mL IPA, neutralized with about 25 drops of concentrated HCl, and the resulting clear but viscous solution was diluted with Et_2O until crystals formed. These were removed by filtration, washed with IPA/Et_2O (1:1), then with Et_2O, and air dried to constant weight. There was thus obtained 2.5 g of 3,4-methylenedioxy-N-allylamphetamine hydrochloride (MDAL) with a mp of 174-176 °C and a proton NMR spectrum that showed that the allyl group was intact. Anal. ($C_{13}H_{18}ClNO_2$) N.

DOSAGE: greater than 180 mg.

DURATION: unknown.

EXTENSIONS AND COMMENTARY: Here is another inactive probe, like MDPR, that could possibly serve as a primer to LSD. The three carbon chain on the nitrogen seen with MDPR is almost identical to the three carbon chain on the nitrogen atom of MDAL. And yet, where an "inactive" level of 180 milligrams of MDPR is a rather fantastic enhancer of LSD action, the same weight of this compound not only does not enhance, but actually seems to somewhat antagonize the action of LSD. All this difference from just a couple of hydrogen atoms. Identical carbon atoms, identical oxygen atoms, and an identical nitrogen atom. And all in identical places. Simply $C_{13}H_{18}ClNO_2$ rather than $C_{13}H_{20}ClNO_2$. So, apparently, almost identical is not good enough!

#102 MDBU; N-BUTYL-MDA; 3,4-METHYLENEDIOXY-N-BUTYLAMPHETAMINE

SYNTHESIS: A total of 30 mL butylamine was introduced under the surface of 33 mL concentrated HCl, and the mixture stripped of volatiles under vacuum. The resulting glassy solid was dissolved in 160 mL MeOH and treated with 7.2 g 3,4-methylenedioxyphenylacetone (see under MDMA for its preparation). To this there was added 50% NaOH dropwise until the pH was at about 6 as determined by the use of external dampened universal pH paper. The solution was vigorously stirred and 2.8 g sodium cyanoborohydride was added. Concentrated HCl was added as needed, to keep the pH constant at about 6. The addition required about two days, during which time the reaction mixture first became quite cottage-cheese like, and then finally thinned out again. All was dumped into 1 L H_2O acidified with HCl, and extracted with 3x100 mL CH_2Cl_2. These extracts were combined, extracted with 2x100 mL dilute H_2SO_4, which was combined with the aqueous fraction above. This latter mixture was made basic with 25% NaOH, and extracted with 3x150 mL CH_2Cl_2. Evaporation of the solvent yielded 4.0 g of an amber oil which, on distillation at 90-100 °C at 0.15 mm/Hg, yielded 3.2 g of a white clear oil. This was dissolved in 20 mL IPA, neutralized with 30 drops of concentrated HCl, and the spontaneously formed crystals were diluted with sufficient anhydrous Et_2O to allow easy filtration. After Et_2O washing and air drying, there was obtained 2.8 g of 3,4-methylenedioxy-N-butylamphetamine hydrochloride (MDBU) as white crystals with a mp of 200-200.5 °C. Anal. ($C_{14}H_{22}ClNO_2$) N.

DOSAGE: greater than 40 mg.

DURATION: unknown.

EXTENSIONS AND COMMENTARY: Straight chain homologues on the nitrogen atom of MDA longer than two carbons are probably not active. This butyl compound provoked no interest, and although the longer chain counterparts were made by the general sodium cyanoborohydride method (see under MDBZ), they were not tasted. All mouse assays that compared this homologous series showed a consistent decrease in action (anesthetic potency and motor activity) as the alkyl chain on the nitrogen atoms was lengthened.

This synthetic procedure, using the hydrochloride salt of the amine and sodium cyanoborohydride in methanol, seems to be quite general for ketone compounds related to 3,4-methylenedioxyphenylacetone. Not only were most of the MD-group of compounds discussed here made in this manner, but the use of phenylacetone (phenyl-2-propanone, P-2-P) itself appears to be equally effective. The reaction of butylamine hydrochloride in methanol, with phenyl-2-propanone and sodium cyanoborohydride at pH of 6, after distillation at 70-75 °C at 0.3 mm/Hg, produced N-butylamphetamine hydrochloride (23.4 g from 16.3 g P-2-P). And, in the same manner with ethylamine hydrochloride there was produced N-ethyl-amphetamine (22.4 g from 22.1 g P-2-P) and with methylamine hydrochloride there was produced N-methylamphetamine hydrochloride (24.6 g from 26.8 g P-2-P). The reaction with simple ammonia (as ammonium acetate) gives consistently poor yields in these reactions.

#103 MDBZ; N-BENZYL-MDA; 3,4-METHYLENEDIOXY-N-BENZYLAMPHETAMINE

SYNTHESIS: To a suspension of 18.6 g benzylamine hydrochloride in 50 mL warm MeOH there was added 2.4 g of 3,4-methylenedioxyphenylacetone (see under MDMA for its preparation) followed by 1.0 g sodium cyanoborohydride. Concentrated HCl in MeOH was added over several days as required to maintain the pH at about 6 as determined with external, dampened universal paper. When the demand for acid ceased, the reaction mixture was added to 400 mL H_2O and made strongly acidic with an excess of HCl. This was extracted with 3x150 mL CH_2Cl_2 (these extracts must be saved as they contain the product) and the residual aqueous phase made basic with 25% NaOH and again extracted with 4x100 mL CH_2Cl_2. Removal of the solvent under vacuum and distillation of the 8.7 g pale yellow residue at slightly reduced pressure provided a colorless oil that was pure, recovered benzylamine. It was best characterized as its HCl salt (2 g in 10 mL IPA neutralized with about 25 drops concentrated HCl, and dilution with anhydrous Et_2O gave beautiful white crystals, mp 267-268 °C). The saved CH_2Cl_2 fractions above were extracted with 3x100 mL dillute H_2SO_4 These pooled extracts were back-washed once with CH_2Cl_2, made basic with 25% NaOH, and extracted with 3x50 mL CH_2Cl_2. The solvent was removed from the pooled extracts under vacuum, leaving a residue of about 0.5 g of an amber oil. This was dissolved in 10 mL IPA, neutralized with concentrated HCl (about 5 drops) and diluted with 80 mL anhydrous Et_2O. After a few min, 3,4-methylenedioxy-N-benzylamphetamine hydrochloride (MDBZ) began to appear as a fine white crystalline product. After removal by filtration, Et_2O washing and air drying, this weighed 0.55 g, and had a mp of 170-171 °C with prior shrinking at 165 °C. Anal. ($C_{17}H_{20}ClNO_2$) N.

DOSAGE: greater than 150 mg.

DURATION: unknown.

EXTENSIONS AND COMMENTARY: The benzyl group is a good ally in the synthetic world of the organic chemist, in that it can be easily removed by catalytic hydrogenation. This is a trick often used to protect (for a step or series of steps) a position on the molecule, and allowing it to become free and available at a later part in a synthetic scheme. In pharmacology, however, it is often a disappointment. With most centrally active alkaloids, there is a two-carbon separation between the weak base that is called the aromatic ring, and the strong base that is called the nitrogen. This is what makes phenethylamines what they are. The phen- is the aromatic ring (this is a shortened form of prefix phenyl which is a word which came, in turn, from the simplest aromatic alcohol, phenol); the ethyl is the two carbon chain, and the amine is the basic nitrogen. If one carbon is removed, one has a benzylamine, and it is usually identified with an entirely different pharmacology, or is most often simply not active. A vivid example is the narcotic drug, Fentanyl. The replacement of the phenethyl group, attached to the nitrogen atom with a benzyl group, virtually eliminates its analgesic potency.

Here too, there appears to be little if any activity in the N-benzyl analogue of MDA. A number of other variations had been synthesized, and none of them ever put into clinical trial. With many of them there was an ongoing problem in the separation of the starting amine from the product amine. Sometimes the difference in boiling points could serve, and sometimes their relative polarities could be exploited. Sometimes, ion-pair extraction would work wonders. But occasionally, nothing really worked well, and the final product had to be purified by careful crystallization.

Several additional N-homologues and analogues of MDA are noted here. The highest alkyl group on the nitrogen of MDA to give a compound that had been assayed, was the straight-chain butyl homologue, MDBU. Six other N-alkyls were made, or attempted. Isobutylamine hydrochloride and 3,4-methylenedioxy-phenylacetone were reduced with sodium cyanoborohydride in methanol to give 3,4-methylenedioxy-N-(i)-butylamphetamine boiling at 95-105 °C at 0.15 mm/Hg and giving a hydrochloride salt (MDIB) with a mp of 179-180 °C. Anal. ($C_{14}H_{22}ClNO_2$) N. The reduction with sodium cyanoborohydride of a mixture of (t)-butylamine hydrochloride and 3,4-methylenedioxyphenylacetone in methanol produced 3,4-methylenedioxy-N-(t)-butylamphetamine (MDTB) but the yield was miniscule. The amyl analog was similarly prepared from (n)-amylamine hydrochloride and 3,4-methylenedioxyphenylacetone in methanol to give 3,4-methylenedioxy-N-amylamphetamine which distilled at 110-120 °C at 0.2 mm/Hg and formed a hydrochloride salt (MDAM) with a mp of 164-166 °C. Anal. ($C_{15}H_{24}ClNO_2$) N. A similar reaction with (n)-hexylamine hydrochloride and 3,4-methylenedioxy-phenylacetone in methanol, with sodium cyanoborohydride, produced after acidification with dilute sulfuric acid copious white crystals that were water and ether insoluble, but soluble in methylene chloride! This sulfate salt in methylene chloride was extracted with aqueous sodium hydroxide and the remaining organic solvent removed to give a residue that distilled at 110-115 °C at 0.2 mm/Hg to give 3,4-methylenedioxy-N-(n)-hexylamphetamine which, as the hydrochloride salt (MDHE) had a mp of 188-189 °C. Anal. ($C_{16}H_{26}ClNO_2$) N. An attempt to make the 4-amino-heptane analogue from the primary amine, 3,4-methylenedioxyphenylacetone, and sodium cyanoborohydride in methanol seemed to progress smoothly, but none of the desired product 3,4-methylenedioxy-N-(4-heptyl)-amphetamine could be isolated. This base has been named MDSE, with a SE for septyl rather than HE for heptyl, to resolve any ambiguities about the use of HE for hexyl. In retrospect, it had been assumed that the sulfate salt would have extracted into methylene chloride, and the extraordinary partitioning of the sulfate salt of MDHE mentioned above makes it likely that the sulfate salt of MDSE went down the sink with the organic extracts of the sulfuric acid acidified crude product. Next time maybe ether as a solvent, or citric acid as an acid. With (n)-octylamine hydrochloride and 3,4-methylenedioxy-phenylacetone in methanol, with sodium cyanoborohydride, there was obtained 3,4-methylenedioxy-N-(n)-octylamphetamine as a water-insoluble, ether-insoluble sulfate salt. This salt was, however, easily soluble in methylene chloride, and with base washing of this solution, removal of the solvent, and distillation of the residue (130-135 °C at 0.2 mm/Hg) there was eventually gotten a fine hydrochloride salt (MDOC) as white crystals with a mp of 206-208 °C. Anal. ($C_{18}H_{30}ClNO_2$) N.

As to N,N-dialkylhomologues of MDA, the N,N-dimethyl has been separately entered in the recipe for MDDM. Two efforts were made to prepare the N,N-diethyl homologue of MDA. The reasonable approach of reducing a mixture of diethylamine hydrochloride and 3,4-methylenedioxyphenylacetone in methanol with sodium cyanoborohydride was hopelessly slow and gave little product. The reversal of the functionality was successful. Treatment of MDA (as the amine) and an excess of acetaldehyde (as the carbonyl source) with sodium borohydride in a cooled acidic medium gave, after acid-base workup, a fluid oil that distilled at 85-90 °C at 0.15 mm/Hg and was converted in isopropanol with concentrated hydrochloric acid to 3,4-methylenedioxy-N,N-diethylamphetamine (MDDE) with a mp of 177-178 °C. Anal. ($C_{14}H_{22}ClNO_2$) N.

And two weird N-substituted things were made. Aminoacetonitrile sulfate and 3,4-methylenedioxyphenylacetone were reduced in methanol with sodium cyanoborohydride to form 3,4-methylenedioxy-N-cyanomethylamphetamine which distilled at about 160 °C at 0.3 mm/Hg and formed a hydrochloride salt (MDCM) with a mp of 156-158 °C after recrystallization from boiling isopropanol. Anal. ($C_{12}H_{15}ClN_2O_2$) N. During the synthesis of MDCM, there appeared to have been generated appreciable ammonia, and the distillation provided a fore-run that contained MDA. The desired product had an acceptable NMR, with the N-cyanomethylene protons as a singlet at 4.38 ppm. A solution of t-butylhydrazine hydrochloride and 3,4-methylenedioxyphenylacetone in methanol was reduced with sodium cyanoborohydride and gave, after acid-basing and distillation at 95-105 °C at 0.10 mm/Hg, a viscous amber oil which was neutralized in isopropanol with concentrated hydrochloric acid to provide 3,4-methylenedioxy-N-(t)-butylaminoamphetamine hydrochloride (MDBA) with a mp of 220-222 °C with decomposition. Anal. ($C_{14}H_{23}ClN_2O_2$); N: calcd, 9.77; found, 10.67, 10.84.

#104   MDCPM;   CYCLOPROPYLMETHYL-MDA;   3,4-METHYLENEDIOXY-N-CYCLOPROPYLMETHYLAMPHETAMINE

SYNTHESIS: A solution of 9.4 g cyclopropylmethylamine hydrochloride in 30 mL MeOH was treated with 1.8 g 3,4-methylenedioxyphenylacetone (see under MDMA for its preparation) followed by 0.5 g sodium cyanoborohydride. Concentrated HCl was added as needed to keep the pH constant at about 6. After several days stirring, the reaction mixture was added to H_2O, acidified with HCl, and washed with 2x100 ml CH_2Cl_2. The aqueous phase was made basic with 25% NaOH, and extracted with 3x150 ml CH_2Cl_2. Removal of the solvent from these extracts under vacuum yielded 2.8 g of a crude product which, on distillation at 90-100 °C at 0.1 mm/Hg, yielded 0.4 g of a clear white oil. This was dissolved in a small amount of IPA, neutralized with a few drops of concentrated HCl, and diluted with anhydrous Et_2O to the point of turbidity. There was obtained a small yield of crystalline 3,4-methylenedioxy-N-cyclopropylmethylamphetamine hydrochloride (MDCPM) which was filtered off, Et_2O washed and air dried. The mp was 218-220 °C, with extensive darkening just prior to melting. Anal. ($C_{14}H_{20}ClNO_2$) N.

DOSAGE: greater than 10 mg.

DURATION: unknown.

EXTENSIONS AND COMMENTARY: The record of the tasting assay of this compound is pretty embarrassing. The highest level tried was 10 milligrams, which showed no hint of activity. But in light of the rather colorful activities of other cyclopropylmethyl things such as CPM and 2C-T-8, this compound might someday warrant reinvestigation. It is a certainty that the yield could only be improved with a careful resynthesis.

#105   MDDM;   N,N-DIMETHYL-MDA;   3,4-METHYLENEDIOXY-N,N-DIMETHYLAMPHETAMINE

SYNTHESIS: To a well stirred solution of 9.7 g dimethylamine hydrochloride in 50 mL MeOH there was added 3.56 g of 3,4-methylenedioxyphenylacetone (see under MDMA for its preparation) followed by 0.88 g sodium cyanoborohydride. A 1:1 mixture of concentrated HCl and MeOH was added as required to maintain the pH at about 6 as determined with external, dampened universal paper. Twenty drops were called for over the first four h, and a total of 60 drops were added over the course of two days at which time the reduction was complete. After the evaporation of most of the MeOH solvent, the reaction mixture was added to 250 mL H_2O

and made strongly acidic with an excess of HCl. After washing with 2x100 mL CH_2Cl_2 the aqueous phase was made basic with 25% NaOH, and extracted with 3x100 mL CH_2Cl_2. Removal of the solvent under vacuum yielded a nearly colorless oil that was distilled at 85-90 °C at 0.3 mm/Hg. There was obtained 1.5 g of a water-white oil that was dissolved in 8 mL IPA, neutralized with concentrated HCl and then diluted with 10 mL anhydrous Et_2O. The slightly turbid solution deposited a light lower oily layer which slowly crystallized on scratching. With patience, an additional 75 mL of Et_2O was added, allowing the formation of a white crystalline mass. This was removed by filtration and washed with additional Et_2O. After air drying there was obtained 1.3 g of 3,4-methylenedioxy-N,N-dimethylamphetamine hydrochloride (MDDM) with a mp of 172-173 °C. The NMR spectrum (60 mH) of the hydrochloride salt (in D_2O and with external TMS) was completely compatible with the expected structure. The signals were: 1.25, 1.37 (d) CCH$_3$, 3H; ArCH$_2$ under the N(CH$_3$)$_2$, 2.96, 8H; CH (m) 3.65; CH$_2O_2$ (s) 6.03 2H; ArH 6.93 (3H). Anal: ($C_{12}H_{18}ClNO_2$) N.

DOSAGE: greater than 150 mg.

DURATION: unknown.

QUALITATIVE COMMENTS: (with 150 mg) " No effects whatsoever."
(with 150 mg) "The effects, if any, were so-so. Perhaps a threshold. But
my libido was non-existent for three days."
(with 550 mg) "I took 550 milligrams of it Saturday night and I had a pretty
bad trip. On a scale of positive 10 to negative 10 it was about a negative 6. It really
downed me. Two other friends took 200 milligrams. They found it very pleasant
after about 20 minutes. It was a plus 3 [on the -10 to +10 scale]. Then it wore off
a little bit; and then, 4 hours later, it hit them even stronger and was about a plus 5."
(with 1000 mg) "I took up to a gram of it and absolutely nothing."

EXTENSIONS AND COMMENTARY: I cannot attest for the actual drug that had
been used in the two larger-dose reports above. These are from an anonymous
source associated with clandestine syntheses. If this material does eventually prove
to be active, it is going to require a pretty hefty dose. But it may well have some
activity, as there have been reports in the forensic literature of its preparation, or at
least its intended preparation, in illicit laboratories. It seems unlikely that much
effort would be directed towards the synthesis of a completely inactive compound.
     The reduced potency of MDDM has been exploited in an unexpected way.
Based on the premise that the dialkylation of the amine group of amphetamine
makes the parent compound intrinsically less active but without interfering with its
ability to enter the brain, a large number of materials have been explored to take
advantage of this very property. There is a need in medical diagnosis for agents that
can allow various organs of the body to be visualized. One of the most powerful
modalities for this work is the positron camera, and the use of the unusual properties
of the positron that allow it to work. In the art of positron emission tomography
(PET), an emitted positron (from a radioactive and thus unstable atom) will quickly
interact with a nearby electron and all mass disappears with the complete conversion
to energy. The detection of the produced pair of annihilation gamma rays will
establish with great exactness the line along which this interaction occurred. So if
one were to put an unstable atom into a compound that went to the tissue of the brain,
and this atom were to decay there, the resulting gamma rays would allow a
"photograph" to be made of the brain tissue. One could in this way visualize brain
tissue, and observe abnormalities.
     But what is needed is a molecule that carries the unstable atom (and
specifically one that emits positrons) and one which goes to the brain as well. One
of the very best unstable atoms for the formation of positrons is iodine, where there
is an isotope of mass 122 which is perfect for these needs. And, of course, the world
of the psychedelic drugs is tailor-made to provide compounds that go to the brain.
But, the last thing that the physician wants, with the diagnostic use of such tools,
would be to have the patient bouncing around in some turned-on altered state of
consciousness.
     So the completely logical union of these requirements is to take a
compound such as DOI (carrying the needed atom and certainly going to the brain)

and put two methyl groups on the nitrogen (which should reduce the chances for conspicuous biological activity). This compound was made, and it does label the brain, and it has shown promise as a flow indicator in the brain, and it and several of its close relatives are discussed in their own separate recipe, called IDNNA.

#106 MDE; MDEA; EVE; N-ETHYL-MDA; 3,4-METHYLENEDIOXY-N-ETHYLAMPHETAMINE

SYNTHESIS: (from MDA) To a solution of 3.6 g of the free base of 3,4-methylenedioxyamphetamine (MDA) in 20 g pyridine, there was added 2.3 g acetic anhydride, and the mixture stirred at room temperature for 0.5 h. This was then poured into 250 mL H_2O and acidified with HCl. This aqueous phase was extracted with 3x75 mL CH_2Cl_2, the extracts pooled and washed with dilute HCl, and the solvent removed under vacuum. The pale amber residue of N-acetyl-3,4-methylenedioxyamphetamine weighed 5.2 g as the crude product, and it was reduced without purification. On standing it slowly formed crystals. Recrystallization from a mixture of EtOAc/hexane (1:1) gave white crystals with a mp of 92-93 °C.

A stirred suspension of 4.8 g LAH in 400 mL anhydrous THF was brought up to a reflux, and then treated with a solution of 5.0 g of the impure N-acetyl-3,4-methylenedioxyamphetamine in 20 mL anhydrous THF. Reflux conditions were maintained for 3 days, and then after cooling in an ice bath, the excess hydride was destroyed with the careful addition of H_2O. The 4.8 mL H_2O (in a little THF) was followed with 4.8 mL of 15% NaOH, and finally an additional 15 mL H_2O. The white, granular, basic mass of inorganic salts was removed by filtration, the filter cake washed with additional THF, and the combined filtrate and washings stripped of solvent under vacuum. The residue was dissolved in 20 mL IPA, made acidic with 40 drops of concentrated HCl, and diluted with 150 mL anhydrous Et_2O. The crystalline product was removed by filtration, washed with 80% Et_2O (containing IPA) followed by Et_2O itself, and then air dried to provide 3.0 g of 3,4-methylene-dioxy-N-ethylamphetamine hydrochloride (MDE) as fine white crystals with a mp of 198-199 °C.

(from 3,4-methylenedioxyphenylacetone with aluminum amalgam) To 40 g of thin aluminum foil cut in 1 inch squares (in a 2 L wide mouth Erlenmeyer flask) there was added 1400 mL H_2O containing 1 g mercuric chloride. Amalgamation was allowed to proceed until there was the evolution of fine bubbles, the formation of a light grey precipitate, and the appearance of occasional silvery spots on the surface of the aluminum. This takes between 15 and 30 min depending on the freshness of the surfaces and the temperature of the H_2O. The H_2O was removed by decantation, and the aluminum was washed with 2x1400 mL of fresh H_2O. The residual H_2O was removed as thoroughly as possible by shaking, and there was added, in succession and with swirling, 72.5 g ethylamine hydrochloride dissolved in 60 mL warm H_2O, 180 mL IPA, 145 mL 25% NaOH, 53 g 3,4-methylenedioxy-phenylacetone (see under MDMA for its preparation), and finally 350 mL IPA. The exothermic reaction was kept below 60 °C with occasional immersion into cold water and, when it was thermally stable, it was allowed to stand until it had returned to room temperature and all the insolubles settled to the bottom as a grey sludge. The clear yellow overhead was decanted and the sludge removed by filtration and washed with MeOH. The combined decantation, mother liquors, and washes, were stripped of solvent under vacuum, the residue suspended in 1500 ml of H_2O, and sufficient HCl added to make the phase distinctly acidic. This was then washed with 2x100 mL CH_2Cl_2, made basic with 25% NaOH, and extracted with 3x100 mL of CH_2Cl_2. After removal of the solvent from the combined extracts, there remained 59.5 g of an amber oil which was distilled at 145-150 °C at 0.5 mm/Hg, producing 40.3 g of an off-white oil. This was dissolved in 600 mL IPA, neutralized with about 20 mL of concentrated HCl and then treated with 300 mL anhydrous Et_2O. After filtering off the white crystals, washing with a IPA/Et_2O (2:1) mixture, with Et_2O and air drying, the final 3,4-methylenedioxy-N-ethylamphetamine hydrochloride (MDE) weighed 37.4 g.

(from 3,4-methylenedioxyphenylacetone with $NaBH_3CN$) To a well stirred solution of 31.0 g ethylamine hydrochloride in 110 mL MeOH there was added 6.6 g of 3,4-methylenedioxyphenylacetone (see under MDMA for its preparation) followed by 3.0 g sodium cyanoborohydride. Concentrated HCl in MeOH was added as required to maintain the pH at about 6 as determined with external, dampened universal pH paper. About 2 days were required for the reduction to be complete as determined by the final stabilization of the pH. The reaction mixture was added to 1 L H_2O and made strongly acidic with an excess of HCl. After washing with 2x100 mL CH_2Cl_2 the aqueous phase was made basic with 25% NaOH, and extracted with 3x100 mL CH_2Cl_2. Removal of the solvent under vacuum yielded 8.3 g of a pale amber oil that was distilled at 85-100 °C at 0.2 mm/Hg. There was obtained 6.0 g of a water-white oil that was dissolved in 65 mL IPA and neutralized with 75 drops of concentrated HCl which produced crystals spontaneously. These were diluted with some 20 mL of anhydrous Et_2O removed by filtration, washed first with IPA/Et_2O (2:1), and then with Et_2O. After air drying there was obtained 6.1 g of 3,4-methylenedioxy-N-ethylamphetamine hydrochloride (MDE) with a mp of 201-202 °C. Anal. ($C_{12}H_{18}ClNO_2$) N.

DOSAGE: 100 - 200 mg.

DURATION: 3 - 5 h.

QUALITATIVE COMMENTS: (with 100 mg) "There was a warm light all about me. And a gentle, almost alcohol-like, intoxication. The drug seems to change my state of awareness, but it does nothing else. The world is as intense or as dull as I choose to make it. At the 1.5 hour point I was clearly dropping, and an hour later yet, completely without residue."

(with 160 mg) "The first effects were felt in forty minutes and I seemed to be completely there by the end of that first hour. There was an initial slightly dizzy intoxication, and then I felt very nice. A good intoxication, with maybe a little motor incoordination. There was absolutely no appetite at all. The next morning there was still some feeling of elation but I was still very relaxed. High marks for the quality of the experience."

(with 160 mg) "Overall this was a wonderful experience. I felt that the effect was stronger and smoother than MDMA, but perhaps the group enhancement may be partly responsible. I felt definitely fewer physiological side-effects than with MDMA, particularly the urinating problem; although there was dehydration, there was less burning annoyance."

(with 160 mg) "I was hard hit, to the extent that there was difficulty in verbalizing and following other people's thoughts. I entered the experience with some cold symptoms, and my sore throat disappeared. I felt quite intoxicated and tranquilized."

(with 200 mg) "Very stoned. There was some nausea in the beginning of the experience. As it developed I found it very difficult to concentrate on what I was thinking or saying simply due to the extraordinary nature of coming on to this material. There is noticeable jaw-clenching and rice crispies in the ears. This is a meditative material not unlike MDMA except there are more difficulties in forming words. And there is a problem in focusing the eyes, what I want to call 'eye-romp.' My anorexia was extremely long-lived — perhaps a total of 72 hours. This may have been too high a dosage."

EXTENSIONS AND COMMENTARY: This immediate homologue of MDMA has a very similar chronology but requires a slightly larger dose. Another similarity is the occasional report of teeth clenching, especially following the use of supplemental dosages intended to extend the effects of the drug. These supplements have been explored in the 50 to 75 milligram range, usually at the two hour point. In one unpublished clinical experiment with MDMA, an extension was attempted at the 1 hour 45 minute point with MDE rather than with MDMA, to see if there was any change in the qualitative character of the experience. The effective time of intoxication was extended, but the group fell surprisingly quiet, with a drop in the usual urge to converse and interact.

The effects of MDE are similar in many ways to those of MDMA, but there are believable differences. The particular magic, and affective transference, does not appear to be there. There is a stoning intoxication, as there is with MDA, and there is a seemingly unrewarding aspect to the upping of the dosages, again similar to MDA, and the properties of unusually easy communication and positive self-viewing of MDMA seem to be absent. Maybe the "S" isomer would have these properties, and they are lost in the racemate due to something coming from a more potent "intoxicating" "R" isomer. The optical isomers have never been evaluated separately in man.

There are only two ways in which two drugs can interact to produce a result that is not obvious from the summing of their individual actions. One is the process of synergism, where two active materials are allowed to interact within a single individual and at one time, and the consequence of this interaction is different than that which would have been expected. The other is the process of potentiation, where only one drug is active, but the presence of the second (and inactive) drug enhances the observed action of the first. MDE seems to fall in the first category.

The "piggy-back" or "window exploitation" studes were first discovered and explored with MDE, and have subsequently been extended most successfully with MDMA. The earliest procedure used was to assay modest quantities of active materials at the drop-off period of MDE, to exploit the open and benign state that was present. Usually, only a fraction of the standard dosage of the following drug was necessary to evoke a full experience. In psychotherapy applications, this sequence has been frequently used with MDMA followed by a second material that has been chosen to modify and expand the opening that the MDMA produced.

With the placement of MDMA under legal control in 1985, MDE occasionally appeared in the illicit street trade. It had been called EVE, which carries some perverse logic in light of the nickname used occasionally for MDMA, which was ADAM. The term INTELLECT has been used for it as well, but there has been no apparent reason advanced for this. And a final note on nomenclature. An old literature use of the code MDE was for the compound 3,4-methylenedioxyethanol-amine. See the discussion on this under the recipe for DME.

I have been told of an analogue of MDE that has been synthesized, and explored by the researcher who synthesized it. It contains the N-trifluoroethyl group common to several pharmaceuticals such as Quazepam. The analogue is 3,4-methylenedioxy-N-(2,2,2-trifluoroethyl)amphetamine hydrochloride (mp 207-209 °C) which was made from 2,2,2-trifluoroethylamine and 3,4-methylenedioxy-phenylacetone and sodium cyanoborohydride in methanol. The best final line for this compound is that it is "possibly active." The most heroic dosage schedule mentioned was a total of 500 milligrams, taken in three approximately equal portions over the course of five or six hours, with only a very mild intoxication and little or no sympathomimetic effects. And what little there might have been was quickly gone. A collection of totally unexplored N-substituted homologues and analogues of MDE is gathered at the end of the recipe for MDBZ.

Another direction that has been used to homologate the MDMA and MDE structure is with the length of the aliphatic chain that carries the phenyl ring and the amine function. "H" shows the two-carbon chain, "I" shows the amphetamine chain length, and MDE can be called ETHYL-I. The four-carbon chain is the "J" group, and this entire Muni-Metro concept is explained under METHYL-J.

#107   MDHOET;   HYDROXYETHYL-MDA;   3,4-METHYLENEDIOXY-N-(2-HYDROXYETHYL)AMPHETAMINE

SYNTHESIS: To a well stirred solution of 25 g ethanolamine hydrochloride in 75 mL MeOH there was added 4.45 g of 3,4-methylenedioxyphenylacetone (see under MDMA for its preparation) followed by 1.1 g sodium cyanoborohydride. Concentrated HCl in MeOH was added as required, over the next few days, to maintain the pH at about 6 as determined with external, dampened universal pH paper. The reaction mixture was added to 300 mL H_2O and made strongly acidic with an excess of HCl. After washing with 3x100 mL CH_2Cl_2 the aqueous phase was made basic with 25% Naoh, and extracted with 4x100 mL CH_2Cl_2. Removal of the solvent under vacuum yielded 3.5 g of a viscous off-white oil that was distilled at 160 °C at 1.3 mm/Hg to give 2.0 g of a white viscous oil. The pot residue remained fluid, but was discarded. This distillate was dissolved in 8.0 mL IPA to give, eventually, a clear solution. This was neutralized with concentrated HCl and diluted with 100 mL anhydrous Et_2O. The loose white crystals of 3,4-methylenedioxy-N-(2-hydroxy-ethyl)amphetamine hydrochloride (MDHOET) that formed were removed by filtration, washed with Et_2O, and air dried. These weighed 2.3 g, and had a mp of 147-148 °C. Anal. $(C_{12}H_{18}ClNO_3)$ N.

DOSAGE: greater than 50 mg.

DURATION: unknown.

EXTENSIONS AND COMMENTARY: Most compounds with bare, exposed polar groups like hydroxyls are not centrally active, as they simply do not have any way of getting into the brain. MDHOET is certainly not very active, if it is active at all.

There was one report that at very high doses some central effects were indeed observed. With quantities in the several hundreds of milligrams a picture emerged of changes in perceived color and depth perception, but without euphoria. It was said to resemble a mild dose of ketamine. This is an interesting comment, in that ketamine has found its major medical use as an anesthetic, and MDHOET is among the most effective of all the N-substituted MDA derivatives assayed in several animal analgesia models.

#108   MDIP;   N-ISOPROPYL-MDA;   (3,4-METHYLENEDIOXY-N-ISOPROPYLAMPHETAMINE)

SYNTHESIS: To a well stirred and cooled solution of 14.75 g isopropylamine in 100 mL MeOH there was added 4.45 g of 3,4-methylenedioxyphenylacetone (see under MDMA for its preparation) followed by a 1:1 mixture of concentrated HCL and MeOH, sufficient to bring the pH to about 4. This was followed with 1.1 g sodium cyanoborohydride, and stirring was continued overnight. When the pH increased to over 6 there was added an additional 0.5 g of the borohydride, and additional methanolic HCl was added as needed to maintain the pH there. When the pH became stable, the reaction mixture was brought soundly acid with the addition of yet additional HCl, and all solvents were removed under vacuum. The residues were added to 500 mL H_2O and washed with 3x100 mL CH_2Cl_2. The aqueous phase was made basic with 25% NaOH, and extracted with 4x100 mL CH_2Cl_2. Removal of the solvent under vacuum yielded 2.8 g of an amber liquid that was distilled at 95-110 °C at 0.3 mm/Hg. There was obtained about 2 mL of a white oil that was dissolved in 10 mL of IPA, neutralized with about 20 drops of concentrated HCl producing spontaneous crystals. These were diluted with some 40 mL of anhydrous Et_2O, removed by filtration, washed with Et_2O, and then air dried. There was obtained 1.6 g of 3,4-methylenedioxy-N-isopropylamphetamine hydrochloride (MDIP) with a mp of 186-186.5 °C with prior sintering at 185 °C. Anal. ($C_{13}H_{20}ClNO_2$) N.

DOSAGE: greater than 250 mg.

DURATION: unknown.

QUALITATIVE COMMENTS: (with 250 mg) "At 35 minutes there was an extremely slight head disturbance which increased over the next few minutes. I would have missed it if there had been any sensory input at all. At the one hour point there was a slight physical malaise, but no 'open window' of any kind, either like MDMA or like LSD. At the most, this was a threshold, and in another half hour, I was completely baseline."

EXTENSIONS AND COMMENTARY: The structure of MDIP can be looked at as exactly that of MDE but with an additional methyl group (one carbon) hanging off the ethyl that is on the nitrogen. And with that slight additional weight, the activity has disappeared. On those occasions where research has shown a compound to be inactive, there has been some study made that could be called a "primer" experiment. Why not take advantage of the fact that an "inactive" compound might well be sitting in some receptor site in the brain without doing anything? Might its presence, wherever it might be, have some effect if only a person were to explore it in the correct way? Might it augment or interfere with the action of another compound? Many experiments of this kind have been performed, geared to milk additional information out of a new trial of a new material.

Here is an example of a primer experiment that involved MDIP. Some five hours following an inactive trial with 120 milligrams of MDIP (maybe a slight disturbance at one hour, nothing at two hours) a calibration dose of 80 milligrams of MDMA was taken. The effects of the MDMA were noted at the 33 minute point, and an honest plus one was achieved at one hour. At this point a second 80 milligrams was added to the inventory that was already on board, and the general intoxication and the eye effects that followed were completely explained by the MDMA alone. It was obvious that the two drugs did not see one-another.

Sometimes an experiment can involve the assay of an unknown material at the supplement time of an active drug. This has been called "piggybacking." Here is an example. At the five hour point of an experiment with 140 milligrams of MDE (this had been a light experience, a plus one which had not laster more than two hours) a dosage of 200 milligrams of MDIP rekindled a +1 experience, a pleasant intoxication of the MDE sort, but one that was quite invested with tremor and some feelings of eye-popping. It was almost as if the physical toxic effects outweighed the mental virtues. Imagine an iceberg, with the bulk of its mass underwater. The MDE had had its own modest effects, and had submerged into invisibility, and the response to a little bit of an otherwise inactive MDIP was to refloat a bit of the otherwise unseeable MDE.

#109   MDMA; MDM; ADAM; ECSTASY; 3,4-METHYLENEDIOXY-N-METHYLAMPHETAMINE

SYNTHESIS: (from MDA) A solution of 6.55 g of 3,4-methylenedioxyamphetamine (MDA) as the free base and 2.8 mL formic acid in 150 mL benzene was held at reflux under a Dean Stark trap until no further H_2O was generated (about 20 h was sufficient, and 1.4 mL H_2O was collected). Removal of the solvent gave an 8.8 g of an amber oil which was dissolved in 100 mL CH_2Cl_2, washed first with dilute HCl, then with dilute NaOH, and finally once again with dilute acid. The solvent was removed under vacuum giving 7.7 g of an amber oil that, on standing, formed crystals of N-formyl-3,4-methylenedioxyamphetamine.

An alternate process for the synthesis of this amide involved holding at reflux for 16 h a solution of 10 g of MDA as the free base in 20 mL fresh ethyl formate. Removal of the volatiles yielded an oil that set up white crystals, weighing 7.8 g.

A solution of 7.7 g N-formyl-3,4-methylenedioxyamphetamine in 25 mL anhydrous THF was added dropwise to a well stirred and refluxing solution of 7.4 g LAH in 600 mL anhydrous THF under an inert atmosphere. The reaction mixture was held at reflux for 4 days. After being brought to room temperature, the excess hydride was destroyed with 7.4 mL H_2O in an equal volume of THF, followed by 7.4 mL of 15% NaOH and then another 22 mL H_2O. The solids were removed by filtration, and the filter cake washed with additional THF. The combined filtrate and washes were stripped of solvent under vacuum, and the residue dissolved in 200 mL CH_2Cl_2. This solution was extracted with 3x100 mL dilute HCl, and these extracts pooled and made basic with 25% NaOH. Extraction with 3x75 mL CH_2Cl_2 removed the product, and the pooled extracts were stripped of solvent under vacuum. There was obtained 6.5 g of a nearly white residue which was distilled at 100-110 °C at 0.4 mm/Hg to give 5.0 g of a colorless oil. This was dissolved in 25 mL IPA, neutralized with concentrated HCl, followed by the addition of sufficient anhydrous Et_2O to produce a lasting turbidity. On continued stirring, there was the deposition of fine white crystals of 3,4-methylenedioxy-N-methylamphetamine hydrochloride (MDMA) which were removed by filtration, washed with Et_2O, and air dried, giving a final weight of 4.8 g.

(from 3,4-methylenedioxyphenylacetone) This key intermediate to all of the MD-series can be made from either isosafrole, or from piperonal via 1-(3,4-methylenedioxyphenyl)-2-nitropropene. To a well stirred solution of 34 g of 30% hydrogen peroxide in 150 g 80% formic acid there was added, dropwise, a solution of 32.4 g isosafrole in 120 mL acetone at a rate that kept the reaction mixture from exceeding 40 °C. This required a bit over 1 h, and external cooling was used as necessary. Stirring was continued for 16 h, and care was taken that the slow exothermic reaction did not cause excess heating. An external bath with running water worked well. During this time the solution progressed from an orange color to a deep red. All volatile components were removed under vacuum which yielded some 60 g of a very deep red residue. This was dissolved in 60 mL of MeOH, treated with 360 mL of 15% H_2SO_4, and heated for 3 h on the steam bath. After cooling, the reaction mixture was extracted with 3x75 mL Et_2O, the pooled extracts washed first with H_2O and then with dilute NaOH, and the solvent removed under vacuum. The residue was distilled (at 2.0 mm/108-112 °C, or at about 160 °C at the water pump) to provide 20.6 g of 3,4-methylenedioxyphenylacetone as a pale yellow oil. The oxime (from hydroxylamine) had a mp of 85-88 °C. The semicarbazone had a mp of 162-163 °C.

An alternate synthesis of 3,4-methylenedioxyphenylacetone starts originally from piperonal. A suspension of 32 g electrolytic iron in 140 mL glacial acetic acid was gradually warmed on the steam bath. When quite hot but not yet with any white salts apparent, there was added, a bit at a time, a solution of 10.0 g of 1-(3,4-methylenedioxyphenyl)-2-nitropropene in 75 mL acetic acid (see the synthesis of MDA for the preparation of this nitrostyrene intermediate from piperonal and nitroethane). This addition was conducted at a rate that permitted a vigorous reaction free from excessive frothing. The orange color of the reaction mixture became very reddish with the formation of white salts and a dark crust. After the addition was complete, the heating was continued for an additional 1.5 h during which time the body of the reaction mixture became quite white with the product appeared as a black oil climbing the sides of the beaker. This mixture was added to 2 L H_2O, extracted with 3x100 mL CH_2Cl_2, and the pooled extracts washed with several portions of dilute NaOH. After the removal of the solvent under vacuum, the residue was distilled at reduced pressure (see above) to provide 8.0 g of 3,4-methylenedioxyphenylacetone as a pale yellow oil.

To 40 g of thin aluminum foil cut in 1 inch squares (in a 2 L wide mouth Erlenmeyer flask) there was added 1400 mL H_2O containing 1 g mercuric chloride. Amalgamation was allowed to proceed until there was the evolution of fine bubbles, the formation of a light grey precipitate, and the appearance of occasional silvery spots on the surface of the aluminum. This takes between 15 and 30 min depending on the freshness of the surfaces, the temperature of the H_2O, and the thickness of the aluminum foil. (Aluminum foil thickness varies from country to country.) The H_2O was removed by decantation, and the aluminum was washed with 2x1400 mL of fresh H_2O. The residual H_2O from the final washing was removed as thoroughly as possible by shaking, and there was added, in succession and with swirling, 60 g methylamine hydrochloride dissolved in 60 mL warm H_2O, 180 mL IPA, 145 mL 25% NaOH, 53 g 3,4-methylenedioxyphenylacetone, and finally 350 mL IPA. If the available form of methylamine is the aqueous solution of the free base, the following sequence can be substituted: add, in succession, 76 mL 40% aqueous methylamine, 180 mL IPA, a suspension of 50 g NaCl in 140 mL H_2O that contains 25 mL 25% NaOH, 53 g 3,4-methylenedioxyphenylacetone, and finally 350 mL IPA. The exothermic reaction was kept below 60 °C with occasional immersion into cold water and, when it was thermally stable, it was allowed to stand until it had returned to room temperature with all the insolubles settled to the bottom as a grey sludge. The clear yellow overhead was decanted and the sludge removed by filtration and washed with MeOH. The combined decantation, mother liquors and washes, were stripped of solvent under vacuum, the residue suspended in 2400 ml of H_2O, and sufficient HCl added to make the phase distinctly acidic. This was then washed with 3x75 mL CH_2Cl_2, made basic with 25% NaOH, and extracted with 3x100 mL of CH_2Cl_2. After removal of the solvent from the combined extracts, there remained 55 g of an amber oil which was distilled at 100-110 °C at 0.4 mm/Hg producing 41 g of an off-white liquid. This was dissolved in 200 mL IPA, neutralized with about 17 mL of concentrated HCl, and then treated with 400 mL anhydrous Et_2O. After filtering off the white crystals, washing with an IPA/Et_2O mixture, (2:1), with Et_2O, and final air drying, there was obtained 42.0 g of 3,4-methylenedioxy-N-methylamphetamine (MDMA) as a fine white crystal. The actual form that the final salt takes depends upon the temperature and concentration at the moment of the initial crystallization. It can be anhydrous, or it can be any of several hydrated forms. Only the anhydrous form has a sharp mp; the published reports describe all possible one degree melting point values over the range from

148-153 °C. The variously hydrated polymorphs have distinct infrared spectra, but have broad mps that depend on the rate of heating.

DOSAGE: 80 - 150 mg.

DURATION: 4 - 6 h.

QUALITATIVE COMMENTS: (with 100 mg) "MDMA intrigued me because everyone I asked, who had used it, answered the question, 'What's it like?' in the same way: 'I don't know.' 'What happened?' 'Nothing.' And now I understand those answers. I too think nothing happened. But something seemed changed. Before the 'window' opened completely, I had some somatic effects, a tingling sensation in the fingers and temples — a pleasant sensation, not distracting. However, just after that there was a slight nausea and dizziness similar to a little too much alcohol. All these details disappeared as I walked outside. My mood was light, happy, but with an underlying conviction that something significant was about to happen. There was a change in perspective both in the near visual field and in the distance. My usually poor vision was sharpened. I saw details in the distance that I could not normally see. After the peak experience had passed, my major state was one of deep relaxation. I felt that I could talk about deep or personal subjects with special clarity, and I experienced some of the feeling one has after the second martini, that one is discoursing brilliantly and with particularly acute analytical powers."

(with 100 mg) "Beforehand, I was aware of a dull, uncaring tiredness that might have reflected too little sleep, and I took a modest level of MDMA to see if it might serve me as a stimulant. I napped for a half hour or so, and woke up definitely not improved. The feeling of insufficient energy and lack of spark that I'd felt before had become something quite strong, and might be characterized as a firm feeling of negativity about everything that had to be done and everything I had been looking forward to. So I set about my several tasks with no pleasure or enjoyment and I hummed a little tune to myself during these activities which had words that went: 'I shouldn't have done that, oh yes, I shouldn't have done that, oh no, I shouldn't have done that; it was a mistake.' Then I would start over again from the beginning. I was stuck in a gray space for quite a while, and there was nothing to do but keep doing what I had to do. After about 6 hours, I could see the whole mental state disintegrating and my pleasant feelings were coming back. But so was my plain, ornery tiredness. MDMA does not work like Dexedrine."

(with 120 mg) "I feel absolutely clean inside, and there is nothing but pure euphoria. I have never felt so great, or believed this to be possible. The cleanliness, clarity, and marvelous feeling of solid inner strength continued throughout the rest of the day, and evening, and through the next day. I am overcome by the profundity of the experience, and how much more powerful it was than previous experiences, for no apparent reason, other than a continually improving state of being. All the next day I felt like 'a citizen of the universe' rather than a citizen of the planet, completely disconnecting time and flowing easily from one activity to the next."

(with 120 mg) "As the material came on I felt that I was being enveloped, and my attention had to be directed to it. I became quite fearful, and my face felt cold and ashen. I felt that I wanted to go back, but I knew there was no turning back. Then the fear started to leave me, and I could try taking little baby steps, like taking first steps after being reborn. The woodpile is so beautiful, about all the joy and beauty that I can stand. I am afraid to turn around and face the mountains, for fear they will overpower me. But I did look, and I am astounded. Everyone must get to experience a profound state like this. I feel totally peaceful. I have lived all my life to get here, and I feel I have come home. I am complete."

(with 100 mg of the "R" isomer) "There were the slightest of effects noted at about an hour (a couple of paresthetic twinges) and then nothing at all."

(with 160 mg of the "R" isomer) "A disturbance of baseline at about forty minutes and this lasts for about another hour. Everything is clear by the third hour."

(with 200 mg of the "R" isomer) "A progression from an alert at thirty minutes to a soft and light intoxication that did not persist. This was a modest +, and I was at baseline in another hour."

(with 60 mg of the "S" isomer) "The effects began developing in a smooth, friendly way at about a half-hour. My handwriting is OK but I am writing faster than usual. At the one hour point, I am quite certain that I could not drive, time is slowing down a bit, but I am mentally very active. My pupils are considerably dilated. The dropping is evident at two hours, and complete by the third hour. All afternoon I am peaceful and relaxed, but clear and alert, with no trace of physical residue at all. A very successful ++."

(with 100 mg of the "S" isomer) "I feel the onset is slower than with the racemate. Physically, I am excited, and my pulse and blood pressure are quite elevated. This does not have the 'fire' of the racemate, nor the rush of the development in getting to the plateau."

(with 120 mg of the "S" isomer) "A rapid development, and both writing and typing are impossible before the end of the first hour. Lying down with eyes closed eliminates all effects; the visual process is needed for any awareness of the drug's effects. Some teeth clenching, but no nystagmus. Excellent sleep in the evening."

EXTENSIONS AND COMMENTARY: In clinical use, largely in psychotherapeutic sessions of which there were many in the early years of MDMA study, it became a common procedure to provide a supplemental dosage of the drug at about the one and a half hour point of the session. This supplement, characteristically 40 milligrams following an initial 120 milligrams, would extend the expected effects for about an additional hour, with only a modest exacerbation of the usual physical side-effects, namely, teeth clenching and eye twitching. A second supplement (as, for instance, a second 40 milligrams at the two and a half hour point) was rarely felt to be warranted. There are, more often than not, reports of tiredness and lethargy on the day following the use of MDMA, and this factor should be considered in the planning of clinical sessions.

With MDMA, the usual assignments of activity to optical isomers is reversed from all of the known psychedelic drugs. The more potent isomer is the "S" isomer, which is the more potent form of amphetamine and methamphetamine. This was one of the first clear distinctions that was apparent between MDMA and the structurally related psychedelics (where the "R" isomers are the more active). Tolerance studies also support differences in mechanisms of action. In one study, MDMA was consumed at 9:00 AM each day for almost a week (120 milligrams the first day and 160 milligrams each subsequent day) and by the fifth day there were no effects from the drug except for some mydriasis. And even this appeared to be lost on the sixth day. At this point of total tolerance, there was consumed (on day #7, at 9:00 AM) 120 milligrams of MDA and the response to it was substantially normal with proper chronology, teeth clench, and at most only a slight decrease in mental change. A complete holiday from any drug for another 6 days led to the reversal of this tolerance, in that 120 milligrams of MDMA had substantially the full expected effects. The fact that MDMA and MDA are not cross-tolerant strengthens the argument that they act in different ways, and at different sites in the brain.

A wide popularization of the social use of MDMA occurred in 1984-1985 and, with the reported observation of serotonin nerve changes in animal models resulting from the administration of the structurally similar drug MDA, an administrative move was launched to place it under legal control. The placement of MDMA into the most restrictive category of the Federal Controlled Substances Act has effectively removed it from the area of clinical experimentation and human research. The medical potential of this material will probably have to be developed through studies overseas.

A word of caution is in order concerning the intermediate 3,4-methylene-dioxyphenylacetone, which has also been called piperonylacetone. A devilish ambiguity appeared in the commercial market for this compound, centered about its name. The controversy focused on the meaning of the prefix, piperonyl, which has two separate chemical definitions. Let me try to explain this fascinating chaos in non-chemical terms. Piperonyl is a term that has been used for a two-ring system (the methylenedioxyphenyl group) either without, or with, an extra carbon atom sticking off of the side of it. Thus, piperonylacetone can be piperonyl (the two-ring thing without the extra carbon atom attached) plus acetone (a three carbon chain thing); the total number of carbons sticking out, three. Or, piperonylacetone can be piperonyl (the two-ring thing but with the extra carbon atom attached) plus acetone (a three carbon chain thing); the total number of carbons sticking out, four.

Does this make sense?

The three carbon sticking out job gives rise to MDA and to MDMA and to many homologues that are interesting materials discussed at length in these Book II comments. This is the usual item of commerce, available from both domestic and foreign suppliers. But the four-carbon sticking out job will produce totally weird stuff without any apparent relationship to psychedelics, psychoactives or psycho-tropics whatsoever. I know of one chemical supply house which supplied the weird compound, and they never did acknowledge their unusual use of the term piperonyl. There is a simple difference of properties which might be of value. The three carbon (correct) ketone is an oil with a sassafras smell that is always yellow colored. The four carbon (incorrect) ketone has a weak terpene smell and is white and crystalline. There should be no difficulties in distinguishing these two compounds. But unprincipled charlatans can always add mineral oil and butter yellow to otherwise white solids to make them into yellow oils. Caveat emptor.

#110 MDMC; EDMA; 3,4-ETHYLENEDIOXY-N-METHYL-AMPHETAMINE

SYNTHESIS: To a solution of 27.6 g protocatechualdehyde (3,4-dihydroxy-benzaldehyde) in 250 mL acetone there was added 57 g finely powdered anhydrous K_2CO_3 and 43 g 1,2-dibromoethane. The mixture was held at reflux for 16 h, and then the acetone removed by evaporation. The remaining tar-like goo was distributed between equal volumes of H_2O and CH_2Cl_2, and the phases separated by centrifugation. The organic phase was washed with 2x50 mL 5% NaOH, and the solvent removed under vacuum. The residue (22.0 g with the smell of the starting halide) was distilled to give a fraction that boiled at 110 °C at 0.25 mm/Hg to yield 3,4-ethylenedioxybenzaldehyde (1,4-benzodioxane-6-carboxaldehyde) as a white oil weighing 6.88 g. This spontaneously crystallized to give white solids that melted at 50-51 °C.

A solution of 6.64 g 3,4-ethylenedioxybenzaldehyde in 40 mL nitroethane was treated with 0.26 g anhydrous ammonium acetate and held at reflux for 3 days. TLC analysis showed that there was much aldehyde remaining unreacted, so an additional 0.7 g ammonium acetate was added, and the mixture held at reflux for an additional 6 h. The excess nitroethane was removed under vacuum. The residue was dissolved in 30 mL hot MeOH which, with patience and slow cooling, finally deposited a heavy yellow-gold powder. This product 1-(3,4-ethylenedioxyphenyl)-2-nitro-propene melted at 95-96 °C and weighed 6.03 g when air dried to constant weight. Recrys-tallization from either MeOH or EtOAc gave the product as a yellow solid, but without any improvement in mp.

A solution of 4.0 g of 1-(3,4-ethylenedioxyphenyl)-2-nitropropene was made in 30 mL warm acetic acid. This was added to a suspension of 16 g elemental electrolytic iron in 75 mL acetic acid. The mixture was heated on the steam bath, and an exothermic reaction set in at about 70 °C. Heating was continued and the reaction allowed to proceed until the mass was a thick gray color and a dirty scum had been formed on the surface. After about 2 h, the entire mix was poured into 2 L H_2O and filtered free of a little residual unreacted iron which was washed with CH_2Cl_2. The filtrate and washes were extracted with 3x100 mL CH_2Cl_2 and the pooled organic extracts washed with 2x50 mL 5% NaOH. Removal of the solvent gave 3.38 g of an amber oil which was distilled. The product 1-(3,4-ethylenedioxy-phenyl)-2-propanone distilled as a white oil, at 105-110 °C at 0.2 mm/Hg. It weighed 2.74 g.

To 2.0 g. of 1 inch squares of light-weight aluminum foil there was added a solution of 50 mg mercuric chloride in 70 mL water. After standing at room temperature for 30 min, the H_2O was drained away, and the amalgamated aluminum washed twice with H_2O, and shaken as dry as possible. There was then added, promptly and in immediate sequence, a solution of 3 g methylamine hydrochloride in 3 mL H_2O, 9 mL IPA, 7.25 mL 25% NaOH, 2.70 g of 1-(3,4-ethylenedioxyphenyl)-2-propanone, and 18 mL IPA. The mixture was heated on the steam bath until an exothermic reaction set in, and then it was continuously swirled as the reaction proceeded. When the aluminum was consumed, there was a colorless gray sludge, and this was filtered and washed with 2x10 mL MeOH. The combined mother liquors and washes were stripped of solvent under vacuum. The two phase residue was suspended in 400 mL H_2O containing sufficient H_2SO_4 to make the resulting water solution acidic to pH paper. This was washed with 3x50 mL CH_2Cl_2, made basic with 25% NaOH, and the product extracted with 3x50 mL CH_2Cl_2. The resulting 3.01 g slightly amber residue oil was distilled at 110-120 °C at 0.25 mm/Hg to give 2.53 g of a white oil, which did not appear to absorb carbon dioxide. This was dissolved in 12 mL IPA, neutralized with 1 mL concentrated HCl and diluted with anhydrous Et_2O to the point of initial turbidity. There separated white crystals of 3,4-ethylenedioxy-N-methylamphetamine hydrochloride (MDMC) which weighed, when air dried to constant weight, 2.53 g.

DOSAGE: 200 or more mg.

DURATION: 3 - 5 h.

QUALITATIVE COMMENTS: (with 150 mg) "A flood of paresthesia at the 30 minute point, and then nothing. There was the development of a plus one-and-a half effect over the next hour with the tendency to drift into a dozing state with hypnogogic imagery. There were colored letters in the periphery of my visual field. There was no appetite loss nor was there any blood pressure rise. And no eye jiggle or teeth clenching. I was out of the experience in 4 to 5 hours. A repeat of this level a few days later gave a bare possible threshold with no other effects."

(with 200 mg) "There was something unmistakable at 45 minutes, with hints of nystagmus. Possibly MDMA-like, with no indicators of anything psyche-delic. Subtle return to baseline, and there were no after-effects."

(with 250 mg) "Alert at 40 minutes, and to a clear ++ at an hour. Slight something in the eye muscles. Dropping thirty minutes later, and baseline at three hours."

(with 250 mg) "I am at a bare threshold at best."

EXTENSIONS AND COMMENTARY: What a strange and completely unsatisfactory compound! In the original run-up from low levels to increasing higher levels, there never was a dosage that was a minus, that had no effect. At every level, something was thought to be there, usually at a level of a single plus or thereabouts. But with different people, different responses. There is no way of guessing what an active level might be, or how consistent that level might be between different people, or for that matter what the responses are that might be expected at that level.

This was yet one more effort to find an MDMA-like substitute by the miniscule manipulation of the MDMA molecule. Perhaps a small molecular change might leave the particular magic of the MDMA action alone, but eliminate the serotonin neuron problem in test animals. Maybe the serotonin neuron change is essential for MDMA to have the action it has. Who can tell?

The original name that this compound got, during the several explorations of MDMA analogues, was based on the nickname for MDMA which was Adam. HAD'EM was mentioned with the hydroxy compound, MADAM with the 6-methyl homologue, and FLADAM with the 6-fluoro analogue. This compound got the sobriquet MACADAM from that horrible black gooey mess generated at the aldehyde stage. This was shortened to "C" and eventually the "C" was added to the MDMA parent name. Thus, MDMC. It doesn't really make sense; EDMA is more reasonable. But then there is no reason why MDMC should make sense.

#111   MDMEO;   N-METHOXY-MDA;   3,4-METHYLENEDIOXY-N-METHYOXYAMPHETAMINE

SYNTHESIS: To a solution of 20.9 g methoxyamine hydrochloride in 75 mL MeOH (a strongly acidic solution) there was added 4.45 g 3,4-methylenedioxyphenylacetone (see under MDMA for its preparation) followed by 1.10 g sodium cyanoborohydride. There was the immediate formation of a solid phase, and the evolution of what appeared to be hydrogen cyanide. To this there were added about 4 mL 5% NaOH which brought the pH to the vicinity of 3 or 4. Another 1.0 g of sodium cyanoborohydride was added (no gas evolution this time) and stirring was continued at ambient temperature for 6 days. All was added to 500 mL H_2O, acidified with 10 mL HCl, and extraction with 3x100 mL CH_2Cl_2 removed almost all the color. The aqueous phase was made basic with 25% NaOH, and extracted with 4x100 mL CH_2Cl_2. Evaporation of the solvent from these extracts yielded 1.8 g of a pale yellow oil which, on distillation at 90-95 °C at 0.5 mm/Hg, gave a 1.6

g fraction of an absolutely white, viscous, clear oil. This was dissolved in 8 mL IPA and neutralized with concentrated HCl. The product was an exceptionally weak base, and appropriate end points must be respected on the external pH paper (yellow to red, rather than purple to orange). Anhydrous Et_2O was added to the point of turbidity, and as soon as crystallization had actually started, more Et_2O was added with stirring, for a net total of 200 mL. After a couple of h standing, the fine white crystalline 3,4-methylenedioxy-N-methoxyamphetamine hydrochloride (MDMEO) was removed by filtration, Et_2O washed, and air dried to constant weight. There was obtained 1.7 g of a product with a mp of 143-146 °C. The proton NMR was excellent with the N-methoxyl group a sharp singlet at 4.06 ppm. Anal. ($C_{11}H_{16}ClNO_3$) N.

DOSAGE: greater than 180 mgs.

DURATION: unknown

EXTENSIONS AND COMMENTARY: Why the interest in the N-methoxy analogue of MDA? There are several reasons. One, this is an isostere of MDE and it would be interesting to see if it might serve as a primer to the promotion of the effectiveness of other drugs (see primer discussion under MDPR). In one experiment, wherein a 60 microgram dosage of LSD was used an hour and a half after a 180 milligram load of MDMEO, there was no augmentation of effects. Thus, it would appear not to be a primer. Another reason for interest was that the material, although having an extremely similar overall structure to most of the active MD-series compounds, is very much a weaker base. And MDOH, which is also a very much weaker base than MDA, still shows the action and potency of MDA. And, as this compound appears to be inactive, base strength is not a sole predictor of activity.

The ultimate reason for making MDMEO was, of course, that it could be made. That reason is totally sufficient all by itself.

#112 MDMEOET; N-METHOXYETHYL-MDA; 3,4-METHYLENEDIOXY-N-(2-METHOXYETHYL)AMPHETAMINE

SYNTHESIS: A crude solution of methoxyethylamine hydrochloride was prepared from 17.7 g methoxyethylamine and 20 mL concentrated HCl with all volatiles removed under vacuum. This was dissolved in 75 mL MeOH and there was added 4.45 g of 3,4-methylenedioxyphenylacetone (see under MDMA for its preparation) followed by 1.3 g sodium cyanoborohydride. Concentrated HCl in MeOH was added as required to maintain the pH at about 6 as determined with external, dampened universal pH paper. About 4.5 mL were added over the course of 5 days, at which time the pH had stabilized. The reaction mixture was added to 400 mL H$_2$O and made strongly acidic with an excess of HCl. After washing with 2x100 mL CH$_2$Cl$_2$ the aqueous phase was made basic with 25% NaOH, and extracted with 4x75 mL CH$_2$Cl$_2$. Removal of the solvent under vacuum yielded 6.0 g of an amber oil that was distilled at 110-120 °C at 0.2 mm/Hg. There was obtained 4.7 g of a crystal-clear white oil that was dissolved in 30 mL IPA and neutralized with 45 drops of concentrated HCl producing a heavy mass of spontaneous crys-tals that had to be further diluted with IPA just to be stirred with a glass rod. These were diluted with 200 mL of anhydrous Et$_2$O, removed by filtration, and washed with additional Et$_2$O. After air drying there was obtained 4.9 g of 3,4-methylenedioxy-N-(2-methoxyethyl)amphetamine hydrochloride (MDMEOET) with a mp of 182.5-183 °C. Anal. (C$_{13}$H$_{20}$ClNO$_3$) N.

DOSAGE: greater than 180 mg.

DURATION: unknown.

EXTENSIONS AND COMMENTARY: This is another example of the replace-ment of a neutral atom out near the end of a chain, with a more basic and a more polar one. MDMEOET would be called an isostere of MDBU in that it has the same shape, with a methylene unit (the CH$_2$) replaced by an oxygen atom. No activity turned up with either compound, so nothing can be learned from this particular example of change of polarity.

#113   MDMP;   α,α,N-TRIMETHYL-3,4-METHYLENEDIOXY-
PHENETHYLAMINE;   METHYLENEDIOXYMEPHENTERMINE

SYNTHESIS: To a well stirred solution of 1.64 g of 1-(N-(benzyloxy-carbonyl)amino)-1,1-dimethyl-2-(3,4-methylenedioxyphenyl)ethane (see under MDPH for its preparation) in 10 mL anhydrous THF there was added a suspension of 0.38 g LAH in 25 mL THF. All was held at reflux for 24 h, the excess hydride was destroyed by the addition of 1.5 mL H$_2$O, and sufficient aqueous NaOH was added to make the reaction mixture basic and flocculant enough to be filterable. The inorganic solids were removed by filtration and, following washing with THF, the combined filtrate and washings were stripped of organic solvent under vacuum. The residue was dissolved in 100 mL Et$_2$O and washed with 2x50 mL saturated aqueous NaHCO$_3$. After drying the organic phase with anhydrous MgSO$_4$, the solvent was removed under vacuum to give a yellow oil. This was dissolved in 50 mL absolute EtOH and neutralized with concentrated HCl. Removal of the solvent under vacuum yielded an off-white solid that was recrystallized from an EtOH/EtOAc mixture to provide 0.84 g of α,α,N-trimethyl-3,4-methylenedioxyphenethylamine hydrochloride (MDMP) with a mp of 206-208 °C. The NMR spectrum showed the α,α-dimethyl pair as a singlet at 1.38 ppm. Anal. ($C_{12}H_{18}ClNO_2$) C,H,N.

DOSAGE: above 110 mg.

DURATION: perhaps 6 hours.

QUALITATIVE COMMENTS: (with 60 mg) "There was a faint, dull alerting at just over a half hour. The time sense was out of order, and an absence of visuals but a generalized attentiveness to my surroundings was suggestive of MDMA. Nothing remained at the six hour point."

(with 110 mg) "There was a light-headedness, and a complete absence of libido. Nothing in any way psychedelic, but there are hints of discomfort (jaw tension) that will bear close watching at higher dosages. It might evolve at higher levels into something like MDMA."

EXTENSIONS AND COMMENTARY: This is one of several candidates for clinical use as a substitute for MDMA, but there will have to be a much broader study of its qualitative action in man. It is clearly not psychedelic at these modest levels, and in *in vitro* animal studies it was apparently inactive as a serotonin releaser. The warped logic for looking at phentermine analogs was discussed in the comments that concerned MDPH. The initials used here have been chosen with care. MDM should not be used as it has found some currency as an abbreviation for MDMA (Methylene-Dioxy-Methamphetamine). MDMP fits neatly with Methylene-Dioxy-Me-Phentermine.

#114   MDOH;   N-HYDROXY-MDA;   3,4-METHYLENEDIOXY-N-HYDROXYAMPHETAMINE

SYNTHESIS: To a well stirred solution of 14.8 g hydroxylamine hydrochloride in 120 mL MeOH there was added 3.6 g of 3,4-methylenedioxyphenylacetone (see under MDMA for its preparation) followed by 1.0 g sodium cyanoborohydride. The oxime, prepared from the ketone and hydroxylamine in MeOH with pyridine, may be substituted for these two components. Concentrated HCl was added over the course of a couple of days, to keep the pH near neutrality. When the reaction was complete, it was added to H_2O, made strongly acidic with HCl, and washed with 3x100 mL CH_2Cl_2. The aqueous phase was made basic with 25% NaOH, and reextracted with 3x100 mL of CH_2Cl_2. The extracts were pooled, and the solvent removed under vacuum to give 1.7 g of an oily residue which, with pumping under a hard vacuum for a few minutes, changed to a white solid. This can be Kugelrohred if the vacuum is sufficiently good to keep the temperature during the distillation below 100 °C. The extremely viscous distillate formed crystals immediately upon wetting with IPA. It was dissolved in 20 mL of warm IPA and neutralized with concentrated HCl, with the titration end-point being red rather than orange on universal pH paper. Modest addition of Et_2O allowed the formation of 3,4-methylenedioxy-N-hydroxyamphetamine hydrochloride (MDOH) as white crystals, which weighed 1.4 g when air dried. If the temperature of distillation exceeded 100 °C, there was extensive decomposition during distillation, with the formation of 3,4-methylenedioxyamphetamine (MDA) and the oxime of the ketone. Under these circumstances, the only base isolated was MDA.

The surest isolation procedure was to obtain MDOH as the free base, as a crystalline solid which could be recrystallized from 5 volumes of boiling IPA. The free base had a mp of 94-95 °C (and should not be confused with the oxime of 3,4-methylenedioxyphenylacetone which has a mp of 86-88 °C since the mixed mp is depressed, mp 56-62 °C, or with the free base of MDA which is an oil). Anal. $(C_{10}H_{13}NO_3)$ N. The hydrochloride salt had a mp of 149-150 °C (and should not be confused with the hydrochloride of MDA which has a mp of 185-186 °C since the mixed mp is depressed, mp 128-138 °C). Anal. $(C_{10}H_{14}ClNO_3)$ N. Acetic anhydride can serve as a useful tool for distinguishing these materials. MDA gives an N-acetyl derivative with an mp of 92-93 °C. MDOH gives an N,O-diacetyl derivative with a mp of 72-74 °C. Methylenedioxyphenylacetone oxime gives an O-acetyl derivative that is an oil.

DOSAGE: 100 - 160 mg.

DURATION: 3 - 6 h.

QUALITATIVE COMMENTS: (with 100 mg) "I felt hampered the first hour by some internal barrier, which prevented total enjoyment. However, this began to break through in a wonderful way just before the supplement was offered. Since I felt I was beginning to move through the barrier, I declined the supplement, particularly since I was anxious to compare the after-effects with my first experience. I had found the first time very remarkable, but felt unusually tired for several days following. I feel it is important to know whether this is a specific drug-induced effect, or the result of psychological phenomena. The experience continued in a rich, meaningful way. There was a marvelous inner glow, the warmth from all the other participants was wonderful to feel, nature was most beautiful. There were no dramatic breakthroughs, or rushes of insight or energy, but just a wonderful contemplative space where things gently unfolded as you put your attention on them."

(with 100 mg) "The material came on fairly rapidly. In about 30 minutes, I was intensely intoxicated, and more deeply than with MDMA. It was a glorious feeling, and beauty was everywhere enhanced. With eyes closed it felt marvelous, and it was appealing to pursue the inner experience. I did notice an internal dryness which was characteristic of MDMA, and I had similar difficulty in urinating, but not as intense as with MDMA."

(with 120 mg) "The colors of the market-place, of all the fresh foods, constituted a beautiful mosaic. Nothing practical, simply a real treasure to be used with individual intention and enjoyment. Everything was seen with new eyes, new meanings, faces, figures, the colors of the rainbow subconsciously individually applied. A 'soul-scape'. The following day very exhausted, tired, back-pain."

EXTENSIONS AND COMMENTARY: The first time that MDOH was synthe-sized, it had inadvertently and unknowingly been converted to MDA. And the search for proper dosage and characterization of effects of this product was, of course, the rediscovery of the dosage and the effects of MDA. It is one of the world's most remarkable coincidences that after the second synthesis of MDOH, when MDOH had really and truly been actually prepared, the brand new search for proper dosage and characterization of effects revealed that they were almost identical to the earlier observations for (the inadvertently produced) MDA.

This reminds me of my speculations in the discussion of both FLEA and the HOT compound where they also showed paired molecular structures with their prototypes that differ only by a single oxygen atom. Again, might there be some metabolic interconversion within the body? The immediate thought would be that the oxygen atom (the hydroxy group) might be metabolically removed, and the effects of either drug are due to the action of MDA. But the opposite direction is in many ways more appealing, the *in vivo* conversion of MDA to MDOH. Why more appealing? For one thing, oxidative changes are much more common in the body than reductive changes. For another, the conversion of amphetamine to N-hydroxyamphetamine is an intermediate in the conversion of amphetamine to phenylacetone, a known metabolic process in several animal species. And that intermediate, N-hydroxyamphetamine, is a material that gives the famous cytochrome P-450 complex that has fascinated biochemists studying the so-called NADPH-dependent metabolism.

I would put my money on the likelihood of MDA going to MDOH if it should turn out that the two drugs interconvert in the body. And in that case, it would be MDOH, or another metabolite on down the line that is common to both MDA and

MDOH, that is the factor intrinsic to the intoxication that is produced. Human metabolic studies are needed, and they have not yet been done.

#115 MDPEA; 3,4-METHYLENEDIOXYPHENETHYLAMINE; HOMOPIPERONYLAMINE

SYNTHESIS: A suspension of 4.0 g LAH in 300 mL anhydrous Et_2O was stirred and heated to a gentle reflux in an inert atmosphere. There was added 3.9 g 3,4-methylenedioxy-ß-nitrostyrene (see under BOH for its preparation) by allowing the condensing Et_2O to leach it out from a Soxhlet thimble. After the addition was complete, the reaction mixture was held at reflux for an additional 48 h. It was then cooled and the excess hydride was destroyed by the cautious addition of 300 mL of 1.5 N H_2SO_4. When both phases were completely clear, they were separated, and the aqueous phase washed once with 50 mL Et_2O. There was then added 100 g potassium sodium tartrate, followed by sufficient base to bring the pH >9. This was extracted with 3x75 mL CH_2Cl_2, and the solvent from these pooled extracts was removed under vacuum. The residue was dissolved in 150 mL anhydrous Et_2O and saturated with anhydrous HCl gas. There was a heavy crystallization of 3,4-methylenedioxyphenethylamine hydrochloride (MDPEA) which weighed 3.0 g and had a mp of 212-213 °C.

DOSAGE: greater than 300 mg.

DURATION: unknown.

QUALITATIVE COMMENTS: (with 200 mg) "It was taken twice at different times in a dosage of 200 milligrams each time, without the slightest peripheral or central effects."
(with 300 mg) "My tinnitus had disappeared. Probably nothing."

EXTENSIONS AND COMMENTARY: How strange. Even more than DMPEA, this cyclic analogue MDPEA is a potential prodrug to dopamine, and would be a prime candidate for central activity. So why is this drug not active? The usual reason advanced by the pharmacologists is that the body is full of potent enzymes known as monoamine oxidases, and this is a monoamine, and so the body simply chews away on it in an oxidative manner, inactivating it before it ever makes it to some target receptor.
    That is the pitch given in the textbooks. Phenethylamines are subject to easy enzymatic oxidation, hence they are not active. The presence of an alpha-

methyl group (the corresponding amphetamines) blocks the compound from easy access to the enzyme, and since that protects them from oxidative destruction, they are active. The oft-quoted exception is mescaline, and even it is largely destroyed, as evidenced by the large amount needed for activity (a fraction of a gram). Sorry, I can't buy it. This entire book is peppered with phenethylamines that are active at the few-milligram area. Why aren't they also destroyed as well? The textbooks simply are not right.

MDPEA was one of the seven compounds evaluated as to toxicity and animal behavior at the University of Michigan under contract from the Army Chemical Center. Its Edgewood Arsenal code number was EA-1297. The number for MDA itself was EA-1298.

The beta-hydroxy analogue of MDPEA is the ethanolamine MDE, standing for methylenedioxyethanolamine. This is an old term, and in the more recent literature, since 1975 certainly, MDE has been used to represent methylenedioxyethylamphetamine. The ethanolamine compound is discussed in the recipe for DME.

There is a family of compounds, to be discussed elsewhere, that is called the Muni-Metro (see under METHYL-J). The simplest member is this compound, MDPEA, and under its chemically acceptable synonym, homopiperonylamine, it can be called "H". Following that code, then, the N-methyl homologue of MDPEA is METHYL-H, and it has been looked at, clinically, as an antitussive agent. N-METHYL-MDPEA, or METHYL-H, or N-methyl-3,4-methylenedioxyphenethyl-amine is effective in this role at dosages of about 30 milligrams, but I have read nothing that would suggest that there were any central effects. I have tried it at this level and have found a little tightness of the facial muscles, but there was nothing at all in the mental area.

#116   MDPH;   α,α-DIMETHYL-3,4-METHYLENEDIOXY-PHENETHYLAMINE;   3,4-METHYLENEDIOXYPHENTERMINE

SYNTHESIS: To 150 mL of THF, under an atmosphere of nitrogen, there was added 11.2 g diisopropylamine, and the solution was cooled with external dry ice/IPA. There was then added 48 mL of a 2.3 M solution of butyllithium in hexane, dropwise, with good stirring. This was warmed to room temperature, stirred for a few min, and then all was cooled again in the dry ice bath. Following the dropwise addition of 4.4 g of isobutyric acid there was added 10.5 mL hexamethyl-phosphoramide. Again, the stirred reaction mixture was brought to room temperature for about 0.5 h. There was then added, drop-wise, 8.5 g 3,4-methylenedioxybenzyl chloride and the mixture allowed to stir overnight at room temperature. The reaction mixture was poured into 100 mL 10% HCl, and the excess THF was removed under vacuum. The acidic aqueous residue was extracted with 2x150 mL Et$_2$O. These extracts were pooled, washed with 10% HCl, and then extracted with 3x75 mL of 4 N Na_2CO_3. These extracts were pooled, made acidic with HCl, and again extracted with Et_2O. After drying the pooled extracts with anhydrous $MgSO_4$, the solvent was removed under vacuum to give a residue that spontaneously crystallized. Recrystallization from hexane yielded 6.5 g of 2,2-dimethyl-3-(3,4-methylenedioxyphenyl)propionic acid as white crystals with a mp of 71-73 °C. The NMR spectrum in $CDCl_3$ showed the alpha-dimethyl groups as a sharp singlet at 1.18 ppm. Anal. $(C_{12}H_{14}O_4)$ C,H.

The triethylamine salt of 2,2-dimethyl-3-(3,4-methylenedioxyphenyl)-propionic acid (5.4 g amine, 11.4 g acid) was dissolved in 10 mL H_2O and diluted with sufficient acetone to maintain a clear solution at ice-bath temperature. A solution of 6.4 g ethyl chloroformate in 40 mL acetone was added to the 0 °C solution over the course of 30 min, followed by the addition of a solution of 4.1 g sodium azide in 30 mL H_2O. Stirring was continued for 45 min while the reaction returned to room temperature. The aqueous phase was extracted with 100 mL toluene which was washed once with H_2O and then dried with anhydrous $MgSO_4$. This organic solution of the azide was heated on a steam bath until nitrogen evolution had ceased, which required about 30 min. The solvent was removed under vacuum and the residue was dissolved in 30 mL benzyl alcohol. This solution was heated on the steam bath overnight. Removal of the excess benzyl alcohol under vacuum left a residue 13.5 g of 1-(N-(benzyloxycarbonyl)amino)-1,1-dimethyl-2-(3,4-methylenedioxyphenyl)ethane as an amber oil. The dimethyl group showed, in the NMR, a sharp singlet at 1.30 ppm in $CDCH_3$. Anal. $(C_{19}H_{21}NO_4)$ C,H. This carbamate was reduced to the primary amine (below) or to the methylamine (see under MDMP).

A solution of 3.27 g of 1-[N-(benzyloxycarbonyl)amino]-1,1-dimethyl-2-(3,4-methylenedioxyphenyl)ethane in 250 mL absolute ethanol was treated with 0.5 g 10% palladium on carbon. This mixture was shaken under hydrogen at 35 pounds pressure for 24 h. The carbon was removed by filtration through Celite, and the filtrate titrated with HCl. The solvent was removed under vacuum, and the residue allowed to crystallize. This produce was recrystallized from an EtOH/EtOAc mixture to provide α,α-dimethyl-3,4-methylenedioxyphenethylamine hydrochloride (MDPH). The white crystals weighed 1.63 g and had a mp of 180-181 °C. Anal. $(C_{11}H_{16}ClNO_2)$ C,H,N.

DOSAGE: 160 - 240 mg.

DURATION: 3 - 5 h.

QUALITATIVE COMMENTS: (with 120 mg) "The alert was felt in forty minutes and I was pretty much there at an hour and twenty. Quite like MDA, simple, with no lines, no colors, no motion, no fantasy. I am pleasantly stoned. The anorexia is real, as is the impotency. The drop from the 4th to the 6th hour was softened by a modest amount of wine, and this proved to be extremely intoxicating. My speech was slurred, and there was later amnesia for the rather aggressive and uninhibited behavior that occurred. I felt that there was more drug than alcohol contributing to this episode. My dream patterns were disturbingly unreal."

(with 160 mg) "A very quiet development. There was no body load whatsoever. And no visual, and I saw it fading away all too soon. This might be a good promoter, like MDPR. I felt refreshed and relaxed on the following morning."

(with 200 mg) "This has an inordinately foul taste. I felt slightly queasy. There were short daydreams which were quickly forgotten. I see no values that are worth the hints of physical problems, a little eye mismanagement and some clenching of teeth, and a tendency to sweat. I was able to sleep at only five hours into it, but there were a couple of darts. This is not as rewarding (stoning) as MDA, and has none of the magic of MDMA. It was a short-lived plus two."

EXTENSIONS AND COMMENTARY: What is the train of thought that leads from the structure of a known compound (which is active) to the structure of an unknown one (which may or may not be active)? Certainly the extrapolations involve many what-if's and maybe's. The path can be humorous, it certainly can be tortuous, and it often calls for special things such as faith, insight, and intuition. But can one say that it is logical?

Logic is a tricky thing to evaluate. One of the earliest approaches was laid down by Aristotle, in the form of the syllogism. In it there are three lines consisting of two premises and a conclusion, a form that is called a "mood." All are statements of relationships and, if the premises are true, there are only certain conclusions that may logically follow. For example:

> Every man is a lover.
> Every chemist is a man.
> Therefore, every chemist is a lover.

Letting lover be the major term "a" and letting chemist be the minor term "b" and letting man be the middle term "m", this reduces to:

> Every m is a,
> Every b is m.
> Therefore, every b is a

and it is a valid mood called Barbara.

Of the 256 possible combinations of all's and some's and none's and are's and are-not's, only 24 moods are valid. The reasoning here with MDPH goes:

Some stimulants when given a methylenedioxy ring are
MDMA-like.
Some ring-unsubstituted 1,1-dimethylphenylethylamines are
stimulants.
Therefore, some ring-unsubstituted 1,1-dimethylphenylethyl
amines when given a methylenedioxy ring are
MDMA-like.

In symbolic form this is:

Some m is a, and
Some b is m, then
Some b is a

and this is not one of the 24 valid moods. Given the first premise as some m is a,
there is only one valid syllogism form that can follow, and this is known as Disamis,
or:

Some m is a, and
Every m is b, then
Some b is a

which translates as:

Some stimulants when given a methylenedioxy group are
MDMA-like.
Every stimulant is a ring-unsubstituted 1,1-dimethylphenyl
ethylamine.
Therefore, some ring-unsubstituted 1,1-dimethylphenylethyl
amines when given a methylenedioxy group are
MDMA-like.

The conclusion is the same. But the second premise is false so the entire
reasoning is illogical. What is the false second premise? It is not a fact that every
stimulant is a phentermine. There are lots of stimulants that are not phentermines.
So much for applying syllogistics to pharmacology.

#117   MDPL;   N-PROPARGYL-MDA;   N-PROPYNYL-MDA;   3,4-METHYLENEDIOXY-N-PROPARGYLAMPHETAMINE)

SYNTHESIS: A solution of 10.5 g propargylamine hydrochloride in 40 mL MeOH was treated with 2.0 g 3,4-methylenedioxyphenylacetone (see under MDMA for its preparation) followed by 0.55 g sodium cyanoborohydride. Concentrated HCl was added as needed, to keep the pH constant at about 6. The reaction seemed to progress very slowly. After about five days, the reaction mixture was added to 400 of H_2O, acidified with HCl, and extracted with 3x100 mL CH_2Cl_2. The aqueous phase was made basic with 25% NaOH, and extracted with 3x100 mL CH_2Cl_2. Evaporation of the solvent from these extracts yielded 1.6 g of a clear amber, strong smelling oil which, on distillation at 105-110 °C at 0.2 mm/Hg, yielded 1.0 g of an almost colorless oil. This was dissolved in 20 mL IPA, neutralized with about 10 drops of concentrated HCl, and the spontaneously formed crystals were diluted with 50 mL anhydrous Et_2O. After filtration, Et_2O washing and air drying, there was obtained 1.1 g white crystals of 3,4-methylenedioxy-N-propargylamphetamine hydrochloride (MDPL) with a mp of 189-190 °C. Anal. ($C_{13}H_{16}ClNO_2$) N.

DOSAGE: greater than 150 mg.

DURATION: unknown.

EXTENSIONS AND COMMENTARY: There is a continuing uncertainty about the name for the three-carbon radical that contains a triple bond. The hydrocarbon is propyne, although it has been referred to as methylacetylene in the older literature. The adjective, going from the triple bond out to the point of attachment, is called propargyl, as in propargyl chloride. When the adjective must be built on the parent hydrocarbon, the triple bond is on the outside and one reads away from it, as in 2-propynyl something. However, when the hydrocarbon is essentially the entire structure, then things get named going towards the triple bond, as in 3-chloro-1-propyne. Wait. I'm not done yet! When the actual hydrocarbon name becomes distorted into the derivative, then the triple bond is again at the high end of the numbering scheme. Propynol is 2-propyn-1-ol, which is, of course, the same as 3-hydroxypropyne, or propargyl alcohol. The code MDPL takes the first and last letter of the two of them, both propargyl and propynyl.

#118   MDPR;   N-PROPYL-MDA;   3,4-METHYLENEDIOXY-N-PROPYLAMPHETAMINE

SYNTHESIS: A total of 20 mL concentrated HCl was added beneath the surface of 20 mL propylamine, and when the addition was complete, the mixture was stripped of volatiles under vacuum. The slightly yellow residual oil weighed 20.7 g and set up to crystals on cooling. It was dissolved in 75 mL MeOH, and there was added 4.45 g of 3,4-methylenedioxyphenylacetone (see under MDMA for its preparation) followed by 1.1 g sodium cyanoborohydride. Concentrated HCl in MeOH was added as required to maintain the pH at about 6 as determined with external, dampened universal pH paper. When the generation of base had stopped, the MeOH was allowed to evaporate and the residue was suspended in 1 L water. This was made strongly acidic with an excess of HCl. After washing with CH_2Cl_2, the aqueous phase was made basic with 25% NaOH, and extracted with 3x100 mL CH_2Cl_2. Removal of the solvent from the pooled extracts under vacuum yielded 3.3 g of a pale amber oil that was distilled at 85-90 °C at 0.2 mm/Hg. This fraction was water-white and weighed 2.3 g. It was dissolved in 10 mL IPA and neutralized with 25 drops concentrated HCl which produced crystals spontaneously. These were diluted with anhydrous Et_2O, removed by filtration, washed with additional Et_2O, and air dried. In this way there was obtained 2.3 g of 3,4-methylenedioxy-N-propylamphetamine hydrochloride (MDPR) with a mp of 190-192 °C. Recrystallization from IPA gave a mp of 194-195 °C. The NMR spectrum was completely consistent with the assigned chemical structure. Anal. $(C_{13}H_{20}ClNO_2)$ N.

DOSAGE: greater than 200 mg.

DURATION: unknown.

QUALITATIVE COMMENTS: (with 200 mg) "There are the slightest hints of physical response, maybe a smidgin of a lightheadedness at the one hour point. Perhaps a slight teeth clench. Certainly there is no central mental effect."

EXTENSIONS AND COMMENTARY: This particular drug, considering that it was without activity, has proven one of the richest veins of pharmacological raw material. Two clues suggested its potential value. A number of reports in the 150 to 200 milligram area suggested that something was taking place in the periphery even without any clear central effects. The term "body window" was used occasionally by experimenters, an outgrowth of the term "window" that was used (at that time, the mid-1970's) to describe the mental effects of MDMA. It was as if the body was opened up and made receptive, instead of the mind. The second clue came from many anecdotal reports that methedrine (a potent central nervous system stimulant) would augment the effects of an LSD dosage which followed it. The putting of a drug on top of an inactive drug is the "primer" concept. It turned out that MDPR was an extraordinary primer to some following psychedelic, especially LSD, even at modest doses. The putting of a drug on top of an active drug, usually during the latter part of its effectiveness is, as previously stated, called "piggy-backing." A third drug-drug interaction has also been studied; the simultaneous administration of two active drugs, to study synergism. There may be an enhancement, or an inhibition, of one with the other. Let's now re-enter the subsection "Qualitative Comments" again, with this primer concept in mind.

QUALITATIVE COMMENTS: (with 160 mg followed at 2 h by 60 µgs LSD) "The visual phenomena were extraordinary. We were at the beach just south of Mendocino. In anything that had ever been living, there was an endlessly deep microcosm of detail. Endless, and forever more microscopic in intricacy. A sea urchin shell, a bit of driftwood, a scrap of dried seaweed, each was a treasure of jewels. I have never had such wealth of visual eroticism and bliss before. Later, we visited the pygmy forest, but these living fossils were not as magical.

(with 160 mg followed at 2 h by 60 µgs LSD) "We both felt the first effects at about 30 minutes, and an hour later we found ourselves in a startling folie-a-deux, involved in reliving the origins of man's arrival on earth. We were deep in a tropic environment, defending ourselves against the nasties of nature (insects, threatening things, blistering heat) and determining that man could indeed live here and perhaps survive. A shared eyes-closed fantasy that seemed to be the same script for both of us."

(with 160 mg followed at 2 h by 100 µgs LSD) "This proved to be almost too intoxicating, and a problem arose that had to have a solution. The entire research group was here, and all were following this same regimen. Two hours into the second half of the experiment a telephone call came that reminded me of a promise I had made to perform in a social afternoon with the viola in a string quartet. Why did I answer the phone? My entire experience was, over the course of about 20 minutes, pushed down to a fragile threshold, and I drove about 10 minutes to attend a swank afternoon event and played an early Beethoven and a middle Mozart with an untouched glass of expensive Merlot in front of me. I could always blame the booze. I declined the magnificent food spread, split, and returned to my own party. Safely home, and given 20 more minutes, I was back into a rolling +++ and I now know that the mind has a remarkable ability to control the particular place the psyche is in."

(with 200 mg followed at 2 h by 60 µgs LSD) "There was a steady climb from the half-hour point to about 2 hours. There was not the slightest trace of anything sinister. There was simply a super tactile person-to-person window. I had an overpowering urge to go out and interact with other people. To see, to talk, to be with others. There are unending fantasies of things erotic. Perhaps being with others should be circumspect. By evening the effects had largely worn off, but this was an incredible day, beautiful and unexpectedly relaxing."

EXTENSIONS AND COMMENTARY: There is need for more commentary. It must be noted that all of the above comments used rather modest dosages of LSD. The notes of this period, some two years of exploring interactions of the MD series of compounds as preludes to true psychedelics, are difficult to distill into a simple pattern. Most of these studies used LSD in the 60-100 microgram range which is fundamentally a modest level. Many trials were made where the challenge of acid plopped right on top of an active residue of another drug was more in keeping with the "piggyback" argument. An illustration of this is a trial in which the primer was MDMA followed at 5 hours (this is at a time of almost no effect) with a larger dose of LSD (250 micrograms). The LSD overwhelmed the residual numbing of the MDMA, and the generated state was overwhelmingly erotic and out of body. There can be no way of analytically organizing such a gemisch of drug-drug interactions with any logic that would allow a definitive interpretation. And LSD is not the only agent that can be used to challenge the "body window" such as that produced by MDPR. 2C-B, 2C-T-2 and 2C-T-7 have all been used with fine success as well.

In general, the use of an MD compound (looking at it as a stimulant and primer) followed by a psychedelic, brings about an exaggeration and enhancement of the latter compound. Much work must be done in this area to make sense of it all.

#119 ME; METAESCALINE; 3,4-DIMETHOXY-5-ETHOXY-PHENETHYLAMINE

SYNTHESIS: To a vigorously stirred suspension of 18.6 g of 5-bromobourbonal in 100 mL CH_2Cl_2 there was added 14.2 g methyl iodide, 1.0 g decyltriethylammonium iodide, and 120 mL 5% NaOH. The color was a deep amber, and within 1 min the top phase set up to a solid. This was largely dispersed with the addition of another 50 mL of water. The reaction was allowed to stir for 2 days. The lower phase was washed with H_2O, and saved. The upper phase was treated with another 100 mL CH_2Cl_2, 50 mL of 25% NaOH, another g of decyltriethylammonium iodide, and an additional 50 mL of methyl iodide. The formed solids dispersed by themselves in a few h to produce two relatively clear layers. Stirring was continued for an additional 3 days. The lower phase was separated, washed with H_2O, and combined with the earlier extract. The solvent was removed under vacuum to give 20.3 g of an amber oil that was distilled at 120-133 °C at 0.4 mm/Hg to yield 15.6 g of 3-bromo-4-methoxy-

5-ethoxybenzaldehyde as a white crystalline solid with a mp of 52-53 °C.

A mixture of 15.6 g 3-bromo-4-methoxy-5-ethoxybenzaldehyde and 10 mL cyclohexylamine was heated with an open flame until it appeared free of H_2O. The residue was put under a vacuum (0.5 mm/Hg) and distilled at 148-155 °C yielding 19.2 g 3-bromo-N-cyclohexyl-4-methoxy-5-ethoxybenzylidenimine as an off-white crystalline solid with a melting point 66-68.5 °C. Recrystallization from 100 mL boiling MeOH gave a mp of 67-68.5 °C. The C=N stretch in the infra-red was at 1640 cm^{-1}. Anal. (C$_{16}$H$_{22}$BrNO$_2$) C,H.

A solution of 17 g 3-bromo-N-cyclohexyl-4-methoxy-5-ethoxybenzyl-idenimine in 200 mL anhydrous Et$_2$O was placed in an atmosphere of He, stirred magnetically, and cooled with an external dry-ice acetone bath. Then 38 mL of a 1.55 M solution of butyllithium in hexane was added over 2 min, producing a clear yellow solution. There was then added 25 mL of butyl borate at one time, and the stirred solution allowed to return to room temperature. This was followed with 100 mL of saturated aqueous ammonium sulfate. The Et$_2$O layer was separated, washed with additional saturated ammonium sulfate solution, and evaporated under vacuum The residue was dissolved in 200 mL of 50% MeOH and treated with 12 mL of 30% hydrogen peroxide. This reaction was mildly exothermic, and was allowed to stir for 15 min, then added to an aqueous solution of 50 g ammonium sulfate. This was extracted with 2x100 mL CH$_2$Cl$_2$, the pooled extracts washed once with H$_2$O, and the solvent removed under vacuum. The residue was suspended in dilute HCl, and heated on the steam bath for 0.5 h. Stirring was continued until the reaction was again at room temperature and then it was extracted with 2x100 mL CH$_2$Cl$_2$. These extracts were pooled and in turn extracted with 2x100 mL dilute NaOH. The aqueous extracts were reacidified with HCl, and reextracted with 2x100 mL CH$_2$Cl$_2$. After pooling, the solvent was removed under vacuum to yield an oily residue. This was distilled at 118-130 °C at 0.2 mm/Hg to yield 7.5 g of 3-ethoxy-5-hydroxy-4-methoxybenzaldehyde as a distillate that set to white crystals. Recrystallization from cyclohexane gives a product with a mp of 77-78 °C. Anal. (C$_{10}$H$_{12}$O$_4$) C,H.

A solution of 7.3 g of 3-ethoxy-5-hydroxy-4-methoxybenzaldehyde in 100 mL acetone was treated with 5 mL methyl iodide and 8.0 g finely powdered anhydrous K$_2$CO$_3$, and held at reflux on a steam bath for 6 h. The solvent was removed under vacuum, and the residue was suspended in H$_2$O. After making this strongly basic, it was extracted with 3x50 mL CH$_2$Cl$_2$, the extracts were pooled, and the solvent removed under vacuum. The residual amber oil was distilled at 110-120 °C at 0.4 mm/Hg to yield 7.3 g of a white oil. This spontaneously set to white crystals of 3,4-dimethoxy-5-ethoxybenzaldehyde which had a mp of 49-49.5 °C. Anal. (C$_{11}$H$_{14}$O$_4$) C,H. This same aldehyde can be obtained, but in a less satisfactory yield, by the ethylation of 3,4-dimethoxy-5-hydroxybenzaldehyde described under the preparation of metaproscaline (MP).

A solution of 7.2 g 3,4-dimethoxy-5-ethoxybenzaldehyde in 100 mL nitromethane containing 0.1 g anhydrous ammonium acetate was held at reflux for 50 min. The excess nitromethane was removed under vacuum producing 6.8 g of a red oil which was decanted from some insoluble material. Addition of 10 mL hot MeOH to the decantings, gave a homogeneous solution that spontaneously crystallized on cooling. The yellow crystals were removed by filtration, washed sparingly with MeOH and air dried yielding 3.5 g yellow crystals of 3,4-dimethoxy-5-ethoxy-ß-nitrostyrene, with a mp of 89.5-90 °C after recrystallization from MeOH. Anal. ($C_{12}H_{15}NO_5$) C,H.

A solution of 2.0 g LAH in 100 mL anhydrous THF under He was cooled to 0 °C and vigorously stirred. There was added, dropwise, 1.3 mL of 100% H_2SO_4, followed by the dropwise addition of a solution of 3.1 g 3,4-dimethoxy-5-ethoxy-ß-nitrostyrene in 50 mL anhydrous THF, over the course of 10 min. The mixture was stirred at 0 °C for a while, and then brought to a reflux on the steam bath for 30 min. After cooling again, the excess hydride was destroyed with IPA in THF, followed by the addition of 20 mL 10% NaOH which was sufficient to convert the solids to a white and granular form. These were removed by filtration, the filter cake washed with IPA, the mother liquor and filtrates combined, and the solvents removed under vacuum. The residue was added to 150 mL dilute H_2SO_4, and the cloudy suspension washed with 2x75 mL CH_2Cl_2 which removed much of the color. The aqueous phase was made basic with 25% NaOH, and extracted with 3x50 mL CH_2Cl_2. The solvent was removed from these pooled extracts and the residue distilled at 103-116 °C at 0.25 mm/Hg to provide 2.3 g of a colorless viscous liquid. This was dissolved in 10 mL IPA, neutralized with about 25 drops of concentrated HCl, which produced an insoluble white solid. This was diluted with 40 mL anhydrous Et_2O added slowly with continuous stirring. The white crystalline 3,4-dimethoxy-5-ethoxyphenethylamine hydrochloride (ME) was isolated by filtration, washed with Et_2O, and air dried, and weighed 2.4 g. It had a mp of 202-203 °C which increased by one degree upon recrystallization from boiling IPA. Anal. ($C_{12}H_{20}ClNO_3$) C,H.

DOSAGE: 200 - 350 mg.

DURATION: 8 - 12 h.

QUALITATIVE COMMENTS: (with 200 mg) "It tasted pretty strong. However, the taste was soon gone, and an energetic feeling began to take over me. It continued to grow. The feeling was one of great camaraderie, and it was very easy to talk to people. Everyone was talking to everyone else. I found it most pleasant, energetic and at the same time relaxing, with my defenses down. This material did not seem to lead to introspection; however, it might if one took it without other people around. Heightened visual awareness was mild, but the audio awareness was quite heightened. The feeling of being with everyone was intense."

(with 250 mg) "Initially I took 200 milligrams of metaescaline, and the experience developed for me very gradually at first, and very pleasantly. After about one half hour I became aware of a wall that seemed to shut me in, not unpleasantly. The wall slowly dissolved, but I was afraid I might get into a negative experience. I felt immediate relief (from this isolation) upon taking the additional 50 mg (at 2:23 into the experiment) as though glad of the decision. I lay down outside on a blanket. There was a marvelous feeling inside, although no imagery. I felt the wall dissolve completely, and I desired to join the group. From this point on the experience was most enjoyable, euphoric. Although not dramatic like some psychedelics, it was most rewarding for me personally. I felt a marvelous bond with everyone present, with clear-headed, excellent thinking, and excellent communication. All in all, a most rewarding and enjoyable experience. Afterwards I felt much strengthened, with good energy and good insight. I have a strong feeling that the group tailored the nature of the experience, and that I and others were most desirous of group interaction. I feel that one could do a lot of other things with it if one turned one's attention to it."

(with 275 mg) "Onset of both physical and mental change was slow relative to other psychochemicals. Very gradual internal stirrings were felt at about the hour-and-a-half point. These were mostly feelingful rather than cognitive, and were quite pleasurable. At about the two-and-a-half hour point I grew quite thirsty, and drank a pint of beer. Almost immediately, and quite unexpectedly, I tomsoed to a much higher level and remained there for another three hours until the whole experience waned. [The verb, to tomso, means a sudden rekindling of the drug-induced altered state with a small amount of alcohol. It is explained in the recipe for TOMSO.] During the experience heights, and in fact before it reached its height, talking was easy and unimpeded. The transference feelings so characteristic of MDMA were basically not there. But for purposes of psychotherapy, there were some advantages: fluent associations, undefended positions, and general bonaise."

(with 400 mg) "Ingested 300 milligrams at about 1:30 in the afternoon. Very quiet climb. Occasional yawns. Matter-of-fact view of the world. No rosy glow. At the end of the second hour, I seem to be stuck at a ++. Take another 100 milligrams at 3:45 PM. Still tastes awful. Feel a small head-rush fifteen minutes after taking the supplement, and within a half hour I am completely +3. For a while this was a sterner mescaline. Saw the eternal, continual making of choices, all opposites continually in motion with each other. Yin and yang everywhere, giving life to every molecule. The universe itself keeps alive by the action-reaction, the yes-no, the black-white, male-female, plus-minus. All life is a continual making of choices on all levels. Then I closed my eyes, and I found myself floating up to the very top of a temple, where there was radiant light and a sense of homecoming. Making love is a clear stream over and through rocks and canyons — the earth and sky make love, and the rocks make love to other rocks, and the water is the teasing, fondling, living and moving actions of loving. To realize that, on some level, all existence makes love to all other existence. The Japanese Garden: a structured way of laying out a small glimpse into cosmic love-making, so that it can be read by other human souls. All loving, when direct and free and undemanding, is a touching of the Source. The hardest lesson, of course, is how to love yourself that same way.

And it remains both the first lesson of Kindergarten and the Ph.D. final. I was able to drift into sleep at about 4:00 AM."

EXTENSIONS AND COMMENTARY: The reorientation of the single ethyl group of escaline (E) to the meta-position produces metaescaline (ME). In cats, in studies of over 50 years ago, the two compounds produced similar effects at similar dosages. In man, ME also appears to be similar to mescaline in potency. However, a subtle difference is apparent between ME and Peyote, the natural source of mescaline. With Peyote itself, the initial taste of the crude cactus is more than just foul; it might better be described as unbelievably foul. But in the middle of a Peyote experience, the taste of the cactus is truly friendly. When ME was retasted in the middle of an experience, the taste was still foul.

There are other distinctions from mescaline. Unlike mescaline or Peyote, there is rarely any body discomfort during the early phase of intoxication, no nausea and only an occasional comment suggesting hyperreflexia. And, also unlike mescaline, most subjective reports on ME claim that music produces little imagery, and the exaggeration of color perception is more reserved. Appetite is normal, the tastes and textures of food are unusually rewarding. No subject has ever expressed a reluctance to repeat the experience. Sleep is easy, refreshing, and the following day seems free from residue.

#120   MEDA;   3-METHOXY-4,5-ETHYLENEDIOXY-AMPHETAMINE

SYNTHESIS: To a solution of 50 g 3,4-dihydroxy-5-methoxybenzaldehyde in 100 mL distilled acetone there was added 70 g ethylene bromide and 58 g finely powdered anhydrous K_2CO_3. The mixture was held at reflux for 5 days. This was then poured into 1.5 L H_2O and extracted with 4x100 mL CH_2Cl_2. Removal of the solvent from the pooled extracts gave a residue which was distilled at 19 mm/Hg. Several of the fractions taken in the 203-210 °C range spontaneously crystallized, and they were pooled to give 18.3 g of 3-methoxy-4,5-ethylenedioxybenzaldehyde as white solids with a mp of 80-81 °C. A small sample with an equal weight of malononitrile in EtOH treated with a few drops of triethylamine gave 3-methoxy-4,5-ethylenedioxybenzalmalononitrile as pale yellow crystals from EtOH with a mp of 153-154 °C.

A solution of 1.50 g 3-methoxy-4,5-ethylenedioxybenzaldehyde in 6 mL acetic acid was treated with 1 mL nitroethane and 0.50 g anhydrous ammonium acetate, and held on the steam bath for 1.5 h. To the cooled mixture H_2O was cautiously added until the first permanent turbidity was observed, and once crystallization had set in, more H_2O was added at a rate that would allow the generation of additional crystals. When there was a residual turbidity from additional H_2O, the addition was stopped, and the beaker held at ice temperature for several h. The product was removed by filtration and washed with a little 50% acetic acid, providing 0.93 g 1-(3-methoxy-4,5-ethylenedioxyphenyl)-2-nitropropene as dull yellow crystals with a mp of 116-119 °C. Recrystallization of an analytical sample from MeOH gave a mp of 119-121 °C.

A stirred suspension of 6.8 g LAH in 500 mL anhydrous Et_2O under an inert atmosphere was brought up to a gentle reflux. A total of 9.4 g 1-(3-methoxy-4,5-ethylenedioxyphenyl)-2-nitropropene in warm Et_2O was added over the course of 0.5 h. Refluxing was maintained for 6 h, and then the reaction mixture was cooled and the excess hydride destroyed by the cautious addition of 400 mL 1.5 N H_2SO_4. The two clear phases were separated, and the aqueous phase was brought to pH of 6 by the addition of a saturated Na_2CO_3 solution. This was filtered free of a small amount of insolubles, and the clear filtrate was heated to 80 °C. To this there was added a solution of 9.2 g picric acid (90% material) in 100 mL boiling EtOH, and the clear mixture allowed to cool in an ice bath. Scratching generated yellow crystals of the picrate salt. This salt was filtered free of the aqueous environment, treated with 50 mL of 5% NaOH, and stirred until the picric acid was totally in the form of the soluble sodium salt. This was then extracted with 3x100 mL CH_2Cl_2, the extracts pooled, and the solvent removed under vacuum. The residue weighed 6.0 g, and was dissolved in 100 mL anhydrous Et_2O, and saturated with dry HCl gas. The white solids that formed were filtered free of the Et_2O, and ground up under 50 mL of slightly moist acetone, providing 4.92 g of 3-methoxy-4,5-ethylenedioxy-amphetamine hydrochloride monohydrate (MEDA) as white crystals.

DOSAGE: greater than 200 mg.

DURATION: unknown.

EXTENSIONS AND COMMENTARY: There are times when the Gods smile in unexpectedly nice ways. Having found the activity of MMDA, the "scientific" thing to do would be to compare it against the other "psychotomimetic" amphetamine that was known at that time (this was 1962), namely TMA. Comparing their structures, the only difference of any kind was that two of the adjacent methoxyl groups of TMA were replaced with a 5-membered ring, called the methylenedioxy ring.

Where does one go next? Some perverse inspiration suggested increasing the size of this ring to a 6-membered ring, the ethylenedioxy (or dioxene) homologue. Well, if you thought that getting myristicinaldehyde was a difficulty, it was nothing compared to getting this 6-membered counterpart. But I huffed and I puffed, and I did make enough to taste and to evaluate. And it was here that I got the divine message! No activity!! So, rather than being condemned forever *a la* Sisyphus to push ever larger rings up my psyche, I gave myself permission to pursue another path. The message was: "Don't change the groups. Leave them as they are, but relocate them instead." And that led directly to TMA-2 and its story.

A couple of diversions may be mentioned here. Before the blessed inactivity of MEDA was established, the 7-membered ring counterpart, 3-methoxy-4,5-trimethylenedioxyamphetamine (MTDA) was prepared by essentially the same procedure. The above 3-methoxy-4,5-dihydroxybenzaldehyde with trimethylene bromide gave 3-methoxy-4,5-trimethylenedioxybenzaldehyde, white solids, with a malononitrile derivative with a mp of 134-135 °C; the aldehyde with nitroethane gave the nitropropene with a mp of 86-87 °C; and this with LAH gave MTDA as the hydrochloride (mp 160-161 °C) again isolated first as the picrate. It had been tasted at up to an 8 milligram dosage (no activity, but none expected) before being abandoned. And, an initial effort was made to synthesize a five-member ring (methylenedioxy) with a methyl sticking out from it. This ethylidine homologue got as far as the aldehyde stage. The reaction between 3,4-dihydroxy-5-methoxy–benzaldehyde and 1,1-dibromoethane in acetone containing anhydrous potassium carbonate gave a minuscule amount of a product that was a two-component mixture. This was resolved by dozens of separate injections into a preparatory gas chromatography system, allowing the isolation of the second of the two components in a quantity sufficient to demonstrate (by NMR spectroscopy) that it was the desired 3-methoxy-4,5-ethylidinedioxybenzaldehyde. Starting with the pre-prepared dipotassium salt or the lead salt of the catecholaldehyde gave nothing. With no activity being found with MEDA, all was abandoned.

There are some comments made under MDA for successful chemistry (using a different approach) along these lines when there is no methoxyl group present. These are the compounds EDA and IDA. But the pharmacology was still not that exciting.

#121   MEE;   4,5-DIETHOXY-2-METHOXYAMPHETAMINE

SYNTHESIS: To a solution of 166 g bourbonal in 1 L MeOH there was added a solution of 66 g KOH pellets in 300 mL H_2O. There was then added 120 g ethyl bromide, and the mixture was held at reflux on the steam bath for 3 h. The reaction was quenched with three volumes of H_2O, and made strongly basic by the addition of 25% NaOH. This was extracted with 3x300 mL CH_2Cl_2, and the pooled extracts stripped of solvent under vacuum. There remained 155 g of 3,4-diethoxybenz-aldehyde as a fluid oil that had an infra-red spectrum identical (except for being slightly wet) to that of a commercial sample from the Eastman Kodak Company.

A solution of 194 g 3,4-diethoxybenzaldehyde in 600 g glacial acetic acid was arranged in a flask that could be magnetically stirred, yet cooled as needed with an external ice bath. A total of 210 g of 40% peracetic acid in acetic acid was added at a rate such that, with ice cooling, the exothermic reaction never raised the internal temperature above 26 °C. The reaction developed a deep red color during the 2 h needed for the addition. At the end of the reaction the mixture was quenched by the addition of three volumes of H_2O, and the remaining acidity was neutralized by the addition of solid Na_2CO_3 (700 g was required). This aqueous phase was extracted several times with CH_2Cl_2, and the solvent was removed from the pooled extracts under vacuum. The residue was a mixture of the intermediate formate ester and the end product phenol. This was suspended in 800 mL 10% NaOH, and held on the steam bath for 1.5 h. After cooling, this was washed once with CH_2Cl_2 (discarded) and then acidified with HCl. There was the formation of an intensely hydrated complex of the product phenol, reminiscent of the problem encountered with 3-ethoxy-4-methoxyphenol. This was worked up in three parts. The entire acidified aqueous phase was extracted with Et_2O (3x200 mL) which on evaporation gave 80 g of an oil. The hydrated glob was separately ground up under boiling CH_2Cl_2 which, on evaporation, gave an additional 30 g of oil, and the aqueous mother liquor from the glob was extracted with 2x200 mL CH_2Cl_2 which provided, after removal of the

solvent, an additional 10 g. These crude phenol fractions were combined and distilled at 1.5 mm/Hg. Following a sizeable forerun, a fraction boiling at 158-160 °C was the anhydrous product, 3,4-diethoxyphenol. It was a clear, amber oil, and weighed 70.0 g. The slightest exposure to H_2O, even moist air, give a solid hydrate, with mp of 63-64 °C. This phenol can be used for the synthesis of MEE (this recipe) or for the preparation of EEE (see the separate recipe). A solution of 2.0 g of this phenol in 5 mL CH_2Cl_2 was diluted with 15 mL hexane. This was treated with 2 g methyl isocyanate followed by a few drops of triethylamine. After about 5 min, white crystals formed of 3,4-diethoxyphenyl-N-methyl carbamate, with a mp of 90-91 °C.

A solution of 26.6 g 3,4-diethoxyphenol in 50 mL MeOH was mixed with another containing 9.6 g KOH pellets dissolved in 200 mL hot MeOH. There was then added 21.4 g methyl iodide, and the mixture was held at reflux for 2 h on the steam bath. This was then quenched in 3 volumes of water, made strongly basic with 25% NaOH, and extracted with 3x150 mL CH_2Cl_2. Evaporation of the solvent from the pooled extracts gave 19.3 g of 1,2-diethoxy-4-methoxybenzene (3,4-diethoxy-anisole) as a clear, pale amber oil that solidified when cooled. The mp was 20-21 °C.

A mixture of 32.0 g N-methyl formanilide and 36.2 g $POCl_3$ was allowed to stand until it was a deep red color (about 0.5 h). To this there was added 18.3 g 1,2-diethoxy-4-methoxybenzene and the exothermic reaction was heated on the steam bath for 2.5 h. This was then poured over 600 mL chipped ice, and the dark oily material slowly began lightening in color and texture. A light oil was formed which, on continued stirring, became crystalline. After the conversion was complete, the solids were removed by filtration producing, after removal of as much H_2O as possible by suction, 26.9 g of crude aldehyde. A small sample pressed on a porous plate had a mp of 87.5-88.5 °C. Recrystallization of the entire damp crop from 50 mL boiling MeOH gave, after cooling, filtering, and air drying, 17.7 g of 4,5-diethoxy-2-methoxybenzaldehyde as fluffy, off-white crystals with a mp of 88-88.5 °C. A solution of 1.0 g of this aldehyde and 0.5 g of malononitrile dissolved in warm absolute EtOH was treated with 3 drops triethylamine. There was the immediate formation of crystals which were filtered and air dried to constant weight. The product, 4,5-diethoxy-2-methoxybenzalmalononitrile, was a bright yellow crystalline material, which weighed 1.0 g and had a mp of 156-157 °C.

To a solution of 14.7 g 4,5-diethoxy-2-methoxybenzaldehyde in 46 g glacial acetic acid, there was added 8.0 g nitroethane and 5.0 g anhydrous ammonium acetate. The mixture was heated on the steam bath for 2 h, becoming progressively deeper red in color. The addition of a small amount of H_2O to the hot, clear solution produced a slight turbidity, and all was allowed to stand overnight at room temperature. There was deposited a crop of orange crystals that was removed by filtration and air dried. There was obtained 7.0 g 1-(4,5-diethoxy-2-methoxy-phenyl)-2-nitropropene as brilliant orange crystals that had a mp of 89-90.5 °C. This was tightened up, but not improved, by trial recrystallization from acetic acid, mp 89-90 °C, and from hexane, mp 90-90.5 °C. Anal. $(C_{14}H_{19}NO_5)$ C,H.

To a gently refluxing suspension of 5.0 g LAH in 400 mL anhydrous Et_2O under a He atmosphere, there was added 6.5 g 1-(4,5-diethoxy-2-methoxyphenyl)-2-nitropropene by allowing the condensing Et_2O to drip into a shunted Soxhlet thimble containing the nitrostyrene. This effectively added a warm saturated solution of the nitrostyrene dropwise. Refluxing was maintained for 5 h, and the reaction mixture was cooled with an external ice bath. The excess hydride was destroyed by the cautious addition of 400 mL of 1.5 N H_2SO_4. When the aqueous and Et_2O layers were finally clear, they were separated, and 100 g of potassium sodium tartrate was dissolved in the aqueous fraction. Aqueous NaOH was then added until the pH was >9, and this was extracted with 3x200 mL CH_2Cl_2. Removal of the solvent under vacuum produced an off-white oil that was dissolved in anhydrous Et_2O and saturated with anhydrous HCl gas. The crystals of 4,5-diethoxy-2-methoxyamphetamine hydrochloride (MEE) that formed were very fine and slow to filter, but finally were isolated as a white powder weighing 5.4 g and melting at 178.5-180 °C. Anal. $(C_{14}H_{24}ClNO_3)$ C,H,N.

DOSAGE: greater than 4.6 mg.

DURATION: unknown.

EXTENSIONS AND COMMENTARY: There were early trials made with MEE, before it became known what direction the ethoxy substitution results would take. A number of progressive trials, up to a dosage of 4.6 milligrams, were without any central effects at all.

There is an instinct in structure-activity studies to think of a change as a success or a failure, depending on whether there is an increase or a decrease in the desired activity. But if one were to look at the effects of putting an ethoxy group onto TMA-2 in place of a methoxy group as a way of decreasing the effectiveness, then the 4-position becomes the worst position (MEM is equipotent to TMA-2), and the 5-position is perhaps a little less bad (MME is almost as potent) and the 2-position is the best by far (EMM is out of it, potency-wise). In other words, in the comparison of the 2- and 5-positions, the lengthening of the 5-position gives modest loss of activity, and the lengthening of the whatever in the 2-position is the most disruptive. With this as a basis for prediction, then MEE (which differs from MEM only by a lengthening of the 5-position substituent) might be only a little less active than MEM and, as MEM is about the same as TMA-2, it is distinctly possible that MEE may show activity in the area at dosages that are not much above the 25 to 50 milligram area. Of all the diethoxy homologues, it would be the most promising one to explore.

Which brings to mind a quotation of a hero of mine, Mark Twain. "I like science because it gives one such a wholesome return of conjecture from such a trifling investment of fact."

#122 MEM; DMEA; 2,5-DIMETHOXY-4-ETHOXYAMPHETAMINE

SYNTHESIS: A solution of 83 g bourbonal (also called ethyl vanillin, or vanillal, or simply 3-ethoxy-4-hydroxybenzaldehyde) in 500 mL MeOH was treated with a solution of 31.5 g KOH pellets (85% material) dissolved in 250 mL H_2O. There was then added 71 g methyl iodide, and the mixture was held under reflux conditions for 3 h. All was added to 3 volumes of H_2O, and this was made basic with the addition of 25% NaOH. The aqueous phase was extracted with 5x200 mL CH_2Cl_2. The pooling of these extracts and removal of the solvent under vacuum gave a residue of 85.5 g of the product 3-ethoxy-4-methoxy-benzaldehyde, with a mp of 52-53 °C. When this product was recrystallized from hexane, its mp was 49-50 °C. When the reaction was run with the same reactants in a reasonably anhydrous environment, with methanolic KOH, the major product was the acetal, 3-ethoxy-α,α,4-trimethoxytoluene. This was a white glistening product which crystallized readily from hexane, and had a mp of 44-45 °C. Acid hydrolysis converted it to the correct aldehyde above. The addition of sufficient H_2O in the methylation completely circumvents this by-product. A solution of 1.0 g of this aldehyde and 0.7 g malononitrile in 20 mL warm absolute EtOH, when treated with a few drops of triethylamine, gave immediate yellow color followed, in a few min by the formation of crystals. Filtration, and washing with EtOH, gave bright yellow crystals of 3-ethoxy-4-methoxybenzalmalononitrile with a mp of 141-142 °C.

A well stirred solution of 125.4 g 3-ethoxy-4-methoxybenzaldehyde in 445 mL acetic acid was treated with 158 g 40% peracetic acid (in acetic acid) at a rate at which, with ice cooling, the internal temperature did not exceed 27 °C. The addition required about 45 min. The reaction mixture was then quenched in some 3 L H_2O. There was the generation of some crystals which were removed by filtration. The mother liquor was saved. The solid material weighed, while still wet, 70 g and was crude formate ester. A small quantity was recrystallized from cyclohexane twice, to provide a reference sample of 3-ethoxy-4-methoxyphenyl formate with a mp of 63-64 °C. The bulk of this crude formate ester was dissolved in 200 mL concentrated HCl which gave a deep purple solution. This was quenched with water which precipitated a fluffy tan solid, which was hydrated phenolic product that weighed about 35 g, and melted in the 80-90 °C. range. The mother liquors of the above filtration were neutralized with Na_2CO_3, then extracted with 3x100 ml Et_2O. Removal of the solvent gave a residue of about 80 g that was impure formate (containing some unoxidized aldehyde). To this there was added 500 mL 10% NaOH, and the dark mixture heated on the steam bath for several h. After cooling, the strongly basic solution was washed with CH_2Cl_2, and then treated with 200 mL Et_2O, which knocked out a heavy semi-solid mass that was substantially insoluble in either phase. This was, again, the crude hydrated phenol. The Et_2O phase, on evaporation, gave a third crop of solids. These could actually be recrystallized from MeOH/H_2O, but the mp always remained broad. When subjected to distillation conditions, the H_2O was finally driven out of the hydrate, and the product 3-ethoxy-4-methoxyphenol distilled as a clear oil at 180-190 °C at 0.8 mm/Hg. This product, 45.1 g, gave a fine NMR spectrum, and in dilute CCl_4 showed a single OH band at 3620 cm^{-1}, supporting the freedom of the OH group on the aromatic ring from adjacent oxygen. Efforts to obtain an NMR spectrum in D_2O immediately formed an insoluble hydrate. This phenol can serve as the starting material for either MEM (see below) or EEM (see separate recipe).

To a solution of 12.3 g 3-ethoxy-4-methoxyphenol in 20 mL MeOH, there was added a solution of 4.8 g flaked KOH in 100 mL heated MeOH. To this clear solution there was then added 10.7 g methyl iodide, and the mixture held at reflux on the steam bath for 2 h. This was then quenched in 3 volumes H_2O, made strongly basic with 10% NaOH, and extracted with 3x100 mL CH_2Cl_2. Removal of the solvent from the pooled extracts under vacuum gave 9.4 g of an amber oil which spontaneously crystallized. The mp of 1,4-dimethoxy-2-ethoxybenzene was 42-43.5 °C, and was used, with no further purification, in the following step.

A mixture of 17.3 g N-methylformanilide and 19.6 g $POCl_3$ was allowed to stand for 0.5 h, producing a deep claret color. To this there was added 9.2 g 1,4-dimethoxy-2-ethoxybenzene, and the mixture was held on the steam bath for 2 h. It was then poured into chipped ice and, with mechanical stirring, the dark oily phase slowly became increasingly crystalline. This was finally removed by filtration, providing a brown solid mat which showed a mp of 103.5-106.5 °C. All was dissolved in 75 mL boiling MeOH which, on cooling, deposited fine crystals of 2,5-dimethoxy-4-ethoxybenzaldehyde that were colored a light tan and which, after air drying to constant weight, weighed 8.5 g and had a mp of 108-109.5 °C. Search was made by gas chromatography for evidence of the other two theoretically possible positional isomers, but none could be found. The NMR spectrum showed the two para-protons as clean singlets, with no noise suggesting other isomers. There was a single peak by GC (for the recrystallized product) but the mother liquors showed a contamination that proved to be N-methylformanilide. A 0.3 g sample, along with 0.3 g malononitrile, was dissolved in 10 mL warm absolute EtOH, and treated with a drop of triethylamine. There was the immediate formation of a yellow color followed, in 1 min, by the deposition of fine yellow needles. Filtering and air drying gave 0.25 g of 2,5-dimethoxy-4-ethoxybenzalmalononitrile, with a mp of 171-172 °C.

A solution of 7.3 g 2,5-dimethoxy-4-ethoxybenzaldehyde in 25 g glacial acetic acid was treated with 3.6 g nitroethane and 2.25 g anhydrous ammonium acetate, and heated on the steam bath. After two h, the clear solution was diluted with an equal volume of H_2O, and cooled in an ice bucket. There was the formation of a heavy crop of orange crystals which were removed by filtration. The dry weight of 1-(2,5-dimethoxy-4-ethoxyphenyl)-2-nitropropene was 4.8 g and the mp was 120-124 °C. Recrystallization of an analytical sample from MeOH gave a mp of 128-129 °C. Anal. $(C_{13}H_{17}NO_5)$ C,H.

To a gently refluxing suspension of 3.3 g LAH in 400 mL anhydrous Et_2O under a He atmosphere, there was added 4.3 g 1-(2,5-dimethoxy-4-ethoxy)-2-nitropropene by allowing the condensing Et_2O to drip into a shunted Soxhlet thimble apparatus containing the nitrostyrene, thus effectively adding a warm saturated ether solution of it to the hydride mixture. The addition took 2 h. Refluxing was maintained for 5 h, and then the reaction mixture was cooled to 0 °C with an external ice bath. The excess hydride was destroyed by the cautious addition of 300 mL of 1.5 N H_2SO_4. When the aqueous and Et_2O layers were finally clear, they were separated, and 100 g of potassium sodium tartrate was dissolved in the aqueous fraction. Aqueous NaOH was then added until the pH was >9, and this was then extracted with 3x100 mL CH_2Cl_2. Evaporation of the solvent from the pooled extracts produced an almost white oil that was dissolved in 100 mL anhydrous Et_2O and saturated with anhydrous HCl gas. There was deposited a white crystalline solid of 2,5-dimethoxy-4-ethoxyamphetamine hydrochloride (MEM) which weighed 3.1 g and had a mp of 171-172.5 °C. Anal. $(C_{13}H_{22}ClNO_3)$ C,H,N.

DOSAGE: 20 - 50 mg.

DURATION: 10 - 14 h.

QUALITATIVE COMMENTS: (with 20 mg) "I experienced some physical discomfort, but doesn't that tell us about the work to be done, rather than the property of the material? The breakthrough I had was the following day (and this seems to be the way MEM operates, i.e., first the energy and expansion, next day insight) was of the highest value and importance for me. I was given a methodology for dealing with my shadow parts. No small gift. And I did it all alone and the results were immediate. I am so grateful."

(with 20 mg, at 1.5 h following 120 mg MDMA) "The transition was very smooth, with no obvious loss of the MDMA experience. I felt less of a need to talk, but the intimate closeness with the others was maintained. The experience continues to grow more profound and euphoric and I prayed, in the latter part of the afternoon, that it wouldn't stop. It continued until midnight with marvelous feelings, good energy, and much hilarity. And it abated very little over the next several days leaving me with the feeling of lasting change with important insights still coming to mind one week later."

(with 25 mg, at 2 h following 120 mg MDMA) "I found that sounds in general were distracting. No, they were out-and-out annoying. I may have been in an introspective mood, but I really wanted to be alone. No body problems at all. Felt good. I developed some color changes and some pattern movement. Not much, but then I didn't explore it much. The wine party afterwards was certainly most pleasant. The soup was a great pleasure. And that hard bread was good. The material was clearly not anorexic, or at least I overcame whatever anorexia there might have been."

(with 30 mg) "I was aware of this in thirty minutes and it slowly developed from there to an almost +++ in the following hour. There were visual phenomena, with some color enhancement and especially a considerable enhancement of brights and darks. The first signs of decline were at about six hours, but there was something still working there after another six hours had passed. A slow decline, certainly."

(with 50 mg) "I came into the experience knowing that yesterday had been a very fatiguing and tense day. I felt this material within the first ten minutes which is the fastest that I have ever felt anything. The ascent was rapid and for the first hour I tended to an inward fantasying with a distinct sensual tinge. There was a persistent queasiness that never left me, and it contrasted oddly with a good feeling of outward articulation and lucidity which succeeded in coming to the fore after the introverted first hour. Sleep was difficult, but the next day was calm and clear."

(with 50 mg) "Lots of energy, best directed into activity. Clear imaging, thinking. Intense yet serene. Good feeling of pleasantness and some euphoria. I felt the need to keep moving. Hard to stay still."

(with 70 mg, in two parts) "The effects of the 40 milligrams were muted by another drug experiment yesterday morning, and I never got much over a plus 1. There is an erotic nature, tactile sensitivity perhaps not as delicate as with 2C-B, but it is there. At the 2 hour point, an additional 30 milligrams increased the body impact (a distinct tremor and sensitivity) but somehow not a lot more mental. I have been compromised by yesterday."

EXTENSIONS AND COMMENTARY: MEM was both a valuable and dramatic compound, as well as a drug that played a watershed role. The completion of all the possible trimethoxyamphetamines (the TMA's) showed that only two of them combined the values of dependability of positive psychedelic effects with a reasonably high potency. Both TMA-2 and TMA-6 are treasures, both active in similar dosages, and both offer methoxyl groups that are begging to be replaced by other things. The first focus was on TMA-2, partly because the needed synthetic chemistry was better known, and partly because I had discovered its activity earlier. But there were three entirely different and distinct methoxyl groups to work on, in TMA-2. There is one at the 2-position, one at the 4-position, and one at the 5-position. The most obvious thing to do, it seemed, was to make each of them one carbon longer. Replace a methoxy with an ethoxy. And a logical naming pattern could follow the use of M for methoxy, and E for ethoxy, in sequence right around the ring from the 2- to the 4- to the 5-positions. The first group to be compared, then, would be EMM, MEM, and MME. And of these three, it was only MEM that was right up there in drama and in potency. But, by the time that became apparent, I had already completed the diethoxy possibilities (EEM, EME, and MEE) as well as the triethoxy homologue, EEE. With the discovery that the 4-position was the magic leverage point, and that the homologues at positions 2- and 5- were clearly less interesting, all emphasis was directed at this target, and this has led to the many 4-substituted families that are now known to be highly potent and felt by many to be personally valuable.

Why put such emphasis on potency, I am frequently asked? Why should it matter how much of a compound you take, as long as the effective level is much lower than its toxic level? Well, in a sense, that is the very reason. There are no guides as to what the toxic levels of any of these many compounds might really be in man. There is simply no way of determining this. Only a few have been explored in animals in the pursuit of an LD-50 level. Most of them are similar to one-another, in that they are, in mice, of relatively low toxicity and, in rat, of relatively high toxicity. But this toxicity appears not to be related to potency in man. So, if one might extrapolate that they are of more or less the same risk to man (from the toxic point of view) then the lower the dosage, the greater the safety. Maybe. In the absence of anything factual, it makes a reasonable operating hypothesis.

Many of the reports of MEM effects have been with experiments in which an effective dose of MDMA had been taken shortly earlier. There has developed a concept, embraced by a number of researchers, that the ease and quietness usually seen with the development of the MDMA experience can mitigate some of the physically disturbing symptoms sometimes seen with other psychedelics. This may be partly due to a familiar entry into a altered place, and partly due to a lessening of dosage usually required for full effects. MEM seems to have had more trials using this combination than many of the other psychedelic drugs.

#123   MEPEA;   3-METHOXY-4-ETHOXYPHENETHYLAMINE

SYNTHESIS: A solution of 10.0 g 3-methoxy-4-ethoxybenzaldehyde in 150 mL nitromethane was treated with 1.7 g anhydrous ammonium acetate, and heated on the steam bath for 1 h. The excess nitromethane was removed under vacuum, yielding a loose, yellow crystalline mass that was filtered and modestly washed with cold MeOH. The 8.0 g of damp yellow crystals thus obtained were dissolved in 50 mL of vigorously boiling CH_3CN, decanted from a small amount of insolubles (probably ammonium acetate residues) and cooled in an ice bath. The crystals so obtained were removed by filtration, washed with 2x5 mL cold CH_3CN, and air dried to constant weight. The yield of 4-ethoxy-3-methoxy-ß-nitrostyrene was 6.3 g of beautiful yellow crystals.

A solution of 2.3 g LAH in 70 mL anhydrous THF was cooled, under He to 0 °C with an external ice bath. With good stirring there was added 2.3 mL 100% H_2SO_4 dropwise, to minimize charring. This was followed by the addition of 6.2 g 3-methoxy-4-ethoxy-ß-nitrostyrene in anhydrous THF. After a few min further stirring, the temperature was brought up to a gentle reflux on the steam bath, and then all was cooled again to 0 °C. The excess hydride was destroyed by the cautious addition of IPA followed by suffecent 10% NaOH to give a white granular character to the oxides, and to assure that the reaction mixture was basic. The reaction mixture was filtered and the filter cake well washed with THF. The filtrate and washes were combined and stripped of solvent under vacuum. The residue was dissolved in dilute H_2SO_4. This was washed with 2x75 mL CH_2Cl_2, which removed the residual yellow color. The remaining aqueous phase was made basic with NaOH, and extracted with 3x75 mL CH_2Cl_2. These extracts were combined and the solvent removed under vacuum. The residue was distilled at 108-115 °C at 0.4 mm/Hg to give 4.2 g of a mobile, colorless liquid. This was dissolved in 12 mL IPA, neutralized with 60 drops concentrated HCl, and diluted with 100 mL anhydrous Et_2O. There was deposited a fine white crystalline product which, after removal by filtration, ether washing, and air drying, yielded 3.8 g of 3-methoxy-4-ethoxyphenethylamine hydrochloride (MEPEA).

DOSAGE: 300 mg or greater.

DURATION: short.

QUALITATIVE COMMENTS: (with 120 mg) "I am at perhaps a +1, a very slight effect of lightness, without any body awareness at all. And then in another hour, I was completely baseline again."

(with 300 mg) "Whatever changes took place were complete at the end of an hour. The effects were very quiet, very pleasant, and very light. There was nothing psychedelic here, but rather a gentle lifting of spirits. No sensory enhancement or other expected changes."

EXTENSIONS AND COMMENTARY: This is one of the very few phenethylamines with only two substituents that shows even a hint of central activity. And there is an interesting story attached. I got a call out of absolutely nowhere, from a Stanislov Wistupkin, that he had discovered a number of new psychedelic drugs which he would like to share with me. Two of them were simple phenethylamines, one with an ethoxy group at the 4-position, and one with an allyloxy group there. Both, he said, were mood elevators active between 100 and 300 milligrams. One of them was this material, here called MEPEA, and the other one was 3-methoxy-4-allyloxyphenethylamine, or MAPEA. When I did meet him in person, he gave me a most remarkable publication which had been authored some ten years earlier, by a person named Leminger, now dead. It was all in Czech, but quite unmistakably, right there on the third page, were the structures of MEPEA and MAPEA, and the statement that they were active at between 100 and 300 milligrams. I have not yet made the allyloxy compound, but I feel that it too might be a gentle mood elevator similar to the ethoxy.

A most appealing extension of these materials would be the amphetamine derivatives, things with a 3-methoxy group, and something small and terse on the 4-position. The immediate analogies of MEPEA and MAPEA would be 3-methoxy-4-ethoxy- (and 3-methoxy-4-allyloxy)-amphetamine. And equally interesting would be the 4-hydroxy analogue. This would be an easily made compound from vanillin, one of our most enjoyable spices in the kitchen cabinet, and it would be directly related to the essential oils, eugenol and isoeugenol. This amphetamine compound has already been synthesized, but it is still unexplored in man.

Some years ago a report appeared in the forensic literature of Italy, of the seizure of a small semitransparent capsule containing 141 milligrams of a white powder that was stated to be a new hallucinogenic drug. This was shown to contain an analogue of DOM, 3-methoxy-4-methylamphetamine, or MMA. The Italian authorities made no mention of the net weight contained in each dosage unit, but it has been found that the active level of MMA in man is in the area of 40-60 milligrams. The compound can apparently be quite dysphoric, and long lived.

In the Czechoslovakian publication that presented MEPEA and MAPEA, there were descriptions of escaline (E), proscaline (P), and the allyloxy analogue (AL). These are all active in man, and have been entered elsewhere. This is the only published material dealing with psychedelic drugs I have ever been able to find, from the laboratory of Otakar Leminger. What sort of man was this chemist? He worked for years in industry, and only at the time of his retirement did he publish this little gem. He lived at Usti, directly north of Praha, on the Labe river (which is called by the better known name, the Elbe, as soon as it enters Germany). Might there be other treasures that he had discovered, and never published? Was young Wistupkin a student of his? Are there unrecognized notes of Otakar Leminger sitting in some farm house attic in Northern Czechoslovakia? I extend my heartfelt salute to an almost unknown explorer in the psychedelic drug area.

#124   META-DOB;   5-BROMO-2,4-DIMETHOXYAMPHETAMINE

SYNTHESIS: The reaction of 2,4-dimethoxyamphetamine (2,4-DMA) with elemental bromine proceeded directly to the formation of 5-bromo-2,4-dimethoxyamphetamine which was isolated as the hydrobromide salt with a melting point of 204.5-205.5 °C and in a 67% yield. A mp of 180-181 °C has also been published.

DOSAGE: 50 - 100 mg.

DURATION: 5 - 6 h.

EXTENSIONS AND COMMENTARY: There is very little synthetic information available, and some of it is contradictory. The initial human report in the medical literature says only that a dosage of about 100 milligrams produced effects that were similar to those produced by MDA. Both the quality of the experience and the potency of the compound have been modified in more recent publications by the originators of this compound. A 40 milligram dose, after an induction period of an hour, produced a vague uneasiness that was interpreted originally as a threshold psychedelic effect. At doses in the 60 to 90 milligram range, there were produced feelings of anxiety and paranoid fantasies, and distinct toxic signs such as flushing, palpitations, and occasional nausea, vomiting and diarrhea. Any psychedelic effects seem to have been blurred by the more obvious toxic actions of the drug. I have been told that their final conclusion was that the drug appears toxic in the 50 to 60 milligram range. I have not personally explored this positional isomer of DOB.

The positional isomer of DOB with the bromine in the ortho-position is 4,5-dimethoxy-2-bromoamphetamine and is called, not surprisingly, ORTHO-DOB. It has been made by the condensation of 2-bromo-4,5-dimethoxybenzaldehyde with nitroethane to give 1-(2-bromo-4,5-dimethoxyphenyl)-2-nitropropene with a mp of 105-106 °C. Reduction to the amphetamine had to be conducted at a low temperature and using only an equimolar amount of lithium aluminum hydride, to minimize reductive removal of the bromo group. The hydrochloride salt of 2-bromo-4,5-dimethoxyamphetamine (ORTHO-DOB) had a mp of 214-215.5 °C, and the hydrobromide salt a melting point of 196-197 °C or of 210 °C. Both have been reported. The yield from the direct bromination of 3,4-DMA was apparently very bad. I do not think that the compound has ever gone into man.

There are three other dimethoxyamphetamine isomers known, and each has been explored chemically as to its reactivity with elemental bromine. With 2,3-DMA, a mixture of the 5-Br-2,3-DMA and 6-Br-2,3-DMA was formed; with 2,6-DMA, 3-Br-2,6-DMA was formed; and with 3,5-DMA, a mixture of 2-Br-3,5-DMA and the 2,6-dibromo product was produced. The bromination of 2,5-DMA is, of course, the preferred procedure for the synthesis of 4-Br-2,5- DMA, or DOB, q.v. None of these positional isomers has ever been put into man, but 3-Br-2,6-DMA and the iodo-counterpart have been explored as potential radio-fluorine carriers into the brain. This is all discussed in the 3,4-DMA recipe.

#125   META-DOT;   2,4-DIMETHOXY-5-METHYLTHIO-AMPHETAMINE

SYNTHESIS: To 27 g 1,3-dimethoxybenzene that was being well stirred, there was added, dropwise, 29 g concentrated H_2SO_4 over a period of 15 min. Stirring was continued for 1 hour, and then the mixture was poured slowly into 250 mL of saturated aqueous K_2CO_3. The precipitate that formed was removed by filtration, and dried at 125 °C to give 59.6 g crude potassium 2,4-dimethoxybenzenesulfonate. This was finely ground, and 30 g of it was treated with 35 g of $POCl_3$ and the mixture heated on the steam bath for 2 h. This was cooled to room temperature, and then poured over 300 mL crushed ice. When all had thawed, this was extracted with 2x150 mL Et_2O. The extracts were pooled, washed with saturated brine, and the solvent removed under vacuum to give a residue which solidified. There was thus obtained 14.2 g 2,4-dimethoxybenzenesulfonyl chloride as white solids with a mp of 69-72 °C. Heating of a small portion with concentrated ammonium hydroxide gave the corresponding sulfonamide which, on recrystallization from EtOH, produced white needles with a mp of 165.5-166.5 °C.

To a stirred and gently refluxing suspension of 11 g LAH in 750 mL anhydrous Et_2O, there was added 13.2 g 2,4-dimethoxybenzenesulfonyl chloride in an Et_2O solution. The refluxing was maintained for 48 h then, after cooling externally with ice water, the excess hydride was destroyed by the slow addition of 600 mL of 10% H_2SO_4. The phases were separated, and the aqueous phase extracted with 2x200 Et_2O. The organics were pooled, washed once with 200 mL H_2O, and the solvent removed under vacuum. The residue was dried azeotropically through the addition and subsequent removal of CH_2Cl_2. Distillation of the residue provided 8.0 g 2,4-dimethoxythiophenol as a colorless oil, boiling at 89-92 °C at 0.5 mm/Hg.

To a solution of 7.8 g 2,4-dimethoxythiophenol in 40 mL absolute EtOH there was added a solution of 4 g 85% KOH in 65 mL EtOH. This was followed by the addition of 5 mL methyl iodide, and the mixture was held at reflux for 30 min.

This was poured into 200 mL H_2O, and extracted with 3x50 mL Et_2O. The pooled extracts were washed once with aqueous sodium hydrosulfite, then the organic solvent was removed under vacuum. The residue was distilled to give 8.0 g of 2,4-dimethoxythioanisole as a colorless oil with a bp of 100-103 °C at 0.6 mm/Hg.

To a mixture of 15 g $POCl_3$ and 14 g N-methylformanilide that had been warmed briefly on the steam bath there was added 7.8 g of 2,4-dimethoxythioanisole. The reaction was heated on the steam bath for an additional 20 min and then poured into 200 mL H_2O. Stirring was continued until the insolubles had become completely loose and granular. These were removed by filtration, washed with H_2O, sucked as dry as possible, and then recrystallized from boiling MeOH. The product, 2,4-dimethoxy-5-(methylthio)benzaldehyde, was an off-white solid weighing 8.6 g. It could be obtained in either of two polymorphic forms, depending on the concentration of aldehyde in MeOH at the time of crystal appearance. One melted at 109-110 °C and had a fingerprint IR spectrum including peaks at 691, 734, 819 and 994 cm^{-1}. The other melted at 124.5-125.5 °C and had major fingerprint peaks at 694, 731, 839 and 897 cm^{-1}. Anal. $(C_{10}H_{12}O_3S)$ C,H.

A solution of 8.2 g 2,4-dimethoxy-5-(methylthio)benzaldehyde in 30 mL nitroethane was treated with 1.8 g anhydrous ammonium acetate and heated on the steam bath for 4 h. Removal of the excess nitroethane under vacuum gave a colored residue which crystallized when diluted with MeOH. Recrystallization of the crude product from boiling EtOH gave, after filtration, washing and air drying to constant weight, 8.3 g 1-(2,4-dimethoxy-5-methylthiophenyl)-2-nitropropene with a mp of 112-113 °C. Anal. $(C_{12}H_{15}NO_4S)$ C,H,N.

A suspension of 6.5 g LAH in 250 mL anhydrous THF was placed under a N_2 atmosphere and stirred magnetically and brought to reflux. There was added, dropwise, 8.0 g of 1-(2,4-dimethoxy-5-methylthiophenyl)-2-nitropropene in 50 mL THF. The reaction mixture was maintained at reflux for 18 h. After being brought to room temperature, the excess hydride was destroyed by the addition of 6.5 mL H_2O in 30 mL THF. There was then added 6.5 mL of 3N NaOH, followed by an additional 20 mL H_2O. The loose, white, inorganic salts were removed by filtration, and the filter cake washed with an additional 50 mL THF. The combined filtrate and washes were stripped of solvent under vacuum yielding a residue that was distilled. The free base boiled at 125-128 °C at 0.1 mm/Hg and was a white oil which solidified on standing. It weighed 5.1 g and had a mp of 47-48.5 °C. This was dissolved in 50 mL IPA, neutralized with concentrated HCl (until dampened universal pH paper showed a deep red color) and diluted with anhydrous Et_2O to the point of turbidity. There was a spontaneous crystallization providing, after filtering, washing with Et_2O, and air drying, 2,4-dimethoxy-5-methylthioamphetamine hydrochloride (META-DOT) with a mp of 140.5-142 °C. Anal. $(C_{12}H_{20}ClNO_2S)$ C,H,N.

DOSAGE: greater than 35 mg.

DURATION: unknown.

QUALITATIVE COMMENTS: (with 35 mg) "There was a vague awareness of something all afternoon, something that might be called a thinness. Possibly some brief cardiovascular stimulation, but nothing completely believable. This is a threshold level at the very most."

EXTENSIONS AND COMMENTARY: Again, as with the studies with ORTHO-DOT, it is apparent that the activity of META-DOT is going to be way down from the most interesting of these isomers, PARA-DOT (ALEPH-1, or just ALEPH). In the rectal hyperthermia assay (which calculates the psychedelic potential of compounds by seeing how they influence the body temperature of experimental animals in comparison to known psychedelics) the three DOT's were compared with DOM. And the results fell into line in keeping with the activities (or loss of activities) found in man. PARA-DOT was about half as active as DOM, but both ORTHO-DOT and the compound described here, META-DOT, were down by factors of 50x and 30x respectively. These animal studies certainly seem to give results that are reasonable with a view to other known psychedelic drugs, in that mescaline was down from DOM by a factor of more than 1000x, and LSD was some 33x more potent than DOM.

I have a somewhat jaundiced view of this rabbit rectal hyperthermia business. One is presumably able to tell whether a compound is a stimulant or a psychedelic drug by the profile of the temperature rise, and how potent it will be by the extent of the temperature rise. But the concept of pushing thermocouples into the rear ends of restrained rabbits somehow does not appeal to me. I would rather determine both of these parameters from human studies.

#126   METHYL-DMA; DMMA;   2,5-DIMETHOXY-N-METHYLAMPHETAMINE

SYNTHESIS: To a stirred solution of 28.6 g methylamine hydrochloride in 120 mL MeOH there was added 7.8 g 2,5-dimethoxyphenylacetone followed by 2.6 g sodium cyanoborohydride. HCL was added as needed to maintain the pH at about 6. The reaction was complete in 24 h, but was allowed to stir for another 3 days. The reaction mixture was poured into 600 mL H_2O, acidified with HCl (HCN evolution, caution) and washed with 3x100 mL CH_2Cl_2. Aqueous NaOH was added, making the solution strongly alkaline, and this was then extracted with 3x100 mL CH_2Cl_2. Removal of the solvent from the pooled extracts under vacuum gave 8.3 g of a clear, off-white oil that distilled at 95-105 °C. at 0.25 mm/Hg. The 6.5 g of colorless distillate was dissolved in 25 mL IPA, neutralized with concentrated HCl, and then diluted with anhydrous Et_2O to the point of cloudiness. As crystals formed, additional Et_2O was added in small increments, allowing clearing crystallization between each addition. In all, 200 mL Et_2O was used. After filtering, Et_2O washing, and air drying, there was obtained 6.2 g of 2,5-dimethoxy-N-methylamphetamine hydrochloride (METHYL-DMA) as fine white crystals with a mp of 117-118 °C. The mixed mp with 2,5-DMA (114-116 °C) was depressed to 96-105 °C. An alternate synthesis gave the same overall yield of an identical product, but started with 2,5-DMA. It required two synthetic steps. The free base amine was converted to the crystalline formamide with formic acid in benzene using a Dean Stark trap, and this intermediate was reduced to METHYL-MDA with LAH.

DOSAGE: above 250 mg.

DURATION: unknown.

QUALITATIVE COMMENTS: (with 250 mg) "There is a slight paresthesia at about 45 minutes, an awareness on the surface of the skin as if I had been touched by a cold draft of air. But nothing more. At three hours, I am completely out, if I was ever in. In the evening I assayed 120 milligrams of MDMA, and it barely produced a threshold effect, so the two materials might be seeing one another."

EXTENSIONS AND COMMENTARY: This is a difficult compound to pin down in the anthology of drugs. For some reason it has intrigued several independent, quiet researchers, and I have accumulated a number of interesting reports over the years. One person told me that he had felt nothing at up to 60 milligrams. Another had found a threshold at 50 milligrams, and had complete and thorough experiences at both 150 and 200 milligrams. Yet another person described two incidents involving separate individuals, with intravenous administrations of 0.2 mg/Kg, which would be maybe 15 or 20 milligrams. Both claimed a real awareness in a matter of minutes, one with a tingling in the genitalia and the other with a strange presence in the spine. Both subjects reported increases in body temperature and in blood pressure. Apparently the effects were felt to persist for many hours.

There is an interesting, and potentially informative, convergence of the metabolite of one drug with the structure of another. Under 4-MA, mention was made of a bronchodilator that has been widely used in the treatment of asthma and other allergenic conditions. This compound, 2-methoxy-N-methylamphetamine is known by the generic name of methoxyphenamine, and a variety of trade names with Orthoxine (Upjohn) being the best known. The typical dosage of methoxy-phenamine is perhaps 100 milligrams, and it may be used several times a day. It apparently produces no changes in blood pressure and only a slight cardiac stimulation. And one of the major metabolites of it in man is the analogue with a hydroxyl group at the 5-position of the molecule. This phenolic amine, 5-hydroxy-2-methoxy-N-methylamphetamine is just a methyl group away from METHYL-DMA; it could either be methylated to complete the synthesis, or METHYL-DMA could be demethylated to form this phenol. There is plentiful precedent for both of these reactions occuring in the body. It is always intriguing when drugs which show distinctly different actions can, in principle, intersect metabolically at a single structure. One wonders just what the pharmacology of that common intermediate might be.

Three additional N-methylated homologues of known psychedelics warrant mention, but do not really deserve separate recipes. This is because they have had only the most cursory assaying, which I have learned about by personal correspondence. All three were synthesized by the reduction of the formamide of the parent primary amine with LAH. METHYL-TMA (or N-methyl-3,4,5-trimethoxy-amphetamine) had been run up in several trials to a maximum of 240 milligrams, with some mental disturbances mentioned only at this highest level. METHYL-TMA-2 (or N-methyl-2,4,5-trimethoxyamphetamine) had been tried at up to 120 milligrams without any effects. METHYL-TMA-6 (or N-methyl-2,4,6- trimethoxyamphetamine) had been tried at up to 30 milligrams and it, too, was apparently without effects. These are reports that I have heard from others, but I have had no personal experience with them. Those that I can describe from personal experience are entered separately as recipes of their own. And there are many, many other N-methyl homologues which have been prepared and characterized in the literature, and have yet to be tasted. So far, however, the only consistent thing seen is that, with N-methylation, the potency of the psychedelics is decreased, but the potency of the stimulants appears to be pretty much maintained.

#127   METHYL-DOB;   4-BROMO-2,5-DIMETHOXY-N-METHYLAMPHETAMINE

SYNTHESIS: To a solution of 6.0 g of the free base of 2,5-dimethoxy-N-methyl-amphetamine (see recipe under METHYL-DMA) in 30 mL glacial acetic acid there was added, dropwise and with good stirring, a solution of 5.5 g bromine in 15 mL acetic acid. The reaction became quite warm, and turned very dark. After stirring an additional 45 min, the mixture was poured into 200 mL H_2O and treated with a little sodium hydrosulfite which lightened the color of the reaction. There was added 20 mL concentrated HCl, and the reaction mixture was washed with 2x100 mL CH_2Cl_2 which removed most of the color. The aqueous. phase was made basic with 25% NaOH, and extracted with 3x100 mL CH_2Cl_2. The removal of the solvent from the pooled extracts under vacuum gave 1.8 g of an oil which was dissolved in 10 mL IPA, neutralized with concentrated HCl, and diluted with 100 mL anhydrous Et_2O. No crystals were obtained, but rather an oily and somewhat granular insoluble lower phase. The Et_2O was decanted, and the residue washed by grinding up under 3x100 mL Et_2O. The original decanted material was combined with the three washes, and allowed to stand for several h. The product 4-bromo-2,5-dimethoxy-N-methylamphetamine hydrochloride (METHYL-DOB) separated as fine white crystals which weighed, after filtering and air drying, 0.3 g and had a mp of 149-150 °C. The Et_2O-insoluble residue finally set up to a pale pink mass which was finely ground under a few mL acetone. Filtration and air drying gave a second crop of product as 0.9 g of pale lavender solids, with a mp of 143-145 °C.

DOSAGE: greater than 8 mg.

DURATION: probably rather long.

QUALITATIVE COMMENTS: (with 8.0 mg) "At an hour and twenty minutes, I was suddenly quite light headed. An hour later I must say that the effects are real, and generally good. I am spacey — nothing tangible. And a couple of hours yet later I am still aware. My teeth are somewhat rubby, and as things have been pretty steady for the last three hours, this will prove to be long lasting. There are a lot of physical effects that may be kidding me into providing myself some of the mental. At the sixth hour, I find that this is almost entirely physical. My teeth are tight, there is a general physical tenseness, my reflexes seem exaggerated, and my eyes are quite dilated. All of these signs are lessened by the eighth hour, and do not interfere with sleep at the twelfth hour. There is no desire to proceed any further, at least at the present time. Mental (+) physical (++). Next day, slight impression of persistence of toxicity."

(with 10 mg) "Nothing psychedelic, but awfully hard on the bod. The next day (24 hours later) I had a severe response to 5 milligrams of psilocybin."

EXTENSIONS AND COMMENTARY: The mention above, of the 10 milligrams of METHYL-DOB followed by 5 milligrams of psilocybin, leads to some interesting speculation. The usual pattern that is seen when two psychedelic drugs are taken too closely together is that the second experience is less effective than would have been expected. This is the property that is called tolerance, and it is frequently seen in pharmacology. The two exposures may be to a single drug, or they may be to two different drugs which usually have some properties in common. It is as if the spirit of the receptor site had become a little tired and needed a while to rest up and recuperate. When there is a demand for a repeat of full effectiveness, the user will customarily increase the dosage of the drug that is used. It is one of the built-in protections, in the area of psychedelics that, after one experience, you must wait for a period of time to lose the refractoriness that has set in.

The measure of the degree of tolerance that can be shared between different drugs, called cross-tolerance, can be used as an estimate of the similarities of their mechanisms of action. In other words, if A and B are somehow seen by the body as being similar, then a normally effective dose of A will make a next-day's normally effective dose of B weaker than expected. Or not active at all. And B will do the same job on A. If two drugs are different in their ways of doing things in the body, there is most often no cross-tolerance seen. This was described for MDMA and MDA, and is the basis of the argument that they act by distinctly separate mechanisms. A person who used what would be held as an active dose of MDMA for several days lost all response to the drug. He was tolerant to its effects. But an exposure to an effective dose of MDA at the time that tolerance to MDMA was complete, provided a normal response to the MDA. The drugs are not cross-tolerant and the body recognizes them as distinct individuals.

But for one drug to promote, or to exaggerate, the effect of another is called potentiation, and can be a clue to the dynamics going on in the brain or body. Here, admittedly in only a single report, METHYL-DOB had somehow sensitized the subject to a rather light dosage of psilocybin. But there have been other reports like this that I have heard of, from here and there. I have been told of an experiment with the dextro-isomer of DOM (this is the inactive optical isomer) at a level that was, not surprisingly, without any effects. The researcher had a severe reaction the following day with what was referred to as "poor" hashish. A similar form of potentiation has been commented upon under the recipe for TOMSO, where an inactive drug, and a most modest amount of alcohol, add together to create an unexpectedly intense intoxication. But note that in each of these cases, it is a phenethylamine interacting with a non-phenethylamine (psilocybin is an indole, hashish is a non-alkaloid terpene thing, and alcohol is, well, alcohol).

The bottom line with METHYL-DOB is, as with the other N-methylated psychedelics, that it is way down in potency, and probably not worth pursuing.

#128   METHYL-J;   MBDB;   EDEN;   2-METHYLAMINO-1-(3,4-METHYLENEDIOXYPHENYL)BUTANE;   N-METHYL-1-(1,3-BENZODIOXOL-5-YL)-2-BUTANAMINE

SYNTHESIS: A solution of 0.12 g mercuric chloride in 180 mL H_2O was added to 5 g aluminum foil that had been cut into 1 inch squares, and amalgamation allowed to proceed for 0.5 h. The gray cloudy aqueous phase was decanted, and the resulting aluminum washed with 2x200 mL H_2O.

After shaking as dry as possible, there was added, in sequence, a solution of 7.6 g methylamine hydrochloride in an equal weight H_2O, 23 mL IPA, 18.3 mL 25% NaOH, 6.72 g 1-(3,4-methylenedioxyphenyl)-2-butanone (see under the recipe of J for its preparation), and finally 44 mL additional IPA. The mixture was occasional swirled, and cooled externally as needed to keep the temperature below 50 °C. After the reduction was completed (no metallic aluminum remaining, only gray sludge), it was filtered and the residues washed with MeOH. The combined filtrate and washes were stripped of organic volatiles under vacuum, the residue treated with 100 mL Et_2O, and this was extracted with 2x50 mL 3 N HCl. After washing the pooled aqueous extracts with 3x100 mL CH_2Cl_2, they were made basic with an excess of 25% NaOH and extracted with 5x50 mL CH_2Cl_2. Drying of these extracts with anhydrous $MgSO_4$ and removal of the solvent gave a residue that was distilled at 88 °C at 0.08 mm/Hg to give a colorless oil that was dissolved in IPA and neutralized with concentrated HCl. The solids that separated were removed by filtration, Et_2O washed, and air dried to provide 6.07 g 2-methylamino-1-(3,4-methylenedioxyphenyl)butane hydrochloride (METHYL-J or MBDB) as white crystals with a mp of 156 °C. Anal. $(C_{12}H_{18}ClNO_2)$ C,H,N. Reductive amination of the butanone with methylamine hydrochloride in MeOH, employing sodium cyano-borohydride, gave an identical product but in a smaller yield.

DOSAGE: 180 - 210 mg.

DURATION: 4 - 6 h.

QUALITATIVE COMMENTS: (with 210 mg) "Generally very, very friendly, very quiet effect. I can read easily, but looking at pictures in most books is relatively meaningless. Distinct de-stressing effect, to the point where it's too much trouble to set out to do anything at all, really. There is just no drive, and it isn't even bothersome to be missing it. Do I like it? Yes, very much. Feel that I've just begun to explore it, though. Would I consider this material in therapy? Well, sure, it's worth trying. Destressing would be excellent, and better than MDMA in some ways, but the empathy and intuition levels have yet to be explored in a therapy setting. I feel that they may be somehow lower."

(with 210 mg) "Onset rapid. Alert 20 minutes, and to a +2.5 at 30 to 35 minutes. No physical symptoms, i.e., teeth clench, no stomach problems. Good visual enhancement; eyes open — bright colors — no visuals with eyes closed. No 'cone of silence' that I get with MDMA (and enjoy), otherwise I'm not sure I could tell which was which if I took them blind."

(with 210 mg and a 50 mg supplement) "Tasted perfectly rotten. Suspect I was getting some type of alert in 5 minutes (I often get one quickly with MDMA) and at 30 minutes, a full blown high developed rather abruptly. It would be difficult to describe the high. I suspect it is the lack of language for the phenomenon. I would describe it somewhat like an alcohol high without the disabling side effects of confusion, slurring, staggering and etc. The high never got any more intense than at that 30 minute point and with a noticeable drop in another hour, I took a 50 mg supplement. I enjoyed the high. I relaxed with the material. However, it did not seem to have the same qualities as MDMA, in that it was not as stimulating, and it had very little visual activity. I talked with others, but found it easy to lie down and relax. There was some jaw-clenching towards the end, and I had considerable nystagmus at the peak which I could control. After the experience, I did not want to drink alcohol very much (sell it as a substitute for EtOH!).''

(with 210 mg and a 70 mg supplement) "I begin to feel the rush at 20 minutes, increasing rapidly. Very much like MDMA, only more intense intoxication. Otherwise same symptoms: intense euphoria that I call a feeling of grace, soft skin, voices, youthful appearance, animated discussions, feelings of great closeness to others. I start to drop noticeably at less than an hour and a half into it, but I delayed a supplement until the hour and fifty minute point. It does not get me back to the original intoxication. However, it is very nice, very much like MDMA. Only difference is that there seems to be more quietness, less inclination to talk than with an MDMA supplement. My conclusion: Seems an excellent substitute for MDMA, Next time may try somewhat lower amount, supplement sooner."

EXTENSIONS AND COMMENTARY: An observer who was familiar with the outwardly apparent effects with groups experimenting with MDMA felt that, although most subjects commented favorably in their comparisons of METHYL-J with MDMA, there was lacking some of the spontaneity, the warmth, and the clear intimacy of the latter drug. The dosage range explored is remarkably tight, attesting to a consistency of response. The typical supplement used, if any, was 70 milligrams or less, just before the two hour point. This indicates a chronology similar to that of MDMA, and about two thirds the potency.

The arguments that weigh the use of the code name of MBDB against the use of METHYL-J are present in the recipe for BDB (or J). But what is the source of this H, I, J, K naming thing that I have called the Muni Metro?

First, a little bit of local color. In San Francisco, there is a public transportation called the S.F. Municipal Metropolitan System complex that has integrated an underground street-car system that emerges above ground and connects with a bus network. A number of the street-car lines fan across the city to the outer reaches which are called the Avenues. These lines are named by sequential letters. There is the J Church Street line, the K Ingelside line, the L Taraval line, the M Ocean line, and the N Judah. And in the pharmacological complex that involved the lengthening of the aliphatic chain, there were two coincidental benchmarks in the names that were proposed. Those without an alpha-substituent (no carbon atoms at the position alpha to the amine group, the phenethylamines) were originally called the H compounds. H stood for "homopiperonylamine." And the first of those with the alpha-ethyl group there (two carbon atoms at the position alpha to the amine group) was familiarly called "Jacobamine" in recognition of a famous chemist who had set the synthetic wheels in motion.

It is quite obvious, that with one carbon atom lying on that alpha-position, you are precisely half-way between no carbons and two carbons. And there was one letter of the alphabet that lies precisely half-way between an H and a J. So, an natural naming pattern developed. The I compounds were already pretty well known by names such as MDA and MDMA and MDE, so I, and METHYL-I, and ETHYL-I, didn't have any appeal. But for the new, the alpha-ethyl compounds, why not call them the J-compounds? If it has a methyl on the nitrogen it will be METHYL-J and if it has an ethyl group it will be ETHYL-J. And in the next longer group, the 3-carbon propyl group on the alpha-position becomes the K family, and the 4-carbon butyl group located there, the L family. Each with its METHYL and ETHYL prefixes, if the nitrogen atoms are substituted with a methyl or and ethyl group. *V'la, comme on dit en Français. Le système Muni Metro. Plus simple.*

#129 METHYL-K; 2-METHYLAMINO-1-(3,4-METHYLENEDIOXYPHENYL)PENTANE; N-METHYL-1-(1,3-BENZODIOXOL-5-YL)-2-PENTYLAMINE

SYNTHESIS: The Grignard reagent of butyl bromide was prepared in anhydrous Et_2O by the dropwise addition of 68 g n-butyl bromide to a well-stirred suspension of 14 g magnesium turnings in 500 mL anhydrous Et_2O. When the exothermic reaction had stopped, there was added a solution of 60 g piperonal in about 100 mL Et_2O, over the course of 1 h. After the exothermic addition was complete, the reaction mixture was held at reflux for several h, then cooled and decomposed by the addition of dilute HCl. The phases were separated, and the aqueous phase extracted with 2x75 mL CH_2Cl_2. The organics were combined and gave, after the removal of the solvents under vacuum, 84 g of 1-hydroxy-1-(3,4-methylenedioxyphenyl)pentane as a yellow liquid. This was used in the following dehydration step without further purification.

A mixture of 52 g of the crude 1-hydroxy-1-(3,4-methylenedioxyphenyl)-pentane and 2 g powdered $KHSO_4$ was heated with a flame until there was no more apparent generation of H_2O. The resulting dark, fluid oil was distilled at 100-110 °C at 0.3 mm/Hg to give 29.5 g of 1-(3,4-methylenedioxyphenyl)-1-pentene as a light yellow liquid. This was employed in the following oxidation step without further purification.

To 120 mL of 90% formic acid there was added, with good stirring, 15 mL H_2O, followed by 23 mL of 35% H_2O_2. To this mixture, cooled with an external ice bath, there was added a solution of 24 g crude 1-(3,4-methylenedioxyphenyl)-1-pentene in 120 mL acetone at a rate slow enough to keep the internal temperature from exceeding 35 °C. At the end of the addition, the temperature was brought up to 45 °C by heating briefly on the steam bath, and then the reaction mixture was allowed to stand and stir at ambient temperature for several h. All volatiles were removed under vacuum, with a bath temperature maintained at 45 °C. The residue was dissolved in 30 mL MeOH, then there was added 200 mL 15% H_2SO_4 and the mixture held on the steam bath for 1.5 h. There was then added an additional 300 ml H_2O, and this was extracted with 2x250 ml of a petroleum ether/EtOAc (5:1) mixture. The extracts were pooled, and the solvents removed under vacuum to give a residue that was distilled at 115-120 °C at 0.3 mm/Hg. This light yellow liquid weighed 13.5 g and was substantially pure 1-(3,4-methylenedioxyphenyl)-2-pentanone by TLC.

To 5.0 g of aluminum foil cut into 1 inch squares, there was added a solution of 150 mg $HgCl_2$ in 200 mL H_2O. The mixture was heated briefly until there were clear signs of active amalgamation, such as fine bubbling for the aluminum surfaces and the beginning of the formation of a gray, amorphous solid phase. The $HgCl_2$ solution was decanted off and the aluminum was washed with 2x200 mL additional H_2O. After shaking as dry as possible, there was added, in sequence and with good swirling agitation between each addition, 10 g methylamine hydrochloride in 10 mL H_2O, 27 mL IPA, 22 mL of 25% NaOH, 5.0 g 1-(3,4-methylene-dioxyphenyl)-2-pentanone, and finally an additional 50 mL IPA. The mixture was heated on the steam bath periodically to maintain the reaction rate at a vigorous boil. When all of the aluminum had been consumed, the cooled mixture was filtered and the solids washed with MeOH. The combined filtrate and washings were stripped of solvent under vacuum. The residue was dissolved in dilute H_2SO_4 and washed with 2x75 mL CH_2Cl_2. After making basic again with 25% NaOH, this was extracted with 2x100 mL CH_2Cl_2, and the pooled extracts were stripped of solvent under vacuum. The residue was distilled at 105-110 °C at 0.3 mm/Hg to give 2.7 g of a colorless liquid. This was dissolved in 15 mL IPA, neutralized with concentrated HCl, and diluted with 75 mL anhydrous Et_2O which allowed a delayed appearance of a fine white crystal. This was removed by filtration, Et_2O washed, and air dried to give 2.45 g 2-aminomethyl-1-(3,4-methylenedioxyphenyl)pentane hydrochloride (METHYL-K) as a white product with a mp of 155-156 °C. Anal. $(C_{13}H_{20}ClNO_2)$ C,H.

DOSAGE: greater than 100 mg.

DURATION: unknown.

QUALITATIVE COMMENTS: (with 100 mg) "There were no effects. I was busy and totally wound up and didn't sleep until 3 AM, but this was probably unrelated to the Me-K."

EXTENSIONS AND COMMENTARY: The well appears to be running dry, with a pentane chain as a basic skeleton. METHYL-J, at this level, was already showing a number of hints and clues, largely physical such as coldness in the feet and a slight mastoidal pressure, that activity was right around the corner. But METHYL-K gave no such hints. The unmethylated homologue, 2-amino-1-(3,4-methylenedioxy-phenyl)pentane (K), was also made, by the reductive amination of 1-(3,4-methylenedioxyphenyl)-2-pentanone with ammonium acetate and sodium cyanoborohydride in methanol. It was a white crystalline solid, mp 202-203 °C, but is given here in the comments only, as its human assaying had never even been initiated. Anal. ($C_{12}H_{18}ClNO_2$) C,H. The N-ethyl homologue, 2-ethylamino-1-(3,4-methylene-dioxyphenyl)pentane (ETHYL-K), is entered with its own recipe, on the other hand, since testing had been started with it.

And the longest chain that has been explored in this Muni Metro series is the six-carbon hexyl chain which is, quite logically, the L-series, sort of the end of the Taraval line (see under METHYL-J for an explanation). The central compound for all the L-compounds was the ketone 1-(3,4-methylenedioxyphenyl)-2-hexanone, which was prepared by the Grignard reagent of (n)-amyl bromide with piperonal to give 1-hydroxy-1-(3,4-methylenedioxyphenyl)hexane, dehydration of this with potassium bisulfate to the olefin, and oxidation of this with hydrogen peroxide and formic acid to the L-ketone which was an orange-colored liquid with a bp of 125-135 °C at 0.3 mm/Hg. This ketone was reductively aminated with ammonium acetate and sodium cyanoborohydride in methanol to produce 2-amino-1-(3,4-methylenedioxyphenyl)hexane hydrochloride (L) as a white crystalline product with a mp of 157-158 °C. Anal. ($C_{13}H_{20}ClNO_2$) C,H. And this ketone was reductively aminated with methylamine hydrochloride and amalgamated aluminum in isopropanol to produce 2-methylamino-1-(3,4-methylenedioxyphenyl)hexane hydrochloride (METHYL-L) as a white crystalline product with a mp of 139-141 °C. Anal. ($C_{14}H_{22}ClNO_2$) C,H. The reduction of this ketone in a similar manner with ethylamine hydrochloride produced 2-ethylamino-1-(3,4-methylenedioxy-phenyl)hexane (ETHYL-L). None of this series has yet been explored either as psychedelic or entactogenic materials.

#130 METHYL-MA; PMMA; DOONE; 4-MMA; 4-METHOXY-N-METHYLAMPHETAMINE

SYNTHESIS: A solution of 20 g methylamine hydrochloride in 150 mL hot MeOH was treated with 10.0 g 4-methoxyphenylacetone and stirred magnetically. After returning to room temperature, there was added 5.0 g sodium cyanoborohydride, followed by cautious addition of HCl as required to maintain the pH at about 6. The reaction was complete after a few days, and the mixture was poured into 800 mL H_2O. This was acidified with HCl (HCN evolution!) and washed with 3x75 mL CH_2Cl_2, which removed most of the yellow color. There was 25% NaOH added to make the reaction mixture strongly basic, and this was extracted with 3x75 mL CH_2Cl_2. The solvent was removed from the pooled extracts under vacuum, and the 10.3 g of residue distilled at 0.3 mm/Hg. The 9.7 g of colorless oil that distilled at 75-90 °C was dissolved in 50 mL IPA, neutralized with 4.5 mL concentrated HCl, and then diluted with 100 mL anhydrous Et$_2$O. There were generated glistening crystals of 4-methoxy-N-methylamphetamine hydrochloride (METHYL-MA or DOONE) that weighed, after washing with Et$_2$O and air drying to constant weight, 11.0 g and which had a mp of 177-178 °C. The same base can be made by the action of ethyl chloroformate on 4-MA in the presence of triethylamine to make the carbamate, or the action of formic acid to make the formamide. These can then be reduced with LAH to this same end product.

DOSAGE: greater than 100 mg.

DURATION: short.

QUALITATIVE COMMENTS: (with 110 mg) "One hour into it, my pulse was up over 100, and I was compulsively yawning. There was some eye muscle disturbance, a little like the physical side of MDMA, but there was none of its central effects. But all the hints of the cardiovascular are there. By the fourth hour, I am pretty much back to baseline, but the yawning is still very much part of it. I might repeat this, at the same level, but with continuous close monitoring of the body."

EXTENSIONS AND COMMENTARY: Why would there be interest in this particular compound? The track record from the comparison of active compounds that are primary amines, and their N-methyl homologues, has shown that, in general, the stimulant component might be maintained, but the "psychedelic" contribution is generally much reduced. MDMA is, of course, an exception, but then, that particular compound is a one-of-a-kind thing which simply defies all the rules anyway, and I drop it from this kind of reasoning. And as 4-MA is a pretty pushy stimulant with little if any sensory sparkle, why bother with the N-methyl compound at all?

For a completely silly and romantic reason. When the MDMA story became front-page news back in mid-1985, the cartoonist-author of Doonesbury, Gary Trudeau, did a two-week feature on it, playing it humorous, and almost (but not quite) straight, in a hilarious sequence of twelve strips. On August 19, 1985 he had Duke, president of Baby Doc College, introduce the drug design team from USC in the form of two brilliant twins, Drs. Albie and Bunny Gorp. They vividly demonstrated to the enthusiastic conference that their new drug "Intensity" was simply MDMA with one of the two oxygens removed. "Voila," said one of them, with a molecular model in his hands, "Legal as sea salt." And what is MDMA with one oxygen atom removed? It is 4-methoxy-N-methylamphetamine or METHYL-MA which, according to the twins, should give the illusion of substance to one's alter ego. So, I called it Doonesamine, or simply "DOONE" for short. Maybe that was also a homonym for Frank Herbert's science fiction book, "Dune," wherein the magical drug "spice" provided a most remarkable alteration of the user's state of consciousness.

This comic strip presentation was the first nationally distributed allusion to the term "designer drugs," and perhaps it lent unexpected support for the passage, just a year later, of the Controlled Substances Analogue Enforcement Act of 1986. This intentionally vague piece of legislation makes the giving of, or the taking of, or even the possession with the intent to take, any drug that in any way alters your state of consciousness, a felony. A shameful and desperate effort by the governmental authorities to maintain the image of control in a lost situation.

Enough editorial. Back to historic technicalities. In truth, METHYL-MA is a well studied drug, at least in animals. In both mice and rats, it is an exceptionally potent agent in creating the state of catatonia. Animal studies, prompted by the clandestine synthesis of METHYL-MA, have shown that there is indeed locomotor stimulation and some central effects, but these effects are somehow different than those of a simple amphetamine-like agent. The experimenter's conclusions, based on its structural resemblance to 4-MA and its proclivity to produce catatonia in some animal species and the ever-present possibility that there might be unsuspected neurochemical changes to be seen with its use, are that human experimentation should be discouraged. I have come to the same conclusion, but in my case this is based on a much more succinct observation: I tried it and I didn't like it.

A brief comment on two of the N,N-dimethylhomologues of methoxy-amphetamine. One was 4-methoxy-N,N-dimethylamphetamine, 4-MNNA. This material, made by the reductive amination of 4-methoxyphenylacetone with dimethylamine, was a colorless oil, which distilled at 70-85 °C at 0.3 mm/Hg. The corresponding 2-methoxy-N,N-dimethylamphetamine was similarly made. 2-MNNA was also a colorless oil and had the same bp. Both of them were fluorinated with ^{18}F labelled acetyl hypofluorite (3% and 6% yields respectively) but neither of them was pursued any further in the search for a brain blood flow indicator.

#131   METHYL-MMDA-2;   2-METHOXY-N-METHYL-4,5-METHYLENEDIOXYAMPHETAMINE

SYNTHESIS: A suspension of 17.4 g electrolytic elemental iron in 100 g glacial acetic acid was heated on the steam-bath until there were the first signs of bubbling and reaction, about 60 °C. There was then added, in small portions, a suspension of 9.2 g 1-(2-methoxy-4,5-methylenedioxyphenyl)-2-nitropropene (see under MMDA-2 for its preparation) in 40 g warm glacial acetic acid. The reaction was extremely exothermic. After the color had lightened as much as possible, there was added an additional quantity of iron sufficient to completely discharge the residual yellow color. Mechanical stirring was maintained as the reaction mixture was allowed to return to room temperature. All was poured into 800 mL H_2O, and the insolubles were removed by filtration. These were washed alternately with H_2O and with CH_2Cl_2, the combined filtrate and washes were separated, and the aqueous phase extracted with 3x100 mL CH_2Cl_2. All organics were combined, washed with 2x75 mL 5% NaOH (which removed most of the color) and the solvent removed under vacuum. The 8.7 g residue was distilled at 90-105 °C at 0.2 mm/Hg to give

6.7 g of 2-methoxy-4,5-methylenedioxyphenylacetone as a pale yellow oil.

To a magnetically stirred solution of 30 g methylamine hydrochloride in 150 mL warm MeOH, there was added 6.5 g 2-methoxy-4,5-methylenedioxyphenylacetone followed by 3.0 g sodium cyanoborohydride. Concentrated HCl was added as was required to keep the mixture at a pH of about 6. When the reaction was complete, it was added to 1 L H_2O and made strongly basic with 25% NaOH. This was extracted with 3x100 mL CH_2Cl_2, and the pooled extracts were, in turn, extracted with 2x100 mL dilute H_2SO_4. This aqueous phase was washed with CH_2Cl_2, made basic with NaOH, and extracted with 3x100 mL CH_2Cl_2. Removal of the solvent from these pooled extracts under vacuum gave 8.7 g of an amber oil. This was distilled at 110-125 °C at 0.25 mm/Hg to give 5.1 g of a colorless oil. This was dissolved in 30 mL IPA, neutralized with about 3 mL concentrated HCl, and diluted with 60 mL anhydrous Et_2O. The clear solution slowly deposited white crystals which were removed by filtration and air dried to give 4.2 g 2-methoxy-N-methyl-4,5-methylenedioxyamphetamine hydrochloride (METHYL-MMDA-2) with a mp of 168-169 °C. Anal. ($C_{12}H_{18}ClNO_3$) C,H.

DOSAGE: greater than 70 mg.

DURATION: unknown.

QUALITATIVE COMMENTS: (with 70 mg) "Maybe a threshold — pleasant but not possible to characterize it."

EXTENSIONS AND COMMENTARY: With the effective dosage of the unmethylated homologue being the range of 25 to 50 milligrams, this N-methyl compound is, as with the other N-methylated materials discussed here, again of reduced activity. The highest dose yet reported was 70 milligrams, and there is no way of estimating what miight be an active level nor, once there, what the quality of the effects might be.

This is the only MMDA analogue that has been explored as an N-methyl derivative. A more highly substituted analogue has also been made, the N-methyl derivative of DMMDA. Isoapiole (see its preparation under DMMDA) was oxidized with formic acid and hydrogen peroxide to the ketone (2,5-dimethoxy-3,4-methylenedioxyphenylacetone, a solid with a mp of 75-76 °C from methanol) which was reductively aminated with methylamine and amalgamated aluminum to give 2,5-dimethoxy-N-methyl-3,4-methylenedioxyamphetamine hydrobromide monohydrate (METHYL-DMMDA, or DMMDMA) as a white crystalline solid with a mp of 91-92 °C. The hydrochloride salt was a hygroscopic solid. Anal. $(C_{13}H_{22}BrNO_5)$ C,H. The above ketone has also been used in the synthesis of another methylated DMMDA, on the beta-carbon. This is described under DMMDA itself. DMMDMA has not yet been launched into an evaluation program, and I wouldn't be surprised if the needed dosage might be up there somewhere over 100 milligrams. I feel quite sure that the answers may be known in the near future. There is a surprisingly large number of inconspicuous chemical explorers out there all over the world, doing their synthetic thing in their private laboratories. They are truly the astronauts of inner space.

#132 MMDA; 3-METHOXY-4,5-METHYLENEDIOXY-AMPHETAMINE

SYNTHESIS: (from protocatechualdehyde) A solution of 18 g commercial protocatechualdehyde (3,4-dihydroxybenzaldehyde) in 200 mL warm acetic acid was filtered free of any insolubles, to provide a very dark but clear solution. With good stirring there was then added 20 g elemental bromine. The reaction spontaneously heated to about 30 °C and solids appeared in about 5 min. Stirring was continued for 1 h, and then the light gray solids that had formed were removed by filtration and lightly washed with acetic acid. These were air dried on the steam bath until free of acetic acid smell. The product, 3-bromo-4,5-dihydroxybenzaldehde, weighed 11.7 g and had a mp of 222 °C.

To a solution of 11.7 g 3-bromo-4,5-dihydroxybenzaldehyde in 36 mL DMSO there was added 29 g methylene iodide followed by 20.8 g anhydrous K_2CO_3. This was heated on the steam bath for 3 h, added to 1 L H_2O, made strongly basic with NaOH, then extracted with 3x100 mL CH_2Cl_2. These extracts were pooled, washed with H_2O, and the solvent removed under vacuum. The dark brown semi-solid residue was distilled with the major fraction (6.0 g) coming over at 120-130 °C at 0.3 mm/Hg. This, upon recrystallization from 35 g boiling MeOH, gave 1.3 g of 3-bromo-4,5-methylenedioxy-benzaldehyde as an off white crystalline solid with a mp of 123-124 °C.

A mixture of 2.2 g 3-bromo-4,5-methylenedioxybenzaldehyde and 3.6 mL cyclohexylamine in a distillation flask was heated to 100 °C to effect solution, and then with an open flame until the signs of H_2O evolution were evident. This was then placed under a hard vacuum to remove the generated water and excess cyclo-hexylamine, and the product distilled at 120-125 °C at 0.2 mm/Hg. There was obtained 2.4 g of the Schiff base of the aldehyde and the amine, melting at 86-96 °C. Recrystallization of an analytical sample from 5 volumes of MeOH gave 3-bromo-

4,5-methylenedioxybenzylidine-N-cyclohexylamine as a white solid with a mp of 97.5-98.5 °C. Anal. ($C_{14}H_{16}BrNO_2$) H; C: calcd, 54.20; found, 53.78.

A solution of 2.2 g 3-bromo-4,5-methylenedioxybenzylidine-N-cyclohexylamine (the above Schiff base) in 50 mL anhydrous Et_2O was placed in a He atmosphere, stirred magnetically, and cooled with a dry ice/acetone bath. A white fine crystalline phase appeared. There was then added 5.2 mL 1.55 M butyllithium in hexane (the fine solids dissolved) followed by 4.0 mL of tributyl borate. After returning to room temperature, the reaction was quenched with 20 mL of saturated aqueous ammonium sulfate. The Et_2O/hexane layer was separated, washed with additional ammonium sulfate solution, and then stripped of volatiles under vacuum. The residue was dissolved in 100 mL 50% MeOH, treated with 2 mL of 30% hydrogen peroxide and, after 15 min swirling, quenched with a solution of 10 g ammonium sulfate in 50 mL H_2O. This aqueous phase (pH about 8) was extracted with 2x50 mL CH_2Cl_2, the extract pooled and stripped of solvent under vacuum, and the residue dissolved in warm, dilute HCl. After all the residue had dissolved (a few min heating was sufficient), the solution was cooled to room temperature and extracted with 2x50 mL CH_2Cl_2. These organics were pooled and extracted in turn with 2x50 mL 5% NaOH. Acidification of the pooled aqueous fractions with HCl, followed by extraction with 2x50 mL CH_2Cl_2 gave, after evaporation of the solvent, a residue that was distilled at 140-150 °C at 0.25 mm/Hg to give 3-hydroxy-4,5-methylenedioxybenzaldehyde. This was recrystallized from toluene (40 mL/g) to give 0.46 g of an off-white product with a mp of 134-134.5 °C. Anal. ($C_8H_6O_4$) C,H.

A solution of 0.44 g 3-hydroxy-4,5-methylenedioxybenzaldehyde in 10 mL dry acetone was treated with 0.5 g methyl iodide and 0.5 g powdered anhydrous K_2CO_3, and was held at reflux for 6 h. All volatiles were stripped under vacuum, the residue dissolved in water, made strongly basic with NaOH, and extracted with 3x50 mL CH_2Cl_2. Removal of the solvent gave myristicinaldehyde (mp 133-134 °C) which, on recrystallization from hexane, gave a final yield of 0.42 g with a mp of 134-135 °C. Care must be taken with two sequential products that have identical mps. A mixed mp with the unmethylated phenol above is strong depressed, whereas that with an authentic sample is not.

A solution of 9.8 g myristicinaldehyde in 35 mL glacial acetic acid was treated with 5.3 mL nitroethane and 3.2 g anhydrous ammonium acetate, and heated on the steam bath for 1.5 h. It was removed, treated with H_2O with good stirring to just short of turbidity, seeded with product nitrostyrene, and allowed to come slowly to room temperature. The bright yellow solids that formed were removed by filtration, washed with a small amount of aqueous acetic acid, and sucked as free of solvent as possible. This material, pressed on a porous plate, had a mp of 107-110 °C. Recrystallization from 60 mL boiling EtOH gave, after filtering and air drying, 5.1 g of 1-(3-methoxy-4,5-methylenedioxyphenyl)-2-nitropropene as light yellow solids with a mp of 109-110 °C.

A suspension of 7.5 g LAH in 500 mL anhydrous Et_2O was magnetically stirred, and heated in an inert atmosphere to a gentle reflux. The condensing Et_2O

leached out a total of 9.8 g 1-(3-methoxy-4,5-methylenedioxyphenyl)-2-nitro-propene from a Soxhlet thimble in a shunted reflux condenser. This, in effect, added the nitrostyrene to the reaction medium as a warm saturated Et₂O solution. When the addition was completed, the refluxing was maintained for an additional 5 h, then the reaction mixture was cooled and the excess hydride destroyed by the addition of 400 mL 1.5 N H_2SO_4 (the first 20 mL a drop at a time and with very good stirring). The phases were separated, and sufficient saturated aqueous Na_2CO_3 was added to the aqueous phase to bring the pH up to about 6.0. This was heated to 80 °C and filtered through a coarse sintered glass funnel to remove some insoluble fines. The clear filtrate was brought up almost to a boil, and treated with a solution of 10.2 g of 90% picric acid in 110 mL boiling EtOH. Crystals of the picrate formed immediately at the edges, and as the reaction flask was cooled in an ice tub, the entire reaction set to a yellow mass of crystals. These were removed by filtration, washed sparingly with 80% EtOH, and air dried to give 14.0 g of the picrate salt of MMDA, with a mp of 182-184 °C. Recrystallization of a small sample from EtOH dropped this to 179-181 °C. This salt was treated with 30 mL 5% NaOH, and the red solution decanted from some insolubles. Additional H_2O and NaOH effectively dissolved everything, and the resulting basic aqueous phase was extracted with 3x50 mL CH_2Cl_2. The pooled extracts were stripped of solvent under vacuum, and the residue dissolved in 200 mL anhydrous Et₂O and saturated with anhydrous HCl gas. There was a heavy precipitation of white crystals, which were removed by filtration, Et₂O washed, and air dried to give 6.37 g 3-methoxy-4,5-methylenedioxyamphetamine hydrochloride (MMDA) with a mp of 190-191 °C. Anal. $(C_{11}H_{16}ClNO_3)$ Cl.

(from Oil of Nutmeg) The careful distillation of Oil of Nutmeg (or the Oil of Mace) allowed the isolation of a number of compounds in varying degrees of purity. The fraction that boiled in the 110-115 °C range at about 1.0 mm/Hg was myristicin (3-methoxy-4,5-methylenedioxyallylbenzene). It constituted some 7% of the original oil of commerce and, in its original isolated form, was obtained with a purity of 87%. The major contaminant was elemicin (3,4,5-trimethoxyallyl-benzene). A solution of 100 g myristicin in 100 g absolute EtOH was treated with 200 g solid KOH and heated on a steam bath overnight. Removal of the volatiles under vacuum, flooding the residue with H_2O, and extraction with 3x100 mL CH_2Cl_2 gave, after removal of the solvent from the combined extracts, a residue of crude isomyristicin (a mixture of the cis- and trans-isomers). This product was distilled, and the fraction boiling at 125-130 °C at 1 mm/Hg gave 63 g of isomyristicin as a pale yellow oil that spontaneously crystallized. The mp was 41.5-42.5 °C. Part of the losses associated with the purification of these solids was due to formation of the cis-isomer of isomyristicin, which was an oil.

A solution of 50 g isomyristicin in 300 mL dry acetone containing 24 g pyridine was vigorously stirred and cooled to 0 °C with an ice bath. To this there was added 54 g tetranitromethane which had been pre-cooled to 0 °C. Stirring was continued for exactly 2 min, and then the reaction was quenched by the addition of a cold solution of 16.8 g KOH in 300 mL H_2O. Stirring was continued until the temperature had again been lowered to near 0 °C. The product was removed by filtration. Extraction of the filtrate with CH_2Cl_2 and removal of the solvent provided additional nitrostryrene, for a combined yield of 50.7 g with a mp of 103 °C due to the presence of a small amount of free myristicinaldehyde. A recrystallization from MeOH produced 1-(3-methoxy-4,5-methylenedioxyphenyl)-2-nitropropene with a mp of 109-110 °C. This material was completely adequate for the above-described reduction to MMDA. The conversion of this nitropropene to myristicinaldehyde is an alternative to the lengthy synthesis given above), and can be used in the preparation of LOPHOPHINE.

A mixture of 50 g 1-(3-methoxy-4,5-methylenedioxyphenyl)-2-nitro-propene and 26 g racemic α-methylbenzylamine was heated on the steam bath. The mixture gradually formed a clear solution with the steady evolution of nitroethane. When the reaction became quiet, there was added a mixture of 20 mL concentrated HCl in 100 mL H_2O. The reaction mixture dissolved completely, and as the temperature continued to rise there was the abrupt solidification as the formed myristicinaldehyde crystallized out. This product was removed by filtration and, when combined with a second crop obtained by the hexane extraction of the filtrate, gave 36.9 g of myristicinaldehyde. The mp of 128-129 °C was raised to 133-134 °C by recrystallization from hexane.

DOSAGE: 100 - 250 mg.

DURATION: moderate.

QUALITATIVE COMMENTS: (with 100 mg) "I felt completely relaxed at one hour. Almost as if I was floating. There were no obvious effects on taste, and the relaxation and composed feeling is much like a small dose, maybe 20 mikes, of LSD. There was some dilation, and in the evening I was a little restless and slightly tired. I slept well, and awoke refreshed and happy."

(with 100 mg) "It seemed to take 45 minutes to work and then it came on very suddenly, as if my eyeballs were being pulled out and my whole head expanding. Soon a cold feeling set in with shivering — this was not unpleasant. My state in about two hours seemed to be one of empathy and passivity, compassion of an impersonal sort. The music sounded artificial and canned and tinny, in contrast to the voices, which sounded rich and full and finely articulated and melodious."

(with 150 mg) "We are on the beach at the river mouth drying seaweed, on split redwood. There is a slight nausea, slight cramps, and then my visual field starts to light up. Still vertigo but only with my eyes open, and heaviness and time stretches out; numbness in the chest as when an opiate is taken. There are geometric patterns, but the excess light on my closed eyelids interferes with this. A dance of the glittering diamond studded sea waves, increasing motion and beauty. More landscapes appear inside. This is a good introductory drug to the drugs of this class, to become familiar with the drug state in as gentle a fashion as possible. This substance seems to have a much gentler action than others of this class; perhaps more like cannabis or psilocybin. There is very little paranoia. I note hallucinations of two types: those which are strictly retinal and more minute and small and influenced by light and focused on the light ahead on the retina or lids; and the other, those deep in the visual tract and occiput which are larger and more global and dream-like and, when solid, are quite dramatic and unforgettable as in meditation."

(with 210 mg) "MMDA tastes awful. The bitter alkaloid taste is followed by a distinctively chemical laboratory flavor as if from old rubber tubing. Nothing seems to happen for about 45 minutes when rather suddenly an anvil seems to lower itself over your head; you feel disoriented, and tend to withdraw from social contact a little. The drug gives less feeling of being ill than mescaline. The effect definitely reaches a climax with a pleasant afterglow following. Apparently there are no profound motor coordination problems. MMDA yields that 'Sunday afternoon' feeling of desiring to lie down and enjoy life; a luxurious feeling of 'layback.' No enhancement of colors in visual scene (except for some greenish tinges in faces) but upon closing eyes hallucinations appear to be quite real in 3-D, like watching a movie. First these dreams appear in black and white, but later colors start appearing. Chartreuse and magenta first appear, then blue and finally red. First I had visions of large numbers on gaming tables, then people. MMDA appears to bring dreams to the conscious level; is a link between the subconscious and the conscious."

(with 225 mg) "I had a strange awareness of my hands in about 20 minutes — not a feeling in them as just that I was attracted to them somehow. Then I began to get fearful, an acute experience of aloneness. I lay face down (a depressed position for me). Next I was talking to the kids at school (an image) or to other teachers. This was very vivid. The scenes at school were more vivid that the real scenes around me here. Those people were much more real. I am actually very sleepy right now during the experiment. Of any experience I have had, this was most like a series of dreams easily remembered. When it was over, I felt as if I had had a long period of sleeping — I had gone to bed and had a series of dream-like states very vivid and colorful and real."

EXTENSIONS AND COMMENTARY: The phrase that had been used by several of the subjects in the early trials with MMDA, again and again, was "brain movies." Apparently the richest of the effects were to be had with the eyes closed. This is the compound that I had first completed in 1962, and had named it MMDA, and had begun the exploring of it when I heard that Dr. Gordon A. Alles, a professor of pharmacology at U. C. L. A. who had his own private laboratory in Los Angeles, had also synthesized it in 1962, had also named it MMDA, and had also begun exploring it. We made a date to meet and share ideas, and then he died, at the age of 62, in 1963.

This is a material that might be a contributing factor to the pharmacology of nutmeg. The major essential oil from that spice is myristicin, and it is the easiest source of MMDA. It has been reported that the passage of this oil through the liver of a rabbit will generate MMDA in that animal. The only difference between the two molecules, structurally, are the elements of ammonia. Myristicin plus ammonia gives MMDA. Another natural source of myristicin is Oil of Parsley, which is also an excellent source of apiole, mentioned under DMMDA. A rumor that had currency in the 1960's, that parsley could get you high, probably had its origins in the reports of myristicin being present, coupled with myristicin being the principal source of MMDA. The relationship to myristicin (an essential oil) led to the classifying of MMDA as a Essential Amphetamine. These relationships are expanded upon, under TMA.

At the time that the FDA issued its proclamation of dangerous drugs (in the mid-1960's), MMDA was being talked about, and in fact it had just become available commercially in England through the Koch Light Industries. But to my knowledge it had never appeared on the street, so its having being swept into the listings of evil drugs was simply a coincidence of bad timing. The close resemblance of initials between MMDA, and the currently notorious MDMA, has led to no small amount of confusion in the popular press. They remain totally separate and completely different drugs.

#133   MMDA-2;   2-METHOXY-4,5-METHYLENEDIOXY-AMPHETAMINE

SYNTHESIS: A solution of 11.5 g pellet KOH (85%) in 75 mL EtOH was treated with 25 g sesamol followed by 27 g methyl iodide. This was brought to reflux on the steam bath. Salt formation was apparent in 20 min, and refluxing was maintained for a total of 4 h. The solvent was removed under vacuum, and residue poured into 400 mL H_2O. This was acidified with HCl and extracted with 3x150 mL CH_2Cl_2. The pooled extracts were washed with 3x100 mL 5% NaOH, which removed most of the color. The solvent was removed under vacuum to provide 24.0 g of 3,4-methylenedioxyanisole as a pale amber oil.

A mixture of 56.4 g $POCl_3$ and 49.1 g N-methylformanilide was allowed to stand for 40 min and then it was poured into a beaker containing 64 g 3,4-methylenedioxyanisole. There was an immediate exothermic reaction with darkening and the generation of bubbles. This was heated on the steam bath for 1 h, then poured into 1 L H_2O with extremely vigorous stirring. The dark brown phase was quite opaque, and then there was a sudden lightening of color with the generation of a fine pale yellow solid. Stirring was continued for 2 h, then these crystals were removed by filtration. This crude product was recrystallized from 400 mL boiling MeOH yielding, after filtering, washing, and air drying to constant weight, 44.1 g 2-methoxy-4,5-methylenedioxybenzaldehyde with a mp of 110-111 °C. Only one positional isomer was visible in the final product by GC, but extraction of the original mother liquors with CH_2Cl_2 produced, after evaporation of the solvent under vacuum, 2 g of a red oil that showed two earlier peaks on OV-17. These were consistent with about 1% of each of the two alternate positional isomers that could result from the Vilsmeier formylation reaction.

A solution of 43 g 2-methoxy-4,5-methylenedioxybenzaldehyde in 185 g nitroethane was treated with 9.3 g anhydrous ammonium acetate and heated on the steam bath for 4.5 h. The excess nitroethane was removed under vacuum to give a residue that spontaneously crystallized. These solids were washed out mechanically with the aid of 200 mL cold MeOH, and the brilliant orange crystals recovered by filtering and air drying to constant weight. There was obtained 35.7 g 1-(2-methoxy-4,5-methylenedioxyphenyl)-2-nitropropene with a mp of 166-167 °C. This was not improved by recrystallization from IPA. Evaporation of solvent from the methanolic washes gave yellow solids (4.6 g melting at 184-186 °C) which, on recrystallization from THF/hexane, melted at 188-190 °C. This showed a molecular weight of 416 by chemical ionization mass spectroscopy (isobutane at 0.5 torr) and is the $C_{20}H_{20}N_2O_8$ adduct of one molecule each of nitrostyrene, aldehyde, and ammonia that frequently appears as a very insoluble impurity in aldehyde-nitroethane condensations that are catalyzed by ammonium acetate.

To a refluxing suspension of 36 g LAH in 1 L anhydrous THF under an inert atmosphere, there was added 44.3 g 1-(2-methoxy-4,5-methylenedioxy-phenyl)-2-nitropropene in hot THF. The solubility was very low, so that it was necessary to use a heat lamp on the dropping funnel to maintain a clear solution for addition. The addition required 2 h and the reflux was maintained for 36 h. The reaction mixture was then cooled in an ice bath and there was added, in sequence and commensurate with heat evolution, 36 mL H_2O, 36 mL 15% NaOH, and finally 108 mL H_2O. The granular solids were removed by filtration and washed with THF. The combined filtrate and washes were stripped of solvent under vacuum yielding 58.8 g of a pale amber oil. This was dissolved in 100 mL IPA, neutralized with concentrated HCl (20 mL was needed) and diluted with 500 mL anhydrous Et_2O. More IPA was required to keep an oil phase from appearing. After the crystalline product was completely formed, it was removed by filtration, washed with IPA/Et_2O, and finally with Et_2O. Air drying gave 31.1 g of 2-methoxy-4,5-methylenedioxy-amphetamine hydrochloride (MMDA-2) with a mp of 186-187 °C.

DOSAGE: 25 - 50 mg.

DURATION: 8 - 12 h.

QUALITATIVE COMMENTS: (with 25 mg) "Had some not-too-pleasant jangly effects — this is not the smoothest of drugs. Duration: onset at 1 1/2 hours (dose after lunch), acute 3 to 4 hours, seconal at 11 hours to stop residual effects so I could sleep. Occasionally from 5 to 10 hours acute abdominal distress, resembling gas pains but unable to defecate. Abdominal muscles tight and hard. This occurred for about 15 minutes every hour or so. Rather unpleasant."

(with 30 mg) "There was the first subtle note at 45 minutes, and the slow development makes the changes easy to assimilate, but difficult to quantitate. My awareness is truly enhanced. Nothing is distorted, so there can be no misrepresentation as a result. This would be a good material to introduce someone to the slow-on slow-off type of experience. It would be impossible for any person, at this level, on this drug, to have a bad experience. This is very much like a slow MDA, perhaps 80 milligrams of it, and fully as controllable. The N-methyl of this is a must."

(with 40 mg) "The chemical is primarily a visual enhancer with only an extremely modest amount of visual distortion. The retinal activity was of a minor and non-threatening nature. The chemical seemed to facilitate empathic communication and the emotions felt strong and clean. Conversation flowed easily, without inhibitions or defensiveness. Anorexia accompanied experience. There was no impotence. There was some restless movement which dissipated with exercise (walking and playing frisbee). Next day woke feeling energetic, no muscular stiffness, alert. I would repeat this experience."

(with 50 mg) "I was coming on within 40-60 minutes, easy and slow, but the body was +3 before the mind. The mental was strange for the first 2-3 hours — I called it 'High Sierras' — realistic, dispassionate, not kind. Some dark areas are persistent. Watched last half of Circus of Dr. Lao and the whole feeling changed from pornographic to erotic. Delightful. Some fantasy. On coming down, sleep was difficult. The body feels unexpectedly depleted. Rubber legs and handwriting jerky."

EXTENSIONS AND COMMENTARY: A comparison of this material to MDA was often made by subjects who were familiar with both. But it is hard to separate that which is intellectualized from that which is felt. An awareness of the chemical structure immediately shows, of course, the close resemblance. There is the complete MDA molecule, with the addition of a methoxy group. And for the non-chemist, the name itself (MMDA-2) represents the second possible methoxy-MDA. Certainly one property that is shared with MDA is the broad variety of opinions as to the quality of its action. Some like it much, and some like it not at all. The N-methyl homologue was indeed made, for direct evaluation in comparison to N-methyl MDA (which is MDMA).

The phenethylamine analog of MMDA-2 has been prepared by the condensation of the above benzaldehyde with nitromethane (in acetic acid with ammonium acetate catalyst, giving an equal weight of the nitrostyrene as deep orange crystals with a mp of 166-167 °C from ethyl acetate) followed by lithium aluminum hydride reduction (in ether). The product, 2-methoxy-4,5-methylene-dioxyphenethylamine hydrochloride (2C-2) melted at 218-219 °C. There were no effects observed at up to 2.6 milligrams, but no higher trials were made. The 4-carbon homologue was made similarly (from the aldehyde and nitropropane but using tert-butylammonium acetate as a reagent in 100% excess and isopropanol as solvent, giving orange crystals melting at 98-99 °C from methanol) followed by reduction (with lithium aluminum hydride in ether) to give 1-(2-methoxy-4,5-methylenedioxyphenyl)-2-aminobutane hydrochloride (4C-2) with a mp of 172-174 °C. This material has never even been tasted.

The Tweetio homologue of MMDA-2 has been tasted, however. This is 2-ethoxy-4,5-methylenedioxyamphetamine, or EMDA-2. The allyl ether of sesamol (3,4-methylenedioxy-allyloxybenzene) was rearranged to the 2-allyl phenol which was, in turn, converted to the ethyl ether. Reaction with tetranitromethane gave the nitrostyrene intermediate which had a mp of 120-121 °C. The final hydrochloride salt of EMDA-2 had a mp of 188-188.5 °C. At 135 milligrams, there have been reported eyes-closed visual phenomena, with intense colors. The overall duration is similar to MMDA-2 (some 10 hours) and there are reported sleep disturbances. At 185 milligrams, the feelings were intensified, there were "marvelous eyes-closed visuals (the colors were incredible), good concentration, but distinct body-tingles and rushes." The time span was about 12 hours from start to finish, but it proved to be impossible to sleep afterwards. This homologue is thus about a third the potency of MMDA-2.

#134   MMDA-3a;   2-METHOXY-3,4-METHYLENEDIOXY-AMPHETAMINE

SYNTHESIS: To a solution of 100 g of 2,3-dihydroxyanisole in 1 L dry acetone there was added 110 g of powdered anhydrous K_2CO_3 followed by 210 g of methylene iodide. This was brought up to a reflux on the steam bath. There was a sudden appearance of a solid phase, and then a gentle reflux was maintained for three days, during which time much of the heavy solid that initially formed had redissolved. The reaction mixture was filtered to remove the insoluble salts, and these were washed with hot acetone. The combined mother liquor and washes were stripped of solvent under vacuum, leaving a solid residue. This was leached with several portions of boiling hexane. These were pooled, and removal of the solvent under vacuum provided 53.6 g of 2,3-methylenedioxyanisole as white crystals with a sharp spicy smell.

A mixture of 120 g N-methylformanilide and 137 g $POCl_3$ was allowed to incubate at ambient temperature for 0.5 h, then there was added 53 g of crude 2,3-methylenedioxyanisole. The dark reaction mixture was heated on the steam bath for 2 h and then poured into a beaker filled with shaved ice. This was stirred until hydrolysis was complete, and the black, almost crystalline gunk that separated was removed by filtration. The 53.6 g of crude product was analyzed by GC using an ethylene glycol succinate column at 190 °C. Three peaks were apparent and had baseline separation. The major peak at 7.8 min constituted 82% of the product and was 2-methoxy-3,4-methylenedioxybenzaldehyde. A minor peak at 12.0 min represented 16% of the product and was the positional isomer 4-methoxy-2,3-methylenedioxybenzaldehyde. A trace component (2%) lay intermediate (at 9.5 min) and was myristicinaldehyde. The mps of the two major benzaldehydes were sufficiently different that they could serve as means of identification. The major product was obtained directly from the black gunk by repeated extraction with boiling cyclohexane which, upon removal of the solvent, gave 33.1 g of a yellow-colored product. This, upon one additional recrystallization from boiling cyclohexane, gave 24.4 g of 2-methoxy-3,4-methylenedioxybenzaldehyde as pale yellow crystals with a mp of 103-105 °C. The mother liquors were pooled and, after removal of all volatiles under vacuum, yielded an amber-colored solid that upon recrystallization provided a yellowish crystals. These, after yet another crystallization from cyclohexane, gave 4.1 g of 4-methoxy-2,3-methylenedioxybenzaldehyde with a mp of 85-86 °C. This latter isomer was used in the synthesis of MMDA-3b.

To a solution of 3.5 g 2-methoxy-3,4-methylenedioxybenzaldehyde in 14 g acetic acid there was added 1.4 g anhydrous ammonium acetate and 2.3 mL of nitroethane. The mixture was brought to reflux and held there for 35 min. It was then quenched by the addition of 40 mL H_2O, knocking out an orange, gummy solid. This was removed by filtration, and recrystallized from 50 mL boiling MeOH. After cooling for a few h in an ice bath, the bright yellow crystals were removed by filtration, washed with MeOH and air dried to constant weight, yielding 2.15 g 1-(2-methoxy-3,4-methylenedioxyphenyl)-2-nitropropene. The mp was 106-107 °C. Recrystallization from EtOH raised this mp to 109.5-110.5 °C.

A suspension of 2.2 g LAH in 300 mL anhydrous Et_2O under an inert atmosphere was brought to a gentle reflux. The reflux condensate was passed through a modified Soxhlet thimble containing 1.95 g 1-(2-methoxy-3,4-methylenedioxyphenyl)-2-nitropropene effectively adding it, over the course of 0.5 h, to the reaction mixture as a saturated Et_2O solution. The mixture was maintained at reflux for 16 h. After cooling to 0 °C with an ice bath, the excess hydride was destroyed by the addition of 1.5 N H_2SO_4. The phases were separated, and the aqueous phase washed with 2x100 mL Et_2O. To the aqueous phase there was added 50 g potassium sodium tartrate followed by sufficient 25% NaOH to raise the pH >9. This was then extracted with 3x100 mL CH_2Cl_2, and the solvent from the pooled extracts removed under vavuum. The residual white oil was dissolved in 250 mL anhydrous Et_2O, and saturated with anhydrous HCl gas. There was produced a crop of white microcrystals of 2-methoxy-3,4-methylenedioxyamphetamine hydrochloride (MMDA-3a) which was removed by filtration, washed with Et_2O, and air dried to a constant weight of 1.2 g. The mp was 154-155 °C.

DOSAGE: 20 - 80 mg.

DURATION: 10 - 16 h.

QUALITATIVE COMMENTS: (with 20 mg) "I became aware at about an hour, and an hour later I found myself suddenly caught up in the marvelous world of insects. Right alongside a pile of bricks I saw a measuring worm, and with great tenderness and patience I picked him up, observed his fore and aft 'feet' and finally replaced him and watched him acclimate himself. There was also a spider on the bricks, and I was compelled to watch him in action. I was grateful that I was not being observed. Time was moving slowly, and I felt I should intentionally move slowly, so as not to exhaust myself."

(with 40 mg) "This developed between one and two hours into it, and there were considerable body tremors. Talking directed the energy outwards, and I became aware of a visually sparkling world about me. I started dropping way too soon; it would have been interesting to have gone higher. By early evening I was left only with an awareness of some residual physical hypersensitivity, and there was light diarrhea. I am not at all sure just what to compare this drug to. It is gentle."

(with 60 mg) "There were visuals of a soft sort — things moved with eyes open, and with eyes closed the music was great. There seemed to be some lasting stimulation, but it didn't get in the way of sleeping. The next morning, however, I was still on. A good compound."

EXTENSIONS AND COMMENTARY: The term MMDA-3a has the feel of being complicated, but there is a reason for the code. As had been mentioned, MMDA was the initials for methoxy (the M) methylenedioxy (the MD) amphetamine (the A). And with a molecule of amphetamine there are six ways of sticking these two groupings on the aromatic ring. The numbers 1-6 had already been assigned to the six ways of sticking three methoxyl groups onto an amphetamine molecule (with the trimethoxyamphetamines, the TMA's) and I decided to hew to the same convention with the methylenedioxy counterparts. However, there are two #3's (the methoxy and the methylenedioxy can go onto the three oxygen atoms in a row in two different ways, whereas the three methoxys can go on in just one way) and there can be no #6 (since a methylenedioxy must, perforce, have two oxygens that are adjacent, and there are none to be so found in the 2,4,6-orientation of TMA-6). So, with two possible MMDA-3's it becomes reasonable, in fact essential, to name one of them "a" and the other "b". The "a" orientation occurs in nature as the essential oil croweacin, or 1-allyl-2-methoxy-3,4-methylenedioxybenzene. It thus can allow MMDA-3a to be classified as an Essential Amphetamine, since it can arise, in principle, by amination in the liver *in vivo*. But in the laboratory, croweacin is certainly not a practical starting material in this synthesis.

I have been told of a number of clinical trials that have explored MMDA-3a at considerably higher levels, but I have no explicit quotations to give, and the details are quite sketchy. Three trials at 80 milligrams, and one at 100 milligrams, all made comparisons, in both quantity and quality of the experience, to 100 micrograms of LSD. However, two events occurred that may or may not be related to these trials; one subject had a spontaneous peak experience five days after the experiment, and another made a symbolic suicide attempt.

And, as with MMDA-2, both the 2-carbon "phenethylamine" analogue and the 4-carbon "ARIADNE" analogue of MMDA-3a have been made. The phenethylamine analog was prepared by the condensation of 7.6 g of the above benzaldehyde with nitromethane (in acetic acid with ammonium acetate catalyst, giving 5.4 g of the nitrostyrene with a mp of 115.5-116.5 °C from methanol) followed by lithium aluminum hydride reduction (in ether). The product, 2-methoxy-3,4-methylenedioxyphenethylamine hydrochloride (2C-3a) melted at 143-145 °C. A series of subjective evaluations were made, and there are reports of marginal effects in the 40 to 120 milligram range. At 40 milligrams, perhaps the hint of a psychic energizer; at 65 milligrams, there was a pleasant mood elevation; at 80 milligrams, there was a brief paresthetic twinge noted at about the hour and a half point, and at 120 milligrams, about the same at one hour, and then nothing. The fact that there can be such a modest change of effect over a three-fold range of dosage suggests that this compound might have some merit as an anti-depressant. It would be interesting to know if it blocks serotonin reuptake!

The 4-carbon analog was made similarly (from the aldehyde and nitropropane but using tert-butylammonium acetate as a reagent in 100% excess and isopropanol as solvent, giving bright yellow crystals melting at 105.5-106.5 °C from 25 volumes of boiling methanol) followed by reduction (with lithium aluminum hydride in ether) to give 1-(2-methoxy-3,4-methylenedioxyphenyl)-2-aminobutane hydrochloride (4C-3a) with a mp of 183-185 °C with prior sintering at 173 °C. This material has been tasted at up to 3.5 milligrams with nothing noted. There have been no trials at any higher dose.

#135   MMDA-3b;   4-METHOXY-2,3-METHYLENEDIOXY-AMPHETAMINE

SYNTHESIS: A solution of 7.0 g of 98% pure (by GC) 4-methoxy-2,3-methylenedioxybenzaldehyde (see under MMDA-3a for its preparation) in 30 mL glacial acetic acid was treated with 5 mL nitroethane and 3 g anhydrous ammonium acetate, and heated on the steam bath for 3.5 h. H_2O was added to the hot solution to the point of turbidity, then it was allowed to cool to room temperature with occasional stirring. A modest crop of yellow crystals formed which were removed by filtration, washed with aqueous acetic acid and air dried to constant weight. There was obtauned 4.6 g of 1-(4-methoxy-2,3-methylenedioxphenyl)-2-nitropropene, with a mp of 95-102 °C. Recrystallization from EtOH tightened this to 97-101.5 °C. The infra-red spectrum is completely different from that of its positional isomer 1-(2-methoxy-3,4-methylenedioxyphenyl)-2-nitropropene.

A suspension of 7.0 g LAH in 1 L anhydrous Et_2O under an inert atmosphere was brought to a gentle reflux. The reflux condensate was passed through a Soxhlet thimble containing 6.15 g 1-(4-methoxy-2,3-methylenedioxyphenyl)-2-nitropropene which was effectively adding the nitropropene as a saturated solution. The mixture was maintained at reflux for 16 h. After cooling to 0 °C with an ice bath, the excess hydride was destroyed by the addition of 800 mL of 1.5 N H_2SO_4. The phases were separated, and the aqueous phase washed with 2x100 mL Et_2O. To this phase there was added 175 g potassium sodium tartrate followed by sufficient 25% NaOH to raise the pH >9. This was then extracted with 3x100 mL CH_2Cl_2, and the solvent from the pooled extracts removed under vacuum. The residual off-white oil weighed 5.4 g and was dissolved in 250 mL anhydrous Et_2O and saturated with anhydrous HCl gas. There was produced a crop of slightly sticky white solids that finally became granular and loose. These were removed by filtration, washed with Et_2O, and air dried to give 5.56 g of 4-methoxy-2,3-methylenedioxyamphetamine hydrochloride (MMDA-3b) with a mp of 196-199 °C. A small sample from propanol had a mp of 199-200 °C, and a sample from nitromethane/MeOH (5:1) had a mp of 201-202 °C.

DOSAGE: greater than 80 mg.

DURATION: unknown.

QUALITATIVE COMMENTS: (with 60 mg) "Definitely active. Qualitatively like MDA; quantitatively perhaps less."
     (with 80 mg) "No more effective than 60 mg."

EXTENSIONS AND COMMENTARY: And that's all there is known as to the activity of MMDA-3b in man. Very, very little. Nothing has ever been tried in excess of 80 milligrams that I know of, and the above trials were made over 20 years ago. There can be little argument that the 3b is less effective than the 3a, but no one can say by how much. The literature statement is that it is threefold less, but that was based on the relative responses at just-above-threshold levels. The effects here are hand-wavingly similar to those reported for MMDA-3a at 20 milligrams, but these are difficult to compare accurately as they were reported by different people. There have been absolutely no animal studies reported with MMDA-3b in the scientific literature. And neither the 2-carbon nor the 4-carbon analogues of MMDA-3b has even been prepared.

     The remaining MMDA-analogue that has been prepared, is the 2,3,6-isomer. The flow diagram started with sesamol (3,4-methylenedioxyphenol) which was methylated with methyl iodide, converted to the aldehyde using butyllithium and N-methylformanilide (putting the new group directly between the two oxygen atoms, giving 2,3-methylenedioxy-6-methoxybenzaldehyde), reaction with nitro-ethane to the nitrostyrene, and its reduction with lithium aluminum hydride in ether. The product, 6-methoxy-2,3-methylenedioxyamphetamine hydrochloride (MMDA-5) is practically unexplored in man. I have heard one report that 30 milligrams was modestly active, but not a particularly pleasant experience. Another person told me that he had tried 15 milligrams, but he neglected to mention if there had been any effects. I have not tried it myself. But, I have succumbed to the pressure of the experimental pharmacologists to give a number for the "Y-axis" of their animal behavior studies. So I said to myself, if this is active at 30 milligrams, and mescaline is active at 300 milligrams, why not say that it is 10x the activity of mescaline? So I did. But I have absolutely no confidence in that number.

And if the information on MMDA-5 is sparse, look at the positional isomer, MMDA-4, which I have discussed under its analogue TMA-4. Here nothing is known at all, since the compound itself is unknown. No one has yet found a way of making it.

#136   MME;   2,4-DIMETHOXY-5-ETHOXYAMPHETAMINE

SYNTHESIS: A solution was made of 166 g ethylvanillin (4-ethoxy-3-methoxy-benzaldehyde) in 600 mL glacial acetic acid and arranged so that it can be stirred continuously, magnetically, and cooled as needed with an external ice bath. There was then added a total of 218 g of 40% peracetic acid in acetic acid, at a rate that permitted the temperature to stay at 25 °C with the continuous application of the ice bath. The temperature should not drop below 23 °C (the reaction stops) but it absolutely cannot be allowed to exceed 29 °C (the reaction can no longer be controlled). The addition takes about 1.5 h.

At the end of the reaction, there was added 3 volumes of H_2O, and all acids were neutralized with solid K_2CO_3. The 3 or so L of black, gooey mess was extracted with 2x400 mL boiling Et_2O which, on pooling and evaporation, provided 60 g of a black oil which was a mixture containing mainly the intermediate formate and the product phenol. This was treated with 300 mL 10% NaOH, and heated on the steam bath for 1 h. After cooling, this was washed with 2x150 mL CH_2Cl_2 (discarded), acidified with HCl, and extracted with 3x200 mL Et_2O. The pooled extracts were washed with 2x200 mL saturated $NaHCO_3$, and then the Et_2O was removed under vacuum. The residual black oil, 41.3 g, was distilled at 1.0 mm/Hg to give a fraction boiling at 140-145 °C as a pale amber oil that set up as crystals. The weight of the isolated 4-ethoxy-3-methoxyphenol was 29.1 g. An analytical sample had a mp of 45.5-46 °C. This product can be used either for the synthesis of MME (see below) or for the synthesis of EME (see separate recipe). A solution of 0.5 g of this phenol, and 0.5 g methyl isocyanate in 10 mL hexane containing 1 mL CH_2Cl_2 was treated with three drops of triethylamine. In about 1 h, there was the spontaneous formation of white crystals of 4-ethoxy-3-methoxyphenyl N-methyl carbamate, with a mp of 104-105 °C.

A solution of 14 g of the distilled, solid 4-ethoxy-3-methoxyphenol in 20 mL MeOH was treated with a solution of 5.3 g KOH in 100 mL hot MeOH. There was then added 11.9 g methyl iodide, and the mixture was held at reflux temperature for 2 h. The reaction was quenched with 3 volumes H_2O, made strongly basic by the addition of 1 volume of 5% NaOH, and extracted with 2x150 mL Et_2O. Pooling the extracts and removal of the solvent under vacuum gave 9.7 g of 2,4-dimethoxy-1-ethoxybenzene as a clear, off-white oil that showed a single peak by GC. An acceptable alternate synthesis of this ether is the ethylation of 2,4-dimethoxyphenol, which is described in the recipe for TMA-4. The index of refraction was $n_D^{25} = 1.5210$.

A mixture of 17.3 g N-methylformanilide and 19.6 g $POCl_3$ was allowed to stand at room temperature until a strong red color had been generated (about 0.5 h). There was then added 9.2 g 2,4-dimethoxy-1-ethoxybenzene and the mixture was heated on the steam bath for 2 h. The black, viscous product was poured onto 800 mL cracked ice, and mechanically stirred. The deep color gradually faded to a yellow solution, and then yellow crystals began to form. After standing overnight, these were removed by filtration and sucked as dry as possible, yielding 16 g of a wet, crude product. This was dissolved in 100 mL boiling MeOH which, on cooling, deposited fluffy, white crystals of 2,4-dimethoxy-5-ethoxybenzaldehyde. The dry weight was 8.8 g and the mp was 107-108 °C. The mother liquor showed no isomeric aldehydes by GC, but there were small suggestions of isomers seen in the CH_2Cl_2 extracts of the original water filtration. A sample of 0.7 g of the aldehyde obtained as a second crop from the methanolic mother liquors was dissolved, along with 0.5 g malononitrile, in 20 mL hot EtOH. The addition of 3 drops of triethylamine generated the almost immediate formation of brilliant yellow crystals, 1.4 g after filtration and EtOH washing, with a mp of 134-135.5 °C. Recrystallization from toluene gave an analytical sample of 2,4-dimethoxy-5-ethoxybenzalmalononintrile with a mp of 135-136 °C.

A solution of 6.7 g 2,4-dimethoxy-5-ethoxybenzaldehyde in 23 g glacial acetic acid was treated with 3.3 g nitroethane and 2.05 g anhydrous ammonium acetate. The mixture was heated on the steam bath for 2.5 h. The addition of a little water to the cooled solution produced a gel which was a mixture of starting aldehyde and product nitrostyrene. The solvent was decanted from it, and it was triturated under MeOH, to provide a yellow solid with a mp of 76-84 °C. Recrystallization from 30 mL boiling MeOH gave, after filtering and air drying, 4.3 g of a yellow solid with a mp of 90-92 °C. There was still appreciable aldehyde present, and this was finally removed by yet another recrystallization from toluene. The product, 1-(2,4-dimethoxy-5-ethoxyphenyl)-2-nitropropene, was obtained as bright yellow crystals with a mp of 96-97 °C. The analytical sample was dried in vacuum for 24 h to completely dispel the tenacious residual traces of toluene. Anal. $(C_{13}H_{17}NO_5)$ C,H.

To a gently refluxing suspension of 1.6 g LAH in 120 mL anhydrous Et_2O

under a He atmosphere, there was added 2.1 g 1-(2,4-dimethoxy-5-ethoxyphenyl)-2-nitropropene by allowing the condensing ether to drip into a shunted Soxhlet thimble containing the nitrostyrene. This effectively added, dropwise, a warm saturated solution of the nitrostyrene to the reaction mixture. Refluxing was continued for 6 h, and after cooling the reaction flask to 0 °C the excess hydride was destroyed by the cautious addition of 1.5 N H_2SO_4. When the aqueous and Et_2O layers were finally clear, they were separated, and 40 g of potassium sodium tartrate was dissolved in the aqueous fraction. Aqueous NaOH was then added until the pH was >9, and this was then extracted with 3x200 mL CH_2Cl_2. Evaporation of the solvent under vacuum produced 1.6 g of an amber oil that was dissolved in 300 mL anhydrous Et_2O and saturated with anhydrous HCl gas. There was an immediate white blush, then there was the generation of an oily solid that upon further administration of HCl became a fine, loose white powder. This was removed by filtration, Et_2O washed, and air dried to give 1.6 g 2,4-dimethoxy-5-ethoxyamphetamine hydrochloride (MME) with a mp of 171-172 °C. Anal. ($C_{13}H_{22}ClNO_3$) C,H,N.

DOSAGE: 40 mg and above.

DURATION : probably 6 - 10 h.

QUALITATIVE COMMENTS: (with 40 mg) "At the one hour point there was a real threshold, and at the second hour, while I was walking down 24th Street, there was an honest 1+. By the third hour it was at, or just under a ++, with the earmarks of a possibly interesting collection of effects, were it just a bit more intense. I had unexpected diarrhea at hour #5, and by #6 I was mending, and by #8 I was largely down. The day was very encouraging, and this must be re-tried at 50 or 60 milligrams."

EXTENSIONS AND COMMENTARY: This is one of the very few compounds with which I actually risked (and took) the lives of experimental animals. I was still impressed by the scientific myth that pharmacological research wasn't really acceptable without animal support data. And I had access to an experimental mouse colony at the University. I injected one mouse with a dose of 300 mg/Kg., i.p. That sounds pretty scientific. But what it really means is that I picked up a mouse by the scruff of the back with my left hand, then turned my hand over so that the mouse was belly-up. I put the ring finger over a hind leg to keep things relatively immobile. Usually at this point there is a little urine evident where there had been none before. And I took a syringe equipped with a very fine needle and containing about 8 milligrams of MME in a fraction of a mL of a water solution and pushed that needle into the mouse at about where the navel would be if one could see the mouse's navel, and then I pulled the needle back just a little so that there should be nothing at the business end but the loose folds of the peritoneum. Then I pushed the syringe plunger home, effectively squirting the water solution into the area that surrounds the intestines. I dropped the mouse back into his cage, and watched. In this case, the mouse went into a twitching series of convulsions (known as clonic in the trade) and in five minutes he was dead.

Fired with the lust for killing, I grabbed another mouse, and nailed him with 175 mg/Kg. Dead in 6 minutes. Another one at 107 mg/Kg. Dead in 5 minutes. Another at 75 mg/Kg. Well, he looked pretty sick there for a while, and had some shakes, and then he seemed to be pretty much OK. One final orgy of murder. I injected 5 mice at 100 mg/Kg i.p., and watched four of them die within 20 minutes. I took in my hands the sole survivor, and I went outside the laboratory and let him loose on the hillside. He scampered away and I never saw him again.

And what did I learn, at the cost of seven precious lives which I can never replace? Not a damned thing. Maybe there is an LD-50 somewhere around 60 or 80 mg/Kg. This is for mice, not for men. I was intending to take an initial trial dose of 300 micrograms of this completely untested compound, and it would have made no difference to me if the LD-50 had been 600 mg/Kg or 6 mg/Kg. I still took my trial dose, and had absolutely no effects, and I never killed another mouse again. No, that is simply out-and-out dishonest. I had an invasion of field mice last winter coming up through a hole in the floor behind the garbage holder under the kitchen sink, and I blocked the hole, but I also set some mouse traps. And I caught a couple. But never again for the simple and stupid reasons of being able to say that "This compound has an LD-50 in the mouse of 70 mg/Kg." Who cares? Why kill?

But there are two very valuable things that have come out of this simple study with MME. One is, of course, that it is an active compound and as such warrants additional attention. And the other, and even more important, is that as one of the three possible ethoxy homologues of TMA-2, it is less active than MEM. The third possible ethoxy compound is EMM and, as will be found elsewhere in this book, it is even less active. Thus it is MEM, only, that maintains the potency of TMA-2, and this was the initial observation that really focused my attention on the importance of the 4-position.

#137 MP; METAPROSCALINE; 3,4-DIMETHOXY-5-(n)-PROPOXYPHENETHYLAMINE

SYNTHESIS: There was mixed 96 g of 5-bromovanillin and 90 mL 25% NaOH. The solution was almost complete, when there was a sudden deposition of a heavy precipitate. This was diluted with 200 mL water. There was then added 300 mL methylene chloride, 85 g methyl iodide, and 3 g decyltriethylammonium chloride. The heterogenous mixture was vigorously stirred for 2 days. The organic phase was separated, and the aqueous phase extracted once with 100 mL CH_2Cl_2. The organic phase and extract were pooled, washed with water and the solvent removed under vacuum The residue weighed 46.3 g and spontaneously crystallized. It was recrystallized from 40 mL of MeOH to yield 34 g of 3-bromo-4,5-dimethoxy-benzaldehyde as white crystals with a mp of 60.5-61 °C. An additional 4 g product was obtained from the mother liquor. Acidification of the aqueous phase above produced, after recrystalization from IPA/acetone, 13.2 g of recovered 5-bromo-vanillin, with a mp of 166-169 °C.

A mixture of 38.7 g 3-bromo-4,5-dimethoxybenzaldehyde and 17.2 g cyclohexylamine was heated with an open flame at about 120 °C until it appeared to be free of H_2O. The residue was put under a vacuum (0.2 mm/Hg) and distilled

at 146-160 °C yielding 44.6 g 3-bromo-N-cyclohexyl-4,5-dimethoxy-benzylidenimine as a clear oil which did not crystallize. The imine stretch in the infra-red was at 1640 cm^{-1}. Anal. $(C_{15}H_{20}BrNO_2)$ C,H.

A solution of 31.6 g 3-bromo-N-cyclohexyl-4,5-dimethoxybenzyliden-imine in 300 mL anhydrous Et_2O was placed in an atmosphere of He, stirred magnetically, and cooled with an dry ice/acetone bath. Then 71 mL of a 1.55 M solution of butyllithium in hexane was added over a 2 min period. The reaction mixture turned cloudy and a light precipitate formed which seemed heaviest at the half-way point. Stirring remained easy and was continued for 10 min. There was then added 35 mL of butyl borate at one time. The precipitate dissolved, and the stirred solution allowed to return to room temperature. There was then added 200 mL of an aqueous solution containing 20 g ammonium sulfate. The Et_2O layer was separated, washed with saturated ammonium sulfate solution, and the organic solvents removed under vacuum. The residue was dissolved in 250 mL of 70% MeOH and 14 mL of 30% hydrogen peroxide added in small portions. This reaction was very exothermic, and stirring was continued for 1 h. The reaction mixture was then added to 500 mL H_2O, which knocked out white solids. A small sample of this intermediate, N-cyclohexyl-3,4-dimethoxy-5-hydroxybenzylidineimine was recrystallized from MeOH to a white crystal with a mp of 148-149 °C and which showed the C=N bond as a doublet at 1635 and 1645 cm^{-1} in the infra-red. These wet solids were suspended in 200 mL 5% HCl and heated on the steam bath for 1 h. Stirring was continued until the reaction was again at room temperature and then it was extracted with 2x100 mL CH_2Cl_2. These extracts were pooled and in turn extracted with 2x75 mL dilute NaOH. The aqueous extracts were reacidified with HCl, and reextracted with 2x100 mL CH_2Cl_2. These extracts were pooled, and the solvent removed under vacuum to yield a brown viscous oil as a residue. This was distilled at 105-120 °C at 0.2 mm/Hg to yield 8.8 g of 3,4-dimethoxy-5-hydroxybenzaldehyde as a distillate that set to white crystals. Recrystallization from toluene/hexane gave a sample with the mp 64-65 °C. The literature mps are several, ranging from at about 60 °C to about 70 °C.

A solution of 4.7 g of 3,4-dimethoxy-5-hydroxybenzaldehyde in 75 mL acetone was treated with 6.0 g powdered KI, 16 mL (21 g) propyl bromide, and 7.0 g finely powdered anhydrous K_2CO_3, and this mixture was held at reflux on a steam bath for 15 h. The reaction mixture was added to 1 L H_2O, made strongly basic, and extracted with 3x100 mL CH_2Cl_2. The extracts were pooled, washed with 5% NaOH, and the solvent removed under vacuum yielding 8.8 g of a yellow oil, undoubtedly containing propyl iodide. This residue was distilled at 133-145 °C at 0.15 mm/Hg to yield 4.5 g of 3,4-dimethoxy-5-(n)-propoxybenzaldehyde as a white oil which did not crystallize. There was an appreciable pot residue. This product was clearly impure, having a minor, slower moving component not the starting phenol, as seen by TLC (on silica gel, with CH_2Cl_2 as a developing solvent). Fusion of a small amount of impure aldehyde with p-anisidine produced a crystalline anil which, on hydrolysis with dilute acid, produced an aldehyde sample free of this impurity. But as this sample also remained as an oil, the above crude product was used in the following preparation.

To a solution of 3.8 g 3,4-dimethoxy-5-(n)-propoxybenzaldehyde in 50 mL nitromethane, there was added 0.5 g anhydrous ammonium acetate. This was held at reflux for 50 min. The excess nitromethane was removed under vacuum and 2 volumes of boiling MeOH were added to the residue. The hot solution was decanted from some residual insolubles, and on cooling spontaneously crystallized. These solids were removed by filtration, washed sparingly with MeOH and air dried yielding 3.3 g yellow crystals of 3,4-dimethoxy-ß-nitro-5-(n)-propoxynitrostyrene as yellow crystals melting at 79-81 °C. Recrystallization from MeOH or cyclohexane neither improved the mp nor freed the product from a residual opalescenceseen in the melt. Anal. $(C_{13}H_{17}NO_5)$ C,H.

A solution of 1.5 g LAH in 30 mL anhydrous THF under He was cooled to 0 °C and vigorously stirred. There was added, dropwise, 1.0 mL of 100% H_2SO_4, followed by the dropwise addition of a solution of 2.3 g 3,4-dimethoxy-ß-nitro-5-(n)-propoxynitrostyrene in 10 mL anhydrous THF, over the course of 5 min. The mixture was stirred at 0 °C for a while, and then brought to a reflux on the steam bath. After cooling again, the excess hydride was destroyed with IPA added dropwise, followed by the addition of about 10 mL of 10% NaOH which was sufficient to covert the solids to a white, granular form. These were removed by filtration, the filter cake washed with IPA, the mother liquor and filtrates were combined, and the solvents were removed under vacuum to yield an amber oil. This residue was added to 75 mL dilute H_2SO_4 which produced a gummy insoluble phase which was physically removed with a spatula. The aqueous phase was washed with 3x50 mL CH_2Cl_2. It was then made basic with 25% NaOH, and extracted with 2x75 mL CH_2Cl_2. The solvent was removed from these pooled extracts and the residue distilled at 106-116 °C at 0.2 mm/Hg to provide 1.3 g of the product as a colorless liquid. This was dissolved in 4 mL IPA, neutralized with about 20 drops of concentrated HCl, and diluted with 4 volumes of anhydrous Et_2O added slowly with continuous stirring. A white crystalline salt crystallized out spontaneously and was isolated by filtration, washed first with IPA, then with Et_2O, and air dried giving 1.3

g 3,4-dimethoxy-5-(n)-propoxyphenethylamine hydrochloride (MP) with a mp of 170-171 °C. Anal. ($C_{13}H_{22}ClNO_3$) C,H.

DOSAGE: greater than 240 mg.

DURATION: unknown.

QUALITATIVE COMMENTS: (with 160 mg) "There might have been some disturbance at the three to four hour point, but it was extremely light if at all." (with 240 mg) "No effects whatsoever."

EXTENSIONS AND EXTRAPOLATIONS: The loss of activity on lengthening the carbon chain on the meta-oxygen from two to three (from metaescaline to metaproscaline) discouraged any further exploration at this specific point of the molecule. The isopropyl analog (3,4-dimethoxy-5-(i)-propoxyphenethylamine, metaisoproscaline, MIP) was started and carried along as far as the aldehyde, and abandoned with the discovery that metaproscaline was without activity. There were other fish to fry.

#138   MPM;   2,5-DIMETHOXY-4-(n)-PROPOXYAMPHETAMINE

SYNTHESIS: To a solution of 68 g 2,5-dimethoxybenzaldehyde in 250 mL glacial acetic acid that had been warmed to 25 °C and well stirred, there was added, dropwise, 86 g of a 40% peracetic acid solution (in acetic acid). The reaction was exothermic, and the rate of addition was dictated by the need to maintain the internal temperature within a few degrees of 28 °C. External cooling was used as needed. The addition took 1 h, and when the reaction had clearly been completed (there was no further temperature rise) the entire reaction mixture was added to 3 volumes of H_2O. The excess acid was neutralized with solid K_2CO_3. The dark solution was extracted with 3x100 mL Et_2O, the extracts pooled, and stripped of solvent under vacuum to give 59 g of crude 2,4-dimethoxyphenyl formate. This was suspended in 200 mL 10% NaOH, and the mixture heated on the steam bath for 1 h. On cooling, the reaction mixture was washed with 2x200 mL methylene chloride, acidified with HCl, and extracted with 3x200 mL CH_2Cl_2. The extracts were pooled and the solvent removed under vacuum. There remained as residue, 47.4 g 2,5-dimethoxyphenol which was deep amber in color, but clear and fluid. It was homogenous by GC and completely correct by NMR. It was used without further purification.

To a solution of 3.08 g 2,5-dimethoxyphenol in 20 g MeOH, there was added a solution of 1.26 g flaked KOH in 20 g hot MeOH. There was then added 2.46 g n-propyl bromide, and the mixture held at reflux for 2 h on the steam bath. This was quenched in 5 volumes H_2O, made strongly basic with 10% NaOH, and extracted with 3x100 mL CH_2Cl_2. Removal of the solvent from the pooled extracts left 2.0 g of 1,4-dimethoxy-2-(n)-propoxybenzene as a clear, amber oil. The IR spectrum was appropriate, no phenol was present, and this residue was used in the following reaction without further purification or characterization.

A mixture of 3.5 g N-methylformanilide and 4.0 g $POCl_3$ was held at room temperature for 0.5 h producing a deep red color. To this there was added 2.0 g 1,4-dimethoxy-2-(n)-propoxybenzene, and the mixture was held on the steam bath for 1.75 h. It was then poured over 400 mL shaved ice, and vigorous stirring was maintained until the dark complex had completely broken up. This aqueous mixture was allowed to stand overnight, and the crude aldehyde solids that had formed were removed by filtration, water washed, and sucked as dry as possible. This 2.0 g damp material was crystallized from 20 mL boiling MeOH giving, after filtering and drying to constant weight, 1.4 g 2,5-dimethoxy-4-(n)-propoxybenzaldehyde as reddish-tan solids, with a mp of 97-98 °C. To the methanolic mother liquors of this crystallization there was added a gram of malononitrile and a few drops of triethylamine. The eventual addition of a little H_2O encouraged the separation of crystals which were removed, and had a mp of 150-152 °C. Recrystallization from toluene gave gold-colored crystals of the benzalmalononitrile with a mp of 153.5-155 °C, but the melt remained slightly cloudy.

To a solution of 1.4 g 2,5-dimethoxy-4-(n)-propoxybenzaldehyde and 0.65 g nitroethane in 4.4 g glacial acetic acid there was added 0.4 g anhydrous ammonium acetate, and the mixture was heated on the steam bath for 5 h. The addition of a modest amount of H_2O and scratching with a glass rod produced crystal seed. The reaction was diluted with about 5 mL H_2O, seeded, and allowed to stand at room temperature overnight. There was generated a crystalline product which was removed by filtration and air dried. There was thus obtained 0.6 g 1-(2,5-dimethoxy-4-(n)-propoxyphenyl)-2-nitropropene as yellow-orange crystals, with a mp of 83-84 °C. The addition of H_2O to the mother liquors provided an additional 0.3 g of an orange solid which proved to be largely unreacted starting aldehyde.

To a stirred, warm suspension of 0.5 g LAH in 20 mL anhydrous Et_2O under a He atmosphere, there was added 0.6 g 1-(2,5-dimethoxy-4-(n)-propoxyphenyl)-2-nitropropene dissolved in a little anhydrous Et_2O. The mixture was heated and stirred for a few h, and the excess hydride decomposed with 30 mL 1.5 N H_2SO_4. The two layers were separated, and 15 g potassium sodium tartrate was dissolved in the aqueous fraction. Aqueous NaOH was then added until the pH was >9, and this was then extracted with 3x50 mL CH_2Cl_2. Removal of the solvent under vacuum gave 0.7 g of an amber oil that was dissolved in anhydrous Et_2O and saturated with anhydrous HCl gas. No crystals formed, and so the ether was removed under vacuum, leaving a residue that set up to crystals that were then no longer soluble in ether. They were, however, very soluble in chloroform. These were ground under dry Et_2O, removed by filtration, and air dried giving 0.35 g 2,5-dimethoxy-4-(n)-propoxyamphetamine hydrochloride (MPM) with a mp of 123 - 125 °C.

DOSAGE: 30 mg or more.

DURATION: probably short.

QUALITATIVE COMMENTS: (with 15 mg) "This is just barely threshold. A marginal intoxication at best. This level is producing less response that the 11 mg. trial of MEM, so the propoxy is off in potency. At four and a half hours I am out of whatever little there was."

(with 30 mg) "By the mid-second hour, I am at a valid plus one. I cannot identify the nature — with eyes closed it would be lost, as it would also be if I were watching a play or movie. It would have been interesting to see where it could have gone. Seventh hour, completely clear."

EXTENSIONS AND COMMENTARY: The 4-propoxy homologue of TMA-2 and MEM is clearly less active, and this has discouraged me from putting too much more effort in this direction. Three additional materials of this pattern were prepared and either shown to be even less active, or simply were not assayed at all. These are the 4-isopropoxy isomer (MIPM), the (n)-butoxy homologue (MBM), and the (n)-amyl homologue (MAM). They scarcely warrant separate recipes as they were all made in a manner similar to this one describing MPM.

For the preparation of MIPM, the above phenol, 2,5-dimethoxyphenol was isopropylated with isopropyl bromide in methanolic KOH giving 2,5-dimethoxy-1-(i)-propoxybenzene as an oil. This formed the benzaldehyde with the standard Vilsmeier conditions, which melted at 77-78 °C from hexane and which gave a yellow malononitrile derivative melting at 171.5-173 °C. The nitrostyrene, from nitroethane in acetic acid was orange colored and melted at 100-101 °C from either methanol or hexane. This was reduced with lithium aluminum hydride in ether to give 2,5-dimethoxy-4-(i)-propoxyamphetamine hydrochloride (MIPM). The properties of the isolated salt were strange (soluble in acetone but not in water) and the microanalysis was low in the carbon value. The molecular structure had a pleasant appeal to it, with a complete reflection symmetry shown by the atoms of the amphetamine side chain and the isopropoxy side chain. But the nature of the actual product in hand had no appeal at all, and no assay was ever started.

For the preparation of MBM, the starting phenol was alkylated to 2-(n)-butoxy-1,4-dimethoxybenzene in methanolic KOH with n-butyl bromide. The benzaldehyde melted at 79.5-81 °C from methanol, and formed a malononitrile derivative that had a melting point of 134.5-135 C. The nitrostyrene from the aldehyde and nitroethane in acetic acid crystallized from methanol with a mp of 71-72 °C. Lithium aluminum hydride reduction in ether gave the ether-insoluble chloroform-soluble product 4-(n)-butoxy-2,5-dimethoxyamphetamine hydrochloride (MBM) with a melting point of 128-130 °C. This product met all tests for structural integrity, and assays were started. At levels of up to 12.0 milligrams, there were no effects noted.

As to the preparation of MAM, the exact same sequence was used, except for the employment of n-amyl bromide. The benzaldehyde crystallized from methanol with a mp of 79-80 °C, and formed a malononitrile derivative which was bright yellow and melted at 103-104 °C. The nitrostyrene, when pure, melted at 57-58.5 °C but proved very difficult to separate from the aldehyde. The final product, 4-(n)-amyloxy-2,5-dimethoxyamphetamine hydrochloride (MAM) was obtained by lithium aluminum hydride reduction in ether and melted at 125-127 °C. It was assayed at up to 16 milligrams, at which level there was noted a heaviness in the chest and head at the 2-hour point, but no cardiovascular disturbance and no mydriasis. This was called an inactive level, and no higher one has yet been tried.

#139   ORTHO-DOT;   4,5-DIMETHOXY-2-METHYLTHIO-AMPHETAMINE

SYNTHESIS: To 26.4 g veratrol that was being magnetically stirred without any solvent, there was added 50 g chlorosulfonic acid a bit at a time over the course of 20 min. The reaction was exothermic, and evolved considerable HCl. The deeply colored mixture that resulted was poured over 400 mL crushed ice and when all had thawed, it was extracted with 2×150 mL CH_2Cl_2. Removal of the solvent under vacuum gave a residue that set up as a crystalline mass. The weight of the crude 3,4-dimethoxybenzene-sulfonyl chloride was 37.1 g and it had a mp of 63-66 °C. Recrystallization raised this to 72-73 °C. Reaction with ammonium hydroxide gave the sulfonamide as colorless needles from EtOH, with a mp of 132-133 °C.

The finely pulverized 3,4-dimethoxybenzenesulfonyl chloride (33 g) was added to 900 mL of crushed ice in a 2 L round-bottomed flask equipped with a heating mantle and reflux condenser. There was then added 55 mL concentrated H_2SO_4 and, with vigorous mechanical stirring, there was added 50 g of zinc dust in small portions. This mixture was heated until a vigorous reaction ensued and refluxing was continued for 1.5 h. After cooling to room temperature and decantation from unreacted metallic zinc, the aqueous phase was extracted with 3×150 mL Et_2O. The pooled extracts were washed once with saturated brine and the solvent was removed under vacuum. The residue was distilled to give 20.8 g of 3,4-dimethoxythiophenol boiling at 86-88 °C at 0.4 mm/Hg.

A solution of 10 g 3,4-dimethoxythiophenol in 50 mL absolute EtOH was protected from the air by an atmosphere of N_2. There was added a solution of 5 g

85% KOH in 80 mL EtOH. This was followed by the addition of 6 mL methyl iodide, and the mixture was held at reflux for 30 min. This was poured into 200 mL H_2O and extracted with 3x50 mL Et_2O. The pooled extracts were washed once with aqueous sodium hydrosulfite, then the organic solvent was removed under vacuum. The residue was distilled to give 10.3 g of 3,4-dimethoxythioanisole with a bp of 94-95 °C at 0.4 mm/Hg. The product was a colorless oil that crystallized on standing. Its mp was 31-32 °C.

To a mixture of 15 g $POCl_3$ and 14 g N-methylformanilide that had been warmed briefly on the steam bath there was added 8.2 g of 3,4-dimethoxythioanisole, the exothermic reaction was heated on the steam bath for an additional 20 min, and then poured into 200 mL H_2O. Stirring was continued until the insolubles had become completely loose and granular. These were removed by filtration, washed with H_2O, sucked as dry as possible, and then recrystallized from 100 mL boiling EtOH. The product, 4,5-dimethoxy-2-(methylthio)benzaldehyde, was an off-white solid, weighing 8.05 g and having a mp of 112-113 °C. Anal. ($C_{10}H_{12}O_3S$) C,H.

A solution of 2.0 g 4,5-dimethoxy-2-(methylthio)benzaldehyde in 8 mL nitroethane was treated with 0.45 g anhydrous ammonium acetate and heated on the steam bath for 4.5 h. Removal of the excess solvent under vacuum gave a red residue which was dissolved in 5 mL boiling MeOH. There was the spontaneous formation of a crystalline product which was recrystallized from 25 mL boiling MeOH to give, after cooling, filtering and air drying, 1.85 g of 1-(4,5-dimethoxy-2-methylthio-phenyl)-2-nitropropene as bright orange crystals with a mp of 104-105 °C. Anal. ($C_{12}H_{15}NO_4S$) C,H,N.

A suspension of 1.3 g LAH in 50 mL anhydrous THF was placed under an inert atmosphere and stirred magnetically. When this had been brought to reflux conditions, there was added, dropwise, 1.65 g of 1-(4,5-dimethoxy-2-methylthio-phenyl)-2-nitropropene in 20 mL THF. The reaction mixture was maintained at reflux for 18 h. After being brought back to room temperature, the excess hydride was destroyed by the addition of 1.3 mL H_2O in 10 mL THF. There was then added 1.3 mL of 3N NaOH followed by an additional 3.9 mL H_2O. The loose, inorganic salts were removed by filtration, and the filter cake washed with additional 20 mL THF. The combined filtrate and washes were stripped of solvent under vacuum yielding a light yellow oil as a residue. This was dissolved in 20 mL IPA, neutralized with 0.9 mL concentrated HCl, and diluted with 200 mL anhydrous Et_2O. There was thus formed 1.20 g of 4,5-dimethoxy-2-methylthioamphetamine hydrochloride (ORTHO-DOT) as a pale yellow crystalline product. This melted at 218-219.5 °C, and recrystallization from EtOH yielded a white product and increased the mp to 222-223 °C with decomposition Anal. ($C_{12}H_{20}ClNO_2S$) C,H,N.

DOSAGE: greater than 25 mg.

DURATION: unknown.

QUALITATIVE COMMENTS: (with 25 mg) "Vague awareness, with the feeling of an impending something. Light food sat uncomfortably. By the late afternoon there was absolutely nothing. Threshold at best."

EXTENSIONS AND COMMENTARY: This material, ORTHO-DOT, can be looked at as the sulfur homologue of TMA-2 with the sulfur atom located in place of the oxygen at the 2-position of the molecule. At what level this compound might show activity is completely unknown, but wherever that might be, it is at a dosage greater than that for the PARA-DOT isomer, ALEPH-1 (or ALEPH), which was fully active at 10 milligrams (ALEPH can be looked at as TMA-2 with the sulfur atom located in place of the oxygen at the 4-position of the molecule). A lot of variations are easily makable based on this structure, but why bother? ALEPH is the much more appealing candidate for structural manipulation.

#140   P;   PROSCALINE;   3,5-DIMETHOXY-4-(n)-PROPOXY-PHENETHYLAMINE

SYNTHESIS: A solution of 5.8 g of homosyringonitrile (see under E for its synthesis), 100 mg decyltriethylammonium iodide, and 10 g n-propyl bromide in 50 mL anhydrous acetone was treated with 6.9 g finely powdered anhydrous K_2CO_3 and held at reflux for 10 h. An additional 5 g of n-propyl bromide was added to the mixture, and the refluxing continued for another 48 h. The mixture was filtered, the solids washed with acetone, and the combined filtrate and washes stripped of solvent under vacuum. The residue was suspended in acidified H_2O, and extracted 3x175 mL CH_2Cl_2. The pooled extracts were washed with 2x50 mL 5% NaOH, once with dilute HCl (which lightened the color of the extract) and then stripped of solvent under vacuum giving 9.0 g of a deep yellow oil. This was distilled at 132-142 °C at 0.3 mm/Hg to yield 4.8 g of 3,5-dimethoxy-4-(n)-propoxyphenylacetonitrile as a clear yellow oil. Anal. ($C_{13}H_{17}NO_3$) C H N.

A solution of 4.7 g 3,5-dimethoxy-4-(n)-propoxyphenylacetonitrile in 20 mL THF was treated with 2.4 g powdered sodium borohydride. To this well-stirred suspension there was added, dropwise, 1.5 mL trifluoroacetic acid. There was a vigorous gas evolution from the exothermic reaction. Stirring was continued for 1 h, then all was poured into 300 mL H_2O. This was acidified cautiously with dilute H_2SO_4, and washed with 2x75 mL CH_2Cl_2. The aqueous phase was made basic with dilute NaOH, extracted with 2x75 mL CH_2Cl_2, the extracts pooled, and the solvent removed under vacuum. The residue was distilled at 115-125 °C at 0.3 mm/Hg to give 1.5 mL of a colorless oil which upon dissolving in 5 mL IPA, neutralizing with

27 drops concentrated HCl, and dilution with 25 mL anhydrous Et$_2$O yielded 1.5 g 3,5-dimethoxy-4-(n)-propoxyphenethylamine hydrochloride (P) as spectacular white crystals. The catalytic hydrogenation process for reducing the nitrile (see under E) also succeeded with this material. The mp was 170-172 °C. Anal. (C$_{13}$H$_{22}$ClNO$_3$) C,H,N.

DOSAGE: 30 - 60 mg.

DURATION: 8 - 12 h.

QUALITATIVE COMMENTS: (with 30 mg) "Proscaline dulled my sense of pain and made the other senses really sharp. Everything felt really soft, and clean and clear. I could feel every hair my hand was touching. I felt so relaxed and at ease. I know that under the appropriate circumstances, this material would lead to uninhibited eroticism."

(with 35 mg) "The whole experiment was very quiet. There was no nystagmus, no anorexia, and insignificant visuals with the eyes closed. I was restless with a bit of tremor for the first couple of hours, and then became drowsy. Would I do this again? Probably not. It doesn't seem to offer anything except speculation about the nature of the high. The high was pleasant, but quite uneventful."

(with 40 mg) "For me there was a deep feeling of peace and contentment. The euphoria grows in intensity for several hours and remains for the rest of the day making this one of the most enjoyable experiences I have ever had. It was marvelous talking and joking with the others. However, I was a little disappointed that there was no enhanced clarity and no deep realizations. There was not a problem to be found. There were no motivations to discuss anything serious. If I had any objection, it would be with the name, not the pharmacology."

(with 60 mg) "The development of the intoxication was complete in a couple of hours. I feel that there is more physical effect than mental, in that there is considerable irritability. This should probably be the maximum dose. Despite feeling quite drunk, my thinking seems straight. The effects were already waning by the fifth hour, but sleep was not possible until after the twelfth hour. There was no hangover the next day."

EXTENSIONS AND COMMENTARY: There is a very early report describing the human use of proscaline tucked away in the Czechoslovakian literature that describes experiments at up to 80 milligrams. At these dosages, there were reported some difficulty with dreams, and the residual effects were still apparent even after 12 hours.

The amphetamine homologue of proscaline, 3,5-dimethoxy-4-(n)-propoxy-amphetamine is an unexplored compound. Its synthesis could not be achieved in parallel to the description given for P. Rather, the propylation of syringaldehyde to give 3,5-dimethoxy-4-(n)-propoxybenzaldehyde, followed by coupling with nitroethane and the reduction of the formed nitrostyrene with lithium aluminum hydride would be the logical process. Following the reasoning given under E, the initials for this base would be 3C-P, and I would guess it would be active, and a psychedelic, in the 20 to 40 milligram range.

#141 PE; PHENESCALINE; 3,5-DIMETHOXY-4-PHENETHYLOXYPHENETHYLAMINE

SYNTHESIS: To a solution of 5.8 g homosyringonitrile (see under E for its preparation) in 50 mL of acetone containing 100 mg decyltriethylammonium iodide, there was added 14.8 g ß-phenethylbromide and 6.9 g of finely powdered anhydrous K₂CO₃. The greenish mixture was refluxed for 3 days, with two additional 4 g batches of anhydrous K₂CO₃ being added at 24 h intervals. After addition to aqueous base, the product was extracted with CH₂Cl₂, the pooled extracts were washed with dilute base (the organic phase remained a deep purple color) and then finally with dilute HCl (the organic phase became a pale yellow). The solvent was removed giving 15.6 g crude 3,5-dimethoxy-4-phenethyloxyphenylacetonitrile which distilled at 165-185 °C at 0.3 mm/Hg to yield 3,5-dimethoxy-4-phenethyloxyphenylacetonitrile as a reddish viscous oil weighing 8.1 g. Anal. (C₁₈H₁₉NO₃) C,H.

A solution of 7.9 g of distilled 3,5-dimethoxy-4-phenethyloxyphenyl-acetonitrile in 15 mL dry THF was added to a 0 °C solution of AH prepared from a vigorously stirred solution of 4.6 g LAH in 160 ml THF which had been treated, at 0 °C with 3.6 mL 100% H₂SO₄ under an atmosphere of He. The gelatinaceous reaction mixture was brought to a brief reflux on the steam bath, then cooled again. It was treated with 5 mL IPA which destroyed the unreacted hydride, followed by sufficient 15% NaOH to give loose, white filterable solids. These were removed by filtration and washed with THF. The filtrate and the washes were combined and, after removal of the solvent under vacuum, there remained 7.8 g of the product as a crude base which crystallized spontaneously. Distillation of this product at 170-180 °C at 0.35 mm/Hg gave 5.1 g white solids, with a mp of 85-86 °C from hexane. This base was dissolved in 20 mL warm IPA and treated with 1.6 mL concentrated HCl. To the resulting clear solution, there was added 75 mL anhydrous Et₂O which gave, after a few moments of stirring, a spontaneous crystallization of 3,5-di-methoxy-4-phenethyloxyphenethylamine hydrochloride (PE) as beautiful white crystals. The weight was 5.4 g after air drying, and the mp was 151-152 °C. Anal. (C₁₈H₂₄ClNO₃) C,H.

DOSAGE: greater than 150 mg.

DURATION: unknown.

QUALITATIVE COMMENTS: (with 150 mg) "At most, there was a bare threshold over the course of the afternoon. A vague unreal feeling, as if I had not had quite enough sleep last night. By late afternoon, even this had disappeared and I was left with an uncertainty that anything at all had occurred."

EXTENSIONS AND COMMENTARY: There is not much there, so there is not much to make commentary on. This response is called a "threshhold" effect, and cannot be used to predict with any confidence just what level (if any) would produce psychological effects.

A similar chain on the 4-position, but with one less carbon atom, deserves special comment. Rather than a phenethyloxy group, this would be benzyloxy group (which in this day and age of Chemical Abstracts purity should probably be called a phenylmethoxy group). If one were to follow the naming philosophy of "proscaline equals P and buscaline equals B" convention, one would call it 4-benzescaline, and give it the code name BZ. The nomenclature purist would probably call the compound PM (for phenylmescaline or, more likely phenyl-methoxydimethoxyphenethylamine), since the term BZ is awkward and mislead-ing. It is a code name that has been given to a potent CNS agent known as quinuclidin-3-yl benzilate, which is a chemical and biological warfare (CBW) incapacitating agent currently being stored by the military to the extent of 20,000 pounds. And, BZ has also recently become the jargon name given to benzodiaz-epine receptors. They have been called the BZ-receptors.

However, let's be awkward and misleading, and call this benzyloxy-base BZ. For one thing, the three-carbon analogue 3C-BZ has already been described in its own recipe using this code. And the 4-fluoroanalogue of it, 3C-FBZ, is also mentioned there. And BZ has already been described synthetically, having been made in exactly the procedure given for escaline, except that the reduction of the nitrile was not done by catalytic hydrogenation but rather by sodium borohydride in the presence of cobalt chloride. It has been shown to be a effective serotonin agonist, and may warrant human experimentation. The serotonin activity suggests that it might be active at the same levels found for proscaline.

All of this says very little about PE. But then, there is very little to say about PE except that it may be active at very high levels, and I am not sure just how to get there safely.

#142 PEA; PHENETHYLAMINE

SYNTHESIS: This compound has been made industrially by a number of routes, with the reduction of benzyl cyanide and the decarboxylation of phenylanaline being the more important. It is offered in the catalogs of all the major chemical supply houses for a few pennies per gram. It is a very strong base with a fishy smell, and rapidly forms a solid carbonate salt upon exposure to the air. It is a natural biochemical in both plants and animals.

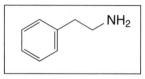

DOSAGE: greater than 1600 mg.

DURATION: unknown.

QUALITATIVE COMMENTS: (with 200, 400, 800 and 1600 mg) "No effects."
(with 500 mg) "No effects."
(with 800 and 1600 mg) "No effects."
(with 25 and 50 mg i.v.) "No effects."

EXTENSIONS AND COMMENTARY: Here is the chemical that is central to this entire book. This is the structural point of departure for every compound that is discussed here. It is the "P" in PIHKAL. It is without activity in man! Certainly not for the lack of trying, as some of the dosage trials that are tucked away in the literature (as abstracted in the "Qualitative Comments" given above) are pretty heavy duty. Actually, I truly doubt that all of the experimenters used exactly that phrase, "No effects," but it is patently obvious that no effects were found. It happened to be the phrase I had used in my own notes.

　　This, the simplest of all phenethylamines, has always been the darling of the psychopharmacologists in that it is structurally clean, it is naturally present in various human fluids and tissues, and because of its close chemical relationship to amphetamine and to the neurotransmitters. These facts continuously encourage theories that involve PEA in mental illness. Its levels in urine may be decreased in people diagnosed as being depressed. Its levels may be increased in people diagnosed as being paranoid schizophrenics. Maybe it is also increased in people under extreme stress. The human trials were initially an attempt to provoke some psychological change, and indeed some clinicians have reported intense headaches generated in depressives following PEA administration. But then, others have seen nothing. The studies evolved into searches for metabolic difference that might be of some diagnostic value. And even here, the jury is still out.

　　Phenethylamine is found throughout nature, in both plants and animals. It is the end product of phenylalanine in the putrefaction of tissue. One of its most popularized occurrences has been as a major component of chocolate, and it has hit the Sunday Supplements as the love-sickness chemical. Those falling out of love are compulsive chocolate eaters, trying to replenish and repair the body's loss of this compound — or so the myth goes. But this amine is voraciously metabolized to the apparently inactive compound phenylacetic acid, and to some tyramine as well. Both of these products are also normal components in the body. And, as a wry side-comment, phenylacetic acid is a major precursor in the illicit synthesis of amphet-amine and methamphetamine.

Phenethylamine is intrinsically a stimulant, although it doesn't last long enough to express this property. In other words, it is rapidly and completely destroyed in the human body. It is only when a number of substituent groups are placed here or there on the molecule that this metabolic fate is avoided and pharmacological activity becomes apparent.

To a large measure, this book has emphasized the "phenyl" end of the phenethylamine molecule, and the "what," the where," and the "how many" of the substituent groups involved. There is a broad variety of chemical groups that can be attached to the benzene ring, at one or more of the five available positions, and in an unending number of combinations. And, in any given molecule, the greater the number of substituents on the benzene ring, the greater the likelihood that there will be psychedelic action rather that stimulant action.

But what can be said about the "ethylamine" end of the phenethylamine molecule? This is the veritable backbone that holds everything together, and simple changes here can produce new prototypes that can serve as starting points for the substituent game on the benzene ring. Thus, just as there is a "family" of compounds based on the foundation of phenethylamine itself, there is an equally varied and rich "families" of other compounds that might be based on some phenethylamine with a small modification to its backbone.

So, for the moment, leave the aromatic ring alone, and let us explore simple changes in the ethylamine chain itself. And the simplest structural unit of change is a single carbon atom, called the methyl group. Where can it be placed?

The adding of a methyl group adjacent to the amine produces phenyliso-propylamine, or amphetamine. This has been exploited already as one of the richest families of psychedelic drugs; and over half of the recipes in Book II are specifically for amphetamine analogues with various substituents on the aromatic ring. The further methylation of amphetamine with yet another methyl group, this time on the nitrogen atom, yields methamphetamine. Here the track record with various substituents on the aromatic ring is not nearly as good. Many have been explored and, with one exception, the quality and potency of human activity is down. But the one exception, the N-methyl analogue of MDA, proved to be the most remarkable MDMA.

The placement of the methyl group between the two carbons (so to speak) produces a cyclopropyl system. The simplest example is 2-phenylcyclopropyl-amine, a drug with the generic name of tranylcypromine and the trade name Parnate. It is a mono-amine oxidase inhibitor and has been marketed as an antidepressant, but the compound is also a mild stimulant causing insomnia, restlessness and photophobia. Substitutions on the benzene ring of this system have not been too promising. The DOM analogue, 2,5-dimethoxy-4-methyltranylcypromine is active in man, and is discussed in its own recipe under DMCPA. The inactive mescaline analogue TMT is also mentioned there.

The dropping of one carbon from the phenethylamine chain gives a benzyl amine, basically an inactive nucleus. Two families deserve mention, however. The phencylidine area, phenylcyclohexylpiperidine or PCP, is represented by a number of benzyl amines. Ketamine is also a benzyl amine. These are all analgesics and anesthetics with central properties far removed from the stimulant area, and are not really part of this book. There is a benzyl amine that is a pure stimulant, which has been closely compared to amphetamine in its action This is benzylpiperazine, a base that is active in the 20 to 100 milligram range, but which has an acceptability similar to amphetamine. If this is a valid stimulant, I think that much magic might be found in and around compounds such as (1) the MDMA analogue, N-(3,4-methylenedioxybenzyl)piperazine (or its N-methyl-counterpart N-(3,4-methylenedioxybenzyl)-N'-methylpiperazine) or (2) the DOM analogue, 2,5-dimethoxy-4-methylbenzylpiperazine. The benzyl amine that results by the relocation of the amine group of MDA from the beta-carbon atom to the alpha-carbon atom is known, and is active. It, and its N-methyl homologue, are described and discussed in the commentary under MDA. Dropping another carbon atom gives a yet shorter chain (no carbons at all!) and this is to be found in the phenylpiperazine analogue 3-trifluoromethylphenylpiperazine. I have been told that this base is an active hallucinogen as the dihydrobromide salt at 50 milligrams sublingually, or at 15 milligrams intravenously in man. The corresponding 3-chloro analogue at 20 to 40 milligrams orally in man or at 8 milligrams intravenously, led to panic attacks in some 10% of the experimental subjects, but not to any observed psychedelic or stimulant responses.

What happens if you extend the chain to a third carbon? The parent system is called the phenyl-(n)-propylamine, and the parent chain structure, either as the primary amine or as its alpha-methyl counterpart, represents compounds that are inactive as stimulants. The DOM-analogues have been made and are, at least in the rabbit rectal hyperthermia assay, uninteresting. A commercially available fine chemical known as piperonylacetone has been offered as either of two materials. One, correctly called 3,4-methylenedioxyphenylacetone or 3,4-methylenedioxybenzyl methyl ketone, gives rise upon reductive amination to MDA (using ammonia) or MDMA (using methylamine). This is an aromatic compound with a three-carbon side-chain and the amine-nitrogen on the beta-carbon. The other so-called piperonylacetone is really 3,4-methylenedioxybenzylacetone, an aromatic compound with a four-carbon side-chain. It produces, on reductive amination with ammonia or methylamine, the corresponding alpha-methyl-(n)-propylamines, with a four-carbon side-chain and the amine-nitrogen on the gamma-carbon. They are completely unexplored in man and so it is not known whether they are or are not psychedelic. As possible mis-synthesized products, they may appear quite unintentionally and must be evaluated as totally new materials. The gamma-amine analogue of MDA, a methylenedioxy substituted three carbon side-chain with the amine-nitrogen on the gamma carbon, has indeed been made and evaluated, and is discussed under MDA. The extension of the chain of mescaline to three atoms, by the inclusion of an oxygen atom, has produced two compounds that have also been assayed. They are mentioned in the recipe for mescaline.

The chain that reaches out to the amine group can be tied back in again to the ring, with a second chain. There are 2-aminobenzoindanes which are phenethylamines with a one-carbon link tying the alpha-position of the chain back to the aromatic ring. And there are 2-aminotetralines which are phenethylamines which have a two-carbon link tying the alpha-position of the chain back to the aromatic ring. Both unsubstituted ring systems are known and both are fair stimulants. Both systems have been modified with the DOM substituent patterns (called DOM-AI and DOM-AT respectively), but neither of these has been tried in man. And the analogues with the MDA substitution pattern are discussed elsewhere in this book.

And there is one more obvious remaining methylation pattern. What about phenethylamine or amphetamine compounds with two methyl groups on the nitrogen? The parent amphetamine example, N,N-dimethylamphetamine, has received much notoriety lately in that it has become a scheduled drug in the United States. Ephedrine is a major precursor in the illicit synthesis of methamphetamine, and with the increased law-enforcement attention being paid to this process, there has been increasing promotion of the unrestricted homologue, N-methylephedrine, to the methamphetamine chemist. This starting material gives rise to N,N-dimethylamphetamine which is a material of dubious stimulant properties. A number of N,N-dimethylamphetamine derivatives, with "psychedelic" ring substituents, have been explored as iodinated brain-flow indicators, and they are explicitly named within the appropriate recipes. But none of them have shown any psychedelic action.

This is as good a place as any to discuss two or three simple compounds, phenethylamines, with only one substituent on the benzene ring. The 2-carbon analog of 4-MA, is 4-methoxyphenethylamine, or MPEA. This is a kissing cousin to DMPEA, of such fame in the search for a urine factor that could be related to schizophrenia. And the end results of the search for this compound in the urine of mentally ill patients are as controversial as they were for DMPEA. There has been no confirmed relationship to the diagnosis. And efforts to see if it is centrally active were failures — at dosages of up to 400 milligrams in man, there was no activity. The 4-chloro-analogue is 4-chlorophenethylamine (4-Cl-PEA) and it has actually been pushed up to even higher levels (to 500 milligrams dosage, orally) and it is also without activity. A passing bit of charming trivia. A positional isomer of MPEA is 3-methoxyphenethylamine (3-MPEA) and, although there are no reported human trials with this, it has been graced with an Edgewood Arsenal code number, vis., EA-1302.

#143 PROPYNYL; 3,5-DIMETHOXY-4-(2-PROPYNYLOXY)-PHENETHYLAMINE

SYNTHESIS: To a solution of 5.8 g homosyringonitrile (see under E for its preparation) in 50 mL acetone containing 100 mg decyltriethylammonium iodide, there was added 12 g of an 80% solution of propargyl bromide in toluene and 6.9 g of finely powdered anhydrous K_2CO_3. This mixture was held at reflux on the steam bath for 12 h, after which the solvent was removed under vacuum. The residues were added to 0.5 L H_2O, acidified, and extracted with 3x75 mL CH_2Cl_2. The extracts were pooled, washed with 5% NaOH, and then with dilute HCl which discharged the deep color. Removal of the organic solvent under vacuum yielded 6.6 g of crude product. This was distilled at 138-148 °C at 0.25 mm/ Hg, yielding 4.3 g 3,5-dimethoxy-4-(2-propynyloxy)phenylacetonitrile which spontaneously crystallized. A small sample from MeOH had a mp of 94-95 °C. Anal. ($C_{13}H_{13}NO_3$) C,H.

A suspension of 2.8 g LAH in 70 mL anhydrous THF was cooled to 0 °C with good stirring under He, and treated with 2.0 g 100% H_2SO_4. To this, a solution of 4.2 g 3,5-dimethoxy-4-(2-propynyloxy)phenylacetonitrile in 30 mL anhydrous THF was added very slowly. After the addition had been completed, the reaction mixture was held at reflux on the steam bath for 0.5 h, cooled to room temperature, treated with IPA to decompose the excess hydride, and finally with 15% NaOH to convert the solids to a white filterable mass. The solids were separated by filtration, the filter cake was washed with THF, and the filtrate and washes were pooled. After removal of the solvent, the residue was added to 100 mL dilute H_2SO_4, and washed with 3x75 mL CH_2Cl_2. The aqueous phase was made basic with dilute NaOH, and the product extracted with 2x75 mL CH_2Cl_2. After removal of the solvent under vacuum, the residue was distilled at 125-155 °C at 0.3 mm/Hg to provide 2.4 g of a light amber viscous liquid. This was dissolved in 10 mL IPA, acidified with concentrated HCl until a droplet produced a red color on dampened, external universal pH paper, and then diluted with 40 mL anhydrous Et_2O with good stirring. After a short delay, 3,5-dimethoxy-4-(2-propynyloxy)phenethylamine hydrochloride (PROPYNYL) spontaneously crystallized. The product was removed by filtration, washed first with an IPA/Et_2O mixture, and finally with Et_2O. The yield was 3.0 g of white needles.

DOSAGE: 80 mg or more.

DURATION: 8 - 12 h.

QUALITATIVE COMMENTS: (with 55 mg) "I have cold feet — literally — I don't mean that in the spiritual or adventurous sense. But also I am somewhat physically fuzzy. I feel that if I were in public my behavior would be such that someone would notice me. Everything was OK without any question at the ninth hour. I could walk abroad again."

(with 80 mg) "There is a body load. The flow of people around me all day has demanded my attention, and when I had purposefully retreated to be by myself, there was no particular reward as to visuals or anything with eyes closed, either. Sleep was easy at midnight (the twelfth hour of the experiment) but the morning was sluggish, and on recalling the day, I am not sure of the events that had taken place. Higher might be all right, but watch the status of the body. There certainly wasn't that much mental stuff."

EXTENSIONS AND COMMENTARY: No experiments have been performed that describe the action of this drug at full level. This compound does not seem to have the magic that would encourage exploration at higher levels.

#144   SB;   SYMBESCALINE;   3,5-DIETHOXY-4-METHOXY-PHENETHYLAMINE

SYNTHESIS: A solution of 15 g 1,3-diethoxybenzene and 15 mL of N,N,N',N'-tetramethylethylenediamine in 200 mL anhydrous Et_2O was placed in a He atmosphere, magnetically stirred, and cooled to 0 °C with an ice bath. Over the course of 10 min there was added 63 mL of a 1.6 M solution of butyllithium in hexane, which produced a fine white precipitate. After an additional 15 min stirring, 20 mL of tributyl borate was added which dissolved the precipitate. The stirring was continued for an additional 15 min. The reaction was quenched by the addition of 50 ml of a concentrated aqueous solution of ammonium sulfate. The resulting "cottage cheese" mass was transferred to a beaker, treated with an additional 300 mL of the ammonium sulfate solution, and allowed to stir until the solids had dispersed to a fine texture. The organic phase was separated and the aqueous phase extracted with 2×100 mL Et_2O. The organic phases were combined, evaporated under vacuum, and the off-white residue dissolved in 100 mL MeOH. This cloudy solution was cooled (ice bath) and, with stirring, 20 mL of 35% hydrogen peroxide was added portionwise, . The reaction was allowed to continue stirring for 15 min, and then with the addition of 600 mL H_2O, crystalline solids were formed. These were removed, washed with H_2O, and upon drying yielded 15.4 g of 2,6-diethoxyphenol with a mp of 79.5-81.5 °C. Efforts to diethylate pyrogallol produced mixtures of 2,6-diethoxyphenol and the isomer, 2,3-diethoxyphenol, and these proved difficult to separate. The pure 2,3-isomer was synthesized from ortho-diethoxybenzene by the process used above, and the product was an oil. Both phenols yielded crystalline 3,5-dinitrobenzoates. This derivative of 2,6-diethoxyphenol, upon recrystallization from CH_3CN had a mp of 161-162 °C. The derivative from 2,3-diethoxyphenol, also upon recrystallization from CH_3CN, melted at 167-168 °C. The mixed mp was appropriately depressed (mp 137-140 °C.).

A solution of 7.6 g 2,6-diethoxyphenol in 40 mL MeOH was treated with 4.9 g of a 40% aqueous solution of dimethylamine followed by 3.6 g of a 40% aqueous solution of formaldehyde. The mixture was heated 1 h on the steam bath, and all volatiles were removed under vacuum. The residual dark oil was dissolved in 36 mL IPA and 10.3 g of methyl iodide was added. There was spontaneous heating, and the deposition of fine white solids. After standing for 10 min, these were removed by filtration, and the filter cake washed with more IPA. The crude product was freed from solvent (air dried weight, 1.7 g) and dissolved in 7 mL hot H_2O. To this hot solution there was added 1.7 g sodium cyanide which slowly discharged the color and again deposited flocculant white solids. After cooling, these were removed by filtration, washed with H_2O, and after thorough drying the isolated 3,5-diethoxy-4-hydroxyphenylacetonitrile weighed 0.5 g and had a mp of 107.5-108.5 °C. Anal. $(C_{12}H_{15}NO_3)$ C,H.

To a solution of 2.1 g 3,5-diethoxy-4-hydroxyphenylacetonitrile in 20 mL anhydrous acetone, there was added 30 mg triethyldecylammonium iodide, 4.6 g methyl iodide, and finally 2.3 g powdered anhydrous K_2CO_3. This mixture was held at reflux for 5 h. The reaction mixture was quenched with 200 mL acidified H_2O and extracted with 3x75 mL CH_2Cl_2. The extracts were pooled, washed with 2x75 mL 5% NaOH, and finally once with dilute HCl. The solvent was removed under vacuum, and the residue distilled at 110-115 °C at 0.3 mm/Hg to provide 3,5-diethoxy-4-methoxyphenylacetonitrile as a solid. This weighed 1.3 g and had a mp of 58-59 °C. Anal. $(C_{13}H_{17}NO_3)$ C,H.

To 30 mL of a 1 M solution LAH in THF that had been cooled to 0 °C with vigorous stirring, under a He atmosphere, there was added dropwise 0.78 mL of 100% H_2SO_4. When the addition was complete, there was added dropwise a solution of 1.3 g of 3,5-diethoxy-4-methoxyphenylacetonitrile in 10 mL anhydrous THF. The reaction mixture was brought to room temperature and stirred an additional 10 min, then refluxed on a steam bath for 1.5 h. After cooling to room temperature the excess hydride was destroyed by the addition of about 2 mL IPA, followed by sufficient 15% NaOH to make the reaction basic to external pH paper and to render the aluminum oxides white and filterable. These were removed by filtration, the filter cake was washed with IPA, then the filtrate and washes were combined. The solvents were removed under vacuum and the residue dissolved in dilute H_2SO_4. This was washed with 2x75 mL CH_2Cl_2, the aqueous phase made basic with 5% NaOH, and extracted with 3x75 mL CH_2Cl_2. The extracts were pooled, the solvent removed under vacuum, and the residue distilled at 120-140 °C at 0.3 mm/Hg to yield 0.9 g of a white oil. This was dissolved in 4 mL of IPA and neutralized with concentrated

HCl to an end-point determined by damp external pH paper. There was the immediate formation of solids which were removed by filtration and washed first with IPA and then with Et_2O. This provided 1.0 g of 3,5-diethoxy-4-methoxy-phenethylamine hydrochloride (SB) as white crystals, with a mp of 186-187 °C. Anal. ($C_{13}H_{22}ClNO_3$) C,H.

DOSAGE: above 240 mg.

DURATION: unknown.

QUALITATIVE COMMENTS: (with 120 mg) "There were no effects. Sleep that evening was strange, however, and I was fully awake at 4:00 AM, alert, and mentally restless. And there was a strange outburst of anger in the mid-morning. Might these be related to the material the previous day?"

(with 240 mg) "There was a slight chill that reminded me that I had taken symbescaline a half hour earlier. There was what might be called a vague threshold for about three hours, then nothing more. This material had a God-awful taste that lingers in the mouth far too long. If ever again, it will be in a gelatin capsule."

EXTENSIONS AND COMMENTARY: It must be concluded that SB is "probably" not active. There was no convincing evidence for much effect at levels that would clearly be active for mescaline. This is the kind of result that puts some potentially ambiguous numbers in the literature. One cannot say that it is inactive, for there might well be something at 400 or 800 or 1200 milligrams. But since it has been tried only up to 240 milligrams, I have used the phrase that the activity is greater than 240 milligrams. This will be interpreted by some people as saying that it *is* active, but only at dosages higher than 240 milligrams. What is meant, is that there was no activity observed at the highest level tried, and so if it *is* active, the active dose will be greater than 240 milligrams, and so the potency will be less than that of mescaline. However you phrase it, someone will misinterpret it.

#145   TA;   2,3,4,5-TETRAMETHOXYAMPHETAMINE

SYNTHESIS: To a solution of 50 g 2,3,4-trimethoxybenzaldehyde in 157 mL glacial acetic acid which was well stirred and preheated to 25 °C there was added 55.6 g 40% peracetic acid in acetic acid. The rate of addition was adjusted to allow the evolved heat of the exothermic reaction to be removed by an external ice bath at a rate that kept the internal temperature within a degree of 25 °C. When the addition was complete and there was no more heat being evolved, the reaction mixture was diluted with 3 volumes of H_2O, and neutralized with solid K_2CO_3. All was extracted with 3x250 mL Et_2O, and the removal of the solvent from the pooled extracts under vacuum gave 42 g of residue that appeared to be mainly phenol, with a little formate and aldehyde. This was dissolved in 200 mL of 10% NaOH, allowed to stand for 2 h at ambient temperature, washed with 2x75 mL CH$_2$Cl$_2$, acidified with HCl, and extracted with 3x100 mL Et$_2$O. The pooled extracts were washed with saturated NaHCO$_3$, and the solvent removed to give 34.7 g of 2,3,4-trimethoxy-phenol as an amber oil which was used without further purification. The infra-red spectrum showed no carbonyl group, of either the formate or the starting aldehyde.

A solution of 11.4 g flaked KOH in 100 g EtOH was treated with 33.3 g 2,3,4-trimethoxyphenol and 21.9 g allyl bromide. The mixture was held at reflux for 1.5 h, then poured into 5 volumes of H$_2$O, made basic with the addition of 25% NaOH, and extracted with 3x200 mL CH$_2$Cl$_2$. Removal of the solvent from the pooled extracts gave about 40 g of a crude 2,3,4-trimethoxy-1-allyloxybenzene that clearly had unreacted allyl bromide as a contaminant.

A 39 g sample of crude 2,3,4-trimethoxy-1-allyloxybenzene in a round-bottomed flask with an immersion thermometer was heated with a soft flame. At 225 °C there was a light effervescence and at 240 °C an exothermic reaction set in that raised the temperature immediately to 265 °C. It was held there for 5 min, and then the reaction was allowed to cool to room temperature. GC and IR analysis showed the starting ether to be gone, and that the product was largely 2,3,4-trimethoxy-6-allylphenol. It weighed 34.4 g.

To a solution of 9.4 g KOH in 100 mL MeOH, there was added 33.3 g of 2,3,4-trimethoxy-6-allylphenol and 21.2 g methyl iodide and the mixture was held on the steam bath for 2 h. This was poured into aqueous base, and extracted with 3x100 mL CH$_2$Cl$_2$. Removal of the solvent from the pooled extracts gave 30 g of an amber oil residue that was distilled at 100-125 °C at 0.5 mm/Hg to provide 23.3 g of nearly colorless 2,3,4,5-tetramethoxyallylbenzene.

The total distillation fraction, 23.3 g 2,3,4,5-tetramethoxyallylbenzene, was dissolved in a solution of 25 g flaked KOH in 25 mL EtOH and heated at 100 °C for 24 h. The reaction mixture was poured into 500 mL H$_2$O, and extracted with 2x100 mL CH$_2$Cl$_2$. The aqueous phase was saved. The pooled organic extracts were stripped of solvent under vacuum to give 13.8 g of a fluid oil that was surprising pure 2,3,4,5-tetramethoxypropenylbenzene by both GC and NMR analysis. The basic aqueous phase was acidified, extracted with 2x100 mL CH$_2$Cl$_2$, and the solvent stripped to give 7.5 g of an oil that was phenolic, totally propenyl (as opposed to allyl), and by infra-red the phenolic hydroxyl group was adjacent to the olefin chain. This crude 2-hydroxy-3,4,5-trimethoxypropenylbenzene was methylated with methyl iodide in alcoholic KOH to give an additional 5.6 g of the target 2,3,4,5-tetra-methoxypropenylbenzene. This was identical to the original isolate above. The distilled material had an index of refraction, n$_D^{24}$ = 1.5409.

A well stirred solution of 17.9 g 2,3,4,5-tetramethoxypropenylbenzene in 80 mL distilled acetone was treated with 6.9 g pyridine, and cooled to 0 °C with an external ice bath. There was then added 14 g tetranitromethane over the course of a 0.5 min, and the reaction was quenched by the addition of a solution of 4.6 g KOH in 80 mL H_2O. As the reaction mixture stood, there was a slow deposition of yellow crystals, but beware, this is not the product. This solid weighed 4.0 g and was the potassium salt of trinitromethane. This isolate was dried and sealed in a small vial. After a few days standing, it detonated spontaneously. The filtrate was extracted with 3x75 mL CH_2Cl_2, and the removal of the solvent from these extracts gave a residue of 20.8 g of crude 2-nitro-1-(2,3,4,5-tetramethoxyphenyl)propene which did not crystallize.

A solution was made of 20.3 g of the crude 2-nitro-1-(2,3,4,5-tetramethoxyphenyl)propene in 200 mL anhydrous Et_2O, and this was filtered to remove some 2.7 g of insoluble material which appeared to be the potassium salt of trinitromethane by infra-red analysis. A suspension of 14 g LAH in 1 L anhydrous Et_2O was stirred, placed under an inert atmosphere, and brought up to a gentle reflux. The above clarified ether solution of the propene was added over the course of 1 h, and the mixture was held at reflux for 24 h. After cooling, the excess hydride was destroyed by the cautious addition of 1 L 1.5 N H_2SO_4 (initially a drop or two at a time) and when the two phases were complete clear, they were separated. The aqueous phase was treated with 350 g potassium sodium tartrate, and brought to a pH >9 with base. This was extracted with 3x150 mL CH_2Cl_2, and the removal of the solvent from the pooled extracts gave a residue that was dissolved in 200 mL anhydrous Et_2O, and saturated with anhydrous HCl gas. An Et_2O-insoluble oil was deposited and, after repeated scratching with fresh Et_2O, finally gave a granular white solid. This product was recrystallized from acetic anhydride, giving white crystals that were removed by filtration, Et_2O washed, and air dried. The yield of 2,3,4,5-tetramethoxyamphetamine hydrochloride (TA) was 1.9 g and had a mp of 135.5-136.5 °C.

DOSAGE: probably above 50 mg.

DURATION: unknown.

QUALITATIVE COMMENTS: (with 30 mg) "Definite threshold. There was eye dilation, and some unusual humor — a completely wild day with chi-square calculations on the PDP-7 that were on the edge of bad taste. But I was definitely baseline in the afternoon during the Motor Vehicle Department interactions."
(with 35 mg) "I had some gastric upset, but nonetheless there was a distinct intoxication. The next morning I had a foul headache."

EXTENSIONS AND COMMENTARY: This is pretty thin stuff from which to go out into a world that is populated by pharmacological sharks and stake out claims as to psychedelic potency. The structure of this molecule has everything going for it. It is an overlay of TMA (active) and TMA-2 (even more active) so it is completely reasonable that it should be doing something at a rational dosage. But that dosage might well be in the many tens of milligrams.

Tens of milligrams. Now there is a truly wishy-washy phrase. There is an art to the assignment of an exact number or, as is sometimes desperately needed, a fuzzy number, to a collection of things. In my youth (somewhere way back yonder in the early part of the century) I had been taught rules of grammer that were unquestionably expected of any well-educated person. If you used a Latin stem, you used a Latin prefix. And if you used a Greek stem, you used a Greek prefix. Consider a collection of things with simple geometric sides (a side is a *latus* in Latin). One would speak of a one-sided object as being unilateral, and a bilateral object has two sides. A trilateral, and quadrilateral, and way up there to multilateral objects, are referred to as having three or four or a lot of sides, respectively. Just the opposite occurs with geometric objects with faces. A face is a *hedra* in Greek, so one really should use the Greek structure. If one has just one face, one has a monohedron, a dihedron has two faces, and there are trihedron, tetrahedron, and polyhedron for things that have three, four, or a lot of faces. Actually, the prefix "poly" swings both ways. It was initially a Greek term, but as was the fate of many Greek words, it wandered its way from East to West, and ended up as a Latin term as well.

But back to the problem of how to refer to something that is more than one or two, but not as much as a lot? If you know exactly how many, you should use the proper prefix. But what if you don't know how many? There are terms such as "some." And there is "several." There is a "few" and a "number of" and "numerous" and "a hand full." One desperately looks for a term that is a collective, but which carries the meaning of an undefined number. There are English gems such as a pride of lions and a host of daffodils. But without a specific animal or plant of reference, one must have a target collective that is appropriate, to let the term "many" or "few" imply the proper size. There were many hundreds of persons (a few thousands of persons) at the rally. Several dozen hunters (a few score hunters) were gathered at the lake. A wonderful prefix is "oligo" which means a few, not a lot, and it means that I am not sure just how many are meant. Say, for example, that you have synthesized something in a biochemical mixture that contains three or four peptides. Di-and tri- and tetrapeptides are exact terms, but they do not describe what you have done. Polypeptide is way too big. However, an oligopeptide means that there are a few peptide units, I'm not sure how many. This may well be the most accurate description of just what you have.

I love the British modesty that is shown by hiding a person's physical weight by referring to it with the dimension known as the stone. This is, as I remember, something like 14 pounds. So, if stones were the weight equivalent of 10 milligrams, the activity of TA would be several stone. And since the synthetic intermediate 1-allyl-2,3,4,5-tetramethoxybenzene is one of the ten essential oils, the amination step from our hypothetical reaction in the human liver would make TA one of the so-called Ten Essential Amphetamines.

#146   3-TASB;   3-THIOASYMBESCALINE;   4-ETHOXY-3-
ETHYLTHIO-5-METHOXYPHENETHYLAMINE

SYNTHESIS: Without any solvent, there was combined 21.7 g of solid 5-bromovanillin and 11.4 mL cyclohexylamine. There was the immediate generation of a yellow color and the evolution of heat. The largely solid mass was ground up under 50 mL of boiling IPA to an apparently homogeneous yellow solid which was removed by filtration and washed with IPA. There was thus obtained about 27 g of 3-bromo-N-cyclohexyl-4-hydroxy-5-methoxybenzylidenimine with a mp of 229-231 °C and which proved to be insoluble in most solvents (EtOH, CH_2Cl_2, acetone). A solution in dilute NaOH was unstable with the immediate deposition of opalescent white solids of the phenol sodium salt. A small scale recrystallization from boiling cyclohexanone yielded a fine yellow solid with a lowered mp (210-215 °C). Anal. ($C_{14}H_{18}BrNO_2$) C,H.

A solution of 32.5 g 3-bromo-N-cyclohexyl-4-hydroxy-5-methoxybenzylidenimine in 60 mL of hot DMF was cooled to near room temperature, treated with 24.5 g ethyl iodide and followed by 14.0 g of flake KOH. This mixture was held at reflux for 1 h, cooled, and added to 1 L H_2O. Additional base was added and the product was extracted with 3x150 mL CH_2Cl_2. These pooled extracts were washed with dilute NaOH, then with H_2O, and finally the solvent was removed under vacuum. The crude amber-colored residue was distilled. The fraction coming over at 118-135 °C at 0.4 mm/Hg weighed 8.7 g, spontaneously crystallized, and proved to be 3-bromo-4-ethoxy-5-methoxybenzaldehyde, melting at 59-60 °C after recrystallization from MeOH. Anal. ($C_{10}H_{11}BrO_3$) C,H. The fraction that came over at 135-155 °C at 0.2 mm/Hg weighed 10.5 g and also solidified in the receiver. This product was 3-bromo-N-cyclohexyl-4-ethoxy-5-methoxybenzylidenimine which, upon recrystallization from two volumes MeOH, was a white crystalline material with a mp of 60-61 °C. Anal. ($C_{16}H_{22}BrNO_2$) C,H. The two materials have identical mps, but can be easily distinguished by their infra-red spectra. The aldehyde has a carbonyl stretch at 1692 cm^{-1}, and the Schiff base a C=N stretch at 1641 cm^{-1}.

A solution of 20.5 g 3-bromo-N-cyclohexyl-4-ethoxy-5-methoxybenzylidenimine in about 300 mL anhydrous Et_2O was placed in a He atmosphere, well stirred, and cooled in an external dry ice acetone bath to -80 °C. There was then added 50 mL of 1.6 N butyllithium in hexane. The mixture became yellow and very viscous with the generation of solids. These loosened up with continuing stirring. This was followed by the addition of 10.7 g diethyldisulfide. The reaction became extremely viscous again, and stirring was continued while the reaction was allowed to warm to room temperature. After an additional 0.5 h stirring, the reaction mixture was added to 800 mL of dilute HCl. The Et_2O phase was separated and the solvent removed under vacuum. The residue was returned to the original aqueous phase, and the entire mixture heated on the steam bath for 2 h. The bright yellow color faded and there was the formation of a yellowish phase on the surface of the H_2O. The aqueous solution was cooled to room temperature, extracted with 3x100 mL CH_2Cl_2, the extracts pooled, washed first with dilute HCl, then with saturated brine, and the solvent removed under vacuum. The residue was an amber oil weighing 20.4 g, and was distilled at 130-140 °C at 0.3 mm/Hg to yield 12.9 g of 4-ethoxy-3-ethylthio-5-methoxybenzaldehyde as a straw colored oil that did not crystallize. Anal. ($C_{12}H_{16}O_3S$) C,H.

A solution of 1.0 g 4-ethoxy-3-ethylthio-5-methoxybenzaldehyde in 20 g nitromethane was treated with about 0.2 g of anhydrous ammonium acetate and heated on the steam bath. TLC analysis showed that the aldehyde was substantially gone within 20 min and that, in addition to the expected nitrostyrene, there were four scrudge products (see the discussion of scrudge in the extensions and commentary section under 3-TSB). Removal of the excess nitromethane under vacuum gave an orange oil which was diluted with 5 mL cold MeOH but which could not be induced to crystallize. A seed was obtained by using a preparative TLC plate (20x20 cm) and removing the fastest moving spot (development was with CH_2Cl_2). Placing this in the above MeOH solution of the crude nitrostyrene allowed crystallization to occur. After filtering and washing with MeOH, 0.20 g of fine yellow crystals were obtained which melted at 75-77 °C. Recrystallization from MeOH gave a bad recovery of yellow crystals of 4-ethoxy-3-ethylthio-5-methoxy-ß-nitrostyrene that now melted at 78.5-79 °C. Anal. ($C_{13}H_{17}NO_4S$) C,H. This route was discarded in favor of the Wittig reaction described below.

A mixture of 27 g methyltriphenylphosphonium bromide in 150 mL anhydrous THF was placed under a He atmosphere, well stirred, and cooled to 0 °C with an external ice water bath. There was then slowly added 50 mL of 1.6 N butyllithium in hexane which resulted in the initial generation of solids that largely redissolved by the completion of the addition of the butyllithium and after allowing the mixture to return to room temperature. There was then added 11.7 g of 4-ethoxy-3-ethylthio-5-methoxybenzaldehyde without any solvent. There was the immediate formation of an unstirrable solid, which partially broke up into a gum that still wouldn't stir. This was moved about, as well as possible, with a glass rod, and then all was added to 400 mL H_2O. The two phases were separated and the lower, aqueous, phase extracted with 2x75 mL of petroleum ether. The organic fractions were combined and the solvents removed under vacuum to give the crude 4-ethoxy-3-ethylthio-5-methoxystyrene as a pale yellow fluid liquid.

A solution of 10 mL of borane-methyl sulfide complex (10 M BH_3 in methyl sulfide) in 75 mL THF was placed in a He atmosphere, cooled to 0 °C, treated with 21 mL of 2-methylbutene, and stirred for 1 h while returning to room temperature. This was added directly to the crude 4-ethoxy-3-ethylthio-5-methoxystyrene. The slightly exothermic reaction was allowed to stir for 1 h, and then the excess borane was destroyed with a few mL of MeOH (in the absence of air to avoid the formation of the dialkylboric acid). There was then added 19 g of elemental iodine followed, over the course of about 10 min, by a solution of 4 g NaOH in 50 mL hot MeOH. The color did not fade. Addition of another 4 mL 25% NaOH lightened the color a bit, but it remained pretty ugly. This was added to 500 mL H_2O containing 5 g sodium thiosulfate and extracted with 3x100 mL petroleum ether. The extracts were pooled, and the solvent removed under vacuum to provide crude 1-(4-ethoxy-3-ethylthio-5-methoxyphenyl)-2-iodoethane as a residue.

To this crude 1-(4-ethoxy-3-ethylthio-5-methoxyphenyl)-2-iodoethane there was added a solution of 20 g potassium phthalimide in 150 mL anhydrous DMF, and all was held at reflux overnight. After adding to 500 mL of dilute NaOH, some 1.4 g of a white solid was generated and removed by filtration. The aqueous filtrate was extracted with 2x75 mL Et_2O. These extracts were combined, washed with dilute HCl, and the solvent removed under vacuum providing 23.6 g of a terpene-smelling amber oil. This was stripped of all volatiles by heating to 170 °C at 0.4 mm/Hg providing 5.4 g of a sticky brown residue. This consisted largely of the desired phthalimide. The solids proved to be a purer form of 1-(4-ethoxy-3-ethylthio-5-methoxy)-2-phthalimidoethane and was recrystallized from a very small amount of MeOH to give fine white crystals with a mp of 107.5-108.5 °C. Anal. ($C_{21}H_{23}NO_4S$) C,H. The white solids and the brown impure phthalimide were separately converted to the final product, 3-TASB.

A solution of 1.2 g of the crystalline 1-(4-ethoxy-3-ethylthio-5-methoxy-phenyl)-2-phthalimidoethane in 40 mL of warm n-butanol was treated with 3 mL of 66% hydrazine, and the mixture was heated on the steam bath for 40 min. The reaction mixture was added to 800 mL dilute H_2SO_4. The solids were removed by filtration, and the filtrate was washed with 2x75 mL CH_2Cl_2. The aqueous phase was made basic with 25% NaOH, extracted with 3x75 mL CH_2Cl_2, and the solvent from these pooled extracts removed under vacuum yielding 6.2 g of a residue that was obviously rich in butanol. This residue was distilled at 138-144 C. at 0.3 mm/Hg to give 0.6 g of a colorless oil. This was dissolved in 2.4 mL IPA, neutralized with concentrated HCl, and diluted with 25 mL anhydrous Et_2O. The solution remained clear for about 10 seconds, and then deposited white crystals. These were removed by filtration, washed with additional Et_2O, and air dried to give 0.4 g 4-ethoxy-3-ethylthio-5-methoxyphenethylamine hydrochloride (3-TASB) with a mp of 140-141 °C. Anal. ($C_{13}H_{22}ClNO_2S$) C,H. The amber-colored impure phthalimide, following the same procedure, provided another 0.9 g of the hydrochloride salt with a mp of 138-139 °C.

DOSAGE: about 160 mg.

DURATION: 10 - 18 h.

QUALITATIVE COMMENTS: (with 120 mg) "This is no more than a plus one, and it didn't really get there until about the third hour. By a couple of hours later, I feel that the mental effects are pretty much dissipated, but there is some real physical residue. Up with some caution."

(with 160 mg) "The taste is completely foul. During the first couple of hours, there was a conscious effort to avoid nausea. Then I noticed that people's faces looked like marvelous parodies of themselves and that there was considerable time slowing. There was no desire to eat at all. Between the eighth and twelth hour, the mental things drifted away, but the body was still wound up. Sleep was impossible until about 3:00 AM (the 18th hour of the experiment) and even the next day I was extremely active, anorexic, alert, excited, and plagued with occasional diarrhea. This is certainly a potent stimulant. The next night I felt the tensions drop, and finally got an honest and easy sleep. There is a lot of adrenergic push to this material."

EXTENSIONS AND COMMENTARY: No pharmacological agent has an action that is pure this or pure that. Some pain-killing narcotics can produce reverie and some sedatives can produce paranoia. And just as surely, some psychedelics can produce stimulation. With 3-TASB we may be seeing the shift from sensory effects over to out-and-out stimulation. It would be an interesting challenge to take these polyethylated phenethylamines and assay them strictly for their amphetamine-like action. Sadly, the potencies are by and large so low, that the human animal can't be used, and any sub-human experimental animal would not enable the psychedelic part of the equation to be acknowledged. If an order of magnitude of increased potency could be bought by some minor structural change, this question could be addressed. Maybe as the three-carbon amphetamine homologs, or as the 2,4,5- or 2,4,6- substitution patterns, rather than the 3,4,5-pattern used in this set.

#147 4-TASB; 4-THIOASYMBESCALINE; 3-ETHOXY-4-ETHYLTHIO-5-METHOXYPHENETHYLAMINE

SYNTHESIS: A solution of 20.5 g N,N,N',N'-tetramethylethylenediamine and 22.3 g of 3-ethoxyanisole was made in 100 mL hexane under a He atmosphere with good stirring. There was added 125 mL 1.6 M butyllithium in hexane, which formed a white granular precipitate. This was cooled in an ice bath, and there was added 24.4 g of diethyldisulfide which produced an exothermic reaction and changed the precipitate to a creamy phase. After being held for a few min at reflux temperature, the reaction mixture was added to 500 mL dilute H_2SO_4 which produced two clear phases. The hexane phase was separated, and the aqueous phase extracted with 2x75 mL methylcyclopentane. The organics were combined, and the solvents removed under vacuum. There was obtained a residue which was distilled under a vacuum.

At 0.3 mm/Hg the fraction boiling at 95-105 °C was a yellow liquid weighing 28.5 g which was largely 3-ethoxy-2-(ethylthio)anisole which seemed to be reasonably pure chromatographically. It was used as such in the bromination step below.

To a stirred solution of 15.0 g of 3-ethoxy-2-(ethylthio)anisole in 100 mL CH_2Cl_2 there was added 12 g elemental bromine dissolved in 25 mL CH_2Cl_2. There was the copious evolution of HBr. After stirring at ambient temperature for 3 h, the dark solution was added to 300 mL H_2O containing sodium dithionite. Shaking immediately discharged the residual bromine color, and the organic phase was separated, The aqueous phase was extracted once with 100 mL CH_2Cl_2, the pooled extracts washed with dilute base, and then the solvent was removed under vacuum to give a light brown oil. This wet product was distilled at 112-122 °C at 0.3 mm/Hg to yield 4-bromo (and/or 6-bromo)-3-ethoxy-2-(ethylthio)anisole as a light orange oil. This was used in the following benzyne step without separation into its components.

To a solution of 36 mL diisopropylamine in 150 mL anhydrous THF under a He atmosphere, and which had been cooled to -10 °C with an external ice/MeOH bath, there was added 105 mL of a 1.6 M solution of butylithium in hexane. There was then added 5.1 mL of dry CH_3CN followed by the dropwise addition of 15.0 g 4-bromo-(and/or 6-bromo)-3-ethoxy-2-(ethylthio)anisole diluted with a little anhydrous THF. There was an immediate development of a dark red-brown color. The reaction was warmed to room temperature and stirred for 0.5 h. This was then poured into 600 mL of dilute H_2SO_4. The organic phase was separated, and the aqueous fraction extracted with 2x50 mL CH_2Cl_2. These extracts were pooled and the solvent removed under vacuum. The residue was a dark oil and quite complex as seen by thin layer chromatography. This material was distilled at 0.3 mm/Hg yielding two fractions The first boiled at 112-125 °C and weighed 3.9 g. It was largely starting bromo compound with a little nitrile, and was discarded. The second fraction distilled at 130-175 °C and also weighed 3.9 g. This fraction was rich in the product 3-ethoxy-4-ethylthio-5-methoxyphenylacetonitrile, but it also contained several additional components as seen by thin layer chromatographic analysis. On standing for two months, a small amount of solid was laid down which weighed 0.5 g after cleanup with hexane. But even it consisted of three components by TLC, none of them the desired nitrile. The crude fraction was used for the final step without further purification or microanalysis.

A solution of LAH in anhydrous THF under N_2 (15 mL of a 1.0 M solution) was cooled to 0 °C and vigorously stirred. There was added, dropwise, 0.40 mL 100% H_2SO_4, followed by about 3 g of the crude 3-ethoxy-4-ethylthio-5-methoxy-phenylacetonitrile diluted with a little anhydrous THF. The reaction mixture was stirred until it came to room temperature, and then held at reflux on the steam bath for 2 h. After cooling to room temperature, there was added IPA to destroy the excess hydride (there was quite a bit of it) and then 15% NaOH to bring the reaction to a basic pH and convert the aluminum oxide to a loose, white, filterable consistency. This was removed by filtration, and washed first with THF followed by IPA. The filtrate and washes were stripped of solvent under vacuum, the residue added to 100 mL dilute H_2SO_4. This was washed with 2x75 mL CH_2Cl_2, made basic with 25% NaOH, and extracted with 2x50 mL CH_2Cl_2. After combining, the solvent was removed under vacuum providing a residue that was distilled. A fraction boiling at 122-140 °C at 0.3 mm/Hg weighed 1.0 g and was a colorless oil. This was dissolved in 10 mL of IPA, and neutralized with 20 drops of concentrated HCl and diluted, with stirring, with 40 mL anhydrous Et_2O. There was the slow formation of a fine white crystalline salt, which was removed by filtration, washed with Et_2O, and air dried. The product 3-ethoxy-4-ethylthio-5-methoxyphenethylamine hydrochloride (4-TASB), weighed 0.5 g, and had a mp 139-140 °C. Gas chromatographic analysis by capillary column chromatography of the free base (in butyl acetate solution on silica SE-54) showed a single peak at a reasonable retention time, verifying isomeric purity of the product. Anal. $(C_{13}H_{22}ClNO_2S)$ C,H.

DOSAGE: 60 - 100 mg.

DURATION: 10 - 15 h.

QUALITATIVE COMMENTS: (with 60 mg) "The compound has a petroleum-refinery type taste. There was a looseness of the bowels as I got into it. Here we have another of these 'What is it' or 'What isn't it' compounds. Somehow I seemed to have to push the erotic, the visual, the whole psychedelic shmeer, to document that this was indeed effective. I am not impressed."

(with 100 mg) "There were some trivial physical problems during the early stages of this experiment. But there was fantasy stuff to music, and some jumpy stuff to music. Is there a neurological hyperreflexia? I was able to sleep at the 12 hour point but I felt quite irritable. I am agitated. I am twitchy. This has been very intense, and I am not completely comfortable yet. Let's wait for a while."

(with 100 mg) "Music was lovely during the experiment, but pictures were not particularly exciting. I had feelings that my nerve-endings were raw and active. There was water retention. There was heartbeat wrongness, and respiration wrongness. During my attempts to sleep, my eyes-closed fantasies became extremely negative. I could actually feel the continuous electrical impulses travelling between my nerve endings. Disturbing. There was continuous erotic arousability, and this seemed to be part of the same over-sensitivity of the nervous system; orgasm didn't soothe or smooth out the feeling of vulnerability. This is a very threatening material. DO NOT REPEAT."

EXTENSIONS AND COMMENTARY: Again, another drug with more physical problems than psychic virtue, but with no obvious structural feature to hang it all onto. Some day this will all make sense!

#148   5-TASB;   5-THIOASYMBESCALINE;   3,4-DIETHOXY-5-METHYLTHIOPHENETHYLAMINE

SYNTHESIS: A solution of 11.5 g 3-bromo-N-cyclohexyl-4,5-diethoxybenzylidinimine (see under ASB for its preparation) in 150 mL anhydrous Et$_2$O was placed in a He atmosphere, well stirred, and cooled in an external dry ice/acetone bath to -80 °C. There was light formation of fine crystals. There was then added 25 mL of 1.6 N butyllithium in hexane and the mixture stirred for 15 min. This was followed by the addition of 4.3 mL dimethyldisulfide over the course of 20 min, during which time the solution became increasingly cloudy and then thinned out again. The mixture was allowed to come to room temperature over the course of an additional h, and then added to 400 mL of dilute HCl. There was the generation of a lot of yellow solids, and the Et$_2$O phase was almost colorless. This was separated, the solvent removed under vacuum, and the residue combined with the original aqueous phase. This phase was then heated on the steam bath for 2 h. The aqueous solution was cooled to room temperature, extracted with 3x100 mL CH$_2$Cl$_2$, the extracts pooled, washed with H$_2$O, and the solvent removed under vacuum to yield 9.4 g of an amber oil which spontaneously crystallized. This was distilled at 125-132 °C at 0.2 mm/Hg to yield 7.1 g of 3,4-diethoxy-5-(methylthio)benzaldehyde as a white oil that spontaneously crystallized. The crude product had a mp of 73-74 °C that actually decreased to 72-73 °C after recrystallization from MeOH. Anal. (C$_{12}$H$_{16}$O$_3$S) C,H.

A solution of 16.2 g methyltriphenylphosphonium bromide in 200 mL anhydrous THF was placed under a He atmosphere, well stirred, and cooled to 0 °C with an external ice water bath. There was then added 30 mL of 1.6 N butyllithium in hexane which resulted in the generation of a clear yellow solution. The reaction mixture was brought up to room temperature, and 7.0 g 3,4-diethoxy-5-(methylthio)benzaldehyde in 50 mL THF was added dropwise, dispelling the color, and the mixture was held at reflux on the steam bath for 1 h. The reaction was quenched in 800 mL H$_2$O, the top hexane layer separated, and the aqueous phase extracted with 2x75 mL of petroleum ether. The organic fractions were combined and the solvents removed under vacuum to give 12.0 g of the crude 3,4-diethoxy-5-methylthiostyrene as a pale amber-colored oil.

A solution of 6.0 mL of borane-methyl sulfide complex (10 M BH$_3$ in methyl sulfide) in 45 mL THF was placed in a He atmosphere, cooled to 0 °C, treated with 12.6 g of 2-methylbutene, and stirred for 1 h while returning to room temperature. To this there was added a solution of the impure 3,4-diethoxy-5-methylthiostyrene in 25 mL THF. This was stirred for 1 h during which time the color deepened to a dark yellow. The excess borane was destroyed with about 2 mL MeOH (all this still in the absence of air). There was then added 11.4 g elemental iodine followed by a solution of 2.4 g NaOH in 30 mL of boiling MeOH, added over the course of 10 min. This was followed by sufficient 25% NaOH to discharge the residual iodine color (about 4 mL was required). The reaction mixture was added to 500 mL water, and sodium hydrosulfite was added to discharge the remaining iodine color (about 4 g). This was extracted with 3x100 mL petroleum ether, the extracts pooled, and the solvent removed under vacuum to provide 25.9 g of crude 1-(3,4-diethoxy-5-methylthiophenyl)-2-iodoethane as a pale yellow fluid oil. Thin layer chromatographic analysis of this material on silica gel plates (using a 90:10 mixture of CH_2Cl_2/methylcyclopentane as solvent) showed largely the iodo-product (Rf 0.9) with no visible starting aldehyde (Rf 0.7).

To this crude 1-(3,4-diethoxy-5-methylthiophenyl)-2-iodoethane there was added a solution of 12 g potassium phthalimide in 90 mL anhydrous DMF, and all was held at reflux in a heating mantle. The reaction progress was followed by TLC, and at 1.5 h it was substantially complete. After adding to 500 mL 5% NaOH, the organic phase was separated, and the aqueous phase was extracted with 2x75 mL Et_2O. The organic fractions were combined, and the solvent removed under vacuum providing 19.3 g of an amber oil. The residual volatiles were removed by distillation up to 170 °C at 0.2 mm/Hg. The distillate weighed 7.0 g and contained little if any phthalimide by TLC. The pot residue was a viscous amber oil, and also weighed 7.0 g. About half of this was employed in the following hydrolysis step, and the rest was rubbed under an equal volume of MeOH providing 1-(3,4-diethoxy-5-methylthiophenyl)-2-phthalimidoethane as a white solid. A small sample was recrystallized from an equal volume of MeOH to give white crystals with a mp of 79.5-81 °C. Re-recrystallization from MeOH produced an analytical sample with a mp of 83-84 °C. Anal. ($C_{21}H_{23}NO_4S$) C,H.

A solution of 3.2 g of the impure 1-(3,4-diethoxy-5-methylthiophenyl)-2-phthalimidoethane in 150 mL of n-butanol there was added 20 mL of 66% hydrazine, and the mixture was heated on the steam bath for 2 h. This was added to 600 mL of dilute H_2SO_4, and the two layers were separated. The butanol layer was extracted with 2x100 mL dilute H_2SO_4. These extracts were added to the original aqueous phase, and this was washed with 3x75 mL CH_2Cl_2. This was then made basic with 5% NaOH, extracted with 3x75 mL CH_2Cl_2, and the solvent from these pooled extracts removed under vacuum. The residue (which weighed 9.7 g and contained much butanol) was distilled at 140-145 °C at 0.3 mm/Hg to give 0.7 g of a colorless oil. This was dissolved in 3.0 mL IPA, neutralized with concentrated HCl, and diluted with 12 mL anhydrous Et_2O to give a solution that immediately crystallized to provide white crystals of 3,4-diethoxy-5-methylthiophenethylamine hydrochloride (5-TASB). These weighed 0.7 g after washing with Et_2O and drying to constant weight. The mp was 182-183 °C, and an analytical sample was dried at 100 °C for 24 h. Anal. ($C_{13}H_{22}ClNO_2S$) C,H.

DOSAGE: about 160 mg.

DURATION: about 8 h.

QUALITATIVE COMMENTS: (with 120 mg) "Maybe there is something at about hour 5. My talking with innocent people had hints of strangeness. And there was the slightest suggestion of some physical effect. Call it an overall (+)."

(with 160 mg) "I am immediately warm at the extremities. An awareness grows upon me for a couple of hours. I am a little light-headed, and I feel that there is more physical than there is mental, and it is not all entirely nice. I am slightly hyperreflexive, and there is a touch of diarrhea. I am happy that I held this at 160 milligrams. I am mentally flat at the eighth hour, although there are some physical residues. The effects are real, but I don't want to go higher. Some trace physical memory seems to stay with me as a constant companion."

EXTENSIONS AND COMMENTARY: There is a ponderousness about adding a couple of ethyl groups and a sulfur that seems to say, "no fun." 5-TASB has something going for it (but not much) and 3-TASB is quite a bit more peppy and, actually, 4-TASB has quite a bit of life. But there is a sense of "why bother?" There were a couple of bouts of light-headedness, but there was no unexpected excitement discovered in this methodical study. No surprises. Keep the chain lengths down.

#149   TB;   4-THIOBUSCALINE;   3,5-DIMETHOXY-4-(n)-BUTYLTHIOPHENETHYLAMINE

SYNTHESIS: A solution was made of 12.1 g N,N,N',N'-tetramethylethylenediamine and 13.8 g of 1,3-dimethoxybenzene in 200 mL 30-60 °C petroleum ether. This was stirred vigorously under a He atmosphere and cooled to 0 °C with an external ice bath. There was added 66 mL of 1.6 M butyl lithium in hexane which produced a white granular precipitate. The reaction mixture was brought up to room temperature for a few minutes, and then cooled again to 0 °C. There was then added 18.7 g of di-(n)-butyl disulfide (this reagent was quite yellow, but was used without any purification) which changed the granular precipitate to a strange salmon color. Stirring was continued while the reaction mixture was brought up to room temperature and finally up to reflux. The reaction mixture was then added to 600 mL of dilute H_2SO_4. The two phases were separated, and the aqueous phase extracted with 2x75 mL Et_2O. The organic phases were combined and the solvent removed under vacuum. The residue weighed 33.0 g and was a dark yellow oil. Efforts to remove this color by reductive extraction of a CH_2Cl_2 solution with aqueous sodium hydrosulfite were futile. The residue was distilled at 0.3 mm/Hg to give two fractions. The first boiled at 95-115 °C, weighed 4.1 g and was largely recovered dibutyl disulfide. The product 2-(n)-butylthio-1,3-

dimethoxybenzene boiled at 115-135 °C and weighed 19.5 g. It was a pale amber oil that could not be induced to crystallize. Anal. ($C_{12}H_{18}O_2S$) C,H.

To a stirred solution of 19.5 g of 2-(n)-butylthio-1,3-dimethoxybenzene in 75 mL CH_2Cl_2 there was added 14.5 g elemental bromine dissolved in 75 mL CH_2Cl_2. The evolution of HBr was evident, but the reaction was not exothermic. The reaction was allowed to stir for 1 h and then heated briefly to a reflux on the steam bath. It was then washed with H_2O containing sodium hydrosulfite which discharged the residual color. After washing with saturated brine, the solvent was removed under vacuum leaving 26.0 g of a pale amber oil. This was distilled at 120-140 °C at 0.4 mm/Hg yielding 4-bromo-2-(n)-butylthio-1,3-dimethoxybenzene as a yellow-orange oil. It could not be crystallized. Anal. ($C_{12}H_{17}BrO_2S$) C,H.

To a solution of 11.5 mL diisopropylamine in 50 mL hexane that was stirred under N_2 there was added 50 mL of 1.6 M butyllithium. After 15 min stirring, the reaction mixture became very viscous, and it was diluted with 150 mL anhydrous THF. After cooling in an ice bath there was added 2.0 mL CH_3CN followed in 1 min with 6.0 g of 4-bromo-2-(n)-butylthio-1,3-dimethoxyanisole a bit at a time over the course of 1 min. There was the immediate formation of a deep red color. After stirring for 0.5 h, the mixture was poured into dilute H_2SO_4. The organic layer was separated, and the aqueous layer extracted with 3x75 mL CH_2Cl_2. These extracts were pooled, dried with anhydrous K_2CO_3, and the solvent was removed under vacuum. The residue was distilled at 0.25 mm/Hg and yielded two fractions. The first fraction boiled at 125-145 °C, weighed 0.8 g and was discarded. The second fraction came over at 145-175 °C as a light yellow oil and weighed 2.2 g. This product, 4-(n)-butylthio-3,5-dimethoxyphenylacetonitrile, was reduced as such without further purification or analysis.

A solution of LAH under N_2 (20 mL of a 1 M solution in anhydrous THF) was cooled to 0 °C and vigorously stirred. There was added, dropwise, 0.53 mL 100% H_2SO_4, followed by 2.0 g 4-(n)-butylthio-3,5-dimethoxyphenylacetonitrile in 10 mL anhydrous THF. The reaction mixture was stirred at 0 °C for a few min, then brought to room temperature for 1 h, and finally to a reflux for 1 h on the steam bath. After cooling back to room temperature, there was added IPA (to destroy the excess hydride) followed by 10% NaOH which brought the reaction to a basic pH and converted the aluminum oxides to a loose, white, filterable consistency. These were removed by filtration, and washed with THF and IPA. The filtrate and washes were stripped of solvent under vacuum, the residue was suspended in 150 mL of dilute NaOH and extracted with 3x100 CH_2Cl_2. These extracts were pooled and extracted with 2x75 mL dilute H_2SO_4. Emulsions required that a considerable additional quantity of H_2O be added. The aqueous phase was made basic, and extracted with 2x100 mL CH_2Cl_2. After combining these extracts, the solvent was removed under vacuum providing a residue that was distilled. The product distilled at 138-168 °C at 0.4 mm/Hg as a white oil weighing 0.7 g. This was dissolved in a small amount of IPA, neutralized with concentrated HCl and, with continuous stirring, diluted with several volumes of anhydrous Et_2O. After filtering, Et_2O

washing, and air drying, 4-(n)-butylthio-3,5-dimethoxyphenethylamine hydro-chloride (TB) was obtained, weighed 0.6 g, and had a mp of 154-155 °C. Anal. $(C_{14}H_{24}ClNO_2S)$ C,H.

DOSAGE: 60 - 120 mg.

DURATION: about 8 h.

QUALITATIVE COMMENTS: (with 35 mg) "I was aware of something at about an hour, and it developed into a benign and beautiful experience which never quite popped into anything psychedelic. At the fifth hour there was a distinct drop, and I made what might be thought of as a foolish effort to rekindle the state with an additional 20 milligrams but it was too little and too late. There was no regeneration of anything additional."

(with 60 mg) "A very subtle threshold, probably, and six hours into it there seems to have been little if any effect. My memory of it is not that certain and now I am not sure that there had been anything at all."

(with 80 mg) "I am vaguely aware of something. The body discomfort may reflect the use of sardines in tomato sauce for lunch, but still things are not quite right. Five hours into it I am still in a wonderful place spiritually, but there seem to be some dark edges. I might be neurologically sensitive to this."

(with 120 mg) "The course of the action of this is extremely clear. The development was from 5 PM to 7 PM [the experiment started at 4 PM] and by 10 PM I was dropping and by midnight I went to bed and slept well. Food was not too interesting, and a glass of wine before sleeping produced no noticeable effect. This was an uneventful experience that never really made it off the ground. It was pleasant, but certainly not psychedelic."

EXTENSIONS AND COMMENTARY: There is a term "dose-dependent" in pharmacology. When there is a complex action produced by a drug, then each of the components of this mixture of effects should be expected to become more intense following a bigger dose of the drug. This is certainly true with most of the actions of psychoactive drugs.

As to the psychedelic aspects of some drugs, there can be visual effects, eyes-open (edge-ripples or colors or retinal games) or eyes-closed (images of the elaborately decorated doors of the mosque, or of an orchestra floating suspended by its music) or fantasy (you are moving beyond the confines of your body and invading someone else's space). The same applies to tactile enhancement, to the anaesthetic component, to the depth of insight realized from a drug. The more the drug, as a rule, the more the effect, up to the point that new and disruptive effects are realized. This latter is called toxicity.

As to the stimulant component, the same is true. The person gets wired up, and there is no sleep because there is no hiding from a cascade of images and meanings, and the body lies there unwilling to yield guard since both the pounding heart and the interpretive psyche are demanding attention. These aspects also intensify with increasingly higher doses.

But an exception to this is the euphoria-producing aspect of a drug. One sees with increasing doses a continuing "threshold" that makes you aware, that fluffs the senses, but which seems not, at any level, to take over or to command the ship. It is truly a catalytic on or off. You are or you are not. In the "Tomso" effect, this action is produced by alcohol. There is disinhibition with alcohol which allows a central intoxication from the drug TOMSO regardless of the amount of drug used (see under TOMSO). One sees again, here with TB, the case of a perpetual series of "thresholds." Never the psychedelic or the stimulant action that increases with increased dose. Always the simple and ephemeral catalyst of euphoria without substance and without body. It is a compound that can never be pinned and labeled in the butterfly collection since it defies an accepted classification.

This action was seen first with the compound called ARIADNE and when it was called an anti-depressant, it proved to be commercially interesting. It is fully possible that TB would be of value to certain depressed people in exactly the same way.

#150   3-TE;   3-THIOESCALINE;   4-ETHOXY-5-METHOXY-3-METHYLTHIOPHENETHYLAMINE

SYNTHESIS: A solution of 10.4 g of 3-bromo-N-cyclohexyl-4-ethoxy-5-methoxybenzylidenimine (see under 3-TASB for its preparation) in 125 mL anhydrous Et_2O, in a He atmosphere, was cooled with an external dry ice acetone bath to -80 °C with good stirring. To this clear pale yellow solution there was added 25 mL 1.6 M butyllithium in hexane (about a 25% excess) which produced a fine white precipitate over the following 15 min. There was then added 4.2 g dimethyl disulfide. At the half-addition point, the generated solids became so heavy that stirring became difficult, but towards the end of the addition the reaction thinned out again and became quite loose. The dry ice bath was removed and the reaction allowed to come to room temperature, which again allowed the formation of a heavy solid phase while warming and, again, a loose and easily stirred mixture when finally at room temperature. All was added to 400 mL H_2O which had been strongly acidified with HCl. The two phases were separated, and the aqueous phase (which contained a small amount of yellow oily matter insoluble in either phase) was heated on the steam bath for 0.75 h. On cooling, the oily component set to a yellow solid, which was removed by filtration and washed with H_2O. This crude product, 5.9 g of yellow solid, was distilled 115-125 °C at 0.3 mm/Hg to give 4.9 g of 4-ethoxy-

3-methoxy-5-(methylthio)benzaldehyde as a pale yellow solid that had a mp of 43-45 °C. Recrystallization from MeOH gave a mp of 47-48 °C. Anal. $(C_{11}H_{14}O_3S)$ C,H. This product can also be prepared from the anion of 3-thiosyringaldehyde (mp 141-143 °C as crystals from MeOH) by reaction with ethyl iodide in the presence of phase-transfer catalyst, but the yield is quite poor.

    To a solution of 4.4 g 4-ethoxy-5-methoxy-3-(methylthio)benzaldehyde in 75 mL nitromethane, there was added 0.5 g anhydrous ammonium acetate and the mixture was heated on the steam bath for 80 min. Care must be taken in the length of time, and there must be frequent TLC montoring, as there is a rapid scrudge buildup (see under 3-TSB for a discussion of scrudge). The reaction mixture was stripped of nitromethane under vacuum, and the residual deep-yellow oil was dissolved in 20 mL of boiling MeOH. This was decanted from a small amount of insoluble matter and, upon cooling, deposited bright yellow crystals of 4-ethoxy-5-methoxy-3-methylthio-ß-nitrostyrene. This was removed by filtration and, after washing with cold MeOH and air drying, weighed 2.4 g. The mp was ambiguous. The above crude material melted at 92-93 °C, which is probably too high! Earlier samples which melted in the low 80's appeared to have a mp, after repeated recrystallization from MeOH, of 87-88 °C. This latter was the property of the analytical sample. Anal. $(C_{12}H_{15}NO_4S)$ C,H. The mp of the TLC low-moving component is always quite high, and might have been a factor in the assignment of this physical property.

    AH was prepared in the usual manner from a suspension of 2.0 g LAH in 75 mL anhydrous THF, cooled to 0 °C, well stirred in an inert atmosphere of He, and treated with 1.33 mL of 100% H_2SO_4 added dropwise. There was added, dropwise and over the course of 10 min, a solution of 2.4 g 4-ethoxy-5-methoxy-3-methylthio-ß-nitrostyrene in 15 mL anhydrous THF. The reaction was exothermic, and was heated on the steam bath at reflux for an additional 10 min. After cooling again, there was added enough IPA to decompose the excess hydride and sufficient 10% NaOH to convert the aluminum oxide solids to a white, easily filterable mass. This was filtered, the filter cake washed with additional IPA, the filtrate and washes combined, and the solvent removed under vacuum. This was dissolved in 100 mL of dilute H_2SO_4 which was washed with 2x50 mL CH_2Cl_2. The aqueous phase was made basic with NaOH, extracted with 2x50 mL CH_2Cl_2, and the extracts pooled and the solvent removed under vacuum to yield a residue of a colorless oil. This distilled at 118-122 °C at 0.4 mm/Hg producing 1.9 g of a colorless oil. This was dissolved in 10 mL IPA, neutralized with 30 drops of concentrated HCl and, with good stirring, diluted with 20 mL anhydrous Et_2O. The product 4-ethoxy-5-methoxy-3-methylthiophenethylamine hydrochloride (3-TE) was removed by filtration, washed with Et_2O, and air dried to provide a white solid that weighed 1.0 g and melted at about 180 °C. Anal. $(C_{12}H_{20}ClNO_2S)$ C,H.

DOSAGE: 60 - 80 mg.

DURATION: 8 - 12 h.

QUALITATIVE COMMENTS: (with 60 mg) "There may well be time slowing. I noticed that the voices on the radio seemed to be of a deeper pitch. And with music there is a most easy flight of fantasy. I tried to keep a logical conversation going on the telephone, but I am pretty sure there were problems. I found myself down sooner than I would have liked."

(with 70 mg) "I found myself in a good, rich place, and thoroughly enjoyed my introspection. I didn't want to talk and interact, and that seemed just fine with everyone else. Several of the others seemed restless, but I lay back and let them do their thing. My appetite was fine towards the end, and I might have actually overeaten. I was able to drive home that evening, but there seemed to be some slight residual something after waking in the morning. I would certainly repeat without hesitation."

(with 80 mg) "Art interpretation and imagery with music are remarkable. This material touches on the psychedelic — rather than just being stoned. The body is higher than the mind, but where the mind is makes it all OK. It's worth the cost. My getting to sleep was easy that evening, but sleep was not too restful and there was something strange about it."

EXTENSIONS AND COMMENTARY: There is a good lesson to be learned in the attempts to predict the potency of 3-TE before it was actually explored. All pharmacological prediction follows pretty much a single mechanism. Find things that are close in some way, and arrange them in a manner that allows comparison. A relates to B in this way, and A relates to C in that way, and since D incorporates both this and that of each, it will probably be such-and-such. The Roman square. Here is the square with the horizontal arrow adding a sulfur in the 3-position and the vertical arrow adding an ethyl group in place of a methyl group at the 4-position:

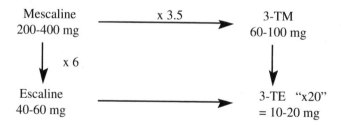

Mescaline   x 3.5   3-TM
200-400 mg   60-100 mg

x 6

Escaline   3-TE "x20"
40-60 mg   = 10-20 mg

and one would predict a potency of some 20x that of mescaline, or something in the range of 15 mg. Here is an equally likely square, based on the horizontal arrow relocating a sulfur from the 4-position to the 3-position, and the vertical arrow again adding an ethyl group in place of a methyl group in the 4-position:

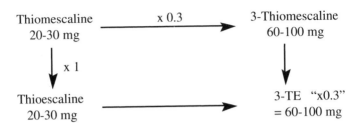

Thiomescaline   x 0.3   3-Thiomescaline
20-30 mg   60-100 mg

         x 1

Thioescaline   3-TE "x0.3"
20-30 mg   = 60-100 mg

and one would predict a potency of some one third of that of thiomescaline, or something in the range of 80 milligrams.

This latter square gave a prediction that was very close to the observed potency, but it would be careless, and probably wrong, to assume that the latter relationships had any more significance than the former ones. As one accumulates the potencies of many compounds it is tempting to draw complex relationships such as these, and to be seduced into believing that they must explain things. And, especially, beware the multivariable power of the computer which can explore monstrous numbers of variables at breakneck speeds, and spew forth fantastic correlations with marvelous ease.

But nothing can ever substitute for the simple art of tasting something new.

#151   TE;   4-TE;   4-THIOESCALINE;   3,5-DIMETHOXY-4-ETHYLTHIOPHENETHYLAMINE

SYNTHESIS: A solution was made of 45.2 g N,N,N',N'-tetramethylethylenediamine and 41.4 g of 1,3-dimethoxybenzene in 300 mL hexane. This was stirred vigorously under a He atmosphere and cooled to 0 °C with an external ice bath. There was added 225 mL of 1.6 M butyllithium in hexane which produced a white granular precipitate. The reaction mixture was stirred for 15 min. There was then added 38 ml of diethyl disulfide which changed the granular precipitate to a creamy character. Stirring was continued for an additional 5 min, then the reaction mixture was poured into 1 L of dilute H_2SO_4. The two phases were separated, and the aqueous phase extracted with 2x150 mL Et_2O. The organic phases were combined, and the solvent removed under vacuum to provide 60 g of 2-ethylthio-1,3-dimethoxybenzene as an off-white oil that spontaneously crystallized. It was distilled nonetheless, boiling at 85-96 °C at 0.4 mm/Hg. This distillate can be recrystallized from hexane to form long needles with a mp of 45-46 °C. Anal. ($C_{10}H_{14}O_2S$) C,H.

To a stirred solution of 60 g of 2-ethylthio-1,3-dimethoxybenzene in 300 ml CH_2Cl_2 there was added 49 g elemental bromine dissolved in 100 ml CH_2Cl_2.

The reaction was not exothermic, and it was allowed to stir for 2 h. The reaction mixture was washed with H_2O, then with aqueous NaOH, and finally with H_2O that contained sodium hydrosulfite. The solvent was removed under vacuum leaving 84 g of an amber oil as residue. This was distilled at 105-115 °C at 0.15 mm/Hg yielding 73.3 g of 4-bromo-2-ethylthio-1,3-dimethoxybenzene as a light yellow oil. Anal. ($C_{11}H_{15}BrO_2S$) C,H.

To a solution of 27 mL diisopropylamine in 150 mL anhydrous THF that was stirred under a N_2 atmosphere and cooled to -10 °C with an external ice/MeOH bath, there was added in sequence 83 mL of 1.6 M butyllithium in hexane, 4.4 mL of dry CH_3CN over the course of 5 min, and finally 12.1 g of 4-bromo-2-ethylthio-1,3-dimethoxybenzene which had been dissolved in 20 mL THF (also added over the course of 5 min). The color progressed from yellow to orange to deep red-brown. Stirring was continued for 10 min, and then the reaction mixture was poured into 300 mL dilute H_2SO_4. The organic layer was separated, and was washed with more dilute H_2SO_4. The aqueous phases were combined, and extracted with 2x100 mL CH_2Cl_2. These extracts were pooled with the original organic phase, and the solvents removed under vacuum. The residue was distilled into two fractions at 0.3 mm/Hg. The first fraction boiled at 95-115 °C and weighed 4.9 g. It was made up of several components, but it contained little nitrile material and was discarded. The second fraction came over at 145->200 °C and weighed 2.9 g. By thin layer chromatography this fraction was largely 3,5-dimethoxy-4-ethylthiophenyl-acetonitrile, and was used as such in the following reduction.

A suspension of 1.25 g LAH in 50 mL anhydrous THF under N_2 was cooled to 0 °C and vigorously stirred. There was added, dropwise, 0.8 mL 100% H_2SO_4, followed by 2.7 g 3,5-dimethoxy-4-ethylthiophenylacetonitrile, neat, over the course of 5 min. The reaction mixture was stirred at 0 °C for a few min, then brought to a reflux for 15 min on the steam bath. After cooling back to room temperature, there was added 15 mL IPA to destroy the excess hydride and 10% NaOH to bring the reaction to a basic pH and convert the aluminum oxide to a loose, white, filterable consistency. This was removed by filtration, and washed with 50 mL portions of IPA. The filtrate and washes were stripped of solvent under vacuum, and the residue suspended between 50 mL CH_2Cl_2 and 50 mL dil. H_2SO_4. The organic phase was separated, and extracted with 2x50 mL dilute H_2SO_4. The original aqueous phase and these two extracts were combined, made basic with aqueous NaOH, and extracted with 3x50 mL CH_2Cl_2. These extracts were stripped of solvent under vacuum. The residue was distilled at 112-135 °C at 0.2 mm/Hg to give 1.1 g of a slightly yellow viscous liquid. This was dissolved in 4 mL IPA, neutralized with 14 drops of concentrated HCl and, with continuous stirring, diluted with 10 mL anhydrous Et_2O. The product was removed by filtration, washed with Et_2O, and air dried to give 1.0 g of 3,5-dimethoxy-4-ethylthiophenethylamine hydrochloride (TE) as white crystals with some solvent of crystallization. The crude mp of 101-106 °C was only slightly improved by recrystallization from CH_3CN (mp 106-109 °C). But upon fusion and resolidification, the melting point was 167-168 °C and this sample was further dried by heating at 100 °C for 24 h before analysis. Anal. $(C_{12}H_{20}ClNO_2S)$ C,H.

DOSAGE: 20 - 30 mg.

DURATION: 9 - 12 h.

QUALITATIVE COMMENTS: (with 20 mg) "I feel it in my ovaries. It is very sensuous. This is total energy, and I am aware of my every membrane. This has been a marvelous experience, very beautiful, joyous, and sensuous. But maybe the dose is a little too high as there is too much body tingling. I am jangly."

(with 20 mg) "The predominant characteristic was the feeling of clean burning, pure energy, a long-lasting clear-headedness and clarity of thought, and an ease of talking and sharing. I did not have a strong feeling of Presence, but more a wonderful feeling of converting energy into action. I found that my initial look inwards was always a look of fear, and I wondered if this might not be the same feeling that others express as excitement. They were certainly of the same nature, they arose at the same point on the fringe of the unknown, and they point to a basic difference in attitude. The excitement is for the new, and is based on trust. The fear is a return to the past, and is defensive, with reluctance to reexperience past pain. The aftermath of this experience was the most profound of any that I have had in a long time. For the following week, I found myself on a new level of functioning, very energetic and very much in the flow of life and free of mental distractions. I have become a great deal more aware of the traps of meditation, and how you can build walls around yourself and around certain concepts, if you are not careful."

(with 22 mg) "Totally developed at 2 hours, to a +++. No clearing of the sinuses, so it is not a decongestant. There is a lot of visual activity. In the group there is good communication, and a lot of laughter."

(with 25 mg) "There is a disconnection, there is complex depth without definition. Without music, this is almost negative, as I can find no definition. But talking gives me some structure. And I got into some pretty extraordinary conversations. About President Hoover, Omni magazine, the colors of spices, and a couple of personal relatives. This is extra-good for ideas and talking. It is indeed a clean experience, and superb for communication."

(with 30 mg) "I was at a plus three for certainly three hours. There were some visuals, some eyes-closed fantasy, but little imagery. Somehow I could at no time interlock with music. It seemed always to get in the way. Sexual activity is an excellent way to relieve the muscular tension and the body's heaviness. There was little hunger and I ate lightly, and I felt somehow depleted. Sleep OK at the twelfth hour. The AM was fine, but on retrospect the experience was overall strangely cloudy, not negative, but there was not enough mental to balance the physical."

(with 30 mg) "My alert was in 40 minutes, and I was completely developed by 2 hours. There was a large measure of erotic fantasy, but the body load was also quite heavy. I had a slight cloak effect, where I was over-energized but somehow under a blanket of quietness. I would certainly repeat this, but at maybe 25 milligrams."

EXTENSIONS AND COMMENTARY: Although the ethyl group (of the ethylthio on the 4-position) is just one carbon atom longer than the methyl group (of TM) that small change already produces hints and indicators of some physical toxicity. The propyl compound (see TP) is still of similar potency, but appears to be yet more difficult, physically. The butyl homolog never made it off the ground at all as a psychedelic, but the physical difficulties seem less as well. All that was left to come through was the euphoria. If this 4-position sulfur analogue series of mescaline is ever to be more carefully explored, it must almost certainly be with the shortest possible chain (TM, as a psychedelic) or with long, long chains (the four-carbon chain of the butyl group in TB), as a feel-good compound.

#152   2-TIM;   2-THIOISOMESCALINE;   3,4-DIMETHOXY-2-METHYLTHIOPHENETHYLAMINE

SYNTHESIS: A short foreword to the synthetic portion is needed. First, although the required thioanisole, 2,3-dimethoxythioanisole, is now commercially available, it is of the utmost importance that it be free of the impurity, veratrole. I know that the material presently available from Aldrich Chemical Company is satisfactory, as I have had a hand in making it. But, if veratrole is present, there are very difficult separations encountered during these preparations. And secondly, the synthesis of 2-TIM and 4-TIM requires a separation of isomers. The first intermediates are common to both. They will be presented here, under this recipe for 2-TIM.

A solution of 150 mL of 1.6 M butyllithium in hexane under N_2 was vigorously stirred and diluted with 150 mL petroleum ether (30-60 °C) and then cooled with an external ice bath to 0 °C. The addition of 26.7 g of veratrole produced a flocculant white precipitate. Next, there was added a solution of 23.2 g of N,N,N',N'-tetramethylethylenediamine in 100 mL anhydrous Et_2O and the stirred reaction mixture was allowed to come to room temperature. The subsequent addition of 20.7 g of dimethyl disulfide over the course of several min produced an exothermic response, and this was allowed to stir for an additional 30 min. There was then added 10 mL EtOH followed by 250 mL of 5% NaOH. The organic phase was washed first with 150 mL 5% NaOH, followed by 2x100 mL portions of 5% dilute HCl. The removal of solvent and bulb-to-bulb distillation of the residue provided 2,3-

dimethoxythioanisole boiling at 72-80 °C at 0.4 mm/Hg as a white oil. This product contained some 20% unreacted veratrole as a contaminant and the isolation of subsequent products from this impure material was extraordinarily difficult. The effort needed for careful purification at this point was completely justified. The product could be obtained in a pure state by distillation at 0.1 mm/Hg through a 6 cm Vigreaux column with collection of several fractions. Those that distilled at 84-87 °C were pure 2,3-dimethoxythioanisole. An analytical sample can be obtained by cooling a concentrated MeOH solution in dry ice, filtering the generated crystals, and washing with cold MeOH. This product melts at 36.5-37 °C. Anal. ($C_9H_{12}O_2S$) C,H,S. The picrate can be formed by treatment with a saturated EtOH solution of picric acid. It formed orange crystals with a mp of 73-78 °C. Anal. ($C_{15}H_{15}N_3O_9S$) N.

To 18 mL of $POCl_3$ there was added 25 mL N-methylformanilide and the solution allowed to stand at room temperature for 0.5 h, until the color had developed to a rich claret. There was then added 25.0 g of 2,3-dimethoxythioanisole and the mixture heated on the steam bath for 2.5 h. This was added to 500 mL H_2O and stirred at ambient temperature for 2 h. The product was extracted with 4x150 mL CH_2Cl_2, the extracts combined, and the solvent removed under vacuum. The residue was distilled through a Vigreaux column under vacuum (0.1 mm/Hg) with the fraction boiling at 125-135 °C being richest in aldehydes, as determined by GC analysis. If the starting 2,3-dimethoxythioanisole contains appreciable veratrole as a contaminant, then this aldehyde fraction contains three components. There is present both 2,3-dimethoxy-4-(methylthio)benzaldehyde and 3,4-dimethoxy-2-(methylthio)benzaldehyde (the two desired precursors to 4-TIM and 2-TIM, respectively), but also present is 3,4-dimethoxybenzaldehyde from the veratrole contamination. The weight of this fraction was 11.9 g and was a white oil free of starting thioether.

Although efforts to separate this mixture were not effective, one of the aldehydes could be isolated in small yield by derivative formation. This was too wasteful to be of preparative value, but it did allow the generation of seed that was of great value in the later separation of the mixed nitrostyrenes that were prepared. If a 1 g portion of this mixture was fused with 0.6 g p-anisidiine over an open flame and then cooled, the melt set up as a solid. Triturating under MeOH gave a yellow solid (0.45 g, mp 77-80 °C) which on recrystallization from hexane appeared to be a single one of the three possible Schiff's bases that could theoretically be prepared. It had a mp of 80-81 °C. Anal. ($C_{17}H_{19}NO_3S$) C,H. Hydrolysis with hot 3 N HCl freed the benzaldehyde which was isolated by quenching in H_2O and extraction with CH_2Cl_2. The extracts were stripped of solvent under vacuum and the residue distilled bulb-to-bulb under vacuum to give white crystals of 3,4-dimethoxy-2-(methylthio)-benzaldehyde (the 2-TIM aldehyde) with a mp of 23-24 °C. A micro-scale conversion of this to the corresponding nitrostyrene provided the seed that was effectively used in the large scale preparation described below.

A solution of 9.0 g of a mixture of 3,4-dimethoxy-2-(methylthio)-

benzaldehyde and 2,3-dimethoxy-4-(methylthio)benzaldehyde in 50 mL of nitromethane was treated with 1.5 g anhydrous ammonium acetate and held at reflux for 5 h. The excess nitromethane was removed under vacuum to yield 10.4 g of a dark orange oil which, upon dissolving in 40 mL hot MeOH and being allowed to cool and slowly evaporate at ambient temperatures, provided dark colored crystals. Filtration (save the mother liquors!) and recrystallization from 40 mL MeOH provided 6.3 g of a yellow crystalline solid. A second recrystallization from 50 mL MeOH gave 5.0 g of lemon yellow plates 3,4-dimethoxy-2-methylthio-ß-nitrostyrene with a mp of 102-103.5 °C. An analytical sample, from IPA, had a mp of 103-104 °C and a single spot on TLC with $CHCl_3$, with an Rf of 0.54. Anal. ($C_{11}H_{13}NO_4S$) C,H. When there had been veratrole left as a contaminant in the original 2,3-dimethoxythioanisole, the nitrostyrene that was isolated by this method had, after recrystallization, a mp of 93-95 °C. This substance acted as a single compound through a number of recrystallization trials, but on TLC analysis always gave two components (silica gel, chloroform) with Rf's of 0.54 and 0.47. It proved to be a mixture of 3,4-dimethoxy-2-methylthio-ß-nitrostyrene and 3,4-dimethoxy-ß-nitrostyrene in an exact molecular ratio of 2:1. This latter nitrostyrene is the precursor to DMPEA, q.v. Anal. ($C_{32}H_{37}N_3O_{12}S_2$) C,H. The mother liquor above is the source of the 4-TIM nitrostyrene, and its isolation is described in the recipe for 4-TIM.

A solution of 4.2 g LAH in 70 mL anhydrous THF was cooled to 0 °C under He and with stirring. There was added, dropwise, 2.8 mL of 100% H_2SO_4, followed by 4.4 g of 3,4-dimethoxy-2-(methylthio)-ß-nitrostyrene dissolved in 25 mL THF. Stirring was continued for a few min as the reaction returned to room temperature, and then it was heated to a reflux for 10 min on the steam bath. The reaction was cooled again, and 25% NaOH was added dropwise until a white granular precipitate was obtained. This was removed by filtration, and the filter cake was washed with 2x50 mL Et_2O. The filtrate was extracted into 100 mL dilute H_2SO_4 which was, in turn, made basic again and extracted with 2x100 mL CH_2Cl_2. The extracts were pooled, and the solvent removed under vacuum to give a residue of crude product. This was distilled from 100-115 °C at 0.3 mm/Hg yielding 3.2 g of a clear white oil. This was dissolved in 25 mL IPA, neutralized with 23 drops of concentrated HCl, and diluted with 75 mL anhydrous Et_2O. There was a deposition of beautiful white platelets of 3,4-dimethoxy-2-methylthiophenethylamine hydrochloride (2-TIM) which were removed by filtration, washed with ether, and air dried. This hydrochloride salt contained a quarter mole of H_2O of crystallization. The mp was 183-184 °C. Anal. ($C_{11}H_{18}ClNO_2S\cdot1/4 H_2O$) C,H,N.

DOSAGE: greater than 240 mg.

DURATION: unknown.

QUALITATIVE COMMENTS: (with 160 mg) "There was perhaps some awareness in an hour or so, but in another hour there was absolutely nothing. A small

amount of wine in the evening was quite intoxicating."
(with 240 mg) "No effects of any kind."

EXTENSIONS AND COMMENTARY: The problems that might be associated
with the making of the three amphetamines that correspond to 2-TIM, 3-TIM and
4-TIM might very well prove quite exciting. These would be the three thio
analogues of TMA-3; vis, 3,4-dimethoxy-2-methylthioamphetamine, 2,4-
dimethoxy-3-methylthioamphetamine, and 2,3-dimethoxy-4-thioamphetamine. The
first challenge would be to name them. Using the 2C-3C convention, they would
be the 3C analogs of trivially named 2-carbon compounds, namely 3C-2-TIM, 3C-
3-TIM and 3C-4-TIM. Using the thio convention (the number before the T is the
position of the sulfur atom), they would be 2-T-TMA-3, 3-T-TMA-3 and 4-T-
TMA-3. The second challenge would be their actual synthesis. The information
gained from the separation of the 2-carbon nitrostyrenes and that most remarkable
mixed-nitrostyrene thing that acted as a single pure material, would not be usable.
But it is intriguing to speculate if there might be some parallel problems in the 3-
carbon world. It seems almost certain that none of the compounds would be
pharmacologically active, so the incentive would be the challenge of the chemistry.
Some day, maybe.

**#153   3-TIM;   3-THIOISOMESCALINE;   2,4-DIMETHOXY-3-
METHYLTHIOPHENETHYLAMINE**

SYNTHESIS: A mixture of 3.1 g $POCl_3$ 2.8 g N-methylformanilide was heated on
a steam bath until it was a deep claret color (about 5 min). To this there was then
added 3.0 g of 2,6-dimethoxythioanisole (see under 4-TM for its preparation), and
heating was continued for 30 min. The reaction mixture was then added to 75 mL
H_2O and stirred overnight. The dark oily mixture was extracted with 3x75 mL

CH$_2$Cl$_2$, the extracts pooled, and the solvent
removed under vacuum. The residue was extracted with 3x20 mL boiling hexane, each
extract being poured off from the insoluble
residue. Pooling and cooling these extracts
yielded 1.5 g of 2,4-dimethoxy-3-(methylthio)-
benzaldehyde as an off-white crystalline solid with a mp of 67-69 °C. Recrystallization from either MeOH or cyclohexane tightened the mp, but lowered it to 67-68
°C and 66-67 °C, resp. Anal. $(C_{10}H_{12}O_3S)$ C,H.
        To a solution of 1.3 g 2,4-dimethoxy-3-(methylthio)benzaldehyde in 60
mL nitromethane there was added 0.3 g anhydrous ammonium acetate and the
mixture was heated at reflux for 3 h. The hot solution was decanted from a little
insoluble material, and the excess nitromethane was removed under vacuum. The

residue dissolved in 10 mL hot MeOH. On cooling, yellow crystals of 2,4-dimethoxy-3-methylthio-ß-nitrostyrene were obtained which were removed by filtration and air-dried, and weighed 0.9 g. The mp was 130-133 °C and could be improved to 136-137 °C following recrystallization from MeOH (10 g/g). Anal. ($C_{11}H_{13}NO_4S$) C,H.

A well-stirred solution of 0.6 g LAH in 10 mL anhydrous THF was cooled to 0 °C under He. There was added, dropwise, 0.4 mL of 100% H_2SO_4, followed by 0.6 g of 2,4-dimethoxy-3-methylthio-ß-nitrostyrene dissolved in a little THF. Stirring was continued for a few min as the reaction returned to room temperature, and then it was heated to a reflux for 5 min on the steam bath. The reaction was cooled again, and 25% NaOH was added dropwise until a white granular precipitate was obtained. This was removed by filtration, and the filter cake was washed with 2x25 mL Et_2O. The filtrate was extracted into 25 mL dilute H_2SO_4 which was, in turn, made basic again and extracted with 2x25 mL CH_2Cl_2. The extracts were pooled, and the solvent removed under vacuum to give a residue of crude product. This was distilled from 120-140 °C at 0.3 mm/Hg yielding 0.25 g of a clear white oil. This was dissolved in 5 mL IPA, neutralized with about 3 drops of concentrated HCl, and diluted with 15 mL anhydrous Et_2O. Scratching with a glass rod instigated crystallization of bright white solids which were filtered, washed with Et_2O, and air dried. The weight of 2,4-dimethoxy-3-methylthiophenethylamine hydrochloride (3-TIM) was 0.2 g and the mp was 204-206 °C with decomposition. This hydrochloride appeared to be a hemihydrate. Anal. ($C_{11}H_{18}ClNO_2S \cdot 1/2 H_2O$) C,H,N.

DOSAGE: greater than 240 mg.

DURATION: unknown.

QUALITATIVE COMMENTS: (with 240 mg) "Briefly I thought that there might have been an alert at the 2 to 3 hour point, but I now think it was nothing. During the following day I had a mild stomach upset off and on, but I can't believe that it was connected with 3-TIM."

EXTENSIONS AND COMMENTARY: Isomescaline itself is not active, but there is no way of knowing just how "non-active" it really is. If it were to be active just beyond the levels assayed, then the introduction of a sulfur into the molecule in place of an oxygen could have increased the potency to where it might have some effect. The absence of any activity from this TIM, and the other two TIMs, might well suggest that isomescaline is really very "non-active," if that makes sense!

#154   4-TIM;   4-THIOISOMESCALINE;   2,3-DIMETHOXY-4-METHYLTHIOPHENETHYLAMINE

SYNTHESIS: The mother liquors from the initial crystallization of the 2-TIM nitrostyrene (see under 2-TIM) was the source and raw material for all 4-TIM chemistry. Once the bulk of the 2-TIM nitrostyrene has been removed, these mother liquors could be processed to give the 4-TIM nitrostyrene. The easier procedure was to evaporate these mother liquors to a residue under vacuum, and hope for a spontaneous crystallization. If this failed, flash chromatography could be used. For reference purposes, the three nitrostyrenes involved in the 2-TIM/4-TIM problem moved on silica gel TLC with $CHCl_3$ solvent in the following manner: 2,3-dimethoxy-4-methylthio-ß-nitrostyrene (leading to 4-TIM), Rf = 0.61; 3,4-dimethoxy-2-methylthio-ß-nitrostyrene (leading to 2-TIM), Rf = 0.54; and 3,4-dimethoxy-ß-nitrostyrene (leading to DMPEA), Rf = 0.47. For flash chromatography, a small portion of the residue from the mother liquor was dissolved in $CHCl_3$, and placed on a silica gel column. $CHCl_3$ was used as the eluding solvent. The first material breaking through from the column was the 4-TIM nitrostyrene and on evaporation of this fraction, seed was obtained as gold-colored crystals that had a mp of 71-73 °C. This, when added to the residues from the described 2-TIM synthesis nitrostyrenes, started the crystallization process. The gummy solid that was produced was triturated under MeOH, and the crystals so revealed were removed by filtration. Recrystallization from 10 mL MeOH gave 1.9 g of solids. A second recrystallization from 5 mL MeOH provided 0.7 g of pumpkin-colored crystals of 2,3-dimethoxy-4-methylthio-ß-nitrostyrene with a mp of 70-71 °C.

A solution of 1.2 g LAH in 20 mL anhydrous THF was cooled to 0 °C under He and stirred. There was added, dropwise, 0.8 mL of 100% H_2SO_4, followed by 0.9 g of 2,3-dimethoxy-4-methylthio-ß-nitrostyrene dissolved in 20 mL THF. Stirring was continued for a few min as the reaction returned to room temperature, and then it was heated to a reflux for 5 min on the steam bath. The reaction was cooled again, EtOAc was added to destroy the excess hydride, followed by 25% NaOH added dropwise until a white granular precipitate was obtained. This was removed by filtration, and the filter cake was washed with 2x35 mL Et_2O. The filtrate was extracted into 50 mL dilute H_2SO_4 which was washed with Et_2O and, in turn, made basic again and extracted with 2x50 mL CH_2Cl_2. The extracts were pooled, and the solvent removed under vacuum to give a residue of crude product. This distilled cleanly from 100-115 °C at 0.3 mm/Hg yielding 0.45 g of a clear white oil. This was dissolved in 6 mL IPA, neutralized with 5 drops of concentrated HCl, and diluted with 25 mL anhydrous Et_2O. There was a deposition of white solids which were removed by filtration, washed with Et_2O, and air dried. The 2,3-dimethoxy-4-methylthiophenethylamine hydrochloride so obtained (4-TIM) weighed 0.3 g and contained a molecule of H_2O of crystallization. The mp was 212-213 °C. Anal. ($C_{11}H_{18}ClNO_2S \cdot H_2O$) C,H,N.

DOSAGE: greater than 160 mg.

DURATION: unknown.

QUALITATIVE COMMENTS: (with 160 mg) "Everything seemed normal. Pulse was under 80, there was nothing with eyes-closed, my appetite was normal. The compound was completely inactive."

EXTENSIONS AND COMMENTARY: There has been much noise made about the effectiveness of an unusual substitution group at the 4-position of the phenethylamine molecule. Here is a methylthio group at this position, and it is an inactive compound. I was just a little bit surprised.

#155   3-TM;   3-THIOMESCALINE;   3,4-DIMETHOXY-5-METHYLTHIOPHENETHYLAMINE

SYNTHESIS: To an ice cold and well stirred solution of 15 g vanillin and 20 g sodium thiocyanate in 150 mL acetic acid there was added, dropwise over the course of 15 min, a solution of 16 g elemental bromine in 40 mL acetic acid. This was followed by the addition of 30 mL of 5% HCl and 300 mL EtOH, and stirring was continued for an additional 30 min. The mixture was heated to its boiling point, and filtered while hot. The mother liquor was diluted with an equal volume of H_2O, which initiated the crystallization of crude 5-formyl-7-methoxy-2-oxo-1,3-benzoxathiole as a flocculant yellow solid. On filtration and air-drying, this weighed 12.5 g. After recrystallization from EtOH, the product was white and had a mp of 164 °C sharp.

A suspension of 12.5 g of crude 5-formyl-7-methoxy-2-oxo-1,3-benzoxathiole in 100 mL MeOH containing 28.4 g methyl iodide was treated with a solution of 12 g NaOH in 100 mL warm MeOH. The mixture was held at reflux for 1 h and then the solvents were removed under vacuum. A solution of 14.2 g methyl iodide in 100 mL DMSO was added and the mixture stirred for 1 h. An additional 2.4 g of NaOH and 16 g methyl iodide were added, and the stirring was continued for another 2 h. The reaction mixture was poured into 800 mL H_2O, acidified with HCl, and extracted with 3x75 mL CH_2Cl_2. The pooled extracts were washed with 5% NaOH, then water, and the solvent removed under vacuum. Distillation at 110-130 °C at 0.4 mm/Hg gave 0.9 g 3,4-dimethoxy-5-(methylthio)benzaldehyde

which had a mp of 57-58 °C after crystallization from EtOH. Anal. ($C_{10}H_{12}O_3S$) C,H.
A solution of 0.9 g 3,4-dimethoxy-5-(methylthio)benzaldehyde in 100 mL
nitromethane containing 0.5 g anhydrous ammonium acetate was held at reflux for
4 h. The excess nitromethane was removed under vacuum, and the deep brown
residue was dissolved in 4 mL hot MeOH. On cooling, the yellow crystals were
removed by filtration, washed with cold MeOH and air dried yielding 0.4 g yellow
crystals of 3,4-dimethoxy-5-methoxy-ß-nitrostyrene, with a mp of 119.5-120.5 °C
after recrystallization from EtOH. Anal. ($C_{11}H_{13}NO_4S$) C,H.

To a solution of 1.0 g LAH in 25 mL anhydrous THF under He, cooled to
0 °C and vigorously stirred, there was added, dropwise, 0.7 mL of 100% H_2SO_4,
followed by a solution of 0.7 g 3,4-dimethoxy-5-methylthio-ß-nitrostyrene in 10
mL anhydrous THF. The mixture was brought briefly to a reflux, cooled again, and
the excess hydride destroyed with H_2O in THF, followed by the dropwise addition
of 15% NaOH until the solids became white and granular. The solids were removed
by filtration, the filter cake washed with THF, the mother liquor and filtrates
combined, diluted with an equal volume of Et_2O, and extracted with 2x40 mL dilute
H_2SO_4. The aqueous extracts were combined, washed with Et_2O, made basic with
aqueous NaOH, and extracted with 2x50 mL CH_2Cl_2. The solvent was removed
from these extracts and the residue distilled to provide 0.4 g of a white oil boiling
at 124-130 °C at 0.2 mm/Hg. This oil was dissolved in 8 mL IPA, neutralized with
concentrated HCl, and diluted with 30 mL anhydrous Et_2O. The white crystalline
product was the monohydrate of 3,4-dimethoxy-5-methylthiophenethylamine hydrochloride (3-TM) which melted at 167-168 °C and weighed 0.29 g. Anal.
($C_{11}H_{18}ClNO_2S \cdot H_2O$) C,H,N.

DOSAGE: 60 - 100 mg.

DURATION: 8 - 12 h.

QUALITATIVE COMMENTS: (with 80 mg) "I went into the experience with the
question of whether it (3-TM) might be a writing aid. I found a considerable color
enhancement (this was at the one hour point) and there seems to be no problem in
writing physical words. But there is no urge to, as there are no new things. This is
progressing into something more complex and there is an interesting shielding
effect. I still have the desire to write and I sense that many things are going on
underneath, but my conscious control suppresses their availability. It is now the
third hour. Music. I would like to try this material at 100 milligrams. Now
awareness seems much more pointed. I have need to build a writing table. This
material is physically relaxing, insisting repose, but with conflicting energy. Seated
in a chair, but I seem unable to find a comfortable position in order to write.

"Pine trees seem a good place
To start. Notwithstanding this table

Of pine, unfinished, unruled,
The pulp upon which we reveal
The unnerved thoughts.
How casual we are at discarding
Our feelings, a rubble we
Leave behind for the living.
Who among us can absorb
The spiritual load we see as
What others carry.

"This material is not poetic, I should say, does not enhance poetry, prose is much more comfortable. I think I should let the experience develop further. It is now the fifth hour. There is something of a violence (emotional) suppressed in all of us, a socially repressed vision of oneself in a direct conflict with oneself. The music has a lot to do with this material. And it changes with time. In the first part there is sublimity, peacefulness, mild intoxication. And a lot more tension in the part that followed the four hour point. There the territories seem much better defined, with the benign shielding of the first half largely dissipated. I have developed a slightly irritated view of myself, probably wanting once again to regain the serenity."

(with 80 mg) "Delightful day. Not insight depth but persistent feeling of pleasant good humor. It is good-natured and very verbal. Everyone talked and the instinct was to express and comment on everything. There were no visuals during the first three to four hours — with the eyes open one could barely detect the intoxication. Eyes closed — quiet lovely window, no images. About +2. And then someone brought in a radio with music on, into the room. There was a tremendous eruption of closed-eyes visual images and fantasy. Bright colors, funny, rich and elaborate. Marvelous. I was suddenly at +3. Next day, no hangover. Pleasant feeling persisted."

(with 100 mg) "I found the day had two halves. The first few hours were characterized by occasional defensiveness (paranoia) and irritability. In interpersonal interactions there was a guardedness, due to a feeling of vulnerability. I went off by myself, and with eyes closed, there was rich imagery and color synthesis to musical imput. And then things smoothed out, and I could express an easy flow of ideas and concepts without always watching my step. And then all too soon, the intensity of the experience began fading away."

EXTENSIONS AND COMMENTARY: The amphetamine which would correspond with this base would be 3,4-dimethoxy-5-methylthioamphetamine (3-T-TMA) and should be an active compound. Its synthesis should be straightforward from the benzaldehyde described above, employing nitroethane rather than nitromethane. It is apparently an unknown compound.

#156　TM;　4-TM;　4-THIOMESCALINE;　3,5-DIMETHOXY-4-METHYLTHIOPHENETHYLAMINE

SYNTHESIS: A solution of 24.2 g N,N,N',N'-tetramethylethylenediamine and 27.6 g of 1,3-dimethoxybenzene was dissolved in 400 mL anhydrous hexane. This was stirred vigorously under a N_2 atmosphere and cooled to 0 °C with an external ice bath. There was added 125 mL of 2.0 M butyllithium in hexane. The stirred reaction mixture became yellow and sludgy, and was briefly warmed back to room temperature to allow easy stirring. After cooling again to 0 °C, there was added 18.8 g of dimethyl disulfide which converted the viscous yellow phase to a loose white solid. Stirring was continued while the reaction mixture was brought up to room temperature, and then all was added to 2 L of dilute H_2SO_4. There was the immediate formation of a white cystalline solid which was removed by filtration, sucked relatively free of water, and recrystallized from 50 mL of boiling MeOH. There was thus obtained 18.9 g of 2,6-dimethoxythioanisole as white crystals with a mp of 81-82 °C. Extraction of the aqueous filtrate with 2x50 mL CH_2Cl_2 and removal of the solvent under vacuum gave a residue which, when combined with the mother liquors from the MeOH crystallization, afforded an additional 3.3 g product with a mp 77-79 °C.

To a stirred solution of 18.9 g of 2,6-dimethoxythioanisole in 200 mL CH_2Cl_2 there was added 16 g elemental bromine dissolved in 75 mL CH_2Cl_2. The initial dark red color gradually faded to a pale yellow color and there was a copious evolution of HBr. The solvent was removed under vacuum leaving 27.5 g of a pale yellow residual oil. This was distilled at 118-121 °C at 0.25 mm/Hg to yield 3-bromo-2,6-dimethoxythioanisole as a white oil weighing 25.3 g. Crystallization from hexane provided white crystals with a mp of 30-30.5 °C. Anal. ($C_9H_{11}BrO_2S$) C,H.

To a solution of 19.3 g diisopropylamine in 150 mL anhydrous THF that was stirred under a N_2 atmosphere and cooled to -10 °C with an external ice/MeOH bath, there was added in sequence 83 mL of 1.6 M butyllithium in hexane, 4.4 mL of dry CH_3CN, and 11.6 g of 3-bromo-2,6-dimethoxythioanisole (which had been dissolved in a little anhydrous THF). The turbid reaction mixture gradually developed color, initially yellow and progressively becoming orange and finally a deep red brown. Stirring was maintained for a total of 20 min, and then the reaction mixture was poured into 1 L H_2O that containing 10 mL concentrated H_2SO_4. This was extracted with 3x75 mL CH_2Cl_2, these extracts pooled, washed with dilute H_2SO_4 followed by saturated brine, and the solvent was removed under vacuum yielding 8.7 g of a viscous oil as a residue. This was distilled at 0.11 mm/Hg yielded two fractions. The first boiled at 115-125 °C and weighed 3.8 g. This material set to an oily crystalline mass which was filtered, washed with cold MeOH and then recrystallized from MeOH. The white solids had a mp of 60-63 °C and were not the desired product. This material has not yet been identified. The second fraction came over at 150-180 °C, weighed 1.8 g and spontaneously crystallized. It was triturated under cold MeOH and filtered yielding, after air drying, 1.1 g 3,5-dimethoxy-4-methylthiophenylacetonitrile, which had a mp of 95-96.5 °C. Anal. ($C_{11}H_{13}NO_2S$) C,H.

A suspension of 1.0 g LAH in 40 mL anhydrous THF under N_2 was cooled to 0 °C and vigorously stirred. There was added, dropwise, 0.7 mL 100% H_2SO_4, followed by 1.2 g 3,5-dimethoxy-4-methylthiophenylacetonitrile in 10 mL anhydrous THF. The reaction mixture was stirred at 0 °C for a few min, then brought to room temperature for 1 h, and finally to a reflux for 30 min on the steam bath. After cooling to room temperature, there was added 1 mL H_2O in 5 mL THF to destroy the excess hydride, followed by 3 mL of 15% NaOH to bring the reaction to a basic pH, and finally 2 mL H_2O which converted the aluminum oxide to a loose, white, filterable consistency. This was removed by filtration, and washed with THF. The filtrate and washes were stripped of solvent under vacuum, the residue was dissolved in 200 mL CH_2Cl_2, and this was extracted with 3x100 mL diute H_2SO_4. These extracts were pooled, washed with CH_2Cl_2, made basic with 25% NaOH, and extracted with 3x100 mL CH_2Cl_2. After combining, the solvent was removed under vacuum providing 1.2 g of a colorless oil as a residue. This was distilled at 122-132 °C at 0.05 mm/Hg to give a colorless oil. This was dissolved in 8 mL of IPA, neutralized with concentrated HCl and, with continuous stirring, diluted with 100 mL anhydrous Et_2O. The product was removed by filtration, washed with Et_2O, and air dried to give 0.95 g. 3,5-dimethoxy-4-methylthiophenethylamine hydrochloride (4-TM) as spectacular white crystals with a mp of 193-194 °C. Anal. ($C_{11}H_{18}ClNO_2S$) C,H.

DOSAGE: 20 - 40 mg.

DURATION: 10 - 15 h.

QUANTITATIVE COMMENTS: (with 25 mg) "I was first aware of any effects as I was sitting in back of the house on a big fluffy pillow. The sun was warm and the grass tall and green, but I felt strange inside. There was distinct uterine cramping, and I could not find a comfortable position for sitting. The others had gone out to the garden leaving me here. It seemed that walking might relieve the physical discomfort, so I went to find them. Walking was easy, but I was a little light-headed and I had to watch my steps with care. They were not there (we had passed on opposite sides of the house) and I returned in some haste to my warm nest behind the house to find my pillow gone. A strange detail, but it perhaps gave me the flavor for my day. The pillow was for me. It was gone. My place was gone. Therefore I am gone. I am dead and yet I can see and think. The small touch of panic at finding myself dead dispelled any internal concerns and I ran inside to find the others; they had brought my pillow in. I was alive again, but the entire day balanced between the alive unreality and the illusion that I was something removed and merely watching the surrounding alive unreality. Everything that happened was completely unlikely.

"Like the soup scene. We decided that some hot soup would be welcome, and so R. brought out three cans of Campbell soup for the three of us. But one was cream mushroom, one asparagus, and one tomato. The discussion as to how to use two cans only, which two, without mixing, and even how to decide to decide was totally beyond any of us. The situation was hopelessly unresolvable, hilariously funny, and distinctly schizophrenic.

"Or like the kite scene. We were returning from a short walk to the back of the property, and I spotted a red thing in the parking area. It had not been there before. None of us could identify it from this distance, and we speculated wildly as to what it was, as we came closer. And at the last approach, we found that there was loose string everywhere about the driveway, all part of a downed kite. The red object had apparently fallen from the sky, right here in front of the garage. There had been no sounds of voices of kite-flyers, and there was no one to be seen in any direction. And then one of us spotted a sheet of paper, torn to the center where there was a small hole, and it was flattened up against the kite. There was a message. Apparently whoever had been flying it had put a message on the string, and let the wind take it up to the kite itself. I reached for the sheet of paper, and removed it. Nothing on either side. The message was that there was no message. Exactly out of Marshall McLuhan. Completely appropriate for this particular day.

"That evening we were to be picked up by my friends for dinner. Choosing what to wear, how to dress myself, how to adjust my persona to fit other people, all this was chaotic. Somehow the dinner succeeded, but I was able to flip in and out of the immediate company easily, but not completely voluntarily. Sleep was comfortable that night, and I feel that the entire day had been very intense, not too much fun, but somehow quite rewarding."

(with 30 mg) "At the one and a half hour point, I was reminded more than anything of LSD, with a distinct feeling of standing just a few feet to the right of ordinary reality. There has been a mild tremor ever since the first effects were evident, but it doesn't bother me except to make my handwriting uncertain. I would not want to double this level. Suddenly the concept of my 5:30's swept over me. I had a penetrating view of myself as a person who had become invested in a pattern of behavior that I had succumbed to, to come home and complete my day with a transition from the work-world to the home-world, by changing the inside clock at 5:30. My wife had been my 5:30 for nearly 30 years and this had been my tacit agreement with her. Never questioned, never challenged, and certainly never violated. And with her death, I have found myself imposing this same 5:30-ness on myself, as some form of an emasculating pattern that is comfortable and stable. No, it is not comfortable, it is simply the course of the least thought and the least disruption. If I were to meet someone else, would I have such a negative image of myself that I would expect her to become my 5:30 so as not to have to disrupt these tired and comfortable patterns? That would be completely unfair to this other person. And I can see where it is completely destructive to me. No new person should ever have to play my wife's old role. I need never again play my old role. And I won't."

(with 30 mg) "At 2:20 PM I ingested 30 mg of TM. It had a mildly alkaloid taste. Since the afternoon was warm, I took a two mile walk with the dog, and with my two companions K.T. and T.T., both also with 30 mg. We talked without any difficulty even after the onset of the first signs of effect. The major emotional and physical effects came on very gradually and quite pleasantly as we sat in the patio. But soon we all grew chilled, and put on more clothing. Nothing really helped the inward chill, and we were to discover that it stayed with us throughout the experience. At 3:30 we went inside where the room temperature was set at 70 degrees, and we all lay down. I launched into an engrossing, somewhat chaotic and erotic reverie, that followed no linear progression, but which lasted perhaps an hour. The ease of talking surprised me; the content was cogent and I felt myself to be articulate. It dawned on me after about two hours had gone by, that the height of the experiment had already passed without any real exhilaration on my part. But my companions suggested that my expectations from the past had been misleading me and, as time went on, they proved to be correct. The clarity and the continued ability to talk, especially with K.T. on a personally difficult topic, were for me the particular genius of this material. When I went inward, which I could do without effort, the sensations were neutral in affect but restful in some way. But coming out was entirely lucid and pleasant. I soon found that I preferred this. I enjoyed a light supper at 8:30 and found the dropoff gentle, and the conversation most amiable until we separated at 1:00 AM. Sleep did not come until 3:00 AM and then only after 10 mg Librium to quell the active mental processes. The next day I awoke around 8:30 AM feeling languid but cheerful."

(with 40 mg) "For quite a while there was some physical concern. Not actual nausea but a generalized uneasiness, with a distinct body tremor. There was little urine produced (500 mL in 18 hours), and I felt the need to search out fluids. There was mild intestinal cramping. I found that my thoughts were able to go in several directions at once, but since they stayed nowhere long enough to structure anything, this was more annoying than constructive. I saw this as a reality shell about me like a Möbius strip, continuous, yet with no consistent side being presented. I was reminded of a similar place with DOB, some few years ago. While lying down with eyes closed, I found the imagery to be very impressive, but my thought processes were quite convoluted and disjointed. Some were most interesting, and some were ugly. I cannot see this as a party drug."

EXTENSIONS AND COMMENTARY: The dosage range has been broadened to include the 20 milligram level, in that several subjects found that even with that small amount there was difficulty in walking and in keeping one's equilibrium. Walking was described as a floating procedure, and one could tilt to one side or the other if care was not taken. Anorexia was occasionally noted, and most people commented on some degree of anesthesia to touch.

All in all, this drug evoked a mixed bag of responses. The most startling and unexpected property was the dramatic increase in potency over the parent prototype, mescaline. The substitution of a sulfur atom for an oxygen atom increased the power of the drug some ten-fold, without any apparent decrease in complexity of action. As there were many materials that were outgrowths of mescaline with the studies of ethyl this and diethyl that, each and all of these would be interesting candidates for synthesis with this or that oxygen atom replaced with sulfur. Most of these have been made, and many of them have proven to be interesting.

What is meaning of the phrase, "sulfur-for-oxygen replacement?" Let me try to explain it for non-chemists.

One of the most exciting bits of architecture in science is the Periodic Table. The principles of electrons and orbitals and different counts of protons in a nucleus gets to be a complex story to try to explain the grid-like structure of the arrangements of atoms. It is easier to simply give the music. And this melody goes: As you look across a row, elements are simple in their binding arrangements on the left, become more complex towards the center where they kind of change polarity, and then get progressively simple again but with the opposite charge as you approach the right-hand side.

And when you look at a column from top to bottom, the bonding complexity stays pretty much the same but the atom gets more and more massive as you go down the column.

The combinations of atoms from the Periodic Table, by and large, is the province of the inorganic chemist. Take one of this, and two of that, and the combination is called a salt, or a complex, or an adduct, and probably has interesting colors, and may even be found in nature as part of a rock somewhere, or coming out of the vent of a volcano.

But if one were to look at just four elements, three in the middle right of the first row, namely carbon, nitrogen and oxygen, and the one up there at the top and the lightest of all, hydrogen, you would find quite a different story. These can be combined in an infinity of ways since there can be dozens of atoms hooked to one-another; this is the territory of the organic chemist, and this is the chemistry of life. With a few exceptions, every molecule within the body, and the food that maintains the body, and the drugs that affect the body, are made up of a bunch of carbons, and an occasional oxygen or two, usually a nitrogen somewhere, and all the remaining loose ends satisfied with hydrogen atoms.

Almost every drug that is to be found in this book is nothing more than a different arrangement of atoms of these four elements.

This compound, thiomescaline, is a byway that takes advantage of one of those vertical columns. Directly below the element oxygen, there is found sulfur, which has much the same binding complexity, but is twice as massive. The prototype of all the phenethylamine drugs being discussed in this book is mescaline, a very simple compound containing these basic four elements of life and pharmacology; it contains eleven carbon atoms, three oxygen atoms, one nitrogen atom, and there are a total of seventeen hydrogen atoms required to balance the books. One of the oxygen atoms holds a central position, and the other two are reflections of one another and cannot be distinguished chemically. The structure of thiomescaline is generated by plucking out that central oxygen atom of mescaline, and putting a sulfur atom back in its place. The definition of the term "thio" is quite simple — it means a sulfur-in-place-of-an-oxygen, with everything else left alone. It is a little awe-inspiring to think that every oxy anything can have a thio something as a spatially similar analogue. And there are a lot of oxy things in the body and in the medicine cabinet. A number of them are discussed in this book.

#157   TMA;   3,4,5-TRIMETHOXYAMPHETAMINE

SYNTHESIS: To a solution of 39.2 g 3,4,5-trimethoxybenzaldehyde in 30 mL warm EtOH there was added 15.7 g nitroethane followed by 1.5 mL n-butylamine. The reaction mixture was allowed to stand at 40 °C for 7 days. With cooling and scratching, fine yellow needles were obtained which, after removal by filtration and air drying, weighed 48 g. Recrystallization from EtOH gave 2-nitro-1-(3,4,5-trimethoxyphenyl)propene as yellow crystals with a mp of 94-95 °C. Anal. $(C_{12}H_{15}NO_5)$ C,H,N. Alternatively, a solution of 20 g of the aldehyde in 75 mL nitroethane was treated with 4 g anhydrous ammonium acetate and heated on the steam bath until a deep red color had been generated. Removal of the excess solvent/reagent under vacuum gave a red oil which dissolved in an equal volume of boiling MeOH. On cooling, yellow crystals of the nitropropene separated. Recrystallization from MeOH gave, after air drying to constant weight, 13.0 g with the same mp.

Under an inert atmosphere, 38 g LAH was wetted with 100 mL anhydrous Et_2O, and then suspended in 1 L dry THF. This was brought up to a gentle reflux, and there was added, slowly, a solution of 43.7 g 2-nitro-1-(3,4,5-trimethoxyphenyl)propene in 160 mL THF. Refluxing was continued for 36 h, and then the reaction mixture was cooled with an external ice bath. The excess hydride was destroyed by the cautious addition of 38 mL H_2O, and this was followed by 38 mL 15% NaOH, and finally another 114 mL H_2O. The inorganic salts which should have ended up as a loose, granular, easily filterable mass, looked rather like library paste, but they were filtered nonetheless. Washing with THF was attempted, but it was not efficient. The combined filtrate and washes were stripped of solvent under vacuum giving 31.5 g of the crude base as an amber oil. This was dissolved in 140 mL IPA, neutralized with concentrated HCl (15 mL was required), and diluted with 650 mL anhydrous Et_2O. There was an initial oily phase which on continued stirring changed to pale pink solids. These were finely ground under CH_3CN to give 15.2 g of 3,4,5-trimethoxyamphetamine hydrochloride (TMA) as white crystals that melted at 195-211 °C. All aluminum salts from everywhere were dissolved in dilute HCl, and 1 Kg of potassium sodium tartrate was added. There as added 25% NaOH allowed the pH to bring the pH to >9 without the precipitation of basic alumina. Extraction of this phase with CH_2Cl_2 was followed by removal of the solvent and salt formation as described above, allowed the isolation of an additional 6.4 g TMA. The product prepared in this manner contains some 10-15% 3,5-dimethoxy-4-hydroxy-amphetamine as an impurity. A solution of 20 g of the TMA made in this manner in 200 mL 5% NaOH was extracted with 2x200 mL CH_2Cl_2. The pooled extracts were washed with 4x100 mL 5% NaOH, and the aqueous washes were pooled with the original base phase. The organic phase was stripped of its CH_2Cl_2 under vacuum to give an oil that was dissolved in 40 mL IPA, neutralized with concentrated HCl, and diluted with 400 mL anhydrous Et_2O. There was the immediate formation of spectacular white crystals of pure 3,4,5-trimethoxyamphetamine hydrochloride, weighing 15.4 g and having a mp of 220-221 °C. The aqueous phase was brought to neutrality, treated with 10 g potassium di-hydrogen phosphate, brought to pH 9.0 with the careful addition of NaOH, and extracted with 5x100 mL CH_2Cl_2. Evaporation of the solvent under vacuum gave an oil that spontaneously crystallized. This product, 3,5-dimethoxy-4-hydroxyamphetamine could be further purified by sublimation at 130 °C at 0.2 mm/Hg. It was a white crystalline solid that slowly discolored in the air. The literature describes a picrate salt with a mp of 225 °C from EtOH.

DOSAGE: 100 - 250 mg.

DURATION: 6 - 8 h.

QUALITATIVE COMMENTS: (with 135 mg) "I had no nausea, although I always vomit with mescaline. Somehow my personality was divided and exposed, and this allowed me to understand my psychic structure more clearly. But maybe others could look in there, too. The psychiatric use of this drug would be interesting to pursue. It is not completely pleasant, maybe because of this personal intimacy."

(with 140 mg) "There were not the color changes of mescaline there, but certainly a good humor and an over-appreciation of jokes. The images behind the eyes were remarkable and tied in with the music, and I became annoyed at other people's conversations that got in the way. I was out of it in eight hours. I would equate this to 300 or 350 milligrams of mescaline and I rather think that I would prefer the latter."

(with 225 mg) "There was quite a bit of nausea in the first hour. Then I found myself becoming emotionally quite volatile, sometimes gentle and peaceful, sometimes irritable and pugnacious. It was a day to be connected in one way or another with music. I was reading Bernstein's 'Joy of Music' and every phrase was audible to me. On the radio, Rachmaninoff's 2nd piano concerto on the radio put me in an eyes-closed foetal position and I was totally involved with the structure of the music. I was suspended, inverted, held by fine filigreed strands of the music which had been woven from the arpeggios and knotted with the chords. The commercials that followed were irritating, and the next piece, Slaughter on Fifth Avenue, made me quite violent. I was told that I had a, 'Don't cross me if you know what is good for you,' look to me. I easily crushed a rose, although it had been a thing of beauty."

EXTENSIONS AND COMMENTARY: TMA was the very first totally synthetic psychedelic phenethylamine that was found to be active in man, for which there had been any attempt to describe such drug effects in any detail. This was the report of research done in Canada, and it appeared in 1955, six years before my own report on the material. There was an earlier report on TMPEA which is mentioned in the appropriate recipe, but there were few details given. Also there had been interest in reports that adrenalin that had become old and discolored seemed to elicit central effects in man. The oxidation products were identified as the deeply colored indolic compound adrenochrome and the colorless analogue adrenolutin. The controversy that these reports created just sort of died away, and the adrenochrome family has never been accepted as being psychedelic. No one in the scientific community today is looking in and about the area, and at present this is considered as an interesting historical footnote. But, in any case, they are not phenethylamines and so not part of this book.

The Canadian studies with TMA involved the use of a stroboscope as a tool for the induction of visual phenomena. These experiments used levels in the 50-150 milligram range, and generally employed pre-treatment with Dramamine for the successful prevention of nausea. There was reported giddiness and light-headedness, and some remarkable flash-induced visualizations. With higher levels, the visual syntheses are present without external stimulation. But there is a thread of negativity that seems to pervade the experience at these higher levels, and the appearance of a publication that emphasized the possible antisocial nature to TMA seemed to discourage further medical exploration. Military interest was maintained however, apparently, as TMA became a part of the chemical warfare studies where it was referred to with the code name EA-1319. It had been used in human trials with psychiatric patients, but no details of these experiments have been published.

The presence of a potentially active impurity in TMA deserves some comment. In the Canadian work, the material used was described as melting at 219-220 °C, which is the property given for the impurity-free material above. If this was the actual material used in those studies, this impurity (3,5-dimethoxy-4-hydroxy-amphetamine) was probably not present. The Army studies use a material of unreported melting point. In my own studies, the lower melting product was used.

There is an intriguing and unanswered question: what contribution did this phenolic component make to the nature of the observed effects of TMA? Assays on the isolated contaminant could answer that, but they have not yet been made.

There is an old saying that has gotten many people into trouble: "If one is good, then two is better." And if a statement of the measure of worth of a compound can be made from its potency, then TMA is a step in the right direction. And this was a chemically simple direction to follow further. Looking at mescaline as a compound with no carbons on its side-chain, and TMA as a mescaline molecule with one carbon on its side chain, then what about a compound with two carbons there, or three, or nine carbons?

Using this pattern of naming, TMA can be seen as alpha-methylmescaline, or AMM. And the two carbon homologue would be alpha-ethyl mescaline, or AEM. Its proper name is 2-amino-1-(3,4,5-trimethoxyphenyl)butane. It and its several higher homologues are discussed in a separate recipe entry called AEM (#1).

A final comment. But maybe a long one! Elsewhere, I have made comparisons between myristicin and MMDA, and between safrole and MDA. And here there is a similar parallel between elemicin and TMA. What are these relationships between the essential oils and the amphetamines? In a word, there are some ten essential oils that have a three carbon chain, and each lacks only a molecule of ammonia to become an amphetamine. So, maybe these essential oils, or "almost" amphetamines, can serve as an index for the corresponding real amphetamine counterparts. I had originally called this family the "natural" amphetamines, but my son suggested calling them the "essential" amphetamines, and I like that. At the time that I had synthesized TMA, back there in the '50s, I had the impulse to explore this body of Essential Amphetamines. As the old folk-wisdom says: "Nature is trying to tell us something."

One of the banes of the archivist is having to choose one pattern of organization over another. The book store owned by a language scholar will have the German poets and playwrights and novelists here, and the French ones over there. Next door, the book store is run by a letters scholar, and the poetry of the world is here, and the plays of the world are there, regardless of the language of origin. The same obtains with spices, and essential oils, and amphetamines. The spice cabinet is a rich source of chemical treasures, each source plant containing a host of compounds, some of which are true essential oils. And the next spice from the next plant has some of the same components and some new ones. Does one organize by plant (spice or herb) or by essential oil (amphetamine)? Let's do it by the ring substitution pattern of the amphetamine, and gather the spices and oils as a secondary collection.

(1) The 4-methoxy pattern. The pivotal essential oil is 4-allylanisole, or methyl chavicol, or estragole (called esdragol in the old literature). This allyl compound is found in turpentine, anise, fennel, bay, tarragon, and basil. Its smell is light, and reminiscent of fennel. The propenyl analogue is called anethole, or anise camphor, and it is found in both anise and camphor. It is a waxy solid, and has a very intense smell of anise or fennel. At low concentrations, it is sweet, as in magnolia

blossoms, where it is also found. The drinks that turn cloudy with water dilution (Pernod-like liqueurs, and ouzo and roki), are heavy with it, since it was the natural flavoring in the original absinthe. That drink was very popular in the last century, as an intoxicant which produced an altered state of consciousness beyond that which could be ascribed to alcohol alone. It contained wormwood, which proved to be neurologically damaging. The flavorings, such as anethole, are still big things in synthetic liqueurs such as vermouth. Old anethole, when exposed to air and light, gets thick and sticky and yellowish, and becomes quite disagreeable to taste. Maybe it is polymerizing, or maybe oxidizing to stuff that dimerizes. Whatever. These changes are why old spices in the cabinet are best discarded. And adding ammonia to any of these natural product oils produces, in principle, 4-methoxyamphetamine, 4-MA.

(2) The 3,4-dimethoxy pattern. The main actor here is methyleugenol, or 4-allyl-1,2-dimethoxybenzene. This is located in almost every item in the spice cabinet. It is in citronella, bay (which is laurel, which is myrtle), pimiento, allspice, pepper, tree-tea oil, and on and on. It has a faint smell of cloves, and when dilute is immediately mistaken for carnations. The propenyl analogue is, not unreasonably, methylisoeugenol, a bit more scarce, and seems to always be that little minor peak in any essential oil analysis. The compounds missing that methyl group on the 4-oxygen are famous. The allyl material is eugenol, 4-allylguaiacol, and it is in cinnamon, nutmeg, cloves, sassafras and myrrh. You taste it and it burns. You smell it and think immediately of cloves. And its property as an anesthetic, in the form of a clove, is well known in the folk-treatment of toothaches. Actually, flowers of clove (the gillyflower, like the carnation) are the small, pointy things that decorate baked hams and, when stuck into apples, make pomander balls. This anesthetic property has recently led to a drug abuse fad, called clove cigarettes. Very strong, very flavorful, and very corrosive things from Southeast Asia. The eugenol that is present numbs the throat, and allows many strong cigarettes to be smoked without pain. The propenyl analogue is isoeugenol, with a smell that is subtle but very long lasting, used more in soaps and perfumes than in foods. The amine addition to the methyleugenol world produces 3,4-dimethoxyamphetamine, or 3,4-DMA. The isomer with the other methyl group missing is chavibetol (3-hydroxy-4-methoxyallylbenzene) and is found in the pepper leaf that is used with betel nut. A couple of positional rearrangement isomers of methyleugenol are known in the plant world. The 2,4-isomer is called osmorrhizole, and the conjugated form is isoosmorrhizole or nothosmyrnol; both are found in carrot-like vegetables. They, with ammonia, would give 2,4-DMA. And the 3,5-dimethoxyallylbenzene isomer from artemisia (a pungent herb commonly called mugwort) and from sage, would give rise to 3,5-DMA. This is an unexplored isomer which would be both an antidote for opium as well as a stimulant, if the classical reputation of mugwort is transferred to the amphetamine.

(3) The 3,4-methylenedioxy pattern. One of the most famous essential oils is safrole, or 4-allyl-1,2-methylenedioxybenzene. This is the mainstay of sassafras

oil, and it and its conjugated isomer isosafrole have a smell that is immediately familiar: root beer! These are among the most widely distributed essential oils, being present in most of the spices, including the heavies such as cinnamon and nutmeg. I am not aware of the 2,3-isomer ever having been found in nature. Adding ammonia to either would give MDA.

(4) The 3-methoxy-4,5-methylenedioxy pattern. The parent compound is myristicin, 5-allyl-1-methoxy-2,3-methylenedioxybenzene, and the source of this is nutmeg (or the botanically parallel material, mace). The nutmeg is the seed of the tree *Myristica fragrans* and mace is the fibrous covering of the seed. The two spices are virtually identical as to their chemical composition. Myristicin and the conjugated isomer isomyristicin are also found in parsley oil, and in dill. This was the oil that was actually shown to be converted to MMDA by the addition of ammonia by passage through an *in vitro* liver preparation. So here is the major justification for the equation between the essential oils and the Essential Amphetamines. Care must be taken to make an exact distinction between myristicin (this essential oil) and myristin (the fat) which is really trimyristin or glyceryl trimyristate from nutmeg and coconut. This is the fat from myristic acid, the C-14 fatty acid, and these two similar names are often interchanged even in the scientific literature.

(5) The 2-methoxy-3,4-methylenedioxy pattern. This is the second of the three natural methoxy methylenedioxy orientations. Croweacin is 2-methoxy-3,4-methylenedioxyallylbenzene, and it takes its name from the binomial for the plant *Eriostemon crowei* from the worlds of rue and the citrus plants. It corresponds to the essential amphetamine MMDA-3a. This oil is found in plants of the Family Rutaceae. My memories of this area of botany are of *Ruta graveolens*, the common rue, whose small leaves smelled to me, for all the world, like cat urine. This plant has always fascinated me because of a most remarkable recipe that I was given by a very, very conservative fellow-club member, one evening, after rehearsal. He told me of a formula that had provided him with the most complete relief from arthritic pain he had ever known. It was a native decoction he had learned of many years eariler, when he was traveling in Mexico. One took equal quantities of three plants, *Ruta graveolens* (or our common rue), *Rosmarinus officinalis* (better known as rosemary), and *Cannabis sativa* (which is recognized in many households simply as marijuana). Three plants all known in folklore, rue as a symbol for repentance, rosemary as a symbol of remembrance, and pot, well, I guess it is a symbol of a lot of things to a lot of people. Anyway, equal quantities of these three plants are allowed to soak in a large quantity of rubbing alcohol for a few weeks. Then the alcoholic extracts are clarified, and allowed to evaporate in the open air to a thick sludge. This then was rubbed on the skin, where the arthritis was troublesome, and always rubbed in the direction of the extremity. It was not into, but onto the body that it was applied. All this from a very conservative Republican friend!

The methoxy-methylenedioxy pattern is also found in nature with the 2,4,5-orientation pattern. The allyl-2,4,5-isomer is called asaricin. It, and its propenyl-isomer, carpacin, are from the Carpano tree which grows in the Solomon

Islands. All these plants are used in folk medicine. These two systems, the 2,3,4- and the 2,4,5-orientations, potentially give rise, with ammonia, to MMDA-3a and MMDA-2.

(6) The 3,4,5-trimethoxy pattern. Elemicin is the well studied essential oil, 5-allyl-1,2,3-trimethoxybenzene, primarily from the oil of elemi. It is, like myristicin, a component of the Oil of Nutmeg, but it is also found in several of the Oils of Camphor, and in the resin of the Pili in the Philippines. This tree is the source of the Oil of Elemi. I had found a trace component in nutmeg many years ago that proved to be 5-methoxyeugenol, or elemicin without the 4-methyl group; it is also present in the magnolia plant. The aldehyde that corresponds to this is syringaldehyde, and its prefix has been spun into many natural products. Any natural product with a syring somewhere in it has a hydroxy between two methoxys. The amphetamine base from elemicin or isoelemicin would be TMA, the topic of this very recipe.

(7) The 2,4,5-trimethoxy pattern. There is an essential oil called asarone that is 2,4,5-trimethoxy-1-propenylbenzene. It is the trans- or alpha-isomer, and the cis-isomer is known as beta-asarone. It is the isomerization analogue of the much more rare 1-allyl-2,4,5-trimethoxybenzene, gamma-asarone, or euasarone, or sekishone. Asarone is the major component of Oil of Calamus obtained from the rhizomes of *Acorus calamus*, the common Sweet Flag that grows wild on the edges of swamps throughout North America, Europe, and Asia. It has been used as a flavoring of liqueurs and, as almost every other plant known to man, has been used as a medicine. In fact, in Manitoba this plant was called Rat-root by the Cree Indians in the Lake Winnipeg area known as New Iceland, and Indian-root by the Icelandic pioneers. It was used externally for the treatment of wounds, and internally for most illnesses. There apparently is no report of central effects. The corresponding propanone, acoramone (or 2,4,5-trimethoxyphenylacetone), is also present in Oil of Calamus. The styrene that corresponds to asarone is found in a number of plants, and is surprisingly toxic to brine shrimp. The older literature describes an allyl-trimethoxy benzene called calamol, but it has never been pinned down as to structure. The isolation of gamma-asarone or euasarone from Oil of Xixin (from wild ginger) has given rise to a potential problem of nomenclature. One of the Genus names associated with wild ginger is *Asiasarum* which looks very much like the name asarone, which comes from the Genus *Acorus*. And a second Genus of medical plants also called wild ginger is simply called *Asarum*. There is an *Asarum forbesi* from central China, and it is known to give a pleasant smell to the body. And there is *Asarum seiboldi* which is largely from Korea and Manchuria. It has many medical uses, including the treatment of deafness, epilepsy, and rheumatism. The amphetamine that would arise from this natural treasure chest is TMA-2.

(8) The 2,5-dimethoxy-3,4-methylenedioxy pattern. The parent allyl benzene is apiole (with a final "e") or parsley camphor, and it is the major component of parsley seed oil. Its conjugated isomer is called isoapiole, and they are valuable as the chemical precurors to the amination product, DMMDA. Whereas both of these essential oils are white solids, there is a green oily liquid that

had been broadly used years ago in medicine, called green, or liquid apiol (without the final "e"). It comes from the seeds of parsley by ether extraction, and when the chlorophyll has been removed, it is known as yellow apiol. With the fats removed by saponification and distillation, the old term for the medicine was apiolin. I would assume that any of these would give rise to white, crystalline apiole on careful distillation, but I have never tried to do it. The commercial Oil of Parsley is so readily available.

(9) The 2,3-dimethoxy-4,5-methylenedioxy pattern. The second of the three tetraoxygenated essential oils is 1-allyl-2,3-dimethoxy-4,5-methylenedioxy-benzene, commonly called dillapiole and it comes, not surprisingly, from the oils of any of the several dill plants around the world. It is a thick, almost colorless liquid, but its isomerization product, isodillapiole, is a white crystalline product which melts sharply. This, by the theoretical addition of ammonia, gives DMMDA-2.

(10) The tetramethoxy pattern. The third and last of the tetra-oxygenated essential oils, is 1-allyl-2,3,4,5-tetramethoxybenzene. This is present as a minor component in the oil of parsley, but it is much more easily obtained by synthesis. It, and its iso-compound, and the amination product, are discussed under the last of theTen Essential Amphetamines, TA.

One must remember that the term "essential" has nothing to do with the meaning of needed, or required. The word's origin is essence, something with an odor or smell. Thus, the essential oils are those oils that have a fragrance, and the Essential Amphetamines are those compounds that can, in principle, be made from them by the addition of ammonia in the body.

There were a few interesting experimental trials that were based on these natural oils. Methoxyeugenol was assayed up to a 10 milligram level, and asarone at up to a 70 milligram level, and neither had any effects at all. And, in an attempt to challenge the "oil-to-amphetamine" concept, I made up a mixture of 1 part MDA, 2 parts TMA and 5 parts MMDA. A total of 100 milligrams of this combination (which I had named the "Pseunut Cocktail" for pseudo-nutmeg) should be equivalent to the safrole, elemicin and myristicin that would be in 5 grams of nutmeg. And 100 milligrams indeed produced quite a sparkle and considerable eye-dilation. But then, I have never taken 5 grams of nutmeg, so I cannot make any comparisons.

#158   TMA-2;   2,4,5-TRIMETHOXYAMPHETAMINE

SYNTHESIS: To a solution of 50 g 2,4,5-trimethoxybenzaldehyde in 175 mL nitroethane there was added 10 g anhydrous ammonium acetate and the mixture was heated on the steam bath for 2 h. The excess nitroethane was removed under vacuum, and the deep orange oily residue was drained out into a beaker, and the flask washed with 3x60 mL boiling MeOH. On stirring the combined decantation and washings, there was a spontaneous formation of crystals. After cooling, these were removed by filtration, washed sparing with MeOH, and air dried to constant weight to yield 35.1 g of 2-nitro-1-(2,4,5-trimethoxyphenyl)propene as yellow crystals with a mp of 98-99 °C. Recrystallization from MeOH increased the mp to 101-102 °C.

A suspension of 31.6 g powdered LAH in 1 L anhydrous THF containing a little anhydrous Et_2O was brought to a gentle reflux, and then there was added a solution of 40.0 g of 2-nitro-1-(2,4,5-trimethoxyphenyl)propene in 200 mL anhydrous THF over the course of 4 h. The mixture was held at reflux temperature for 24 h, cooled to 0 °C with external ice, and the excess hydride destroyed by the addition, in sequence, of 32 mL H_2O (which had been diluted with a little THF), 32 mL 15% NaOH, and finally with 96 mL H_2O. The white inorganic solids were removed by filtration, and the filter cake was washed with THF. The combined

filtrate and washings were stripped of solvent under vacuum to give 48 g of an impure amber oil. This was dissolved in 180 mL IPA, neutralized with 30 mL concentrated HCl, and the mixture diluted with 1500 mL anhydrous Et_2O. After a short induction period, an oily precipitate separated, which on stirring changed into a loose crystalline phase. This was removed by filtration, washed with Et_2O, and air dried to yield 29.0 g of 2,4,5-trimethoxyamphetamine hydrochloride (TMA-2) as fine white crystals with a mp of 188.5-189.5 °C. Anal. $(C_{12}H_{20}ClNO_3)$ C,H,N. A 4.0 g sample of the free base was dissolved in 15 mL pyridine, treated with 2.5 mL acetic anhydride, heated on the steam bath for 20 min, added to 400 mL H_2O, acidified with HCl, and extracted with 3x75 mL CH_2Cl_2. After washing with H_2O the pooled extracts were stripped of solvent under vacuum to give 4.5 g of flakey, off-white solids which, on recrystallization from MeOH, were white, weighed 2.3 g, and had a mp of 132-133 °C. Recrystallization from this acetamide from MEK did not improve its quality. Anal. $(C_{14}H_{21}NO_4)$ C,H,N.

DOSAGE: 20 - 40 mg.

DURATION: 8 - 12 h.

QUALITATIVE COMMENTS: (with 20 mg) "I took it in two 10 milligram doses, spaced by two hours. There was a slight movement of surface textures, my hearing was deepened and spatially defined. The body was relaxed and stretching seemed necessary. The further I got into it the more I realized that I was totally lazy. Very lethargic, to the point of laughter. At the sixth hour, I was seeing more life in the woodwork, and the wooden angel hanging on the ceiling was flesh and feathers when I stared at it. Great vision. But by no means overwhelming. Sleep was fine."

(with 20 mg) "The first two hours seemed like an eternity, with time passing slowly. Then it settled into a very calm and enjoyable event (not that it wasn't already). The material seemed somewhat hypnotic. I suspect that I would believe suggestions, or at least not challenge them too much. I had a little confusion but it was not troublesome. On reflection, the material was quite good. It was benign in the sense that there appeared to be no dark spots. I would try it again, perhaps at 30 milligrams. Almost base-line after 12 hours, but not quite."

(with 24 mg) "I took the dosage in two halves, an hour apart. Initially, I was a little nauseous, with light tremors and modest eye dilation. But after another hour, there was the entire package of mescaline, missing only the intense color enhancement. The world is filled with distorted. moving things. Then my little fingers on both hands got periodically numb. And there was an occasional light-headedness that hinted at fainting. The two phenomena alternated, and never got in each other's ways. Both passed, once I realized that I would recover from this experience. Then the humor and joy of the world returned. The drop-off was quite rapid from the fifth to eighth hour, and no effects remained at all by the twelfth hour."

(with 40 mg) "Very slow coming on. Didn't feel it for an hour, but then at a full +++ in another hour. Beautiful experience. Erotic excellent. Eyes-closed imagery and fantasy to music. No dark corners. Benign and peaceful and lovely. There were brief intestinal cramps early, and a little diarrhea, but no other problems. I was able to sleep after eight hours, but had guarded dreams."

(with 40 mg) "Beautiful plus 3. Some visuals, but not intrusive. Moderate, good-mannered kaleidoscopic imagery against dark. Music superb. Clear thinking. Calmly cosmic. This is a seminal, or archetypal psychoactive material. A very good experience and good for repeats. About 10-12 hrs. Sleep difficult but OK."

EXTENSIONS AND COMMENTARY: There was absolutely no reason to suspect that the simple rearrangement of the methoxy groups of TMA from the classic 3,4,5-positions to this new, 2,4,5-orientation, would dramatically increase potency like this. Mescaline, 3,4,5-trimethoxyphenethylamine, is an extraordinary compound, but it is not particularly potent, requiring hundreds of milligrams for a trip. And going from its 3,4,5-pattern to the 2,4,5-pattern of TMPEA makes the compound even less potent. There was essentially nothing reported in the scientific literature about central activity of 2,4,5-substituted stuff, so there could not have been any logical preparation for the activity of TMA-2. My very first trials were with a rather liberal 400 micrograms, and the levels being explored leaped up in fairly large steps, mostly on separate days. On November 26, 1962, at 6:00 AM, when 12 milligrams proved to be inactive, another 12 milligrams went in and down an hour later. This was the 24 milligram discovery experiment, a fragment of which is given above. The anxiety of being thrust into the unknown certainly played a role in what can now be seen as obvious psychosomatic difficulties.

The unexpected ten-fold increase of effectiveness uncovered by the simple relocation of a single methoxy group of TMA gave the further juggling of methoxy groups a very high priority. There are a total of six arrangements possible for the three groups, namely, 3,4,5- (the original TMA), 2,4,5- (the present TMA-2), and then and in systematic sequence, 2,3,4-, 2,3,5-, 2,3,6-, and 2,4,6. These compounds were totally unknown at that time, and they could and would be assigned the sequential names TMA-3, TMA-4, TMA-5 and TMA-6, respectively. I made them all, and they are all included in this book.

Having found the treasure of 2,4,5-ness, it is instructive to look back at nature, to see what its plant equivalents might be. There are indeed a few essential oils that have their methoxy groups in this arrangement. TMA-2 is thus one of the Essential Amphetamines, and most of the botanical connections are discussed under TMA. The natural skeleton is found in asarone, with alpha-asarone being trans-propenyl, beta-asarone the cis-propenyl and gamma-asarone (also called euasarone) being the allyl-isomer. I had mentioned, in the spice cabinet discussion under TMA, the tasting of asarone at up to 70 milligrams without any effects.

A couple of additional experiments involving TMA-2 had been set up and started, but somehow never had enough fire to get completed. Studies on the optical isomers had gotten up to assays of 6 milligrams on each of the separate isomers, but had never been taken higher. The "R" isomer is much the more potent in rabbit assays, but the human comparisons remain unknown at present. Also, a study of the ^{14}C labeled racemate (5 microcuries in 40 milligrams) was conducted with a view to metabolite analysis, but again, the project was abandoned before any results were obtained. In the rat, the 4-methoxyl carbon appeared as expired carbon dioxide to the extent of about 20%. And this is some four times the amount seen from either of the other two methoxyl carbon atoms.

One final memory in the TMA-2 area. About twenty years ago I co-authored a rather thorough review article in the British journal Nature, that described the structure-activity relationships between the simpler one-ringed psy-chotomimetics. It also quietly served as a vehicle for mentioning a number of newly-discovered compounds and their human activities. But as a magnificent attestment to youth and brashness, we proposed a complex compound that embraced each and every clue and hint that might tie it to the neurological process. This hybrid monster was 2,ß-dihydroxy-4,5-dimethoxyphenethylamine. It had everything. The 6-hydroxydopamine hydroxy group and the rest of the dopamine molecule intact as represented by the two methoxyl groups. And the beta-hydroxy group gave it the final "norepinephrine" touch. And, with due modesty, we proposed that it might be "an endogenous psychotogen." Why not "*the* endogenous psychotogen?" And then, to compound the picture, what should arrive in the mail a month or two later, and from a most respected scientist, but a sample of just this stuff, synthesized for our investigations. I must have bought a little of my own promotion, as I noted that even after my first four graded dosages with the compound, I was still only up to a 250 microgram dose. And then, as the sample became increasingly brown and was clearly decomposing, the project was finally abandoned.

A sad note on how things have changed since that time. I recently queried the editors of Nature, about their thoughts concerning a twenty year retrospective of this area, written by the three authors of the original review. We had each followed quite divergent paths, but each of us was still keenly the researcher. It would have been a marvelous paper to put together, and it would have delighted the reading audience of Nature, had it been the audience of twenty years ago. But not today. The journal is now dedicated to neutron stars and x-ray sources. The respected old English journal of interdisciplinary interests is not the grand and curious lady she used to be. The Editor's reply was polite, but negative. "Such an article would be unsuitable for publication in Nature at present," they said. And, I am sad to say, they're right.

And I am afraid that the American counterpart journal, Science, has suffered a similar deterioration. It, too, has abandoned multidisciplinary interest, but in a different direction. They are now dedicated to chromosomes, and nucleotide identification, and are totally captivated by the attention paid to, and the apparent importance of, the human genome project. There is where you automatically go to publish, now, if you have unraveled some DNA sequence from the Latvian cockroach.

#159   TMA-3;   2,3,4-TRIMETHOXYAMPHETAMINE

SYNTHESIS: To a solution of 12.4 g 2,3,4-trimethoxybenzaldehyde in 45 mL glacial acetic acid, there was added 7 mL nitroethane and 4.1 g anhydrous ammonium acetate, and all was held at reflux temperature for 1.5 h. To the cooled and well stirred reaction mixture, H_2O was added slowly, dropping out an oily crystalline solid mass. This was separated by filtration, and ground under a quantity of 50% aqueous acetic acid, and re-filtered. The 6.5 g of crude product was recrystallized from boiling MeOH to give, after air drying to constant weight, 5.0 g of 2-nitro-1-(2,3,4-tri-methoxyphenyl)propene, with a mp of 56-57 °C. Anal. $(C_{12}H_{15}NO_5)$ C,H.

To a gently refluxing suspension of 3.0 g LAH in 300 mL anhydrous Et_2O under a He atmosphere, there was added 3.65 g 2-nitro-1-(2,3,4-trimethoxy-phenyl)propene by allowing the condensing Et_2O drip into a shunted Soxhlet thimble containing the nitrostyrene and effectively adding a warm saturated solu-tion of it dropwise. Refluxing was maintained for 5 h following the completion of the addition of the nitrostyrene. The milky reaction mixture was cooled and the excess hydride destroyed by the addition of 200 mL 10% H_2SO_4. When the aqueous and Et_2O layers were finally clear, they were separated, and 75 g of potassium sodium tartrate was dissolved in the aqueous fraction. NaOH (25%) was then added until the pH was >9, and this was then extracted with 3x75 mL CH_2Cl_2. Evaporation of the solvent under vacuum produced 2.5 g of a nearly colorless clear oil that was dissolved in 300 mL anhydrous Et_2O which was saturated with anhydrous HCl gas.

The product, 2,3,4-trimethoxyamphetamine hydrochloride (TMA-3) separated as a fine white solid. This was removed by filtration, Et_2O washed, and air dried to constant weight. The yield was 1.65 g of a product which, after recrystallization from IPA, had a mp of 148-149 °C. Anal. $(C_{12}H_{20}ClNO_3)$ C,H.

DOSAGE: greater than 100 mg.

DURATION: unknown.

QUALITATIVE COMMENTS: (with 100 mg) "There were no effects at all. No eye dilation, no believable diversion from complete normalcy. Appetite was normal, as well."

EXTENSIONS AND COMMENTARY: There is a small lesson to be learned from this completely inactive compound. There is no way of saying that it is or is not inactive. All that can be said is that trials were made (in this case using three separate individuals) at an oral level of 100 milligrams. And, at this level, nothing happened. And since a bottom threshold for mescaline would be perhaps 200 milligrams, it can be honestly said that the activity of this compound, if expressed relative to mescaline (using mescaline units) is less than 2 M.U. Had 200 milligrams been inactive, it would have been less than 1.0 M.U. If 2 grams had been inactive, it would have been less than 0.1 M.U. But the actual printed form, activity < 2.0 M.U. was accepted by many readers as indicating that TMA-3 was active, but at dosages greater than 100 milligrams. All that can be said is, *if* there is activity, *then* it will be at oral levels greater than 100 milligrams At the moment, as far as I know, this compound is not active in man, but then I know of no trials in excess of 100 milligrams.

This admonition applies to all the published M.U. values that are preceded by the "less than" sign, the "<."

#160   TMA-4;   2,3,5-TRIMETHOXYAMPHETAMINE

SYNTHESIS: To a solution of 68 g 2,4-dimethoxybenzaldehyde in 250 mL glacial acetic acid that had been warmed to 25 °C and well stirred, there was added, dropwise, 86 g of a 40% peracetic acid solution (in acetic acid). The reaction was exothermic, and the rate of addition was dictated by the need to maintain the internal temperature within a few degrees of 28 °C. External cooling was used as needed. The addition took 1 h, and when the reaction had clearly been completed (no further temperature rise) the entire reaction mixture was added to 3 volumes of H_2O. The excess acid was neutralized with solid K_2CO_3 (283 g were required). This was extracted with 3x100 mL Et_2O, the extracts pooled, and stripped of solvent under vacuum to give 66 g of crude 2,4-dimethoxyphenyl formate. This was suspended in 125 mL 10% NaOH, and the mixture heated on the steam bath for 1.5 h. On cooling, the reaction mixture set to a heavy black solid. This was removed by filtration, washed with H_2O, and dissolved in 250 mL CH_2Cl_2. The organic phase was washed with dilute HCl, and then with aqueous $NaHCO_3$, which removed much of the color. Removal of the solvent under vacuum gave a deep red goo that was dissolved in 200 mL anhydrous Et_2O and filtered through paper. The resulting clear solution was stripped of solvent, yielding 34.4 g of 2,4-dimethoxyphenol as a red oil that crystallized on cooling. A 1.0 g sample in 4 mL pyridine was treated with 0.9 g benzoyl chloride and heated on the steam bath for a few min. The addition of H_2O gave a pasty solid that was isolated by pressing on a porous plate. The yield of crude 2,4-dimethoxyphenyl benzoate was 1.1 g. Recrystallization from cyclohexane gave a white product with a mp of 86-87 °C. A second recrystallization from cyclohexane raised this to 89-90 °C, which is in agreement with the literature value.

To a solution of 31.0 g crude 2,4-dimethoxyphenol in 60 mL absolute EtOH there was added a solution of 11.25 g KOH in 90 mL boiling EtOH. To this, there was then added 28 g allyl bromide which produced an immediate white precipitate of KBr. The mixture was held at reflux for 2 h and then quenched in 3 volumes of H_2O. Sufficient 10% NaOH was added to make the reaction strongly basic, and this was extracted with 3x100 mL Et_2O. Removal of the solvent under vacuum gave 33.2 g of 1-allyloxy-2,4-dimethoxybenzene, shown to be free of phenol starting material by GC analysis. Analyses must be carried out at low column temperatures (below 180 °C) on an ethylene glycol succinate substrate. If a silicone column is used, even at these low temperatures, there is considerable Claisen rearrangement taking place on the column. Low temperature distillation can be used for further purification (107-110 °C at 1.0 mm/Hg).

A 31.0 g sample of 1-allyloxy-2,4-dimethoxybenzene was gently heated with a soft flame until the internal temperature reached 215 °C. An exothermic reaction took place, with the temperature rising to 270 °C. The residue left in the flask was largely 2-allyl-4,6-dimethoxyphenol, that contained perhaps 10% of 2,4-dimethoxyphenol which resulted from the pyrolytic loss of the allyl group. This mixture was methylated without further purification.

To a solution of 30 g impure 2-allyl-4,6-dimethoxyphenol in a little absolute EtOH there was added a boiling solution of 8.7 g KOH in 75 mL absolute EtOH followed, immediately, by 22.4 g methyl iodide in a little EtOH. The mixture was held at reflux for 3 h, then added to 4 volumes of H_2O. Sufficient 10% NaOH was added to make the mixture strongly basic, and this was extracted with 4x100 mL Et_2O. Removal of the solvent gave 28 g of 1-allyl-2,3,5-trimethoxybenzene. GC analysis showed some 10% of the expected impurity, 1,2,4-trimethoxybenzene.

To a solution of 26 g crude 1-allyl-2,3,5-trimethoxybenzene in an equal weight of absolute EtOH there was added 52 g of flaked KOH. The mixture was heated on the steam bath overnight, and then quenched with much H_2O. This was extracted with 3x100 mL Et_2O which, on removal under vacuum gave 24.6 g of product. This contained, by GC analysis, largely cis- and trans-1-propenyl-2,3,5-trimethoxybenzene and the expected 1,2,4-trimethoxybenzene. This mixture was dissolved in an equal volume of pentane, and cooled in dry ice. Quick filtration gave 9.2 g of an amber solid which had a melting point of 39-41.5 °C. Recrystallization from hexane provided pure trans-1-propenyl-2,3,5-trimethoxybenzene with a mp of 44-45 °C. Evaporation of the original pentane mother liquor provided an impure sample of mixed cis- and trans- isomers.

A solution of 7.2 g trans-1-propenyl-2,3,5-trimethoxybenzene in 41 g dry acetone was treated with 3.3 g dry pyridine and, with good stirring, cooled to 0 °C. There was then added 6.9 g of tetranitromethane over the course of 1 min, and the reaction mixture was allowed to stir for an additional 2 min. The reaction mixture was then quenched with a solution of 2.2 g KOH in 40 mL H_2O. After the addition of more H_2O, the product was extracted with 3x50 mL CH_2Cl_2. Removal of the solvent under vacuum yielded 7.0 g of an impure product which would not crystallize. This was distilled under vacuum to give four fractions, all of which crystallized spontaneously. Cuts #1 and #2 (bp 100-120 °C and 120-130 °C at 2 mm/Hg) were combined, weighed 0.8 g, and after crystallization from hexane yielded white crystals with a mp of 62-63 °C. The NMR spectrum (in $CDCl_3$) was in agreement with 2,3,5-trimethoxybenzaldehyde, and the literature mp has been reported as being 62-63 °C. Cuts #3 and #4 (bp 130-170 °C and 170-175 °C at 2 mm/Hg with the bulk coming over in the latter fraction) were combined to give 3.0 g of yellow crystals. These were triturated under a little cold MeOH, and then recrystallized from MeOH to give 1.15 g of yellow crystals of 2-nitro-1-(2,3,5-trimethoxyphenyl)propene, with a mp of 87-88 °C. The forerun of the distillation contained considerable unreacted trans-1-propenyl-2,3,5-trimethoxybenzene and some 1,2,4-trimethoxybenzene, by GC analysis.

To a refluxing and stirred suspension of 1.1 g LAH in 150 mL anhydrous Et_2O and under an inert atmosphere, there was added a solution of 1.1 g 2-nitro-1-(2,3,5-trimethoxyphenyl)propene in 50 mL anhydrous Et_2O. The creamy mixture was held at reflux for 4 h, cooled, and then the excess hydride cautiously destroyed by the addition of 1.5 N H_2SO_4. There was then added 20 g potassium sodium tartrate followed by sufficient aqueous NaOH to raise the pH to >9. The Et_2O phase was separated, and the remaining aqueous phase extracted with 3x75 mL CH_2Cl_2. The organic phase and extracts were combined, and the solvent removed under vacuum yielding 0.9 g of a colorless oil. This was dissolved in 200 mL anhydrous Et_2O which was saturated with anhydrous HCl gas. There was generated a thick oil that did not crystallize. The Et_2O was decanted from this, and allowed to stand for several days in a sealed container at room temperature. There was the deposition of fine white needles of 2,3,5-trimethoxyamphetamine hydrochloride (TMA-4) weighing, after Et_2O washing and air drying, 0.31 g. The mp was 118-119 °C. Anal. ($C_{12}H_{20}ClNO_3$) C,H. The residual oil was dissolved in H_2O, made basic with NaOH, and extracted with CH_2Cl_2. Evaporation of the solvent gave 0.40 of a white oil which was dissolved in a little MeOH containing 0.22 g oxalic acid. There was the immediate deposition of crystals of the oxalate salt of 2,3,5-trimethoxyamphetamine, with a mp of about 110 °C.

DOSAGE: greater than 80 mg.

DURATION: perhaps 6 h.

QUALITATIVE COMMENTS: (with 80 mg) "I was concerned about life issues, with much introspection, for about 6 hours. There were no subjective physical symptoms. It was comparable to about 50 micrograms of LSD, or to 120 milligrams TMA, for me."

EXTENSIONS AND COMMENTARY: That is the sum total of the knowledge of subjective effects that exist. There was such a precious small amount of the final hydrochloride salt that, by the time the needed build-up of dosage had been completed, there was just enough left for this single trial, which was conducted in South America. Based upon the volunteered comparisons to LSD and TMA, a potency for this compound has been published that states that it is 4x the potency of mescaline, or 4 M.U. The material must be re-synthesized, and re-evaluated with the now-accepted protocol.

In the future re-synthesis, there will be a considerable improvement made with the several steps that are described above. The products from the preparations of the phenol, the allyl ether, the Claisen rearrangement, the methylation of the new phenol, and the isomerization to the mixture of cis- and trans-propenylbenzenes were all conducted without the benefit of a Kugel-Rohr apparatus. The products became progressively thick and blacker, and it was only by the grace of getting a solid at the trans-propenyl stage that some degree of purity could finally be obtained. All of the intermediates are certainly white oils, and when this preparation is repeated, they will be distilled at each and every stage.

This 2,3,5-orientation of the methoxy groups on the aromatic ring is far and away the most difficult tri-substitution pattern known to chemists. There just isn't any simple way to put it together. The 2-carbon phenethylamine (2,3,5-trimethoxy-phenethylamine) had been synthesized quite a while ago. Its role as a substrate for liver amine oxidase in *in vitro* studies has been explored, but it has never been tried in man. Even more bizarre is the amphetamine with this oxygenation pattern, in which a methylenedioxy ring has replaced the two adjacent methoxyl groups. This is the material 2,3-methylenedioxy-5-methoxyamphetamine, or MMDA-4. Despite its theoretical appeal (being one of the six possible MMDA derivatives) and it's synthetic challenge (as with the 2,3,5-trimethoxy things above, everything is simply in the wrong position) the compound is of unknown pharmacology. This follows, quite logically, from the fact that it has never been synthesized. No one has yet put together a workable procedure that would make it. In the course of making all possible positional isomers of MMDA explicitly Schedule I drugs, the DEA has named this compound, and since it was specifically named, it was entered into the Chemical Abstracts. So it is listed in the literature, at least it is in the Chem. Abstracts. But it is in reality completely unknown. Some day, some one somewhere will have a light bulb go on over his head, and find a synthetic process that will make it. Of course, the moment it is made, an illegal act will have occurred, at least in the United States as long as the present laws remain unchanged, as it is currently a Schedule I drug.

Needless to say, the 2-carbon analog of MMDA-4, 2,3-methylenedioxy-5-methoxyphenethylamine (would 2C-MMDA-4 be a reasonable name?) is also unknown.

#161 TMA-5; 2,3,6-TRIMETHOXYAMPHETAMINE

SYNTHESIS: A solution of 100 g 1,2,4-trimethoxybenzene in 1 L hexane was cooled to 15 °C and treated with 400 mL of a 15% solution of n-butyllithium in hexane. A white precipitate formed immediately, and stirring was continued for an additional 2 h while the reaction returned to room temperature. There was then added a solution of 40 g freshly distilled propionaldehyde in 100 mL hexane. The reaction was exothermic and, as the stirring was continued, the precipitate gradually dissolved. Stirring was continued overnight at room temperature. There was then added 1 L H_2O, and the reaction was acidified with HCl. The hexane phase was separated, and the remaining aqueous phase was extracted with hexane, then with Et_2O. The pooled organic extracts were stripped of solvent under vacuum, and the residue distilled to give 60 g ethyl 2,3,6-trimethoxyphenyl carbinol, with an index of refraction $n_D^{20} = 1.5192$. Anal. $(C_{12}H_{18}O_4)$ C,H. From the Et_2O extracts above, additional carbinol was obtained, containing a small amount of the starting 1,2,4-trimethoxybenzene. The two materials were readily separated by vacuum distillation, providing an additional 21 g of carbinol.

The above alcohol, 60 g of ethyl 2,3,6-trimethoxyphenyl carbinol, was stirred without solvent and cooled to 0 °C with an external ice bath. There was then added 80 g PBr_3 at a rate that maintained the temperature below 60 °C. At the end of the addition, there were added quantities of chipped ice, followed by H_2O. The reaction mixture was extracted with 3x100 mL Et_2O, and removal of the solvent provided 60 g of 1-bromo-1-(2,3,6-trimethoxyphenyl)propane which was used in the following dehydrobromination step without further purification.

A solution of the above 60 g of 1-bromo-1-(2,3,6-trimethoxyphenyl)propane in an equal weight of EtOH was treated with 120 g of flaked KOH. The exothermic reaction was allowed to run its course with stirring continued overnight. The mixture was then quenched in H_2O and extracted with 3x200 mL CH_2Cl_2. Removal of the solvent from the pooled extracts gave a crude product which contained no starting bromo material, but which was contaminated with an appreciable quantity of the ethoxy analogue, 1-ethoxy-1-(2,3,6-trimethoxyphenyl)propane. This impure product was heated briefly to 80 °C with 50% H_2SO_4. Cooling, dilution with water, and re-extraction with 3x100 mL CH_2Cl_2 gave, after removal of the volatiles under vacuum, 1-(2,3,6-trimethoxyphenyl)propene. This was distilled to provide 7.0 g of a clear oil that was a 12:1 ratio of the trans- and cis-isomers.

A well-stirred solution of 6.8 g of the mixed isomers of 1-(2,3,6-tri-methoxyphenyl)propene in 40 g of dry acetone was treated with 3.2 g pyridine and cooled to 0 °C with an external ice bath. There was then added 6.5 g tetranitro-methane over the course of 1 min, the stirring was continued for an additional 2 min, and then the reaction mixture was quenched by the addition of 2.2 g KOH in 40 mL H_2O. There was additional H_2O added, and the organics were extracted with 3x75 mL CH_2Cl_2. The solvent from the pooled extracts was removed under vacuum, and the 5.3 g residue distilled at 0.2 mm/Hg. A fraction boiling at 150-170 °C proved to be largely 2,3,6-trimethoxybenzaldehyde. A second fraction (170-200 °C at 0.2 mm/Hg) also spontaneously crystallized to a yellow solid. This was recrystallized from MeOH to provide, after drying to constant weight, 2.8 g of 2-nitro-1-(2,3,6-trimethoxyphenyl)propene with a mp of 73-74 °C. Anal. ($C_{12}H_{15}NO_5$) C,H.

To a refluxing and stirred suspension of 2.4 g LAH in 300 mL anhydrous Et_2O and under an inert atmosphere, there was added a solution of 2.4 g 2-nitro-1-(2,3,6-trimethoxyphenyl)propene in 100 mL anhydrous Et_2O. The mixture was held at reflux for 4 h, cooled, and then the excess hydride cautiously destroyed by the addition of 1.5 N H_2SO_4. There was then added 40 g potassium sodium tartrate followed by sufficient aqueous NaOH to raise the pH to >9. The Et_2O phase was separated, and the remaining aqueous phase extracted with 3x100 mL CH_2Cl_2. The organic phase and extracts were combined, and the solvent removed under vacuum yielding 1.8 g of a colorless oil. This was dissolved in 200 mL anhydrous Et_2O which was saturated with anhydrous HCl gas. There was generated a thick oil that slowly crystallized. The resulting white crystalline solid was removed by filtration, providing 2.2 g 2,3,6-trimethoxyamphetamine hydrochloride (TMA-5). The mp was 124-125 °C. Anal. ($C_{12}H_{20}ClNO_3$) C,H.

DOSAGE: 30 mg or more.

DURATION: 8 - 10 h.

QUALITATIVE COMMENTS: (with 20 mg) "There appeared to be a slight stimulation. Modest eye dilation, but normal pulse. If this is the marginal edge of intoxication, then it is not a psychotomimetic, but a stimulant. Go up with care."

(with 30 mg) "Intense introspection. Comparable to about 75 micrograms of LSD, or more."

EXTENSIONS AND COMMENTARY: TMA-5, as was the case with TMA-4, has only been superficially explored. The above two quotations are from two different people, and together no more than hint at the possibility that it might be active in the several tens of milligrams.

Pharmacologists have developed quite an art in the design and evaluation of animal behavior models for the study of psychedelic drugs. They have always faced two formidable tasks, however. There is the qualitative question: is the drug a psychedelic? And there is the quantitative question: how potent is it?

The first question is addressed by taking a number of known psychedelic drugs, and searching for some animal responses that are common to all. Since there is little logic in the argument that animals can experience, let alone reveal, altered states of consciousness or fantasy fugues or colored imagery, the investigator must look for objective signs such as conditioned responses to stimuli, or unusual behavior. If one explores ten drugs that are known psychedelics, and all ten produce, say, bizarre nest-building behavior in mice, and an eleventh drug of unknown pharmacology does exactly the same thing, then the eleventh drug can be suspected of being a psychedelic drug.

And the second question, how potent, is answered by seeing how much of the drug is required to evoke this standardized behavior. This is called the dose-response curve, in which the more drug you give, the more response you get. This curve gives confidence that the drug is indeed responsible for the activity that is seen, as well as giving a quantitative measure of that activity.

But this entire discipline depends on the acceptance of the fact that the first ten drugs are indeed psychedelic materials. And these inputs can only come from human trials. What is the validity of these assumptions with TMA-5? Not very good. The statement that it is psychedelic has actually been published in reviews solely on the basis of the above two studies; the potency has been put at some ten times that of mescaline. Mescaline is certainly an effective psychedelic drug in the 300-500 milligram range, and this factor of ten implies that TMA-5 is also a psychedelic drug and is active in the 30-50 milligram range. And indeed, both statements may be true, but confidence in these conclusions must await more extensive trials.

The two-carbon analogue of TMA-5 is 2,3,6-trimethoxyphenethylamine (or 2C-TMA-5 or 2,3,6-TMPEA). This is a known material, although there has been some controversy as to its physical properties. It has been studied in monoamine oxidase systems, and appears to be either a competitive substrate or an inhibitor of that enzyme. But as far as I know, no one has nibbled it, so its human activity is unknown.

#162   TMA-6;   2,4,6-TRIMETHOXYAMPHETAMINE

SYNTHESIS: To a solution of 100 g phloroglucinol dihydrate in 320 mL MeOH there was added 55 mL of concentrated H_2SO_4, and the clear solution held under reflux conditions overnight. After cooling, there was added 500 mL H_2O, and the bulk of the MeOH was removed under vacuum. The residual oil was extracted with Et_2O, and the removal of this left 60 g of a red oil as residue. This was dissolved in 300 g methyl sulfate (caution, this is extremely toxic through skin contact, and any exposure must be flushed thoroughly with dilute ammonium hydroxide). With good stirring, this was cautiously treated with 500 g of 40% aqueous KOH, and the exothermic reaction allowed to run its course. Extraction with 3x100 mL Et_2O gave, after evaporation of the solvent from the pooled extracts, an oil that became largely crystalline. This was suspended in 100 mL hexane, and filtered through a coarse fritted funnel. With evaporation there was obtained 57 g of 1,3,5-trimethoxybenzene as a pale amber solid that melted at 44-50 °C. A sample purified by recrystallization from EtOH had the proper mp of 54-55 °C.

A mixture of 62.9 g N-methylformanilide and 71.3 g of $POCl_3$ was allowed to stand for 0.5 h producing a light claret color. There was then added 30.9 g of 1,3,5-trimethoxybenzene and the mixture heated on the steam bath for 2 h. The reaction mixture then was poured into chipped ice, and allowed to stir for several h. The dark gummy mess was extracted with 2x100 mL Et_2O (this was discarded) and then with 4x200 mL CH_2Cl_2. The latter extracts were pooled, and stripped of solvent under vacuum yielding 14 g of an amber solid. This was recrystallized from 80 mL boiling MeOH (with decolorizing charcoal employed and filtration of the boiling solution through paper) to give 10.0 g of 2,4,6-trimethoxybenzaldehyde as a white crystalline solid with a mp of 115-116 °C. The literature values are generally one-degree ranges, and they are reported as high as 121 °C. The malononitrile adduct was prepared from a solution of 0.5 g aldehyde and 0.5 g malononitrile in 10 mL warm MeOH treated with a drop of triethylamine. There was an immediate formation of a yellow crystalline mass which was removed by filtration, washed with EtOH, and air dried. The yield of 2,4,6-trimethoxybenzalmalononitrile was 0.5 g and the mp was 174-175 °C. Anal. ($C_{13}H_{12}N_2O_3$) N.

A solution of 5 g 2,4,6-trimethoxybenzaldehyde in 20 g nitroethane was treated with 1.0 g of anhydrous ammonium acetate and held on the steam bath for 24 h. The excess solvent/reagent was stripped from the deep-red colored solution under vacuum yielding a residue that spontaneously set to a crystalline mass. This was well triturated under 5 mL MeOH, filtered, and washed with 3 mL additional MeOH to give 5.4 g of 2-nitro-1-(2,4,6-trimethoxyphenyl)propene as yellow crystals. The mp of the crude material was 135-142 °C which could be raised to 147-148 °C by recrystallization from EtOH. The use of an alternate procedure for the synthesis of this nitrostyrene, using acetic acid as solvent and a stoichiometric amount of nitroethane (and ammonium acetate as catalyst), gave very poor yields. The use of butylamine as catalyst gave considerably better results.

A suspension of 50 g LAH in 1 L anhydrous THF was placed under an inert atmosphere, stirred magnetically, and brought to a gentle reflux. There was added a total of 56.9 g 2-nitro-1-(2,4,6-trimethoxyphenyl)propene as a saturated solution in THF. This was achieved by letting the condensed THF drip through a Soxhlet thimble containing the nitrostyrene with direct addition to the reaction mixture. The solubility was extremely low. The stirred mixture was maintained at reflux for 36 h, generating a smooth creamy gray color. After being brought to room temperature, the excess hydride was destroyed by the patient addition of 50 mL H_2O, followed with 50 mL 15% NaOH (still some heat evolved) and then 150 mL additional H_2O. Stirring was continued until the insoluble salts were white and loose. These solids were removed by filtration, and the filter cake washed with additional THF. The combined filtrate and washes were stripped of solvent under vacuum, and the 73 g of pale amber residue dissolved in 200 mL IPA, neutralized with approximately 50 mL concentrated HCL, and diluted with 2 L anhydrous Et_2O. A lower, oily phase separated slowly set up as a crystalline mass. This was removed by filtration, Et_2O washed, and allowed to air dry to constant weight. The weight of 2,4,6-trimethoxy-amphetamine hydrochloride was 41.3 g and the color was an off-white. There was a tendency to discolor upon air exposure. The mp was 204-205 °C which was increased to 207-208 °C upon recrystallization from IPA. The literature gives a mp of 214-215 °C for this salt after isolation and purification as the picrate salt (with a mp 212-213 °C from EtOH).

DOSAGE: 25 - 50 mg.

DURATION: 12 - 16 h.

QUALITATIVE COMMENTS: (with 25 mg) "I was outside at the California-Washington State football game, which was completely nutty. As was I. With the crowd activity, it was impossible to separate the drug's action from the environment. Later I simply sat in the car, and tried to define what the effects really were. Things were completely benign, there was ease with concepts, and writing was good and smooth. At twelve hours, comfortably down. Maybe a plus two."

(with 35 mg) "My body was tingling all over, and there were times when walking was unsteady. Thinking was a little difficult, as I was quite intoxicated most of the day (all of the day, now that I think that over). To accomplish anything, such as toasting the toast in the toaster, was difficult. And things were so funny most of the time. Setting the table for supper, six hours later, proved to be hilarious. I like to think of the day as a mixture of the mad hatter's tea party, and a trip to the moon. We were all still intoxicated at bedtime, whatever time that was. Had difficult time sleeping. If I were to repeat, would go lighter in dosage, I feel."

(with 40 mg) "This experiment was begun at noon of a cool rainy day. Almost all of the day had to be spent indoors, without benefit of sunshine, This is worth mentioning because there was, for the first eight hours of the experiment, a decided feeling of inner chill which might not have occurred so strongly had it been a warm day. Most, if not all, of the other eight subjects also reported the same chill. There was some visual sparkle which persisted throughout. At the two hour point a minor but persistent stomach queasiness came on, preceded by a diarrhea-like bowel movement. There was no impairment of speech, but there was some halting quality to all thought processes. It was easy to talk about personal matters, but there did not seem to be a significant insight increase. Appetite for food was lessened. Sleep was decidedly difficult after the effects of the material seemed otherwise gone."

(with 40 mg) "As the experience grows in intensity for the first four hours, I feel a strange mixture of plateaus, exuberance, and strong negative feelings, all replacing each other. I found myself inside a stout, hemispherical shell, curled up in the solid part, thoroughly walled off but absolute master within the shell, calling all shots, making all decisions, in complete control. Moving beyond the half-shell meant becoming vulnerable, which I refused to do. Consequently my difficulty in hearing what other people say, becoming involved in their perceptions and lives. I keep relationships shallow, pull away inside my shell rather than become involved. I like to be by myself. This was a great revelation; I had never seen it before. This material had an enormous drive. I feel extremely grateful for exposing a very deep personal problem."

(with 50 mg) "My previous try at this level produced a record that said, 'alteration of consciousness, but no visual, no anything,' and oh my, surprise! It was very, very active, visual, colorful, etc., etc. Good talking, clear and steady control of body, despite intense energy flow. Extremely funny — great humor, wonderful laughter."

EXTENSIONS AND COMMENTARY: Here is a simple and easily made compound that might well bid fair to be one of the most rewarding and pleasurable of the methoxylated amphetamines. It is fully as potent as its counterpart, TMA-2. This latter compound, with its 2,4,5-trisubstitution pattern, has served as a template from which an immense family of very active and fascinating drugs have arisen. The 2,5-dimethoxy aspect has been kept intact, and modifications in the 4-position have given rise to treasures such as DOM, DOB, DOET, DOI, and the Aleph compounds. And, of course, the entire world of the 2C-X's has exploited this same orientation.

Here, there is the blatant, parallel call from TMA-6. It can serve, as the 2,4,6-counterpart, as a similar template compound. And the first indicators are that, in keeping the 2,6-dimethoxy aspect intact, a completely analogous series could be made, again with modifications of the 4-position. These have been named the psu-series, or psi-series, as an abbreviation for the prefix, pseudo, and can be differentiated from the 2,4,5-things with the use of the Greek letter "Ψ". Thus there is the Ψ-DOM (called Z-7 in this book, and certainly an active compound), and Ψ-DOB, Ψ-DOET, Ψ-DOI, and the Ψ-ALEPH compounds. And, of course, the Ψ-2C-X counterparts. I would expect all of them to be active and, certainly, some of them interesting. They will be considerably more difficult to synthesize. However, some of them, specifically things such as Ψ-2C-T-4, have already been prepared, and are being evaluated.

One of the guiding premises of this Book II was to make all recipes employ commercially available materials as starting materials. And in the case of TMA-6, the required benzaldehyde (2,4,6-trimethoxybenzaldehyde) is an easily obtained trade item from any of several supply houses. Why not start the recipe there? Why tell how to make it from 1,3,5-trimethoxybenzene (also presently available from commercial sources) and how to make the ether in turn, from phloroglucinol? This simply reflects a valid paranoia of our times. Today the aldehyde is available (at $2/ g) and can be easily purchased. But tomorrow? What about in the year 2003? Who can tell what will, or will not, be easily available then? There might be a world-wide acknowledgment that the "war on drugs" is more destructive than any drug itself could ever be, and every law that had been written in the attempt to dictate human behavior will have been transformed into a force that truly educates and allows choice. This might really happen. But maybe, on the other hand, no fine chemicals may be permitted to be held in any hands, at any price, except for those of licensed chemists and in authorized laboratories. The black market price for the aldehyde might be $1000/g with another $1000 for protection.

But, it will be impossible to remove phloroglucinol from availability. It is available as a natural component in the free form, in sources as diverse as the cones of the *Sequoia sempervirens* (the coast redwood tree) and species of *Camillia* (that provides the leaves of our morning tea). And combined with a molecule of glucose in the form of its glucoside, it is called phlorin, and it is present in the discarded rinds of almost all citrus fruits as well as the resins from many of the *Eucalyptus* species. And one step yet further back into nature, there is a dihydrochalcone glucoside called phloridzin which practically drips out of all parts of the apple and pear trees except for the apple or pear itself. It, on base hydrolysis, gives phlorin, which on acid hydrolysis gives phloroglucinol, which when dissolved in methanol and sulfuric acid gives —. Nature is indeed most bountiful.

The phenethylamine homologue of TMA-6 is well known, but is virtually unexplored pharmacologically. The above benzaldehyde with nitromethane in glacial acetic acid containing ammonium acetate gave the appropriate beta-nitrostyrene as yellow crystals with a mp 177-177.5 °C. This, with LAH in ether, gave 2,4,6-trimethoxyphenethylamine (2,4,6-TMPEA, or 2C-TMA-6) as the picrate salt (mp 204-205 °C) or the hydrochloride salt (mp 234-235 °C). It has been shown not to be a substrate to the soluble amine oxidase from rabbit liver, a property it shares with mescaline, but whether it is or is not active in man is at present unknown.

#163   3-TME;   3-THIOMETAESCALINE;   4,5-DIMETHOXY-3-ETHYLTHIOPHENETHYLAMINE)

SYNTHESIS: A solution of 13.0 g of 3-bromo-N-cyclohexyl-4,5-dimethoxy-benzylidenimine (see under MP for its preparation) in 125 mL anhydrous Et_2O in a He atmosphere was cooled with an external dry ice acetone bath to -80 °C with good stirring. To this clear pale yellow solution there was added 32 mL 1.55 M butyllithium in hexane (about a 25% excess) which was stirred for 10 min producing a fine white precipitate. There was then added 7.0 g diethyl disulfide. The dry ice bath was removed and the reaction stirred as it came to room temperature. This was then added to 300 mL dilute HCl and the aqueous phase separated and heated on the steam bath for 45 min. A yellow oil was formed with a nearly colorless aqueous over-head. This was removed by decantation, and the remaining oil was diluted with a little MeOH and additional concentrated HCl. After further heating on the steam bath, this was added to the separated phase, all was cooled and extracted with 2x50 mL CH_2Cl_2. Removal of the solvent from these pooled extracts gave 11.8 g of a residue that was distilled. The product, 3-ethylthio-4,5-dimethoxybenzaldehyde boiling at 106-125 °C at 0.4 mm/Hg and was an almost colorless oil weighing 8.3 g. Anal. ($C_{11}H_{14}O_3S$) C,H.

To a solution of 8.2 g 3-ethylthio-4,5-dimethoxybenzaldehyde in 125 mL nitromethane, there was added 1.0 g of anhydrous ammonium acetate and the mixture was heated on the steam bath for 1.5 h. The reaction mixture was stripped of nitromethane under vacuum, and the residual red oil was dissolved in 20 mL of boiling Meoh. This was decanted from a small amount of insolubles, and allowed to cool to room temperature. After considerable manipulation of a small sample with dry ice cooling, a seed of crystal was obtained, which successfully promoted crystallization of the entire Meoh solution. After standing for 1 h, the product 3-ethylthio-4,5-dimethoxy-ß-nitrostyrene was removed by filtration and, after air drying, weighed 3.2 g with a mp of 96-98 °C. Upon recrystallization from Meoh, the mp was tightened to 98-99 °C. Anal. ($C_{12}H_{15}NO_4S$) C,H.

AH was prepared in the usual manner from a suspension of 2.0 g LAH in 75 mL anhydrous THF, cooled to 0 °C and well stirred in an inert atmosphere of He, and treated with 1.33 mL of 100% H_2SO_4 added dropwise. There was added, drop-wise and over the course of 10 min, a solution of 3.1 g 3-ethylthio-4,5-dimethoxy-ß-nitrostyrene in 15 mL anhydrous THF. At the end of the addition, the reaction mixture was returned to room temperature, and finally heated on the steam bath for 10 min. After cooling again, there was added enough IPA to decompose the excess hydride and sufficient 10% NaOH to convert the aluminum oxide to a white, easily filterable mass. This was removed by filtration, the filter cake washed with additional IPA, and the filtrate and washes combined and the solvent removed under vacuum. This was dissolved in 100 mL of dilute H_2SO_4, which was washed with 2x50 mL CH_2Cl_2. The aqueous phase was made basic with NaOH, extracted with 2x50 mL CH_2Cl_2, and the extracts pooled and the solvent removed under vacuum to yield a residue of a colorless oil. This was distilled at 160-170 °C at 1.0 mm/Hg yielding 2.6 g of a colorless liquid. This was dissolved in 12 mL IPA, neutralized with 24 drops of concentrated HCl and diluted with 25 mL anhydrous Et_2O. The clear solution was decanted from a little solid material, and the decantings diluted with a further 50 mL anhydrous ether. The still clear solution became cloudy after a few min, and then there was the slow formation of 3-ethylthio-4,5-dimethoxy-phenethylamine hydrochloride (3-TME) as a fine white crystalline product. Removal by filtration, washing with Et_2O, and air drying yielded 2.8 g of white granular solids that melted at 171-172 °C. Anal. $(C_{12}H_{20}ClNO_2S)$ C,H.

DOSAGE: 60 - 100 mg.

DURATION: 10 - 15 h.

QUALITATIVE COMMENTS: (with 60 mg) "As important as the experience was, itself, I feel that it was in the two or three days that followed that it had the most profound impact on me. It was at the time of the death of my wife's mother, and I found that I could look directly towards death and its ramifications. Including my own death. I felt very close to the Higher Powers that seemed to make their presence felt all around. And there was still the deep internal strength that was the direct product of the 3-TME experience. I feel it very strongly, still, but I have no desire to repeat the experience right away. It is almost as if the effects are still in evidence, and one should take one's time in letting it manifest all its ramifications. But it is certainly an experience one should have once a year, if not oftener."

(with 100 mg) "I was aware of the development quite early, and by the end of an hour and a half, I was in quite a remarkable state. I was extremely disinhibited, with easy verbal play and easily self-revealing, but not at too deep a level. There was great fun with a set of water colors but, when a used Kleenex became my canvas, the others failed to share my humor. I drove home at midnight with considerable care and was unable to sleep for another two hours. I would be very willing to repeat this experiment, at this level, to see if the good humor of it all was a consistent property."

(with 100 mg) "I had a sudden revelation — what I called the wet-paint theory of Christ. How does one find and identify the Messiah? It is most simple. All of life is nothing more than a freshly painted fence separating us from the rest of the world. And the fence has many, many signs on it that say: Beware. Don't Touch. Wet Paint. And if you touch too soon, indeed you get a dirty finger because the paint really is still wet. But the very first man to touch it and find it dry? There is your natural leader, your Son of God, and all those who touch later than He are the followers of the leader who first touched and found the paint dry."

EXTENSIONS AND COMMENTARY: A short unraveling of the codes used here for the various materials is very much needed. There are 3's and 4's and M's and I's and incipient confusion. Mescaline is mescaline. That much is simple. All homologs are the first letter of the homolog. Escaline is E, Proscaline is P, etc. If the group is at the three-position, then the term "meta" is used and an M preceeds the name of the homolog, i.e., ME is Metaescaline. The number (3- or 4- or 5-) gives the position of the sulfur, which is represented by the prefix "Thio" so this compound, 3-TME, has the sulfur at the 3-position, and by chance, the ethyl group there as well.

Here is a brief presentation of the needed Rosetta Stone:

Number of ethyl groups	all three are oxygen atoms	One oxygen is replaced with sulfur
none	M	3-TM
		4-TM
one	E	3-TE
		4-TE
	ME	3-TME
		4-TME
		5-TME
two	SB	3-TSB
		4-TSB
	ASB	3-TASB
		4-TASB
		5-TASB
three	TRIS	3-T-TRIS
		4-T-TRIS

#164   4-TME;   4-THIOMETAESCALINE;   3-ETHOXY-5-METHOXY-4-METHYLTHIOPHENETHYLAMINE

SYNTHESIS: A solution of 5.1 g N,N,N',N'-tetramethylethylenediamine and 6.8 g of 3-ethoxyanisole was dissolved in 80 mL hexane. This was stirred vigorously under a He atmosphere and cooled to 0 °C with an external ice bath. There was added 27.5 mL of 1.6 M solution of butyllithium in hexane. The stirred reaction mixture deposited a fine white precipitate. It was warmed to room temperature and stirred for 15 min. After cooling again to 0 °C, there was added 4.6 mL of dimethyl disulfide which converted the precipitate to a creamy white material. Stirring was continued while the reaction mixture was brought up to room temperature, and continued for an additional h. All was then added to 200 mL dilute H_2SO_4. The solids dissolved and there was the formation of two phases. These were separated, the aqueous phase extracted with with 2x75 mL Et$_2$O, the organic phases combined and evaporated under vacuum. The residue weighed 11.1 g and set up to a waxy solid. This was ground under 1 mL of hexane, filtered, washed sparingly with hexane, and air dried yielding 7.6 g of 3-ethoxy-2-(methylthio)anisole as white crystals. The mp was 35-36 °C which was not improved following recrystallization from hexane. Anal. (C$_{10}$H$_{14}$O$_2$S) C,H.

To a stirred solution of 7.6 g of 3-ethoxy-2-(methylthio)anisole in 100 mL CH$_2$Cl$_2$ there was added 6.2 g elemental bromine dissolved in 50 mL CH$_2$Cl$_2$. The initial dark red color gradually faded to a pale yellow and there was a steady evolution of HBr. An added crystal of iodine did not appear to increase the rate of reaction. After 4 min the color was a pale orange. The reaction mixture was extracted with H$_2$O containing sufficient dithionite to remove most of the residual color. The solvent was removed under vacuum leaving 12.2 g of a pale yellow fluid oil. This was distilled at 100-110 °C at 0.3 mm/Hg to yield a mixture of 4-bromo-3-ethoxy-2-(methylthio)anisole and 6-bromo-3-ethoxy-2-(methylthio)anisole as a pale yellow, highly refractory oil that was used as such in the following reaction. Anal. (C$_{10}$H$_{13}$BrO$_2$S) C,H.

To a solution of 12 mL diisopropylamine in 75 mL anhydrous THF that was stirred under an N$_2$ atmosphere and cooled to -10 °C with an external ice/MeOH bath, there was added in sequence 35 mL of 1.6 M butyllithium in hexane, 1.8 mL of dry acetonitrile, and 5.0 g of 4-bromo- (and 6-bromo)-3-ethoxy-2-(methylthio)-anisole. The reaction mixture changed color from yellow to red to reddish brown. Stirring was maintained for an additional 0.5 h, and then the reaction mixture was poured into 80 mL of dilute H$_2$SO$_4$. The phases were separated, and the aqueous phase was extracted with 100 mL CH$_2$Cl$_2$. The organic phases were combined, and the solvent was removed under vacuum. The oily residue was distilled at 0.2 mm/Hg yielded two fractions. The first fraction boiled at 90-115 °C and weighed 1.7 g. This material proved to be largely the unreacted bromo starting materials. The second fraction came over at 140-170 °C, weighed 1.7 g, and it crystallized when seeded with a small crystal obtained externally with dry ice. This fraction was recrystallized from 10 mL MeOH, filtered, and washed sparingly with cold MeOH. After air drying, there was obtained 0.5 g 3-ethoxy-5-methoxy-4-methylthio-phenylacetonitrile which had a mp of 65-66 °C. Anal. (C$_{12}$H$_{15}$NO$_2$S) C,H.

A suspension of 0.5 g LAH in 50 mL anhydrous THF under N$_2$ was cooled to 0 °C and vigorously stirred. There was added, dropwise, 0.35 mL 100% H$_2$SO$_4$, followed by 0.45 g 3-ethoxy-5-methoxy-4-methylthiophenylacetonitrile in 10 mL anhydrous THF. The reaction mixture was stirred at 0 °C for a few min, then brought to a reflux for a few min on the steam bath. After allowing the mixture to return to room temperature, there was added IPA sufficient to destroy the excess hydride followed by 10% NaOH to bring the reaction to a basic pH and to convert the aluminum oxide to a loose, white, filterable consistency. This was removed by filtration, and washed with 50 mL IPA. The filtrate and washes were stripped of solvent in vacuo, and the residue suspended in dilute H_2SO_4. This was washed with 2x75 mL CH_2Cl_2, made basic with aqueous NaOH, and the product extracted with 2x75 mL CH_2Cl_2. After combining these extracts, the solvent was removed under vacuum providing 1.2 g of a residue which was distilled at 132-140 °C at 0.4 mm/ Hg to give 0.35 g of a colorless oil. This was dissolved in 7 mL of IPA, neutralized with 7 drops of concentrated HCl and diluted with 3 volumes of anhydrous Et_2O. The product was removed by filtration, washed with Et_2O, and air dried to give 0.30 g 3-ethoxy-5-methoxy-4-methylthiophenethylamine hydrochloride (4-TME) as white crystals with a mp of 164-165 °C. Anal. $(C_{12}H_{20}ClNO_2S)$ C,H.

DOSAGE: 60 - 100 mg.

DURATION: 10 - 15 h.

QUALITATIVE COMMENTS: (with 60 mg) "There was a strange off-baseness for several hours in the middle of the day, which was replaced by a mild gastric upset in the evening. The mild mental disturbance is neither visual nor particularly interesting."

(with 100 mg) "A benign and gentle altered state became progressively sad and morbid. Nothing went together well — I could not empathize with anyone, and trying to write at the typewriter was useless. So were efforts to sleep at midnight, but this was totally relieved with 200 milligrams of Miltown. In the morning I seemed still to be off baseline, and I was extremely sleepy, with much lethargy. Even several days later there were problems trying to integrate my emotions and feelings. I am not yet completely at peace."

EXTENSIONS AND COMMENTARY: Sometimes things work well in their mysterious ways. The reports with 4-TME were more to the toxic than to the joyous side, and this by chance with a compound that could only be obtained in an atrociously small yield.

#165   5-TME;   5-THIOMETAESCALINE;   3-ETHOXY-4-METHOXY-5-METHYLTHIOPHENETHYLAMINE

SYNTHESIS: A solution of 10.4 g of 3-bromo-N-cyclohexyl-4-methoxy-5-ethoxybenzylidenimine (see under ME for its preparation) in 150 mL anhydrous Et_2O in a He atmosphere was cooled with an external dry ice acetone bath to -80 °C with good stirring. The addition of 52 mL 1.6 M butyllithium in hexane produced a thick precipitate which was stirred for 5 min. There was then added 8.5 mL of dimethyl disulfide and the reaction mixture gradually became thinner and lighter. The dry ice bath was removed and the reaction allowed to come to room temperature over the course of 15 min. This was then added to 400 mL of dilute HCl. The two phases were separated, and the aqueous phase was heated on the steam bath for 1 h which generated a separate yellow oily phase. On cooling, this set to a yellow solid, which was removed by filtration, washed with H_2O, and sucked relatively free of H_2O. These yellow solids weighed 14.4 g and were ground under 20 mL of cold cyclohexane which removed almost all the color and, after filtering and air drying, there remained 12.9 g of an off-white crystalline solid that melted at 83-84 °C. Recrystallization from cyclohexane produced 3-ethoxy-4-methoxy-5-(methylthio)benzaldehyde as a white fluffy crystalline material with a melting point of 84-85 °C. Anal. ($C_{11}H_{14}O_3S$) C,H.

To a solution of 8.0 g 3-ethoxy-4-methoxy-5-(methylthio)benzaldehyde in 100 mL nitromethane, there was added 0.5 g anhydrous ammonium acetate and the mixture was heated on the steam bath for 1.5 h, at which time most of the aldehyde had disappeared and there was a sizeable quantity of nitrostyrene as well as a cascade of wrong things down to the origin, as seen by TLC on silica gel, with CH_2Cl_2. The excess nitromethane was removed under vacuum, and the residual red oil was dissolved in 25 mL of hot MeOH and decanted from a small amount of insoluble material. With cooling in an ice bath for 20 min, bright yellow crystals were formed which were removed by filtration, washed with MeOH and air dried, producing 4.1 g 3-ethoxy-4-methoxy-5-methylthio-ß-nitrostyrene which melted at 80-82 °C. This sample, on resolidification and remelting, melted at 109-110 °C. This higher-melting polymorphic form was also produced by recrystallization of the product from cyclohexane. The two polymorphs were chromatographically and analytically identical. Anal. ($C_{12}H_{15}NO_4S$) C,H.

AH was prepared in the usual manner from a suspension of 3.0 g LAH in 100 mL anhydrous THF, cooled to 0 °C, well stirred in an inert atmosphere of He, and treated with 2.0 mL of 100% H_2SO_4 added dropwise. There was then added a solution of 2.4 g 3-ethoxy-4-methoxy-5-methylthio-ß-nitrostyrene in 20 mL anhydrous THF. The reaction was exothermic, and had come nearly to a boil at the half-addition point. The reaction was cooled again to 0 °C and the remaining nitrostyrene then added. This was brought to a reflux briefly on the steam bath, then cooled again and stirred for an additional 1 h. IPA was carefully added to decompose the excess hydride followed by sufficient 10% NaOH to convert the aluminum oxide to a white, easily filterable mass. This was filtered, the filter cake washed with additional IPA, and the filtrate and washes combined and the solvent removed under vacuum. This was dissolved in 100 mL of dilute H_2SO_4, which was washed with 2x50 mL CH_2Cl_2. The aqueous phase was made basic with sodium hydroxide, extracted with 2x50 mL CH_2Cl_2, and the extracts pooled, dried over anhydrous K_2CO_3, and stripped of solvent under vacuum to yield a nearly colorless residue. This was distilled at 125-135 °C at 0.3 mm/Hg producing 2.0 g of a water-white oil. This was dissolved in 8 mL IPA, neutralized with 23 drops of concentrated HCl and, with good stirring, diluted with 20 mL anhydrous Et_2O. The product 3-ethoxy-4-methoxy-5-methylthiophenethylamine hydrochloride (5-TME) was removed by filtration, washed with Et_2O, and air dried to provide a white solid that weighed 2.0 g and melted at 168-169 °C. Anal. ($C_{12}H_{20}ClNO_2S$) C,H.

DOSAGE: greater than 200 mg.

DURATION: unknown.

QUALITATIVE COMMENTS: (with 200 mg) "There was a noticeable tinnitus, but then that comes and goes at odd times without any reason needed. There was perhaps a brush of light-headedness at the third hour point, but other than that, nothing. No effect that can be ascribed to today's drug trial."

EXTENSIONS AND COMMENTARY: Nothing comes to mind. This, along with most of the di- and triethylated thiomescaline analogues, represents a lot of synthetic effort without useful qualitative data. If there is any activity, it would only be seen with monster dosages, and why put the body through such potential impact?

#166   2T-MMDA-3a;   3,4-METHYLENEDIOXY-2-METHYLTHIOAMPHETAMINE

SYNTHESIS: A solution of 30 g piperonal in 25 mL cyclohexylamine was brought to a boil on a hot plate, until there was no more water apparently being evolved. The resulting melt was distilled giving 45 g of N-cyclohexyl-3,4-methylenedioxy-benzylideneimine boiling at 114-135 °C at 0.2 mm/Hg as a light yellow oil.

In 400 mL anhydrous Et_2O there was dissolved 40.3 g N-cyclohexyl-3,4-methylenedioxybenzylidenimine and 30 mL N,N,N',N'-tetramethylethylenediamine (TMEDA). This solution was put under an inert atmosphere, and with good stirring brought to -78 °C with an external dry ice/acetone bath, which produced a light white crystalline precipitate. There was then added 120 mL of 1.55 M butyllithium, which produced an immediate darkening and a dissolving of the fine precipitate. After 10 min stirring, there was added 20 mL of dimethyl disulfide. The color immediately vanished and there was the formation of a white precipitate. The temperature was allowed to return to ice bath temperature, and then all volatiles were removed under vacuum. The residue was poured into 500 mL H_2O and acidified with HCl. After heating for 1 h on the steam bath, the reaction mixture was cooled, producing a gummy solid that was shown to be a complex mixture by TLC. But there was a single fluorescent spot that was the product aldehyde and it was pursued. Extraction with 3x75 mL CH_2Cl_2 gave, after pooling and stripping of the solvent, a residue which was extracted with four separate passes, each with 75 mL boiling hexane. The deposited crystals from each were separated, and all recrystallized from boiling MeOH to give 3.3 g of 3,4-methylenedioxy-2-(methylthio)benzaldehyde, with a mp of 77-80 °C.

To a solution of 3.0 g 3,4-methylenedioxy-2-(methylthio)benzaldehyde in 25 mL IPA there was added 2 mL nitroethane, 0.11 mL ethylenediamine and 0.1 mL acetic acid. This was held at reflux temperature for 18 h, and the solvents removed under vacuum. The residue showed a total of eight spots on TLC analysis, extending from the origin to the spot of the product nitrostyrene itself. Trituration of this residue under 25 mL MeOH gave a crude nitrostyrene which was, after separation, recrystallized from 20 mL of boiling MeOH. The final isolation of 1-(3,4-methylenedioxy-2-methylthiophenyl)-2-nitropropene gave 0.5 g of a product that had a mp of 94-95 °C. The mixed mp with the nitrostyrene from piperonal (mp 97-98 °C) was soundly depressed (mp 67-79 °C).

A solution of AH was prepared by the treatment of a solution of 0.5 g LAH in 10 mL THF, at 0 °C and under He, with 0.32 mL 100% H_2SO_4. A solution of 0.45 g 1-(3,4-methylenedioxy-2-methylthiophenyl)-2-nitropropene in 10 mL THF was added dropwise, and the stirring was continued for 1 h. After a brief period at reflux, the reaction mixture was returned to room temperature, and the excess hydride destroyed by the addition of IPA. The salts were converted to a filterable mass by the addition of 5% NaOH, and after filtering and washing with IPA, the combined filtrate and washings were stripped of solvent under vacuum. The residue was dissolved in dilute H_2SO_4 which was washed with 3x75 mL CH_2Cl_2. After alkalinification with 25% aqueous NaOH, the product was extracted with 2x75 mL CH_2Cl_2. The extracts were pooled, and the solvent removed under vacuum. Distillation of the residue gave a fraction that boiled at 137-150 °C at 0.3 mm/Hg and weighed 0.3 g. This was dissolved in 1.6 mL IPA, neutralized with 6 drops of concentrated HCl, warmed to effect complete solution, and diluted with 4 mL of anhydrous Et_2O. The formed crystals were collected by filtration, and after Et_2O washing and air drying to constant weight, gave 0.3 g 3,4-methylenedioxy-2-methylthioamphetamine hydrochloride (2T-MMDA-3a).

DOSAGE: greater than 12 mg.

DURATION: unknown.

EXTENSIONS AND COMMENTARY: And visions of sugar-plums danced through their heads. There are many trisubstituted amphetamine analogues that have been documented with varying degrees of activity. There are six TMA's and if one were to systematically make every possible thio-analogue of each of these, there would be a total of sixteen thio-analogues of the TMA. Let's go for it, said I to myself. Let's get the 16 thio analogues in hand. That is where the action's at. But hold on a minute. Each and every MMDA isomer has, by definition, three possible thio analogues, so there are eighteen more possible thio compounds just with them. Sure, let's make them all! It will be an unprecedented coup for students of structure-activity relationships. Let's whip out some 34 compounds, and test them all, and maybe we will begin to understand just why those which are active are, indeed, active. And maybe not.

Anyway, this was the most manic of all manic programs ever, involving thio-analogues. And it was totally compelling. Another synthetic clue stemmed from the fact that vanillin also formed the cyclic carbonate with sodium thiocyanate and it could, in principle, be brought around in time to 3-methoxy-5,4-methylene-thiooxyamphetamine, or 5T-MMDA. That made two of the magic analogues, and only some 32 to go. What a marvelous task for a graduate student. (What a horribly dull task for a graduate student.) But in any case there was no graduate student, and this appeared to be the end of the line. Some day, let's make all these possibilities. A magnificent tour-de-force, but at the present time, not worth the effort. Other directions are more exciting and more appealing.

A last note of simple humor. One of the compounds used in this preparation was N,N,N',N'-tetramethylethylenediamine, which has been abbreviated TMEDA. There is a pattern, within any active inner clique of research chemists intently pursuing a goal, to begin condensing complex concepts into deceptively simple terms. We "MOM-ed the hydroxy group of the T-BOC-ed amine." I have recently heard the above tetramethyl monster referred to in the chemist's jargon as a pronounced, rather than a spelled out, word. It sounds very much like "tomato" spoken by a native of the Bronx.

#167   4T-MMDA-2;   6-(2-AMINOPROPYL)-5-METHOXY-1,3-BENZOXATHIOL;   2-METHOXY-4,5-METHYLENETHIOOXYAMPHETAMINE

SYNTHESIS: To a well-stirred solution of 120 g thiourea in 800 mL 2N HCL, there was added a solution of 100 g benzoquinone in 500 mL acetic acid over the course of 15 min. Stirring was continued for an additional 0.5 h at room temperature, and then the reaction mixture was heated on the steam bath for 1 h. With cooling in ice water, a heavy crop of crystals separated. These were removed by filtration and air dried to provide 90.1 g of 5-hydroxy-1,3-benzoxathiol-2-one (2-mercaptohydro-quinone cyclic carbonate ester) with a melting point of 170.5-172.5 °C.

To a suspension of 100 g finely powdered anhydrous K_2CO_3 in 400 mL acetone containing 50 g methyl iodide there was added 41 g 5-hydroxy-1,3-benzoxathiol-2-one, and the mixture stirred overnight at room temperature. The solids were removed by filtration, and the solvent removed under vacuum. The residue was distilled to give a fraction subliming over as a solid at an oven temperature of 110 °C at 0.1 mm/Hg. This was a yellowish solid, weighing 27.4 g and having a mp of 66-72 °C. Recrystallization from MeOH gave 5-methoxy-1,3-benz-oxathiol-2-one as a white solid with a mp of 75.5-76.5 °C.

To a solution of 30 g 85% KOH in 75 mL warm H_2O, there was added an equal volume of warm MeOH followed by 16 g 5-methoxy-1,3-benzoxathiol-2-one, and the mixture was held under reflux conditions for 2 h. After cooling to room temperature, the mix was acidified with HCl and extracted with 2x100 mL CH_2Cl_2. Removal of the solvent from the pooled extracts gave a yellow oil that crystallized on standing. The product, 2-mercapto-4-methoxyphenol, weighed 14 g and had a mp of 56-57 °C.

A solution of 10 g 2-mercapto-4-methoxyphenol in 100 mL MEK was added over the course of 1 h to a vigorously stirred suspension of 25 g finely powdered anhydrous K_2CO_3 in 200 mL MEK that contained 14 g methylene bromide. The reflux was maintained for 48 h. After cooling, the mixture was freed of solids by filtration and the filter cake washed with 50 mL additional MEK. The combined washes and filtrate were stripped of solvent under vacuum, and the product distilled to give 3.3 g of 5-methoxy-1,3-benzoxathiol as a yellowing oil that had a bp of 110-120 °C at 1.7 mm/Hg. There was considerable residue in the pot, which was discarded. The NMR spectrum was excellent, with the methylene protons a two-hydrogen singlet at 5.6 ppm.

To a mixture of 3.2 g $POCl_3$ and 2.8 g N-methylformanilide that had been heated briefly on the steam bath (to the formation of a deep claret color) there was added 2.3 g 5-methoxy-1,3-benzoxathiol, and steam bath heating was continued for an additional 5 min. The reaction mixture was poured into 100 mL H_2O, and after a few minutes stirring, the insolubles changed to a loose solid. This was collected by filtration, H_2O washed and, after sucking as dry as possible, recrystallized from 30 mL boiling MeOH. This provided 1.9 g of 6-formyl-5-methoxy-1,3-benzoxathiol as brownish needles that melted at 119-120 °C.

A solution of 1.5 g 6-formyl-5-methoxy-1,3-benzoxathiol in 50 mL nitroethane was treated with 0.3 g anhydrous ammonium acetate and heated on the steam bath for 5 h. Removal of the solvent under vacuum gave a residue that crystallized. This was recrystallized from 110 mL boiling EtOH providing, after filtering and air drying, 1.3 g 5-methoxy-6-(2-nitro-1-propenyl)-1,3-benzoxathiol as San Francisco Giants-orange-colored crystals.

A solution of AH was prepared by the treatment of a solution of 1.3 g LAH in 10 mL THF, at 0 °C and under He, with 0.8 mL 100% H_2SO_4. A solution of 1.1 g of 5-methoxy-6-(2-nitro-1-propenyl)-1,3-benzoxathiol in 25 mL THF was added dropwise, and the stirring was continued for 1 h. After a brief period at reflux, the reaction mixture was returned to room temperature, and the excess hydride destroyed by the addition of IPA. The salts were converted to a filterable mass by the addition of 5% NaOH and, after filtering and washing with IPA, the combined filtrate and washings were stripped of solvent under vacuum. The residue was dissolved in dilute H_2SO_4 which was washed with 3x75 mL CH_2Cl_2 and then, after being made basic with 25% NaOH, the product was extracted with 2x75 mL CH_2Cl_2. The extracts were pooled, and the solvent removed under vacuum. Distillation of the residue gave a fraction that boiled at 140-155 °C at 0.3 mm/Hg which weighed 0.7 g. This was dissolved in 4 mL IPA, neutralized with 14 drops of concentrated HCl, heated to effect complete solution, then diluted with 10 mL of anhydrous Et_2O. The white crystals that formed were removed, Et_2O washed, and air dried to give 0.6 g 6-(2-aminopropyl)-5-methoxy-1,3-benzoxathiol hydrochloride (4T-MMDA-2).

DOSAGE: greater than 25 mg.

DURATION: unknown.

QUALITATIVE COMMENTS: (with 25 mg) "At three hours after having taken the material, I felt that there might have been a little exhilaration. And maybe a hint of tremor and of teeth clench. Perhaps this is a threshold dose."

EXTENSIONS AND COMMENTARY: There is no logical way to try to guess where the active level of this might be. In a comparison of 4-oxy with 4-thio- and with 4-alkyl (as, for example, TMA-2, PARA-DOT and DOM) the analogue with the sulfur atom lies intermediate in potency between the oxygen atom and the carbon atom. Then, perhaps, 4T-MMDA-2 should be somewhat more potent than MMDA-2. Which is where the trials have gone to, and the absence of effects therefore declares that line of reasoning invalid. What else could be used for clues? The whole benzofuran project, which had the same cyclic nature, was without activity. They had a carbon where the sulfur was of 4T-MMDA- 2, so, by that reckoning, this compound should be even less active. Maybe that is the formula to follow. The bottom line is inescapable. None of these extrapolations can hold a candle to the only experiment that can give believable findings, the actual trial of a new compound in man.

　　　The positional isomer of the heterocyclic carbonate used here is also known. Instead of using benzoquinone as a starting material with thiourea as the sulfur source (giving the 1,4- oxygen orientation), one can start with resorcinol in reaction with ammonium thiocyanate as the sulfur source (in the presence of copper sulfate) and get the positional isomer with a 1,3- oxygen orientation. This material (also known as thioxolone, or tioxolone, or 6-hydroxy-1,3-benzoxathiol-2-one, and which is commercially available) should follow the same chemistry shown here for the 5-hydroxy analogue, and give 5T-MMDA-2 (5-(2-aminopropyl)-6-methoxy-

1,3-benzoxathiole or 2-methoxy-5,4-methylenethiooxyamphetamine) as a final product. I would guess, based on the findings that compare 5-TOM with DOM, that this would be a relatively low-potency compound. At least it should be an easy one to make!

#168   TMPEA;   2,4,5-TRIMETHOXYPHENETHYLAMINE

SYNTHESIS: To a solution of 39.2 g 2,4,5-trimethoxybenzaldehyde in 160 mL nitromethane there was added 7.0 g anhydrous ammonium acetate, and the mixture was heated on the steam bath for 2 h. The excess solvent/reagent was removed under vacuum, leaving a deeply colored residue that spontaneously crystallized. This was mechanically removed and triturated under 60 mL cold MeOH. Filtration, washing with cold MeOH and air drying, gave 49.3 g of bright orange crystals. Trial recrystallizations from EtOAc gave a mp of 132-133 °C; from CH$_3$CN, 130.5-131.5 °C. The entire product was recrystallized from 1.1 L boiling IPA to provide, after filtration, IPA washing, and air drying, 34.5 g of ß-nitro-2,4,5-trimethoxystyrene as yum-yum orange crystals with a mp of 132-133 °C. Literature values are usual one-degree ranges, anywhere in the area of 127-130 °C.

To a suspension of 30 g powdered LAH in 800 mL of well stirred and refluxing anhydrous THF there was added a solution of 34.9 g ß-nitro-2,4,5-trimethoxystyrene in 200 mL anhydrous THF. The mixture was maintained at reflux for an additional 36 h, cooled, and the excess hydride activity destroyed by the addition of 30 mL H$_2$O followed by 30 mL 15% NaOH, and finally with another 90 mL H$_2$O. The solids were removed by filtration, washed with THF, and the pooled mother liquor and washings stripped of solvent under vacuum. The residue was dissolved in CH$_2$Cl$_2$, washed with both 5% NaOH and then H$_2$O, removing much of the color. It was then extracted with 3x75 mL N HCl. The pooled red-colored acid extracts were washed with CH$_2$Cl$_2$, made basic with 25% NaOH, and extracted with 3x75 mL CH$_2$Cl$_2$. Removal of the solvent gave some 25 g of residue which was dissolved in 100 mL IPA and neutralized with concentrated HCl. The crystalline mass that formed was diluted with an equal volume of Et$_2$O, and the solids removed by filtration. Washing with cold IPA, followed by Et$_2$O and air drying, gave 17.7 g of 2,4,5-trimethoxyphenethylamine hydrochloride (TMPEA) as a white product. The reported melting point was 187-188 °C.

DOSAGE: greater than 300 mg.

DURATION: unknown.

QUALITATIVE COMMENTS: (with less than 300 mg) "Since it was not easy, however, to judge the extent of a 'Rausch'-action from experiments on animals, some injections of beta-2,4,5-trimethoxyphenethylamine were administered to the author, and finally a control test was carried out with an equal quantity of mescaline. The action of both these substances in these experiments agreed only to a limited extent with the effects described for mescaline by, for example, Beringer. It must be remembered, however, in this connection, that the quantities used by Beringer were larger than the doses administered in these experiments. Nevertheless, it may be concluded that the pharmacological action of beta-2,4,5-trimethoxyphenethyl-amine agrees to a large extent with that of mescaline. However, the new compound had more unpleasant secondary effects (nausea) and did not bring about the euphoristic state caused by mescaline."

(with 300 mg) "Under double blind conditions, I was unable to distinguish this from a placebo. Both were without any of the changes described after the ingestion of psychotomimetic drugs."

(with 200 mg, followed after 45 minutes, with 100 mg mescaline) "The normally modest effects known to be due to mescaline alone at this level, were strongly potentiated with the earlier taking of 2,4,5-TMPEA. The effects were stronger as well as longer lived."

EXTENSIONS AND COMMENTARY: The code letters used for this drug are not as ambiguous as they might seem at first glance. A large number of the 2-carbon homologues are given names based on the code for the 3-carbon compound. On that basis, this should be 2C-TMA-2, since it is the 2-carbon counterpart of TMA-2. But since the first of the trimethoxyphenethylamines already had a trivial name, mescaline, the code TMPEA was unassigned. So, here is the logical place to use it.

There have been just two reports published of self-experimentation with TMPEA, and these comments are taken from them.

The first is presented here, word for word, as it was originally published (this was in 1931). It leaves much to be desired. The administration was by injection (intramuscular injection?). The dose was not given, but it was less than those reported by Beringer in his studies with mescaline, and this latter experimenter's published levels were all between 300 and 500 milligrams. What can one conclude from all this? Only that TMPEA apparently did not measure up to mescaline in his comparisons.

The second, reported some 40 years later, is not really contradictory. Here the TMPEA was administered orally, and the subject surrounded himself with a battery of psychological tests. This might allow statistics to provide an aura of validity to the observations. But the comments are pretty self-explanatory. The drug was not active in its own right, but when employed preliminary to mescaline, greatly enhanced the effects of the latter.

This is an area of research that deserves more attention. The simple compound that results from the stripping of all three of the O-methyl groups from

TMPEA is the extremely potent neurotoxin, 6-hydroxydopamine. When it is administered to an otherwise intact experimental animal, it produces sympathectomy, effectively destroying the sympathetic nervous system. And some of the methyl groups of TMPEA are known to be stripped off through the normal metabolic processes that occur in the liver. There are many fascinating psychedelics that have a signature of methoxyl groups para to one-another. It is known that they, too, can lose a methyl group or two. It would be intriguing to see if there was some biochemical overlap between the metabolism of some of these centrally active drugs and the metabolic fate of 6-hydroxydopamine. But in a test animal, of course, rather than in man.

#169   2-TOET;   4-ETHYL-5-METHOXY-2-METHYLTHIOAMPHETAMINE

SYNTHESIS: A mixture of 24.4 g ortho-ethylphenol and 18.9 mL methyl iodide was added to a solution of 15.6 g 85% KOH in 100 mL hot MeOH. The mixture was kept at reflux temperature overnight, stripped as much as possible of the MeOH, and poured into 1 L H_2O. An excess of 5% NaOH was added and this was extracted with 3x75 mL CH_2Cl_2. The pooled extracts were washed with 1% NaOH, and the solvent removed under vacuum to give 32.8 g of a pale amber oil. This was distilled at 55-65 °C at 0.4 mm/Hg to yield 22.0 g of 2-ethylanisole as a colorless oil.

To a 21.7 g sample of 2-ethylanisole, well stirred but without solvent, there was added, 1 mL at a time, 21 mL of chlorosulfonic acid. The color progressed from white to yellow, and finally to deep purple, with the evolution of much HCl. The exothermic reaction mixture was allowed to stir until it had returned to room temperature (about 0.5 h). It was then poured over 400 mL cracked ice with good mechanical stirring, which produced a mass of pale pink solids. These were removed by filtration, washed well with H_2O, and air dried to give about 27 g of 3-ethyl-4-methoxybenzenesulfonyl chloride as an off-white solid that retained some H_2O. A sample recrystallized from cyclohexane had a mp of 44-46 °C. A sample treated with ammonium hydroxide provided white crystals of 3-ethyl-4-methoxybenzenesulfonamide which could be recrystallized from H_2O to give tufts of crystals with a mp of 97-98 °C. Anal. ($C_9H_{13}NO_3S$) C,H.

In a 2 L round bottomed flask equipped with a mechanical stirrer there was added 200 mL cracked ice, 45 mL of concentrated H_2SO_4, 26.7 g of still moist 3-ethyl-4-methoxybenzenesulfonyl chloride, and 45 g elemental zinc dust. With external heating, an exothermic reaction set in and the temperature was maintained at reflux conditions for 4 h. After cooling to room temperature, the reaction mixture was filtered and the insolubles washed alternately with H_2O and with CH_2Cl_2. The mother liquors and washings were diluted with sufficient H_2O to allow CH_2Cl_2 to become the lower phase. These phases were separated, and the aqueous phase extracted with 3x100 mL CH_2Cl_2. The original organic phase and the extracts were pooled, washed with H_2O, and the solvent removed to give 15.7 g of a smelly amber oil. This was distilled at 72-84 °C at 0.3 mm/Hg to give 12.1 g of 3-ethyl-4-methoxythiophenol as a water-white oil. The infra-red was perfect (with the SH stretch at 2562, OCH_3 at 2837 and 1061, and with fingerprint peaks at 806, 880, 1052, (1061), 1142 and 1179 cm^{-1}). Anal. ($C_9H_{12}OS$) C,H.

To a solution of 11.7 g of 3-ethyl-4-methoxythiophenol and 6.5 mL methyl iodide in 100 mL MeOH there was added, with good stirring and a bit at a time, a solution of 5.5 g 85% KOH in 25 mL hot MeOH. The mixture was held at reflux on the steam bath for 1.5 h, and then stripped of volatiles under vacuum. The residues were added to 400 mL H_2O, made strongly basic with 5% NaOH, and extracted with 3x75 mL CH_2Cl_2. The pooled extracts were back-washed with 1% NaOH, and the solvent removed under vacuum. The 13.2 g residue was distilled giving 2-ethyl-4-(methylthio)anisole as a fraction boiling at 78-85 °C at 0.2 mm/Hg. The weight was 11.6 g for an isolated yield of over 90% of theory. The mp was at about 0 °C. The infra-red showed no SH or other functionality, but an OCH_3 at 2832 and 1031, and a fingerprint spectrum with peaks at 808, 970, (1031), 1051, 1144 and 1179 cm^{-1}. Anal. ($C_{10}H_{14}OS$) C,H.

A solution of 11.2 g 2-ethyl-4-(methylthio)anisole and 9 g dichloro-methyl methyl ether in 200 mL dry CH_2Cl_2 was treated with 13 g anhydrous aluminum chloride, added a bit at a time. The color progressed from pink to claret to deep claret, with a modest evolution of HCl. Stirring was continued for 1 h, then the reaction was quenched by the cautious addition of 250 mL H_2O. The two phase mixture was stirred an additional hour and then separated. The aqueous phase was extracted with 2x100 mL CH_2Cl_2. The organics were pooled, washed with 5% NaOH, then with saturated brine, and the solvent removed under vacuum. The residue was an amber oil weighing 13.7 g. This was distilled at 0.2 mm/Hg. A first fraction was a yellow oil boiling at 90-100 °C, and weighing 2.9 g. It was a mixture of starting anisole and the desired benzaldehyde. A second fraction, boiling at 100-130 °C was a viscous yellow oil weighing 4.8 g. By TLC it was free of starting anisole, and contained a sizeable quantity of a second benzaldehyde. From this fraction, seed crystal was obtained, and when the oil was dissolved in an equal volume of MeOH, the seed took, producing a yellow solid. This was filtered and air dried, to give 2.2 g of 4-ethyl-5-methoxy-2-(methylthio)benzaldehyde with a mp of 62-63 °C. A small sample from MeOH was almost white, and melted at 61-62 °C. The mixed mp with 4-ethyl-2-methoxy-5-(methylthio)benzaldehyde (57-58 °C) was severely depressed (37-44 °C). A cooled solution of the first fraction of the distillation, in MeOH, provided an additional 1.6 g product, with a mp 59-61 °C. The combined mother liquors gave additional product for an overall weight of 5.3 g. Anal. ($C_{11}H_{14}O_2S$) C,H.

A solution of 1.9 g 4-ethyl-5-methoxy-2-(methylthio)benzaldehyde in

75 mL nitroethane was treated with 0.3 g anhydrous ammonium acetate, and held on the steam bath for 2.5 h. The excess solvent/reagent was removed under vacuum, and the deep orange oil residue was dissolved in 10 mL boiling MeOH. As this cooled, there was the spontaneous generation of crystals. After cooling in an ice bath for a few h, these were removed by filtration, washed with MeOH, and air dried to constant weight. A total of 1.4 g of 1-(4-ethyl-5-methoxy-2-methylthiophenyl)-2-nitropropene was obtained as canary-yellow crystals melting at 83-84 °C which was not improved by recrystallization from MeOH. Anal. ($C_{13}H_{17}NO_3S$) C,H.

To a solution of 1.5 g LAH in 30 mL anhydrous THF that was cooled to 0 °C and stirred under a He atmosphere, there was added, slowly, 1.05 mL freshly prepared 100% H_2SO_4 (prepared by adding 0.9 g 20% fuming H_2SO_4 to 1.0 g 96% concentrated H_2SO_4). This was followed by the addition of a solution of 1.4 g 1-(4-ethyl-5-methoxy-2-methylthiophenyl)-2-nitropropene in 20 mL THF, over the course of 10 min. The color of the nitrostyrene solution was discharged immediately upon addition. With continued stirring, this was allowed to come to room temperature, and then to a gentle reflux for 2 h. After cooling again to room temperature, the excess hydride was destroyed by the addition of IPA. Sufficient 5% NaOH was added to generate the inorganic salts as a loose filterable mass, and these were removed by filtration. The filter cake was well washed with additional IPA, and the combined mother liquors and washes were stripped of solvent under vacuum. The residue was dissolved in 100 mL dilute H_2SO_4, washed with CH_2Cl_2, made basic with 5% NaOH, and extracted with 2x75 mL CH_2Cl_2. Removal of the solvent gave a residue that was distilled at 102-117 °C at 0.15 mm/Hg. The colorless liquid that distilled (0.7 g) was dissolved in 6 mL IPA and neutralized with 11 drops of concentrated HCl. The solids that formed were dissolved by heating the mixture briefly to a boil, and this clear solution was diluted with 20 mL anhydrous Et_2O. The white crystals of 4-ethyl-5-methoxy-2-methylthioamphetamine hydrochloride (2-TOET) weighed 0.6 g and had a mp of 164-167 °C. Anal. ($C_{13}H_{22}ClNOS$) C,H.

DOSAGE: greater than 65 mg.

DURATION: unknown.

QUALITATIVE COMMENTS: (with 50 mg) "After about an hour and a half, I found myself a little light-headed. And maybe a feeling of being physically a bit fragile. I ate something, but there was not much joy in eating. And the next day there was some residual fragility, whatever that means. Ahead with caution."
(with 65 mg) "During the day this was barely noticeable, but pleasant."

EXTENSIONS AND COMMENTARY: It seems as if the sulfur in the 2-position makes things less interesting, and less potent, than when it is in the 5-position. 2-TOM required twice the dosage of 5-TOM, and here it appears that it could well take a dosage of twice that required for 5-TOET, to get 2-TOET off the ground. There is an understandable reluctance to push on upwards in dosage with a new and unknown compound, when there are feelings of physical discomfort that outweigh the mental effects. There is nothing tangible here. In the complete report of the 50 milligram trial, there is a mention of an inability to effect erection, and this with the light-headedness and disinterest in food, all suggest some involvement with the sympathetic nervous system. And with these subtle effects persisting into the next day, why push higher? Instinct said to leave it alone. So I left it alone.

The 2-carbon analogue, 2C-2-TOET, was made from the same aldehyde intermediate. The appropriate nitrostyrene came smoothly from the aldehyde and nitromethane, and gave glistening pumpkin-orange crystals from methanol, that melted at 93-94 °C. Anal. ($C_{12}H_{15}NO_3S$) C,H. The final phenethylamine hydrochloride salt was prepared from its reduction with aluminum hydride in THF, and was isolated in the usual manner. It was a white crystalline mass that melted at 226-227 °C. It, as with the other 2-carbon analogues of the TOMs and TOETs, remains untasted as of the moment.

#170   5-TOET;   4-ETHYL-2-METHOXY-5-METHYLTHIO-AMPHETAMINE

SYNTHESIS: A solution of 25 g 3-ethylphenol in 100 mL Et_2O was equipped with a magnetic stirrer, and cooled to 0 °C with an external ice bath. There was added 16 mL DMSO. Then, a total of 15 mL chlorosulfonic acid was added dropwise, over the course of 30 min. The reaction was allowed to return to room temperature and stirred overnight. The overhead Et_2O phase was removed by decantation, and the light-colored residue was dissolved in 100 mL IPA. The clear solution spontaneously generated white crystals which were allowed to stand for 1 h, removed by filtration, and lightly washed with IPA. After air-drying, this crop of dimethyl-(2-ethyl-4-hydroxyphenyl)-sulfonium chloride weighed 20.0 g and had a mp of 168-170 °C without obvious effervescence. A solution of 19.8 g of this sulfonium salt in 200 mL H_2O was diluted with 500 mL MeOH, and there was added 30 g NaOH. This was heated to reflux on the steam bath. There was an initial deposition of some white solids, but after 36 h the solution was almost clear. The excess MeOH was removed under vacuum, and the non-volatiles were poured into 1 L H_2O. This was acidified with HCl, and extracted with 3x100 mL CH_2Cl_2. The extracts were pooled, and the solvent removed under vacuum. The residue, 12.6 g of an amber oil, was distilled at 95-120 °C at 0.3 mm/Hg to give 10.0 g of 3-ethyl-4-(methylthio)phenol as an off-white oil. This spontaneously crystallized to a solid that had a mp of 47-49 °C. Recrystallization of an analytical sample from cyclohexane gave a mp of 47-48 °C.

To a solution of 9.7 g 3-ethyl-4-(methylthio)phenol in 50 mL MeOH there was added a solution of 4.6 g 85% KOH in 50 mL hot MeOH. There was then added 5.4 mL methyl iodide and the mixture was held at reflux on the steam bath for 18 h. Removal of the solvent under vacuum gave a residue that was poured into 1 L H_2O and made strongly basic by the addition of 5% NaOH. This was extracted with 3x75 mL CH_2Cl_2, and the extracts were pooled and the solvent removed under vacuum. There remained 11.0 g of an almost white oil with a startling apple smell. This oil was distilled at 78-88 °C at 0.3 mm/Hg to give 7.9 g 3-ethyl-4-(methylthio)-anisole as a white oil. Anal. ($C_{10}H_{14}OS$) C,H.

A mixture of 7.8 g $POCl_3$ and 6.9 g N-methylformanilide was heated on the steam bath for a few min, until there was the development of a deep claret color. This was added to 7.7 g 3-ethyl-4-(methylthio)anisole and the mixture was heated on the steam bath for 2 h. This was poured into 400 mL H_2O and stirred overnight, which produced an oily phase with no signs of crystals. The entire reaction mixture was extracted with 3x75 mL CH_2Cl_2, and the pooled extracts washed with H_2O. Removal of the solvent under vacuum gave 9.2 g of a residue. This was suspended in 25 mL hexane, and after 1 h standing, the overhead clear solution was decanted from the settled sludge. This hexane solution was stripped of solvent under vacuum, giving 7.7 g of an oil that by TLC was a mixture of starting ether and desired aldehyde. This was distilled at 0.25 mm/Hg to give three fractions, the first boiling at 75-100 °C (2.7 g) and the second at 100-115 °C (2.6 g). These were largely starting ether and aldehyde, and were chemically processed below. A third fraction, boiling at 120-140 °C, solidified in the receiver, weighed 1.6 g, and was largely the desired aldehyde. Cuts #1 and #2 (5.3 g of what was mostly recovered aldehyde) were resubmitted to the Vilsmeier reaction. A mixture of 5.4 g $POCl_3$ and 4.7 g N-methylformanilide was heated on the steam bath until it became claret-colored. The recovered aldehyde was added, and the mixture was heated overnight on the steam bath. This was poured into 500 mL H_2O. The heavy tar that was knocked out was extracted with 3x75 mL CH_2Cl_2, and the solvent was removed from the pooled extracts under vacuum. Some 5.8 g of residue was obtained, and this was heated to 120 °C at 0.2 mm/Hg to remove all materials lower boiling than the desired aldehyde. The very dark pot was extracted with 3x50 mL boiling hexane, and removal of the solvent from these pooled extracts under vacuum gave 0.9 g of a yellow oil. This was distilled at 0.2 mm/Hg to give a fraction boiling at 130-140 °C which spontaneously crystallized. This pressed on a porous plate gave almost white crystals with a mp of 55-57 °C. Recrystallization from 0.3 mL cyclohexane provided 0.3 g of 4-ethyl-2-methoxy-5-(methylthio)benzaldehyde with a mp of 57-58 °C. The total yield was 1.9 g. Anal. ($C_{11}H_{14}O_2S$) C,H.

To a solution of 1.2 g 4-ethyl-2-methoxy-5-(methylthio)benzaldehyde in 25 mL nitroethane there was added 0.25 g anhydrous ammonium acetate and the mixture was heated on the steam bath. The initial color was green, but this quickly changed to the more usual yellow which darkened as the reaction mixture was heated. After 1.5 h heating, the excess solvent/reagent was removed in vacuo. The yellow residue was dissolved in 10 mL hot MeOH and allowed to stand in the refrigerator overnight. There was an orange oil layer formed underneath the MeOH. A small sample of this was scratched externally with dry ice, and seed was obtained. The orange oil layer slowly set to crystals which, after a few h, were removed by filtration to give 1.3 g of a slightly sticky orange solid with a mp of 43-45 °C. This was recrystallized from 8 mL boiling MeOH to give, after cooling, filtering, and air drying to constant weight, 1.1 g of 1-(4-ethyl-2-methoxy-5-methylthiophenyl)-2-nitropropene as electrostatic yellow crystals melting at 59-60 °C. Anal. ($C_{13}H_{17}NO_3S$) C,H.

A solution of 1.0 g LAH in 25 mL tetrahydrofuran was cooled, under He, to 0 °C with an external ice bath. With good stirring there was added 0.6 mL 100% H_2SO_4 dropwise, to minimize charring. This was followed by the addition of 1.1 g of 1-(4-ethyl-2-methoxy-5-methylthio)-2-nitropropene in a small amount of THF. After 10 min further stirring, it was brought up to room temperature and allowed to stand for several days. The excess hydride was destroyed by the cautious addition of IPA followed by sufficient 15% NaOH to give a white granular character to the aluminum oxide, and to assure that the reaction mixture was basic. This was filtered, and the filter cake washed first with THF and then with IPA. The filtrate and washings were pooled and stripped of solvent under vacuum providing a pale amber residue. This was dissolved in 50 mL of dilute H_2SO_4 and washed with 2x50 mL CH_2Cl_2. The aqueous phase was made basic with 5% NaOH, and extracted wit 2x50 mL CH_2Cl_2. These extracts were pooled, stripped under vacuum, and distilled at 0.15 mm/Hg. The fraction with a bp of 102-128 °C weighed 0.4 g and was a colorless liquid. This was dissolved in a small amount of IPA, neutralized with concentrated HCl and diluted with anhydrous Et_2O to provide the 4-ethyl-2-methoxy-5-methylthioamphetamine hydrochloride (5-TOET) which weighed 0.6 g and melted at 146-147 °C. Anal. ($C_{13}H_{22}ClNOS$) C,H.

DOSAGE: 12 - 25 mg.

DURATION: 8 - 24 h.

QUALITATIVE COMMENTS: (with 8 mg) "After my totally freaky experience on the very closely related compound in this series, 5-TOM, I intended to approach this with some caution. Three milligrams was without effects, so I tried eight milligrams. I was a little light-headed, and saw sort of a brightness around trees against the blue sky. Noticed movement on couch in living room, and there was some activity in the curtains, almost 2C-B like. In the evening writing was still difficult, and there was eye dilation but minimal nystagmus. My sleep was fitful, but certainly there was no hint of the 5-TOM storm."

(with 18 mg) "This was too much. There was an exhausting visual hallucinatory tinsel, continuous movement, and there was no escape. It popped into an LSD-like thing, strong, restless, constantly changing, with too much input. I had to take a Miltown to calm down enough for an attempt at sleep. In the morning, a day later, I was still 1.5 + and tired of it. It was the next day after that before I was completely clear."

(with 20 mg) "This has the makings of a superb, extraordinary material. I didn't get to a full plus two, maybe something around a plus one and three quarters. The eyes-closed fantasy was exceptional, with new dimensions. The nature of the fantasy, the feeling that one had about the fantasy figures and landscapes, was the essence of joy, beauty, lovingness, serenity. A glimpse of what true heaven is supposed to feel like. Or maybe a button in the brain was pushed which has not been pushed by previous chemicals. Insight? Don't know yet. I was able to function without difficulty with eyes closed or open. Erotic absolutely exquisite. In fact, the entire experience was exquisite. Next day, same sense of serene, quiet joy/beauty persisted for most of the day. A true healing potential. Onwards and upwards. This one could be extraordinary."

(with 30 mg) "Tried to focus on cosmic questions, and succeeded. Very little fantasy images for the first 2-3 hours. After that, lovely interacting, music okay but not vital. On this compound the Brahms Concerto #1 gave vivid 'memory' impressions of house and vegetable garden, like a primitive painting. Tremendous nostalgia for a place I've never seen."

EXTENSIONS AND COMMENTARY: With the extraordinary experience that had been observed with one person with 5-TOM, this ethyl homologue was not only run up with special caution, but that individual ran his own personal titration. And he proved to be perhaps twice as sensitive to 5-TOET than any of the other subjects. An approach to what might just be some unusual metabolic idiosyncrasy on the part of his liver, is discussed in the recipe for TOMSO.

The initials of TOET progressed quite logically from TOM, in an exact parallel with the relationship between the corresponding sulfur-free analogues, where the ethyl compound is DOET and the methyl counterpart is DOM. "T" for "thio" which is the chemical nomenclature term for the replacement of an oxygen atom with a sulfur atom. And, as has been discussed in the text of this volume, the peculiarities of pronunciation in this series are interesting, to say the least. TOM is no problem. But TOET could have any of several pronunciations such as "Two-it", or "Tow-it", or "Too-wet", but somehow the one syllable term "Twat" became regularly used, and the family was generally referred to as the "Toms and Twats." The almost-obscene meaning of the latter was progressively forgotten with usage, and has led to some raised eyebrows at occasional seminars when these compounds are discussed. And not only at seminars. Once at the between-acts intermission at the Berkeley Repertory Theater, the topic came up and the phrase was used. There was a stunned silence about us within the circle of hearing, and we seemed to have been given a little extra room immediately thereafter.

As with the other members of the TOM's and TOET's, the phenethylamine homologue of 5-TOET was synthesized, but had never been started in human evaluation. The aldehyde from above, 4-ethyl-2-methoxy-5-(methylthio)-benzaldehyde, was condensed with nitroethane (as reagent and as solvent) and with ammonium acetate as catalyst to give the nitrostyrene as spectacular canary-yellow electrostatic crystals with a mp of 91-92 °C. Anal. $(C_{12}H_{15}NO_3S)$ C,H. This was reduced with aluminum hydride (from cold THF-dissolved lithium aluminum hydride and 100% sulfuric acid) to the phenethylamine 4-ethyl-2-methoxy-5-methylthiophenethylamine (2C-5-TOET) which, when totally freed from water of hydration by drying at 100 °C under a hard vacuum, had a mp of 216-217 °C. Anal. $(C_{12}H_{20}CINOS)$ C,H.

#171   2-TOM;   5-METHOXY-4-METHYL-2-METHYLTHIO-AMPHETAMINE

SYNTHESIS: To a solution of 64.8 g of o-cresol and 56 g dimethyl sulfoxide in 300 mL Et$_2$O, cooled with an external ice bath with vigorous stirring, there was added 40 mL chlorosulfonic acid dropwise over the course of 30 min. The cooling bath was removed, and the two phase mixture was mechanically stirred at room temperature for 12 h. The Et$_2$O phase was then discarded, and the deep red residue that remained was thoroughly triturated under 300 mL IPA, producing a suspension of pale pink solids. These were removed by filtration, washed with an additional 150 mL IPA, and allowed to air dry. The yield of dimethyl (4-hydroxy-3-methylphenyl)sulfonium chloride was 31.6 g and, upon recrystallization from aqueous acetone, had a mp of 155-156 °C, with effervescence. Anal. $(C_9H_{13}CIOS)$ C,H,S. This analysis established the anion of this salt as the chloride, whereas the literature had claimed, without evidence, that it was the bisulfate. The thermal pyrolysis of 31.0 g of dimethyl (4-hydroxy-3-methylphenyl)sulfonium chloride resulted first in the formation of a melt, followed by the vigorous evolution of methyl chloride. The open flame was maintained on the flask until there was no more gas evolution. This was then cooled, dissolved in 200 mL CH$_2$Cl$_2$, and extracted with 3x100 mL of 5% NaOH. The aqueous extracts were pooled, acidified with concentrated HCl, and extracted with 3x75 mL CH$_2$Cl$_2$. The solvent was removed under vacuum, and the residue distilled at 100-110 °C at 0.5 mm/Hg yielding 22.0 g of 2-methyl-4-(methylthio)phenol as a white crystalline solid with a mp 36-37 °C.

To a solution of 25.5 g 2-methyl-4-(methylthio)phenol in 100 mL MeOH there was added a solution of 12 g 85% KOH in 60 mL hot MeOH, followed by the addition of 12.4 mL methyl iodide. The mixture was held at reflux for 16 h. The solvent was removed under vacuum, and the residue added to 400 mL H$_2$O. This was made basic with 25% NaOH and extracted with 3x100 mL CH$_2$Cl$_2$. The extracts were pooled, the solvent removed under vacuum giving 28.3 g of a light, amber oil as residue. This was distilled at 72-80 °C at 0.5 mm/Hg to provide 2-methyl-4-(methylthio)anisole as a pale yellow oil. Anal. ($C_9H_{12}OS$) C,H. The same product can be made with the sulfonyl chloride and the thiol as intermediates. To 36.6 g 2-methylanisole there was added, with continuous stirring, a total of 38 mL chloro-sulfonic acid at a modest rate. The exothermic reaction went through a complete spectrum of colors ending up, when the evolution of HCl had finally ceased, as deep amber. When it had returned again to room temperature, the reaction mixture was poured over a liter of cracked ice which, on mechanical stirring, produced a mass of white crystals. These were removed by filtration, washed with H_2O, and sucked as dry as possible. The wet weight yield was over 40 g and the mp was about 49 °C. Recrystallization of an analytical sample of 4-methoxy-3-methylbenzenesulfonyl chloride from cyclohexane gave white crystals with a mp of 51-52 °C. A small sample of this acid chloride brought into reaction with ammonium hydroxide produced the sulfonamide which, after recrystallization from EtOAc, melted at 135-136 °C. To a slurry of 300 mL cracked ice and 75 mL concentrated H_2SO_4 in a round-bottomed flask equipped with a reflux condenser, there was added 43 g of the slightly wet 4-methoxy-3-methylbenzenesulfonyl chloride followed by 75 g elemental zinc dust. The temperature was raised to a reflux which was maintained for 2 h. The reaction mixture was cooled and filtered, with the finely ground filter cake being washed alternately with H_2O and with CH_2Cl_2. The combined mother liquor and washings were diluted with 1 L H_2O, the phases separated, and the aqueous phase extracted with 100 mL CH_2Cl_2 which was added to the organic phase. This was washed with 100 mL H_2O, and the solvent removed under vacuum. The residue was a pale amber oil weighing 27.3 g and it slowly set up to a crystalline mass that smelled of banana oil. A portion of this, pressed on a porous plate, gave a waxy solid with a mp of 39-43 °C which, on recrystallization from MeOH, gave 4-methoxy-3-(methyl)thiophenol with a mp of 45-46 °C. Anal. ($C_8H_{10}OS$) C,H. A solution of 24 g of the crude thiol in 100 mL MeOH was treated with a solution of 17 g KOH 85% pellets in 100 mL hot MeOH, and to this there was added 16 mL of methyl iodide. This was held at reflux on the steam bath for 1.5 h, then stripped of solvent under vacuum, added to 1 L H_2O, and made strongly basic with 25% NaOH. Extraction with 3x100 mL CH_2Cl_2, pooling of the extracts, and removal of the solvent, gave an amber oil weighing 22.6 g. This was distilled at 70-80 °C at 0.7 mm/Hg to give 16.3 g of 2-methyl-4-(methylthio)anisole as a white oil, identical in all respects to the product that came from the sulfonium salt pyrolysis above.

A solution of 22.1 g 2-methyl-4-(methylthio)anisole and 17.5 g dichloro-methyl methyl ether in 600 mL CH_2Cl_2 was vigorously stirred, and treated with 24.5 g anhydrous aluminum chloride added portion-wise over the course of 1 min. Stirring was continued for 20 min while the color developed to a dark red. There was added 500 mL H_2O with caution, and stirring was continued until the initial yellow solids redissolved and there were two distinct phases formed. These were separated, and the aqueous phase was extracted with 3x100 mL CH_2Cl_2. The original organic phase and the pooled extracts were combined and washed with 5% NaOH. The organic solvent was removed under vacuum. The residue was distilled, giving two major fractions. A forerun (85-95 °C at 0.5 mm/Hg) proved to be largely starting ether. The major fraction (8.4 g, boiling at 95-120 °C) consisted of two materials, both benzaldehydes. Crystallization of this fraction from 30 mL cyclohexane provided, after filtering, washing and air drying, 2.9 g of 5-methoxy-4-methyl-2-(methylthio)benzaldehyde as a pale yellow crystalline solid with a mp of 69-70 °C. Anal. $(C_{10}H_{12}O_2S)$ C,H. The mother liquor from this crystallization contained a slower-moving component, 2-methoxy-3-methyl-5-(methylthio)benz-aldehyde, which was best separated by preparative gas chromatography. The proof of the structure of the major aldehyde above was obtained by its reductive conversion to 2,5-dimethyl-4-(methylthio)anisole with amalgamated zinc and HCl. The details are given in the recipe for 5-TOM.

To 4 mL glacial acetic acid there was added 1.0 g 5-methoxy-4-methyl-2-(methylthio)benzaldehyde, 0.35 g anhydrous ammonium acetate, and 0.8 g nitroethane, and the mixture was heated on the steam bath for 4 h. Another 0.5 g of nitroethane was added, and the heating continued for an additional 4 h. Standing at room temperature overnight allowed the deposition of spectacular orange crystals which were removed by filtration, washed lightly with acetic acid, and air dried. This product melted at 82-83 °C. Recrystallization from 10 mL boiling MeOH gave 0.7 g of 1-(5-methoxy-4-methyl-2-methylthiophenyl)-2-nitropropene with a mp of 83-84 °C. Anal. $(C_{12}H_{15}NO_3S)$ C,H. The alternate method for the formation of nitrostyrenes, the reaction of the benzaldehyde in nitroethane as both reagent and solvent, with ammonium acetate as a catalyst, gave a gummy product that could be purified only with severe losses. The overall yield with this latter method was 24% of theory.

A solution of 1.5 g LAH in 75 mL THF was cooled, under He, to 0 °C with an external ice bath. With good stirring there was added 1.0 mL 100% H_2SO_4 drop-wise, to minimize charring. This was followed by the addition of 3.0 g 1-(5-methoxy-4-methyl-2-methylthiophenyl)-2-nitropropene in 20 mL anhydrous THF. After a few min further stirring, the temperature was brought up to a gentle reflux on the steam bath, and then all was cooled again to 0 °C. The excess hydride was destroyed by the cautious addition of IPA followed by sufficient 5% NaOH to give a white granular character to the oxides, and to assure that the reaction mixture was basic. The reaction mixture was filtered, and the filter cake washed first with THF and then with IPA. The filtrate was stripped of solvent under vacuum providing a light yellow oil. This was dissolved in 100 mL dilute H_2SO_4 and then washed with 2x50 mL CH_2Cl_2. The aqueous phase was made basic with 5% NaOH and extracted with 2x50 mL CH_2Cl_2. These were pooled, the solvent removed under vacuum, and the residue distilled at 105-130 °C at 0.25 mm/Hg to give 1.6 g of a white oil. This was dissolved in 8 mL IPA, neutralized with 24 drops of concentrated HCl which formed crystals spontaneously. Another 20 mL of hot IPA was added to effect complete solution, and then this was diluted with anhydrous Et_2O. On cooling fine white crystals of 5-methoxy-4-methyl-2-methylthioamphetamine hydrochloride (2-TOM) separated. These weighed 1.55 g and had a mp of 195-196 °C. Anal. ($C_{12}H_{20}ClNOS$) C,H.

DOSAGE: 60 - 100 mg.

DURATION: 8 - 10 h.

QUALITATIVE COMMENTS: (with 60 mg) "There is a superb body feeling, and food tasted excellent but then it just might have been excellent food. By the tenth hour, there were absolutely no residues, and I had the feeling that there was no price to pay. Venture up a bit with confidence."

(with 80 mg) "For me this was excellent, in a down-to-earth, humorous, matter-of-fact universe-perspective sense. Very pleasant feeling, although there was a strong body awareness below the waist (not the erotic thing, but rather a slight heaviness, and the next day I came down with a G.I. cold). Very good feeling, and I sense that the depth of the experience is way out there where the big questions lie. I found it easy to go out of body (in the good sense) into a warm, loving darkness. Sliding down by 6, 7th hour, and had no trouble sleeping. Fully scripted dreams, vivid. Very, very good. Want to try 100 mg."

(with 80 mg) "Completely foul taste. The effects were quite subtle, and I found this to be a strange but friendly ++. There was much eyes-closed fantasizing to music, even to Bruchner, whom I found unexpectedly pleasant. There was a feeling of tenseness at the twilight of the experience."

EXTENSIONS AND COMMENTARY: There is a most extraordinary loss of potency with the simple substitution of a sulfur atom for an oxygen atom. DOM is fully active at the 5 or so milligram area, whereas 2-TOM is active at maybe the 80 milligram area, a loss of potency by a factor of x15 or so. And the duration is quite a bit shorter. It might take a fair amount of learning to become completely at peace with it, but it might be worth the effort. And there are none of the disturbing hints of neurological and physical roughness of 5-TOM.

Again, as with the other TOM's and TOET's, the two-carbon homologue of this has been synthesized but not yet evaluated. The common intermediate benzaldehyde, 5-methoxy-4-methyl-2-(methylthio)benzaldehyde was condensed with nitromethane and ammonium acetate to give the nitrostyrene which, upon re-crystallization from ethanol, had a melting point of 118-118.5 °C. Anal. ($C_{11}H_{13}NO_3S$) C,H. Reduction with aluminum hydride in THF gave the crystalline free base which, as the hydrochloride salt, melted at 233-234 °C. Anal. ($C_{11}H_{18}ClNOS$) C,H. Quite logically, it has been called 2C-2-TOM.

#172   5-TOM;   2-METHOXY-4-METHYL-5-METHYLTHIO-
AMPHETAMINE

SYNTHESIS: To a solution of 6.6 g KOH pellets in 100 mL hot EtOH there was added a solution of 15.4 g methylthio-m-cresol (3-methyl-4-(methylthio)phenol, Crown-Zellerbach Corporation) in 25 mL EtOH. This was followed by the addition of 17 g methyl iodide, and the mixture was held at reflux on the steam bath for 16 h. The reaction mixture was poured into 400 mL H_2O, acidified with HCl, and extracted with 4x50 mL CH_2Cl_2. These were pooled, washed with 3x50 mL 5% NaOH, once with dilute HCl, and then the solvent was removed under vacuum. The residue was 3-methyl-4-(methylthio)anisole, a clear pale yellow oil, weighing 12.7 g. Distillation at 150-160 °C at 1.7 mm/Hg, or at 80-90 °C at 0.25 mm/Hg, did not remove the color, and gave a product with no improvement in purity.

To a mixture of 82 g $POCl_3$ and 72 g N-methylformanilide that had been heated on the steam bath for 10 min, there was added 33.6 g 3-methyl-4-(methylthio)phenol, and heating was continued for an additional 2 h. This was poured into 1.2 L H_2O, producing a brown gummy crystalline mass that slowly loosened on continued stirring. This was filtered off, washed with additional H_2O, and sucked as dry as possible. This was finely ground under 60 mL of cold MeOH, refiltered, and air dried to give 17.8 g of a nearly white crystalline solid with a mp of 94-96 °C. Recrystallization from 50 mL boiling MeOH gave a product of higher purity, but at some cost in yield. With this step there was obtained 13.4 g of 2-methoxy-4-methyl-5-(methylthio)benzaldehyde with a mp of 98-99 °C. An additional recrystallization from IPA increased this mp by another degree. From this final recrystallization, a small amount of material was left as an insoluble residue. It was also insoluble in acetone, but dissolved readily in CH_2Cl_2. It melted broadly at about 200 °C and was not identified. Proof of the structure of 2-methoxy-4-methyl-5-(methylthio)benzaldehyde was obtained by its successful reduction (with amalgamated Zn in HCl) to 2,5-dimethyl-4-(methylthio)anisole. This reference convergence compound was prepared separately from 2,5-dimethylanisole which reacted with chlorosulfonic acid to give the 4-sulfonyl chloride derivative, which was in turn reduced to the 4-mercapto derivative (white crystals from MeOH, with a mp of 38 °C sharp). This, upon methylation with methyl iodide and KOH in MeOH, gave 2,5-dimethoxy-4-(methylthio)anisole (white crystals from MeOH, with a mp of 67-68 °C). The two samples (one from the aldehyde reduction, and the other from this independent synthesis), were identical in all respects.

A solution of 1.9 g 2-methoxy-4-methyl-5-(methylthio)benzaldehyde in 40 mL nitroethane was treated with 0.5 g anhydrous ammonium acetate and heated under reflux, with stirring, with a heating mantle for 3.5 h, at which time TLC analysis showed no unreacted aldehyde and only a trace of slow moving materials. Removal of the excess nitroethane under vacuum gave a yellow plastic film (the wrapping of the magnetic stirrer had dissolved off) which was extracted first with 35 mL boiling MeOH, then with 2x35 mL boiling IPA. Separately, the MeOH extract and the combined IPA extracts, on cooling, deposited 0.6 g each of fluffy needles. The mother liquors were combined and allowed to evaporate to about 15 mL final volume, providing another 0.4 g crude product. All three samples melted at 101-102 °C. These were combined, and recrystallized from 50 mL boiling MeOH to provide, after filtering and air drying, 1.4 g of 1-(2-methoxy-4-methyl-5-methyl-thiophenyl)-2-nitropropene as bright yellow crystals with a mp of 102-102.5 °C. Anal. ($C_{12}H_{15}NO_3S$) C,H.

A solution of 2.0 g LAH in 100 mL anhydrous THF was cooled, under He, to 0 °C with an external ice bath. With good stirring there was added 1.28 mL 100% H_2SO_4 dropwise, to minimize charring. This was followed by the addition of 1.35 g 1-(2-methoxy-4-methyl-5-methylthiophenyl)-2-nitropropene in 50 mL anhydrous THF over the course of 5 min. After a few min further stirring, the temperature was brought up to a gentle reflux on the steam bath, and then all was cooled again to 0 °C. The excess hydride was destroyed by the cautious addition of 5 mL IPA followed by sufficient 5% NaOH to give a white granular character to the oxides, and to assure that the reaction mixture was basic (about 5 mL was used). The reaction mixture was filtered, and the filter cake washed first with THF and then with IPA. The combined filtrate and washings were stripped of solvent under vacuum and the residue dissolved in 150 mL dilute H_2SO_4. This was washed with 3x50 mL CH_2Cl_2 (the color stayed in the organic layer), made basic with aqueous NaOH, and extracted with 2x50 mL CH_2Cl_2. After the solvent was removed under vacuum, the residue was distilled at 110-125 °C at 0.4 mm/Hg to give 0.9 g of a colorless oil. This was dissolved in 4 mL IPA, neutralized with about 11 drops of concentrated HCl, and then diluted with 20 mL anhydrous Et_2O. After about a ten second delay, white crystals formed. These were removed by filtration and air dried, to give 0.6 g of 2-methoxy-4-methyl-5-methylthioamphetamine hydrochloride (5-TOM) as white crystals with a mp of 156-157 °C. A second crop obtained from the mother liquors on standing weighed 0.3 g and melted at 150-156 °C. Anal. ($C_{12}H_{20}ClNOS$) C,H.

DOSAGE: 30 - 50 mg.

DURATION: 6 - 10 h.

QUALITATIVE COMMENTS: (with 35 mg) "There was an awful lot of visual activity, and in general I found the day quite good, once I got past the early discomfort."

(with 40 mg) "I knew that I was sinking into a deep reverie after an hour into it. I was not totally unconscious since I seemed to respond to external stimuli (at least most of the time). But I certainly wasn't all that much there. The experience dominated completely. At one point (perhaps the peak?) I remember seeing a very quiet sea with a horizontal shoreline and a clear sky. This image seemed to come back rather frequently. At other times I would see a set of disjointed horizontal lines on this beach. These lines reminded me of spectral lines. For a short period of time I thought they were some kind of expression of my energy levels that I didn't understand. In retrospect, I suspect the horizontal lines were only expressions of how my mind was reacting to the material. I don't remember talking to anyone until I had started to come down from the experience. I eventually could see real images, but they were greatly distorted. It was as if I was looking at Cubism paintings by Picasso, having intense and strange colorations. As I came back into the real world, I realized that I had had an extraordinary trip. I had not been afraid at any time. The experience seemed unique, but quite benign. The experience for my fellow travelers was probably much more anxious. I wasn't particularly interested in food when I came down. I slept well. I was quite lethargic the next day. It really took me another day to integrate back into normal life. Would I repeat it? Possibly, but at a way smaller dose."

(with 50 mg) "The body was complete whacked, and the mental simply didn't keep up with it. There was some early nausea going into it, and my sinuses never cleared, and I somehow became irritable and angry. In fact, the impatience and grimness lasted for a couple of days. There were some visual events that might have been interesting to explore, but too much other stuff got in the way."

(with 50 mg) "There was much eyes-closed fantasy, and quite a bit of it with erotic undertones. In efforts to direct my actions, I found it difficult to find the point of initiation of a task. Reading and writing both impossible. I am somehow de-focused. But art work became quite rewarding. The experience was heavy going in, but rich coming out. Good dosage."

EXTENSIONS AND COMMENTARY: The bottom line is that 5-TOM is a pretty heavy-duty experience, with more negative reports than positive ones. I have received no mentions of a completely ecstatic time, and not even very many neutral experiences. The consensus is that it wasn't worth the struggle. Some cramping, some nausea, and a generalized discomfort. And that one case of a catatonic response. An approach to possible individual variation in the metabolic handling of the sulfur atom is the rationale for the preparation of the compound TOMSO, and it is discussed there.

The two-carbon homologue of 5-TOM has been prepared. It uses, of course, the same aldehyde, but the condensation was with nitromethane which yielded the nitrostyrene as an orange powder with a melting point of 118-119 °C from methanol. This was reduced with LAH in ether containing anhydrous $AlCl_3$, giving 2-methoxy-4-methyl-5-methylthiophenethylamine hydrochloride as white crystals with a melting point of 257-258 °C. It has been named 2C-5-TOM, but it has not yet been entered into the screening program so it is pharmacologically still a mystery.

#173 TOMSO; 2-METHOXY-4-METHYL-5-METHYLSULFINYLAMPHETAMINE

SYNTHESIS: A suspension of 12.7 g 1-(2-methoxy-4-methyl-5-methylthiophenyl)-2-nitropropene (see under 5-TOM for its preparation) in 50 mL warm acetic acid was added to a suspension of 22.5 g electrolytic grade elemental iron in 100 mL warm acetic acid. The temperature was raised cautiously until an exothermic reaction set in, and the mixture was maintained under reflux conditions as the color progressed from yellow to deep brown to eventually colorless. After coming back to room temperature, the somewhat gummy mixture was poured into 1 L H_2O, and all insolubles were removed by filtration. These were washed with CH_2Cl_2, and the aqueous filtrate was extracted with 3x100 mL CH_2Cl_2. The washes and extracts were combined, washed with 5% NaOH until the bulk of the color was removed and the washes remained basic, and the solvent was then removed under vacuum. The residue, 11.6 g of a pale amber oil that crystallized, was distilled at 110-120 °C at 0.4 mm/Hg to give 9.9 g 2-methoxy-4-methyl-5-methylthiophenylacetone with a mp of 41-42 °C. This was not improved by recrystallization from hexane. Anal. $(C_{12}H_{16}O_2S)$ C,H.

To a solution of 7.3 g 2-methoxy-4-methyl-5-methylthiophenylacetone in 35 mL methanol there was added 7.3 mL 35% hydrogen peroxide, and the mixture held under reflux conditions for 40 min. All volatiles were removed under vacuum, and the residue suspended in 250 mL H_2O. This was extracted with 3x50 mL CH_2Cl_2, the extracts pooled, and the solvent removed under vacuum. The residue, 8.6 g of an oily solid, was recrystallized from 10 mL boiling toluene to provide, after filtering and air drying, 5.4 g of 2-methoxy-4-methyl-5-methylsulfinylphenylacetone as a white solid with a mp of 89-89.5 °C. Anal. $(C_{12}H_{16}O_3S)$ C,H.

To a vigorously stirred solution of 5.2 g of 2-methoxy-4-methyl-5-methylsulfinylphenylacetone in 70 mL MeOH there was added 17 g anhydrous ammonium acetate followed by 1.0 g sodium cyanoborohydride. HCl was added as needed to maintain the pH at about 6 as determined with damp universal pH paper. No further base was generated after 3 days, and the reaction mixture was poured into 500 mL H_2O. After acidification with HCl (caution, highly poisonous HCN is evolved), this was washed with 2x100 mL CH_2Cl_2, made strongly basic with NaOH, and then extracted with 3x100 mL CH_2Cl_2. The pooled extracts were stripped of solvent under vacuum, and the residue weighed 7.1 g and was a pale amber oil. This was distilled at 150-160 °C at 0.3 mm/Hg to give a colorless oil weighing 4.4 g. A solution of this in 13 mL IPA was neutralized with 30 drops of concentrated HCl and the resulting solution warmed and diluted with 20 mL of warm anhydrous Et_2O. White crystals separated immediately and, after filtering, ether washing and air drying, provided 4.4 g of 2-methoxy-4-methyl-5-methylsulfinylamphetamine hydrochloride (TOMSO) that melted at 227-229 °C after vacuum drying for 24 hrs.

Anal. ($C_{12}H_{20}ClNO_2S$) C,H. The presence of two chiral centers (the alpha-carbon of the amphetamine side chain and the sulfoxide group at the 5-position of the ring) dictates that this product was a mixture of diastereoisomeric racemic compounds. No effort was made to separate them.

DOSAGE: greater than 150 mg (alone) or 100 - 150 mg (with alcohol).

DURATION: 10 - 16 h.

QUALITATIVE COMMENTS: (with 100 mg) "There were no effects at all, and it was at the so-called surprise pot-luck birthday lunch for the department chairman that I ate a little and had two glasses of Zinfandel. I shot up to an immediate ++ and this lasted all afternoon. I went to San Francisco by BART, and walked up Market Street and saw all the completely bizarre faces. I was absolutely unable to estimate the age of anybody who was female, at least by looking at her face. All aspects, both child-like and old, seemed to be amalgamated into each face, all at the same time. There was remarkable time-slowing; overall the experience was favorable. That certainly was not the effect of the alcohol in the wine. Food poisoning? No. It must have been the TOMSO that had been kindled and promoted to something."

(with 150 mg) "At best there is a threshold and it is going nowhere. At the third hour I drank, over the course of an hour, a tall drink containing 3 oz. of vodka. Soon I was clearly somewhere, and three hours later I was a rolling plus three. This lasted until well after midnight, and was not an alcohol response."

EXTENSIONS AND COMMENTARY: This entire venture into the study of TOMSO was an outgrowth of the extraordinary response that had been shown by one person to 5-TOM. There were two obvious approaches that might throw some light on the reason for this dramatic sensitivity. One would be to see if he was unusually capable of metabolizing sulfur-containing molecules, and the second would be to assume he was, and to try to guess just what product he had manufactured with his liver.

The individual sensitivity question was addressed in a tidy and direct manner. Why not study a simple sulfur-containing model compound that would probably be metabolized only at the sulfur and that would itself probably be pharmacologically inactive in its own rights? Sounded OK to me, so I made up a goodly supply of 4-tert-butyl thioanisole, which proved to be a gorgeous white crystalline solid. It seemed quite logical that this would be metabolized at the sulfur atom to produce either or both the sulfoxide and the sulfone. So I treated a methanol solution of this with a little hydrogen peroxide and distilled the neutral extracts at 100-115 °C at 0.2 mm/Hg to give the sulfoxide as a solid that melted at 76-77 °C from hexane: Anal. ($C_{11}H_{16}OS$) C,H. On the other hand, if a solution of the thioanisole in acetic acid containing hydrogen peroxide was heated on the steam bath for a few hours and then worked up, a new solid was isolated that proved to be the sulfone (a negative Fries-Vogt test). This was obtained as white crystals with a mp of 94-95 °C from aqueous methanol. Anal. $(C_{11}H_{16}SO_2)$ C,H. And I found that these three compounds separated well from one another by GC, and that they could be extracted from urine. Everything was falling into place. My thought was to determine a safe (inactive) level of the parent thioanisole, and determine the distribution of metabolites in my urine, and then in the urine of several other people, and then finally in the urine of the person who was the intense reactor to 5-TOM. I found that there were no effects, either physical or psychological, at an oral dose of 60 milligrams of 4-tert-butyl-thioanisole. But then everything fell apart. There was not a detectable trace of anything, neither parent compound nor either of the potential metabolites, to be found in my urine. The material was obviously being completely converted to one or more metabolites, but the sulfoxide and sulfone were not among them. It would be fun, someday, to methodically trace the fate of this compound.

So, on to the second approach. What might the active metabolite of 5-TOM actually be? The sulfoxide seemed completely reasonable, and that encouraged the synthesis of TOMSO. This name was given, as it is the sulfoxide analogue (SO) of 5-TOM. And since only one of these analogues has been made, the "5" distinction is not needed. But it is apparent that this approach to the finding of an explanation for the idiosyncratic sensitivity to 5-TOM also failed, in that TOMSO itself appeared to be without activity.

But the fallout of this study was the uncovering of an unusual property that alcohol can occasionally have when it follows the ingestion of certain inactive drugs. Or if it is used at the tail end of an experience with an active drug. Usually some alcohol has been employed as a softener of the residual effects of the day's experiment, or as a social habit to accompany the post-mortem discussions of a day's experiences, and perhaps as a help to sleeping. But if there is a rekindling of the effect, rather than the sedation expected, then the verb "to tomso" can be used in the notes. It represents the promotion of an inactive situation into an active one, with the catalysis of alcohol. But the effect is not that of alcohol. Might the extreme sensitivity of some alcoholics to even a small amount of alcohol be due to some endogenous "inactive" factor that is promoted in this way into some centrally florid toxicity? I remember seeing proposals of some tetrahydroisoquinolines as potential mis-metabolites in efforts to explain the toxicity of alcohol. Maybe they are nothing more than psychedelics that are thought to be inactive, but which might be ignited with a glass of wine. And the person is tomsoing with his small amount of alcohol.

#174 TP; THIOPROSCALINE; 3,5-DIMETHOXY-4-(n)-PROPYLTHIOPHENETHYLAMINE

SYNTHESIS: A solution was made of 12.1 g N,N,N',N'-tetramethylethylenediamine and 13.8 g of 1,3-dimethoxybenzene in 200 mL 30-60 °C petroleum ether. This was stirred vigorously under a He atmosphere and cooled to 0 °C with an external ice bath. There was added 66 mL of 1.6 M butyllithium in hexane which produced a white granular precipitate. The reaction mixture was brought up to room temperature for a few minutes, and then cooled again to 0 °C. There was then added 15.8 g of di-(n)-propyl disulfide which changed the granular precipitate to a creamy appearance. Stirring was continued while the reaction mixture was brought up to room temperature and finally up to reflux. The reaction mixture was then added to 600 mL of dilute H_2SO_4. The two phases were separated, and the aqueous phase extracted with 2x75 mL Et_2O. The organic phases were combined, and the solvent removed under vacuum. The residue was 24.2 g of a pale amber liquid which was distilled at 0.35 mm/Hg to give two fractions. The first boiled at 85-90 °C, weighed 0.5 g and appeared to be recovered dipropyl disulfide. The product 2-(n)-propylthio-1,3-dimethoxybenzene boiled at at 105-125 °C, and weighed 20.8 g. A small sample recrystallized from hexane had a mp of 27-28 °C. Anal. ($C_{11}H_{16}O_2S$) C,H.

To a stirred solution of 19.8 g of 2-(n)-propylthio-1,3-dimethoxybenzene in 200 mL CH_2Cl_2 there was added 15.4 g elemental bromine dissolved in 100 mL CH_2Cl_2. The reaction was not exothermic, and it was allowed to stir for 1 h. The reaction mixture was washed with H_2O containing sodium hydrosulfite (which rendered it nearly colorless) and finally washed with saturated brine. The solvent was removed under vacuum leaving 33.5 g of a pale yellow liquid. This was distilled at 112-120 °C at 0.3 mm/Hg to yield 4-bromo-2-(n)-propylthio-1,3-dimethoxy-benzene as a pale yellow oil. Anal. ($C_{11}H_{15}BrO_2S$) C,H.

To a solution of 16.8 g diisopropylamine in 100 mL anhydrous THF that was stirred under a N_2 atmosphere and cooled to -10 °C with an external ice/MeOH bath, there was added in sequence 75 mL of 1.6 M butyllithium in hexane, 3.0 mL of dry CH_3CN, and 8.7 g of 4-bromo-2-(n)-propylthio-1,3-dimethoxybenzene which had been dissolved in 20 mL THF. The bromo compound was added dropwise over the course of 5 min. The color became deep red-brown. Stirring was maintained for a total of 30 min while the reaction came to room temperature. It was then poured into 750 mL dilute H_2SO_4, the organic layer separated, and the aqueous phase extracted with 2x100 mL CH_2Cl_2. These extracts were pooled, washed with dilute H_2SO_4, and the solvent was removed under vacuum yielding a residue that was distilled. Two distillation cuts were taken at 0.3 mm/Hg. The first fraction boiled at 110-138 °C and weighed 0.7 g and was discarded. The second fraction came over at 148-178 °C and weighed 3.0 g. By thin layer chromatography this fraction was about 80% pure, and was used as such in the following reduction. A small sample was ground under methyl cyclopentane yielding white crystals of 3,5-dimethoxy-4-(n)-propylthiophenylacetonitrile with a mp of 35.5-37.5 °C.

A solution of LAH in THF (15 mL of a 1 M solution) under N_2 was cooled to 0 °C and vigorously stirred. There was added, dropwise, 0.4 mL 100% H_2SO_4, followed by 2.7 g 3,5-dimethoxy-4-(n)-propylthiophenylacetonitrile dissolved in 10 mL anhydrous THF. The reaction mixture was stirred at 0 °C for a few min, then brought to a reflux for 30 min on the steam bath. After cooling back to room temperature, there was added IPA to destroy the excess hydride and 10% NaOH to bring the reaction to a basic pH and converted the aluminum oxide to a loose, white, filterable consistency. This was removed by filtration and washed with both THF and IPA. The filtrate and washes were stripped of solvent under vacuum, the residue added to 1 L dilute H_2SO_4. This was washed with 2x75 mL CH_2Cl_2, made basic with aqueous NaOH, extracted with 3x75 mL CH_2Cl_2, the extracts pooled, and the solvent removed under vacuum. The residue was distilled at 137-157 °C at 0.3 mm/Hg to give 1.3 g of a colorless oil. This was dissolved in 10 mL of IPA, neutralized with 20 drops of concentrated HCl and, with continuous stirring, diluted with 50 mL anhydrous Et_2O. The product was removed by filtration, washed with Et_2O, and air dried to give 1.4 g of 3,5-dimethoxy-4-(n)-propylthiophenethylamine hydrochloride (TP) as bright white crystals with a mp of 164-165 °C. Anal. ($C_{13}H_{22}ClNO_2S$) C,H.

DOSAGE: 20 - 25 mg.

DURATION: 10 - 15 h.

QUALITATIVE COMMENTS: (with 18 mg) "There was very little effect until more than two hours, when I came inside out of the cold and jumped to an immediate +1. It is hard to define, and I am quite willing to have it develop more, and if not, quite willing to go higher next time. I got into several quite technical conversations, but through it all I was aware of a continuous alteration. There was a drop at the seventh hour, and nothing at all was left at twelve hours."

(with 27 mg) "My body feels heavy. This is not a negative thing, but it is there. I feel a heavy pressure at the back of the neck, which is probably unresolved energy. The nervous system seems to be somehow vunerable. Towards the end of the experience I considered a Miltown, but settled on an aspirin, and I still couldn't sleep for about 24 hours. The imagery is extremely rich and there is quite a bit of eyes-open visual, but mostly eyes closed. I think the rewards are not worth the body price. Sometime again, maybe lower?"

EXTENSIONS AND COMMENTARY: There is a high potency here, but clearly there are signs of increased toxicity as well even over the ethyl homologue, TE. The butyl compound (see TB) was the last of this series of phenethylamines and as is noted there, the physical problems lessen, but so do the psychedelic properties. The three-carbon amphetamine homologues are completely unexplored. The most reasonable starting material for these would be 4-thiosyringaldehyde, with S-alkylation and then the conventional nitroethane coupling followed with LAH reduction. The most appealing target as a potential psychedelic would be the methylthio homologue (3,5-dimethoxy-4-methylthioamphetamine, 3C-TM) or, as a potential euphoriant, the butylthio homologue (3,5-dimethoxy-4-(n)-butylthio-amphetamine, 3C-TB). I am not sure that these alkylthio analogues would justify the labor needed to make them.

#175   TRIS;   TRESCALINE;   TRISESCALINE;   3,4,5-TRIETHOXYPHENETHYLAMINE

SYNTHESIS: A solution of 16.9 g of ethyl 3,4,5-triethoxybenzoate in 25 mL THF was added to a well stirred suspension of 8 g LAH in 150 mL THF. The mixture was heated at reflux for 24 h and and, after cooling, treated with IPA to destroy the excess hydride. There was then added sufficient 25% NaOH to produce a granular, white form of the aluminum oxide. This was removed by filtration, the filter cake washed with IPA, and the filtrate and washes were combined and stripped of solvent

under vacuum. The residue weighed 12.2 g and was distilled at 120-140 °C at 0.4 mm/Hg to yield 8.6 g of 3,4,5-triethoxy-benzyl alcohol that spontaneously crystallized. It had a mp of 29-30 °C and was free of the parent ester carbonyl absorption at 1709 cm^{-1} in the infra-red.

This product 3,4,5-triethoxybenzyl alcohol was suspended in 30 mL concentrated HCl, heated briefly on the steam bath, cooled to room temperature, and suspended in a mixture of 75 mL CH_2Cl_2 and 75 mL H_2O. The phases were separated, and the aqueous phase extracted with another 75 mL CH_2Cl_2. The organic fractions were combined, washed first with H_2O and then with saturated brine. Removal of the solvent under vacuum yielded an off-white oil that was distilled at 112-125 °C at 0.4 mm/Hg to provide 7.5 g of 3,4,5-triethoxybenzyl chloride that spontaneously crystallized. The crude product had a mp of 34-37 °C which was increased to 37.5-38.5 °C upon recrystallization from hexane. Anal. ($C_{13}H_{19}ClO_3$) C,H.

A solution of 4.5 g 3,4,5-triethoxybenzyl chloride in 10 mL DMF was treated with 5.0 g sodium cyanide and heated for 1 h on the steam bath. The mixture was then poured into 100 mL H_2O and the oily phase that resulted immediately crystallized. This was filtered off, washed well with H_2O, air dried, and distilled at 128-140 °C at 0.25 mm/Hg to yield 3.7 g of 3,4,5-triethoxyphenylacetonitrile which melted at 54-56.5 °C. There was a sharp nitrile band at 2249 cm^{-1}. Anal. ($C_{14}H_{19}NO_3$) C,H.

To 18.8 mL of a 1 M solution of LAH in THF under N_2, vigorously stirred and cooled to 0 °C, there was added, dropwise, 0.50 mL 100% H_2SO_4. This was followed by 3.6 g 3,4,5-triethoxyphenylacetonitrile in 10 mL anhydrous THF over the course of 5 min. The reaction mixture was brought to room temperature and stirred for a few min, and finally held at reflux on the steam bath for 1 h. After cooling back to room temperature, there was added about 2 mL IPA (to destroy the excess hydride) followed by sufficient 15% NaOH to make the aluminum oxide granular and white, and the organic solution basic. The solids were removed by filtration, and washed with IPA. The filtrate and washes were stripped of solvent under vacuum, the residue added to 400 mL dilute H_2SO_4. This was washed with 2x75 mL CH_2Cl_2, the aqueous phase made basic with aqueous. NaOH, and the product extracted with 2x75 mL CH_2Cl_2. These extracts were pooled, the solvent removed under vacuum, and the residue distilled at 115-135 °C at 0.4 mm/Hg to give a white oil. This was dissolved in a few mL of IPA, neutralized with concentrated HCl, and diluted with anhydrous Et_2O to the point of turbidity. When the crystal formation was complete, the product was removed by filtration, washed with Et_2O, and air dried to give 2.8 g 3,4,5-triethoxyphenethylamine hydrochloride (TRIS) as white crystals with a mp of 177-178 °C.

DOSAGE: greater than 240 mg.

DURATION: unknown.

QUALITATIVE COMMENTS: (with 240 mg) "No effects were noted at any time following 240 milligrams of trisescaline. This would have been a thoroughly active level of the trimethoxy counterpart, mescaline."

EXTENSIONS AND COMMENTARY: With the progressive diminution of human potency with increased ethylation of the mescaline molecule, there is no suprise in finding that this base is devoid of activity. Studies done years ago in the cat at a dosage of 25 mg/Kg (i.m.) gave none of the expected, and looked for, signs of behavioral changes (pilomotor activity, pupillary dilation, growling, hissing, aggressive behavior, withdrawal, or salivation) that are often seen with the less bulky substituents. It was without action.

More lengthy substituents in the 3,4,5-positions (with combinations of ethyls and propyls, for example) are presently unknown compounds, and there is small incentive to make them.

#176   3-TSB;   3-THIOSYMBESCALINE;   3-ETHOXY-5-ETHYLTHIO-4-METHOXYPHENETHYLAMINE

SYNTHESIS: A solution of 13.4 g 3-bromo-N-cyclohexyl-4-methoxy-5-ethoxy-benzylidenimine (see under ME for its preparation) in 150 mL anhydrous Et_2O was placed in a He atmosphere, well stirred, and cooled in an external dry ice/acetone bath to -80 °C. There was the formation of a granular precipitate. There was then added 28 mL of 1.6 N butyllithium in hexane over the course of 5 min, and the mixture (which had turned quite creamy) was stirred for 15 min. This was followed by the addition of 5.5 g diethyl disulfide over the course of 1 min. The mixture was allowed to come to room temperature over the course of 1 h, and then added to 100 mL of dilute HCl. The Et₂O phase was separated and the solvent removed under vacuum. The residue was dissolved in 50 ml Meoh, combined with the original aqueous phase, and the entire mixture heated on the steam bath for 0.5 h. The aqueous solution was cooled to room temperature, extracted with 3x100 mL CH₂Cl₂, the extracts pooled, and the solvent removed under vacuum. The residue was distilled at 132-140 °C at 0.3 mm/Hg to yield 9.1 g of 3-ethoxy-5-ethylthio-4-methoxy-benzaldehyde as a white oil that, on standing for several months, spontaneously crystallized. A small bit of the crystalline solid was wastefully recrystallized from MeOH to provide white crystals with a mp of 31.5-32.5 °C. Anal. ($C_{12}H_{16}O_3S$) C,H. The crude distillate was used in the following reactions.

Several attempts were made to prepare the nitrostyrene from this aldehyde and nitromethane. The most successful, but still inadequate, procedure is described here. A solution of 1.0 g 3-ethoxy-5-ethylthio-4-methoxybenzaldehyde in 10 mL nitromethane was treated with about 150 mg of anhydrous ammonium acetate and heated on the steam bath. The course of the reaction was followed by TLC. The bulk of the aldehyde had disappeared in 45 min, and there were several UV-absorbing spots visible. Removal of the excess nitromethane under vacuum gave an orange oil which, when rubbed under cold MeOH, gave 200 mg of yellow solids. This was (by TLC) a mixture of nitrostyrene, starting aldehyde, and several slow-moving scrudge impurities. Recrystallization from MeOH gave a poor recovery of a yellow solid with a mp of 102.5-104 °C but this was still contaminated with the same impurities. Several repetitions of this synthetic procedure gave little if any of the desired 3-ethoxy-5-ethylthio-4-methoxy-ß-nitrostyrene.

A suspension of 5.4 g methyltriphenylphosphonium bromide in 30 mL anhydrous THF was placed under a He atmosphere, well stirred, and cooled with an external water bath. There was then added 10 mL of 1.6 N butyllithium in hexane which resulted in the generation of a bright pumpkin color. The initial heavy solids changed into a granular precipitate. There was then added 2.4 g of 3-ethoxy-5-ethylthio-4-methoxybenzaldehyde in a little THF. An initial gummy phase became granular with patient swirling and stirring. After 30 min, the reaction was quenched in 500 mL H₂O, the top hexane layer separated, and the aqueous phase extracted with 2x75 mL of petroleum ether. The organic fractions were combined, washed with H₂O, dried over anhydrous K₂CO₃, and the solvents removed under vacuum to give the crude 3-ethoxy-5-ethylthio-4-methoxystyrene as a yellow mobile liquid.

A solution of 2 mL of borane-methyl sulfide complex (10 M BH₃ in methyl sulfide) in 20 mL THF was placed in a He atmosphere, cooled to 0 °C, treated with 4.2 mL of 2-methylbutene, and stirred for 1 h while returning to room temperature. To this there was added a solution of the impure 3-ethoxy-5-ethylthio-4-methoxy-styrene in a little anhydrous THF. This was stirred for 1 h. The excess borane was destroyed with 1 mL MeOH, followed by the addition of 3.8 g elemental iodine, followed in turn by a solution of 0.8 g NaOH in hot MeOH added over the course of 5 min. The color gradually faded, and became a pale lime green. This was added to 300 mL dilute aqueous sodium thiosulfate which was extracted with 2x100 mL petroleum ether. The extracts were pooled, and the solvent evaporated under vacuum to provide crude 1-(3-ethoxy-5-ethylthio-4-methoxyphenyl)-2-iodoethane as a residue.

To this crude 1-(3-ethoxy-5-ethylthio-4-methoxyphenyl)-2-iodoethane there was added a solution of 3.7 g potassium phthalimide in 50 mL anhydrous DMF, and all was heated on the steam bath. The reaction seemed to be complete after 15 min (as seen by TLC) and the addition of a second batch of potassium phthalimide in DMF produced no further change. After adding to 500 mL of dilute NaOH, the aqueous phase was extracted with 2x75 mL Et_2O. These extracts were combined, washed first with dilute NaOH and then with dilute H_2SO_4, dried over anhydrous K_2CO_3, and the solvent removed under vacuum which provided an amber oil as residue. This was triturated under cold MeOH giving white solids which were recrystallized from 20 mL MeOH. Thus there was obtained 0.9 g of 1-(3-ethoxy-5-ethylthio-4-methoxyphenyl)-2-phthalimidoethane as white crystals that melted at 79-80.5 °C. A small sample was recrystallized from EtOH to give large flat needles with a mp of 81-82 °C. Anal. $(C_{21}H_{23}NO_4S)$ C,H.

A suspension of 0.8 g of the crystallized 1-(3-ethoxy-5-ethylthio-4-methoxyphenyl)-2-phthalimidoethane in 25 mL of n-butanol was treated with 2 mL of 66% hydrazine, and the mixture was heated on the steam bath for 0.5 h. Initially all went into solution, and then there was the separation of solids that resembled cottage cheese. The reaction mixture was added to 150 mL dilute H_2SO_4. The solids were removed by filtration, and the filtrate was washed with 3x50 mL CH_2Cl_2. These washes were discarded. The H_2O phase was then made basic with aqueous NaOH, extracted with 2x75 mL CH_2Cl_2, and the solvent from these pooled extracts removed under vacuum. The residue was distilled at 135-155 °C at 0.3 mm/Hg to give 0.45 g of a colorless oil. This was dissolved in 2.5 mL IPA, neutralized with 5 drops of concentrated HCl, and diluted with 10 mL anhydrous Et_2O. The solution became cloudy, and then deposited lustrous white plates. These were removed by filtration, washed with additional Et_2O, and air dried to give 0.4 g of 3-ethoxy-5-ethylthio-4-methoxyphenethylamine hydrochloride (3-TSB) with a mp of 153.5-154.5 °C. Anal. $(C_{13}H_{22}ClNO_2S)$ C,H.

DOSAGE: greater than 200 mg.

DURATION: unknown.

QUALITATIVE COMMENTS: (with 200 mg) "No effects whatsoever, neither mental nor physical."

EXTENSIONS AND COMMENTARY: The elephant labored and brought forth a mouse. A lot of work for a material without activity.

I have used the term "scrudge" in this and other recipes, without defining it. With this aldehyde, as with most aldehydes in this nitrostyrene synthesis reaction where there is no ortho-substituent on the benzaldehyde, the reaction progress should be carefully followed by thin-layer chromatography. As the aldehyde disappears from the reaction mixture, the nitrostyrene appears, but there is usually the development of one or more slower moving components as seen by TLC. Such a wrong-product is called scrudge. The reaction should be continuously titrated, and stopped when there is a favorable balance between the aldehyde being mostly gone, the nitrostyrene being mostly made, and the slower-moving scrudge components being not yet too plentiful. Methylene chloride is an excellent solvent to try first, with silica gel plates and UV detection. The nitrostyrene is always the fastest moving component of the reaction mixture and often fluoresces a dull purple. The starting aldehyde is the second spot and usually fluoresces white or pale yellow. The scrudge spots then occur in a cascade from the aldehyde to the origin. A maddening property is that they are yellow or brown colored, and in the probe mass spectrograph they can crack to give rise to what appears to be the right nitrostyrene. Usually, they are high melting.

In this preparation, there was not one but several scrudges, and little if any nitrostyrene. The same was true for the other of the diethyl compounds such as 3-TASB, 5-TASB and 3-T-TRIS. Thus, it is preferable to circumvent this usual synthetic step by using the Wittig reaction instead, as described here.

#177   4-TSB;   4-THIOSYMBESCALINE;   3,5-DIETHOXY-4-METHYLTHIOPHENETHYLAMINE

SYNTHESIS: A solution of 12.1 g N,N,N',N'-tetramethylethylenediamine and 16.6 g of 1,3-diethoxybenzene was made in 200 mL 30-60 °C petroleum ether. This was stirred vigorously under a N_2 atmosphere and cooled to 0 °C with an external ice bath. There was added 66 mL of 1.6 M butyllithium in hexane. The stirred reaction mixture became a little cloudy and then gradually formed a white granular precipitate. This was brought to room temperature, stirred for 0.5 h, and returned again to 0 °C. There was added 9.45 g of dimethyl disulfide which converted the loose precipitate to a creamy texture. The reaction was exothermic. After being held 0.5 h at reflux temperature, the reaction mixture was added to 600 mL dilute H_2SO_4. There was the immediate formation of white solids which were insoluble in either phase. The petroleum ether phase was separated, and the aqueous phase extracted with 3x100 mL Et$_2$O. The organics were combined, and the solvents removed under vacuum. There was obtained as residue 24.8 g of a slightly oily crystalline solid that, after trituration under 30 mL cold hexane, filtering, and air drying, weighed 16.9 g. This product, 2,6-diethoxythioanisole, had a mp of 71-72 °C which was not improved by recrystallization from methylcyclopentane. Anal. (C$_{11}$H$_{16}$O$_2$S) C,H.

To a stirred solution of 16.7 g of 2,6-diethoxythioanisole in 175 mL CH$_2$Cl$_2$ there was added 13 g elemental bromine dissolved in 100 mL CH$_2$Cl$_2$. After stirring at ambient temperature 1 h, the dark solution was added to 150 mL H$_2$O containing 1 g of sodium dithionite. Shaking immediately discharged the residual bromine color, and the organic phase was separated. The aqueous phase was extracted once with 100 mL CH$_2$Cl$_2$, the pooled extracts washed first with H$_2$O, and then with saturated brine. Removal of the solvent under vacuum provided 28.6 g of a pale yellow oil with several globs of H$_2$O present. This wet product was distilled at 118-125 °C at 0.25 mm/Hg to yield 3-bromo-2,6-diethoxythioanisole as a white oil weighing 21.5 g. It could not be crystallized. Anal. (C$_{11}$H$_{15}$BrO$_2$S) C,H.

To a solution of 19.3 g diisopropylamine in 75 mL hexane under a He atmosphere there was added 100 mL of 1.6 M butyllithium. The viscous mixture was loosened by the addition of 200 mL anhydrous THF, and this stirred mixture was cooled with an external ice bath. There was then added 4.0 mL of dry CH$_3$CN, and 11.6 g of 3-bromo-2,6-diethoxythioanisole (which had been diluted with a little anhydrous THF). The deep red brown reaction mixture was stirred for 0.5 h, and then poured into 1 L dilute H$_2$SO$_4$. This was extracted with 3x75 mL CH$_2$Cl$_2$, the extracts pooled, washed with H$_2$O, dried with anhydrous K$_2$CO$_3$, and the solvent was removed under vacuum. The residue was distilled at 0.3 mm/Hg yielding two fractions. The first fraction boiled at 120-140 °C and weighed 1.2 g. This fraction partially crystallized, but was not investigated further. The second fraction was 3,5-diethoxy-4-methylthiophenylacetonitrile, which came over at 135-160 °C, was a yellow liquid, weighed 3.2 g, but did not crystallize.

A solution of LAH in anhydrous THF (30 mL of a 1.0 M solution) under N$_2$ was cooled to 0 °C and vigorously stirred. There was added, dropwise, 0.78 mL 100% H$_2$SO$_4$, followed by 3.0 g 3,5-diethoxy-4-methylthiophenylacetonitrile diluted with a little anhydrous THF. The reaction mixture was stirred at 0 °C for a few min, then brought to reflux on the steam bath for 1.5 h. After cooling back to room temperature, there was added IPA to destroy the excess hydride and 10% NaOH to bring the reaction to a basic pH with the conversion of aluminum oxide to a loose, white, filterable consistency. This was removed by filtration, and washed first with THF followed by IPA. The filtrate and washes were stripped of solvent under vacuum, the residue added to 1 L dilute H$_2$SO$_4$. This was washed with 2x75 mL CH$_2$Cl$_2$, made basic with 25% NaOH, and extracted with 3x100 mL CH$_2$Cl$_2$. After combining, the solvent was removed under vacuum providing an orange oil. This was distilled at 135-160 °C at 0.4 mm/Hg to give a light yellow oil. This was dissolved in 20 mL of IPA, and neutralized with 32 drops of concentrated HCl producing white crystals spontaneously. These were dissolved by bringing the IPA suspension to a boil on the steam bath and, with stirring, diluted with 80 mL of warm anhydrous Et_2O. There was the immediate formation of crystals which were removed by filtration, washed with an IPA/Et_2O mixture, and then with Et_2O. After air drying there was obtained 1.5 g of 3,5-diethoxy-4-methylthiophenethylamine hydrochloride (4-TSB) as white crystals. The mp was 194.5-196 °C. Anal. $(C_{13}H_{22}ClNO_2S)$ C,H.

DOSAGE: greater than 240 mg.

DURATION: unknown.

QUALITATIVE COMMENTS: (with 80 mg) "There was a real effect about three hours into this experiment — a little bit spacey while I was talking to Mr. X. But the talk went well, and we were all really friendly. There was no hint that he suspected anything. A couple of hours later, nothing."

(with 160 mg) "Twinges at a couple of hours, but the rest of the day disappointing as to any effect from the drug."

(with 240 mg) "No effects at all."

EXTENSIONS AND COMMENTARY: Here is an excellent presentation of a report that shows false positives or maybe false negatives. Something at low levels. Nothing at higher levels. Always tend to trust the absence of an effect in preference to the presence of an effect, if one of the two observations is presumed to be in error.

#178   3-T-TRIS;   3-THIOTRESCALINE;   3-THIOTRISESCALINE;
3,4-DIETHOXY-5-ETHYLTHIOPHENETHYLAMINE

SYNTHESIS: A solution of 11.5 g 3-bromo-N-cyclohexyl-4,5-diethoxy-benzylidenimine (see under ASB for its preparation) in 150 mL anhydrous Et_2O was placed in a He atmosphere, well stirred, and cooled in an external dry ice acetone bath to -80 °C. There was light formation of fine crystals. There was then added 25 mL of 1.6 N butyllithium in hexane and the mixture stirred for 15 min. This was followed by the addition of 5.8 g diethyl disulfide over the course of 20 min during which time the solution became increasingly cloudy with the eventual deposition of an insoluble gummy phase. The mixture was allowed to come to room temperature over the course of 1 h, and then added to 400 mL of dilute HCl. The organic phase was separated and stripped of solvent under vacuum. This residue was combined with the original aqueous phase, and the mixture was heated on the steam bath for

2 h. The aqueous mixture was cooled to room temperature, extracted with 3x100 mL CH_2Cl_2, the extracts pooled, washed with H_2O, and the solvent removed under vacuum to yield 11.0 g of an amber oil. This was distilled at 130-150 °C at 0.2 mm/ Hg to yield 7.2 g of 3,4-diethoxy-5-(ethylthio)benzaldehyde as a white oil that spontaneously crystallized. The crude product had a mp of 52-57 °C that increased to 57-58 °C upon recrystallization from EtOH. Anal. $(C_{13}H_{18}O_3S)$ C,H.

A solution of 14.9 g methyltriphenylphosphonium bromide in 200 mL anhydrous THF was placed under a He atmosphere, well stirred, and cooled to 0 °C with an external ice water bath. There was then added 27.6 mL of 1.6 N butyllithium in hexane which resulted in the generation of a yellow color which was at first transient, and then stable. The reaction mixture was brought up to room temperature, and 6.8 g

3,4-diethoxy-5-(ethylthio)benzaldehyde in 50 mL THF was added dropwise dispelling the color, and the mixture was held at reflux on the steam bath for 1 h. The reaction was quenched in 800 mL H_2O, the top layer separated, and the aqueous phase extracted with 2x75 mL of petroleum ether. The organic fractions were combined and the solvents removed under vacuum to give 12.0 g of the crude 3,4-diethoxy-5-ethylthiostyrene as a deep yellow oil.

A solution of 5.6 g of borane-methyl sulfide complex (10 M BH_3 in methyl sulfide) in 45 mL THF was placed in a He atmosphere, cooled to 0 °C, treated with 11.6 g of 2-methylbutene, and stirred for 1 h while returning to room temperature. To this there was added the crude 3,4-diethoxy-5-ethylthiostyrene in 25 mL THF and the stirring was continued for 1 h. The excess borane was destroyed with about 2 mL MeOH. There was then added 11.4 g elemental iodine followed by a solution of 2.2 g NaOH in 40 mL hot MeOH. This was followed by sufficient 25% NaOH to minimize the residual iodine color (about 4 mL was required). The reaction mixture was added to 500 mL H_2O containing 4 g sodium hydrosulfite. This was extracted with 3x75 mL petroleum ether, and the pooled extracts stripped of solvent under vacuum to yield 24.5 g of crude 1-(3,4-diethoxy-5-ethylthiophenyl)-2-iodoethane as a viscous yellow oil.

This crude 1-(3,4-diethoxy-5-ethylthiophenyl)-2-iodoethane was added to a solution of 11.1 g potassium phthalimide in 80 mL DMF, and all was heated on the steam bath for 1.5 h. It was then flooded with 600 mL H_2O, made basic with NaOH, and extracted with 3x100 mL Et_2O. Removal of the solvent under vacuum provided 18.5 g of a residue that was dried to a constant weight by heating under vacuum (0.2 mm/Hg). The solid residue was ground under MeOH, and then recrystallized from MeOH providing 1-(3,4-diethoxy-5-ethylthiophenyl)-2-phthalimidoethane as white granular crystals, with a mp of 86.5-87.5 °C. Anal. $(C_{22}H_{25}NO_4S)$ C,H.

The recrystallized 1-(3,4-diethoxy-5-ethylthiophenyl)-2-phthalimido-ethane was dissolved in n-butanol, treated with 66% hydrazine, and the mixture heated on the steam bath for 1.5 h. This was then added to dilute H_2SO_4, the butanol separated, the aqueous phase washed with 2x75 mL Et_2O. After being made basic with aqueous NaOH, the aqueous phase was extracted with 3x75 mL CH_2Cl_2 and the solvent removed under vacuum to provide a pale amber oil. This was distilled at 140-155 °C at 0.25 mm/Hg to give about 1 g of a white oil. The distillate was dissolved in 5 mL IPA, neutralized with concentrated HCl, and treated with 10 mL anhydrous Et_2O to give a solution from which a white crystalline product slowly separated. These crystals, 3,4-diethoxy-5-ethylthiophenethylamine hydrochloride (3-T-TRIS) weighed 1.1 g and had a mp of 161-162 °C. Anal. $(C_{14}H_{24}ClNO_2S)$ C,H.

DOSAGE: greater than 160 mg.

DURATION: unknown.

QUALITATIVE COMMENTS: (with 160 mg) "There were no effects. At the 9th or 10th hour after having taken the material I was aware of some neurological irritability. I will not try this at any higher dosage, and let me stretch things a bit by a few percent in good conscience and say that this is less active than mescaline. This would allow it to be reported as < 1 M.U."

EXTENSIONS AND COMMENTARY: The term "M.U." pops up here and there in a lot of the earlier literature on these phenethylamines. It stands for "mescaline units" and was used to give a quantitative measure for the relative potency of a compound. Since it became obvious quite early in these studies that mescaline, although the prototypic compound, was probably going to remain the least potent, it seemed reasonable to use it as a bench mark of unity. By dividing the dose needed of mescaline (to produce central effects) by the dose needed of another drug, one would generate a number that represented just how many times more potent this new drug was than mescaline. I used this term in a very early review of the one-ring psychotomimetics, and it served satisfactorily for quite a while.

Its intrinsic worth proved, however, to be its very limitation. It was quickly apparent that the principal value, to behavioral researchers, of the reports of new hallucinogenic drugs, was not in the nature of their action but in the amount of stuff needed to produce that action. This was an essential axis against which the animal pharmacologist could plot his findings. A number was wanted, and the mescaline unit was just that number. Sadly, the major question that is asked by most academic researchers in their evaluation of the psychedelic materials is, "How much does it take," rather than "What does it do." The marvelous nuances of action, the subtle variations of effect, are dismissed as being hopelessly subjective and thus without scientific worth. But they are, I believe, of great worth. That is exactly what this book is all about.

#179   4-T-TRIS;   4-THIOTRESCALINE;   4-THIOTRISESCALINE;
3,5-DIETHOXY-4-ETHYLTHIOPHENETHYLAMINE

SYNTHESIS: A solution of 12.1 g N,N,N',N'-tetramethylethylenediamine and 16.6 g of 1,3-diethoxybenzene was made in 200 mL 30-60 °C petroleum ether. This was stirred vigorously under a He atmosphere and cooled to 0 °C with an external ice bath. There was added 66 mL of 1.6 M butyllithium in hexane. The stirred reaction mixture became a little cloudy and then gradually formed a white granular precipitate. This was brought to room temperature, stirred for 0.5 h, and returned again to 0 °C. There was added 12.8 g of diethyl disulfide which seemed to produce an exothermic reaction. After being held for a few min at reflux temperature, the reaction mixture was added to 600 mL dilute H_2SO_4 which produced two clear phases. The petroleum ether phase was separated, and the aqueous phase extracted with 2x75 mL Et_2O. The organics were combined, and the solvents removed under vacuum. There was obtained as residue 24 g of a viscous oil. This was distilled at 93-110 °C at 0.3 mm/Hg yielding 21.5 g 1,3-diethoxy-2-ethylthiobenzene which spontaneously crystallized. Grinding under a small amount of hexane, filtering, and hexane washing provided 18.5 g of white crystals with a mp of 26-27 °C. Anal. ($C_{12}H_{18}O_2S$) C,H.

To a stirred solution of 17.3 g of 1,3-diethoxy-2-ethylthiobenzene in 175 mL CH_2Cl_2 there was added 11.8 g elemental bromine dissolved in 100 mL CH_2Cl_2. There was an immediate loss of color, and the obvious evolution of HBr gas. After stirring at ambient temperature for 1 h, the dark solution was added to 150 mL H_2O containing 1 g of sodium dithionite. Shaking immediately discharged the residual bromine color, and the organic phase was separated, The aqueous phase was extracted once with 75 mL CH_2Cl_2, the pooled extracts washed first with H_2O, and then with saturated brine. Removal of the solvent under vacuum provided 34.2 g of a pale yellow oil with several globs of H_2O that were mechanically removed. This wet product was distilled at 105-125 °C at 0.35 mm/Hg to yield 4-bromo-1,3-diethoxy-2-ethylthiobenzene as an off-white oil weighing 21.6 g. It could not be crystallized. Anal. ($C_{12}H_{17}BrO_2S$) C,H.

To a solution of 20.2 g diisopropylamine in 200 mL anhydrous THF that had been cooled to -10 °C under a He atmosphere with an external ice/MeOH bath, there was added 125 mL of a 1.6 M solution of butyllithium in hexane. There was then added, in sequence, 5.1 mL of dry CH_3CN followed by the dropwise addition of 15.3 g 4-bromo-1,3-diethoxy-2-ethylthiobenzene diluted with a little anhydrous THF. There was only a modest color development. Analysis by thin-layer chromatography showed that the reaction components were largely starting bromide and only a little product nitrile. An additional 2.5 mL dry CH_3CN was added, followed immediately by a solution of lithium diisopropylamide prepared separately from 14 mL isopropylamine in 50 mL hexane treated with 60 mL butyllithium solution. There was an immediate darkening of color. After 15 min stirring, the bromo starting material was gone, by TLC analysis. The reaction mixture was then poured into 1 L dilute H_2SO_4. The organic phase was separated and the aqueous fraction extracted with 2x100 mL CH_2Cl_2. These extracts were pooled, washed with H_2O, dried with anhydrous K_2CO_3, and the solvent was removed under vacuum. The residue was distilled at 0.3 mm/Hg yielding two fractions. The first fraction boiled at 124-145 °C and gave an amber liquid weighing 2.4 g. It was largely starting bromo compound with a little nitrile, and was not processed further. The second fraction distilled at 140-190 °C and weighed 6.2 g. Although this was largely product nitrile, it was quite complex by chromatographic analysis. It was redistilled at 0.3 mm/Hg and several fractions taken. The material collected at 145-165 °C weighed 3.2 g and was approximately 80% 3,5-diethoxy-4-ethylthiophenylacetonitrile by TLC assay. This was used in the subsequent reduction. The earlier fraction in this second distillation (130-145 °C) weighed 2.1 g but contained only 50% product nitrile by TLC analysis, and was discarded.

A solution of LAH in anhydrous THF under N_2 (20 mL of a 1.0 M solution) was cooled to 0 °C and vigorously stirred. There was added, dropwise, 0.53 mL 100% H_2SO_4, followed by 3.0 g 3,5-diethoxy-4-ethylthiophenylacetonitrile diluted with a little anhydrous THF. The reaction mixture was stirred at room temperature for 1 h, and then at reflux on the steam bath for an additional 0.5 h. After cooling back to room temperature, there was added IPA to destroy the excess hydride and 10% NaOH to bring the reaction to a basic pH and convert the aluminum oxide to a loose, white, filterable consistency. This was removed by filtration, and washed first with THF followed by IPA. The combined filtrate and washes were stripped of solvent under vacuum, the residue added to 1 L dilute H_2SO_4. This was washed with 2x75 mL CH_2Cl_2, made basic with 25% NaOH, and extracted with 3x100 mL CH_2Cl_2. After combining, the solvent was removed under vacuum providing a residue that was distilled. A fraction boiling at 135-150 °C at 0.3 mm/Hg weighed 1.2 g and was a light yellow oil. This was dissolved in 20 mL of IPA, and neutralized with 17 drops of concentrated HCl which produces white crystals spontaneously. These were dissolved by bringing the IPA suspension to a boil on the steam bath and, with stirring, there was added 40 mL of hot anhydrous Et_2O. There was the immediate formation of crystals which were removed by filtration, washed with an IPA/Et_2O mixture, followed by Et_2O. After air drying there was obtained 1.0 g of 3,5-diethoxy-4-ethylthiophenethylamine hydrochloride (4-T-TRIS) as sparkling white crystals. The mp was 177-178 °C. Anal. ($C_{14}H_{24}ClNO_2S$) C,H.

DOSAGE: greater than 200 mg.

DURATION: unknown.

QUALITATIVE COMMENTS: (with 120 mg) "Maybe there is some physical effect? There is a slight tingling or numbing of my hands and fingers, and a certain amount of gas. It is certainly negative on the mental side, but go up slowly due to the physical."

(with 200 mg) "There was a passing awareness at the third hour. Otherwise, no effects, either mental or physical."

EXTENSIONS AND COMMENTARY: As with the sulfur-free counterpart, the phenethylamine with three ethyl groups hanging out from it is not active in man. It doesn't matter where the sulfur is, since the 3-T-TRIS isomer is also without action. The labor of making the amphetamine analogues of these triethylated things seems hardly worth the effort.

There are no differences but differences of degree
between different degrees of difference
and no difference.

William James, under nitrous oxide; 1882

APPENDIX A: LONG INDEX TO BOOK II

Apiole *see under* DMMDA, #58
Apiolin *see under* TMA, #157
APM *see under* AEM, #1
ARIADNE #8 page 475
Artemisia *see under* TMA, #157
Asaricin *see under* TMA, #157
Asarone (α,ß, and γ)*see under* TMA, #157
ASB #9 page 480
ASM *see under* AEM, #1
4-Astito-2,5-dimethoxyphenethylamine *see under* 2C-I, #33
Asymbescaline *see* ASM, #9
AUM *see under* AEM, #1
B #10 page 484
Basil *see under* TMA, #157
Bay *see under* TMA, #157
BDB *see* J, #94
BEATRICE #11 page 486
Benzescaline *see under* PE, #141
1-(1,3-Benzodioxol-5-yl)-2-butanamine *see* J, #94
1-(1,3-Benzodioxol-5-yl)-2-ethanamine *see* MDPEA, #115
1-(1,3-Benzodioxol-5-yl)-2-hexanamine *see under* METHYL-K, #129
1-(1,3-Benzodioxol-5-yl)-2-pentanamine *see under* METHYL-K, #129
1-(1,3-Benzodioxol-5-yl)-2-propanamine *see* MDA, #100
Benzylamines *see under* PEA, #142
4-Benzyl-2,5-dimethoxyamphetamine *see under* DOAM, #61
N-Benzyl-2,5-dimethoxy-4-iodoamphetamine *see under* IDNNA, #90
N-Benzyl-2,5-dimethoxy-4-iodo-N-methylamphetamine *see under* IDNNA,
     #90
N-Benzyl-3,4-methylenedioxyamphetamine *see* MDBZ, #103
N-Benzyl-MDA *see* MDBZ, #102
4-Benzyloxy-3,5-dimethoxyamphetamine *see* 3C-BZ, #21
4-Benzyloxy-3,5-dimethoxyphenethylamine *see under* PE, #141
N-Benzylpiperizine *see under* PEA, #142
BETA-D *see* ß-D, #51
Beta-deuteromescaline *see* ß-D, #51
Betel pepper *see* under TMA, #157
Beth State *see under* ALEPH-7, #7
2,5-bis-(methylthio)-4-methylamphetamine *see* BIS-TOM, #12
2,5-bis-(methylthio)-4-methylphenethylamine *see under* BIS-TOM, #12
BIS-TOM #12 page 487
BL-3912 *see* ARIADNE, #8
BOAD *see under* BOHD, #16
BOB #13 page 490

2,4-DNNA *see under* 2,4-DMA, #53
2,6-DNNA *see under* 3,4-DMA, #55
3,5-DNNA *see under* 3,4-DMA, #55
DOA *see under* DOC, #64
DOAA *see under* DOC, #64
DOAM #61 page 617
DOB #62 page 620
DOBU #63 page 622
DOBZ *see under* DOAM, #61
DOC #64 page 626
DOCPM *see under* DOBU, #63
DOEF #65 page 628
DOEH *see under* DOEF, #65
DOET #66 page 631
DOF *see under* 2C-F, #26
DOHE *see under* DOAM, #61
DOI #67 page 633
DOIB *see under* DOBU, #63
DOIP *see under* DOPR, #71
DOM #68 page 637
Ψ-DOM #69 page 643
DOM-AI *see under* PEA, #142
DOM-AT *see under* PEA, #142
DON #70 page 646
DOONE *see* METHYL-MA, #130
DOPR #71 page 647
DOSB *see under* DOBU, #63
DOT *see* ALEPH, #3
DOTB *see under* DOBU, #63
E #72 page 650
4-EA *see under* 4-MA, #97
EA-1297 *see* MDPEA, #115
EA-1298 *see* MDA, #100
EA-1302 *see under* PEA, #142
EA-1306 *see* M, #96
EA-1316 *see* 3,4-DMA, #55
EA-1319 *see* TMA, #157
EA-1322 *see under* ARIADNE, #8
Ecstasy *see* MDMA, #109
EDA *see under* MDA, #100
EDEN *see* METHYL-J, #128
EDMA *see* MDMC, #110
EEE #73 page 654

APPENDIX B: GLOSSARY

This is a dictionary of terms that have commonly been used in and about the area of psychedelic drug experimentation. Many of these are common words, but in immediate application to this particular area of inquiry, they can carry different meanings than usual. These are our definitions of terms we have used in this book.

Ambrose Bierce composed a Devil's Dictionary over the course of 25 years, at the turn of the last century. His definition of a dictionary is most apt:

DICTIONARY, n. A malevolent literary device for cramping the growth of a language and making it hard and inelastic. This dictionary, however, is a most useful work.

We hope that our little dictionary, too, will prove useful, and that our efforts to give simple descriptions of what can be complex concepts will serve to clarify what we have written.

ACUTE, adj. A single exposure to a drug.

AFTERGLOW, n. A state of total peace and contentedness that can follow on the heels of a psychedelic experience. There is a well-known term, POT, or post-orgasmic tranquility, that implies a drifting, a de-stressed period of inattention and reflection, calmness and placidity; this can also be a major part of the drop-off and recovery period following the use of a psychedelic. It is the smile on the face of the Buddha.

ALERT, n. The first clue that a drug will show activity. Each researcher, with experience, comes to recognize his own personal alert. It may be a tinge of lightheadedness, a chill, or a brief raising of the hair on his neck, and simply serves as a reminder that he took something half an hour (or a couple of hours) ago. Sometimes an alert can follow very soon after the taking of the drug, without any further effects becoming apparent until some time later. Each person's alert tends to be experienced consistently, regardless of the nature of the drug being researched.

ANOREXIC, adj. (Or anorectic.) Related to anorexia, meaning loss of appetite. Some of the psychedelic drugs, especially those with a considerable stimulant component, can quite effectively wipe out all desire to eat. Unfortunately (for most of us), there are others, especially those with a strong sensory component, which achieve quite the opposite effect.

ASC   Altered state of consciousness.

ASSAYING, see RUNNING UP.

AWARENESS, see ALERT.

BASELINE, n. The normal psychological and physical state of a person prior to the start of an experiment which, once regained, marks the end of that experiment.

BODY LOAD, n. Any sense of unease in the physical body, such as nausea, aching, heaviness, or the feeling of being "wired," or over-stimulated. For some people, diarrhea is considered a form of body load, while for others it is an expected part of most psychedelic experiments, and is regarded as a welcome cleaning out of the system. One elderly and very experienced psychologist considered nausea and vomiting to be a positive event; he welcomed it as a sign that the experimental drug was active, and for him, it meant the beginning of his experience. His attitude, however, was very much the exception and we haven't heard of anyone else doing this research who regards nausea quite that fondly.

CENTRAL NERVOUS SYSTEM   The part of the nervous system that involves the brain, the brain stem, and the spinal column. It is to this system that all senses connect (the afferent pathways) and it is from this system that all motor commands emanate (the efferent pathways).

CHRONIC, adj. Repeated exposure to a drug.

CLEAN, adj. To be in that state of body which results from having declined the use of any psychoactive drug for a period of time. For some people, that might well be months, or even years, but for those who are continuously experimenting with new materials, and who are primarily worried about the masking of effects due to tolerance or refractoriness, it is more likely to mean a period of four or five days.

CNS, *see* CENTRAL NERVOUS SYSTEM

CONSCIOUS, adj. Used most commonly in phrases such as "the conscious mind," or "being conscious of." It is the term applied to that part of the human psyche which is aware of its surroundings, and is capable of being aware of its own existence and observing its own functioning. It has been speculated that the conscious mind also serves as a filter, to prevent the activities of the unconscious psyche from flooding the field of waking awareness. In sleep, the conscious, self-aware mind is usually, for the most part, at rest, and the unconscious part of the psyche becomes activated.

CONTACT HIGH, n. A common occurrence in a group experiment with a psychedelic drug is that a drug-free observer becomes aware that he is experiencing some effects of the material being used by the others. The altered state has become contagious. Animals in the household are especially prone to this kind of unintentional participation, usually appearing to enjoy it immensely. There is no known scientific explanation for this phenomenon.

CROSS-TOLERANCE, n. The decrease or loss of response to a drug due to recent (or prolonged) exposure to a different drug that displays some pharmacological similarities. *see also* TOLERANCE.

DARTING, n. A sudden and unexpected neurological firing that produces a momentary contraction of the musculature. It may occasionally occur when falling asleep while still at a plus two level of effect. It also occurs under normal conditions involving no drug at all.

DECLINE, n. or v. The period that follows the plateau, during which there is a loss of the drug's effects and an eventual recovery of one's baseline state. From person to person, this is the most variable of the time periods in a drug experiment. It has also been called recovering, tapering off, or dropping off.

DEVELOPING, v. The period of change from the onset of effects to the achievement of the plateau. It is also called the transition. The temporal sequence terminology is: taking the drug, alerting, developing, plateauing, declining, and reestablishment of (or being at) baseline.

DROPPING, *see* TAKING, *also see* DECLINING.

DRUG-DRUG INTERACTIONS, *see* PIGGYBACKING, PRIMER *and* SYN-
ERGISM.

DRUG-FREE, *see* CLEAN.

ENERGY TREMOR, n. A sensation of heightened responsiveness and sensitivity which may be actually experienced as a fine body tremor with visible shaking, or simply felt as excitement.

EUPHORIA, n. "Eu-" is a prefix that means "normal." Euphoria is from the Greek, euphoria, literally a "bearing well," from eu, meaning well, and pherein, to bear. The original meaning is a normal state of feeling, as opposed to dysphoria, which means an abnormal state of feeling. In the field of medicine, to give another example, the term euthyroid means a normal, healthy state of the thyroid gland, as opposed to dysthyroid, which indicates an abnormal condition of that gland (usually either hyper- or hypothyroid).
    The fact that the word euphoria has come to mean a state of feeling better — or much, much better — than usual, should give us pause. The implication is that our customary state is one of dysphoria, and that what has come to be considered the proper and normal way to feel in our everyday life is, in actuality, a state of depression.
    This term must not be confused with U-4-E-uh, a name given to the drug 4-methylaminorex.

EXPERIENCED TRAVELER A person who can remember to feed the cats while under the influence of a psychedelic drug.

FANTASY, n. The eyes-closed construction of an interior world which can become believable to the point where the subject confuses it with objective reality, until and unless he opens his eyes. At high dosage levels of a psychedelic drug, some subjects may forget to open their eyes occasionally, and may find themselves totally captured by and immersed in the fantasy landscape and interactions, as happens in normal dreaming.

FLASH-BACK, n. The rare but not unknown recapitulation of a psychedelic experience at a time when there is no drug present. A reasonable explanation is that there had been, during a past psychedelic experience, some unusual stimulus which had become associated with it, and that, at some subsequent time, a re-experiencing of that unusual stimulus could reprecipitate the psychedelic state. The main reason that the average man views this phenomenon as something negative, is that the average man has been taught to view the psychedelic state as something negative.

FUGUE STATE, n. As used in this book, a transient disorientation that separates the cognitive part of oneself from the sensory part. There is a loss of understanding of the symbolic interpretations of words and things, with only the literal and tangible meanings left for personal use. This is our definition of the word, not that of the medical profession.

GRAM, n. The basic unit of weight on the metric scale, a system used for weights and distances and volumes in all countries other than the United States and, I believe, Brunei. The common subdivisions of the gram is into a thousand parts called milligrams, or a million parts called micrograms. Imagine that you are sitting down to eat a couple of eggs over easy. You take the salt shaker, and give three or four light shakes of salt over the surface of your breakfast. That is about a fourth of a gram of salt, or 250 milligrams. This is equivalent to the weight of a typical dose of mescaline. And in that 250 milligrams of salt there are maybe 5,000 grains, or individual crystals. Each grain weighs maybe 50 micrograms, which is equivalent to the weight of a low-level dose of LSD.

HALLUCINATION, n. An extremely rare phenomenon, in which a completely convincing reality surrounds a person, with his eyes open, a reality that he alone can experience and interact with. The inducement of hallucinations is a property that is commonly attributed to psychedelic drugs, but in reality is virtually non- existent in the use of such materials. In almost all psychedelic experiences undergone by normal, healthy people, there is an awareness of real surroundings. Visual distortions are common, but they are not confused with objective reality by the subject; they are known to be visual distortions and appreciated as such. The delusional anesthetic drugs, such as scopolamine and ketamine, on the other hand, can and do produce true hallucinations.

HALLUCINOGENS, n. A misleading and inaccurate synonym for psychedelic drugs.

HAND IN THE AIR In any psychedelic experience involving two or more people, there can be a shifting of one's reality reference point and a concomitant potential for mental game-playing. In our research group, a phrase that is unquestioned as being a prelude to a not-game comment is, "Hand in the air." It means that whatever follows is a serious, non-stoned, non-mind-fuck statement. "I smell smoke" could be the entry to an editorial on cigarette smoking or a remark on some aspect of politics. But, "Hand in the air; I smell smoke," is intended to cut right through any fantasy or game and must be taken seriously. This particular agreement, or rule, is never violated.

HARDHEAD, n. There is an occasional person who requires 200 milligrams of MDMA, or 300 micrograms of LSD, just to get some beginnings of effect. Whatever the drug might be, he will need twice or five times the dosage required by most other people. This may be due to psychological barriers that must be overcome, or it may be due to the fact that he was born with a nervous system and physical chemistry which is unusually insensitive to the effects of drugs. The term hardhead implies a thick, tough skull, of course, and is often used by such subjects to describe themselves, always with a certain amount of pride.

HITCHHIKING, v. Sometimes an innocent, drug-free person will find himself strangely disturbed or uncomfortable in the presence of an experimental subject who is, unknown to him, experiencing the effects of a psychedelic drug; for instance in the checkout line at the supermarket. This unconscious awareness (or contact high) can produce a feeling of irritation, or even overt hostility, in the inadvertent hitchhiker, and his or her distress is all the worse for having no apparent or understandable cause. The responsible psychedelic researcher does not go out in public when under the influence, or if he must do so, he takes care not to risk such intrusion on the unconscious psyches of strangers.

IDIOT, n. A person of either sex who drives a car, motorcycle, or even a bicycle, for that matter, on a public road while under the influence of a psychedelic drug. Most researchers in this area have done it at least once, sometimes in an emergency, but only in a life-and-death situation is it excusable.

IMAGERY, n. Figures, lines and shapes of all kinds, including fine filigree and intricate patterns, superimposed on the dark visual field behind closed eyes. Music can serve as a template for the construction of these images. There is no confusion of realities as can happen with fantasy, but instead, a continuing complexity and richness of design. Such images disappear upon the opening of the eyes. To be precise, they should be referred to as eyes-closed imagery. Patterns and movements seen with the eyes open are called visual changes or visual images.

INFLATION, n. An exhilarating sense of self-importance, self-validation and fearless power. It is essential that any researcher seeking insight into the workings of the human mind experience this radiant state at least once, in order to learn its nature and, by contrast, the nature of a normal, well-balanced state of integration and self-validation. It is also important to his/her under-standing of psychological inflation in emotionally disturbed people and in the rulers of certain nations.

INGESTION, *see* TAKING

INTOXICATION, n. This word has the same general meaning in the psychedelic area as it has among drinkers of alcohol and people in love.

KETAMINE STATE Used to indicate a state of consciousness alteration which involves a large degree of dissociation from the body. Users of ketamine can become adept at remaining integrated with their physical world by carefully monitoring their dosage levels and keeping them low, but most ketamine use tends to result in separation from the body and its concerns. We are strongly prejudiced against psychedelic drugs which cause such mind-body separation, as we are against any drug which causes separation from feelings and emotions. However, we acknowledge that the ketamine state can be highly instructive for researchers trying to understand the functions of the human mind.

LAUNCHING, *see* TAKING

MACHO, adj. This describes a person of either sex who pushes his limits too much in experimentation with psychedelics. He always strives to take a higher and yet higher dosage, to prove that he can weather the storm. Such a person should be encouraged to do some intensive insight work into his compulsion, which is essentially self-destructive.

MINUS, n. On the quantitative potency scale (-, ±, +, ++, +++), there were no effects observed.

MYDRIASIS, n. Enlargement of the pupil of the eye.

NAIVE, adj. An adjective used to describe a person who has had no personal experience with any psychedelic drug. More properly, the term used should be "drug-naive."

NIBBLING, v. This is a jargon term for running up, in small increments, the human evaluations of a new compound. (See under "running up")

NOISE, n. A term used in describing the inner busyness of the mind, the excessive or annoying mental input, produced by certain psychedelic drugs, or characteristic of the initial — transition — stages of some drug experiments. It can also result simply from too high a dosage level.

OFF BASELINE, *see* ALERT

PARESTHESIA, n. A peripheral response to a drug which can be felt as tingling, pins-and-needles, or hair standing on end; it might take the form of a chill (even if the air is warm), or a feeling that one's skin is crawling.

PIGGYBACKING, v. A study of the interaction of two different drugs, the second being administered in place of a supplement to the first. Any deviation from the effects that would have followed a supplement of the original drug will give additional information as to the nature of the second drug.

PLATEAU, n. or v. The period of time spent at the level of maximum effect of whatever drug has been ingested, at the particular dosage given. It is preceded by the transition and development, and is followed by the decline. As a verb, "to plateau" means to reach that level of drug effect.

PLUS/MINUS, n. (±) The level of effectiveness of a drug that indicates a threshold action. If a higher dosage produces a greater response, then the plus/minus (±) was valid. If a higher dosage produces nothing, then this was a false positive.

PLUS ONE, n. (+) The drug is quite certainly active. The chronology can be determined with some accuracy, but the nature of the drug's effects are not yet apparent.

PLUS TWO, n. (++) Both the chronology and the nature of the action of a drug are unmistakably apparent. But you still have some choice as to whether you will accept the adventure, or rather just continue with your ordinary day's plans (if you are an experienced researcher, that is). The effects can be allowed a predominent role, or they may be repressible and made secondary to other chosen activities.

PLUS THREE, n. (+++) Not only are the chronology and the nature of a drug's action quite clear, but ignoring its action is no longer an option. The subject is totally engaged in the experience, for better or worse.

PLUS FOUR, n. (++++) A rare and precious transcendental state, which has been called a "peak experience," a "religious experience," "divine transformation," a "state of Samadhi" and many other names in other cultures. It is not connected to the +1, +2 and +3 of the measuring of a drug's intensity. It is a state of bliss, a *participation mystique*, a connectedness with both the interior and exterior universes, which has come about after the ingestion of a psychedelic drug, but which is not necessarily repeatable with a subsequent ingestion of that same drug. If a drug (or technique or process) were ever to be discovered which would consistently produce a plus four experience in all human beings, it is conceivable that it would signal the ultimate evolution, and perhaps the end of, the human experiment.

POTENTIATION, n. The influence of an inactive drug on the effects realized from an active drug.

PRIMER, n. A word used in the study of the interaction of two different drugs, one of them without activity. The inactive, "primer," drug is administered and, while it is still in the system, the second, "primed," drug is given. Any activity observed which is different from that expected from the primed drug alone will be a measure of potentiation. The effect may be one of enhanced action; it may be that of decreased action; it may be a change in either quality or duration of activity.

PRIMING, see PRIMER

PRODRUG, n. A chemical that is intrinsically without activity at a receptor site, but which is converted (activated) by the metabolic processes of the body.

PSYCHE, n. A term used to encompass the non-physical human mind, conscious and unconscious, including feelings and emotions. The word, psyche, has come into modern use as a substitute for the more ancient, but scientifically unapproachable, concept of soul.

PSYCHEDELIC, n. or adj. As an adjective, meaning pertaining to a change in the normal state of consciousness, usually with some accompanying changes in the acuity of the senses. Also, "mind-manifesting." As a noun, a drug that can allow such changes to occur. The word was coined by Doctor Humphrey Osmond in the 1950's.

PSYCHOTOMIMETIC, n. or adj. A name given to the psychedelic drugs to emphasize some supposed similarities between certain of their effects and the psychotic state. The word unites the prefix *psychoto-* (referring to psychosis) with the suffix *-mimetic* (meaning imitation). It was one of the earliest terms used for these drugs, and one which implied medical approval of the use of such drugs, at least as research tools.

RECOVERY, *see* DECLINE

REFRACTORY, adj. The state of showing a reduced response to the action of a drug. This may be due to tolerance resulting from recent exposure, the action of some inhibitor, or a condition of health or expectation that interferes with the expected action.

RUNNING UP, v. The process of searching for activity in a new drug by a strategy of taking incrementally larger and larger doses, at time intervals which are calculated to minimize the development of tolerance. A usual pattern is an increase of either 60% or 100% of the previous dosage, following a clean period of several days, until activity is detected. There are many popular terms for this titration process, such as nibbling, assaying, or tasting.

SAMADHI, n. A word in the terminology of the Yoga which represents a direct union with ultimate reality, allowing the dissolving of the ego and an achievement of a state of bliss. Used by western researchers, the word does not necessarily imply a dissolving of ego, but a transformation of it.

SCRUDGE, n. (Defined in Book II, entry #176)

STARTING, see TAKING

STONED, adj. This generally means being under the influence of a psychoactive drug. It is a widely used word, and we have employed it in our story as carelessly as most people do. However, in writing a report on the effects of an experimental drug, there is actually an important difference between being "stoned" and being "turned-on," and the researcher should make a distinction between them. A stoning effect is one in which there is awareness of a strongly altered state of consciousness; it may be pleasurable or unpleasant. It is characterized, usually, by a general inability and disinclination to deal with concepts or to employ insight. In other words, one finds it difficult to learn anything of value. On the other hand, being turned on is simply to be aware of a change in one's mind and/or body in the direction of an increased sense of physical and mental energy. Being turned on is usually thought of as positive, whereas there are many researchers who do not enjoy being stoned at all.

STRAIGHT, adj. The state of being at baseline, with no psychedelic drug present in the body,

SUBACUTE, adj. An occasional or short-term exposure to a drug.

SUPPLEMENT, n. or v. The administration of a second dose of an active drug, during the drop-off phase of the activity of an initial dosage. The usual consequence is a prolongation of effect, with a concomitant increase in signs of toxicity.

SYNERGISM, n. The interaction of two drugs, often administered at the same time, which produces a response that is not simply additive. The summed responses may be exaggerated (positive synergy), or attenuated (inhibition).

SYNESTHESIA, n. An activation of two or more senses simultaneously; for instance, sound may be "seen" in the mind as being composed of color and shape, or a color may be "heard" as a musical note or harmony. There are innumerable examples of this melding together of the senses, and the experience is generally considered one of the most treasured effects of a psychedelic drug. There are many people who live in a world of synesthesia continuously, without benefit of drug, having been born with this ability. For the most part, they regard themselves as profoundly blessed.

TAKING, v. The actual ingestion of a drug. When there are several persons involved, any of several rituals can be followed; a toasting and clinking of glasses, the recital of an favorite prayer, or a touching of hands and brief silence. The taking of a drug has also been called "launching," "dropping," "taking off" or, simply, "starting."

TAPERING OFF, see DECLINE

TASTING, see RUNNING UP

THRESHOLD, n. A dosage of a drug that gives some detectable change from baseline. A minimum detectable effect of a drug.

TIME-DISTORTION A mis-perception or distortion concerning the subjective passage of time. With psychedelic drugs, there is almost always a sense that time is passing more slowly than usual. This may be recognized at the global level (you mean it's only been an hour since we took this stuff?), at the clock-watching level (I've been watching the second hand and I've found I can really slow it down), or at the afferent level (where, for instance, the radio pitch and the pulse rate might appear to have dropped considerably).

TITRATE, v. To determine the effective level of a drug by the sequential taking of graded doses, at separated intervals. see RUNNING UP.

TOLERANCE, n. The decrease or loss of response to a drug, due to recent or prolonged exposure to it.

TOMSO, n. or v. Used as a noun: a sulfur-containing drug, described in detail in Book II, entry #173. Used as a verb: to instigate or promote an altered state of consciousness during exposure to an ineffective dosage of a psychedelic drug, by the absorption of a modest amount of alcohol.

TRANSITION, see DEVELOPING

TRAVELER, n. A person who explores the effects of psychedelic drugs.

TURNED-ON, *see* STONED

UNCONSCIOUS, n. or adj. As an adjective, this is a simple word, meaning not being conscious. As a noun, it is a most complex word, meaning that part of the psyche which contains the building blocks of each individual identity, not accessible for most people in the everyday waking state. The sources, shapes and origins of these blocks, these components, are — to varying degrees — available to us in sleep, in certain states of mental disturbance, in hypnotic trance, meditation, artistic inspiration, and with the use of certain drugs. Intentional and conscious access to unconscious material can be achieved with the aid of psychedelic drugs, which is one of the values — and risks — of such exploration.

VISUALS, n. Changes in the visual area that are usually among the effects of a psychedelic drug. There may be an enhancement of colors, an exaggeration of light-dark contrast, a sparkling of lights, or a change in the visible texture or quality of an object. Some of the changes may reflect the mydriasis (enlargement of pupils) that is often one of the effects of such a drug. The term "visual effects" is also used to describe the apparent movement of objects in one's surroundings which may be seen with the eyes open, usually at higher than plus-two dosage levels of a psychedelic drug. These are not hallucinations, since they are known by the subject to be apparent and not objectively real, which is not the case in an hallucinatory experience.

WIRED, adj. A condition of intense neurological alertness, which suggests that the response to a given stimulus might be exaggerated by an overly sensitive nervous system.

APPENDIX C: ACKNOWLEDGEMENTS

There are here acknowledged the many sources upon which we have called for the information presented in this book. Much of it is from the scientific literature, and these citations are listed here. But as much is from the unpublished findings of a large number of individuals who have generously shared their information with us. These contributions have come from many quarters, from the crime labs of law enforcement to the seminar rooms of academia. They have included facts and suggestions ranging from drug law, to pharmacological effects, to book-writing procedures. An observation here and a comment there, when combined together, have enriched this presentation beyond what we could have done alone. Our sincere thanks to all of you, not only to those who have allowed us to list them with an acknowledgement of "personal communication" but also to those who, for whatever reason, have chosen to remain unnamed. We appreciate your contributions and respect your privacy.

Aldous, F.A.B., Barrass, B.C., Brewster, K., Buxton, D.A., Green, D.M., Pinder, R.M., Rich, P., Skeels, M. and Tutt, K.J., J. Med. Chem. **17**, 1100-1111 (1974).
Aldrich, M., personal communication.
Allen, A., personal communication.
Alles, G.A., J. Am. Chem. Soc., **54**, 271-274 (1932).
Alles, G.A., Neuropharmacology, Transactions of the Fourth Conference, The Josiah Macy Jr. Foundation, 1959, p 181-268.
Alter, J., personal communication.
Anderson III, G.M., personal communication.
Anderson III, G.M., Castagnoli Jr., N. and Kollman, P.A., NIDA Research Monograph #22, U.S.G.P.O, 1978, p 199-217.

Angrist, B.M., personal communication.
Angrist, B.M., Rotrosen, J. and Gershon, S., Psychopharmacologia **36**, 203-207 (1974).
Angrist, B.M., Schweitzer, J.W., Friedhoff, A.J. and Gershon, S., Nature **225**, 651-652 (1970).
Anon. Microgram **20**, 96 (1987).
Anon. Microgram **21**, 1 (1988).
Autun, F.T. and Kurkjian, R. Brit. J. Psychiat. **140**, 611-614 (1982).
Badiner, A., personal communication.
Bailey, K., By, A.W., Legault, D. and Verner, D., J.A.O.A.C. **58**, 62-69 (1975).
Bailey, K., Gagne, D.R. and Pike, R.K., J.A.O.A.C. **59**, 1162-1169 (1976).
Bakalar, J., personal communication.
Barfknecht, C.F. and Nichols, D.E., J. Med. Chem. **14**, 370-372 (1971).
Barfknecht, C.F., Caputo, J.F., Tobin, M.B., Dyer, D.C., Standridge, R.T., Howell, H.G., Goodwin, W.R., Partyka, R.A., Gylys, J.A. and Cavanagh, R.L., NIDA Research Monograph Series #22, 1978 p 16-26.
Battersby, A.R., Dobson, T.A., Foulkes, D.M. and Herbert, R.B., J. Chem. Soc. Perkins Trans. p 1730 (1972).
Beck, J., personal communication.
Beck, J., Harlow, D., McDonnell, D., Morgan, P.A., Rosenbaum, M. and Watson, L., Exploring Ecstasy: A description of MDMA Users, NIDA Report, September 1989.
Beck, W.S., Modern Science and the Nature of Life, Harcourt Brace, New York 1957, p 302.
Benington, F., personal communication.
Benington, F., Batelle Technical Review, 1960, p 2.
Benington, F. and Morin, R.D., J. Med. Chem. **14**, 375 (1971).
Benington, F., Morin, R.D. and Clark Jr., L.C., J. Org. Chem. **19**, 11 (1954).
Benington, F., Morin, R.D. and Clark Jr., L.C., J. Am. Chem. Soc. **76**, 5555-5556 (1954).
Benington, F., Morin, R.D. and Clark Jr., L.C., J. Org. Chem. **20**, 102 (1955).
Benington, F., Morin, R.D., Clark Jr., L.C. and Fox, R.P., J. Org. Chem. **23**, 1979 (1958).
Beringer, K., Der Meskalinrausch Seine Geschichte und Erscheinungsweise, Verlag von Julius Springer, Berlin (1927).
Braun, G., personal communication.
Braun, G., Shulgin, A.T. and Sargent III, T., J. Labelled Compounds and Radiopharm. **14**, 767-773 (1978).
Braun, U., personal communication.
Braun, U. and Kalbhen, D.A., Deut. Med. Wochen. **42**, 1614-1615 (1972).
Braun, U., Shulgin, A.T., Braun, G., J. Pharm. Sci. **69**, 192-195 (1980).
Braun, U., Shulgin, A.T., Braun, G., Arzn. Forsch. **30**, 825-830 (1980).
Braun, U., Shulgin, A.T., Braun, G. and Sargent III, T., J. Med. Chem. **20**, 1543-

1546 (1977).

Brown, W.T., McGeer, P.L. and Moser, I., Can. Psychiat. J. 13, 91-92 (1968).

Bruckner, V., J. Prakt. Chem. 138, 268-274 (1933).

Buffum, J., personal communication.

Bunnell, S., personal communication.

By, A.W., Duhaime, R. and Lodge, B.A., For. Sci. International 49, 159-170 (1991).

Callaway, E., personal communication.

Callaway, J., personal communication.

Campbell, H., Cline, W., Evans, M., Lloyd, J. and Peck, A.W., Europ. J. Clin. Pharmacol. 6, 170-176 (1973).

Carlino, J., personal communication.

Carlino, L., personal communication.

Carlsson, A., Corrodi, H. and Magnusson, T., Helv. Chim. Acta 46, 1231-1235 (1963).

Cash, L., personal communication.

Cass, H., personal communication.

Cassels, B.K., personal communication.

Cassels, B.K. and Gomez-Jeria, J.S., J. Psychoactive Drugs 17, 129-130 (1985).

Castagnoli Jr., N., personal communication.

Charalampous, K.D. and Tansey, L.W. J. Pharm. and Exptl. Therap. 155, 318-329 (1967).

Charalampous, K.D., Orengo, A., Walker, K.E. and Kinross-Wright, J., J. Pharm. Exptl. Therap. 145, 242-246 (1964).

Charalampous, K.D., Walker, K.E. and Kinross-Wright, J., Psychopharmacologia 9, 48 (1966).

Cheng, A.C. and Castagnoli Jr., N., J. Med. Chem. 27, 513-520 (1984).

Cheng, H.C., Long, J.P., Nichols, D.E. and Barfknecht, C.F., J. Pharm. Exptl. Therap. 188, 114-123 (1974).

Cimbura, G., J. Can. Med. Assn. 110, 1263-1267 (1974).

Clark Jr., L.C., Benington, F. and Morin, R.D., J. Med. Chem. 8, 353-355 (1965).

Clark, C.C., J. Forensic Sci. 29, 1056-1071 (1984)

Cohn, R., personal communication.

Collins, C., personal communication.

Cooper, P.D. and Walters, G.C., Nature 238, 96-98 (1972).

Coutts, R.T and Malicky, J.L., Can. J. Chem. 51, 1402-1409 (1973).

Cozzi, N., personal communication.

Dal Cason, T.A., personal communication.

Dal Cason, T.A., J. Forensic Sci. 34, 928-961 (1989).

Dal Cason, T.A. and Janesko, J.L., National Meeting of the American Academy of the Forensic Sciences, San Diego, CA February, 1987.

Davis, B.A. and Boulton, A.A., Eur. J. Mass Spec. Biochem. Med. Environ.

Res. **1**, 149-153 (1980).

Devgan, O.N. and Bokadia, M.M. Austral. J. Chem. **21**, 3001-3003 (1968).

de Zan, P., Microgram **4**, 5-11 (1971).

de Zorzi, C. and Cavalli, A. Zacchia, **10**, 3-11 (1974).

Dittrich, A. Psychopharmacologia **21**, 229-237 (1971).

Doblin, Rick, personal communication.

Domelsmith, L.N., Eaton, T.A., Houk, K.N., Anderson III, G.M., Glennon, R.A., Shulgin, A.T., Castagnoli Jr., N. and Kollman, P.A., J. Med. Chem. **24**, 1414-1421 (1981).

Downing, J., personal communication.

Duberman, J. personal communication.

Dudlettes, S.D., personal communication.

Ehrlich, B., personal communication.

Ely, R., personal communication.

Entel, J., Ruof, C.H. and Howard, H.C., J. Am. Chem. Soc. **73**, 2365 (1951).

Fairchild, M.D., Doctorate Thesis, Department of Pharmacology, University of California at Los Angeles, 1963.

Fentiman Jr., A.F. and Foltz, R.L., J. Labelled Compounds Pharmaceut. **12**, 69-78 (1976).

Ferguson, M., personal communication.

Fijusawa, T. and Deguchi, Y., J. Pharm. Soc. Japan **74**, 975-977 (1954).

Fischer, E., Biological Mechanisms of Schizophrenia and Schizophrenia-like Psychoses, Mitsuda and Fukuda, Eds. Georg Thieine, Stuttgart, 1975 p 177.

Freye, H., personal communication.

Friedhoff, A.J. and Schweitzer, J.W., Dis. Nerv. System **29**, 455-456 (1968).

Friedhoff, A.J. and Van Winkle, E., Nature **194**, 897 (1962).

Fritscher, R., personal communication.

Garfinkel, S., personal communication.

Gerdes, J.M., personal communication.

Gerdes, J.M., Mathis, C.A. amd Shulgin, A.T. Tetrahedron Lett. **29**, 6537-6540 (1988).

Gill, S., personal communication.

Glennon, R.A., Life Sciences **39**, 825-830 (1986).

Glennon, R.A., Ismaiel, A.E-K.M., Martin, B., Poff, D. and Sutton, M., Pharmacol. Biochem. Behav. **31**, 9-13 (1988).

Glennon, R.A., Liebowitz, S.M. and Anderson III, G.M., J. Med. Chem. **23**, 294-299 (1980).

Glennon, R.A., Liebowitz, S.M. and Mack, E.C., J. Med. Chem. **21**, 822-825 (1978).

Glennon, R.A., Seggel, M.R., Soine, W.H., Herrick-Davis, K., Lyon, R.A. and Titeler, M., J. Med. Chem. **31**, 5-7 (1988).

Glennon, R.A., Young, R., Benington, F. and Morin, R.D., J. Med. Chem. **25**, 1163-1168 (1982).

Gomez-Jeria, J.S., Cassels, B.K., Clavijo, R., Vargas, V., Quintana, R. and Saavedra-Aguilar, J.C., Microgram **19**, 153-161 (1986).
Gomez-Jeria, J.S., Cassels, B.K. and Saavedra-Aguilar, J.C., Eur. J. Med. Chem. **22**, 433-437 (1987).
Greer, G., personal communication.
Grinspoon, D., personal communication.
Grinspoon, L., personal communication.
Grof, S., personal communication.
Gross, D., personal communication.
Gross, P., personal communication.
Grotjahn, D., personal communication.
Hammond, M.L., Zambias, R.A., Chang, M.N., Jensen, N.P., McDonald, J., Thompson, K., Boulton, R.J., Kopka, I.E., Hand, K.M., Opas, E.E., Luell, S., Bach, T., Davies, P., MacIntyre, D.E., Bonney, R.J. and Humes, J.L., J. Med. Chem. **33**, 908-918 (1990).
Hansen, K., personal communication.
Hardman, H.F., Haavik, C.O. and Seevers, M.H., Toxicol. Appl. Pharmacol. **25**, 299-309 (1973).
Harley-Mason, J., J. Chem. Soc. 200-203 (1953).
Harlow, D., personal communication.
Harris, R., personal communication.
Henderson, G., personal communication.
Herbert, P., personal communication.
Hey, P., Quart. J. Pharmacy Pharmacol. **20**, 129-134 (1947).
Hipkiss, D., personal communication.
Ho, B.T., Tansey, L.W., Balster, R.L., An, R., McIsaac, W.M. and Harris, R.T., J. Med. Chem. **13**, 134-135 (1970).
Hoffman, A., personal communication.
Hofmann, A., personal communication.
Hollister, L.E. and Friedhoff, A.J., Nature **210**, 1377-1378 (1966).
Hope, T., personal communication.
Horowitz, M., personal communication.
Ishii, H., Ueda, E., Nakajima, K., Ishida, T., Ishikawa, K.I., Harada, K.I., Ninomiya, I., Naito, T. and Kiguchi, T., Chem. Pharm. Bull. **26**, 864 (1978).
Jacob III, P., personal communication.
Jacob III, P., Anderson III, G., Meshul, C.K., Shulgin, A.T. and Castagnoli Jr., N. J. Med. Chem. **20**, 1235-1239 (1977).
Jacob III, P., Kline, T. and Castagnoli Jr., N., J. Med. Chem. **22**, 662-671 (1979).
Jacob III, P. and Shulgin, A.T., Syn. Commun. **11**, 957 (1981).
Jacob III, P. and Shulgin, A.T., Syn. Commun. **11**, 969 (1981).
Jacob III, P. and Shulgin, A.T., J. Med. Chem. **24**, 1348 (1981).
Jacob III, P. and Shulgin, A.T., J. Med. Chem. **26**, 746-752 (1983).

Jacob III, P. and Shulgin, A.T., J. Med. Chem. **27**, 881 (1984).

Jansen, M.P.J.M. Rec. Trav. Chim. **50**, 291-312 (1931).

Jones, H.B. and Jones, H.C., Sensual Drugs, Cambridge University Press, Cambridge, 1977.

Jones, R., personal communication.

Joy, D., personal communication.

Kahn, R.S., Wetzler, S., Asnis, G.M., Kling, M.A., Suckow, R.F. and van Praag, H.M., Psychopharmacology **100**, 339-344 (1990).

Kaiser, C., Trost, B.M., Beeson, J. and Weinstock, J., J. Org. Chem. **30**, 3972-3975 (1965).

Kantor, R., personal communication.

Kaplan, D., personal communication.

Karoum, F., Potkin, S., Chuang, L.W., Murphy, D.L., Liebowitz, M.R. and Wyatt, R.J., Biol. Psychiat. **19**, 165-178 (1984).

Karoum, F., Potkin, S.G., Murphy, D.L. and Wyatt, R.J., Noncatecholic Phenethylamines, Ed. Mosnaim and Wolf, Marcel Dekker, New York, 1980, p 178-191.

Kennedy, A., personal communication.

Kline, T., personal communication.

Klug, E. Deut. Apoth.-Ztg. (1971), Chem. Abst. **74**:115965p.

Kornfeld, H., personal communication.

Kulkarni, A.S., Biol. Psychiat. **6**, 177 (1973).

Lemaire, B., personal communication.

Lemaire, D., personal communication.

Lemaire, D., Jacob III, P. and Shulgin, A.T. J. Pharm. Pharmacol. **37**, 575-577 (1985).

Leminger, O., Chem. Prum. **22**, 553 (1972).

Lenz, B., personal communication.

Li, W.Y. and Lien, E.J., Bull. Oriental Healing Arts Inst. of the U.S.A. **8**, 23-30 (1983).

Lindeke, B., Paulsen-Sörman, U., Hallström, G., Khuthier, A-H., Cho, A.K. and Krammerer, R.C. Drug Metab. Disp. **10**, 700-705 (1982).

Love, W., personal communication.

Lloyd, D., personal communication.

Lombrozo, L., personal communication.

Lopez, I., personal communication.

Luduena, F.P., C.R. Soc. Biol. **121**, 368 (1936).

Mannich, C., Arch. Pharm. **242**, 506 (1919).

March, D.F. and Herring, D.A., J. Pharm. Exptl. Therap. **100**, 298-308 (1950).

Mathis, C.A., personal communication.

Mathis, C.A., Shulgin, A.T. and Sargent III, T., J. Labelled Compounds Radiopharm. **23**, 115-125 (1986).

Mathis, C.A., Shulgin, A.T., Yano, Y. and Sargent III, T., Appl. Radiat. Isot.

37, 865-972 (1986).
Matin, S.B., Callery, P.S., Zweig, J.S., O'Brien, A., Rapoport, R. and Castagnoli Jr., N., J. Med. Chem. **17**, 877-882 (1974).
Matsuhiro, B. and Furst, A., J. Med. Chem. **13**, 973 (1970).
Mauthner, F., Ann. **499**, 102 (1926).
McKay, G., Cooper, J.K., Hawes, E.M., Roy, S.D. and Midha, K.K., Xenobiotica **13**, 257-264 (1983).
McClure, M., personal communication.
McKenna, D.J., personal communication.
McKenna, D.J., Mathis, C.A., Shulgin, A.T., Sargent III, T. and Saavedra, J.M., Eur. J. Pharmacology **137**, 289-290 (1987).
McKenna, T., personal communication.
McKinney, H., personal communication.
Merchant, J.R. and Mountwala, A.J., Current Sci. (India) **26**, 211 (1957).
Merchant, J.R. and Mountwala, A.J., J. Org. Chem. **23**, 1774 (1958).
Metzner, R., personal communication.
Michaux, R., Experimental Brain Research **3**, 178-183 (1967).
Midha, K.K., Cooper, J.K., Bailey, K. and Hubbard, J.W., Xenobiotica **11**, 137-146 (1981).
Millay, J., Personal communication.
Mitchell, R., The Beaver, Spring, 1968 p 24-26.
Mohandas, J., Slaytor, M. and Watson, T.R., Austral. J. Chem. **22**, 1803-1804 (1969).
Moore, J., personal communication.
Moore, M.M., personal communication.
Morin, R.D., Benington, F., Mitchell, S.R., Beaton, J.M., Bradley, R.J. and Smythies, J.R., Experientia **31**, 93-94 (1975).
Mueller, E.A., Sunderland, T. and Murphy, D.L., J. Clin. Endocrinol. Metab. **61**, 1179-1184 (1985).
Muller, A., Meszaros, M., Kormendy, K. and Kucsman, A., J. Org. Chem. **17**, 787-799 (1952).
Naranjo, C., personal communication.
Naranjo, C., The Healing Journey, Pantheon Books, Random Press, New York, 1973.
Naranjo, C., Shulgin, A.T. and Sargent III, T., Med. Pharmacol. Exp. **17**, 359-364 (1967).
Naylor, D.A., personal communication.
Nichols, D.E., personal communication.
Nichols, D.E., Barfknecht, C.F., Long, J.P., Standridge, R.T., Howell, H.G., Partyka, R.A. and Dyer, D.C., J. Med. Chem. **17**, 161-166 (1974).
Nichols, D.E., Barfknecht, C.F., Rusterholz, D.B., Benington, F. and Morin, R.D., J. Med. Chem. **16**, 480-483 (1973).
Nichols, D.E., Brewster, W.K., Johnson, M.P., Oberlender, R. and Riggs, R.M.,

J. Med. Chem. **33**, 703-710 (1990).

Nichols, D.E. and Dyer, D.C., J. Med. Chem. **20**, 299-301 (1977).

Nichols, D.E., Hoffman, A.J., Oberlender, R.A., Jacob III, P. and Shulgin, A.T., J. Med. Chem. **29**, 2009-2015 (1986).

Nichols, D.E., Hoffman, A.J., Oberlender, R.A. and Riggs, R.M., J. Med. Chem. **29**, 302-304 (1986).

Nichols, D.E. and Kostuba, L.J. J. Med. Chem. **22**, 1264-1267 (1979).

Nichols, D.E., Lloyd, D.H., Hoffman, A.J., Nichols, M.B. and Yim, K.W., J. Med. Chem. **25**, 530-535 (1982).

Nichols, D.E., Oberlander, R., Burris, K., Hoffman, A.J. and Johnson, M.P. Pharmacol. Biochem. Behav. **34**, 571-576 (1989).

Nichols, D.E. and Shulgin, A.T., J. Pharm. Sci. **65**, 1554 (1976).

Nichols, D.E., Shulgin, A.T. and Dyer, D.C., Life Sciences **21**, 569-576 (1977).

Nichols, D.E., Weintraub, J.R., Pfister, W.R. and Yim, G.K.W., NIDA Research Monograph #22 QuaSAR of Analgesics, Narcotic Antagonists and Hallucinogens, U.S.G.P.O., 1978, p 70-83.

Nichols, D.E., Woodard, R., Hathaway, B.A., Lowy, M.T. and Yim, G.K.W., J. Med. Chem. **22**, 458-460 (1979).

Nooteboom, L. Proc. R. Acad. Amsterdam **37**, 562 (1934).

Oberlender, R.A., personal communication.

Oberlender, R.A., Kothari, P.J., Nichols, D.E. and Zabik, J.E., J. Med. Chem. **27**, 788-792 (1984).

Olender, B., personal communication.

Olender, I., personal communication.

Orfali, S., personal communication.

Pace, D., personal communication.

Palmer, C., personal communication.

Patra, A. and Mitra, A.K., J. Natl. Prod. **44**, 668-669 (1981).

Peretz, D.I., Smythies, J.R. and Gibson, W.C., J. Men. Sci. **101**, 317-329 (1955).

Peroutka, S.J., personal communication.

Perry, A., personal communication.

Perry, B., personal communication.

Perry, J., personal communication.

Perry, W., personal communication.

Peterson, M., personal communication.

Pitas, A., personal communication.

Quincy, C., Personal communication.

Repke, D., personal communication.

Rheingold, H., personal communication.

Ricaurte, G.A., personal communication.

Riedlinger, J., personal communication.

Riedlinger, T.J., personal communication.

Ross, D., personal communication.

Saiki, Y., Sano, S. and Fukushima, S. Yaku. Zasshi **90**, 103-106 (1970).

Sager, R.K., personal communication.

Santos, W., personal communication.

Sapienza, F., personal communication.

Sargent III, T., personal communication.

Sargent III, T., Braun, U., Braun, G., Kusubov, N. and Bristol, K.S., Nucl. Med. Biol. **16**, 91-99 (1989).

Sargent III, T., Kalbhen, D.A., Shulgin, A.T., Braun, G., Stauffer, H. and Kusubov, N., Neuropharmacology **14**, 165-174 (1975).

Sargent III, T., Shulgin, A.T. and Mathis, C.A., J. Labelled Compounds Radiopharm. **19**, 1307-1308 (1982).

Sargent III, T., Shulgin, A.T. and Mathis, C.A., J. Med. Chem. **27**, 1071-1077 (1984).

Sargent, V., Personal communication.

Sayigh, A.A.R., Ulrich, H. and Green, M., J. Chem. Soc. 3482 (1964).

Schoenfeld, E., personal communication.

Schoonover, S., personal communication.

Schwartz, J., Personal communication.

Schweitzer, J.W. and Friedhoff, A.J., Am. J. Psychiatry **124**, 1249-1253 (1968).

Schweitzer, J.W., Friedhoff, A.J., Angrist, B.M. and Gershon, S., Nature **229**, 133-134 (1971).

Sepulveda, S., Valenzuela, R. and Cassels, B.K., J. Med. Chem. **15**, 413-415 (1972).

Seymour, R., personal communication.

Shulgin, A.T., unpublished findings.

Shulgin, A.T., Nature **201**, 1120-1121 (1964).

Shulgin, A.T., Experientia **20**, 336 (1964).

Shulgin, A.T., Can. J. Chem. **43**, 3437-3440 (1965).

Shulgin, A.T., J. Med. Chem. **9**, 445-446 (1966).

Shulgin, A.T., Can. J. Chem. **46**, 75-77 (1968).

Shulgin, A.T., British Patent 1,147,739 (1969).

Shulgin, A.T., U.S. Patent 3,547,999 (1970).

Shulgin, A.T., J. Psychoactive Drugs **18**, 291-304 (1986).

Shulgin, A.T. and Carter, M.F., Psychopharm. Commun. **1**, 93-98 (1975).

Shulgin, A.T. and Dyer, D.C., J. Med. Chem. **18**, 1201-1204 (1975).

Shulgin, A.T. and Jacob III, P., J. Anal. Tox. **6**, 71 (1982).

Shulgin, A.T. and Jacob III, P., Clinical Toxicology **19**, 109 (1982).

Shulgin, A.T. and Sargent III, T., Nature **215**, 1494-1495 (1967).

Shulgin, A.T., Bunnell, S. and Sargent III, T., Nature **189**, 1011-1012 (1961).

Shulgin, A.T., Sargent III, T. and Naranjo, C., Nature **212**, 1606-1607 (1966).

Shulgin, A.T., Sargent III, T. and Naranjo, C., Ethnopharmacologic Search for Psychoactive Drugs. Public Health Publication #1645, D. Efron, Ed. 1967 p 202-214.

Shulgin, A.T., Sargent III, T. and Naranjo, C., Nature **221**, 537-541 (1969).

Shulgin, A.T., Sargent III, T. and Naranjo, C., Pharmacology **5**, 103-107 (1971).

Shulgin, A.T., Sargent III, T. and Naranjo, C., Pharmacology **10**, 12-18 (1973).

Shulgin, L.A., unpublished findings.

Shulgin, T.A., personal communication.

Siegel, R.K., personal communication.

Slotta, K.H. and Muller, J., Z. physiol. Chem. **238**, 14 (1936).

Smythies, J.R., Personal communication.

Snyder, J., personal communication.

Spath, E. and Bruck, J., Chem. Ber. **70**, 2446 (1937).

Spath, E. and Bruck, J., Chem. Ber. **71**, 1275 (1938).

Spencer, J., personal communication.

Stafford, P., personal communication.

Standridge, R.T., Howell, H.G., Gylys, J.A., Partyka, R.A. and Shulgin, A.T., J. Med. Chem. **19**, 1400-1404 (1976).

Stanley, A.O., Personal communication.

Stevens, J., personal communication.

Stolaroff, J., personal communication.

Stolaroff, M., personal communication.

Strassman, R., personal communication.

Tarcher, J., personal communication.

Tolbert, R., personal communication.

Tozman, S., Schweitzer, J.W. and Friedhoff, A.J., Life Sciences **11**, 1069-1078 (1972).

Trampota, M., personal communication.

Trudeau, G.B., Doonsbury, Universal Press Syndicate, August 12-24, 1985.

Turek, I.S., Soskin, R.A. and Kurland, A.A., J. Psychedelic Drugs **6**, 7-14 (1974).

van der Schoot, J.B., Ariens, E.J., van Rossum, J.M. and Hurkmans, J.A.Th.M., Arzn. Forsch. **12**, 902-907 (1962).

Wang, Z.W., Ma, W.W. and McLaughlin, J.L., J. Nat. Prod. **51**, 382 (1988).

Weintraub, H.J.R., Nichols, D.E., Makriyannis, A. and Fesik, S.W., J. Med. Chem. **23**, 339-341 (1980).

Weiss, J., Personal communication.

Weiss, L., personal communication.

Weinstock, J. J. Org. Chem. **26**, 3511 (1961).

Williams, P., personal communication.

Winek, C.L., Collom, W.D. and Bricker, J.D., Clinical Toxicology **18**, 267-271 (1981).

Wolfson, A., personal communication.

Wolfson, P., personal communication.

Zeff, L., personal communication.

Zhingel, K., personal communication.